Wines of the World

With contributions by

Julius Barratt   Ian Jamieson MW
Nathan Chroman   Julian Jeffs
Noel Cossart   Jan Read
Philip Dallas   Ron Small
Len Evans   David Stevens MW
Wyndham Fletcher   Serena Sutcliffe MW
Bill Gunn MW   Jack Ward

André Simon's
Wines of the World

Second edition by Serena Sutcliffe

McGraw-Hill Book Company
New York   St Louis   San Francisco
Hamburg   Mexico   Toronto

This book was designed and produced by
The Rainbird Publishing Group Limited
36 Park Street
London W1Y 4DE
for McGraw-Hill Book Company, Inc.
1221 Avenue of the Americas
New York, 10020

House editor: Fiona Roxburgh
Cartographer: Eugene Fleury
Indexer: Vicki Robinson

Library of Congress Cataloging in Publication Data
André Simon's wines of the world.
Editions for 1967-1972 edited by A. L. Simon.
Bibliography: p.
Includes index.
1. Wine and wine making.   1. Sutcliffe, Serena.
II. Simon, André Louis, 1877-1970, comp. Wines of the world.
III. Title: Wines of the world.
TP 548.S68 1981   641.2'22   80-24441
ISBN 0-07-057432-5

The text was set by Oliver Burridge and Company Limited
Crawley, England
Printed by R. R. Donnelley & Sons Company
Chicago, United States of America

Contents

List of Colour Plates

*The page numbers given are those opposite the colour plates
or, in the case of a double-page spread, those either side of the plate.*

List of Maps

Foreword to
the Second Edition

HARRY YOXALL

When it was first published in 1967 *Wines of the World* was recognized as a remarkable book, edited by the leading oenophile of the day and covering, in its 700 pages, all the wine-producing areas of the world in authoritative sections written by recognized experts. But what was perhaps its most remarkable feature was the fact that its editor, who had also personally written 205 of its pages and co-written another 120, was ninety years of age.

It is now over ten years since André Simon died, having already outlived most of his contemporaries; and the roll of those who personally knew him is rapidly getting shorter. His books, of course, remain to be read. Several are still available for purchase, and the rest can be consulted in libraries, and should be studied by all who are interested in their subject. Some of his descriptions of technical processes are admittedly out of date. But his encyclopedic knowledge and his sure sense of comparative values remain permanently useful to the student.

Yet not all his learning, not all the sagacity of his judgments, and certainly not just the prolific volume of his writing can explain the authority that he wielded in his time. This came also, perhaps primarily, from his person and personality. I was one of those privileged to know him long and well, and I can never forget the lovely white hair, the blue eyes, the *rusé* smile, the pink complexion, fresh as a child's, that he retained to the day of his death, aged ninety-three. I remember too what the French would tactfully call *son léger embonpoint*, his moderate corpulence that was consoling to other gastronomes who found that alcohol contained calories. Then there was his seductive French accent, curiously (indeed I think, carefully) preserved despite his many years of residence in England. Add too, his flawless memory for scent and taste (which made him an extraordinary exponent of the art of blind tasting). And there were his fluent style of writing, his compelling enthusiasm and his constant good humour, and you will readily understand not only his authority, but also the devotion of his contemporaries, to the man and his opinions, that his survivors still pay. He laid the foundation of that authority with his pioneer work in the education of young members of the wine-trade. He then extended it to amateur wine-lovers not only through his many non-technical books on wine but particularly through his foundation, when he had himself left the trade, of The Wine and Food Society, with its quarterly magazine *Wine and Food*, and his expansion of both throughout the world. (It is now The International Wine & Food Society, and has 250 branches in 35 different countries.) André, as everyone called him *tout court*, André (there was only one André) extended a general appreciation of good wine and food in innumerable places where before they had been the perquisites only of limited coteries.

But despite his missionary enthusiasm he was always a realist, and he moved with the years. Though he had an extraordinary knowledge of the past, he lived in the present. When it came to the republication of his book, half a generation after its original appearance, he would have been the first to realize that patching and pruning were not enough. In the last fifteen years there have probably been greater changes in the scenes of wine-growing and -making than had occurred in the whole of his long life-time. He would, I am sure, have agreed to the almost complete re-writing of the book, with only his own contributions on Champagne and Cognac left virtually intact. And knowing both of them, I am sure he would have approved of the choice of the new editor. That this choice fell on a female Master of Wine would, I think, have given him additional pleasure; André (and I write this with no mischievous *sous-entente*) had a great appreciation of attractive, intelligent women.

The team of contributors has been changed, but it retains a level of expertise equal to that of the original one. Naturally the newcomers bring to their writing a knowledge of contemporary conditions that their predecessors could not have possessed. Yet they write in the spirit of the original book. They follow André's doctrine that to get the fullest possible enjoyment out of wine you must learn as much as possible about its various methods of production and the differences of its regional characteristics. But they know too that wine-making is not just a matter of botany and chemistry; it is an expression of the devotion of the vintners, and is above all an aesthetic achievement. They know also that, even in the New World, behind the continuous process of experimentation, there is the solid body of tradition. They reflect too André's attitude towards the enjoyment of wine. Living at the period when he lived, and commanding the resources (more of friendship than of money) that he possessed, André probably drank as much great wine, and particularly as varied a selection, as anyone has ever enjoyed. Yet he always stood for moderation. To know the highest and at the same time to value the humble was the essence of his gospel.

He advocated indeed the occasional feast, with its generous succession of fine dishes and great bottles; but he insisted that this should be occasional. For the regular pleasures of the table he asked for simple food and soundly made wine, insisting only that the first should be fresh and the second mature. (To this he would have made one exception: the meat and game must be well-hung.) As to maturity, many unpretentious wines are now ready in a year, some indeed in a few weeks. Our new authors endorse these attitudes. And though they may not feel quite as André did, on the basis of his profound if simple Christian faith, that the knowledge and enjoyment of wine is a manifestation of our duty towards God, in gratitude for the good things He has given us, the contributors to the new edition do see the appreciation of decent wine as an essential part of the fullness of life.

These current writers give sufficient technical information for the professional student; but I am glad to note they add history to their geography, and have been provided with sufficient space for the expression of personal preferences, so that their text will interest the amateur no less. One gets from these pages, as their editor intended, a fair sense of the taste of numerous wines, which will encourage readers to make their own experiments and form their own opinions.

Reading the proofs of the new edition, I have again been impressed by the immense difficulty and laboriousness of viticulture, vinification and maturation if consistent standards of wine, at whatever level, are to be regularly maintained, particularly in the difficult economic circumstances of our time. How much knowledge and care go to the making of even a secondary *appellation*. This book makes me not only more appreciative of the best, it makes me more tolerant of the modest quality of the bottles that most of us are now forced by price to drink most of the time. But any wine can please, however unassuming it is, if it has been soundly made.

So though this is in fact a new book, the spirit of André hovers over it. Even those contributors who did not know him personally were students of his writing. He was the most prolific of all writers on wine, and the most influential. He left his personal mark on two generations of pupils, indirectly influenced a third, and now, with this new edition, will convince a fourth. I see him, in the terms of his own faith, as a patron saint in heaven, smiling benignly in blessing on this Revised Version of his Authorized Gospel. For those to whom such imagery does not appeal, let me simply describe him as the tutelary genius of the new edition. Genius in this sense, as the inspirer and propagator of a tradition, André certainly was.

I conclude my Foreword with a quotation from his Introduction of 1967. 'There is now wine made', he wrote, 'in more places than ever before, most of it, of course, of the plainer sorts, but none as bad as the bad wines of the "good old days". Modern science and a greater number of better educated wine-makers leave no excuse for making as bad wines as were sometimes made by ignorant or unlucky growers. The bad wines of today are always drinkable. Unfortunately, economic conditions have been mainly responsible for great wines being fewer and not as great as great wines were made occasionally in the past. . . . But let us be grateful that there is as much and as good wine as there is throughout the world, wines of many different types and styles, wines to suit every taste and occasion, wines which may be dear but are worth more than any money that we have to pay for them: joy and health are the gifts of wine, and they are priceless.' This seems to me to be not only prophetic, but an endorsement of the continuity of the original work in this new edition.

Introduction to the Second Edition

SERENA SUTCLIFFE MW

I never met André Simon before he died, but I am close to many who knew him well. The strongest impressions of this great man that have been passed on to me are his tasting perception, his *joie de vivre* and his literacy. I hope that this book perpetuates his philosophy of life and does him honour.

How does one communicate the character of a wine when there is no glass between the reader and the writer? We have to conjure up and catch taste, the sight of a vineyard and the wisdom of a wine-maker by mere words. In the past these were sometimes too romantic, now they are perhaps too clinically technical. In this book, we have all tried to use the vocabulary of the wine-makers themselves, which naturally varies from country to country, and again from continent to continent.

Wine takes pride of place in this book, and we have eschewed history and tourism in an effort to cover as many as possible – after all, historical background can be found in abundance in the first edition of *Wines of the World*. Similarly, we do not mention restaurants and gastronomy, near as they are to the hearts of most lovers of wine.

This is a book about wine, how it tastes, how it is made, how it ages. Much time is spent on grape varieties, because without the grape there would be no wine, and once the characteristics of the main grape varieties are known, a clear idea of the type of wine to expect can be formed, even if the reader is a complete newcomer to a particular area or property.

A greater proportion of space is given to the descriptions of fine wines than of ordinary wines, on the assumption that the latter are there for drinking, when the pocket or concentration cannot reach higher, but the former are those people wish to read about. Since one pays a great deal more for fine wine, it is also more important that errors are not made. So, we have dared to recommend wines, preferring not to linger on the bad or dull ones but to point out the good and exciting ones. Wine is a great gift to life. Enjoyed in moderation, and with all the senses, it is also a voyage of discovery.

Viticulture, Vinification and the Care of Wine

SERENA SUTCLIFFE MW

Growing and making wine, from the vine to the bottle, is a judicious mixture of art and science, with the emphasis on science. It is true to say that pure technicians *can* make poor wine, and peasant growers with very little book-knowledge *can* make delicious wine, but on the whole, the best results are obtained with a blend of experience and training. The balance veers more towards science where conditions for making wine are not ideal, such as in very hot countries, or those with not enough sun. Man can juggle with Nature to a certain extent, blasting slopes so that they face the right way, spray irrigating to compensate for lack of rain, but he must always respect the basic terrain and climate.

At the basis of all wine-making lies the grape itself. It is amazing how often this can be overlooked, but miracles cannot be worked with poor raw material. Climate, soil and site all reflect on the grape, and the resulting health or otherwise of this most fascinating fruit is the answer to whether man has got the configuration right.

The ultimate taste and character of your wine will depend on a multitude of factors, embracing viticulture, vinification, right through to such mundane things as transport conditions and shelf-life. At the heart of it all lies the grape, and the way it *tastes*. The nobler the grape variety the more its basic quality will assert itself. Nothing will elevate a poor grape variety, not even the cleverest vinification, although poor vinification can ruin the noblest grape, with only glimpses of what the wine might have been peeping through. Quite apart from the inherent quality of the individual grape variety, no good wine can ever be made from unhealthy must. The grapes must be picked at optimum point (easier in a small vineyard than in a large one) and be free of rot and bacteria. It is here that the deadly sins of Sloth and Greed come in. If the vineyard owner has been lax in going through his vines with sprays against mildew, oidium and botrytis (the mould only becomes 'noble' when it attacks *ripe* grapes), if he has been less than energetic in watching leaf growth and encouraging good air circulation to avoid excess humidity, if he has neglected to spray insecticide against the dreaded red spider, particularly harmful to the Merlot in Bordeaux, and if he is too greedy to sort and throw out rotten or unripe grapes from the final harvest, the must will never make great wine.

Enormous progress has been made in judging the best moment to pick the grapes in order to extract all the help that nature can give. The right balance between rising sugar content and falling acid content must be found for each region and grape variety, and the pH has to be watched. Inclement weather and contract labourers do not necessarily wait for grapes to reach perfect maturity, but increased scientific knowledge of the composition of the grape has enabled better harvesting decisions to be made. These run into high-risk areas with all late-harvested grapes, *Spätlese*, *Auslese*, and especially with *Eiswein*. The extensive use of the harvesting machine in certain parts of the world has dramatically shortened the picking time and reduced the risk element.

There exist more than 3,000 known grape varieties and nomenclature is an enormous problem. Local terminology is at its most fertile in viticulture, and one rather insignificant grape variety can sail under at least half a dozen names in different parts of the world. Some varieties are indigenous to their areas, and have been since time immemorial, others get transported across countries, and even oceans, and turn up newly baptized in some far-flung new vineyard. Others change somewhat in the move, become mutations of their original selves, but confusingly cling to family names that bear little resemblance to the original plant. Yet others are given endearing local nicknames which remain endearing only as long as one is drinking, not writing about, them. Some are named after the areas of their, supposed, birth (the Traminer after the village of Tramin in Süd Tirol/Alto Adige), some after their inventors (to this family belong many new German varieties, such as Müller-Thurgau after Herr Müller from Thurgau in Switzerland, Morio-Muskat after Doktor Morio, and Scheurebe after the late Mr Scheu), and some names are what the French would term *fantaisie*. An idea of the multiplicity of names for the same grape variety can be given by a brief trip round Europe, hardly venturing to the other continents. You might not have come across the Abruzzo Bianco of Central Italy, but it is none other than the Trebbiano of Orvieto and one of the grapes making Soave – a small proportion can also be added to Chianti to give it lightness. But the Trebbiano is also none other than the Ugni Blanc of Southern France, which is known as the St Emilion in Cognac, where it makes the thin, acid wine so suitable for distillation. The one place it has never been near is St Emilion! The Sauvignon grape is known as the Blanc Fumé at Pouilly-sur-Loire (and sometimes in Napa, where it becomes the Fumé Blanc), but that name would not get you any-where if you used it in Graves. The Chasselas of Pouilly-sur-Loire and Alsace is the Gutedel of Germany, which becomes the Fendant in Switzerland – and also becomes a better wine in the transition. The Elbling of the Upper Mosel and Luxembourg is almost unrecognizable as the sweet Pedro Ximénez of Jerez. But Germanic countries also call it the Räuschling or Kleinberger. The Muscadet of Muscadet is a refugee from Burgundy, where it is the Melon de Bourgogne and rather *ordinaire*. The Malbec of the Médoc becomes the Pressac in St Emilion, the Côt in the Loire and, quite inexplicably, the Auxerrois in Cahors. At St Emilion they also see fit to rechristen the Cabernet Franc the Bouchet. Pinots abound everywhere, some of doubtful parentage and of all colours. The Chardonnay is not strictly a Pinot, although some would claim a distant connection for it with Pinot Blanc. Then there is Pinot Gris (or Pinot Grigio, Pinot Beurot or Ruländer), Pinot Meunier (red, and one of the three grapes used for Champagne), and the ubiquitous Pinot Noir, which also masquerades under the names of Spätburgunder or Blauer Burgunder in Germany, and Rotclevner in Switzerland: Clevner or Klevner being a sort of all-purpose name for Pinot. The Pineau de la Loire is not a Pinot at all, but another name for Chenin Blanc – in South Africa they call it Steen. The Rhein-riesling is the classic Riesling of Germany and the same as Johannisberg Riesling of California, but the Wälschriesling (or Olaszriesling or Laski Riesling or Italico Riesling) of Austria, Middle Europe and Northern Italy is probably not a Riesling at all in origin and came from France. The red Trollinger, chiefly grown in Austria, the Italian Tyrol and Germany, and useful for wine-making or eating, must take pride of place for the sheer diversity of its names. It also appears as the Gross-Vernatsch, the Blauer Malvasier, the Black Hamburg (of Hampton Court fame), the Frankenthaler, the Schiava-Grossa, to name but a few.

This is exhausting but, unfortunately necessary, as without the possibility of 'decoding' grape variety names, it is impossible to establish the relationship between grape varieties and the wines they produce, and to have some idea of what to expect when tasting. Tracking 'families' of vines across the world is difficult, especially before the grapes appear, as most grape varieties are extremely hard to identify from the leaf structure, even for the locals. All these grapes are varieties of *Vitis vinifera*, which originally came from the Middle East. The wild *Vitis vinifera sylvestris* of Europe cannot produce crops suitable for wine-making. *Vitis vinifera* is susceptible to that devastating aphid, phylloxera, and that is why nearly all European vines are grafted on to immune American root stocks. The three main American varieties are *Vitis riparia* (from river banks), *Vitis rupestris* (from rock and mountain) and *Vitis berlandieri* (a Texan vine) – all from the central, temperate zone of America. Many crossings of these original root stocks have been evolved and are now produced in Europe. The root stock must be chosen with great care with regard to the soil and to the marriage with the chosen European grape variety. The basic health and quality of the vine depends on the choice of both graft and root stock, and the failure rate can be high if due care and analyses are not employed. Only in a few places in Europe can the *Vitis vinifera* grow ungrafted and unaffected – in the Arenas area of Jerez, near Chipiona, where the sand prevents the aphid from harming the vine, and for the same reason at Colares near Lisbon, and in some parts of the Mosel and the Douro (especially at Quinta do Noval) where the slate and schist are equally inhospitable.

There should not be any confusion (and not surprisingly, there often is) between a hybrid and a cross-bred grape. Hybrids, in viticultural terms, are crossings between American and European vines. Very few are permitted to be grown in European vineyards, and in fact their presence can now be detected by atomic absorption machines. These ungrafted vines are also known as *producteurs directs*. Some of these hybrids are very resistant to disease, but it is generally accepted that they do not produce the very best wines. Crossings of European varieties are not hybrids, and are grafted on to American stocks.

In the Vineyard

Grafting can take place in a nursery or directly in the vineyard, rather depending upon the clemency of the regional climate. Spacing of the vine plants is obviously of paramount importance, bearing in mind such things as mechanization and slope – in cool climates, slopes are preferred as they give better exposition to the sun. Drainage is vital everywhere, and apart from using slopes to this end, the natural make-up of the soil can sometimes be assisted, such as adding more pebbles. Use of stones in the vineyard helps heat reflection. As the viticultural year progresses, foliage must be watched, as too much leaf surface in humid conditions leads to rot. The age of the vines has a direct effect on the quality of red wine, increasing the concentration noticeably – young vines give lighter wine and usually more of it. To compensate for this thinness some wine-makers add *vin de presse* to the produce of young vines, but this is often unhappy, as the press wine does not 'marry' well with the soft, light yield from the young vines. The result is a hard wine, still hollow, but with a stalkiness in the background. The best thing with young red vines is to delay picking as long as possible, to get maximum ripeness, and reduce yield as much as possible by reducing the amount of fertilizer used at the time of planting and pruning with severity. This age factor is not nearly so important for white wines. There are optimum points in the life of a vine, varying with the region and climate – but it could be said that vines of fifteen to twenty-five years old give generously and well, while thirty-five to forty-year old vines make greater wine. However, vines in hot countries, like the inhabitants, tend to mature faster.

Cleanliness of soil is all-important, and 'fatigued', overworked soil seldom gives of its best and is prey to disease. It remains to be seen what the long-term effects of heavy non-organic fertilization will bring. Fertilizer should go into the soil soon after the vintage, so that it has time to go down deep into the ground before the new growing season starts. Minerals in the soil are a boon to the wine-maker, when the roots can go down deep, and these 'trace elements' in a wine can greatly contribute to complexity in the final result. Mineral deficiencies or excesses can be corrected in the soil. After the aphid phylloxera – for a graphic description and diagrams of its life cycle, see *Sherry*, by Julian Jeffs, published by Faber, London (1971) – never beaten but outmanoeuvered, the fungoid diseases are always a danger. These include the dreaded oidium or powdery mildew, which affects all parts of the leaf, young shoots and grapes. A white, dusty covering is to be seen and the grapes subsequently split and rot, ultimately drying up. Spraying with sulphur, or sulphur dusting when applied regularly in warm and humid conditions will protect against oidium. There are other chemical, patent sprays, but some of these can produce side effects. Mildew (the downy variety) or *Peronospora* is another dangerous fungus. Once it has taken a hold, it can destroy the leaves, vital in the assimilation process of vines and, if not observed and treated, the grapes can be affected and shrivel, ruining the flavour of the resultant wine, if anyone is foolish enough to try to make wine from such sick material. The young leaves must be protected, and careful watch should be kept to see that oily patches are not appearing on them. Regular spraying with Bordeaux Mixture (basically copper sulphate) is a reliable preventive measure, and it has a good effect on other diseases such as black rot at the same time.

Pourriture grise, or grey rot, is the same fungus as *Botrytis cinerea*, the name also applied to *pourriture noble*. Botrytis is a danger to all grapes that are already not healthy due to bad weather or oidium. The stalks can also be affected, causing the berries to drop prematurely. When this rot attacks healthy ripe white grapes of certain varieties (such as Riesling, Sémillon, and sometimes Sauvignon), the desirable effect of noble rot occurs. The fungus punctures the skin of the grape, the water content evaporates, and the sugar and concentration of the grapes increase. There is also a specific flavour to grapes attacked by *pourriture noble*, without which, for instance, a top Sauternes is not really true. The fungus is not desirable on unripe grapes or on red grapes, and copper sulphate spraying can increase resistance. Good husbandry in the vineyard is another general precaution. *Court Noué* or fan leaf, is a virus, for which the only cure is uprooting. It is not something which is readily admitted by vine-growers who may have it, but it is a degeneration, often encouraged by overtired soil. Changes become visible on the leaves, and the vines' yield decreases. Until resistant root stocks are found, uprooting and thorough cleansing of the soil before replanting are the only remedies. Chlorosis of the vine is caused by incorrect soil balance, and when serious, can affect the shoots and the grapes. Correcting additions of sulphate of iron can restore the balance, as well as careful selection of root stocks. Moths, cochylis, eudemis and pyrpalis, can be devastating, but should not be so with strict observation for the first signs and good insecticide spraying. Red Spider is more common now in certain places of the world than it should be (prematurely browning leaves is often a sign), and requires early treatment. In some areas, birds are a problem, particularly where the grapes are the most enticing food in the radius.

Vines are also susceptible to conditions uniquely arising from the weather. Bad weather at flowering can cause the blossoms to fall, or the embryonic berries immediately afterwards. *Coulure* such as this is responsible for small vintages. *Millerandage* is caused by unequal flowering and will result in a bunch of grapes having some berries that are normal, and others that remain small and green and never ripen. These unripe berries should not be made into wine and should remain unpicked (the best machines now do this) or be selected out by human hand. Frost is a danger in some areas of the world, and always looms over vineyards near woods and on plains. The most serious winter frosts freeze the sap in the vine, and can in extreme cases destroy the vine – this only happens with prolonged temperatures at well below freezing. Spring frosts are dangerous when there has been a mild winter and the vines are in advance. Hail is often very localized, but can be so fierce as to shred a whole area of vineyard. The whole plant is damaged, and can also impart a taste to the grapes. Rockets are sometimes used to disperse hail cloud formations, and aircraft can intercept the clouds to cause only rain to fall.

Pruning in a vineyard directly affects the yield, and therefore has to be slightly prophetic, since the ensuing climatic conditions of the year are not known. An experienced pruner is the most valuable member of the vineyard staff, as he will sense how strong a plant is and will adjust his pruning accordingly. Methods vary with the viticultural area and the training method employed, which will be discussed in individual areas. Generous pruning, to encourage high yield, will probably 'dilute' the final quality of the wine, but on the other hand, the grower has to prune for all eventualities. An old vine, which produces little quantity anyway, needs the help of an understanding pruning hand, but a vigorous, young vine probably needs restraining. When pruning, it is also necessary to know what is being done in the way of fertilization, for the general replacement of organic manures by chemical products has often pushed production too far. One hundred days is usually counted as the time necessary between flowering and harvesting (although Bordeaux is now averaging 110), but late-ripening varieties or top-sweet wines will obviously need up to a month more. After picking, automatically or by hand, the aim is to get the grapes to the winery or *cuvier* as quickly as possible. In hot countries this is particularly necessary, and in some areas of the world, night picking is practised in order to avoid the heat of the day. Most picking is done once only per vineyard, but in the case of top Sauternes/Barsac or *Beerenauslese* or *Trockenbeerenauslese* wines, pickers might go through the same vineyard three or four times, gathering each bunch, or sometimes berry, at its optimum point.

Vinification

The wine-maker's work begins in the vineyard; the picking must be organized with the aim of filling each vat with the most homogeneous material possible. This applies to grape variety, situation of the vine, size of the harvest, level of ripeness, and health of the grapes gathered. It is no use thinking that the deficiencies of one component can be made up by the qualities of another – all that happens is that the really good ingredients are lost in the whole. Later on, careful tasting of each vat can control those that do not quite make the grade, but if the first rule of homogeneity is followed, there are far fewer nasty surprises. Professeur Ribéreau-Gayon of the University of Bordeaux particularly stresses this point.

Red grapes usually go through a crusher-stemmer, unless the additional tannin from the stems is required and they are conserved. The crushing process is extremely light, with the aim of getting enough juice to run to start the fermentation. Fermentation either starts naturally, with natural yeasts, or selected, cultivated yeasts are used, if absolute control is desired. In a natural fermentation, the wild yeasts begin the process, and then the *Saccharomyces ellipsoideus* take over. A small amount of sulphur dioxide is used to cleanse the must and kill off bacteria. Fermentation can take place in wooden *cuves*, in lined or unlined concrete vats, or, more normally nowadays, in closed stainless-steel vats, where it is far easier to control the temperature – a vital necessity if real quality is to be attained. Normal temperatures for the fermentation of red wine are between 28°C and 30°C maximum, but sometimes this is lower, thereby prolonging fermentation. As the sugar is transformed into alcohol and carbonic gas (but there are also many other side-products of fermentation, such as glycerine, succinic and acetic acid, lactic acid and acetaldehyde), the solid matter of grapes, skins and pips is forced to the top of the vat or other fermenting vessel to form a cap – or *chapeau*. This cap is dangerous if exposed undisturbed to the air (if the vats are open), as it attracts bacteria with great ease when dry. It is also necessary that the skins remain in parmanent contact with the fermenting must in order to get good colour extraction. The cap can also cause the middle of the vat to rise alarmingly in temperature. The most successful way of keeping the cap in contact with the must, ensuring good colour extraction and an even working of the yeasts, is to practise the system of *remontage*. This is quite simply drawing off must from the bottom of the vat and pumping it over the top or spraying it over the top, or even pushing the pipe through the hat and pumping direct into the liquid. Open vats can also have a system of a permanently submerged cap, but *remontages* are still necessary.

Chaptalization (and deacidification if necessary) takes place during the process of *remontage*. More nonsense is probably written about chaptalization than anything else in the vinification process. Chaptalization is the addition of sugar to the must, therefore increasing the potential alcohol level. Ironically, Chaptal did not develop the process in 1801 for this reason, but to help in the conservation of wine. There are, of course, other ways of raising alcoholic level, such as the Italian method of adding concentrated must. For red wines, sugar from cane or from beetroots can be used, but the former must be used for white wines. Chaptalization cannot be envisaged unless the must in question already has the minimum alcoholic level required by the *appellation contrôlée* laws in France. It is totally erroneous to attribute sweetness in a wine to chaptalization – there are other methods of sweetening wine, such as the addition of *Süssreserve*, called back-blending in some parts of the New World, or the process of stopping a wine's fermentation before all the sugar is converted – *mutage*. Sometimes when a dry wine appears to have sweetness to it it is because of the sheer ripeness of the grapes – unripe grapes can taste sour and green, just as grapes from a really ripe year give a really ripe, almost sweet, taste to the wine they make. But chaptalization does change the balance of a wine. It slightly lowers the fixed acidity (yet another reason why a chaptalized wine might appear softer than a non-chaptalized one), although the addition of concentrated must raises the fixed acidity level. The alcohol/extract ratio is also higher in chaptalized wines, and when tests are made for excessive chaptalization, this is taken into account. It is particularly important to control fermentation temperatures when wines have been chaptalized usually during the *remontage* process. Stainless-steel vats can have cold water which runs down the sides of the vats to cool them, or there is a system resembling a milk cooler through which the must passes.

It is essential that the alcoholic fermentation should pass steadily. It should not career forward, nor should it 'stick' as this attracts bacteria. If it is cold, it may be necessary to heat the surroundings of the *cuvier* in order to start the fermentation. Some wine-makers resort to heating red grapes before fermentation when colour and ripeness are deficient – this is usually applied to the produce of young vines.

With white wines, things are a little different. The stalks are not removed, as this makes quick and efficacious pressing easier. However, with automatic harvesters the stalks are removed, and care must be taken when pressing that blocks of the *marc* do not form. Luckily, the newest cylindrical presses (either pneumatic or screw-type) are very effective in making this fall to the 'carpet' at the bottom of the press. The juice is then run off, and usually goes through a cleansing process or *débourbage*, when it rests in a vat for twenty-four hours in order for the solid matter to fall to the bottom. Sometimes a centrifuge can be used for this purpose. A small amount of sulphur dioxide (SO_2) prevents fermentation from starting immediately, but when the *débourbage* is complete, fermentation will start with a cleaner must and probably result in fewer 'rackings' at a later stage. This is useful for light, dry white wines where minimum handling is advisable to guard against oxidation. White wine fermentation is usually between $15°$ and $20°C$ when elegant wines with strong bouquet are desired, but some very low temperatures are being practised in some parts of the world. After fermentation, red and white wine can be run off into barrels or kept in vat. With red wine which has only undergone fermentation but not pressing the correct term is 'free run' wine. This *vin de goutte* can be mixed with a proportion of *vin de presse* – the amount will vary with the characteristics of the year in fine wine regions, as *vin de presse* is not quite of the same composition as the *vin de goutte* – it is, for example, higher in volatile acidity and tannin, as well as mineral content.

In certain areas of the world, carbonic maceration is practised in cases where red wine is intended for young drinking. Here the grapes are put whole into a closed vat in a carbonic gas atmosphere. The grapes undergo an intercellular fermentation, with a small quantity of sugar within the berry itself being converted into alcohol without the need of yeasts. Some of the grapes are crushed by the natural weight of the volume, and their normal fermentation also creates carbon dioxide. This maceration can go on for five to ten days, followed by pressing, with the *moût de presse* being added to the *vin de goutte*. The fermentation is then finished within forty-eight hours. Carbonic maceration wine is less rich in extract, acidity, colour and tannin than classically fermented wine.

Cellar Work – or Elevage

'Bringing up' a wine is precarious business, requiring particular attention when wine is aged before selling. Many wines for quick consumption (Beaujolais and many dry white wines) have a short stay in vat and are bottled a few months after their birth. Serious red wines will go into cask (usually oak) after their alcoholic fermentation. This results in significant evaporation, and regular 'topping up' is necessary to prevent oxidation. This should be done under very hygenic conditions, with wine of top quality, itself kept in perfect conditions. However, the tendency seems to be leading to earlier three-quarter bung (the bungs to the side of the cask) – in Bordeaux this is often now in May after the vintage. The malolactic fermentation will take place either, in some cases, almost concurrently with the alcoholic fermentation, or usually a little time afterwards. Basically, this is the transformation of the rather green malic acid in the wine into the milder lactic acid. Malolactic fermentation nearly always takes place in red wine, sometimes in white.

If wines are stored in vat, they can be protected from the air by means of a covering of carbon dioxide or of nitrogen. Wines in cask are always subject to a small amount of oxidation through the wood, but this is desirable in the maturation process. If the casks are new oak, flavour and tannin will certainly be imparted to the wine. If a wine is big and solid, this can add a new dimension, but a light wine can be enveloped by new oak. Wines in cask must be racked, or periodically removed from the old lees of one cask to go into another, clean one. At all stages of cellar work, sulphur dioxide is used as a cleanser. A delicate wine should not be racked as much as a robust one, as it is a tiring process. In Bordeaux, during the first year of its life, a wine will be racked four times. No wine, even in vat, should remain in contact with old lees for too long, as the wine then begins to taste stale.

Wine also has to be clarified, or fined, removing the unstable elements in it. There are many products used to achieve this, including white of egg (for very fine wines), gelatine, fish glue (isinglass), and casein. For a wine to be stable, it should contain free and bound sulphur dioxide, but the free sulphur can be very low in certain types of wine. Heating, refrigeration, sorbic acid, ascorbic acid, metatartaric acid, citric acid, and bentonite (against excess protein) are other stabilizing treatments. Refrigeration is used to cause precipitation of potassium bi-tartrates. The temperature has to be lowered to $-3°$c or $-5°$c for table wines and $-8°$c or $-10°$c for fortified wines, and it is vitally important that this temperature should be held for an absolute minimum of five days, rising to twenty days in some cases. The addition of metatartaric acid (dehydrated tartaric acid) can only prevent tartrate formation for a limited amount of time, and thereafter can even aggravate the problem. It is a pity that a crystalline tartrate deposit is not acceptable to many consumers (probably because the crystal looks like sugar, or even glass), as it does not indicate that the wine is in any way impaired, and acceptance of a few crystals would mean that yet another wine treatment could be avoided.

In Germany, it has been noticed that in some years when there is a great deal of *Botrytis cinerea*, a slime acid called very unprettily *Schleimsäure* and which is a form of oxidized glucose, can occur. It can be tolerated up to 2 grams/litre in must, but above this it forms an insoluble calcium salt which tends later to throw a white opaque crystal deposit in bottle – again, nothing to worry about.

Choosing the right bottling time for individual wines is of paramount importance. This can vary from a few months after the vintage for light, fresh white wines, to two years for top red Bordeaux, or even three years for Yquem. Wines bottled too late for their particular composition and qualities can tend to lack vigour. Most wines now are bottled at their place of origin, although certain mass-market wines are transported in bulk and bottled by the customer. Certain grape varieties, such as Cabernet Sauvignon and white Chardonnay, need good bottle-ageing to reach their full potential and breed. Bottling should be carried out in conditions of great hygiene, and should be homogeneous – bottling from cask to cask is not advisable, for example. Wine is usually assembled in a bottling tank, given a light, final filter, and then bottled. In some areas of the world, notably California, there is a vogue for unfiltered wines from specialist wineries – the wines are meant to retain more character and fruit when unfiltered. If a totally sterile wine is desired (and this is usually not the case in fine wines intended to develop in bottle, but in wines sold for mass-consumption), pasteurization, flash-pasteurization, or hot bottling can be employed. If all this seems daunting, it is certainly meant to show that wine-making is not for the dreamy poet, surveying his vineyards glass in hand, but for the informed professional, alert to the dangers constantly threatening the ultimate quality of his wine, but perceptive enough to see the real and realistic potential of his wine and intelligent enough to develop it. Each region has its nuances in wine-making, and within each region there are people attempting different things. It should always be remembered that there are producers who are striving for the best, and others who are looking for the short-cuts. There are also areas which are not designed for top wines, and here the aims are for pleasant wines at accessible prices, with resulting modifications to 'classic' practice.

A really good cellar is almost as precious a commodity as a great wine; very often, the cellar is the rarer. The best advice is probably to look at what constitutes ideal cellar conditions, and then choose the best place in the house, flat or garden shed that most nearly corresponds to them. If no corner of one's abode is suitable, it is really better to keep only everyday wine to hand, and either share good cellar accommodation with someone luckier, or rent cellar space with a wine merchant. This obviously entails charges, but they will invariably be lower than ruined fine wine. The most dangerous thing for wine is a large fluctuation in temperature. Anything between 7°C and 12°C is ideal, the lower figure preferable for white wines (they can be put below the red wines, because heat rises). It would matter less for the temperature to be slightly higher than for there to be a considerable seasonal change. The higher the temperature, the faster your wine will tend to age. If wine gets too cold, it can throw tartrates – not in itself harmful to the wine, but worrying when people do not know what they are. Half bottles mature faster than bottles; and magnums more slowly. Choose a place that is dark, or make it dark, as light can harm wine. Clear bottles (Sauternes, some Champagne) are very vulnerable to sunlight. A damp atmosphere is preferable, as the corks stay in better condition. Wine matures more slowly in damp conditions which are totally beneficial, except sometimes to the labels. A humidifier can be used if excessive dryness is a danger, or sometimes a large bowl of water placed in the middle of the cellar can be sufficient. 16°C relative humidity is a good guideline, but you could go above this – I have seen a cellar with a humidity level around 25°C and there was no damage to the labels. Another solution to a lack of healthy humidity in a cellar is to put some small gravel on the floor of the cellar and sprinkle it with water occasionally – gravel retains humidity. Alternatively, this could be done with gravel in a wide tray. No storage place should be near a heating system, or have a strong smell, as this can eventually permeate the bottle. Reverberation should be avoided. Wine bottles should be stored horizontally so that the liquid is always in contact with the cork to prevent it from drying and shrinking and thus letting in air. You can stack bottles on their side in a small space or specially-made bin, or in a metal or wooden rack, which makes the bottles easy to remove. Sherry and Madeira can be left upright, as the spirit in the wines can eat into the cork over a long period, and if air does penetrate the drying cork, this is not harmful to a wine (with the exception of Fino Sherry, which should be drunk young and fresh and would not be stored anyway) whose production process protects it from oxidation. Vintage Port should be stored horizontally, with no change in the bottle's position so that the 'crust' or deposit can form evenly.

Many people worry about the journey from the cellar to the table – how should the wine be carried. Should it travel in style in a basket, or should it go 'deck class', unadorned? The logical answer is that if the bottle is likely to have sediment, it is best to draw the cork with it lying horizontally in the same position as it was in the cellar – standing upright and waiting for the wine to clear can take days, and in a few cases, the wine never completely clears. Therefore, a basket to keep the bottle in the same position is a great aid. Baskets in a restaurant, when the wine is either young with no deposit, or when the wine has already been carried around vertically, are just an affectation. First, remove the metal capsule to below the ring of the bottle-neck. Drawing a cork horizontally, from a bottle reclining in a basket, can be tricky. The patented, plastic Screwpull makes even this easy, and has even proved its worth on old, crumbly corks. When a bottle is vertical, the kind of corkscrews with 'wings' are just as simple and again involve no strength on the part of the bottle opener. When decanting from your horizontal bottle, put a candle in a candlestick, lift the bottle out of the basket so that the shoulder is lit up by the candle behind it, and pour slowly and steadily until you begin to see cloudiness or sediment enter the neck of the bottle – then stop, and use the 'silt' for marinating or in a stew!

To decant or not to decant – a most complicated question. In Bordeaux, it is a common occurrence, in Burgundy a rare one, for Vintage Port it is a necessity. It is the best thing to do when a wine has thrown some sediment in bottle. The very action of pouring the wine from one receptacle to another aerates it and releases the esters and aldehydes, perhaps trapped in the bottle for years, to intoxicate your nose and palate. A young wine can soften with this contact with the air, an old wine will release its complexity. The general rule is that the younger a wine is, the longer time the wine should be decanted before a meal. A very old wine often needs to be decanted and then drunk almost immediately, before it 'dies in the glass'. However, there are exceptions, largely due to the character of certain years (the 1945s in Bordeaux, for example, usually need time in decanter to open out) and certain grape types are more fragile than others. When in doubt, 'under-decant' rather than decant too soon – if the wine has not had enough time since the cork was drawn and you suspect it can open out further, just leave it in the glass, coming back to it at intervals to see how it is getting on. On the other hand, a wine that was decanted too soon and literally dies in the glass before you, cannot be revived. The same rule applies to the temperature at which wine should be served. A red wine served too warm or *chambré* is unrecoverable – if it is on the cool side, put your hand round the glass and warm it a little and coax out the bouquet. A wine too warm is a tragedy – it takes the edge off the flavour and makes it go 'soupy'. Never drink fine red wine in hot weather, unless you have air conditioning. White and rosé wines should be served slightly chilled – a few hours in the door of the refrigerator (the warmest part) is usually ideal. Certain light, fresh red wines are delicious cool – some reds from Provence, some straight Beaujolais, young quaffing wines. When decanting, always smell the decanter first, to see if any off-odours have entered it. Unobtrusive checks on glasses in restaurants are also worthwhile, because wine for which one has paid dearly will hardly improve when mixed with unrinsed detergent. Ideally, water only should be used for washing all decanters and glasses. If a decanter becomes stained, the simplest remedy is to scatter some denture powder on the bottom of the vessel and fill it with cold water. After some hours, the water is usually pink, and the decanter can then be rinsed out and will be bright.

Ideal tasting glasses, and also ones which are suitable for drinking just about everything, are those designed and approved by the Institut National des Appellations d'Origine (INAO). They have a nice stem which can be held without contact with the wine, the bowl is sufficiently wide for a certain volume of wine, and the long glass tapers towards the rim, thereby 'trapping' the bouquet, and enabling one to swirl the wine, to release this same bouquet, without wine spilling. Variations of this tulip theme are always suitable, sometimes larger, wider versions for fine Bordeaux, and squatter versions for rich Burgundy, almost Cognac *ballons*. The traditional Sherry *copita* is a smaller version of the INAO glass, and an elegant Champagne *flûte* is narrower and longer. Never fill glasses more than two-thirds full.

The general order for both tasting and drinking wines is young before old, and dry before sweet. I, personally, do not like mixing very different types of wine at a meal (say, Bordeaux with Burgundy), but prefer a graduated escalation of quality, or wines of the same class of varying age. One can also mix countries, but stay with the same grape types – perhaps showing a Cabernet from California, followed by a Cabernet-dominated wine from the Médoc. But care must always be taken that too assertive a wine does not immediately precede a delicate one, otherwise the latter may not do itself justice.

1

The Wines of France

SERENA SUTCLIFFE MW

Senera Sutcliffe MW, General Editor of the Second Edition of André Simon's *Wines of the World* and an independent wine consultant and broker, frequently contributes articles on wine to leading magazines and newspapers in the United States and in the United Kingdom and has made television and radio appearances on both sides of the Atlantic. She also does much work on tasting panels and as a wine judge. At the invitation of Les Amis du Vin, she has made two month-long lecture tours of the United States.

Guide to the Appellation System in France

The *appellation contrôlée* system in France is an attempt to see that the wines come from the place they say they do, and gives basic viticultural and vinification instructions that are meant to lead to better quality. The laws do not guarantee quality, but they lay down specifications that are more conducive to making pleasantly drinkable wine than vinegar. The rules cover the area of production; the grape varieties permitted (sometimes divided into principal and accessory grape varieties); the minimum alcohol level of the wine (which should be achieved before chaptalization); the maximum yield allowed per hectare; the method of planting, pruning and treating the vines; the vinification of the wine; and conditions of ageing.

Vins Délimités de Qualité Supérieure (VDQS) have the same laws, but they are wider than Vins à Appellation d'Origine Contrôlée, i.e. greater yields, less strict conditions to the zones of production, sometimes less 'noble' grape varieties. However, in one way, the VDQS rules were tighter than the AOC laws, and this was in respect to tasting. Wines could only obtain the VDQS label after official tasting, while no such thing existed for *appellation* wines, unless local bodies set up their own forms of tasting. Now *appellation* wines must also go before a tasting panel, and although one cannot say that this has been completely set up all over France, it is undoubtedly on the way. Of course, no tasting panel is infallible, and the few wines that are refused, can represent themselves. Tasting panels are usually composed of a grower, a *négociant* and a broker, but there is, naturally, a certain reluctance to refuse wines when they are tasted blind in one's own region.

There is often the possibility of the wine taking a lesser classification if it fails to meet all the requirements for the higher one. However, this does not mean that the *cascade* system can operate – officially abolished in the *appellation* decrees of 1974. This involved making much more than the maximum allowed, obtaining the classification up to the limit, and a lesser classification for everything over that. This did not, obviously, improve the quality of the higher classified wine, it only maintained its high price. Now, the grower must opt for the classification he desires for the crop in its entirety at the time of his declarations of the vintage. With the best laws in the world, *and* the inspectorate to control them, it is impossible to follow every drop of wine in the cellar. The figures and papers must tally at the end of the day, but the cards can be shuffled *entretemps*. Perhaps not every vintage year is purer than pure, but who complains when a poor vintage gets a helping hand from a prolific, good one that had the intelligence to follow? Conversely, it is a pity when something very good becomes just good through being stretched by the addition of something that needed improving.

Vins de Pays do have approved grape varieties, but they are very wide, and maximum yield is set at 90 hectolitres per hectare. Some people making wine within this framework very much follow their own inclinations and set themselves far higher standards, and others take advantage of the greater freedoms, especially in prolific years. The Midi of France has a mass of Vins de Pays every year, but a Vin de Pays such as Jardin de la France in the Loire would be virtually unobtainable in a year of low yields. Below Vins de Pays, there are Vins de Table, which must conform to certain standards of palatability and say from whence they come. Vins de Table are at the bottom of the pyramid as far as classifications go. The EEC groups wines into two classes: Vins de Table and Vins de Qualité Produits dans une Région Déterminée (VQPRD). In France, each of these categories subdivides, with *appellation* and VDQS wines both falling into the European classification of VQPRD, and Vins de Pays and other Vins de Table both falling into the Vins de Table classification.

Like all laws, those of the *appellation contrôlée* work best when there is the will to see them work. Above all, they should allow the best possible wines to be made in each category, and marry tradition with innovation.

The four organizations listed below carry out between them the work of controlling the quality of and marketing French wines.

1. The INAO (Institut National des Appellations d'Origine)
2. The ONIVIT (Office National Interprofessionnel des Vins de Table)
3. The SRFCQ (Service de la Répression des Fraudes et du Contrôle de la Qualité)
4. The DGI (Direction Générale des Impôts)

BORDEAUX

Bordeaux is a pivotal word for wine-makers and wine-drinkers all over the world. Bordeaux would never have been able to make this impact were it not for its size. It is the largest fine-wine producing area in the world, and that, in the vernacular, counts for something. Over 110,000 hectares are under vine, one-tenth of the Gironde, the largest *département* in France. In a good year, Bordeaux is now producing over two million hectolitres of *appellation* red wine and 1 million of white. It will also produce just under 2 million hectolitres of red and white *vin de table* or *vin de consommation courante*. 1979 produced a record quantity of red *appellation* wine: 3,315,124 hectolitres compared with 2,479,382 in 1973, an increase of no less than 33 per cent. It is noticeable that some of the largest increases are to be found in the Médoc and Haut Médoc *appellations*, while St Emilion and Pomerol are both below the 1973 level, an indication perhaps of the damage done by the 1977 frosts. With the decrease in the area under vine, similar results were hardly to be expected for the white wines. The total for white *appellation* wine was 1,124,048 hectolitres, which was the largest figure since 1974, but should be compared with the 1,313,553 made in 1970. This still brings the total of *appellation* wine for 1979 to the remarkable figure of 4,439,172 hectolitres, which is 17.5 per cent larger than 1973. This is not only the largest vintage since the Second World War, it is the first time since 1939 that more than six million hectolitres have been harvested in the Gironde, the total for *appellation contrôlée* and *vin de table* being higher than in that poor year, but still falling short of the prodigious 1934 yield.

It was during the 1850s that the disease of oidium struck the vineyards. No sooner was this blow assimilated than phylloxera and mildew followed, causing a viticultural depression throughout Europe. However, invention born of necessity triumphed, and with the vines grafted on to American root stocks, the nineteenth century ended with some fine vintages and the restoration of Bordeaux's reputation, if not her complete economic health. The fact that the troubled times of the beginning of the twentieth century, culminating in the First World War and its implications both for France and her customers (obviously still European), did not create a stable market for Bordeaux wines, only served to underline that economic difficulties for those in the wine trade were not over. The glowing vintages of the late 1920s might have heralded a new horizon, but the between-the-wars slump arrived soon afterwards and, as if to reflect the depression, the weather did not assist a series of vintages in the 1930s. The 1950s did see prices slowly rising and a more healthy chain of distribution forming, with a solid basis of Bordeaux-loving customers spread out over many countries, and a little more money in their pockets with which to indulge their predilection. The very serious frost of 1956 did affect the vineyard area and cost a great deal of money in new plantings and lost sales. After the excellent and prolific 1970 vintage, things seemed set fair for a successful decade for Bordeaux. People bought the 1970s and the small but good 1971s as fast as they appeared on the market, and wine changed hands rapidly and unseen (or untasted). Wine was regarded as a commodity, not for drinking, but for making a profit. For the first time substantial investment was being made by people outside the trade who alighted on wine from Bordeaux simply as another way to make money. No blame can be attached uniquely to any group of people in these transactions. It is easy to criticize the 'philistine' outsider, but the fact remains that while the going was good, both merchant and château-owner were quite willing to sell at ever spiralling prices. This would not have been enough in itself to bring about the dramatic slump in the Bordeaux wine trade of 1973/4. When prices continued to rise on a poor vintage, 1972, the danger lights were on. No one ever makes a bad buy on a really good vintage, especially if one is not pressed to sell. But buying bad vintages at all, let alone at high prices, is ill-advised. And some of the top, classified Bordeaux châteaux, which is where the heavy investment was taking place, were bad in 1972 and should never have appeared under their château names. At the same time, the oil crisis hit the Western world, and the 'advanced' nations, those who drink fine wine, came down to earth with a crash.

The recovery was slow, but lessons have been learned. The problem is essentially one of supply and demand, and the Comité Interprofessionnel des Vins de Bordeaux (CIVB) has done much work to stabilize prices and review stocks. It introduced a *fourchette* system of maximum and minimum prices for the basic *appellations* and, in prolific years, blocks some of the yield for release at a later date in order to keep prices steady. No one can say that all its efforts succeed, agreements are not always adhered to, and growers, brokers, and merchants or *négociants* do not always have the same aims or needs, but everyone is now aware of the problem.

The *négociants* of Bordeaux suffered a great deal from this unhappy period, and the newer ones, without reserves of stock and capital, crumbled under the blow – often rather unfairly, as some of them were not the worst offenders in encouraging the exaggerated prices. Some disappeared from the scene, and others became less of a *négociant* and more of a broker (*courtier*) – working on commission and eschewing stocks. The recovery was slow, both in Bordeaux and in the customer markets, as there was an immense amount of stock lying heavy on people's hands, some of it 'dumped' by companies that fell by the wayside. The Bordeaux market is now on a more even keel. Prices can still go high, but they tend to do this on excellent vintages, such as 1975 and 1978. The market has also had to come to terms with large vintages, the product of greatly increased plantings and avoidance of the worst disasters dealt by the vagaries of the weather.

The balance between red and white wine in Bordeaux has changed, with many white vines being replaced by red. Dry white wine is now in demand all over the world, especially at a reasonable price, and this shortage could be felt in the future, now that Bordeaux has learnt how to vinify well this type of wine. There are also periodic shortages of Bordeaux Rouge at *négociant* level, as the small properties that used to furnish the merchants with this basic *appellation* now often prefer to bottle under their château name. Buying of generic wine, such as Médoc, St Julien, St Emilion, has certainly become more difficult and very much more expensive for this same reason, and well-chosen small properties are often better value.

The top twenty exporting Bordeaux Négociants are: D. Cordier, Barton & Guestier, C.V.B.G. (Maison Dourthe), A. Delor & Cie, Alexis Lichine & Cie, Sté Distribution des Vins Fins, Calvet, Castel Frères & Cie, Cruse & Fils Frères, A. de Luze & Fils, Maison Sichel, Gilbey de Loudenne, J. Lebègue & Cie, Schroder & Schyler & Cie, Dulong Frères & Fils, Les Fils de Marcel Quancard, Borie Manoux, Louis Eschenauer, De Rivoyre & Diprovin/Dubroca and R. Joanne & Cie.

Classifications in Bordeaux

The very word 'classification' can sometimes sound rather terrifying, as if Bordeaux wines are in rigid groups and failure to know by heart the exact placings of all the important growths will result in awful drinking mistakes. It will not. In fact, personal experience or reliable recommendation is the surest way to find the best wines. But, with all the reservations brought out below, the 1855 classification of top châteaux did produce a quality structure, at least a standard at which to aim.

1855 Classification of the Médoc

FIRST GROWTHS

Lafite-Rothschild (Pauillac)	Margaux (Margaux)
Latour (Pauillac)	Haut-Brion (Pessac, Graves)

SECOND GROWTHS

Mouton-Rothschild* (Pauillac)	Gruaud-Larose (St Julien)
Rausan-Ségla (Margaux)	Brane-Cantenac (Cantenac-Margaux)
Rauzan-Gassies (Margaux)	Pichon-Longueville-Baron (Pauillac)
Léoville-Las-Cases (St Julien)	Pichon-Lalande (Pauillac)
Léoville-Poyferré (St Julien	Ducru-Beaucaillou (St Julien)
Léoville-Barton (St Julien)	Cos d'Estournel (St Estèphe)
Durfort-Vivens (Margaux)	Montrose (St Estèphe)
Lascombes (Margaux)	

THIRD GROWTHS

Giscours (Labarde-Margaux)	Palmer (Cantenac-Margaux)
Kirwan (Cantenac-Margaux)	La Lagune (Ludon-Haut-Médoc)
d'Issan (Cantenac-Margaux)	Desmirail (Margaux)
Lagrange (St Julien)	Calon-Ségur (St Estèphe)
Langoa-Barton (St Julien)	Ferrière (Margaux)
Malescot-St-Exupéry (Margaux)	Marquis d'Alesme-Becker (Margaux)
Cantenac-Brown (Cantenac-Margaux)	Boyd-Cantenac (Cantenac-Margaux)

FOURTH GROWTHS

St-Pierre (St Julien)	La Tour-Carnet (St Laurent-Haut-Médoc)
Branaire (St Julien)	Lafon-Rochet (St Estèphe)
Talbot (St Julien)	Beychevelle (St Julien)
Duhart-Milon-Rothschild (Pauillac)	Prieuré-Lichine (Cantenac-Margaux)
Pouget (Cantenac-Margaux)	Marquis-de-Terme (Margaux)

FIFTH GROWTHS

Pontet-Canet (Pauillac)	du Tertre (Arsac-Margaux)
Batailley (Pauillac)	Haut-Bages-Libéral (Pauillac)
Grand-Puy-Lacoste (Pauillac)	Pédesclaux (Pauillac)
Grand-Puy-Ducasse (Pauillac)	Belgrave (St Laurent-Haut-Médoc)
Haut-Batailley (Pauillac)	de Camensac (St Laurent-Haut-Médoc)
Lynch-Bages (Pauillac)	Cos Labory (St Estèphe)
Lynch-Moussas (Pauillac)	Clerc-Milon-Rothschild (Pauillac)
Dauzac (Labarde-Margaux)	Croizet-Bages (Pauillac)
Mouton-Baronne-Philippe† (Pauillac)	Cantemerle (Macau-Haut-Médoc)

*Decreed a First Growth in 1973.   †Formerly known as Mouton Baron Philippe.

This classification was not just decided upon overnight. It was based on the prices that these top châteaux had fetched for approximately a hundred years, and on previous assessments. It was largely the work of brokers who sold the wine *en primeur* or when very young. The fact that these châteaux consistently fetched high prices did establish that this is what people were ready to pay for them – in short, they were worth it. The proof of the general accuracy of the classification is that, with few exceptions, the châteaux listed are still the best in Bordeaux, largely because they occupy the best sites. Obviously, the best site, most ideal soil and potential is not always well-exploited, and châteaux have their good and bad epochs. Consistency is really the crux of the matter – if a château not in the classification regularly makes very fine wine, it should be considered for entry should it ever be revised, or in the case of a château already in the listing, it should go further up the ladder.

There is no doubt that the price gap between the First Growths and the others is extremely wide and entrenched, and to some, inexplicable. If this is felt strongly enough, there is nothing like 'voting with one's palate' – in other words, desist from buying. Much depends on needs and requirements – if you do not want to age wine before seeing it at its best, do not choose a First Growth. There is no use in denying that the classification is controversial. And certainly it needs reviewing. Some châteaux have disappeared (Château Desmirail, for example, has been swallowed by Château Palmer), and others have fallen too f-r by the wayside, or really do not have the potential to be top flight – one must here put into question at least two of the wines of St Laurent. There are also some top *bourgeois* growths waiting in the wings.

The *crus bourgeois* are the step just below the classified growths and in 1978 the Syndicat des Crus Bourgeois du Médoc produced an up-to-date assessment of these properties, dividing them into *grand bourgeois*, with 18 *crus exceptionnels* amongst them, and into *bourgeois* growths. It is intended periodically to keep this under review, which shows admirable flexibility.

THE GRAPES OF BORDEAUX (RED)

Cabernet Sauvignon: Cabernet Sauvignon must take pride of place in the list of red grape varieties. It is the dominant grape variety in the Médoc and Graves and, combined with the gravelly soils and superlative drainage of the best sites, can produce wines of some of the greatest breed in the world. It is a grape variety that needs time to develop complexity, although it always has a depth of fruit. When young, it can be austere and tannic and for this reason it is nearly always blended with a proportion of Cabernet Franc and Merlot. Cabernet Sauvignon is a late ripener, but this can have its advantages at the beginning of the season when spring frosts can wreak havoc. It is, however, a strong grape, resistant to *coulure* and rot. The berries are small, with thick skins, resulting in a lowish yield. It is less successful and less used in St Emilion and in the cooler soil of Pomerol, where it is known as the Gros Bouchet.

Cabernet Franc: This grape variety is a slightly muted version of Cabernet Sauvignon, less tough in youth and less concentrated, but with a lovely 'grassy' perfume. It is an important part of Médoc and Graves; but much more widely planted in St Emilion, Pomerol and Fronsac, where it is, logically, known as the Bouchet.

Merlot: Merlot is a vital part of Médoc and Graves wines, and the dominant grape variety in St Emilion and Pomerol. Many small properties in other regions of the right bank, such as Bourg and Blaye, also have a good proportion of it. The yield is generous, and the Merlot gives more alcohol than both the Cabernets, varying between one and 1.5 per cent more. The grape flowers earlier than the Cabernet and is picked earlier. But *coulure* can be a problem and rot can race through Merlot if not checked in time. The grape is also prone to attacks from red spider. But the wines are very commercial, tending to mature earlier than Cabernet-dominated wines, and they are softer and rounder in character. The wines have good colour when young, but tend to brown earlier than Cabernet Sauvignon.

Malbec: The Malbec plantings are less than they used to be in Bordeaux, and probably no vineyard wants more than 5-10 per cent now. In St Emilion, it is known as the Pressac. The wines from this grape variety can be very pleasant, if not really distinguished, but the dangers from *coulure* in the vineyard are considerable.

Petit Verdot: This grape variety has never had more than a tiny share of the Bordeaux vineyard, but a small proportion (especially in the Médoc) can add much-needed concentration to a soft wine. It needs a great deal of sun to ripen to its full degree, but can add real body to a wine.

THE GRAPES OF BORDEAUX (WHITE)

Sémillon: By far the most distinguished of the white grape varieties, when made in the proper way, the Sémillon is a vital component of great Sauternes and Barsac, and also in top Graves dry white wines. It is resilient and gives a good yield. However, in the right conditions, it is also a good recipient of *pourriture noble*, or noble rot. It is blended with the white Sauvignon for both the sweet and dry wines. When made into a sweet wine, it can impart great lusciousness and richness, and in dry wines this same richness can be a revelation – full, high in glycerine and smoothness, with wonderful, subtle flavours.

Sauvignon: This grape variety has taken an increasing hold on the Bordeaux area. As well as being a vital part of the blend in the above wines, it is also used alone, or as the most important part, in light dry white wines for early drinking, as in Entre-Deux-Mers. It is an aromatic grape variety, with a pungent smell and taste. The yield is moderate, and the sun is needed if Sauvignon wines are not to be too acid.

Muscadelle: This is a reliable grape variety, producing a great deal of lesser sweet wine in such areas as the Premières Côtes, but is found in smaller quantities in Sauternes and Barsac. It is scented and yields well, but has a tendency to maderize relatively early unless great care is taken. Too much can give a coarse flavour.

There are a few other peripheral white grape varieties which may feature in basic Bordeaux Blanc and in the Côtes de Blaye – Colombard, Merlot Blanc and Folle Blanche. Ugni Blanc can sometimes be grown in the lesser sweet white wine areas; it is a late-ripening grape that gives acidity, and when blended with Sauvignon, can

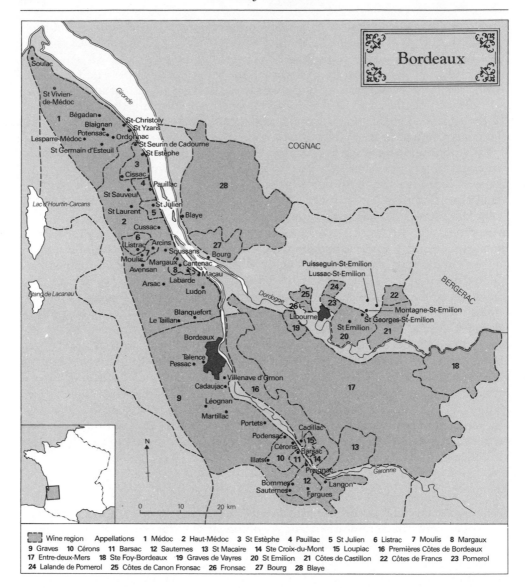

Bordeaux

Wine region   Appellations   **1** Médoc   **2** Haut-Médoc   **3** St Estèphe   **4** Pauillac   **5** St Julien   **6** Listrac   **7** Moulis   **8** Margaux
9 Graves   **10** Cérons   **11** Barsac   **12** Sauternes   **13** St Macaire   **14** Ste Croix-du-Mont   **15** Loupiac   **16** Premières Côtes de Bordeaux
17 Entre-deux-Mers   **18** Ste Foy-Bordeaux   **19** Graves de Vayres   **20** St Emilion   **21** Côtes de Castillon   **22** Côtes de Francs   **23** Pomerol
24 Lalande de Pomerol   **25** Côtes de Canon Fronsac   **26** Fronsac   **27** Bourg   **28** Blaye

also produce a pleasant dry white Bordeaux in areas such as Entre-Deux-Mers.

As an indication of what can be produced from a good quality red-wine château, a yield of between four to five *tonneaux* per hectare would indicate a policy of careful wine-making, aiming for high standards. Obviously, this can vary according to the age of the vines in the vineyard (old vines producing less than young ones) and the nature of the vintage. A *tonneau* is not an actual barrel, but is the traditional measure in which the Bordeaux trade buys and sells – it 'contains' 900 litres of wine. The Bordeaux barrel or *barrique* is what you see in all the *chais* – they each contain 225 litres, and four of them make a *tonneau*.

Which Wines to Drink When

It is essential to treat the different strata of Bordeaux wines differently. Basic Bordeaux Rouge is delicious in the year after its birth, capturing all the fruit and charm of the Cabernet family. This applies also to *appellations* like Premières Côtes de Bordeaux, with some of the St Emilion 'satellites' and red wines from Bourg and Blaye needing a year or two more. However good, a small château wine will not improve beyond about five years of age as a general rule. They can be excellent after eighteen months. However, a *cru bourgeois* of a good year will only really give of its best after five years, and a *cru classé* after ten to fifteen years, again, in a good to a very good year. Very good, balanced years have a tremendous life-span. Even a *cru classé* in a light year, such as 1973, will not benefit from extensive keeping, and may even be more delicious relatively young. So, when deciding when to drink one's Bordeaux, the intrinsic quality of the property must be considered, and its position in the hierarchy, as well as the individual composition of the wine in a given year.

With Bordeaux white wines, the simple dry white Entre-Deux-Mers and other predominantly Sauvignon wines are usually best in the eighteen months after vinification. Sauvignon here is not quite so well constructed as in, say, Sancerre, and is usually quite a bit lighter. Dry white Graves of a certain quality category, going on to the top Graves châteaux, benefit from bottle age, round up and become more interesting. Top Sauternes and Barsac, with classic noble rot, keep for a very long time indeed, and their luscious qualities can become more subtle with time.

THE MEDOC

The topography of the whole Bordeaux region differs widely, having a great effect on the individual micro-climates. Rivers dominate the area, with the majestic Gironde coming in from its wide estuary at the Pointe de Grave and dividing into the Dordogne and the Garonne rivers near Bordeaux itself. The Atlantic Ocean is a very real presence in the vineyard area, especially in the Médoc, more directly under the influence of its moods and changeability. The first thing that is striking about the Médoc is its severity, the main *appellation* area being bare and gravelly, not pretty and soft. Here there is no polyculture, and a very gentle slope slides down to the Gironde. The best plateau areas are only for the vines.

There are eight *appellations* in the Médoc, all for red wine: Haut Médoc, Margaux, Moulis, Listrac, St Julien, Pauillac, St Estèphe, and Médoc (formerly the Bas Médoc). Below, there is Bordeaux Supérieur and Bordeaux, the two basic *appellations*. Apart from the *appellation* Haut Médoc, which encompasses all the list aside from Médoc, near the estuary of the Gironde, the *appellations* are named from a south to north direction, with the city of Bordeaux in the south. It could be said that the wines in the south tend to have more delicacy and less body than those in the north, but there are other factors, such as wines from nearer the river generally having more finesse than wines further inland, which can be more robust. Everything in the Médoc depends on depth of gravel, and good drainage. The fertile, alluvial *palus* next to the river is not suitable for fine wines.

HAUT MEDOC

Haut Médoc was the first, basic *appellation*, along with Bas Médoc, before the six other *appellations contrôlées* were formed. Thus, a bottle of 1947 Château Margaux, for example, is labelled Château Margaux, Appellation Haut Médoc. Pauillac received its *appellation contrôlée* before this, however, as 1945 Lafite has the Pauillac *appellation*, not Haut Médoc. There are five classified châteaux that still have the *appellation* of Haut Médoc. La Lagune is the first classified château you come to, going north from Bordeaux. A Third Growth, in the village of Ludon, this is a more than worthy introduction to the fine wines of the Médoc. La Lagune is a very beautifully run property, with the vineyards and *chais* always impeccable. The vineyard was almost totally replanted in the late 1950s, and so the wine was light at first. Ludon has a good deal of the excellent gravelly soil of more northerly Margaux communes, and so one can expect, and will get, finesse here.

The present owners of La Lagune are the Champagne house of Ayala, and the remarkable Madame Boyrie is the manager. The 1970s began magnificently for La Lagune, with a 1970 of full fruit and good breeding. 1971, 1973, 1975 are all excellent examples of their respective vintages, and the 1976 is a most exciting wine, with almost exotic fruit. The 1978 is very perfumed, with a bigger structure than usual, beautifully matched by high glycerine. La Lagune is a very good buy.

Château Cantermerle, a Fifth Growth, is in the commune of Macau, just south of where the *appellation* Margaux begins. The château, bought by Cordier in 1980, has long associations with Holland, as it was owned by the Bordeaux *négociants*, Beyerman, who are of Dutch origin. The two men who will be forever associated with Cantemerle are the great M. Pierre Dubos and, after his death, his son-in-law M. Henri Binaud. The vineyards are on good, gravelly soil in the Ludon direction. The 1953 is superlative and the 1959 very good. Naturally enough, there is a resemblance to Margaux, but the wines are fuller and plumper. There were some nice vintages up to 1966, but latterly the wines do not seem to have the true Cantemerle class.

The other three Haut Médoc *appellation*-classed growths, Château Belgrave, Château de Camensac and Château La Tour Carnet, are all in the commune of St Laurent, inland from St Julien. At the moment, I cannot see at least one of them retaining this status if there was a reassessment.

Other wines to look out for with the Haut Médoc *appellation* are: Château d'Agassac, Château d'Arcins and Château Barreyres. Château Beau Rivage, in fact, only has the Bordeaux Supérieur *appellation contrôlée*, because it is on the alluvial *palus* near the river. Managed by the firm of Borie-Manoux, it is a nice, easy wine – the 1967 was most acceptable. Château Bel-Orme-Tronquoy-de-Lalande, north of St Estèphe, makes a very good wine, and there are some remarkable old vintages that I have been lucky enough to taste. A *grand bourgeois*.

Château Le Breuil, near St Estèphe, is a good *bourgeois* wine and Château Caronne Ste-Gemme in St Laurent is a very good *grand bourgeois exceptionnel*. Château Cissac and its good solid wine is well known in the United Kingdom and the United States. Château Citran, inland from Soussans and Margaux, is generally dependable. Château Coufran at St Seurin-de-Cadourne makes pleasant, lightish wines and Château La Dame Blanche at Le Taillan makes dry, white Bordeaux. Château Dillon at Blanquefort is owned by the regional agricultural school and the wines of the 1970s have improved greatly. Other châteaux to look out for are: Château Lamarque, Château Lanessan at Cussac, Château Larose-Trintaudon at St Laurent, Château Liversan and Château Peyrabon at St Sauveur, Château du Taillan at Le Taillan and Château Villegeorge at Avensan.

BAS MEDOC

This is the area north of St Estèphe, beginning at St Yzans in the south and running up to Soulac near the sea, but the vineyards stop before then between Lesparre and St Vivien. The *appellation* is Médoc, but it should be remembered that, when speaking, people often refer to the Médoc when they mean the whole of the Haut and Bas Médoc together. There are many cooperatives, supplying beefy, full wines to the *négociants*. The best areas are round Bégadan, Blaignan, St Christoly, Ordonnac and Potensac, St Yzans and St-Germain-d'Esteuil.

Château Loudenne is the Gilbey/International Distillers & Vintners property. A beautiful château is surrounded by vineyards on gravel, unusually going almost down to the river's edge. Vinification is modern and efficient, and there is now an interesting wine museum. Wine of great character, with the best vintages ageing beautifully. A delicious, Sauvignon-based white wine is also produced. Credit for much of what Château Loudenne is today must go to Martin Bamford of Gilbeys, France. Loudenne is also the headquarters of Gilbey's Bordeaux *négociant* business which is responsible, amongst other things, for the selection and distribution of La Cour Pavilion. The red is an excellent blend of wines from the area of Loudenne itself, bearing the Médoc *appellation* and showing the marked character of the communes around St Yzans. The white is *appellation* Bordeaux and is dry and crisp. There is also a highly recommended *appellation* Bordeaux Rouge, rather delightfully called La Bordelaise. Château La Cardonne at Blaignan is owned by the Lafite-Rothschilds and makes wine with character. Château du Castéra at St Germain-d'Esteuil is relatively unknown but good. Château Greysac at Bégadan is a *grand bourgeois* of good standard and much distributed in the United States. Château Livran at St-Germain-d'Esteuil is a wine worth looking for. Other reliable châteaux are: Château Patache d'Aux and Château La Tour de By at Bégadan, Château Potensac, and Château St Bonnet, Château La Tour Blanche and Château La Tour St Bonnet at St Christoly.

MARGAUX

Margaux is one of the great names of the Haut Médoc. The *appellation* includes wines from the commune of Margaux itself, as well as Labarde, Arsac, Cantenac, and parts of Soussans. Margaux wines can attain great breed and finesse, with an intense, poignant scent and a real silky texture. They are not as 'fleshy' or big as, say, Pauillac wines. The very best parts of Margaux are covered in white pebbly gravel, and these *croupes* or ridges give the wines with most delicacy. The village of Margaux is the kernel of the *appellation*, with its meagre soil so beloved of vines. Many properties in this *appellation* have small parcels of vineyards in several different places.

CHATEAU MARGAUX (Margaux)

This is a First Growth that, at its best, conjures up all that is most elegant, scented and refined in top Bordeaux. Apart from approximately eighty hectares under vine, Château Margaux is also an important farm. Château Margaux was bought by M. and Mme André Mentzelopoulos in 1976. Determined that the property should regain the peak of its marvellous potential, M. Mentzelopoulos brought the same dynamism he applied in his business life to the resuscitation of both the wine and the beautiful neo-classical château. Sadly he died at the end of 1980. The celebrated and experienced Professeur Peynaud, who has done so much in consultancy work in improving the quality of many top Bordeaux wines, was called in to oversee operations. The improvement has been dramatic. The 1978 in cask is a splendid wine, fully perfumed and beautifully constructed, filling out enormously between May 1979 and September 1979 tastings. The 1979 looks very well made. This is a real achievement, as in the short time so far afforded the new owners and their adviser, not much could have been done in the vineyard – but enormous care has been taken in selection. There has been a tendency to bottle earlier in some vintages, shown in the 1977, when some of the other First Growths were not at their best. The 1975 is good, but not amongst the greatest in this context. The wines of the 1960s and early 1970s did not really show the best that Margaux can do, which is quite remarkable, although the 1970 and 1966 are very honourable. The 1971 is not for keeping. But the 1961 is very fine, absolutely delicious, scented wine, not too tannic – not quite as luscious as Palmer, but showing great breed. The 1953 Margaux was probably the best wine of the vintage, incredibly elegant and distinguished. The 1950 was a great success, and the 1947 is still glorious.

The property also makes some white *appellation* Bordeaux, called Pavillon-Blanc du Château Margaux. Now entirely made of Sauvignon, the wine is very respectable, grown as it is on ten hectares of 'black sand' vineyard outside the Margaux *appellation* in the commune of Soussans.

Château Rausan-Ségla, a Second Growth, is now part of the international combine, Lonhro. Sometimes bottles from good vintages are rather disappointing from this property, lacking the breed they should have. The 1975, however, has very good fruit and is well-made wine, if not amongst the deepest in weight. The Second Growth 'twin' of Rausan-Ségla is Château Rauzan-Gassies. The wine can have the best qualities of Margaux and Cantenac, and take time to show at its best. However, too many wines show rather thin. The 1976 seems one of the best in recent years, with a very fruity nose, lovely silky texture and nice fullness. Château Durfort-Vivens is owned by M. Lucien Lurton, who also owns Château Brane Cantenac. The wine produced is very firm, partly due to a fairly small proportion of Merlot, but there are changes afoot, and a more elegant Margaux wine could be emerging.

Another Second Growth, Château Lascombes, is now owned by the brewery and wine and spirits group, Bass Charrington. Alexis Lichine did much to restore the vineyard in the 1950s and 1960s, after a long period of neglect, but since his sale of the property in 1971, the château perhaps lacks tight personal control. The vineyard area has been greatly increased, but this is a property where the plots are very scattered. The 1970 is full and plump, but other vintages in the 1970s have tended to dryness and are rather light for the class of wine. Château Brane Cantenac is a large property, possessing a magnificent plateau of very white, chalky-gravelly soil. This can produce Margaux *appellation* wine *par excellence*. The 1961 and the 1970 are both beautiful wines, appearing elegant and not too weighty, but with the balance to go on for a long time. M. Lurton is a very careful proprietor, and his 1978 is showing great potential, a wine that is perhaps bigger than usual, with great structure, and still at a very young stage. Château Kirwan is currently disappointing.

Château d'Issan is another Third Growth, and is owned by Mme Emmanuel Cruse. Unfortunately, the distribution of the wine is not very general, which is a pity, as d'Issan can produce big, rich, fruity wines, rather a typical Margaux. 1966 and 1970 both produced good wines. The 1964 is extremely good for the year. Château Giscours is a very important Third Growth, owned and managed by the energetic and conscientious Tari family. Although the area under vine is large, about 70 hectares, the estate is much bigger, and includes forest, farm and horses. The wine of Giscours is distributed by Gilbeys of Loudenne, and the reputation at the moment is justifiably high. The bouquet can often be aromatic, and the texture of the wine silky. The 1976 is rich and full, and the 1975 quite excellent, with an intense, fruity nose, real breed and a cedary flavour, married to good 1975 tannin – all pointing to a very harmonious future. The 1973 was very good indeed for the year. Château Cantenac-Brown is not exceptional at the moment.

Château Palmer is a property at its zenith, on occasions rivalling the First Growths in spite of its classification as a Third. Palmer is internationally owned by the firms of Mahler-Besse (with Dutch connections), Sichel (English) and the Miailhe family (French). Production is meticulous, both in the vineyard and in the *chais*, and every detail is known and followed by M. Chardon, the *régisseur*, whose family have a great hand in the reputation Palmer now enjoys. Palmer 1978 has a wonderful colour, richness and structure, perhaps following the 1961 style, but lighter in weight. Château Margaux's 1978 is bigger. The 1979 looks set on an excellent course. The 1977 is pleasant, although Palmer's Merlot grapes (of which there are approximately 40 per cent) were badly hit by the frost on the last two days of March. The 1976 is sweet and ripe, with the softness of Merlot, with depth of fruit and a lovely velvet texture. The 1975 wine is very fine indeed, with an almost exotic nose that Palmer can attain in its great years, great fruit and persistence, acidity and tannin – all the ingredients for a long life. One has to mention the 1973, 1971 (one of the best in the Médoc), 1970, 1966 (incredible depth of scent and individuality),

1962, 1961, 1960, 1959 (absolutely superb in magnum in January 1980, still youthful, and rich as a 1961), 1957, 1955 and lovely 1953. The 1961 is legendary, and is a quite glittering wine of immense opulence and beauty, a taste one recalls for ever.

Château Malescot-St-Exupéry is a Third Growth, very well managed by the owners, the Zuger family. The wine has delicacy and class, with the scent of Margaux and good balance, qualities needing time to show themselves. The 1970 and 1961 are very good. The 1975 has a classic Margaux nose and a lot of body, and the 1978 shows great promise. Owned by Alexis Lichine since 1952, Château Prieuré-Lichine, a Fourth Growth, is witness to what great care and personal pride can do in restoring a property. With 52 hectares now under vine, some of them are necessarily young. The 1978 in cask has elegance and tannin, a medium-weight wine. The 1977 has a nice blackcurrant flavour and is full of fruit. The 1970 shows an exotic, blackcurranty nose, and is rich and high in glycerine. The 1967 is perfect to drink now, twelve to thirteen years after its birth. The 1974 is well above average. Château Marquis-de-Terme, a Fourth Growth, has a high production but the wine is sound and ready to drink relatively quickly.

Château Le Tertre is owned by one of the well-known Gasqueton family, Médocains par excellence. The vineyard is in one parcel, which is unusual for the Margaux *appellation*, and there is a great deal of Cabernet Sauvignon. The wines thus have a great deal of body, but with the perfumed bouquet of Margaux.

Other châteaux of note are: Château Boyd-Cantenac, Château Marquis d'Alesme-Becker, Château Siran, Château La Tour de Mons, Château Bel-Air-Marquis d'Alegre, Château d'Angludet, Château Paveil-de-Luze, Château de Labégorce, Château l'Abbé-Gorsse-de-Gorsse, Château Labégorce-Zédé and Château Ferrière. Château Martinens is a *grand bourgeois* in the 1978 classification, and Château Tayac is a *cru bourgeois*. A further twenty-five or so châteaux regularly make wine, none in very large quantities. Margaux is an expensive *appellation*, and no château with that on its label is ever going to be cheap. But good Margaux can give really refined and elegant drinking, and should be savoured.

ST JULIEN

The wine of St Julien represents very precious liquid. It is the smallest of the four great communes in the Haut Médoc, with a high proportion of properties in the top category, especially among the Second, Third and Fourth Growths. The very best sites are along the river slopes, gravel over clay outcrops, and attract all the available sun. Further inland there is more variety in the soil, which can include sand and silicate. St Julien might be the easiest to appreciate at all stages of its development of the four great Haut Médoc *appellations*. The wines can have great suppleness and lusciousness of fruit, and a generous, distinguished, tempting scent. They can be gloriously glossy. Perhaps they do not always have the sheer finesse of top Margaux, or the backbone of top Pauillac – St Julien could be described as a stepping-stone between the two styles. All St Julien *appellation* wines are in the same commune.

Château Léoville-Las-Cases, a Second Growth, makes uncompromisingly excellent wine. The main part of the vineyard is a walled forty-hectare enclosure, aristocratic vine territory. The soil is such that the wines of Léoville-Las-Cases have weight combined with their St Julien fruit. There is also a high proportion of Cabernet Sauvignon, more reminiscent of neighbouring Pauillac than a classic St Julien vineyard make-up. The direction of the property has now passed to M. Michel Delon, whose wine-making intelligence and enormous attention to detail are second-to-none. Throughout this century, Léoville-Las-Cases has made magnificent wines, and with every vintage now this reputation is consolidated. There was, however, a transient period in the 1950s, following extensive replanting. The

(Above) Devatting at Château de Lamarque, Lamarque-au-Médoc
(Below) Last phase of racking during the 1979 vintage at Château Margaux
when the clarity of the wine is checked

great 1928 is still, in 1980, outshining all else from that year, with its characteristic power, but with much more fruit than some of the tannic, dry examples of the vintage. The late 1940s produced fine wines, and then the 1959 marked the end of the young-vine stage. The 1961 is enormous, still with a distance to go, but the 1962 is a glorious wine that is now showing all its paces. The 1966 is the other great wine of the 1960s, but very honourable wines were made in 1964 and 1967, the former perhaps the best wine of the vintage in the Médoc. The 1970 is a classic, but it should be emphasized that this wine really needs time to come out. In the context of their vintages, one cannot fault 1971, 1973, 1976 (superb), a 1977 with charm, and a full, rich 1978. The 1979 is right up with the First Growths. The 1975 is a classic in the making, distinguished, intense, with a concentration of fruit and body that takes it into the very front ranks. It is this combination of unctuous fruit, breed, and weight that singles out Léoville-Las-Cases as top Claret. Clos du Marquis is a second label of the property, often exceptional in good years.

Château Léoville-Poyferré, a Second Growth, was a real rival of Léoville-Las-Cases during the 1920s and 1930s, but recent vintages are strangely disappointing. Both 1928 and 1929 were rightly famous for this château. There was a perfectly lovely 1961, sweet and ripe, with that St Julien lusciousness of fruit. The 1966 had a classic blend of fruit and tannin, so typical of this year. The 1973 is most pleasant drinking without much more delay. Château Léoville-Barton is another of the fine collection of St Julien Second Growths and has been in the hands of the Barton family since 1826. The current long era of Ronald Barton has seen some very fine vintages make their appearance, and happily the wine is ably distributed internationally by his nephew, Anthony. In 1978, Léoville-Barton made a big, tannic wine, *charpenté*, and with almost a flavour of fennel. The 1977 very much follows the style of the property, but in lighter vein. The 1976 excels, with good youthful astringence for the year – much needed in a year of low acidity. The 1975 is a classic, with a *grand vin* nose, enormous flavour and tannin, a worthy successor to the glorious 1970, a great, glossy mouthful of wine, rich with enormous body. The 1961 has always showed as really fruity St Julien whenever I have seen it. In great years, one feels the Cabernet in these wines.

Château Gruaud-Larose is a large property, but that does not deter the Cordiers from running it with great attention to detail. A feature of all the Cordier properties is the presence of sixty-hectolitre wooden *cuves* or vats, alongside the normal 225-litre *barriques* or casks. The maturing wine spends time in both receptacles, and this is seen as especially beneficial in light years, when this type of vintage benefits from being part of a greater 'mass' of wine in a large *cuve* and can keep its fruit better. The wines are now generous and fruity, showing well comparatively young, but having the balance to last with grace. There is a high proportion of Cabernet Sauvignon, and approximately eighty hectares are under vine. The 1977 has charm and more 'extract' than most, showing the effect of its time in large vats. The 1976 is really rich, and the 1975 has great *race* and style, with a juicy acidity balancing the great tannin. The 1974 is to be complimented for the year, the 1973 is admirable, and the 1971 good. The 1970 is a beauty, classic and showing good acidity and fruit and the 1969 is one of the best of a mean bunch. The 1967 has an excellent reputation in this charmless year, the 1966 is to be savoured, and the 1961 is superlative.

It is always with immense pleasure that one writes about Château Ducru-Beaucaillou, as when a man of integrity and modesty succeeds in what he intends to do, it is a cause for celebration. M. Jean-Eugène Borie owns and lives at Ducru-Beaucaillou, and he and his family have put the property at the forefront of Bordeaux wine. The vineyard is situated in the best ridge, not far from the river, near Léoville-Las-Cases and Beychevelle. Ducru's wines are 'breed' exemplified, the opposite of 'coarse', elegant and silky-textured. They usually do not have the weight of Léoville-Las-Cases (the soil changes even between neighbouring properties), but are refined, 'classy', and distinguished. In blind tastings and in good vintages Ducru can rival the First Growths. The property built up its redoubtable modern reputation throughout the 1950s, with 1953 a star in the decade (perhaps tiring now), and triumphed in 1961. This decade included many fine vintages, and the next began with a magnificent 1970. The 1971 is delicious in the Médocain context (a vintage where St Emilion and Pomerol usually eclipsed the Médoc), and the 1975 has great finesse, with harmony and breed. The 1976 is elegant rather than big. The 1977 looks charming, the 1978 rich, full and well-structured, and the 1979 totally consistent.

Château Langoa-Barton, a Third Growth in the Barton stable, can produce some quite remarkable wines. The 1974 is probably the best I have seen in the Médoc, quite leaving the rather dull standard of the main body of wines, and showing a deep, aromatic nose, with a flavour somewhere between cassis and mint, rich and fruity. The 1971 is also quite exceptionally good, a lovely fruity, 'chewy' wine, and and the 1977 scores heavily and is remarkable drinking value. The 1975 and 1970 are on very good form, true to their respective vintages. Château Lagrange is a Third Growth that was for long solely distributed by one *négociant* and so was not seen everywhere. But now it is once again on the open market, and the excellent 1978 vintage heralds this new era. The wine always has body and backbone, perhaps a cross between St Julien and St Laurent style, and the 1978 certainly represents very good value. The owners, the Cendoya family, are Spanish. Château Branaire-Ducru is a Fourth Growth that would most certainly be classed higher in a new list. Owned by the dynamic M. Jean Tapie, the wine is often excitingly good, full of exotic flavours and nuances. Since 1952 when M. Tapie bought the property, the vineyard has been gradually replanted and innovations in the cellar have taken place. The wine is part-stored in new oak and part in old oak, and the final result is a judicious blend of the two. I always think Branaire has great individuality, with an almost chocolate flavour on the nose, great colour and depth, and strong body and richness. Branaire par excellence is the 1975 – a fantastic wine of enormous interest, a whole span of flavours, and a great future ahead of it. The 1979 and 1978 look outstanding, the 1976 is excellent, the 1971 is delicious, and the 1970 is a classic wine. The 1960s produced a very high standard throughout, with 1966 outstanding, although the poor vintages of 1963, 1965 and 1968 did not appear under the vintage label. A small part of the vineyard is on the plateau of St Laurent, but because of historic usage, all the wine is under the St Julien *appellation*.

Château Talbot is another Cordier property, this time a Fourth Growth. The same large oak vats have the same effect as at Gruaud-Larose. The attention to detail, and quality rather than excessive quantity for the area of vineyard, is followed throughout the properties. Larger than Gruaud-Larose, it can also afford to knock off some bunches about three weeks before the harvest, to give the remaining bunches more chance to retain real ripeness. Cordier also make a practice of removing the bottom leaves on the vine to let the sun get at the grapes for optimum sugar gain. Although a neighbour of Gruaud-Larose, the wines are always different when tasted side-by-side, with Talbot usually the lighter. The proportion of Cabernet Sauvignon is relatively high. The 1976 will make very supple drinking, and the 1975 will not take as much time to come round as some wines. 1973 is highly drinkable, and the 1970 has every quality in good proportions and is intensely perfumed. The 1959 and 1961 drink beautifully in 1981.

The production of Château Beychevelle is, luckily, large. Beychevelle makes supple, fruity wines that can come forward more quickly than comparable growths, but which offer a wonderful, ripe St Julien flavour. The 1961 is a great wine, so complex and scented, and showing beautifully from now on. 1962, 1964 and 1966 all really showed the very best that these respective years could offer, and this pattern has followed in the 1970s, picking out especially the 1971, 1975, 1976, 1978 and 1979. Amongst old vintages, the 1928 is still a great and pleasurable experience to drink. Beychevelle gives us wines that delight the nose and palate, and could be a wonderful introduction to top St Julien. Château St Pierre-Sevaistre and Château St Pierre-Bontemps, both Fourth Growths, are now one property. Château St Pierre is producing good standard, straightforward wine at the moment, but its classified status would be disputed nowadays by several properties which did not appear in the 1855 classification, notably Château Gloria. The 1975 St Pierre is, however, fruity and scented, and will make a most rewarding bottle of Bordeaux.

Château Gloria has been built up during the last thirty years, gradually acquiring very good parcels of land from classed growths nearby. M. Henri Martin is a man of immense experience, and he has established the solid reputation of Gloria on a very genuine basis. The wine is fleshy and fruity, and shows a very commendable consistency. One can safely say that, apart from the acknowledged poor vintages, Gloria has made good wines throughout the last twenty years. Personally, I find the 1978 and 1975 quite the best Glorias I have tasted, albeit at a very early stage. Château Peymartin is a subsidiary *marque* that is used for the product of the less mature vines. There is also Château Haut-Beychevelle Gloria, usually lighter than Gloria itself. Château du Glana was built up during the twentieth century and has recently been classed as a *grand bourgeois exceptionnel*. Production is high, but the wines can be good.

In St Julien, there is not the mass of lesser châteaux that one finds in, say, St Estèphe. Château Terry Gros Caillou is worth looking out for, but St Julien is not a happy hunting ground for a 'good little château wine'. One needs to save up for the glamorous beauties. M. Meffre, at Château du Glana, makes very good generic St Julien. However, there is one very welcome addition to the list of St Julien properties, and that is M. Jean-Eugène Borie's Château Lalande-Borie. He bought eighteen hectares of land from Château Lagrange in 1970, and with the 1979 vintage, supple and fruity, but with good backbone, we have much drinking pleasure ahead.

PAUILLAC

To some, Pauillac is the king of the Médoc. It can often be magisterial, powerful and definite. Its fame rests on its great growths, which carry the weight of responsibility with honour. There is immense variety between the top châteaux, but they all have good body and firmness when young. Sometimes they do not have the intense bouquet of the other communes in the Médoc, nor the sheer flowery elegance of, say, Margaux, but they have flesh and great character, and age to perfection. It is perhaps more of a crime to drink top Pauillac too young than any other wine. There is a great deal of gravel in Pauillac, sometimes mixed with heavier soil, especially further away from the Gironde, and there is good mineral content below. Pauillac embraces quite a few sub-communes, all with their small differences of micro-climate and soil.

CHATEAU LATOUR (Pauillac)

Latour is only just in the area of Pauillac on the southern limit, bordering St Julien. The vineyard occupies some of the choicest sites of the Médoc, on marvellous gravelly outcrops near the river front, but there are parcels further inland. The site to see is not so much a handsome château, but a very impressive and modern *cuverie*. Huge, tall stainless-steel fermenting vats tower over the human beings below and minute attention is paid to temperature. Enormous care is taken with the raw material, and the grapes themselves are checked for every flaw before being allowed into the *fouloir-égrappoir*. A very well-planned underground cellar ensures ideal conditions for the wine during its life in cask.

For three centuries Château Latour was the property of connected families. In 1962, majority control of Latour was sold to the English, predominantly to a company headed by Viscount Cowdray, with Harvey's of Bristol acquiring 25 per cent, and the last French owners, the Beaumonts, maintaining an interest. Harry Waugh, then of Harvey's, became a director, and has done a great deal for the reputation of Latour. He was instrumental in bringing in both M. Henri Martin and M. Jean-Paul Gardère, two very knowledgeable Girondins, steeped in experience and pride in their work, and Latour has benefited enormously from their attentions.

The total *encépagement* of the vineyard is 80 per cent Cabernet Sauvignon, 10 per cent Cabernet Franc and 10 per cent Merlot, which includes some Petit Verdot and Malbec. It is certainly true to say that the wines of Latour bear the character of Cabernet Sauvignon in as much as they are slow to mature, and have firm body, and astringency, when young. But it is not only the grape variety that marks the wine – after all, Mouton Rothschild has almost the same proportion of Cabernet Sauvignon, and the two wines do not taste at all alike, especially when mature and 'nosed' and tasted side-by-side. The differences in soil, distribution of vineyard parcels, drainage and micro-climate are much more important. Latour wines of good vintages are very deep coloured, big and powerful, tannic when young, but fleshy enough to give lovely texture and flavour when smoothed out with bottle age.

I have drunk Latour 1928 in both half-bottles and bottles during the latter part of the 1970s, and it seems to keep its character very constantly albeit a severe rather than soft wine, but lovely, deep and 'meaty'. The 1931 is an amazing example of what Latour can do in an 'off' year – in 1980 it had a beautiful, typically Latour nose, and intricacy of taste coupled with silky fruit. The 1944 is an unheralded delight. The 1955 is very great, far more distinguished than the run of the vintage, and looking superb in 1979. Latour made a great success of the light 1960, probably the best wine of the year, but it should have been drunk by 1980. The 1929, a fabled wine, is tiring now.

The 1961 is very top Claret, certainly in the league of the greatest one will see. In 1978, when I saw it twice, it had still not entirely opened out, but it is quite one of the most complete wines I have ever tasted, promising a long and glorious future. The 1962 is excellent and distinguished. The 1966 is very fine Latour indeed, and although still tannic, might well head the list of the vintage in the end. The 1968 is light and pleasant, and still drinking well in 1980 – I much prefer it to the 1969. The 1970 is tight and dumb at this 'adolescent' stage, but the fruit will come through. The 1973 is satiny and has style. The 1975 is absolutely superb – not so massive as Mouton, but with a better finish at this youthful stage. It has an immensely interesting, complex, cedar-wood nose (but this can always close up again temporarily in young Latour), with great grip on the finish. The 1976 has class but is still tannic and 'hidden', the 1977 is very light indeed, and the 1978 in cask looks like one of the 'greats' – a wine of fine structure and rich fruit.

The other wine of Latour, Les Forts de Latour, launched with the 1966 vintage, is made up of younger vines (generally speaking, those up to twelve years) and from the produce of certain sections of the property. Fermentation usually takes twelve days, whereas it is up to three weeks for Latour. In all cases, the individual blend of the year is the decision of M. Gardère, and it is based on sound experience. The 1970 is a great delight, the 1976 forward and delicious, and the 1978 the best Les Forts I have tasted – scented and fat in cask.

CHATEAU LAFITE-ROTHSCHILD (Pauillac)

Probably the most magic name in the whole of Bordeaux is right at the other end of Pauillac, on the northern limit, just across the Jalle du Breuil from St Estèphe and Château Cos d'Estournel. *Jalles* are streams in *bordelais* parlance, and much used as borders between the communes in the Gironde. Lafite became Rothschild property in 1868, when Baron James de Rothschild acquired it, and has passed down ever since. The shares are always divided in the family, with one member having particular responsibility for the running of the property. Between the end of the Second World War and 1977, this person was Baron Elie de Rothschild, but now Baron Eric de Rothschild has assumed responsibility.

Perhaps the previous regime was not the happiest time for Lafite, with some superb highlights, but too many disappointments. And with that potential, this was tragic, especially so for some who paid very high prices. In 1975 the ubiquitous Professeur Emile Peynaud was asked to advise at the château. In the same year, the extremely able M. Jean Crété, formerly *régisseur* of Château Léoville-Las-Cases, was appointed to the post of *régisseur* at Lafite. The results were immediate, even with the 1975 vintage, not controlled throughout by the new regime, but brought up by them. Since then, it would be difficult to find fault with anything. Much is made of the Merlot content of Lafite's wines, in an attempt to explain the extraordinary finesse of its great vintages. In fact, nowadays, an average of a sixth of the blend would be from the softer Merlot grape variety, with variations of anything from 10 to 24 per cent in recent years. Thus, the almost lyrical delicacy of flavour must be put down to other factors, by far the greatest of which being the unique *assemblage* of wines coming from forty different *parcelles* of land. These different plots of vines have different soil compositions, face in different directions, receive different doses of sunlight and experience different drainage conditions. When their produce is blended, the result can be fascinating complexity. The total land under vine is around ninety hectares. Fermentation is still in oak vats.

There has been a proliferation of tastings of old Lafites, and I shall not add to extensive notes on vintages that are largely academic. The 1940s produced a string of good Lafite years, 1945, 1947, 1948 and 1949, still superb. Some of the 1953s were wonderful, some were not, and this could be applied to the 1961s. 1962 was excellent at the château, but then one has to wait until 1970 for real First Growth Claret again. However, I do not think it as great as the 1975, and the 1976 may turn out in the top three of the vintage, an astoundingly distinguished wine. The 1977 has charm, 1978 looks lovely, and the 1979 is dense and powerful.

The second wine of Lafite was Carruades de Lafite but, to avoid confusion, this name was last used in 1967. There was an interim period when the property used an extremely discreet label 'Bordeaux Supérieur' with, in very small letters, 'Mise en bouteille au Château Lafite-Rothschild', but legislation changes stopped this. Now the label 'Moulin des Carruades' is used for the second wine of Lafite.

CHATEAU MOUTON-ROTHSCHILD (Pauillac)

Mouton was elevated to First Growth status in 1973, after long being at that level in price and quality. While one could have wished that this had been part of an overall reassessment, no one could grudge the need for Mouton's achievement to be recognized. Baron Philippe de Rothschild worked tirelessly for this honour, and the estate has been in his hands for nearly sixty years. The enhancement of Mouton has included the creation of a unique museum and the commission of famous artists to design the labels. Mouton is large, with about seventy-five hectares of vineyard, most of which is planted in Cabernet Sauvignon. The character is unmistakable, especially in comparative youth, and there is a deep, cassis-like concentration about the wine, broadening out as it gets older, but always retaining an intensity and almost exotic opulence about it. The nose is definite and impact-making, and the deep blackcurrant nature of its unadorned fruit can sometimes remind one of a forceful top Californian Cabernet Sauvignon, usually without quite that alcohol. No two

First Growths taste less alike than Mouton and Lafite, and yet their vineyards almost touch in parts – proof of the finely differing soil types in the Médoc.

I have been charmed by the delicious 1933, and impressed by the harder 1934. The 1947 and 1949 are superb, and the 1953 one of the most beautiful bottles of mellow, opulent Claret I have drunk. The 1959 is excellent, and the 1961 has everything, enormous cassis flavour, wonderful youthful acidity, a wine to go on and on, not austere and tough, but fleshy and full and really distinguished. 1962 and 1966 are very fine, but the rest of the 1960s provided some poor or mediocre wines, and it could be argued that a First Growth should make wines of a certain standard, even with difficult weather conditions. One could say the same for the 1970s – when Mouton hits the bull's eye, it is terrific, but there are perhaps too many misses. However, the 1970 is a classic, with excellent fruit and acidity balance, the 1975 is still very young and tannic (in 1979), the 1976 showed enormous promise, and the 1978 will surely be amongst the best. The 1979 is in the classic mould. Mouton Cadet is not related to the First Growth but is a branded Appellation Bordeaux Contrôlée.

Second Growths are: Château Pichon-Longueville, often known as Pichon Baron, now belongs to the Bouteiller family of Château Lanessan. Pichon Baron makes big, beefy Pauillac wines, needing time to attain a fine bouquet and softer texture. There were some fine wines in the 1940s and 1950s, but in the last twenty years the property has perhaps not had either the intimate care or the consistent distribution that goes with top-class wine. 1962 and 1966 were solid and good, but many vintages were on the dull side – the material was there, but perhaps the direction was lacking. However, the 1979 is excellent, *fin* and distinguished, which is most encouraging. Across the road is Château Pichon-Longueville-Lalande, owned by the Miailhe family. Pichon Lalande has a beautiful, custom-built underground cellar, and a skilful, young *régisseur*, M. Godin, trained by M. Paul Delon of Léoville-Las-Cases. M. Godin has firm views, great enthusiasm and talent, and he is making excellent wine at Pichon-Lalande. About a third of the vineyard lies in St Julien, but now the *assemblage* or final blend of the Grand Vin all has the right to the Pauillac *appellation*. There is no doubt that the St Julien contribution adds its share of finesse and fruit to the wine, with Pauillac backbone behind it. The vintages of the 1960s were admirable in the different conditions of the years, with 1961 outstanding, but the 1967 is a most successful example of this rather 'dry' year. Consistency in the 1970s is remarkable, with a run of vintages, 1975, 1976, 1977, 1978 and 1979 all showing what trained and devoted wine-making can make of nature's varying gifts. Pichon-Lalande is a wine to recommend unhesitatingly.

There is quite a jump in dimension between the First and Second Growths of Pauillac, and the Fourth (Duhart-Milon) and Fifths – there are no Third Growths in the commune. In 1964, the Lafite-Rothschilds bought Château Duhart-Milon, a geographically logical extension to their first property, and have done extensive replanting. Some of the *croupes* or gravelly ridges are really fine vineyard, and the scene is now set for some excellent wine. Rigorous selection is practised and the wine-making is as well done as it is now at Lafite – the 1978 is very good indeed, already quite supple when still in cask. There is the opportunity to make a 'second' wine when necessary (when only the best selections will go into the Grand Vin), and this will be named Moulin de Duhart.

In the 1855 classification, Château Pontet-Canet was the first of the many Pauillac Fifth Growths. The property belonged to the Cruse family of owners and *négociants* for over one hundred years, but in 1975 was sold to M. Guy Tesseron of Château Lafon-Rochet, who is married to a Cruse. There were some legendary Pontet-Canet wines, such as the 1929 (and I have enjoyed the 1917, the balanced 1948 and a 1953 which is still excellent), but the latter part of the Cruse ownership saw some dull wines. The yield is probably the largest of the classed growths. The vintages made under the new ownership are good, without being exciting. The 1978 is nice, but seemed a bit short, the 1977 seems good for young drinking, with a very Pontet-Canet nose mixed with new oak, but the 1975 is very good, showing the high percentage of Cabernet Sauvignon in the vineyard. Château Batailley is owned by the Borie family and very ably managed by a son-in-law, M. Emile Castéja. I do not see as many vintages as I would like, as often happens when a classed growth is sold uniquely through one *négociant* (in this case, Borie-Manoux), but the 1953, 1961, 1962 and 1966 were all very good indeed in their different ways, and the wines are big, firm Pauillacs, not with ultimate finesse, but good body and fruit. Château Haut-Batailley is another Borie property, but here M. Jean-Eugène Borie of Ducru-Beaucaillou is administrator and in charge of wine-making. The difference in style between Batailley and Haut-Batailley is as much due to the individual style of the wine-making as anything else, as both properties are 'inland' wines, towards the woods. The wines have elegance and charm at Haut-Batailley. The 1970 is a delicious example of these qualities. I liked the 1976 which was quite solid when in cask, and the 1978 is stylish. Cabernet Sauvignon in the vineyard is about 65 per cent.

Château Grand-Puy-Lacoste is another property that has now come under the wine-making control and part-ownership of Jean-Eugène Borie, and the beneficial effect is immediate. The other owner is the legendary M. Raymond Dupin, a man of great stature, much loved in Bordeaux circles, and a great gastronome. Grand-Puy-Lacoste is predominantly Cabernet Sauvignon in style (we may see this gradually change, to give more finesse), and tends to be big, straightforward Pauillac. The 1979 is absolutely excellent, and the 1978 will be very fine, with perfume and intensity. The area in production has increased to fifty-five hectares, as Léoville-Poyferré sold some of its Pauillac vineyard land to Grand-Puy-Lacoste. The 1953 was very good, not quite up to Grand-Puy-Ducasse when compared together in 1978. The 1960s produced very dependable wines, and the 1980s look very promising indeed. The wine of Château Grand-Puy-Ducasse has always been a personal favourite, with its glossy fruit and long-lasting flavour, and I am glad I have renewed acquaintance with its recent vintages, after a period of changing ownership and lack of availability on foreign markets. In 1971 it was sold by the Bouteiller family to a group in which the Bordeaux *négociants*, Mestrezat Preller, are involved. After tasting wines made under this new direction, I am extremely impressed. The 1978 has that lovely, thick purple colour of good Grand-Puy-Ducasse, an almost aromatic nose that reminded me of the wonderful 1961 and 1962 at the same time, masses of *fond* or depth, and very rich and interesting. The 1977 has the same style of nose, and exceptional fat and length for the year. The 1976 has real richness and ripeness, married with backbone, and the 1975 was still extremely tannic in 1979, barely out of the embryonic stage. Even the 1974, not a favourite vintage, had good fruit and acidity and was most charming. The vineyard is now thirty hectares.

Château Lynch-Bages has one of the wines that are easiest to recognize on the nose alone, as usually there is enormous intensity of Cabernet Sauvignon (in spite of only 65 per cent planted in the vineyard) and an overwhelming 'blackcurrant' flavour. It has wonderful, tempting fruit, and is nearly always excellent drinking. The 1978 looks fine, the 1977 is too Cabernet and drying (95 per cent Cabernet, as the Merlots went with the frost at the end of March that year), and the 1975 displays the best qualities of the year. Between then and 1970 I have not been very impressed, but the 1970 is a very good wine for the future. The 1962 is nice, and the 1961 has body and power, and a lovely cedary flavour, without being complex – beware the English bottlings of this vintage, incidentally. Lynch-Bages is owned by the Cazes family, now run by M. André Cazes and his son Jean-Michel. Château Lynch-

Moussas, a very small Fifth Growth, is a Castéja family property. The vineyard suffered considerably in the 1956 frosts, and new planting meant light wines for some years. The wines are, naturally, difficult to find, and perhaps difficult to place in the classified bracket. But the 1979 points to a big improvement. Château Mouton-Baronne-Philippe belongs to Baron Philippe de Rothschild of Mouton, and has been called Mouton d'Armailhacq, Mouton-Baron-Philippe from 1956, and Mouton-Baronne-Philippe from the 1975 vintage, in honour of Baron Philippe's late wife. There is considerably more Merlot here than at Mouton-Rothschild and, with the differences in vineyard site, the wine is softer and matures a little earlier than the First Growth, but the family resemblance is there. I do not see it very often, but the 1962 and 1966 are very good indeed, and the 1975 is big, straightforward, classic Pauillac. Château Clerc-Milon is under the same ownership.

Situated near Lynch-Bages, Château Croizet-Bages is owned by the Quie family. With a high proportion of Cabernet Franc, the wine has quite an assertive flavour, and maintains a good, consistent standard, usually maturing well. The 1960 had the most amazing deposit in bottle and the 1966 is very good. The classed growths of Pauillac end here, but immediately after them, and surpassing a few, must come Château La Couronne, another property ably managed by the indefatigable Jean-Eugène Borie. This is good fruity, balanced Pauillac wine – always a good buy. Châteaux Haut-Bages-Monpelou, Haut-Bages-Averous, Pibran and Fonbadet are also in evidence on foreign markets and are reliable. The Pauillac cooperative is called La Rose Pauillac, and it has a good reputation.

ST ESTEPHE

There is a wide variety of wine in St Estèphe, some great long-maturing ones, and some *petits vins* from the backwoods. There are fewer classified growths here than in Pauillac, St Julien or Margaux, but a large number of *bourgeois* growths which, when selected carefully, can give great pleasure. Perhaps St Estèphe, at the northern end of the Médoc, needs really ripe years to produce wines of top quality – then they can have richness, class and style, with a bouquet of great definition when mature. They can have marked flavour and individuality which, in lesser wines, can be a real *goût de terroir*. The fault with some St Estèphe wines is sometimes a lack of flesh, leaving rather a dry, thin wine. The wines need time to soften, and the heavier soil, with a little more clay and less gravel than elsewhere in the Haut-Médoc top three communes, leads to a robust character rather than finesse. Châteaux of note are: Château Cos d'Estournel, a Second Growth, has probably given me more pleasure than any other in St Estèphe. The wines tend to be the fattest and most fruity, in good years even opulent, with a firm backbone. The 1970s have seen a run of fine vintages, including 1970, 1971, 1973, 1975, 1976, and a much finer 1977 than the normal standard for the year, especially in St Estèphe, where the wines were particularly mean. The 1979 is very good. The 1961 is magnificent and rich, but the 1950s were on the whole better than the 1960s. Cos's (and the 's' is pronounced) return to making great wine thus can be dated from when the Prats family took over in 1971, and M. Bruno Prats put all his training and skill into the wine. The wonderful oriental exterior of the property's buildings does not, in fact, front a château at all, but masks the *chais*. The proportion of Merlot is high for the Médoc, which partly explains the rich, fruity taste of Cos. Maître d'Estournel is a nonvintage branded wine with only a Bordeaux *appellation*, which is slightly misleading. The quality, however, is good.

Château Montrose is the other St Estèphe Second Growth, owned by the Charmolüe family. It has a high amount of Cabernet Sauvignon which, when combined with the heavier soil, can make for rather hard wines in youth. The 1979 looks very good. The 1977 suffered from being almost entirely Cabernet, as the Merlots were, unusually for the property, hit by frost. However, the 1976 is a lovely wine, fruity and supple, and the 1970 is very good indeed, cedary, fruity and balanced. The 1966 is much harder, and needs to soften a bit more before the fruit comes out.

Château Calon-Ségur is a Third Growth of imposing history, part-owned and managed by a member of a very old Bordeaux family, M. Philippe Capbern-Gasqueton. There is a considerable amount of Cabernet Franc and Merlot in the vineyard, which contributes to its different character when compared to Montrose. The vineyard of sixty hectares is in one piece, almost surrounded by a wall, and the château is very handsome. The 1948 in 1977 was still lovely and rich, even improving all the time in the glass, a sure sign that a wine is still vigorous. I am afraid I have not been impressed by the 1961, but the 1970s have shown Calons of consistently high standard. 1970, 1971, 1973, 1975 and 1976 can all be thoroughly recommended, but the 1977 was very light. The 1979 looks most elegant. The one St Estèphe Fourth Growth is Château Lafon-Rochet. Now owned by M. Guy Tesseron, who did much replanting during the 1960s, the wine is mostly very reliable and good Claret, if a bit on the light side. The 1978 is light, elegant and fruity, the 1977 is another unsuccessful St Estèphe in this year, the 1976 is a bit thin, but flavourful, for early drinking, the 1975 combines fruit and tannin, even if it lacks individuality, and the 1974 is good for the year. St Estèphe finishes its classed growths with one Fifth Growth, Château Cos-Labory. Opposite Cos d'Estournel, the wine is good without being extraordinary. The 1975 has fruit, but also youthful, austere tannin and, as so often with this château, the character is really St Estèphe.

The top *bourgeois* growths of St Estèphe command attention. Château Phélan-Ségur is a *grand bourgeois exceptionnel*, usually robust and satisfying. They made a particularly good 1964, in that difficult year, but recent vintages are lighter. Château de Pez is very well run by M. Robert Dousson, who has been making wine there since 1959. There is a huge, very good 1970, a delicious 1971 for drinking over the next years, an outstanding, concentrated 1975, and a lovely 1976. M. Dousson told me he never adds in *vin de presse*. The large Château Meyney belongs to Cordier, and produces very well-made wines. I have admired the 1976, an excellent 1975, a delicious 1973, a really interesting, fat 1971, and a big, full 1970. The wines have a backbone of good St Estèphe *terroir*, and should be drunk when reasonably young to get the full benefit of their fruit.

Other wines to be recommended are Château Marbuzet, Château Pomys, Château Beau Site (belonging to the *négociants* Borie-Manoux), Château Tronquoy-Lalande, Château Haut-Marbuzet, Château Capbern (a London-bottled 1962, drunk in 1973, still had some way to go) and Château Les Ormes-de-Pez (owned by the Cazes of Lynch-Bages). There is a good cooperative which sells its wines as Marquis de Saint Estèphe, or under individual château names.

MOULIS AND LISTRAC

Although Moulis lies north-west of Margaux and inland, the wines have their own *appellation*, and generally combine firmness and fruit, without being in the top bracket of elegance. The best is Château Chasse-Spleen: the 1978 is good and very true to the *appellation*, the 1977 is pleasant and forward, the 1976 quite tannic, and the 1975 very concentrated and still a bit rough at four years old. Other châteaux to look out for are Château Poujeaux-Theil, the tongue-twisting Château Gressier-Grand-Poujeaux, Château Dutruch-Grand-Poujeaux, Château Maucaillou (owned by the *négociants* Dourthe), Château La Closerie, Château Brillette, Château Moulin à Vent and Château Pomeys. Listrac in some ways resembles Moulis, just to the south, and if there is one property today making classified-standard wine, (although a *grand bourgeois exceptionnel*), it is not because the soil is the very best gravel of the communes near the river (it has more clay and sand), but because of perfect wine management and clever composition of the vineyard. This château is Fourcas-Hosten, since 1972 owned by a group of French and Americans, headed by M. Bertrand de Rivoyre, the well-known *négociant* and owner. The wine-maker is M. Crèvecoeur, and the results of the new direction were immediate. Even the 1972 turned out much better than most classified growths and, with the exception of the 1974, every vintage has been really good of its kind. The body and fruit of Listrac have at last been married with some breed and finesse. Other châteaux are Fourcas-Dupré, with well-made wines and equally a *grand bourgeois exceptionnel*, Pierre-Bibian, Fonréaud, Lafon and Lestage. Château Clarke, which belongs to Baron Edmond de Rothschild, is now being replanted. The cooperative in Listrac produces very good wines under the name of Grand Listrac.

GRAVES

Graves is a huge area of vineyard land, stretching from the outskirts of Bordeaux southwards to round Langon, with two sweet white wine areas, like islands, lying within the region near its southern limit – Sauternes/Barsac, and Cérons. Graves is not an area (like the Médoc) with a high proportion of classified châteaux – it is more a large region of small proprietors, most of whom sell their wine to Bordeaux *négociants* who will blend it for generic red and white Graves. Obviously, small 'châteaux', or properties selling their wine under their own name, are increasing, but those of importance are few. The communes producing the best wines are those of Pessac and Talence, but unfortunately these are also the communes nearest Bordeaux, and precious vineyard land has been, and is being, eaten up by houses, railway lines and roads. Some of this ideal wine-producing land (Graves implies pebbles, and it is here where they go deepest) has gone for ever, and fighting for what remains is a constant battle. Léognan also produces top quality wines, and happily this is further south and further away from urban marauders, although they have left their mark here too. Graves, not so long ago, was producing one-third red wine to two-thirds white, and rather indifferent white at that, but the gap has narrowed considerably. The communes round Bordeaux concentrate on really fine red wines, with a tiny amount of absolutely exceptional dry white wine. Many important properties throughout the region make both a red and a white Graves.

The style of top red Graves is rich, even slightly spicy, with a faint earthiness in the finish. The nose can be fruit mixed with a whiff of tobacco, and the wines can have a firm grip to them when young, developing to a mass of subtle flavours when mature. Some of the top wines can seem quite Médocain in character, particularly La Mission Haut-Brion, but often there is something that is more exotic and less 'classic' about the flavour – now and again, a mature Graves can even, mysteriously, look like a Pomerol, which is strange when one considers that the *encépagement* is more Médoc than right bank of the Gironde.

The basic white wines have improved out of all recognition in recent years. White Graves can be fairly sweet or completely dry, which is slightly confusing for the consumer. There could be a decision to put dry wines in green bottles and sweet in clear white bottles, which would make things clearer, but organization for the merchants more difficult. The combination of sulphur and residual sugar in Graves white wines was certainly far from attractive, but now drastic measures are being taken to ensure healthier wines. White Bordeaux has always had to fight *pourriture grise*, or grey rot, leading directly to oxidation. Advice is given as to the best moment to pick and the best equipment to use, such as less fierce presses. The importance of reducing contact with the air is stressed as well as better selection and cold fermentation. Growers are encouraged to seek advice and have samples analysed at all stages of vinification, and the wine has become both fresher and more stable, with markedly less sulphur dioxide. The 1855 Classification of the Médoc contained one Graves wine, that of Château Haut-Brion, classed as a First Growth. In 1953, Graves made its own classification, which was confirmed in 1959.

CLASSIFIED RED WINES OF GRAVES

Haut-Brion (Pessac)
Bouscaut (Cadaujac)
Carbonnieux (Léognan)
Domaine de Chevalier (Léognan)
de Fieuzal (Léognan)
Haut-Bailly (Léognan)
La Mission-Haut-Brion (Pessac)

La Tour-Haut-Brion (Talence)
La Tour-Martillac (Martillac)
Malartic-Lagravière (Léognan)
Olivier (Léognan)
Pape-Clément (Pessac)
Smith-Haut-Lafitte (Martillac)

CLASSIFIED WHITE WINES OF GRAVES

Bouscaut (Cadaujac)
Carbonnieux (Léognan)
Domaine de Chevalier (Léognan)
Couhins (Villenave-d'Ornon)
La Tour-Martillac (Martillac)

Laville-Haut-Brion (Talence)
Malartic-Lagravière (Léognan)
Olivier (Léognan)
Haut-Brion* (Pessac)

*Château Haut-Brion Blanc did not present itself for inclusion in 1959, but was added to the list in 1960.

CHATEAU HAUT-BRION (Pessac)

Since 1935, Haut-Brion has had a very special link with the United States, as in that year Clarence Dillon bought the property. It is now owned by his son, Douglas Dillon, and the President of the domain is his daughter, the Duchesse de Mouchy. The vineyard sites at Haut-Brion are very good, often enabling them to vintage relatively early, as the grapes have already reached maturity.

The nose of Haut-Brion is of the most extraordinary intensity, really rich, somehow reminding me of damp earth and lush vegetation. The wine can be velvety and glycerine smooth, with great flavours opening out in the mouth. Apart from the 1921, I have only seen the vintages made after the Second World War, which seem gradually to be developing a lighter style, only really becoming apparent with the wines of the 1960s and 1970s. The 1953 was delicious, the 1955 good, and the 1959 a most honourable example. The 1961 is definitely more advanced than many other Second, Third and Fourth Growth wines. But a bottle drunk in 1978 had a wonderful, taut, 'tobacco' nose, and a taste of enormous richness and an incredible tobacco-wood flavour. There was great concentration, without overpowering tannin, excellent balance, and it 'packed a punch' – there was no doubt that this would last. 1962, 1964 and 1966 were all most successful, with the 1966 having a beautiful flavour, less opulent but tighter than La Mission, and terribly Graves.

The 1970s have, regrettably, seen some light, dull vintages – not worthy of a First Growth. The 1975, however, had all the breed of Haut-Brion, with a concentrated, rich taste and great Graves flavour, but it was very forward in development in 1979. The 1976 looks very pretty. Haut-Brion produces more wine on average than the other classed growths of the Graves. At its best it is a revelation of bouquet and taste. There is a very rarely seen white wine at Haut-Brion – I have only seen it on a few occasions. It tends to be lighter than Laville-Haut-Brion, fresh, but will round up with time. The grape variety combination is 50 per cent Sémillon and 50 per cent Sauvignon.

Only across the road from Haut-Brion lies Château La Mission Haut-Brion, but you could not get more different wines in the same area. In reality, the vines lie in both Pessac and Talence. The Woltner family bought La Mission in 1918, and for fifty years M. Henri Woltner contributed both love and immense skill to the property, founding its unassailable position today in the hierarchy of fine wine. M. Fernand Woltner also played a valuable part in this work, and his daughter and son-in-law, M. and Mme Francis Dewavrin, now administer the property carefully.

The gravelly soil of La Mission is really exceptional, sometimes descending fourteen metres in depth. There is approximately 65 per cent Cabernet Sauvignon, 10 per cent Cabernet Franc and 25 per cent Merlot. I have tasted a great many vintages of La Mission, and what a repertoire it is. In 1978 and 1979 the 1919 was gone, but the 1920 and 1921 were still there. The following were magnificent: 1924 (rich and excellent), 1926, 1928, 1929, 1933 (light, but excellent balance), 1934 (unbelievably elegant), 1936 (interesting and spicy), with a remarkable 1940. 1945 was big, 1947 is supple and harmonious, 1948 is very rich and still young, 1949 has real elegance, and the 1950 is terrific for the year. The 1952 is surprisingly good, and the 1953 very fine, but perhaps tiring a bit, the 1955 is classic Claret, the 1957 is very Graves, the 1958 fragrant and deep, and the 1959 has wonderful complexity.

The 1960s gave us some more outstanding wines: 1961 is one of the greatest in Bordeaux, intense, with a concentrated kernel to it and enormous lasting power. 1962 is most drinkable, 1964 is fruity for the year, 1965 was light but remarkable for the year, and 1966 a superlative wine, with a wonderful, fully-blown 'tobacco' nose, a really exotic taste and still great youth. The 1970 has great power and richness and is for the long-term, the 1971 is not one of my favourites, and the 1973 was caught by hail. The 1975 is very big indeed, with great fruit and a chewy, long finish. The 1974, 1976 (very deep and complex), and 1977 all make the most of their respective years, but the 1978 is absolutely magnificent.

Château La Tour Haut-Brion is the second wine made by the property, and as the selection for La Mission is becoming even stricter, the La Tour is looking more and more classy. It is a separate property, but there is movement between the two. I have liked the 1959, the 1962, 1964, 1966, 1971, 1974, a marvellous 1975, 1976, 1977 and a big, excellent 1978. On the whole, La Tour should be drunk earlier than La Mission.

Château Laville Haut-Brion is one of the most exciting dry white wines of the world. Its development in bottle to a great, unctuous richness, coupled with a panorama of tastes and subtleties, is a meal and a nourishment in itself, demanding your entire attention. It is tragic to think that many bottles must be drunk too young, remaining delicious, but lacking that great experience for the senses. The white wine area of La Mission, never big, has recently become a little smaller, as some old vines have recently been uprooted, and the construction of a railway line did not improve matters. The soil is slightly richer than the pure pebbly gravel for the reds. The grape variety mixture is about half Sauvignon and half Sémillon, but emphasis is moving towards the latter, as giving that wonderful richness and class.

Fermentation is, unusually, carried out in cask and not in vat, and this no doubt contributes to the final flavour. Only very basic filtration is used, thereby retaining maximum texture and taste in the wine. Bottling is relatively early – the 1978 was bottled in May 1979. The 1978 looks as if it will be very fine and beautifully balanced, the 1977 is more austere with more acidity, the 1976 is very ripe, very rich and lanolin smooth, the 1975 very youthful in 1979, but one sensed the alcohol and the need for time in bottle, and the 1971 and 1970 both very fine, with the 1971 perhaps the more elegant. The 1969 is very smooth, the 1967 needs time, the 1966 is lovely, the 1962 exceptionally beautiful, with that lovely lemony Graves nose, glorious balance and elegance, with 1961 much more concentrated and seemingly alcoholic. In 1979, the 1960 was full, round, and only *just* beginning to show age.

Château Pape-Clement is, to me, Graves *par excellence* – its bouquet and flavour are textbook red Graves, full, earthy rich, with that strange, almost exotic tobacco overtone. M. Montagne had completely to resurrect the property after he bought it in 1939, and the 1955 is the first great vintage here after its revival, still lovely in 1979. However, the 1950 has remained youthful and blackcurranty, and I have been very impressed by the 1962, the 1964 (quite one of the best Bordeaux wines of the year) and the 1966. The 1961 is outstanding, with great interest and spiciness, already drinking well in 1978. Good wine-making has continued throughout the 1970s, and if one wants to try archetypal top Graves, this is the property to sample.

Domaine de Chevalier is in more rural Léognan, the commune that produces the greatest number of fine red and white Graves in the whole *appellation contrôlée* area. It is modest in appearance, but produces a small amount of aristocratic wine. The Ricard family, the current owners, have long connections with the domain, and manage it with minute care. When the wines are not from excessively tannic years, Domaine de Chevalier matures relatively quickly, and goes for breed and style rather than sheer power. There is 30 per cent Merlot in the vineyard, but this is not unusual for the Graves, where the proportion is usually slightly higher than in, say, Pauillac. Delicacy and softness are the keywords here, especially in the old Domaine de Chevalier red wines; the few I have tasted, in the 1920s, were ethereal. Frost damage in 1945 caused some replanting, and the 1953 was the first top vintage after this setback. There really have been few errors since then, and I particularly remember the 1964 and 1966 as showing the elegance of the property. The 1973 is delicious drinking at six years old, with the 1970 and 1975 more long term and exceptionally promising. The 1977 was a bit marked by oak, but the 1978 looks outstanding, a very big wine. The 1976 is excellent. The white Domaine de Chevalier is made much in the same way as Laville Haut-Brion, with the very big differences of bottling time – Domaine de Chevalier bottles about a year later than at Laville. The quantity is about half that of Laville, and so, unfortunately, one does not see it at all often. It is definitely lighter than Laville. The intense bouquet and fruity, yet taut, flavour need time to open out. There is more evidence of oak here than at Laville, where all the maturation is essentially in bottle. The 1976 and 1970 are marvellous. The 1979 shows superbly at a very early stage. Château Haut-Bailly is hidden away in the backwoods of Léognan, but the gravelly soil is ideal for red wine. It is owned by the Sanders family, who are Belgian. The 1961 is, justifiably, famous, and the 1960s were successful for the château, which continued to make rich wines with a true Graves flavour about them. The 1970s were less consistent, and only the 1975 and the superb 1979 were of the class that Haut-Bailly should attain.

I have some very happy drinking memories of Château Malartic-Lagravière, as one of my first Graves experiences, although the wines tend to be on the hard, austere side. Both red and white wines are made, but only a small amount of the latter. The 1955 red has stood the test of time very well. The 1970s have produced very good wines in the good vintages, perhaps less hard than in the past; the 1979 looks good. The 1978 has great individuality, as indeed has the white 1978, an extremely interesting wine. It has an intriguing, slightly spicy nose, with a great freshness in the mouth and an almost cinnamon flavour. Normally, it is not as rich as Laville and needs a little less time to reach full maturity, but there is great elegance and breed in it. The 1979 white is equally well-made. Château Carbonnieux is a very large property in Léognan, producing good red and white wines, the latter predominating in terms of output. The white is predominantly Sauvignon, and tends to be light and straightforward, rather than rich and complex. This is in a dry, light, crisp style, for relatively early drinking, but this is the good commercial white wine that M. Perrin and his son are looking for. The red wine is good, without being exciting – a bit one-dimensional, but with some regional Graves 'earthiness', which gives character. Château Olivier is controlled by the *négociants* Eschenauer, and white wine production is about eight times that of red. It has to be said that the château itself is more interesting than the white wine (I have never seen the red), which is sound, commercial white Graves, inclined to have too much sulphur showing through. The red of Château de Fieuzal is classified, but the white is not. The wines are well-made, going for lightness and elegance.

Château Larrivet-Haut-Brion is also in Léognan, producing dependable red and white wines – the red 1966 is still young, and will develop well. Château La Louvière makes red and white wines, but currently the white wines appear much better than their stablemate. I have much admired the 1970 and 1971 whites, and the wines of 1974 through to 1978 are all really well-made and quite excellent in their different ways. I liked the red 1970, but since then have found some off-flavours and tannin imbalance that did not enchant. M. André Lurton makes the wine here, as well as at the small Château Neuf. Château Le Pape makes good wine.

The commune of Martillac has some good properties, with the wines not quite in the top rank. Château Smith-Haut-Lafitte is owned by Eschenauer – the red is classified, but the white is not, but then production of white only started in the late 1960s. The red wines tend to be solid and to age quite well, without having much breed. The 1959 was still young in 1972, the 1962 was very tannic, but rich and earthy in 1974, and the 1967 combined fruit and tannin when drunk at the same time. Château La Tour-Martillac is owned by the Kressmann family, and both red and white wines are classified – white wine production is very small. The 1978 red La Tour-Martillac looks good, although I was not impressed by the 1976. The white wine, from very old vines, is most interesting, when you can get it. Château La Garde is owned by Eschenauer, and is better known for its red wine. Château Ferran, distributed by Dourthe, should be mentioned, and I have heard good reports of Domaine La Solitude.

At Villenave d'Ornon, Château Couhins makes only white wines. M. André Lurton also manages this property, and now the wine is lighter and earlier maturing than in the past. Château Baret makes red and white wine, both good but the white especially so. I would also highly recommend Château Pontac-Monplaisir – the white wine has real distinction. Château Graville-Lacoste in Pujols also makes very good dry white wine.

The commune of Cadaujac possesses Château Bouscaut, very well-known in the United States due to its American ownership for more than a decade. However, in 1980 this passed to M. Lucien Lurton. The style of both red and white wines is fresh and fruity, rather than distinguished, but Bouscaut is nevertheless a good bottle. At St-Morillon, there is the excellent dry white Graves of Château Piron. In the commune of Portets, Château de Portets and Château Rahoul are interesting, particularly the latter, now under Australian ownership and undergoing great changes in wine-making techniques, especially very cold, slow fermentations. Both make red and white wine. I have also liked Château Le Tuquet in Beautiran and Château La Tuilerie in Illats. Château Magence in St-Pierre-de-Mons makes a fair amount of good red and white wine; the white is really pleasant and reliable, very Sauvignon in character. Château Archambeau at Illats deserves special mention. Dr Jean Dubourdieu here makes excellent dry white Graves, perfumed and flowery. Illats is, of course, within the *appellation contrôlée* area of Cérons, itself an enclave in the larger area of Graves. Proprietors within the communes of Cérons, Illats and Podensac call their wines Cérons, Graves Supérieures or Graves for white wines, and Graves for red. In reality, owners do not keep changing, but opt for one of the white *appellations* according to what type of wine they are making – Cérons if it is sweet (weather permitting), and Graves or Graves Supérieures if it is dry. The minimum alcoholic level for Graves is 11 per cent and for Graves Supérieures 12 per cent – the latter would be more likely to have a small amount of residual sugar. Cérons itself is indistinguishable from Barsac, although lacking its top properties.

SAUTERNES AND BARSAC

Sweet white wines can be wonderful or dreadful, just like red wines, only perhaps more so. Some of the greatest in the world come from Sauternes and Barsac, and if you have never appreciated them to the full, it is probably because they were not drunk at the right time or with the right things. Barsac and Sauternes are small, adjoining areas and *appellations* within the larger *appellation* of Graves, at the southern end of the latter, near the town of Langon and on the left bank of the Garonne. There are five communes entitled to the *appellation* of Sauternes: Sauternes, Barsac, Preignac, Bommes and Fargues. If you have a property in Barsac, you may call it 'Sauternes' but not vice-versa, and there is even provision for the description 'Sauternes-Barsac'. Occasionally, Haut Sauternes or Haut Barsac can be seen, but this does not mean that the wine is any 'higher' than the others – it is just a relic of the past. Barsac is the flattest of the communes, and the soil is gravel mixed with clay or sand. The other four communes are hillier, with more pebble, gravel and calcareous soil. Bommes and Sauternes have some beautifully exposed, pebbly hills, ideal for catching maximum sun in the long autumns.

Classic Sauternes and Barsac is not just sweet, luscious white wine – it should have the unique smell and taste of *pourriture noble* – noble rot or *Botrytis cinerea*. Unfortunately, this natural phenomenon does not happen every year, and a simply sweet wine from this area without noble rot is not particularly special. Equally unfortunately, it is still made and sold as Sauternes and Barsac, when to my mind, it would be better to 'cut one's losses' and make a dry or dryish 'Graves', never using additional sugar. (At the moment, a dry white wine from this area can only carry the cheap *appellation* Bordeaux Blanc.) This is quite logical, since Sauternes and Barsac are within the Graves area, there is a good, strong market for well-made white wine, more quantity could be made in this way, and economically it would be much more sensible for the owner. Then, all Sauternes and Barsac made would have a chance of being as great as its potential even if it could not be made every year. The weather conditions of heat and humidity in the autumn that give noble rot, and very small yields, are not conducive to healthy economics in wine-making. Some owners have given up, and others have compromised with quality. Some finance their Sauternes and Barsac with other ventures, which is all too precarious. It must always be remembered that *Botrytis* or rot is disastrous in other areas, and it is only when it attacks *ripe grapes* that the right conditions prevail for making classic top sweet white Bordeaux. This amazing fungus or mould can run rampant in humid weather, but if it does not start until the grapes are already full of sugar and ripe, it imparts an intoxicating flavour and smell to the resultant wine. The fungus gradually attacks the grape skin, finally piercing it, evaporating the water in the grape, and thereby increasing the sugar ratio. The grape shrivels (and looks most unappetizing), and the sugar concentrates.

All this produces wines of unctious body, immense flavour, with essence-like aromas and concentration. But, even if nature is kind, minute care has to be given to the picking to obtain grapes at the optimum point – in the top vineyards, they go through the vineyard again and again, hardly an inexpensive process. Vinification problems are immense, with high sugar content often demanding a considerable amount of sulphur, although with the high alcohol of Sauternes, this is not as fragile a product as *Beerenauslese* and *Trockenbeerenauslese*. The grapes themselves must be in perfect condition when picking takes place, and it is also important that they are not overripe – a must should be somewhere between 20° and 22° Baumé

for the fermented wine to stop naturally at 13.5 per cent or 14 per cent leaving sugar of about 5° Baumé. This is balanced, luscious Sauternes. Oxidation is an ever-present problem in wines that are kept for some years in wood, but with the exception of Yquem, this period is generally down now to between eighteen months and two years (a few even less), and the sheer alcohol of a Sauternes is an additional protection against oxidation. The grape varieties permitted are Sémillon, Sauvignon and Muscadelle, but the best vineyards concentrate on the first two, as Muscadelle can have a slightly vulgar taste. Sémillon is the key grape variety in Sauternes and Barsac, and its wonderful style, fat and lusciousness when really ripe and attacked by *pourriture noble* is one of the world's great tastes. Top wine from a good year needs time to marry all these qualities – an optimum point for drinking would probably be between twenty and thirty years, with some pleasant experiences on either side of this. The wines from hot, really concentrated years (1945, 1961) tend to darken very early, but this looks a healthy amber-brown colour.

In 1855, there was a classification of the best properties of Sauternes and Barsac. As there have been important changes since then, both in the names of châteaux and in sub-divisions, the full table of 1855 is given below, with the current names of the classified châteaux beside it.

1855 Classification of Sauternes and Barsac

Name of classed growth in 1855	Name of classed growth today	Name of classed growth in 1855	Name of classed growth today
SUPERIOR GROWTH		**SECOND GROWTHS**	
Yquem (Sauternes)	d'Yquem	Mirat (Barsac)	Myrat
FIRST GROWTHS		Doisy (Barsac)	Doisy-Daëne, Doisy-Védrines and Doisy-Dubroca
Latour-Blanche (Bommes)	La Tour-Blanche		
Peyraguey (Bommes)	Lafaurie-Peyraguey, Clos-Haut-Peyraguey	Pexoto (Bommes)	Part of Rabaud-Promis
		d'Arche (Sauternes)	d'Arche
		Filhot (Sauternes)	Filhot
Vigneau (Bommes)	Rayne-Vigneau	Broustet-Nérac (Barsac)	Broustet and Nairac
Suduiraut (Preignac)	Suduiraut		
Coutet (Barsac)	Coutet	Caillou (Barsac)	Caillou
Climens (Barsac)	Climens	Suau (Barsac)	Suau
Bayle (Sauternes)	Guiraud	de Malle (Preignac)	de Malle
Rieussec (Sauternes)*	Rieussec	Romer (Preignac)†	Romer and Romer du Hayot
Rabeaud (Bommes)	Sigalas-Rabaud, Rabaud-Promis	Lamothe (Sauternes)	Lamothe and Lamothe-Bergey

*The château of Rieussec is in the commune of Fargues.
†The château of Romer is in the commune of Fargues.

CHATEAU YQUEM (Sauternes)

Château Yquem stands on its own, in both price and quality, and sets the standards for everyone else. Of course, being able to command high prices brings with it the possibility of affording extra care and nurturing of the wine, but the property first had to attain this position at the summit before being able to rise significantly above the rest when it came to selling. Here, Yquem was helped by a wonderful situation of sloping vineyards, and the fact that the same family, the Lur-Saluces, has owned the property since 1785. The present owner, Comte Alexandre de Lur-Saluces,

The Château of Gevrey-Chambertin showing a typical Burgundian wall enclosure with the slope of the Côte de Nuits in the background

directs with aplomb and flair. Only about ninety hectares of vineyard are used for production, although more is entitled to the *appellation*, and the final amount of wine made is about eighty *tonneaux* on average, more than three times less than a top red-wine producing château in the Médoc would be producing.

The grape variety proportions at Yquem are 80 per cent Sémillon and 20 per cent Sauvignon. Enormous care is taken at all stages, from rigorous pruning and the use of organic manure in the vineyard, to picking in ten or eleven stages, often until late November. This carries its own risks, and in 1964 the whole crop was lost through autumn rain. The grapes are first crushed and then undergo three pressings – the immensely concentrated must is then fermented in new oak casks. Yquem still stands by its principle of keeping the wine three years in cask before bottling, which involves immense topping up and racking work.

Great Yquems were 1921, 1928 and 1937, but in the 1980s it is safe to say that their greatest moments are past, albeit remaining splendid. The 1945 is great Yquem, in the style of the 1961 – both are highly coloured, with slightly volatile noses and huge concentration. The high alcohol is evident in both, but the flavour of the 1961 is lighter and has more balance. The 1955 is big, with a luscious nose, but not the elegance of the best years; in 1980 it was still splendid drinking, but just beginning to go 'raisiny'. The 1959 is very volatile, but the 1962 has lovely balance and elegance. 1963 and 1968 were disasters, and should never have appeared under the name of Yquem – a trap for the uninitiated, which is hardly fair at very high prices. The 1967 is the ultimate in finesse married to luscious fruit, and will last for many a day. The 1970 is big and deep, but the 1971 is superb, with the elegance of 1967 but its own character. The 1975 is way out on its own at the top of this massive, alcoholic, overripe vintage – a wine of sheer class and great, tight flavour, with exotic over-tones. Yquem also sometimes makes a dryish white wine, Ygrec. Made from 50 per cent Sémillon and 50 per cent Sauvignon, the nose is unctuous and resembles the 'true' Yquem, but the taste is a surprise, full but dry.

First Growths:

Château La-Tour-Blanche is now under the auspices of the Ministry of Agriculture, and is run as a school for viticulture and vinification. As such, there is continual experimentation, and this has sometimes perhaps not led to consistent quality. Sémillon predominates, and the wine is good rather than distinguished. The attractive château and vineyard of Lafaurie-Peyraguey are now owned by the important *négociants*, Cordier. The vineyard is composed of three-quarters Sémillon, a quarter Sauvignon, and the wine spends half its time before bottling in cask, half in vat. The whole style is much lighter than Lafaurie-Peyraguey of yore, and many of the vintages bear no trace of botrytis characteristics. The 1970 was pleasant but no more, and the 1975 immensely sweet without seeming to have balancing acidity or real style. However, I have been lucky enough to taste some superb older vintages, amongst them (in 1978) the 1922, which had a very dark colour and not a great deal of nose, but immense fruit in the mouth. The taste was like a bouquet of flowers, and the marvellous acidity, after all this time, kept the wine in perfect condition with terrific balance. In 1977, I also greatly admired the 1928, 1929, 1945 and 1947 – some of which were better than their counterparts at Yquem at the same stage. At Clos-Haut-Peyraguey production is small, predominantly Sémillon, and the wine is bottled after two years, with time in cask and vat beforehand. It is not often seen, but now and again can produce very pleasant surprises. Château Rayne-Vigneau is now owned by a group and, although the site is one of the best in the whole region, wines are not being made to their true potential here. It is a very large estate, producing a fair amount of wine – an aspect of the management that shows in the style of the end product. 1976 is, however, quite excellent, a true Sauternes, luscious, but with lovely acidity – not heavy, but balanced. The 1975 was too alcoholic, and did not seem to have that magic *pourriture noble* nose. I have been fortunate enough to taste a still sweet and interesting 1900, and some halves of the 1923, which is still excellent and harmonious – unlike some 1921s which, because of the great heat, coloured up tremendously and eventually lost some of their sweetness through the effects of volatile acidity. There is also some dry Raynesec.

Château Suduiraut is capable of making some of the very greatest wines of Sauternes, and if rigorous selection and care continue, we will have some splendid drinking ahead of us. The vineyard is almost entirely Sémillon. The 1970s brought a few lapses – notably the 1971 and the 1975, which were not as good as they should be, when judged at the highest level. The 1970 is splendid, and the 1976 is quite excellent. I like the elegant 1969, the stylish 1967 and 1962, and the bigger 1961. The 1959 is absolutely classic and rich. The 1899 was quite outstanding and amazingly youthful, sweet and gentle in 1979. Château Coutet is always 'twinned' with the other great Barsac property, Climens, and they vie with each other to top the vintage in the commune. Coutet 1975 is exceptionally big, rich without being really luscious (anyway, in youth), but with lovely length and good balance. The 1973 has a nose of apples and peaches, with a surprising amount of concentration on the middle palate – most successful for the year. 1962 and 1971 are outstanding in their years. Château Climens is making superlative wine at the moment, combining finesse with luscious fruit. M. Lucien Lurton now owns Climens – perhaps the losses of some years at Climens are offset by his ownership of Château Brane-Cantenac. Mme Janin is the experienced *régisseur*. The *encépagement* is Sémillon, on chalky soil, and the wines are generally bottled at two and a half years after maturation in cask. I remember the 1962 with great pleasure, and the 1970s have given some classic Climens: a 1971 with some way to go, but an amazing finish, with a great opening out of flavours and esters; a wonderfully elegant 1975, with real *pourriture noble* character, perfect weight and balance; and a 1976 of distinction.

Château Guiraud is a very large property, now also making dry white wine called Pavillon Sec and some red Pavillon Rouge. However, Guiraud is capable of making really good Sauternes, even if I have sometimes found it clumsy – such as with the 1975, which was heavy and alcoholic. The 1976 looks much more balanced. I have very much liked the 1966, but found the 1967 completely dried out. Château Rieussec is actually in Fargues, but as the vineyards are mostly in Sauternes, this is how the 1855 classification settled it. It always used to be amongst the 'drier' of the top Sauternes, but since new ownership in 1971, there is a certain overripeness and lack of balance, and the elegance seems to have been sacrificed. The 1975 at first seemed to have recaptured this, but in 1979 it was dark and ageing fast. The 1976, also, is much too dark at this early stage, too advanced, with some lovely lusciousness, but without balancing acidity. The 1970 has fruit, and is relatively much less overblown – it needs time. The 1969 combines elegance with richness. Château Sigalas-Rabaud is predominantly Sémillon, and the wine matures in cask and vat. The 1975 is an excellent wine, balanced and stylish.

The list of the *deuxième crus classés* includes the good, the bad, and the totally disappeared – sadly, Château Myrat has been uprooted. However, the trio of Doisy châteaux are very much in existence. Doisy-Daëne, owned by the talented M. Pierre Dubourdieu, is renowned both for its sweet white Barsac and for its stylish dry white wine. Doisy-Védrines is administered by M. Pierre Castéja and is a fuller Barsac than Doisy-Daëne, resulting from more 'traditional' methods of sweet white wine-making. There is also a small amount of red Bordeaux Supérieur made, Château Latour-Védrines, a predominantly Merlot wine. Château Doisy-Dubroca is small, but under M. Lucien Lurton it is now producing very fine wines.

Château d'Arche in Sauternes can be rich and full, but a bit clumsy – Château d'Arche-Lafaurie is its second wine. Château Filhot in Sauternes produces carefully made wine, not quite in the top class. The 1975 is immensely fragrant, delicious and soft, while the 1976 has the same floweriness, sweetness – both have a hint of tar on the finish. But the sheer elegance of past years is missing.

There are four more *deuxième crus* in Barsac: Châteaux Broustet, Nairac, Suau and Caillou. Broustet's 1975 was good in this second category. Château Nairac, under Mr Tom Heeter, is predominantly Sémillon, and going from strength to strength; the 1975 is excellent, lighter than most. Château Caillou is not sold much to the trade. Château de Malle in Preignac is an enchantingly beautiful property, and the Comte Pierre de Bournazel is making his wines with immense attention to detail. The wines are not really rich and luscious, but intriguing and elegant. There is also a good, lightish red wine called Château de Cardaillan, and a dry white Sauvignon wine, Chevalier de Malle – the red has the Graves *appellation contrôlée* as the vineyards are in the commune of Toulenne. There are, in fact, two Châteaux Romers, of which the most important is now known as Château Romer du Hayot. The 1976 is exceptionally good and elegant. There is also Château Lamothe and Château Lamothe-Bergey. Much property wine in Sauternes and Barsac finds its way into *négociants'* generic blends. But a few châteaux are known individually. I liked the 1975 of Château Haut-Bommes and Château Saint-Amand – the latter has another wine, Château de La Chartreuse, with a very good 1971. In Barsac, there is the very good Château Liot, and Château Cantegril and Château Piada are reliable. Château Bastor-Lamontagne in Preignac, and Château Raymond-Lafon (owned by M. Meslier, the manager at nearby Yquem) should also be mentioned. Château du Mayne and Château Roumieu, both in Barsac, are usually good buys.

STE-CROIX-DU-MONT AND LOUPIAC

These are very small *appellations*, just across the river Garonne from Barsac and Sauternes. The lovely, hilly countryside is worth a lingering visit, even if you do not like sweet white wines. The wines are very similar to Sauternes and Barsac, with lusciousness in years of noble rot, and a sugary, cloying quality in poor years. The best are excellent, and these would include Domaine de Fonthenille, Châteaux Ricaud and Loupiac-Gaudiet in Loupiac, and Loubens, Terfort and de Tastes in Ste-Croix-du-Mont. Côtes du Bordeaux St Macaire is a diminishing *appellation*, next door to Ste-Croix-du-Mont. The wines are white and semi-sweet, often suffering from liberal doses of sulphur dioxide.

CERONS

Cérons is next door to Sauternes and Barsac, on the same side of the river. Here again, the wines resemble those of their neighbour, and good value can be found here – however, the sweet wines are not classy, and probably do not have the marked character of the best Ste-Croix-du-Mont and Loupiac wines. But Cérons has the luck of being able to make dry white wines under the label of Graves, and this gives them more commercial advantage.

PREMIERES COTES DE BORDEAUX

This is a large *appellation* on the right bank of the Garonne, producing both red and white wines. The red wines are at their nicest drunk young when they can be very quaffable indeed. Those sweet wines produced in the communes closest to Loupiac can have the name Cadillac added to the *appellation*, but this is rarely used nowadays. Most of the whites are medium-sweet to sweet, and form a good base of reasonable wine for the Bordeaux trade.

ENTRE-DEUX-MERS

This is a huge *appellation*, covering only white wines. The red wines produced in the area become Bordeaux or Bordeaux Supérieur. During the 1970s, Entre-Deux-Mers replied to the demand for dry white wine, and concentrated more on Sauvignon-based, light, fresh wines, made by modern methods. Some of these are extremely palatable, especially when there is some Sémillon, and perhaps Ugni Blanc, in the blend. The wines are bottled young and fermented cold in the best establishments – cooperatives are important here, and the brand name of La Gamage is one to look for. Now it is not possible to find sweetish Entre-Deux-Mers, as in the past, because a maximum residual sugar limit was set for the *appellation*. Entre-Deux-Mers is now the second largest *appellation* for white wine, after Bordeaux Blanc itself, and it must be admitted that the quality of the individual wine being tasted is more important than the difference between the *appellations*. This applies also to the Bordeaux Rouge produced here and elsewhere, in that a well-made wine with this simple *appellation* can be better than a wine carrying a classier title.

To the north of Entre-Deux-Mers there is the tiny *appellation* of Graves de Vayres, producing both red and white wines. I have liked Château Cantelaudette here. In the north-east corner of Entre-Deux-Mers there is another small *appellation*, Sainte-Foy-Bordeaux. The whites are better known, being traditionally sweet from Sémillon, Sauvignon and Muscadelle, but the Sauvignon and dry wines are now taking over. The reds are mostly Cabernet and Merlot mixtures.

ST EMILION

If Médoc wines can sometimes be haughty, austere and aristocratic, St Emilion wines are more attainable, more warm and welcoming. The best of them have immense breed, tempered with luscious accessibility and generous fruitiness. Lesser wines are giving from the start, a seductive invitation to Claret drinking. We are in quite different land in St Emilion. There are no huge, imposing châteaux – the properties are more country manor-houses or even farms. Now, St Emilion trade has prospered to a point where the wines are not channelled through Bordeaux – the bustling town of Libourne serves them just as well.

The range of wines is very wide indeed. Firstly, there are two distinct groups of wine within the St Emilion *appellation* itself – the Côtes area around the beautiful old town, and the Graves area on the plateau bordering Pomerol. Both soil and site differ, the Côtes vineyards naturally enjoying some kind of slope, with the plateau Graves exactly what it says. As well as the gravel here, there are pockets of much more sandy soil, while the Côtes vineyards are a mixture of silica, clay and chalk. In both areas every spare centimetre is covered with vines. The rocky nature of the land round the town has provided some magnificent natural cellars, like rabbit warrens in the hillside. Archetypal Côtes wines are Ausone, Magdelaine, Belair and La Gaffelière, with great scent, breed and style, intense but also delicate when mature. Archetypal Graves wines are Cheval Blanc, Figeac, and the Figeac 'family' – bigger, fuller, richer. The soil differences account for differences in weight, flavour and character, with fascinating nuances within each area.

Eight communes, including that of St Emilion itself, enjoy the right to call their wine St Emilion *appellation contrôlée*. There are also a few outlying communes, now reduced to four, who have the right to add the magic words 'St Emilion' to their name. Thus we have: Lussac-St Emilion; Montagne-St Emilion; St Georges-St Emilion; and Puisseguin-St Emilion. However, it must be admitted that, in the main, the wines from the other seven communes entitled to the St Emilion label are really no better than the 'satellite' communes – the *appellation* should really reflect the more accurate picture of the wines of the commune of St Emilion itself, and the rest. Tasting certainly makes this division. On the whole, these wines are delicious when drunk relatively young, generous and fruity and without much complication.

In St Emilion, the Merlot and Cabernet Franc grapes predominate, and there is also some Malbec – the Cabernet Franc is traditionally called the Bouchet here and the Malbec, the Pressac. Cabernet Sauvignon does not do so well on this side of the river, and there are ripening problems mostly due to colder soil. Its relative absence makes for less tannin in the wine, but it is wrong to assume that for this reason the top St Emilions do not last as well as top Médocs. The same rule applies here as elsewhere – if there are class and balance, wines live to great ages, provided they are nurtured at all stages of their life. But Merlot contributes a full character, a richness and seeming softness, and a respectable amount of alcohol – all of which serve to make good St Emilions seem rounder, sooner, than Médocs. Merlot ripens before Cabernet Sauvignon, and thus the vintage in St Emilion usually begins a week to ten days earlier than in the Médoc. Exceptionally, in 1978, the two vintages began together. The Merlot is, however, highly susceptible to rot, and three terrible vintages in the 1960s (1963, 1965 and 1968) led to improved vigilance in the vineyard and to a more perfect spraying technique. Its viticultural precocity, too, makes it vulnerable to spring frosts.

The best St Emilion growths offer an immense life-span of drinkability, opening out earlier than Médocs, and retaining their richness and charm for considerable time. The nose is often rather heady, exciting, more difficult to pin down than a pure, classic St Julien, for example. You are almost enveloped in fruit and ripeness, the whole backed up with a vinuous softness that is distinctly 'more-ish'. The classification of St Emilion also has its own individuality. This was not achieved until 1955, with a slight modification in 1969. At least, this shows flexibility in comparison with the Médoc, but perhaps in the future one could wish for the occasional downgrading to match the promotions. There are twelve First Great Growths, with Château Ausone and Château Cheval Blanc set apart at the head of this section. Then there are now seventy-two *grands crus classés*. Naturally, these vary considerably, both in quality and general availability. Both categories are subject to tasting. Below this, there is the somewhat armorphous category of *grand cru* which, to the uninitiated, can sound grander than it is. The title of *grand cru* is only awarded after tasting and for that particular vintage – so one year a château might have it, the next it would disappear from the label.

List of Classified Growths in St Emilion

FIRST GREAT GROWTHS

1.

Ausone　　　　　　　　Cheval-Blanc

2.

Beauséjour Duffau-Lagarrosse)	Belair	La Gaffelière
	Canon	Magdelaine
Beauséjour (Société-Bécot)	Clos Fourtet	Pavie
	Figeac	Trottevieille

GREAT GROWTHS

L'Angélus	Fonplégade	La Tour-du-Pin-Figeac (Belivier)
L'Arrosée	Fonroque	
Baleau	Franc-Mayne	La Tour-du-Pin-Figeac (Moueix)
Balestard-la-Tonnelle	Grand-Corbin	
Bellevue	Grand-Corbin-Despagne	La Tour-Figeac
Bergat	Grand-Mayne	La Châtelet

Cadet-Bon
Cadet-Piola
Canon-la-Gaffelière
Cap-de-Mourlin
 (R. Capdemourlin)
Cap-de-Mourlin
 (J. Capdemourlin)
Chapelle-Madeleine
Chauvin
Clos des Jacobins
Clos la Madeleine
Clos St-Martin
Corbin (Giraud)
Corbin-Michotte
Coutet
Couvent-des-Jacobins
Croque-Michotte
Curé-Bon
Dassault
Faurie-de-Souchard

Grand-Pontet
Grandes-Barrail-
 Lamarzelle-Figeac
Grandes-Murailles
Guadet-St-Julien
Haut-Corbin
Haut-Sarpe
Jean-Faure
La Carte
La Clotte
La Clusière
La Couspaude
La Dominique
Lamarzelle
Laniote
Larcis-Ducasse
Larmande
Laroze
Lasserre

Le Couvent
Le Prieuré
Matras
Mauvezin
Moulin-du-Cadet
L'Oratoire
Pavie-Decesse
Pavie-Macquin
Pavillon-Cadet
Petit-Faurie-de-Soutard
Ripeau
St-Georges-Côte-Pavie
Sansonnet
Soutard
Tertre-Daugay
Trimoulet
Trois-Moulins
Troplong-Mondot
Villemaurine
Yon-Figeac

CHATEAU AUSONE

This is the top *premier grand cru classé* of the Côtes area, with vineyards on a steep south-east escarpment below the town of St Emilion, looking out over the plain. There is something very miniature about Ausone, and the compact nature of its seven hectares producing under 3,000 cases of wine a year on average makes it appear quite manageable! The vines look gnarled, showing their average age of forty years, and the calcareous, crumbly soil is much in evidence, allowing the roots of the vines to reach down as much as six metres. Deep-rooted vines gain the maximum from the soil, all possible minerals and trace elements greatly contributing to the ultimate interest and subtlety of the wine. Ausone has the potential of being perhaps the most exciting wine of Bordeaux – a wine like the 1928 demonstrates the point admirably. The soil and site are perfect, only the right management was missing. Owned by the Dubois-Challon family and M. Alain Vauthier, the firm of J. P. Moueix has long sold part of the crop. After some really disappointing years since the Second World War, during the 1970s M. Christian Moueix was asked to involve himself more with the running of the property. A new *régisseur*, Pascal Delbeck was installed, and there were immediate differences with the marvellously complex and exciting 1975 vintage. Certainly the very damp cellars in the rock at Ausone posed problems for the maintenance of casks, and the wine seemed to suffer from its time in wood, often losing that heady flavour and richness of Ausone and beginning to lighten, and even dry out, far too rapidly. The wine is now kept under impeccable conditions, and the results have been immediate. The vineyard is also run with the great precision of all the Moueix-directed properties, with great attention to health of the vine and optimum picking-point at vintage time – always easier to stage-manage in a small property like Ausone. The grape variety balance here is soon to become 50 per cent Merlot and 50 per cent Cabernet Franc. Ausone at its best recalls both opulence and finesse. I think this magic combination will be seen at its zenith in the 1976 and in the remarkable 1978 and 1979.

CHATEAU CHEVAL BLANC

Cheval Blanc is put on a par with Ausone at the top of the classification, and this greatest wine of the Graves area of St Emilion provides a fascinating contrast in style and definition. The wines of Cheval Blanc are bigger and fleshier than Ausone, for me often characterized by a slightly 'roasted' nose of super ripeness and richness. On the Graves plateau adjoining Pomerol, the surface is gravelly with irony clay beneath it. This is a very large property for St Emilion, thirty-five hectares, but unfortunately this does not seem to have much steadying influence on the price!

The predominant grape variety is the Cabernet Franc (two-thirds), but it is the complexity of the soil that gives the wine its unique stamp. A magnificent new, white *chais* built in 1974 permitted far better control over the whole wine-making process and also enabled Cheval Blanc to château-bottle – before that it was allowed to take place at Libourne. The descendants of the Fourcaud Laussac family own the property, and M. Jacques Hebrard is co-proprietor and manager. The 1921 and 1947 Cheval Blanc are legendary. The grim February 1956 frost hit the St Emilion and Pomerol plateau with enormous ferocity, and only the 1961 marked a return to top form, if not exquisite Cheval Blanc. In 1978, I wrote of the 1961: 'Particularly dense colour, very tight, almost "roasted" nose to be found in Cheval Blanc of dry, hot years; totally different from other wines, a lot of grip and backbone and underlying hidden flavours – almost "oriental" and very far from straight-forward, Médocain fruit.' The 1966 in the same year had a deep brown colour, and was big, rich and sweet – a weighty wine, classic of its type, slightly one-dimensional. This wonderful Cheval Blanc sweetness was also present in massive quantity in the 1970, with its lovely acidity and fruit, while the fabulous 1964 had opened out to real opulence in 1980. Really good wines have also been made in 1975 (lusciously fruity), 1976 (incredibly rich and exotic), 1978 and 1979.

Châteaux of Note in the Côtes Area of St Emilion are:

Château Belair shares ownership with Ausone, and also the same steep vineyards near the town of St Emilion with their clayey-calcareous soil, but facing southwards rather than south-east. There are also vineyards on chalky plateau. The wine is no longer kept in the cellars of Ausone, but in another very beautiful old cellar. Belair can sometimes be a bit 'thin', often with a light colour, but its breed and elegance is most evident. The 1976 is very fine indeed, and sweetness and elegance are both present in the 1970, although the length did not indicate a great keeper. A 1947 drunk in 1974 still had enormous fruit and life. The grape variety composition is 50 per cent Merlot and 50 per cent Cabernet Franc on thirteen hectares of vineyards.

Château Magdelaine is another property on the slopes of St Emilion, adjoining Belair on one side and facing south. The exact composition is five hectares on the clayey slope, which gives depth to the wine, and six hectares on chalky plateau, which contributes finesse to the final blend. Owned by M. Jean-Pierre Moueix, it enjoys the same attentions as the rest of their properties. The vineyard includes a high proportion of Merlot, 70 per cent, with 30 per cent Cabernet Franc, and those ripe years for Merlot, such as 1971, obviously show Magdelaine at its best. Intelligent wine-making helps give Magdelaine the little bit more body that it sometimes needs – vines of between twenty-eight and thirty years' average age, a small pro-portion of stalks included in the vinification, picking as late as possible. I have been very impressed by the wines of the 1970s, which all show scent and delicacy.

There are now two Châteaux Beauséjours, one belonging to the Duffau-Lagar-rosse heirs, and the other to M. Michel Bécot. The vineyards adjoin, and the tasting qualities are not dissimilar. They are typically full St Emilion wines, and improve greatly from ageing in good years. M. Bécot has improved his property considerably and is very forward-looking. Château Canon is again, another full wine, sometimes a little coarse, but with a supple and fruity character. 1966 is a good example of these qualities. The 1978 shows some class. Château Canon is owned by the Fourniers.

Owned by the Lurton family, Clos Fourtet has some remarkable cellars in the calcareous rock near the town. There is both Cabernet Franc and Cabernet Sauvignon in the vineyard, as well as over 50 per cent of Merlot. The wines are perhaps a little lighter now than they were, but the real tasting characteristic of Clos Fourtet was a certain toughness when young, but with remarkable ageing potential, when it developed an exceptionally delightful bouquet. The 1970 is good, and the 1979 looks promising. Very much the family château of the Comtes de Malet-Roquefort, Château La Gaffelière was known as La Gaffelière-Naudes until the 1964 vintage. Fuller and rounder than some wines of the Côtes, the wine has the potential to be superb, rather than just good, should ideal wine-making techniques be used. I have much liked the 1966 and the 1970. Château Pavie is a large property, very well-managed (with advice from Professor Peynaud now) and owned by the Valettes. The 1970 is lovely, full and plummy – delicious, fruity drinking. The 1975 seemed to show its alcohol in a slightly unbalanced way, but the future will reveal all. Owned by the family firm of Borie-Manoux, Château Trottevieille's wine is generous and full, rather than elegant; but Trottevieille makes consistently good bottles.

There is a mass of *grands crus classés* in the Côtes area of St Emilion. Amongst them, Château L'Angélus is very well-known, both for its large production and the consistent pleasant wines it gives. Château Curé-Bon, or Curé-Bon-la-Madeleine, has something of the character of Belair about it, a wine of breed, often with a light colour; the 1979 is lovely. Château Balestard-La-Tonnelle is making excellent wine at the moment, with really careful vinification by the owners, the Capdemourlin family. Sometimes, in years of small production, the quality is exceptional. Nearby, at Château Villemaurine, the wine has finesse and ages well. Château Cadet-Piola is a real Côtes wine of breed and elegance, at its best ageing admirably, but unfortunately not always living up to this. Château Soutard is very well run, and the wine is of good, dependable quality, even if it does not show its breed in every year. Château Fonplégade has both generosity and class, and is beautifully sited. Further down the hill below St Emilion, there is Château Canon-La-Gaffelière, a property of some size, producing consistently pleasurable St Emilion wines of charm. Right beside the town, Château La Clotte is a particular favourite, sometimes giving wines of immense generosity and fruit, full and deep and memorable – the 1970, 1966 and 1959 are examples. Château Fonroque, to the north of St Emilion, is a Moueix property, with a marked character of the soil in the wine, giving it great individuality.

Château Grand Pontet is now owned by M. Bécot of Beauséjour. It is very honourable wine, grown in the vicinity of the Châteaux Beauséjours and Clos Fourtet. Château Laroze is quite easily found and extremely dependable; the 1979 is delicious. Château Moulin du Cadet is Moueix-owned, and near to Soutard and Cadet-Piola. It has the Côtes elegance, with pronounced flavour and definition. Château Pavie-Macquin, near Pavie, makes wines of some style, as befits its situation. Château Tertre-Daugay is always a good buy, as is Château Troplong-Mondot, important both for its size and consistent quality. The excellent Château Larcis-Ducasse is not far away, but in fact lies outside the commune of St Emilion and in that of St-Laurent des Combes. This is also the case with Château Haut-Sarpe, which lies just inside St-Christophe des Bardes. Clos des Jacobins now belongs to the *négociants* Cordier, and makes softish wines of charm, with the exception of a remarkably tannic 1975.

The St Emilion Graves area has only two First Great Growths; Château Cheval Blanc has its place right at the top, but the other is a worthy partner indeed.

Although adjoining Château Cheval Blanc on the gravelly plain near the border with Pomerol, Château Figeac's wines have a very different taste. The *encépagement* is obviously partly responsible for this, since there is about 70 per cent of the two

Cabernets, equally divided between the two types, with 30 per cent Merlot. This high amount of Cabernet Sauvignon is very unusual for St Emilion and is part of Figeac's individuality. The owner is M. Thierry Manoncourt.

I do not find that Figeac has the slightly *rôti* bouquet that Cheval Blanc can sometimes demonstrate. It usually has gloriously velvety elegance, rich without being overpowering. Throughout the 1960s and 1970s the wine has been consistently excellent, with a remarkably good, balanced 1970, and what looks like a very fine, classy 1978. The 1975 has a fascinating, scented, exotic nose, still dry and tannic, but a distinguished wine. The 1976 has intensity and depth.

There are not many *grands crus classés* in this Graves area of St Emilion, but a few of note. Five of them include the name 'Figeac' in their names, but they are certainly not of the class of the pivotal château. During the 1970s, the two properties in this group that impressed me most often were Château Grand-Barrail-Lamarzelle-Figeac and Château Yon-Figeac. The others are Château La Tour-du-Pin-Figeac (one part is owned by the Belivier family and the other by A. Moueix), and Château La Tour Figeac – I have found a casky taste in some of the latter's wines of the 1970s.

Corbin is another word that crops up again and again in St Emilion. By far the most famous property is Château Corbin in this Graves area of St Emilion. It is well vinified – an excellent *bourgeois* wine. Château Croque-Michotte, Château La Dominique and Château Ripeau are all worth finding and drinking, all capable of making exceptionally good wines in certain years. Following this, there is a mass of St Emilion *grands crus*, from both the main *appellation* area and the 'satellite' communes. Any château can aspire to *grand cru* status if it passes the annual tasting and has a minimum of 11.5 per cent alcohol. Many of these properties practise a flourishing direct sale trade to private customers in France, others such as Château Fombrauge and Château Lyonnat are regularly seen on export markets. Château Haut-Pontet has much impressed me. There are also important cooperatives.

POMEROL

The wines of Pomerol should not be linked with those of St Emilion as right-bank wines, as even though some of the greatest vineyards of the two districts are contiguous, the tastes are very different and totally individual. This is mainly due to soil fluctuations and the fascinating bearing they have on the final product. The soil of Pomerol is predominantly clayey gravel – a mixture of quite deep clay and a superficial layer of gravel giving the best wines. The proportion of clay and gravel changes with the growths – thus, Château La Fleur Pétrus, which is almost entirely gravel, gives a much lighter wine than some of the other great Pomerols, but is very elegant, while Château Pétrus has about 80 per cent clay and 20 per cent gravel, giving a much deeper, more powerful wine, at the same time as being supple and full. Château Trotanoy is somewhere between the two, mixing equally clay and gravel, and combining elegance with body.

Pomerol is Merlot land *par excellence*. Perhaps even more so than in St Emilion, the Cabernet Sauvignon does not do well here, due to the colder, more acid soil, preventing good ripening. Clay holds cold, and it is significant that the growths with the most clay specialize almost entirely in Merlot. This high proportion of Merlot, inter-related with the soil, helps give Pomerol that full, luscious, almost exotic flavour. Pomerol is important for quality and its special taste, not for its quantity, which is the smallest of the main Bordeaux regions. This small production has certainly prevented some of the finest wines attaining the reputation and recognition accorded to the top Médoc wines – so few people can see exactly what is meant by supreme class in Pomerol terms. Ownership is also very split up – 110 owners possess less than one hectare and ninety proprietors between one and two hectares. This limited production has also contributed to the system of direct sales to the French public which many small Pomerol properties practise.

There is no official classification for Pomerol, so any hierarchy has to be made on informed opinion and experience. Pomerol trade is channelled through the market town of Libourne, and the firm of J. P. Moueix on the quay there has always been a monument to integrity and quality, and a rich source of fine wines at all levels. The best growths are on the plateau between the church of Pomerol and the St Emilion Graves area. Here is all vine-growing, the actual châteaux or manor houses are often very modest, and the atmosphere is very rural. To the south-west and west there are some bigger properties, good but not with the finesse of the greatest.

CHATEAU PETRUS

Pride of place must go to Château Pétrus, the epitome of all that is exciting and exotic in Pomerol. First launched into the international arena when it won a gold medal at the Paris Exhibition of 1878, Pétrus is now considered a First Growth, even in the absence of anything official. The prices are certainly in the First Growth stratosphere. The peculiarity of the soil at Pétrus has already been discussed, and there are certainly traces of iron deep down in the clay, lending its mineral influence to the wine. The other critical factors of this small vineyard (average output is forty *tonneaux*) are the forty-year average age of the vines, and the 95 per cent Merlot – 5 per cent Cabernet Franc grape variety combination. Another insight into the immense ripe, super-mature taste of Pétrus is the late picking. The vintage is always as late as possible at Pétrus, usually mid-October.

The joint Loubat/Moueix ownership of Pétrus has over the years ensured proper recognition for this highly individual wine. Rigorous selection takes place for the final *grand vin*, which is all the more astonishing in such a small property. The taste of Pétrus is perhaps more difficult to describe than any other Bordeaux growth, encompassing as it does a massive range of flavours and nuances, combining the exotic with traditional power, and fining down to elegance with maturity.

The 1947 and 1949 were Pétrus at its most exciting, and there is no reason to suppose that either are not still showing this class. The 1946 was surprisingly good, if unfashionable, and the 1950 is magnificent. The 1960s produced very fine wines indeed, but I have had the opportunity to study the 1970s more closely. The 1970 has the property's big colour, with a bouquet that was still closed in 1978, a deep, herby flavour and an obvious very far distance to go before maturity. At the same time I tasted the 1971, which was even more crimson than the 1970, wonderfully developed and *épanoui*, with extreme ripeness and almost vegetal fruit. Already there were lovely subtleties and complexity – Pétrus at its most opulent. However, in 1980 I had the wine again, and it seemed rather overpowered by its enormous ripeness and had temporarily lost its balance – something that can happen at an intermediate stage. I have felt that this wine is potentially the best 1971 in the Bordeaux area. The 1975 has big colour, very great depth of fruit on the nose, and is complex and many-layered, but still very tannic and tight. The 1976 is very aromatic and fine – in 1975 and 1976, no chaptalization was needed, a not uncommon occurrence at Pétrus. The 1977, when very young, had a slightly salty taste and lots of dry extract, and the 1978 in cask had immense, purple colour, great character, and a wonderful, ripe, almost cassis-like after-taste. The 1979 had twenty-four days of fermentation, tannin, and 12.6 per cent of natural alcohol.

CHATEAU TROTANOY

On current showing, and intrinsic merit of the property, this has to be the best wine of Pomerol after Pétrus. Trotanoy is a sumptuous wine of quite dazzling quality. It is owned by the family of Jean-Pierre Moueix, and the vineyard is unfortunately small – nine hectares. The taste of the wine is of intense fruit with a velvety texture, backed by firm body, richness and fat. Sometimes it does not smell of Pomerol at all, but more of the Médoc, which is astonishing when one considers its proportion of grape varieties – 80 per cent Merlot and 20 per cent Cabernet Franc. The whole composition of the wine does not seem to fit our idea of the right bank. The vines are as old here as at Pétrus – with an average age of between thirty-five and forty years. 1961 Trotanoy is immense and amazingly good, 1962 is delicious, and 1966 very good indeed. 1970 is big and straightforward, with 1971 outstanding. 1975 is very classic, 1976 has class, ripeness and a long aftertaste, and 1978 is big, full and tannic – a huge wine. The 1979 is also big and rich – the result of long vatting.

CHATEAU LA CONSEILLANTE

I would put La Conseillante on the same level as Trotanoy, a wine of immense breed, perhaps without the glossy fat of Trotanoy, but nevertheless the wines can age with the utmost elegance. Owned by the Nicolas family, the vineyard is superbly placed on the plateau, opposite Cheval Blanc. Here the Merlot is balanced by an equal amount of Cabernet Franc, with a small amount of Malbec. There are some fabled vintages of the past, but unfortunately I only started to see La Conseillante regularly with the vintages of the 1960s, which were consistently fine, although the one time I saw the 1961 it appeared dull and dry. 1970 is incredibly good – one of the really big La Conseillantes. There is a wonderful depth and intensity of fruit, almost tactile, quite stunningly good. I found the 1971 a bit thin, the 1973 exceptionally good, and the last years of the 1970s are all unmitigated successes, with a 1976 of great finesse and distinction, and a 1979 that looks a winner.

Other Châteaux are:

Vieux Château Certan makes some of the wines that last the longest in Pomerol. It is owned by the Belgian Thienpont family and lies near La Conseillante. There is Cabernet Sauvignon as well as Franc here, but half the total is made up of Merlot. There is distinguished breed at Vieux Château Certan, and the wines have a pronounced, individual bouquet. For the last twenty years, there has been great consistency at this château, and I have particularly admired a very flavoury, spicy 1970, and a 1978 with ripeness, 'attack' and character. Again, near La Conseillante, the wines of Château l'Evangile can often require some time to age. Unfortunately, the wines do not often come my way (or I theirs), but the 1970 and 1971 are impressive. It is a predominantly Merlot wine. Château Lafleur is a little gem of a property, only four hectares of it, and should never be missed if an opportunity for tasting presents itself. The Robin sisters own it, and the wine is of exceptional quality, full and ideally suited to ageing. Château La Fleur-Pétrus is confusingly nearby, on what is known as the Graves de Pomerol. The wine has finesse and breed and nobility. I have never had anything less than a superb bottle, and will long remember the magnum of 1961 drunk at the generous Moueix table, as well as a remarkable 1948. The 1970 has tannin and concentration and is for the future. The 1976 will be for much earlier drinking, the 1977, with greatly reduced quantity because of frost, has a lovely scent and balance, and the 1978 is aromatic, but does not appear to have the body to be a great keeper. Merlot predominates here, and therefore showed very well in 1979 – a great year for this grape variety. Château Petit-Village has wines of great quality, but unfortunately the few I have seen have not lived up to this potential. However, the 1945, drunk in 1980, was quite outstanding. Bruno Prats of Cos d'Estournel now manages the property. Owned by Madame Lacoste-Loubat who part-owns Pétrus, Château Latour-Pomerol wines can be both *gras*, or fat, and solidly constructed, with good penetration of taste. The 1970 has good fruit combined with a fair amount of tannin, and the 1978 has a projected nose and good character. The 1979 is very powerful wine. Château Certan de May made some splendid vintages before the 1956 frost, but suffered since then. However, the excellent site has huge potential. The 1978 had body and tannin, but perhaps could have been made in a way so as to give more finesse. Château Gazin's wine has a good reputation and is well known on the British market, but I have to say that I have never tasted a really distinguished Gazin – the breed always seems to be sacrificed to a certain coarseness. However, it ages well, and the 1945 was deep and remarkable in 1980. I have preferred the 1966 in more recent years. The 1970 is rather forward but very ripe tasting, the 1964 I found a bit 'jammy' and plummy, and the 1957 had a fragrant nose and fruit, but rather a short finish. The 1976 has good depth of fruit. The site of Clos L'Eglise is excellent, but the wine-making sometimes did not live up to expectations. At its best, it is delicate and fine, epitomized in the 1979, and it is evident that now the two Moreau sons are vinifying with great care. The wine of Château L'Eglise Clinet is very well made, and the taste full and charming. Worth finding, but production is small – about twenty *tonneaux*. Château Lagrave is now owned by Christian Moueix, and the wine is elegant and has breed, with less body than some so can be appreciated to the full earlier. I have found the 1976 delicious and glossy, with an enticing minty flavour, and the 1979 will be beautiful, fruity wine. Château Lagrange makes wine that is more powerful, perhaps with less finesse. But it is beautifully situated on the plateau of Pomerol, and the wines have a delicious flavour and are of remarkable quality. Situated on the boundaries of Pomerol and St Emilion, the wines of Château Beauregard have breed and a supple character, and are very highly regarded. The wines often show well when comparatively young. Château Nenin is a wine that is often seen in the United Kingdom. It is good, but I have never seen a Nenin of ultimate finesse or breed, although with time very high quality bottles emerge. I have admired both the 1967 and the 1961, which both needed time to soften the tannin in them. Château La Pointe is a large property that produces wines with a lovely bouquet and great charm. The 1970 should last well, the 1971 has a delicious, intense Pomerol nose, but the last time I saw it I felt it was drying up a bit.

There are other properties in Pomerol that have good distribution and are really worthwhile. Château Close René made a fruity, but rather light 1970, but excellent 1976, 1978 and 1979. Château Rouget has given me a lot of pleasure, particularly a stunning 1964 and a still lively, rich 1959. The largest property in Pomerol, Château de Sales, makes reliable wines, not in the top flight. I have liked the 1961 and 1962, and the 1976 shows promise. Château Plince is really rewarding Pomerol – the 1947 is fabled, and the 1971 could well turn out like that, warm and rounded, with a nose of truffles that I have also noticed at Lagrange. Château Moulinet is most honourable, and the 1970 and 1971 are both fine examples. Château Le Gay is a personal favourite, with wines of the 1960s outstanding, especially the 1964 and 1966 – the 1970s continue the good work. Château La Croix-de-Gay is also very good drinking, as is Château Vraye-Croix-de-Gay. Château Lafleur-Gazin is also recommended.

There is also the neighbouring *appellation* of Lalande de Pomerol. The wines of the commune of Néac can now use this *appellation*, which is certainly more advantageous for them.

FRONSAC

Fronsac has quite one of the most beguiling tastes of Bordeaux, extremely marked by the Cabernet Franc, with that lovely grassy, 'sappy' freshness about it which almost jumps out of the glass. These red wines have a slightly earthy finish, and when young can be quite tannic – although much less so nowadays, with a slightly less *artisan* approach to wine-making in the area. There are two *appellations*, Fronsac and Côtes de Canon Fronsac. Given time, good châteaux can develop real interest and finesse with six years or more of age – providing, of course, the vintage is good. I have particular admiration for the really tempting Canon de Brem from Canon-Fronsac, but I have also seen really good wines from La Dauphine and Rouet, both in the Fronsac *appellation*. Mention must also be made of Châteaux Canon (Canon-Fronsac), du Gaby, Junayme, Vrai-Canon-Bouché, Vray-Canon-Boyer, Mayne-Vieil, La Valade, La Venelle, Toumalin and Bodet.

BOURG AND BLAYE

Both these right-bank regions give wines that are a great standby for those who like to drink reasonable Claret on a regular basis. Uncomplicated red wines, for the greater part made of the Cabernet Franc and Merlot grapes, give much pleasure when drunk relatively young. The best growths of Bourg come from slopes near the Gironde, and have the most weight and character of this area. They have more body than the lighter Blaye wines, which are nevertheless full of fruit and charm. There is a mass of small properties in both regions ('château' would be too grand a word), and although they produce good base material, it is sometimes safer if a reliable *négociant* does the bottling. Bourg produces more wine than Blaye. The white wine of these areas tends to be somewhat common, although there are good Côtes de Blaye. The countryside is pretty, green and hilly, with mixed farming and an unspoilt feeling of rustic France. Cooperatives play a large part in wine-making, selling a great deal of their produce to the Bordeaux *négociants*.

There are some properties that are large enough to have made their mark, and every good Bordeaux merchant has a good choice of *petits châteaux* from Bourg and Blaye. In Bourg, mention must be made of the excellent châteaux of de Barbe and Guerry, both of which have good ageing properties. Du Bousquet is also most reliable, and others of note are Coubet, de La Croix-Millorit, Guionne, Mille-Secousses, Poliane, Rousset and Tayac. In Blaye, Haut Sociondo and Le Menaudat have given really pleasant drinking, as have Segonzac and Mondésir-Gazin. Taste any small châteaux offered to you from these regions – they often provide a lesson in what Bordeaux can produce at a reasonable price. You can also find Bordeaux or Bordeaux Supérieur Côtes de Castillon, from around the small town of Castillon-la-Bataille – Château Lardit is a good example. These wines resemble 'satellite' St Emilions, and can be very good wine to quaff. There is also a small amount of Bordeaux Supérieur Côtes de Francs, which is again Merlot-type wine. However, the overall *appellation* of Bordeaux Supérieur is now usually used alone. The wines from around St André-de-Cubzac are only entitled to be called Bordeaux or Bordeaux Supérieur, but there are important properties here – Château de Terrefort-Quancard, Château Timberlay and Château du Bouilh.

Bordeaux Vintages

Nowhere else in the wine-making world are vintages more relevant than in Bordeaux. This Atlantic-influenced region is at the mercy of the weather, and although man can mitigate its ravages, spray in hand, he cannot provide what is not there. Vintage characteristics are not there by accident – they are the direct result of the weather prevailing during the growing and ripening season. Above all, in Bordeaux, the month of September is all-important – September can make or break a vintage. 1977 was an example of a vintage 'made' in September, 1963 an illustration of a vintage 'killed' by rain in September. Even when events are not so dramatic, sun, warmth and dry conditions can make the difference between good and great.

The Bordeaux vintages that are most likely to be drunk now are those from the last two decades (some older wines are described under individual châteaux):

1960: A light vintage, with some pleasant wines, that should be drunk by now.

1961: Probably the best vintage that I have seen – it *may* even be that elusive chimera so beloved of the media, the 'vintage of the century'. A tiny, concentrated vintage – the product of perfect summer and autumn weather. Wonderful balance, fruit and extract. The wines have great individuality, even in lesser growths and are an experience to drink at all stages of their life. Some of the top wines will remain at their peak for years. The sweet white wines are famous, but are perhaps not the most elegant of their kind – alcoholic and concentrated rather than honeyed finesse.

1962: A large vintage of wines that have given more and more pleasure over the years. High acidity has maintained a wonderful clean, classic flavour and deep, youthful colour in the top wines. Wines were good from all areas, with most of the St Emilions and Pomerals now fully recovered from the 1956 frost. Lovely wines of breed in Sauternes and Barsac.

1963: Terrible wines that should never have been sold under illustrious labels.

1964: Unfortunately, over a week of continuous rain in the Médoc during the vintage took its inevitable toll, and some wines are rather dry and short, either because the whole crop was not picked before the rain started, or because careful selection of the grapes did not follow. However, the good wines are supple and fruity, and many St Emilions, Pomerols and Graves are superb – the right bank wines, picked well before the rains, can be really full and luscious. It is certainly not worth keeping Médoc wines any longer. The October rain demolished nearly all the sweet white wines.

1965: A miserable year, and the grapes never ripened. *A oublier.*

1966: A very classic vintage – in the Médoc, the best of the decade after the 1961s. The wines are beautifully constructed, deep-coloured with ample fruit and tannin. The best are splendid keeping wines; it is difficult to find any fault with the 1966s. There are some really good Sauternes, even if not quite top class.

1967: Some worthy wines from a large vintage, but there are many with a characteristic dry, somewhat hard finish, especially as they get older. Even the best will not benefit from further keeping. St Emilion and Pomerol tend to be fruitier. There were really outstanding Sauternes and Barsac, rich wines with great style and elegance.

1968: Rain did much damage again, but with careful selection there were a few light, drinkable wines, all of which should have been drunk. Sauternes was ruined.

1969: Happily, it is a small vintage, as the wines turned out to be exceptionally mean, dry and charmless. Frankly, I have had more pleasure from the best of the 1968s. Light, not very consequential Sauternes.

1970: An exceptional year, combining abundance with quality. The grapes everywhere were perfectly healthy – many wine-makers said they had never seen such ideal conditions. From the start, the 1970s had wonderful colour, and all the qualities of fruit, acidity and tannin. The top wines went through a rather dumb stage of adolescence, and the 1980s will see them opening out and showing their full potential. Lesser growths also needed time, and although this vintage does not have the sheer beauty of the 1961s, it has richness and depth that reward keeping. The Sauternes are good and consistent.

1971: A much smaller amount of wine made, with the wines possessing a very different structure. They have ripeness and fruit, with a seductive bouquet, but the low acidity augurs a shorter life for them than the 1970s. A few Médocs can be slightly dry, and some took on a brown colour relatively early. More selection has to be exercised in 1971 than in 1970, but the St Emilions and Pomerols are superb, rich and fascinating. White Graves, Sauternes and Barsac were all magnificent, with wines of the utmost finesse and distinction.

1972: There is a nasty, unripe, greenish quality about the 1972s that completely obliterates charm and makes most of them singularly unattractive to drink. It was a pity that many classified châteaux bottled under their own name – more modest properties often made better wine than the big stars.

1973: A large vintage with many wines of immense charm – on the light side, but with a flowery attractiveness that made delicious Bordeaux drinking. Some were too weak, or too heavily chaptalized, results of a high yield. Only the top properties are set for lasting into the 1980s – in general, it was a vintage to drink young and enjoy. Rather an ordinary year for Sauternes.

1974: A poor September ensured that these wines would not be anything special. I find them very dull, with neither districts nor châteaux possessing individuality. Apart from the odd exception, this is a vintage that lacks charm and fruit and any form of complexity. Really poor for Sauternes.

1975: A very great vintage, stamped with the heat of the summer and ideal conditions in September. The wines are concentrated and tannic. At first, it appeared that they might have too much tannin for balance, but at the end of the 1970s, the fruit was beginning to glow through, and the splendid, individual bouquet of the properties was promising magic to come. The quality is superb at all levels, and the greatest wines will be world-beaters. All appreciators of fine Claret should have some. They have a very long life ahead at top level. The Sauternes were very rich and alcoholic.

1976: The vintage was very early, after an extremely hot and dry summer, but it rained during picking. The wines combine as much tannin as 1975 (although of a different kind), but with very low acidity – a point always worth bearing in mind when projecting length of life. There are some very good wines for early drinking at modest levels, and some really elegant, fruity wines at the top end. The First Growths shine, and there are particularly lovely St Juliens and Pomerols. But these are obviously early assessments for top wines. Some exquisite white Graves and Sauternes, with finesse rather than sheer power.

1977: September saved this vintage from disaster, and there are some charming wines for relatively young drinking. Others are somewhat mean and thin (northern area of Haut Médoc and Médoc), and the warmth of the Merlot (hit by the frost at the end of March) was missing. With careful selection, there are some good buys. No great hopes for Sauternes – the ingredients were just not there.

1978: A splendid autumn imbued the wines with some extraordinary qualities. They have great depth and structure, and a velvety texture, full of 'fat' and glycerine. Anticipation runs high for the 1978s, and there are certain to be top, rich wines of great class. A few St Emilions are not quite up to this level. Otherwise, there is great consistency of quality right down to the most modest wines in the hierarchy. The Sauternes were picked very late, as the weather was superb and the grapes ripe, but the lack of humidity precluded any *pourriture noble*.

1979: A huge vintage, picked in October for the third year running. The Merlot was splendid, and Pomerol and St Emilion look especially favoured. As in any large vintage, selection will be necessary, but there undoubtedly will be many fine wines. The colour is good and there is much more tannin than was expected with a large vintage. But the figures are deceptive: the vineyard area has increased tremendously during the 1970s, the actual grapes in the bunches were nothing like as large as they were in 1973, and the top châteaux made good, but far from excessive, yields. Very good signs of classic Sauternes.

1980: Far too early to predict, but the colour everywhere looks good.

BURGUNDY

Good Burgundy is difficult to make – it is also difficult to buy. There are probably more pitfalls in Burgundy for both the amateur and the professional buyer than in any other fine wine area of the world. It has to be remembered at the outset that, for red wine, Burgundy is at the very northern limit of feasible production. Certainly, neither England, with its attempts at a pale red wine, nor Germany with its 'curiosity' red wine of Assmannshausen, would claim to be in the fine wine league. The problem, here, when so far north, is largely one of colour – what the French call *véraison*. But the special slopes that make up so much of Burgundy help to counteract this by attracting all the sun there is available, and the continental nature of the climate ensures drier weather than, say, in southern England. Eastern France becomes very cold in winter, often freezing with a dusting of snow, but the summers and autumns can be very warm.

One is talking in very general terms when one talks of 'Burgundy', as the word encompasses such disparate wines as Chablis, Romanée-Conti and Beaujolais. The worst climatic hazards occur, naturally enough, in the most northerly vineyard area, Chablis – a viticultural 'island' in the *département* of the Yonne, about 175 kilometres southeast of Paris, Continuing southeast, one arrives at Dijon, the start of the kernel of Burgundy, the Côte d'Or. This Golden Slope encompasses the Côte de Nuits in the north and the Côte de Beaune in the south, stretching for sixty kilometres down to Chagny. This town marks the beginning of the Côte Chalonnaise, which ends at Buxy and Montagny. Here the vineyards merge into the Mâconnais, they in turn give way to the Beaujolais, and the Burgundian road comes finally to an end above Lyon. The Burgundian area is elongated, but not wide, and unfortunately the narrowest point, the Côte d'Or, is also the finest. Total production can be only one-third of that of Bordeaux, and by far the greatest part of the Burgundian figure is made up of Beaujolais. The figures for 1979, a prolific year, show how the *appellation contrôlée* total is broken down:

Département	Declared production in hectolitres
Côte d'Or (Côte de Nuits, Côte de Beaune)	343,000
Saône et Loire (Côte Chalonnaise, Mâconnais)	518,000
Rhône (Beaujolais)	1,150,000
Chablis	114,728
Total	2,125,728

The 1978 total for Burgundian *appellation contrôlée* wines was 1,882,649 hectolitres. This amount has to supply the entire world and, to complicate matters, not all this *appellation contrôlée* wine is good. Although this is true of any wine area of the world, the problem is particularly acute in Burgundy, due to the distribution of the vineyards and their complicated ownership. Unlike Bordeaux, the Church played an enormous part in the development of the Burgundian vineyards and its importance cannot be enough stressed. Unfortunately, what remains of the Benedictine Abbey of Cluny can give no idea of its former magnificence and size. However, the Revolution put an end to both Church and noble ownership, and the parcelling out of vineyards literally changed the face of Burgundy, particularly in the Côte d'Or. But the Burgundian *négociants* were already established, and began to build up their businesses and domains. Vineyard ownership multiplied, with single domains being divided into little plots. In many cases, this splintered still further owing to the French inheritance laws, where property is divided amongst all the children equally. When a single *appellation*, often not large in size in Burgundy, is in the hands of many different owners, there is an obvious variation in quality, and only careful and experienced tasting will prevent buying accidents. There is also

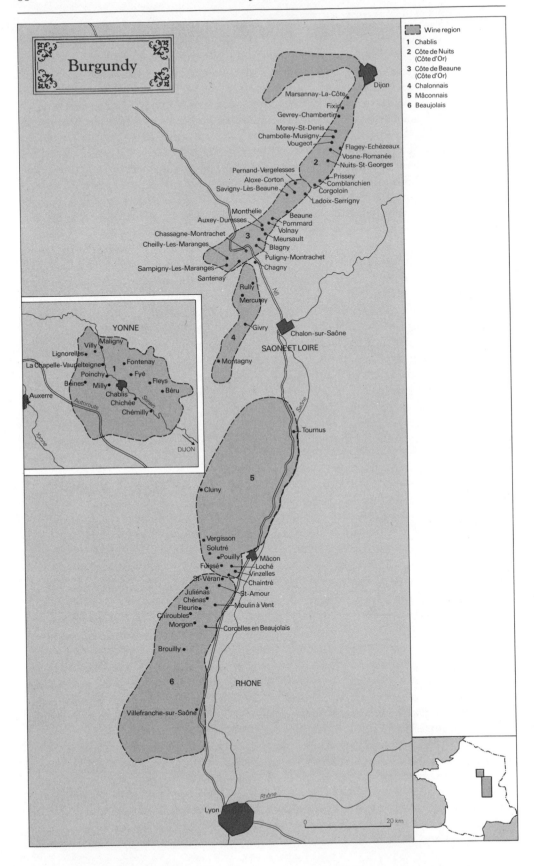

Burgundy

Wine region
1 Chablis
2 Côte de Nuits (Côte d'Or)
3 Côte de Beaune (Côte d'Or)
4 Chalonnais
5 Mâconnais
6 Beaujolais

Dijon

Marsannay-La-Côte
Fixin
Gevrey-Chambertin
Morey-St-Denis
Chambolle-Musigny
Vougeot
Flagey-Echézeaux
Vosne-Romanée
Nuits-St-Georges
2
Prissey
Pernand-Vergelesses
Comblanchien
Aloxe-Corton
Corgoloin
Savigny-Lès-Beaune
Ladoix-Serrigny
Monthelie
Beaune
Auxey-Duresses
Pommard
Volnay
Chassagne-Montrachet
Meursault
Cheilly-Les-Maranges
Blagny
3
Puligny-Montrachet
Sampigny-Les-Maranges
Chagny
Santenay
Rully
Mercurey
Givry
Chalon-sur-Saône
4
SAONE ET LOIRE
Montagny

YONNE
Maligny
Villy
Lignorelles
Fontenay
La Chapelle-Vaupelteigne
1
Fyé
Poinchy
Fleys
Beines
Milly
Béru
Auxerre
Chablis
Chichée
Chémilly
DIJON

N6
Saône
Tournus

5
Cluny

Vergisson
Solutré
Pouilly
Mâcon
Fuissé
Loché
Vinzelles
St-Véran
Chaintré
Juliénas
St-Amour
Chénas
Fleurie
Moulin à Vent
Chiroubles
Morgon
Corcelles en Beaujolais
Brouilly

6
RHONE

Villefranche-sur-Saône

Rhône
Lyon

0   20 km

the practical problem of vinifying very small amounts of wine. It is extremely difficult, if not impossible, to do this well with only a *pièce* or two – wine needs a certain 'mass' to ferment and develop smoothly. (A *pièce* is a hogshead of 228 litres.) Another contributory factor to variable quality in Burgundy is the comparative lack of experience in *élevage* and bottling on the part of some growers. Growers are just that, people who grow and tend vines, and most of them do it very well. But that does not mean they are automatically expert in the difficult art of cellar work.

For various socio-economic reasons, more growers are bottling their own wines than ever before in Burgundy – it is estimated that 40 per cent of the wine produced is now domain bottled and sold direct to the consumer. This is partly due to the depression of the market in 1973/4, when the *négociants* did not require so much wine from growers, who thus had to devise other means of selling their production. Direct sale to the public filled a large gap, and had the added advantage of being highly profitable – the grower took the *négociant*'s margin, as well as his own. The development of this type of selling has obviously made the *négociant*'s life more difficult, with more limited choice, especially in years where there is a small crop, and those *négociants* who are also domain owners are better placed to ride this particular change in market conditions. There are also many vineyards *en métayage* in Burgundy. This is the system, still very much alive in France, whereby a vineyard owner has an arrangement with a grower who undertakes to 'farm' his vines in return for what is usually half of the crop. This further complicates the issue, as legally the same wine from the same plot can be sold estate bottled under the name of the *vigneron* and under the name of the owner.

Much is made of the changed yields in Burgundy, and the effect of this on the style of the wines. It is certainly true that for the first twenty or thirty years of this century yields were much lower (fifteen hectolitres to the hectare were considered good generally), and this contributed to a more concentrated, bigger wine. And it is also true that some *appellations* tend to overcrop. But often Grand Cru owners do not make the maximum allowed under the *appellation contrôlée* laws, and if they are aiming for high quality and keep a good proportion of old vines in their vineyard, could not hope to. It could be said that the *appellation contrôlée* limits are not properly adjusted to what is really feasible in Burgundy: normally, a Grand Cru of real class on the Côte d'Or will not produce the maximum production per hectare of thirty hectolitres, a Premier Cru at thirty-five hectolitres might be right, but a straight village wine with a limit of thirty-five hectolitres in a healthy year could easily be lifted – there is too little difference between the great and the pleasant.

What has certainly changed for everyone is the nature of the grapes themselves. Clonal variations in Burgundy are very marked, and these have a direct impact on the taste of the wine. In one experiment alone at Echevronne in the Hautes-Côtes-de-Beaune the following clones of Pinot Noir were being studied: type fin; types moyens; type droit; type Jura; type Côte Chalonnaise; and type Champagne. The Pinot Noir of old was smaller, with a thicker skin and less flesh in relation to the skin. This meant less water in relation to solid, colouring matter, and the resultant wine was tougher, deeper and more concentrated. The grape has evolved, and does not make wine of the weight of yore, but tends to make wines of a more supple character. In the white wines, the Chardonnay has developed local characteristics that entirely suit the soil it is in. The grape is not the same in the Mâconnais, on the Côte de Beaune or in Chablis – in fact, if you transplanted the slightly muscat-flavoured Chardonnay of Mâcon to Meursault, your Meursault would taste very different. In Chablis, the Chardonnay is referred to as the Beaunois, the same word, incidentally, as one would use to describe a citizen of Beaune. With the exception of the modest Bourgogne Passetoutgrain (two-thirds Gamay and one-third Pinot

Noir), the wines of Burgundy are made of a single grape variety. The red wines of the Côte d'Or and the Côte Chalonnaise are made from the Pinot Noir, while the reds of the Mâconnais and Beaujolais are made from the Gamay. The Pinot Beurot, or Pinot Gris, is still permitted and occasionally used in very small proportions. The Chardonnay is responsible for all the white wines that are not named Bourgogne Aligoté – the Aligoté is a more lowly grape variety making a simple white wine, delicious in ripe years, much too acid in sunless years.

The Chardonnay has shown itself beautifully both in California and in Australia, and only the very best wines of the Côte de Beaune and Chablis have something individual, a sheer class, that makes their drinking not just another dimension of a varietal taste, but a distinct, inimitable addition to the repertoire. The Gamay is an amazing grape, capable of being so common on the wrong soil, and so very delicious on its chosen territory. This happens to be the granite of northern Beaujolais, the home of the nine Beaujolais *crus*. It also does well on more chalk-based soil, as in southern Beaujolais, but it does not rise above a very ordinary level in rich, more fertile soil. The Gamay is a much more productive plant than the Pinot, and pruning should be quite severe. The Gamay is grown in bushes round a single stake, with no wire – *à gobelet*. The Pinot Noir and the Chardonnay (as well as some Gamay in basic Beaujolais) are trained along low wires – *taille guyot*. In the Mâconnais, it is the *taille à queue du Mâconnais*, where the fruit-bearing branch is bent over and attached to the lower wire. Frost is an ever-present risk in the Burgundian vineyard, especially on the plain, and growers always have this in mind when pruning – unfortunately, as this takes place long before the latest spring frosts can occur, the tendency is to take the risk into account and accordingly prune less severely. Hail is much more of a danger in Burgundy than in Bordeaux. It is usually patchy and localized, as in parts of the Côte de Beaune in 1971, parts of Mercurey in 1976, and in 1979 when there was a June hailstorm which seriously affected Nuits-St-Georges and Vosne-Romanée, and in July another attack which touched Gevrey-Chambertin. In spite of rockets and aeroplanes disturbing cloud formations so that rain falls instead of hail, it can be seen that there is no 'cure' for hail.

How Burgundy is Classified

Classification is perhaps a misleading word, because in Burgundy it in no way resembles the 1855 classification of Bordeaux châteaux. Burgundy now has Grands Crus and Premiers Crus, followed by the village wines, e.g. Volnay, Nuits-St-Georges. A First or Fifth growth in Bordeaux will only have one owner, but a Grand Cru in Burgundy, e.g. Bonnes-Mares, can have several owners. In Burgundy it is the plot of land that is classified, and even if an owner is negligent, his mediocre wine will still be Grand Cru. A Grand Cru is the *appellation* itself, and does not have to show the name of the village it is in, e.g. Clos de la Roche does not have to be followed by the village name of Morey-St-Denis.

With Premiers Crus, however, the name of the village must appear with similar-sized letters, e.g. Pommard les Epenots. If two or more Premiers Crus are blended together, the wine is simply known as a Premier Cru, e.g. Beaune Premier Cru. Sometimes this is also done because the name of the village *appellation* carries a great deal of weight and the name of a slightly unknown Premier Cru would mean little outside the region. Beneath Premier Cru, a grower is permitted to put a *clos* or vineyard name, provided it is not more than half the size of the lettering of the village *appellation* name.

The ladder begins with the basic *appellation* wines of Burgundy, such as Bourgogne Grand Ordinaire (rarely seen on the export markets, probably because of the pejorative sound of *ordinaire*), Bourgogne, Bourgogne Passetoutgrain and Bourgogne Aligoté. Then there are *appellations* such as Beaujolais, Beaujolais Villages, Mâcon, Bourgogne Hautes-Côtes de Beaune and Hautes-Côtes de Nuits, Côte de Beaune Villages and Côte de Nuits Villages. Then there are the village names, such as Fleurie, Chassagne-Montrachet and Gevrey-Chambertin. Finally, Premiers Crus and Grands Crus top the ladder. For red wines, Grands Crus should attain 11.5 per cent alcohol minimum, without chaptalization, Premiers Crus 11 per cent, and village wines 10.5 per cent. For white wines, the figures are 12, 11.5, and 11 per cent for straight commune wines.

The 1974 legislation (see page 22) did decree that within five years all wines wishing to have *appellation contrôlée* status should be analysed and tasted. In Burgundy this was regarded as a near impossible task, with the mass of different owners and wines, but in 1979 the mechanics of these analyses and tastings were set in action. Before presenting his wines, a grower may have the option of choosing which *appellation* to ask for, but he has to make this decision for his *whole* crop. For instance, in a poor year a grower may decide that his wine is not up to Beaune standard, and decide to declassify his entire crop to Côte de Beaune, but this would be a last resort, when a wine was really inferior to its true *appellation*, as there would be an inevitable loss of revenue. A Grand Cru *could* declassify right down the scale, to Premier Cru, or to village status, Bourgogne, or finally to Bourgogne Grand Ordinaire. The need for it is rare, however. It must be said clearly that the classification of Burgundy, the choice of Grands Crus and Premiers Crus, is extremely accurate. These are really the vineyards with the best potential, capable of producing the most distinguished wines. Of course, occasionally a very well-made village wine, sometimes beautifully blended from various vineyards by an experienced shipper, will surpass a badly made Premier Cru from an unskilled producer, but this is the same thing as a really good Cru Bourgeois sometimes surpassing a *cru classé* in decline. The basically marl-stone soil of the Côte d'Or, mixed with calcareous soil, with more limestone where the white wines are grown, has many nuances within a very short space – sometimes a tiny track in the vineyard can mark a change of emphasis in the soil. All this has been noticed in the classification of the vineyards, together with the exact angle of the slope and the micro-climate. The Grand Cru vineyards tend to be in the middle of the Côte, facing southeast, neither near the scrubby top of the hill, nor in the fertile 'plain' near the Route Nationale that runs the length of the Côte d'Or. There are a few Premiers Crus that could be elevated to Grand Cru status, based on their sheer, persistent greatness – such as Clos St-Jacques and Les Véroilles in Gevrey-Chambertin, les Epenots and les Rugiens in Pommard and Les Caillerets in Volnay.

There are certain discrepancies in Burgundian spelling of place-names (Dominode and Dominaude, Véroilles and Varoilles), but these are usually self-evident, especially when pronounced out loud. The word *climat* means 'vineyard'.

Which Wines to Drink When

Burgundy offers a whole range of wines, those to keep for many years, or as long as you can hold out, and those to drink while waiting. You can start drinking Beaujolais a few weeks after the grapes are picked from the vine, but Beaujolais Villages has more to offer in the following year, and the Beaujolais *crus* have a longer life altogether. Mâcon wines are usually best with the fruity freshness of youth, and this could be said for most of the basic *appellations*. On the Côte d'Or and Côte Chalonnaise, village red wines vary with the year and the commune, but three to ten years would be a generalization. Premier Cru and Grand Cru wines, when superb examples of their kind, often prove to have limitless lives when they are from excellent vintages, but it would be a pity to guzzle them at under five years, even in the lightest of vintages.

Many top white Burgundies are drunk far too young, and much of their glory is thus missed. The Chardonnay takes some time to develop in bottle, especially in a northern clime. Young Grand Cru Chablis is as nothing beside a mature ten-year-old, and Corton Charlemagne remains very closed for the first four to five years of its life. However, white Mâcon and the Pouilly family are meant for relatively young, fresh drinking.

COTE D'OR: COTE DE NUITS

The Côte de Nuits makes the most majestic wines in the whole of Burgundy, wines of great breed and structure, often of great richness and opulence. They are almost entirely red. The complexity and depth of flavour in the best is a reflection of the mineral-rich soil, the geological deposits of ages past, and the exposure of the slopes. The Côte de Nuits is both narrower and steeper than the Côte de Beaune. The slopes are mostly east-facing, with variations of east-south-east or east-north-east, and therefore the weather is less southwest orientated than the Côte de Beaune and is more under the influence of the continental weather type, with its extremes of a drier cold in the winter and hotter summer. Some of the alluvial deposits are near the foot of the slope, and generally the best growths are lower down in the Côte de Nuits than they are on the Côte de Beaune, from mid to lower slope. Some of these deposits also gather in folds in the slope. Geological debris, silt and scree, blend with marl over calcareous soil to make the perfect combination. Marl (clay and carbonate of lime) would be to rich and fertile on its own, and needs to be mixed with poorer soil for high quality wine production. On the other hand, thin limestone soil on its own really is too meagre for the best wines, and in some parts of the Côte de Nuits there have been earth additions. However, the structural aspect of the slope is all important. Parts of the marl-rich soil of the Côte de Nuits appear almost red in colour, indicative of the exciting shades and tints in the wine to come. Production in the Côte de Nuits is smaller than in the Côte de Beaune. Starting from Dijon and working southwards down the Côte, these are the main villages.

Marsannay-La-Côte: This is a real Burgundian village, with some fine houses (and fine cellars) nestling away in their unshowy manner, solid and reassuring behind their walls. Marsannay should be one of the villages producing Côte de Nuits Villages, but the matter is still under discussion, hotly opposed by some growers from villages which already have the right to this *appellation*. Some red Bourgogne Marsannay is produced, but the commune is particularly known for its Bourgogne Rosé Marsannay, a pleasant curiosity, rather than a 'must', on a drinking itinerary. The famous grower, Bernard Clair, who lives in Marsannay, also has a small amount of Bourgogne Aligoté in the commune.

Fixin: This commune marks the southernmost part of what was the Côte Dijonnaise. Fixin is entitled to use the *appellation* Côte de Nuits Villages (and, exceptionally, can be declassified into that *appellation*), but the best *climats* are much more likely to be sold as Fixin itself. Fixin also includes neighbouring Fixey, and with true Burgundian individuality, the 'x's are pronounced as double 'ss'.

There are six Premier Cru vineyards in Fixin, of which the most distinguished is certainly the Clos de la Perrière – it is also the largest. The other Premier Cru wines are Clos du Chapitre, Les Hervelets, Les Arvelets, Aux Cheusots (more often known as Clos Napoléon) and Les Meix-Bas. I have always found Fixin wines deep in colour, slow to mature, and somewhat rustic if you compare them to the top wines from the Côte de Nuits. However, Clos de la Perrière can certainly share many characteristics with a Premier Cru from Gevrey-Chambertin. These robust wines are always well-made by the Domaine Pierre Gelin and, outside the Premier Cru category, Domaine Marion.

Gevrey-Chambertin: Where does one begin in a village capable of making some of the greatest wines on the Côte de Nuits and some of the most sad. The village *appellation* of Gevrey-Chambertin extends over the Nationale road, well into the plain, where the soil is vastly different from that of the slope, and the wine considerably more common. Some of the produce of this area has not done a great deal of good to the name of Gevrey-Chambertin, and one hopes the new tasting commissions will be courageous and will throw out wines not worthy of the name.

Gevrey-Chambertin is a typical example of a Burgundian village that enhanced its status by tagging on the name of its most famous vineyard (Chambertin) to the name of the village – Gevrey. It has done it no harm. Chambertin and Chambertin-Clos de Bèze are the two most prestigious vineyards in the commune, Grands Crus in a special, outstanding category of their own. Production is limited to thirty hectolitres to the hectare, but rarely reaches that quantity. Chambertin-Clos de Bèze can call itself Chambertin, but Chambertin *tout court* cannot become Chambertin-Clos de Bèze. Both should be majestic, the essence of the Côte de Nuits, beautifully constructed, generous and perfectly balanced. Bottles of these Grands Crus should not be broached within a few years of their birth – much will be lost if they are drunk at too embryonic a stage.

With more than two dozen owners, Chambertin and Chambertin-Clos de Bèze will not produce wine of a uniform quality. But there are some very meticulous growers in these magic 'fields', and their wines are worth saving for. Domaine Clair-Daü makes some of the biggest wines – its Clos de Bèze always needs years to show at anywhere near its best. As Bernard Clair makes firm wines that are slow to mature, even the so-called 'lighter' vintages such as 1973 are different things in his domain. This is partly explained by old vines, and partly by more lengthy vatting than some growers. The structure of the Clair-Daü Clos de Bèze 1978 is magnificent, and the wine is firm, big and rich. But at this level of *cru*, there should always be breed and elegance beneath the structure – top wines should never be clumsy. Drouhin-Laroze is also known for his Clos de Bèze, but this is quite a different style. This grower makes delicious flowery and fragrant wines, very pretty when young – perhaps tailing off a bit when older in light years. But when youthful, it is like having a mouthful of flowers on the palate.

Other owners in Chambertin and Chambertin-Clos de Bèze are: Domaine Armand Rousseau (M. Charles Rousseau makes superb wines); Pierre Gelin; the *négociant* Louis Latour (whose Chambertin 1971, Cuvée Héritiers Latour, is all silky elegance); Marion; Trapet; Camus, whose wines have disappointed recently; Domaine Damoy (some of whose wines have appeared over-chaptalized and unbalanced); and Tortochot. There are six other Grands Crus, which differ from the 'top two' in that they are allowed to produce up to thirty-two hectolitres to the hectare. Latricières-Chambertin must be considered on the same level as Chambertin itself – it is indeed on the same level on the slope. The 1978 Latricières from Bouchard Père et Fils is a gem of a wine, concentrated, with a mass of ripe Pinot Noir in it. I remember having a 1952 from Jules Régnier in 1973 that hardly showed any signs of age, had a beautiful bouquet and was balanced, lightish and elegant. This finesse is very typical of Latricières, and Trapet also makes perfect examples of the *appellation*. The other Grands Crus are Charmes-Chambertin (or Mazoyères-Chambertin), excellent at Domaine Dujac, and the 1969 of Bouchard Père is wonderful, Chapelle-Chambertin, Griotte-Chambertin, Mazis-Chambertin (or Mazys or Mazy) and Ruchottes-Chambertin. Mazis-Chambertin is the only lot of Côte de Nuits wine appearing at the Hospices de Beaune sale (this began in 1977), and although the first year's offering was poor, the 1978 and 1979 Hospices wines were superb.

There is a magnificent array of Premiers Crus in Gevrey-Chambertin, at least two of which stand out as being on a par with the Grands Crus: Clos St-Jacques and Les Varoilles (or les Véroilles). One of the best Burgundies I have ever experienced was the Clos St Jacques 1969 of Fernand Pernot – unfortunately, the family does not make wine like that any more. Clair-Daü's Clos St-Jacques 1976 is very dense in colour, has a deep bouquet, and is huge and tannic, full of scent and flavour. Overall, the Domaine Clair-Daü is the largest private domain in Burgundy – all the larger domains are owned by *négociants*. Bernard Clair has over forty hectares of vineyards, and no fewer than eighteen hectares of these are in the Grands Crus and Premiers Crus, nearly all in the Côte de Nuits. The Domaine des Varoilles of Jean-Pierre Naigeon is also highly respected. This is a relatively small domain of twelve hectares, nearly all of which is Premier or Grand Cru. It takes its name from the most important holding, the Clos des Varoilles – the whole six hectares is owned by the domain. Varoilles has a micro-climate, which enables picking to take place up to eight days later than elsewhere. The Clos des Varoilles 1976 is big and tannic, with a spicy nose – here, M. Naigeon had only vatted for one week, as given the conditions of the year, a normal vatting would have produced altogether too much tannin. The very fine 1972 is only just coming into its own. The 1978 Varoilles is outstanding, with a fantastic colour, wonderful nose of violets and glorious structure. This means that all the component parts were there in all the right proportions, giving a fine framework to the wine. The 1977s at this domain are very good value. Amongst the other Premiers Crus, look out for Cazetiers, Etournelles, Fonteny, Combe-aux-Moines, Clos-Prieur and Champonnets.

Straight village Gevrey-Chambertin should be warm and generous, with a lovely scent. Much depends on the maker and where the vineyards are. Some parts of the commune of Brochon are entitled to the Gevrey-Chambertin *appellation*. Two other domain names are Louis Rémy and Henri Rebourseau.

Morey-St-Denis: Here, the modest village of Morey opted for the addition of St-Denis, from the name of its famous Clos. The four Grands Crus of the commune are comparatively little vaunted, when put against the other big names of the Côte de Nuits. Apart from the Clos St-Denis, there is the Clos de la Roche, bigger in area and body, Clos de Tart, and a small part of Bonnes-Mares – by far the greater part is in the commune of Chambolle-Musigny. A maximum yield of thirty hectolitres to the hectare is permitted for these *appellations*. The Clos de la Roche and the Clos de Tart tend to be the biggest wines of the commune, the Clos St-Denis combines charm and *mâche*, and Bonnes Mares has much of the character of the neighbouring commune.

M. Jacques Seysses of Domaine Dujac lives at Morey, and in his cellars you can see the fine differences between the growths. The domain has eleven hectares of vines, comprising ten *appellations* – an indication of the 'parcelling' in Burgundy.

In November 1979, the Morey-St-Denis Premier Cru 1978 had already been bottled, and had a fine strawberry nose, a long finish and silky texture, almost a Chambolle character. The 1978 Clos St-Denis was deceptively charming, but with firm backbone behind it (as it should have at this young stage), while the Clos de la Roche filled the mouth with luscious fruit. A Clos St Denis 1969 was very *racé*, full of breed, stylish, fruity and elegant. At this domain, bottling is done entirely by gravity, as M. Seysses is convinced that pumping oxidizes and tires the wine and, when in vat, the wine is kept under nitrogen gas. The entire domain is vintaged in a week, thereby managing to pick all the different parcels of vineyard more or less at the optimum moment.

The Clos de Tart, exceptionally in Burgundy, has one owner, the Beaujolais *négociants*, Mommessin. The wines are good, although perhaps not as good as they might be, judged by the highest standards. There is a Premier Cru Morey-St-Denis, Clos des Lambrays, or Les Larrets, that could conceivably be a Grand Cru – the plot

Imminent storm over the old village of Santenay in the Côte de Beaune
(Overleaf) The vineyards at Fuissé, one of the villages making up the Pouilly-Fuissé
'appellation', with the rolling hills of the Mâconnais in the background

of land is right, the *direction* is missing. Under Mme Cosson, there were some amazingly good wines up until the 1950s. The property was for sale for many years, and in 1979 was finally sold to a group founded on Lazards Bank. It remains to be seen whether this is just a short-term adventure, because the property itself needs twenty years of devotion to reach its full potential – complete replanting is required, for a start. The Premiers Crus most likely to be seen are Les Sorbés, Le Clos-des-Ormes, and Clos-Bussière; Roumier makes a good example of the latter. Important domains include Amiot, Ponsot and Lignie.

Chambolle-Musigny: Le Musigny is a great wine, in the right hands. A Grand Cru of enormous elegance, subtle, with a hidden, almost 'irony' backbone. Le Musigny should have a sorcerer's bouquet when mature. Comte de Vogüé's wines have this magic. The 1976 Musigny of Louis Latour has real class, and their 1971 is absolutely impeccable, with restrained breed that opens out, great ripeness, and ultimate elegance. I have also tasted a Musigny 1969 Vieilles Vignes from Remoissenet, but although this had interest, there was a trace of clumsiness at the end which one should not find in this Grand Cru. Owners of note in this Grand Cru include Domaine Jacques Prieur, Domaine Comte Georges de Vogüé, Domaine Mugnier, Joseph Drouhin, Roumier and Hudelot. A tiny amount of white Musigny is made.

Bonnes-Mares is the other Grand Cru of Chambolle-Musigny, and I have never seen a classier example than that of Bouchard Père in the 1969 vintage – with a scent which permeated the whole taste, and an almost 'irony' flavour and backbone which characterizes Bonnes-Mares. This wine has a great future, and must be admired as a feat of buying and *élevage*, as Bouchard Père do not own in Bonnes-Mares. A Bonnes-Mares 1970 from Drouhin-Laroze, tasted at the beginning of 1980, was deeply scented and very consistent and still solid. Comte de Vogüé, Clair-Daü and the Domaine des Varoilles make outstanding Bonnes-Mares. Most owners of Musigny have a plot in Bonnes-Mares. I have also admired a 1976 Bonnes-Mares from the shipper Louis Jadot. The Domaine Roumier is important. The Premiers Crus of Chambolle can be silky, satiny, elegant wines. Les Amoureuses and Les Charmes must be considered at the top; the rest are nearly always sold as Chambolle-Musigny Premier Cru.

Vougeot: With the fifty hectares of Clos de Vougeot (or Clos Vougeot), Burgundy has a Grand Cru of Bordelais proportions! Unfortunately, the wall-enclosed Clos does not have one owner, but around eighty, and one does not have to be psychic to see that this means variations in quality. These variations are not only due to where exactly in the Clos the owner has his plot, but also to the amount he has, because it is much more difficult to make fine wine with just a tiny quantity. However, exact vineyard site is of paramount importance, and it has to be admitted that were it not for the historical creation of the Clos by the Cistercians, by no means all of the area would be classified as Grand Cru, especially those vineyards bordering the Route Nationale 74. In fact, one of the choicest parts of the Clos slope is occupied by the famous Château du Clos de Vougeot, but I am sure no one would consent to its destruction to make way for more vines, especially if they were in the habit of attending the boisterous Chevaliers du Tastevin dinners within its walls.

The name is certainly illustrious enough to encourage some high yields within the Clos, and it is comparatively rare to taste a Clos de Vougeot of real distinction. At its best it should be a big, rich wine, with a complex, scented nose. Just about every owner from the neighbouring communes has a slice of Clos de Vougeot, as well as many of the shippers, such as Morin, who has Château de la Tour de Clos Vougeot, Faiveley and Joseph Drouhin. The Domaine des Varoilles which now vinifies its wine with another owner in order to get a better 'mass' of wine, has made an outstanding 1977 and a 1976 of immense *ampleur* and richness. A 1972 Clos de

Nylon netting is used in the Champagne region to protect the grapes from birds

Vougeot from René Engel, tasted in December 1979, had a rich smell, great concentration and a lovely flavour – perhaps it could have been even better had it been picked a little later, in this unripe year, but it was still a fine bottle. Other owners are Drouhin-Laroze, Charles Noëllat, Jean Grivot, Jacques Prieur and Henry Lamarche.

The Confrérie des Chevaliers du Tastevin is a brotherhood of wine which has done a miraculous feat of promotion for Burgundy, its wines and its *joie de vivre*. Many other *confréries* have followed, but none have the world-wide influence and impact of the Chevaliers du Tastevin. The Confrérie also awards its label to wines submitted and found to be truly good and representative examples of their *appellation* and vintage. The wines are tasted blind by a panel consisting of different aspects of the wine trade and consumers, and there is no doubt that the award of a Tastevin label adds *cachet* to a wine. There are occasional lapses in judgement here, as there are everywhere, and certain tasteviné wines have had a tendency to go on for ever, but generally it is an indication of a wine that is honourable, and often very good indeed. The *tastevin* itself is a shallow, fluted cup, often silver, which is traditionally used by Burgundians, to look at the colour and clarity of a young wine. It is, however, more difficult to judge the bouquet of a wine in a wide-surfaced container, and many wine professionals like to use a classic tasting glass, even if it looks less picturesque.

The commune of Vougeot consists of nearly thirteen hectares, and so is naturally overshadowed by the great Clos. But its Premiers Crus can produce very fine wines, such as the Vougeot Clos de la Perrière 1962 from Domaine Bertagna, perhaps then making more outstanding wines than nowadays, partly because there was new planting later in the 1960s. The other Premiers Crus are Clos Blanc, les Petits-Vougeots and part of Les Cras; the Clos Blanc makes white wine from Chardonnay.

Flagey-Echézeaux: The village of Flagey-Echézeaux is stranded on the wrong side of the Route Nationale 74, far from its main vineyards, which are up behind the Clos de Vougeot. Flagey-Echézeaux is not a commune *appellation*, and if the great vineyards of Grands Echézeaux and Les Echézeaux are declassified, they become Vosne-Romanée, the neighbouring commune. Grands Echézeaux is a Grand Cru of enormous quality, full and rich and complex. Les Echézeaux is more than three times the size, and therefore more variable – it does not have the sheer class of Grands Echézeaux, but can be very fine wine. It is made up of a number of vineyards, including Les Rouges, and Les Champs Traversins. Owners are the Domaine de la Romanée-Conti, René Engel, and the Gros family. Well-chosen Echézeaux can be at a relatively good price for a Grand Cru.

Vosne-Romanée: The Grands Crus of this commune are the greatest names of Burgundy, mostly justifying their reputation, if not always their astronomical price. This kind of price spiral is difficult to avoid when the quantities are tiny and the *renommée* is international, but there should always be some relation between the two. Romanée-Conti is just under two hectares of red-earthed grandeur. It is solely owned by the Domaine de la Romanée-Conti (the de Vilaine and Leroy families), who market the wine with vigour. At its best, Romanée-Conti is an unrepeatable drinking experience. The 1971 is a vintage like this, a scented wine, with beautiful balance, big with lovely fruit, almost chewy in its body and texture. Now, the Pinot Noir vines are on American, phylloxera-resistant root stocks, but until 1945 the Romanée-Conti owners persevered with French root stocks, in spite of a severely deteriorating yield.

The Domaine de la Romanée-Conti is also the sole owner of the six-hectare La Tâche. The 1971 La Tâche was exquisite, soft and scented in 1974, with a glorious ripe finish; the 1962 is as great. Romanée-Conti can age even more splendidly than La Tâche on occasions. A comparison between the two was made with the 1952 vintage, but here La Tâche was the easy winner, a great and noble wine in

1979, for this was the first vintage, made with young vines, from Romanée-Conti after the replanting. The 1970 La Tâche seemed to me good, but not great. The 1969 had a deep colour in 1974, was much racier and nervier, and seemed set to last to perfection. However, five years later the wine was browning and seemed clumsy and unbalanced. Occasionally, the domain grapes seem to be picked too late, giving a slight taste and smell of over-ripeness to the wine, almost a roasted flavour sometimes. Apart from being sole owners of Romanée-Conti and La Tâche, the Domaine also owns in Richebourg, Grands Echézeaux and Echézeaux, as well as in Le Montrachet. In addition, the Domaine produces and sells about half of Romanée-St-Vivant, the part which forms the Domaine Marey-Monge.

Richebourg can be big, fat and velvety, a most seductive Grand Cru. The 1971 Richebourg from the Domaine de la Romanée-Conti was massive and concentrated. I tasted this against a 1971 Grands Echézeaux from the Domaine, which has a big 'masculine' style, and the rather delightful rich, minerally earthiness that I often find in top Vosne-Romanée wine – almost a spiciness on the nose. The 1978 Riche-bourg of Bouchard Père is really *gras*, rich and full, with immense backbone, and their 1971 is a great wine now and for the future, enormous and spicy. I have also been impressed by the Richebourg 1971 of Remoissenet, which has class – again, a big wine, with a lot of scent, power and strength, with the opulence of the *appellation*. Remoissenet have as well a very good Grands Echézeaux 1969, Cuvée Jacquinot de Richemont, with some tightness and concentration as befits this great year.

Romanée-St-Vivant is under ten hectares and has a monastic background. Part of the vineyard is called Les Quatre Journaux and belongs to the *négociant*, Louis Latour. The 1971 shows immense class and breed, a beautifully made wine from this very ripe vintage. Magnums of the 1966 drunk in 1979 were superb, as is the 1978.

La Romanée is the smallest *appellation* in area in France, producing an average thirty hectolitres of wine per crop. Lying just above Romanée-Conti, it is inevitable that the wines should be compared, but really they are very different. This difference is attributable to nuances in the soil and to different ownership, and therefore to varying methods of vinifying and *élevage*. La Romanée is entirely owned by the family of Liger-Belair, but the distribution and *élevage* is now effected by the Beaune shippers Bouchard Père et Fils. This has been the case since the 1976 vintage, as with Vosne-Romanée Les Reignots. The 1978 La Romanée is top-class, with a vast range and depth of flavours and great silkiness.

Commune Vosne-Romanée wines can give immense pleasure, and their heady perfume and generous nature are very individual. There is a very respectable list of Premiers Crus: Aux Malconsorts (I remember a magnificent 1935 from the Barolet collection), Les Beaux-Monts, Les Suchots, La Grand'Rue, Les Gaudichots, Aux Brûlées, Les Chaumes, Les Reignots, Le Clos-des-Réas and Les Petits-Monts. The wines of Lamarche and Noëllat often look better in cask.

Nuits-St-Georges: There may be no Grands Crus in Nuits-St-Georges, but it is rich in Premiers Crus. If the name is full of imagery, the taste is no less so, incisive, earthy and plummy. There is a kind of irony backbone about good Nuits that is extremely evocative, and the flavour lives long in the mouth. Nowhere is Nuits better than at the Domaine Gouges. The late M. Henri Gouges was one of the very first growers to bottle his wine himself. The domain is over ten hectares, which is less than it sounds when one calculates that this is spread over many *climats* and must satisfy the world. Gouges own in Les Vaucrains, Les Saint-Georges, Les Porrets (they have the Clos des Porrets, which is the best part of the first growth), Les Pruliers, Aux Chaignots, and have white wine in La Perrière, as well as having village wine.

The vineyards north of Nuits, towards Vosne-Romanée, are not quite as famous as those Premiers Crus south of the village, but remain very good sites – they tend not to be so big and are more supple than those *climats* to the south. The best of this group of Premiers Crus are probably Aux Boudots, Aux Murgers and Aux Chaignots. South of Nuits there is a succession of very fine Premiers Crus: Les St-Georges, probably the wine with the most finesse – there is a little sand in the soil; Les Vaucrains, the most solid of all and the slowest to mature; Les Cailles; Les Porets (or Les Porrets); La Perrière and Les Pruliers.

The neighbouring commune of Prémeaux can also use the *appellation* Nuits-St-Georges, and there are Premiers Crus here too, notably the Clos de la Maréchale (sold by Faiveley), Les Didiers, Clos-des-Forêts, and Clos des Corvées. Faiveley is a big owner throughout Nuits, as is Lupé-Cholet – they have the Château Gris. Commune Nuits-St-Georges is, unfortunately, expensive, but at its best you are promised a bottle of considerable interest – the wine is bound to have a pronounced nose and a strong flavour coupled with a velvety texture.

Bourgogne Hautes-Côtes de Nuits: Up behind this southern part of the Côte de Nuits, from the hills behind Nuits-St-Georges itself down to south of Corgoloin, a considerable revival has taken place in the vineyards and some pleasant wine is being made under the Bourgogne Hautes-Côtes de Nuits *appellation*. These Arrière-Côtes are very charming, with small Burgundian villages dotted around on the rolling hills amidst mixed farming. Pinot Noir, Chardonnay, Gamay and Aligoté are planted in these hills, and the wines have to pass a Commission de Dégustation (tasting panel) before achieving the *appellation*. The problem in these Arrière-Côtes is lack of sun, as many of the slopes do not face in the right direction. Much of the wine is made at the Cave Coopérative des Hautes-Côtes just outside Beaune. The house of Geisweiler own seventy hectares of Pinot Noir and Chardonnay round the village of Bévy. There is much less Hautes-Côtes de Nuits than Hautes-Côtes de Beaune, and it could hardly be called cheap. But sometimes bottles can be surprisingly good and fruity; especially those from Delaunay.

The Côte de Nuits peters out with the three communes of Prissey, Comblanchien and Corgoloin, all of which can produce Côte de Nuits Villages. Much of Comblanchien and Corgoloin seems to be eaten up by marble quarries, but Corgoloin has a single vineyard of some note, the Clos des Langres. The vineyards of the Côte de Nuits run almost straight into those of the Côte de Beaune but there is a clear division in the two slopes, and it is not one continuous Côte.

COTE D'OR: COTE DE BEAUNE

Ladoix-Serrigny: The first commune on the Côte de Beaune is Ladoix-Serrigny, an *appellation* in its own right, but not often seen on labels. Most of the vineyards are very good, but they have the right to the Grand and Premier Cru *appellations* of the neighbouring commune of Aloxe-Corton. What is left is more often than not declassified into Côte de Beaune Villages, thereby incorporating the magic name of Beaune. Red and white wines are made. I have admired the Ladoix Côte de Beaune 1976 of the Prince de Mérode, who makes wines with real Pinot Noir character.

Aloxe-Corton: The *appellations* and vineyards within this commune are some of the most confusing (and confused) in Burgundy. The wine of the commune can be soft (like the sound of the 'x' in Aloxe), but full and ripe. The nub of the whole area is the impressive hill of the Grand Cru Corton. Here are the best and most magnificent red wines of the Côte de Beaune, and some would argue that the best whites are also made on these slopes too – about 30 per cent of the production is in white wine. The *appellation* of Corton is made up of several vineyards which can add their name to that of Corton itself, e.g. Corton Bressandes. Any wine with a label that features the name 'Corton' is a Grand Cru. But some of these vineyards are only in part classified as Grand Cru, and the other part is Premier Cru, therefore becoming an Aloxe-Corton-Maréchaudes, for example. The part of this vineyard that is Grand Cru would be labelled Corton-Maréchaudes, or just simply Corton. Le Corton is just one of these vineyards making up the Grand Cru of Corton. It, like any other, can be sold separately, or blended with other vineyards within the Grand Cru, but of course two vineyard names would not appear – it would just be Corton.

The great red wines of Corton have some of the majesty of the Côte de Nuits, taking time to soften and open out, but eventually combining body with enormous seduction. Probably the Corton Clos du Roi wines need the greatest time to reach their apogee, with Corton Bressandes often showing lovely fruit earlier. The wines of M. Daniel Senard are excellent, as are those of M. Antonin Guyon at the Domaine de la Guyonnière – his Corton-Bressandes 1971 has a wonderful, ripe, Pinot nose, and is rich and completely balanced. Bouchard Père have wonderful Le Corton and Tollot-Beaut is reputed, with a very good 1976 Bressandes. Louis Latour also make excellent wine in Corton, namely their Château Corton-Grancey, their domain wine which is not named after a vineyard but after their Château de Grancey. Louis Latour's Clos de la Vigne au Saint produces superb bottles. A Corton-Bressandes 1969 from Joseph Drouhin had a ripe nose, and was rich and full with good length – a Burgundy for cold climates. On the other hand, a Corton Clos du Roi 1971 from Michel Voarick was really very light, but most flowery, which proves that the hand of the wine-maker can prevail over the intrinsic character of the respective *climat*. The Prince de Mérode has Corton-Maréchaudes and Clos du Roi, and makes commendable wine. Some very good Corton-Pougets come from Louis Jadot. A white Corton Vergennes 1976 Hospices de Beaune from Chanson looked superb in 1979.

The great white wine, Corton-Charlemagne, comes from round the bluff of the Corton hill, facing the little road going into Pernand-Vergelesses and below the tree-line of the hill-top. These upper slopes have more limestone in the soil, and lend much to the splendour of the bouquet. Corton-Charlemagne owes nothing to anyone; it is aristocratic, subtle wine that will take its time to show its full beauty. So often it is drunk too young, when all the complexities of nose and taste are still hidden. There is a wonderful firmness, even a tautness, about Corton-Charlemagne when young, breaking out into glorious Chardonnay scent and elegance when mature. The best sites are not those nearest Pernand, but to the south of the slope. One of the most famous owners is the *négociant* Louis Latour – it was the great-grandfather of the present Louis Latour who started planting white grapes at Corton. The 1978 already has that mysterious, unmistakable slightly peppery nose that is Corton-Charlemagne, and a waxy texture that makes for a great future – the 1976 drunk in 1979 had a lot of body behind it. The 1974 when young was already scented, but not really developed, with many flavours and that Chardonnay-almondy finish, but in the background the firmness of the *appellation*. The 1973 was obviously much more forward, crisp and utterly drinkable relatively young. The 1972 had more acidity and firmness, and the 1971 had an overwhelming nose, very big and 'giving'. The 1961 was superb in 1980. Other important owners are the shippers Louis Jadot and Bouchard Père, and the Domaine Bonneau de Martray, the latter also having red Corton. Corton-Charlemagne can, in fact, be produced from part of the *climat* called Corton, and vice versa, but note of the exact composition of the soil will indicate whether Pinot Noir or Chardonnay is most suitable. With the demand for top white Burgundy, there has been, perhaps, a tendency to plant Chardonnay in plots more suited to red-wine production.

Pernand-Vergelesses: The village of Pernand lies in a fold in the hills, in the shelter of the great Corton hill. Where the vines end, the woods begin, and there are some lovely walks into the Arrière-Côtes from here. The wines of Pernand can have a lovely, flowery bouquet, delicate and subtle – some say of violets. Nowadays they tend to be light, and their charm lies in their youthful fruit. I even drank a straight village 1977 in 1979 with much pleasure, although one would obviously not take this course of action with the 1976s and 1978s. Although there are five Premiers Crus in Pernand-Vergelesses, one stands out – Ile des Vergelesses – which generally has more body and elegance than the others. Louis Latour makes a good example of this Premier Cru, as do Dubreuil-Fontaine, the Domaine Chandon de Briailles, and the Domaine de la Guyonnière, whose 1973 was a memorable wine. The Rapet family are big owners in Pernand and the shippers Chanson own in another Premier Cru, les Basses-Vergelesses, although the word *Basses* is dropped on the label (following a tendency in place-names all over France – gone are the Basses Pyrénées and the Basses Alpes). Chanson also produce a little white wine from the Caradeux vineyard, and I can recommend the Pernand Vergelesse (the final 's' is sometimes dropped) Blanc 1976 from Guyon which, at the beginning of 1980, was excellent, with a very perfumed nose. The whites in Pernand tend to be soft but full, totally without the nervy class of Corton. Good Aligoté comes from Laleure-Piot.

Chorey-Lès-Beaune: The flat vineyards here are not particularly favoured, and much of the wine is sold to the Beaune shippers for Côte de Beaune Villages, a pleasant bottle of Burgundy to be drunk relatively young. There is some white wine too, but much of that would go into straight Bourgogne in the shippers' cellars.

Savigny-Lès-Beaune: The *appellation* Savigny covers red and white wine, with the emphasis very much on reds. The best can be really attractive wines, with great charm, delicacy of flavour and persistence. In style, they are perhaps between Pernand-Vergelesses and Beaune, which is in fact where the small town is situated physically. The greatest bottles of Savigny that I have tasted have been from the Premiers Crus of La Dominode and Les Lavières. The 1976 Dominode from Clair-Daü is excellent, rich and long, as fat as the 1964. The 1978 is also juicy and fat, but not big or tannic. Fine wines are also made by Chanson Père et Fils, Joseph Drouhin, and Champy Père et Fils. The Lavières of Bouchard Père et Fils has enormous charm and seduction, as does the same *climat* from Robert Ampeau, although it is perhaps lighter; however, that could not be said about the 1978. The shippers Henri de Villamont are a strong force in this *appellation*, owned as they are by the large and well-run Swiss firm of Schenk. The wines of M. Pierre Petitjean are also good. The red wines of Savigny can also be Côte de Beaune Villages.

Beaune: Beaune is a beautiful old walled town with wine in its stones. Many of the most important shippers of Burgundy have their headquarters here, and vineyard ownership in the *appellation* is dominated by these *négociants*. Over twenty times as much red wine is made as white, and there are no Grands Crus. This is an indication of the nature of the wines, which are straightforward and frank but do not have great hidden depths or complexity. Red Beaune has a full-bodied approach, uncomplicated and fruity. The fascination lies in comparing the top Premiers Crus, which show consistent and marked differences. I have often had the opportunity to do this at Bouchard Père, and the vineyards keep their individuality while holding the respective vintage characters. One leads in with a restrained Clos de la Mousse, then goes into a more robust Teurons, followed by a fuller, fatter Marconnets, almost Côte de Nuits in its assertiveness (Marconnets is the Premier Cru that lost so much land to the autoroute coming down the Côte), finishing with the beautiful elegance, scent and finesse of the Grèves Vigne de l'Enfant Jésus. The Clos de la Mousse, on a rocky base, will always be the first to develop, some would call it feminine, while the other, better, Premiers Crus will need time to show their nuances of flavour. In 1977, I enjoyed the 1962 l'Enfant Jésus and 1947 Marconnets, both in perfect condition. In 1979, the 1961 l'Enfant Jésus was rich and concentrated. At Bouchard Père, their Cent Vignes often goes into their splendid non-vintage Premier Cru blend, Beaune du Château, one of the most reliable and best value bottles of Burgundy you can buy – the white blend is equally good, rustic rather than complex. Clos du Roi is usually bigger in character than Cent Vignes. The other top Premiers Crus are les Fèves, much of which belongs to the shippers Chanson, who sell it under the name of Beaune Clos des Fèves. Les Vignes Franches from Louis Latour is always splendid, with the 1976, 1978 and 1979 wines showing great promise. Louis Jadot's Clos-des-Ursules is an enclave within Vignes-Franches. Les Bressandes is another top Premier Cru, usually very good from Chanson, and red and white Clos des Mouches from Joseph Drouhin are recommended; the 1976 white, seen in 1979, was delicious. Other noted Premiers Crus are Champimonts, Cras and Toussaints.

The Hospices de Beaune is a very important owner in the Beaune Premiers Crus. The top vineyards donated to this charity, devoted to looking after the sick and old, supported the good works, and still play a significant role in the welfare of Beaune's citizens. The lots of wine sold at the famous Hospices de Beaune auction on the third Sunday of every November are named after vineyard workers connected with the wines or the benefactors of the Hospices, so where it is not evident in the title, it is necessary to know from which vineyard the wine originated. With one exception, all the wines sold at the auction come from the Côte de Beaune, and they bring a prestige value which is not a weather-vane for the prices in the ordinary marketplace, although it can indicate a trend.

Côte de Beaune and Côte de Beaune Villages: The Côte de Beaune *appellation* is both red and white, but is rarely seen. It only applies to wine from the Beaune vineyard area. However, Côte de Beaune Villages is for red wines only, and very much in evidence. The villages that have the right to the *appellation* are: Auxey-Duresses; Blagny; Chassagne-Montrachet; Cheilly-les-Maranges; Chorey-lès-Beaune; Dézize-les-Maranges; Ladoix; Meursault; Monthelie; Pernand-Vergelesses; Puligny-Montrachet; St-Aubin; St-Romain; Sampigny-les-Maranges; Santenay and Savigny.

Pommard: If Gevrey-Chambertin is where the side is let down in the Côte de Nuits, Pommard is the Achilles heel of the Côte de Beaune. Somehow the name is a password to success, especially in the United States, and there has been much abuse. However, now that is less possible and the risk is more of paying a great deal of money for mediocrity. Pommard should have a fine, sturdy character, firm and rich, but the best of the Premiers Crus go way beyond that into finesse and delicacy, with underlying backbone. Top wines from Les Epenots and Les Rugiens exemplify this, perhaps none more so than Les Epenots from the Domaine de Courcel – the 1976 is set for a very long life indeed. Other top domains are Comte Armand (with superb Clos des Epeneaux), Michel Gaunoux, Parent (with both Epenots and their Clos Micault) and the Domaine de la Pousse d'Or. Jaboulet-Vercherre, the shippers, own the Château de la Commaraine and its Clos, and the Château de Pommard is commercial without being sought-after for its quality. The Domaine Billard-Gonnet makes fine wines.

Volnay: Volnay at its most distinguished presents a different picture of charm, scent and delicacy, not highly-coloured, but lingering and flowery. Working upwards, and using the marvellous range of Bouchard Père wines as a yardstick, one can begin with a delicate Volnay Taille-Pieds, go on to a flowery Frémiets, and then to a more complete, powerful, rich Caillerets. This combines the seductive charm of the *appellation* with something much more lasting – the superb domain of the Marquis d'Angerville also makes wines that show these qualities. Another owner in Caillerets is Jean Clerget. Champans and Chevret are the other top Premiers

Crus of Volnay – there is also the splendid Santenots, which is in Meursault but which is allowed to use the Volnay *appellation* for the red wines. Robert Ampeau makes excellent Volnay-Santenots, even in the less impressive years – the wines have real grace. The Domaine des Comtes Lafon produces excellent Santenots-du-Milieu. The Domaine de la Pousse d'Or makes really distinguished wines, and I have admired, amongst others, the Volnay Clos de la Bousse d'Or 1970 and the Volnay les Caillerets, Clos des Soixante Ouvrées 1972. Delagrange, Henri Boillot and Louis Glantenay are other owners, and the Volnay Clos des Chênes of the Domaine du Château de Meursault must be mentioned.

Monthelie: This is a lesser-known name of Burgundy, but the best wines speak for themselves. They tend to mature somewhat faster than the best Volnays. De Suremain makes some of the finest wines and owns the Château de Monthelie, and the Domaine A. Ropiteau-Mignon makes excellent wine from the Clos des Champs-Fulliot, one of the Premiers Crus. The Domaine Parent and the Deschamps family are also owners in Monthelie.

Auxey-Duresses: This is an *appellation* of both red and white wines (considerably less), and some of the whites are quite remarkable, especially in youth, when they have a charming, biscuity quality. I particularly admire those of Bouchard Père, which show great character when drunk comparatively young. Domains of great note are the Duc de Magenta and Roland Thévenin's Domaine du Moulin aux Moines. There are worthy wines to be found amongst growers here, treading, as always, with care. The shipper Leroy is based in Auxey.

St-Romain: There are more white wines than red here, due to the higher location, and careful choice can produce some fine examples. Roland Thévinin is well-known here, under the Domaine du Château de Puligny-Montrachet label.

St-Aubin: Red wines, and about half as much white are produced here. Unlike St-Romain, there are some Premiers Crus here. The *négociant* Raoul Clerget has his headquarters in St-Aubin, and the best-known growth is Frionnes.

Meursault: To many, Meursault is archetypal Côte de Beaune white wine, rich, fat and with a glorious, full-blown Chardonnay nose and generous colour. The top Premiers Crus are Les Perrières, Les Charmes and Genevrières, followed by Poruzot and La Goutte-d'Or. There are some big owners in Meursault, as well as the multitude of small growers evident in every Burgundian commune – beware those with land down in the plain near the N74 road. This will either be marketed by the grower himself or sold to a shipper as straight village Meursault, and it will be a disappointment. The firm of Ropiteau have important holdings in Meursault, as do Patriarche, who now own the Château de Meursault. They produce wines of high repute. The Domaine des Comtes Lafon makes remarkable Meursault-Perrières and the less expensive Clos de la Barre – the 1969 of the latter was wonderful in 1980. Other top producers are the Domaine Jacques Prieur, Bernard Michelot, Domaine Joseph Matrot, Darnat, Guy Roulot and Raymond Javillier. J. P. Gauffroy has excellent Les Poruzots under the Selection Jean Germain label, and one of the greatest Meursaults I have drunk for sheer balance and finesse (rather than obvious lushness) was the Genevrières 1973 from Jean Monnier, drunk in 1979. Naturally enough, Louis Latour and Bouchard Père both produce classic Meursaults, wines with a long finish and almost a lanolin texture. There are also the Meursault-Blagny vineyards, the best being La Pièce-sous-le-Bois and Sous le Dos d'Ane. These whites are very like Meursault, sometimes a bit firmer. Ampeau is a good grower.

Puligny-Montrachet: The greatest vineyards and *appellations* of this commune are on the border with Puligny-Montrachet and Chassagne-Montrachet. The great Le Montrachet itself has its seven and a half hectares divided between the two communes, and although the direction of the slope changes slightly, one tends to believe that the differences in Le Montrachet are more due to the different owners. The main owners are the Marquis de Laguiche (the shipper Joseph Drouhin distributes this), the Domaine Baron Thénard (distributed by the shippers Remoissenet), and Bouchard Père et Fils. Other owners are the Domaine Jacques Prieur, the Domaine de la Romanée-Conti (their 1971 is magnificent), the Domaine René Fleurot and Comte Lafon. Montrachet should never be drunk too young – it cannot begin to show its incredible breed and layers of taste until eight to ten years of age.

Bâtard-Montrachet is also divided between the two communes, and it can rival Le Montrachet for sheer splendour, in the right hands. These can be the hands working at the Domaine Leflaive, or Delagrange-Bachelet, Albert Morey or the Domaine Ramonet-Prudhon. I remember some magnificent wines from Jean-Noël Gagnard in the 1960s, wines that were so full of body and flavours that they replaced a meal. The 1976 Bâtard from Jadot is good. Chevalier-Montrachet, which lies completely in Puligny, is about the same size as Le Montrachet, and again can rival it for quality at its peak. It might not have quite the same power as Le Montrachet. Bouchard Père own the greater part here, but there is also Leflaive, Louis Jadot, Louis Latour. A Domaine Jacques Prieur Chevalier 1970, drunk in 1980, was superb. There is also Criots-Bâtard-Montrachet and Bienvenues-Bâtard-Montrachet, with similar owners. As one is paying so much for these wines, it is best to go for the owners with the very best credentials.

The commune of Puligny-Montrachet has some excellent Premiers Crus, amongst which Le Cailleret, Les Combettes, Les Pucelles and Les Folatières. Logically enough, those vineyards near the Montrachet family have some of their characteristics (Le Cailleret, Les Pucelles, Folatières and Clavoillons), while Champ Canet, Les Combettes and Les Referts are nearer Meursault, and are perhaps more mellow – commune Puligny wines in youth often have more 'attack' than young Meursaults, which are soft sooner. The top Premiers Crus can, and should, be slightly austere in extreme youth, and as they become less 'green', they develop richness and complexity. Names to trust are Leflaive, Etienne Sauzet, Domaine du Duc de Magenta, Roland Thévenin's Domaine du Château de Puligny-Montrachet, Joseph Drouhin, Bouchard Père, Louis Latour and Domaine J. Pascal.

Chassagne-Montrachet: Producing both red and white wines, at *village* level, they often reach readiness for drinking quicker than the next-door commune. However, the red wines from the Premiers Crus of Clos-St-Jean, Morgeot, Abbaye-de-Morgeot and La Boudriotte need some years in bottle to show their full interest. The top white wines come from Cailleret and Les Ruchottes, but some of the red wine Premiers Crus make fine white too. The Beaune shippers, the de Marcilly family, make excellent red Clos-St-Jean, of the traditional, full, rich kind much loved in the United Kingdom. Indeed, many of their wines have this quality, with rich Pinot Noir nose and influence of oak. They have small holdings also in Beaune and Gevrey Chambertin, and use these wines as a base for excellent *appellation* Bourgogne blends going under the names of Marcilly Première and Marcilly Réservé which always give very good value. Albert Morey, Delagrange-Bachelet, André Ramonet, Domaine du Duc de Magenta and the Château de la Maltroye (Marcel Picard) are names to trust. Bachelet-Ramonet's Caillerets is excellent.

Santenay: Virtually all the wines produced are red, and they can have a nice, fruity, earthy character about them. This is less attractive when the wines are thin, and generally, they are not made for long keeping. The best Premiers Crus are Les Gravières, Clos-de-Tavannes and La Comme, followed by Maladière. The domain that stands out is that of La Pousse d'Or and the manager, Gérard Potel, must be congratulated on the consistent fine quality of his wines. The Clos Tavannes 1976 has a deep, soft Côte de Beaune nose (and even the Côtes can be difficult to tell apart in the hands of some houses!), velvet fruit, youthful attack and a lovely earthy finish. There are also the domains of Mestre, Lequin-Roussot, Roux and Prieur-Brunet, and the wines of the *négociant* Prosper Maufoux.

Bourgogne Hautes-Côtes de Beaune: The *appellation* of Bourgogne Hautes-Côtes de Beaune can be used by twenty villages in the Arrière-Côtes. In an effort to revive the area, Pinot Noir and Chardonnay have been planted to augment the Aligoté and Gamay, and the wine is often made at the Cave Coopérative des Hautes-Côtes at Beaune. The firm of Henri de Villamont at Savigny sells much of this, but there are individual domains where the owners sell their own wine, such as Jean Joliot at Nantoux and the Domaine Louis Jacob of Echevronne. The Château Mandelot wines are vinified and distributed by Bouchard Père. These areas tucked away in the hills do need sun to produce wines of charm and interest, but under the best circumstances, it is one of the best value bottles of Bourgogne one can buy.

COTE CHALONNAISE

The 1970s have seen a great revival of interest in the wines of the Côte Chalonnaise, an interest which is solidly based and sure to continue and grow. It is unlikely that the region will ever regain the size of pre-phylloxera days, but replanting has been steady and well thought out. In general, the red wines can have quite an earthy flavour, strongly marked by the region (the locals often say of a wine, *il terroite*), with the weight varying with the actual *appellation*. The whites can be light and delicate, elegant rather than full and fat in the Côte de Beaune sense. On the whole, one would not keep Côte Chalonnaise wines as long as their counterparts on the Côte d'Or. The vineyards are not all along a clear slope, or Côte, but they tend to cluster round the four *appellation* villages of Rully, Mercurey, Givry and Montagny, and break out in patches where the site is particularly advantageous. There has been considerable new planting in the area during the 1970s, which shows the confidence that both big shippers and small growers have in the region. Apart from the four main *appellations* of the Côte Chalonnaise, the area is a good source of supply for Bourgogne Rouge and Bourgogne Blanc. The former is often relatively light in colour but full of flavour, and in this area will come from the Pinot Noir. Bourgogne Blanc will come from the Chardonnay.

Bourgogne Passetoutgrain: A deal of Bourgogne Passetoutgrain also comes from the Côte Chalonnaise. When made carefully by people who understand the different nature of the grape varieties (Passetoutgrain is a blend of Gamay and Pinot Noir, never less than a third of the latter), it can be very good, but too young, or badly blended, the marriage can be unhappy, with dominating acidity.

Rully: This first *appellation* of the Chalonnais region produces predominantly white wines of great finesse. They have delicacy and interest, and a clean, incisive taste. The young oenologist and vineyard-owner, Jean-François Delorme, has done a great deal for the reputation of Rully wines, both white and red, and his modern cellars and equipment have kept pace with the growing new vineyards. His Rully-Varot and Rully La Chaume have great complexity and nutty finesse, and all wines from the Delorme Domaine de la Renarde inspire confidence. The wine-making emphasis is always on bringing out the fruit character of the grape and achieving balance, and bottling is done early. Jean-François Delorme owns about forty-two hectares at Rully (twenty hectares in Rully Blanc and twenty-two in Rully Rouge), including all Varot (eighteen hectares in one parcel), and parts of Monthelon, Les Cloux, La Fosse and Grésigny.

Rully is a great centre for Bourgogne Mousseux wines, and Crémant de Bourgogne, both of which must be made by the Champagne method. The crisp acidity of the Aligoté grape is needed with Pinot Noir, Chardonnay and Gamay. Some of the red wine is also turned into sparkling Burgundy by the Champagne method and, although decried by wine 'purists', can be extremely pleasant drinking. Delorme is a top name for 'sparklers'. The still wines from the Domaine de la Folie are admirable, and I have been impressed by their red Rully Clos de Bellecroix 1976 and 1978. Jean Coulon makes excellent Rully Blanc Grésigny.

Mercurey: Mercurey makes almost entirely red wine, and it is the most solid, definite of the reds of the Chalonnais. Those vineyards facing southeast and well-exposed can give wines of good colour, body and concentration. The production is large enough to have attracted Côte d'Or shippers, amongst them Faiveley, who has the Clos des Myglands, and Bouchard Aîné. The Protheau family own the Clos des Corvées, la Fauconnière, les Vellées and Clos l'Evêque, and also run a *négociant* business from the Château d'Etroyes. Another leading shipper, Antonin Rodet, owns the Château de Chamirey, and there is also the superb Mercurey les Crêts from de Suremain. The Mercurey Clos des Barraults of Michel Juillot maintains an excellent standard, and Voarick is a strong name in Mercurey. The other *climats* to look out for are Clos du Roi, Clos Voyen, Clos Marcilly, Clos des Fourneaux and Clos des Montaigus. Mercurey can keep well, but has a tendency to dry out if this is exaggerated, especially if the cask ageing was too long.

Givry: The wines from Givry are nearly all red, and can have a fruity delicacy, if not the body of Mercurey. I have admired the Givry Cellier aux Moines from the domain of Baron Thénard, as well as the almost floral, fruity Clos du Cellier aux Moines from Delorme. There is also Givry Clos St-Pierre from the Domaine Baron Thénard, distributed by Remoissenet, Clos Salomon and Clos St-Paul.

Montagny: The white wine from Montagny tends to be fuller than that from Rully, sometimes with more fat, but with less finesse and elegance. The shipper Louis Latour always chooses excellent *cuvées* in the region. The Cave Coopérative de Buxy, one of the communes within the *appellation*, has a wide range of wines, with varying qualities, as befits an establishment whose sales have grown enormously in the 1970s. But good Bourgogne Rouge and Blanc, as well as Aligoté, can be found there together with the Montagny – the name can also be the Cave des Vignerons de Buxy.

COTE MACONNAISE

The Mâconnais is a prolific wine region, dominated by the power of the co-operatives, and specializing in white wines on chalky soil from the Chardonnay grape. Some of this is pretty basic stuff, and some is quite delicious, but none is great. The red wine from the Gamay grape is more everyday, but well made it can produce very useful and reasonable drinking, and there has been a considerable improvement in the quality of Mâcon Rouge in recent years. The Cave Coopérative 'Les Vignerons de Mancey', for example, make their wines with great care. The Gamay grapes for the red are not crushed, and a semi-*macération carbonique* fermentation takes place. They also make a good Bourgogne Rouge from Pinot Noir which has some wood age. The area of the Mâconnais is very beautiful, with rolling hills, white cattle and Romanesque churches. In spite of the huge production of the Mâconnais, vineyards are often not very visible – but they are to be found between the lovely town of Tournus, what remains of the historic Cluny, and the riverside town of Mâcon. There are also areas of vines round Mancey and Chapaize. The cooperatives of the Mâconnais have strong links with *négociants* for white wines, taking a large part of their production. Louis Latour always offers superb Mâcon-Lugny les Genièvres, and Piat has very reliable Mâcon-Viré. Georges Duboeuf's Mâcon-Prissé is always full and interesting. Duboeuf makes excellent selections of white wine in the Mâconnais, including St-Véran and Pouilly Fuissé.

Pouilly-Fuissé: The *appellation* of Pouilly-Fuissé reigns supreme in the area, and popularity has sometimes helped sell wine that was no more than ordinary. The villages of Pouilly, Fuissé (where you can find the Château Fuissé of Marcel Vincent), Solutré, Vergisson and Chaintré are included in the *appellation*, and the weight of the wine depends on the exposition of the slopes (some really catch the sun, by now becoming more southerly than on the Côte d'Or) and the style of wine-making. Small growers still have a good deal of wood and oxidation can be the result of careless handling, while the top cooperatives are equipped to modern standards.

Pouilly-Loché and Pouilly-Vinzelles: Pouilly-Loché and Pouilly-Vinzelles are neighbouring *appellations* for which one does not have to pay so much – they can lack the finesse of the very best Pouilly-Fuissés, and have a slightly more earthy character about them, but in the right hands, they can be excellent wines. These *appellations* are not for keeping, but, as with all Chardonnay, drunk *en primeur* the wines lack any dimension to them. A few years of bottle age for this top category of Mâconnais wine can sometimes produce wines of more depth of flavour than would first appear.

St-Véran: The *appellation* of St-Véran was created in 1971 and, confusingly, some of the communes entitled to the name also make red Beaujolais, notably St-Amour, and I drink regularly good Beaujolais-Villages Domaine de la Citadelle from the village of Leynes, which is also entitled to call its white wines St-Véran. The village of St-Vérand is also within the *appellation* St-Véran. St-Véran wines usually mature slightly faster than Pouilly-Fuissé, but nevertheless, often show more complexity after two years than after one. The St-Véran Cuvée les Crais from M. Roger Tissier gives an indication of the chalky soil.

Mâcon Villages, Mâcon Supérieur, Mâcon and Pinot-Chardonnay-Mâcon: The *appellation* of Mâcon Villages, or Mâcon followed by the name of a village, is for white wines. Good examples are Mâcon-Clessé from the Domaine of Jean Thévenet, the Mâcon-Viré Clos du Chapitre of Dépagneux, and Joseph Drouhin's Mâcon-Villages Laforêt. Adrien Guichard's Mâcon-Villages is always good. The use of the words Mâcon followed by the village name and then Villages is for red wine, which is somewhat more earthy than Beaujolais, with less zingy Gamay fruit and almost a nuttier taste. Mâcon Supérieur is for red or white wines, and Mâcon for red, white and rosé. There is also the rather strange Pinot-Chardonnay-Mâcon which can be made of Pinot Blanc or Chardonnay, as can Mâcon itself, but it is nearly always Chardonnay, the rather sweet-soft tasting clone of the area.

BEAUJOLAIS

If there is one instantly recognized wine word in the world's vocabulary, this is it. It encompasses the good, the bad and the beautiful, and the wine-growers are some of the luckiest of the *métier*. They live in delightful, hilly countryside, they usually sell their wine within the year after it is made and usually there is plenty of it. There are some growers who do honour to their *métier*, others who are careless and greedy, and large establishments who take the product of these lax growers and 'arrange' it in their fashion. If you have once had 'good' Beaujolais, it is easy to know when you are not getting it.

The nine Beaujolais *crus*, or top growths, are all in the north of the area, in very hilly country of granitic origin. The Gamay Noir *à jus blanc* grape shows *race* or breed when planted on a granitic base, and this is not repeated when the soil becomes more chalky, for instance. Gamay grown on granite with clay topsoil also changes character with age, and can take on Pinot Noir characteristics that are quite astonishing. The nine Beaujolais *crus* can be declassified into Beaujolais Villages. It is less widely known that they can also be labelled Bourgogne Rouge, so not all the wines of this *appellation* will be made from Pinot Noir.

Moulin-à-Vent: Old Moulin-à-Vent can taste surprisingly like Côte d'Or wine. The soil has volcanic origins here, and a good deal of manganese has been traced in it. These mineral trace elements add to the complexity of the wine and its indubitable longevity. Moulin-à-Vent should have a deep colour, good backbone and a velvety texture if it is to last any time successfully. Wines to look out for are the Château du Moulin-à-Vent owned by the Bloud family, Château Portier, Les Carquelins and Château des Jacques.

Morgon: Morgon produces the most robust of the nine Beaujolais *crus*, often showing the most closed at the outset, big and beefy, and opening out with some years in bottle and showing individuality and strength. The soil is almost schistous here, *roche pourrie* as it is known locally. The distinctive bouquet has created a verb in the area – *morgonner*. Apart from Brouilly, more wine is made in this *cru* than in any other. Jean Descombes, who has his vineyards on the Mont de Py, is a reputed grower, and the Château de Bellevue produces excellent wine.

St-Amour: St-Amour is a small *appellation*, right on the border in the north with the Mâconnais region. The wines are sprightly, fruity and delicate, needing sunny years, and at their best when two to three years old. The Château de St-Amour, which is commercialized through Piat, is worth looking for, as is the Domaine des Billards from Jean Loron. St-Amour can be the epitome of Beaujolais.

Juliénas: Nearby there is Juliénas, with its wonderful sturdy, purple fruit. This crushed-grapes character makes it delicious to drink young, but the fullness behind promises more. Here there is the Château de Juliénas owned by the Héritiers Condemine, les Capitans, the Clos des Poulettes of Paul Loron and the Domaine de Beauvernay sold by Piat.

Chénas: Chénas has an even smaller production than St-Amour and is not as well known as it should be. The wines repay keeping a few years and have a lot of character, though perhaps they lack the silkiness of Moulin-à-Vent. Château Bonnet, Domaine des Journets and Les Rougemonts are worth looking for.

Fleurie: Fleurie's great charm, generous fruit and extreme drinkability, combined with a picturesque name, make this *appellation* much sought-after. It lasts well, and is large enough to have made its mark in many countries. The Château de Fleurie is owned by Jean Loron, and there is also La Chapelle des Bois and Clos de la Roilette.

Chiroubles: Chiroubles is the highest of the *crus*, perched up on dipping, rolling hills that often become sprinkled with snowflakes in winter. As befits the height, Chiroubles is light, airy, deliciously tempting, graceful wine. At early comparative tastings of all the *crus*, it often looks the prettiest youngest, while some of the bigger wines look more earth-bound and clumsy. The Domaine de Raousset and the Domaine Cheysson-les-Farges are important.

Côte de Brouilly and Brouilly: The wines of the Côte de Brouilly, high up on Mont Brouilly, are considered as slightly better than the far larger Brouilly. However, that is not to denigrate Brouilly, which produces 'textbook' Beaujolais, fruity, giving and mouth-filling. They are delicious from the outset, while some Côte de Brouilly wines will build up a bit more character with a year or two more in bottle. The Château Thivin is well respected in Côte de Brouilly, and the Château de Pierreux and Château de la Chaize in Brouilly. Bouchard Père's Domaine de Saburin is also worth looking for.

Cooperatives play a very important part in the whole of Beaujolais, including the area of the *crus* in the north. One singles out particularly the Cave Coopérative de Fleurie (which makes excellent Morgon, Moulin-à-Vent, and Chiroubles, as well as Fleurie), not only because it is run by a wonderful, old lady, Mlle Chabert, with whom I have had the pleasure of sitting on a tasting panel. The cooperatives of both

Chénas (which also has Moulin-à-Vent) and Juliénas (which also has St-Amour) must also be singled out.

At Corcelles-en-Beaujolais there is an excellent *groupement* of growers called the Eventail de Vignerons Producteurs. The forty members make their wine themselves, and only send it to the Eventail cellars for bottling. Many of the members are in the *crus*, others make Beaujolais Villages, and there is also Pouilly Fuissé, St-Véran and Mâcon. Each grower's wine is kept apart and labelled differently, and, together with the wines of Duboeuf, they tend to sweep the board at the Concours of Paris and Mâcon. The Brouilly of M. Bassy, the Morgon le Clachet of M. Brun, the Juliénas of M. Monnet, the Côte de Brouilly of M. Verger, the Chiroubles of M. Passot and M. Savoye, the St-Amour of M. Patissier, the Fleurie of M. Brugne and the Moulin-à-Vent of the Héritiers Finaz-Devillaine, are just the flagships of a group of growers who really bring out the individual characteristics of the Beaujolais *crus*. The Eventail also has a range of individual Beaujolais Villages, such as the Vignoble de Chêne and the Domaines de la Citadelle and des Esservies.

Beaujolais: Beaujolais as an *appellation*, or what is sometimes called Beaujolais *tout court*, can be red, white or rosé; a tiny amount of white Beaujolais is produced in the north, on the borders of the Mâconnais. The Beaujolais Blanc of Louis Jadot is well-known, as is the Château de Loyse of Thorin. The red is mostly produced in the south of the region, above Lyon and south of Villefranche and is for drinking quickly and young; it is in this category that one can find some horrid, thin, acid examples, or some equally noxious, over-chaptalized (in spite of the controls that grow stricter), heavy brew. If the wine is very young, in a good café or bar in Lyon or Paris, the chances are that youthful charm will disguise faults, but in the year following the vintage, if you want to drink straight Beaujolais, it is better to go for a reputable and well-tried shipper's wine. The lightest wines are those suitable for making Beaujolais Nouveau, the fly-by-night wine released normally on November 15 after the vintage. Obviously, very careful vinification must take place if the wine is to be palatable, with the most modern techniques of stabilization. Wines from acid years rarely make good Nouveau, and it is equally tragic when the current fashion 'creams off' some would-be fine, more serious wines for instant transformation into Nouveau. There is also Beaujolais Supérieur, which just means 1 per cent more of alcohol – but it is rarely used, and in fact, both *appellations* always sell their wines at more than the minimum level required.

Beaujolais Villages: Beaujolais Villages is an *appellation* made up of over forty communes who have the right to use it, some in the north on the border of the Mâconnais in the *département* of Saône-et-Loire, and the majority in the *département* of the Rhône which is, confusingly, still in the north of the Beaujolais region. Romanèche-Thorins is the most important county town. When buying wine outside the area, and without a clear recommendation, it is always safer to go for Beaujolais Villages rather than just plain Beaujolais.

The serried ranks of Beaujolais-Mâconnais *négociants* must be led by Georges Duboeuf, who has done so much for the area as a whole. Loron and Dépagneux are also highly respected, as are Piat, Trenel and Louis Tête. Mommessin, Pasquier-Desvignes, Ferraud, Sapin, Thorin, Aujoux, and David & Foillard are other names. The Côte d'Or *négociants* of Louis Latour, Joseph Drouhin, Bouchard Père and Louis Jadot, among others, also sell honourable Beaujolais. A final plea for Beaujolais – drink it cool, but not too chilled. And if you ever come across an old Moulin-à-Vent or Morgon, treat it as you would a wine from the Côte d'Or.

Burgundy Shippers

The *négociants* form a very important part of the commercial activity of this great wine region. They buy in wine, mature it and prepare it for sale. Some of them also own vineyards (Bouchard Père is the largest domain of Grand and Premier Cru vineyards on the Côte d'Or). Undoubtedly, in the current climate of many growers bottling their own wines, those *négociants* with a solid proportion of their own vineyards are better placed. I would put Louis Latour and Bouchard Père at the top of my list of *négociants*, followed by Louis Jadot and Joseph Drouhin. Many good wines can be found amongst the following:

Bouchard Ainé	Clerget	Leroy	Ropiteau
Champy	Delaunay	Marcilly	Thévenin
Chanson	Faiveley	Remoissenet	

Others include:

Belin	Doudet-Naudin	La Reine Pédauque	Patriarche
Bichot	Dufouleur	Les Fils de Marcel	Ponnelle
Boisseaux-Estivant	Geisweiler	Quancard	Poulet
Boisset	Henri de Villamont	Lupé-Cholet	Viénot
Calvet	Héritier-Guyot	Maufoux/Marcel Amance	
Chauvenet	Jaboulet-Vercherre	Moillard	
Cruse (Bruck and	Labouré-Gontard	Morey	
Hasenklever are in	(sparkling wines)	Morin	
the group)	Labouré-Roi	Morot	

On the Côte Chalonnaise, the *négociant* that stands out is André Delorme (or Delorme-Meulien). There are also Antonin Rodet, Chandesais, Picard, and Protheau.

Burgundy Vintages

Vintages really matter in Burgundy, logically enough for a wine-producing area not so far from the northern limit for growing vines successfully. Burgundians have to cope fairly regularly with both rain and hail, and often have to play a 'dicing with death' game with those last few days before the vintage in order to gain maximum ripeness. A general rule is that poor red wine vintages can make better white wines – warmth at the last moment is not quite so vital for white grapes as for red.

1945: Very good, small vintage. They still look big.

1947: The extreme heat made the fermentations difficult to handle, and some wines inevitably 'went over the top'. The best have lasted beautifully.

1948: Some great wines have lasted well to start the 1980s.

1949: Some excellent 'finds' still with this vintage.

1950: Whites very good, reds not.

1952: Good wines, but they cannot last much longer. Excellent whites.

1953: These wines had the balance to last, and many have. Very good whites.

1955: Wines with style and character. Some are still showing well – excellent whites.

1957: Wines with good body and flavour which have generally lasted well.

1959: Generous, popular wines. The heat made the acidities low, so they will not go on improving. Can be lush. Whites mostly too old now.

1961: Very good wines indeed, and still tasting marvellous. Small crop.

1962: Again, very good wines, sometimes with less concentration, but more acidity balance, than the 1961s. Still excellent. Wonderful whites.

1963: Poor – it is rare to find something drinkable now.

1964: Some very good sturdy bottles, most of them at their prime. This applies to white and red.

1965: Best forgotten.

1966: A generous vintage, from all points of view. Lovely fruit and delicious drinking. Elegant, stylish whites.

1967: Very mixed vintage – the best have elegance, but many reds were over-chaptalized and now look totally out of balance and brown. Whites often have a good deal of breed.

1968: The reds were a write-off, but a few whites were drinkable.

1969: A simply superb vintage – the only complaint is the small size! The reds have great nerve, backbone, and fruit upheld by good acidity. Will last exceptionally well – the vintage to show off wines with *race* and breed. The whites are splendid.

1970: A big vintage of soft, fruity, thoroughly attractive wines. Both reds and whites looked lovely when comparatively young, and at ten years old they are mostly at their apogee.

1971: An extremely ripe vintage, producing wines of great concentration and richness. Some were too ripe for balance and lack complete harmony. They are heady wines, intoxicating at their best, sometimes too top-heavy to be 'classic'. The low acidity sometimes causes the reds to brown earlier than would be expected. The whites are very full-blown. There were patches of hail on the Côte d'Or.

1972: The wines have developed beautifully, those rather green and acid reds softening and gaining great character in bottle. One almost never makes a bad buy with a 1972 red now. The whites had unpleasant acidity when young, but the best made now look more in balance, even if they lack luscious fruit.

1973: Very large vintage, producing light wines of charm and fruit. If they were not too chaptalized, they retained that charm. Low natural acidity in the whites, but delicious young drinking.

1974: Good colour reds, often quite straightforward and dependable, but lacking any charm or great individuality. The whites are more interesting.

1975: Rot ruined this vintage, and it is rare to find a red wine free from taint. Some presentable whites, but do not keep them.

1976: An abnormal year producing abnormal wines for Burgundy. The reds are extremely tannic, and necessitated slightly different treatment if they were to emerge with their fruit intact. In 1981 they are just beginning to open out, but have a long way to go – some of the Beaujolais *crus* will give a big surprise to drinkers ten years or more on! The whites are very good, if the acidities did not get too low – they should not be kept for too long.

1977: A 'miracle' vintage, saved by the fine September weather. The reds are mostly light, but make good, young drinking. The whites are commercially useful, and some have real finesse.

1978: An exceptionally lovely vintage, better balanced than either 1971 or 1976. Lovely fruit, with excellent backbone behind. The wines will mature in great style. Both whites and reds will need a bit of time for their full complexity to emerge.

1979: A large vintage. The wines have charm and fruit and often class.

1980: Variable, depending on whether the grower treated against rot. The best reds and whites will make good, medium-term drinking.

CHABLIS

Chablis could be considered as an island, almost equidistant between Paris and Dijon, and is in the *département* of the Yonne. 2,000 hectares of vines produce white wines with a quality spectrum ranging from the banal to the very great. The secret to the greatness is the combination of Kimmeridgian clay soil and Chardonnay, and where this does not exist, the wines are merely run-of-the-mill. It is regrettable that in 1976 the area of Chablis was considerably enlarged, with plantings on soil that was not purely Kimmeridgian being accepted as *appellation contrôlée* Chablis. These new plantings should never have been elevated beyond the status of Petit Chablis, which is itself unfortunate as a name (created in 1944, while the Chablis *appellation* area was delimited in 1938) as the wine bears little relation to the aristocratic real thing. Apart from the difference in soil type, planting on the plain cannot rival that on the slopes.

The most marked slopes are those of the seven Grands Crus, over the little Serein river from the sleepy town of Chablis, and regally facing south and southwest. The Premier Cru vineyards are scattered on both sides of the river, in villages such as Fyé, Fleys, Poinchy, Fontenay, Maligny, Milly, Beine and Chichée. At one time, it looked as if Chablis might cease to exist as a vineyard area. The first blow was phylloxera. Then the exposed, northern aspect of the viticultural region attracted remorseless frosts in spring, and time after time whole crops were ruined, with every little valley a prime target area. However, during the 1960s, effective methods of combating frost were developed, starting with smoking pots amongst the vines to raise the air temperature, with gas, oil and irrigation systems following. In the 1970s, with more predictable crops, relatively speaking, and the growing export demand in the United States and in Britain for dry white wine, the region has come into its own. Smaller crops inevitably lead to steep price increases, with market resistance hardening as a result (1978 was an example of this), but Chablis has a much-loved place in the English-speaking world.

The Chardonnay grape is called the Beaunois at Chablis, and it thrives on the sub-soil of Kimmeridgian clay, mixed with chalky and stony matter. The chalk element helps warm up the soil. This combination is ideal for the production of white wine, and it reappears north of Chablis in the valleys of Bar-sur-Seine and Bar-sur-Aube which produce Champagne, and at Pouilly-sur-Loire and Sancerre, here combined with the Sauvignon grape. Kimmeridgian clay is also found in Hampshire, and English vineyards growing white vines have taken advantage of it.

The vines are trained low on wires, so that the grapes can benefit at night from the warmth that the soil can pick up in the day during the ripening period. Traditionally, Chablis growers often left their vineyard land fallow (or planted with a fodder crop like lucerne) for up to fifteen years after pulling out old vines and before re-planting, but chemical disinfectants have obviously shortened the time. The greatest change in vinification at Chablis over the last decade is the diminishing use of wood as a material for keeping wine. Small, peasant growers still have the traditional Chablis *feuillettes* which hold 132 litres, but many cellars have gone over to glass-lined vats or stainless steel. Bottling is also now much earlier, with Chablis and Premier Cru Chablis normally being bottled in the early spring after the vintage, and Grand Cru Chablis a few months later. All this has made for wines that are lighter in colour than, say, twenty years ago, and the cold, controlled fermentations have led to delicate bouquet and finesse. Development is now necessary in the bottle for the Grands and Premiers Crus, as they would have had little or no oxidation in the maturing process before bottling.

Grands Crus: The seven Grands Crus, starting upstream and going downstream, are: Blanchot, Les Clos, Valmur, Grenouille, Vaudésir, Les Preuses, and Bougros. Sometimes you will see Blanchots, Vaudésirs and Grenouilles, but the spellings are interchangeable. The name of Moutonne was given separate identification in 1951, and is made up of parcels in Vaudésir and Preuses. All the Grands Crus are within the commune of Chablis, except for Blanchot which is in that of Fyé. Les Clos is the largest of the Grands Crus, and sometimes the one that requires the most bottle age to open out fully, but, as always, this depends on individual wine-making methods.

Premiers Crus: Originally, there were about twenty-five Premiers Crus, but these have been amalgamated to form a dozen or so that are used regularly. If two Premier

Cru wines are blended, only Chablis Premier Cru appears on the label. The main Premiers Crus are: Monts de Milieu; Montée de Tonnerre; Fourchaume (or Fourchaumes); Vaillons; Montmains; Mélinots; Côte de Léchet; Beauroy; Vaucoupin; Vosgros; Les Fourneaux; Vaulorent; Les Forêts; Beugnons; and Les Lys.

In poor vintages, the difference between Grand and Premier Cru is small. However, in good vintages, and unbelievably so in great vintages, there is a large difference between straight Chablis and Premier Cru, and an equally large gap between Premier and Grand Cru. Perhaps the most astounding Premiers Crus I have drunk have been Fourchaume, combining finesse with great flavour, but the *cru* is extensive and there are favoured parts, especially on mid-slope. Vaillons can produce excellent wine (although always it should be remembered that Premier Cru Chablis does not last as long or as superbly as Grand Cru Chablis), and Montée de Tonnerre and Vaulorent are neighbours of the Grands Crus, although the vineyard is not contiguous in either case.

Chablis: This is the wine to drink while biding one's time for the Premiers and Grands Crus! When young, it should have a good acidity (otherwise it will rapidly become 'flabby'), a green-straw colour, and a certain 'flinty' attack. Often it needs a little time in the glass for the nose to come out. Sometimes, Premier Cru wine is declassified into Chablis – if Chablis itself is declassified for some reason, it becomes Bourgogne (if the wine has a minimum of 10.5 per cent alcohol) and Bourgogne Grand Ordinaire – an *appellation* which is hardly sold on the export markets, but has its place in France. Villages such as Beine, Chemilly and Béru are important.

Petit Chablis: A simple *appellation*, with no pretences – or it should not have. The wine should be drunk within a year or two of being made. Villages such as Maligny, Lignorelles, La Chapelle-Vaupelteigne and Villy are known for their Petit Chablis. However, it is being phased out.

Some Wines and their Wine-makers

TESTUT

Some of my greatest *souvenirs chablisiens* have been wines from the Testut family. The Société Testut Frères now produce wines from fifteen hectares and young Philippe Testut is in charge of vinification. He is a most careful wine-maker, who has become convinced that no wood-ageing at all can lead to wines with a short finish. The 1979 Fourchaumes, under Philippe Testut's own label, is superb and set to develop over several years. The family also own a part of Grenouille.

JEAN DURUP

The biggest private domain in Chablis is that of Jean Durup at Maligny. Up to 1973, the wine was sold in bulk to *négociants*, but the bottle sales have greatly increased, as elsewhere in Chablis. Most of the wine is plain Chablis, and the standard is high. Various domain names are used, such as Domaine de l'Eglantière, Domaine de la Paulière and Domaine des Valéry. The Premiers Crus include Montée de Tonnerre, Montmain, Fourchaume and Côte de Léchet.

LOUIS MICHEL

The Chablis of Louis Michel are always excellent. M. Michel owns eighteen hectares, of which two are Chablis, two and a half are Grand Cru and all the rest is Premier Cru – about thirteen and a half hectares. The 1978 vintage was excellent.

ALBERT PIC

The *négociants* Albert Pic (who are also Régnard) vinify extremely well. All the wine sold by Albert Pic is bought as grape juice from growers with whom they have long standing contracts, and the whole process, from fermentation to bottling, is personally supervised by M. Michel Remon, the head of the firm. Of the total 60,000 hectolitres produced by the Chablis vineyards in an average year, Albert Pic are responsible for 8,000 hectolitres, or 13 per cent of the total. Of an excellent range of 1976 wines, I particularly liked a Côte de Léchet and a Montée de Tonnerre, and the 1979 Fourchaume showed style. Régnard has produced excellent Beugnons.

RENE DAUVISSAT

A grower who makes superb wine is René Dauvissat, who usually finished his wines in *feuillettes*, giving them richness and complexity, and bottles some as late as the November after the vintage. Because of the influence of wood, Dauvissat's wines often have more colour than others. The Grand Cru Les Clos 1973 was easily one of the best of this vintage, and the 1973 Premier Cru 'La Forest' was equally fine.

Other Producers

The Domaine Laroche wines can be very good, as well as the Domaine la Jouchère, and they are marketed by the *négociants* Bacheroy-Josselin; old labels show the name of Dupressoir. These *négociants* specialize in a variety of Yonne wines. A wine-maker whose wines I have often admired is William Fèvre, of the Domaine de la Maladière. He made an excellent 1970 Montée de Tonnerre, and also has Grand Cru Les Preuses and Premier Cru Vaulorent, amongst other good things. His Vaudésir 1977 was excellent. Moreau is now a huge firm of *négociants*, but with domain wines, which include Les Clos and Vaillons. Forceful marketing in North America also includes the sale of white *vin de table*. Long-Depaquit is a respected name in Chablis – it is now owned by the Beaune *négociants* Albert Bichot. They are the sole proprietors of the 2.35 hectare enclave of Moutonne. Simonnet-Febvre are well-established *négociants* (for all the wines of the Yonne) as are Lamblin, *négociants* at the Château de Milly. The Domaine Robert Vocoret has a totally deserved reputation, producing excellent wines from *crus* such as Les Clos, Blanchot, Valmur and La Forêt. Other growers of note are Louis Pinson, Jacques Philippon, René Rey, Filippi, Servin, Ravenaux, Gérard Rottiers, Defaix and Gérard Tremblay.

The cooperative at Chablis is called La Chablisienne, and its *adhérents*, or members, own in the Grands Crus, Premiers Crus and in the straight Chablis and Petit Chablis area. In the last decade, quality has risen to a good general standard. However, as at all Caves Coopératives, there are *cuvées* and *cuvées*, and the buyer should choose carefully. Much wine is still sold in bulk to *négociants* in Beaune and elsewhere, but a new, greatly improved bottling line will increase the tendency to bottle *sur place*. The cooperative manager is Jean-Michel Tucki, and he has encouraged the increased bottlings of Grands and Premiers Crus – in Grand Cru, the cooperative has members who bought parcels of Grenouille from the Crédit Agricole when the Testut family sold some of their estate to the bank, and there is also a good part of Les Preuses, together with Fourchaume in Premier Cru.

Other Wines of the Yonne

A certain amount of red and white Bourgogne is produced in the Yonne, as well as Bourgogne Grand Ordinaire. Additional grape varieties are allowed in this *département* – the César and the Tressot for red wines, which are on the decline, and the Sacy for the white (but not for Bourgogne Blanc). There is also good Aligoté in the Yonne, often suitable for making sparkling wines, when mixed with the Chardonnay, César or Tressot. I have very much liked still Bourgogne Aligoté de St-Bris from Robert Defrance, a grower in St-Bris-le-Vineux, near Auxerre. There is also a small amount of Bourgogne Passetoutgrain from Pinot Noir and Gamay.

There are two good Bourgogne Rouges in the Yonne, at Irancy and at Coulanges-la-Vineuse. An Irancy would be labelled, Bourgogne-Irancy Appellation Bourgogne Contrôlée. These wines can be a bit acid when young, but soften in bottle. A good Bourgogne-Irancy is made by Cyprien Vincent, a grower at Irancy, and Simonnet-Febvre has Bourgogne-Irancy Côte de Palotte. These villages are really Burgundy, with grey stone and steep roofs and wood-smoke curling along the village street. Tonnerre and Joigny also produce local wines, classic Pinot Noir and Chardonnay near the former, and an unusual *vin gris* from Joigny. The village of Epineuil has both *vin gris* and solid red. Proximity to Paris means that the wine is quickly bought by the buyer at the door. In 1974, a new VDQS was created at St-Bris-le-Vineux – Sauvignon de St-Bris. Obviously, the Sauvignon gives a more Loire-like taste than a Burgundian, but the wine is very quaffable. Jean-Louis Bersan is a reliable grower at St-Bris itself. The other communes making this wine are Chitry, Irancy and Vincelottes.

Chablis Vintages

Vintages in the region of Chablis do not always correspond with those on the Côte de Beaune; the most glaring example being 1975, which was very good indeed in Chablis, and only of medium quality (when rot was avoided) for the white wines of the Côte. Great old vintages of Chablis would include 1949, 1953, 1955, 1957, 1959, 1961 and 1964, but the oldest here would only represent academic interest, although Grands Crus of the 1960s can sometimes give one a splendid surprise.

1966: Elegant and with a lovely bouquet when at their peak – almost all have passed this stage.

1967: There were some very good wines, but they could be risky now.

1968: Very slight at the time, and now only history.

1969: Big, powerful, ripe wines – some have gone 'over the top'.

1970: Really attractive, but very soft, and most now show age.

1971: A classic vintage, great body and flavour. The greatest live on into beautiful maturity.

1972: Mostly acid and harsh. A few improved in bottle, especially the top *crus*.

1973: A very tempting, delicious vintage, abundant, and with little Chablis acidity, even in youth. Therefore, most should have been drunk relatively young, but a few had more 'bite' to them and are ageing beautifully.

1974: Very inhospitable when young, but took on some character and more fruit when in the bottle.

1975: Really well-balanced wines that had all the ingredients – easily the best vintage since 1971. The great wines have real breed.

1976: Wines that are very 'fat' for the region, but the best have the composition to make mature bottles. Rich and luscious, but not as blowsy as some on the Côte de Beaune. The Grands Crus with bottle age will fool some into thinking of Puligny!

1977: Very honourable wines, with some finesse and length when the initial acidity softened out.

1978: Small vintage, but very good indeed, with wines of great flavour and individuality, depth and harmony. It is a pity to drink the Premiers and Grands Crus in the early 1980s. Splendid wines. Unfortunately, they were scarce and expensive – one producer said he got forty-five hectolitres to the hectare in 1978, and sixty-five hectolitres in 1979.

1979: A big vintage, giving wines of immense attraction and charm. Lovely fruit, very generous and scented. Drink them before the 1978s, but the Premiers and Grands Crus show great style.

1980: Small quantity. Quality much better than expected.

Depending on the character of the year, Premiers Crus taste delicious when between three and six years old, the Grands Crus between six and ten, and exceptionally, and when there is body and good acidity, long after that. Essentially, when one thinks of the crisp Chablis taste, the wine to go with oysters, one is imagining a straight Chablis or a Premier Cru – in years of any stature, Grand Cru Chablis is a different wine altogether – rich, complex and mysterious.

CHAMPAGNE

Champagne is, today, the festive wine *par excellence*, the most lively and one of the most expensive of quality wines, a joy and a luxury. But it was not ever thus. During many centuries the wines of the great Champagne province, stretching from Flanders in the north to Burgundy in the south, and from Lorraine in the east to the Ile de France in the west, were plain, still table wines, mostly red. Whether better or not than the wines of Bordeaux and Burgundy is anybody's guess, but they can certainly claim, without fear of contradiction, to have been French much longer. The wines of Champagne had no other competitors in Paris except those of Orléans and Touraine until the seventeenth century, when both Bordeaux and Burgundy also sent in their wines. The wines of Burgundy were the more dangerous competitors of the two; they were of the same grape, the Pinot, and of the same type as the wines of Champagne, and they were very likely better wines, to judge from the still table wines of Champagne made today compared to the still table wines of Burgundy of the same vintages. There is, therefore, every reason to assume that the *vignerons* of Champagne sought to produce a wine that would be, if not better than, at least different from any wine that had ever come out of Burgundy, and eventually sparkling Champagne proved to be the right answer. This is where Dom Pérignon comes in.

Dom Pérignon was born at Sainte-Menehoulde in January, 1639. He renounced the world at the early age of nineteen and never regretted it. In 1668 he was appointed to the post of Cellarer of the Benedictine Abbey of Hautvillers, near Epernay, in the Champagne country. During forty-seven consecutive years, until the day of his death, in September, 1715, Dom Pérignon was in charge of the cellars and of the finances of the Abbey. He had a remarkably keen palate and knew how to use it to good purpose. He had great experience in all matters pertaining to viticulture and wine-making; he was hardworking and shrewd; he made better wines than had ever been made before at Hautvillers; he also made some sparkling wine. He was a good man, he loved the poor. So much, and very little more, is tolerably certain. Dom Pérignon has been hailed as the discoverer, inventor or creator of sparkling Champagne. He has been described as the wizard who first put the bubbles into Champagne. This is mere romance. Dom Pérignon did not discover, invent or create sparkling Champagne. He never claimed to have done so, nor did any of his contemporaries claim any such honour for him. He would certainly have greatly resented being hailed as the first to have put bubbles into Champagne, when neither he nor anybody else ever put bubbles into Champagne. The bubbles of sparkling Champagne are the same as the bubbles of bottled beer: they are tiny drops of liquid disturbed, chased and whipped by escaping carbon dioxide or carbonic acid gas. This carbon dioxide is an inevitable by-product of a most natural phenomenon known as fermentation.

Champagne is a cold-blooded northener. It begins fermenting cheerfully enough, but thinks better of it and settles down to a long sleep during the winter months. In the following spring or early summer it wakes up and takes up its half-finished job where it had left it. There is still some of the original grape-juice sugar left to be

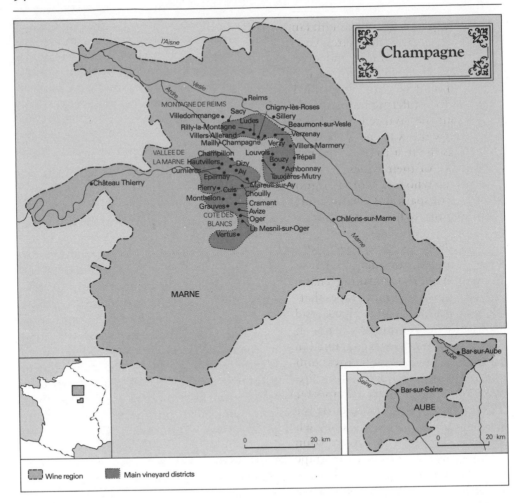

Champagne

MONTAGNE DE REIMS

l'Aisne

Vesle

Ardre

Reims
Chigny-lès-Roses
Sacy
Villedommange
Sillery
Rilly-la-Montagne
Ludes
Beaumont-sur-Vesle
Villers-Allerand
Verzenay
Mailly-Champagne
Verzy
Villers-Marmery

VALLEE DE
LA MARNE
Champillon
Louvois
Hautvillers
Dizy
Bouzy
Trépail
Cumières
Ay
Arbonnay
Epernay
Tauxières-Mutry
Château Thierry
Mareuil-sur-Ay
Pierry
Cuis
Chouilly
Monthelon
Cramant
Grauves
Avize
Oger
Châlons-sur-Marne
COTE DES
BLANCS
Le Mesnil-sur-Oger
Vertus

MARNE

Marne

Aube
Bar-sur-Aube

Seine

Bar-sur-Seine

AUBE

0   20 km   0   20 km

☐ Wine region   ▨ Main vineyard districts

fermented, and after their long winter rest the saccharomycetes will now get busy again and supply the necessary zymase. In fact, to make sure that they will have plenty to do, a little more sugar is added to the wine, which is then bottled and corked securely down. Exactly the same thing goes on within the bottle as in the cask, but with this difference, that the carbonic acid gas can no longer lose itself in the air; it remains in solution in the wine, a most amenable prisoner so long as there is no hope of escape. But once that gate of its prison, the cork, has gone, it rushes out of the wine with joy, carrying along in its haste thousands of dewdrops of wine; these are the Champagne 'bubbles'. Dom Pérignon did not create sparkling Champagne, but he did a great deal for its fame. He made better wines than had been made in Champagne before, both still and sparkling. The excellence of Dom Pérignon's wines was due to the art with which he blended the grapes from various vineyards. It was due also to the fact that the Abbey of Hautvillers owned more vineyards and received by way of tithes a greater variety of grapes than any private vineyard owner.

Situated as they are so close to the northern latitude beyond which grapes will grow but will hardly ever fully ripen, the vineyards of Champagne are not blessed, nor were they blessed in the seventeenth century, with their full quota of sunshine year after year. They only enjoy a really fine summer now and again, and they produce then, but only then, grapes which give wonderful wine, wine truly deserving to be enjoyed and remembered as a vintage wine. Such years are the exception; other years, poorer years, years of acid, sun-starved wine, are the rule.

Judicious blending has brought fame and riches to the old province of Champagne. By saving wines of the better years and by finding out which blends of various vineyards will harmonize and give the best results, a very much higher level of average excellence has been reached and stocks of wines of fairly uniform quality have been built which have enabled the Champagne shippers to dispense for years and years to a suffering humanity that most exhilarating form of relaxation known throughout the civilized world as sparkling Champagne. Dom Pérignon was the first to show the way; he was not the first to make sparkling wine nor to use corks, but he was the first to show the people of Champagne what was the best use they could make of their wines. It is not only the wine-growers and wine shippers of Champagne who owe Dom Pérignon a deep debt of gratitude but all who appreciate the charm of sparkling Champagne, all those to whom Champagne has brought at some time that which is worth more than gold and silver: health and joy.

The Making of Sparkling Champagne

It is now time to consider in what way the making of sparkling Champagne differs from the methods for making a natural wine. Sparkling Champagne is a white wine made mostly from Pinot grapes that we call black, but they are not black; their juice is white and their skin is blue outside and red inside. To make a white wine from black grapes is not done by magic, but by care and skill. The colouring pigment of so-called black grapes is contained in the lining of their skin, so that grapes must be picked and brought to the press unbruised and without delay if their white juice is not to be dyed pink before they are pressed. In Champagne the grapes are picked with care as soon as they are ripe, but before being sent to the *pressoir* to be crushed they are first examined at the roadside nearest the vineyard of their birth by a team of women, mostly elderly ones who have had their full share of back-breaking grape-picking when they were younger: they sit in a row with a wide osier tray at knee height before them; the grapes gathered by the pickers are brought to the women at the roadside in baskets, which are tipped over on to the osier tray. The women quickly take up and look over bunch after bunch, removing expertly with a pair of long pointed scissors all defective berries, if and when there happen to be any, either unripe or mildewy, or otherwise undesirable for any cause whatsoever. All such rejects are dropped in a refuse bin, while the bunches with none but sound and ripe grapes go into great osier baskets known as *caques*. These are then loaded on lorries and driven to the nearest *vendangeoir* of the person or firm who owns the vineyard or who has bought the grapes from the *vignerons*. At the *vendangeoir* the grapes are weighed in their *caques* and tipped out into the *pressoir* until there is enough for a pressing or 'charge', usually of 4,000 kilograms. The bunches are kept whole, not *égrappées* nor *foulées* as in Burgundy or the Gironde, and the grapes remain whole when tipped in the *pressoir*. This consists of a square wooden floor with four adjustable open-work wooden rails which make a sort of cage in which the grapes are heaped. The *pressoir* has a heavy lid of oak boards which is lowered and raised at will by a screw, now driven, as a rule, by electricity, but until recently by muscle and sweat. When the lid is clamped on the heaped grapes in the *pressoir*, and slowly but relentlessly driven down, its crushing pressure bursts the grapes, and their sweet juice immediately runs off through the rails into a slightly sloping wide groove that leads it to a collecting 'station' without having been in contact for any time with the skins of the grapes; these are left behind in the cage of the press. The first flow pressed out of the grapes is either led or pumped into a vat which holds 2046 litres of this, the best grape juice or *cuvée*. Greater pressure is then applied and more juice is squeezed out of the wet husks still in the cage of the *pressoir*, but it is neither as white nor as sweet nor as good as the *cuvée*, and it is not mixed with it. Very soon after the *cuvée* has been vatted, it begins to ferment in a rather boisterous manner, throwing off an ugly 'head' or scum, thus getting rid of any dirt or dust or anything else which is not wanted; some of which, the heavier stuff, falls to the bottom of the vat as lees. When the must, as this working grape-juice is called, returns to a more normal temperature, in twenty-four or thirty-six hours as a rule, all that is clear is drawn into ten clean oak casks holding two hundred litres each, and these casks are sent at once by lorry to Reims, Epernay, Ay or wherever the persons or firms who own the wine-to-be have their cellars. All through the vintage, which may be long or short according to the more or less favourable weather conditions from year to year, lorries are busy day and night fetching casks to put the new wine in and delivering full ones at the *celliers* from all parts of the Champagne vineyards. During the next eight to ten weeks the must will be left alone to become new wine, most of the grape-sugar present in the must having become alcohol, which stays put, and carbonic acid gas, which loses itself in the air.

The new wines are then racked, that is transferred into new casks, leaving behind the sediment cast off during the process of fermentation. After being racked the new wines of different pressings or *marcs* of each vineyard are 'assembled' or blended together, in order to obtain one standard wine from each place, irrespective of whether the wine was made at the beginning of the vintage or at the end, from grapes which might have been hardly fully ripe in the first instance and from what may be slightly overripe grapes in the second. The newly racked and 'assembled' wine is given another four or five weeks to rest and to proceed a little further with its slow fermentation, if it has a mind to do so. It is then racked another time, which serves the double purpose of separating it from any lees it may have cast off and to give it plenty of fresh air. Then comes the all-important business of making-up the *cuvées*. The *chef de caves*, whose responsibility it is, must taste with the greatest keenness the wines of all the different vineyards or sets of vineyards, and he has to decide how much or how little of the wines of each different district he ought to blend together to secure the approximately right quantity and quality of each one of the different brands which his firms sells on different markets, in competition with other Champagne shippers. The *chef de caves* may also decide to add to his *cuvées* more or less of older wines which have been kept in cask for that very purpose. When, after many tastings and much hesitation, his choice has been made, the chosen wines are mixed and blended together in great *foudres* or vats with an electrically actioned mechanical arm churning the wines; after which they are tested for sugar, liqueured and bottled.

The style of each *cuvée* depends entirely upon the skill and taste of the *chef de caves*, but the quality of the wine depends in the first place upon the quality of the grapes which, in Champagne as everywhere else, varies with the soil, sub-soil and aspect of different vineyards. No *chef de caves*, however skilled he may be in the art of blending, can possibly make a first-quality wine out of second-quality grapes. A Champagne *cuvée* made from different wines from none but the very best vineyards would not be an economic or commercial proposition, but the best *cuvées* are always those in which there is a greater proportion of *premiers crus* grapes, a smaller proportion of *deuxièmes crus* and no *troisièmes crus* at all.

The quantity of *liqueur de tirage* which is added at bottling time to the *cuvées de tirage* is such that the newly bottled wine will have just the right proportion of carbonic acid gas to make it as sparkling as it should be, no less and no more, after fermentation will have intervened. This *liqueur de tirage* is plain sugar candy melted in Champagne wine. When the *cuvée de tirage* is bottled its cork is held by a strong clamp which will keep it safely in the bottle at the *prise de mousse*, that is, when fermentation does its job. As soon as it is bottled, the *cuvée de tirage* is laid to rest in the deep, damp, cold, chalk cellars of Reims, Epernay and Ay, to be left alone for two

View of Riquewihr, Alsace, taken from the famous hill of Schoenenberg

or three years: long before that, the wine will have fermented out any of the sugar that was in it when it was bottled. It will be sparkling Champagne right enough, but not fit to drink. During its bottle fermentation the wine throws off small but none the less objectionable pieces of tartaric acid, mucilage and other matters of either mineral or vegetable origin. This sediment lies quietly enough in the safely corked bottle, but it would foul the look and taste of the wine the moment glasses were filled. So it must be taken out of the wine somehow, and this is done most skilfully by the *remuage* and *dégorgement*. The *remuage* consists in giving each bottle, day after day, a twist sharp enough to make the sediment slide down towards the neck of the bottle, but not hard enough to make it rise into the wine. The process begins with the bottle in a horizontal position, but when completed the bottle stands vertically, neck downwards, and by that time the whole of the sediment has been gathered upon the inside face of the cork.

The next move is the removing of the cork with its wad of sediment, so that the wine is absolutely 'star bright' and will remain like it to the last drop. This must be done, and it is done, with practically no loss of wine and very little loss of the precious gas in it. The man who does it, *le dégorgeur*, is a skilled and valuable man indeed. He is the first of a team who deal with the bottle of sparkling Champagne when the time has come to make it ready to leave the depths of the cellars and go into the world. Next to the *dégorgeur* comes the *doseur*, the man who adds to the bottle of wine more or less *liqueur d'expédition*, a very sticky mixture of sugar, still Champagne wine and brandy: the wine to melt the sugar, the sugar to sweeten the wine and the brandy to stop the sugar fermenting. The object of this addition of *liqueur d'expédition* is to give to the wine just the degree of sweetness which is to the taste of the customer; it may be as little as half a per cent if the wine is for people who like *brut* Champagne, 1 per cent for those who prefer *extra sec*, 3 per cent for those who prefer *sec* and 5 per cent for the *demi-sec* connoisseurs. All such proportions are only approximate, since each Champagne shipper has his own technique in preparing the *liqueur d'expédition* and using it. When the *doseur* has done his job he passes on the bottle to the *boucheur*, who drives into the neck of the bottle a long and fat branded cork, which has to be forcibly squeezed to half its natural size for half its length to fit in the neck of the bottle. Next to the *boucheur* sits the *ficeleur*, who squashes down the half of the cork jutting out of the neck and makes it fast to the ring of the bottle neck with a three-branch or four-branch wire. The bottle of sparkling Champagne is then ready; when the call comes it is sent up from the cellars to the *cellier*, where it is washed and packed up.

Vintage and Non-vintage Champagne

A vintage Champagne is, or ought to be, the wine made from permitted grapes grown in Champagne vineyards in the same year, the date of which it bears printed on its labels and branded upon its corks. The vineyards of Champagne are very near the northern limit beyond which grapes will not mature in the open, and Champagne grapes do not ripen fully unless there has been a particularly hot summer. There are, unfortunately, a number of years when the weather is not all that it should be, and the wines made in such years are likely to be somewhat tart and thin. Then it is that those wealthy Champagne shippers with immense reserves of wines of past good vintages bring forth the right quantity of soft and fat wine to blend with the others, and they often do produce in this manner very nice wines indeed which cannot be sold under the date of any one particular year, but they are none the less quite good wines, often better value than vintage wines.

Vintage wines possess, naturally, a greater degree of personality, and they age more graciously, especially when they are really self-wines – not assisted or 'bettered' by the addition of older wines. They also invariably cost more than non-vintage

Storm over the vineyards at Vallet in the Loire-Atlantique,
the heart of the Muscadet area of Sèvre-et-Maine

Champagne; in the first place because they are, or ought to be, better wines, and in the second because there is a limited quantity of any vintage *cuvée*; sooner or later the time must come when there will be no more; when that time approaches the scarcer and dearer the wines become.

The Champagne District

The old Champagne province was divided in 1790 into four *départements*, Aisne and Haute-Marne in the north, Marne in the centre and Aube in the south. There are vineyards in all four *départements*, but the fact that the roots of their vines are in Champagne soil is not sufficient to give to the wine made from their grapes the right to the name of Champagne. The soil, sub-soil and aspect of the vineyards must be such that the noble grapes can thrive and produce a wine worthy to bear the honoured name of Champagne. This is why the limits of the *région délimitée*, the only area allowed to call its wines Champagne, have been drawn and fixed by law. This official *région délimitée* covers (in 1981) a total of roughly speaking, 24,200 hectares, of which 18,700 are in the Marne *département*, 3,700 in the Aube and 1,800 in the Aisne. Obviously, although these vineyards are legally entitled to call their wines Champagne, there are very great differences in the quality of their wines. We can, without any hesitation, discard, to begin with, the wines of the Aube and Aisne vineyards. They produce none but the cheaper qualities of Champagne which are drunk either locally or in Paris night-clubs. All the better-quality Champagne comes from the vineyards of the Marne *département*, which does not mean, unfortunately, that all the vineyards of the Marne *département* produce automatically very high quality wines.

There are in the Marne, as in the Côte d'Or and the Gironde, vineyards which are either very much better or just a little better than others. It depends chiefly upon the nature of soil and sub-soil, and also on the altitude and aspect of each vineyard. The climate is the same for all, although some may be more sheltered than others. In Champagne the weather is often bitter in winter, but the vines do not mind hard frost when dormant; spring is the most dangerous time of the year, as late frosts may do and often do do incalculable damage. Summers are often very hot, with occasional thunderstorms and hailstorms; autumn, vintage time, is often warm and sunny, which makes everybody very happy; a wet and cold vintage spells disaster. It was ever thus, or, at any rate, for the past thousand years; we can be fairly certain of the age-long uncertainty of the weather in Champagne, because records still exist of the prices paid at the vintage time from the tenth century to our own day, and they show that prices soared when spring frosts had brought about a shortage of wine, but slumped badly when there was a glut.

All the better vineyards of the Marne have been divided into many classes or categories, according to the quality of the wine which may be expected from their grapes. The best are in what is called the *catégorie grand cru*, and the next three in *première*, *deuxième* and *troisième catégorie*. When vintage time is at hand the Champagne shippers and the growers, whose grapes the shippers are going to buy, meet and agree upon what shall be the right price to pay for the grapes of the *catégorie grand cru* vineyards, and that settles the price of the grapes of the remaining categories; they are paid for according to an agreed descending scale, from 100 to 90 per cent of the maximum price for *première cru* wines (the wines of this category rated at 100 per cent are the *grands crus*); wines below 90 per cent are of lesser quality. The margin allows for paying more or less according to quality, since all the wines of the same *catégorie* are not likely to be identical. Some *vignerons* may have taken greater care, or they may have had better luck than others.

Nearly all the better growth vineyards are in the *arrondissements* of Reims and

Epernay, and a few only in the Canton of Vertus, of the *arrondissement* of Châlons-sur-Marne. They cover the approaches to the Montagne de Reims and its lower slopes facing Reims and Châlons-sur-Marne; the hillside upon the right bank of the River Marne above and below Epernay; and the approaches and lower slopes of a range of gentle hills some distance to the left of the Marne, above Epernay, known as the Montagne d'Avize or Côte des Blancs.

The Montagne de Reims is a cliff of tertiary formation and in the shape of a flat iron with its sharp end pointing eastwards towards Châlons-sur-Marne; it rises sharply from the billowing plain crossed by the little River Vesle, on the north-east, and from the banks of the Marne, on the south-west. A great forest and wild-boar sanctuary covers the broad crest of the Montagne de Reims, but its sides and approaches are covered with closely planted vineyards on all sides. That part of the Montagne de Reims on the Vesle side, and farthest away from Châlons-sur-Marne, is known as La Petite Montagne and its vineyards produce the less distinguished wines entitled to the name of Champagne; the best of them, however, those of Sacy and Villedommange, are in good demand, being cheaper than most and considered to be very good value. Leaving La Petite Montagne and La Montagne and proceeding eastwards, we shall pass through the vineyards of Villers-Allerand, Rilly-la-Montagne, Chigney-les-Roses, Ludes, Mailly-Champagne, Verzenay, Verzy and Villers-Marmery, all of them hillside villages and vineyards, while we shall survey from our vantage point – none of greater beauty than the Moulin de Verzenay – a wonderful panorama of flourishing vineyards, including those of Sillery and Beaumont-sur-Vesle stretching to the main road from Reims to Châlons-sur-Marne.

All these 'Montagne' vineyards are practically back-to-back with the 'Marne' vineyards on the other side, but there are others at the eastern end, or turning-point of the Montagne, forming a sort of connecting link between the two: they are the vineyards of Trépail, Tauxières and Louvois, on the Châlons-sur-Marne side, and Bouzy and Ambonnay on the Marne side. We shall then turn our backs on Châlons-sur-Marne, and, facing Château-Thierry and Paris farther west, we shall pass through the riverside vineyards of Bisseuil, Mareuil-sur-Ay, Avenay and Ay, a little town as quaint as its name and well worth a visit. Beyond Ay, the vineyards of Dizy-Magenta and Cumières, and those of Champillon and Hautvillers much higher up, all produce very fine wines but the same cannot be said of the wines made from grapes grown farther west upon the right bank of the Marne, practically as far as Château-Thierry.

The two great grape varieties of the Champagne district are the red Pinot and the white Chardonnay. The black grape varieties dominate, with about 80 per cent of the vineyard area either under the Pinot Noir grape variety, or the Pinot Meunier, or other clonal variations of Pinot. The Pinot Noir is the nobler of the two main varieties, and predominates in the Montagne de Reims region. The robust Pinot Meunier, which produces wines that are not so suitable for ageing and with less finesse, is much to be found in the Vallée de la Marne. The aristocratic Chardonnay predominates in the Côte des Blancs area, where there is both chalk and marl. The wines are delicate with a light emphasis and an enticing bouquet. But for all the grape varieties, the calcareous soil is an absolutely vital element in the distinctive breed of a Champagne, as against other sparkling wines.

On the left bank of the Marne the better wines are those of Chouilly and Pierry, close to Epernay, to the right and left of the town, but the best wines are those of a range of gentle hills a little farther back from the river; they rise soon after one leaves Pierry and stretch as far as Vertus. This is the part of the Champagne *viticole* known as La Côte des Blancs, or the hill of the white grapes, where the white Chardonnay grapes are grown almost exclusively. The most important township of the Côte des Blancs is Avize, with Cramant on higher ground to its right, or west, Le Mesnil, Oger and Vertus to its left, or east. The other vineyards of La Côte des Blancs, those of Monthelon and Cuis, on the Pierry side of Cramant and Grauves on the other side of the same hill, also produce white wines from white grapes, 'Blanc de Blancs', entitled to the name of Champagne, but they are of plainer quality.

M. André Simon's wonderful account of Champagne is reproduced, with minor alterations, because no one describes the setting as well as he does. He knew Champagne intimately, its wines, land, history and people, and it is amazing, after nearly two decades, how much of what he says remains a true and clear picture of why Champagne tastes as it does.

Obviously, there have been some changes or modifications in the Champagne-making process, gradual developments made necessary by changing socio-economic conditions. Right at the early stages of picking, there is the process of sorting through the grapes for any damaged fruit – *épluchage*. This is much less usual nowadays, largely because greater protection of the vineyards from rot, by means of efficient spraying, has greatly improved the health of the grapes. The traditional wooden presses are still much in evidence, although some very large concerns and coopera-tives use the horizontal press with a rubber bag inside which swells up and gradually presses the grapes against the sides of the machine. This is a gentle way of pressing, very necessary in the making of Champagne. The following fermentation is now nearly always carried on in stainless-steel vats, and selected yeasts are the order of the day, thus ensuring a more easily controlled fermentation. The Champagne houses have done much research on the cultivation and selection of strains of yeast, and even export some of the results of their work.

Nothing has diminished the importance of the head blender of a Champagne house, and in a non-vintage wine he will seek to maintain continuity of house style, choose his wines to set aside for a future vintage wine if the year is good enough, and separate the very finest wines, if nature made it possible to produce them, for a top *cuvée*, if this is the policy of his house. Stocks are still the basis of a fine Champagne house, and a minimum of three years of stock is regarded as 'security' level, with top quality houses infinitely preferring to have five years of stock behind them.

The *liqueur de tirage* is still sugar dissolved in the base wine of Champagne, and the sugar is very carefully calculated according to what is already in the wine, and the pressure ultimately wanted in the final Champagne. Six atmospheres is what is required normally, as this goes down a little after disgorging – *crémant* Champagnes are usually about four atmospheres. Extra yeasts are usually also added at this stage, to help complete a satisfactory second fermentation. Nowadays, this fermentation in bottle, the *méthode champenoise*, is nearly always held in its container by means of a crown cork, not a cork held by a clamp or *agrafe*. The crown cork is metal and plastic, with only a strip of cork between that and the wine, and the resultant savings in cost have been marked.

Remuage has obviously become very costly, with its intensive hand-labour and the difficulty of finding young people to take the places of the retiring *remueurs*. Experiments with rotating metal frames holding quantities of bottles are being undertaken and inevitably it is the way of the future for much of the production of Champagne. No mechanical method has yet been found entirely satisfactory, especially in years when the deposit formed in the bottle proves exceptionally difficult to move, but undoubtedly ways of doing this will be perfected. But in 1981, *remuage* by hand is still very much part of the work of a Champagne cellar. *Dégorge-ment* before consumption, removing the deposit which has gathered on the first cork, is now rarely done completely by hand – *à la volée*. Now, the neck of the upturned bottle is plunged into a freezing solution, and the sediment near the cork solidifies, making it easy to remove in a small block of ice. Before the Champagne receives its second cork, the *liqueur d'expédition* is added, with various degrees of sweetness. The *brut* and *extra sec* might have a little more sugar than indicated, and there is also a *doux* category, a rich Champagne, delicious in the right context. Totally *brut* wines would not appeal to all, but when completely balanced, they can have great finesse. Non-vintage Champagne is the wine on which a house builds its reputation. Vintage Champagnes (and it has to be admitted that there is sometimes a certain amount of flexibility with the year featured) usually have more pronounced character, and can be marvellous with some bottle age. Rosé or pink Champagne, made by extra grapeskin contact or by adding red, still wine from Champagne, can be both non-vintage or vintage, and the strengthened influence of the black grapes can give more body. With age a rosé Champagne takes on a beautiful, subtle, tawny colour, and exciting flavours all of its own. Houses that make rosé Champagne include: Taittinger, Perrier-Jouët, Veuve Clicquot, Moët & Chandon (there is also Dom Pérignon Rosé), Heidsieck Monopole, Giesler, Pommery & Greno, Laurent Perrier, Piper-Heidsieck, Roederer, Pol Roger, Charles Heidsieck and Mumm. As with other Champagne, there are different house styles; Roederer, for instance, has depth and great length, while Charles Heidsieck is delicious, light and fragrant, and Dom Ruinart Rosé ethereal.

Blanc de Blancs Champagne is simply Champagne made only from the Chardonnay grape, with no red Pinot in it. Consequently, it is usually a lighter, very delicate wine – ideal *apéritif* Champagne. The rarely encountered Blanc de Noirs is logically enough made entirely from black grapes, but is white in colour – a full-bodied wine with marked bouquet. *Crémant* Champagnes can have tremendous finesse, with a real taste of the wine coming through. There are also single vineyard Champagnes, notably from villages in the Montagne de Reims area, but perhaps they lack the balance of the best Champagnes, thereby proving the benefit of astute blending.

Some houses make a 'luxury' *cuvée*, a wine that they consider the very best blend possible, whether vintage or non-vintage. This is usually highlighted by a specially shaped or designed bottle. Some are magnificent, others are disappointing, especially at such a very high price level. It is also rather impudent for such luxury wines to be sold (as some are) when still very young indeed, and very far from their complex best – when asking very high prices, there should be some element of financing by the producer. These de luxe Champagnes include: Dom Ruinart (a wine of great elegance), Dom Pérignon, La Grande Dame from Veuve Clicquot, Roederer's Cristal in the clear glass, Perrier-Jouët's Belle Epoque (with beautiful enamelled flowers fired on to the bottle) and Blason de France, Heidsieck Dry Monopole's excellent and often unsung Diamant Bleu, Taittinger's Comtes de Champagne, Laurent Perrier's Cuvée Grand Siècle, Charles Heidsieck's Cuvée Royale, Mumm's René Lalou, Canard-Duchêne's Charles VII Brut, Piper-Heidsieck's Florens-Louis, Abel Lepitre's Prince A. de Bourbon Parme, De Venoge's Vin des Princes, Mercier's Réserve de l'Empéreur, Irroy's Cuvée Marie Antoinette, and Deutz & Geldermann's Cuvée William Deutz. Bollinger have two unusual Champagnes, the Vieilles Vignes from ungrafted vines, and the Bollinger Tradition RD – the recent disgorging giving the wine more maturity.

The main Champagne houses are the following: (The non-vintage wines apply to *brut* style)

Ayala: Reliable non-vintage, slightly sweeter style.
Besserat de Bellefon: Reliable Champagne, much seen in France.
Bollinger: Distinguished house and wines, finesse and style rather than sheer weight.

Deutz: A big-flavoured non-vintage. Marvellous Blanc de Blancs Vintage.

Canard Duchêne: Light non-vintage, with a good deal of breed, although not great length.

Giesler: Non-vintage on light side, with Chardonnay flavour.

Gosset: Charming non-vintage, and a remarkable 1961 in the past!

George Goulet: Beautifully balanced non-vintage and Crémant Blanc de Blancs.

Alfred Gratien: Flowery, quite full non-vintage.

Heidsieck Dry Monopole: Marvellous de luxe Cuvée Diamant Bleu – perfect for laying down. Pleasant non-vintage.

Charles Heidsieck: Extremely pleasant non-vintage, and vintage wines that age beautifully. In 1980, the 1966 was still most distinguished, as was the 1966 Cuvée Royale.

Piper-Heidsieck: A light, fresh, apéritif-style non-vintage.

Krug: This is aristocratic Champagne *par excellence*, always outstanding by its sheer breed. The non-vintage Grande Cuvée is charming, heady, refreshing and distinctive. The vintage has much more weight and great class. A chance to drink Krug is never to be missed.

Lanson: The non-vintage is pleasant, perfect apéritif Champagne.

Abel Lepitre: Good vintage, non-vintage and Crémant.

Mercier: Under the same ownership as Moët. The non-vintage has a nice flavour – good, straightforward Champagne, often underrated.

Moët & Chandon: Non-vintage quite concentrated, vintage naturally has more character. Considering amounts sold across the world, standards kept remarkably high, with only occasional lapses. De luxe brand Dom Pérignon combines elegance with body.

Mumm: The non-vintage is now considerably lighter than it was. Delicious Blanc de Blancs Crémant.

Joseph Perrier: A family firm making really flowery, delicate non-vintage, delicious apéritif wine, and impressive vintage.

Laurent Perrier: A lightish, refreshing non-vintage – all-purpose and ages beautifully.

Perrier-Jouët: A full, really interesting non-vintage. The de luxe blends go under different names for different markets – Belle Epoque, Fleur de Champagne, and Blason de France. Excellent house.

Philipponat: A light, very *brut* non-vintage.

Pol Roger: Lightish, easy-to-drink non-vintage, weightier, classic vintage.

Pommery & Greno: Rather a one-dimensional non-vintage. Vintage has more class and finish.

Louis Roederer: Outstanding non-vintage, full and with immense class – if you like Champagne with meals, this is it. Also sublime Rosé and really good Rich, which is not cloying but just rounder. Excellent vintage.

A. Rothschild: Very good Champagne. This house also supplies many Buyer's Own Brands (BOBS).

Ruinart: Under the same ownership as Moët. Incredibly elegant and aristocratic non-vintage called Tradition, delicious Dom Ruinart Blanc de Blancs and Dom Ruinart Rosé.

Salon: Only vintage wine, and only from Chardonnay grown in the finest vineyards at Le Mesnil. Some wonderful old vintages.

Taittinger: A really good, complex non-vintage. Comtes de Champagne Vintage Rosé and Vintage Blanc de Blancs are both distinguished wines.

De Venoge: Extremely reliable Champagne – this *marque* is made by the house of Trouillard, which is responsible for many good Buyer's Own Brand (BOB) Champagnes. Now part of Charles Heidsieck.

Veuve Clicquot: The Widow herself, with quite an assertive non-vintage, and really distinguished vintage wines that age beautifully.

There are also cooperative wines, such as Mailly, and cooperative brands such as St Gall and St Simon, the latter very good. St Marceaux is a noteworthy small house. Of course, it has to be remembered that the dosage in non-vintage Champagnes can vary a little from country to country, but this is hardly detectable. Differences in Champagnes from the same house are far more likely to be caused by different storage conditions and the influence of temperature. No wine suffers more than Champagne from poor storage, and cool conditions away from light are essential. Half-bottles can suffer very quickly from this, in particular, and they should always be drunk as young as possible. If you like Champagne with a little bottle age, magnums are ideal for laying down for some special occasion or party. The very large bottles have delightful names, but take some remembering:

Magnum	2 bottles	Salmanazar	12 bottles
Jeroboam	4 bottles	Balthazar	16 bottles
Rehoboam	6 bottles	Nebuchadnezzar	20 bottles
Methuselah	8 bottles		

Champagne, being a very northerly vineyard area, has enormous fluctuations in the size of the annual crop. The following table showing the harvest yield over a period of ten years proves this point. It will be seen that the 1979 harvest broke the previous all-time record obtained in 1970, but two consecutive good crops are really needed to restore stocks, that vital ingredient of good Champagne.

HARVEST YIELD (IN BOTTLES)

Year	Bottles	Year	Bottles	Year	Bottles
1969	91,264,000	1973	210,189,067	1977	186,660,533
1970	219,017,200	1974	169,751,467	1978	79,297,600
1971	84,945,467	1975	175,324,000	1979	226,666,667
1972	154,896,267	1976	211,675,667		

Champagne will never be cheap. Firstly there is the cost of the grapes themselves, which spirals ever upwards (the 1979 harvest saw more than a 20 per cent rise, in spite of the size of the crop), and then there is the long, complicated process that is the *méthode champenoise.* That is why standards in Champagne must be kept high. But good Champagne has a taste and complexity that cannot be achieved elsewhere, due almost entirely to the difference in the base wine, and above all it has a bouquet that is quite inimitable to the area.

Good vintages in Champagne have included:

1952, '53, '55, '59   1961, '62, '64, '66, '69   1970, '71, '73, '75, '76, '77

Still Wine from Champagne

These non-sparkling wines used to be called Champagne Nature, but this was naturally very confusing and even open to abuse, so in 1974 a new *appellation* was created for them, Coteaux Champenois. The amount made is strictly controlled, and although the *appellation* covers white, red and rosé wines, white still wines made from the Chardonnay grape are the most common. Some well-known Coteaux Champenois names are Ruinart Chardonnay, Moët's Saran still wine and that of Laurent Perrier. These white wines are never as great as white Burgundy, but can provide simple enjoyment and the added tinge of excitement when drinking something of a curiosity – albeit at far from simple prices.

The same could be said of the red still wines made from black Pinot grapes, mostly in the villages of the Montagne de Reims – the wine suffers if compared with red

Burgundy. However, if staying in Champagne for a length of time, an occasional change of colour is welcome. These Coteaux Champenois red wines come from vineyards round Bouzy, Ay, Ambonnay, Dizy and Cumières, Verzenay and Rilly, between Reims and Epernay.

ALSACE

The chequered history of Alsace has forged an individuality in the people and the wines that is good enough reason for getting to know the region through the glass. From the reign of Louis XIV to 1870 Alsace was French, from 1870 to 1918 it was German, the Riesling and the Traminer (as it then was) were forbidden, and the Alsations were forced to make cheap wines, from 1918 to 1940 Alsace was French again and the region once again opted for quality, always a long, slow business of replanting, from 1940 to 1944 Alsace was again German and greatly devastated as well, and from 1944, happily, to this day Alsace is French again. Since the end of the Second World War, when Alsace once more became French, her entire policy has been to maintain quality standards, and it is no accident that Alsace has the most stringent anti-fraud squad operating in France. The, at the time, startling decision in 1972 to bottle all Alsatian wines in the area of production was also taken with quality standards and respect for professional integrity in mind, and although its reversal has been discussed, the reasons for keeping this decision still hold good.

There are 11,500 hectares of *appellation contrôlée* vineyards in production, from which there are 800,000 hectolitres average annual production of *appellation contrôlée* wines – or 115 million bottles. Wine is very important to the whole region of Alsace, as it represents 25 per cent of the total agricultural production – and here it should be remembered that we are in a very fertile area, particularly renowned for its fruits. Alsace has 20 per cent of the total French production of *appellation contrôlée* white wines, and the very high figure of 45 per cent of the French market of white *appellation* wines drunk at home. Exports are very important to Alsace, and in 1979, 20 million bottles were exported, or 21 per cent of the total sales of Alsatian wine in bottles. The large houses of *producteurs-négociants*, in particular, are heavily dependent on export sales – Hugel export 80 per cent of its wines, Trimbach 65 per cent. The home market tends to be more supplied by *propriétaires-viticulteurs* and cooperatives, although the latter are now well represented on export markets too.

The whole pattern of Alsace wine production is one of small units. 9,200 separate producers declare *appellation contrôlée* Alsace wine, of which only 2,900 have more than one hectare – 1,000 have between one and two hectares, 1,450 between two and five hectares, 450 have more than five hectares, with only the tiny number of forty-five having more than ten hectares. So, the highly individual character of the Alsatians is reflected in the manner in which they divide their vineyard area. Obviously, very small owners have other jobs – three hectares is probably the minimum viable size. There is one *appellation* Alsace, which went on the statute books in 1945, about a decade later than most of the other *appellations* in France, but it only became a decree in 1962. This governed such things as the area of cultivation, the species of grape, the processes involving the improvement and preparation of wine and the date on which the grapes are gathered. The bottle used is the traditional green *flûte*. There is also the *appellation* Alsace Grand Cru, which must be completed by the name of the grape variety used. The grape varieties grown are the Gewürz-traminer (21%), Muscat (3.7%), Riesling (17.9%), Pinot Noir (4.5%), Pinot Gris or Tokay d'Alsace (4.6%), Pinot Blanc, sometimes called Clevner, (16.8%) and Syl-vaner (22.4%) – the *cépages nobles*. The *cépages courants* are the Knipperlé, the Chasselas (ennobled in the early 1970s), the Goldriesling and the Müller-Thurgau, all of which are gradually being phased out. So, *appellation contrôlée* Alsace Grand Cru or Grands Vins will be of superior quality, and must also have a higher degree of natural sugar (when converted into alcohol) before any chaptalization – for instance, a minimum of 11 per cent for the Gewürztraminer and 10 per cent for the Riesling.

The main points to note in the choice of grape variety today is the growth of the Riesling (which the Alsatians consider their top grape) and the Pinot Blanc, and the drop in quantity of the Sylvaner and the lesser Chasselas, or Gutedel. To the Alsatians, the essential part of their duty as wine-makers is to bring out the individual characteristics of each grape variety. They lay particular emphasis on the nose of a wine, saying it should project the essence of the grape used, and look for harmony, freshness and clean fruitiness on the palate. Except in rare years, when the weather conditions are particularly favourable, the wines are always fermented out to dryness.

Riesling: The epitome of delicacy and finesse, elegant rather than big or overblown, although in years like 1971 and 1976 it can be rich. Riesling should have marvellous, full fruit, and length of finish. It is less steely-fruity than German Riesling from, say, the Saar, and more aromatic, earthy and heady.

Gewürztraminer: This is perhaps the grape variety that beginners in wine like best, because of its wonderful 'come and get me' nose of spiciness and fruit, with a strong positive taste. It makes immensely attractive wine, although occasionally, in the hands of vulgarians, it can be a bit blowsy, and one would perhaps tire of the taste faster than one would of Riesling. The grape has a reddish hue when ripe. The Gewürztraminer can be rather fragile to grow, with berries falling off in poor weather conditions.

Tokay d'Alsace or Pinot Gris: Rather the dark horse among the Alsatian varieties, as people first get seduced by the more widely planted, better-known grapes. With Tokay, one gets rather an earthy taste, which has real *typicité* as the Alsatians say – the taste is one of *terroir* and richness, rather than straightforward fruit. Ideally, it should have over 88° Oechslé to be good – the great ones are over 100°. (In Alsace, sugar is measured in Oechslé degrees, as in Germany.)

Muscat: Muscat has a lovely, unmistakable 'catty' nose when young, followed by a pronounced, pungent taste. Unlike the wines of the south of France from this grape variety, in Alsace Muscat is vinified completely dry. The main clone in Alsace is the Muscat Ottonel, perhaps the most delicate, and the Muscat Blanc d'Alsace which is very grapy. Unfortunately, the Muscat is very susceptible to flowering problems (*coulure* and then *millerandage*) and very small yields can follow.

Pinot Blanc: Perhaps growing in popularity, as it is more reasonable in price than the foregoing varieties, Pinot Blanc has a fresh fruit taste in abundance and is delicious drinking, but lacks a long, complex finish.

Sylvaner: A pleasant grape variety, without 'breed' (except when grown very high in the Alto Adige, right on the Italian-Austrian border), but in Alsace, nice young drinking. It can go a bit flattish and 'fat' if left too long in the bottle.

Chasselas: A grape variety without much character – the best one can hope for is a round fruitiness, without distinction. Usually goes into wines for quick, local consumption, or in the blends of *Edelzwicker*, which has to contain noble varieties. *Zwicker* ended its life as a wine term in 1972.

Pinot Noir: Some would say that it is hardly worth trying to make red wine in Alsace, as the northerly climatic zone does not favour extraction of any colour or depth. Occasionally, cleverly vinified and with a good year to back it, the wines can have a fruity charm and taste somewhat like a Sancerre Rouge. The words *rouge* and *rosé* are often interchangeable.

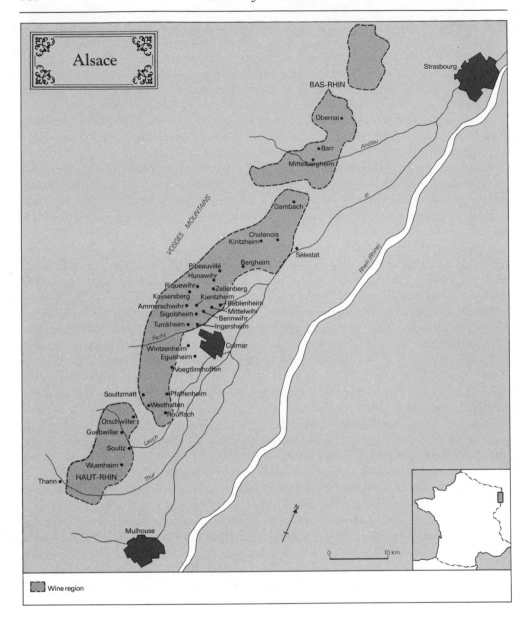

At vintage time, the Chasselas and the Sylvaner are picked first, with the Riesling and the Gewürztraminer coming in last. Picking usually starts at the beginning of October and lasts about a month, with rare exceptions when there is a real *Vendange Tardive* very late in the season. When a wine is labelled with a grape variety, it is 100 per cent that variety. The same principle applies to the use of the vintage year. The climate of Alsace is a very continental, as opposed to a temperate, one, befitting a region far away from the sea. The area is protected by the Vosges mountains, and the rain falls on the western side of the range, causing Alsace to be one of the driest regions of France. The summers tend to be hot and sunny, and the winters can be bitter, sometimes with snow, and there is always the danger of frost until late spring. There is the plain of Alsace, and the vine-covered sub-Vosges hills running east to west – the best vine-bearing slopes face south and southeast, to gain the best possible micro-climate. The very best sites are usually mid-slope, and do not go too far up the Vosges. There is such multiplicity of soil that it allows for the ideal sites for each grape variety to be chosen – this also applies to site and position on the slope, particularly with regard to the shy, late-ripening Riesling, which must have a particularly favoured slice of the land. Tokay and Pinot Blanc are hardier, but obviously the Pinot Noir must have shelter from cold and winds. The very best soil is *argilo-calcaire* or calcareous clay, but there is also sandy soil, loamy soil, and combinations of all. The two *départements* where vines are grown in Alsace are the Bas-Rhin, the northern part towards the border with Germany, and the Haut-Rhin, the southern part, with Colmar as its centre. In fact, the area round Colmar perhaps marks the high point of quality in Alsace, with villages such as Ribeauvillé, Hunawihr, Riquewihr, Kientzheim, Bennwihr, Kaysersberg, Ammerschwihr, Turckheim, Wintzenheim and Eguisheim. In the Bas-Rhin above Sélestat there is Dambach, Barr and Obernai, but Sylvaner and Chasselas are grown more in this area, and the wines generally do not have the same breed. Way south of Colmar, there are Rouffach and Guebwiller, which should not be forgotten.

Alsace combines modern with traditional, using up-to-date presses and methods of vinification, but still keeping wood in the cellar, especially in the smaller establishments, where it is a delight to come upon large carved casks, German-fashion, with painted quotations from Goethe on the walls! But large houses like Hugel also have old, often historical wooden casks, usually encrusted with tartrates inside so wood/wine contact is minimal. The great wines are sometimes vinified in wood, others in stainless steel, and temperatures at fermentation are usually around 20°C. It is desirable to have casks of all sizes as, with a wide range of grape varieties, some of them producing very small amounts, it is necessary to have adaptability – a wide selection of cask sizes is also vital where racking is concerned. So you can see huge casks holding seventy hectolitres, or small ones with anything between 250 and 650 litres of wine in them. Some houses have centrifuges to clarify the must, and bentonite fining to remove excess proteins is usually done at must, rather than at wine state. The malolactic fermentation is usually encouraged in lesser years, although it is not needed in great, ripe years, and bottling takes place from April to September, with the great Gewürztraminers and Tokays being bottled last.

After the vintage, the vines are usually cut back to two sprigs and the earth mounded up round the base. Vines can be led up to the height required on wires, to about 1.8 metres high, with frost being taken into account and when maximum sun is desired. Training is lower in the Bas-Rhin. A very top vineyard, aiming for the greatest quality, might have 5,000 vines per hectare and the pruning might limit production to twenty-four buds per square metre. There are quite high yields in Alsace by comparison, say, with Burgundy – 100 hectolitres per hectare for *appellation* Alsace (plus sometimes the *plafond limite de classement* of 20 per cent), and seventy hectolitres per hectare for Alsace Grand Cru. The top grape varieties tend to produce less than the maximum allowed, and it must be remembered that quantity affects white wines less than red.

There are a number of historical site names in Alsace, that have always been used locally, but which have rarely been used on labels. It was felt that this might muddle the customer, especially on the domestic French market, as the site names are more Alsatian than French. However, now it is felt that the consumer is more sophisticated, and would like to know when his wine comes from a special, usually very favoured, site. So, a top echelon of Grands Crus is proposed, and these would be true Grands Crus (or *climats*) based on certain proven vineyards, not only on a superior natural sugar strength, as at present. Some of the best-known sites, many of which could be in line for Grand Cru status, should the project ever come to fruition, are:

Haut-Rhin

Ammerschwihr 'Kaefferkopf'; Beblenheim 'Sonnenglanz'; Bergheim 'Kanzlerberg'; Colmar 'Hardt'; Eguisheim 'Pfirsigberg' and 'Eichberg'; Guebwiller 'Kitterlé' and 'Wanne'; Hunawihr 'Muhlforst'; Ingersheim 'Florimont'; Kaysersberg 'Schlossberg'; Kientzheim 'Schlossberg' and 'Clos des Capucins'; Mittelwihr 'Mandelberg'; Ribeauvillé 'Osterberg'; Riquewihr 'Sporen' and 'Schoenenberg'; Rouffach 'Langenzug' and 'Bollenberg'; Sigolsheim 'Mamburg'; Soultzmatt 'Zinnkoepfle'; Thann 'Le Rangen'; Turckheim 'Brand'; Voegtlinshoffen 'Hatschburg' and 'Grosskohlausen'; Westhalten 'Clos St Landelin'; Wettolsheim 'Steingrubler'; Wintzenheim 'Hengst'; Wuenheim 'Ollwiller'; Zellenberg 'Buergen'.

Bas-Rhin

Andlau 'Kastelberg' and 'Moenchberg'; Barr 'Kirchberg', 'Zisser' and 'Rotluf'; Chatenois 'Hahnenberg'; Mittelbergheim 'Zotzenberg' and 'Brandluft'.

Some of these sites, according to their soils and expositions, are particularly suitable for certain grape varieties; for example, the Schoenenberg at Riquewihr specializes in Riesling and Muscat (both are late-ripening), the Sporen, also at Riquewihr, in Tokay and Gewürztraminer, and the Eichberg at Eguisheim produces excellent Gewürztraminer.

The Wines and Who Makes Them

The large houses of Alsace, many of which concentrate on exporting, usually own a proportion of their vineyard needs, and buy in other grapes. This gives them total control over the wine-making process and ensures quality. Some of the larger houses will charge higher prices than the cooperatives, but their reputation is high and you buy with complete security. They are also, with financial and technical power, able to take full advantage of great years, when they make exceptional wines.

HUGEL (Riquewihr)

A house that must come first for many Britons and Americans, as they form the main export market for Hugel. The family tradition of this firm is typical of Alsace, where ties are strong and people faithful to their land and customs. With the death in 1980 of the great Monsieur Jean Hugel, his three sons, Jean, Georges and André carry on the fine aims of the firm, which is to make wines as naturally and as well as possible. In Alsace as a whole, wine-makers like to treat wine as little as possible, letting the true identity of the fruit speak for itself. Hugel own twenty-five hectares, composed of 48 per cent Riesling, 47 per cent Gewürztraminer, 3 per cent Pinot Gris and 2 per cent Muscat, including a good part of the Sporen and the Schoenenberg. They own no Pinot Blanc, Sylvaner or Chasselas, and only buy in grapes, not wine. In common with most growers and wine-makers in Alsace, they use Vaslin horizontal presses, but with special non-standard stainless-steel parts to the machines. Since the 1979 harvest, Hugel have the newest version of the Vaslin press, which has not only a rotating outside cylinder, but also a counter-rotating central screw to avoid pressure problems with easily crushed grapes like Sylvaner. It is this kind of detail which tells.

Hugel's basic wine is Couronne d'Alsace, or Flambeau d'Alsace, which is fruity and frank and for young drinking. Les Vignards is a delicious Pinot Blanc. With Riesling, there is the straight wine with a vintage year, then the Riesling Cuvée Tradition from a better exposed slope, more smoky and with a fantastic fullness, and finally the Riesling Réserve Exceptionnelle or Réserve Personnelle from the very best slopes. The same graduation can apply to Gewürztraminer and Tokay and

Muscat, and most other houses have similar names to show differences in quality – the choice of names is personal and not enshrined in law. The Pinot Noir of Hugel is one of Alsace's best red wines. Some of the truly grand wines of recent years have been the marvellous ripe ones of the 1976 vintage, when the weather was so clement.

TRIMBACH (Ribeauvillé)

Hubert Trimbach is as astonishing an ambassador for Alsatian wines as Johnny Hugel, both of them travelling indefatigably, but still very much in touch with the vine-roots. Hubert's brother, Bernard, controls vineyard and cellar. The family has owned vines since 1626, and you do not trifle with traditions as strong as these. Trimbach produce one of the most stately wines to come out of Alsace, perhaps the most subtle and complex I have ever tasted – the Riesling Clos Ste Hune, a small, sheltered vineyard above Hunawihr. This should be kept in bottle for as long as you can resist it for the full dimension of the wine to come out – from six to ten years would bring its rewards. Their Gewürztraminer Cuvée des Seigneurs de Ribeaupierre, and Riesling Cuvée Frédéric Emile are other top wines.

LEON BEYER (Eguisheim)

Like all the big houses, there are a great many *cuvées* of different qualities to choose from, but the top wines of Léon Beyer rank with the finest. In 1980, their Gewürztraminer 1978 was impressive, as was the Gewürztraminer Cuvée des Comtes d'Eguisheim 1975, while the 1971 Gewürztraminer Vendange Tardive was superb.

DOPFF & IRION (Riquewihr)

An extremely large firm, where perhaps commerce sometimes reigns over real individuality. But I usually like their Gewürztraminer Les Sorcières and their Muscat Les Amandiers, and in 1980 I saw an astoundingly beautiful Gewürztraminer 1976 Domaine du Château de Riquewihr, unfortunately, like all these special wines, in very limited supply. A 1975 Tokay Sélection also tasted well. Their Les Murailles Riesling comes from the Schoenenberg.

DOPFF AU MOULIN (Riquewihr)

Usually very pleasant wines. In 1980, I particularly liked their 1976 Gewürztraminer Eichberg, Propre Récolte Tardive, Réserve Spéciale.

LOUIS GISSELBRECHT (Dambach-La-Ville)

Comparatively, not a large or world-known house, but one which produces wines of outstanding quality, most consistent over the whole range of grape varieties. A Riesling Cuvée Réservée 1977 was the first wine of this house I was conscious of seeing, and it was immensely elegant. I have since admired their Gewürztraminer 1977, a charming (and cheap) Pinot Noir 1979, a Riesling Cuvée Réservée 1979, again remarkable value, a Riesling Cuvée Spéciale 1979, and a Gewürztraminer Cuvée Réservée 1979. This house represents some of the best buys in Alsace.

ZIND-HUMBRECHT (Wintzenheim)

A small, family enterprise, owned and run personally by M. and Mme Léonard Humbrecht. Their wines are made to a very high quality, and what makes them especially interesting is the fact that most come from definite sites with well-defined tastes of their own. They make superb Tokay du Rangen, Clos St Urbain, which usually needs time in bottle to come out. The Riesling du Rangen (the famous site at Thann) is impressive – here the soil is schistous, the same as in the Moselle, but rare in Alsace. The Rangen faces south, and M. Humbrecht owns five of the total six hectares. Some of the Humbrecht wines have considerable natural carbon dioxide when young, as well as some acidity, as there is no malolactic fermentation here. Humbrecht also have vineyards at Hengst (Wintzenheim), Brand (Turckheim) and at Gueberschwihr, where the deep clay makes for wines with less finesse than the granite at Brand or the quite heavy *argilo-calcaire* at Hengst.

SCHLUMBERGER (Guebwiller)

Schlumberger at Guebwiller make rather different wine, exclusively from their own vineyards (140 hectares, making them the largest owners in Alsace) on steep slopes with rather red sandy soil. The wines have a special flavour, rather earthy and highly individual. The vines are on narrow terraces here, difficult to work, and producing less yield than normal in Alsace, giving Schlumberger wines a certain body and concentration. The steeply sloping Kitterlé vineyard produces Gewürztraminer and Riesling of great interest, and the Gewürztraminer Cuvée Christine Schlumberger is justly renowned for its grand *pourriture noble* character. Fermentation is in wood, and there is a wide variety of casks of different sizes from 17,000 to 7,000 litres for different qualities. Top quality wines are stored in 7,000-litre barrels, and these wines tend to be stored for a year or two in bottle before sale.

I have also liked a delicious Gewürztraminer 1979 from Laugel, and a good Riesling Cuvée Réservée 1978 from Kuentz-Bas. Willm's Grande Réserve Exceptionnelle Clos Gaensbroennel Gewürztraminer 1976 is a fine wine, as is Boeckel's straight Gewürztraminer 1979. Other houses that export, and which produce reliable wines, are: Bott, Ribeauvillé; Heim, Westhalten; Charles Jux, Colmar; Klipfel, Barr; Kuehn, Ammerschwihr; Lorentz, Bergheim (both Gustave and Jérome); Muller, Bergheim; Preiss-Henny, Mittelwihr; Preiss-Zimmer, Riquewihr; Louis Sipp, Ribeauvillé; and Sparr, Sigolsheim.

Small growers in Alsace abound, and I know of none better than M. Wiederhirn of Riquewihr. He sells mostly direct to the customer in France, but exports a little, including to England. The SYNVA is a Syndicat of Négociants/Viticulteurs that works from the Chamber of Commerce in Colmar. Their 1976 Gewürztraminer Réserve Exceptionnelle certainly lived up to the name. The Gewürztraminer from Pierre Ritzenthaler, Cellier du Muhlbach at Guémar is also good. The cooperatives, on the whole, hold up the reputation for quality that Alsace guards with so much care and they are very important because of the mass of small growers. The main ones are:

Haut-Rhin

Cave Coopérative de Ribeauvillé; Cave Coopérative Vinicole de Gueberschwihr et environs Gueberschwihr; Cave Coopérative Vinicole de Bennwihr à Bennwihr; Cave Coopérative Vinicole d'Eguisheim (one of the most reputed); Cave Coopérative Vinicole de Hunawihr; Cave Coopérative Vinicole de Kientzheim-Kayserberg à Kientzheim; Cave Coopérative Vinicole de Pfaffenheim; Cave Coopérative Vinicole du Vieil Armand; Cave Coopérative Vinicole de Turckheim; Cave Coopérative Vinicole de Westhalten; Cave Coopérative des Viticulteurs d'Ingersheim et des environs dans la région des Trois-Epis à Ingersheim; Coopérative Vinicole d'Alsace Réunies 'Codival' à Beblenheim; Société Coopérative Vinicole de Beblenheim; and Société Coopérative Vinicole de Sigolsheim.

Bas-Rhin

Cave Coopérative Vinicole d'Andlau; Société Coopérative Vinicole d'Orschwiller; and Union Vinicole pour la Diffusion des Vins d'Alsace, Obernai.

Crémant d'Alsace

A relatively new *appellation* for sparkling wines made by the Champagne method from grapes grown in Alsace. Dopff au Moulin in Riquewihr and the cooperative in Eguisheim are well-known for their *Crémant*. The quality is always good, and it should be remembered that the price can never be cheap for wines such as these from expensive base material and where the method requires financing. Like Crémant de Bourgogne, this is a really good alternative to Champagne.

Vintages in Alsace

The vital things to remember about Alsace vintages are that the great years keep well, the lesser ones should be drunk young, and certain years favour certain grape varieties. As examples of longevity, in 1978 a Gewürztraminer Hugel Sélection de Grains Nobles 1945 (an exceptionally good year) was still rich and interesting, while a magnum of Gewürztraminer Vendange Tardive Hugel 1945 was superb in 1975. At the 1978 tasting, a 1947 Riesling Hugel Réserve Exceptionnelle (in magnum, which helps) was in good form. In 1975, a magnum of 1953 Tokay Hugel was still young with great finesse, and three years later a magnum of 1953 Tokay Hugel Vendange Tardive elicited perfect marks for its wonderful smoky taste, typical of the Tokay, its breed and its young elegance. Vendange Tardive averages 100° Oechslé and Sélection de Grains Nobles 115°.

1959: A very great year, and in 1979, a 1959 Gewürztraminer Hugel Sélection de Grains Nobles combined delicate fruit, with elegance and fullness, with the great richness not yet fully out.
1961: A very great year, as shown by a magnum of 1961 Tokay Vendange Tardive Hugel, which got near perfect marks in 1976 for its characteristic smoky taste, its balance and its richness.
1964: A very fine year.
1966: This year produced some remarkable wines, especially Riesling and Gewürztraminer, as evidenced in a memorable 1966 Riesling Vendange Tardive from Hugel tasted in 1976.
1967: Excellent, especially for the Gewürztraminer and the Tokay – in 1979, a 1967 Hugel Tokay Vendange Tardive was very rich and ripe and *grand vin*.
1968: A poor year, and not worth considering after a few years.
1969: A very good vintage indeed, combining richness with marked acidity.
1970: Good, plentiful year, with some wines having *pourriture noble*.
1971: A great year, the best since 1961. At this time, record Oechslé readings, especially in the Gewürztraminers. The wines are lasting beautifully, if chosen with care – some are at their apogee.
1972: Mediocre – tended to be harsh and green. Muscats were the best.
1973: Pleasant, fruity wines, excellent for drinking relatively young.
1974: Reliable and good, without having great charm – some very nice Gewürztraminers, the low yield giving some concentration.
1975: Very good vintage, with wines showing breed and elegance. They have very good balance.
1976: This is a really exciting year, a great rarity. Exceptionally high Oechslé degrees giving wines of real berryish character. In other years (1934, 1945, 1959, 1961 and 1967) there was a small amount of wines of comparable quality, but 1976 had them in abundance. *Enfin*, a vintage of the century! The late-harvested wines literally reek of noble rot, and these are the ones to treasure for the future.
1977: Good, average quality, with the Gewürztraminers and Tokays particularly attractive – Rieslings and Muscats are lighter.

1978: Very small harvest, very nice wines made which show well their grape character. Rich and fruity Gewürztraminers.

1979: Very good quantity and quality. Some wines will even attain quality of 1976 (the wines from the Sporen look that way), even if they do not quite reach the same Oechslé readings.

1980: Quality good, especially for Pinot Gris (Tokay) and Pinot Blanc, but Gewürztraminer and Muscat are virtually wiped out through *coulure*.

LOIRE

While the Loire is hardly of Amazon length, it certainly dominates a good deal of France and offers a challenging diversity of scenery, history and, happily, of wines. Kings and monks have enjoyed and fostered the product of the vine from the Atlantic to the Massif Central, and a goodly number of saints have passed into Loire wine lore. But although great monasteries have played their vital part in the unbroken tradition of wine-making along this great river and its tributaries, this is not a progress of aristocratic domains – it is rather a paean of praise for the small peasant grower. In a few instances the ancestral château has been turned into a fine wine property, or sometimes a dynamic marketing enterprise, but it is an army of *petits vignerons* who make the wines of the Loire. There are important cooperatives, some of which sell to the Loire *négociants*, a powerful group, while a few operate their own efficient direct selling business, especially to Paris restaurants. In 1978, the Loire valley produced 682,131 hectolitres of red and rosé *appellation contrôlée* wine, and 708,382 hectolitres of white *appellation contrôlée* wine, making a total of 1,390,513 hectolitres. This made the Loire the fourth largest *appellation contrôlée*-producing area in France, after Bordeaux, the Côtes-du-Rhône and the South, and Burgundy.

MUSCADET

Muscadet is mostly drunk within the year, it is perfect bistro and café wine, and there is lots of it. The international demand for light, dry white wine has boosted exports to a high level. The generally large yields have led to certain rather supple interpretations of the *appellation contrôlée* law in the area with regard to wines to be released and wines to be 'blocked' – only to be deblocked some time later – it was amazing how long the 1976 vintage lasted in Muscadet, and how rarely one saw the 1977; small as the latter was, it did exist! There was also a good deal of recent concern over the misuse of the term *Mis en bouteille sur lie* – which is bottling the wine directly off its lees, thereby imparting a particularly fruity flavour and sometimes a touch of carbon dioxide gas. When correctly fulfilling the proper procedures for a bottling off the lees, now much better controlled, only Muscadet and the VDQS of the region, Gros Plant du Pays Nantais, can benefit from the extra descriptive qualification of *sur lie – vins de pays* are excluded.

The Muscadet grape variety itself bears a mysterious name. People used to speak of the Melon *musqué* de Bourgogne, and it is certain that the grape did come west from Burgundy. The roots are strong and the vine stock thick, the branches are short, the leaves are big and the bunches are small and dumpily shaped. The juice is a greeny white with quite a pungent taste. The Muscadet should be harvested early to preserve its acidity and give the wine finesse, but it is naturally early ripening, with the vintage usually in the second half of September, which is just as well since October is the wettest month in the area. Although the Muscadet area can be very sunny, especially in winter, the influence of the Atlantic can bring down the temperature at the same time. There are, in fact, three *appellations* for Muscadet, of

Château des Fines Roches is situated on one of the best sites
of Châteauneuf-du-Pape; stones or 'galets' cover most of the soil

which by far the most important from a quantity point of view is Muscadet de Sèvre-et-Maine. This *appellation* covers communes in the cantons of Clisson, Loroux-Bottereau, Vallet, Vertou and Aigrefeuille-sur-Maine. The *appellation* of Muscadet des Coteaux de la Loire covers communes on both sides of the river in Loire-Atlantique, and some communes in Maine-et-Loire. The straight *appellation* of Muscadet covers the wine produced from the area of production not mentioned in the two other categories. The total surface of all the Muscadet *appellations* covers 9,400 hectares, with an average production of 350,000 hectolitres. Nearly 85 per cent of the total volume comes from the area of Sèvre-et-Maine. The latter area is very intensively planted with vines, whereas the other two *appellation* areas have vines planted more patchily. The maximum yield for Sèvre-et-Maine is forty hectolitres per hectare, the same for the Coteaux de la Loire, with fifty hectolitres per hectare for Muscadet *simple*. However, this is often increased on an annual review basis, and sixty hectolitres per hectare would be allowed in Sèvre-et-Maine in a good year. It cannot be denied that sometimes very high yields indeed are attained.

Generally speaking, the wines of the Coteaux de la Loire are drier with perhaps less fruit than those of Sèvre-et-Maine, but they stand up quite well in bottle. Muscadet de Sèvre-et-Maine has charm and fruit, and is extremely attractive young drinking – obviously, those producers making wines with more flavour and body find that their wines last better in bottle than those which have a flowery, attractive nose, but not much behind that. In Sèvre-et-Maine, the triangle between Vallet, Mouzillon and La Chapelle-Heulin is supposed to produce the best wine – it is certainly the heart of the region. The wines coming from Le Landreau are also highly prized. There are different characteristics between communes – the excellent wines from Mouzillon stand up well in bottle, while those from La Chapelle-Heulin are supple and delicious young. When the wine does not come from a single domain, a blend of the two can produce a very complete wine.

Methods of vinification vary according to the size of the enterprise and the capital available. The governmental body of the SAFER tends to prevent too large holdings, preferring that the land should be held by a larger number of small growers. The installations of a domain such as Pierre Lusseaud's Château de la Galissonnière at Le Pallet near Vallet (the vineyards of Château de la Jannière and Château de la Maisdonnière are also within the estate) are of the most modern, with fermentations of three to four weeks at 18 to 22°C giving wines of enormous character and flavour for the region. At La Chapelle-Heulin, the Fleurance family at the Domaine des Gautronnières relies much more heavily on wood throughout the whole wine-making and keeping process, and the result shows in the wine, full-bodied and concentrated. Casks can be large, many of 600 litres.

The soil of the Sèvre-et-Maine region has a great deal of sand, from 60 to 80 per cent, with clay making up from 10 to 30 per cent. At Galissonnière, the soil is siliceous clay, on a base of granite – there is no calcareous soil in Sèvre-et-Maine. Malolactic fermentations are usually prevented in Muscadet, as the acidity is necessary to give some backbone to the wine. On the other hand, chaptalization is needed, but Muscadet must never be more than 12 per cent, the only *appellation contrôlée* to have an upper alcohol limit. The wines must all pass tasting and analysis, and there is no doubt that in the 1970s the amount of badly produced wines, be they oxidized or suffering from excessive sulphur dioxide, diminished dramatically. Machine picking is becoming more usual in the Muscadet, especially on the large domains such as Galissonnière. The vines have traditionally been trained very low on one wire, but probably for the future a compromise between high and low training is best, as always walking the tightrope between too much vegetation, or leaves, leading to *pourriture* when it is humid, but with enough to nourish the ripening grapes.

Roussillon vineyards near Thuir in the Pyrénées-Orientales
with the distinctive shape of Mont Canigou in the distance

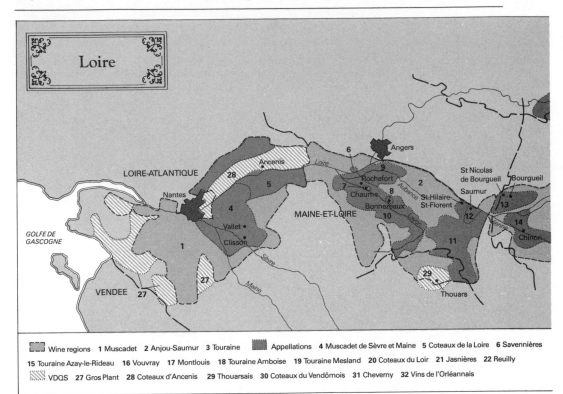

Estates such as Galissonnière/Jannière/Maisdonnière, and Henri Poiron's Les
Quatre Routes are of the very top quality, and completely bely the view that
Muscadet is pleasant, but neutral. The Fleurance Domaine des Gautronnières and
La Berrière at Barbechat, La Chapelle-Basse-Mer, belonging to the de Bascher
family, are examples of two very good domain wines. M. Gabriel Thébaud at
Saint-Fiacre is also a most careful wine-maker and *négociant*, with his Domaine de
la Hautière usually very good, and M. Léon Boullault at his own Château la Touche
near Vallet has a justifiably high reputation. The very erudite Comte de Malestroit
has the Château La Noë, which perhaps needs a little more technical expertise to
fulfil its true potential. The *négociant* Drouet at Vallet produces wines to a very
high standard, as does the house of Pierre Guéry, whose great experience at choosing
wines both for straight Muscadet de Sèvre-et-Maine and specific domains (such as
the much acclaimed Domaine de la Plaize and the Domaines des Pierres Blanches)
is now well known. Martin at Mouzillon is well distributed, as is Sautejeau (M.
Jean Beauquin) at La Chapelle-Heulin; both make wines that are good value but
need to be drunk when very young. Donatien Bahuaud is a very large concern
indeed, and their wines include their own Château de la Cassemichère. They have
also planted a little Chardonnay, which they sell as Vin de Table, Le Chouan. The
Marquis de Goulaine has made a great success of his Muscadet business round the
world. Sauvion is a reliable *négociant* and Métaineau can be recommended.

Muscadet should always be drunk young. 1975 and 1976 were both good, but
should have disappeared down thirsty throats by now. 1977 was hardly seen, and
1978 and 1979 were both fruity and good, with 1978 perhaps firmer and 1979
fruitier. 1980 needs careful selection – the best are attractive, some are acid.

Gros-Plant du Pays Nantais: This VDQS wine is often, justifiably, criticized for its
high acidity, and it is only in ripe years, such as 1976, that it attains really pleasurable
proportions. In other years, it is necessary to pick as late as possible to give the acidity

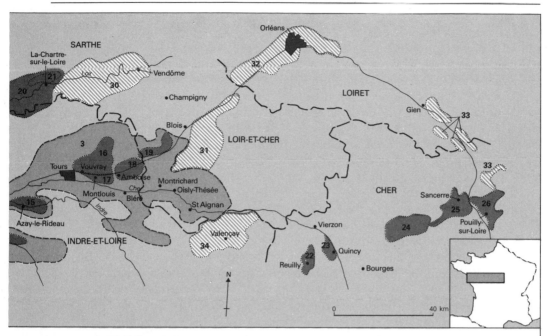

7 Quarts de Chaume 8 Bonnezeaux 9 Coteaux de l'Aubance 10 Coteaux du Layon 11 Saumur 12 Saumur-Champigny 13 Bourgueil 14 Chinon

23 Quincy 24 Menetou-sur-Loire 25 Sancerre 26 Pouilly-sur-Loire

33 Coteaux du Giennois 34 Valençay

a chance to fall. Known as the Folle Blanche in the Charente, the wine produced from the Gros Plant grape variety has a rustic freshness and a low alcohol reading. It is grown on poor, acid soil, often with schist as a base. The area covered by the VDQS includes a great many communes in the Loire-Atlantique, the Vendée and in Maine-et-Loire. The total surface area is 2,400 hectares, and the average production 80,000 hectolitres. Some of the best Muscadet producers also have a Gros Plant on their list, and the wine is well-known for its diuretic qualities.

Coteaux d'Ancenis: The right bank of the Loire round Ancenis produces some light but pleasant Gamay wines, rather acid in poor years, but benefiting from those with more sun. There is also a little Cabernet, and some rather surprising patches of less usual grape varieties. Jacques Guindon at St-Géréon makes some excellent, full Malvoisie (which is really the Pinot Gris). In the same village Joseph Toublanc is even making some dry white Verdelho. Auguste Athimon is another good *vigneron*, with Gamay and Cabernet. The VDQS Coteaux d'Ancenis covers red, rosé and white wines, but the name must be followed by the grape variety.

ANJOU-SAUMUR

This large area, on either side of the Loire, produces a wide variety of wines for all tastes. The Chenin (Pineau de la Loire) is responsible for the white wines (occasionally, now, mixed with a small proportion of Sauvignon or Chardonnay when dry), be they sweet or dry or hovering in between, and the reds are made predominantly from the Cabernet Franc, occasionally mixed with a little Cabernet Sauvignon. The Cabernet Franc is also the grape behind the rosés of superior quality The Groslot, the Gamay and the Côt (or Malbec) are also used for lesser rosé wine, the rockbed of Rosé d'Anjou. The Chenin Noir, or Pineau d'Aunis, is less seen.

Savennières: Going upstream, the first important Angevin *appellation* is Savennières, an enclave on the right bank of the Loire, within the Anjou Coteaux de la Loire *appellation*. Savennières, like Quarts de Chaume, Bonnezeaux and Vouvray, is a wine that makes history; people talk tantalizingly about bottles of up to fifty years old with rare richness and complexity. Unfortunately, when Savennières is young, it gives little indication of its greatness – the Chenin grape is rather crude when young, the wines often have a whiff of sulphur and seem rather acid, and one wonders what all the fuss is about. Savennières is usually dry, attaining some richness in very ripe years, but often with that Chenin characteristic of appearing very full, but ending dry in the mouth – bottle age always makes the wine more ample. These slopes of Savennières are really rocky spurs advancing towards the Loire, beautifully exposed to the south, giving the late-ripening Chenin the sun it so much needs. The yield is usually small, the soil on the slopes thin and with fragmented blue volcanic rock, together with some pebbles.

Within Savennières, there are two Grands Crus: La Roche aux Moines (about twenty planted hectares), and La Coulée de Serrant (less than five hectares). The Vignoble de la Bizolière belongs to Baron Marc Brincard with eighteen hectares of vineyard, mostly in small parcels. The estate includes vineyard in La Roche aux Moines which is more fertile than Savennières Clos du Papillon, another site along this slope, but can become very dry in summer. These wines really need time to 'marry' and become harmonious – the 1947s are still fresh here. In 1980, the 1976s were still too young, the 1971s only just coming into their own. Frost can be a problem on these slopes, and 1945 and 1977 bear witness to that. There is a second white wine of the property, Clos des Fougeraies, with *appellation* Anjou. A dry white Savennières has to have 12.5 per cent minimum alcohol, and 5 grams acidity would give good balance for this type of wine, suitable for ageing. Savennières is limited to a yield of twenty-five hectolitres per hectare, but is often less.

Another Savennières proprietor making wines of the very highest quality is Yves Soulez at Château de Chamboureau, and there is also the Château d'Epiré, the property of M. Armand Bizard, with the cellars in the church behind the château. The Domaine du Closel is also a most worthy property. The Château de la Roche aux Moines and vineyard of Coulée de Serrant belong to Madame Joly, who has made a very prestigious niche for her wines. She also owns part of La Roche aux Moines, and has a red Cabernet, Château de la Roche. I cannot help feeling that the wines are somewhat overpriced now, somehow promising a bit more than one gets, whether one tastes an embryonic 1978 or a mature 1964. The 1976 should be better than either. Monsieur Jean Baumard from across the river also produces Savennières and Savennières Clos du Papillon. The Baumard domain own nearly half of the four hectares which make up the vineyard of Clos du Papillon.

Coteaux-du-Layon (Bonnezeaux and Quarts de Chaume): Across the river, and this can be difficult when it floods in winter, one arrives at Rochefort-sur-Loire. Somehow the wines from around Rochefort itself are between Savennières and Layon in character. Here, along the Layon river, the overall *appellation* is Coteaux-du-Layon, and within it two distinct *appellations*, Bonnezeaux (approximately 100 hectares) and Quarts de Chaume, about half that size. The Layon river, running from the south-east towards the Loire, has made a sheltered valley for itself and the surrounding vineyards, protecting them from the north and the east. It is a real micro-climate, and six communes were recognized in a decree of 1955 as Coteaux-du-Layon-Villages – Beaulieu, Faye-d'Anjou, Rablay-sur-Layon, Rochefort-sur-Loire, St-Aubin-de-Luigné, St-Lambert-du-Lattay, together with the hamlet of Chaume. Bonnezeaux, near Thouarcé, and Quarts de Chaume are *grands crus*, classified in 1951 and 1954 respectively. At their greatest, these wines are a subtle and magic blend of scents and fruits, with an uncloying complexity that makes one almost question whether the grape alone has gone into their making. People talk of quince and peach and honey, but underlying all there is the lively spirit of the Chenin grape itself. However, this is Layon wine at its pinnacle. When the fermentations are stopped with sulphur, racking and sometimes refrigeration, the wines can be merely common.

The vintage can be very protracted, usually beginning during the first days of October and sometimes lasting until about 10 November. Occasionally, when the autumn is hot but dry, the *Botrytis cinerea* cannot develop; here, the must becomes rich by a simple concentration of all the ingredients. This concentration of sugar, whether it be due to the influence of *pourriture noble* or a simple evaporation of the water in the grapes, obviously makes for a reduced yield. Fermentations can last from four to six weeks, sometimes requiring the cellars to be warmed so that they proceed continuously. The alcohol in these wines can reach 14 or 15 per cent or more, contributing to their longevity. The wines do not need ageing in cask, many of which are the large 600-litre type, and benefit from being bottled in the spring after the vintage.

Quarts de Chaume can produce the most concentrated and rich wines of all. The soil is hard schist, and the situation particularly protected from the winds from the north, the east and the west, helping the grapes ripen more quickly than elsewhere. The maximum yield is 22 hectolitres per hectare, but is often less. It must have 13 per cent alcohol minimum. I have tasted excellent Quarts de Chaume from the Domaine Baumard (the 1959 was remarkable) – the Baumard domain has one of the three main holdings in the *grand cru*, although there are five proprietors in all. Monsieur Lalanne at the Château de Bellerive produces excellent wine, as does the Laffourcade family with their two properties, Suronde and Echarderie.

The Bonnezeaux vineyard is within the commune of Thouarcé on the right bank of the Layon. The wines are perhaps softer and gentler than Quarts de Chaume, but still golden and unctuous. No one makes better Bonnezeaux than M. Jean Boivin at the Château de Fesles – he also makes the wine of Madame Fourlinnie, his sister. The Raimbault family at Thouarcé also makes very good Bonnezeaux. M. Jean-Paul Tijou, with his cellars right on the quayside at Rochefort always at the mercy of the rising waters, makes the very fine Château de Bellevue and excellent Coteaux-du-Layon Chaume, as does M. Jaudeau at the Château de la Roulerie. Two Chaumes from the higher part of the slope, and easily the equal of Quarts-de-Chaume, are the Château de Plaisance of M. Henri Rochais, and La Guimonière of M. Doucet. M. Jacques Lecointre at the Caves de la Pierre Blanche has very good Coteaux-du-Layon Rablay, and M. Jean Petiteau at St Lambert-du-Lattay is worth visiting. The Clos de Ste Catherine, Coteaux-du-Layon Rochefort of Jean Baumard is also recommended – it is a very well-placed site. At Beaulieu, there is the Domaine de la Soucherie.

Other Anjou appellations: The *appellation* Cabernet d'Anjou is only for rosé wine made from Cabernet Franc with or without Cabernet Sauvignon (a grape which is more fragile here) – the same applies to the *appellation* Cabernet de Saumur. The skins are left in contact with the juice from anything between a few hours to a day, according to the depth of colour preferred. Rosé d'Anjou is of inferior quality, and usually rather sweet, giving a wine much appreciated in the United Kingdom and in Germany and Scandinavia; it can also be *pétillant*. Rosé d'Anjou is commercially very important to the region – production was 219,309 hectolitres in 1978, and 317,491 in 1979. It is interesting to note that the wines of Anjou and Saumur, after Bordeaux, Burgundy and the Côtes du Rhône, take fourth place in the list of *appellation contrôlée* wines exported from France. Three-quarters of this amount is rosé. A little more than half is exported in bottle. Rosé de la Loire is a recent (1974) *appellation* producing dry wines, but it has been slow to make its mark. It is a blend of Cabernet (30 per cent), Groslot, Côt, Gamay and Pineau d'Aunis. There are also the *appellations* of Anjou (Blanc et Rouge), Anjou-Gamay, Saumur (Blanc et Rouge), Anjou (Blanc) *pétillant*, and Saumur (Blanc) *pétillant*. Brissac is regarded as a very good area for the Cabernet, with good finds amongst small growers and the large cooperative. Good red Cabernet, sappy and fruity, will be found under the *appellation* Anjou. The Saumur whites are usually nervier, more acid and perhaps drier than the Anjou whites. Anjou certainly has a soft and gentle climate for much of the year. From April to September, the average temperature at Angers is a degree higher than that in Paris. However, Anjou and the Saumurois have many differences, although they both come under the Anjou 'umbrella'. The Saumur area is predominantly calcareous, while to the west and at Layon the soil is predominantly hard schist, with occasional sandstone. Saumur produces *vin de tuffeau*, Anjou *vin d'ardoise*. The soil has a direct influence on the types of wine produced – lighter on chalky soil, heavier on the schist where the blackish soil stores the heat better. Calcareous and siliceous soils give good red wine; on schist, red and rosé wine are thicker, with less breed. Apart from the rosé Cabernet de Saumur, the Saumur growers can choose between the Anjou or Saumur *appellation* when they declare their harvest.

Coteaux de l'Aubance: Coteaux de l'Aubance wines are white from the Chenin, and most successful when *demi-sec*. Running parallel to the Layon *appellations*, they can be very good value. Biotteau at St-Jean-des-Mauvrets is highly recommended, as is M. Papin at St-Melaine-sur-Aubance.

Anjou Coteaux de la Loire: Anjou Coteaux de la Loire is an *appellation* that includes villages on both sides of the river, nearly all to the west of Angers. The vineyards cling to the slopes near the river, as the plateaux behind them are mostly clayey, with the soil too humid for good ripening of vines. As with all Chenin white wines, poor years can give rather mean, acid wines, but kinder vintages can give a nervy lusciousness that is most tempting. Villages that produce a good deal of wine are Bouchemaine, St Georges-sur-Loire, Champtocé and Ingrandes – and on the left bank, Montjean, La Pommeraye and a part of Chalonnes, where there is a wine fair towards the end of February.

Saumur Appellations: The best rosé wines originate from around Saumur, Tigné and Brissac. The wonderful *craie tuffeau* soil gives seemingly endless underground cellars, which serve the large *négociants* and cooperatives well. After the devastation of phylloxera in the Saumurois region, the reconstitution of the vineyard, always difficult in calcareous soil, was not always helped by the choice of root stocks which would favour maturation of the grapes. Saumur concentrated too much on its sparkling wines, and neglected its still wines, particularly in the case of white wines, where Bas Anjou gave formidable competition – at that time, the area round Saumur was 'Haut Anjou'. In many ways, the Saumur region is more akin to Touraine, with its *tuffeau* and Vouvray-like caves. The *appellation* Coteaux-de-Saumur is for white wines only, made from the Chenin, and includes villages like Montsoreau, Bizay, Brézé, Parnay, St-Cyr-en-Bourg, Turquant and Dampierre, but now the Saumur *appellation* is normally used. The wines are nearly always dry or *demi-sec*, with a great deal of youthful vivacity. In poor years, they can be 'green'. Locally, they say that they have a *goût de tuf*, which is picturesque, if difficult to identify.

Occasionally, when the year permits, there are rich wines from these communes, and these are the bottles that last. In days past, they were often labelled with the name of the village and the *lieu dit* or site, with no mention of the word 'Saumur' – I remember one such marvellous bottle, which simply announced itself as Brézé 1959, Baron Brancard. I admire the wines of M. Chauvat at the Château Fouquet at Brézé, and have seen good wine from Le Floch-Ernoult at Turquant. At Parnay, the Château de Parnay wines of M. Jacques Collé are excellent, with the reputed

Clos des Murs, and in the same commune M. Bertholet also has a fine reputation. At Bizay, there is the estimable Domaine Bougoin, and at Souzay-Champigny, M. Chevallier at the Château de Villeneuve produces very well-made wine. Two Saumur Blanc wines to look out for are those of M. Pichot at the Clos de Bois-menard at Tourtenay, Thouars, and M. Claude Daheuiller at Les Varinelles, Var-rains. Of course, many of these producers also make excellent red Saumur-Champigny, which became very popular indeed in France during the 1970s. The wines are made almost entirely from the Cabernet Franc, which gives a sappy, somewhat 'grassy' nose, and a lot of life and fruit on the palate. Many of the wines are nice drunk comparatively young, within a few years of their birth, but there are exceptions. One is M. Paul Filhatreau at Chaintres, in the Dampierre area, who makes wines with more body, colour and depth than is usual for the region, with more tannin; his wines need more time to smooth out – it is worth waiting. He also has a plot of very old vines, which he keeps separate. There is also the Château de Chaintres at Dampierre, belonging to the de Tigny family, making consistently good wine. Apart from many of the producers mentioned above for white wine, one can add the wine of M. Maurice Rebeilleau and the Domaine des Roches Neuves of Denis Duveau at Varrains, where there is more gravel and less tufa, the Château de Targé of M. Pisani-Ferry at Parnay, and M. André Sanzay in the same commune. This part of the Loire is lucky to have two excellent cooperatives. The Vignerons de Saumur at St Cyr-en-Bourg work with great seriousness, and all their wines can be relied upon – Saumur Blanc et Rouge, Saumur-Champigny, Crémant de Loire and Mousseux made by the Champagne method. The under-ground cellars cover three hectares, and can be visited by car! The other large cooperative, Les Caves de la Loire at Brissac, is nearer Angers, to the west – it also is most reliable. There is also the INRA at Montreuil-Bellay, which has helped raise the standard of the red wines of the area and does not neglect to make a good one itself.

Sparkling Wine

The Saumur area is also famous for its Champagne-method Mousseux, or sparkling wine – 80 per cent of the total is made by the Champagne method, the rest is non-*appellation contrôlée*. Saumur Mousseux is white, Anjou Mousseux can be white or rosé. The acidity of the Chenin lends itself to *champenisation*, and the wines are very carefully made, often by firms with connections in Champagne. They lack the breed on the nose that the grape varieties of Champagne impart (occasionally at Saumur there is a bit of Chardonnay in the blend), but they are good alternatives when the occasion calls for something light-hearted. Up to 60 per cent *blanc de noirs* can be added, essentially from the Cabernet. The *appellation* wines must always be made using the method of a second fermentation in bottle, not in vat. The house of Gratien-Meyer (the same family ownership as Alfred Gratien Champagne) has a justifiably high reputation, only buying in grapes not wine, and Ackerman-Laurance, Bouvet-Ladubay (belonging to Taittinger), and Veuve Amiot are also most reliable. These firms tend to give their wines a couple of years of rest before disgorging. The houses at St Hilaire-St Florent benefit from marvellous natural cellars in the tufa. The laws for the production of Crémant de Loire, an *appellation* dating from 1975, are stricter than for Mousseux, with regard to grape varieties permitted. *Pétillant* wines also have a second fermentation in bottle, but the pressure in the bottle is two times less and the cork can be held in place by a simple *agrafe*. *Vins du Thouarsais:* Right to the south of Anjou-Saumur, round the town of Thouars, there is the VDQS called Vins du Thouarsais. The whites are Chenin and sweetish and there are light, fruity reds, and some rosé. Michel Gigon at Oiron is a good producer.

Vins du Haut-Poitou: South-east of here, towards Poitiers, there is another VDQS of great note, the Vins du Haut-Poitou. The production is virtually entirely in the hands of the Cave Cooperative du Haut-Poitou at Neuville-de-Poitou, which now has about 300 grower members. This cooperative is surely one of the best run in the whole of France, and has a formidable history of enterprise behind it. The area, which looks more suitable for cereals than for the vine, used to supply a large amount of low-alcohol white wine, mostly from hybrids, to the Cognac producers. After the Second World War, the remarkable director of the cooperative, M. Gavid, began a policy of persuading the growers to plant good grape varieties, and gradually he built up the quality to a standard today that is more worthy of many *appellations*. M. Gavid also developed a clever selling plan which reduced the sale of wine *en vrac*, in bulk, and bottled his wines young and well for direct sale to the best restaurants in France. His successor, M. Raffarin, has continued all these ideas and the Cave has gone from strength to strength, with excellent modern installations. The wines made are dry, crisp Sauvignon, Chardonnay, and a red produced mostly from Gamay.

TOURAINE

Touraine shares the soft light and gentler climate of Anjou with that region, and a good deal of the *tuffeau* soil of Saumur. It shares with both a preponderance of Chenin and Cabernet Franc, but also makes a speciality of Sauvignon and Gamay in certain areas of the region. Touraine itself is not very large, with the total vineyard surface area not as much as 24,000 hectares, with an average production of 1,000,000 hectolitres. However, the area is quite diverse. The most famous *appellations*, Chinon, Bourgueil, Vouvray, and Montlouis, are in the *département* of the Indre-et-Loire, less famous wines, such as Touraine Mesland, are in the Loir-et-Cher (it is a muddling fact that a tributary of the Loire is called the Loir), and the vineyard even stretches into the Sarthe with the Coteaux du Loir and Jasnières. It is the sides of the valleys that give the best vineyard sites in Touraine, and Touraine is rich in rivers – the Loir, the Loire, the Cher, the Indre, the Vienne and the Creuse, to name the most important.

Chinon and Bourgueil: Going upstream, the first vineyards of Touraine that one encounters are those red *appellations* of Chinon and Bourgueil. Both are predominantly produced from the Cabernet Franc grape, that zingy, sappy, fruity varietal that gives a tempting, almost 'grassy' or 'herby' nose and a definite and generous taste. It has neither the astringence nor the tannin of the Cabernet Sauvignon, nor its long life. The two *appellations* of Bourgueil and St-Nicolas-de-Bourgueil are only for red and the rarely met rosé wine, made almost entirely from the Cabernet Franc (or the Breton, as it is often known in the region), although the Cabernet Sauvignon is allowed. The same applies to Chinon, although the *appellation* exists for white wine as well, made from the Chenin. However, the wines that count are red.

Bourgueil and St-Nicolas-de-Bourgueil, north of the Loire, are on banks or terraces of ancient alluvia, giving very well-drained gravelly soil. Wines from this alluvial mixture of sand and large gravel are very scented and refined and develop quite early. But above these pebbly gravel soils, higher up, the soil is more clayey-calcareous on a sub-soil of *craie tuffeau*. Here the wines are slightly harder, take time to show their fruit, and keep better. The vine covers 870 hectares in *appellation* Bourgueil and 470 hectares in *appellation* St-Nicolas-de-Bourgueil. The communes of the Bourgueil *appellation* are Benais, Bourgueil, La Chapelle-sur-Loire, Chouzé-sur-Loire, Ingrandes, Restigné and St-Patrice. St-Nicolas-de-Bourgueil is only produced in the commune of the same name. In both Bourgueil and Chinon, the grapes are de-stalked, often on the vine, vatting is long, and the cellars in the rock are cold. Cutting the grape from the stalk in the vineyard leaves the grape intact, while mechanical *égrappage* is more brutal – thus, *égrappage manuel* helps give supple wines, without astringence, in spite of the long vattings. Obviously, the process can only be followed in relatively small holdings. Fermentation can be for twenty to twenty-eight days in Bourgueil and Chinon, without making the wines tough, but giving them bouquet and character. Obviously, the temperature must be watched carefully, and in 1976 there were some 'accidents' in the region at this stage. But normally, the cold cellars give long, cool fermentations, and morning and evening the growers push down the *chapeau* or hat that has formed on top of the fermenting vat. This 'floating hat' method, often dangerous in hotter climes, suits the wines of Chinon and Bourgueil, and helps in the extraction process. These red wines usually have good tannin balance and alcohol levels of between 11 and 12 per cent. Their bouquet seems to draw out an imaginative vocabulary, with that of Chinon likened to violets or wild strawberries, and Bourgueil to raspberries.

Some remarkable St-Nicolas-de-Bourgueil is made by M. Claude Ammeux at the Clos de la Contrie. Perhaps it is not altogether typical, because there is an *égrappoir* here, the soil is stony and flinty and, very unusually, they use a yeast from the Côte d'Or, which, whether real or imagined, for me seems to have an influence on the nose and taste. There is no fining or filtering, just racking, and bottling is at about eight months – many growers bottle a bit later. The result is big wines with depth and body. The Amirault family also make excellent St-Nicolas, as does M. Pierre Boireau, a small, welcoming grower. Other really good Bourgueils are made by Paul Maître at Benais, Lamé-Delille-Boucard at Ingrandes-de-Touraine, La Hurolaie by Caslot-Galbrun, and the Clos de l'Abbaye of the GAEC de la Dime.

Chinon scatters her vineyards over a wider area, between the Loire and the Vienne and all along the valley of the Vienne. The most densely planted communes are on the best exposed sites of the right bank of the Vienne. The soil is more diverse than in Bourgueil, mixing sand, gravel and pebbly slopes. The vineyard covers 1,060 hectares and includes eighteen communes. Cravant-les-Coteaux is often regarded as the best, and has some good gentle slopes. The Loire *négociant* of Aimé Boucher makes some excellent selections in Cravant, and also chooses robust Bourgueil. Couly-Dutheil and his domain of Clos de l'Echo are well known, if expensive (as are Audebert in Bourgueil). The Angelliaume family at Cravant has very good value wines as does M. René Gouron, and M. Paul Zéja at Ligré has Chinon of character. Different members of the Raffault family at Savigny-en-Véron are recommended. The wine of M. Raymond Desbourdes at Panzoult is very carefully made, and the *négociant* Langlois-Château always has very good Chinon. M. Jean Baudry of the Domaine de la Perrière at Cravant has a good reputation. Good years for Bourgueil-Chinon are: 1979, 1978, 1976, 1975, 1971, 1970, 1969, 1964, 1959, 1955, 1953, 1949, 1948 and the great 1947s.

Vouvray: Great Vouvray is a remarkable experience of long-lasting flavour in the mouth, and a wonderful contrast of honey and fruit flavours, backed with Chenin firmness. But the wines made in this *appellation* are also very pleasurable when they cannot be rich and luscious, just smooth and slightly sweet. The vineyard area is to the north of the Loire river, very near Tours, and produces *tuffeau* wine *par excellence*, with its chalky soil and incredible natural cellars. Well away from the river the soil becomes more clay/flint. Here the Pineau Blanc de la Loire, or Chenin, reigns supreme, and the wines can be still, *pétillant*, or *mousseux*. These latter are made by the Champagne method and the whole process is frequently looked after by *champenisateurs*, specialists who visit the growers' cellars at the propitious moments to carry out the various manoeuvres necessary for the *appellation* Vouvray-Mousseux. On the whole, the less well-placed sites provide wines that are dry or that are suitable for base wine for Mousseux (low alcohol), and the best sites give *demi-sec* or *moelleux*

Vouvray. Mousseux wines throughout Touraine are sold at 4.5 kilograms of pressure, Crémant de Loire 3.5 kilograms, and *pétillant* 2.5 kilograms. The vineyard area covers 1,550 hectares, and includes the communes of Chançay, Noizay, Parçay-Meslay, Reugny, Rochecorbon, Tours-Ste-Radegonde, Vernou-sur-Brenne and Vouvray itself. The area is criss-crossed by little valleys, such as the Vallée Coquette, the Vallée Chartier, the Vallées de Cousse, de Vaux and de la Brenne. The best sites are still referred to locally and much recorded in old volumes, but unfortunately, very few wines are now sold under their site names.

The art of making good Vouvray is careful selection – choosing the best grapes for the great sweet wines, and then going down the scale to the totally dry wines and the sparkling wines. The wines always have a good balance of malic acidity, with no malolactic fermentation taking place, to give freshness, and are not too vulnerable to oxidation – a great advantage. Some years give conditions for *pourriture noble*, which always requires a certain amount of humidity with the sun, and others, such as 1947, were rich through great ripeness, *surmaturité*, with no *pourriture noble*. Obviously, quality differs according to the communes and sites, and there are wines of the Côtes (nearly all in the case of Rochecorbon) and those of the Arrières Côtes.

A Vouvray house that has a justifiably very high reputation for blending marvellous wines is that of Marc Brédif, at Rochecorbon. The large Pouilly-Fumé firm of Ladoucette bought Marc Brédif in 1980. The late Marc Brédif's son-in-law, M. Jacques Cartier, has great experience of the wines of Vouvray, and makes wines to last when vintage conditions permit. The wines are blended in glass-lined vats (Brédif buys wine, not grapes), and only receive about a month in wood. I have had generous tastings with M. Cartier, seeing satiny *moelleux* 1971 wines, a *moelleux* 1953 with *pourriture noble* character but not really *liquoreux*, and a magnificent 1928 Rochecorbon, rich, old and venerable, with that noble rot taste, silky texture and a lightness of touch that was sheer joy. M. Gaston Huet at the Haut-Lieu in Vouvray is a renowned producer of fine Vouvray. Amongst many wines, I particularly recall a *demi-sec* of great breed from the small yielding 1969 vintage, and a wonderful *moelleux* wine from the 1973 vintage, giving the impression of a bouquet of flowers in the mouth. The sites are often kept separate here, Clos du Bourg, Le Haut-Lieu, Le Mont. Other top producers are M. Foreau at the Clos Naudin, M. Allias at the Petit Mont, M. Delaleu who has the Clos Dubois, M. Raoul Diard, M. Maurice Audebert with his Coteau Chatrie, M. Jean Bertrand at Rochecorbon, and Prince Poniatowski at Le Clos Baudoin, with his wine, L'Aigle Blanc. And I have a particular affection for the Huguet family at Le Grand Ormeau, who make all types of Vouvray, still, sparkling, sweet and dry, with honesty and warmth. The Château Moncontour makes quite stylish wines with very modern methods of vinification. Vouvray of great years is almost indestructible. 1979 and 1978 were good, 1976 was great, 1975 good, 1973 good with some really ripe wines, excellent *moelleux* wines in 1971, good in 1970, great 1969s, wonderful 1964, 1961, 1959, 1955, 1953, 1949, 1947, 1945, 1943, 1937, 1934, 1933 (rather curiously, but some great surprises), 1928, 1924, and the fabled 1921. The 1947 and 1921 years are the great rivals – both were high in alcohol. The years with marked *pourriture noble* character are 1933, 1934, 1937 and 1949. It might seem esoteric to cite these old vintages, but great old Vouvray has a habit of turning up occasionally in a wine-lover's life.

Montlouis: Just across the river from Vouvray is Montlouis, a slightly lighter wine, sometimes with marked acidity when dryish and young, and never attaining the great lusciousness of the very best Vouvray. The climate and soil are the same, but the sites less well exposed in the main. Only the very best have the definition and 'edge' of good Vouvray, but they can be really pleasant, soft, and very good value. I have admired the wines of MM. René-Pierre Dardeau, Moyer, Berger, Denis, Leblois,

Tessier and Levasseur. As at Vouvray, the site names have all but disappeared, although I still have a very old label from the Clos de Cangé at St-Martin-le-Beau. The vineyard is about 260 hectares and covers the communes of Lussault, Montlouis-sur-Loire, and St-Martin-le-Beau.

Touraine Azay-le-Rideau: Touraine Azay-le-Rideau is rather an outpost of vines – the wines of the commune of Saché used to be famous, even rivalling Vouvray in great years. It is rare that these white products of the Chenin become rich and complex, but they can. Otherwise, they are fresh and crisp. M. Gaston Pavy makes the very best of the *appellation* at Saché itself, as does M. Francis Paget at Rivarennes. There are also rosé wines made from the Grolleau, and some red wines from Gamay, *appellation* Touraine.

Touraine Amboise: Touraine Amboise gives white wines from a sub-soil of *craie tuffeau*, but also red and rosé wine from the Côt (or Malbec), Gamay and Cabernet. M. Yves Moreau at Cangey and M. Jacques Bonnigal of Limeray both have a range of Touraine-Amboise, as well as M. Hubert Dennay at Le Breuil and M. Dutertre at Limeray. These wines are always reasonable and so, if well made, good bargains.

Touraine Mesland: Touraine Mesland is for white, red and rosé wines grown in the Mesland area on the right bank of the Loire in the Loir-et-Cher. Much bigger than the previous two *appellations*, it concentrates on red and rosé. The Domaine Girault-Artois and the Domaine Lusqueneau of M. Brossillon are worthy producers.

Gamay de Touraine: Gamay de Touraine (the *appellation* is Touraine with the grape variety name) is a very good buy in sunny years. The Gamay flourishes along the valley of the river Cher, and the left bank, around St Aignan, is particularly noted. In years with high acidity, some Gamays are made by the *macération carbonique* method, and bottling is in the January or February after the vintage, with some people even doing a November bottling to catch the Primeur market. There are good cooperatives at Francueil and Civray, and the area as a whole is cooperative orientated.

Sauvignon de Touraine: The Sauvignon de Touraine of the cooperative at Oisly-Thésée had made its mark; all the whites here have quite a firm acidity, as there is no malolactic fermentation. The most 'aristocratic' Sauvignon de Touraine wines I have seen in the Oisly area (if that is a term that can be applied to this grape variety) belong to M. Maurice Barbou, whose grandfather introduced the grape variety to the region from Pouilly/Sancerre. His Vignoble des Corbillières is quite excellent, and all his wine-making is of the most intelligent. He also has some Chardonnay and Pinot Noir (experimentally), Gamay, and Cabernet. There is flint in this area, which is ideal for the Sauvignon. The Janvier family at Thésée is also known for quality. The much-respected *négociant* Aimé Boucher makes a speciality of these wines, working from his cellars near Chambord at Huisseau-sur-Cosson. At Montrichard, the *négociant* Monmousseau specializes in *mousseux*.

Coteaux du Loir: The area of the Coteaux du Loir (white, red and rosé) is due north of Tours, round La Chartre-sur-le-Loir.

Jasnières: The white wines of Jasnières can become quite rich with age in bottle – this can be proved with the good wines of MM. Legreau, Gigou or Pinon – but when young they are more often hard and austere.

There are a few VDQS wines in Touraine, some of more than passing interest, particularly Valençay. All the grape varieties are found here, as well as the local Arbois (nothing to do with the Jura) which is related to the Chenin. M. Paquier at Chabris and M. Berthonnet are both honourable producers, and the prices are good. I have my doubts about Cheverny, as I find the local white grape variety, the Romorantin, acid in all but the ripest years. Two other VDQS are the Coteaux du Vendômois and the greatly diminished Vins de l'Orléannais.

POUILLY FUME AND SANCERRE

These are very important *appellations* for lovers of French dry white wine, although in years when quantity is affected, their prices tend to go higher than their intrinsic worth. But their teasing, smoky flavour and glancing elegance will always attract those who dislike neutral wines – these make a statement. Happily, their great popularity has helped encourage the *vigneron* to stay and cultivate his vines, because many became disenchanted with spring frosts and other bad weather, particularly hail at Pouilly, giving very irregular harvests.

Pouilly : In fact, there are three *appellations* at Pouilly : Blanc Fumé de Pouilly, Pouilly Fumé (which are none other than the crisp Sauvignon wine we know and love), and Pouilly-sur-Loire, a wine lower in alcohol made from the Chasselas grape, with or without an admixture of Blanc Fumé (Sauvignon), it should be consumed young. The communes included are Pouilly-sur-Loire, St-Andelain, Tracy-sur-Loire, St-Laurent, St-Martin-sur-Nohain, Garchy and Mesves-sur-Loire. Here, as at Sancerre, the small *vigneron* is 'roi', producing about 200,000 cases of the two Fumé wines a year, whereas at Sancerre the quantity is nearer 500,000 cases. Pouilly Fumé wines are very similar to Sancerre, although the former can be fuller and more complex, and tend to improve still further with a year or two in bottle, whereas Sancerre is delicious and fragrant when really young. Both are on chalky, flinty soil – the vineyards of Pouilly rise from the river Loire and go into rolling hills and plateaux.

I have always enjoyed the attack and sheer definition of M. Maurice Bailly's Fumé wines, and M. Serge Dagueneau at Les Berthiers is a master at his craft. Also recommended are M. Michel Redde, M. Georges Guyot, M. Robert Penard at Les Loges, M. Blanchet of Les Berthiers, M. Paul Mollet of Tracy-sur-Loire, MM. Robert Minet and Seguin of Le Bouchot, M. Marcel Laugoux of Le Soumard, M. Paul Figeat of Les Loges and M. Jacques Foucher of Pouilly. I have drunk older wines of the Château de Tracy which were really complex. The very dynamic Baron Patrick Ladoucette has enlarged and expanded his business in an enviable way. The Château du Nozet now has one single holding of fifty hectares, but of course a very large part of the production is bought in. Vinification is of the most modern, enabling encouragement of the malolactic fermentation in acid years, such as 1977, and inhibition of it in ripe, full years such as 1976. In the 1970s, a *tête de cuvée* Pouilly Blanc Fumé was also launched, the Baron de 'L'. Comte Lafond Sancerre, also from the Ladoucette enterprise, is entirely bought in, but the same attention to detail goes into the *élevage*. Ladoucette is also behind the Baron Briare *appellation* Touraine wines.

Sancerre : Sancerre is all hills and dipping valleys, with fine, chalky well-exposed slopes. Limestone and the Sauvignon grape give great finesse and a lingering flavour. The communes in the *appellation* are Bannay, Bué, Crézancy, Menetou-Râtel, Ménétréol, Montigny, St-Satur, Ste-Gemme, Sancerre, Sury-en-Vaux, Thauvenay, Veaugues, Verdigny and Vinon. A big name at Sancerre is the Clos de la Poussie of Cordier, but the quality does not always match the price. One of the truly great Sancerres was the Clos du Chêne Marchand of Picard-Crochet, but that does not seem to have retained the real class it had ; however, that of M. Lucien Picard *tout court* has. High quality Sancerres come from MM. Marcel Gitton, Prieur, Vacheron, Vatan, Carobolante, Marcel Boin, Bernard and René Laporte, Reverdy, Henri at Chavignol, and the Cotats, who have Les Monts Damnés at Chavignol. Les Montachins of the Domaine Henri Brochard is always good, as is M. Gustave Fouassier's Les Groux. The cooperative has a serious reputation at Sancerre. Pouilly Blanc Fumé and Sancerre should always be drunk young ; 1979 and 1978 are very good and 1977 a little acid. Other good years were 1976, 1975, 1974, 1973 and 1971. There is also some red and rosé Sancerre made from Pinot Noir.

Menetou-Salon: Just to the south-west of Sancerre there is the small *appellation contrôlée* area of Menetou-Salon, where there is more white wine from the Sauvignon than red from the Pinot Noir. As throughout this region, Kimmeridge clay adds character and 'zip' to the wines. Good growers are Jean Teiller, Bernard Clément at the Domaine de Châtenoy, and the delightful small growers' cooperative of Les Vignerons Jacques-Coeur; the area is certainly 'on a revival'.

Quincy and Reuilly: Further away to the west, around Vierzon, there is Quincy and Reuilly, the former only producing crisp Sauvignon wines, but the latter also branches out into red and rosé. The wines can have great mouth-watering charm given favourable weather conditions. In Quincy, I have enjoyed the wines of M. Raymond Pipet, M. Pierre Mardon, M. Maurice Rapin and M. Marcel Fragnier. In Reuilly, M. Robert Cordier makes white wine from Sauvignon, red from Gamay and a delicate rosé from the Pinot Gris. The Renaudat family, M. Pierre Beaujard and the delightfully named M. Olivier Cromwell are other reliable growers.

Châteaumeillant: Way to the south of Bourges, there is the VDQS of Châteaumeillant. Here the wines are red or *gris* – the grapes are Pinot Noir, Pinot Gris and Gamay. The cooperative is good, and M. Maurice Lanoix is a very conscientious producer.

Coteaux du Giennois: The Coteaux du Giennois VDQS, along the Loire between Pouilly and Gien, has all the colours, and Gamay, Pinot Noir, Sauvignon and Chenin. The area does not produce much, but at St-Père, MM. Carroué, Jarreau and Nérot make honourable wines.

St-Pourçain-sur-Sioule: In the Bourbonnais and Auvergne, there are a clutch of VDQS wines that are eminently quaffable. Pride of place must go to St-Pourçain-sur-Sioule, residing on a tributary of the Loire, and greatly appreciated by those taking the cure at Vichy. The red and rosé wines are predominantly Gamay, but the dry white has up to 50 per cent Tressallier, a very local grape variety, mixed with Sauvignon, Chardonnay and even Aligoté. The result is an interesting, fresh taste. The cooperative is most reliable, as are MM. Maurice Faure, Joseph Laurent, Jean Cherillat and Jean Ray.

Côtes d'Auvergne, du Forez and Roannaises: In the Massif Central, the Côtes d'Auvergne are white (Chardonnay), red and rosé (Gamay and Pinot Noir), round the town of Châteaugay. The Côtes du Forez make red and rosé wine from the Gamay – the cooperative and M. Paul Gaumon at Chozieux, Leigneux are good producers here. The Côtes Roannaises are very similar – MM. Chargros and Servajean at Changy, M. Désormières at Renaison and M. Villeneuve at Champagny, St-Haon-le-Vieux make delicious wines for young drinking.

RHONE

The Rhône is one of France's main arteries, dividing *départements*, fostering trade and commerce, and nurturing agriculture. The Romans used it on their way north, and holidaymakers in the 1980s use it on their way south. It rises in Switzerland and meets the sea at Marseille, and has forged for itself in parts a deep ravine to challenge the Massif Central. The vine follows the river spasmodically, sometimes clinging to steep sides, as in the northern Rhône immediately below Lyon, or spreading out over flat, stony terrain, as around Avignon in the south. This difference between the Rhône Septentrional and the Rhône Méridional should be emphasized. The climate is often dissimilar, the land is different, and the grape varieties, although largely the same, vary greatly in proportion between the two areas. One can separate the vinous north and south Rhône very clearly, because although there are about 200 kilometres between Lyon and Avignon, the grape is not planted without a break

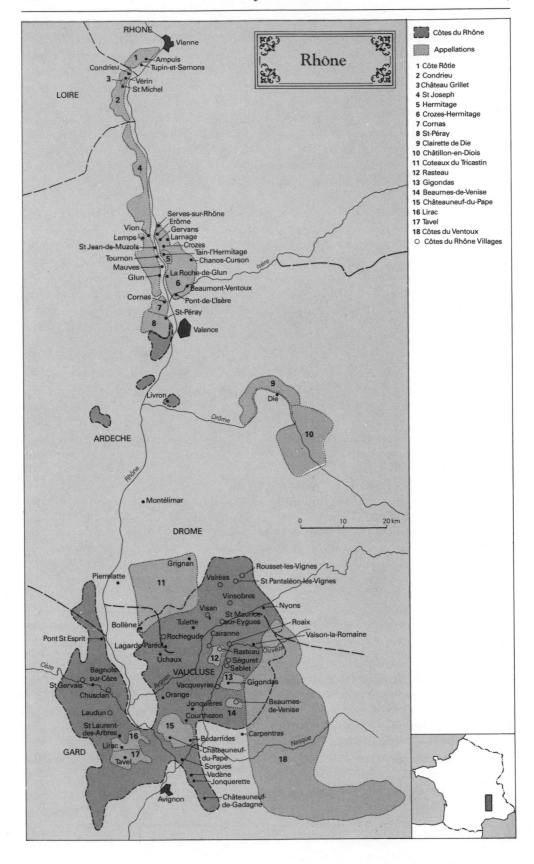

RHONE

Vienne

1 Ampuis
Tupin-et-Semons
Condrieu
3 Vérin
St Michel
2

LOIRE

4

Serves-sur-Rhône
Erôme
Vion Gervans
Lemps Larnage
St Jean-de-Muzols Crozes
Tain-l'Hermitage
5 Chanos-Curson
Tournon
Mauves La Roche-de-Glun
Glun 6 Beaumont-Ventoux
Cornas Pont-de-L'Isère
7 St-Péray
8
Valence

Isère

9
Die
10

Livron

Drôme

ARDECHE

Rhône

Montélimar

DROME

0   10   20 km

Grignan
Rousset-les-Vignes
Pierrelatte Valréas
11 St Pantaléon-les-Vignes
Vinsobres
Visan Nyons
St Maurice
Bollène Tulette sur-Eygues Roaix
Rochegude Cairanne Vaison-la-Romaine
Pont St Esprit
Lagarde-Paréol Ouvèze
Uchaux Rasteau
12 Séguret
Bagnols- Sablet
sur-Cèze VAUCLUSE 13
St Gervais Vacqueyras Gigondas
Chusclan Orange
Jonquières Beaumes-
Laudun 14 de-Venise
St Laurent- 15 Courthezon
des-Arbres Carpentras
16 Bédarrides
Lirac Châteauneuf- Nesque
17 du-Pape 18
GARD Tavel Sorgues
Vedène
Jonquerette
Avignon Châteauneuf-
de-Gadagné

Cèze

Aygues

VAUCLUSE

Nesque

Rhône

Côtes du Rhône
Appellations

1 Côte Rôtie
2 Condrieu
3 Château Grillet
4 St Joseph
5 Hermitage
6 Crozes-Hermitage
7 Cornas
8 St-Péray
9 Clairette de Die
10 Châtillon-en-Diois
11 Coteaux du Tricastin
12 Rasteau
13 Gigondas
14 Beaumes-de-Venise
15 Châteauneuf-du-Pape
16 Lirac
17 Tavel
18 Côtes du Ventoux
○ Côtes du Rhône Villages

down the river. At Valence, the vineyards virtually stop, apart from an outpost at Die about sixty-four kilometres south-east of Valence, and the river continues vineless past Montélimar. The vineyards begin in earnest again round Bollène, and from thence one can hardly ignore them. The Rhône and south-east France produce about 3 million hectolitres of *appellation* wine each year. Of this, about $1\frac{1}{2}$ million hectolitres is Côtes du Rhône, and about 90,000 hectolitres Châteauneuf-du-Pape. The area entitled to the Côtes du Rhône *appellation* falls into six *départements*, which are, in order of volume: Vaucluse, Gard, Drôme, Ardèche, Rhône and Loire. The Vaucluse is particularly known for its red wines, the Gard for fine rosés and good whites, with the others mostly pleasant red wines, including some of the great ones.

Most classical historians consider that it was on the Côtes du Rhône that vines were first planted in France. One thing is certain and that is that they would have had to contend with the relentless Mistral wind in the same way that the inhabitants have to today. It blows down the Rhône valley from the north, icy in winter and sometimes drying and scorching in summer, and psychologically very trying in its persistence. Occasionally, its drying properties can be useful after rain, but more often the vines need protecting from its influence, either by pruning low or by having rows of trees as barriers. The climate, as befits an area for the most part far from the sea, is continental, with dry, cold winters, and often very hot summers. The rain mostly comes in spring and autumn, and is not very equally distributed. Different grape varieties are given predominance according to the prevailing soil and the type of wine required. The Rhône, in fact, provides virtually every type of wine that one could want, from deep, long-lived reds, to more light, quaffing versions, dry rosé wines, dry white wines, luscious dessert wines and dry sparkling wines. The north is dominated by the red Syrah grape variety and the hard granite of the Massif Central, while the south has a veritable fan of grape varieties and soils to match, from stony, to alluvial, and even chalky. The art is in the matching. Pruning, equally, depends upon the terrain and its protection from the dreaded wind. In the south, there are a great deal of 'bush' vines, often round one stake – *taille gobelet*. The vine can often do without the stake when it is older and more resistant. There is also Guyot pruning along wires. On the very steep slopes of Côte Rôtie, special measures have to be taken, described on page 128.

GRAPE VARIETIES

Syrah: This red grape variety, often known as the Sérine in the Rhône, produces deep, long-lived aristocratic wines on the granite of Hermitage, Côte-Rôtie and Cornas, but used on its own in the south, it would be much too tannic. It gives wines of deep, intense scent, great colour, structure and body, eminently suitable for ageing.
Grenache (Noir): The great grape variety of the southern Rhône, and indeed, of the south of France (the Midi). The main type of this red grape is the same as the Spanish Garnacha. The grape produces wines with good colour, high alcohol levels and all-round strength. But for real longevity, it should be blended with the Syrah. There is also Grenache Rouge, Grenache Gris and Grenache Blanc.
Mourvèdre: An excellent red variety, which blends well – it contributes very good colour, generosity, and has ageing properties.
Cinsault: The Cinsault has a good deal of fruit and, when grown on stony soil, is ideal in red blends of class.
Viognier: A great, aristocratic white grape variety, unique of bouquet and flavour – the former is sometimes likened to mayblossom. Grown only in the northern Rhône of France, it is full but vinified dry. It is shy yielding and can oxidize if not handled with care. A great experience at its best.
Marsanne and Roussanne: These white grape varieties of the northern Rhône are

related, but the Marsanne is the better and more widely planted. There is also an improved version of the Roussanne called the Roussette, which appears to be a cross between the Clairette and the Roussanne. They tend to make white wines of high alcohol which are full and assertive, but can have a classy austerity when older, if made in the traditional way. Vinified fresher, they are for younger drinking.

The Bourboulenc, Clairette, Picpoul (Folle Blanche), Grenache Blanc, and Ugni Blanc are grape varieties used for white wines in the southern Rhône; the first three also go into red Châteauneuf-du-Pape. The red Carignan is good when blended with Grenache, but common on its own. The Muscat à petits grains is responsible for some of the best dessert wines.

In the north, starting at Vienne, the first vineyard reached is on the right bank of the Rhône.

Côte-Rôtie: This is one of those rare red wines which contain a proportion of white grapes – in this case, the predominant red grape variety is the Syrah (minimum 80 per cent), and this is softened by a small proportion of the fragrant Viognier. The result is intriguing, combining the power of the Syrah with the tempting scent of the Viognier, often now added in rather small proportion. The south-east facing 'Roasted Slope' certainly attracts all the sun-rays it can, from its terraces and supporting walls. The steepness of the terrain necessitates special pruning and training, with the Syrah vines trained together in groups up sticks, in a pyramid-like form, stretching the vines out in order to gain maximum exposure. Explosives are sometimes used to make an impression on the granite. Work in the vineyards is often done by cable and winch, and at harvest time, when the grapes are gathered in *bennes* (large baskets), they are winched up to the tracks at the summit for transport to the press house. Mules are sometimes still used where even this is not possible.

Above Ampuis, there are two individual slopes within the *appellation*, the Côte Brune, and the Côte Blonde, just to the south. The feudal Seigneur of Ampuis apparently once had two daughters, a blonde and a brunette, who were each given a vineyard as a dowry. The Côte Brune is, in fact, a dark brownish clay, while the Côte Blonde is of a silico-calcareous nature and lighter, more suitable for the Viognier grape. Nowadays, the two slopes are nearly always blended, giving a harmonious whole. Vinification tends to be traditional, although stainless-steel vats are to be seen now. Time in cask varies, but is usually two years or more. The wines thereafter need time in bottle to attain the great complexity of which they are capable, becoming the most subtle red wines of the northern Rhône.

Some of the greatest wines are made by the Guigal family, who blend Côte Blonde and Côte Brune, but also produce La Mouline, which only comes from the Côte Blonde. Guigal both own, and buy in grapes from small growers. Robert Jasmin makes magnificent Côte Rôtie La Chevalière d'Ampuis. More tannic, the Côte Rôtie of Emile Champet is also of majestic character. M. Albert Dervieux is also a highly recommended grower. The great house of Ampuis is that of Vidal-Fleury, which makes an excellent blended Côte Rôtie of the two main Côtes, which they call La Rolande. The Côte Rôtie Les Jumelles from Paul Jaboulet Ainé is always of depth and class, with the 1979 quite magnificent, and the houses of Chapoutier and Delas also own at Côte Rôtie. The wines of M. Alfred Gérin, the mayor of Ampuis, are also recommended.

Condrieu: Just south of Côte Rôtie, these could be called the strangest white wines of France, springing from the rare Viognier grape, and grown on steep slopes with a topsoil of soft, powdery *arzelle*, which is decomposed rock. This meagre soil can easily be washed down the slopes after rain, and has to be laboriously replaced. The vines are again trained up poles, usually two. The Viognier is one of those rare grapes that actually has a pungent smell at must stage, most varieties only attaining their particular character when made into wine. The attractive mayblossom flavour is most evident when young, but if the wine is very carefully treated and there is no oxidation, you can find really complex old wines. The area is very small, seven hectares, and the Viognier yields shyly, rarely going over 25 hectolitres per hectare and often well below. Unfortunately, this has led to many of the terraces being abandoned, even with the high price that Condrieu can command. Condrieu used to be bottled when there was still unfermented sugar in the wine, thereby producing a second fermentation in bottle and a wine that was just slightly sparkling, or *perlé*. Nowadays, nearly all the wine is vinified dry, so the real essence of the Viognier can be seen more clearly, uncluttered by sugar. The undoubted *roi* of Condrieu is M. Georges Vernay, who makes wine under modern methods with great style. There is also the Château du Rozay belonging to M. Paul Multier. Other owners are Delas Frères, now linked with Champagne Deutz, and M. André Dézormeaux, one of the last exponents of sweet Condrieu. Domaine Guigal buy in grapes and make an excellent example. Robert Jurie-Descamier has a good reputation.

Château Grillet: There are less than two hectares of vines in this *appellation*, an enclave within Condrieu and, like it, made entirely from the Viognier grape. There is only one owner, M. Neyret-Gachet, and he has gradually reclaimed terraces, which often carry only one row of vines. South-facing, the grapes can attain great power and alcohol. Again, the topsoil is decomposed mica. A pneumatic press and stainless-steel vats are concessions to today, but the wine still stays several months on the lees. As at Condrieu, the wine undergoes malolactic fermentation, and the bottling date has been reduced from three years to about half that time or eighteen months, while at Condrieu it is usually in the spring following the vintage. When young, the wine can have great charm and finesse, and honeylike aromas. It darkens considerably with age, and then the alcohol can take over from the youthful fragrance. It is a drinking experience, but is perhaps overpriced.

St-Joseph: Still on the right bank of the river, this scattered vineyard area can produce some of the best value of the northern Rhône. The reds are made from the Syrah, and the whites from the Marsanne and the Roussanne. The *appellation* is comparatively modern, having been granted in 1956. The vineyards of St-Joseph lie round the town of Tournon, and they produce mostly red wine, but with a small quantity of white. One of the seven St-Joseph villages forming the *appellation* is Mauves, and since the eighteenth century its wine has been imported into England – Victorian enamel wine labels with the name can still sometimes be found. The red wines have an earthy flavour and pronounced nose, and should be drunk comparatively young. The growers here are carefully replanting some areas, as at one time St-Joseph wines were used for blending and, instead of the Syrah, hybrid vines were grown. Opposite Hermitage, St-Joseph echoes its slopes, hewn out of the Massif Central. Vines are trained up one stake, and there is some clay and sand on the granite. The red wines may not be given the same time in cask as a Hermitage, but they will be robust enough and in good years, startlingly good. The white wines are vinified dry, but yet can be rich and full. The red St-Joseph Le Grand Pompée of Jaboulet is impressive, and the marvellous 1979 was probably the best wine since 1969. Delas own vineyards in St-Joseph and make deep red wines, which can be a bit one-dimensional in youth, but open out with time. M. Gustave Coursodon of Mauves has a justifiably high reputation, as has M. Jean-Louis Grippat at Tournon. Chapoutier also own at St-Joseph, and the Trollat family at St Jean-de-Muzols makes fine wines.

Hermitage: Standing on top of the great hill of Hermitage, by the chapel of St Christopher, one cannot help but be reminded of the Mosel. Far below, the Rhône makes a great turn, and all around are steep terraced slopes. Only here, the terraces are called *chalais*, and the red Syrah grape predominates, wedded to its granite-based soil, covered with a thin, loose, decomposed flinty/chalky topsoil. Legally, the red wine here can have up to 15 per cent white Marsanne and Roussanne added to it, but nearly always does not. The 130-hectare Hermitage slope, in spite of being on the left, or eastern bank, of the Rhône, is really part of the Massif Central, and faces full south. The huge, deep red wines of Hermitage have, with top Claret and the Grands Crus of the Côte de Nuits, the longest life of all red wines in France. In the first half of the nineteenth century, Bordeaux used to be sold as 'hermitaged', and this cost more than the non-hermitaged variety! The granite reflects heat and the sun beats down on the slope. Winds are high, however, and the bush *gobelet* vines are tied to one stake. Young Syrah, grown with this intensity and concentration, can carry with it a wonderful peppery flavour. At Hermitage, all the special problems of vine cultivation in the northern Rhône can be easily seen. Since pre-Roman times the ground has been worked here, and the soil on the higher slopes is very thin. When it rains, what soil there is gathers at the foot of the hill and piles up against the iron gates at the entrance to the vineyards – only to be laboriously carried up the slope again. The slopes are often not worked, but anti-weed products are used to avoid disturbing the soil still further. The Syrah is grown on the higher and middle slopes and the plots for the best white wines are Chante Alouette, les Rocoules, les Murets, Maison-Blanche and les Greffieux. The Marsanne is more robust than the Roussanne and therefore usually preferred, but white Hermitage is a mixture of both. Annual production in Hermitage averaged about 3,500 hectolitres over the 1970s, with approximately 80 per cent red, 20 per cent white.

La Chapelle, near the top of the slopes, is probably the most renowned growth, and in the hands of the Jaboulet family, has to be one of the best red wines of the whole Rhône, its long vatting giving great depth and character. Wines of this calibre deserve ageing in bottle if their real nobility is to emerge. Dense, rich and strong, the complexity and style have to come through the tannin. But rarely is the fruit not there to combat the tannin, and it is a strange wine indeed that eventually dries up without first unfolding into great splendour. Wine-making tends to be traditional, often with a minimum two years in barrel, although La Chapelle is bottled after a year. Paul Jaboulet Aîné are not only *négociants* of repute, but very big vineyard owners. (They are also known as Jaboulet-Isnard.) They own twenty-four hectares at Hermitage, including the chapel of St Christopher. The Chapoutiers are also *négociants* and owners, with thirty-one hectares at Hermitage. La Sizeranne is their top red wine. The house of Delas has seventeen hectares at Hermitage, and their best red is the Marquise de la Tourette. M. Gérard Chave is another top owner, with highly regarded wines. Léon Revol is also a name in Hermitage.

Great white Hermitages are Jaboulet's Le Chevalier de Stérimberg, now made in a modern way, with no malolactic fermentation or keeping in wood, and bottled early in the spring after the vintage, and Chapoutier's Chante Alouette, more traditional and longer lived, with great fullness. Gérard Chave also makes excellent white Hermitage. When these wines age, they can have a similar *noisette* finish to them as a mature Meursault, but they are more powerful than white Burgundy, with a more austere, alcoholic backbone. The cooperative at Tain does not always produce wine of character.

Crozes-Hermitage: There are some who think that it is a pity that Crozes ever hyphenated Hermitage to its name, since the vineyards are not in such a good position as Hermitage, being to the north, and there is much more clay in the soil. This can, of course, produce wines of depth and power, but without perhaps the added grace and nobility of more granitic Hermitage. It is, however, bigger than Hermitage, with 600 hectares. The wines tend not to last as long as Hermitage, but have an individual *goût de terroir*. Most of the vines are planted on gentle slopes and mechanization can be used, making this *appellation* less of an endangered species than others in the northern Rhône. The steepest slopes, though, make the best wines. The grape varieties are the same as for Hermitage. Having been rather severe with Crozes-Hermitage, one has to say that the twenty-hectare Domaine de Thalabert of Jaboulet is a magnificent wine, with even the unremarkable vintage of 1977 incredibly good. Chapoutier have Les Meysonniers. One of the villages in the Crozes *appellation* is Gervans, and it is here where the best and steepest sites are to be found – M. Raimond Roure and M. Jules Fayolle (on slightly gentler slopes) both make fine wine in this area. M. Albert Bégot of Serves-sur-Rhône also produces wines with a high reputation, and I have very much admired Crozes-Hermitage from the Domaine Bruno Thierry (Vidal-Fleury). Amongst white Crozes-Hermitage, there is Jaboulet's La Mule Blanche.

Cornas: A little further south, and on the other side of the river, there is the seventy-five hectare *appellation* of Cornas, on some of the steepest terrain in the northern Rhone. The wine is only red, from the Syrah. It is some of the blackest wine of the area when young, needing time in bottle to throw off its initial coarseness. The best wine comes from the very steepest slopes, not the flatter strip at the foot of the hill. These slopes are away from the river and the Mistral, and the grapes, therefore, can attain great ripeness and are vintaged before the other *appellations*. It must be for this reason that Cornas, a Celtic word, means burnt or scorched earth. Near St-Péray, there is more sand in the granite-based clay soil, and the wines are consequently lighter. But true Cornas is made traditionally, with long vatting and ageing in wood, and the bottles should be kept patiently before drinking. Delas' Chante-Perdrix always repays keeping. M. Auguste Clape makes wine of real depth and power, in the most traditional manner. Other owners are the Lionnet, Michel and Verset families and M. Guy de Barjac.

St-Péray: The last *appellation* of the northern Rhône, just south of Cornas, is made mostly from the white Marsanne, but also from the Roussanne/Roussette. It can be still but is more often made *mousseux* by the Champagne method, even using Champagne yeasts. There the similarity ends, though, as the wine is richer, fuller and heavier than Champagne, and the different grape varieties naturally cannot emulate the ultimate finesse of top Champagne. Ideally, the wine should have a few years of bottle age, and then it can be interesting and most pleasant. The sub-soil is granitic, covered with sand, stones and pebbles, and the vineyard covers about fifty hectares. M. Jean-François Chaboud is a well-known grower, as is M. Milliand. Some good Cornas growers, such as MM. Clape, Juge and Voge, also have holdings in St-Péray, and they must make their sparkling wine here to obtain the *appellation* St-Péray.

Before going into the well-defined southern Rhône, there are two other areas, the Ardèche, that wild country of the Massif Central to the west of the Rhône, and Die, about sixty-four kilometres south-east of Valence.

Côtes du Vivarais and Coteaux de l'Ardèche: The Ardèche is poor, and many of the villages are depopulated, but there is a revival of its wine, which one hopes will encourage those who stayed. The VDQS of the Côtes du Vivarais is made from Grenache, Cinsault and Carignan, with some Syrah and Gamay. The wines are made for young drinking, vinified to bring out youthful fruit. The best sources are the cooperatives at Orgnac and Ruoms, and an extremely conscientious grower is M. André Marron at Vallon Pont d'Arc. M. Léon Brunel at St-Remèze is in the same mould. The *négociant* Amédée Dubourg at St Péray is also a source of reliable wine. There is good Gamay de l'Ardèche, Vin de Pays, officially Coteaux de l'Ardèche, from the cooperative of St Désirat-Champagne, between Condrieu and Tournon, which also makes St-Joseph.

Clairette de Die and Châtillon-en-Diois: Before the sparkling wines took over, Clairette de Die was a still white wine from that grape variety. However, now one goes to Die for its traditional sparkling wine made by the *méthode Dioise* – which will be labelled Tradition or Demi-Sec, and made from varying proportions of Clairette and Muscat à petits grains. There is also Clairette de Die Brut, made by the Champagne method, entirely from the Clairette, which does not have the bloomy fruit of the Muscat; it has rapidly gained popularity. The *méthode Dioise* consists of centrifuging the must to clarify after pressing, then lightly filtering the juice to remove some of the yeasts and delay fermentation. Eventually, fermentation starts, and advances slowly – if it speeds up, a light filtering slows things down. Then, when the wine is bottled in the New Year, there is some residual sugar left and this ferments slightly inside the bottle. No yeasts or extra sugar are added. Before sale, the wine is filtered under carbon dioxide pressure and re-bottled. The cooperative at Die is important, as are Buffardel Frères, who sometimes give their wine a vintage when exceptionally good. There are a quantity of growers, with M. Vincent of Ste-Croix making attractive wine.

In 1974 the new *appellation* of Châtillon-en-Diois was created, but it should, on intrinsic merit, have remained VDQS. The reds and roses are predominantly Gamay, with Syrah and Pinot Noir, and the whites are produced from Aligoté and Chardonnay and are marginally better. The sole producer is the cooperative.

Vintages in the Northern Rhône

Really good earlier vintages are, 1929, 1945, 1947, 1949, 1952, 1953, 1955, 1957, 1959, 1961 (superb), 1962, 1964, 1966, 1967, 1969, 1970 (particularly good) and 1971. 1972 produced some surprisingly good wines, given the vintage in general in France, especially in Hermitage. There were some good wines in 1973, but 1974 was only moderate. 1975 suffered from rot, as everywhere on this side of France, and the 1976 reds look set for a long life, if the low acidity holds out. 1977 produced light, rather green, wines, but 1978 was magnificent, with exceptional extract and concentration. The abundant 1979s are also astonishingly good, with some of the right-bank wines rivalling the 1978s.

In the Southern Rhône, the first *appellation* reached is about twenty kilometres north-east of Orange.

Rasteau: Apart from being one of the communes entitled to produce Côtes du Rhône Villages, Rasteau's *appellation* covers Vins Doux Naturels and Vins de Liqueur made from a minimum of 90 per cent Grenache grapes and a maximum of 10 per cent of grape varieties that have the right to the Côtes du Rhône *appellation*. Nearly all this fortified wine is made as white, although the colour is amber or caramel. The Grenache has high natural alcohol and takes on a taste of age comparatively quickly, so it is regarded as ideal fortified wine material, even though it lacks the lusciousness of the Muscat. It can be a little crude when young, and that is why aged Rasteau is prized; some is even kept in cask for anything up to ten years, when it is called Rancio and has a distinctly maderized taste. For the Vins Doux, the Grenache grapes are picked as late as possible, in order that they can attain 15 per cent alcohol naturally. The grapes are pressed, fermented up to 15 per cent or more, away from the skins to avoid colour tinting, and then alcohol is added to arrest the fermentation and retain residual sugar. The resulting Vin Doux has 21.5 per cent alcohol. Vins de Liqueur do not have to start with quite such high natural sugar, and the alcohol can be added before, as well as during, the fermentation – these wines are not as good as the Vins Doux. Both are sold without a vintage, and are mostly appreciated locally as apéritifs, or digestifs at the end of a meal. There is a cooperative, and MM Bressy, Charavin and Vache are all important producers.

Beaumes-de-Venise: Also a Côtes du Rhône Villages, the special *appellation* of this commune is Muscat-de-Beaumes-de-Venise, Vins Doux Naturels and Vins de Liqueur, only made from the Muscat à petits grains, also called the Muscat de Frontignan. The Muscat makes particularly tempting fortified wines, delicious drunk slightly chilled both as a pre- and post-prandial glass. Unlike the Grenache-based Rasteau, Muscat-de-Beaumes-de-Venise is at its most delectable when young. The method of vinification is similar to Rasteau. Apart from the cooperative's good example, in screw-topped bottle, the Domaine des Bernardins of M. Louis Castaud is truly rich and aromatic and Jacques Leydier of Domaine de Durban makes delicious wine. M. Guy Rey of Domaine St Sauveur is also recommended. All have good red wine as well.

Gigondas: Before the days when *appellation* rules were strictly followed, a great deal of Gigondas found its way into the better-known Châteauneuf du-Pape, and those 'in the know' bought Gigondas for themselves at very good value prices. Nowadays, this impish behaviour is no more, and Gigondas itself, granted its *appellation* in 1971, justifiably sells for a fair sum. Nestling in the Dentelles de Montmirail, the foothills of the majestic, often snow-peaked, Mont Ventoux, the dark wine of Gigondas is made principally of Grenache, with some Syrah and Cinsault, Mourvèdre and Clairette. The best vineyards are mid-slope on terrain that is markedly stony; above the soil is clay, and below more sandy. Vinification is traditional, and barrel-ageing varies from under a year to two years, mostly depending on the size of the enterprise. Bottle-ageing is also important, if one is to enjoy these wines fully. When they are young they are often almost purple in colour, have a strong, assertive taste and a good deal of alcohol. The best also add breed to this list. In a good year, it will keep well, with perhaps maximum fruit at about six to eight years, but one should expect flavour, rather than complexity.

The two big grower/*négociants* of the region are Gabriel Meffre (Domaine des Bosquets, Domaine St Jean and Domaine La Chapelle) and, less giant-like, Pierre Amadieu. Top domains are Roger Meffre's Domaine St Gayan, the Archimbauds' Château de Montmirail, M. Henri Barruol's Domaine St Cosme, M. François Ay's Château de Raspail, Hilarion Roux's Domaine Les Pallières, Roger Combe and M. Burle's Les Pallieroudas. The cooperative is highly respected, and Paul Jaboulet Ainé's selections are always first-class.

Châteauneuf-du-Pape: Châteauneuf has a lilting name, a fascinating history and very special soil. Unfortunately, not all the growers of Châteauneuf have always honoured their legacy, and some of the wine is not as good as it should be, failing to bring out the unique character of the *appellation*. This character partly comes from the incredibly stony soil, often formed of enormous *galets*, flattish, smooth stones of a pinkish colour. During the day these stones absorb and reflect a good deal of heat, and continue to radiate heat even at night, ensuring that the grapes ripen almost all round the clock, and even from below. These stones take their toll in machinery and implements, with a high replacement rate. But their presence gives the grapes of Châteauneuf great ripeness and thick skins, so that the result in the wine, if nature takes its course, is a dark colour and great tannin.

Within the *appellation* rules, thirteen varieties of grape are permitted, including some white grapes. Most growers usually settle for about nine varieties, choosing grapes to suit different plots (as estates are often scattered), and those listed first predominate: red – Grenache, Syrah, Mourvèdre, Cinsault, Terret Noir, Muscardin, Vaccarèse, Counoise; white – Clairette, Bourboulenc, Roussanne, Picpoul, Picardan. Each grape adds something to the blend – Grenache ensures good alcohol, Mourvèdre good colour, Cinsault and Syrah give fruity mellowness and backbone, respectively. The addition of white grapes undoubtedly helps the bouquet and provides an intriguing finesse hidden in the structure of the wine which takes it out of the merely robust category. Each variety ripens at a different time, which is an aid to the *vigneron*; the Cinsault is usually picked first, the Grenache last. The grapes are in bushes, *gobelet* fashion, except for the Syrah, which is trained on to wires.

The disparity between styles of Châteauneuf and, it must be admitted, the difference in quality between the best and the worst (much of it bottled outside the area, which is unwise in the circumstances), make it essential to have a list of the best domains. This applies to red Châteauneuf – although there is a tiny amount of white wine made as a curiosity – about 4 per cent of under 100,000 hectolitres' average annual yield. The *appellation* area is about 3,000 hectares, completely planted. Château Rayas is often regarded as the king of the area, for its wine of great longevity and depth, partly due to small yields, long wood ageing, and also to the grape variety combination of Grenache, Syrah and Cinsault. The Reynauds also make a very good Côtes du Rhône, Château de Fonsalette. The Domaine de Mont Redon is the largest estate at Châteauneuf, run most efficiently by M. Jean Abeille and other descendants of the Plantin family. The wine is big, tannic and robust, the produce of some of the stoniest terrain. The Domaine de Beaucastel lasts well, as does the excellent Chante Cigale of M. Noël Sabon, the Clos de l'Oratoire des Papes and Château La Nerte. The Château des Fines Roches is one of the best-placed properties in the *appellation*, producing wine of class, and nearby Château Fortia has very good traditional character. Other highly recommended properties are the Domaine du Vieux Télégraphe, Clos du Mont-Olivet, Domaine de la Terre Ferme, Clos des Papes, and Les Clefs d'Or, excellent both for red and white. Domaine de Beaurenard, Domaine de la Solitude and Domaine de Nalys make lighter, 'new style' wines. *Négociants* include the Caves St-Pierre, the Caves Eugène Bessac, Louis Mousset and Père Anselme. Paul Jaboulet have their Les Cèdres Châteauneuf and Chapoutier La Bernardine. There are two associations of growers who bottle and store their wines together, Les Reflets, and Prestige et Tradition.

Very good years in Châteauneuf-du-Pape are 1945, 1947, 1949, 1955, 1957, 1959, 1961 (superb), 1962, 1964, 1966, 1967 (tannic and full), 1969, 1970 and 1971. It should be remembered that sometimes these wines of the south do not keep with quite the same consistency as the top reds of the northern Rhône. The 1972s are somewhat 'patchy', but some have improved in bottle to a great extent, the 1973s were too diluted by the quantity produced to hold much interest, and the 1974s are not much better than moderately good. 1975 is to be avoided altogether, 1976 can be good, but depends on whether the property vintaged before the rainstorms, and 1977 is a 'fill-in' vintage while waiting for the 1978s, although some are drying out a bit. The 1978s are quite magnificent, a much-needed classic year for the region. The wines have structure, opulence and fruit, and will make splendid bottles in the future. The 1979s are very good, without the overall *charpente* and body of the 1978s, but immensely attractive. On the whole, these vintage notes can be applied to the southern Rhône *appellations*, bearing in mind that as the *appellations* get more modest, their keeping time shortens.

Tavel: From a quality point of view, this is the most famous rosé wine in France. Dry, full-bodied and alcoholic, this is not a pretty little holiday wine to toss back, but something more serious to accompany food with a definite taste. On the western side of the river, Tavel has the same large, flat stones as at Châteauneuf-du-Pape, and roughly the same grape varieties, with a preponderance of Grenache and Cinsault. Some of the best soil is chalky on slopes, and the whole terrain is hot and arid. The *appellation* area is about 1,000 hectares, completely planted, and average annual production is between 35,000 and 40,000 hectolitres. The rosé colour is extracted by a maceration of the grapes in their juice for one to two days, before fermentation starts. Then the grapes are pressed lightly, and fermentation is away from the skins. Bottling is in the New Year after the vintage, and Tavel is best appreciated relatively young, when the colour is pink and not tawny and there is youthful freshness and fruit added to the character of the wine. The cooperative at Tavel has a high reputation and is one of the most conscientiously run in France. Top domains are Château Aquéria, Domaine de la Genestière, Domaine de la Forcadière, Le Vieux Moulin de Tavel, Château de Trinquevedel, Domaine de Tourtouil, the Prieuré de Monté-zargues, de Lanzac, and the Château de Manissy which is run by the Pères de la Ste-Famille.

Lirac: Just to the north of Tavel, this *appellation* covers red, rosé and white wines, although it is the red that takes pride of place. The rosé is delicious drunk young, often more supple than Tavel. The main grape varieties are the Grenache, followed by the Cinsault, Syrah, Mourvèdre and Clairette. There is also a small amount of the unusual Maccabéo. The soil is mixed, sometimes pebbly, with some clay, and the western part of the plateau of Roquemaure has large stones. The *appellation* area is about 3,500 hectares, of which only 2,000 are planted and only 500 are declared *appellation* Lirac; the rest are Côtes du Rhône. Current annual production is about 20,000 hectolitres, and it is clear that there is room for expansion. These red wines have fruit, charm and body and represent some of the very best value in the southern Rhône. There are some exceptionally well-run domains, some of them bought by ex-settlers in Algeria, and it is well worth finding them. The Pons-Mure family have two separate properties of great note, the Domaine de Castel-Oualou and the Domaine de La Tour-de-Lirac, and a relation has the excellent Domaine Rousseau. The Château de Ségriès has old vines and can be rich and concentrated, and the Domaine du Devoy belonging to the Lombardo family makes delicious wine. A more recent estate is that of Philippe Testut, of the well-known Chablis family, whose wines show immense skill and whose red is a very fine bottle indeed. The Domaine du Château St-Roch has a justifiably high reputation, and Jean-Claude Assémat's Les Garrigues makes delicious, fresh wines. M. Maby's La Fermade is always good, as well as M. Bernard's Domaine de la Genestière and the wine of M. Gabriel Roudil, who actually lives at Tavel. The cooperative at St Laurent-des-Arbres is not recommended.

Côtes du Rhône Villages: Initially, there was just Côtes du Rhône, but in 1953 the INAO decided that four villages could add their name to that simple *appellation*: Gigondas, Cairanne, Chusclan and Laudun. In 1955, Vacqueyras was added to the list, and two years later Vinsobres entered the ranks. In 1967, this group of wines was officially baptized Côtes du Rhône Villages, and now there are seventeen communes which fall into this category, Gigondas now being full *appellation* on its own. If there is inter-communal blending, it is just plain Côtes du Rhône Villages. The Côtes du Rhône Villages are: in the Drôme – St Maurice-sur-Eygues, Rousset-les-Vignes, Rochegude, St Pantaléon-les-Vignes and Vinsobres; in the Vaucluse – Cairanne, Vacqueyras, Rasteau, Valréas, Visan, Roaix, Sablet, Beaumes-de-Venise, and Séguret; in the Gard – Chusclan, Laudun and St Gervais. The alcohol level of Côtes du Rhône Villages must be 12.5 per cent for reds, and 12 per cent for rosé or white, and yield is more limited than plain Côtes du Rhône. The grape varieties are those of the main *appellations* of the southern Rhône, and although red, white and rosé are made, it is the red that is the important wine. This is an area dominated by the cooperatives, most of which are very good, especially when their best wines are chosen. There are a few domains that are becoming known for their quality and, where possible, it is worth finding these two categories, rather than *négociant* wine, which often suffers in less than perfect years. Cooperatives that can be thoroughly recommended are those of Cairanne, La Cave des Vignerons de Chusclan (excellent red, rosé and white and a superb example of what a cooperative can do), Beaumes-de-Venise and Vinsobres.

It is worth noting a few characteristics of the main Villages wines. Cairanne is often grown on clayey slopes, where the wines have body and roundness, combined with the colour and tannin of wine from the *garrigues* area, where it is stony. These are lovely, full wines. L'Oratoire St-Martin and the Domaine des Travers are very good. Laudun makes red, rosé and white wine – the latter is good, from the Clairette and the Roussanne. But the red dominates, usually quite big wine, and the best producers are the Cave des Quatre Chemins, the Domaine Rousseau (the same ownership as at Lirac) and the Domaine Pélaquié, the latter making really powerful, long-vatted wines. Rochegude has a good cooperative making supple wines, and Sablet has the excellent Domaine de Verquière. The village of St-Gervais has the Domaine Ste-Anne, where the wines are made by a *semi-macération carbonique* method of eight to twelve days and have great attraction.

Vacqueyras is certainly one of the best Côtes du Rhône Villages, and its red wine has depth of bouquet, fruit and body. The best domains are: La Fourmone of Roger Combe, Domaine des Lambertins, Pascal Frères, the Clos des Cazaux of Archimbaud Frères, Le Vieux Clocher, and the Domaine des Garrigues of Bernard Frères. Valréas has a good cooperative and the Domaine du Val-des-Rois of M. Romain Bouchard, who is Burgundian by origin, as well as the Domaine des Grands Devers of M. Sinard. Vinsobres has several good domains, amongst which that of M. Jean Vinson, Le Moulin, and Jaume Père et Fils. Visan is dominated by its cooperative, where the red is easily the best wine.

Côtes du Rhône: This is the basic generic wine of the Rhône, and its financial rock. About $1\frac{1}{2}$ million hectolitres are made each year of red, white and rosé wine, which must reach 11 per cent alcohol. It can also contain a higher proportion of Carignan than the Villages wines. The red is the most reliable, and the following are domains of note: Domaine de la Chapelle at Châteauneuf-de-Gadagne – M. Marcel Boussier here grows big, long-lasting wine on the same stony soil as at the 'other' Châteauneuf; the aristocratic Château de Fonsalette (at Lagarde-Paréol) of M. Reynaud of Château Rayas fame; Château de l'Estagnol at Suze-la-Rousse; Château St-Estève at Uchaux near Orange; Château des Roques at Sarrians; Château Malijay at Jonquières, if you like light wines; Domaine Mitan-Fabre at Vedène; and La Vieille Ferme, at Jonquières, which is not a single domain but buys in grapes and young wines to make a light Côtes du Rhône. *Négociants* include the reliable Bellicard at Avignon, Le Cellier des Dauphins at Tulette, which sells wine from eight cooperatives, David et Foillard at Sorgues, and Ogier at Sorgues. Paul Jaboulet have the full-bodied Côtes-du-Rhône Parallèle 45.

Coteaux du Tricastin: Elevated to *appellation* status in 1974, this vineyard area expanded with great speed, and now is about 1,500 hectares. As a result, for a time the red wines often showed the influence of young vines, but as we go into the 1980s, the quality has improved enormously. Vineyards were planted with difficulty in the stony terrain, and everything is highly mechanized, again with the dynamism behind it of some former settlers in Algeria who returned to France in the 1960s. The grape varieties are Grenache, Cinsault, Syrah and Mourvèdre. Production of Coteaux du Tricastin red and rosé in 1979 was 64,422 hectolitres – white wine production is practically non-existent in this area. The best domains in Tricastin are those of the Bour family, with their wonderful Domaine de Grangeneuve and Domaine des Lônes, and M. Pierre Labeye with his Domaine de la Tour d'Elyssas, producing the Cru du Devoy, the Cru de Meynas and the Cru des Echirouses. I have also liked Tricastin wines from the Tricastin cooperative at Richerenches.

Côtes du Ventoux: This is another young *appellation* (1974), with predominantly red, but also rosé and a tiny amount of white wine. The dominant grape varieties are Grenache, Syrah, Carignan and Cinsault, but they are mostly vatted for a very short time with resultant light freshness and palish colour. 1979 production was 195,520 hectolitres of red and rosé wine. The two best domains are the Domaine des Anges and the Domaine St Sauveur at Aubignan; otherwise, the cooperatives hold sway. I have liked Côtes du Ventoux from the *négociants* Louis Mousset, Pascal, and Les Caves St Pierre.

Côtes du Lubéron: This VDQS wine has great charm, not the least of which is the beautiful country from which it comes around the Lubéron hills inland from Marseille. Red and rosé come from Grenache, Carignan and Cinsault, while the white is from the Bourboulenc and Grenache Blanc; red predominates. The Cellier de Marrenon at La Tour d'Aigues makes a good wine, as do the Caves St Pierre.

PROVENCE

Provence is a ray of sunlight in a gloomy world, but sometimes sunshine comes expensive. However, this large area provides enough wine to suit all pockets, from really inexpensive rosés and reds, the house wine of local restaurants and some of the most reasonable at the supermarket, to expensive estates. Some of the latter may not be worth it, relying on their *renommée* or, in some cases, small *appellation* area for justification, but some offer real value in the quality/price balancing act. Côtes-de-Provence was elevated to *appellation* status in 1977, continuing a trend to upgrade a number of good VDQS wines that perhaps were more realistically placed in their former category. But once the spiral has started, no one wants to be left behind – or very few. Annual production is approximately 700,000 hectolitres from 17,000 hectares of vines. About a third of the production comes from individual domains, while two-thirds comes from about sixty cooperatives. 60 per cent of the wine is rosé, that delectable holiday wine when it is too hot to appreciate a red (unless chilled), about 35 per cent is red, and rising, and 5 per cent white. Many of the domains doing their own bottling now concentrate mainly on reds, while cooperatives, and the *négociants* buying from them, are the great rosé producers. It must be admitted that much of this rosé could be a deal more interesting, and in some cases, more palatable and *sain*. On the whole, the vintages are the same as the southern Rhône, but with more regularity and fewer failures. The grape varieties are the same: Carignan is preponderant, and must certainly fall in proportion if quality is the aim; Grenache; Cinsault; Mourvèdre; Syrah; Tibouren (Provençal); and, more recently introduced, the Cabernet Sauvignon. The vines are trained on to wire and pruned on the 'Cordon de Royat' system. The best white wines are made from the Rolle, Sémillon, and Clairette in small quantities. There are three main zones: the coastal zone, between the Massif des Maures and the sea (St Tropez, La Londe-les-Maures and up to Pierrefeu); the area inland between Toulon and Fréjus, particularly good for reds, round Pierrefeu, Cuers and Puget-Ville, and also Le Luc, Le Cannet-des-Maures, Vidauban, Les Arcs-sur-Argens and La Motte; and further inland again, round Correns (whites) and Cotignac (reds). There is also the area near Aix, around Puyloubier and Trets, good for reds, the area round Bandol (when the wines are not Bandol), and the area behind Nice.

The following are recommended domains and wines: Château Minuty at Gassin (its Cuvée de l'Orotaire is expensive but the tops); the Domaine des Paris from the excellent cooperative Les Maîtres-Vignerons de la Presqu'île de St Tropez; at Cogolin the Domaine des Garcinières and the Domaine de St-Maur; at Bormes-les Mimosas the Domaine des Campaux; and at La Londe-les-Maures, the Clos

Mireille of Domaines Ott, a very expensive white wine, the Domaine du Carrubier, and the Domaine St-André-de-Figuière. At Pierrefeu there is the Domaine de l'Aumérade, at Le Luc the Domaine de la Bernarde, at Le Cannet-des-Maures the Domaine de la Bastide-Neuve, the Domaine des Bertrands, the Château de Roux, and the Domaine de Reillanne. At Vidauban there is the excellent Domaine des Féraud of the Laudon family, with reds and rosés of character, and at les Arcs-sur-Argens, Château Ste Roseline. At Lorgues there is Castel-Roubine and at Trets-en-Provence, Château Grand'Boise. Taradeau has the Château de Selle and the Château de St Martin, the former belonging to Domaines Ott. The Domaine de la Croix also has a considerable reputation. *Négociants* whose Côtes de Provence give confidence are Pradel, now belonging to Cordier of Bordeaux, especially their Impérial Pradel, Bagnis (Rouge Estandon), Cauvières (Mistral) and Bernard Camp-Romain (Bouquet-de-Provence Réserve).

Palette: Palette, on the outskirts of Aix-en-Provence, is a tiny *appellation* with an excellent micro-climate revolving round one property, Château Simone. Fifteen hectares of old vines on calcareous soil here produce red wines aged in wood and capable of lasting for years. They have great complexity and unique flavour. The rosés and white are highly individual, and the quality and originality of all the wines go a long way to justify the high price. The grape varieties are Grenache, Mourvèdre and Cinsault for the reds and rosés, and Clairette for the whites, but there are some old Provençal varieties in smaller quantities.

Cassis: Cassis is another small *appellation*, again making all three 'colours' of wine, but famed for its white. When this is well-made and not oxidized, it has a very interesting taste indeed, influenced by the Marsanne in the blend of more usual varieties of the southern Rhône area. There are four domains of note, all making wines of class that will revive memories of *bouillabaisse* round the port of Cassis: Domaine de la Ferme Blanche; Domaine du Paternel; Clos Ste-Magdeleine; and the Château de Fontblanche.

Bandol: Bandol is a really 'serious' *appellation* – here the red wines are the greatest. The Mourvèdre contributes the greatest part to the blend, when elsewhere it is usually only a small component part of the whole. The Grenache and the Cinsault complete the picture. The vines are grown on terraces, locally called *restanques*. The fault of many Bandol wines in the past was a too-long life in cask, sometimes up to four or five years, which succeeded in drying out the wine before it got to the consumer. Legally, the red wines have to spend eighteen months in cask before being sold (this is an unusual stipulation for an *appellation*), and their main qualities are richness, structure, an array of intoxicating tastes and the capacity to age with interest and grace. About 20,000 hectolitres are produced annually, but there is much room for expansion within the *appellation* area, which can only be a good thing for the consumer, and should help to keep the price within bounds. Recommended properties are: the Domaine Tempier, possibly the best; Château des Vannières; the two domains of the Bunan brothers, the Moulin des Costes and the Mas de la Rouvière; the Domaine du Val d'Arenc; the Domaine de Pibarnon; the Château Pradeaux, perhaps not as consistent as some; La Laidière; and the cooperative, the Moulin de la Roque, which produces excellent wines at a very keen price. Domaines Ott has Château Romassan.

Bellet: Bellet is almost a forgotten *appellation*, forty hectares behind Nice, and sold mainly in the smart hotels and restaurants of Nice and Monte-Carlo. On the whole, the whites are more consistent than the reds and rosés. There are some curious grape varieties in the blends – the Braquet and Folle Noire in the reds and rosés, mixed with Cinsault and Grenache, and the Rolle in the whites, mixed with a very little Roussanne, Chardonnay, Clairette and Bourboulenc. The Château de Bellet and the Château de Crémat are the two best domains.

Coteaux-d'Aix-en-Provence: The Coteaux-d'Aix-en-Provence are VDQS wines from around Aix and made in red, rosé and white. In fact, they are just as good as the wines of Côtes-de-Provence, and should follow their path towards an *appellation*. It is certain that M. Georges Brunet of Château Vignelaure, who planted a high proportion of Cabernet Sauvignon at his domain and eschewed chemical treatments (quite a tendency now in Provence amongst good domains), encouraged others to go for quality. The soils are rather chalky, and the wines often have finesse and can be utterly delicious. There are properties which follow the Cabernet Sauvignon trend (mixed with Syrah and Grenache), and others which prefer to stick to the all-traditional recipe of Grenache, Cinsault, Carignan, Syrah, Mourvèdre, with a touch of Cabernet Sauvignon. The other VDQS of the area, the Coteaux-des-Baux-de-Provence, is now more or less merged with Coteaux-d'Aix.

Good domains are, obviously, Château Vignelaure at Rians, now rather expensive, Château de Fonscolombe at Le Puy-Ste-Réparade of the Marquis de Saporta, which has great charm and quality, together with another good property, the Domaine de la Crémade, Domaine de Lauzières at Mouriès, the Mas de la Dame at Les Baux-de-Provence, the Château de Calissanne at Lançon-de-Provence, Château La Coste at Le Puy-Ste-Réparade, Château de Beaulieu at Rognes, and the Domaine de la Semencière at Les Milles.

CORSICA

Corsican wines are of little interest to those not on the island, for few of them escape in bottle, but it is worth knowing what to hunt down when holidays are taken on this scented isle, where there is mountain and sea, forest and vineyard. A good deal of the two million hectolitres' annual production goes to reinforce weak table wine made elsewhere. But, after the overall Vin de Corse *appellation*, there are seven delimited areas: Patrimonio; Coteaux d'Ajaccio; Sartène; Calvi (Balagne); Coteaux du Cap Corse; Figari; and Porto-Vecchio. These represent only six per cent of the total output of Corsica. Apart from the scent of the herb-filled *maquis*, which seems to impart something to the wine, the distinctive aromas and tastes of Corsican wine are more due to the grape varieties, predominantly indigenous. At Patrimonio, the reds and rosés are largely made from the Nielluccio, a relation of the Sangiovese of Tuscany, with the Sciacarello, which is also found at Sartène, in both cases mixed with the Grenache. White grape varieties are Malvoisie, Ugni Blanc (Trebbiano, again the Italian influence) and Vermentino.

Good domains are: Clos de Bernardi and Clos Marfisi at Patrimonio; the Couvent d'Alzipratu, Clos Landry, Colombu and the Coopérative de Calenzana et de Balagne in the Calvi area; Domaines Péraldi, Martini and Capitoro at Ajaccio; Poggio d'Oro and Domaine de Canella at Figari; and the Domaine de Torraccia and Fior di Lecci at Porto-Vecchio. In the Cap Corse area there is the Clos Nicrosi, with its interesting dry white wine, and the unique Muscatellu, Muscat Doux Naturel. At Ponte-Leccia, there is the Domaine Vico, making *appellation* Vin de Corse wines. The Margnat family (now separate from the table-wine firm) have important holdings on Corsica, amongst which there are the good-value Domaine de Fontanella and the Domaine de Furgoli, *appellation* Vin de Corse, from the Domaines de Tizzano round the Golfe de Tizzano on the south-east of the island. The wines are well made from the Nielluccio, Grenache and Carignan, and sometimes shipped in bulk for bottling in the United Kingdom. The Vin de Pays L'Ile de Beauté is also beginning to be seen in the United Kingdom and the Domaine de Musoleu at Folelli makes excellent examples.

LANGUEDOC-ROUSSILLON

To a certain extent, these are wines to be drunk (after taking due advice) and not read about and the best, it is to be hoped, will continue to give an example to the worst, of which there is a larger proportion than any government would want. Originally, the vineyards were on the slopes, with cereals on the plains, but in the nineteenth century these flatlands were planted with the Alicante and the Aramon which, on clay and alluvial soils, produced astonishing yields of 200 hectolitres per hectare. The highlands followed suit, and the result was the 'wine lake'. The situation is hardly helped by the high price paid for poor wine at the distillery. Since 1960, various government bodies and the most far-sighted producers have been searching for ways to improve matters. Obviously, the grape varieties had to improve and they in turn have to be adapted to the multitude of soils, mini-regions and micro-climates that lie in the slopes and valleys of the *coteaux*. There is every type of soil, from terrain of huge stones left by the retreating Rhône, to clay-calcareous slopes, to schist, granite and sandstone. The zones gradually have to be redefined, so that they do not necessarily follow the communes, but the more logical viticultural plots. The cooperatives have to be helped to improve their methods and techniques and to have equipment conducive to the production of healthy wine.

The Carignan grape is still *roi*, with its high alcohol and big yield, but when the vines are old and the vineyard is high, the results can be good. The Grenache and Cinsault are added in varying quantities, followed by the Syrah and Mourvèdre, with some Cabernet Sauvignon. But we are talking about those properties that really care about quality and are prepared to make sacrifices to get it.

Costières du Gard: Travelling from the east, the first VDQS of note is Costières du Gard, south of Nîmes. Good red and rosé wines are made, rather similar to Côtes du Rhône, fruity, with some body, but uncomplicated wines. There are cooperatives at Vauvert, Générac and Beauvoisin and, at Gallician, two properties which make worthy wine – the Mas de la Tardine and the Mas Aupellière.

Vins des Sable: Down in the Camargue, there are the Vins des Sables, and at Grau-du-Roi, the Domaine de l'Espiguette, Sicarex-Méditerranée. This is the main centre of practical research of the Institut Technique de la Vigne et du Vin, with regard to clonal selection, viticultural and vinification methods. Some of the wines, naturally, are perfect technically without being exciting, but there are individual lots to be selected of real interest.

Much the same could be said of the Domaines Viticoles des Salins du Midi at Montpellier, whose vast range of wines is made with great technical ability and in the most 'natural' way possible, i.e. no chemical products in the soil, no pasteurization. Nearly all the domains which belong to the Compagnie des Salins du Midi are in the production area of the Vins de Pays des Sables du Golfe du Lion and, as the phylloxera louse does not develop in sand, the vines are largely ungrafted and are on French root stocks. The hot sun of the south is also here tempered by the breezes from the sea and the salt marshes. Listel is a trade mark of the Salins du Midi, and well-known domains are Domaine du Bosquet (red), and Domaine du Château de Villeroy (red and white). For whites, they often judiciously blend the Clairette with the Ugni Blanc and the Sauvignon; for some soft red wines they remove the grapes from the skins, heat the skins to extract colour, which is then added to the juice and fermented – the result is colour and not tannin.

Coteaux du Languedoc: The Coteaux du Languedoc VDQS wines cover a vast area between Nîmes and Béziers – thirteen areas within this region can add their name to the overall title. On the whole, reds and rosés are better than whites, wine-makers often lacking the equipment and technique for the latter. There is quite a bit of *macération carbonique* in the reds, which was often the original way of vinification on the farms, putting the grapes whole into the *cuve* without crushing, as well as some Vin d'Une Nuit, a very light, fruity red achieved by maceration overnight – the rosés take a matter of hours. The most important areas are Faugères and St-Chinian, both awaiting the award of *appellation* status. Faugères red wine can have real richness with good backbone, while St-Chinian, with its two zones of schist and clay-chalk, usually blended together, has style and a scented bouquet. Berlou St-Chinian comes from a high valley and is made from Carignan. St-Saturnin is also important, with a good cooperative and Vin d'Une Nuit. Quatourze is small but with some good properties, while La Clape has an unfortunate name but is producing some remarkably good wines.

Before going further west, there are three *appellation* Vins Doux Naturels made from the Muscat grape, along the lines of Beaumes-de-Venise – Muscat de Lunel, Muscat de Mireval and Muscat de Frontignan. If you like the grapy taste of Muscat and its rich aromas, you will like these. Well-chilled, they can be good apéritifs, but they are also good digestifs, with nuts and fruit. The *appellation* Clairette du Languedoc is dry white wine or Vin de Liqueur, made from the Clairette grape. The VDQS Picpoul de Pinet is small enough to jump over – light dry white wine.

Minervois: Minervois VDQS, between St-Chinian and Carcassonne, encompasses valley and hills, and it is the produce of the latter you want, particularly round St Jean-de-Minervois and Minerve. Another candidate for *appellation* status, the wines from the hills have a full fragrance and body and provide excellent, gulpable bottles.

Corbières and Corbières Supérieures: These cover a huge area of the Aude, VDQS with *appellation* ambitions. There is the coastal zone, where a high alcohol content is obtained, the middle zone round Lézignan, Lagrasse, St Laurent de la Cabrerisse, with supple wines, and the Hautes-Corbières, behind and to the south of the foregoing, with very assertive wines. Corbières can be rounder and more velvety than Minervois, which can have more structure. There is a good deal of *macération carbonique* and Carignan, Cinsault, Grenache, and now some Syrah. The vines are trained *en gobelet*.

Fitou: The *appellation* Fitou falls within this greater area of VDQS of Corbières, and is for red wine only, mostly made of Carignan and Grenache, with other varieties that can be added up to 25 per cent: Cinsault, Terret-Noir, Malvoisie, Maccabéo, Muscat and Picpoul. They have to spend at least nine months in wood before being sold, but that does not improve the mediocre quality of many of them. An exception is the Chateau de Nouvelles at Tuchan.

Blanquette-de-Limoux: Blanquette-de-Limoux, made both still (unexciting) and *mousseux*, is produced from the Mauzac grape, formerly known as Blanquette (see Gaillac), and the Clairette in very small proportion. Made by the Champagne method, it is a really fine sparkling wine and the local cooperative does it honour, with the most modern techniques and the greatest care. I would rank Blanquette-de-Limoux with the very best Champagne-method wines of the Loire and Burgundy.

The Roussillon appellations: The Roussillon encompasses three *appellations* – Côtes-du-Roussillon, Côtes-du-Roussillon-Villages and Collioure, and the Carignan is perhaps at its best here. There is also Grenache and Cinsault, Syrah and Mourvèdre. The Villages area is around the basin of the Agly, on slaty hills, and the best communes are Estagel, Maury, Cases-de-Pène, Rasiguères, Montner, Caramany, and Latour-de-France. The red wines have great impact on the palate, but are at their most giving when they are young. Amongst the whites, there is Vin Vert, from early picked grapes, and consequently lively with good acidity, but, on the other hand, 'green' and a bit empty. Collioure is mostly made of Grenache Noir.

Banyuls, Rivesaltes and Maury: Banyuls, Rivesaltes and Maury are *appellations* enormously appreciated in France, but hardly known on the export markets. They are Vins Doux Naturels and Vins de Liqueur, red, white, rosé and *rancio* – that peculiar taste that comes with age and maderization. The main grape varieties that make them are the same – Muscat, Grenache, both Noir and Rouge, Maccabéo and Malvoisie. In Banyuls-Grand-Cru, the Grenache must be 75 per cent. There is also Muscat de Rivesaltes, made only from the Muscat.

Where to find good wine in such a sea of liquid? Four *départements* – Gard, Hérault, Aude and Pyrénées Orientales – make up the region known as Languedoc-Roussillon, where 450,000 hectares are devoted to wine-growing. This represents 35 per cent of the entire wine-growing regions of France and 5 per cent of the total wine-growing area of the whole world. Total annual production in Languedoc-Roussillon (*appellation*, VDQS, Vins de Pays and Vins de Table) is between 25 and 30 million hectolitres, of which Corbières produces about 650,000 hectolitres, Minervois 240,000, and Côtes-du-Roussillon and Côtes-du-Roussillon-Villages about the same on average.

The area is dominated by the cooperatives, which produce and market 55 to 65 per cent of the entire wine output. Cooperatives and smaller producers of the region have also joined together to form about twenty marketing organizations. This cooperation is absolutely necessary in a region where there are as many as 80,000 wine growers – of these, 60 per cent cultivate less than five hectares and 25 per cent over fifty hectares. The cooperatives handle a great range of wines, *appellation*, VDQS and Vins de Pays, with top *cuvées* for those willing to pay a bit more. They, and a few of the top *négociants* of the area, also market some of the best domains, keeping them separate and maintaining their identity. The *négociants*, of course, use the cooperatives as sources of supply.

The huge French firm of Nicolas was one of the first into Languedoc-Roussillon, and worked with oenologists to bring up the quality. Château Les Palais (Corbières) and Faugères are good examples of Nicolas' ability to select. Jean Demolombe is a Narbonne *négociant* with a great deal of talent for searching out the best. He is also responsible for Château Les Palais, Château de Pech-Redon (La Clape), Domaine de Rivière-le-Haut (La Clape), and the Sélections l'Epervier. Chantovent also makes good selections throughout the region – their Minervois is always good value. Paul Rouanet at Béziers makes honourable selections, especially of St-Chinian. Various SICA (or agricultural collectives) do careful work – the SICA du Val d'Orbieu is one. The firm of Jeanjean at St-Félix-de-Lodez makes good selections of Corbières and Coteaux-du-Languedoc, much sold in the better French supermarkets. The Vignerons Catalans at Perpignan have done a very great deal to raise the level of the Roussillon wines, and export with gusto. They also have good *cuvées de propriétaires*. The cooperative at Baixas pursues a policy of quality, as does that of Tautavel, both producing Côtes-du-Roussillon-Villages. In Corbières, the Cave Coopérative Agricole des Viticulteurs at Paziols produces extremely modest-priced wines of good quality. Other reputed domains are Domaine de Fontsainte at Boutenac, Chateau Le Bouis at Gruissan, the Domaine de Villemajou, St-André-de-Roquelongue, and the Domaine de l'Ancien Prieuré de St-Amans, at Bizanet. Foncalieu at Carcassonne produce very good Corbières from different properties as well as delicious Vins de Pays de l'Aude. At Minervois, there is the Château de Villerambert-Julien at Caunes-Minervois, the cooperative at the same place, the Château de Blomac near Capendu, the Domaine Ste-Eulalie at La Livinière, and the cooperative at Trausse-Minervois.

Amongst the mass of producers in the Coteaux-du-Languedoc, time must be spent at Faugères and St-Chinian. At Faugères, the Cave Coopérative Les Vignerons Réunis pursues a path of real quality, and any wine from the Vidal family at La Liquière, Cabrerolles, is worth hunting down. At St-Chinian, the Domaine des Jouglas at Prades-sur-Vernazobres, the Château Coujan at Murviel, and the co-operatives at Roquebrun and Berlou are all excellent producers of wine.

SOUTH-WEST FRANCE

South-west France in the 1980s is one of the best hunting grounds for wines that give interest and pleasure for an acceptable sum. Some of the wines are almost satellites of Bordeaux, using the same grape varieties and following the same styles, but others, further away, have a character and individuality all of their own. The wines must keep standards high because, with Bordeaux and its huge diversity of properties and prices on the doorstep, comparisons are inevitable when looking at value.

Côtes du Marmandais: Coming out of Bordeaux through Sauternes/Barsac and into the Lot-et-Garonne, the first wine area reached is that of the Côtes du Marmandais, right at the top of the VDQS ladder. Production is dominated by two good coopera-tives, of which the one at Cocumont is a model of intelligent organization and careful vinification. The *encépagement* is now mostly of Bordeaux varieties, Cabernet, Merlot and a bit of Malbec, with the vestiges of a few, old local varieties. Production is nearly all of red wines, soft and fruity, delicious when two to three years old, but the rosé and tiny amount of white (basically Sauvignon/Sémillon) are now also delicious.

Côtes-de-Buzet: South-east of the Côtes du Marmandais lies the *appellation* area of Côtes-de-Buzet, dominated by the cooperative called Les Vignerons Réunis des Côtes-de-Buzet. The reds, made from Cabernet Sauvignon, Cabernet Franc and Merlot, are aged in oak and can take a few years of age in bottle – but not too much, otherwise they tend to dry out. At two to three years the fruit is delicious, and the top wine of the cooperative is the excellent Cuvée Napoléon. The rosé and white wines are bottled four to five months after the vintage. Mechanical harvesting is now greatly used in the area. Another excellent source of Côtes-de-Buzet has emerged in the completely replanted Château de Padère at Ambrus.

The Bergerac Appellations: Round the county market town of Bergerac, there are a cluster of *appellations*: Bergerac and Côtes-de-Bergerac (reds, rosés and whites, both dry and sweet); Pécharmant (reds); Monbazillac (sweet white wine); Côtes de Saussignac (sweet white); and Côtes de Montravel, Haut-Montravel and Montravel, all white and varying from dry to sweet. The *appellation* Rosette for sweet white wines has virtually disappeared.

　　Bergerac Rouge and Côtes-de-Bergerac Rouge are made of a combination of the two Cabernets, Merlot and Malbec, with the latter diminishing in many properties. The wines can be fresh, fruity and 'sappy', often reminiscent of right-bank Bordeaux wines. Côtes-de-Bergerac must have one per cent more minimum alcohol level than Bergerac. As much of the area has been changing from unfashionable sweet whites to red, some of the vines are young, so the wines should not be kept too long. Vintages are much the same as the St Emilion area. Bergerac-Sec is made principally from Sauvignon, Sémillon and Muscadelle with Sauvignon tending to predominate – however, it should not take over, as the mixture gives a more complex wine which, when vinified in a modern way, is quite delicious and good value. Côtes-de-Bergerac *moelleux* is made from the same grape varieties, as are Côtes-de-Saussignac white wines. Monbazillac is made from the same trio of grapes. Un-fortunately, the name became tainted with some of the over-sulphured examples sold in bulk to *négociants* for conversion to loftier *appellations*, but those producers who have persevered through the 'bad times' are making a real effort to make their wine correctly, and when this is done, Monbazillac can be a luscious wine of fragrance and peachy charm, drunk relatively young when chilled as an apéritif, or given the years of ageing it deserves and drunk more seriously with fine fruit or Roquefort cheese.

The Cave Coopérative de Monbazillac manages the Château de Monbazillac; their wines can last beautifully. Other good wines are made at the Château Lades-vignes, the Château Treuil-de-Nailhac, the Château Thieulet and Vieux Vignobles de Repaire. An Englishman, Nick Ryman, at the Château de la Jaubertie at Colombier, has an array of stainless-steel *cuves* and vintages mechanically. His Bergerac *blanc sec* is delicate and classy, with a fine bouquet, and his reds, made predominantly of Merlot and Cabernet Sauvignon, will improve as the age of his vines increases. The Château Court-les-Mûts at Razac-de-Saussignac is owned by oenologist M. Sadoux, who has very good red Côtes-de-Bergerac, Bergerac *blanc sec* and Côtes-de-Saussignac *moelleux*. Further good producers of Bergerac wines are the Château de Fayolle at Saussignac, always impressive, the Domaine Constant at Lamonzie-St-Martin, Maxime Prouillac at St-Laurent-des-Vignes, the Domaine de Bouffevent in Lamonzie-St-Martin, Château le Caillou at Rouffignac, and the Château La Rayre at Colombier. Two châteaux producing Bergerac *blanc sec* are Panisseau and la Reynaudie. Panisseau has great finesse and a long and successful record of exporting. Pécharmant can produce the finest red wines on its chalky plateau to the north-east of Bergerac. The best are made at the Domaine du Haut-Pécharmant, the Château de Tiregand, owned by the Comtesse de St-Exupéry at Creysse, who also has the Clos de la Montalbanie, and the Domaine du Grand-Jaure. I have also had good Pécharmant from Paul Pomar, and from the SICA Producta at St-Laurent-des-Vignes. The Montravel wines (Côtes-de-Montravel and Haut-Montravel just require a higher alcohol level) are made from the Sauvignon, Sémillon and Muscadelle, and the best are crisp and dry and very good value indeed. Good examples come from the cooperative and through the Bordeaux *négociant*, Louis Dubroca (Rineau Wines).

Côtes de Duras: The Côtes de Duras *appellation* is to the south of Bergerac, making red and white wines which are very similar to their neighbours'. The whites are predominantly Sauvignon, and are at their best when very young. The cooperative is important. The Côtes de Duras Sauvignon from the Cave de Berticot is recommended.

Cahors: Cahors is an important *appellation* (created in 1971), now finding its feet again after a period when it did not quite know where it was going. In the days when it was the real 'black' wine of Cahors (reputedly, due to heating of the must), it went to 'fortify' weaker cousins in Bordeaux. When this ceased, and people were said to appreciate lighter wines, there were many Cahors made that lacked character and regional definition. Now, there are a number of producers who make wines of real interest and, in good years they have the ability to age. The frost of 1956, which so affected St Emilion and Pomerol, did grave damage here too, but it did give the chance to those searching for real quality to rethink the *encépagement* of their vineyards. The ideal is thought to be 70 per cent Auxerrois Rouge (the Malbec, Côt, or Pressac, as it is known in St Emilion), 15 per cent Tannat and 15 per cent Merlot. The Syrah is also allowed in small proportion. The high proportion of Malbec was one of the reasons why the vineyard was so difficult to reconstruct after the devastation of phylloxera – the new root stocks did not suit the grape variety and aggravated its tendency to develop *coulure*, or poor development after flowering. Hybrids were planted in their place, and it took only the most persistent growers to insist on replacement with 'noble' varieties. Now this is established, and the vines are on suitable root stocks, pruned on the Guyot method, whereas it used to be *gobelet*.

Over half the *appellation* wine is sold through the cooperative Les Côtes d'Olt at Parnac, which has done so much to revive the region. The Caves, which buy in grapes, are very well equipped, with wooden vats of eighty hectolitres and *barriques* of 600 litres. It is a region of 'polyculture', and the thorough management of the cooperative enables the growers to combine grape growing with tobacco and fruit production. The cooperative's wines are always reliable (much more so than *négoce* wines of the area), and some of its top *cuvées*, such as the non-vintage Vieille Réserve, or the vintaged Cahors Comte André de Monpezat, are very good indeed. Les Côtes d'Olt also produce the Vin de Pays, Coteaux du Quercy. Good domains include: the Château de Cayrou of M. Jean Jouffreau at Puy l'Evêque – he also has the excellent Clos de Gamot; the Clos Triguedina of M. Baldès also at Puy-l'Evêque; the wines of the Gayraud family at Soturac and the Burc family at Leygues; Domaine de Pailhas; the wines of the Pontié family at Gamot, Prayssac; and Clos La Coutale and Domaine du Cèdre at Vire, Puy-l'Evêque. The Château de Haute-Serre of M. Vigourroux is on the light side, but his vines are ageing and depth will come.

Côtes du Frontonnais: North of Toulouse, there is the relatively unknown (except to the Toulousains) new *appellation*, Côtes du Frontonnais, mostly making red wine, predominantly from the local grape variety Négrette, with some Cabernet and Syrah. The cooperative at Villaudric is very well run, and good domains include the Château Bellevue-La Forêt, which is run with the greatest technical efficiency and which can only improve as the vines age, the Domaine de la Colombière, the Domaine de Bel-Air and Ferran. The Coopérative de Lavilledieu at La Ville-Dieu-du-Temple makes the very respectable VDQS Vin de Lavilledieu.

Gaillac: Gaillac, almost next door, is proving a source of reasonably-priced wine, perhaps lacking real definition, but very pleasant to drink. The traditional grape variety for white wines is the Mauzac, which has plenty of bouquet and taste but lacks acidity. Blending with Sauvignon also adds acidity, and there is also a local grape variety, L'En de L'El. There is another oddity in the Ondenc, but also the more familiar Sémillon and Muscadelle. The Mauzac is, however, ideally suited to making sweet white wines, whether sparkling or not, but these are more difficult to sell at the beginning of the 1980s. The reds are made from the Gamay (used by those who want to make lighter wines), combined in greater or lesser proportions with the Syrah, the Braucol and the Duras, local varieties both, with sometimes some Merlot. The vines are trained *en gobelet*.

There is a good cooperative in the area, which rejoices in one of the longest names yet conceived for one of these worthy institutions: Cave Coopérative de Vinification des Côteaux de Gaillac et du Pays Cordais – you can find it at Labastide-de-Lévis. They have a good range of wines, including the Sec Perlé, which obtains its slight prickle from being left on the lees after the malolactic fermentation. They also have a Gaillac Crémant which, for the moment, they can sell only in the European markets, not in France until it is passed by the INAO, and a Mousseux. This last can be made by the Champagne method or the *méthode gaillaçoise*, or *méthode rurale*, which is similar to the method employed for Clairette de Die. The Cave also has good Vins de Pays des Côtes du Tarn vinified at the Cave de Cunac – the red is made by the *macération carbonique* method and is quite delicious. The Côtes du Tarn Blanc is very fresh, like spring water. Good domains are: Domaine de Labarthe, Domaine Très-Cantoux, Château de Rhodes, Château Larroze. There is another good cooperative, the Cave Coopérative de Técou.

Madiran: Madiran is a really 'serious' *appellation* for lovers of red wine. The local Tannat grape predominates (usually about 60 per cent), and the name gives the, correct, impression of tannin. This is mixed with Cabernet of both types (the Cabernet Franc is here called the Bouchy), but if it is too pervasive, the wine loses its real Madiran character. There is another local variety called the Pinenc or Couhabort. When the producer adheres to the traditional proportion of Tannat in his wine, Madiran keeps superbly, its deep purple colour of youth and tannin developing richness and great diversity of flavour. About 600 hectares are under vine.

Pacherenc-du-Vic-Bilh: The white *appellation* wines of Pacherenc–du–Vic–Bilh are only seen locally. They are made from the Ruffiat, the Gros and Petit Manseng, the Courbu, Sémillon and Sauvignon. It has no finesse, but is usually dry, with good acidity, and pleasant 'on the spot'.

The Coopérative Vinicole du Vic-Bilh-Madiran at Crouseilles produces a marvellous Madiran Rôt du Roy, which has complexity, backbone and generosity. This is their *tête de cuvée*; their straight Madiran is good, but does not last as well as the Rôt du Roy. They also have good *appellation* Béarn Rouge and Rosé, and a rare Pacherenc *moelleux*. The cooperative at Bellocq also specializes in Béarn wines.

Good domains are the Château de Peyros, Domaine Barréjat, Domaine Lalanne, Domaine Labranche-Laffont, and the Vignobles Laplace, which make more 'Bordeaux-style' wines, but good, and also Pacherenc of quality. There is also the Union de Producteurs Plaimont at Riscle which has, apart from Madiran, the Vin de Pays, Côtes de St-Mont, a robust red.

Jurançon: Jurançon is a white wine 'with a past', at least as far as Henri IV is concerned. There are about 500 hectares under vine, to the south of Pau. The wines are made dry or *moelleux*, from a battery of strange grapes – the Gros Manseng (generous yielding, and good for the *sec*), Petit Manseng, Courbu, Camaralet and Lauzet – the first three are the most important, with the Petit Manseng largely responsible for the special character of the classic Jurançon *moelleux* wines. It yields little and has a rich, aromatic flavour. The climate is influenced by the Pyrenees and the ocean, and the harvest for these great *moelleux* wines begins about 15 October, when it is usually warm and sunny. However, the vintage may not end until end November-beginning December, after the first falls of snow on the Pyrenees and the first frosts. The combined effect of sun in the day and freezing at night leads to a concentration of the grape pulp which gives musts of a richness up to potential alcohol of 16–18 per cent. Thus, the grape is concentrated on the vine – described as *passerillage*. Pickers go through the vineyard several times, to ensure picking each bunch at the right moment. When the beginning of the winter is mild, with the south wind from Spain during the end of the vintage towards the end of November, there is also *pourriture noble*, as well as the *passerillage*. Fermentations are at a cold temperature and they stop of their own accord when the alcohol reaches 13 per cent. It can be seen why total production of these wines is about 7,000 hectolitres annually, while Jurançon *sec* produces about 20,000 hectolitres. When climatic conditions are not favourable, only a small amount of the *moelleux* can be made from those small plots of Petit Manseng which undergo this process; the rest makes Jurançon *sec*, which is floral and full. The taste and aromas of these wines have been compared to acacia flowers, honey and grilled hazelnuts, apparently bestowed by the relationship of mineral and organic acids with the sugar. Although attractive when young, these wines age beautifully, becoming the colour of amber and taking on a bouquet of cinnamon, guavas and nutmeg, depending on the exact origin of the wine. Two excellent sources of Jurançon *moelleux* are M. Chigé at La Chapelle-de-Rousse, with his Cru Lamouroux, and M. Alfred Barrère at Lahourcade with his Clos Cancaillaü. The Clos Uroulat is also recommended. A good Jurançon *sec* is the Clos de la Vierge from the Cave Brana. The Coopérative Vinicole de Gan-Jurançon has a good range of wines, going up to the greatest.

SAVOIE AND BUGEY

The wines of the mountains of Savoie always seem delicious and tempting, perhaps because one is often drinking them after a hard day's skiing, which is hardly fair on other viticultural regions. But the wines do bear vinous exploration, even if in less-favoured years they illustrate the difficulties of growing vines in a mountain climate. 80 per cent of the wines of Savoie are white, with some light red and rosé, and sparkling and *pétillant* wine. Although the wines of Savoie have risen to *appellation* status, it is worth considering at the same time their VDQS neighbours, the wines of Bugey to the west nearer Lyon, because they are very similar and are certainly not inferior to their more elevated, in all senses of the word, cousins in the mountains. The *appellations* and grape varieties in Savoie and Bugey are extremely, and unnecessarily complicated. Overall, there is the *appellation* Vin de Savoie for red, white and rosé wines, which covers a mass of communes, fifteen of which can add their name to the title Vin de Savoie on the label. There are also three white wine *appellations*, Seyssel, Crépy and Roussette-de-Savoie.

The great danger in Savoie wines is acidity, as when the ripening conditions are not sufficient, the reds are thin and the whites horribly acid. The Jacquère white grape variety is the most commonly planted in Savoie, with acidity and not much alcohol, often bottled from the lees, giving it a *perlant* character – it should be drunk in the year after its birth. It is mostly grown between Aix-les-Bains and Montmélian. The Altesse, or the Roussette, is by far the best grape variety in this terrain, giving wines of character and great flavour. The Gringet is of the Savagnin or Traminer family, the Mondeuse, white and red, is very local, the Chasselas is well-known over the Swiss border where it makes Fendant, and the Roussanne is a high-class refugee from the northern Rhône. The Molette is a local variety used in sparkling wines, and the Cacaboué is reputed to come from St-Péray, but its presence is almost academic now. Among the red varieties, the character of the Gamay and the Pinot Noir is well-known, while the Persan is very rare and has a hint of Pinot Noir about it.

The best wines are considered to be Vins de Savoie from Abymes and Apremont, the rare Chignin-Bergeron made from the Roussanne, the Roussette-de-Savoie, with village name, made from the grape of the same name (the Altesse) and the Roussette-du-Bugey with village name, both medium dry – if it is just Roussette-du-Bugey *tout court*, it can be made purely of Chardonnay. Crépy, made between Thonon and Geneva, can have a touch of bubble about it and, if not too acid, be very refreshing. Seyssel from the Roussette, can aspire to complexity.

Good wines are produced by: the Domaine des Granges Longes at St André-les Marches, Montmélian (Abymes); Yves Ollivier at Chambéry (Abymes and Apremont); Jean Masson and M. Simiand at Apremont; the Coopérative Le Vigneron Savoyard at Apremont; Jean Perrier at St-André-les Marches (Apremont) and Pierre Boniface at Montmélian (Apremont). The Quénard family at Torméry, Montmélian, have Chignin-Bergeron and others, the Château-Monterminod at St-Alban-Leysse has Roussette and Mondeuse, while François Vial in the same village has Vin-de-Savoie Persan. Good Bugey producers are Eugène Monin at Vongnes, Camille Crussy at Flaxieu, and Jean Peillot also makes good Roussette-du-Bugey Montagnieu. Goy at Ballaison has good Crépy. The Château de Ripaille, overlooking Lake Geneva, makes good Vin de Savoie from the Chasselas. Wines that come from the *négociant* houses of Donati, Maison Mollex, or through M. Claude Marandon, a broker who specializes in the wines of Savoie, will be good. Mercier at Douvaine has Crépy, as well as Fichard at Chens-sur-Léman.

The sparkling wines of Savoie and Bugey are mostly drunk locally, as production cannot satisfy export demand. The famous Varichon & Clerc sparkling wine is now just Champagne-method Mousseux Blanc de Blancs, when it started as Seyssel. Seyssel-Mousseux must have their second fermentation in bottle, Champagne-method. Sparkling Cerdon from Bugey must be made by the Champagne-method or the *rural* method to have the VDQS title. However, there is a great deal of artificially carbonated wine in the area, mostly drunk in Lyon.

JURA

This beautiful mountain region near the French/Swiss border was particularly devastated by the phylloxera, and reconstruction was hard work because of the slopes and the difficulty of attracting labour. Although one does not want all wines to taste alike, the original character of the local grape varieties, which are much used, does not attract everyone. The red Ploussard, or Poulsard, lightly tinted rosé, can give fruity, delicate light reds or rosés, but it can also be acid and thin. The red Trousseau has more colour and body, and both these are usually mixed with the Gros Noirien, which is the local name covering Pinot Noir or Pinot Gris. The white wines are dominated by the Savagnin (or Naturé, or Traminer of Alsace), mixed with the Melon d'Arbois (or Chardonnay) and the Pinot Blanc. About 600 hectares are under vine.

Côtes-du-Jura is the overall *appellation*, and covers the red, rosé or *gris*, white, yellow wines, as well as *vins de paille* and sparkling wines by the Champagne method. The *appellation* Arbois covers the same categories, while the *appellation* L'Etoile omits red and rosé, and the *appellation* Château-Chalon must be made from the Savagnin alone; this last is the archetypal *vin jaune*. The soil is basically chalky, the vineyards are high, and the climate very continental, with severe winters. The heart of the region is between Lons-le-Saunier and Arbois. As in Alsace, there is often little distinction between red and rosé; the name on the label is more the personal decision of the wine-maker than anything else. There are the wines from around Arlay-Voiteur, quite light and supple, but with more body when occasionally made with 100 per cent Pinot Noir, and those from Arbois made from the Ploussard which mix a certain fruity delicacy with tannin. But when the wines are just light, with drying tannin, they lack charm. The reds from the Trousseau can be almost Burgundian in character. Both reds and rosés can be acid if there is not enough sun. The whites can be made almost entirely of Chardonnay, when they taste nicer when young, or almost entirely of Savagnin, when they need ageing – the best of both can have a complex flavour.

Vin jaune is a very special category of wine, and the slightly maderized taste will appeal to Sherry lovers. It is made with the Savagnin grape grown on marly soil and picked very late, fermented slowly over several months, and then left in old oak casks for a minimum of six years. There is no topping up, and a film of *flor*, the yeast cells found in fino Sherries in Spain, protects the wine from the worst aspects of oxidation, while imparting its own special taste. *Vins jaunes* are bottled in the 65-centilitre *clavelins*. They can be kept for years, and have a curious taste which combines a honey-like flavour with dryness, and a *goût de terroir* common to all the white wines of the region, but exaggerated in *vins jaunes*. The finish can resemble walnuts. The esterization of these wines can be of real interest, although perhaps an acquired taste. *Vin de paille* obtains its name from the fact that the red and white grapes are dried on straw mats to increase the sugar content, but now also by hanging up the bunches in a dry, well-ventilated attic or room. This process must last a minimum of two months, before the grapes are vinified with extremely long fermentations, and three to four years in cask. These are dessert wines of complexity and class, with the special taste of the area. *Vins jaunes* and *vins de paille* are both, necessarily, expensive.

After Pasteur, Henri Maire is the best-known *fils d'Arbois*. This huge commercial enterprise also comprises important domain holdings in the Jura, and examples of all types of wine. The Rolet family at Montigny-les-Arsures also produce very good wines of all types, as do Roger Lornet, Lucien Aviet and Jacques Puffeney in the same village. Other good producers are the Château d'Arlay, Marius Perron at Voiteur (especially for Château-Chalon), the Château de la Muyre at Domblans for its Château-Chalon, as well as Jean Bourdy at Arlay. The Caveau des Byards at Voiteur is a good source of supply for most types of wine, as is the prettily named Fruitière Vinicole d'Arbois, while Joseph Vandelle at L'Etoile makes good Etoile Blanc and *vin jaune*.

The Wines of Germany

IAN JAMIESON MW

Ian Jamieson MW has worked in the wine trade for the past twenty years; since 1961 he has been with Deinhard and Company Limited of London, specializing in the buying of German wines. He is a past chairman of the Master of Wine Education Committee and a trustee of the Wine and Spirit Education Trust. He also contributes magazine articles on German wines.

'Age cannot wither her, nor custom stale her infinite variety.' If this is true of a woman, it is also true of wine, and certainly of German wine. Its individuality and character are greatly valued, even if a product based on a more predictable crop than grapes grown in a northern climate might reduce the uncertainties for those who do business with it. Germany, however, with its unreliable climate, has the possibility in a good year to produce white wines of a quality quite unlike those made elsewhere in the world. After an indifferent or inferior summer, the skills of the vine-grower and vintner today are such that when used to their utmost, the disastrous vintages of the past no longer occur. The improvements in wine-making and vine-growing during the last thirty-five years have won an increasing appreciation for German wine, and how and why this is I have attempted to show in the sections that follow. To many, wine is rather more than just another drink, but its continued production depends, of course, on hard commercial and economic suppositions. Fortunately for the consumer, Germans are convinced that the future of their wine industry and their own best interests depend on an emphasis on quality. The intention is to continue to improve the standard of the cheaper wines, whilst maintaining that of the finer. A glance at wine-trade history will show that German wine has changed much over the years, and often practices that we assume to be long established are, in fact, of relatively recent origin. Whatever happens in the future, real quality will always begin in the vineyard, and therefore it is with the vine that the German chapter of *Wines of the World* must also start.

The main factors affecting the style of wine are the climate, the soil, the type of vine grown, the cellar technique, to which can also nowadays be added the taste and preference of the consumer. There is not a great deal that can be done about the climate. The soil may be improved and enriched but it is the grower's privilege to choose what vine he will grow from a considerable list of possibilities available to him. That said, it must be added that the choice is restricted, by EEC Regulation 816/ 70, which created the following categories for German vines: (a) Recommended (b) Authorized (c) Temporarily authorized. However, there are exceptions allowed to the rule, in certain circumstances, for what are called 'new crossings'.

Apart from the limitations of choice imposed on the grower by law, there are, naturally, strong commercial and technical considerations that must be borne in mind when a vine type is selected. The statistics for 1977 given below show that, though the choice might be wide, there was considerable unanimity amongst growers as to what type of vines was to form the backbone of their vineyards.

White wine varieties	In hectares	% of total area
Müller-Thurgau	24,705	30.8
Riesling	18,308	22.9
Silvaner	12,684	15.8
Kerner	3,374	4.2
Ruländer	3,322	4.2
Scheurebe	2,941	3.7
Morio-Muskat	2,821	3.5
Other white wine varieties	11,998	14.9
Total	80,153	100.0

The varieties of vine named above obviously meet certain requirements that the growers must have, and in order to find out what these requirements might be, it is worth considering the performance of the individual vines in some detail.

Müller-Thurgau

This vine dates from 1882, and was produced at the Viticultural School at Geisenheim by Professor Dr H. Müller from the canton of Thurgau in Switzerland. Originally, it was thought to be a crossing between Riesling as the mother, and Silvaner as the father, but that has been disputed by various authorities in recent years. However, the point is mainly of academic interest, as the success and value of the Müller-Thurgau vine is widely recognized. It may be found growing in Czechoslovakia, Austria, Hungary, Luxembourg, East Germany, amongst other countries, but nowhere in such profusion as in West Germany. Its success has not always been so great. In the 1930s many of the more conservative members of the wine trade in Germany felt that it represented a threat to the true, traditional character of German wine, and attempts were made to prevent its further plantation. For many years its wine was sold without the grape type being mentioned on the label, or in wine lists. Recently this has changed, and it may now be found, particularly in the south of the Palatinate, being sold rather in the manner of Alsatian wines, simply under the name Müller-Thurgau, without any close geographical description. The following chart clearly shows the development of the distribution of the Müller-Thurgau vine since 1954 in West Germany.

	Müller-Thurgau	Riesling	Silvaner
1954			
Hectares	4,647	15,546	22,406
% of total area under vine	8	26	38
1964			
Hectares	14,702	17,701	18,992
% of total area under vine	21	26	28
1977			
Hectares	24,705	18,308	12,684
% of total area under vine	27	20	14

The Müller-Thurgau needs a deep soil, rich in humus, that retains humidity well if it is to give of its best. It is, in this respect, more demanding than the Riesling, but it is more resistant than the Silvaner to chlorosis (a vine disease often caused by an excess of calcium in the soil). The wood does not ripen particularly well, and therefore, after two or three winter days with temperatures of less than −15°C, damage to the eyes of the vine is likely to occur. On the other hand, it holds its fruit well in the early summer, and can produce good quality wine with a yield per hectare of up to 130 hectolitres. (A maximum yield commensurate with good quality for the Riesling vine would be about 110 hectolitres per hectare.) The Müller-Thurgau may also have its grapes left on the vine until well into October, to develop extra sugar which, it is hoped, will produce a superior wine. When this is done, the grower must be careful that the level of acidity in the grape does not drop too low, otherwise the wine it makes will be flat and lifeless. The young wine itself is likely, as well, to lose a lot of its acidity, with incorrect vinification, through the action of bacteria. To avoid this happening, it must be removed from the yeast immediately after the first fermentation is complete. It is also necessary to guard against the tendency of Müller-Thurgau wines to oxidize, which would result in an unwanted darkening of the colour, and damage to the bouquet, or 'nose', as the wine trade likes to call it. However, to ensure these faults do not occur is part of the German wine-makers' science and craft in which they are consistently so successful.

Riesling

'From the juice of its grapes, stems our noblest wine,' writes Walter Hillebrand in his *Taschenbuch der Rebsorten*, and nobody would dispute this. It is upon the Riesling grape that the reputation of German wine has been built. The chief characteristic of the wine is not a high alcoholic content, but its fine fruity acidity and elegance. (The first syllable of 'Riesling' should be pronounced so as to rhyme with 'geese', rather than 'rice'.)

The success of the German Riesling has meant that its name has sometimes been misappropriated, particularly in the United States, Canada, Australia, and South Africa. It has been given to other vines, which may be admirable in themselves, but are not the same as the Riesling vine found in West Germany and cannot be compared with it. There is also a variety of 'Riesling' found principally in Eastern Europe, correctly known as the Welsch, or Wälsch Riesling, which some experts believe originated in France. It produces fruity, good wines, that lack the character or elegance of the German Riesling.

The true Riesling has been grown in Germany certainly since the fifteenth century. One of the reasons that it has stayed the course so well is no doubt connected with its ability to withstand the cold German winters. This was made clear yet again in the winter of 1978-79, when frost damage to non-Riesling vines on the Moselle was very serious, while the Riesling showed that it could survive temperatures well below freezing point. (At −20°, or even −25°C, the Riesling can escape serious damage, if its wood has ripened well the previous season, which is often the case.) In spite of its strong survival instinct, the Riesling does require a good south-west-, or south-facing site, and, therefore, in less favoured vineyards it has been replaced by the Müller-Thurgau. It is not at all demanding about the type of soil in which it should be grown, and can live productively in the driest of German soils.

One of the principal characteristics of the Riesling is the fact that it ripens so late, not being gathered until the end of October, well into November, and sometimes still in December. This brings with it the risk of unripe grapes being attacked by early frosts, which can produce a bitter flavour in the wine that is made from them. From ripened, frozen grapes, *Eiswein* can be made (see page 172).

Silvaner

In the last century, the Silvaner ousted the Elbling from a large part of the Rhineland. Now, it is the turn of the Silvaner to make way for the Müller-Thurgau, as was shown by the statistics on page 151. The origin of the Silvaner is obscure, to say the least, and different authorities seem to have different opinions about it. It has been known in Germany since the eighteenth century and, up to a few years ago, was Germany's most widely grown vine. Like the Müller-Thurgau, it is found throughout Eastern Europe, but Germany still has the largest area in the world under the Silvaner vine.

Its requirements, and performance in the vineyard, lie halfway between that of the Riesling and the Müller-Thurgau. It cannot be grown successfully on a site where ripening is likely to be delayed. Whilst the Riesling wine can tolerate a high acidity, that can be reduced by de-acidification, such treatment to a Silvaner apparently leaves it with a 'green' and unripe flavour. A very dry soil also does not suit the Silvaner, for at the first signs of a shortage of water, the lower leaves on the vine start to turn yellow. Severe winter frosts, which the Riesling will survive, can totally destroy the Silvaner and, therefore, the micro-climate has to be examined very carefully before a site for its plantation is selected. Much work has been carried out this century at the viticultural school at Alzey in the Rheinhessen on improving the quality of the Silvaner vine, by selection of the best clones. As a result, the Silvaner today produces a high yield, although not as much as that of the Müller-Thurgau.

The Silvaner can show real quality, but ultimately lacks the elegance of the Riesling. However, in areas such as the vineyards on the slopes facing the Rhine at Nierstein and Oppenheim, the style of the Silvaner, combined with the character that comes from the soil, can produce wines of a very considerable distinction.

As I have indicated earlier, the Müller-Thurgau, the Riesling and the Silvaner vines cover just under 70 per cent of the total vineyard area, and I have mentioned some of their merits, and disadvantages. It is in consideration of these characteristics, that the viticultural institutes at Geisenheim, Weinsberg, Würzburg, Alzey, Freiburg and Geilweilerhof in the Palatinate, are heavily engaged in producing new crossings of European vines, to which I shall return later. In the meantime, there remain four more vines worthy of individual attention.

Kerner

This vine is a crossing of Trollinger and Riesling, from Weinsberg in south Germany. Vines are notorious for the number of synonyms from which they suffer. This is not just simply a matter of each country having its own name for a vine, but even within the frontiers of one state, many alternative names may be found for the same vine. Trollinger, which is said to be a corruption of Tirolinger (the vine originates in the South Tirol), is referred to in the United Kingdom as the Black Hamburg. The famous old vine at Hampton Court, near London, is known by this name.

The wine trade in Germany has great faith in Kerner, which explains why from 5 hectares in 1964, the vineyard area it occupied had grown by 1977 to 3,374 hectares. It is happiest in the type of vineyard site suitable for the Silvaner, and prospers on all types of soil. It is as resistant to winter and spring frost as the Riesling. However, it must be said, no vine can be expected to escape unscathed from bad frosts late in the spring, which fortunately do not occur often.

In flavour and bouquet, the wine is not unlike the Riesling, which is much in its favour. The yield is normally 10 to 15 per cent greater than that of the Riesling, whilst the leaves have the ability to remain green long into the autumn, and so continue to play their part in assimilation. The harvest can be delayed almost as long as that of the Riesling. What is also of great significance is that the must weight of the Kerner is 10–15 degrees greater than that of the Riesling, grown in similar conditions. Must weight, its vinous and commercial importance, and how it is measured, I shall discuss when writing of new crossings.

Ruländer

The Ruländer, named, so it is said, after an eighteenth-century merchant from Speyer, who promoted its plantation, is one of the great Burgundian Pinot family. It is known in France as the Pinot Gris, amongst other names, and in Italy as the Pinot Grigio. Clonal selection has much improved the quality of the vine in recent years, and its plantation is spreading. The Ruländer needs a site with a good exposition to the sun to do well, as, if the wine is to be successful, the must weight should be considerable. Indeed, in this respect, the Ruländer is somewhat unlike most German wines, whose character depends on their fresh acidity and relatively low alcohol content. It is often a 'big' wine, broad in flavour, which is to say that it has, for a German wine, low acidity. Its colour is deep gold, and its bouquet is strong and full of interest. These characteristics are possibly emphasized by the fact that for the most part the Ruländer is grown in the Palatinate and south Germany where, in any case, the wines are fuller, and contain less acidity than those of the more northerly vineyards. The Ruländer is well suited to making fine wines from late picked (*Spätlese*) grapes, as well as sweet full dessert wines (*Auslesen*).

Scheurebe

The Scheurebe, with the Müller-Thurgau, is one of the older of the 'new crossings' that one finds in Germany. It is a crossing of Silvaner and Riesling, and dates from 1916, though its year of registration was not until 1956. Before being accepted by the registration authorities, new vines must undergo lengthy tests to prove their worth, which usually take from twenty to thirty years. No doubt the Second World War delayed registrations. The Scheurebe was known by the trade for many years as 'Sämling 88' – its original reference number as a seedling.

The Scheurebe likes a well-sited vineyard, at least as good as that in which the Silvaner would be planted. It is happy in most soils, and is very resistant to chlorosis. The Scheurebe harvest takes place shortly before that of the Riesling, but in the same vineyard conditions it will produce a must of greater weight than the Riesling by as much as 10 degrees. Even with a low must weight, the Riesling can produce a perfectly acceptable wine, given the right cellar technique, but this is not so with the Scheurebe. An unripe Scheurebe has an unpleasantly sharp acidity, and cannot be made into a good wine, so the extra must weight compared to the Riesling, and the reduction in acidity that goes with it, is very necessary.

In the United Kingdom wine trade in the late 1950s, interest in the Scheurebe was considerable. The pungent, flowering-currant type of bouquet, with the well-balanced fruit and acidity that one finds in a good and sun-blessed vintage, made it immediately appealing. Georg Scheu, the creator of the vine, has described the wine as having a *Rieslingbukett*, but frankly it is a little difficult to share this view. Interestingly enough, it seems that the richer, and more concentrated the Scheurebe wine, the less pronounced is its own special bouquet. So, if you wish to discover the bouquet for yourself, do not buy a fine dessert wine (*Auslese*, or *Beerenauslese*), but rather look for a less expensive wine, possibly of not greater than late-picked (*Spätlese*) quality. Nevertheless, fine, rich Scheurebe wines can be superb.

Morio-Muskat

Although the area of vineyard covered by the Morio-Muskat vine in West Germany is nearly as great as that of the Scheurebe, it is much less well known. Until about

1976, Morio-Muskat was used mostly for blending purposes, rather than being kept as a single vine wine, so its name did not appear very often on wine labels or lists. The Morio-Muskat, which the growers know simply as the Morio, is a crossing of Silvaner and Weisser Burgunder (Pinot Blanc) and, as in the case of so many of the new crossings, is found mainly in the Palatinate and south Germany. Like the Scheurebe, the Morio needs to be planted in a well-sited vineyard to avoid producing excessively 'green' and sharp wine. Provided the grapes have not been attacked by rot, the Morio harvest will normally be gathered a week after that of the Müller-Thurgau. In a vintage with high must weights, it will produce wine with a powerful Muskat bouquet, and a well rounded Muskat flavour.

These, then, are the vines that covered in 1977 just over 85 per cent of the area in West Germany from which white wine was made. The standard, by which all other German wines seem to be judged, if they have any pretensions to quality, has been set by the Riesling. It is probably true to say that what the breeders of new vines would like to find would be a crossing very similar to the Riesling, and yet one that would ripen, even in less favoured sites, as early as the Müller-Thurgau. If this heaven-sent vine would yield a crop as large as the Müller-Thurgau as well, then their prayers would be fully answered.

From a marketing point of view, the new crossings can present a problem. Germany is not a wine-drinking country to the same extent as countries such as France, Portugal, Italy, or even Luxembourg, in terms of consumption per head of the population. According to the official statistics, West Germany has, after a steady increase since 1955, when 8.9 litres of wine were drunk per head of the population, now settled down since 1975 to a figure of about 23 litres. (The figure for beer in 1977 was 148.7 litres.) The consumption in the south-west of Germany, is on average twice as high as that in the north, a recent publication by the 'Stabilisier-ungsfonds für Wein' tells us. All this seems to suggest that in the north of Germany the population's awareness of its country's wine is not very great. German wine names are sometimes rather lengthy and not easy to understand, although they must be amongst the most informative in the world. If, therefore, the name of a new crossing is added to what might seem an already sufficiently long wine name, confusion can result. It takes time for the consumer to get used to new grape names. As it is not obligatory that the type of grape from which the wine is made should appear on the label, it will probably be some time before some of the more obscure names will become widely known. In many instances, it is said, the lesser-known new crossings seem to have the most interest for the grower who bottles and sells his wine himself. They provide him with something different to sell, with which he can catch the imagination of his customer. They also have rarity value, as the quantity produced will most likely not be great. This, of course, is a disadvantage to the large concern with many selling outlets, for which anything, where the supply is too limited, is not worth the time spent trying to promote it.

It is important, as Professor Dr Becker has pointed out, that the range of German wine offered should not be continuously extended by an ever increasing number of new crossings. However, the whole process of developing a new crossing, to the point where its wine is ready to be sold commercially, is such a slow one, that it is most unlikely that the German wine trade will suddenly find that it has a larger choice of wine from different grapes than it really needs. By the nature of things, the less good vine gives way to the better specimen, as the years pass, and ultimately it is the consumer who decides the style of wine for the future.

When writing about the Kerner vine, I referred to the importance of must weight in establishing the quality of German wine. Must is heavier than water, and its specific gravity is measured on a scale invented by Ferdinand Oechsle, a German inventor who died in 1852. (Apart from interesting himself in the weight of must, Herr Oechsle is also credited with the creation of the first German harmonium and mouth organ, and a primitive form of cinematography.) The readings on the Oechsle scale indicate the approximate sugar content. Now it has been found that the quality of German wine should be judged more by the harmonious balance of alcohol, acidity and, in many cases, residual sugar, than simply by the alcoholic content alone. The fact remains, however, that for general purposes, the potential alcohol of the must, as represented by the sugar content, is a very good guide to the future likely quality of the wine. This thinking has been built into the wine laws of the wine-producing regions. Under EEC law, all wines produced in the Community fall into two categories – (1) table wine and (2) quality wine.

Germany further divides the second category into simple quality wine, and quality wine with distinction. In a later section, German and EEC wine law will be dealt with in greater detail. There is, nevertheless, one aspect of the legislation that is very relevant to the subject of new crossings. If a grower on the Moselle, for example, wishes to make a quality wine with the distinction *Kabinett*, from the Riesling grape, it is necessary that the must should have a minimum weight of 70° Oechsle. However, if the must comes from a new crossing, then the minimum weight should be not less than 73° Oechsle. As a new crossing may well produce a must, under normal conditions, of 10° more weight than the Riesling, it does seem that the new crossing is placed at a commercial advantage over the Riesling vine in this particular instance. Expressed in this way, the problem may be somewhat over-simplified, as quality does not rest on must weight alone. Indeed, after a certain point, an increase in must weight from a new crossing may not be an advantage at all, if it is also accompanied by too heavy a drop in the acidity, as the wine merely risks being heavy and clumsy. From the point of view of the interested consumer, new crossings, with their sometimes unusual bouquet and flavour, have a definite appeal of their own. Few people would wish to drink the same wine day after day, no matter how good the quality, so that to taste a wine from a new type of vine is always worthwhile, even if it only confirms your preferences for, or prejudices against, wines to which you are already accustomed. Anybody, who is not a professional wine taster or buyer, has a perfect right to be prejudiced, but the more open your mind, the greater will be your reward.

Unfortunately, as many wine-lovers will know, a section about the vine that deals only with the European *Vitis vinifera* is sadly incomplete. In 1863, the vine louse, *Phylloxera vastatrix*, arrived on the European mainland in the Languedoc region of France, and by 1874 it had reached Germany. With the roots and leaves of the vine being attacked, it was found that the only way to prevent the vineyards of the world from being totally destroyed was to graft the European *Vitis vinifera* on to American root stocks which were more or less resistant to phylloxera. Today, grafting is still the only remedy, and for those who would like detailed information on the subject, as it applies to West Germany, I would recommend a booklet sponsored by the German Federal Ministry of Food, Agriculture and Forestry, called *The Wine Industry in the Federal Republic of Germany*. The root stocks that may be used in West Germany are established by law, and to some extent vary from one viticultural specified region, such as the Rheingau or the Palatinate, to another. Apart from these legal limitations, the grower will consider the following factors when selecting a root stock for his vines:

1. The type of soil in the vineyard.
2. The method of training of the vine.

3. The distances between rows.
4. The yield of the European vine.

The actual grafting takes place on the bench in nurseries, rather than in the vineyard, where the climatic conditions would produce uncertain results, and too great a rate of failure of the grafts to 'take'. The whole process of the selection of the best clones is strictly controlled, even when the root stocks are grown in France or Italy. The Germans have put as much care and energy into selecting the most suitable root stocks as they have in developing the best clones for their grape-bearing vines. The maintenance of quality, and an increase in the yield, have been major targets for which the growers have aimed, with great success.

The Vineyard

Modern vine-growing must be one of the most extreme forms of monoculture. If a farmer were always to grow his cabbages in the same field, he would soon find disease rampant amongst his crop. Yet vines are not only grown year after year on the same site, but century after century, and that, in a most unnatural way. Left to nature, the vine, which is a climber, would spread in a disorderly fashion, and finding the right host, would reach the top of the highest tree. However, as we know, commercially grown vines are dragooned into rows, and by severe pruning forced into a viticultural equivalent of factory farming. The price that has to be paid for this is constant attention to the condition of the soil and the health of the vine.

In the past, before the Second World War, it was the standard practice to allow some years between the grubbing out of old vines and the planting of new. In most cases nowadays, a long period of regeneration is not economically possible, so that unless care is taken, the soil can easily become tired, and unsuited to commercial vine growing. Part of the problem lies in the fact that, other than in deserts, rocky landscapes, or areas of extremely low temperatures, nature does not wish the soil to remain uncovered. An unweeded garden may be possessed by 'things rank and gross in nature', but it will be green. In a few years, the surface of the soil will bear a layer of dead plant material, and an umbrella of shade provided by living plants. The constant bouncing of the rain on bare soil damages its structure, and turns it to mud. This is of great significance in West Germany, where over 60 per cent of the vineyards are found on slopes – many of extreme severity. Under such conditions, erosion can easily start. At the same time it is said, that the direct rays of the sun on the unprotected soil hinder the life in the soil, and can lead to a decrease in humus. To counteract such effects, growers may mulch the soil with straw, although unless it can be mixed with the top soil, it brings with it the risk of fire, particularly in steep vineyards. There is a shortage of organic fertilizer. When horse manure was readily available, it helped to maintain the structure of the soil in good order. In its absence, there is the possibility, unless care is taken, that after rain the soil will form a hard 'pan' on its surface, which will need to be broken up by machinery. This operation itself can cause the tractor to enter the vineyard once more, and compaction results, so that the cure of the disorder becomes father to the complaint. To avoid such ecological catastrophes, the grower has his soil regularly analysed, and follows a balanced manuring programme. Good vineyard husbandry is one of the main reasons why the Germans successfully produce such a high yield from their vines. Having ensured that all is well for his vines, on and below the soil, the German vine-grower has to cope with all the potential diseases and pests common to vines throughout Europe.

The aim of the grower is to produce the maximum quantity of liquid from his vines, commensurate with quality. To do so, he has available to him advice from viticultural institutes, government departments, and companies which produce and distribute spray material. This advice will relate to the spray to be used, frequency of its use, concentration of the liquid, and so on. The laws concerning the protection of the environment must be observed, as well as regulations dealing with matters such as the use of the local water supply. There is a wide range of ways in which spraying may be carried out, and the method selected depends on economic factors, the terrain, the size of the parcel of vineyard to be treated, and the number of persons available to work in the vineyard. This last point may well be, in the event, somewhat theoretical. In Germany in 1972–73, the average size of vineyard per holding actually planted under vine was only 0.84 hectares. From this it seems clear that for many, vine-growing is very much a peasant or part-time occupation. A vineyard worker sick or just absent, in some enterprises equals a big staff problem. In these circumstances, the small family-run vineyard may suffer a 50 per cent cut in its labour force, if one worker is ill. To try to rationalize this situation has been something in which the various states (*Länder*) have been actively engaged for a number of years, and which I shall discuss later. Because of the shortage of manpower, new methods of spraying vines have had to be employed, such as the use of helicopters, or by pumping the spray material through the vineyard overhead watering system, where it exists, and by high-powered mechanized spraying machines. These methods, from the point of view of the treatment of the individual vine, do not necessarily result in a better spread of the spray material than that achieved by hand spraying. However, according to figures calculated at the Viticultural School at Bad Kreuznach, spraying by hand involves 200 to 250 man hours per hectare per season, whilst a fully mechanized method of spraying reduces the time spent to 25 to 50 man hours per hectare. These figures speak for themselves.

Spraying in winter is no longer so widespread as it was, as it has been replaced, in many instances, by a first spraying at bud burst, in the spring, against various pests. The first preventative sprays against such diseases as oidium and peronospora will be carried out early in June, before the flowering towards the end of the month. The last spraying of the season will probably be against botrytis in September.

Amongst the more instantly recognizable pests of the vine are wasps, birds, hares and deer. Wasps are very difficult to control, if one is not going to destroy insect life on a wide scale. Their inroads into the very early ripening crop of the Siegerrebe vine, supported by bees as well, may reveal their appetites, but can mean a serious financial loss for the grower. Birds can be frightened into the neighbouring vineyards by percussive effects, but it is rather anti-social. It has been found that birds get accustomed to loud bangs after a while, so only human nerves suffer from the noise, and the birds remain. Hares are regarded as rather cuddly animals in Germany, but they can be the cause of the destruction of many young vines, unless the stem of the vine is adequately protected. Deer, whose population in the forests by the vineyards is very large, can also inflict damage to the wood of the vine, when they are not actually helping themselves to the grapes.

Probably the greatest enemy of the vine is frost, as it is both difficult and expensive to protect the vineyards against its effect. The massive winter frost that occurs from time to time is something against which vine-growers can do very little. If the wood of the vine has ripened well during the previous season, it will be in a better condition to withstand very low mid-winter temperatures than would otherwise be the case. However, it is the much less severe spring frost that the growers fear the most, for the devastation it can cause when the sap has started to rise in the vine and the buds have begun to swell, is very great. In the twelfth century, it used to be the custom to drive flocks of sheep through the vineyards when a spring frost seemed imminent. The movement of the animals would stir the atmosphere, so that the cool layer of air lying just above the surface of the ground would be mixed with the warmer air above. Presumably also, the warmth of the bodies of the sheep would contribute a small measure of protection. Nowadays, whatever is done to overcome frost damage must be related to cost, and should possibly be best regarded as a form of insurance. To avoid cold air building up, trees or shrubs that will break the force of a wind blowing across the vineyard can be removed. Where there is a lake or river, certain protection against frost is likely, as the water, heated by the sun in the daytime, gives off warmth at night, and creates a circulation of cold and warm air. The darker the soil, the warmer it is, so that it is sometimes recommended to add to it coal dust, or basalt slack. Where the vines are trained to grow high, their branches will avoid the cold air on the ground. Where there is an overhead watering system, spraying the vines in spring, before a frost is expected, will also give protection. It is more common, however, to try to warm the air in the vineyard by using oil or solid fuel heaters, though this may not be possible without special permission, if the vineyard is sited near houses. The protection of the environment is taken very seriously in this respect. Only the minimum amount of heating is allowed, and certain specific types of heating oil must be used. The oil must not be permitted to escape into the vineyard, and if solid fuel is burnt, it should be smokeless. To some extent, these are not exclusively German problems, for all the northern European vineyards are at the risk of spring frost from time to time. The German vineyards, though, are the most northerly of all, with due respect to the small but growing English wine industry, and the record of their losses through the frost is formidable.

The way in which vines are grown, and pruned, is a highly technical business. Until the recent past, many of the different wine-producing regions of Germany had their own particular preferred methods of vine-growing, which were said to take into account local conditions. The shortage of labour in the vineyards has meant that vines have to be planted so that the maximum use can be made of mechanization. Naturally, the growth capacity of the different types of vine, and the micro-climate, will also have to be considered before a vineyard is planted. Vines on steep slopes often grow less vigorously than those on the plain, or on gentle slopes. Therefore, the distance between each vine will be probably about 1 metre to 1.6 metres in a steep vineyard, and 1.6 metres to 1.8 metres in others. The distance between rows will, where the terrain permits the use of mini tractors, be sufficiently large to allow them to pass without damaging the plants. Considerable driving skill seems to be required, for in many cases the room to manoeuvre between the harrow, being dragged behind the tractor, and the vines, is much less than the 40 centimetres on each side recommended by the technicians.

The trunks of vines are now allowed to grow much higher than used to be the case, in order to make the vineyard work easier, and therefore cheaper. The height of the leaf area of the vine is also of significance, and from the point of view of vineyard maintenance, a maximum height of 2.2 metres is recommended. In order to save water through transpiration in hot and dry years, such as 1976, the growth of the leaves will be restricted. Within the 2.2-metre height limit mentioned above, it is said that experiments have shown that the higher the leaf area, the better the growth, the ripening of the wood, the yield, and the quality. Not all vines perform in the same way, however, and therefore, such statements do not necessarily hold good in all circumstances.

In certain areas, use has been made in Germany of a system of growing vines originally developed at Krems in Austria by Lenz Moser, by which the rows are as much as 3.5 metres apart. The advantages of this system seem to be a reduction of some 45 per cent in man hours per hectare per year spent in the vineyards, the possibility to use standard sized tractors, etc., and a reduction in winter and spring frost damage. This is because the system also involves growing the vines and the fruit higher than normal, so that the sensitive fruit-bearing parts of the vine are lifted clear of the cold air close to the ground. The disadvantages, on the other hand, are that the vine grown in this way comes into full production a year later than normal, and that frost damage to the stem of the vine is likely to take longer to be overcome. It is also claimed that those who do not fully understand the system obtain a crop of reduced size.

By pruning, an orderly plant is achieved which produces a regular crop of good quality in an economic way. Vines can be grown relatively close to one another, and yet still receive the light and air they need to remain healthy. The aim of pruning is to create a balance between the supply of minerals to the stem of the vine, through the root system, and the leaves, through which the assimilation takes place. The normal winter pruning should ideally start after the winter frosts have passed. It may be necessary, though, to begin pruning earlier, depending on the size of the available labour force. Pruning vines in winter conditions is very unpleasant and unhealthy work, which nobody likes doing. Experiments have been made in recent years with pneumatic shears, which seem to produce less physical fatigue, and therefore the concentration of the operator is greater. The time taken in pruning is also said to be reduced by 30 per cent when pneumatic shears are used, and as there are accompanying overall savings in cost, we shall no doubt hear more of them in the future.

During the pruning, one or two fruit canes only are left, each with a specific number of buds which, in Germany, will probably amount to about 8-12 per square metre. The actual number of buds left on the vine will depend on such factors as the type of vine, the richness of the soil, the width of the rows between the vines, and the distance of the vines, one from another, within the rows. In the very steep vineyards, such as those one finds in the Mosel-Saar-Ruwer, or the Mittelrhein regions, the vines are trained up single stakes, whereas on more gently sloping terrain, rows of vines supported by wires are preferred.

I should now like to mention briefly some of the problems related to growing vines in the very steep vineyard. The vineyard areas in the EEC, are divided into zones, named A, B, CIa and Ib, CII and CIII. Before we ask ourselves what happened to the romance of wine, let me say that these zones are used simply for administration and legal purposes only, and from the point of view of the consumer, have little commercial significance. Therefore, we are not going to find reference to 'zones' on wine labels, or in lists. All the German vineyards fall into zone A, with the exception of North and South Baden which, with their warmer and more southerly climate, are included in zone B, with such areas as Alsace. To ripen grapes in zone A is not always easy, and in some ways, the great achievement of the German wine producer is not the magnificent wine he makes in years with many hours of sunshine, such as 1976 or 1971, but more the exceptionally refreshing, crisp, and fruity wine that can be produced following cooler summers. To be able to continue to do so, and make a reasonable living, is the problem of the grower whose vineyard may be not far from the vertical. Unless he is producing top quality wine that can demand a good price, he is faced with an increasingly difficult situation. His production costs in the vineyard are greater, and the yield per hectare is probably less, than that of the grower on the plain. It is generally accepted in Germany that much of the world-wide reputation of its wines has been built upon those coming from steep vineyards. However, one can certainly gain the impression that rationalization, and modernization of techniques, has in recent years been greater in vineyards on the level. In fact, the region in which the viticultural area has shrunk the most in the last twenty years,

Bacharach is one of the many beautiful Mittelrhein villages situated on the banks of the Rhine; it has over 80 per cent Riesling planted in its vineyards

has been the Mittelrhein, that runs through the famous Rhine gorge, from just south of Bonn upstream to the confluence of the Nahe and Rhine at Bingerbrück. Many of the vineyards, here, are steep in the extreme, and it is probably the mental picture of them that most of us who have visited the area will have, when drinking a glass of Hock. To better the lot of the grower in such terrain, and make his vineyards viable, improvements need to be made to the provision and retention of water in the soil. Where possible, roads need to be built, so that the vineyards may be more easily worked. If this is not feasible, consideration should be given to small, single-rail systems for carrying personnel and material up the vineyards. The improvement in clonal selection of the vines must continue, and root stocks must be suited to the dry soils of the steep vineyard. All this amounts to a very considerable undertaking, which can possibly only be carried out within the context of *Flurbereinigung*. By this word, the Germans understand the rebuilding of vineyards, and their amalgamation and redistribution amongst the growers. It is a massive undertaking, that really began during the country's period of reconstruction after the Second World War. The traditional method of growing vines on steep slopes, throughout Europe, was through the use of terraces that formed steps up the hillsides. On each step there might be room for three, or even fewer, rows of vines, grown up stakes. From one step to another, there would be a drop of two metres or so, with the soil being held back by a wall of stone, that was time-consuming to maintain. Mechanization of work in such a vineyard was impossible, and to reach some of the terraces the worker was confronted with a long walk, loaded with his tools for tilling the soil, as it had been done for hundreds of years. Such vineyards were picturesque, but uneconomic. The only way to make them viable has been to remove the terraces, re-landscape the hillside, and replant the vineyard with rows of recommended vines. It has given the grower the impetus to use the most suitable clones only, and to restudy his vineyard methods and organization. By the construction of roads through the vineyards, labour costs have been reduced. This work of reconstruction has not been restricted to terraced vineyards alone, though where these have been previously sited, the change has been the most dramatic to the casual observer. The total vineyard area, some of which was unplanted, was 101,162 hectares at the beginning of 1978, and of this, 45,564 hectares had been reconstructed to a greater, or lesser extent. Though naturally the economics of viticulture have been the main stimulus to *Flurbereinigung*, the aesthetic implications have not been ignored, nor has the possibility of encouraging tourism, and ultimately sales of wine, by well signposted paths through the vineyards.

The laws of inheritance in West Germany have resulted in the ownership of vineyards being split up, on some occasions to an almost ludicrous point. Along with the physical reconstruction of the vineyards has gone an exchange of ownership of individual parcels of land, with the aim that the grower should have as large an area of vineyard to work as possible. This sometimes may enable him, for example, to have his vineyard sprayed by helicopter, which a too small parcel of land would make impractical. It will also reduce the time spent by the workers moving from one small strip of vineyard to another. This is not an unimportant consideration, for it was calculated some years ago that in one part of the Palatinate region, 12.5 per cent of the workers' day was spent in transit.

The cost of rebuilding vineyards is, of course, enormous and is said to range from DM. 15,000 to DM. 100,000, per hectare, depending on the terrain. The owners of the vineyards may have to cover a good percentage of these costs, and to do so various schemes providing low interest rates have been set up. Subsisidies can also be obtained from the EEC. It is interesting to note that many growers and wine-makers feel that they have done all they can to contain costs through rationalization and

View of the village of Mayschoss in the Ahr Valley,
the home of the first cooperative wine cellar in the world

improvement in their vine-growing. Certainly, when we consider by how relatively little the cost of wine from the place of production in Germany has increased over the last ten years, compared to that of wine from some other European countries, we can see the value of *Flurbereinigung*. If prices have climbed more rapidly abroad, it is because of the weak performance of other currencies against the Deutsche Mark, or because of increased import taxes.

German Vineyard Organization

If a grower wishes to plant, or replant, a vineyard, he will take into consideration the various relevant factors that have been discussed in the last two sections. His choice of vine type will depend on:

1. The market in which he intends to sell his wine, or grapes.
2. The characteristics of the viticultural area.
3. The characteristics of the available vine types.
4. The quality of the vineyard, and economic factors involved in working the vineyard.

The quality of the vineyard will depend on its position in relation to the sun (preferably south-south-east to south-west in Germany), and its height above sea level. Its ability to retain warmth and moisture, the proximity of large areas of water to warm the atmosphere, and its susceptibility to frost or excessive wind, will also have a direct bearing on the type of vine to be selected.

This, unfortunately, is not the end of the story, for the German wine-grower is subject to much legislation, some of which he may feel is designed more for those growing vines in a Mediterranean climate, than for himself. Since 1970, the EEC regulations for wine have become law, and they cover all aspects of vine-growing, wine-making and marketing. There has been what the media referred to as a wine lake within the Community. An imbalance between production and consumption has resulted in an excess of lesser quality wine in the south of France and Italy. In an attempt to reduce the surplus, there has been a ban on the planting of new vineyards since 1 December 1976, which has already been extended beyond its initial period of duration of two years. As a generalization, it is probably true that this restriction has not caused much hardship in West Germany, but concern has been expressed that if it were to continue for too long, it could be said to be an undemocratic interference with the natural development of the German wine industry. The Germans do not have a problem in disposing of their stocks of wine, though, of course, with a crop that can vary so considerably in size from year to year, there can be shortages or temporary surpluses from time to time. After a year such as 1976, when an outstanding summer produced large quantities of fine wine, the cheaper qualities were hard to find. The reverse situation was true following two sound, but not top quality vintages, in 1977 and 1978, when the superb rich *Auslese* wines made from selected bunches of grapes started to become scarce. There have been some exemptions to the ban on planting vineyards. Where authorization had already been given for development plans in line with EEC regulations, before the planting restrictions came into effect, they could go forward as intended. Re-plantings, as part of the *Flurbereinigung*, (see page 161), have also been possible. Further, where vineyards have lain fallow for not more than four years, replantation has been allowed.

Apart from any short-term restrictions under EEC law, permission has to be obtained from the local state authority, before a vineyard may be planted, or replanted. It will have to be convinced that the proposed vineyard is capable of producing must with a sufficient sugar content, averaged over a ten-year period, to meet the minimum legal requirements for the particular grape variety in the district in question.

Many growers who vinify their crop may well sell the wine in bulk, rather than involve themselves in the technically and financially demanding business of bottling. Others do not make wine themselves, but deliver their grape crop to larger establishments who are well equipped to do so. Such growers, who are really operating as fruit farmers, must, of course, have a close working relationship with those to whom they sell their grapes, particularly when it is a matter of the choice of variety of vine to grow. The grower who makes and bottles his own wine must concentrate on producing the best quality wine possible over the whole of his range, which should be as wide as he can manage, without becoming too fragmented. In some cases, a grower will bottle part of his crop only, and sell the remainder in bulk. He must obviously react to the requirements of the market. There is an attraction for many German wine drinkers in buying their wine in bottle directly from the grower, often collecting it themselves from the cellar by car. A visit to the vineyards makes a pleasant outing. Buying from the grower, discussing and tasting the wine with him, is more glamorous than a purchase from the supermarket and, in fact, it is said that 39 per cent of the German's requirement of his own country's wine is bought in this way. A wine bought from a grower may or may not be better than one supplied by a wine merchant or supermarket. It depends on many factors, which can vary from year to year, and grower to grower.

On page 158 I wrote that the average vineyard holding in West Germany was very small (0.84 hectares), although it has increased in size a little over the last few years. In 1972-3, 58 per cent of the holdings grew vines as a side line only, and in spite of the excellence of the German viticultural schools, were in most cases managed by persons without formal viti-vinicultural training. Clearly, a highly qualified viticulturalist is not likely to be employed to look after one hectare of vineyard. People of this calibre will always be found in the larger, privately or state-owned enterprises, or in the very important cooperative cellars.

Concentrating too much on the small average size of vineyard holding can give us a somewhat false picture, as only a quarter of the total number of holdings work over 70 per cent of the total area under vine. It may be just about possible to make a living from growing grapes, vinifying and bottling wine from two to three hectares of vineyard, provided that members of the family all help out, but the income will be low. It is probably better in such circumstances to sign a contract with a cooperative cellar, and look for a second source of income.

The first vintager cooperatives (*Winzergenossenschaften*) were formed at the end of the nineteenth century, rather as children of necessity. Nowadays they handle the crop from 34,500 hectares, which is more than a third of the total German vineyard area. As its name implies, the aim of a cooperative cellar is that the lot of its members should be improved by cooperation. It does not involve itself directly in grape-growing, and pays the member for his crop at an established price based on the quality and variety of grape, and the vineyard from which it comes. Over the last twenty years, the cooperatives have increasingly bottled and marketed their wines, whereas before they were mainly suppliers of wine in bulk to the trade. In fact, 90 per cent of the wine from the cooperatives is now sold in bottle. It is not surprising that they therefore discuss with their members the types of vines to be grown, the maintenance of their vineyards and ways of improving the crop. The cooperatives are in a particularly strong position in south Germany, where the average size of vineyard holding is very small indeed. In Baden-Württemberg, over 80 per cent of production is in their hands. Their achievement can well be judged by the relatively high price of Baden-Württemberg wines compared to those of other regions further north. They have a well-developed marketing policy, and expenditure on advertising is greater than in any other vine-growing region in Germany.

The weakness of the German wine trade has been the unbalanced situation that exists in the state of Rheinland-Pfalz, which includes principally the viticultural regions of Mosel-Saar-Ruwer, Nahe, Rheinhessen and Rheinpfalz (Palatinate). Here the cooperative cellars are not so powerful as in Baden-Württemberg, and a very large number of growers try to do business with a small number of buyers. Seventy-five per cent of German wine comes from Rheinland-Pfalz, and to produce a more equitable relationship between grower and trade buyer, the state government has produced a *Weinbauplan*, a plan for the vine-growing industry. A central part of this plan is the formation of producer associations, known as *Erzeugergemeinschaften*. These were made legally possible in 1969, and it is their aim to adapt production and marketing to the needs of the EEC. The structure of a producer association is more flexible than that of a vintager cooperative. There is also one important difference. Under certain circumstances, a buyer who has signed a contract with a producer association will be able to benefit from state subsidies. The producer associations have already been able to obtain better prices too for their wines than those achieved on the open market. Their continuing development seems, therefore, absolutely necessary for the health of the German wine trade. The growers feel this even more keenly, when they contemplate the extension of the EEC to include still more wine-producing countries.

The lover of German wine might well be wondering at this point whether an increase in price paid to the grower, cooperative, or producer association is going to be to his advantage. The probable answer to this may be 'no' in the short term, but certainly 'yes' in the long term. If a fair income cannot be earned from growing grapes, then it will be slowly replaced by other forms of agriculture.

The German State owns wine-producing establishments, known as *Domänen*. In addition, there are various state-owned viticultural institutes also making wine. Whilst it would be impertinent for the writer to attempt to discuss their relative merits, there is little doubt that the State cellars at Niederhausen-Schlossböckelheim do set a standard of vine-growing and wine-making that is of great benefit to the reputation of the wines of the Nahe valley. It seems that because the cellars are owned by the State, and in spite of the fact that they are selling their wine on a commercial basis, they have a special relationship with many of their neighbouring growers. Their expertise and experience they share with others, and their advice is often sought. As it happens, the Niederhausen-Schlossböckelheim Domäne is one of the smallest, with forty hectares of vineyard. Others may be found in the Rheingau at Eltville, in Franconia at Würzburg, in the Rheinhessen at Mainz, in Trier on the Moselle, at Meersburg by Lake Constance and in the Ahr Valley.

There are still wine-producing estates of some size, principally, but not exclusively, in the Rheingau whose origins are noble. In some instances, although the family name will be used in connection with its wine, the ownership of the estate may well be out of the family's hands. It would be incorrect to say that a *von* or *zu* added to a grower's name on a label will improve the quality of the wine in the bottle, but it may add to its attraction, human nature being what it is.

No matter how big or how small the holding, the harvest is likely to find the vineyard and cellar workers at full stretch. As in all vine-growing areas, additional help is necessary at harvest time, and the staff has to be temporarily increased, at least four-fold. The owner of a small vineyard, who works in it mainly at the weekends, will almost certainly rely on the help of relatives and friends. The larger estates will have arrangements with many of their pickers to gather the harvest each year. Some will come from the towns, rather in the way that the hop pickers in Kent used to be supplied by the East End of London. Students are also widely used. The time the harvest takes to be brought in depends on various factors, including the yield per vine, and its method of training, the quality and condition of the grapes, the terrain, the weather, and the number of pickers available. Some years ago, it was calculated that whilst 240 man hours were sufficient to pick the crop in a vineyard on the level, 324 to 356 hours were needed in a steep vineyard of the same size, such as one finds on the Moselle. Nothing is likely to be able to speed the actual picking of the grapes in the steep vineyard, though a good system of roads created by *Flurbereinigung* can reduce the time taken to deliver them to the press house. This is technically important, as I shall explain later. In the vineyard on the plain, or in the gently sloping vineyard, much interest has been shown in the last three years in the possibility of using harvesting machines. They would not be able to gather the harvest in stages at different degrees of ripeness, as has often been the case in Germany up until now. Neither are all grapes suitable for picking by machine, for some have too thin a skin. The weight of a harvesting machine prevents it being used when the soil is damp, and there is undeniably a loss of grape juice in mechanical harvesting. Nevertheless, in five to seven hours, a harvesting machine can pick the crop in a hectare of vineyard, which is very considerably quicker than would normally be managed. A limiting factor could be the ability of the press house to handle the arrival of the grapes in such volume. Whilst it seems highly unlikely that harvesting machines will become a regular part of the vintage scene in the top quality producing vineyards, they may be of use in the less good vineyard areas. The cost of harvesting by hand certainly makes mechanization worth considering.

The preparations for the harvest in the press house are as important today as they were a hundred years ago, although in a well-run establishment they may now be less time-consuming. The replacement of wood by inert man-made materials has meant that a high standard of hygiene can quickly be reached by the use of steam and the usual cleaning materials. In making wine, cleanliness and orderliness in the press house and cellar are essential to obtain the best results, and this is particularly true of the light, elegant German wines. The pneumatic horizontal press seems to be found more widely than any other in Germany. Down its centre there is a rubber bladder which, on being filled with compressed air, swells and forces the grapes, the skins and the stalks against the perforated stainless-steel sides of the press.

According to the German Wine Law, grapes may only be harvested if they have reached the attainable degree of ripeness in that particular year, bearing in mind the grape variety, the weather and the locality. As a rule, this actual time will be made known after discussion with a board of experts, probably by a public notice. Grapes which are harvested before the earliest time laid down for the start of the harvest, without the presence of circumstances which make an exception necessary, may not be used for the production of must or wine. In Rheinland-Pfalz, before the beginning of the harvest, the vineyards are officially closed and only certain persons with authority to do so may enter them. One might well feel that that was the end of the matter, and that the State had taken over the responsibility from the grower of decision-making. This would not be true.

To find out when grapes are likely to begin to be ripe, it is necessary to go back to the end of the flowering period. The difference between the two dates may be about fifty-two days for the Müller-Thurgau and sixty-eight days for the Riesling, but this can vary considerably, depending on the weather. As the sugar content of the grapes is formed by the assimilation in the leaves, the acidity will drop. A state of over-ripeness sometimes develops, caused by water in the grape permeating the outer skin and escaping so that the grape becomes like a raisin, with an increased sugar content. The fungus, *Botrytis cinerea*, can also damage the skin on the grape. If this happens, when the grapes have developed the correct degree of ripeness, not only is the water content reduced, but also the acidity. The sugar content increases greatly, and the wine that is made from such dried grapes should have a particularly fine, honeyed bouquet and flavour. At the same time, it will have lost, to some extent, the bouquet associated with the grape from which it has been made. The glucose in the grape will have decreased under the influence of the *Botrytis cinerea*, and the balance will have swung in favour of fructose, which tastes much sweeter. Such grapes will either be used to increase the overall sugar content of the must pressed from grapes not attacked by *Botrytis cinerea*, or will be harvested separately to produce fine, rich wines. *Botrytis cinerea*, appearing at the right time, is known as *Edelfäule*, or noble rot. Some might feel that it is at its most effective and most positive in the Rheingau, although it can also help towards the production of very fine wines in all the German wine-producing regions. Wherever it occurs, and wherever grapes benefiting from noble rot are vinified separately, a high quality product is likely to be found. Nothing else will justify the expense of making fine sweet wine in such limited quantities as grapes with noble rot have to offer.

As has already been explained, a board of experts will have decided when the harvest may start, but the individual grower does not have to begin picking actually on that day, although he cannot start before it. In any vineyard, it is difficult to decide when to begin the harvest. This is not peculiar to Germany. A delay may prove costly if the weather breaks, and the crop becomes diluted with water. In discovering when the grapes have reached the required degree of ripeness, it is essential that the part bunches that are picked and measured for their sugar content and acidity should be representative. The condition of the grapes and their ability to ripen further will be probably the most important factors that the grower will have to consider. If the weather turns bad before the official start of the harvest, an early picking of the damaged grapes will be allowed. This can happen after a hail storm that may leave a significant part of the crop on the ground. Fortunately such disasters do not occur frequently.

An early gathering of the grapes is known as a *Vorlese*, the main harvest as the *Hauptlese*, and the late-picked crop as the *Spätlese*. The main harvest will probably last about ten days, and the *Spätlese* gathering will follow immediately afterwards. The grower does not only have to concern himself with the decision as to when his grapes have reached their peak of quality, but he must stage-manage his harvest correctly, bearing in mind the number of pickers available and the time it will take to bring in the crop. Good planning and organization is very important in a German vineyard at harvest time, where different grape varieties are grown, and different qualities of wine with different harvesting dates are produced. As a general rule, the vines in south Germany ripen before those further north. The 'stage-management' problem is more or less the same throughout Germany at the time of the harvest, but it is obviously greater where the grower is trying to produce different qualities of wine from the same vine variety, i.e. Riesling QbA, Riesling Spätlese, etc.

The picking of the grapes will probably start between nine and ten o'clock. To gather the grapes earlier is to risk harvesting the morning dew as well, which could reduce the must weights by several degrees. The pickers may pass through the same vineyard a number of times during the harvest. Each visit will have a definite individual purpose, or combination of purposes. There may be a *Vorlese*. There may be rotten grapes to be gathered with grapes that have fallen to the ground, which need to be handled separately from the healthy crop. Grapes may be left on the vine for the *Spätlese* crop, and some with noble rot will be picked at the same time as the rest of the harvest but kept apart from it to make rich *Auslese* wine. It is not essential that the selection of the bunches of grapes for the *Auslese* wine be made actually in the vineyard. It can also take place in the press house, if this is more convenient. In all events, the selecting of an *Auslese* crop in the vineyards presupposes a well-disciplined and trained force of grape pickers. This is essential for the German type of harvest, which requires the selection or rejection of bunches of grapes for the various reasons I have discussed. To achieve the necessary high standard of picking, one will probably find an experienced worker or foreman supervising every ten pickers.

In the best years, exceptionally concentrated musts will be produced from individually selected and picked grapes, and they will be converted into the extraordinarily rich *Beerenauslese* or even *Trockenbeerenauslese* wines. If the grapes are sufficiently ripe and healthy, and the weather sufficiently cold towards the end of the year, it may be possible to produce fine, sweet concentrated *Eisweine* from grapes picked early in the morning. Some growers prefer to crush the grapes lightly in the vineyard, rather than in the press house, before the residue is put in the press itself. There are various technical reasons for this about which experts hold different opinions. One of the main advantages must be a more economic use of the transport from the vineyard to the press house. On the other hand, there is a risk of oxidation, which must be avoided. Whatever system is used to crush the grapes, as opposed to pressing them, which follows later, they must be delivered quickly to the press house, particularly in warm weather.

The character of German wine depends on its freshness, its fruit and its acidity. Slight oxidation, which might be regarded as a virtue in a well-matured white Burgundy or Champagne, is abhorrent to a German wine, unless its presence is so small as to make it totally insignificant. The aim of German white-wine vinification, therefore, is to develop to the full those characteristics upon which its individuality, and world-wide reputation depend.

Categories of Wine

In writing about the principal vines that are found in the German vineyards, I explained that the EEC divided its wine into table wine and quality wine. Germany further sub-divided this second category into simple quality wine, and quality wine with distinction. The last three sections have dealt with matters concerning the vineyard. Before leaving this subject to discuss vinification, it seems a good moment to consider the various categories of German wine. If the skill of the cellar master can produce something good, wholesome and attractive even in an indifferent year, it is the quality of the grape that really decides the real value of the future wine. Were it not so, the risky, protracted German vintage would be unnecessary, and the crop could be gathered in the span of a fortnight.

There is a fundamental difference in approach to wine between the attitude of Germany and Luxembourg on the one hand, and France and Italy on the other. The German says that any of his vineyards can produce wine varying in quality from simple table wine to the finest quality wine with distinction. No one vineyard has a monopoly of all the virtues, and there are no vineyards reserved exclusively for quality wine production. A German quality wine is only recognized as such once it has been objectively tasted by the control authorities and has passed their tests. The quality is judged, therefore, on the contents of the bottle – not on the origin of the wine. The Frenchman in Burgundy, for example, takes another view, and declares that this vineyard can produce Gevrey-Chambertin, whilst another, next door to it, can only make Bourgogne Rouge. Such a system does not seem to take fully into account the differences of the micro-climate in any one year, or the skill, or otherwise, of the wine-maker, who may not be able to create a fine wine out of poor material, but can certainly mar a good one by bad handling.

Quality is very difficult to define. As we have seen, for practical purposes, the German wine-producer judges the quality of his must in the first instance by its sugar and acid contents. Later there will be a chemical analysis and objective tastings of the wine which will lead him to a professional judgment. It is not difficult for the amateur, who drinks wine with some frequency, to pass a fair judgment on it. Good style in a mature wine is easily recognizable and is probably the result of the various elements that form the wine being delicately balanced. Unfortunately, in some ways, German wine is pleasant to drink when it is very young. Because of this, many *Auslese* wines will have been consumed long before they have had an opportunity to develop the character and depth of flavour that comes with proper ageing. The cheaper simple quality or table wine from Germany has a lot of refreshing charm almost from the moment that it is bottled. To keep such a wine until it has acquired six months' bottle age or more is to miss the attraction of its youth. However, a few weeks after bottling a fine wine may be a little tired, as a result of the process of filtration and filling into bottle, but this should soon pass. Between the time when maturation begins to show and the merits of bottle age become obvious, and the end of the few months immediately after bottling, wine can often taste, frankly, a little boring. Generally speaking, the better the quality of a German wine, the longer it will take to taste to its best advantage. Thus, a year after a fine vintage, *Kabinett* quality wines of that vintage may show more character and style than the basically finer *Spätlesen*, which may need several years in bottle if their residual sugar and acidity are to harmonize perfectly. Whilst the generally accepted view of a wine is most likely to be the 'right' one, it would be a shame if individual preference and opinion were not to exist, although the professional taster always tries to be as objective as possible. Wine is full of contradictions, and each vintage brings a further supply to arouse interest, and stimulate curiosity. For example, it is remarked from time to time that the *Kabinett* wine in an average year is a finer wine than that of the same quality in an exceptionally sunny year. This is said to be the result of the long, slow period of ripening that one finds in the more ordinary summer. Hot summers can and do produce fine rich wines, but they can also make some fairly ordinary flabby wines with little acidity. For that reason, the simple quality wine in an average year will often show the typical German characteristics of balanced fruit and acidity better than a simple wine in a great year. In such circumstances, much depends on the skill of the cellar master. It is a long time since the 1959 vintage was made. The summer was scorchingly hot and all the wines had more than their usual share of alcohol. The autumn was also very warm, and the natural breakdown of acidity, in grape first, and in must and wine second, led to many charmless wines of lesser quality being made. In subsequent hot years, and I think particularly of 1971 and 1976, wine-makers have been able to prevent this happening again on any wide scale, although their knowledge and skills must have been stretched for the Müller-Thurgau wines to retain their freshness.

German Table Wine (Deutscher Tafelwein – DTW)

German table wine must be made from recommended, authorized or temporarily authorized vine varieties, and from grapes grown exclusively in Germany. The minimum must weight required is 44° Oechsle, except for the south German region of Baden, where 50° Oechsle is needed. There is also a minimum acidity content laid down. The addition of sugar to increase the alcohol content (chaptalization) is permitted. In most years only some 5 per cent or so of the total German wine harvest falls into the table-wine category. Germany, therefore, does not suffer from the superfluity of crop that one finds in certain areas of the south of France. In order to give some of the French table wines an identity of their own, the *vin de pays* category has been created. The all-embracing EEC regulations have required that Germany should follow suit and create *Landweine*. So far there has not been much enthusiasm to do so, for in practical terms they seem to be unnecessary. Some regions have produced proposed *Landweine* names, such as Moselländischer Landwein, Pfälzer Landwein, but whether they will ever be used, or, if used, mean very much to the consumer, is another matter.

In some circumstances, because of the EEC regulations, it is possible for a grower to sign a contract that will give him a guaranteed price for his table wine. This could mean, in theory, that it might pay him to concentrate on table-wine production rather than to produce simple quality wine, for which no price guarantees are given. Were this to happen, the German vineyards might then be divided, like the French, into separate quality and table-wine producing areas. However, this is not likely to occur, as the whole emphasis in Germany is on producing the best quality wine possible. The costs of growing grapes in a northerly climate, and the high cost of labour in Germany, compared to Italy, for example, makes this essential.

Quality wine from a specified region (Qualitätswein eines bestimmten Anbaugebietes – QbA)

Quality wine must be made from recommended and authorized vine varieties only, grown in one of the eleven specified regions. Minimum must weights are laid down for the production of quality wine, depending on the vine variety and the region in which it is grown. The actual alcohol content must be at least 7 per cent. Concentrated grape must may not be used in the production of QbA, although it may be chaptalized, (have sugar added). Possibly most important of all, a German quality wine may only be sold as such when it has been analysed and tasted by an official control centre, and given a control number. I shall discuss this system and other effects of the 1971 German Wine Law in a later section.

The QbA category forms the backbone of the German wine harvest, and can amount to 74 per cent or more of the total crop. Some regions, such as Baden, Württemberg, or Franconia, seem traditionally to produce a higher proportion of simple quality wine than others. (By simple quality wine, I mean quality wine without any added distinctions.) This is a result to a certain extent of the marketing policy of those specified regions that wish to promote energetically their own geographical identity, rather than the use of such terms as *Kabinett* or *Spätlese*. In many ways, a well-made QbA provides the consumer with the happiest blend of all the most appealing characteristics of German wine. It has fruit, acidity, and sufficient body or alcohol. QbA category wine, particularly that made from the Riesling grape, can benefit from two or three years' bottle age, and in many cases will keep to advantage even longer.

Quality wine with distinction (Qualitätswein mit Prädikat – QmP)

Quality wine with distinction must meet all the conditions for simple quality wine, but must be made from grapes grown in a smaller geographical area than a specified region, called a *Bereich* or district. The intention to make a quality wine with distinction has to be reported in writing to the appropriate state authorities before the vintage. The minimum must weight levels are much higher than those of simple quality wines, but for the finest, rich wines (*Beeren-* and *Trockenbeerenauslesen*), the actual minimum alcohol level can be lower by 1.5 per cent. This again shows, incidentally, that the Germans by no means regard alcohol as the all-important factor in deciding the quality of their wines. Another great difference in approach to wine between, say, the French and the Germans, is illustrated by the fact that the QmP may not have sugar added to them. This is perfectly legal when making a fine red Bordeaux wine, for example, but not in Germany, in spite of its northern climate, and what some French or Italians might well regard as feeble summers.

Kabinett

This is the lowest category of QmP. Some might feel that some wines from Baden-Württemberg in EEC zone B could be matched by certain white wines from Switzerland, or even Austria. Nobody would claim, surely, to be able to produce anything closely resembling a *Kabinett* quality wine from the Moselle, Nahe or Rheingau in any other country. They are the lightest and most delicate wines in the world, and fine though the better quality *Spätlese* and *Auslese* wines may be, they do not, for the writer, epitomize all that is most individual in German wine so effectively as do the best *Kabinett* quality wines.

The legal requirements for *Kabinett* wines are as described in the opening paragraph about QmP. There are occasions when a grower has to make the difficult decision as to whether to produce a *Kabinett* wine, or whether to add sugar to his must and make a simple quality wine. Apart from any commercial considerations, the total balance of the wine will have to be taken into account, for it can be that a simple quality wine, judiciously sugared to increase the alcohol content, will be a better wine than a *Kabinett*, that has 'only just made it'. Strangely enough, there have been reports from Germany from time to time of difficulties in selling *Kabinett* wines. They seem on occasions to have been somewhat overshadowed by the demand for the better known *Spätlese* category wines. This sort of situation can arise and disappear, as a result of different styles of vintage.

Spätlese

There is a traditional and charming story of the delayed return in 1775 of the messenger from the Prince Abbot of Fulda to Schloss Johannisberg. As he was bearing permission for the harvest to start, the grapes were left on the vine for longer than usual, and greatly increased in sugar. However, late harvesting has been recorded elsewhere long before 1775.

A date is announced each year after which a late-picked or *Spätlese* crop may be gathered. The must weight has to reach a certain level, and the grapes have to be fully ripe. The weight of the must is really all important, as fully ripe is a term that is open to different interpretations. Bunches of grapes rarely ripen as a whole, except in very hot summers such as those of 1976 or 1971. Frequently, while the majority of grapes on a bunch are ripe, there will be others that remain the size of small peas, and contain virtually no sugar. To assess which bunch is fully ripe and which is not, requires considerable supervision and discipline at the harvest. After the intention to pick a *Spätlese* crop has been reported, the wine-control authorities may well wish to check on the maturity of the grapes, or to test the weight of the must, before fermentation sets in.

Within the *Spätlese* group one finds big differences in quality, and this applies to all categories of German wine. A fine *Spätlese* wine from the Rheingau will probably be a much better wine than a *Spätlese* from a less prestigious district. Nature and the weather being what they are, no two vintages are identical, and within the legal categories there are many variations of flavour, style and quality. The standards established in law represent the minimum requirements, but it is the endless difference in flavour and bouquet which singles wine out from other alcoholic drinks.

Spätlese category is probably better known than any other. The names of German wines are, frankly, many and various, and even to the German consumer can appear somewhat confusing. However, *Spätlese* he has heard of, and *Spätlese* is a name he can remember, and for which he is prepared to pay a little bit extra. It is not surprising, therefore, that in the lesser-known vineyard areas, to be able to harvest a *Spätlese* is of great importance to the grower, for the prices he receives for his ordinary QbA may be minimal.

Auslese

If an *Auslese* crop of selected bunches of grapes is to be picked, it can take place at any time during the main harvest or the *Spätlese* harvest. By the nature of things, for the sugar to develop in the grape, time is needed, so *Auslesen* are usually gathered late in the season. After a sunny summer and a good autumn a grower will certainly consider making an *Auslese* wine, although it is possible on a straight costing basis, which ignores the prestige of producing an *Auslese*, that it might be more financially rewarding to produce a *Spätlese* only. The selling price to the consumer of an *Auslese* does not depend on production costs, but rather on what the market will stand, to put it crudely. The reduction in liquid within the grape as the sugar content increases can be very considerable indeed. At the same time, the labour costs arising from the individual attention that the making of an *Auslese* requires are high.

These comments refer to a fine Riesling *Auslese*, which can only be made by allowing the grapes to remain on the vine until late into November. There is a short-cut to producing a wine legally entitled to be called *Auslese*, through the use of some of the new varieties of vine, such as Optima and Kanzler. These will quite frequently produce grapes with sufficient must weight to make an *Auslese* wine, but the fine fruit and acidity of the Riesling affected by noble rot will be missing. However, the wine will, of course, have to measure up to the standards of the control authorities. As I have mentioned in an earlier section, weight is not enough. If the must has insufficient acidity, the wine will taste clumsy and flabby. Not all of the new varieties, by any means, produce inferior rich wines, but the grower of Riesling *Auslese* in a fine vintage such as 1976 can be forgiven for feeling that there should be some way of differentiating his *Auslese* from those of less noble grapes.

Beerenauslese and Trockenbeerenauslese

These must be just about the easiest wines in the world to enjoy, but amongst the most difficult to judge. Their enormous concentration of flavour finds weaknesses in the taster's vocabulary. Up to the level of an *Auslese*, the normal comments applied to wine should be fully adequate to give some idea of what the wine actually tastes like. Above that level, most tasters either fall back on well-worn clichés, or give way to laudatory, inarticulate grunts.

The richness of a *Beerenauslese* is extraordinary and, when combined with the fine acidity of the Riesling grape, it represents, for many, the peak of German wine-making. With all peaks, there is always another higher still to be climbed, and this is really the case with the *Trockenbeerenauslese*. It is like a *Beerenauslese* only much more so. It is richer, even more concentrated, and even more difficult to describe.

The cost to the grower who bottles his own *Beerenauslese* wine is at least seven times greater than that of a simple QbA, whilst, in straight costing terms, a *Trockenbeerenauslese* is probably often not worth producing. To make these very rich wines, the grapes are individually selected and picked. A *Trockenbeerenauslese* is made from grapes not only affected by noble rot, but dried out on the vine to the consistency of raisins. Wet weather would easily ruin grapes in this condition, so the risks are high. The vines have to comply with the general regulations concerned with the production of QmP. Because they can only be produced in very small quantities, they are allowed to be picked in more than one vineyard site, and blended together. In such a case, the wine will bear the name of the vineyard from which more than 50 per cent of the grapes originate.

Eiswein

The term *Eiswein*, or ice wine, may only be used when the wine is made exclusively from grapes that are frozen at the time of picking, and frozen when they are pressed. It cannot be used by itself, but must be combined with a term of distinction such as *Auslese*. Ice wines have been produced at irregular intervals for many years, and records in the Rheingau show them to have been made as long ago as 1858. However, it is really only in the last nineteen years or so that they have achieved the reputation that they now hold.

To make ice wine it is necessary to pick the grapes at a temperature of at least $-5°C$. This will involve harvesting early in the morning, in exceptionally tough conditions. The grapes will be brought as quickly as possible to the press house, and probably passed through a widely set crusher, though some growers will omit this stage. From the crusher, the still frozen grapes will be placed in a pneumatic horizontal press. In pressing, a large amount of the water in the grapes will be held back in the form of ice crystals, so that the must becomes proportionately very concentrated. The exact degree of concentration depends on various factors, but it is said that the increase in must weight can be between 20° and 50° Oechsle. As it happens, this could mean an increase of 20–50 per cent in weight, dependent on the potential must weight before freezing.

Before the 1971 wine law came into force, ice wine made from grapes harvested on 6 January could be called *Dreikönigswein*, or Three Kings' Wine. This and similar *appellations* relating to late harvesting dates are no longer permissible. The making of ice wine is every bit as expensive, if not more so, than the production of a straightforward *Beerenauslese*. The effect on costs of the reduction in liquid that ice-wine making brings with it is, of course, most easily absorbed in years when the general crop is large, such as 1973. Most of the ice wines that one finds on the market are either *Auslese Eisweine* or *Spätlese Eisweine*. A *Kabinett Eiswein* is legally possible, but is rare as the acidity in a *Kabinett* wine does not usually lend itself well to ice-wine production, being already fairly high. *Beerenauslese Eisweine* are made, though the manual selection of individual frozen grapes is not really practical in the short time available if the grapes are not to thaw.

Leaving the all-important question of production costs to one side, one might wonder if the making of ice wines was worth while. Does the end justify the means? The answer must be that when ice wine is well made from well-ripened grapes, it has a life and style about it that is unique. The best way to realize this is to taste an *Auslese* and an *Eiswein Auslese* from the same vineyard, in the same vintage. Whilst the *Auslese* may be an excellent wine when drunk by itself, in comparison with the ice wine it will seem a little dull, even a little ordinary.

In Bordeaux, the classified growths of the Médoc maintain the reputation of Claret, although the largest part of the production in the area is in humbler wine. Similarly, it is the fine QmP wine of Germany that attracts attention by reason of its quality and individuality. Sun is not everything in wine production. If it were, the Corsican and Tunisian wine would be valued more highly than Bordeaux or Burgundy. The apple grown in Kent, England, is said to be a better, crisper product than the apple from the Loire Valley in France. So it is with German wine. The growers have turned the possible misfortune of their cool climate to their advantage, and thanks in particular to the Riesling grape, have developed a style of wine that seems to appeal to wine lovers everywhere.

Vinification

There can be few processes so outwardly simple and yet inwardly so very complex as vinification. That is certainly the impression one can have of white-wine vinification, and it is probably not very far from the truth. In the 1971 German Wine Law, wine is defined as being the product of the alcoholic fermentation of the juice of freshly gathered grapes. In grape juice, water is the largest constituent, and sugar and acids the most important in deciding the style of the future wine. The proportion present of one to another depends on the vine variety, the vintage, the vineyard, and the quantity of grapes borne by the vine. This last factor is one over which different countries have different views. It is generally agreed that a vine can only produce a limited number of bunches of grapes without the juice becoming too diluted. What is not agreed by Europe as a whole is the exact point at which the dilution becomes unacceptable. Under EEC law, maximum allowable yields must be established for quality wine production. This is a concept that is foreign to the German grower. However, it must be admitted that white-wine production can certainly support higher yields than red.

The most important acids in a German must in terms of quantity present are tartaric and malic. The first of these, which the Germans call *Weinsäure*, or wine acid, as if to emphasize its significance, gives their wine character. Its presence is highly valued as it brings with it balance, freshness and staying power. A fine Riesling wine in a good quality vintage will have a high proportion of tartaric acid, while in a poor vintage the malic acid will be relatively high. Malic acid is what the wine-maker in a Mediterranean climate will be seeking when he harvests early in order to have freshness in his white wine, providing, of course, that he then prevents a malolactic fermentation. It can add what is known as 'greenness' to a German wine, and providing it is not too pronounced, has its own attraction. Fermentation of a wine must is caused by the action of yeast in converting the sugar into ethyl alcohol and carbon dioxide. In the past, great reliance has been put on the 'natural' yeasts found in the skins of the grapes to ferment the must. They have not always performed successfully, with faulty or spoilt wine as the result. To avoid this happening, and a year's work in the vineyards being wasted, selected dried yeast cultures, which ensure that fermentation begins quickly and continues satisfactorily, have been used to an increasing extent in recent years.

Some ten years ago, sulphur dioxide was frequently used to excess in the handling and bottling of white wine. The sweet white wines of Bordeaux, in particular, and white wines with 10 per cent of alcohol or less and residual sugar were often over-sulphured by bottlers in the United Kingdom and elsewhere. Sulphur dioxide is an antioxidant, and inhibits fermentation. It was this second property that encouraged bottlers with inadequate expertise or equipment to use more than was necessary to the detriment of the wine, and possibly the consumer. An oversulphured wine is a vile-smelling thing, with a rough throat-aching taste. EEC regulations have reduced the amount of sulphur dioxide that may be legally present in wine to such levels that it becomes unnoticeable on the palate. Used correctly, its effect is entirely beneficial. Sulphur dioxide is a gas that is widely found not only in wine production, but also in the soft drinks industry, in jam-making and in the preservation of fruit. It can easily be pressurized to form a liquid, and is also available in tablet form as potassium bisulphite. For centuries, it has been used in wine-making, though nowadays, from the moment the grapes are brought to the press house, as little is added as possible. Small additions will be made immediately after fermentation to prevent the young wine becoming brown in colour and oxidized. In a vintage when there are many rotten grapes, more sulphur dioxide will be added at the early stages of vinification than when the grapes are clean and healthy. However, care must always be taken to keep the sulphur dioxide content within the legal limits, which in many years is not always easy. These limitations have had an influence on the making of German wine, and have encouraged the use of fast-acting yeast cultures. To delay fermentation is to risk oxidation, and to suffer oxidation to any great extent is to lose the freshness of the wine.

The sun does not shine strongly enough every year in Germany to avoid the necessity of adding sugar to the must or wine to increase the alcohol content and improve the balance. This is common to both France and Germany, although as I have explained earlier, Germany only allows additions of sugar to table wine or simple quality wine. In the case of table wine, saccharose or concentrated grape juice may be added, but only saccharose may be used to increase the alcohol content of a potential quality wine. The whole process is strictly controlled and the intention to enrich or add sugar to a must or wine has to be reported in advance to the appropriate official authority. This announcement will have to include the name and address of the cellar, the date and time of the proposed operation, the cask or reference number, the quantity to be enriched, the weight of the must or the alcohol content of the wine, and so on. Nothing can remain a secret. The normal method of adding sugar is similar to that used for most fining materials. The sugar is thoroughly mixed or whisked with a small quantity of the liquid to which it is to be added. Sufficient room must be left in the container in which the must or wine is lying to allow for the increase in the total quantity of liquid after the addition of sugar, as well as the foam caused by fermentation. The law allows enrichment up till 15 March in the year following the vintage. The advantage of enrichment of a must or young wine that is still fermenting, as opposed to an older wine, is that there is no necessity to restart the fermentation, and therefore it is technically easier. On the other hand, in a poor vintage when the acidity is higher than one would like, an addition of sugar to wine and the fermentation that follows, brings with it a desirable drop in the acid content. If the acidity of a wine or must is too high, it may be reduced by the addition of calcium carbonate, but this only precipitates tartaric acid. In a less than top quality vintage, when dealing with musts with high acidity, it will be necessary to reduce the malic acid content by treatment with a double salt called Acidex. Such an operation is every bit as subject to legal controls and procedures as the enrichment of a must. Apart from these two chemical ways of reducing acidity, some wines undergo a natural or biological reduction of acidity, in which the sharp-tasting malic acid is converted into the milder lactic acid during a natural malolactic fermentation. There is always a risk that a must or wine can turn acetic. It is most important to prevent this happening by a high standard of hygiene, and a judicious use of sulphur dioxide. Unfortunately, excessive acetic acid cannot be removed by methods of deacidification mentioned above, and an acetic wine can only be used for vinegar or distillation.

One of the complaints that the merchant will receive about his wines from the consumer from time to time is that there is 'glass in the bottle'. Were this to be true, it would be a very serious matter, but almost always what is mistaken for glass is a tartrate deposit. If an excessive amount of tartrates are present, they will form crystals which do not impair the quality of the wine at all, but nevertheless spoil its appearance to a certain extent. This crystallization process will occur more readily at low winter temperatures. Therefore, the wine-maker with the appropriate equipment may chill his wine to a temperature of $-3°$ or $-5°C$ for five days or more. The results of this cooling are not always entirely successful, and alternative methods of considerable variation are being studied throughout the world. Regardless of whether a grower has the possibility of chilling his wine artificially or not, he will allow the ambient temperature of his cask or bulk cellar to drop in winter, as the weather outside becomes increasingly cool. This is true of wine-makers in all countries. On economic, and on technical grounds, it is much better to let nature do your work for you, providing it does it properly. Recently a new method of tartrate stabilization has been tested in Germany, known as the contact process. The largest possible tartrate crystals are added to the wine, and cause a precipitation of the excessive amount of soluble tartrates. This method appears to be both effective and economic, but as yet has not been given legal approval.

So far in this section, I have discussed some of the techniques used in the making of German wine, but it would be incomplete if mention was not made of the machinery employed. As far as possible, the grapes are transferred from the containers in which they have been brought from the vineyard to the presses by mechanical means. The crop may first be placed in a specially designed container, having passed through a crusher, to allow some of the juice liberated from the grapes to escape, before the residue is placed in the press itself. Up to some 40 per cent of the must may be obtained in this way before the grapes are pressed. This speeds the process of obtaining all the juice from the grapes, and reduces the risk of oxidation. It is extremely important that all the machinery that comes into contact with the grapes, the juice and the stalks should be thoroughly cleaned daily, so as to avoid the risk of acetic bacteria developing.

Earlier on, I wrote that the pneumatic horizontal press with its rubber bladder seemed to be found more widely than any other in Germany today. Its main advantage over other presses of similar size is that it extracts the juice more quickly, and avoids oxidation. Some large establishments use modern continuous presses which produce a must with a greater amount of dirt in it than the horizontal press. This is not a great problem in most cellars, as the must from the press passes into a centrifuge for clarification. However, the small cellar may not have a centrifuge, in which case the freshly pressed juice will be pumped into a vat to allow the gross dirt to settle. The danger with this system is that fermentation may start at this point, and any hope of clarification will then be temporarily lost. Now is the time that the enrichment of the must, and the various possible treatments mentioned earlier, will be given. The fermentation should last for at least eight days, and not more than three weeks. The Germans like the fermentation to take place slowly and at relatively low temperatures. A too hurried fermentation results in a fat wine without any delicacy. If, on the other hand, the fermentation is too protracted, there is a risk that too much sulphur dioxide will be needed to maintain the quality of the wine.

The traditional picture of a German wine-cellar is of rows of nicely polished casks, possibly with the ends or heads of the casks, as they are known, heavily decorated with carvings of Father Rhine and Mother Moselle. Such a cellar lit by candle provides a charming and romantic atmosphere. Wooden casks, though, are expensive to buy, and expensive to maintain. To ensure that they are sufficiently clean inside is time-consuming and unpleasant work. To a great extent, wood is therefore being replaced by stainless steel, fibreglass, and other inert man-made materials. Whilst wood is essential in the development of quality red wine, its benefit to white wine is more debatable. This is particularly true of white wines that must contain as little sulphur dioxide as is good for them, and one of whose principal characteristics is their freshness. For fermentation, stainless-steel tanks are excellent, as they transfer temperature so easily, and allow the fermenting must to be simply cooled by spraying the outside of the tank with cold water. Once the first fermentation is complete and after about four to eight weeks, the wine is racked. That is to say, it is transferred from the lees, or deposit, left by the fermentation. It will be given either a light filtration or passed through a centrifuge into a container in which it can mature. Additions of sulphur dioxide will be made. During the next few months the wine will be stabilized against tartrate deposits, as described earlier, and given whatever treatments are necessary to ensure that it is in perfect condition when the time for bottling arrives. A table or simple quality wine will be bone dry a week before bottling, and yet the German wine that most of us know has a pleasant amount of sweetness in it. How does this change take place and why?

The answer to the first question is technical and simple, but the second deals with taste, social customs and possibly fashion, and must therefore be considered later. There are two ways in which sweetness is achieved in German wine. The first depends on the sugar in the grape from which the wine is made, and the second on the addition of unfermented grape juice. As we have seen, after a fine summer some of the grapes will have sufficient sugar in them to make rich *Auslese* wines, with an adequate amount of alcohol, without the addition of any sweetening. The natural tendency of most German musts, however, is to ferment to such a point that virtually no sugar remains. In order to produce a wine with a certain amount of residual sugar, it used to be the custom to stop the fermentation before it was complete. To do so, it was necessary to filter the still fermenting must into yeast-free casks or containers, and to inhibit any further fermentation by ensuring that the sulphur dioxide content remained relatively high. A slowing down of the fermentation could also be achieved by a reduction in temperature of the must, or by the pressure of carbon dioxide gas. Frankly, which method, or combination of methods, was chosen depended on available cellar equipment or installations. The disadvantage of this way of retaining sweetness in the wine is that it requires close and continuous surveillance to avoid fermentation re-starting and, more seriously, involves the use of more sulphur dioxide than may be legally possible. Economics and legality aside, it can produce most attractively balanced wines with a high proportion of fructose in their sugar content. By far the greater amount of German wines today, other than the finest and richest, are fully fermented and have virtually no sugar in them when they are stored in bulk. Immediately before bottling, they will be sweetened with *Süssreserve* or sweet reserve. In effect, sweet reserve is unfermented grape juice. At the time of the harvest, a part of the crop will be treated in any of the following ways:

1. The grape juice will be passed through filter sheets that will remove the yeast, and be stored under carbon dioxide pressure. (At a pressure of eight atmospheres fermentation cannot take place.)
2. The grape juice will be passed through filter sheets as above, and stored in sterilized (yeast-free) containers.
3. The grape juice will be heated to 90°C for two minutes, and stored in sterilized containers.
4. The grape juice will be given a large dose of sulphur dioxide, that will prevent any fermentation starting.

This last method seems to have much to recommend it. It is not time-consuming, which is most welcome when the cellar staff is already fully engaged handling the new vintage. It is also said to compare favourably with the other methods of sweet reserve production from the point of view of cost. Naturally, the high sulphur-dioxide content will have to be reduced before the sweet reserve is added to the wine. Whatever method of production is followed, sweet reserve must be stabilized in the normal way against excessive protein or heavy metals. This stabilization will be carried out as quickly as possible before the grape juice is converted into sweet reserve. The laws concerning the geographical origin of unfermented grape juice and its quality category (simple quality, *Kabinett* quality, etc.) are similar to those for table and quality wine. This means that the unfermented grape juice used to sweeten a *Kabinett* wine, for example, must be of *Kabinett* quality itself.

If there is a point of no return in wine production, it is the moment of bottling. Good bottling cannot improve a wine, but bad bottling can ruin it and destroy all

The steep terraced vineyards of the Mosel region as seen at Zell-am-Mosel

the good work that has gone into its making. Bottling is, therefore, of great importance in the life of a wine, and the losses in good will and the costs that have arisen through technical failures or ignorance in the past must have been enormous. German wine is delicate, light in alcohol, and usually contains residual sugar. To bottle it correctly requires discipline and absolute attention to detail, of a standard that is unnecessary when bottling wines with high alcohol content and no residual sugar. The aim when bottling German wine is to ensure that when the wine is in the bottle, it is yeast-free. Obviously, not only must the liquid filling the bottle contain no yeast, but neither must the cork or closure, or the bottle itself be contaminated. In a perfect world, each wine would be bottled when the time was ripe. On a good estate, 'bottling ripeness' will be taken very much into account, and as far as the capacity of the machinery allows, the estate will try to put the wine into bottle at exactly the right moment. It is particularly important to do so where the wines are stored in wood, and are liable to mature fairly quickly. Where a cellar is equipped with tanks or vats, the urgency to bottle at a particular moment is less, for they themselves are little more than big bottles – maturation is slow in them. Exactly what is meant when one says a wine is ready for bottling is difficult to describe; it is recognizable only by tasting, and cannot therefore be established by chemical analysis, other than through the detection of obvious faults before bottling.

There are three systems in regular use for bottling German white wine: 1. Cold sterile-bottling. 2. Cold sterile-bottling with the addition of sorbic acid. 3. Warm bottling. Under ideal conditions, all three systems will apparently produce a satisfactory result. However, conditions are not always perfect, and neither is the personnel employed in bottling. If one takes the view that the less a wine is treated or handled the better, the cold sterile-method of bottling has much to recommend it.

A bottling plant will probably consist of a filter for the wine, a bottle sterilizer, a machine for filling the bottles, and a corking machine. The machinery and filter will be sterilized with steam, and the bottles and corks with sulphur dioxide gas, or an aqueous solution of sulphur dioxide. This is the cold sterile-process of bottling. Naturally, in terms of machinery, and its capacity and lay-out, there are a great many possible variations. Many bottlers follow this system, but add sorbic acid which will prevent any yeast development should there have been a breakdown in the sterilizing process. Sorbic acid is widely used throughout the world as a sterilizing agent. How much should be added to a wine depends on the alcohol content of the wine, and the number of yeast cells present, if any. The maximum additions of sorbic acid that are allowed, are covered by EEC regulations. The use of warm bottling, in which the wine is heated to about 55°C, is rather more controversial. If incorrectly carried out, it can cause a wine to taste flat through a loss of carbon dioxide, and an albumen haze can develop if the fining has been insufficient. It would seem that for German wine, whose character depends on freshness, the cold sterile-process is, on balance, the most suitable method of bottling. Its only real disadvantage is that it does require a very high standard of cellar procedure, but this the Germans can provide.

The Law

The Germans feel that the future of their wine industry must lie in quality production. To some extent, this undoubtedly reflects their national approach to almost any activity, from making cars, to football, and to the music of the Berlin Philharmonic Orchestra. The standard of living and the costs of labour are both high. As a result, even ignoring the difference in climatic conditions, wine made in Germany cannot be as inexpensive as that in Italy, for example. The German wine trade realizes that to remain successful in an EEC that includes Greece, and possibly

The old monastery of Kloster Eberbach in the Rheingau is used by the German Wine Academy for seminars and for wine auctions

one day Spain, the emphasis must be on the individuality and quality of their wines. For the first they should thank their climate, and for the second, they can thank themselves. In countries with warm and reliable climates, excellent wine is produced that changes little from vintage to vintage. On commercial grounds, such lack of variation would seem to have much to recommend it. Consistency of style is only achieved in a northern European climate by blending. When it is well done, it is an excellent thing, for it combines the characteristics of a vintage with the quality and style expected of that particular wine. Blending is a skilled craft which is responsible for many of the most distinguished wines of the world, from Sherry, Port and Champagne to fine red Bordeaux. The individuality of German wine is both its strength and its weakness. It is interesting, but also confusing, and where there is confusion in the mind of the consumer, he is likely to look for something simpler. That Germany has faced up to this potential problem and turned it to its advantage is clear from the success of its wine in export markets in recent years. How then has the great well of individual German wines been given a semblance of cohesion? The answer must lie to some extent in the law, and while all German wines are born under one law, there are many regulations which sometimes come, sometimes go, and sometimes evolve. The principle behind the German Wine Law is that only that is permitted which is expressly stated in the law. This means, for example, that the contact process of stabilization of tartrates, described on page 173, cannot be used commercially until it is 'enshrined', as the EEC jargon will have it, in the Wine Law.

The reunification of Germany in 1871 provided the opportunity for a common national German law. It was not, though, until 1892 that the first Wine Law actually came into force. The French *Lois Administratives* took effect in 1905, and the first successful Italian attempt to pass regulations for controlling place names of origin became law in 1963. The German Wine Law of 1892 was succeeded by further laws in 1901 and 1909. Each got closer to grips with the complexities of wine production and its marketing, which emphasized the growing commercial importance of wine. The fourth German Wine Law of 1930 continued the efforts to be both comprehensive and comprehensible. From 1930 onwards there were advances in the improvement of wine production which, because of their novelty, were neither legal nor illegal – such as the introduction of the use of sweet reserve after the Second World War. In 1930, they were simply unthought of and technically impossible. During the years following the war, the immediate need for the German wine trade was to rebuild its house, and develop its business once more. The changes in the structure of the trade were considerable, and the channels through which wine was sold had altered greatly since the 1930s. The creation of the EEC in 1957 gradually removed the protection to the German grower of import duties on French and Italian wines, and today the German seems to drink roughly equal quantities of imported and home-grown wine. Though Germany, as we have seen, produces a very high proportion of quality wine, its total production represents some 7 per cent only of that produced in the EEC as a whole. With the formation of the EEC, it seemed that the competition to German wine would become steadily stronger. To meet this competition it was even more necessary to have a wine law that was positive and up to date. To this end, a new law was announced on 19 July 1969. It was never to become effective, for it was overtaken in April 1970 by the EEC Regulations 816/70 and 817/70. Such regulations take precedence over national law and, therefore, Germany published on 19 July 1971 its own German Wine Law, which took into account all the Common Market requirements at that time. Since 1971, there have been many additions to the EEC regulations, and doubtless there are still more to come. Possibly the most significant of these have been those concerned with the labelling and description of wine. By their sheer complexity and great number, they have been difficult for the wine trade to absorb and to put into effect. There have been criticisms of the regulations themselves and the timing of their introduction. It seems that the most difficult period of assimilation for the wine trade is over, even if there are still areas of uncertainty in the regulations that are disputed and awaiting clarification. In fact, though, one of the principal aims of the 1971 German Wine Law was the establishment of *Klarheit und Wahrheit*, clarity and truth. The consumer is the benefactor. The protection of his health through the elimination of any method of treatment of the vine or handling of wine that might remotely be harmful to him, is an important part of German wine law.

It is not only the consumer's good health that is the concern of the German Wine Law, but also that of his pocket. The consumer is not to be disappointed when he buys a bottle of German wine. To understand this, it is necessary to know a little about the naming of German wine, and the quality control by the state authorities. The viticultural area, as we have already seen, forms part of two EEC wine-producing zones. Zone A comprises all the German viticultural areas, with the exception of North and South Baden. In zone A are also found the vineyards of Luxembourg and the United Kingdom, as well as those of the Netherlands and Belgium, these last being devoted almost exclusively to the growing of table grapes under glass. Zone B, besides North and South Baden, includes the viticultural areas in the French departments of Alsace and Lorraine amongst others. Any of the German vineyards *may produce quality wine or quality wine with distinction, or indeed table wine.* Quality wines must come from any one of the eleven specified regions, with an exception which I shall discuss later. These specified regions have not developed their identity through any economic or political factors, but simply through the style of wine that they produce as a result of their individual climates, soil and geological conditions. The following table shows how the specified regions for quality-wine production equate to the table-wine regions and sub-regions.

TABLE WINES		QUALITY WINES AND QUALITY WINES WITH DISTINCTION
Regions	*Sub-regions*	*Specified regions*
Rhein und Mosel	Rhein	Ahr
		Hessische Bergstrasse
		Mittelrhein
		Nahe
		Rheingau
		Rheinhessen
		Rheinpfalz (Palatinate)
	Mosel	Mosel-Saar-Ruwer
Main		Franken (Franconia)
Neckar		Württemberg
Oberrhein	Römertor	Baden
	Burgengau	

The specified regions for quality wine and the table-wine regions and sub-regions are further divided into *Bereiche* or districts. That the *Bereich* names may be used for quality wines or table wines can be confusing to the consumer, if not to the international wine trade as a whole. Naturally, a *Bereich* quality wine must meet all the technical requirements necessary for a quality wine in terms of grape type, original must weight, and so on, and must have been tested (analytically and by tasting) and approved by an official control centre. It might be noted that a German quality

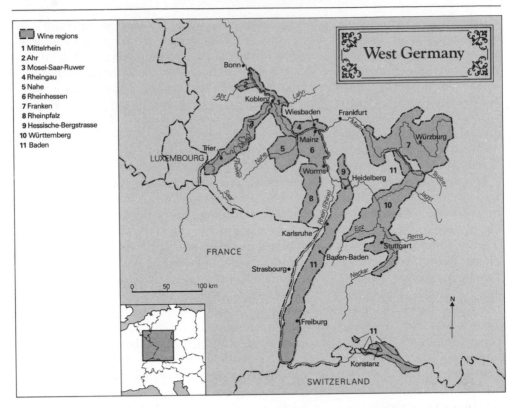

wine nowadays always has a control number on its label, usually consisting of ten or eleven figures, whereas a table wine with a *Bereich* name has no control number.

The names of the *Bereiche* are as follows, and on the left of the table are shown the specified regions to indicate the geographical areas from which they come.

Quality wine specified region	Bereich
Ahr	Walporzheim
Hessische Bergstrasse	Starkenburg, Umstadt
Mittelrhein	Bacharach, Rheinburgengau, Siebengebirge
Mosel-Saar-Ruwer	*Zell*, *Bernkastel*, Obermosel, Saar-Ruwer
Nahe	Kreuznach, *Schloss Böckelheim*
Rheingau	*Johannisberg*
Rheinhessen	Bingen, *Nierstein*, Wonnegau.
Rheinpfalz (Palatinate)	Südliche Weinstrasse, Mittelhaardt-Deutsche Weinstrasse
Franken (Franconia)	Steigerwald, Maindreieck, Mainviereck
Württemberg	Remstal-Stuttgart, Württembergisch-Unterland, Kocher-Jagst-Tauber
Baden	Badische Bergstrasse-Kraichgau, Badisches Frankenland, Bodensee, Markgräflerland, Kaiserstuhl-Tuniberg, Breisgau, Ortenau

Wines from the *Bereiche* that are in italics are most likely to be found under their Bereich names on the export market. The rest of the names, some of which seem to lack any charm for the English-speaking reader (or drinker), illustrate clearly one of the difficulties which has to be overcome to sell German wine in non-German-speaking countries.

A table wine, besides being able to bear a *Bereich* name, may also, if it is geographically entitled to do so, bear the name of a village. It cannot be given the narrower description of a large or individual vineyard name, to which only a quality wine is entitled. So the following type of descriptions on labels are possible.

1. *For table wine*
   (a) Bereich Johannisberg, Deutscher Tafelwein Rhein
   (b) Johannisberger, Deutscher Tafelwein Rhein

The second example assumes that the wine comes from within the boundaries of the vineyards of the village of Johannisberg, and the first that the wine comes from the larger district of Johannisberg.

2. *For quality wine*
   (a) Bereich Johannisberg, Qualitätswein Rheingau, A.P. Nr. 12 345 678 79
   (b) Johannisberger Erntebringer, Qualitätswein Rheingau, A.P. Nr. 12 345 678 79

Both table and quality wine may also bear a vintage, and indicate the grape variety from which the wine is made. The German Wine Law lays down that if a vintage or grape type is named, at least 85 per cent of the wine must be made from the vintage or grape type stated. The style of the grape variety shown on the label must be immediately apparent when the wine is tasted. The actual control numbers, or A.P. numbers, shown above are, of course, fictitious. If the quality wine has a distinction, such as *Spätlese*, then this will also be shown on the label. The word *Erntebringer* in the second quality wine appellation indicates that the wine comes from the Erntebringer vineyard at Johannisberg.

There are two sorts of 'vineyard' – *Grosslagen* and *Einzellagen*. A *Grosslage* consists of a collection of *Einzellagen*, or individual vineyard sites. Under EEC law, a vineyard site must not be less than five hectares. Some *Grosslagen* will consist of up to forty *Einzellagen*, covering an area of 100 hectares or more, whilst others may be very much smaller. The climatic conditions, the soil and the terrain will be the same throughout any one *Grosslage*. Wines from a *Grosslage* will have to reach the same standards as those from an *Einzellage*, so that whichever vineyard name is chosen really depends on commercial considerations. If the *Grosslage* name is better known than the *Einzellage* name, a grower may well decide to make use of it. It is not possible to say, therefore, that wines from individual vineyard sites are either 'better' or 'worse' than wines from a collection of vineyard sites. To the casual reader, the system may seem like anarchy. It is undoubtedly complex, but very well controlled, and the origin and treatment of wine has to be meticulously recorded in the cellar register, which is subject to unannounced spot checks by the wine-control authorities.

To get the most out of wine it is helpful to understand the main part of the label. Somebody who buys a bottle labelled simply Margaux expecting it to be Château Margaux will be disappointed. It is the same in Germany as in France. The one word on a label can mean the difference between a fine and a good, but not outstanding, wine. The information given on a German wine label is concise and comprehensive. The formula remains the same, and the following examples of wines from the Moselle village of Graach show what some of the variations can mean.

	Vintage	Village name	Vineyard name	Grape type	Distinction
1.	1976	Graacher	Himmelreich	Riesling	Auslese
2.	1975	Graacher	Himmelreich	Riesling	Spätlese
3.	1977	Graacher	Himmelreich	Riesling	—
4.	1977	Graacher	Himmelreich	—	—

Example 1: This will be a splendid wine with fine rich fruit and balancing acidity, which will just be starting to show its real quality in 1980, but can best be kept for another three years at least.

Example 2: An excellent, crisp wine, with a long lingering flavour, in a very good vintage. Not so much weight as the 1976 Auslese above. Ready to be drunk from 1979 onwards.

Example 3: A good example of a Moselle. Crisp, refreshing, pleasant to drink as from about the autumn of 1978.

Example 4: Makes no claim to be a Riesling wine, and therefore may not have the typical elegant Moselle characteristics. Should nevertheless be a good, attractive wine.

The examples also show that wines would not necessarily be drunk in chronological order, but more with regard to the type of vintage and the quality category of the wine. The advice has always been given to the consumer outside Germany to look for the shipper's name on the bottle, for it is he whose reputation is at stake when the wine is drunk. This is possibly even more true today than it was some years ago. It is not that wines imported by other means than a traditional shipper are of necessity inferior, but simply that not so much of a commercial reputation is at stake when they are sold. Shippers such as Deinhard, Hallgarten, Langenbach, Sichel and Siegel cannot afford to make mistakes. Great individual estates obviously stand on their own merit.

One of the most remarkable innovations of the 1971 Wine Law was the establishment of the quality-control system in Germany. It is unique, in that it is far more comprehensive than any other official control system found elsewhere. As we have seen, it concerns itself with vine varieties, harvesting, must weights, the treatment and analysis of the wine, and finally and most importantly, the christening of the wine. After bottling a quality wine, three samples must be sent to the control centre of the district in which the grapes were grown, accompanied by a chemical analysis carried out by an officially recognized laboratory. The application for a control number will include information about the origin of the wine, any additions of sugar that have been made in the case of a simple quality wine, and certain other relevant factors. If the analysis and the details about the wine are in order, it will then be tasted, and awarded points for colour, clarity, bouquet, and flavour. Each control centre has a large number of qualified tasters upon whom it can call. They will be drawn from all sides of the wine trade, as well as the administrative branches of the civil service concerned with wine. The tastings take place in ideal conditions permitting total concentration. The name of the wine for which application is being made, such as 1978 Winkeler Hasensprung Riesling Kabinett, has obviously to be revealed to the tasters. The name of the grower or bottler remains a secret. Because the cost of obtaining the required chemical analysis and a control number is quite significant, it is not surprising that most applications for the right to use a quality wine name are successful. Frivolous applications are unlikely. Of the three original samples sent to the control centre, two will be kept in case of need as reference samples for two years, should there be any complaints about the wine in the future. The system is therefore excellent. Criticisms have been made occasionally that the basic standards – let us say, for example, the minimum must weight for a particular category of wine – are not severe enough. But with the best producers, these are minima and are often exceeded. Wine, with its different balance from one year to another, is a very complex product, and the fact that this is so adds enormously to its attraction. Its worth cannot be judged each year by entirely the same rigid standard. The best objective tasters will nearly always agree on the fundamental quality of a wine, but the subtlety of it will often bring dissension. The task of the control centres is to see that the basic qualities of German wine in their different categories are maintained, and most will agree that theirs is a job well done.

MITTELRHEIN

There are two specified regions in Germany whose area under vine has decreased in the last twenty years – the Mittelrhein and the Ahr Valley. The Mittelrhein follows the course of the Rhine from Trechtingshausen opposite the vineyards of Lorch in the Rheingau on the other side of the river, down the left bank as far as Koblenz. On the right bank, the Mittelrhein vineyards stretch from Kaub to Königswinter near Bonn. The vine is grown on the south-, south-west and west-facing slopes, many of which are very severe indeed and have a grey and austere appearance from the slate of the soil when the leaves are absent in winter. If one travels up the side valleys that lead down to the Rhine, one finds more vineyards, but only on the slopes with good exposure to the sun. The part of the region near Königswinter in the Grosslage Patersberg has the most northerly vineyards on the mainland of Europe. Here the decline is obvious and many vineyards have been abandoned and have become overgrown, as usual with coarse grass and gorse.

There was a time when the vineyards of Germany stretched up to Lübeck on the Baltic – a town now known principally for its marzipan. Their disappearance was not only the result of climatic changes, but it was more that the quality of the wine could not compare with that of the vineyards further south. This might not be quite so true today, for if good, balanced wines can be produced in the south of England from carefully chosen vine varieties, no doubt Hildesheim near Hanover could once again become a centre of viticulture. The problem would lie in selling a Hildesheimer wine, for whereas English wines still have a curiosity value which looks as though it will be replaced by a proper appreciation of their true worth, the consumer would probably lack the impetus to go out and buy a north German wine, so the process of selling and trading would never have a chance to develop. The continuing reduction in the area under vine in the Mittelrhein has been caused mainly by a shortage of labour. The towns of Koblenz, Bonn, and others along the river offer much easier, better paid and often pleasanter work than tending a vineyard. *Flurbereinigung* has helped to rationalize viticulture in the region, but the lie of the land makes it necessary in many places to retain terracing and the lack of true mechanization that that implies. Some 70 per cent of the region's vineyards have been rebuilt or re-allocated, and today there are about 900 hectares under vine.

The Mittelrhein climate, with a spring that starts early and positively, so that you know that it has arrived, suits the Riesling well, and it is said to give an unwonted elegance to the Müller-Thurgau. As in the Rheingau, the new varieties of vine that have been planted are relatively few in number. A Riesling must with a low sugar content often makes a better wine than a heavier must from a new crossing, as I explained earlier in this section. The Mittelrhein Riesling wines should have time to develop in bottle. The amount of bottle age needed depends on the quality of the wine and the balance of the wine produced by the vintage. In fact, even a simple quality Mittelrhein Riesling wine, with no special attributes, benefits from a year's bottle age or so. Apart from good classic wines, the Riesling from the region also lends itself well to conversion into sparkling wine, and Riesling style in German sparkling wine is highly regarded.

The vineyards of the Mittelrhein must be the most photographed in Germany and possibly the world. The Rhine Gorge from Koblenz to Bingerbrück is a real centre of tourism, and the vineyards form the background to the attractive villages along the river banks. Much of the wine is consumed on the spot by the visitors, but though villages such as Hammerstein and Leubsdorf have a local reputation for excellent wine, beyond the region they are little known, and on the export market they are virtually not found at all. In spite of the difficulties in growing vines in the region, it would be quite wrong if an impression were to be given of total decline. The region can easily sell all the wine it produces and the thirst of the tourists forces the cafés and restaurants to import wine from outside the Mittelrhein. There are flourishing family businesses that combine vine-growing and wine-making with a restaurant of a simple sort, whose main function is to be an aid to selling the wine. Such establishments, well equipped with reproduction 'old German' furniture, and a genuinely serious approach to their wine, do provide an atmosphere in which the German customer is happy to sit for hours and relax. They demand, however, a long working day from the owning family that provides the personal attention and interest that is not often found outside the family business.

Sixty per cent of the Mittelrhein vineyards do not create the main source of income for their owners. Statistics also show that whilst the yield per hectare has greatly increased since the start of the century, the time spent working in the vineyards has dropped in the last twenty-five years from 2,500 to 1,500 hours per annum. This is the result of *Flurbereinigung* and the increased use of machinery that comes with it. Even if the small grower cannot afford personally to own a relatively expensive piece of viticultural machinery, he can join a *Maschinenring* and share its cost with others. There are three *Bereiche* in the Mittelrhein, eleven *Grosslagen*, fifty-nine villages or communities and 112 *Einzellagen*. None of the villages are internationally known, neither are the growers who make wine in them.

AHR

The little region of the River Ahr is one of those areas of great beauty that make visiting Germany's vineyards so rewarding. Its wines, on the other hand, do not reach the highest levels, and many who are accustomed to wines with more sun in them will no doubt declare Ahr wines quite unimportant. But they are mainly consumed in the region or in the neighbouring towns, and, after years of unsensational and irregular decline, the area actually planted with vines has begun to increase a little. In spite of its northern situation, there is a larger percentage grown of red-vine varieties in the form of Spätburgunder and Portugieser than of the white Riesling and Müller-Thurgau. The Ahr rises in the Eifel Mountains and from Altenahr in the middle section down to near Bad Neuenahr-Ahrweiler, not far from the Rhine, the vineyards attend the twists of the river, occupying only the best situated sites. At Bad Neuenahr-Ahrweiler the valley is crossed by a bridge carrying the motorway to Koblenz and the Rheinhessen, some two hours' motoring further south-east. The region is well supported by the diplomatic community in Bonn and business people from Cologne, who enjoy the medieval atmosphere of some of the villages and restaurants. The Ahr Valley has suffered more than most regions from wars and economic problems and, in 1868, at a very difficult time for growers, it claims to have founded the first cooperative cellar in the world at Mayschoss. A less welcome first appearance in Germany was the arrival of phylloxera near Heimersheim in 1881.

Today, the vineyard holdings are for the most part very small, with ten hectares counting as a big estate. The cooperative cellars handle the largest proportion of the crop and the State owns nineteen hectares of vineyard. It would seem from statistics that the future for the region is now more hopeful than it was some thirty years ago. The poorer vineyards have been abandoned and only the best remain. Competition from sunnier regions and countries does not appear to be a threat to the future of viticulture in the Ahr Valley. There are one *Bereich*, one *Grosslage*, eleven villages or communities and forty-three *Einzellagen*.

MOSEL-SAAR-RUWER

The Mosel-Saar-Ruwer region is as pretty as its wine. Its 11,769 hectares of vineyard are just over half as extensive as those of the Rheinhessen. They are crowded on to the truly steep slopes of the Moselle, apparently making use of every site suitable for vine-growing. As if to emphasize the northerly latitude, any slope on the twisting river that faces away from the sun is left to be taken over by gorse and coarse undergrowth. Useless for viticulture, such land, shaded for much of the day, seems to have no other purpose than to separate one long stretch of vineyard from another. It is the length of the Moselle vineyards of which one is aware when driving from the confluence of the river with the Rhine at Koblenz upstream to Trier. By motorway the journey takes not much more than an hour, but some five hours or longer must be allowed if the course of the river is to be followed. On the one bank the vineyards climb up to the plateau of the Hunsrück that separates the Moselle from the Rhine and Nahe, and above the other lies the plain that leads to the Eifel hills, and on to the Low Countries.

It is sometimes difficult to remember that the Mosel-Saar-Ruwer is only one of eleven specified regions in West Germany for making quality wine. It is traditionally given equal importance with the Rhine by the wine trade, which sometimes speaks as though there were two categories of German wine only – namely Rhine and Moselle. Thus Moselle wine has a very clear identity of its own, no doubt much helped by the traditional slender green bottle in which the wine is sold. It seems so perfectly to express the cool elegance of the wine, its lightness and charm. Nowadays it is unsafe to assume without close inspection of the label that every wine from Germany in a green bottle of normal size (0.70 litres or 0.75 litres) comes from the Moselle, for such a bottle could contain a blend of wine from various EEC countries. If it does, though, it should say so quite clearly on the label in the language of the country in which it is being sold. Such blends are not necessarily bad, but by definition they will not have much character and very little of the style one expects in a German wine of even simple origin. Their reason for existing at all is the high cost of viticulture in Germany, and particularly in the steep vineyards of the Moselle. Wine can be made very cheaply in Italy, sent in bulk to Germany, blended to some extent with the cheapest German wine and offered to the public under a Germanic brand name. Blends of this type can also be found in Rheinwein bottles. *Caveat emptor*! Of course, highly respectable wines of excellent quality are found in Moselle-type bottles in countries all over the world, and whilst some may try to masquerade as being of German origin, this is by no means always the case. It is interesting, however, how often the lighter and drier white wines in many countries may be found in Moselle-type bottles, with which lightness and freshness seem such natural partners.

Until recent years, the Moselle has not always been a very helpful waterway to trade. The river lacked the depth of the Rhine and was unsuited to heavy barge traffic. In 1958, following an agreement between France, Luxembourg and West Germany, a start was made on the construction of thirteen dams to make the river navigable upstream as far as Thionville. Inevitably, the character of the Moselle has changed as a result. Whilst the villages by the river still have their attractions, they are now sharing them amongst a great many more people than before. It is said that the increased depth of water produced by the dams has raised the average temperature of the valley. This seems logical, though whether it has been scientifically proved or not I cannot say.

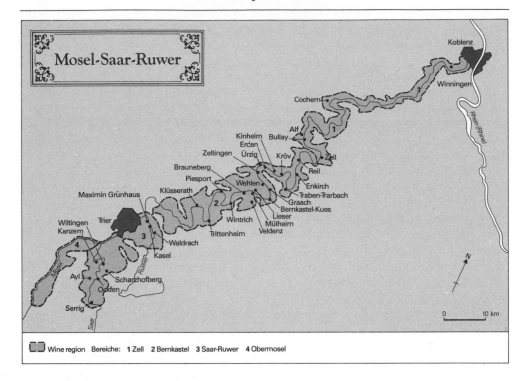

The Romans brought viticulture to the Moselle valley, as they did to so many other parts of Europe. Much evidence has been found of their interest in vine-growing, and possibly none is more striking than the tomb of a Roman wine merchant found at Neumagen, near Piesport. It depicts a ship, laden with casks of wine, and is now in a remarkable state of preservation in the Landesmuseum at Trier.

Phylloxera or vine louse has not established itself so strongly on the Moselle as in some other regions, partly because of the slaty soil there. Because of this, in the middle of the 1970s some 45 per cent of the vines on the Moselle were still growing, ungrafted, on their own root stocks, but *Flurbereinigung* has brought more grafted vines. Phylloxera did not arrive until 1912, and in 1975, sixty-four of the 143 Moselle villages were free of the pest. Like other regions, the Moselle has seen its vineyards expand and contract over the years in response to economic conditions. Since 1950, the growth has been considerable, and possibly not always in the right direction. To obtain a truly objective opinion about any viticultural area, wherever it may be, is often difficult, for most growers will have a personal view that supports their commercial interests. So we find that some will say that the Müller-Thurgau on the Moselle will produce wine of almost Riesling quality, whilst others affirm that it is a threat to the future of the Moselle crisp style that is widely known and easily identified. Its success is certainly clear, in that it now covers 21 per cent of the viticultural area. Those not so enthusiastic about the Müller-Thurgau claim that it has been planted in vineyards at the foot of the slopes where potatoes might be a better crop. Whether this is prejudice speaking or not is another question, but statistically it is true that the Moselle has shared the general tendency for a move-ment of the vineyards from the very steep slopes to the plain. The reasons, as we have already seen earlier, are economic and based on the high cost of maintaining the steepest vineyards, of which the Moselle had some 2,500 hectares in 1966 (27 per cent of the total area under vine).

Whatever statistics may tell us, only a visit to the region can give a true concep-tion of what the steepest vineyards are really like. Where the new motorway from the Eifel to the Rheinhessen and beyond crosses the Moselle near Winningen there is an elegant bridge, a hundred metres or so high, spanning the deep valley. Below and on either side of the bridge there are some of the most vertiginous vineyards on the Moselle. The soil is apparently, technically speaking, very diverse, though to the non-expert it all looks like slate. Whatever, it may be, it has the ability for the most part to remain where it is, retaining warmth and not sliding down into the valley below.

As in other regions of West Germany, the proportions of the various vine varieties, one to another, have altered on the Moselle over the years. From what one hears, one might suppose that the Riesling has always predominated, but that is not so. At the end of the nineteenth century, its plantation increased from 42 per cent in 1880 to 88 per cent in 1910. Whilst the Riesling was gaining so much ground, the Elbling vine was disappearing, so that today it is found to any great extent only in the Bereich Obermosel beyond Trier. Here the Elbling produces 'neutral' wine with good acidity that lends itself to conversion into pleasant sparkling wine. Neutrality is not always a negative characteristic in a wine, for a crisp, refreshing flavour without too overpowering a bouquet can often be enjoyed in greater quantity than can a scented wine, such as a Morio-Muskat, which can cloy. The Riesling now covers 61 per cent of the vineyard area and a much greater percentage of the best vineyard sites. A red Moselle wine seems almost a contradiction in terms, but it existed until the start of the 1930s. Even today, north of the Moselle in the Ahr Valley, red wine is still made, though on a decreasing scale as we have seen.

After the Second World War, the *Flurbereinigung*, or re-allocation and reconstruction of the vineyards, began. Because of the terrain, the reconstruction could not be so obvious or dramatic to the casual eye as at Rüdesheim in the Rheingau, for example. Nevertheless, roads have been built where only paths existed before and drainage has been improved to reduce soil erosion. In the very steep vineyards, the vines are still grown up wooden poles, but where possible they are trained on wires nowadays in order to keep costs down. In the Upper Moselle and on the Saar, where vine-growing is mixed to a greater extent with other forms of farming, machinery for the vineyards is often shared amongst a number of growers. From Schweich near Trier down to Koblenz, where the vineyards are at their steepest, the use of machinery is of necessity limited. One finds lifts of a simple design for carrying materials and tools to the top of the slopes. Ploughs are pulled by winches attached to vehicles stationed at the headland and guided by a worker who follows on foot, rather as though the plough were drawn by a horse. It is a slow and expensive procedure, but it is difficult to see how it can be radically improved.

The proportion of growers who sell their wine in bulk to the trade without firm long-term contracts, is said to be very high. When commercial strength seems to lie very much with the buyer rather than the grower, this is not a happy situation and some feel that the cooperative movement should develop even more rapidly than has been the case. Each year, the number of part-time growers with holdings of less than half a hectare decreases, and the average-size holding, therefore, slowly increases. The absolute need for quality production to justify a selling price that will meet the high costs of cultivating steep vineyards is often mentioned when growers meet. One advantage the Moselle grower who bottles his own wine has over his counterpart in some other vine-growing areas is the sheer beauty of the countryside. This, and the continuing improvement of the road system, encourages tourism and, therefore, the consumption of wine. It is virtually impossible to resist the temptation if one is in the Moselle Valley to stop at a wine bar or restaurant and drink a glass or more. The sort of simple wine sold by the glass will be pleasant, refreshing and light in alcohol. The vine is everywhere, and in every village there are signs outside growers' houses advertising the sale of wine in bottle. There are not the same number of wine festivals as one finds in the Palatinate. Attempts to organize such functions have sometimes failed, surprisingly, through lack of support. In the tourist season the towns of Bernkastel and Cochem, to name but two, seem to be the scene of a permanent festival with their restaurants full of people enjoying wine, so perhaps official festivals are unnecessary.

Although the first cooperative cellar was founded in 1896 at Gondorf near Koblenz, it is really only recently that the movement has greatly increased its strength. Between 1961 and 1963, three large district cooperatives were formed, and a central cooperative cellar was built at Bernkastel-Kues in the heart of the Middle Moselle.

In spite of the fact that the river is now navigable throughout its journey in West Germany, the Moselle remains different to the Rhine. The freight traffic is not as heavy, the water is cleaner, the scene more rural. Whereas it is just not possible to believe in Rhine salmon, Moselle eel, pike and even trout do not immediately appear to be claiming a false origin. The cooking on the Moselle is, for the most part, standard West German, with which the crisp Moselle wine, served in an elegant Treviris glass, goes well. The richer and sweeter *Auslese* wines are best drunk by themselves or with the minimum of food of the dry biscuit variety. It is most unusual for a Moselle *Auslese* to have the fullness of even a Rheingau *Auslese*, and it certainly does not have the body to accompany a dessert in the manner of a sweet white Bordeaux. The subtlety of a fine Moselle with its delicate fruit, acidity and sweetness is at its most rewarding when given individual attention. I hope this does not sound too much like a deterrent to pleasure or too over-serious, for the Moselle is the most easily enjoyed of wine. Subtle it is, withdrawn it is not.

Possibly the wines that seem in a good year to embody more than any other the qualities one looks for in a Moselle do not, strictly speaking, come from the Moselle at all but from its tributary, the Saar. The professional may on occasions be expected to taste as many as fifty wines or more in a morning. Even with wines so easily accessible as Moselles, the concentration required is very tiring, so that to have included in the tasting a range of Saar wines is always welcome. Their particularly strong combination of fruit and acidity is immediately obvious from the bouquet. The flavour is stronger than that of a wine from the Middle Moselle, possibly less delicate, but nothing if not positive. Their disadvantage is that they are so appealing when young that they often do not have an opportunity to reach maturity. This is a pity, for at maturity one finds the balance of flavour and the elegance of form and sheer style that is missing in the young wine. In less than good years, the wines of the Saar tend to be rather ordinary, although, of course, there are always exceptions to every generalization. German does not have a sparkling wine-producing area in the way that France does in Champagne. There are, though, a number of districts that produce the type of neutral wine with good acidity that lends itself to being made into sparkling wine, and much of the wine from the Saar is treated in this way in 'off' vintages.

The Saar is not a river that one would make a special effort to visit unless there was an interest in wine as an encouragement. Where the vineyards are found, it is pleasant and rural, but no more. The best known wine-producing villages are Ockfen, Ayl and Wiltingen, but even upstream as far as Serrig, in a good year, splendid wines can be made. Trier claims to be the oldest city in West Germany and, with some 110,000 inhabitants, is almost as large as Koblenz at the opposite end of the river. It is the centre of many of the wine trade's activities in the region. In 1910, the first wine auctions were held in Trier, when a number of growers formed the *Grosse Ring* to promote their better quality wines. Most of the estates that put up some of their wines for auction in 1910 are still members of the *Grosse Ring* today.

The first school on the Moselle for training people in matters to do with the wine trade was opened in Trier in 1893, and now there are similar establishments in Bernkastel and Bullay. It is not, though, the trade and growers alone that can nowadays receive some sort of formal training in wine on the Moselle. In 1972, an instructional path some three kilometres in length was opened through the vineyards on the outskirts of Trier. By means of a brochure printed in English and in Dutch, as well as in German, the visitor can learn about vine-growing as he walks through the vineyards. At the end of the walk there is a visit to a cellar and a tasting. Similar instructional tours can be made at Reil and at Winningen near Koblenz. Seminars in English are held at certain times of the year in Trier and elsewhere on the Moselle, providing basic information about the local wine. More detailed information can be obtained from: Weinwerbung Mosel-Saar-Ruwer, Neustrasse 86, 5500 Trier, West Germany.

In spite of its importance to the wine trade, Trier does not produce wine of great reputation throughout the world. For this, one must move downstream to the Middle Moselle where the best known villages may be found. Before reaching this point, one passes the little Ruwer river, a tributary of the Moselle. Its wines are in a very similar position to those of the Saar. They can be full of character and firm in a good year, but are not of great interest in an indifferent one. Nevertheless, there are some excellent estates in the district whose wines are amongst the best that the Moselle can produce.

It is something of a paradox that much of the interest in wine lies in its variety, and yet at the same time we wish to categorize it, to be able to make positive statements about it, to understand it. The commercial pressures for doing so are obvious. There must be some relationship between the flavour of the wine in the bottle and what we expect it to be, otherwise the purchase of a bottle of wine becomes a thing of chance. A grower in village 'A' may be able instantly to differentiate between the wines of that village and those of the adjacent village 'B', but others may not. Often, though, the differences between two wines will be the result of different cellar techniques as much as a change of locality. Where there are many individual growers making and bottling a small production of wine, as in Burgundy or West Germany, one has within the general style of a particular district a great variety of flavour. Therefore, some villages by common consent will have a reputation for fine wine, but the best wine from lesser known villages may be better than the more ordinary wine from the best known villages. Not all the geese are swans, but some of the swans may be geese. For all the good wine that comes from the Middle Moselle villages of Bernkastel, Piesport or Wehlen, how much equally fine wine is left behind at Pölich, Wolf or Pünderich? Probably nobody knows the answer to this, but no doubt the better known wine villages have, for good reason, won their reputation over many years.

Bernkastel is one of the larger towns in the Middle Moselle, and from its population of under 6,000 inhabitants one has an idea of the rural character of the district. It has narrow streets, overlooked by medieval half-timbered houses, dominated by its most famous vineyard – the Bernkasteler Doktor. Between Bernkastel and Zeltingen there is a large sweep of vineyard, forming a gentle curve and rising as though it were part of a huge amphitheatre from the Moselle. In it there lie the vineyards of the Bernkasteler Bratenhöfchen, the Graacher Himmelreich, and the Wehlener Sonnenuhr, to name some of the best known. Similar stretches of vineyard continue the length of the river, into the district known as the Lower Moselle and down to the Rhine at Koblenz. Most of the villages by the Moselle are full of charm and places where the traveller may quench his thirst, as the guide books would put it. The Moselle is consistently the prettiest of rivers. There are four *Bereiche* in the Mosel-Saar-Ruwer region, nineteen *Grosslagen*, 192 villages or communities and 525 *Einzellagen*. Amongst the better known villages are:

BEREICH ZELL

Alf, Cochem, Winningen, Zell.

BEREICH BERNKASTEL

Bernkastel-Kues, Brauneberg, Enkirch, Erden, Graach, Kinheim, Klüsserath, Kröv, Leiwen, Lieser, Mülheim, Piesport, Reil, Traben-Trarbach, Trittenheim, Ürzig, Veldenz, Wehlen, Wintrich, Zeltingen.

BEREICH SAAR-RUWER

Ayl, Kanzem, Kasel, Maximin Grünhaus, Oberemmel, Ockfen, Scharzhofberg, Serrig, Waldrach, Wiltingen.

As we have seen, Trier is the home of a number of estates of outstanding quality, amongst which the following deserve individual attention, together with a few away from the town.

VERWALTUNG DER STAATLICHEN WEINBAUDOMÄNEN (Trier)

Also known in English as the State Cellars. There are four individual estates administered from Trier, at Trier itself, Trier-Avelsbach, Ockfen, and Serrig, of which that at Ockfen is the oldest, dating from 1896. The vineyards consist of 88 hectares, of which 80 per cent are on steep and 20 per cent on moderate slopes. On the four estates mentioned above, the best known vineyard sites are at Ockfen (Bockstein, Herrenberg), and at Serrig (Vogelsang). The vine varieties are 85 per cent Riesling, 3 per cent Müller-Thurgau, 1 per cent Ruländer, 1 per cent Spätburgunder and 10 per cent others. This is Saar wine at its very best, as one finds from all the big Trier-based estates. Matured in wood, crisp, often naturally slightly *spritzig* (sparkling), with fine fruit and acidity.

GÜTERVERWALTUNG VEREINIGTE HOSPITIEN (Trier)

A charitable institute, founded in the Middle Ages, supported by the income from 1,400 hectares of land in Trier, and its vineyards. The cellars are the oldest in Germany, part dating from the Roman period. There are 40 hectares of vineyards, of which 70 per cent are on steep slopes, and the rest on moderate slopes. Many of the vineyard sites are at Serrig (Vogelsang), at Wiltingen (Kupp, Braunfels, etc.), at Kanzem, at Trier, at Piesport (Goldtröpfchen, etc.) and at Zeltingen (Sonnenuhr, Himmelreich, etc.). The vine varieties are 93 per cent Riesling, 5 per cent Müller-Thurgau, 1 per cent Ruländer and 1 per cent Kerner. There is a concentration on quality wines with distinction (QmP), showing the expected virtues for wines of the region of elegance, fruit, and a stylish acidity. Twenty-five per cent of the sales are in dry wines, suitable for diabetics.

VERWALTUNG DER BISCHÖFLICHEN WEINGÜTER (Trier)

In 1966, three estates with ecclesiastical origins combined to form the present large estate. They were the Bischöfliches Konvikt, the Bischöfliches Priesterseminar and the Hohe Domkirche. The grapes are pressed in eight press houses amongst the vineyards, and the must is brought to the central cellar in Trier for fermentation. There are 96.4 hectares of vineyards, practically all on very steep slopes. The vineyard sites are at Ürzig (Würzgarten), at Erden (Treppchen), at Trittenheim, Kasel,

Kanzem, Wiltingen, Ayl, Piesport (Goldtröpfchen), Eitelsbach, Avelsbach and at
Scharzhofberg. The vine varieties are 95 per cent Riesling and 5 per cent new
crossings. Emphasis is laid on producing typical, fine Riesling wines, matured in
wood. A considerable amount of dry wine is made. In good years, the wines need
time to mature to their full beauty.

STIFTUNG STAATLICHES FRIEDRICH-WILHELM-GYMNASIUM (Trier)

The foundation dates from 1563. The central cellar is situated in Trier, and there are
six estate houses in the vineyards on the Moselle and the Saar. The vineyards consist of 46 hectares, of which 65 per cent are on steep and 15 per cent on moderate
slopes. Many of the vineyard sites are situated at Falkenstein, Pellingen, Ockfen,
Mehringen, Trittenheim, Neumagen, Dhron, at Graach (Domprobst and Himmelreich), at Zeltingen (Sonnenuhr and Schlossberg) and at Bernkastel (Bratenhöfchen and Graben). The vine varieties are 87 per cent Riesling, 11 per cent
Müller-Thurgau with 2 per cent new crossings. These are typical top quality
Riesling wines, which have been matured in wood, and are well differentiated one
from another.

REICHSGRAF VON KESSELSTATT (Trier)

This is one of the largest and older estates on the Moselle, having been established
over 600 years ago. The administrative offices and cellar are in Trier, and there are
four estate houses/cellars in the vineyards at Graach, Piesport, Kasel and Oberemmel. The vineyards consist of 94 hectares, mainly on steep and moderate slopes.
Many of the vineyard sites are at Graach (Josephshöfer, Himmelreich, etc.), Zeltingen, Wehlen (Sonnenuhr), Bernkastel (Doktor, Bratenhöfchen, etc.), Piesport
(Goldtröpfchen, Treppchen, etc.), Brauneberg (Juffer), Neumagen, Dhron, Trittenheim, Leiwen, Kasel, Waldrach, Oberemmel, Niedermennig, Scharzhofberg,
Wiltingen, Kanzem and at Ockfen. The vine varieties are 98 per cent Riesling and
2 per cent new crossings under trial. The high percentage of Riesling in outstanding
sites shows where the aim of this estate lies. Riesling wines, matured in wood, of the
classic Mosel-Saar-Ruwer type are produced.

C. VON SCHUBERT'SCHE GUTSVERWALTUNG (Grünhaus Bei Trier)

This estate is first known to have been mentioned on 7 January 996(!), and was
acquired by the great grandfather of the present owner, Andreas von Schubert, in
1882. The setting of the estate on the Ruwer is delightful. There are 22 hectares of
vineyards, of which 30 per cent are on steep and the rest on moderate slopes. The
vines are mainly grown on wires, which is unusual in this region. The vineyard
sites are at Bruderberg, Herrenberg, Abtsberg – all at Maximin Grünhaus, and all
in the sole ownership of the estate. The vine varieties are 95 per cent Riesling, and 5
per cent Müller-Thurgau. These are stylish, fruity wines, typical of the Ruwer at
its best.

KARTHÄUSERHOF EITELSBACH (Trier-Eitelsbach)

The estate dates from the early thirteenth century. The present owner, Werner
Tyrell, is president of the Deutsche Weinbauverband, the German Wine Growers'
Association based in Bonn. There are 19 hectares of vineyards, of which 30 per cent
are on steep and 70 per cent on moderate slopes. The vineyard sites are all at Eitelsbach. Sole owners of the Eitelsbacher Karthäuserhofberg Stirn. One hundred per
cent Riesling is used. These are powerful, firm wines, often *spritzig* (slightly sparkling) that keep their freshness for years in bottle, and are frequently dry in flavour.
Wines of great character.

WEINGUT WWE. DR H. THANISCH (Bernkastel-Kues)

A fine, family-owned estate of about 13 hectares, planted with 93 per cent Riesling with outstanding vineyard sites at Bernkastel (Doktor, Graben), at Wehlen (Sonnenuhr), and at Graach (Himmelreich).

GUTSVERWALTUNG DEINHARD (Bernkastel-Kues)

An estate owned by Deinhard & Co. of Koblenz, producing classic, fine Riesling wines from 10.9 hectares of prime vineyard sites at Bernkastel (Doktor, Graben and Bratenhöfchen), at Graach (Himmelreich and Domprobst).

WEINGUT JOH. JOS. PRÜM (Wehlen)

A family estate whose wines have a world reputation, particularly those from the Wehlener Sonnenuhr vineyard, of which the estate is the largest single owner. The Riesling QmP wines are famous for their extremely elegant fruit/acidity balance.

WEINGUT EGON MÜLLER (Scharzhofberg)

This ancient estate, dating back to the eighth century, has been in the hands of the present family since the end of the eighteenth century. There are 8.5 hectares of vineyards, of which 63 per cent are on steep slopes and 37 per cent on moderate. The sites are Scharzhofberger Braune Kupp, Klosterberg and Braunfels, all at Wiltingen. The vines are over 90 per cent Riesling with some new crossings on a trial basis. Perfect examples come from this fine estate of Saar wine at its finest. Superb fruit and acidity keeps the wine fresh for years.

RHEINGAU

The Rheingau is one of the smaller of the specified regions. Its countryside is pleasant but compared with those of Baden, many of its villages lack charm. The grey roofs of the houses, the rather ordinary little cafés with the ubiquitous rubber trees and aluminium-framed doors and windows can have a lowering effect on the spirits. At least it cannot be said that the beauty of the landscape interferes with the objective judgments of those who appreciate Rheingau wine. Most countrysides appear better seen from a slight elevation, however, so that the view from the upper parts of the vineyards looking towards the Rhine and across to the Rheinhessen is

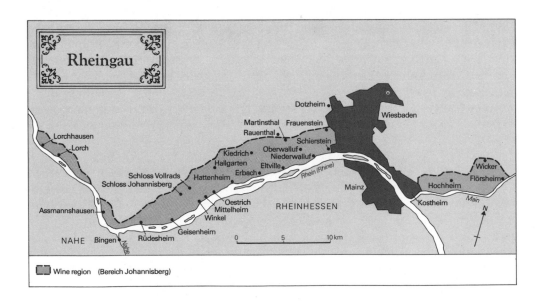

enjoyable but not sensational. It is made far more interesting if it is remembered that the Rheingau produces some of the finest white wine in the world. It is a region of monoculture, and it seems in the central part of the Rheingau that every possible plot is either planted or waiting to be replanted with vines.

The region is only forty kilometres long and divided into two unequal parts by the town of Wiesbaden. Downstream, the Rheingau starts near the village of Assmannshausen. This part of the region lies in the Rhine Gorge, where the scenery is impressive and the area capable of supporting vines is very limited in extent. The red wines of Assmannshausen, made from the Spätburgunder grape, have a considerable local reputation. The State owns vineyards here, and undoubtedly one of the best places to taste the wine would be at the Hotel Krone overlooking the river. Even in such charming old-world surroundings, the visitor will find the wine rather insignificant if he is used to red wine from a more southern climate. The central and largest part of the Rheingau begins at Rüdesheim and ends at Wiesbaden. Between these two towns, most of the great Rheingau wines are made, though on the far side of Wiesbaden lies the well-known village of Hochheim. The majority of the Rheingau vineyards can be worked by small tractors, and only in the Rhine Gorge is the terrain too steep to make this possible. Some 25 per cent of the vineyards are on level territory and 50 per cent on moderate slopes. Terracing has largely disappeared from the region as a result of *Flurbereinigung*, and this is particularly noticeable on the large hill above Rüdesheim. In the last twenty years this has been rebuilt, and the lay-out of the vineyards, which had remained almost intact since the eleventh century, completely altered. The Rüdesheimer vineyards usually produce grapes with a higher sugar content than those from elsewhere in the region. Their exposition to the sun is ideal, whilst the Rhine at the foot of the vineyards and the hill above Bingen opposite improve the micro-climate. Rüdesheim is very much a resort, and not a place for anyone looking for solitude in the summer, or on public holidays. It has many, very many, wine bars, and its *Drosselgasse* – a narrow lane filled with *Weinstuben*. It is possible to pass over the vineyards by a chair lift from the town to the top of the hill, from where there is a panoramic view over to Bingen and the mouth of the Nahe River.

Whilst in the other ten specified regions of West Germany there are many wine-producing villages that are virtually unknown outside the immediate district, this is not true of the Rheingau. All the villages can and do produce good wine, and most are capable of great wine in a fine year. Therefore, in spite of the fact that the region only covers just over 2,800 hectares, its wines are found in better quality wine lists throughout the world. One might wonder if Rheingau wines are not over-represented, but it is more that wines from some other regions are undoubtedly under-represented. Both the Rheingau, and its neighbouring specified region, the Mittelrhein, have a high proportion (75 per cent) of Riesling growing in their vineyards. The Mittelrhein can produce fine Riesling wine that will be as good as a Rheingau, and yet there is hardly one village in the Mittelrhein that is known outside the region. I suspect that the reasons for this unbalanced situation are commercial, not vinous.

There is a 'Rheingauer Riesling Route' marked in the vineyards that runs through the best known villages or by the best known estates. Many of these have a noble origin, and the name of the titled family will still be used even if the vineyards are no longer in their hands. One of the most impressive buildings in the Rheingau is undoubtedly Schloss Johannisberg, which overlooks the vineyards of Geisenheim and Winkel. It is visible up on its hill above the Riesling vines from miles around. The wines of Schloss Johannisberg should not be confused with those of the Bereich Johannisberg which covers the whole of the Rheingau. The name 'Johannisberg', in fact, is one that can lead to misunderstandings, for in Switzerland a wine is produced in the canton of the Valais called Johannisberger made from the Sylvaner grape. In the United States, a Johannisberger Riesling is also grown, which is, in fact, the true Riesling from Germany, transported to the New World. The label is worth more than a hurried glance when buying wine.

Geisenheim is best known for its Viticultural Institute already mentioned earlier in this section, which was founded in 1872. Apart from its investigative work, it has an important role training students to various different levels of knowledge and expertise. Whilst the Geisenheim wines are very good indeed, those of neighbouring Winkel can be finer still. Even where footpaths are not signposted, it is possible to walk through the vineyards away from the small service roads that lead to the Taunus Hills at the back of the Rheingau vineyards. Given the time, it is clearly the best way to get to know the region, though it is very difficult to identify the individual vineyard sites or, indeed, to distinguish those of one village from another. To do so, it is probably best to seek the help of one of the local vine-growers. The Rheingau vineyards are only about two kilometres in depth, so that, when walking from Winkel towards the woods above the vineyards, it is not long before one reaches Schloss Vollrads. Like all the best Winkeler wines, those of Schloss Vollrads have great elegance and breeding. To compare the wines of one Rheingau village with another in a general way is only possible up to a certain point. Within any one village there will be a multiplicity of growers, probably each with his own concept of what a Rheingau wine should be. As a result of this, and because of minute variations in micro-climate and soil, there will be many different wines bearing the same village and vineyard name. In some instances, the differences may well be very subtle, but it is the minute variation in flavour of bouquet that may separate a great from a good wine. The wines of Oestrich have possibly a little more flavour and a shade less delicacy than those of its neighbour Winkel, but both are among the best produced in the Rheingau. On the river front at Oestrich, apart from a charming old hotel, there is still an ancient crane that was at one time used to load wine casks on to boats for shipment downstream to Cologne.

The State has its largest vineyard holding in the Rheingau based on the village of Eltville, and certainly one of its most widely known vineyards is the Steinberg, above the small and attractive village of Hattenheim. One of the advantages to the visitor of the Steinberg is that it is easily located, for the Cistercian monks who planted the vines surrounded them with a high wall. Nearby is the old monastery of Kloster Eberbach, now used for wine auctions and wine trade functions of national importance. It is in many ways the home of the wine trade in the Rheingau and has a fine and much photographed cellar. In recent years, Kloster Eberbach has provided a base for the German Wine Academy, which runs seminars and courses in English on all aspects of the German wine trade and wine production.

Hattenheim is the headquarters of the Schloss Schönborn estate which, like Schloss Johannisberg, uses the title of *Domäne*. Usually, when one speaks of a *Domäne* nowadays in Germany one means a state-owned property, such as the Domäne Trier, or the Domäne Niederhausen. As both Schloss Johannisberg and Schloss Schönborn had state responsibilities in the past, it became customary to call them *Domäne* as well. The holdings of the large estates in the Rheingau, for the most part, are not concentrated in the immediate vicinity of the producing cellar and press house. Thus the Koblenz-based company of Deinhard has its Rheingau *Gutshaus*, or estate house and cellar, at Oestrich, but its vineyards are found at Rüdesheim, Johannisberg, Geisenheim, Winkel, Mittelheim, Hallgarten and Oestrich itself.

Nearer the Taunus Hills than the Rhine, and above Eltville, are the villages of

Kiedrich and Rauenthal. In terms of quality, the Kiedricher wines are probably not amongst the very finest in the Rheingau, but still very much in the First Division. The church at Kiedrich was remarkably well endowed by an Englishman in the nineteenth century, and has a great musical reputation as a bastion of the Gregorian chant, so that attendance at High Mass is quite an experience, no matter what one's view of religious faith may be. Rauenthaler wines are exceptionally elegant and have a wonderful fruity acidity.

Travelling in a more or less easterly direction through the Rheingau from Eltville and before reaching Hochheim on the River Main, one must first pass through the outskirts of Wiesbaden. It is an elegant city and spa with over 250,000 inhabitants. To take a cure is still very much part of the German way of life, though in most cases today the cost will be met by a health insurance scheme. The city escaped serious damage in the Second World War and has a reputation for great prosperity.

Hochheimer wine has a more earthy flavour than that of the central Rheingau, but a very positive style that combines well with the firm Riesling flavour. Queen Victoria seems to have done a great deal for the promotion of Hochheimer, although it is a little difficult to believe, as has been reported, that she actually said 'Good hock keeps off the doc'. However, she did allow her name to be given to a vineyard, the Hochheimer Königin Victoria Berg. In fact, the use in English-speaking countries of the word Hock, an abbreviation of Hochheimer, antedates Queen Victoria by several centuries. It may now legally be used for a table wine from the Rhein 'district', or for a quality wine from any of the Rhineland specified regions, with the exception of Franconia, Baden and Württemberg.

In comparison with other regions, there is a greater number of big estates in the Rheingau, but the average size holding still remains small. It is, however, slowly becoming larger, with the greatest increase being found in the number of holdings between one and five hectares. Of the 2,250 growers today, 800 have no cellars of their own but deliver their grapes to cooperative cellars or to the wine trade for processing. *Strausswirtschaft*, whereby the grower is permitted to serve his wine from his own house accompanied by cold food, is strong amongst those whose wines are not of the best. One sees many signs while passing through the region advertising wine for sale in bottle directly to the consumer – *Flaschenwein Verkauf*. It may not be very charitable to write it, but many wines that are offered to the consumer in this way will be depending on the reputation of the Rheingau wines from the famous estates to secure their sale. In the last thirty years or so there has been a decline in the number of wine merchants in the region, in Frankfurt am Main and Wiesbaden, which may be related to the increase in sales from the grower.

The first Rheingau cooperative cellars were founded at the end of the nineteenth century and, as elsewhere, were the result of hard times. Over the years the number of cooperative cellars has decreased, but the vineyard area whose crop is vinified by cooperatives has increased. Today it accounts for 17 per cent of the total area. Some would say that it is a pity that the percentage is not greater, as a strong cooperative movement helps price stability.

West Germany is said to be the home of the Riesling, and the Rheingau claims to be its actual birthplace. Certainly, it is of the Riesling that one thinks first of all in connection with Rheingau wines and their vine varieties. There are other vines growing in the region, and from the thirteen hectares of Scheurebe some excellent stylish wines are produced. The Müller-Thurgau covers 283 hectares, the Silvaner 125 hectares, and the Ehrenfelser sixty-seven hectares. This last vine, a product of the Viticultural School at Geisenheim, is a crossing of Riesling and Silvaner, dating from 1929. It has the advantage of producing a larger yield than the Riesling, a heavier must weight, and it ripens some eight days before the Riesling.

Unlike those of Württemberg, the majority of Rheingau wines are sold in restaurants in the region in bottle, or sometimes in the half-bottle, and the quantity served when it is offered by the glass is 0.2 litres – not 0.25 litres. The Rhinelanders put a lot of effort into their public holidays. It is a predominantly Roman Catholic part of the country and all the religious festivals are observed and celebrated. The consumption of wine in Rüdesheim on such occasions is formidable and begins in the morning, but starts to peter out early in the evening as saturation point is approached. There are no great regional dishes to be eaten, but the good and essentially meaty types of *Wurst* go admirably with Rheingau wine up to *Kabinett* quality. Above this level, as the wine becomes more and more 'important', the necessity for food diminishes. When wines of Riesling *Auslese* quality are reached, food begins to be an intrusion, and a Rheingau *Trockenbeerenauslese* should be drunk on its own with the smallest and most insignificant dry biscuit you can find. The finesse of the best quality Rheingau Riesling wine is, therefore, most easily enjoyed and appreciated with no accompaniment, no distractions. This advice may seem somewhat precious, if not downright tiresome, but it is the advice a Rheingauer would give as to how to get the best out of his wine, and nobody knows how to do this better than he.

The Rheingau has one *Bereich*, ten *Grosslagen*, twenty-eight villages or communities and 120 *Einzellagen*. The names of the *Grosslagen* are: Burgweg, Daubhaus, Deutelsberg, Erntebringer, Gottesthal, Heiligenstock, Honigberg, Mehrhölzchen, Steil and Steinmächer. The villages or communities of the Rheingau, practically all of which are well known for their wine are: Assmannshausen-Aulhausen, Böddiger, Dotzheim, Eltville, Erbach, Flörsheim, Frankfurt, Frauenstein, Geisenheim, Hallgarten, Hattenheim, Hochheim, Johannisberg, Kiedrich, Kostheim, Lorch, Lorchhausen, Martinsthal, Mittelheim, Niederwalluf, Oberwalluf, Oestrich, Rauenthal, Rüdesheim, Schierstein, Wicker, Wiesbaden, and Winkel. In the Rheingau, many of the villages lie within the boundary of more than one *Grosslage*, and though their reputations may be spread throughout much of the world, in some instances it is the individually owned estate that is the best known of all. Amongst a number of these, the following should be mentioned.

SCHLOSS VOLLRADS (Winkel)

The oldest wine-producing estate in the Rheingau, still in the hands of the original owning family, the Matuschka-Greiffenclaus. The earliest buildings date from the start of the fourteenth century, and part will be opened in 1981 as a tasting centre for Rheingau wines, and restaurant. The setting is truly picturesque. There were 47 hectares of vineyards in production in 1980, of which 60 per cent lie on moderate slopes and 20 per cent on steep slopes. Most of the vineyard sites are in the immediate vicinity of the Schloss near the village of Winkel. The vine varieties are 95 per cent Riesling, 3 per cent Müller-Thurgau and 2 per cent others. The wine is classic, stylish Rheingau Riesling wine with good acidity. Interest is being shown in the production of dry and medium dry wines as an accompaniment to food. The wines are sold under the name Schloss Vollrads, 65 per cent being exported.

VERWALTUNG DER STAATSWEINGÜTER ELTVILLE

These are also known in English as the State Cellars. The vineyards are spread throughout the Rheingau and into the Hessische Bergstrasse, some dating back to the twelfth century. There are today seven individual estates administered from Eltville, as well as the famous Kloster Eberbach mentioned earlier. The director of the estate, Dr Hans Ambrosi whose information on individual estates has been invaluable in the writing of this section, is a leading authority on German wine. There are 196 hectares of vineyards – the largest individual wine estate in Germany, two-thirds being on slopes. There are many vineyard sites at Assmannshausen, Rüdesheim, Hattenheim, the Steinberg, Rauenthal, Kiedrich, Eltville, Hochheim and at Bensheim (Bergstrasse). The vine varieties are 74.6 per cent Riesling, 10.5 per cent Spätburgunder (Black Pinot), 8.4 per cent Müller-Thurgau and 6.5 per cent others. Because of the wide area from which the wines originate, the estate produces an equally wide variety of Rheingau wine. Emphasis is laid on full Riesling wines with fine fruit, particularly suited for development in bottle over many years.

SCHLOSS REINHARTSHAUSEN (Erbach)

Parts of the estate buildings date from the eighth century. The present owners are great-grandchildren of Kaiser Wilhelm II. There are 67 hectares of vineyards, of which 80 per cent are on moderate slopes. The vineyard sites include the world-famous Erbacher Marcobrunn and the neighbouring Erbacher vineyards of Schlossberg, Hohenrain and Honigberg, as well as the Hattenheimer vineyards of Wisselbrunnen, Nussbrunnen, Rheingarten, amongst others, and sites at the villages of Kiedrich. Rauenthal and Rüdesheim. The vine varieties are over 80 per cent Riesling. There is an interesting plantation of Chardonnay (from clones imported from the Chablis region and California) in the Erbacher Rheinhell – a site on an island in the Rhine with a particularly favourable micro-climate. Spätburgunder, Traminer and Kerner are also grown. Powerful, fruity Riesling wines, which have excellent keeping qualities, are made and matured in wood.

G. H. VON MUMM'SCHES WEINGUT (Johannisberg)

The estate dates from the early nineteenth century, and now falls under the same ownership as the Wiesbaden firm of sparkling wine producers, Söhnlein. There are approximately 55 hectares of vineyards, of which 40 per cent are on steep slopes and 30 per cent on moderate slopes. There are many vineyard sites at Johannisberg (30 hectares), Rüdesheim (10 hectares), Geisenheim, Winkel, as well as 10 hectares of the recently purchased Assmannshäuser Höllenberg. The vine varieties are 85 per cent Riesling, 12 per cent Spätburgunder and 3 per cent others. The estate concentrates on the traditional, wood-matured, fine Riesling wines. Excellent opportunity exists to taste the wines from this estate at the restaurant Burg Schwarzenstein near Schloss Johannisberg.

GUTSVERWALTUNG DEINHARD (Oestrich)

The estate dates from the late nineteenth century, and is now particularly well represented on the German export markets. The administration is also responsible for estates in the Palatinate (at Forst, Ruppertsberg and Deidesheim), and on the Moselle (at Bernkastel and Graach). There are approximately 56 hectares of vineyards, of which 42 per cent are on moderate and 25 per cent on steep slopes. There are many vineyard sites at Hallgarten, Oestrich, Mittelheim, Winkel, Johannisberg, Geisenheim and Rüdesheim. Most are of top quality, with Oestricher Lenchen, Winkeler Hasensprung and the two Rüdesheim sites of Berg Rottland and Berg Roseneck being particularly well known. The vine varieties are 86 per cent Riesling, 6 per cent Müller-Thurgau, 2 per cent Scheurebe, 1.5 per cent Ruländer, 1.5 per cent Gewürztraminer and 3 per cent others. An above-average quantity of top quality wine is produced, with great attention being given to the maintenance of the individual vine-variety characteristics.

WEINGUT KÖNIGIN VICTORIA BERG (Hochheim)

A small estate of 5 hectares originally laid to vine in 1846, now planted in 100 per cent Riesling. The origin of the name has been explained in the main text of this section. The wines have a very positive character, firm and full of flavour and individuality.

SCHLOSS JOHANNISBERG (Johannisberg)

Vines are said to have been grown in the Schloss Johannisberg vineyards since the eighth century. The Schloss itself commands a view of much of the Rheingau, and its detailed wine-making records date from 1716. The estate is one of the best known in Germany and is now administered by the Firma Oetker, the owners of the Mumm'sche Weingut. There are 35 hectares of vineyards, of which 30 per cent are on moderate slopes and 25 per cent on steep slopes. The vineyards surround the Schloss under whose name the wine is sold. 100 per cent Riesling is used. Very fruity wines are produced with strongly pronounced Riesling characteristics.

DOMÄNENWEINGUT SCHLOSS SCHÖNBORN (Hattenheim)

The von Schönborn family, who still own the estate today, were active as vineyard owners in the fourteenth century in Winkel. There are 90 hectares of vineyards, of which 55 hectares are at present in production. 58 per cent are on moderate and 8 per cent on steep slopes. The estate is sole owner of Hattenheimer Pfaffenberg. Also owners of vineyards at Oestrich, Erbach, Rauenthal, Hallgarten, Mittelheim, Johannisberg, Winkel, Geisenheim, Rüdesheim, and Hochheim. The vine varieties are 89 per cent Riesling, 4 per cent Müller-Thurgau, 2.5 per cent Spätburgunder and 4.5 per cent new crossings. An estate producing fine traditional Rheingau wines.

LANDGRÄFLICH HESSISCHES WEINGUT (Johannisberg)

The von Hessen family bought this estate in 1958, and further purchases have increased its size since then. The old estate buildings have been retained but have been modernized internally. There are 30 hectares of vineyards, of which 80 per cent are on moderate slopes. There are top quality sites at Johannisberg, Geisenheim, Winkel, and Rüdesheim. The vine varieties are 80 per cent Riesling, 10 per cent Müller-Thurgau, 5 per cent Scheurebe and 5 per cent crossings. Because of the wide variety of soils, an interesting range of flavours is produced. The fine Scheurebe wines are a speciality.

WEINGUT DR WEIL (Kiedrich)

A well known Rheingau estate, dating from 1867, with its cellars and administrative offices adjacent to one of the best known churches in the region. There are some 18.5 hectares of vineyard, of which 80 per cent lie on moderate, and 10 per cent on steep slopes. The main grape is the Riesling (94 per cent), with a small quantity of Müller-Thurgau (4 per cent) and Spätburgunder (2 per cent) being found. A fine range of typical Rheingau wines is offered that benefit from traditional Rheingau maturation in cask, and the personal attention of the owner, Robert Weil.

SCHLOSS GROENESTEYN, WEINGUT DES REICHSFREIHERRN VON RITTER ZU GROENESTEYN (Kiedrich)

An estate dating from the fourteenth century that has been in the family of the present owner, Heinrich Freiherr von Ritter zu Groenesteyn, since 1640. There are 15 hectares of vineyard around Kiedrich. 30 per cent are on steep and 60 per cent on moderate slopes. The estate owns 18 hectares of vineyard in well known sites at Rüdesheim (Berg Rottland, Berg Roseneck, etc.). A high proportion of Riesling is grown (92 per cent), and the rest is in Müller-Thurgau. The wines show all the character that one would expect from a long established 'Weingut' dedicated to fine, Riesling wine production.

NAHE

In terms of quality, the Nahe seems to divide itself into three parts. Firstly, there is the central area, upstream from Bad Kreuznach to Schlossböckelheim. Then comes the Lower Nahe near Bingen, and finally there is the rest. The rest spreads out in varying distances through the whole of the region in an irregular circle outwards from Niederhausen, the source of some of the finest Nahe wines. In describing Nahe wines, it is often said that they lie in style somewhere between those of the Rheingau or Rheinhessen, and those of the Saar River. This is a loose but fair description, for the range of flavour offered by the Nahe will not allow a close definition. The best wines often have a particularly delightful, flowery bouquet. The region has some 5,000 hectares of vineyard, of which a little over 500 hectares are not in production at present. It stretches from the confluence of the Nahe River with the much larger Rhine at Bingerbrück, some forty kilometres upstream, straying up side valleys where it seems profitable for viticulture to do so. Much of the country is undiscovered by the majority of tourists who are trapped by the splendid and obvious scenery of the Mittelrhein, and are not encouraged to branch into the Nahe valley by its rather unpromising start at Bingerbrück. From here to Bad Kreuznach on the north bank of the river lie vineyards in pleasant, but somewhat characterless country, very similar to that of the Rheinhessen on the far side of the river. The wines they produce are meaty and well rounded in flavour and quite different from those made further upstream. The State *Domäne* has vineyards in both parts of the region but vinifies its entire crop in its cellars at Niederhausen. So, in tasting the *Domäne* wines from Dorsheim or Münster-Sarmsheim against those of the vineyards of Schlossböckelheim, one is making as fair a comparison as possible. The treatment of the vineyards and the vinification is the same. The difference lies purely in the varying soils of the two areas and their micro-climates. In these circumstances, starting a tasting with a Dorsheimer, one appreciates its meaty, earthy flavour, and is only persuaded that it might not represent the best wine on the Nahe when it is followed by a Niederhäuser Hermannsberg or a Schlossböckelheimer Kupfergrube from the same stable. The growers concentrate their efforts on the Riesling grape in the best vineyard sites, while elsewhere the Müller-Thurgau and Silvaner predominate.

There seems to be quite a large gap in quality between the finest wines from the best vineyards of the Nahe, and the worthy but more ordinary wines made from the outlying areas. In other words, the aristocracy and the artisans are numerous, but the middle classes more difficult to find. The finest Nahe Riesling is the equal to the best that the Rheingau can produce, but the Rheingau, though it has a much smaller area under vine, has the larger amount of top quality wine to offer. The Nahe, like all regions whose reputation is built on the Riesling vine, has seen an increase in the plantation of the Müller-Thurgau over the last twenty years, but it is not likely to provide a home of any real size for the new varieties of vine from which strongly perfumed wines are made. The wines from such varieties prove much more satisfactory when grown in the Rheinhessen or Palatinate.

The town of Bad Kreuznach has its attractive parts, appropriate to a spa, but much of it is modern with no special architectural merit. Its vineyards produce top quality wine, and it is the largest town (45,000 inhabitants) in the Nahe Valley. It is also the home of a number of wine-trade institutions, and the scene of wine auctions each spring. The real importance of these auctions to the German wine trade is probably debatable. Certainly, they do not have the same relevance as the Hospices de Beaune auction does to the Burgundy trade, and they have no significant effect on the level of prices of wine as a whole. At the German auctions, the wine is offered to the public, who may bid only through brokers. They will often

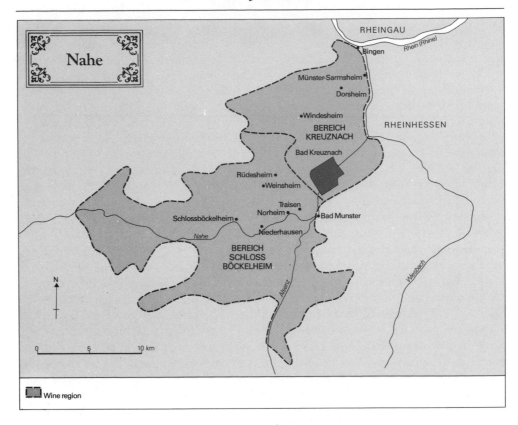

share lots between their customers and one can have the impression that there is little competition in the bidding. Normally, all the brokers will come from the same district and know each other well, but occasionally a broker from further afield will make a counter bid against his colleagues and tension will enter the proceedings. This can quickly turn into something stronger, for each wine is tasted immediately before being auctioned. By the end of the day much has also been consumed and feelings are more freely expressed. The auctions do provide a quite remarkable opportunity to taste a full range of wine from one region, and to note and compare the overall quality of one grower's wine with that of another. It is also a good public relation exercise.

The job of the wine broker in Germany is one that seems to arouse strong opinions. His principal function is to act as a liaison between the grower and the wine trade. Wine brokers are known to have been active since the fourteenth century and today their *raison d'être* is the same as ever. The number of growers is vast, even if some of the holdings are minute, and it is quite impossible for a busy wine buyer, working for a firm selling a large range of wine, to know exactly what is available in every wine village. The function of the 365 wine brokers in Germany today is to understand the needs of the buyers and to show where they can be met. A good broker will also be able to give growers impartial advice about the quality of their wines, changes in the taste of the consumer, and so on. The criticism of the broker arises when the grower feels, particularly after a good vintage, that he does not need the help to which he is contracted in selling his wine, or simply when the grower believes that his broker is not working as well as he should. No doubt there are lazy and inefficient brokers just as there are inadequate doctors, shoe-makers or soldiers.

Moving upstream from Bad Kreuznach, one passes the strange high walls made

St Hildegard Abbey, surrounded by the Klosterberg vineyard in the Rheingau
(Overleaf) Burrweiler on the Deutsche Weinstrasse in the Rheinpfalz

from the small branches of trees over which the salty spring water is passed to spread ozone amongst the visitors to the spa. By the high rocks at neighbouring Bad Münster, one finds top quality vineyards that have been abandoned for years. They are small, in some cases steep, and defy economic working. That they could make fine wine there is no doubt, for a little further on, from the Traisener and Norheimer vineyards, in an almost confusingly similar situation, splendid wine is made. It has a particular flavour that comes from the porphyry rock, the experts claim. The situation of these vineyards is remarkable. At the rear of narrow and sometimes terraced rows of vines, the rock face rises several hundred feet up to the woods and into the sky. At the foot of the vineyards there is a minor road and a minor railway and then the Nahe. The micro-climate benefits from the rocks and the river but the soil is dry, and the yield small.

Germany is rich in panoramic views, but not many can be better than the vertiginous sight of the Niederhausen and Schlossböckelheim vineyards on looking down from the hill on the opposite side of the Nahe. They appear as a relief map, with the effect of height greatly reducing the famous Schlossböckelheimer Felsenberg and Kupfergrube vineyards in scale. The Kupfergrube vineyard is entirely artificial, having been built by convict labour at the start of the twentieth century on the site of an old copper mine – the Kupfergrube. After Schlossböckelheim, there are no more famous wine villages, though names such as Meddersheim and Monzingen are locally respected. The remainder of the wines of the district fall mainly into the 'also ran' category, although, as in all the German specified regions, exceptions can be found. The Müller-Thurgau (31 per cent of the vineyard area) and the Silvaner (23 per cent of the vineyard area) provide the bulk of the cheaper Nahe wines and are most intensively grown in the less well-known villages. Even if they will not have the elegance of the Riesling, they should still have the grip that comes from a good balance of acidity.

The area under vine in the Nahe Valley has more than doubled in the last thirty years, with the number of farmers concentrating exclusively on viticulture increasing as well. Formal vini-viticultural training is much more usual than it was, and 40 per cent of the crop each year will be bottled and sold by the grower, while 20 per cent is handled by the cooperative cellars. The remainder is sold as bulk wine, with a small amount reaching the market as table grapes. Apart from the State Vini-Viticultural Institute, advice on technical wine matters can be obtained in Bad Kreuznach from the famous Seitz-Werke on the banks of the Nahe. Seitz cellar machinery is found all over the world, and the company has been pioneering new cellar techniques since the last century. As in so many other German factories, one is conscious of the thoroughness of training. Qualifications are highly regarded and bring status with them, and a proper respect for one's job. The results of this healthy state of affairs are clear from the high technical standard of German wine, not only in the years when the sun shines well, but also in the off vintages.

In the Nahe, there are two *Bereiche*, seven *Grosslagen*, eighty villages or communities and 321 *Einzellagen*. Amongst the best known village or community names are: Münster-Sarmsheim (whose wines omit 'Sarmsheim' in the name), Bad Kreuznach, Dorsheim, Niederhausen, Norheim, Schlossböckelheim, and Traisen. From a relatively small list of leading growers in the Nahe, the following certainly deserve mention:

VERWALTUNG DER STAATLICHEN WEINBAUDOMÄNEN
(Niederhausen-Schlossböckelheim)

These are also known in English as the State Cellars. An outstandingly well-equipped establishment, dating from 1902. The viticulture is particularly advanced

Schloss Johannisberg, once a Benedictine cloister, overlooks its Riesling vineyards in the Rheingau

in technique. The setting is perfect. There are 45 hectares of vineyards on steep slopes. The vineyard sites are at Schlossböckelheim (Kupfergrube and Felsenberg), Niederhausen (Hermannsberg Hermannshöhle, etc.), Traisen, Altenbamberg, Ebernburg, Dorsheim (Burgberg) and at Münster (Dautenpflänzer, Pittersberg, etc.). The vine varieties are 80 per cent Riesling. This is modern wine-making at its best; Riesling wines with fine acidity, and charming, positive bouquet are produced.

WEINGUT HANS CRUSIUS (Traisen)

A small but superbly run estate, dating from the middle of the seventeenth century. There are 8 hectares of vineyards, of which 30 per cent are on steep, and 40 per cent on moderate slopes. The vineyard sites are at Traisen (Bastei) and at Schlossböckelheim (Felsenberg). The vine varieties are 65 per cent Riesling, 20 per cent Kerner and 15 per cent Müller-Thurgau. These are excellently produced, wood-matured Riesling wines, with the flavour that derives from the soil of the district. The wines are well represented on the export market.

WEINGUT AUGUST ANHEUSER (Bad Kreuznach)

The name Anheuser has long been linked with viticulture in the Nahe Valley. This estate dates from 1869. There are 57 hectares of vineyards, of which 35 per cent are on steep slopes and 50 per cent on moderate slopes. There are many vineyard sites at Kreuznach (Brückes, Narrenkappe, etc.), Niederhausen (Hermannshöhle), Norheim, and at Schlossböckelheim (Felsenberg, etc.). The vine varieties are 70 per cent Riesling, 13 per cent Silvaner, 10 per cent Müller-Thurgau, 4 per cent Ruländer and 3 per cent others. A wide range of wines is produced, matured in wood, each typical of its grape type and vineyard of origin, with particularly successful stylish, fruity Rieslings. The estate is able to offer a number of fine wines of great age.

RUDOLF ANHEUSER'SCHE WEINGUTSVERWALTUNG (Bad Kreuznach)

Founded in 1888, now run by the grandson of the original owner, Rudolf Peter Anheuser. There are 65 hectares of vineyards, of which 54 hectares are at present in production. Some of the vineyards are found in the Rheinhessen. Fifty per cent are on steep slopes and 30 per cent on moderate slopes. The vineyard sites are at Kreuznach (Krötenpfuhl, etc.), Schlossböckelheim (Königsfels, etc.), Niederhausen, Norheim, Altenbamberg, Monzingen, Roxheim, and at Oppenheim and Dienheim in the Rheinhessen. The vine varieties used are 70 per cent Riesling, 5 per cent Müller-Thurgau, 8 per cent Ruländer, 10 per cent Weissburgunder and Scheurebe, and 7 per cent Kerner and others. A considerable range of wine types and vintages are available. The wines are matured in wood and, like those from a number of other cellars on the Nahe, benefit from fermentation at low temperatures. They have elegance and fine fruit.

REICHSGRÄFLICH V. PLETTENBERG'SCHE VERWALTUNG (Bad Kreuznach)

An estate whose vineyards are spread over much of the Nahe Valley. There are 40 hectares of vineyards, of which 29 per cent are on steep and 58 per cent on moderate slopes. Many of the vineyard sites are at Winzenheim, Kreuznach, Bretzenheim, Roxheim, Schlossböckelheim (Kupfergrube and Felsenberg) and Norheim. The vine varieties used are 65 per cent Riesling, 20 per cent Müller-Thurgau, and Ruländer, Silvaner, Huxelrebe, Kanzlerrebe, Siegerrebe, Optima, Kerner, etc. An exceedingly modern and careful cellar technique produces balanced, clean wines with a well-developed bouquet. A wide range of wines is offered from several vintages by this estate.

STAATSWEINGUT WEINBAULEHRANSTALT BAD KREUZNACH (Bad Kreuznach)

A leading viticultural school, owned by the state of Rheinland-Pfalz, with vineyard sites in Kreuznach and Norheim. Many different vine varieties are grown, some on a trial basis. The wines are expertly made, and the individual characteristics of each grape type are carefully guarded.

RHEINHESSEN

The Rheinhessen is certainly not as attractive as some of the German specified regions. There are parts that are really rather dull and flat, where one is conscious of the proximity of industry and the Autobahn system that feeds it. Compared to the steep vineyards of the Moselle or the Middle Rhine, the slopes of the Rheinfront in the Bereich Nierstein lack drama. The lover of unsophisticated villages will find them in the less well-known parts of the region, where vine-growing is only one of the forms of agriculture that are practised. At harvest time in the latter part of October, the country lanes are just as likely to be blocked by tractors bringing in the sugar-beet crop as by growers queueing to deliver their grapes to the local co-operative cellar.

Many of the names of the vine-growing villages are unknown outside the immediate locality. If their wines are ever exported, in most cases it will be either under a brand name, or the name of the local *Bereich*. It seems reasonable to wonder if such anonymity is deserved. However, compared to the Rheingau, the Rheinhessen has only a few villages that produce wine of world class or reputation. Those that are known outside Germany, such as Nackenheim, Nierstein, Oppenheim or Dienheim on the Rheinfront south of Mainz, can produce fine wine, softer in style than Rheingauer wine, with charm and lots of flavour. Though the Riesling wines from the Rheinfront can be stylish and yet have a taste that comes from the rich red soil, it is somehow the Silvaner that seems to produce a wine that is most typical of the Rheinhessen. By its nature, a Silvaner is soft in flavour and sometimes has a rather vegetable-like bouquet. Agreeable seems to be a good description of it, which may sound a little tame. Its virtues, though, are positive, and it is certainly not flabby. Up until a few years ago, the Silvaner was grown more widely than any other vine variety in the Rheinhessen, and the Riesling, as now, was found only in the best-suited sites. The Silvaner, unfortunately, has a tendency to suffer from chlorosis, and today it covers some 22 per cent only of the viticultural area, compared to about 70 per cent before the Second World War. It is, however, a vine that produces wine of quality, and it would be a pity for the consumer were it to disappear altogether from the Rheinhessen. Not surprisingly, it has been replaced in many places by the ubiquitous Müller-Thurgau, and other crossings such as Scheurebe and the recently developed Kerner. This illustrates the desire of growers to plant vines that will ripen earlier than the old varieties, and to produce *Spätlese* wines from them, possibly before the main Riesling harvest has even begun. Whereas this is all very understandable on economic grounds, warnings have been given that too great a variety of new crossings in the Rheinhessen vineyards could confuse the consumer and his palate. Nevertheless, the Kerner is well thought of in the Rheinhessen, for if it is planted in an average-to-good vineyard site, it can produce fruity, powerful and well-balanced wine. Even in a year without much sunshine, Kerner can still make a wine that is acceptable to the consumer.

Apart from this range of vine varieties for white wine, under 5 per cent of the Rheinhessen vineyard area produces red wine. German red wine is totally different to the red wine of France or Spain. It is so different, in fact, that it is almost impossible to make a comparison, although there is, of course, no doubt which is best. Whilst the German grower, with considerable justification, may say that he

Rheinhessen

makes the best white wine in the world, he will not make a similar claim for his red, which often tastes as though it should be white. In other words, it has a certain amount of residual sugar, and is a light and agreeable drink. Taken with game such as boar, hare, or venison, it can be very pleasant, for with such dishes sweetness in the form of blackcurrant jelly or cranberries is often associated. The best German red wine is usually made from the Spätburgunder vine, better known elsewhere as the Pinot Noir. In the Rheinhessen, the plantation of Spätburgunder is limited to the area around the small town of Ingelheim, in the north, where it has been grown for many years. It seemed recently that the future of German red wine production would be threatened by blending restrictions imposed by the EEC, but this no longer appears so likely. It has never been a major part of the total Rheinhessen wine production, and at the start of the twentieth century only 8 per cent of the area under vine was making red wine.

The terrain in the Rheinhessen, with either level or gently sloping vineyards for the most part, allows maximum use to be made of mechanization. It offers the type of vineyards in which mechanical harvesters can operate and, indeed, here and there one can see them in action. Their use, though, is not widespread and some hold strong views against them. It is claimed that they brutalize the vine, collect leaves as well as grapes, whilst damaging the grapes themselves, although the most refined avoid all these faults. In the south of the region, the slopes become steeper, and the countryside seems to have more character. Even the villages are more attractive, and one finds old half-timbered houses that escaped the Second World

War. One can often be mistaken in this, though, for in many cases old buildings, destroyed in the war in West Germany, have been rebuilt with enormous care and faithfulness to the original. The new can therefore be easily confused with the old, and what may look like a town hall from the days of Hans Sachs may well have been built within the last thirty years.

The climate of the Rheinhessen is gentle, for the region is protected from the west by the hills of the Hunsrück and the Pfälzer Wald, and from the north and east by the Taunus mountains and the Odenwald forest. The soil varies from area to area, with loess deposits predominating.

The Rheinhessen is the largest of the German specified viticultural regions and covers 21,144 hectares, producing about 22 million dozen bottles per year, most of which, of course, is drunk outside the district. In fact, the Rheinhessen claims to be the German region with the greatest success on the export market. As elsewhere, the number of growers is declining and has been doing so throughout the twentieth century. The very small vineyard holding cannot be run economically, so that we find that in 1907 the average holding was 0.57 hectares, whilst in 1977 it was almost three times this figure. Averages can be misleading, but today certainly two-thirds of the total area under vine is owned by growers with holdings of more than two hectares. This may still seem pretty small beer, if one can use that phrase of a vineyard, to anybody familiar with other forms of farming. Of the 14,700 growers in the Rheinhessen, under 800 actually bottle their entire crop themselves. The cost of bottling machinery is such that it is simply not worth the capital outlay unless there is a reasonable amount of wine to be bottled. In these circumstances, it is not surprising that one finds a number of cooperative cellars. The first cooperative or *Winzergenossenschaft* in the Rheinhessen was founded in the east of the region in 1897 at Gau-Bickelheim, not far from Bad Kreuznach in the Nahe Valley. It was quickly followed by others, and by 1903 six cooperative cellars were in existence, although it soon seemed as though their future would be threatened. There were disputes between the members and the board of management of the cooperatives, both about the amount to be paid for the grapes and also about the timing of the payment. The member wished to be paid in full when he delivered his grapes at the harvest to the cooperative, and to finance such payments the cooperative had to borrow heavily. In some instances, the price that would be obtained for the wine in the future was misjudged and some of the cooperatives became heavily in debt. It was clearly a state of affairs that could not be allowed to continue, so that in 1905 a new system was set up by which the members would be paid for their grapes in stages throughout the year. On joining, the grower hands over to the cooperative a sum of money based on the size of his vineyard holding. At the time of the harvest the cooperative announces the price it will pay for the different types of grapes that its members will deliver to it. These prices are related to a precise must weight. If the grapes are below the required standard, then a penalty is imposed, and if they are above, the member receives a bonus. This naturally encourages good vineyard husbandry. The cooperative cellars in the Rheinhessen have increased their storage capacity considerably in the last few years, and claim that they can now receive even the largest vintage without running short of vat space. This enables them to have a steadying effect on prices to the benefit of all concerned, including the consumer. Also, more and more, the cooperatives are bottling their wine, as opposed to selling it in bulk to the wine trade. The cooperative at Gau-Bickelheim, now the Zentralkellerei Rheinischer Bezirkswinzergenossenschaft, handles almost half of the total cooperative output in the Rheinhessen and sells virtually all its wine in bottle.

In visiting a modern cooperative cellar, one may miss the charm of the traditional wine cellar with its low vaulted roof and rows of shining casks. This traditional type of cellar still has its place in villages or towns such as Oppenheim or Nierstein, where the finest wine is made. To justify the high cost of running such a cellar, an appropriately enhanced selling price must be more or less guaranteed, for without that the storage of individual parcels of wine in wooden casks becomes quite uneconomic. Whilst a Riesling wine with good acidity may well benefit from a period in wood, and build itself up, as the Germans say, a Müller-Thurgau wine might taste fresher and better if stored in a vat, protected from the slightest oxidation. The Riesling covers just over 4 per cent of the Rheinhessen vineyards only, and the Müller-Thurgau over 32 per cent. The conclusion is obvious, even if I have over-simplified the question a little. In the cooperative at Monsheim near Worms, three cellarmen provide all the labour involved in running a cellar with a capacity of 14.5 million litres in which no bottling takes place. The lay-out and techniques are of the most modern type, and hygiene and orderliness is everywhere apparent. It is this sort of cellar, which is by no means unique in the Rheinhessen or in West Germany as a whole, that helps to keep the price of wine stable. A great deal of the work in an old-type cellar is unattractive and carried out, by the nature of things, in cold and damp conditions. Cellar staff are not always easy to find and wages in West Germany are comparatively high. Much of the future of the trade, it would seem, must lie in the large, efficient, modern establishment, with the old, traditional cellar being found mainly in the areas producing the most prestigious wines in limited quantities.

If one looks at the map of the Rheinhessen, one will find the town of Bingen at the top left-hand corner. It is an old and busy place from which much wine used to be shipped on the Rhine. Unfortunately, the river is an uncertain route that periodically suffers from low or high water, so that consignments can be delayed. For this reason, wine being exported overseas from West Germany usually finds its way nowadays to a northern port in a container by road. The Autobahn system is such that large areas of the country can be covered in the shortest possible time, and moving container loads of wine quickly and, therefore, still relatively cheaply, is not a problem. At Bingen the Nahe flows into the Rhine opposite the hill at Rüdesheim in the Rheingau, whilst across the Nahe by the banks of the Rhine, the vineyards of the Mittelrhein soon start. Bingen produces meaty wine, possibly firmer and less delicate than that of the Rheinfront, rather reminiscent of some of the neighbouring Nahe wines of Münster or Dorsheim. The best known vineyard at Bingen is the Scharlachberg, in whose wine one can smell and taste the influence of the porphyry rock that is also found in some of the wines of the Middle Nahe. Besides many local vine-growers, a number of large, internationally known wine firms have their seat in Bingen, and one is therefore very conscious of the importance of wine to the town. Though it has some solid town houses, Bingen is not a beautiful place. The hills of the Rhine seemed to have compressed factory buildings, a railway junction and private houses into rather too close contact one with another. However, it is as good a spot as any from which to start a tour of the Rheinhessen, and at the same time allows a quick visit to the Nahe or Rheingau for wines of another sort.

The largest town of the Rheinhessen is Mainz, once known as the 'golden' city because of the prosperity of its trade, with some 178,000 inhabitants. Like so many of the large German towns, it is situated on the banks of a river, the Rhine. As Bingen has a second river in the Nahe, so has Mainz in the Main that flows from the wine region of Franconia and past the vineyards of Hochheim at the east end of the Rheingau before joining the Rhine. Mainz is the capital of the state of Rhein-land-Pfalz, and one finds here a number of official bodies such as the Stabilisierungs-fonds für Wein, concerned with the promotion and protection of German wine. The city was very damaged in the Second World War, but it has been imaginatively rebuilt and there is much to see. Apart from the cathedral, there is a university, several museums, palaces and town houses. If this gives an impression of great earnestness, then it must be corrected by a mention of the annual Mainzer Karneval that rises to its noisy climax on Rosenmontag, the day before Shrove Tuesday. The carnival sees the consumption of large quantities of wine and sparkling wine and is, indeed, an important part of the drinks-trade year in Germany. There is an understood freedom and licence allowed to the participants, which permits the sober citizen to behave in a manner which would be unthinkable at other times. It is all pretty harmless for the most part, and very teutonic.

Besides the town of Mainz, the Rheinhessen has another old city in Worms. To reach it by road from Mainz, one can drive the length of the Rheinfront, passing all the most famous wine towns and villages in the Rheinhessen. In fact, Worms lies so far south that it almost finds itself in the Palatinate. It is an old city that is principally associated with Martin Luther, the Jewish faith in Germany, and Liebfraumilch. Liebfraumilch nowadays has no special connection with Worms or, indeed, the Rheinhessen, but it is of very great importance to the German export trade. Originally, Liebfrau(en)milch came from the vineyard that still, surprisingly, exists to this day close to the centre of Worms by the Liebfrauenkirche – the Church of our Lady. It is said that this wine has a smoky character which some may regard as a fault, whilst others will claim it as part of the natural style of the wine. These are the sorts of questions that are debated year after year wherever German wine with a positive character is drunk. How dull it would be if it were not so and wine became a standard product, bland and tailor-made to suit an average taste, never giving offence and never arousing interest. There is a place for that which is solid, constant and reliable, but it is not necessarily amongst the fine wines of the world.

To make a general statement about the wine of any area is to risk being accused of dogmatism, and the people who are closest to it are sometimes those the least well placed to make an objective judgment. The grower knows his wine as the parent knows his child, and may just as easily be prejudiced in his opinion. It is ultimately the consumer who decides the value of a wine, for it is what he is prepared to pay for it. The fact that through lack of experience he may know the price but not the value, simply shows how complex is the buying of wine. If it were otherwise, it would be much less fascinating and much less fun. An inexpensive Rheinhessen wine is as straightforward as wine can be. Its virtue is that it is not excessively anything. Neither too sweet, nor too dry, it is balanced and soft but yet not flabby. It is not characterless, but at the same time is not so positive that it cannot be enjoyed, slightly chilled, with most dishes other than the sweetest. For many, it is what they understand by a glass of Hock, and as such it is appreciated far beyond the small villages from which it comes.

In the Rheinhessen there are three *Bereiche*: Bereich Bingen, Bereich Nierstein, and Bereich Wonnegau near Worms. These *Bereiche* are subdivided into twenty-four *Grosslagen* (collective sites), 167 villages or communities, and 446 *Einzellagen* (individual vineyard sites). The best known village or community names in the Rheinhessen are as follows: Alsheim, Alzey, Bechtheim, Bingen, Bodenheim, Dienheim, Guntersblum, Ingelheim, Mainz, Mettenheim, Nackenheim, Nierstein, Oppenheim, Westhofen and Worms. There is only a small number of internationally known estates in the Rheinhessen, and practically all of these are found in the vicinity of Nierstein on the Rheinfront. Amongst the best known are:

GUSTAV ADOLF SCHMITT'SCHES WEINGUT (Nierstein)

An estate established in 1618 and also a leading export house for German wine. The vineyards consist of about 65 hectares, mainly on flat or gently sloping terrain, and the sites are at Nierstein (Pettenthal, Heiligenbaum, Ölberg, Hipping, Bildstock and Paterberg), at Oppenheim (Herrenberg) and at Dienheim (Tafelstein). The vine varieties are 50 per cent Silvaner, 25 per cent Riesling, 20 per cent Müller-Thurgau, and 5 per cent others. Well-balanced, well-rounded, stylish Rheinhessen wines are made. Many top quality wines are produced.

WEINGUT GESCHWISTER SCHUCH (Nierstein)

A family-owned estate, established in 1817. The vineyards consist of 16 hectares, of which 60 per cent are on the level. The vineyard sites are at Nierstein (Hipping, Ölberg, Spiegelberg and Orbel), at Oppenheim (Sackträger), and at Dienheim (Falkenberg). The vine varieties are 35 per cent Riesling, 25 per cent Silvaner, 10 per cent Scheurebe, 8 per cent Müller-Thurgau, 4 per cent Ruländer, and 18 per cent others. A wide range of vine varieties permits an interesting selection of wines with body, character and good Rheinhessen style.

WEINGUT LOUIS GUNTRUM (Nierstein)

A family business established in 1824, well known on the export markets for German wine. The vineyards consist of approximately 67 hectares, 65 per cent on level or rolling land and 35 per cent on steep slopes. Many of the vineyards are situated at Nierstein (Findling, Ölberg, etc.), at Oppenheim (Schloss, Sackträger, etc.), at Dienheim, and at Nackenheim. The vine varieties are 30 per cent Riesling, 25 per cent Silvaner, 25 per cent Müller-Thurgau, 9 per cent Ruländer, and 11 per cent others. Carefully and individually made wines show well the character of the different vine varieties and vineyard sites.

WEINGUT J. u H. A. STRUB (Nierstein)

An old-established family business, which has 17 hectares of vineyards. The vineyards are situated at Nierstein (Hipping, Ölberg, Heiligenbaum, Orbel, Brückchen, Paterberg, and Bildstock) and at Dienheim (Falkenberg). The vine varieties are 30 per cent Riesling, 30 per cent Silvaner, 30 per cent Müller-Thurgau, and 10 per cent others. The wines are gentle, appealing, soft in style and excellently made.

WEINGUT BÜRGERMEISTER ANTON BALBACH ERBEN (Nierstein)

A family business established in the seventeenth century. There are 18 hectares of vineyards. The vineyard sites are Pettenthal, Hipping, Ölberg, Kranzberg, Rosenberg, Klostergarten, and Bildstock, all at Nierstein. The vine varieties are 70 per cent Riesling, 15 per cent Silvaner, 10 per cent Müller-Thurgau, and 5 per cent others. The interest in firm wines, matured in bottles, is clear from the relatively high proportion of Riesling grown for this region. Outstanding quality wines are produced.

WEINGUT FRANZ KARL SCHMITT (Nierstein)

An old estate, in the hands of the Schmitt family since 1549. There are 15 hectares of vineyards, of which 50 per cent are on the level, 30 per cent on gentle slopes and 20 per cent on steep slopes. The vineyard sites are at Nierstein (Hipping, Pettenthal, Orbel, Kranzberg and Ölberg). The vine varieties are 70 per cent Riesling, 15 per cent Silvaner, 7 per cent Müller-Thurgau, 4 per cent Ruländer, 2 per cent Gewürztraminer, and 2 per cent others. Full bodied, carefully made, fruity wines are produced with the Riesling grape being particularly successful.

WEINGUT WINZERMEISTER HEINRICH SEIP, KURFÜRSTENHOF (Nierstein)

The owning family has lived in Nierstein since the Middle Ages, and has been a vineyard proprietor since 1696. There are 35 hectares of vineyards, of which 30 per cent are on steep slopes and the balance on moderate slopes or flat terrain. The vineyard sites are at Nierstein (Paterberg, Bildstock, Kirchplatte, Findling, Rosenberg, Klostergarten, Pettenthal, Hipping, Kranzberg, Ölberg, Heiligenbaum, Orbel, Schloss Schwabsburg, and sole owners of the Goldene Luft), at Oppenheim (Schloss), at Dienheim (Tafelstein, Kreuz and Falkenberg), and at Nackenheim (Engelsberg). The vine varieties are 20 per cent Silvaner, 20 per cent Müller-Thurgau and 20 per cent Riesling. Many others are also grown and in particular the Jubiläumsrebe, a new crossing, whose wine is similar to the Ruländer in flavour, and of considerable weight. A large amount of top quality wine is made from the many new crossings that are grown, as well as the more traditional styles of wine usual to the region. 3,800 litres of *Trockenbeerenauslese* and 17,990 litres of *Beerenauslese* were produced in 1976!

WEINGUT CARL SITTMANN (Oppenheim)

A large family business with about 75 hectares, in the prime vineyard sites on the Rheinfront at Nierstein, Oppenheim, Dienheim and Alsheim. A wide range of typical Rheinhessen wines, are produced, well made, gentle and clean flavoured.

FRANCONIA (Franken)

In Franconia, the visitor from the United Kingdom may well begin to feel how small is the island from which he comes. There is a sense of space about the rolling vineyards that suggests to the untrained eye that their 3,847 hectares could be much extended, as is indeed the case. Looking at leafless rows of Franconian vines in the spring of 1979 it was clear, though, that frost can cause as much damage here as anywhere, and that one was very much in the land of the continental climate. As well as the hard winter frosts, the region is familiar with hot and dry summers. However, there are many differences of climate within the region, caused by the lie of the land, the presence of water, the proximity of woods, or, indeed, the effect of *Flurbereinigung*. The River Main, which twists across the breadth of Franconia, does not impress itself on the viticultural landscape as does the Rhine, or indeed the Moselle, but it is not an inconsiderable river and must be crossed many times if the vineyards are to be systematically visited. Not only do the vineyards allow themselves room, unlike those of the Rheingau which crowd one upon another, but there are large areas where no vines are seen at all.

The region owes much of its development in the ninth and tenth centuries to the church and ecclesiastical establishments. Apart from the usual causes for a decline in viticulture, disease and war, one authority claims that taxation on wine and an increasing beer consumption in the seventeenth century helped to reduce the extent of the vineyards even further. The more things change, the more they are the same, and a high level of taxation on wine still has an inhibiting effect on wine consumption in some of Germany's export markets.

The size of the Franconian viticultural area seems to be now determined as much by economic factors as by purely viticultural considerations, although there is always a link between the two. Since 1965, the area under vine has been increasing once more, and the yield per hectare is vastly greater than it was at the start of the twentieth century. As usual, this has been the result of better vineyard husbandry and good clonal selection. In order to ensure the future of vineyards, many of which are on steep slopes, an increase in production was essential. Franconian wine has great individuality and much character, but is, unfortunately, expensive when compared with the wine from other German regions, such as the Palatinate or Rheinhessen. It is easily identifiable in a store or supermarket for it is bottled into the flagon-shaped Bocksbeutel. This dumpy bottle or flask is of antique origin and is said to derive its shape from the scrotum of a goat. Goat skins were, at one time, converted into containers. Whatever the origin of the Bocksbeutel, although it is used for all Franconian quality wine today, not every wine in a flagon-shaped bottle comes from Franconia. A close examination of the label is always essential, for the Portuguese use a similar, but not identical, bottle for some of their rosé and white wines, and the shape has been adopted by other countries as well.

Comparison is the major part of tasting. Either a wine is compared with another that is to be tasted at the same time, or as the wine trade would rather curiously say, 'looked at', or the memory is used of a wine 'seen' on a previous occasion. In general, it is necessary to compare like with like, for it is relatively minor differences of quality that are of interest or importance. Therefore, to compare a young Moselle with a mature white Burgundy would be rather meaningless, but to taste a Franconian Silvaner against an Alsatian Sylvaner is to find points of similarity between the two. If the wines are typical examples, the style of the grape will be very clear – soft but not flabby. The Alsatian may be the firmer, but the Franconian will have a pleasant taste of the soil. Neither wine will normally be overstocked with charm, which is a quality more easily found in the Riesling. They will, though, have positive character and, in some opinions, will represent the Silvaner at its best.

The Müller-Thurgau is now the most widely grown vine variety in Franconia, having overtaken the Silvaner in the early 1970s. The regional character is strong, however, so that a Müller-Thurgau from Franconia has more in common with the local Silvaner than it would with a Müller-Thurgau from the Rheinhessen. It seems that the shape of a wine is decided in outline by the grape from which it is made, but it is the soil of the region that gives substance to the picture. Between them, the Müller-Thurgau and Silvaner occupy some 78 per cent of the vineyards. For the rest, there is the usual collection of new crossings grown on a small scale, and after the Riesling, in terms of size of area covered, comes the Perle which has met with a certain success in Franconia. It is a crossing of Gewürztraminer and Müller-Thurgau and originates from Alzey in the Rheinhessen, where it was developed by Georg Scheu, the father of the Scheurebe. The Viticultural Institute in Würzburg (the Bayerische Landesanstalt für Weinbau und Gartenbau, Würzburg) has produced a clone that is more disease resistant. The main attraction of the Perle to the grower lies in its ability to withstand frost. Whatever the grape variety, it is the overriding Franconian character that predominates and this, with the eyecatching Bocksbeutel, has secured a strong marketing position for all Franconian wine.

In Germany, Franconian wine is regarded as a speciality. It separates itself from other German traditional wines by its dryness, strong local flavour and its Bocksbeutel. It is a wine that many have come to buy direct from the grower, particularly in the last ten years or so, and sales to the passing motorist from the grower's cellar are said to be considerable. Some 28 per cent of the Franconian crop is sold by growers who make and bottle their wines themselves, while 50 per cent is sold by cooperative cellars. The initial impetus to form cooperative cellars at the start of the twentieth century was the same as in other regions. Low prices and an increasing inability to turn over stock at an economic pace made vine-growing hardly worthwhile. As cellar technique developed, the small grower often realized that he had neither the means nor the training to make the most of his grapes. To join a cooperative cellar was the only solution.

The State today has over 180 hectares of vineyard based on the Viticultural Institute in Würzburg. The quality and reputation of the state-owned Hofkellerei or Court Cellar under the Residenz in Würzburg are very high. A somewhat unwanted compliment is paid to it on the international market by a South African wine that is sold in a flagon-shaped bottle bearing a label whose resemblance to that of the Hofkellerei can hardly be the result of chance. The actual cellars of the Hofkellerei must be amongst the best known in Germany. They are maintained in superb order and are much used for civic and wine trade functions. Their atmosphere is traditional and full of the romance of wine. Besides the Hofkellerei, there are also two other cellars in Würzburg whose antecedents go back several hundred years. The oldest, dating from the fourteenth century, is the Bürgerspital zum Heiligen Geist which still functions today as a home for old men as well as a wine-producing establishment. The Juliusspital was founded later in the sixteenth century, and is now one of the largest and best known estates in Franconia.

Würzburg is an exceptionally beautiful city of great style. The vineyards reach down from the Marienberg that overlooks the Residenz and are visible from much of the city. One is very aware of the importance of wine to Würzburg in its history today as well. The best known *Einzellage* in Würzburg is called Stein, and for years Franconian wine was referred to as *Steinwein*. The use of the word *Steinwein* is no longer permitted in this way, and has been replaced by *Frankenwein*. The Residenz was built in the first part of the eighteenth century and provides a major focal point of attention in the centre of the city. Not as large as Versailles, its fore-court is every bit as crowded in the tourist season. It is a truly palatial building. The villages of Franconia are attractive, and their half-timbered restaurants and cafés provide just the sort of subjective atmosphere that a serious wine-trade buyer should avoid like the plague if his heart is not to rule his head. Even the most ordinary of table wines gains a glamour, given the right local atmosphere, that needs to be firmly discarded in the sterile conditions of the tasting room. Franconia has two *Bereiche*, seventeen *Grosslagen*, 125 villages or communities and 155 *Einzellagen*. Most of the village or community names are seldom heard of outside the region, but the following are met from time to time: Würzburg, Randersacker, Escherndorf, Castell and Iphofen.

FÜRSTLICH CASTELL'SCHES DOMÄNENAMT (Castell)

The family of the present owner of this estate, Fürst zu Castell-Castell, is known to have been connected with vine-growing at Castell since the thirteenth century. It also founded the Castell Bank in 1774. Records of the vintages on the estate going back to the sixteenth century are still in existence. There are 45 hectares of vineyards, of which 85 per cent are on moderate and 15 per cent on steep slopes. The vineyard sites are at Schlossberg, Reitsteig, Bausch, Trautberg, Hohnart, Kirchberg, Kugelspiel and Feuerbach, all at Castell. The vine varieties are 40 per cent Müller-Thurgau, 30 per cent Silvaner, and a wide variety of other vines including Perle, Rieslaner, Scheurebe, Traminer, Auxerrois, Ortega, Siegerrebe, Morio-Muskat, Kerner, Albalonga, Bacchus, Mariensteiner and Spätburgunder. The wines are powerful, earthy, lively and fruity with good acidity. Superb wines of top quality are produced in fine years.

BÜRGERSPITAL ZUM Hl. GEIST (Würzburg)

The wine estate of this old people's home dates from the fourteenth century, and was the first estate to bottle its wine into the Bocksbeutel. There are 130 hectares, of which 89 are in production, 70 per cent on steep and 30 per cent on moderate slopes. The vineyard sites are mainly at Würzburg (Absleite, Stein, Pfaffenberg and Innere Leiste), and at Randersacker (Teufelskeller, etc.), Thüngersheim, Michelau, Himmelstadt, and Gössenheim. The vine varieties are 15 per cent Silvaner, 21 per cent Müller-Thurgau, 25 per cent Riesling, 10 per cent Kerner, 7 per cent Ruländer, 4 per cent Traminer, 3 per cent Spätburgunder and 15 per cent others. These are big wines, well balanced with good depth of flavour and expertly made.

BAYERISCHE LANDESANSTALT FÜR WEINBAU UND GARTENBAU (Würzburg)

A large state-owned estate, with an eighteenth-century cellar described earlier in the text of this section, established in its present form in 1952. There are 186 hectares of vineyards, 60 per cent on steep and 40 per cent on moderate slopes. Many of the vineyard sites are in leading Franconian wine villages or communities such as at Würzburg and at Randersacker. The vine varieties are 18 per cent Silvaner, 16 per cent Müller-Thurgau, 13 per cent Rieslaner (Silvaner x Riesling), 13 per cent Riesling, 12 per cent Perle and others. This is fine Franconian wine, particularly the Rieslings, matured in wood, made to the highest standards.

JULIUSSPITAL-WEINGUT (Würzburg)

A fine estate mentioned in the text of this section already, still functioning as a hospital, an old people's home, and a wine-producing concern. The vineyards consist of 120 hectares, 60 per cent on steep and 40 per cent on moderate slopes. Many of the vineyard sites are in the leading Franconian wine villages or communities such as at Würzburg (Stein) and at Randersacker (Teufelskeller). The vine varieties are 42.3 per cent Silvaner, 23.5 per cent Müller-Thurgau, 12.5 per cent Riesling, 4.4 per cent Scheurebe, 3.7 per cent Traminer, 3.4 per cent Ruländer and others. The wine is of excellent quality, powerful, and wood-matured.

PALATINATE (Rheinpfalz)

Whilst much of the Rheinhessen is pretty uninteresting to visit except to the student of wine, no such complaint can be made of the Palatinate. Although its rolling vineyards do not impress as do those on the near vertical slopes of the Moselle or Middle Rhine, their tidiness and concentration tell you that here wine is a major and successful part of the local economy. In spite of the tourists, the *Deutsche Weinstrasse* and the notices advertising wine for sale to the passing traffic, the risk seems to have been avoided that visitors, by their over-numerous presence, would have spoilt the land they came to see. As elsewhere, most do not wander far from their cars and the rambler, dressed as if to climb the Matterhorn and to sing in the chorus of *Der Freitschütz* all at once, is easily persuaded to follow the clearly marked footpaths. These, like so many things in West Germany, work well, so that with the aid of a map and easy-to-read signs on trees and rocks, a walk of whatever length one feels one wants to attempt can be made without difficulty. To stand on the edge of the woods above the vineyards in the northern part of the Palatinate is to enjoy a view uncannily similar to that of the Côte de Beaune from above the Burgundian plain. The hills overlooking the Palatinate are more mountainous, but the long slope down to the flat land that eventually leads to the Rhine could just as well find its way to the busy treelined N74 that runs from Chagny to Dijon. The similarities do not end there, for the best vineyards of the Bereich Mittelhaardt Deutsche Weinstrasse are almost all in the seemingly obligatory position, halfway up the slope. Evidently, the peoples of the two regions have a common outlook on many things. A merchant in the Côte de Beaune, speaking of the German occupation during the Second World War, said that life had been tolerable for much of the time in his village, for the local occupying forces came from the Palatinate and understood wine. When there was a subject to be discussed, a bottle would be opened and common sense would reign. Unfortunately, this sensible human contact came to an end when the Palatinate wine men were replaced with others of a different sort.

The history of the Palatinate is confused and confusing. Over the years, the land has been fought over, occupied by foreign forces, had its boundaries moved, and it is really only today that the wines have a clear regional identity. According to one authority, interestingly enough, much Palatinate wine used to be sent to Bacharach in the Middle Rhine, where it was sold as 'Bacharacher'. In other words, it took the name of the place at which it was sold rather than that of the locality in which the grapes were grown. A similar practice used to be followed at Pommard in Burgundy, which was also an important market for selling wine. Growers seem, by the nature of things, to be very independent in their outlook. They have often been very proud of their own wine and unwilling to share their views and knowledge with others in the past. A more open approach can be found nowadays compared to only twenty or so years ago. This has been encouraged by the *Weinbauplan* and what it represents, described earlier, and the realization that to survive in the EEC, pooling of ideas and cooperation is necessary. Though the cooperative cellars may not be quite so powerful as those in Baden-Württemberg, they still receive the crop from 27 per cent of the Palatinate vineyards.

According to Hans Siegel in his *Guide to the Wines of Germany*, the name 'Palatinate', which is the English version of *Pfalz*, comes from the Latin word *palatium*, meaning a palace or seat of government where the Roman Governor stayed. The Germans speak of the Rheinpfalz and also of the Rheinland-Pfalz. The latter is one of the states in West Germany of which, as we have already seen, Mainz is the capital. The Rheinpfalz forms part of the Rheinland-Pfalz, and lies in the south of that state bordering on France or, more precisely, Alsace. The vineyards are mainly either on the level or on gentle slopes, with only some 5 per cent being able to be described as truly steep. In this region possibly more than any other in West Germany the work in the vineyards has been able to be mechanized, and the man hours spent tending

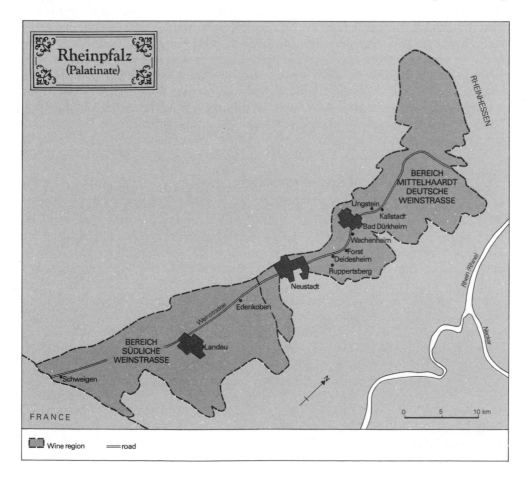

the vines have been reduced. At the start of the twentieth century each hectare of Palatinate vineyard required, on average, 2,000 hours' work spent in it per year. Today, the figure has been reduced to 700 hours. At the same time the yield has been much improved. In 1903, for example, the area under vine amounted to 15,267 hectares and produced 59,000 hectolitres (1 hectolitre = 11 dozen bottles approximately). In 1977 there were 20,920 hectares from which 2,400,000 hectolitres were made.

The big increase in area under vine has been in the Bereich Südliche Weinstrasse where the yield per hectare is very large. Though the prices paid to the grower in this *Bereich* are very much less than those for the better quality wines produced in the central part of the Palatine, in such villages such as Forst, Deidesheim or Ruppertsberg, he is not necessarily at a financial disadvantage. The overheads involved in producing a high yield are almost the same as those for a small yield. Presumably the grower in the Bereich Südliche Weinstrasse considers that it is quantity that will bring him the best return on his investment rather than involving himself in the battle to produce the finest wine possible. There is, of course, absolutely nothing wrong at all with cheap wine, providing that it is sound and honest. In the nineteenth century, when the growers had difficulty in selling their wines, they blamed the trade that existed at that time in artificial wines whose origin was more closely related to the potato than the grape. That wine consumption has risen by some 400 per cent since then may well be connected with the improvement in quality. A cheap wine from the south of the Palatinate today may be marketed in a bottle with a screw-top and a dressing or label similar to that of some brands of German beer. It will be very light, clean, and a pleasant drink, principally made for consumption on the home market. Because of the shipping, distribution costs and the high rate of duty imposed on wine in the United Kingdom, even cheap wine cannot be regarded there as an everyday alternative to soft drinks, but in the wine-producing regions of West Germany this is exactly how it has to compete. Not all wines from the Bereich Südliche Weinstrasse come into this category, but if the country has an area of mass production then it is in the south of the Palatinate. That the old trade in artificial wines died out years ago is not surprising, for in 1903 the first wine controller in Germany began his work in the Palatinate. It was, though, the wine trade itself that had already been fighting for many years to stop the production of artificial wine.

As in the Rheinhessen, the financial difficulties of the many growers with small holdings of vineyard forced them to form cooperative cellars. In Deidesheim in 1898, one year after the formation of the first Rheinhessen cooperative at Gau-Bickelheim, the first Palatinate *Winzergenossenschaft* was created. The movement spread, and by 1903 a further sixteen cooperative cellars had been started. Today, particularly in the Bereich Mittelhaardt, the cooperatives have a reputation for combining high technical excellence with the production of really fine wine. Indeed, many of their members have holdings in the best vineyard sites in the region. It should possibly be pointed out that technical expertise can be used to produce good cheap wine as well as the most expensive qualities. Many of the cooperatives manage to do both. Nearly 50 per cent of the Palatinate vineyards sell their produce in the form of grapes, must, or wine in bulk to the wine trade. In other words, the wine is not bottled by the grower. From the point of view of the consumer and the quality of wine that is sold to him, this does not necessarily have any special implications. The ability to bottle a wine well has nothing to do with being a grower, but depends on there being good bottling facilities and the correct expertise in the bottling establishment. On the other hand, some wines that are light in alcohol and with a delicate character, certainly benefit if they are bottled not too far away from their source. A journey in a bulk container, with the pumping operations that are necessary to fill and then empty the container at its destination, does tire a delicate wine. The old saying that a wine does not seem to 'travel well' does not really make much sense nowadays. The enjoyment of wine is very subjective. A bottle of crisp, refreshing Moselle consumed on a hot day by the banks of the river in summer may taste quite differently when another bottle of the same wine is opened on a wet winter day in a northern climate. The wine has remained the same, but the circumstances have changed and the mood is not what it was on the Moselle. This is not, though, the end of the story, for I recall a professor at the Viticultural School at Geisenheim telling me that all good wines should be rested at least three weeks after a journey. On being asked the reason for this, the professor, who knew as much about the chemistry of wine as anybody, said that he had no idea. Some may feel that it is nice that wine still has its mysteries, even if the mystique has diminished.

In the Bereich Mittelhaardt Deutsche Weinstrasse, the crop from 22 per cent of the vineyard area is sold by the grower in bottle, whilst in the Bereich Südliche Weinstrasse the figure is 18 per cent. Amongst the wines of the Bereich Mittelhaardt Deutsche Weinstrasse are some of the finest in the Rhineland. In these circumstances, the demand is greater, and the incentive for involvement in the expensive business of bottling on a relatively small scale is only there if the final selling price warrants it. Overall, one senses a slight disappointment that *Pfalzwein* is not better known, and that some other regions appear to be more successful in promoting their wines in the northern part of Germany. However, in most of the wine-producing regions, one can be aware of a feeling that the regional name, be it Rheinpfalz, Rheinhessen, or what you will, must be promoted in order to secure a place in the EEC. A few years ago, this was much less obvious.

The Deutsche Weinstrasse runs from the north of the region to the French border near Schweigen in the south, and is eighty kilometres in length. There is a southern atmosphere about the region that the motorist will notice if he drives into it from the Rheinhessen. The soil is varied and, as in the Rheinhessen, the grape types grown are numerous, which a glance at any local restaurant wine list will confirm. The Müller-Thurgau covers over 24 per cent of the vineyard area, the Silvaner 18 per cent and the Riesling 13 per cent. The Traminer vine, which used to be more widely grown in the nineteenth century than now, produces an interesting wine, more delicate but less powerful than the Alsatian Gewürztraminer from over the border. It is another of those disturbing vines, like the Ruländer, whose skin is positively red, but from which white wine is consistently made. The Ruländer in the Palatinate is very much at home, and produces splendid, full-flavoured wines of *Auslese* quality in the best vineyards, such as one finds at Forst. It is not, though, just in the well-known villages that the Ruländer performs well, for I can recall a quite amazing *Beerenauslese* from the hardly prestigious village of Edenkoben, towards the south of the Palatinate. The vintage was the 1967, a year abundant in noble rot. The colour resembled a beech tree in late autumn, blazing in the sunshine. The flavour was almost too powerful, and the must weight had been enormous. This was a wine from the area now known as the Bereich Südliche Weinstrasse, not normally recognized as producing the finest quality. It is this ability to produce wine of this quality from an area where you least expect it that makes German wine such a continuously fascinating subject for study.

As usual in West Germany, given a really good site for a vineyard, it is the Riesling that most growers would choose to plant. The best vineyards are around the villages and towns of the Bereich Mittelhaardt Deutsche Weinstrasse, such as Deidesheim, Forst, Ungstein, Kallstadt and Bad Dürkheim, and it is there that the highest proportion of Riesling will be found. A Palatinate Riesling should have the elegance associated with the wine that this grape produces in the northern regions of the Rheingau, Nahe and Mosel-Saar-Ruwer, plus a particular flavour that comes from the Palatinate soil. Sometimes it can have a slight earthiness on the nose and finish. If it is a quality wine with a distinction, it will most likely have a little more alcohol than a northern Riesling, and less acidity. There will be nothing retiring about its flavour and it should be easily 'understood'. A more negative way of expressing this is to say that a Palatinate Riesling is less subtle than one from the Rheingau. Which is the best is a matter of personal choice. In general, it can be said that the style of a Palatinate wine is halfway between that of Baden wine in the south, which is broad in flavour, and the firm, stylish wine from the Rheingau.

Some 10 per cent of the Palatinate vineyards are planted in Portugieser for the production of red wine of no distinction, and of Weissherbst – a rosé wine that must be made from one grape variety only. It may be made in any of the following specified regions: Ahr, Baden, Franconia, Rheingau, Palatinate and Württemberg. Weissherbst can only be a quality wine, not a table wine. As the Portugieser produces a must without much colour, its rosé wine is rather more successful than its red. The Portugieser is the sort of wine to taste if you come upon it in Germany, for little is likely to be found on the export market. Because the Palatinate has a warmer climate than the Rheingau or Mosel-Saar-Ruwer, it produces quality wines with distinction much more frequently, and in almost all years some *Spätlesen* will be made. On the other hand, *Eisweine* are less common, as the really cold weather necessary for their production seldom occurs early enough in the winter.

West Germany is not renowned for the delicacy or variety of its kitchen. Too often, hotel and restaurant menus are long and pretentious, whilst the food itself seems to suffer from the misapprehension that a *dicke Sosse*, or thick sauce, will save the day. However, there are good German dishes which should not be discarded with the endless veal scallops and the vegetables out of a tin, or salad. The wild boar can be found in Palatinate restaurants and its habitat is in the extensive woods above the vineyards, where there are also deer in large herds. With game, the full-flavoured Palatinate wines can be happily drunk and enjoyed. There are many pleasant wine bars in the villages where one can either sit or eat, or do both, for as long as one likes. The usual measure of wine served, other than in a bottle of 0.70, or more recently, 0.75 litres, is a quarter of a litre. Some restaurants offer a range of wines in smaller glasses served on a revolving frame or roundabout that is placed on the table. This is an excellent system, for it enables one to enjoy a tasting of the local wines at minimum cost.

There are no major towns in the Palatinate, but a number of attractive small towns with many half-timbered buildings and much wrought-iron work, a lot of which is modern. The conifer forests above the vineyards provide a dark backcloth for the greenery of the vines and the setting for many old castles, as well as the summer residence of King Ludwig I of Bavaria, Schloss Ludwigshöhe. One of the larger towns in the region is Bad Dürkheim, with a population of 15,000 only, where the *Wurstmarkt* takes place each September. This is not simply a celebration of the German sausage, first rate as this is in all its various forms, but a major wine festival at which the possibility exists to taste as many wines as you can manage. The Palatinate has many such festivals at different times of the year, that are not only enjoyable but do much for the promotion of wine. The wine student visiting the Palatinate for the first time will automatically be drawn to the Bereich Mittelhaardt Deutsche Weinstrasse as the source of the best-known wines of the region, but the scenery further south is possibly even more attractive and picturesque and the variety of wine as great as ever. Dividing the two *Bereiche* is the principal town in the Palatinate, Neustadt, which, with its 51,000 inhabitants, is still not large. It is very much a wine town, where viti-vinicultural machinery is made and the regional viticultural institute may be found. Further south at Siebeldingen is another viticultural institute at the Geilweilerhof, where all manner of experiments are carried out on vines, often in artificially created conditions. One of the best known new crossings from the Geilweilerhof is the Morio-Muskat, described in an earlier chapter. A mere interest in gardening is sufficient to make a visit to such a viticultural institute extremely worthwhile. The enthusiasm of those carrying out the experiments is catching, and one can gain the wrong impression that it is only a matter of time before the whole of Germany is once more growing vines, even up to the Baltic. The limitations in the long term to an extension of the present viticultural area are probably more commercial than technical. The Palatinate has benefited greatly from the improvements in vines and viticulture in Germany during the twentieth century. Its best wines are known wherever German wine is exported in any significant quantity. The main commercial task for the area is to increase the awareness of *Pfalzwein* as a whole, both in West Germany north of Mainz, and on the quickly developing export markets.

Within the Bereich Mittelhaardt Deutsche Weinstrasse and the Bereich Südliche Weinstrasse, there are twenty-six *Grosslagen*, 170 villages or communities, and 335 *Einzellagen*. Most of the village and vineyard names are seldom met on wine lists, although the following villages and towns in the Bereich Mittelhaardt are well-known amongst wine drinkers, for they consistently produce the finest wines of the region: Bad Dürkheim, Deidesheim, Forst, Kallstadt, Neustadt, Ruppertsberg, Ungstein, Wachenheim. Amongst the best known estates of the Palatinate are:

GEHEIMER RAT DR V. BASSERMANN-JORDAN'SCHES WEINGUT (Deidesheim)

The Bassermann-Jordan family, into whose hands the estate came in 1816, is widely respected in Germany for its services to the wine trade over the centuries. The estate has built up a comprehensive wine museum, and has a remarkable, extensive cask cellar. There are 50 hectares of vineyards, described as being on lightly rolling country. Many of the vineyard sites are at Deidesheim (Grainhübel, Herrgottsacker, etc.), at Forst (Ungeheuer, Jesuitengarten, etc.), at Ruppertsberg (Reiterpfad, Linsenbusch, etc.), at Dürkheim and at Ungstein. The vine varieties are 95 per cent Riesling, 2 per cent Gewürztraminer, and 3 per cent new crossings. The preceding figures show that a very high proportion of Riesling is produced which is individually vinified and matured in wood. This is top quality Palatinate wine.

WEINGUT DR BÜRKLIN-WOLF (Wachenheim)

This is probably the largest privately owned estate in Germany. The Bürklin family has been connected with wine-growing from at least 1579. The estate is technically very advanced, both in vineyard and cellar. The vineyards consist of 100 hectares, in ideal situations, in which the maximum use is made of mechanization, commensurate with top quality production. Many of the vineyards are situated at Wachenheim (Gerümpel, Goldbächel, etc.), at Forst (Kirchenstück, Ungeheuer, Jesuitengarten, etc.), at Deidesheim (Hohenmorgen, Kalkofen, etc.) and at Ruppertsberg (Hoheburg, Geisböhl, etc.). The vine varieties are 88 per cent Riesling and 12 per cent others. Very fine Palatinate Riesling wines are matured in wood to the highest standards, and in all qualities up to *Trockenbeerenauslese* – weather permitting.

WEINGUT K. FITZ-RITTER (Bad Dürkheim)

The Fitz family, of Scottish origin, has been engaged in vine-growing in Bad Dürkheim since the eighteenth century. It was one of the earliest producers of

German sparkling wine. The vineyards consist of 22 hectares, of which 50 per cent are on moderate slopes and 50 per cent on level ground. The vineyard sites are at Dürkheim (sole owner of the Abtsfronhof 3.2 hectares), at Ungstein and at Wachenheim. The vine varieties are 65 per cent Riesling, 5 per cent Ruländer, 4 per cent Silvaner, 1 per cent Spätburgunder, and 25 per cent others, mostly new crossings. These are fine fruity wines with great variety of flavour, matured in wood.

WEINGUT REICHSRAT VON BUHL (Deidesheim)

A large, well-known estate, dating from the eighteenth century. The vineyards consist of nearly 100 hectares, mainly on level ground. Many of the vineyard sites are at Deidesheim (Herrgottsacker, Kieselberg, etc.), at Forst (Ungeheuer, Pechstein, etc.), at Ruppertsberg (Linsenbusch, Reiterpfad, etc.) and at Wachenheim. The vine varieties are 70 per cent Riesling and 30 per cent various. The estate is renowned for top quality Palatinate Riesling wine which, as on all the best estates, is matured in wood. Magnificent range of wines.

EUGEN SPINDLER WEINGUT LINDENHOF (Forst)

The Spindler family has been growing vines since 1620. There are 13.5 hectares of vineyards. The vineyard sites are at Forst (Jesuitengarten, Ungeheuer, etc.), at Deidesheim and at Ruppertsberg. The vine varieties are 65 per cent Riesling, 15 per cent Müller-Thurgau, 8 per cent Ruländer, 4 per cent Gewürztraminer, 3 per cent Scheurebe and 5 per cent new crossings. Excellent quality, traditional wines are made and matured in wood, that benefit from a few years in bottle.

HESSISCHE BERGSTRASSE

This is the smallest of the German specified regions. North of Heidelberg, south of Darmstadt, east across the Rhein from Worms, one cannot help wondering if it justifies its status as a separate specified region. A great deal of wine is consumed within the region in the cafés and restaurants. As a result of the large sale of wine by the glass, much is bottled into litre rather than 0.70-litre or 0.75-litre bottles. As the ratio of wine to cork, glass, handling costs and so on is marginally greater in the case of the larger bottle, the cost of the wine by the glass to the restaurateur sold in this way is also lower. In most regions, the litre bottle is kept for the cheaper wines, but even *Spätlesen* can be found in litre bottles in the Hessische Bergstrasse.

The region is variously described as having 300 or 450 hectares of planted vineyard. In a country where precision is so usual and highly regarded, such a variance is certainly uncommon. Most of the vineyards are on steep slopes, a few still terraced, and the Riesling vine predominates, covering 55 per cent of the vineyard area. This combination suggests immediately that we are dealing with a region that produces good, interesting wine. The average annual temperature of Bensheim in the Bereich Starkenburg of 10.2°C is higher than that of any other specified region, with the exception of the Middle Rhine and Baden. It was here that in 1904 the State cellars were founded, and in the same year the first cooperative cellar was built at Heppenheim. Today, most of the region's production is handled by two cooperative cellars who sell all their wine in bottle and thus obtain the maximum profit. In some instances, where a vineyard is owned by more than one member of a family, the shareholders in the vineyard may each have a private stake in the cooperative cellar. The result of this is that there are more members of the cooperative cellars than there are establishments growing grapes. At the same time, some of the growers in the adjacent part of Baden have elected to deliver their grapes to one of the Hessische Bergstrasse cooperatives to the further confusion of those reading statistics.

Nine of the growers practise the old custom of *Strausswirtschaft*. In the Epilogue to *As You Like It*, we read that a 'good wine needs no bush', and it was to the custom of *Strausswirtschaft* that Shakespeare was presumably referring. A small branch of a tree or bush is hung outside the grower's house to indicate that he has the right to sell his wine on the premises for a limited period, accompanied by cold food only. By the nature of things, in a small village where everybody knows everybody else, where there is *Strausswirtschaft* or 'bush trading' there is a party. The Germans like to drink sitting down in groups of four or more and to take their time about it. It is this type of social drinking that is portrayed and promoted in Germany by the wine trade. There is a loose formality about such occasions, with glasses being raised in unison and toasts being drunk. To leave early, in under two or three hours, is to risk mild disapproval. Pleasure is sometimes taken almost as seriously as work.

In a region as small as the Hessische Bergstrasse, it is not likely that one will find wine brokers, and indeed there are none. The exact function of the broker I discussed on page 200, but suffice it to say that they are persons with expert local knowledge who can 'place', or sell a grower's wine, collecting a commission by so doing. In the last few years, the size of the viticultural area has started to expand once more. In most respects, the history of the vineyards mirrors that of other regions. The wars, the diseases, and the economic pressures have been much the same. To taste Hessische Bergstrasse wine, it may well be necessary to visit the district. In the late autumn of each year, the State Cellars at Bensheim auction a certain amount of their wine, when there is an opportunity to taste everything that is being offered for sale at the auction. There are two *Bereiche*, three *Grosslagen*, ten villages or communities and twenty-two *Einzellagen* in the Hessische Bergstrasse.

WÜRTTEMBERG

Württemberg, like Baden, is one of those regions of West Germany whose vineyards are not concentrated in an easily defined area. On the contrary, their distribution seems to lack system, and they do not always have the proximity of a river to explain their presence. No one part of the region can really claim to make vastly better wine than another, but the standard is high and the wines have the south German virtues of breadth and length of flavour. That little is exported is a pity, but understandable, for consumption of wine greatly exceeds supply in Württemberg, and imports into the region have to be kept at a high level to meet the demand.

There are 9,451 hectares of vineyard in production, with as much as 47 per cent of the area being planted in red-wine varieties, the principal of which is the Trollinger. This vine, as I have mentioned earlier, is known in the United Kingdom as the Black Hamburg. It covers over 1,900 hectares of vineyard in Württemberg and very little elsewhere in West Germany, although it used to be grown quite widely for use as a table grape. It is said that the Romans brought the Trollinger to the Rhineland, but the Schwabians imported it into their homeland in Württemberg as late as the sixteenth century, directly from the Tyrol. The Trollinger requires a good site to ripen well, and in this respect is even more demanding than the Spätburgunder. It is also not very resistant against winter frost. When one considers that it ripens even later than the Riesling, one cannot help wondering if a more suitable vine variety might not have been found. Nevertheless, as the Trollinger has almost disappeared from most other regions of Germany, it has become a speciality of Württemberg. The wine is fresh in flavour through its relatively high acidity, whilst its colour is somewhat light. It is pleasant to drink but usually not much more than that. The Müller-Rebe, known in France as the Pinot Meunier and in the United Kingdom as the Wrotham Pinot, is another red-vine variety found more in Württemberg than in any other region of Germany. Its wine has more colour than that of the Trollinger but is in other respects inferior to it. Nevertheless, it is a wine to taste if the opportunity occurs, and can be enjoyed with the local dumplings (*Knöpfle*) or the *Spätzle* that are also found in Baden.

Of the white varieties of vine, the most widely grown is the Riesling, covering 2,048 hectares. As always, it will only be found in the vineyards with the best microclimate. The Müller-Thurgau is planted in the less favoured sites, and the new Kerner, a locally developed vine, has also been planted in 557 hectares of land unsuited to the Riesling. One of the most reliable vines in Württemberg is the Ruländer, which regularly produces fat, rather heavy wine that does not appeal entirely to the modern taste on any wide scale. Throughout the wine-producing world, the consumer seems to appreciate freshness and the acidity that causes it, but it would surely be a pity if the demand for light, crisp wines, however attractive these may be, were to bring about the disappearance of white wine whose only fault was that it did not meet this description.

Württemberg wine is much less well known than Franconian and, of course, it lacks the Bocksbeutel. The vineyard holdings are very small and, as we have seen in Baden, a large part of the production is sold by the cooperative cellars, and only 10 per cent of the wine is bottled and sold by the grower. At Weinsberg, there is one of the best viticultural schools in West Germany. Its former pupils are found all over the country making wine in the most modern way and up to the highest standards. Naturally, there are more of them in Württemberg than in other regions and the standard of orderliness in the vineyards is exemplary. Even those vineyards that do not produce the finest grapes are still well tended and show the care that goes into their upkeep.

The capital of the state of Baden-Württemberg is Stuttgart, which lies in the viticultural region of Württemberg In spite of the size of the industrial part of the town, where the factories of Daimler-Benz and Bosch may be found, the vines grow close to the centre of the city. German sources of reference are never short of statistics, and it is interesting to read that of the city's 625,000 inhabitants, there are 400,000 who are *trinkfähig* – capable of drinking. These capable 400,000 consume 44 litres of wine each per year, compared to the national average of about 23 litres. Apart from the local population, the visitor to Württemberg also adds to the wine-consumption figures, and this must be particularly true when Stuttgart is holding its 'Intervitis' exhibition. Though Intervitis claims to be an international exhibition, the emphasis is very much on the home market, but this is no matter. It provides an opportunity to examine the latest in vini-viticultural machinery, and to taste an enormous range of German wines and a smaller selection of imported wines. It was last held in May 1979 and the next one is scheduled for May 1983. There are many trade functions that take place in Stuttgart at the same time as Intervitis, and one can attend lectures on all manner of matters connected with wine, but an understanding of German is essential if these are to be survived. Though the exhibition is principally aimed at the trade rather than the consumer, the wine enthusiast will find that there is much that will interest him. The city of Stuttgart, with its two universities, is attractive rather than beautiful. It has some fine buildings and is a cultural centre, renowned for its music. It lies in a valley surrounded by woods and vineyards, with eighteen natural springs producing eighteen million litres of mineral water per day. The population bathe in it as well as drink it.

The cafés and restaurants of Württemberg serve most of their wine by the glass with a content of 0.25 litres. A speciality in the region is *Schillerwein*. It is a quality wine produced by the fermenting together of red and white grapes to produce a form of deep-coloured rosé wine. The wine cannot be made by simply blending white and red wine. Whatever the quality of the wine they produce, the Württemberg vineyards are every bit as well cared for as those of the internationally known

Rheingau. The sloping vineyards of the Neckar River are very similar in appearance to those on the Rheinfront near Nierstein in the Rheinhessen. There is an air of prosperity that is emphasized by the new service roads that run through the vineyards as a result of the *Flurbereinigung* plan. The countryside has much rural charm and of course is easily reached, thanks to the Autobahn system. Württemberg has three *Bereiche*, sixteen *Grosslagen*, 230 villages or communities and 205 *Einzellagen*. None of the names are well known outside the region.

BADEN

Most of the German specified regions for wine-growing are easily identifiable on the map. They follow the course of a river with varying degrees of tenacity and an apparent sense of corporate feeling that is not shared by Baden. Its vineyards are often not far from the Rhine, yet they do not relate to it as do those of the more northerly regions. Whilst they may benefit from proximity to the river at certain points, one cannot help feeling that they can manage well without it. This characteristic of being different may also be found in Baden's wine. It in some ways resembles Swiss more than northern German wine, for it is broad in flavour and often strong in alcohol compared to the wine of the Rheingau or Mosel-Saar-Ruwer. To some, its relatively low acidity may make the wine too bland, and others will find the earthiness that runs through the wines of the Bereich Kaiserstuhl-Tuniberg almost overpowering. It is perhaps for good reason that in south Germany one hears a reference to *drei Männerwein*. The wine is so potent that if one man drinks it, two other men are needed to hold him down afterwards. At the vini-viticultural exhibition at Stuttgart in 1979, a computer was demonstrated that would carry out the complete analysis of a wine that was necessary when applying for an official control number. I was told it could handle all German wines but that when given a Baden wine, it would shake most dreadfully. This may have been an example of a rather ponderous sense of humour, but it showed the reputation that Baden wine enjoys. 'Spoilt by the sun' is the slogan for promoting Baden wines in Germany. 'Spoilt' is, of course, being used here in the sense of pampered or coddled, and there is certainly no doubt that the Baden wines have much sun in them.

The region stretches from the river Main in the north to the Swiss border just under 300 kilometres away to the south, with excursions from the main vineyard areas to follow the course of the Neckar or to the banks of Lake Constance. In many areas, the vineyards are dispersed and their wines largely unknown except to the local inhabitants. For much of the region the Black Forest overlooks the vineyards, fulfilling all the romantic notions that one can possibly gain from travel brochures of what a southern German vineyard should really be.

Like so many of the specified regions for wine, the history of the Baden vineyards, though ancient, is not one of steady development. The Thirty Years War much reduced the area under vine, and where war failed to finish the destruction, disease carried on the work, if not quite bringing it to a conclusion. There was a time when Baden was the largest producing region of Germany. Early in the nineteenth century, the vineyards covered some 26,600 hectares, while today they are just under 13,000 hectares in extent. The vineyard area was at its smallest in recent years, in 1950, when it covered less than 6,000 hectares. Its expansion since then is undoubtedly connected with the success of the cooperative movement in promoting the identity of Baden as a region. As elsewhere in Germany, one cannot but notice how greatly the yield per hectare of vineyard has increased in Baden over the last seventy years or so. It is certainly true that the vine today is much more productive than it was in the nineteenth century. The effect of disease and the damage caused by pests of the vine were catastrophic in some years.

In 1913 the average yield per hectare was 3.2 hectolitres, whilst in 1910 it had fallen to 2.7 hectolitres. As a comparison, the yield per hectare for the whole of West Germany in 1977 was 118.4 hectolitres. A positive effect of such poor vintages was the abandoning of the vine in unsuitable sites and its replacement by corn. The First World War and the shortage of labour that it caused brought a further reduction in the vineyard area, which was slowly made up after the return of peace. Phylloxera did not appear in Baden to any great extent until 1913, and the replacement of the old vines on their own root stocks began in 1924. At first, the State was the only provider of grafted vines, but gradually the growers learnt the technique of grafting for themselves. Even so, the supply of grafted vines was insufficient and many were imported after the Second World War from France and neighbouring Switzerland. In the early part of the twentieth century, a considerable number of American and hybrid vines were planted that were disease resistant and produced an abundant crop. The quality of the wine was poor, but even as late as 1933, 26 per cent of the Baden vineyard area was planted in hybrids. These have since been removed, often as part of a *Flurbereinigung* plan, previously described. By 1977, the *Flurbereinigung* had been carried out in some 60 per cent of the viticultural area.

In the Bereich Ortenau, the Riesling is the most widely grown vine and is known locally as the Klingelberger. The Gutedel or Chasselas predominates in the Bereich Markgräflerland. The Chasselas is often grown to provide grapes for the table rather than wine-making, although under the name of Fendant it produces the good white wine of the Canton of Vaud in Switzerland. In all the districts of Baden, the Müller-Thurgau may be found growing in profusion, and it occupies more of the vineyards than any other vine, followed by the Spätburgunder or Pinot Noir.

To those used to the red wines of France, the red wine of Baden will surprise as much as any other German red wine. The principal problem in German red-wine vinification seems to be the absence of sufficient colour. In a well-equipped Baden cellar, the must may be heated rapidly to between 70° and 80°C, and after a short time cooled to 40°C. If the heating process is too slow, there is the possibility that between 45° and 55°C a negative effect will develop and instead of gaining colour, the must will actually lose it. Red-wine sweet reserve will be added before bottling, which may have been made from a new crossing with much colour. This will also help to darken the wine to which it is added, of course. Normally, bottling will take place in the spring following the vintage. Badisch Rotgold is a quality wine produced by the blending of the grapes or must (not wine) of Ruländer and Spätburgunder grown in Baden, and the names of the two varieties must appear on the bottle label.

The better quality Baden wines will usually be sold in 0.70 litre or 0.75 litre bottles, and the cheaper wines in litre bottles. In the local cafés, a glass of wine amounts to 0.25 litres, as opposed to the 0.20 litres served in the wine regions to the north. This, and the increased alcoholic content of a Baden wine compared to a Moselle, is something the visitor to the region should not overlook. If one lives in a wine-producing area, one very quickly becomes used to the style of the local wine, and that which is well known is often liked. Wines from outside the area whose virtues are different may not appeal to the same extent. That this is not always the result of misplaced nationalistic feeling can be judged by the great quantity of Alsatian wine that is imported into Baden, with its powerful bouquet. It is very much to the taste of the Baden wine-drinker. Strangely enough, though, one often finds that the South German will not care for the Rheinhessen or Palatinate wine, but the fruit and acidity of a Moselle, so different to his own wine, will attract him. All one can say to this is that it shows once again how dangerous it is to make generalized statements. Dogmatism and wine make a bad blend.

Because of the difficulties which the growers suffered at the end of the nineteenth century and the beginning of the twentieth, the cooperative movement is very strong in Baden. The first cooperative cellar was founded in 1881 at Hagnau by Lake Constance. Today there are 123 cooperative cellars, which together handle the crop from no less than 84 per cent of the vineyard area. The huge central co-operative at Breisach, not far from Colmar in Alsace, receives just under 50 per cent of this total quantity, either in the form of grapes or must. To do so it now has a storage capacity of 150 million litres and a daily bottling output of 200,000 bottles. It is one of the largest cellars in Europe. The standard of Baden wine is high, but with the type of production described above, it is difficult not to suppose that with a general improvement in quality, there has not also been a certain loss of individuality. Whatever opinion one may have of this, it must be remembered that growers need to live and wine is to be sold, and the cooperative movement in Baden is meeting these two requirements well.

Those who wish to diet should no doubt spend as little time as possible enjoying the Baden kitchen. It seems to be pleasant in the best culinary sense, but one does meet *Spätzle* rather frequently. (For brevity's sake, *Spätzle* may be described a little inaccurately as homemade pasta.) There are good flavours in the Baden kitchen and not everything comes out of a packet, can or bottle. The broad, soft wines with their strong bouquet go well with the game dishes, followed by the splendid Black Forest Cherry cream cakes.

The wines from the north of Baden from the Bereich Badisches Frankenland are very similar to those previously discussed in the rest of Franconia. They are also sold in the flagon-shaped bottle known as a Bocksbeutel, and the Müller-Thurgau predominates. In the Bereich Badische Bergstrasse Kraichgau, there is the city of Heidelberg, which needs no further mention here. The landscape is pleasant without being outstandingly beautiful. The Bereich Ortenau is, on the other hand, well worth a detour for anybody, and the spa of Baden-Baden has elegance and a somewhat nostalgic atmosphere of the past. The Ortenau, which is known for its high quality Riesling wine, is a land of many orchards and vineyards that reach to the foothills of the Black Forest. Here, as in other districts of Baden, there are instructional wine paths through the vineyards, similar to those on the Moselle. There are also wine festivals, seminars and guided tours for those who wish to acquire more than a superficial knowledge of the region.

I must confess to very little personal experience of the wines of Lake Constance in the Bereich Bodensee in the far south of Baden. Most writers mention their fairly high acidity which, in a region known for wines with relatively low acidity, obviously makes them required tasting at the first opportunity. The state owns 52 hectares of vineyard at Meersburg am Bodensee. The wines of the Bereich Markgräflerland are somewhat more widely met, especially in Switzerland over the border. The Bereich Kaiserstuhl-Tuniberg, whose volcanic soil transmits its flavour so effectively to the wine produced on these slopes, makes powerful Ruländer wines that seem to be at their best with food, unlike some of the delicate wines from the Moselle or Nahe rivers. Baden has seven *Bereiche*, sixteen *Grosslagen*, 315 villages or communities and 306 *Einzellagen*. None of the villages or communities are well known outside the region.

German Sparkling Wine

In 1824, sparkling wine was produced on a commercial scale for the first time in Germany at Esslingen am Neckar by Georg Christian Kessler. He had worked for a number of years in the Champagne district, where he learnt as much as was then possible of the conversion of a still base wine into sparkling wine. The process was not fully understood, and the losses through bottles exploding while the secondary fermentation was taking place amounted regularly to between 20 and 40 per cent. It was the discovery of how to measure the sugar content of a wine that made fermentation in bottle, which was then the only known method of producing sparkling wine, commercially more interesting. Others soon followed Kessler. In 1836, Carl Burgeff joined forces with Ignatz Schweickardt, who had begun to produce sparkling wine at Hochheim three years previously, and in 1838 the firm was founded in Eltville that was later to become known as 'MM'. The wine merchants in Koblenz, Deinhard, who had been in business since 1794, started sparkling-wine production in 1843. Kupferberg followed in 1850, Henkell in 1856, and Söhnlein in 1864. The foundations of the German sparkling-wine trade had been firmly established. By the end of the nineteenth century, there were over 220 cellars producing sparkling wine, but since 1900 this number has decreased greatly. The competition in Germany amongst sparkling-wine manufacturers is exceedingly fierce and many have not been able to survive. Today, over 77 per cent of the production is in the hands of eight concerns, which have been able to increase their share of the German market in spite of the success of sparkling wines imported from France, Italy, and the Soviet Union. The consumption of sparkling wine in Germany of some 275 million bottles per year is the highest of any country in the world. It is drunk on all sorts of occasions, both formal and informal, and much is sold in quarter bottles as an alternative to beer or still wine.

Market research has shown that the consumer in Germany buys sparkling wine much more on the brand name rather than on geographical origin. The production of sparkling wine from delimited areas in Germany is very small, so that there is no German equivalent to the Champagne district. Any German vineyard, as we have seen, can produce quality wine of distinction (QmP) depending on the vintage, so that growers are naturally reluctant to make a standard wine each year for conversion into sparkling wine. In some hot years German wine, admirable as it is as a still wine, is quite unsuited to sparkling wine production, so the large brand owners keep their options open and buy their base wine where the quality, style and price best meet their aims. It can well be that a North Italian wine with a good acid content, or a wine from the Loire Valley in France, may be able to be made, with sufficient expertise and care, into a better sparkling wine than a German base wine. Nature does not necessarily always favour one country more than another, and neither do the manufacturers of German sparkling wine. Wine-growers, not surprisingly, tend to vary their prices from year to year depending on the quality and quantity produced by the vintage, but this the owner of a brand of sparkling wine cannot do, other, of course, than in the case of Champagne which seems to become ever more expensive. 'Produce of Germany', in the case of sparkling wine, refers to the country where the sparkling wine was produced – not where the base wine was made. The grapes for the best German sparkling wine are in fact grown in Germany, for it is there that the Riesling is at its most elegant. The steely wines of the Mittelrhein or the fresh wines of the Saarland when made from the Riesling grape convert marvellously into sparkling wine, taking their typical bouquet and style with them.

The German sparkling-wine industry began at the very early stages of its career to engage in the export market, usually using English names such as Sparkling Hock and Sparkling Moselle. It would seem that though German still wine is unique, the sparkling wine has many competitors and therefore can be easily replaced on the export market. Two World Wars have allowed cheap sparkling wine from elsewhere to become firmly established as a cheaper alternative to Champagne. The German word for sparkling wine is *Schaumwein* but the bulk of their production is technically *Qualitätsschaumwein*, or quality sparkling wine. Instead of using the

A view from the porphyry rocks above the Traisener Rotenfels vineyard near Bad Kreuznach in the Middle Nahe

word *Qualitätsschaumwein*, the Germans somewhat uncharacteristically use a shorter word, *Sekt*, whose detailed origin is rather involved and possibly uncertain. It is said to date from 1825 when an actor playing Henry IV in Berlin was regularly served Champagne on stage when he called for Sack. *Sekt* now means quality sparkling wine but unless the Germans are speaking in strict legal terms, they often use the word somewhat imprecisely to include both quality and ordinary sparkling wine.

There are various factors that have a major effect on the quality of a sparkling wine, starting from the selection of the base wine. As I have explained, this may come from outside Germany, but whatever the origin, maintenance of an established standard will be the intention. Some German sparkling wines, it is claimed, still reflect the style that was established when Alsace Lorraine belonged to Germany and was the source of much *Sekt* base wine. Others depend more on the fresh, crisp style associated with the German Riesling or the Elbling. Blind tastings would suggest, however, that it is not simply a matter of a good acid content being the foundation of a good sparkling wine, though this is an essential ingredient. Wines that have a high acidity but a rather pronounced bouquet, such as those made from Scheurebe, Morio-Muskat or Bacchus, do not make attractive sparkling wines, and soft wines with a pronounced bouquet, such as those made from Reichensteiner, are the least successful of all in terms of quality. One should not forget, however, that the consumer is not always interested in quality as the wine-trade taster understands it, for if he were, the imports of cheap sweet sparkling wine with a residual sugar content of 55 g/l or more into Germany, and for that matter, the United Kingdom and elsewhere as well, would not be as large as they are. Sugar can mask a multitude of imperfections. If we wish to make a good quality German sparkling wine, a neutral-tasting and crisp base wine must be obtained. There are various ways in which *Sekt* can be produced. They all have their different characteristics, and the most successful are those that combine the achievement of quality with economy, and in practical terms allow themselves to be carried out with exactitude and control. Up until thirty years ago, a secondary fermentation in bottle was the only permissible way of producing *Sekt*. It is the oldest method of sparkling-wine production, but has the disadvantage of not allowing the precise control of the development of the sparkling wine during the secondary fermentation when the gas is being formed. One well-known *Sekt* producer employs this system, but when the sparkle has developed in the bottle, he transfers the contents under pressure into a vat where it then receives an addition of wine and sugar to achieve the appropriate amount of sweetness. Bottling then follows, under pressure, via a filter.

It is difficult to find out which, ignoring economics, is the 'best' method of making sparkling wine. Nevertheless, it is probably safe to assume that one is as good as another if all are perfectly carried out with the same attention to detail and an equal amount of maturation. However, making sparkling wine is a commercial undertaking in which there is no doubt much to be said for reducing the possibility of human error to a minimum, and for this reason the precision method of tank fermentation has much to recommend it. Let us assume that we wish to produce *Sekt* and this is the method we have chosen.

Our crisp base wine is one year old and is lying in a pressurized vat. A cultured yeast able to ferment to five atmospheres is added with about 20 g/l of beet sugar. Fermentation starts and the fermenting wine is roused by a propeller within the vat for thirty minutes each day. This process releases amino acids which contribute greatly to the bouquet of the final *Sekt*. Fermentation should proceed slowly at a temperature of 15°C. The advantage of this method of tank fermentation is that the fermenting wine is all at the same stage of development at the same time, and that

Vineyards near the Black Forest in the wine region of Baden

this can either be speeded up or slowed down as necessary. This degree of control cannot be achieved if the fermentation is taking place inside individual bottles amongst which there are liable to be variations. During the six months when the *Sekt* is harmonizing it is regularly roused and tasted. Eventually it is passed through a Kieselguhr filter under pressure, and via K10 filter sheets into chemically cleaned tanks. A small dose of sulphur dioxide (about 30 mg/l) is added, as is a liqueur made of mature wine and sugar. The quality of the liqueur is very important for it must reflect the character of the *Sekt* to which it is blended. Normally, it will be made at a strength of one kilogram of sugar to one litre of wine. After further maturation, the *Sekt* is transferred to vats that allow it to be chilled over a period of twenty-four hours to −3°C. At this temperature the pressure in the *Sekt* is reduced to 1.5-2 atmospheres. The carbon dioxide gas is now bound in the *Sekt* and bottling takes place, preceded by a final filtration. As the temperature slowly rises in the bottles, the pressure returns to about five atmospheres. The *Sekt* now rests for at least six months, before being released for sale to the trade. This method of making *Sekt* goes beyond the minimum legal requirements, which are as follows:

1. The sparkle in the wine must be the result of secondary fermentation.
   The Sekt must:
2. Be on the yeast for a minimum of twenty-one days.
3. Achieve an actual alcohol content of not less than 10 per cent by volume.
4. Have a maturation period of a minimum of nine months at a pressure of at least 3.5 atmospheres.
5. Be granted an official control number.

The European Courts of Justice, against the wishes of the Germans, decided in 1975 that the word *Sekt* could be used for sparkling wines of non-German origin. However, the legal requirements outlined above relate only to German *Sekt* (Deutscher Sekt). Therefore, a sparkling wine from Italy or France, sold in a German-speaking country as 'Italienischer Sekt' or 'Französischer Sekt', will not have to comply with the same conditions of production.

Apart from the question of standards of production, German *Sekt* must, like a quality still wine, bear a control number. This is granted after the *Sekt* has undergone an analysis and passed a 'blind' tasting in which a minimum number of marks has to be exceeded for the type of sparkle, colour, clarity, smell, taste, balance of acidity, sweetness and alcohol. If the *Sekt* claims to originate from a specified region, the base wine must have been made exclusively from grapes grown in that region. Not every bottling of a brand of *Sekt* has to be examined by the control authorities. A control number will be granted to a particular style or brand of *Sekt* each year and only if there are changes from the original blend during the year does a further official examination have to take place.

The technical requirements laid down for ordinary *Schaumwein* as opposed to *Qualitätswein* (*Sekt*) are less demanding. The sparkle in a German *Schaumwein*, or in *Sekt*, may not be achieved by the first fermentation, as in the case of Italian Asti Spumante, or what the French refer to as the *méthode rurale*.

The Germans produce on a limited scale a type of sparkling wine called *Perlwein*. It has a carbon dioxide pressure between 1.5 and 2.5 atmospheres measured at the usual temperature of 20°C. Generally, *Perlwein* derives its sparkle from an injection of carbon dioxide rather than through the development of the gas by fermentation, and its label and style of bottle must not cause it to be confused with *Schaumwein*.

One of the genuinely rather than politically difficult problems that the European sparkling-wine industry has had to consider in recent years has been that of sweetness in sparkling wine. How sweet a sparkling wine tastes does not simply depend on its sugar content but on its other constituents as well, and in particular on its acid content. A wine with a higher level of acidity will taste drier than one with less acidity. This has sometimes produced a curious situation in which a *brut* (the most 'dry' of sparkling wines) has actually contained as much sugar as a *demi-sec* (or medium dry) sparkling wine. In preparing a *cuvée* or blend of base wine for conversion into sparkling wine, the taster is exceedingly important for the choice simply cannot be made by analysis alone. In spite of the uncertainty of sugar content as a guide to sweetness, the following terms to describe sparkling wine only, have been able to be established by law in the EEC.

French	German	Equivalent Sugar Content
Brut	Herb	0–15 g/l
Extra Sec Extra Dry	Sehr Trocken	12–20 g/l
Sec, Dry	Trocken	17–35 g/l
Demi-Sec Medium Dry	Halbtrocken	33–50 g/l
Doux	Süss or Mild	over 50 g/l

Some 49 per cent of *Sekt* is produced in the state of Hessen and 44 per cent in Rheinland-Pfalz. A brief look at the statistics for 1978 produced by the central authorities in Rheinland-Pfalz gives an indication of the importance of some of the various types of *Sekt* produced in Germany. Of 440 applications for a control number, nine were unsuccessful. 228 applications were made to the control centre for *Sekt* bearing a vintage, geographical origin or grape type, representing 11.3 million litres. For *Sekt* without an indication of a geographical origin, etc., there were 212 applications for 72.2 million litres. 8.7 million litres had been produced by a secondary fermentation in bottle and 74.7 million litres by vat fermentation. 97.3 per cent of the total quantity of *Sekt* produced in Rheinland-Pfalz and for which control numbers were applied was white, 2.6 per cent red, and the balance rosé. 44 per cent was *trocken* (dry), and 38 per cent medium dry or sweet. Possibly surprisingly when there seems to be a move towards dry still wine in Germany, the sweeter sparkling wines appear to be becoming more popular, though whether this tendency will continue or not it is too soon to say.

As a general rule the more one pays for a bottle of *Sekt*, the more rewarding is the purchase likely to be. This is especially true in countries outside Germany where shipping costs and import duty may be high and form a disproportionate share of the selling price. Whilst one would hope that the cheapest *Sekt* would be perfectly drinkable if undistinguished, the finer examples offer very much more. A good German Riesling *Sekt* should combine all the virtues of that grape with the finesse that is associated with the best sparkling-wine production.

German wine as others know it

The export market is important to the producers of German wine for it absorbs some 12 per cent of the average crop each year. The United States and Britain are Germany's two largest customers, and take over 60 per cent of the total amount exported. In both countries, consumption of wine is not great; as neither drinks more than 7 litres per head of the adult population each year, a further increase in their wine imports could quite easily be achieved. It has not always been the quality or, indeed, the price that has determined the success of German wine abroad. In the last eighty years, two World Wars, and the understandable reluctance to buy a German product that was their residue, the loss of the Russian market through the

1917 revolution, and prohibition in the United States from 1918 to 1933, all had a depressing effect on German wine exports.

What then is responsible now for the increase in the consumption of German wine abroad? The style is easily appreciated. German wine is uncomplicated. Other than being slightly chilled, it needs no special treatment. It does not normally require time to breathe, as does a red wine, but may be opened and served on impulse, as a refreshing drink, pleasant by itself but also agreeable with food. The flavour is usually not too strong and the acidity is balanced by an appropriate sweetness. The alcohol is never high, which makes German wine an easy part of social life. A light elegance distinguishes it from wines from other countries and this may seem strange, for elegance is not, generally speaking, a German virtue. Most German products are well made, solid, reliable, but often somewhat heavy in design, as may be seen in German furniture and food. The wine of Germany, though, is as elegant as the tall, slim bottle in which it is sold. The increases in price to the consumer on the export market have been less than those from some other EEC countries over the last ten years, in spite of the strength of the Deutsche Mark, though nothing can prevent the effect of increased taxes, shipping and distribution costs that occur beyond the German frontier.

The main disadvantage that German wine has to overcome abroad is the German language. To many it sounds harsh and aggressive and, when written, a word such as the *Bezirkswinzergenossenschaft* is quite beyond the understanding of anybody who has not some knowledge of the language. Whereas French is the first foreign language that many are taught in school, German is usually regarded as a 'second language'. Because of the language difficulty, the use of brand names for wine has been very strong on the German export market. If there is one type of wine more than any other that with, or without, a brand name has contributed to the success of German wine, it is Liebfraumilch, which now accounts for 60 per cent of all German wine exports. As mentioned earlier, Liebfraumilch, or Liebfrauenmilch as it was called originally, came from the small vineyard in the middle of Worms in the Rheinhessen by the Church of Our Lady – the Liebfrauenkirche. Over the years, the use of the name Liebfraumilch was widened, and it almost became synonymous with Northern Rhine wine. The principal export houses over the last 150 years or so have developed markets for their own particular brands of Liebfraumilch. These major brands, whilst having an individual 'house style', have always reflected their area of origin and it is of them that many will think first when German wines are mentioned. Unlike the wine trade in some other countries, the German exporter has not had the benefit of a large national advertising budget to promote his wines and, therefore, his success has almost entirely been the result of his own efforts and expenditure. Today, Liebfraumilch is a quality wine within the sense of the EEC regulations, which must be made predominantly from Riesling, Silvaner, or Müller-Thurgau grapes, though the grape variety may not be indicated on the label. Before 1971, it was possible to find Liebfraumilch wines with a distinction such as *Spätlese*, but this is no longer permitted. That is, of course, not to say that *Spätlese* or even *Auslese* grapes may not be included in a Liebfraumilch blend, for in the case of a top quality Liebfraumilch this may indeed happen. It is simply that no distinctions are allowed on the label, no matter how justified or factual they may be. To be honest, one must say that there are some rather ordinary Liebfraumilch wines on the market and one might wonder if they were really worth their quality wine status. To avoid an inferior wine, it is probably advisable to buy a Liebfraumilch from an established exporting house which will have everything to lose, including its reputation, if its wine is not acceptable. At present, Liebfraumilch may come from the Rheingau, the Nahe, the Rheinhessen, or the Palatinate, and may be blended from wine from those regions, though at the moment of writing at the end of 1979 this is being questioned. The dispute, for such it has become, is regrettably a political rather than a wine matter. The exporting houses wish to obtain and sell their Liebfraumilch wines as they have done for many years, buying from sources in the four regions mentioned above, though very little wine for sale as Liebfraumilch will be bought in the Rheingau. EEC regulations say that a quality wine must come from one specified region only and cannot be blended with wine from another. It has been suggested that in order to comply with EEC regulations, a specified region for Liebfraumilch should be created, which would more or less cover the same areas as the present Liebfraumilch-producing regions. A similar arrangement exists in the Bordeaux region, which has within its boundaries smaller *appellation contrôlée* areas such as Médoc, St Emilion and within the Médoc still further *appellation contrôlée* areas such as St Julien, Pauillac and so on. The wine from the whole district may be sold as *appellation contrôlée* Bordeaux. However, some growers feel that their best interests would be served if within the area for Liebfraumilch the blending of wine from one region with that of another was banned. Therefore, one would always find printed on labels Liebfraumilch Rheinhessen, Liebfraumilch Rheinpfalz (Palatinate), and so on. The problem for Germany would then be that it would become less easy to object to the use of the word Liebfraumilch in connection with wines from other countries. The matter is not yet settled, and whether Liebfraumilch is to become merely an indication of a type of wine in future, or continue still to be an indication of origin as in the past, is not known. Fortunately, the German climate at least cannot be transported elsewhere, so that for true German wines we must continue to look to Germany.

The adoption of German wine names for wines of non-German origin, particularly in English-speaking countries outside the EEC, is the cause of a perpetual battle for the responsible wine authorities in Mainz – the Stabilisierungsfonds für Wein. It is a battle that is often complicated by extraneous political questions and sometimes a total lack of comprehension by the offender of what he has done wrong. If a Wiener Schnitzel does not have to come from Vienna and a Brussels sprout from Belgium, why cannot a Moselle wine be made in Australia or New Zealand? The Germans are not flattered by imitations, but rightly worried. Their wines are inimitable, but their names are not. If the consumer in Australia buys a bottle of locally made Moselle and is disappointed, it can well be that he will not be prepared even to consider buying the genuine product. In finding and preparing a wine for sale under a brand name, it is necessary to be able to provide continuity of style, and if one is wise, of price as well. To achieve this end, blending will certainly be essential, and yet the description 'blended wine' has a disparaging meaning for many, suggesting as it seems to do a reduction to the lowest characteristic common to all its constituents. Wines from different vines are blended together to make the fine red wines of Bordeaux, and this is also true of Chianti, Rioja, Châteauneuf-du-Pape and nearly all the solid red wines from the south of France. Where a wine is blended, the aim is to make up the deficiencies of nature in not creating a vine variety that will produce a perfectly balanced wine by itself. It also often adds complexity to a wine. In the case of Champagne, the blender will be aiming to maintain a house style when he selects his base wines, and so it is with the maker of a top quality German brand wine. Such an operation is entirely different from stretching a wine of a limited production with a wine from elsewhere, in order to make an illegal sale. Apart from the traditionally blended wines, to produce a balanced product, which is not necessarily a brand wine, it is often sensible to blend one wine with another that has in excess some of the qualities that are missing from the original wine. Providing such a blend does not contravene any of the strict laws of nomenclature, it is to be thoroughly recommended. The principle of such a blend must be that the end product is better than the individual wines from which it was made.

The German Wine Law lays down exactly what is permitted when wines or must of different geographical origin, grape type or vintage are to be blended. That part of the blend that is to give its name to the final wine must equal at least 85 per cent of the whole. Naturally, the resultant wine must taste true to the name it carries, otherwise it will not be granted a control number by the authorities after bottling. This attitude to the necessity to blend in certain years and conditions, as stated in the German Wine Law, is really a formal expression of a practice that occurs in some other European countries, where blending is legally not possible but in fact frequently happens when the grape harvest is deficient in one way or another.

In recent years in Germany there has been a lot of interest in dry and medium dry wines. A dry wine, according to EEC regulations, is one with a sugar content of not more than 4 grams per litre, or at the most 9 grams per litre, with a total acid content of 2 grams per litre less. To put these figures into perspective, a Liebfraumilch will normally have a sugar content of about 20 g/l to 24 g/l. A medium dry German wine must not contain more than 18 g/l sugar and have a total acid content of 10 g/l less. There does not seem to be one sole reason why dry wines are now becoming increasingly popular, nor is it yet clear whether there has been a real change in the German consumer's taste. Certainly, some Germans are aware of *Esskultur*, or in other words, the art of eating. Previously they have been thought of more as a people interested in quantity than quality in matters of food, but the idea of the marriage of food and wine associated with the French kitchen has gained a lot of ground. It must be remembered that the Germans usually drink their wine without food of any substance and a touch of sweetness in these circumstances is welcome. Dry German wines are now being recommended by the German catering trade which might otherwise offer an imported wine to its customers. Totally dry wines are often also necessary for diabetics.

The wine trade is responding to this trend towards drier wine with a mixture of caution and enthusiasm. In 1978, nearly 8 per cent of all the wines submitted to the authorities for the award of a control number were dry, although the actual volume of liquid represented by dry wines was probably much less. Many cellars include a few bottlings of dry wine in their programme, possibly in order to test the market and their customers' reaction. Whether dry German wines will really become popular is certainly not known at present, and market research in Germany suggests that many, if not most, people still prefer their wine to contain a little sugar. The further north one goes in Germany, the more sweetness seems to be appreciated. It is true of the United Kingdom and Scandinavia, where those living nearest to the North Pole prefer the sweeter wines. Many of the dry German wines that have been offered for sale so far are not really as attractive as one would like them to be. To make a dry wine it is not simply a question of neglecting to add sweet reserve before bottling. The wine must be balanced and have sufficient body for presentation in this way. Such wines are less likely to be found in those regions where the acid level of the wine is normally highest. In the northern wine regions of Germany, therefore, it may be that in most years medium dry wines will be more successful. There is a general European move towards light, dry, refreshing white wines and we shall have to wait to see what role Germany plays in it.

Some German dry wines will have a yellow paper seal on the bottle bearing the words *Deutsches Weinsiegel Trocken*, whilst medium dry wines may carry a similar seal in green with the word *Trocken* or dry, being replaced by *Halbtrocken* or medium dry. There are a number of such awards that are given by the Deutsche Landwirtschafts-Gesellschaft, or DLG. The DLG is a society that was founded in 1885 to promote all forms of agriculture. The status of its various awards is now established by EEC regulations. If a wine is to be submitted to a DLG examination board, it must already have obtained a number from the control authorities, so that it has been officially baptized. The standard of the DLG examination is said to be higher than that of the control authorities whose function is, of course, to see that minimum standards of wine production are met. In this way, the DLG could be compared to a Consorzio in Italy. There is no doubt that to the consumer the wide variety of German wine is confusing but, as we have seen, the trade tries to simplify matters by the use of brand names. At the same time the German growers and wine trade do regard theirs as a speciality amongst the wines of the world. The struggle for an individual identity is great, and the use of DLG awards helps to differentiate one wine from its neighbours on the shop shelf. If all the wines in the shop were to be 'specialities', then the problem of choice for the consumer would remain as great as ever. What the trade and the consumer both need is to have available reasonably large quantities of good but not great wine for what is hopefully called 'every day' drinking, and smaller quantities of finer wine for the special occasion. The real specialities amongst German wine can only be produced in limited quantities, so that supply and demand for these is fairly well balanced. The present tendency in the wine-drinking world is for the consumption of the cheapest wines to decrease in favour of that of better quality wine. Germany, with its dedication to quality-wine production, therefore, seems to be well placed to enjoy a good vinous future.

The Good and the Great in the 1950s and the 1960s

Time, like nothing else, sorts out the great from the more ordinary vintages. Any deficiencies that may be hidden in a young wine are liable to become more apparent with age. Incorrect storage at too high a temperature, or with the cork being allowed to dry out through the bottle being left upright over a period, can ruin the finest wine. Therefore, it is advisable to find out something of an old wine's history before actually making a purchase. Better than this is to lay young wine down yourself and, if you can, to buy more than one bottle so that you may taste it at intervals over the years and enjoy its development.

1952

Area under vine in hectares: 53,391
Yield per hectare: 50.9 hectolitres
Total yield in 1000 hectolitres: 2715
This year was above average in quality with wines of good acidity and some of top quality.

1953

Area under vine in hectares: 54,520
Yield per hectare: 45.1 hectolitres
Total yield in 1000 hectolitres: 2457
Truly great vintage. The right balance of sun and rain encouraged noble rot, and superb, top quality wine was the result.

1959

Area under vine in hectares: 60,995
Yield per hectare: 70.5 hectolitres
Total yield in 1000 hectolitres: 4303
A very dry summer produced wines that were high in alcohol, and often short of charm and acidity. Their weight was impressive. *Beerenauslesen* and *Trockenbeeren-auslesen* were made, although there was little noble rot. Those that have lasted until now will be well worth tasting.

1961

Area under vine in hectares: 66,265
Yield per hectare: 53.9 hectolitres
Total yield in 1000 hectolitres: 3574
Some very successful Moselles were made in 1961, as well as excellent ice wines – particularly on the Nahe. Attractive cheaper wines of pleasant fruit and acidity were produced. A goodish vintage, but certainly not great as was the case in Bordeaux and Burgundy.

1964

Area under vine in hectares: 68,623
Yield per hectare: 104.7 hectolitres
Total yield in 1000 hectolitres: 7185
A very good vintage with, on average, lower acidity than usual. Well-kept Moselle *Auslesen* taste splendidly today, whilst the Rhine wines do not seem to have the same charm.

1966

Area under vine in hectares: 69,166
Yield per hectare: 69.5 hectolitres
Total yield in 1000 hectolitres: 4809
A very good vintage of stylish, crisp wine, usually slightly lighter than the 1964s. Top quality wine-makers produced fine Riesling of charm but not great weight.

1967

Area under vine in hectares: 69,460
Yield per hectare: 87.4 hectolitres
Total yield in 1000 hectolitres: 6069
Dampness and warmth in the autumn made 1967 a difficult vintage to vinify. Rotten grapes were numerous but with careful handling, good quantities of top quality wines were produced, particularly in the Palatinate. Many of the Moselle and Rheingau wines were somewhat coarse in comparison with those of the 1966 vintage, and showed the difficulties of making clean, stylish wine in a year with an excessive amount of noble rot.

1969

Area under vine in hectares: 71,336
Yield per hectare: 83.4 hectolitres
Total yield in 1000 hectolitres: 5947
A successful vintage on the Moselle in particular, with excellent wines, typical of the region, being made. Elsewhere the quality of the vintage was felt to be not up to the standard of the 1967 or 1966 vintages. Good quality Riesling *Kabinett* wines were made in the Rheingau and Nahe regions, but very little *Auslesen* and upwards.

The 1970s offered us two really outstanding vintages in 1976 and 1971, with a very good runner-up in the 1975. The 1960s were not so generous, although the 1964 could be compared with the 1975 in some regions, and some 1967s were excellent. The best of the 1950s was represented by the 1953 vintage, with the controversial 1959 vintage sometimes producing the biggest wines since 1921. Amongst the really poor vintages, the 1965 was particularly bad. The musts, after a wet and sunless summer, contained too little sugar and too much malic acid. But, through good cellar technique drinkable ordinary wine was made, and the State Cellars at Niederhausen managed against all odds to produce a light but stylish ice wine in the Schlossböckelheimer Kupfergrube vineyard. Often the satisfaction of finding a good wine in a poor vintage is greater than that of finding a good wine in a great vintage.

Vintage Report for the 1970s

1970

Area under vine in hectares: 73,700
Yield per hectare: 134.2 hectolitres
Total yield in 1000 hectolitres: 9889

A big vintage whose quality sometimes suffered through overproduction. The Palatinate produced many Riesling wines of *Auslese* quality, but a shortage of noble rot in the Rheingau made *Auslesen* uncommon. 'Typical', light, elegant *Kabinett* wines could be found on the Moselle and a yield of as much as 200 hectolitres per hectare for the Müller-Thurgau was reported from certain parts of the Nahe. Unless the wine is exceptional, any remaining bottles of the 1970 vintage that may be found should be drunk soon.

1971

Area under vine in hectares: 75,514
Yield per hectare: 79.8 hectolitres
Total yield in 1000 hectolitres: 6027

The smallest vintage of the decade, and one of the very best (so far) in the century. Finely balanced wines were produced in all regions, with the Riesling in the Rheingau, in particular, showing its quality. Even the lesser wines had an excellent concentration of fruit, whilst the *Spätlesen* and *Auslesen* benefited from much noble rot. A well-constituted vintage, the best of which will continue to improve. Riesling *Beerenauslesen* and *Trockenbeerenauslesen* should not yet be drunk. Wines of supreme class were made by the top producers.

1972

Area under vine in hectares: 77,551
Yield per hectare: 96.1 hectolitres
Total yield in 1000 hectolitres: 7456

A poor year with a higher proportion than usual of table wines (16.4 per cent) reported at the time of the harvest and only 11.5 per cent quality wines with distinction. Wines with high acidity made pleasant drinking. Where they still exist, they are now fully mature and should not be kept longer.

1973

Area under vine in hectares: 80,622
Yield per hectare: 132.7 hectolitres
Total yield in 1000 hectolitres: 10,697

The largest vintage of the present century found a shortage of storage space in the Rheinhessen and Palatinate. Must weights were heavier than in 1972 or 1970, and many *Kabinett* wines were made. Certainly not a great vintage but much superior in quality to 1972, with pleasantly balanced wines up to *Spätlese* quality being produced. A few outstanding *Beerenauslesen Eisweine* were made. Apart from these and similar specialities that are still too young, the wines should be drunk now – they were for consumption in the 1970s, rather than in the 1980s.

1974

Area under vine in hectares: 83,028
Yield per hectare: 82.0 hectolitres
Total yield in 1000 hectolitres: 6805

A small harvest with a high proportion of simple quality wine and very few quality wines of distinction. *Spätlesen*, in particular, were rarer than usual. The Riesling crop was almost half that of 1973, but the Müller-Thurgau showed only a 16 per cent drop on the previous year. In general, the wines were sound and unexciting, but superior to those of 1972.

1975

Area under vine in hectares: 84,970
Yield per hectare: 108.8 hectolitres
Total yield in 1000 hectolitres: 9241

A charming vintage. A good proportion of *Spätlesen*, welcomed by the growers, and many *Auslesen* on the Moselle. The typical German wine virtues of fruit and acidity nicely balanced makes the Riesling wines very attractive five years after the vintage. Somewhat overshadowed by the amazing 1976 vintage, but their lovely elegance should not be overlooked, especially on the Moselle.

1976

Area under vine in hectares: 86,296
Yield per hectare: 100.3 hectolitres
Total yield in 1000 hectolitres: 8659

A good sized vintage overall, but much smaller than in 1975 in the Mosel-Saar-Ruwer and Mittelrhein regions, with a general shortage of simple quality and *Kabinett* wines. Relatively large quantities of superb *Auslesen* and even finer wines, that benefited from ideal weather conditions for noble rot. The fine quality wines with distinction that taste well in 1980 should improve for many years – many are outstandingly rich.

1977

Area under vine in hectares: 87,730
Yield per hectare: 118.4 hectolitres
Total yield in 1000 hectolitres: 10,389

A very large vintage in Franconia, Baden, and Württemberg in particular, principally of simple quality and a certain amount of *Kabinett* wine. A good partner for the 1976 vintage, when the cheaper wines were so scarce. Some of the lesser wines are somewhat hollow.

1978

Area under vine in hectares: 88,917
Yield per hectare: 82.1 hectolitres
Total yield in 1000 hectolitres: 7297

Bad weather during the flowering resulted in a small crop, particularly in the Mosel-Saar-Ruwer, Nahe and Baden districts. Little wine of *Spätlese* quality and upwards produced, but good simple-quality Riesling wine made which benefited from fine autumn weather.

1979

Area under vine in hectares: 87,592
Yield per hectare: 94.0 hectolitres
Total yield in 1000 hectolitres: 8330

Very variable results, e.g. the 1979 crop was 70 per cent larger than in 1978 in the Mittelrhein, and 50 per cent smaller in Franconia. The quality also varied very much from region to region and even vineyard to vineyard, but generally a good quantity made of quality wine with distinction. The Müller-Thurgau suffered very much from frost damage, but the Riesling survived well. A good quality, but not outstanding vintage to end the 1970s.

The Wines of Italy

PHILIP DALLAS

Philip Dallas has lived in Italy since 1948. Founder and past chairman of the Rome branch of the International Wine and Food Society, he is the author of many books and articles on Italian wines and gastronomy, including *The Great Wines of Italy*, published in 1974 by Doubleday, New York, and of *Italian Wines*, published by Faber, London, also in 1974.

Recent grape harvests in Italy have been getting larger every year. In 1973, when I was writing a book about Italian wines, 1979's yield of 78 million hectolitres would have been a disaster rather than a gift from God. Then, it would have been difficult to market such an abundance: today, the situation is vastly changed, and nearly 25 per cent of that wine may be exported. The world market for wine has increased, and Italy is not only playing a large role in supplying it, but is even supplying the raw materials to France and to Germany so that they, too, may meet their increased demands.

In 1973, although already the world's largest wine-producer, Italy had no great reputation abroad for fine wines; that this was a long-standing prejudice abroad and not based on pragmatic tasting of wines available in Italy is by the way. The situation has not changed so much due to a relaxation of prejudice but to the turn of events. Up until 1974, the world – and perversely, Italy, as well – enjoyed Italian wine scandals which made headlines in the newspapers, no matter how flimsy were the facts of the case. In the late 1970s, there has not been one worth a column-inch, and I feel sure that this has not been for lack of trying. Among the changes has been the rapid ascent of Californian wines and their prices; and the unexpected setbacks of prestige suffered by the French at a time when their wines were on the crest of the wave and selling for sums which ultimately priced them out of a lot of their traditional markets. The Italians over the last two decades have made enormous investments in their vineyards, replanting with DOC-approved vines, and in their wineries with the most modern, and usually remote-controlled, processing equipment. *Denominazione d'origine controllata* (DOC) is a close equivalent to the French *appellation d'origine contrôlée* (AOC) status for wines. It ensures that the wine is from the area named; that it is produced from the laid-down proportions of specific grapes by the traditional methods and has been properly aged; that the vineyards have been surveyed and their maximum grape-production and wine yield not exceeded; that the sales of the wine have been recorded in ledgers that are subject to inspection; that the vintage year on the bottle is wholly accurate, and that no misleading information is printed. A consortium neck-seal may be found on some bottles, such as the Chianti

Classico's rooster or Black Cockerel, which is a further local guarantee of quality and, if there is a serial number, it indicates the limited production.

The major mockery of the Common Market Wine Policy – at least *vis-à-vis* Italy – comes through the completely licit export of wine in 10,000-tonne tankers which leave Italy for France loaded to the Plimsoll line. Much of this wine is fine, strong, full-bodied and rich-coloured cutting wine which is required to give clout to France's better non-AOC wines. The French wine probably comes from the southern Midi region, and needs the addition of both the alcohol and the body in the Italian wine. The resultant blend will be sold as *vin de table* coming from more than one country in the EEC. Some Italian wine, undoubtedly, returns to its country of origin with a French label, a sop to Italian snobbery.

I do not wish to denigrate the inexpensive bulk wines, just because they may be made in vats rather than numbered barrels; after all, it is just old-style *vin de pays*, and is usually processed nowadays very well. In every event, I am a supporter of the theory (and practice) that the working man has a right to his litre at a price that he can afford. Taxation, if taxation there must be on wine, should be on luxury and aged wines. The crux of the problem is that these basic wines can sail under false colours and, with a pretty label, trick far more than they are worth out of the pockets of innocents. This, however, rarely is imputable to the Italian shipper, who has sold at rock-bottom prices and paid the Common Market levy (compensatory tax) for the export of non-DOC wines. It is often in the other continental European lands that the wine is bottled, distributed, and sometimes even ennobled. This juggling trick, fortunately, according to all reports, is not practised in the United Kingdom, nor in the United States.

One of the criteria of a good wine is the number of quintals per hectare of yield. The yield is, for fine wines, held down by pruning back the vines; thus a great wine will rarely come from a yield of more than 120 quintals per hectare, and sometimes from one as low as forty. The high-sugar 'cutting' or blending wines of southern Italy are, for example, produced on vines cropped back to one-metre high bushes that produce around fifty quintals per hectare; if allowed to grow on long trellises with irrigation and fertilization on the plains of the south, they can yield as much as 400 quintals per hectare, which is a very different story. The quality, of course, plummets. Naturally, Italian vines, due to the warmer climate, tend to have a greater productivity than those of northern Europe.

Much of our buying is by trust and by habit; but with a new labelling law, 'EEC Regulation 355/1979 for the designation and presentation of wines', that has come into force in the EEC, we are all going to find ourselves a trifle confused because it means that many wine producers must redesign their old familiar labels, some of which are classics and recognized all over the world at a glance. The new legislation requires that the varietal name of the particular wine (if not the name of the DOC group) must be as large as the producer's trade-name. Many producers have made their reputation for a wine under a trade-name or the name of their castle or villa. For example, the *fattoria* producers of Tuscany have put in second place, or even ignored entirely, the fact that their wines are, say, Chianti Classico: their labels give the trade-name only. Now, in some cases, fifty years and more later, they must make up their labels informing the public – in large capital letters – that the contents of the bottle are Chianti Classico. Many producers have thought of going non-DOC to save their labels, but study of the new European laws has shown that, in that case, they must print RED TABLE WINE in large characters on their label – which, if anything, is worse. However, if people are paying more for a DOC wine, the name of that DOC should appear boldly, especially for foreign customers who may not be conversant with the Italian language or mere place-names.

When one tries to conceive of the vastness of the transport of nearly 50 million hectolitres of bulk wine to France from Italy each year (which, along with some bottled wines, added up to close to half of Italy's 1978 total world exports) or of the 550,000 hectolitres of stabilized must that goes to Germany every year, one is brought up short and almost incredulous at the leaps of technology and the immensity of the wine industry. In 1977, Germany imported 77,000 hectolitres of must – in 1979, the quantity is estimated to be 700,000 hectolitres. In 1979, Italy exported 18 million hectolitres (of which 1.5 million hectolitres went to the United States), a 63 per cent increase over 1978.

Looking at the statistics, one finds that Italy is the only country which is in a position to face the new demand for wines at all levels; that is to say, Italy can export Pinot grapes or must for making Champagne and *mousseux* wines; it can sell cutting-wines and inexpensive wines in bulk with almost no limit to quantity; it can sell DOC and non-DOC wines in bulk and in two-litre bottles. It can sell Superiore wines in corked bottles with all the criteria of the finest of wines and, lastly, it can sell well-aged wines of great dignity and top quality Champagne-method sparklers. It is this complete quality and price range which tends to be mind-boggling and confusing, particularly as the prices all down the line are well-contained, which is remarkable when one considers that Italy no longer has the advantage of inexpensive labour or of other facilitations. The generous yields and the high technology are the basis of Italy's growth in wine-production and, as viewed today, the increase will continue in the next decade, both in quality and quantity. I myself admit to having been taken aback by the change between 1973 and 1980. The cooperatives today, for example, sell half a million litres of bulk wine abroad when, in 1973, they sold next to nothing. And, of course, the Lambrusco figures are of fable – ten million cases alone to the United States. That is 120 million bottles, mostly sold in New York and New Jersey.

In contrast to the fifty or so DOC wines of 1968, today there are over two hundred. Yet, of these, scarcely a dozen hold a near monopoly on the export market; while, of over one thousand exporting companies, the number of exporters which can be considered major and do between ten to twenty thousand dollars worth of business yearly, can be counted on one's fingers and toes.

Virtually all quality Italian wines are now bottled in the country of origin. The wine industry relies on the following names – Chianti, Soave, Valpolicella, Bardolino, Verdicchio, Orvieto, Barbera and Frascati, and, to a lesser degree, Barolo, Gattinara, Brunello di Montalcino, Amarone di Valpolicella, Vin Nobile di Montepulciano, Merlot, Tocai, Corvo, Barbaresco, Merlot, Tocai and Pinot Grigio of Friuli, EST! EST! EST! and Ghemme have entered the lists. It is a useful range, but little in comparison with the two hundred DOC categories, which extend from high in the Alps to Pantelleria, the island lying a few miles off Tunis; and for a grand total of 7.8 billion, repeat, billion litres.

Great Aged Wines

The EEC DOC legislation has been of great service to the wine world, to both producers and to wine-lovers. It has tidied up a lot of promiscuous vineyards and promiscuous drinkers. With careful reading of labels, we can be sure of drinking honest wine from a specific source. It has been a factor in the increase in the cost of wine, but only one of several; others, such as inflation, energy, labour, and taxation have been more pressing. And it can be said that Italian wines, due to their abundance and the consequent competition, have risen in price less dramatically than those of some other countries. In fact, many importing countries have turned to Italy for high and medium quality wines at practical prices.

I have always wanted to set into high relief a side of Italian wine-production that, though covered by the DOC regulation, if incompletely, cannot be stressed without putting lesser wines into the shade. It is the category of well-aged wines.

Italy, in contradistinction to France, which matures its wines for, say, eighteen months in the wood and for much longer periods in the bottle, ages wines in the barrel for many years. The purpose is to soften wines that, at birth, are harsh but which, with age, mellow in the wood. After that, they are refined in the bottle, lying in a quiet cellar for a year or two. In some cases, the oenologist will keep his wines in the wood for as many as eight to ten years. In any event, he will choose the moment he thinks right to bottle, which will be before any sign of oxidation sets in. The DOC ageing-norms, then, as with all the other DOC norms, are to be considered minimum requirements for categorizing a wine as old or as Riserva, or whatever other term of maturity.

A wine that has been aged two or more years in the wood is obviously considered by its producer as his best and, as such, is a wine that will justify the trouble, the work, the expense and the ultimate risk, not to mention the tied-up capital and cellar space. I think it can be fairly said that such wines can be confidently recommended as Italy's finest; also because only the most distinguished producers lay down their best wines in this manner. There are also a number of non-DOC wines which equally come into this category, although they are essentially proprietary wines belonging to specific producers rather than wines that can be made according to an approved formula by any producer who meets the specifications. Immediately come to mind such masterpieces as the Conte Sella winery's Lessona which has, in fact, only just and very belatedly joined the DOC club; the Venegazzù of Conte Loredan of Treviso; the Castello di Roncade by Barone Bassetti, also from near Treviso; Giorgio Odero's Gran Cru Frecciarossa from the Oltrepò Pavese; Conte Bossi Fedrigotti's Fojaneghe from the Trentino; and Principe Francesco Caracciolo's Sant'Eramo from near Taranto. It is these wines that I would ask connoisseurs to compare with the fine wines of other countries, for it is on these that Italy rests its reputation, not on a flask of cheerful young Chianti.

Let us look first at the DOC categories that require ageing in the wood before marketing. One should remember that a wine that has had such loving care expended upon it is a wine that, with similar loving care in its future, will continue maturing in the bottle – some for five years, some for a decade, some for many decades. It is, of course, ready and at its first optimum condition for drinking from the day it is sold, but if you are not in a hurry, a delay of months or years will repay the patience and restraint.

I have extracted 120 names of DOC wines which, by law, are required to rest in the wood from one to five years. These are mostly dry, red table wines, but there are a few sweet and dry dessert wines, some of which are fortified (*liquoroso*) and come into the same category of wines as Sherry and Port. On the whole, Italian dessert wines have a naturally high alcoholic content (14 per cent and over) because either the grapes have been semi-dried before pressing, or because the wines have been produced in warm areas such as Sardinia, Puglia, Sicily, or on offshore islands of Sicily, such as Pantelleria and the Lipari.

This list is not just another wine list; it is one from which can be deduced what the producers and the DOC committee of experts think about Italian aged wines. Those that mature will have earned the various designations – Superiore, Vecchio, Riserva, Riserva Speciale etc – which may, therefore, be included in their title on the label. One can thus identify the areas which are most favourable for fine wines, the vines that are most successful, and the wines that are the best bets for laying down in your cellar. One can get an overall view of the top bracket of Italian red wines and of the sweet and dry dessert wines from this listing. The latter are not enjoying a rising parameter of production and exports like the other wines, which is a pity because they are excellent and make an enjoyable apéritif at any time of the day.

In the listings that follow, I have added the figure for the number of quintals-per-hectare to accustom the reader to think in these terms. And, against each wine, I have put a letter of the alphabet – from A to I – which gives an idea of the total quantity of wine produced by that DOC zone. This is an imprecise reckoning, as it does not take into consideration that a DOC zone may have a red, a white and a rosé, various matured categories, and even several types of vine permitted. However, it is a sort of guideline so that the reader can note that very little (under 1,000 hectolitres – i.e. 100,000 litres) is produced of Carema in the Aosta Valley; that somewhere between 10,000 hectolitres and 30,000 hectolitres covers the Brunello di Montalcino output; and that Chianti and Chianti Classico is the major DOC zone, with a production of over 100,000 hectolitres. The letters A to I noted against each wine name refer to the quantity of wine expressed in hectolitres produced for that specific DOC zone and not to that of the particular wine. The letter, therefore, will refer to the total production of the group.

A less than 1,000	D from 10,000 to 30,000	G from 100,000 to 500,000
B from 1,000 to 5,000	E from 30,000 to 60,000	H from 500,000 to 1,000,000
C from 5,000 to 10,000	F from 60,000 to 100,000	I more than 1,000,000

Wines for 5-year ageing	*No. of quintals per hectare*	*Output*
Aglianico del Vulture Riserva	100	A
Barolo Riserva Speciale	80	E
Brunello di Montalcino Riserva	100	D
Marsala – Vergine Riserva, (also fortified) dessert wine (*solera* system)	100	G
Vin Santo Trentino Riserva, (also fortified) dessert wine	120	E

This first list provides one major surprise for most wine-lovers, even those of Italy. The Aglianico del Vulture is a sort of ghost wine – many have heard of it, few have drunk it. It comes from the slopes of an extinct volcano, the Vulture, in Lucania – the instep of the boot of Italy. A few years ago, the major producer was acquired by the Winefood Company, a large Milan holding company, currently owned by the Crédit Suisse bank. This should tend to make this remarkable and most delectable wine better known, and even its obscure home-town, Rionero. It is no surprise to find Barolo and Brunello at the top of the list nor, for that matter, the *solera* system Marsala. However, the Italian *vin santos* are always well-aged, according to the traditions of the respective houses, which often entail the arcane mystery being passed, even secretly, from one generation to another. In this category, one must never, of course, exclude the possibility that a Chianti Classico from one of the famous *fattorie* has been aged for five or more years; but, in this listing, we refer only to the minimum period according to DOC norms for reaching the specification Riserva or Riserva speciale.

Wines for 4-year ageing	*No. of quintals per hectare*	*Output*
Brunello di Montalcino	100	D
Carema	80	A
Gattinara	90	B
Vin Santo Trentino (also fortified)	120	E
Ghemme	100	B
Vin Nobile di Montepulciano Riserva Speciale	100	D

The wines that have four years of maturation in wood are not, perhaps, a surprise at all, except for Carema. The Carema, a small production wine which comes from the snowline, high in the Aosta Valley, is probably little known abroad as it is little known in Italy. The Ghemme and Gattinara sturdy reds are from the Novara area in Piedmont and are close rivals to the Barolo–Barbaresco duet of fine wines, also from Piedmont. The Vin Nobile of Montepulciano, from southern Tuscany, like the Brunello, is a historic wine and fairly well known abroad.

Wines for 3-year ageing	*No. of quintals per hectare*	*Output*
Aleatico di Puglia Riserva (dessert wine)	80	D
Aglianico del Vulture Vecchio	100	B
Barbaresco Riserva Speciale	100	D
Barbera d'Alba Riserva Speciale	90	D
Barolo Riserva	80	E
Boca	90	A
Bramaterra	80	A
Cabernet de Pramaggiore Riserva	100	A
Carmignano Riserva	80	A
Cannonau di Sardegna Riserva (Oliena – Capo Ferrato)	110	B
Chianti – Chianti Classico Riserva	110	I
Cirò Riserva	115	E
Colli Berici Cabernet Riserva	120	D
Colli Bolognesi Riserva	120	D
Donnaz	75	A
Piave Cabernet Riserva	110	G
Sizzano	100	B
Taurasi Riserva	110	A
Torgiano Rubesco Riserva	120	C
Trentino Lagrein	90	E
Vernaccia di Oristano Superiore	80	D
Vin Nobile di Montepulciano Riserva	100	D

Three years, however, is normally sufficient to age a wine in the barrel. In this group, the DOC categories begin to extend to cover a variety of Italian zones. The Barbaresco, Barbera d'Alba, Barolo, Chianti and Chianti Classico, and Vin Nobile di Montepulciano wines keep up the tradition of Piedmont and Tuscany, abetted by the magnificent Donnaz, a Nebbiolo from the Aosta Valley, and the Sizzano and the Bramaterra, big Nebbiolos from near Gattinara. The Boca is also a good Nebbiolo from just north of the Sizzano zone. The Carmignano is a Chianti that, over the centuries, has always been a sort of independent wine-state with its own legislation. The Cabernet of Pramaggiore is the first swallow from the eastern part of the Veneto, an area that is growing in importance yearly, both for its increased yield and its unexpectedly high quality. The Cabernet of the Piave River is also one of the many eastern Veneto wines, most of which are based on French and German vines to excellent effect. Cirò takes us to Calabria and to a 'Greek' wine that has a different basic taste – it is in the same spirit as that of the Aglianico del Vulture. Much the same can be said of the Taurasi which comes from just south of Naples, at which point the 'Greek' wines begin. The Greek wines are unlike the other Southern Mediterranean wines and have their own particular personality.

The Colli Berici Cabernet (south of Vicenza and towards Venice) is a newcomer that will have to stand in the queue to gain a reputation at home and abroad; but the Colli Bolognesi have already made a nice little reputation in Bologna, renowned as the home of good food in Italy. Both follow the new trend of using French vines.

The Trentino Lagrein – and for that matter, all the DOC wines of the Trentino

The Nebbiolo vines at Carema in the Aosta Valley are trained
to grow on trellises to make maximum use of the steep slopes

area – are very well made and with exceptional raw materials. It has always surprised me that they have not become favourites in the United States and United Kingdom, just as the Valtellina wines long ago gathered their following of enthusiasts abroad. Sardinia produces large quantities of strong, fine wines, much of which is destined to serve as cutting-wines in France. However, the Oliena-Capo Ferrato areas age and bottle some of these formidable table wines; those from the mountain areas of Oliena reach 18 per cent of alcohol, and are suited best for drinking accompanied by roast wild boar or venison. The Capo Ferrato wines are made by former wine producers of Tunisia who settled in Sardinia, to the not inconsiderable advantage of Italian wines, some twenty years ago. Lastly, we have the Vernaccia of Oristano from the west coast of Sardinia: it is a strong, full-bodied white suited as an apéritif or whenever the cockles of one's heart need warming.

Wine for 2-year ageing	*No. of quintals per hectare*	*Output*
Alto Adige Cabernet Riserva	110	F
Barbaresco Riserva	80	D
Barbera d'Alba	100	D
Barbera d'Asti	90	G
Barbera di Monferrato	100	E
Cannonau di Sardegna Superiore secco (Oliena – Capo Ferrato)	110	B
Chianti Vecchio – Chianti Classico Vecchio	125	I
Colli Orientali del Friuli	110	D
Merlot Riserva		
Cabernet Riserva		
Pinot Nero Riserva		
Refosca Riserva		
Picolit Riserva	40	A
Colli Tortonesi Barbera Superiore	90	B
Girò di Cagliari Riserva Liquoroso (dessert)	90	B
Lessona	90	A
Malvasia di Bosa (secco; dolce naturale; dolce liquoroso; secco liquoroso)	80	B
Malvasia di Cagliari Riserva Liquoroso (dessert)	90	B
Marsala Superiore (SOM – Superior Old Marsala; GD-Garibaldi Dolce; LP-London Particular)	100	C
Merlot di Pramaggiore Riserva	110	A
Monica di Cagliari Riserva Liquoroso (dessert)	90	B
Nasco di Cagliari Riserva Liquoroso (dessert)	90	A
Montepulciano d'Abruzzo Vecchio (also Cerasuolo)	140	G
Piave Merlot Vecchio	130	G
Primitivo di Manduria (dolce naturale liquoroso; liquoroso-dessert)	90	A
Rosso di Cerignola Riserva	140	G
Sangiovese di Romagna	110	G
Teroldego Rotaliano	130	E
Trentino		E
Cabernet Riserva	110	
Lagrein Riserva	120	
Marzemino Riserva	90	
Merlot Riserva	125	
Pinot Nero Riserva	110	
Pinot Riserva	120	
Moscato Riserva	100	
Valtellina Superiore (Sassella; Grumello; Inferno; Valgella)	100	E
Vin Nobile di Montepulciano	100	D

Barbera vines near Canelli in the province of Cuneo, Piedmont

In this group of wines, we have a lot of repeats because the oenologist has decided that a wine is ready for the bottle at two years of age due to its mature taste and chemistry rather than that it would improve with another year or two in the barrel to reach a higher category. We also have extensions of recommended red wine vineyards to Friuli, the Abruzzo, the Romagna, the Valtellina, and to the Trentino.

From this list of two-year-olds – and it should be said that the producers have the practice of keeping the wine after bottling in their cellars for another year and, in some special cases, even for two – first let us extract the dessert wines: the Girò of Cagliari, the various Malmseys of Bosa and Cagliari, the Marsala, the Monica of Cagliari, and the Nasco about which it can equally well be said that, as with the Vernaccia of Oristano, they warm the cockles of the heart in a twinkle with their rich, velvety taste of the elixir of life. Though they will travel, due to their high alcohol making for stability, unless fortified they may not age for long, and risk breaking up due to oxidation.

Then we have the Piedmont wines – the Barbaresco, the Lessona and the three Barberas. Barbaresco is always a fine, limited-production wine, but Barbera is the *vin de pays* wine available in enormous quantities in northern Italy; it is the carafe wine of Turin and Milan. Therefore, one must make the clear distinction between Barbera (which is just the name of the grape variety) and Barbera d'Alba, di Asti and di Monferrato, which are produced under DOC regulations and which, particularly when aged by one of the distinguished Piedmont wineries, reach a peak of quality that puts them in the top rank. In fact, only in the last decade or two have DOC Barberas and Dolcettos become wines of which to take serious note.

From Tuscany, we have the Chianti and Chianti Classico, the Vin Nobile of Montepulciano and, though the Tuscans would not like to see them put together, we have the Sangiovese of the Romagna which has a close varietal connection, as has also the Montepulciano of the Abruzzo region with its stern, tannic characteristics. The Valtellina quartet of wines are from the same Nebbiolo vine which gives us Barolo, Gattinara and Carema; from a little plateau with a perfect southern aspect we are offered the thoroughly reliable and widely-known Sassella, Inferno, Grumello and Valgella wines. The Colli Orientali del Friuli (eastern hills of Friuli) first made their contemporary claim to fame with their whites, particularly Tocai and Pinot Grigio. Their deep straw-coloured Picolit dessert wine is a rarity which made its reputation in Vienna under the Emperor Franz Joseph and which, in its old age, is not too generous with its yield, as you may observe – forty quintals only per hectare. Only later did they present us with their reds, almost all of which are made with French vines. The best red from the area is the Piave Merlot; but all the varietals used in Claret seem to have settled into Italy cosily, offering warm, rounded and full-flavoured wines. There is also the Merlot of Pramaggiore (an excellent growing zone) to add to the list of new names from this rugged area bordering Yugoslavia.

The Trentino starts south of Trento and leads up a valley of vineyards to Bolzano in the Alto Adige and even higher. It is divided into two zones: the Trentino, which is more Italian, and the Alto Adige or South Tyrol which is distinctly Austrian in character and whose vines are mostly from northern Europe. Despite the bitter winters, the vines flourish through the long Italian summers to produce some of Italy's most enjoyable and full-bodied wines. The Teroldego is considered the best of the Trentino group and, as with the Valtellina, you never meet a bottle that disappoints expectations.

Most wines are ready to bottle twelve months after they are fermented: it is quite enough that they rest during that year in a large resined or stainless-steel vat. In fact, there are oenologists who think that this is the best way to get the precise taste of the fermented wine, rather than one conditioned by the overtones that are picked up from the wood and the continuous, if slow, oxidation of wine through the pores of the wood and the interstices of the staves of the barrel.

Wines for one-year ageing	*No. of quintals per hectare*	*Output*
Aglianico del Vulture (also *spumante*)	100	A
Alto Adige		F
Lagrein de Gries Riserva	100	
Malvasia Riserva	110	
Merlot Riserva	130	
Pinot Nero Riserva	120	
Bardolino Classico Superiore	80	F
Cannonau di Sardegna (dessert – Superiore amabile; Superiore dolce; Liquoroso secco; Liquoroso dolce)	110	B
Cinque Terre 'Sciacchetra' (dessert – also Liquoroso)	90	B
Colli Euganei Rosso Superiore	120	D
Dolcetto d'Acqui Superiore	80	B
Dolcetto d'Alba Superiore	90	B
Dolcetto d'Asti Superiore	80	B
Dolcetto di Dogliani Superiore	80	B
Dolcetto delle Langhe Monregalesi Superiore	70	B
Dolcetto d'Ovada Superiore	80	B
Enfer d'Arvier	50	A
Freisa d'Asti Superiore	80	A
Monica di Sardegna Superiore	100	D
Moscato di Cagliari Riserva	90	
Moscato Passito di Pantelleria Extra (dessert)	70	A
Moscato di Trani (dessert)	80	A
Nebbiolo d'Alba	90	B
Parrina	110	B
Rossese di Dolceacqua Superiore	90	B
Rosso Piceno Superiore	140	B
Trentino		E
Lagrein	120	
Marzemino	90	
Merlot	125	
Pinot Nero	110	
Pinot	120	
Traminer Aromatica	100	
Valpolicella Superiore	120	G
Valpantena Classico	120	
Vernaccia di San Gimignano	100	

Producers and the DOC committee experts have required of thirty types of wine that they be aged in the wood for one year. As you will see from the list, it is made up of a block of Alto Adige wines, the whole range of the seven Dolcettos, and the remainder of the Trentino wines. There is also a group of dessert wines – Moscato di Cagliari, Moscato Passito di Pantelleria, Moscato di Trani and the Sciacchetra of the Cinque Terre. After that, we have the 'young' Aglianico del Vulture, the Bardolino Superiore, the Colli Euganei Superiore (from the volcanic hills which grow out of the plains to the south of Padua), the Enfer d'Arvier cultivated at 600 metres in the foothills of the Alps, and the Freisa of Asti, a traditional strong wine which is also bottled while still *pétillant*, and sometimes with a trace of sweetness – a delightful wine which seems to be disappearing from the market-place. The Monica di Sardegna is a 'stretched' form of the Monica dessert wine that has had an

	'61	'62	'63	'64	'65	'66	'67	'68	'69	'70	'71	'72	'73
Amarone*	8c	8c	7c	10c	6c	8c	8c	8b	9b	7a	8a	7a	8a
Barbaresco	9c	8c	2e	10c	6d	2e	8c	6d	7b	8b	10a	2d	6c
Barbera d'Asti	8d	8d	4e	9c	6d	2e	7c	6d	7c	8c	10c	2d	5d
Bardolino**	6e	9e	6e	8e	6e	6e	7e	7e	9e	7e	8e	5e	7e
Barolo	10c	8c	4e	10c	8c	2e	8c	6d	7b	8b	10a	2c	6c
Brunello di Montalcino	6e	—	—	10b	6c	7c	8b	6b	7b	10a	10a	4d	6c
Cabernet Trentino	6d	4d	6d	10b	2d	6d	6d	4d	10c	10b	8b	4c	4c
Carema	—	—	—	—	—	—	—	—	—	8c	8c	4d	6b
Chianti	4e	8d	2e	6e	4e	4e	6d	8c	8c	8c	8c	4e	4c
Chianti Classico (Riserva)	5d	9d	3e	9c	6c	6c	9c	9c	9c	9b	10b	5d	5c
Ciro' Rosso	8d	4e	8d	4e	6d	—	6d	10b	2d	6c	6b	6b	8a
Corvo Rosso	—	—	—	—	—	—	—	—	—	9c	8c	8c	
Gattinara	8c	6d	2c	10c	6c	4e	6c	8c	8b	8b	4d	2e	4c
Ghemme	6d	8c	2e	10c	6c	4e	6c	8c	8b	8b	4d	2e	4c
Grignolino	8d	4e	2e	6	4e	4e	4e	4e	6d	6d	8c	2d	6c
Grumello	8c	4e	4e	10d	2e	4e	6d	4d	8c	8c	8c	4c	6c
Inferno	8e	4e	4e	10c	2e	4e	6d	4d	8c	8c	8c	4c	6c
Lambrusco di Sorbara	10e	2e	6e	2e	4e	2e	4e	6e	6e	8c	10c	4c	6c
Merlot Trentino	8d	6d	2d	8c	2d	6d	6d	4d	10c	6d	8c	2d	2c
Montepulciano d'Abruzzo	6e	6e	8e	2e	8d	6d	6d	10c	2d	4d	4d	4c	8c
Nebbiolo d'Alba	10d	8d	4e	8d	6d	2e	8c	6c	6c	6c	10b	2d	4c
Sassella	8e	4e	4e	10	2e	4e	6d	4d	8c	8c	8c	4c	6c
Sfursat	8d	4e	4e	10b	2e	4e	6c	4c	8c	8c	8b	4c	6c
Taurasi	10	2e	2e	8d	6e	8d	8d	10c	6c	8c	8c	6b	8b
Torgiano	—	—	—	—	—	—	—	—	—	9c	8c	8c	
Valpolicella***	7e	8e	7e	9e	6e	7e	8e	7e	8e	8e	9e	8d	8
Vino Nobile di Montepulciano	6d	8d	2e	8c	2e	6d	10c	8c	8c	10b	4c	4d	8c

unexpected success as an introductory wine, in the sense that even those people who have never drunk wine in their lives find it most attractive – it is not a stern wine full of character but therein, perhaps lies its charm and its success. The Nebbiolo joins the Barolo-to-Dolcetto group of southern Piedmont, and the Parrina is the only Tuscan wine made near the Argentaria peninsula but, for all that, it is in the traditional Chianti style. The Rossese is among the last of the wines made on the Ligurian Riviera; the Rosso Piceno is a good Sangiovese from the Marches region overlooking the Adriatic and, to finish up, we have three well-known labels – the Valpolicella Superiore, the Valpantena Classico and the Vernaccia di San Gimignano white which, unlike its Sardinian namesake, is not a dessert wine but a sturdy Tuscan wine to accompany a hearty meal. This list, then, includes not only wines from the Alps to the southernmost islands of Italy, but wines that originate from different

'74	'75	'76	'77	'78	'79	All-time greats
9a	9a	6a	8a	10	9	1964
9a	5b	5a	5a	10	8	1964 1971
8b	5b	4a	2c	10	8	1971
7e	8d	8c	8c	8	8	
9a	5b	5a	5a	10	8	1957 1964
6b	10a	4a	7a	10	8	1947 1958
4c	6a	6a	6a	8	6	
8b	6b	4b	2b	8	6	
8c	8c	2b	8b	10	6	
9b	9b	5a	9a	10	8	1947 1949
8a	6a	2c	8a	8	8	
8b	8b	6b	7b	10	8	
10a	6a	8a	4a	8	6	1952
10a	6a	8a	4a	8	6	1947 1964
8c	2c	6b	2c	8	6	
4c	6c	4b	2b	8	6	1964
4c	6c	4b	2b	8	6	1964
6c	8b	6b	6a	8	8	1961
6c	4b	6a	4a	8	6	1947 1959
8c	8c	4c	8b	10	8	
6c	4c	4b	4b	10	8	
4c	6b	5b	2a	8	6	1947 1952
4b	6a	3b	5a	10	8	1947 1952
6b	8a	6b	10a	8	8	1961 1968
7b	7b	4a	6a	10	6	
7c	8b	6b	8a	8	6	
6c	10a	2a	8a	10	6	1958

Ratings of vintages for Italian red wines of the 1960s and 1970s

Key to reading table:

2	less than average vintage
4	average vintage
6	good vintage
8	very good vintage
10	exceptional vintage

Additional qualifications are listed by the letters:

a	best with further ageing
b	can improve with ageing
c	ready for drinking
d	caution advised if aged further
e	wine may be too old to drink

And by the asterisks:

*	Normal ageing – about 10 years
**	Ideal ageing – about 1–2 years
***	Ideal ageing – about 2–3 years

These numbers and letters should not be taken as absolutes. Within each region each year there is a variation in quality from vintner to vintner, from vineyard to vineyard, and even during the harvest period if the weather breaks.

vine sources. We have the traditional Italian vines, such as the Nebbiolo, the Sangiovese and the Montepulciano, we have French vines such as Cabernet, Merlot and the Pinot brothers, along with Greek vines in southern Italy, and vines in Sardinia of unknown provenance, though I suspect they came from Spain and/or Portugal several centuries ago. There is also a range of German vines, happily acclimatized in Italy, but they offer us only white wines. With this roundup, we have not touched whites (except for some dessert wines and the odd Pinot), which include 100 million bottles of Spumante and Champagne-method sparklers, and over eighty DOC denominations from top to toe of Italy.

During the last two or three years, the Ministry for Agriculture has approved DOC legislation, including ageing-in-the-wood for two years for the following zones: Morellino di Scansano, Rosso Barletta, Squinzano, Pollino and Savuto; and

	'70	'71	'72	'73	'74	'75	'76	'77	'78	'79
Corvo Bianco	—	—	7	7	8	8	6	7	8	10
Frascati	7	7	4	6	8	7	5	6	8	8
Greco di Tufo	8	6	6	8	8	8	6	10	8	6
Lacryma Christi del Vesuvio	6	6	4	6	8	6	6	10	8	8
Orvieto	6	8	4	8	8	6	2	8	8	8
Pinot Bianco	8	8	6	6	8	6	6	8	8	8
Pinot Grigio	8	8	8	8	8	8	6	8	8	8
Riesling	6	8	6	6	8	8	6	8	8	8
Soave	8	9	7	8	7	8	8	8	8	8
Tocai	6	6	8	8	8	4	8	6	8	8
Trebbiano di Romagna	10	8	6	6	8	8	6	10	6	6
Tuscan Whites	8	8	4	4	8	8	6	7	8	8
Verdicchio	6	6	4	6	2	6	2	10	8	8
Vernaccia di S. Gimignano	10	8	6	8	8	8	6	8	10	8

Ratings of vintages for Italian white wines of the 1970s

The consumer should note that in general Italian whites should be drunk as young and fresh as possible. This is true for all of the wines listed here, except Greco di Tufo which improves with a few years' ageing.

Key to reading table:

2	less than average vintage
4	average vintage
6	good vintage
8	very good vintage
10	exceptional vintage

for one year in the barrel for Carignano di Sulcis, Riviera di Garda Bresciana, and Dolcetto d'Alba. As a postscript, I should add that the names mentioned above are far from being all-inclusive; dozens of wines that are aged in the wood are missing from this DOC listing. For example, the red Corvo di Salaparuta and Regaleali of Sicily, though the law does not require it as they are non-DOC wines, are aged for a year or two in the wood. In the gazetteer (see pages 281–332), the regulations for ageing and for alcohol content are included; but there are occasional minor modifications published in the Official Gazette by the Ministry.

Among the details printed on labels, I think that the vintage date is not sufficient to help one evaluate a wine; one needs to know also the bottling-date and some information as to how the wine passed its time, and where, between those two dates. A new zone like the Colli Bolognesi di Monte San Pietro becomes immediately more interesting when one learns that the Barbera they produce must be aged for three years to be called Riserva. It means that not only is the terrain good, but the possibilities of further maturing in the bottle are most favourable.

The Future of Italian Wines

The whole range of Italian wines will probably not, of course, change more rapidly in the future than it has in the past; but change it has and change it will. Not only has technology and oenology improved the quality of wines, but the taste of the general public, and particularly that of foreign lands, has had a profound influence.

Due to the climate, Italian wines tended, in the past, to be high-alcohol ones, often 13–14 per cent and full-bodied: full-bodied often due to the addition of some cutting-wines or concentrated must from the south. They also tended to be rather tannic and with a high total acidity – all characteristics of wines that travel and age.

When the DOC legislation was written up in collaboration with the other EEC countries, the Italians did not look into the future at all. They treated the European Wine Policy as an extension of their own internal wine policy, which had never allowed chaptalization for the good reason that they wished to support the producers of cutting-wine in the deep south. Even when the new Wine Policy generally excluded the use of cutting-wines in DOC wines, it did allow anything up to 15 per cent of grapes, must, concentrated must, or wine from outside the respective DOC area to be added to some DOCs. The Italian negotiators were thus convinced that all would go well, as they had left this little loophole to increase the alcohol content of wines by a half per cent in poor years. This, however, has turned out to be very expensive. A neutral-tasting concentrate from Sicily is the least costly method; to make the concentrate with the same wine as the one to which it is to be added is far better, but uneconomic, and puts the Italian product at a severe disadvantage *vis-à-vis* the chaptalizing countries such as France and Germany, which can chaptalize up to 2 per cent and more.

Among the evolutions initiated by the Italian wine-producers was that of harvesting a little earlier to give the Italian wines a more 'northern' taste. Picked at full Mediterranean maturity, the wines were very Italian and the grapes overripe, whereas the French and German grapes rarely reach full maturity, and the world has accustomed itself to the sharp taste which is softened by chaptalization. The trouble here, naturally, was a drop in the sugar content of the Italian grape which could not be made up with a teaspoonful of sugar. At all events, an equilibrium and a compromise was found that gave the Italian wines the northern chic that they searched for. This coincided with the broad-based success of the Verona wines, red, white and rosé, throughout the world.

Then came the rise of the Emilia-Romagna wines, the Lambrusco reds, but also a variety of whites, some sparkling, others not. This trend, which is still highly active, required wines that had a low total acidity and a touch of sweetness. Italy found no difficulty in tooling up immense wine-making plants to supply what was required abroad; fortunately, one of the characteristics of this trend was that the wine should be low in alcoholic content. The taste for light, fresh and soft Italian wines extended to Frascati, which equally adjusted itself, with changes in the vineyard systems and in the processing to meet the demand. The wine became drier but not excessively so. In the long past, Frascati had often been *amabile*, or very dry with a full body and rich bouquet.

The Sicilian situation arose a few years ago; economic surveys had told the oenologists what was needed on the world markets, and they set themselves to make it, shifting vineyards from the plains to the hills, building great temples of processing plants in the countryside, and organizing the smallholders into cooperatives. Here again, we find the soft, light, fresh wines which, though meeting world taste, are a far cry from the rumbustious wines of Sicily in the past. The legislation for the DOC discipline for the various zones always arouses a wry smile when I read the following phrases repeated in each section: 'the wines must be cultivated in the traditional manner and in traditional conditions so as to provide traditional characteristics. The system of cultivation or pruning must be traditional to the area and be such as not to alter the characteristics of either the grape or the wine.' The stickler for precision will justly point out that the new vineyards in the hills of Sicily are mostly non-DOC and therefore have no traditions to follow; however, the practice of altering the style of cultivation and processing is not unusual anywhere in Italy.

The stretching of a vineyard to produce far more than the traditional 50 to 140 quintals per hectare is the major means of meeting the demand for soft, fresh and light wines. On the hot plains, even of Lazio, one can obtain 300 quintals a hectare and produce a wine that does not require chaptalization. However, the chaptalization issue will, inevitably, arise in the 1980s and Italy will ask for a change in the EEC Wine Policy to permit it. Whether the French and the Germans will be willing to grant Italy the use of this overwhelming weapon to increase exponentially its output is still to be seen. By nature, wine comes from between 5 and 18 per cent of alcohol; we can make the choice of what we want through cultivation and processing methods. The standard 12 per cent was laid down by custom and then by law. But in fact, in recent years, the alcoholic content of some popular wines is much less: and this could become a major trend.

The factors conditioning Italian wines are various. The traditional stern and robust wines have also been conditioned – even the Barolo and Chianti Classico which, a quarter of a century ago, often had a little rugged cutting-wine from Puglia or Sardinia added to give them more authority. One could compare the addition, in the past, of Hermitage to Claret, to give the latter body. Other factors are the cultivation of the vines and the methods of processing to reach an 'ideal' wine to suit contemporary taste. Economic costs have inevitably played a major role, too. One interesting trend has begun recently to cut costs in ageing fine old wines. Traditionally, the reds are put into casks of Slavonian oak; these have a median capacity of around 4,000 litres. The wines do not draw much by way of flavour from the casks as they are very old ones and have nothing more to offer, unlike the brand-new 225-litre casks used by the French. The purpose is to leave the wines to precipitate most of their sediment and then to mellow. This process is costly and also a lengthy one. A major Tuscan producer has started a system to age his traditional Sangiovese wines more rapidly, which may well be a sound one. He has acquired a number of secondhand French 225-litre barrels. These have been well used by the French, in the sense that they no longer have sufficient tannin which can be transferred to the wines and thus are in the right state for use by the Italian producers for their wines, which do not need tannin. Technically, it is contact with the wood that facilitates the whole operation of ageing – thus, more wine is in contact with the wood in a small vat than in a large one, so the ageing is speeded up. In all, this Tignanello is aged seventeen months in the wood and a year in the bottle, and is reckoned to have a long cellar-life.

Although the aged vintage Italian wines have altered their character slightly (some, like Barbera and Dolcetto DOC, have been vastly improved), they still represent a mine that has not been worked by the importers nor even by the Italians; even though, in the last ten years, the domestic market for quality and fine aged wines in Italy has risen sharply. But, like Italian Champagne-method Spumante, they cost appreciably less than those of their rivals abroad, and cede little or nothing in quality. Despite that, Italy buys around 45 million US dollars of French Champagne and aged reds (mostly the former) every year, though surprisingly almost no German wine at all.

It is odd that, in a country that has the largest percentage of public sector industry in Western Europe, the wine business is almost entirely free enterprise. Though the cooperative movement is very large, and often supported by facilitated government and para-government loans, most of the wine world consists of small and medium companies. The multi-nationals and banks which are owners in the field, for the most part, seem to have become involved by chance as often as by choice. The Crédit Suisse bank found itself, by chance, the owner of the Winefood empire, worth 800,000,000 US dollars. The Monte Paschi di Siena Bank, one of Europe's oldest established banks dating back to medieval times, is the owner of the Fontana-fredda winery, famous for its Barolo. The Fiat motor company, through its Cinzano subsidiary, is a major Marsala- and brandy-producer through Florio of Sicily and makes Champagne-method and Charmat sparkling wines under the Cinzano label. The Martini and Rossi company, over and above its vermouths and apéritifs, makes wines and even has its own whisky distillery in Scotland.

The Italian scene is not, therefore, ruled simply by a few giants and those that are present in the vineyard have been very discreet, almost shy, of exposing themselves and have left the wine policy of their subsidiaries to the experts and managers on the spot. The Winefood holding company keeps a very low profile, despite the great prestige, and production, of its subsidiaries: Bigi of Orvieto, Vini Vaja of the South Tyrol, Val Panaro of Modena (Lambrusco), Umano Ronchi of the Marches (Verdicchio), Santi of Verona (Soave), Pelizzati of the Valtalline and Nino Negri of the Valtelline (Inferno etc), Lamberti of Lazise sul Garda (Soave etc), Fontana Candida of Frascati, D'Ambra of Ischia, Melini of Tuscany (Chianti), Luigi Calissano of Alba (Piedmontese wines), and Folonari, which is a major *négociant* of non-DOC wines. The other major foreign investor is Seagram Distillers which is present in the Ricasoli Brolio and Bersano companies, the INVEST conglomerate group is a major shareholder of Sella e Mosca's Sardinian operation, and Villa Banfi cellars is part-owner of Bruzzone and investing heavily in Montalcino for the production of Brunello and Moscadello di Montalcino, a rare sparkling wine.

Some Italian *négociants* have grown to become economic powers during the 1970s boom of exports and domestic consumption. The Riunite is a consortium of cooperatives of the Emilia-Romagna region that has been the major producer of Lambrusco. Among the others that have risen on the tide of the Lambrusco boom are Giacobazzi, Zonin and Cella. Bolla and Folonari, with Bertani a close runner-up, have dominated the Verona wine market. The Winefood group, in this competition for world outlets, owns the Fontana Candida Frascati winery and Melini of Tuscany, both of which have been highly successful. In the Brunello field, Biondi-Santi is the major name, although Poggio alle Mura, imported into the United States by Villa Banfi, is the larger seller; it should also be recalled that the Villa Banfi has a project, now well under way, involving 800 hectares of vineyards.

The Use of Foreign Vines

Five years ago, the Italian producers, at least so it seemed, were still facing the issue of exporting their wines from a traditional fixed point of view. They were confident of the quality of their wines, but the problem was to persuade the foreigners to like them. The Italian taste was different from that of France and Germany, which ruled the worthwhile markets. The Italian basic wines were more forceful and perhaps drier in character, whether Nebbiolo, Sangiovese or Trebbiano. It was, in fact, a difficult, if not almost impossible, task that could take half a century at enormous cost. Where and when it was that the Italians decided to meet their potential clients half-way, or all-the-way in some cases, would be difficult to say; inevitably it varies from zone to zone and winery to winery. Some may change, others may survive anyhow, and even flourish, without changing. DOC legislation, of course, was a major step as it initiated change. The improved technology was a much greater stride. The shock of the success of Lambrusco must also have demonstrated that people buy what they like rather than what you think is good for them and their aesthetic sensibilities. And the ever-growing popularity of Verona wines was a lesson, too.

Today, there is a new trend in the use of French and German vines; on the surface, this might be read as the Italians deciding to use their rivals' materials to break into their market, but that would be both an unkind and incorrect view. Italy's vines come from many sources, French, German, Greek and Spanish, acclimatized and with full citizenship of long standing. The major French vine in use in Italy is the Cabernet Sauvignon. During the nineteenth century, it was cultivated throughout Italy. Its partial eclipse may have been caused by the phylloxera which hit Italy in the 1920s and 1930s. The Italian government supplied farmers, who stripped their vineyards bare, with new Italian vines grafted onto American roots free of charge.

One of the advantages of foreign vines, particularly of Cabernet Sauvignon and Cabernet Franc, is that, in Italy, they have proved themselves to be economically convenient in more ways than one. The most important advantage is that they yield best on the plains and on low, rolling ground. Though Italy's tradition for cultivating fine grapes has always been 'the higher the better', there is a tendency to look for easier ways of producing equally fine wines and on land that can be worked with tractors and, one day soon, mechanical harvesters. Along with the Merlot, these French vines are nowadays yielding best in the Veneto, the Breganze and the Berici hills, the Piave and Pramaggiore zones going east, in the Trentino and along the coast from Treviso and up to the Friuli hills. They are being made up mostly as single-grape wines, but also as composites. The Friuli wines, in particular, do not run to type, their personalities vary, and most of them are memorable. The composite Bordeaux-style wine, Venegazzù, which has been on the market for many decades, has been followed by several others made in the same fashion in the Veneto, in Lombardy, and now in the low-lying Bologna hills.

These 'foreign' vines have impressed the other Italian producers and we can expect to see them playing a far greater role in the future. There is even talk of having the DOC legislation for Chianti and Chianti Classico altered so that Cabernet Sauvignon may be included to replace the Trebbiano and the Malvasia in its composition. Already the Carmignano autonomous Chianti zone is doing precisely this. The Frescobaldi winery is using 10 per cent Cabernet Sauvignon in its Pomino red, DOC permission having been specially obtained because the Cabernet had traditionally been produced on the property. Antinori has gone out on a limb in praise of and in production of Cabernet Sauvignon. Of their two new wines – Tignanello and Sassicaia – the latter is an 80 per cent Cabernet Sauvignon, 20 per cent Cabernet Franc of small production; however, this latter picked up the laurels at a recent (1979) international tasting in London of thirty-five Cabernets from eleven countries, which is an unprejudiced demonstration that Cabernet Sauvignon is a wine with a future in Italy. This Sassicaia, for the record, is aged for two years in small oak barrels and one in the bottle, and is reckoned to have another, and useful, ten years of cellar-life before broaching.

I suspect that the trend has firmly set in and that Cabernet Sauvignon will make itself felt throughout Italy in the 1980s. The growers are persuaded that here lies one of the many new means of improving their wines and making them more acceptable abroad; and, at the same time, it gives them the welcome opportunity of making good use of their flat-lands which are not suited to the traditional Italian vines and, in fact, where cultivation is prohibited for DOC wines. As major wine-producing areas with plenty of extensive plains to plant out, Puglia and Sardinia could cause a profound change in the style of Italian wines in the 1990s were they to opt for the French vines, or just add them to their present production. They are experimenting. A warning note, however, has been sounded from the EEC. This trend is giving Italy a new and upsetting economic and productive strength, and a move is afoot to force the Italians back into their hills.

The producers, so far, are not worrying whether the French vines are DOC-approved: they know they will be good and that they can sell them or use them in non-DOC wines. Permission to use them in composite wines or as a varietal, when and if it comes, is all the better. For the time being, growing Cabernet and, for that matter, Chardonnay is a sound proposition.

The greatest change, however, is that modern technology and oenology have made a goodly part of our acquired knowledge of wine completely obsolete. Pronounced colours, odours and flavours induced by wood, oxygen and volatile acidity can now be avoided completely, leaving only the essential taste, aroma and other characteristics of the grape. Wines are now clear as they have never been in history: cloudy wine is as dated as black-and-white television. Ageing-in-the-wood, though it will never be discarded for the finest of wines, is likely to be used less and less, with the possible use even of glass barrels coming into fashion. The use of sulphur in wine-processing is already at a minimum in Italy, and only used for sterilizing the must at the fermentation stage.

Italian Champenois-and-Charmat-method Sparkling Wines

It was the shortage of French Champagne in Italy, caused by the various vine diseases of the nineteenth century, that encouraged Italian oenologists to go to Reims and Montpellier to study the art of making Champagne. Not only was the art learned, but the black and grey Pinot and Chardonnay vines were brought back to Italy. The two former were acclimatized in the rolling hill-country of the Oltrepò Pavese, south of Pavia, and the Chardonnay (and subsequently all the Pinots, too) in the Trento area at a height of 500–800 metres in the mountains.

The resulting product was usually labelled Champagne but, in 1948, the French succeeded in establishing their sole right to the use of this zonal denomination and the Italians then called their product Spumante, unfortunately making no distinction between the Champagne and Charmat methods, as the French had wisely done with Champagne and *mousseux*. It is, therefore, necessary to search carefully on the Italian label for the words *metodo champenois* to be sure that one has the correctly bottle-fermented article that used to go under the name of Champagne.

The autonomous group of Italian 'Champagne' producers (the Italian Spumante Institute) formed in 1975, set themselves higher standards than those required by the EEC Wine Policy. All Spumante Classico Metodo Champenois – as Italian Champagne is now called – must be vintage-dated, no *cuvée* mixture of wines from different years is permitted, and all the bottles must be fermented for three years before being disgorged and marketed. EEC policy permits a one-year fermentation in the bottle, but the Italians insist that the natural and correct cycle for a complete fermentation is of three years to reach the ideal product. However, it is important to note that not all producers of *brut* are members of the Institute.

Like its French counterpart, the Italian Spumante Classico Metodo Champenois is made from gently handled and lightly pressed Pinot grapes; although, in Italy, a small proportion of Cortese, Riesling, Malvasia or Prosecco grapes may be added, according to zonal legislation. The wine is made under a strict quality control, and then bottled with the addition of selected yeasts, sugar in liquid form, some bentonite and other mineral salts – this is the *liqueur de tirage* – and a complete re-fermentation cycle of three years, at a pressure of six atmospheres, takes place. At the end of this second fermentation, the seventy-day *remuage* and *frisson* process is carried out, whereby the sediment is sent to the neck of the bottle and frozen. After the disgorgement of the frozen sediment, the *liqueur d'expédition*, consisting of wine-concentrate, aqua-vitae, some citric acid and, except in the case of the *bruts* – but even there perhaps a little – a percentage of liquid cane-sugar, is added to each bottle. This *liqueur d'expédition* is the secret of each producer and serves to stabilize the wine, to encourage the bubbling *perlage* and to regulate the dryness or sweetness. The bottles are then stored in a cold cellar for at least six months.

With Champagnes and Spumante, it is important to know that a *brut* or a *nature* means that there is from 0 to 1.5 per cent of sugar-content, and that 1.5 per cent is a perceptible sweetness. There is no legal way of knowing if a wine is 100 per cent dry, but the Institute's members tend to make it completely so: 1.5-2.8 per cent of sugar is labelled extra sec, extra secco or extra dry (when it is *abboccato* or *amabile*); 2-5 per cent is sec, secco or dry (when it is distinctly sweet); 5-8 per cent is demi-sec, and 8-15 per cent is dolce.

The producers of Italian *brut* Spumante Classico Metodo Champenois are distinguished, respected, and even revered. In alphabetical order they are: Antinori, of Chianti fame, offering Gran Spumante Nature; Calissano, producing a *brut*; Carpene Malvolti, the famous Veneto producer of brandy, grappa and *prosecco* sparkling wines – a *brut*; Conzano, known throughout the world for its vermouths – a *brut*; Contratto, an old-established company noted for its fine Piedmont wines – a *brut*; the Sabauda Riserva, Riserva for England, and Riserva Bacco d'Oro; Equipe 5, a more recent group of perfectionists specializing in *metodo champenois* – a *brut*; Ferrari of Trento, perhaps the most distinguished of this distinguished company, and said to have been admired by André Simon himself – a *blanc de blanc brut* and a *brut rosé*; Fontanafredda, a subsidiary of the Monte dei Paschi di Siena bank founded in medieval times – Contessa Rosa; Carlo Gancia – a *brut* and Gran Cremant *secco*; Girelli of Trento with their new Cesarini Sforza Brut Riserva; the Cantina Sociale di Santa Maria della Versa, a cooperative in the middle of the great Pinot-growing area near Pavia – its La Versa *brut*; Maschio of Treviso – *bruts*; Martini and Rossi with their Riserva Montelera and *bruts* and, finally, Riccadonna, noted for its vermouths and apéritifs – President *brut*.

The quantities of these excellent wines imported into the United States and the United Kingdom are negligible, mainly because the production is small and because, I suspect, no notable effort has ever been made to launch them on any foreign market, with the possible exception of Switzerland who is an old customer. After all, four million bottles can be drunk at home with a few friends; and they cost half the price of the imported article.

Of the above list of producers, Carpene Malvolti, Cinzano, Contratto, Gancia, Martini and Rossi, Maschio of Treviso and Riccadonna, together with Angoris of Gorizia, Cora of Turin, Cantina Viticoltori of Trento, Valdo of Treviso, Bertani and Bolla (these last two make magnificent red Recioto Spumante in Verona), Berlucchi of Franciacorta, the Cantina Sociale of Valdobbiadene, Bruzzone of Piedmont, Salaparuta of Palermo, Kettmeir and Klosterkellerei of the South Tyrol, and the Santa Margherita winery of Friuli produce an ever-increasing quantity of Italian Spumante, from *brut* to slightly-sweet, by the variously called Charmat, autoclave, *cuve close* or *mousseux* method. And these cost about one-half of the Italian *classico* Champagne-method wines.

Mousseux Wines

Some people tend to denigrate Asti Spumante and Moscato Spumante and all the other sparkling *mousseux* wines of Italy as commercial wines. This is far from the truth. Asti and Moscato Spumantes have been among the prides of Piedmont's wine-makers for a hundred years. Foaming, yet consistently bodied wines, full of verve and heady aroma, issue from the bottle with a festive spirit. A fine Asti *mousseux* first requires grapes in perfect condition, grown in favourable soil, with a sunny aspect and on well-drained hillsides and picked just before maturity – and a yield of not more than 100 quintals per hectare – when the sugar and the acidity balance is just right. In fact, the grapes are delicate and require much tending to prevent spoiling from various causes. The grapes flourish, however, in favourable micro-climates and the big producers go to these vineyards every year and bid for their crops. Having got the grapes in perfect condition to the winery, they are horizontally pressed and treated as white wines; it is, however, their high sugar-content which permits the transformation in the autoclave of the wine into sparkling wine. Now that the Charmat plant and equipment, which is expensive and complicated, has been brought to perfection, the producers' problem has changed to being a shortage of grapes. About 10 million bottles of Asti Spumante were produced every year in the 1950s; today, the output is over 40 million, of which over 30 million bottles are exported, and the availability of grapes is approaching its limits.

Under consideration is the use of a percentage of Pinot grapes which could best meet the situation organoleptically, but the problem is not as simple as that. Spumante have moved from being inexpensive tipples to being internationally established quality *mousseux* with a serious following and a considerable reputation to maintain. Those who bought them because they were relatively cheap have found cheaper sparkling wines elsewhere.

There are two other prime-producing zones for Champagne-method and *mousseux* wines. One is the Oltrepò Pavese, south of Pavia, in the hills that extend to Piedmont. Here, there are vast vineyards of Pinot which furnish not only the great winery of Santa Maria della Versa, but the *négociants* of Lombardy, Piedmont, and even of other countries. The third prime-producing zone is around Treviso, close to Venice, where the Prosecco is made. This is a delightful, cheering wine, made from the grape of the same name, usually slightly *abboccato* and suited for a wide variety of occasions – in Venice they dine with it. This *mousseux* also comes as a *brut* when it is made with a good percentage of Pinot grapes. As with the Astis, it can be said that the high technology and oenology give us sparklers of a delicacy, bouquet and attraction that was not previously possible except with the Champagne-method. And, for the record, the Cartizze *brut* made by the Champagne-method and with Pinot grapes is also available in these parts.

Vins de Primeur

Thirty years ago and more, Chianti was customarily fermented with the *governo* process and marketed shortly after and, in wine-tasting terms, was called prickly. It bubbled 'pétillantly' with youthful zest, tickled the palate, and was most enjoyable. Hot-bottling or pasteurization put an end to that, and the *governo* process became less common: young Chianti took on a maturity that was premature, but a notable advantage in the long run, even though at the expense of the wine's first few months of youthful frivolity. This prickliness was also produced – but, unintentionally on small farms – by inefficient pressing of the grapes by foot, whereby some grapes escaped being pressed at all and started up a private and immediate fermentation of their own. Then came Beaujolais. In the early 1950s, this vivacious characteristic was developed with a new and better *governo* system called Flanzy, after the oenologist who laid down its specifications. This *primeur* wine was an immediate success, and put the provincial area of Beaujolais, not only on the map, but into magnificent orbit.

In the last few years, Beaujolais Primeur has been arriving in Italy, and the fashion has spread amongst Italian producers, particularly in the Veneto, Tuscany, Piedmont and the Oltrepò areas, where they have suitable light red wines for the process. The first to try was Antinori, back in 1975, with a Chianti-style *primeur* called San Giocondo: in 1979 they had a production of about 350,000 bottles and began exporting. The Italian *primeurs*, like the French ones, are made by mid-November and should be drunk by April of the following year.

Antinori was followed by Angelo Gaja of Piedmont with his Nebbiolo Vinot that has now reached a production of 28,000 bottles. Lamberti of Bardolino came next with its Novello, which was not a Flanzy wine but used their own accelerated fermentation method made with DOC grapes – they have reached a 150,000-bottle output. Frescobaldi now produces 95,000 bottles of Nuovo Fiore. The Cantina Volpe has marketed its San Martino (in honour of the Saint whose feast-day is 10 November, when the wine is released); this is made with Freisa and Dolcetto, both of which reds were traditionally processed as slightly *frizzante* to great advantage. The Ca' del Bosco winery of Franciacorta has made a Flanzy from a Merlot, Nebbiolo and Barbera composite called Vino Novello, while the South Tyrol has come up with Pinot Nero and Pinot Bianco Flanzies with notable success, particularly appreciated in Milan . . . in fact, these *primeurs* are being sold almost exclusively in north Italy. These wines are all outside the DOC legislation, except for Lamberti's. Some people are quietly saying that the *primeur* characteristics – fruitiness, youth and effervescence – have been in Lambrusco for a long time and at half the price.

The trend, however, is growing, and those in the wine and catering trades feel that it is something which is here to stay. Certainly, with the modern taste for the young, the fresh, the light, these *primeurs* fit such requirements to perfection. The total production, however, cannot be much over a million bottles, and the price is sustained.

PIEDMONT, LOMBARDY AND THE VALTELLINE

The Nebbiolo vine, which is grown in central Piedmont, the Novara hills, the Aosta Valley and the Valtellina of Lombardy, without doubt yields some of Italy's best traditional wines. Its juices, when nursed and nurtured by an equally distinguished winery to make an aged-in-the-wood Barolo, Barbaresco, Carema, Gattinara or Sassella, can stand up to any fair criticism. I would recommend that anyone who doubts that Italian red wine can compare favourably with the world's best, acquires a bottle of one of the Riserva or Riserva Speciale Barolos that has been properly cellared all its life: 1958, 1961, 1964, 1971, or 1974 would be good vintage choices; the fact is that the Piedmont producers tend to lay down more wines in good years so that the bottles you find available on the market are almost always from vintages that have been successful. To be sure that you are drinking the best, buy a bottle by one of the distinguished producers such as Prunotto, Paolo Cordero di Montezemolo, Ratti, Borgogno, Contratto, Pio Cesare, Luigi Einaudi Ceretto, Giacosa or Bersano – there are many other excellent producers (listed in the Gazetteer on page 283), but I am just suggesting a test with certain criteria. Since the bottle may be an old one, it may not have DOC printed on the label which involves certain guarantees from 1966 onwards, but the name of an honoured producer is more important than a DOC symbol.

When young, all Nebbiolo is bitter, overly tannic and unattractive. It requires at least one year in the wood to soften its acerbities. A fine Barolo, however, needs two years in the wood and one in the bottle before it can be called harmonious. Selected *crus* are matured for three years in the barrel and one in the bottle, when they are called Riserva, while prime wine is matured for four and five years in the wood. A Barolo Riserva Speciale is usually ready for drinking by its sixth year, but warrants more cellaring.

In the past, these Nebbiolo wines were never exported extensively, with the exception of Valtelline wines to Switzerland. This was because these wines are not ones to drink during summer as they are too strong: and because most foreigners come to Italy in that period, they have never been able to demonstrate their natural proclivities for marrying perfectly with roast meats, steaks, venison and game birds, to be followed by mature cheeses, such as Gorgonzola.

The DOC legislation draws a line delimiting an area in which a certain type of DOC wine can be produced. In the case of Barolo, the area is small and fully planted – that is to say, all the favourable hillsides are planted; valley bottoms and northern-

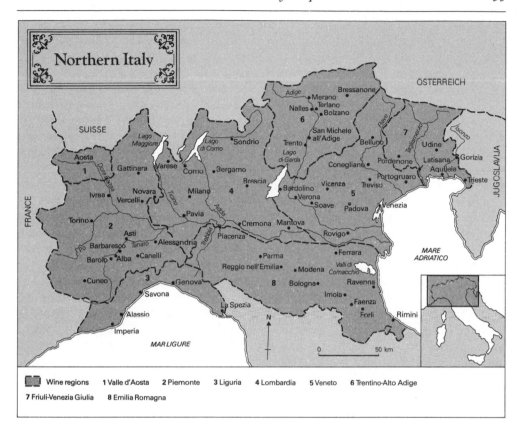

Northern Italy

Wine regions 1 Valle d'Aosta 2 Piemonte 3 Liguria 4 Lombardia 5 Veneto 6 Trentino-Alto Adige
7 Friuli-Venezia Giulia 8 Emilia Romagna

aspect slopes, for example, are not permitted. The only way that the Barolo producers can keep up with inflation and rising costs, therefore, is to produce finer
(and more expensive) wines – they cannot plant more vineyards. If all the world
decides to drink Barolo, the price will go through the roof. The big Piedmont
producers, however, can extend their interests to the other nearby DOC categories
which, in most cases, they produced before but at a more modest level. Today,
these new DOC zones – Barbera d'Alba, Barbera del Monferrato, Barbera d'Asti,
Dolcetto d'Acqui, Dolcetto d'Ovada, Dolcetto d'Alba, Dolcetto d'Asti, Dolcetto
di Piano d'Alba, Dolcetto di Dogliani, Dolcetto delle Langhe Monregalesi – have
been given the investment and the ageing that previously was available and worthwhile only for Barolo and Barbaresco.

The Barolo and all the other Nebbiolo-based wines are distinguished for their
body. Nowadays, those who talk of wine tend to stress the nose and the freshness of
the wine. Body is rarer. Though an aged Barolo has a fine and subtle bouquet, its
strength of character lies in its full and harmonious body and its natural alcoholic
content of 13 per cent and more. This high alcoholic content does not produce,
however, the inebriating sensation that a badly chaptalized wine does. In addition,
its tannic astringency, attenuated with age, and its lingering aftertaste provide the
palate with an unusually satisfying taste experience when confronted with roasted
meats and cheeses. Barolo producers are proud of their reputation for integrity. In
1972, after a miserable and rainy summer, the grape crop offered little over 10.5 per
cent alcohol. Instead of employing technological tricks to save the vintage and their
bank accounts, the Barolo producers unanimously decided that the 1972 crop would
not be bottled as Barolo.

In the Aosta Valley, the Nebbiolo vine grows up to 2,000 metres above sea-level
and is known as Picoutener or Pugnet. It is sold as Carema, with 12 per cent alcohol

after two years in the barrel and two more in the bottle. The Donnaz, at 1,000–2,000 metres in the same Alpine valley, is also a small-production wine by Luigi Fernando and requires two years in the wood and one in the bottle before being considered mature. These mountain wines with their long refinement in the bottle develop a bouquet that can offer a unique experience to most wine-lovers.

The Novara hills is also a relatively small production area, though not as limited as the Aosta Valley. Except for the Gattinara, which is already producing at 90 per cent capacity of its DOC legislation, this area is one likely to develop. The Ghemme could double its production, while the Boca, Fara and Sizzano group could do much more. The contiguous and historic Lessona winery is building up stocks of fine old aged wines with a view to the future, rather than to current sales.

These Novara hills produce robust wines in true Barolo spirit. On labels the Nebbiolo wine is often called Spanna, its local dialect name; however, this name is used almost exclusively for non-DOC wines from peripheral vineyards, which should by no means be ignored because they, in my experience, are of equal quality when aged. Names like Travaglini, Antoniolo, Ravizza, Vallana, Ponti, Sebastiani, Brugo, Uglioni and Sella are worthy of being noted down by those who buy on the reputation of old-established producers. And, for those who like unique wines that are produced on small farms, I would personally recommend the miniscule production of MOTZ SIFLON by Luciano Brigatti of Suno. The unusual name, I believe, means in Lombardy dialect something like the breeze that comes over the mountains, but I would not guarantee it. All I would guarantee is that Signor Brigatti, his wife, his mother-in-law and a couple of hired hands make excellent wine.

The Valtelline, the valley of the River Adda close to the Swiss frontier, has been producing fine wines since the time of the ancient Romans. Today, the DOC zone produces over 90 per cent of its capacity. Here, the 1968 regulations, requiring one year's ageing in the wood and one in the bottle, are customarily surpassed by the major producers for their Valtelline Superiore, which they process to appreciably higher standards than required. They have retained four of their traditional zonal names, Sassella, Inferno, Grumello and Valgella, but have had to give up Castel Chiuro to abide by the DOC regulations. They have, however, been allowed to keep their Sfurzat, which is a speciality wine, made with grapes that have been semi-dried. The wine provides a high alcoholic content of 14.5 per cent and has a notably rich body. Perhaps, this is a good wine to recommend for those who are looking for big wines in Italian traditional style.

These wines are grown in ideal, southern-aspect conditions, 700 metres up in the hills. They are strong in body and with a bouquet that takes on an ethereal quality of mountain air. There is, however, an inevitable loss, as in the Aosta Valley, of some alcoholic content in comparison with the Barolo, but the Valtellina Superiore reaches 12 per cent which is sufficient for a fine table wine and sufficient for ageing.

Here, the Nebbiolo vine goes under yet another name – Chiavennasca: and the producers' names to remember are Bettini, Tona, Negri, Polatti, Rainoldi, Pellizzati, Balgera and Enologica Valtellinese, none of which is likely to disappoint.

All Nebbiolo-based wines should be brought from the cellar and opened an hour or so before serving in order to let them adjust to the ambient temperature. The biggest of them might be uncorked three or four hours before serving, unless they are twenty or more years old when the breathing period should be shortened to half an hour as the wine risks fading. The world of big, red wines of Piedmont offers, surprisingly, from its very centre, two large growing areas of white *moscato* grapes which are the source of the Asti Spumantes; grapes so full of sweetness and light that it is hard to believe they come from the same soil as crusty old Barolos. A little to the south, towards the Ligurian coast, one finds Piedmont's only dry white wine, the Cortese, which is in the same spirit as the reds – elegant, bone-dry and unrelenting in its classic spirit. Bruzzone is making it *pétillant* to fine effect.

The same rolling moors, covered with vines, accompany one as one goes east into Lombardy. There, one finds another great wine-producing district but far less known, called the Oltrepò Pavese, which, interpreted, means the land on the other side of the River Po, south of Pavia. It is a great Pinot vineyard that supplies all the big Champagne- and Charmat-method makers of sparkling wine in both Piedmont and Lombardy. It is also the producing area of a lot of the quality wines that Milan drinks (over and above the great quantities of Piedmontese carafe Barbera) for they are rarely seen elsewhere. After the large and highly qualified Cantina Sociale Santa Maria della Versa (expert in all manner of sparkling wines), there are many old-established firms with long reputations for their Barbera-and-Bonarda wines; those I have drunk have been both vigorous and harmonious. But their range is now far wider, including Rieslings and Pinots.

The other major growing area of Lombardy is around Brescia and towards Lake Garda. Franciacorta is the best known, not only for its Pinots and Cabernets but also for its sparkling wines. The Botticino, Cellatica reds and the San Martino della Battaglia Tocai whites are also old established but, like the well-known wines such as Sangue di Giuda and Balestriere of the Oltrepò, seem to be consumed locally with no trouble.

The Lugana and the Riviera del Garda wines, and especially the Chiarettos, are much more familiar territory. They are all well-appreciated for their gentle nature and fragrant air of old-world romance; they were, I think, the first Italian wines to win favour abroad due to tourism – the tourism of the 1920s and 1930s that took its visitors to Lake Constance and to Lake Garda, to the music of palm-court orchestras. But the charm of Lake Garda lives on. The wines on both sides of the lake – we move into the Veneto on the other side with Bardolino, Valpolicella and Soave – have lost none of their delights, as the production parameters demonstrate so persuasively.

TRENTINO AND THE SOUTH TYROL

The Germans and the Austrians have known all about the South Tyrol (Alto Adige) for centuries and, for a people who have always been leaders in the art of wine-making, the choice of these wines is a compliment. I am told that Caldaro – or, better, Kalterersee as it is called in German – wines are counted as local production in Munich. The whole Trento valley, up to the snowline, is covered with vine terraces; not even the most pernickety wine connoisseur could say that South Tyrol wine has a heavy Mediterranean taste; it must be as cold in Merano as in Berlin. And there are eight DOC zones to be indulged in; five of them include several varietals (one even has seventeen), and there is a wide assortment of non-DOC wines. The most distinguished, to my taste, is the Santa Maddalena; a perfumed yet robust red wine that comes from high in the mountains.

The whites run to Müller-Thurgau, Pinot Grigio – called Ruländer in those parts – Sauvignon Bianco, Sylvaner, Pinot Bianco, Riesling Renano and Riesling Italico, Gewürztraminer, and Moscato Giallo in the Alto Adige zone; and to Pinot Bianco, Riesling Italico and Renano, Sauvignon and Sylvaner in the Terlano zone of the Trentino. The Alto Adige group also includes a formidable range of reds – Pinot Nero, Cabernet Franc, Cabernet Sauvignon, Lagrein, Malvasia, Merlot, Moscato Rosa and Schiava – the last being the indigenous vine of the valley. To finish off this cornucopia, there are the Valle Isarco whites – Gewürztraminer, Müller-Thurgau, Pinot Grigio, Sylvaner and Veltliner.

Go where you please – from Novacella, Bressanone and Merano, with their long views of the Dolomites, to Bolzano, Caldaro and Terlano a little lower in the valley, and you will find wine and more wine. Further down again, there is a similar abundance of much the same French and German wines but, in the Trentino, they tend to be a little stronger in alcohol and richer in style; the Blauburgunder – the Pinot Nero burgundy from either part of the valley – is a formidable drink. The economic situation in the whole valley is conditioned by the growing of vines on hillside terraces, often at considerable heights. What is produced must be of top quality to command prices which make the cultivation and processing a viable proposition.

In the hills of the Trentino, there is a great deal of Pinot-growing which goes for making Champagne-method and *mousseux* wines. Ferrari and Equipe 5 are recognized as fine producers of the former. The rest of the grapes are sold to the Treviso-Conegliano area near Venice, where they are used to make the Cartizze champagnes. In the Trento names like Bossi Fedrigotti, Endrizzi, the Cantina Viticoltori (Italy's best cooperative, rivalled only by the Santa Maria della Vcrsa cooperative for its sparkling wines) leap to mind as great producers, and, in the South Tyrol, the Klosterkellerei, Kettmeir, Carli, Novacella Abbey and Hofstatter. The visitor to the valley might well make the oenological and viticultural institute, San Michele all'Adige, both a goal and a point of departure for further studies. Not only can it offer guided tours and technical information, it produces five excellent wines that can be tasted as an introduction to the delights of the area.

THE VENETO AND FRIULI-VENEZIA GIULIA

Wine has been produced in the Veneto since time immemorial; archaeologists have dug up prehistoric wine jars from the shores of Lake Garda. The Veneto has a natural vocation for producing wine – rolling hills, a relatively mild climate without great heat or excessive frost, and rare snowfalls. However, there is a lot of difference between making wine for two or three millennia, and making good, dry wine today. There is also a difference between knowing how to make fine wine in favourable circumstances, and having a market that is ready and willing to buy it. The Veneto, and the provinces that stretch towards the Brenner Pass, have throughout history been economically and often politically connected to both Austria and Germany. Between 1814 and 1866, most of the Veneto was part of the Austro-Hungarian Empire and is, today, one of the favourite holiday spots for Austrians and Germans. These Austrians and Germans have always been, and still are, big importers of Verona wines, but they have not been the greatest of connoisseurs and brought the best only in relatively small quantities.

Valpolicella

It is perhaps something of a surprise to find that the major importer of Valpolicella Superiore is the United States, and that well over half of all Valpolicella is exported. Although Valpolicella has been made for well over a century, the producers have tasted success only in the last two decades. This is due to what they call the quality explosion, which was also enhanced by the DOC legislation. This has become highly visible on the charts which show the quantity produced of Valpolicella and of Valpolicella Superiore. In the past, more Valpolicella was produced, but today Valpolicella Superiore has risen so fast that the two will soon balance.

The Valpolicella zone lies to the north of Verona, stretching toward the Bardolino zone on Lake Garda in the west and to the Soave zone in the east. Most of it is rolling hills between 200 and 250 metres high. The best grapes come from hills that rise from 300 to 600 metres. These are customarily used for the Recioto Amarone Valpolicella, the special reserve wine of the country. The soil has a high calcium carbonate content which also is favourable for growing vines.

The four major vines employed to make Valpolicella and, to a great extent also, Bardolino, are planted nowhere else in Italy and would appear to be indigenous to the region. They are Corvina, Molinara, Negrara and Rondinella; Corvina for its *finezza*; Rondinella for its strength; Negrara for its colour and body; and Molinara for *beva*. *Beva* is a term that means its pure and simple drinkability, a characteristic that leaves behind it the desire to take another glass of the same wine. There are also half a dozen other vine varieties that may be added in very small quantities – 10 per cent in all: Rossignola for its almondy aroma; Corvinone for its bouquet and Barbera and Sangiovese for body. These grapes give Valpolicella ample fixed acidity for ageing and sufficient alcoholic strength also. This alcoholic strength may be increased by half a per cent, if required, through the Ripasso process which I shall explain later. Some years ago, the DOC discipline was modified to give the producers greater opportunity to personalize their wines within the limits of remaining Valpolicella – that is to say, they have greater leeway in the percentages of each wine they use. The experts insist that the soil and other ambiental conditions vary from valley to valley, so that a Valpolicella from Marano will have a bouquet of roses, while that of Negrar tends to violets, and that of Fumane to a perfume of irises. The Valpantena of Bertani fame (Valpantena is a valley due north of Verona) tends to be more robust, tannic and forceful than the others. These local characteristics, therefore, are being accentuated although, by and large, one can say that a good Superiore is a medium red ruby wine, dry but with the slightest hint of sweetness, with an elegant finish and an almondy aroma.

The whole production structure of Valpolicella is rather different from that of Italy as a whole, where estate-bottling is mostly the rule. An understanding of this structure helps to understand the wine. There are fourteen major Verona *négociants*, with Bolla and Lamberti leading in production quantity. They are followed by Sartori, Montresor, Castagna and Pasqua, with Bertani and Peternella close behind.

Among the smaller producers are Boscaini, Masi, Santa Sofia and Villa Gerardi. Most of these market both Valpolicella and Valpolicella Superiore. The former, a wine that has been improved greatly in the last decade, is mostly bought by the *négociants* in the form of wine from the cooperatives, processed in part and bottled. The Superiore, however, is made by these same *négociants* from grapes grown in their own vineyards with the addition of grapes purchased from the smallholders, then processed, aged for two years in the wood (although the DOC does not require more than one year) and bottled. The Superiore, therefore, is not only a superior wine in every sense, but its character will vary and depend essentially on the skill in growing vines and in the purchasing and processing ability of the individual *négociant*. The next stage is to find out who does what. Masi and Bertani make only Superiore; over half of Bolla's production is Superiore; Lamberti and Castagna are around 35 per cent and the remainder less than 25 per cent, which is much the same as that produced by the big cooperatives, such as Illasi, Negrar, Soave and Valpantena.

The third category of producers is that of the *artigiani*, which in Italian means the small producers, the artisans. These make between 50,000 and 500,000 litres a year, almost all of which is Superiore. Connoisseurs like to encourage and support these producers whose wines have the strong local characteristics that wine-lovers appreciate. This is particularly true of the Recioto Amarone, which is made with as much as three or four more per cent alcoholic content than is required by DOC legislation. This means a higher customs duty, but it can be considered money well spent. Such strong local characteristics tend to get, if not lost, at least attenuated by bigger production. In this artisan group you will find producers such as Allegrini, Quinterelli, Tedeschi, Speri, Pule, Tommasi, Farina and Arturo Scamperle. Despite the larger production, I would add Masi, with his excellent Campo Fiorin label, to this list of highly personalized wines. These artisans' wines, of course, may not necessarily be as well stabilized as those of the big *négociants*. If, for example, you are going to drink your Valpolicella Superiore or Amarone in Venezuela or Lagos, it may not stand up to the trip, but that is not to say that it is not worth trying.

There is a curious process in Valpolicella production which is used widely to turn a Valpolicella into a Valpolicella Superiore; it is called the Ripasso system. Valpolicella by nature and with due regularity comes up with an 11.5 per cent of alcoholic content. This can be increased to make Valpolicella Superiore with 12 per cent alcoholic content by a more discriminating selection of grapes or by the Ripasso method. This last is a by-product of the Recioto Amarone process, which must first be explained.

The Recioto is a strong 14–18 per cent full-bodied red wine, of which about 20 per cent is processed as a sweet sparkling wine, mostly for local consumption. The Amarone, the dry Recioto, the production of which doubles every year, is made from *passito* grapes which are dried on racks and pressed after Christmas, then fermented for forty-five days and given a further slow fermentation for eighteen months. After eighteen months in the wood, it is ready for bottling and another rest in the bottle before being drunk. It can be a remarkable autumn-coloured wine with fascinating nuances of bouquet and taste, quite unlike any other wine-drinking experience. New legislation will not permit Amarone to have more than one per cent of sugar residue. This Recioto is made from choice grapes, grown on metre-high vines at around 500 metres and above, which are called 'ears' because the bunches stick out and pick up most of the sunshine. *Orecchie* is the Italian word for ears, and it was presumably so centuries ago too, when it was said to have been transformed into Recioto.

To carry out the Ripasso system, the semi-dried grapes of the Recioto are pressed very lightly, the grape-skins are then passed to big vats and the Valpolicella, made three months previously, is poured in. A second fermentation is set up for two weeks, which not only increases the alcoholic strength by half a per cent, but puts more body and mineral salts into the wine.

The lifespan of the various wines differ. Simple Valpolicella should be drunk within a year; it will last much longer, but will not improve with keeping. Valpolicella Superiore, after reaching its peak in its third year, will appreciate a little more ageing, but on the whole it is better to drink it. Valpolicella Recioto Amarone, after three or so years maturing in the winery, is best drunk between its fourth and seventh years and, on the whole, advisedly consumed by its eighth. My final recommendation is to serve Valpolicella Superiore at a warm room temperature and to uncork it at least half-an-hour before serving. The Amarone will benefit from an hour's wait or more, so that it can expand its bouquet.

The Veneto stretches from Lake Garda and Verona in the west to Padua and Venice in the east, then north to the Dolomite Alps. It is a land of great natural beauty, fine cities and civilized living. Unlike its heavily industrialized neighbours, Lombardy and Piedmont, the Veneto is still mainly an agricultural region. Though Verona, for example, is an efficient modern city, it is also a Renaissance city of antique elegance – a delight to the eye and a tranquillizer to the turbulent spirit – while that unique marvel, Venice, with its improbable gondolas and tracery palaces, is a short drive down the *autostrada*.

In brief, it can be said that the Veneto is the producer of large quantities of high quality table wines, some of which are suited for ageing, many excellent Champagne and Charmat sparklers, and many superb white wines. Soave is quite the best known, and needs no introduction since it is drunk the world over. It is a white wine with a delightful bouquet, provided you do not freeze it into insignificance. Especially for a Pieropan or a Masi Superiore, a short rest in the ice-bucket is enough to give the right balance between temperature and aroma and bring out the full character of the wine. Equally well-known is the Bardolino – an ever-ready and willing partner at table and most suited for buffet meals; the Superiore, however, can demonstrate its worth and, particularly from *artigiani*, is to be taken very seriously. In 1974, the new DOC zone of the Colli Berici (Berici hills) was established near Vicenza; its range includes Tocai, Sauvignon, Pinot Bianco, Merlot, Tocai Rosso, Garganega and Cabernet wines. Of these, the Cabernet has risen above the others with a three-year aged Riserva permitted. But the delights to be found to the north of Venice, around Treviso and Conegliano, are more interesting. Here, there is a munificent supply of Charmat- and Champagne-method sparkling wines called Prosecco when slightly sweet, and Cartizze or Prosecco Brut when fully dry. Cartizze is the classic zone of Prosecco. In Italy, the Charmat sparklers such as Prosecco are fresh, effervescent wines much drunk at receptions, weddings, cocktail parties and extensively at table. They prepare the palate better for fine cooking and fine wines to follow at the table than any conventional or harder apéritif.

The Cartizze Champagne-method wines are made by the Valdobbiadene Cooperative and the Prosecco Brut by the well-known Carpene Malvolti company, as well as by De Bernard and Valdo Vini. These *bruts* are, nowadays, mostly made from black Pinot grapes from the Trentino to give them that classic dry taste; Charmat *bruts* are also available. These producers and the noted Soligo cooperative all make the slightly sweet Prosecco and in far larger quantities. However, it should be said that this Spumante is not aggressively sweet; certainly much less so than many regular apéritifs, 'dry' fortified wines and even some Champagnes and *mousseux*.

This area around Treviso is highly expert in the subtleties and art of wine-making, possessing one of Italy's three oenological research institutes, Conegliano. One of the most distinguished wines of Italy has been produced here for decades, a wine you are likely to meet if you stay at Grand and Excelsior hotels when in Italy. It is Conte Piero Loredan's Venegazzù, made from Cabernet Franc, Cabernet Sauvignon, Merlot, Malbec and Petit Verdot, and given three years' maturing in the cask. Another interesting wine from this area is the Raboso red which, with four years' ageing, acquires a remarkable strength of character. It comes from the Soligo cooperative.

Further to the east, near Portogruaro, the well-known Santa Margherita winery produces high-quality table wines, particularly the Tocai di Lison – a dry white of considerable personality, astringent full-bodied and with a most generous bouquet. Other distinguished producers in this area include Conte Antonio Verca Falzacappa, Luciano Cannella and Italo Maccari.

The wines of Friuli-Venezia Giulia are still a little difficult to come by. This is chiefly because the production is split up into hundreds of small holders and small companies. But people's eyes light up as conversation turns to Pinot Grigio, Traminer or Tocai from those parts. This small province has made the problem of knowing its wines better even more difficult by arranging to have thirty – I repeat thirty – DOC denominations approved. I do not know how to explain the magic of Friuli-Venezia Giulia's wines, but it exists.

There are three major groups of DOC wines – Collio, Eastern Hills of Friuli (Colli Orientali) and the Grave Hills. The Collio area is considered the best and is distinguished for its Tocai, a white of character and body, and not to be limited to marrying only with fish and light dishes. The Pinot Grigio has become a success story, not only in Italy but abroad, which should encourage wine-lovers to investigate this whole province more closely, as Pinot Grigio is not alone as a fine wine. The Merlot red has become very popular too, as it comes soft, round and attractive and very easy to drink. None of the producers are big operators and many are 'craftsmen', but all are highly skilled in modern oenology; here are some of their names – Conte Attems, Barone Roncada, Marco Felluga and Conti Formentini, to mention the better known.

Among the offerings of the Eastern Friuli Hills is the Picolit, a sweet white dessert wine of 15 per cent alcohol, much admired in Vienna at the time of the Austro-Hungarian empire. The grape variety suffers from a floral-abortion malady and yields very poorly; however, it is the dowager duchess of Italian wines and, as such, is treated with respect – particularly in view of her price.

The red that has most impressed me is the Refosco which, unlike most of the vines grown in this area, would seem to be indigenous. It is a virile, aggressive wine, full-bodied, bitter yet warm and dry, a maverick of no mean dimensions. It is best made by Conti di Maniago and Ronchi di Manzano. The wines of the smaller Grave zone are classic Merlot, Cabernet and Tocai, best made by Pighin and Antonio Furchir.

The Friulans, over a decade ago, started planting out their low hills and flatlands along the coast where they, first of all, found out that the French vines responded to such, often damp, terrain with generosity and good quality yields; this, since 1975, is the DOC zone of Aquileia, behind the holiday island of Grado. The Cantina Sociale of the Eastern Friuli Hills is the major processor of wine in this area.

The last two years have been hard for the residents of Friuli-Venezia Giulia, with literally dozens of earthquakes, large and small. There has not been, fortunately, an exodus of the population fearing further earthquakes; perhaps they love their vineyards too much and the good wine they produce.

Turning to the south of Venice and Padua, one finds the little group of Euganean Hills. They are of volcanic origin, which is always a promising augury for good wine. There are two producers here of note; one, the Cooperative at Vo' which makes, as well as local wines for local consumption, an inexpensive but good *Charmat moscato*. The other producer is the long-established Luxardo company that invented Maraschino cherry liqueur over a century ago when their winery was in Yugoslavia, then part of the Austro-Hungarian empire. The present Marchese Nicolo Luxardo is particularly proud of the dry red called Sant'Elmo Superiore made from Merlot, Cabernet Franc and Barbera. This is aged two years in the wood and one in the bottle before marketing.

THE VALLEY OF THE PO AND EMILIA ROMAGNA

Most people think of Milan and Turin as the driving force of Italy – the factories, the efficiency, the money – but I cannot help feeling that the real economic wisdom and the real wealth, and, for that matter, the real efficiency, is in the Valley of the Po. When the rest of Italy, a few decades ago, willy-nilly dumped its agriculture as a shame-and-disgrace to man in favour of a policy of industrialization, the Emilia-Romagnans ignored propaganda and invested their last lira in their land, in orchards, in cows, pigs and vineyards, to make it one of the most fruitful and profitable areas of all Europe. The spin-off from agriculture has been great food-processing industries, including Parmesan cheese, Parma hams and salamis from Bologna and, above all, wine. Throughout history, the great cities of the Po Valley – Piacenza, Parma, Reggio nell'Emilia, Modena, Bologna, Ferrara, Forli, Faenza, Ravenna and Rimini – have been synonymous with wealth, abundant food and hard work.

Starting in the north-west corner of Emilia Romagna, one finds the same hills that lead over into the growing areas of the well-known Piedmont wines and which also stretch north into another growing area, the Oltrepò Pavese, on the south side of the Po River, after Pavia. Here are to be found robust Bonarda reds, and a great deal of white Pinot used for making sparkling wines. Emilia Romagna's slice of this traditional wine-producing area offers a little known but sturdy, dry red called Gutturnio, made from 60 per cent of Piedmontese Barbera and 40 per cent of Lombardy Bonarda, the latter noted for its lively bouquet and its softening effect on the masculine Barbera. This wine is often aged but there is no ruling on this.

Then, we enter the home of Trebbiano, the wine that has invaded all central Italy. It has no exaggerated characteristics, yet is strong and firm-bodied. Nowadays, however, it is seldom used alone, because of the unending search for more delicate and more attractive characteristics. It is the ubiquitous Ugni blanc, used for making cognac and, in fact, the Trebbiano is widely used in Italy for distilling into brandy.

In the Piacenza hills, we have two new DOC whites; the Monterosso Val d'Arda made from Malvasia di Candia, Trebbiano and some Sauvignon Bianco; the other is Trebbianino di Val Trebbia, with a slightly different but basically the same make-up. Like so much of the wine produced within a reasonable distance of Milan, these whites are not found outside the region.

More likely to meet a broader market in due course is the Parma Lambrusco; this rosé differs from the already established ones, partly by being reinforced by some Merlot, which gives the wine greater body and character. This has, as yet, not got its DOC licence. Lambrusco Reggiano DOC, also, is new and offers a light 11 per cent alcohol wine with a generous foam. In this area we find also part of the vast quantities of non-DOC *amabile* Lambruscos which have had such an effect abroad. Despite the lack of DOC controls and the consequent opportunities for being less than honest, especially considering the remarkably modest prices, the quality standards and the use of natural fermentation rather than carbonation are well maintained. Also produced in this area are large quantities of non-DOC white which is a very light, *amabile* and *frizzante* wine.

Modena is the centre for the traditional Lambruscos, Grasparossa di Castelvetro, Salamino di Santacroce and that of Sorbara. All three come as dry and *amabile*. They are all light in alcohol – 10.5 to 11 per cent – fresh, easy to drink and with a pleasant wine bouquet and taste. Though the success abroad of these wines has been of considerable satisfaction to Italy and has served as an introduction for many more, and better wines, there is an underground sense of concern at Lambrusco's domination of the export market. No economist likes to see so many of his eggs in one basket. This is particularly the case with the United States, which imported 120 million bottles of Lambrusco in 1979. However, so successful has Lambrusco been in breaking down international barriers that there is an EEC move to promote it to the status of being a Spumante, with the consequent Champagne taxes.

In line with the new trend for the Sauvignon, there is a new DOC wine in the Lambrusco area, south-west of Modena, dating from 1977, called Scandiano Bianco and which, given the talent of the wine-producers of those parts, is not likely to remain hidden under a bushel. It is a light, *abboccato* wine made with 85 per cent of Sauvignon which they are also making sparkling by the Charmat system, something which should surprise nobody. Slightly older, 1975, is the new zone just south of Bologna. This, too, has stressed the new prestige of French and German vines that have also demonstrated themselves so useful in flourishing where the native vines do not. The zone is called Colli Bolognesi (Monte S. Pietro e Castelli Medioevali). There is a long-established Barbera (a vine that is also travelling south and finding favour – even in Sicily and Sardinia) and a Merlot. The whites are Sauvignon, Pinot, Riesling Italico and an Albana-and-Trebbiano mix. The white Sauvignon is notably successful as an all-purpose apéritif and table wine.

After this little sally into the exotic, we return to the classic Italian tradition with three old favourites, the Sangiovese of Romagna, the Trebbiano of Romagna, and the Albana of Romagna. It was on a visit to Bologna and Rimini years ago, to the Italian Academy of Cuisine, that I was shown how good a young red wine is with cooked seafood, or, perhaps, I should say how well a young Sangiovese di Romagna goes with clams and crayfish and all the other delights that come out of the Adriatic because I have never met a better and more unconventional marriage between land and sea. Sangiovese Superiore is, however, less promiscuous and, after due ageing, is a respectable member of society. The Trebbiano white is a staunch old reliable that is treated with friendly disrespect only because it is so familiar; its virtues are, in fact, many. The Albana white, long ago, was rather a chameleon because every winery had its own way of processing it. It turned up sparkling, dry, *amabile*, but more often a strange bitter-sweet. The production has settled in the main now for a conventional dry; but *amabile* and sparkling can still be found locally.

TUSCANY

Chianti

Tuscany, although beautiful countryside to the eye, is mostly poor agricultural land. But the vine, like the olive, welcomes this very lack of fertility. Paradoxically, it somehow finds the nourishment from meagre soil to produce its best wine. There seems little doubt that the Tuscans, in Renaissance times, were the first Europeans to produce a completely dry red wine such as we would accept today. They also used the *governo* process, causing a second fermentation with a must made from semi-dried grapes (5–10 per cent of the total harvest picked before the general crop). This gave the young wine a smoothness and well-formed body such as could not normally be obtained without long ageing in the cask. In the light of modern oenology and in view of the labour required, this system has now become less usual, but is still practised by some estates, convinced of its value in adding extra body to a wine.

The prospective purchaser of Chianti should know the trademarks of the two major consortia whose members produce a great deal of the wine in their respective areas, and which offer certain extra guarantees of quality; the Black Rooster of the Chianti Classico zone, and the Cherub of the Putto zone, which is a naked child holding three bunches of red grapes. The Gallo Nero (the Black Rooster, Cockerel or Cock as it is variously translated into English), the symbol of the Classico consortium, was chosen because it was the crest of the thirteenth-century Chianti Defence League. There are over 700 producers in the consortium, of which more than 200 estates bottle and market their products under their own, registered labels. Their wines are subjected to extensive tests and tastings, over and above the DOC. There is a small number of world-famous *négociants* – Ricasoli, Antinori, Melini, Serristori and Bertolli – whose private wine-production is limited and who purchase grapes and wine from the small producers and the cooperatives, which they process, mature and bottle. Of these distinguished names, two – Ricasoli and Antinori – have resigned from the consortium considering that the DOC legislation for Chianti Classico and their own well-founded reputations are nowadays sufficient guarantees of the quality of their wines.

The Tuscan wineries, or *fattorie*, are based mainly in ancient castles or country villas, and many have been in the same family's hands for centuries. In recent years, a number have been sold totally or in part. Among the more notable of such changes of proprietorship is the Seagram Distillery's interest in Ricasoli, and Winefood's (a Swiss-based conglomerate) in Melini. These have all had the largely beneficial effect of bringing in new investment capital for modernization and expansion.

The current production of the Chianti Classico consortium is around 2.25 million

Wine regions   1 Toscana   2 Marche   3 Umbria   4 Abruzzo   5 Lazio   6 Molise   7 Sardegna   8 San Marino

hectolitres, while that of Chianti Putto from all the other zones is approaching 12 million hectolitres. The latter category includes Montalbano, Rufina, Val d'Elsa, Colli Empolesi, Colli Fiorentini, Colli Senesi, Colli Aretini, Colline Pisane, and the Colli Pistoiesi. These divisions are enough to make a wine-lover's head spin without taking a drop. However, a grand simplification of sorts has taken place. All Chianti producers, except those of Chianti Classico and Carmignano, are now centralized under the aegis of the Putto consortium, with the further exception of the *négociant* Folonari with his Ruffino, who has opted out. The Carmignano zone has succeeded in re-establishing its independent status as it once was under the Grand Duchy in 1716. However, this rationalization will not stop people, for the next half-century, talking about Montalbano, the Florentine hills, the Siena hills and Arezzo hills as being Chianti.

Chianti Classico and Chianti, as we know them today, are, like Claret, composite wines made up of several different grapes, each contributing to make a harmonious whole. The Chianti Classico proportions are, roughly, 70 per cent of Sangiovese, 10–15 per cent of Canaiolo Nero, 10–15 per cent of Trebbiano Bianco and Malvasia Bianco (this can be much less in newer vineyards), and up to 5 per cent of Colorino may be added if necessary to strengthen the colour. It is also useful for the *governo*. The Sangiovese is a noble, full-bodied wine of strong character, but harsh when young; it therefore can take long barrel-ageing. The Canaiolo Nero mitigates the Sangiovese's youthful asperities and enhances the colour. The reader may be surprised to see the white grapes among the components, but Trebbiano is employed for its astringency, and the Malvasia for its bouquet and for its softening effect, which is especially important when the wine is to be drunk young. Interesting, and successful, experiments have been made replacing the whites with Cabernet Sauvignon.

The Chianti Classico consortium wine, in Bordeaux-style bottles that carry a neckband showing a black rooster on a silver or gold ground, have been aged, respectively, for a minimum of two years (marked Vecchio) and three years (marked Riserva) before being bottled and rested. It is a curious fact that neither the DOC nor the consortium insist that the wines are actually aged in wood, as they are in fact aged. Perhaps the DOCG legislation, when it comes, will settle this equivocation.

There is, however, a theory afoot that the highly tannic wines of Italy – in contradistinction to the 'softer' Cabernets, Merlots, and Pinots of France and Italy, which actually need to draw tannin from the new wood of the barrel – could mature better in glass, stainless-steel or fibreglass vats and be more true to type. With wood-ageing, there is a risk of or a tendency to oxidation, and some of the larger Chianti Classico *négociants* have made a compromise, ageing their Riservas a year or so in the wood, followed by a year or so in vats and another in the bottle before marketing. On the other hand, fine Chianti Classicos with a high total acidity may be aged to advantage for as much as eight years before bottling, although some would say this was an acquired taste. Five years is quite customary. However, long ageing in wood like this can lead to bacterial spoilage, and great care is taken to avoid this.

Bottles and flasks carrying the Black Rooster neck-seal with a red ground (or those not marked Vecchio or Riserva in the case of non-consortium members) contain wine that has been aged for only between six and twelve months and is not intended for long maturing in the cellar. It should, normally, be drunk by its third or fourth year, preferably much earlier. Very approximately, it can be said that 90 per cent of the production of the big *négociants* is of this young Chianti, and 10 per cent is reserved aged Chianti or Chianti Classico.

Most Chianti Classico is already of considerably higher quality and made under stricter controls than those required by the DOC legislation. Soon, all Chianti may be governed by the new and more rigid DOCG (Guaranteed Controlled Denomination of Origin) regulations, see page 281. Though this could further improve quality on a broad front, it is altogether too all-embracing a legislation to interest the real connoisseur, who will find that he must still use his discrimination and nose out the *fattoria* with the best raw materials and the best ageing. With minor changes, these will tend always to be the same producers. For all the *fattorie* and *négociants* who have worked hard and contained their production to maintain the highest international standards, the DOCG may turn out to be a disadvantage, putting, as does also, in fact, the DOC system, every winery on a common denominator basis, even if that denominator has been raised to notably high levels. In fact, the Chianti Classico growers are continually tightening their own discipline. They often reduce the maximum permitted crop of 115 quintals a hectare to 60 quintals, thus producing a better grape with plenty of sugar and yeasts to reach the required 12.5 per cent of alcohol needed for a Riserva.

The average *fattoria* is a small operation dedicated to aged-in-the-wood wine. There are only, for example, about 15,000 bottles of the famous Fonterutoli Riserva Chianti Classico bottled each good vintage year; Castello di Uzzano is much larger and bottles 185,000, but nobody would say that that was a lot of wine. For example, San Felice of San Gusmè bottles around 150,000; Badia a Coltibuono 100,000; Castello di Gabbiano 150,000 and Tizzano 50,000. I know a Lambrusco company – and not the biggest by any means – that would consider 185,000 bottles just two days' work. None of these small *fattorie* produce much young red-seal wine; this is left to the world-famous *négociants* and to the smaller producers of the other zones. 'Young' wine, provided it is made under DOC regulations, should be reliable, but quality does differ from winery to winery. It is therefore best to buy from producers who have a reputation to maintain, and to remember that a young Chianti Classico will always be superior to a young Chianti.

The Chianti Classico growers, in fact, can only survive by making quality wines – wines that are finer and more expensive than those of other zones because their vines are grown on hillsides between 250 and 500 metres above sea-level where cultivation and harvesting are difficult and costly. The easier-to-run vineyards on the rolling hills of other zones can undercut them for price but not for quality. Classico Riserva, given proper cellaring, can age and improve in the bottle as long as any Claret, if not longer. Only a few producers of the other zones are in the same quality bracket; distinguished names such as Biondi Santi (Fattoria I Pieri), Conte Contini Bonacossi (Villa Capezzana), Marchesi De' Frescobaldi (Fattorie Nipozzano and Pomino), Conte Guicciardini (Castello di Poppiano), Melini (Tenute Piana di Terrasano, La Selvanella, Terrarossa and Granaio), Conte Spaletti (Fattoria Poggio Reale), Conte Gotti Lega (Villa Capannoli), Marchese Emilio Pucci di Barsento (Fattoria Granaiolo), Duca Amedeo di Savoia (Fattoria Il Borro), Guicciardini Principe Strozzi (Villa Cusona), Conte Pasolini dall'Onda (Villa Pasolini), and Il Conte Giuntini (Villa Selvapiano) are in the front rank. Umberto Navarro also produces a fine Chianti but it is less widely known that part of his production is kosher and made under the supervision of the Chief Rabbi of Rome. The Cantina Sociale of Pitigliano also is a kosher supplier. To the best of my knowledge, the difference is little more than a ritual cleansing of casks.

The owners of the *fattorie* in the classic zone, in the main the old landed aristocracy of Tuscany, were in no way prepared to face the horse-trading that went on in the use of the name of Chianti, which as a result deteriorated in prestige disastrously. This damage began early in the twentieth century and, in 1924, the owners of the *fattorie* set up the 'Black Rooster' consortium in an effort to save the boat. But the trade considered it a vanity and anti-commercial. And since there had always been plenty of producers outside the Classico zone – and even in distant parts of Italy – ever ready and willing to meet the demands of the foreign importers for any inexpensive red wine provided it was bottled in Chianti's famous straw-covered flasks and marked Chianti, the *fattorie* lost the battle.

They lost out, also, because the phylloxera pest reached Tuscany only in the 1920s. Although the Italian government's agricultural experts facilitated the replanting of the vineyards with American roots grafted with traditional vines, it harmed the quality of the Chianti, just as it had done in Bordeaux in the 1870s and 1880s. It was some years before quality returned to its previous standards. At all events, the Black Rooster associates, facing these double troubles, concluded that the word Chianti was, for them, a dead-weight and tended to stress on their labels the names of their wineries, printing Chianti in small type or omitting it completely. They left the good name of Chianti in the hands of those who did not respect it or its traditions.

However, the 1970s has seen the members of the various consortia, with DOC legislation as their ally, return to the battle and most of their enemies are being put to flight. The production of the Bordeaux-style bottle Riserva Chianti Classico, for example, has been increasing since the DOC legislation came into force in 1967.

Vineyards now extend over 12,000 hectares and this, surprisingly, with an exodus of 25 per cent of the population from the zone in the last twenty years. Greater rationalization has overcome the shortage of physical labour though, in Tuscan hill country, full-scale mechanization will never be a practical possibility.

There are only three dozen or so of *fattoria* exporters to the United States and United Kingdom, but I hope that more of these Tuscan delights will find their way abroad in future. These Riserva Chiantis offer fascinating nuances of difference in taste, bouquet and body, due to the exposure and altitude of the vineyards, the nature of the soil, the cultivation, the processing and maturing methods and, of course, the vintage and age. Above all, they all have a consistent body and sturdy legs which, to my mind, is essential, if not the essence, of a fine aged red wine, without which bouquet and taste count for little.

There will rarely be much sediment in a reserve wine, unless it is very very old, since it will have precipitated during its barrel-ageing, but with all old wine particular care should be taken. The bottles should be brought to a warm, 22°C temperature, even a day or more before the bottle is broached. An hour or two, some say more, should elapse between the uncorking and the serving at table, to give the wine time to expand its bouquet after long confinement in the bottle.

The world is nowadays saying that Italian wines are much better; in fact that they are really very good. This is quite true, but the other truth is that these fine wines were always there in lesser quantities and fewer people knew about them. Only in the last thirty years, during which time I have been in Italy, has the home market for fine wines – and particularly for fine aged-in-the-wood wines – grown to a size sufficiently consistent to form a springboard for sales abroad.

Three decades ago, there were a few major wine-producers and tens of thousands of small wineries. These latter were often inexpert but many – such as the *fattorie* of Tuscany – made superb wine. Today, these small producers have almost all improved out of all recognition and grown to the extent that they have even conditioned the major wine-makers into offering far better wines and they have taken a remarkable share of the market. There are also dynamic new wineries such as Villa Calaggio, which has, incidentally, one of the two must-concentrators in the Classico zone. Thus, if the alcohol level of a Chianti Classico needs to be raised, it can be done now by the addition of concentrated must made from Chianti Classico grapes, until the day that the EEC permits a half per cent increase of alcoholic content by inexpensive chaptalization.

This growth and success, encouraged by DOC legislation and modern oenology and technology, is a fine example of the virtues of private enterprise, know-how and good taste, along with a profound sense of history, civilization and love of the land. A fuller list of recommended producers of both Chianti Classico and Chianti – with particular stress on the *fattorie* – will be found on pages 313-5.

Brunello of Montalcino

The Brunello of Montalcino is today the most expensive and among the most prestigious of Italian wines. It is a kissing cousin of the Sangiovese vine, which is the most important ingredient of Chianti. Brunello, one might say, was invented a hundred years or so ago by Biondi Santi (the grandfather), and its quality and reputation have been nursed and nurtured since then with utmost care by subsequent generations of Biondi Santis. Over and above being a fine red wine with all the characteristics in high relief for a mature wine to accompany roasts and game, it has a fabulous proclivity for ageing for decades and decades. In the last ten or so years, three or four other wineries of Montalcino, having noted the worldwide success of Brunello, have entered the lists.

Perhaps the greatest shock to this sleepy medieval township just south of Siena has been the arrival of Villa Banfi, the American importers, not only as buyers, but as producers. This company has acquired about 800 hectares, and planted out already 400 of them with Brunello, Moscadello, Cabernet Sauvignon, and Pinot Chardonnay. The company is investing over a period of five years the sum of about 35 million US dollars in land, wineries, bottling plants and everything needed, from the land on which to plant the vine to the crates for stowing in the sea-containers for export. It is a courageous investment at a time when Italy is in economic jitters; at the same time, it is a good one, in as much as the Montalcino DOC zone is not yet overcrowded and the soil is noted for its fine production. However, Villa Banfi is not only planning to produce Brunello di Montalcino, but has resurrected a white sparkling wine traditional to the area, Moscadello di Montalcino, which had been allowed to lapse by the local producers, perhaps because of the difficulty in production, and perhaps because they lacked a market due to the brisk competition in this field from the makers of Spumante throughout all of north Italy. Villa Banfi, however, has its own market ready for a fine *mousseux* wine and the technology to make it. They report that they will have a total annual bottling capacity of three million cases. The chairman of the Italian Oenologists Association, Ezio Rivella, designer and consultant of this major operation, is overseeing the progress of the construction and the planting out of vineyards, and will subsequently be responsible for the processing of the wines, so there is an atmosphere of serene confidence in a successful outcome.

Montepulciano (Siena)

No work about Italian wines should omit Vin Nobile of Montepulciano, one of Italy's oldest traditional wines. It is produced from Sangiovese vines grown high in the hills, as high as 700 metres. It is a good, strong Chianti Classico-style wine with three years' maturing, two in the wood and one in the bottle. It is called Riserva Speciale after three years in the barrel and one in bottle. It is a *cru* to lay down in the cellar to earn more bottle-age, and due compliments in years to come when broached.

Tuscan Whites

Tuscany has basically the same whites today as it had when the Signoria was built in Florence at the beginning of the fourteenth century from local taxes. Most of it, nowadays, is bottled by the big *négociants* such as Toscano Bianco and, though the provenance is either Tuscany or Umbria, it is not from a specific DOC zone; in all events, these whites are well-made with a good body that nobody has spurned for centuries.

More specifically, from the lonely Pitigliano area, volcanic and bare, comes a very dry white that is making a modest reputation: even its screw-top bottle wine is of good quality and, inevitably, made chiefly from the old reliable Trebbiano. The Virgin White (Bianco Vergine) of the Chiana Valley comes from the hills that spread happily into Umbria's Trebbiano growing areas. This is near Arezzo, noted for the vigour of its red wines which, historically, used to be cut into the Chiantis of other areas to give them some clout and stiffening. The island of Elba again, offers a Trebbiano, but the sea-breezes seem to soften it. The producers there complain of fraudulent rivalry, so perhaps it is wise to settle for estate-bottled wine with an address on the island. The Vernaccia di San Gimignano is a solid, dry, golden wine which seems to fit the term White Chianti very well. It is not ideal for accompanying a full-blooded Tuscan meal, but for most lighter lunches or dinners, a San Gimignano is far more than just adequate. The simple character of central Italian whites, based as they are all to some extent on the faithful Trebbiano, is found dull by those accustomed to the multi-faceted French whites and consequently, many are being slightly altered by blending to meet this criticism.

The last two white wines in Tuscany are the Parrina and the Montecarlo. The former is a bone-dry white from by the sea near the elegant resorts of Porto Ercole and Porto Santo Stefano; it is good Trebbiano and is now being exported. The other is a small production wine of very high quality which, despite its rarefied ingredients – Trebbiano, Sémillon, Pinot Grigio, Pinot Bianco, Vermentino, Sauvignon and Roussane – has well earned its DOC status which goes to demonstrate that many other special cases of exotic components could be granted DOC status too. Without the DOC, their loss is having to pay a small EEC duty on each case of wine exported and in being excluded from any publicity abroad which is paid for by public funds. On the plus side, they have fewer authorities breathing down their necks and looking through their books.

Vin Santos

A last word should be added in praise of Tuscan *vin santos*. Every *fattoria* and every *négociant* has his own speciality – strong, full-bodied, smooth and so relaxing. They might be called the 'sherries' of Italy, with a full range of styles from the bone-dry to the luscious sweet. The details of making *vin santo* vary from winery to winery. Generally, however, it is a wine that is not made year-by-year but requires a basic proportion of well-aged *vin santo* to start with – this is called the *madre*, a long-aged wine that has reduced itself in quantity by evaporation and consequently increased its alcoholic content to perhaps 18-20 per cent. To this is added a new *passito* wine i.e. made with semi-dried grapes (and optionally a little concentrated must); this is left to ferment slowly at its own convenience without the hand of man. It may ferment a little in summer and lie dormant in winter. After several years of benign negligence, the barrel is broached and a wondrous, golden liquid is found in it for our delectation.

UMBRIA

Umbria, with its natural vocation for producing large quantities of fine grapes, is to all intents and purposes an extension of Tuscany, culturally, agriculturally, gastronomically and scenically; and it has usually been dominated by the Florentines. Orvieto wines used to be the only named wines of Umbria but even they were mostly owned by Florentines. The great production of Umbrian red Sangiovese and white Trebbiano found its way to the big *négociants* of Tuscany in bulk to be bottled and labelled as Tuscan non-DOC specialities. Today, there is a Lake Trasimeno cooperative that sells Umbrian wines under their own name, and DOC, Colli del Trasimeno, though I imagine that still the majority of Umbrian grapes and wine move north to Tuscany for the traditional purpose. The subtle and delicate Orvieto wines are a delight that one tends to forget – like Umbria itself, they are too shy to make a fuss and a clamour about their reputation and charms. The slightly sweet-*abboccato* Orvieto is the real and traditional wine; it reflects all the gentleness of Umbria. There is, however, a fully dry version available too.

The only relatively new and important arrival on the Umbrian scene is the production of the Torgiano winery, a few kilometres or so outside Perugia. Over the last thirty years, the winery has gained a solid reputation for its impressive Sangiovese Rubesco and for its white Trebbiano due to the far-sightedness of its owner, Dr Giorgio Lungarotti. Both wines are, in fact, composites; the red is Chianti-like with small proportions of Canaiolo, Trebbiano Toscano and Montepulciano and the white has a softening touch of Grechetto and Malvasia di Candia. Incidentally,

Dr Lungarotti and his wife have set up a fascinating museum of wine-making implements which can make a visit more interesting.

The newest arrival, expected for 1980, is not in the same class, though in thirty years' time it may be; and sooner, if the producers find the huge sums of money to buy avant-garde plant for the processing of their white wines. The wine of the Upper Tiber Hills (Colli Altotiberini as the new DOC zone is to be called) is basically of excellent quality and has always been. The only problem is money. I wish the producers luck; after all, in only a few years the Trasimeno has succeeded in making itself felt even as far away as Canada.

There is another DOC zone in arrival, Montefalco which, though miniscule, is offering some good, strong country wine called Sagrantino. You are unlikely to find any unless you tour Umbria and there are many worse things to do in this valley of tears. The ancient cities of Orvieto, Assisi, Perugia and Spoleto, not to forget Gubbio, are lovely to look at and the food is simple, yet imaginative and always well prepared. There is still a certain old-style muddle in Umbrian vine cultivation and in the consequent local wines, but this, too, is not without its charms. You may come across all sorts of unexpected wines. Trebbiano and Malvasia of course lead the whites, after which one finds Grechetto and Greco, Verdicchio, Riesling, Tocai, Pinot Bianco and Sauvignon Bianco and, among the reds, the occasional Merlot, Cabernet Sauvignon and even Gamay which has a tendency to pop up in the most improbable parts of Italy. *Vin santo* is made in fair quantities in Umbria – a sweet but more often bone-dry dessert wine, rich, luxurious and velvety in taste, body and finish with a sherry-like alcoholic content of around 16–18 per cent. It is made from semi-dried grapes and matures in the wood over many years. Lungarotti makes a nice one.

THE MARCHES AND THE ABRUZZO

The Marches, with the exception of its Verdicchio di Jesi, only started serious wine production on a fully professional basis a decade ago. The progress has been very considerable and many new DOC zones have been set up. The style of the Marches' wines is a traditional central-Italian one based on the Sangiovese, Montepulciano, Malvasia Toscana and Trebbiano vines, and their own Bianchello and Verdicchio. There are no romantic Chardonnays, Rieslings, and Gamays.

This province, like Umbria, was recognized as having good prospects as a major wine-producing area by the EEC authorities, and consequently has had their encouragement and incentives to tidy up their vineyards and get down to producing a good bottled product, which has been done.

The Verdicchio di Jesi, an old Italian favourite, has been subjected to modern oenological methods and made in a sparer, cleaner style with no loss in bouquet and taste. The Verdicchio of Matelica is no second fiddle; it can stand up to Jesi criteria. If anything, it is drier and, therefore, makes a good Spumante, though I have never seen this, even in the *enotecas* of Rome; however, I am assured that it can be found in the Adriatic towns.

The three new DOC zones for whites are Bianchello di Metauro, the Falerio of the Ascoli hills and the white of the Macerata hills. They are dry, all-purpose whites to be drunk young, either as an apéritif or with light cooking. The Bianchello is a light but hard wine that concedes nothing to the aromatic, harmonious and velvety world, a wine with an alert personality. The Falerio is 80 per cent Trebbiano along with some local grapes to make it more interesting and to give it a delicacy that the Trebbiano lacks. The Macerata hills wine is also a Trebbiano composite, fresh, dry and pleasing.

The red I am more at home with, as my neighbour serves them when I dine with him and, above all, the Monte Conero with a little ageing is more than just pleasant; it has a certain Tuscan strength and vigour from its Montepulciano grape. The Piceno Rosso, like the Pesaro Hills wines, are not neatly tamed for a well-behaved society; they still have a certain independent, combative spirit, which after lots of harmonious, rounded, smooth and velvety wine, can come as a welcome relief.

The Vernaccia di Serrapetrona is something of a fossil wine. It is a sweet red Spumante which, despite its local fame, said little to me, and what it said I did not agree with. However, perhaps, the dry version, which I have not been able to nail down, is more enjoyable.

The Abruzzo region is even more mountainous than the Marches, and equally a relative newcomer even to the national wine market. In both cases, the vineyards are in the valleys which run down eastward to the Adriatic sea; and the style is again classic – Montepulciano and Trebbiano. The Trebbiano production, from around Chieti, is most pleasing, but would seem to be drunk *in toto* on the coast there, accompanying their fabulous *bouillabaisses* – one can only envy them. The Montepulciano di Abruzzo, however, is gaining a real reputation among connoisseurs. It was always a well-made wine of character, stronger when aged, and had a small but dedicated following. It has a level-eyed mountaineer's authority about it, and the best of it goes under the name Cerasuola. These Abruzzo and Marches reds are out-of-doors wines, suited to accompany a good barbecue or a hunter's meal of hare and game birds on the spit. Like mountain air, they are invigorating rather than luxuriant.

From here southwards, there is nothing to mention till one reaches Puglia which is another, and much more complex, world, that of southern Italy; a civilization of the plains, and with a softness and wealth of an easier life which, strangely enough, reflects itself in the wine.

ROME AND LAZIO

The success in the last decade of Roman Castelli wines can perhaps best be judged by there having been made recently – I am assured on the best of authority – five most generous and flattering offers for the acquisition of the Fontana Candida winery at Frascati, coming not only from Italy but also from abroad.

Also in the last ten years, the Marino Gotto d'Oro winery has also moved into the realm of advanced oenology and enjoys a new international life to which it was not accustomed. It is not up for sale, as it is a cooperative and also doing fine since the Marino grape is considered the best of the Castelli's offerings. In 1979, the Colli Albani cooperative opened up its new and technologically up-to-date winery with renewed optimism.

The wines of the Roman *castelli* – the towns of the hills south of Rome – were, once upon a time, an oenologist's nightmare: mildew, oxidation, a distaste for travelling – even to Rome, a tendency to re-ferment in summer and much else. The Romans' traditional Sunday outing was to go to the *castelli* for lunch and have a bottle of wine in its natural habitat where it somehow was always a joy, particularly on a sunny day.

Most of the Roman castle towns now have their own DOC legislations: Frascati Marino, the Alban hills (including Castelgandolfo, Ariccia and Albano Laziale), Montecompatri and Colonna (with Roccapriora and Monte Porzio), Zagarolo, Velletri and Lanuvio (with Genzano and Nemi). This has entailed a major replanting of vineyards and, what is more, their extension right down to Cori which lies in the hills beyond Velletri above the one-time Pontine Marshes. The whole area is chiefly a white-wine land based on the Tuscan Malvasia and the Trebbiano vines which produce a neutral and balanced wine that is undemanding. It makes a pleasant apéritif and one that can satisfy a wine-lover faced with a goodly Roman luncheon. The Frascati Superiore is particularly to be recommended and there are various *amabile* and sweet versions of these wines available. There is a great deal of non-DOC wine from the area, made by the cooperatives, which meets a need both for quantity and price; these wines may be strengthened and stretched also with some Sicilian and Sardinian whites which, with today's high quality production in those two islands, should worry nobody.

Reds are harder to come by in the *castelli*. Velletri has a Cesanese and Cori a Montepulciano. One must go down to the plains of Aprilia to find the Merlot and the Sangiovese which, though well-made and inexpensive, are not wines to eulogize over. In any event, the expert wine-makers there know precisely what they are doing – meeting two different markets: the screw-top city market and the strong cutting-wine market in north Italy.

In the hinterland, beyond Zagarolo, there is a new interest, this time in red wines – the Cesanese triplets: Affile, Piglio and Olevano Romano. The Cesaneses are wines which have not yet been given the full courtesies of the oenologists, yet they deserve it. They are good robust wines which, added to their coming from high in the hills (from 250 to 800 metres), giving them their character, react well to ageing in the barrel. A single year does far more than it does elsewhere – and five years in the wood can do miracles with a good *cru*. However, the sources are few and not all production methods recommended. La Selva winery, at 250 metres up near Colleferro, has made a good reputation for its aged wines, both for its Cesanese del Piglio but more for its proprietary non-DOC wine labelled as 'La Selva'. This latter is made from the same Cesanese varietal but with minor touches from other wines produced on the same estate to make a more subtly balanced wine. Their 1979 harvest has been handled by their new 1.5 million US dollar winery from which expectations are high.

Lazio has also several minor wines of Simple Denomination (DOS), the more important of which is the Cecubu, grown in vineyards prized long ago by the ancient Romans. If, by chance, the famous Roman Cecubus vine had lived for so long, it was certainly killed off by the phylloxera in the twentieth century; at all events, the wine is now made with Negromaro (a sturdy cutting-wine vine from Puglia) and Sangiovese. There is also the Maccarese estate (which belongs to the State Holding Company, the IRI) close to Rome airport, which makes a Merlot-Montepulciano red and a Tuscan Malvasia white; both are pleasing wines while their Superiore Red, labelled San Giorgio, is excellent.

SARDINIA

Sardinia should always be considered separately from mainland Italy. There are species on the island, such as rabbits and donkeys, that are far smaller than the European average, the birds are different, honey is bitter instead of sweet, and, in fact, it was the only part of Europe where the Phoenicians of Tyre and Carthage set up home with no fear of attack, so good were their relations – some 2,500 odd years ago – with the Sardinians. In the last decade, the cooperatives have set up efficient bottling plants and a fairly wide variety of local wines is now available in the grocery stores; there is also some export to the mainland and to the rest of Europe, but not much. The first company to set itself up as an international supplier was Sella and Mosca of Alghero which has aligned itself with the most up-to-date technology and, which is equally important, marketing methods and delivery deadlines. This firm is of Piedmontese origin, of the Sella family of statesmen, economists and bankers and its present capital and executives are from Piedmont, too. Piedmont was until 1870 a part of the kingdom of Sardinia which explains the connection, especially as the Piedmontese also liked the wild-boar hunting in Sardinia. At all events, Sella and Mosca is moving to place Sardinian wines on the shelves of the wine shops of the world.

If you ask anybody where the surplus wine goes to, you will get the quick reply – France. In the past, much of the strong wine of Sardinia was cut into Barolo and other fine Piedmontese wines to their great benefit; it also had the reputation for doing the same service for France's best wines. But with the AOC and DOC regulations, this is not possible, except for wines which do not come within these new legislations. Today, Germany has become a major importer of these bulk wines.

The two great wines – the Nuragus white from the broiling plains of the south and the Cannonau red, a subtle yet forceful wine from the north of the island – were the main wines used, and still are. Today, however, much bottled Cannonau di Sardegna is available also under the name Mandrolisai, when it comes up with a natural 13.5 per cent alcoholic content; if aged in the wood, it may be called Riserva, and if it has 15 per cent of alcohol (without chaptalization, of course), it may be called Superiore.

There are four mountain wines – at Oliena (Deina winery), Tortoli (Mereu winery), Jerzu (Cooperative) and Capo Ferrato (Cooperative) – which specialize in these big, stern and strong Cannonaus. They are by nature 'black' wines but also produced as rosé so as not to frighten the children. The alcoholic content ranges from 15–18 per cent and their aroma and stimulating effect is unforgettable. One can easily understand the contribution they can make to the overall character of other wines. The other great Sardinian wine is the Nuragus. It has been tamed for direct public consumption to 12 per cent but it must have saved many northern (including Roman) and foreign wines from anaemia in its role as a full-bodied cutting-wine. The bottled DOC version, today, is made from vines grown in the hills *a spalliera* and with cool and slow fermentation and other new processes to give a more delicate wine. Unlike the Cannonau but like the mainland Trebbiano, it is a neutral wine which makes it a good all-purpose wine.

Sardinia has one particularly delicate wine, the Vermentino of Gallura, from the north of the island. It makes a most welcome apéritif and partner for light dishes; however, the Superiore at a minimum of 14 per cent alcoholic content is by no means as 'light' as it seems, as it often has only a minimum of 14 per cent which may well turn out to be over 15 per cent. Another two whites which have suave and enticing personalities are the Torbato and the Dorato di Sorso, the latter being a red Cannonau processed *in bianco*.

Better known in Italy and even abroad is the Vernaccia di Oristano. A Superiore Vernaccia is a dry dessert wine, aged in the wood for three years and with a natural 15.5 per cent, or often more, of alcoholic content. It makes a good drink at any time and those with good heads enjoy it as a table wine, accepting the risk of not being able to get up from the table afterwards.

The Sella and Mosca company has its own dessert wine called the Red Angel (Anghelu Ruju in Sardinian), which is sweet (7 per cent of residual sugar) *passito*, fortified so that it has an 18 per cent alcoholic content, after which it is aged for three to four years in the wood; it is well suited for cocktails and for being passed around the table at the end of a convivial dinner. It is made from the Cannonau grape.

The Monica di Sardegna has made great strides in the late 1970s as a light dry red, such as is fashionable nowadays; an undemanding wine with a low acidity and requiring little attention. However, the Monica Superiore, at 14 per cent and a little ageing, is something to take more seriously. The Sardinians also have a Sibiola from the Cantina Sociale di Monserrato which they like but which probably has never been seen far beyond Cagliari; for the record, it is a Barbera, Monica, Cannonau blend and most successful at that. Relatively new are the Terralba and Carignano DOC zones for red wines, made by the three local cooperatives of the south-western plains; but these will have to stand in line and wait their turn for some recognition. The Carignano is a formidable black wine of full body and delicate bouquet, but lacks the acidity necessary for long ageing.

The wines, however, that have been recognized for decades, and perhaps centuries, are the dessert wines; their origin surely lies somewhere during the three hundred years of Spanish domination of the island between the fifteenth and seventeenth centuries. On pages 322–5, the reader will find many details of the Malvasia di Bosa, the Malvasia di Cagliari, the Moscato di Cagliari and the Nasco di Cagliari which are all liquid gold; while the Giro di Cagliari and the Monica di Cagliari are deep, luxuriant, velvety reds. In the general contemporary stampede away from hard drinking (especially on an empty stomach), it surprises me that the world has not caught up with these wines. The regular style is a straight unchaptalized 14 per cent of alcohol; the *liquoroso* version (i.e. fortified like a Port or Sherry with wine alcohol) runs to 17–18 per cent which is also the same strength as a Sherry. However, the straight edition is full and warm enough to know that you have had a drink; unlike the Vernaccia, even the *secco* has a certain sweetness but this is in no way cloying. The ladies of Cagliari do not go out when it rains; instead they enjoy, for example, a Nasco – which is alleged to be the wine alive today closest in character to the one-time famous Imperial Tokay dessert wine of the Austro-Hungarian empire where even sabre-rattling cavalry officers drank it with relish. At all events, Sardinia offers a lot of pleasures, intriguing discoveries and many liquid subjects upon which to meditate.

THE BAY OF NAPLES AND THE CAMPANIA

On the way to Naples from Calabria we traverse unending miles of mountainous countryside, of subsistence-farming with very little useful agricultural land. The hinterland of the bay of Salerno is the beginning of economic sanity and, therefore, activity. The Campania is a large producer of wines but with few great and famous ones: 300 million litres (a little more than Lombardy's production); but it produces very little DOC wine. Despite that, the Campania's wines are unusual ones and worth seeking out, also because they are little known. The hinterland in this case is Avellino, land of emigration and ungenerous soil. Here, Mastroberadino wineries have, over the decades, built up an unchallengeable reputation based on vines of Greek origin, of a 'northern type' and excellent quality control.

There are two fine whites, the Greco di Tufo and the Fiano (the former perhaps the better) both 12 per cent wines with a lithe but firm body, persistent, delightful bouquets and an affectionate finish. The Taurasi is, however, the giant – a big Aglianico which needs three years ageing in the wood and some vintages enjoy as much as fifteen years in the wood and the bottle to reach their optimum.

Mastroberadino has, one might say, nailed down the Lacryma Christi and got the copyright. For decades, any producer could and did put a Lacryma Christi label on any sweet *frizzante* wine he had to hand, but this era of Neapolitan levity is over. Lacryma Christi must now come from vineyards on the lower slopes of Vesuvius and the results today, under Mastroberadino's label, are most satisfactory. There is a red and a rosé, both fresh, dry and with a heady aroma. The rosé is traditionally the correct style for this historic wine.

Before the DOC legislation, there was some considerable confusion with Ischia and Capri wines; it was not that they were not good and enjoyable, but that often they were mainland wines hiding under false colours. But things seem to have changed even in Naples and the wines also are much better now. This is particularly so of the Ischia Superiore white at 12 per cent alcohol, made from the island's indigenous vines grown there. It is a good seafood partner.

Capri has at last joined the DOC club and has been given a little leeway in its production, probably in view of the flood of thirsty tourists that arrives every summer. They may use wine from certain communes on the slopes of Vesuvius under the Capri label. These wines, and those of Capri, are from the excellent Greco and Piedirosso vines used by Mastroberadino in his distinguished wines.

The delicate, but remarkably strong red, white and rosé Caruso wines made in the hills above Amalfi at Ravello have always succeeded in enchanting, particularly when dining there with a long view over the Bay of Salerno. On the other side of the Lattere mountains, which make the spine of the Sorrento peninsula, there is a wine of a very different nature – the Gragnano. It is a fine red and even better well-aged. It is a great wine in need of a master oenologist and producer to bring it to the fame it deserves. Saviano, a producer of Ottaviano-Vesuvius (you have not seen the

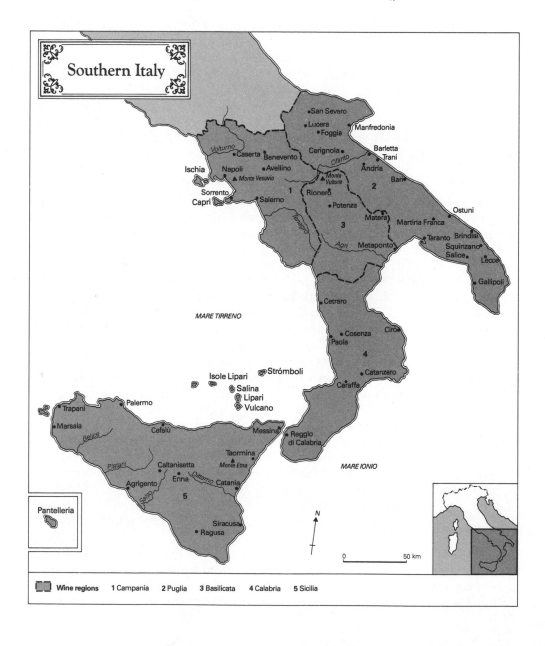

Wine regions   1 Campania   2 Puglia   3 Basilicata   4 Calabria   5 Sicilia

real Naples till you have been there), buys it and bottles it. The Ravello and Gragnano wines are non-DOC. The Fiano of Avellino, a new DOC wine, is making its reputation as a partner to accompany fish and seafood, due to its good body and fragrance. To wind up, there is the famous non-DOC Per'e' Palummo; a ruby red wine which the Ischians enjoy with all well-spiced seafoods, such as stewed octopus, and the 'ancient' Roman Falernum white, still well-made by Cena Tiempo of Formia. The initial gloom at looking at the Campania's vinous offerings, on closer observation, like the sun burning out the morning mist, turns to a certain anticipatory desire to indulge in a little *dolce-far-niente*, sipping wine while sitting comfortably on a terrace overlooking the sea. This is certainly a region to watch.

PUGLIA

The flood of wine, a thousand million hectolitres, that Puglia can and does produce is formidable. It is, for the most part, wine of good quality. There are many wineries with long-standing and high reputations for their bottled table wines; most of the wine used in making vermouth is from Puglia as is much of the cutting-wine sent to north Italy and across European borders; huge quantities of inexpensive wine are bottled locally in two-litre flagons and demijohns, and still there is a surplus of some 100 million litres of perfectly good wine in most years which is destined to end its days at cost-price as industrial alcohol. With a growing and richer local market, in the last ten to fifteen years, the bottling of wine has at last become commonplace; previously, the wineries loaded tanker trucks and tanker ships as it was their easiest way of marketing their wines, given their lack of infrastructure, both commercial and technical.

Today, most of the producers are thoroughly conversant with the new oenology and have equipped their wineries accordingly; particularly to face the problem of the broiling summer heat which causes a violent fermentation of the grapes, and the problem of excessive oxidation due to the outdated equipment and the consequent southern taste so much denigrated at home and abroad. Many of the top producers long ago planted their table-wine vineyards in the hills with notable success.

Here, in the past, the problem lay in the grapes maturing too soon (even in August and with a second crop in October!) and with an excess of sugar for table wines. Cultivation in the plains was suited best for cutting-wines and for the sweet table grapes for which Puglia is famous and a major supplier of the European markets.

The names of Sansevero (from the D'Alfonso del Sordo winery at Sansevero), Castel del Monte (from Premiovini of Torre Sveva), Torre Quarto (from Farrusi of Cerignola), Rivera (the Rivera winery at Andria) and the Salento wines (from Leone de Castris of Salice and Renna of Squinzano) are a traditional part of Italian eno-gastronomy and, as such, nobody who knows his way around Italian wines would spurn any of them. An aged Torre Quarto is a particularly fine dinner wine which I would feel confident in having served to the most critical of guests, sure that they could not fault me in my choice or taste. The Rivera rosés are something on their own – they are apéritifs, blending with all sorts of light food especially lobsters, crayfish, shrimps and prawns and also with strawberries and icecream – try it, and plenty of other unusual combinations will come to mind. It is dry, velvety and round and a fabulous pink.

The Salento wines, when dry, are big, full-bodied and something to remember. When the fermentation has been switched off early and they leave a part of their sugar in its natural state, you have the most luxuriant of *amabile* dessert wines which are the symbol of the deep Italian south. If a natural dessert wine, it will have 15 per cent of alcohol and if fortified (*liquoroso*), around 18 per cent which is equal to a Port or a Sherry. The Moscato of Trani (by the Gennaro Marasciulo and Picardi wineries of Trani) are well known in this discreet tippling field, as are some of the products of Signor Leone de Castris. These above-mentioned producers all have their whites and rosés which are now made to fit the European taste and can be fully recommended. However, there is another type of white, less known but with more fight in it. It is the full-bodied wine that goes to make most of the white vermouth in Europe. This has been further refined as a table wine and I would say that it is the only type of white that can really stand up to a jumbo plate of well-garlicked and peppered *bouillabaisse*: these wines are now DOC'd under the names Locorotondo, Martina Franca and Ostuni-and-Ottavianello. The most renowned winery of this zone is Miali of Martinafranca.

BASILICATA

Moving from the Adriatic to the mountains of the west, one finds the great loner of Italian wines – the Aglianico del Vulture, a major producer of which, of all improbabilities, is the Crédit Suisse bank. The Basilicata province where it is found is among the most forgotten and ignored of all Italy, and even the volcano on the slopes of which Aglianico vines grow is extinct. The Basilicata (also called Lucania) has been through history a colony of Puglia, but has recently awakened to its possible independence in the wine field, especially at Metaponto on the shores of the Gulf of Taranto. We shall hear more of these wines, but not immediately. The proof that the area has a vocation for fine wines is the Vulture wine which is superb; not only a wine for roasts of beef, lamb and pork but a wine for roast venison, hung pheasants and quail, wild boar and any other strong meat. Its vine of Greek origin, the volcanic soil and the ageing-in-the-wood present a wine-style subtly yet profoundly different from the claret-Chianti-Burgundy-Barolo world. It still speaks Italian with a slight foreign accent, even after millennia of residence, and there, too, lies a lot of its charm and, at the same time, like the Magna-Graecia philosophers of of these parts they would never have reached their paramount wisdom, had they not been transplanted to Italy.

CALABRIA

Like the Aglianico del Vulture, the Cirò is also a wine of Greek origin. The production is fairly large and reaches its apex in the classic zone and with its three-year-old Riservas. The town of Cirò is on the instep of the foot of Italy at the mouth of the Gulf of Taranto where the Ionian Sea begins. We are, of course, in a land of ancient Grecian and Bacchic myth where one finds the recently excavated ruins of Sybarus, the Greek city which lived life up so well that it earned itself a place as an adjective in the English language for its luxury. A little further down the coast – under Italy's big toe, so to speak – there is the town of Gerace which would probably have passed unnoticed by most travellers and *cognoscenti* in these parts were it not for its two remarkable wines – the Greco of Gerace (or Greco di Bianco) and the Mantonico, both whites. The former is a 16–18 per cent alcohol dessert wine, sweet when young, that quickly becomes dry with ageing. It is best made by Umberto Cerratti of Caraffa del Bianco. It is expensive because each vine only yields one bottle of golden wine from the sunbaked soil – but what a bottle! The other wine is the Mantonico, equally amber coloured and with an intense bouquet which requires a little ageing, but not too much for oxidation reasons. They are not party or gossip-group wines but, rather, at most to be shared with one other person, and a fond one, in moments of supreme tranquility.

Wine production on the Tyrrhenian coast of Calabria was tidied up by the Ente Sila; this is a para-governmental corporation capitalized for the purpose of the agricultural and animal-husbandry development of the whole mountainous hinterland of Calabria. These wines, due in part to the fact that they are grown at 700 metres above sea-level, and because of high quality, are inevitably not inexpensive and, since they are little known, do not find an easy market. Most impressive to me are the bright rosé Pellaro, a wine with a hint of *abboccato*, considerable body and a big bouquet, and the Enotria white with a nose that is redolent of fresh sea-breezes and the mountain pines. Not to be discounted are the Savuto and Pollino reds, the Donnici, the Melissa Ciro and the Sant'Anna, all dry-dry wines produced in the Sila highlands. When I first met these wines over five years ago, I reported that some could justify a year or two of ageing and I am happy to see that the Savuto and the Pollino, by DOC legislation, now have a Superiore rating requiring two years in the wood. This 'little Switzerland' in the heart of the Mediterranean has, only in the last two decades, been opened up with roads and the odd hotel. Naturally, these mountain wines do not have the defect of the 'southern' taste and are processed, in any case, according to modern criteria.

SICILY

At the end of the Second World War Sicily nearly succeeded in seceding from Italy to make itself an independent state, but it finally opted for autonomy within the Italian republic. However, this outburst of new energy had its effect in arousing this land of antique civilization to come to terms with the present. Economically speaking, Sicily was not, in modern terms, viable. Except for half a dozen large estates owned by the old aristocracy – the Tascas, the Villagrandes and the Salaparutas – the land was split up into small homesteads. Today, 70,000 of such little farms are members of cooperatives to which they supply grapes. This has been one of the most remarkable changes in the social life of Sicily in 3,000 years: the small-holder can at last protect himself and get the proper market price for his product.

The Sicilian soil was eroded, compacted and back-breaking to work. By the grace of God, and with the aid of tractors, the task of giving new life to the soil became a practical proposition on a large scale. The Regional Vine and Wine Institute of Palermo (Instituto della Vita e del Vino) chose new vines to plant, counselled on the setting up of the cooperatives which, in turn, acquired farm machinery and the latest in wine-making plant. The most inspired of the Wine Institute's recommendations was that of slowly letting a large part of the old vine-yards on the plains die and of setting up new ones with the new vines in the hills.

This concept requires some explanation. The old vineyards on the plains were planted with vines for making cutting-wines – that is, high-alcohol, high-colour wines that come from pruning back the vine to a bush so that it produces a few five-kilogram bunches of very sweet grapes. Since the new DOC legislation was going to make it largely illegal for north Italian wine producers to add cutting-wines to their DOC wines, Sicily was going to lose its market, at least in part; they could still sell their produce for non-DOC wines and for export. It was concluded that Sicily would be better off producing table wines for export. However, the vineyards on the plains are not entirely suitable for this role; the soil is poor and the summer heat, torrid. The Vine Institute, therefore, recommended that the hill-land behind the coastal plains should be ploughed up deeply and planted in modern style, leaving room for tractors and trucks to pass between the lines of vines. Further, small dams and reservoirs were constructed in the hills to ensure irrigation through-out the long, rainless summer.

The ultimate step, so as to make table wine of a normal 11–12 per cent alcoholic content rather than a cutting-wine of 18 per cent alcohol, was to set up the vines so that, instead of being cropped back as low bushes (*ad alberello*), they grew up 1.5-metre high cement stakes and then along wires; this system is called *a spalliera* and *a tendone*: and when there is a complete roof over the vineyard it is called *a pergola*.

All in all, the Sicilians have reached now a total of 200,000 hectares of renovated vineyards, producing 800 million litres of wine which even the Gallos of California would consider quite a lot of wine. Almost all of this restructuring has taken place in western Sicily in the provinces of Palermo, Trapani and Agrigento. Today, half of this considerable production is exported. Much of the remainder is sold for making vermouths and the wine concentrates that northern Italian producers are allowed to add in very modest quantities to their wines to bring up the alcoholic percentage, normally half a per cent, in poor years.

These wines made by the cooperatives, on the recommendation of the Vine Institute, have been selected and processed to meet contemporary taste abroad more than at home. This may not bring joy to old-style wine-lovers but there is still plenty of old-style wine available for them, in Sicily also. The new wines are light, fresh and soft ones and it must also be said that they are genuine. They are wines that can be tossed back cheerfully and without requiring too much aesthetic and intellectual concentration. They are wines to be enjoyed. Gone is the southern taste – heavy, maderized and too alcoholic; today, Sicilian table wine retains its individual taste and is a well-stabilized and thoroughly conventional wine from all other aspects.

The fact is that Sicily, Puglia and Sardinia are the inexhaustible cellars of Europe. Sicily has now fifty-five cooperatives, thirty-seven of which are in the province of Trapani. However, their production being to a great extent on virgin lands or on former cornfields, cannot get into any DOC category since one of the criteria is that the land must have a long tradition of producing a certain type of wine, in a certain manner and with the winery within the boundaries of the growing area. It will, of course, be some many years before these requirements can be met and, for that matter, before we can cope mentally and gastronomically with the abundance that they are producing. There is the astonishing grand total of 150 different wines, bottled and labelled in Sicily – DOC and non-DOC – and of all types, from table wines to highly alcoholic dessert wines of which latter the Sicilians have been specialists over the centuries.

Sicily still has its well-known fine wines which also have been modernized in their vineyard and processing operations; these include the various Marsalas, the Corvo of Salaparuta, the Regaleali of Tasca d'Almerita and the Etna wines of Barone Villagrande. Less known are the d'Angelo winery of Alcamo, the Di Giuseppe of Partinico, the Diego Rallo of Marsala (a producer also of table wines), Faustus of Casteldaccia, the Florio, producer of Marsala and also an excellent brandy.

On the subject of Marsala, it can be said that it represents, along with Madeira, Port and Sherry, nineteenth-century imperial Britain's sally into the wine-producing field. The sun may never have set on the Empire, but England itself remained a very chilly place where a glass of well-aged wine, elegantly fortified with wine-alcohol and processed in a complete but basically economical way – the *solera* system – was most welcome at any time of the day or night. All four wines are full-bodied, Mediterranean-style, made from grapes which have completely matured in a broiling heat. The addition of wine-alcohol guaranteed the stability of the wine, thus ensuring that it would arrive in the London docks or in any part of the far-flung empire in prime condition; this was very important in a period of history when oenology had not overcome the stability problems, particularly those which involved taking casks of wine in sailing ships across the equator and around the Cape of Good Hope.

With the years, the ownership of Marsala left British hands and the tradition was continued by Sicilian growers and shippers. Today, one might say that Giovanni Agnelli, the chairman of the FIAT motor company, has taken the place of

Bardolino vineyards near Lake Garda in the Veneto
(Overleaf) Harvesting grapes at Castell'in Villa, a 'specializzata' vineyard,
near San Gusmè in the south east of the Chianti Classico zone

Mssrs Woodhouse and Ingram through the Florio Marsala company, a subsidiary of the Cinzano Vermouth company which, in turn, is a subsidiary of FIAT. Marsala is still popular as an apéritif and as a post-prandial drink, and it is probably made far better today than it was when Lord Nelson used to buy it for his fleet in the 1790s. It comes dry and sweet, long aged and less aged. The younger and more inexpensive Marsalas are particularly useful in the kitchen for enhancing many recipes.

Among the offerings of other wineries, the following DOC and non-DOC labels can be recommended – Segesta, Normanno, Castelvecchio, Donzelle, Draceno, Saturno, Settesole, Solunto, Gebbia, Alcamo Bianco, Moscato of Pantelleria, Moscato of Syracuse, Faro, Cerasuola of Vittoria, Alberello, Birgi Bianco, Mamertina, Vespri Stravecchio, Ciclopi, Eloro Rosso, Fenicio Stravecchio, Rapitala and Zibibbo. On pages 330–2 the wines and suggested producers are listed in greater detail.

A GAZETTEER OF ITALIAN WINES

This is a list of DOC zones and relative wines, with names of recommended producers of each wine. The list is divided into regional sections.

You should prefix all addresses with Azienda Vinicola (wine company) but in the case that the address given is insufficient, it is suggested that, to communicate with any of the following wine producers, contact be made through the Italian Trade Commissioners or through the provincial Chambers of Commerce (Camere di Commercio). For more detailed information (geographical, chemical, organoleptic, and prohibitions) regarding specific DOC legislation, the Italian State Official Gazette is the ultimate authority; the serial number and the date of relative publication is printed against each DOC zone section. The gazettes are available for reference at Italian consulates.

DOC: The Italian wine law of 1963 regulated production and labelling of wines of 'particular reputation and worth', aiming to protect these specific wines produced in specifically defined areas and under clearly laid-down disciplines. This legislation is called Denominazione di Origine Controllata, hence DOC.

DOCG (Guaranteed DOC): In the first instance, 'select wines of particular excellence' will be subject to more rigorous controls. The 'guaranteed' refers to a direct government control and the sealing of each bottle with a government stamp as is already the case with spirits. Brunello di Montalcino was included in this new category in 1980 and Barbaresco, Barolo, Chianti and Vin Nobile di Montalcino are expected to be included in 1981. The description given under each DOC zone that follows are the barebones requirements of the law and do not take into account the myriad subtleties and nuances of the various wines caused by the infinite factors involved in their production. Alcohol is expressed in per cent by volume and refers to the minimum total alcoholic content for the DOC.

VAL D'AOSTA

1979 vintage – good quality and ample yield.

Donnaz (87–5.6.1971)

A Nebbiolo, with a maximum yield of 75 quintals per hectare, produces a dry red wine; minimum alcohol 11.5 per cent. Ageing at least three years, two in the wood being obligatory. Produced by:

Caves Cooperatives de Donnaz, Donnaz, Aosta   Luigi Ferrando, Ivrea, Torino

The Institute of San Michele all'Adige in the Trentino is one of the foremost oenological schools in Italy; it specializes in viticulture but now also makes and sells its own wine

Enfer d'Arvier (112–10.8.1972)

A Petit Rouge vine, maximum yield 50 quintals per hectare, produces a dry red wine; minimum alcohol 11.5 per cent; one year ageing in the wood obligatory.
Also recommended non-DOC wines: Blanc de Morgex produced by both Luigi Ferrando and Les Riboteurs, La Salle, Aosta; and Blanc de la Salle by Les Riboteurs, La Salle, Aosta.

PIEDMONT

1979 vintage – good quality and ample yield.

Barbaresco (145–14.6.1966 and 244–26.9.1970)

A Nebbiolo vine (sub-species Michet, Lampia and Rosé), at 80 quintals per hectare, produces a dry red wine; minimum alcohol 12.5 per cent. Two year's ageing obligatory. If three years in the wood, the wine can be called Riserva; if four years, Riserva Speciale. To be categorized DOCG in 1981. Produced by:

Antica Casa Scarpa, Nizza Monferrato, Asti
Barbaresco Societa Cooperativa, Barbaresco, Cuneo
Bersano, Nizza Monferrato, Asti
Borgogno, Barolo, Cuneo
Luigi Bosca, Canelli, Asti
Bruzzone, Strevi, Alessandria
Luigi Calissano, Alba, Cuneo
Cantina del Parroco di Neive, Neive, Cuneo
Giorgio Carnevale, Rocchetta Tanaro, Asti
Castello di Neive, Neive, Cuneo

Giacomo Conterno, Monforte d'Alba, Cuneo
Giuseppe Contratto, Canelli, Asti
Franco Fiorina, Alba, Cuneo
Angelo Gaja, Barbaresco, Cuneo
Bruno Giacosa, Neive, Cuneo
La Brenta d'Oro, Vezza d'Alba, Cuneo
La Spinona, Barbaresco, Cuneo
Lorenzo Lodali, Treiso, Cuneo
Marchesi di Barolo, Barolo, Cuneo
Fratelli Oddero, La Morra, Cuneo
Alfredo Prunotto, Alba, Cuneo
Francesco Rinaldi, Alba, Cuneo

Barbera d'Alba (228–9.9.1970; 15–16.1.1978)

This dry red wine is obtained exclusively from the Barbera grape, at a yield of 100 quintals per hectare; to produce a wine of a minimum alcohol content of 11.5 per cent. If this is 12 per cent and the wine has been aged for at least two years, one of which must be in the bottle, it may be called Superiore. Produced by:

Giacomo Ascheri, Bra, Cuneo
Bersano, Nizza Monferrato, Asti
Giacomo Borgogno, Barolo, Cuneo
Cantina del Parroco di Neive, Neive, Cuneo
Adorno Cattaneo Gabiano, Monferrato, Asti
Cavallotto, Castiglione Falletto, Cuneo
Riccardo Ceretto, Alba, Cuneo
Pio Cesare, Alba, Cuneo
Giacomo Conterno, Monforte d'Alba, Cuneo

Eredi di Luigi Einaudi, Dogliani, Cuneo
Fontanafredda, Serralunga d'Alba, Cuneo
Bruno Giacosa, Neive, Cuneo
Kiola, La Morra, Cuneo
La Brenta d'Oro, Vezza d'Alba, Cuneo
Marchesi di Barolo, Barolo, Cuneo
Fratelli Oddero, La Morra, Cuneo
Mario Savigliano, Diano d'Alba, Cuneo
Giuseppe Sordo, Castiglione Falletto, Cuneo
Valletti, La Morra, Cuneo
Vietti, Castiglione Falletto, Cuneo

Barbera d'Asti (73–23.3.1970; 9–10.1.1978)

A Barbera that produces a dry red wine with a minimum alcohol content of 12 per cent. If aged for two years, of which one must be in the wood, and with 12.5 per cent of alcohol, the wine may be labelled Superiore. Produced by:

Guido Acuto, Grana Monferrato, Asti
Giuseppe Baldo, Bionzo di Costigliole, Asti

Carlo Baldovino, Boglietto di Costigliole, Asti
Pietro Barbero, Moasca, Asti

Fratelli Baucheri, Cocconata, Asti
Bava Cantine, Cocconata, Asti
Bersano, Nizza Monferrato, Asti
Boidi di Borgogno Dante, Calosso d'Asti, Asti
Luigi Bosca, Canelli, Asti
Enoteca Braida, Rocchetta Tanaro, Asti
Bruzzone, Strevi, Alessandria
Luigi Calissano, Alba, Cuneo

Cantina Sociale Cooperativa di Canelli, Asti
Cantina Sociale di Casorzo, Casorzo, Asti
Giuseppe Contratto, Canelli, Asti
Amilcare Gaudio, Bricco Mondalino, Vignale Monferrato, Alessandria
Scarpa Antica Casa, Nizza Monferrato, Asti
Luigi Trinchero, San Martino Alfieri, Asti
G. L. Viarengo, Castello d'Annone, Asti

Barbera del Monferrato (72 – 21.3.1970; 162 – 14.6.1979)

A Barbera, with up to 15 per cent of Freisa, Grignolino and Dolcetto, produces a dry red wine; minimum alcohol 12 per cent. With two years' ageing and 12.5 per cent alcohol, it may be labelled Superiore. Produced by:

Lorenzo Bertolo, Torino
Bruzzone, Strevi, Alessandria
Luigi Calissano, Alba, Cuneo
Castello di Lignano, Frassinello Monferrato, Alessandria
Amilcare Gaudio, Bricco Mondalino, Vignale Monferrato, Alessandria

Livio Pavese, Treville Monferrato, Alessandria
Giovanni Rossi, Pratochiuso, Vignale Monferrato, Alessandria
Tenuta dei Re, Castagnole Monferrato, Asti

Barolo (146 – 15.6.1966 and 244 – 26.9.1970)

This dry red wine is derived from the sub-species of the Nebbiolo vine called Michet, Lampia and Rosé. It is produced at 80 quintals per hectare and must offer a minimum alcohol content of 13 per cent. It must have three years' ageing, of which two must be in the wood. If matured for over four years, it may be called Riserva and if for more than five years, Riserva Speciale. It is one of the wines which will be included in the DOCG legislation in 1981. Produced by:

Bersano, Nizza Monferrato, Asti
Giacomo Borgogno, Barolo, Cuneo
Luigi Bosca, Canelli, Asti
Bruzzone, Strevi, Alessandria
Luigi Calissano, Alba, Cuneo
Carretta, Piobesi d'Alba, Cuneo
Olivio and Gildo Cavallotto, Castiglione Falletto, Cuneo
Riccardo Ceretto, Alba, Cuneo
Consorzio Agrario Asti, Bobbio, Piacenza
Pio Cesare, Alba, Cuneo
Giacomo Conterno, Monforte d'Alba, Cuneo

Giuseppe Contratto, Canelli, Asti
Franco Fiorina, Alba, Cuneo
Fontanafredda, Serralunga d'Alba, Cuneo
Bruno Giacosa, Neive, Cuneo
La Brenta d'Oro, Vezza d'Alba, Cuneo
Marchesi di Barolo, Barolo, Cuneo
Fratelli Oddero, La Morra, Cuneo
Alfredo Prunotto, Alba, Cuneo
Renato Ratti, La Morra, Cuneo
Francesco Rinaldi, Alba, Cuneo
Scarpa Antica Casa, Nizza Monferratto, Asti
Vielti, Castiglione

Boca (226 – 5.9.1969)

A Nebbiolo, with some Vespolina and Bonarda, produces a dry red wine; minimum alcohol 12 per cent. Ageing at least three years, two of which are in the wood. Produced by:

Cantina Sociale di Fara, Fara, Novara
Ermanno Conti, Maggiora, Novara
Podere ai Valloni, Boca, Novara

Ronchetto Cantine, Boca, Novara
Vallana e Figlio, Maggiora, Novara

Brachetto d'Acqui (282 – 7.11.1969)

A Brachetto, with up to 10 per cent of Aleatico and Moscato Nero and a yield of 80 quintals per hectare, produces a sweet red wine which is *pétillant* if bottled young;

minimum alcohol 11.5 per cent. Produced by:

Abbazia di San Gaudenzo, Santo Stefano Belbo, Cuneo

Bersano, Nizza Monferrato, Asti

Brama Antiche Cantine, Incisa Scapaccino, Asti

Cantina Sociale Maranzana, Maranzana d'Asti, Asti

Bramaterra (285 – 18.10.1979)

A Nebbiolo, with a little Cabernet and Bonarda, produces a dry red wine; minimum alcohol 12 per cent. With 13 per cent and three years' ageing in the wood, it may be labelled Riserva. Produced by Sella Bramaterra, Villa del Bosco, Lessona, Vercelli.

Carema (199 – 9.8.1967)

A Nebbiolo (Picutener, Pugnet, Nebbiolo-Spanna), at 80 quintals per hectare, produces a dry red wine; minimum alcohol 12 per cent. At least four years' ageing, of which two in the wood are obligatory. Produced by:

Lorenzo Bertolo, Torino

Cantina dei Produttori 'Nebbiolo di Carema', Torino

Luigi Ferrando, Ivrea, Torino

Colli Tortonesi (68 – 13.3.1974)

Two wines are covered by this legislation – a white and a red. The former is a Cortese, at 100 quintals per hectare and 10 per cent of alcohol. The red is Barbera, with 15 per cent of Freisa, Bonarda Piedmontese, Dolcetto, at a yield of 90 quintals per hectare. Minimum alcohol 11.5 per cent; if alcohol content is 12.5 per cent and wine aged for two years, one of which in the wood, the wine may be labelled Superiore. Produced by:

Sergio Borasi, Villaromagnano, Alessandria

Cantina Sociale di Tortona, Tortona, Alessandria

Cantina Volpi, Tortona, Alessandria

Cortese di Gavi or *Gavi* (294 – 12.11.1974)

The Cortese, with 100 quintals per hectare, produces a dry white wine; minimum alcohol 10 per cent. It may be used to make a sparkling wine. Produced by:

Bersano, Nizza Monferrato, Asti

Luigi Bosca, Canelli, Asti

Bruzzone, Strevi, Alessandria

Cantina del Gavi, Gavi, Alessandria

La Brenta d'Oro, Vezza d'Alba, Cuneo

La Piacentina, Gavi, Alessandria

La Scolca, Gavi, Alessandria

Olivari Pastorino, La Giustiniana, Rovereto di Gavi Ligure, Alessandria

Pinelli-Gentile, Tagliolo Monferrato, Alessandria

Raggio d'Azeglio, Gavi, Alessandria

Cortese dell'Alto Monferrato (322 – 26.11.1979)

A Cortese, with a 100-quintal yield per hectare, produces a dry white wine; minimum alcohol 10 per cent. May be transformed into a sparkling wine. Produced by Bruzzone, Strevi, Alessandria.

Dolcetto d'Acqui (308 – 27.11.1972)

A Dolcetto, at 80 quintals per hectare, produces a dry red wine; minimum alcohol 11.5 per cent. With a minimum alcohol content of 12.5 per cent and one year's ageing, the wine may be labelled Superiore. Produced by:

Bruzzone, Strevi, Alessandria

Cantina Sociale Canelli, Canelli, Asti

G. B. Merlo, Acqui Terme, Alessandria

Dolcetto d'Alba (276 – 23.10.1974)

A Dolcetto, at 90 quintals per hectare, produces a dry red wine; minimum alcohol

11.5 per cent. With a minimum alcohol content of 12.5 per cent and one year's ageing, the wine may be labelled Superiore. Produced by:

Giacomo Ascheri, Bra, Cuneo
Giacomo Borgogno, Barolo, Cuneo
Luigi Bosca, Canelli, Asti
Luigi Calissano, Alba, Cuneo
Cantine del Parocco di Neive, Cuneo
Carretta, Piobesi d'Alba, Cuneo
Cavallotto, Castiglione Faletto, Cuneo
Ceretto, Alba, Cuneo
Giacomo Conterno, Monforte d'Alba, Cuneo

Franco Fiorina, Alba, Cuneo
Fontanafredda, Alba, Cuneo
Bruno Giacosa, Neive, Cuneo
Kiola, La Morra, Cuneo
La Brenta d'Oro, Vezza d'Alba, Cuneo
Renato Ratti, Abbazia Annunziata, La Morra, Cuneo

Dolcetto d'Asti (269 – 15.10.1974)

A Dolcetto, at 80 quintals per hectare, produces a dry red wine; minimum alcohol 11.5 per cent. To be labelled Superiore, one year's ageing and 12.5 per cent alcohol content are required. Produced by:

Bava Cantine, Cocconato, Asti
Bersano, Nizza Monferrato, Asti
Borgogno Dante, Calosso, Asti
Brema Antiche Cantine, Incisa Scapaccino, Asti
Cantina Sociale Canelli, Canelli, Asti

Cantina Sociale Maranzana, Maranzana, Asti
Castelvero Antica Contea, Castelboglione, Asti

Dolcetto di Diano d'Alba (269 – 15.10.1974)

A Dolcetto, at 80 quintals per hectare, produces a dry red wine; minimum alcohol 12 per cent. With a minimum alcohol content of 12.5 per cent and one year's ageing, the wine may be labelled Superiore. Produced by:

Mario Savigliano, Diano d'Alba, Cuneo

Terre del Barolo, Castiglione Falletto, Cuneo

Dolcetto di Dogliani (299 – 16.11.1974)

A Dolcetto, at 80 quintals per hectare, produces a dry red wine; minimum alcohol 11.5 per cent. With a minimum alcohol content of 12.5 per cent and one year's ageing, the wine may be labelled Superiore. Produced by:

Cantina Sociale del Dolcetto, Clavesana Cuneo

Eredi di Luigi Einaudi, Dogliani, Cuneo
Mirella Luzi Donadei, Clavesana, Cuneo

Dolcetto delle Langhe Monregalesi (276 – 23.10.1974)

A Dolcetto, at 70 quintals per hectare, produces a dry red wine; minimum alcohol 11 per cent. To be labelled Superiore, one year's ageing and 12 per cent alcohol content are required. Produced by:

Giacomo Borgogno, Barolo, Cuneo
Giuseppe Contratto, Canelli, Asti

Marchesi di Barolo, Barolo, Cuneo

Dolcetto d'Ovada (311 – 30.11.1972)

A Dolcetto, at 95 quintals per hectare, produces a dry red wine; minimum alcohol 11.5 per cent. With a minimum alcohol content of 12.5 per cent and one year's ageing, the wine may be labelled Superiore. Produced by:

Agostino Pestarino, Silvano d'Orba, Alessandria
Giuseppe Luigi Ratto, Cascina Oliva, Ovada, Alessandria

Savoia, Roccagrimalda, Alessandria
Terre del Dolcetto, Cantina Sociale, Presco, Alessandria

Erbaluce di Caluso, Caluso Passito, Caluso Liquoroso (203 – 14.8.1967)

The Erbaluce vine, with 5 per cent Bonarda, at 120 quintals per hectare, produces a sweet dessert wine; minimum alcohol 13.5 per cent through the use of semi-dried grapes. Five years' ageing in the wood is obligatory. It is also made as a white table wine with an 11 per cent alcohol content. Produced by:

Lorenzo Bertolo, Torino

Renato Bianco, Caluso, Torino

Luigi Ferrando, Ivrea, Torino

Maria Boux Passera, Caluso, Torino

Instituto Carlo Ubertini, Caluso, Torino

Fara (279 – 5.11.1969)

A Nebbiolo (locally called Spanna), with Vespolina and Bonarda, at 110 quintals per hectare, produces a dry red wine; minimum alcohol 12 per cent. Three years' ageing are obligatory, of which two must be in the wood. Produced by:

Cantina Sociale Colli Novaresi, Fara
  Novarese, Novara

Luigi Dessilani, Fara Novarese, Novara

Attilio Rusca, Fara Novarese, Novara

Freisa d'Asti (311 – 30.11.1972)

A Freisa, at 80 quintals per hectare, produces both a dry and a sweet red wine; minimum alcohol 11 per cent. With 11.5 per cent alcohol and one year's ageing, the wine may be labelled Superiore. Produced by:

Pietro Barbero, Moasca, Asti

Bava Cantine, Cocconato, Asti

Bersano, Nizza Monferrato, Asti

Biletta, Casorzo, Asti

Dante Borgogno, Cascina Boidi, Calosso,
  Asti

Luigi Calissano, Alba, Cuneo

Cantina Sociale di Canelli, Canelli, Asti

Alfredo Prunotto, Alba, Cuneo

Freisa di Chieri (27 – 29.1.74)

A Freisa, with 100 quintals per hectare, produces a dry and a sweet red wine; minimum alcohol 11 per cent. Both may be refermented naturally to produce a sparkling wine. With 11.5 per cent of alcohol and one year's ageing, the wine may be labelled Superiore. Produced by:

Melchiorre Balbiano, Andezeno, Torino

Lorenzo Bertolo, Via del Carmine 32,
  Torino

Alfredo Prunotto, Alba, Cuneo

Gattinara (200 – 10.8.1967)

The Nebbiolo (locally called Spanna), at 90 quintals per hectare, produces a dry red wine; minimum alcohol 12 per cent. Four years' ageing is required, of which two in the wood. Produced by:

Mario Antoniolo, Gattinara, Vercelli

Brugo, Gattinara, Vercelli

Consorzio del Gattinara, Gattinara,
  Vercelli

E. Conti, Maggiora, Novara

L. and F. Nervi, Gattinara, Vercelli

Ugo Ravizza, Gattinara, Vercelli

Giancarlo Travaglini, Gattinara, Vercelli

Antonio Vallana, Gattinara, Vercelli

Ghemme (292 – 19.11.1969)

The Nebbiolo (locally called Spanna), with some Vespolina and Bonarda, at 100 quintals per hectare, produces a dry red wine; minimum alcohol 12 per cent. Ageing for four years is obligatory, three of which are in the wood. Produced by:

Brugo, Ghemme, Novara

Cantina Sociale di Sizzano and
  Ghemme, Sizzano, Novara

Guido Ponti, Ghemme, Novara

G. and F. Sebastiani, Ghemme, Novara

Uglioni dei Bertinetti, Ghemme, Novara

Grignolino d'Asti (218 – 24.8.1973)

The Grignolino, with 10 per cent of Freisa, at 80 quintals per hectare, produces a dry red wine; minimum alcohol 11 per cent. This wine is customarily aged, although this is not required by the DOC legislation. Produced by:

Carlo Baldovino, Boglietto di Costigliole, Asti

Baucheri, Bava, Cocconato, Asti

Bersano, Nizza Monferrato, Asti

Giacomo Bologna, Braida, Rocchetta Tanaro, Asti

Luigi Bosca, Canelli, Asti

Cantina della Porta Rossa, Diano d'Alba, Cuneo

Cantina Sociale di Canelli, Asti

Cantina Sociale di Casorzo, Casorzo, Asti

Giorgio Carnevale, Cerro Tanaro, Asti

Riccardo Ceretto, Alba, Cuneo

Bruno Giacosa, Neive, Cuneo

Vincenzo Ronco, Moncalvo, Asti

Scarpa Antica Casa, Nizza Monferrato, Asti

Tenuta dei Re, Castagnole Monferrato, Asti

G. and L. Viarengo, Castel di Annone, Asti

Grignolino del Monferrato Casalese (266 – 11.10.1974)

A Grignolino, with a yield of not more than 74 quintals per hectare, produces a dry red wine; minimum alcohol is 11 per cent. This wine is customarily aged for one year. Produced by:

Castello di Lignano, Frassinello Monferrato, Alessandria

Amilcare Gaudio, Bricco Mondalino, Vignale Monferrato, Alessandria

Livio Pavese, Podere Sant'Antonio, Treville Monferrato, Alessandria

Giovanni Rossi, Cascina Pratochiuso, Vignale Monferrato, Alessandria

Vietti, Castiglione Falletto, Cuneo

Lessona (58 – 2.3.1977)

The Nebbiolo (locally called Spanna), with up to 25 per cent of Vespolina and Bonarda, at 80 quintals per hectare, produces a dry red wine; minimum alcohol is 11.5 per cent. The wine must be aged for two years, one year of which is in the wood. Produced by: Sella, Lessona, Vercelli.

Malvasia di Casorzo d'Asti (267 – 19.10.1968)

The Malvasia di Casorzo, with 10 per cent of Freisa, Grignolino and Barbera, and at a yield of 110 quintals per hectare, produces a sweet red wine; minimum alcohol is 10.5 per cent. Produced by:

Cantina Sociale di Casorzo, Casorzo, Asti

Livio Pavese, Podere Sant'Antonio, Treville Monferrato, Alessandria

Malvasia di Castelnuovo don Bosco (26 – 28.1.74)

A Malvasia di Schierano, produces a light aromatic sweet wine at a minimum alcohol level of 10.5 per cent. This may be made sparkling by natural methods.

Moscato Naturale d'Asti (199 – 9.8.1967)

This wine, which is used for making Asti Spumante, is no longer marketed as a still wine in bottles.

Moscato d'Asti, Asti Spumante, Asti (199 – 9.8.1967; 201 – 7.8.69; 38 – 12.2.70; 192 – 25.7.72; 155 – 18.6.73; 20 – 7.1.78)

The Moscato, at 100 quintals per hectare, produces a sweet white wine which is subjected to the Charmat process to make it sparkling; minimum alcohol 11.5 per cent. Produced by:

Arturo Bersani, Nizza Monferrato, Asti

Luigi Bosca, Canelli, Asti

Bruzzone, Strevi, Alessandria

Luigi Calissano, Alba, Cuneo

Cantina Sociale di Canelli, Canelli, Asti
Giorgio Carnevale, Rocchetta Tanaro, Asti
Francesco Cinzano, Torino
Cora, Torino
Giuseppe Contratto, Canelli, Asti

Fontanafredda, Serralunga, Cuneo
Fratelli Gancia, Canelli, Asti
Kiola, La Morra, Cuneo
Martini e Rossi, Pessione, Torino

Nebbiolo d'Alba (228 – 9.9.1970)

The Nebbiolo, at a yield of 90 quintals per hectare, produces a red wine which, when young, is dry but with ageing becomes sweet. The minimum alcohol content is 12 per cent. One year's ageing is required. Also made as an *amabile* sparkling wine. Produced by:

Arturo Bersani, Nizza Monferrato, Asti
Luigi Bosca, Canelli, Asti
Carretta, Piobesi d'Alba, Cuneo
Cavallotto, Castiglione Falletto, Cuneo
Riccardo Ceretto, Alba, Cuneo
Giacomo Conterno, Monforte d'Alba, Cuneo
Franco Fiorina, Alba, Cuneo

Bruno Giacosa, Neive, Cuneo
La Brenta d'Oro, Vezza d'Alba, Cuneo
Marchesi di Barolo, Barolo, Cuneo
Fratelli Oddero, La Morra, Cuneo
Alfredo Prunotto, Alba, Cuneo
Terre del Barolo, Castiglione Falletto, Cuneo

Rubino di Cantavenna (71 – 20.3.1970)

A Barbera, with up to 25 per cent of Grignolino and Freisa, at a yield of 100 quintals per hectare, produces a dry red wine; minimum alcohol is 11.5 per cent. Produced by Cantina Sociale di Cantavenna, Cantavenna, Alessandria.

Sizzano (225 – 4.9.1969)

A Nebbiolo (locally called Spanna) with some Vespolina and Bonarda, at 100 quintals per hectare, produces a dry red wine; minimum alcohol 12 per cent. Ageing for three years is obligatory, two of which are in the wood. Produced by:

Cantina Sociale di Sizzano e Ghemme, Sizzano, Novara

Francesco Fontana, Sizzano, Novara
Ponti, Ghemme, Novara

LIGURIA

1979 vintage – excellent quality but limited yield.

Cinque Terre and *Cinque Terre Sciacchetra* (217 – 23.8.1973)

The Albarolo (Erbarola) and Vermentino vines, at 90 quintals per hectare, produce a dry, white wine; minimum alcohol content 11 per cent. The Sciacchetra dessert wine is customarily fortified to 17 per cent of which 13 per cent is developed into alcohol, making a dry-*amabile* wine after one year's ageing in the cask. Produced by:

Cantina Crespi, Imperia
Cooperativa Cinqueterre, Riomaggiore, Imperia

Giuliano Crovara, Monarola, Imperia

Rossese di Dolceacqua or *Dolceacqua* (125 – 15.5.1972)

The Rossese vine, at 90 quintals per hectare, produces a dry red wine with a hint of sweetness; minimum alcohol 12 per cent. May be labelled Superiore with 13 per cent alcohol and one year's ageing. Produced by:

Cantina del Rossese Crespi, Dolceacqua, Imperia
Eno Val d'Arroscia, Pieve di Teco e Imperia, Imperia

Enzo Guglielmi, Soldano, Imperia
Michele Guglielmi, Soldano, Imperia
Produttori Associati, Dolceacqua, Imperia
Lelio Tornatore, Dolceacqua, Imperia

Giuseppe Viale, Soldano, Imperia   Antonio Zino, Dolceacqua, Imperia

LOMBARDY

1979 vintage – good-quality and generous-yield.

Botticino (140 – 3.6.1968)

Produced by the Barbera, Schiava Gentile, Marzemino and Sangiovese vines, at 100 quintals per hectare, the Botticino is a dry red wine with a minimum alcoholic content of 12 per cent. Produced by:

Pietro Bracchi, Botticino Sera, Brescia   Emilio Franzoni, Botticino Sera, Brescia
Contessa Cazzago, Botticino, Brescia

Cellatica (141 – 4.6.1968)

From the Schiava Gentile, Barbera, Marzemino and Terzi vines, the Cellatica, with a yield of 120 quintals per hectare, offers a dry red wine, with minimum alcohol at 11.5 per cent. Produced by:

Cooperativa Cellatica 'Gassago',   Fratelli Tonoli, (Tenuta Santella),
  Cellatica, Brescia   Cellatica, Brescia
Bernardo Corti, Cellatica, Brescia

Colli Morenici Mantovani del Garda (224 – 25.8.1976)

A dry white wine is produced by the Cantina Sociale dell'Alto Mantovano, Ponti sul Mincio (Mantua), at minimum 11 per cent of alcohol. The legislation permits a broad variety of grapes that may be used – Garganega, Trebbiano, Trebbiano dei Castelli Romani, Soave, Pinot Bianco, Malvasia di Candia and Riesling Italico.

Franciacorta Pinot (209 – 21.8.1967)

The white Pinot produces a dry white wine with a minimum alcohol content of 11.5 per cent: it is much used for making Champagne- and Charmat-method sparkling wines. Produced by:

Bersi Serlini, Timoline di Cortefranca,   Monti della Corte, Nigoline di
  Brescia   Cortefranca, Brescia
Giampaolo and Giovanni Cavalleri,   Giacomo Ragnoli, Colombaro di
  Erbusco, Brescia   Cortefranca, Brescia
Cooperativa Vitivinicultura Cellatica –   Gualberto Ricci Curbastro, Capriolo,
  Gussago, Cellatica, Brescia   Brescia
Del Mosnel, Barzano Barboglio,
  Camignone, Brescia

Franciacorta Rosso (209 – 21.8.1967)

The Cabernet Franc, with some Barbera, Nebbiolo and Merlot, with a yield of 125 quintals per hectare, produces a dry red wine; minimum alcohol content of 11 per cent. Suitable for ageing but not required by legislation. Produced by:

Guido Berlucchi, Borgonata di   Cooperativa Vitivinicultura Cellatica-
  Cortefranca, Brescia   Gussago, Cellatica, Brescia
Bersi Serlini, Timoline di Cortefranca,   Bernardo Corti, Cellatica, Brescia
  Brescia   Giacomo Ragnoli, Colombaro di
Cantina del Bosco, Franciacorta, Brescia   Cortefranca, Brescia
Giampaolo and Giovanni Cavalleri,   Gualberto Ricci Curbastro, Capriolo,
  Erbusco, Brescia   Brescia

Lugana (210 – 22.8.1967; 201 – 7.8.1969 and 38 – 12.2.1970)

The Trebbiano di Lugana vine, with a yield of 125 quintals per hectare, offers a dry white wine; minimum alcohol 11.5 per cent. Produced by:

Aziende Agricole del Lugana, Pozzolengo, Brescia

G. Frassine, Moniga, Brescia

Lamberti, Lasize del Garda, Verona

Vincenzo Marsadri, Raffa del Garda, Brescia

Lodovico Montresor, Peschiera, Brescia

Andrea Pasini, San Zeno s/Naviglio, Brescia

Pellizzari di San Girolamo, Desenzano, Brescia

Prandell, San Martino della Battaglia, Brescia

Premiovini, San Grato, Brescia

A. and C. Salvalai, Bagnolo Mella, Brescia

Fratelli Zenato, San Benedetto di Lugana, Verona

Oltrepò Pavese (273 – 27.10.1970; 300 – 13.11.1975; 9 – 10.1.1978)

When not otherwise qualified, Oltrepò' Pavese refers to a dry red wine, produced from the Barbera, Croatina Uva Rara and Vespolina grapes at 110 quintals per hectare and 11.5 per cent minimum of alcohol. Produced by:

Bagnasco, Santa Maria della Versa, Pavia

Balestriere, Casteggio, Pavia

Broglio Podere, Borgo Priolo, Casteggio, Pavia

Lino Maga, Proni, Pavia

Mairano, Le Fracce, Casteggio, Pavia

Mazza, Tenuta Genestrello, Montebello della Battaglia, Pavia

Monsupello, Carlo Boatti, Torricella Verzate, Pavia

Tenuta Nazzano, Rivanazzano, Pavia

Barbera dell'Oltrepò Pavese: The Barbera, with up to 20 per cent of Uva Rara and Croatina and a yield of not more than 120 quintals per hectare, produces a dry red wine; minimum alcohol 11.5 per cent. Produced by:

Carlo Boati, Monsupello, Torricella Verzate, Pavia

Cantina Sociale Santa Maria della Versa, Santa Maria della Versa, Pavia

Mazza, Montebello della Battaglia, Pavia

Edmondo Tronconi, Rovescala, Pavia

Vilide, Stradella, Pavia

Bonarda dell'Oltrepò Pavese: The Bonarda, with a small percentage of Uva Rara and Barbera, and a 90-quintal yield per hectare, produces a dry red wine; minimum alcohol 11 per cent. Produced by:

Giovanni Agnes, Rovescala, Pavia

Balestriere, Casteggio, Pavia

Luigi Buscaglia, Rovescala, Pavia

Cantina Sociale, Casteggio, Pavia

Cantina Sociale Santa Maria della Versa, Santa Maria della Versa, Pavia

Cortese dell'Oltrepò Pavese: A Cortese, with maximum yield of 100 quintals per hectare, produces a dry white wine; minimum alcohol 11 per cent. Produced by: Cantina Sociale Santa Maria della Versa, Santa Maria della Versa, Pavia.

Moscato dell'Oltrepò Pavese: A Moscato, with a yield of 110 quintals per hectare, produces a sweet white wine; minimum alcohol 10.5 per cent. This is much used for the making of sparkling wines.

Pinot dell'Oltrepò Pavese (white, red and rosé): These three Pinots (the rosé being made from Pinot Nero grapes) produce dry wines at 11 per cent minimum alcohol. They are much used for the production of sparkling wines. The Oltrepò Pavese wines are produced by:

Whites

Baruffaldi, Castello di Stefanago, Borgo Priolo, Pavia

Cantina Sociale, Casteggio, Pavia

Cantina Sociale Santa Maria della Versa, Santa Maria della Versa, Pavia

Mairano, Le Fracce, Casteggio, Pavia

Reds

Balestriere, Casteggio, Pavia

Cantina Sociale di Versa, Santa Maria della Versa, Pavia

Maga Lino, Broni, Pavia

Mairano, Le Fracce, Casteggio, Pavia

Reds

Mazza, Tenuta Genestrello, Montebello
    della Battaglia, Pavia
Monsupello, Carlo Boatti, Torricella
    Verzate, Pavia

Rosés

Mairano, Le Fracce, Casteggio, Pavia
Monsupello, Carlo Boatti, Torricella
    Verzate, Pavia

Under the Oltrepò banner there are many fine producers and fine wines of long tradition, which merit a fuller discussion for which there is no room here. However, names like Balestriere, Tronconi and Frecciarossa, are amongst them.

Riesling dell'Oltrepò Pavese: A Riesling Italico or Riesling Renano (or both) with a yield of 100 quintals per hectare, produces a dry white wine; minimum alcohol 11 per cent. Produced by:

Balestriere, Casteggio, Pavia
Cantina Sociale Casteggio, Casteggio,
    Pavia
Cantina Sociale Santa Maria della Versa,
    Santa Maria della Versa, Pavia

Mairano, Le Fracce, Casteggio, Pavia
Mazza, Montebello della Battaglia, Pavia
Giuseppe Riccardi, San Damiano al Colle,
    Pavia
Vilide Vitivinicultura, Stradella, Pavia

Riviera del Garda Bresciano (282 – 15.10.1977)

A red and a rosé (*chiaretto*) are included in this legislation. The former is a dry red wine produced mostly from the Gropello vine, with smaller proportions of Sangiovese, Barbera and Marzemino. The yield per hectare is 125 quintals and the minimum alcohol content is 11 per cent. With one year's ageing and 12 per cent minimum alcohol, the wine may be labelled Superiore.

    The *chiaretto*s are made from the same grapes, which may also include small quantities of Trebbiano, Nebbiolo, Schiava, and Cabernet Franc. The *chiaretto* has no ageing legislation; minumum alcohol content 11.5 per cent. Produced by:

Avenzi, Manerba del Garda, Brescia
Azienda Bertanzi, Moniga, Brescia
Francesco Bertelli, Raffa del Garda, Brescia
Fabio Bottarelli, Picedo di Polpenazze,
    Brescia
Gerardo Cesari, Quinzano, Brescia
Azienda Colombaro, Cunettone di Salo,
    Brescia

Frassine, Moniga del Garda, Brescia
Andrea Pasini, San Zeno Naviglio, Brescia
Pellizzari di San Girolamo, Desenzano,
    Brescia
Fattoria Saleri, Polpenazze, Brescia
San Grato – Selezione Premiovini, Brescia

Tocai di San Martino della Battaglia (131 – 27.5.1970)

The Friuli Tocai vine, with a yield of 125 quintals per hectare, produces a dry white wine; minimum alcohol 12 per cent. Produced by:

Andrea Guetta, Cascina La Torretta Spia
    d'Italia, Lonato, Brescia
Pellizzari di San Girolamo, Desenzano,
    Brescia

Prandell, San Martino della Battaglia,
    Brescia
Zenato, San Benedetto di Lugana

Valcalepio (308 – 18.11.1976)

The Merlot vine, with the support of much less Cabernet Sauvignon, produces a dry red wine; minimum alcohol 12 per cent. Two years' ageing in the wood is obligatory. Produced by:

Cantina Sociale Bergamasca, San Paolo
    d'Argon, Bergamo

Castello di Grumello del Monte Tenuta,
    Grumello del Monte, Bergamo

The Valcalepio white is made with mostly Pinot Bianco and the balance with Pinot Grigio, with a resulting minimum 11 per cent of alcohol content. Produced by Cantina Sociale Bergamasca, San Paolo d'Argon, Bergamo.

Valtellina and *Valtellina Superiore* (244 – 25.9.1968)

The Nebbiolo vine (locally called Chiavennasca) for 70 per cent of the total, and Pinot Nero, Merlot, Rossola, Pignola Valtellinese and Prugnola for 30 per cent, with a yield of 120 quintals per hectare, produces a dry red wine; minimum alcohol 11 per cent.

The Chiavennasca with only 5 per cent of the other varietal vines, with a yield of 100 quintals per hectare, produces the Superiore at 12 per cent minimum alcohol. Both Valtellina and Valtellina Superiore must be aged, the former for one year, the latter for two. If the wine is made from semi-dried grapes, has an alcohol content of over 14.5 per cent and is suitably aged, it may be called Sfursat. Produced by:

Franco Balgera, Chiuro, Sondrio

Fratelli Bettini, San Giacomo di Teglio, Sondrio

Enologica Valtellinese, Sondrio

Nera Casa, Chiuro, Sondrio

Nino Negri, Sondrio, Sondrio

Pellizzatti, Sondrio, Sondrio

Fratelli Polatti, Sondrio, Sondrio

Rainoldi e Figlio, Chiuro, Sondrio

Triacca, Villa di Tirano, Sondrio

Tona 1892, Villa di Tirano, Sondrio

Villa Bianzone Cantina Cooperativa, Villa di Tirano, Sondrio

Amongst recommended non-DOC wines are: Frecciarossa (St George, Grand Cru, La Vigne). San Colombano, Barbacarlo, Buttofucco, Sangue di Giuda, Balestriere and Clastidium, all of the Oltrepò Pavese, and Fracia of the Valtelline.

VENETO

1979 vintage – good quality and generous.

Bardolino (186 – 23.7.1968 and 324 – 4.12.1976)

A blending of the grapes from the Corvina Veronese, Rondinella, Moninara and Negrara vines, with a maximum yield of 130 quintals per hectare, produces Bardolino, a dry red wine; minimum alcohol content 10.5 per cent. Produced by:

Bertani, Verona

Fratelli Bolla, Soave, Verona

Cantina Sociale della Valpantena, Quinto Valpolicella, Verona

Cantina Sociale di Soave, Soave, Verona

Cantine Fabiano, Verona

Castagna, San Bonifacio, Verona

Colle dei Cipressi, Calmasino di Bardolino, Verona

Guerrieri-Rizzardi, Bardolino, Verona

La Vinicola del Garda, Cavion, Verona

Lamberti, Lazise del Garda, Verona

Masi, Cantina di Affi, Marano Valpolicella, Verona

Giacomo Montresor, Verona

Naiano, Cavaion Veronese, Verona

Pasqua, Verona

Pegaso Premiovini, Brescia

A. and G. Piergriffi, Bardolino, Verona

Fratelli Poggi, Affi, Verona

Santi, Illasi, Verona

Pietro Sartori, Negrar, Verona

Bianco di Custoza (142 – 5.6.1971)

A composite wine made from grapes from the following vines: Trebbiano, Garganega, Friuli Tocai, Cortese, Tuscan Malvasia, and Riesling Italico. It is dry and white and with a minimum alcohol content of 11 per cent. Maximum yield per hectare is 130 quintals. Produced by:

Belcamin, Bussolengo, Verona

Giacomo Montresor, Verona

Breganze

The DOC legislation permits six different types of wine to be made under this discipline. They are all made by the Cantina Sociale 'Beato Bartolommeo da Breganze' at Breganze, Vicenza. The maximum yield per hectare for the red Breganze wines is 140 quintals and 130 for the whites.

Breganze Bianco: This dry white wine is made with at least 85 per cent Tocai grapes and has a minimum alcohol content of 11 per cent.

Breganze Rosso: A dry red wine made from Merlot grapes. It has a minimum alcohol content of 11 per cent.

Breganze Cabernet: Made from Cabernet grapes, this dry red wine has a minimum alcohol content of 11.5 per cent.

Breganze Pinot Nero: This dry red wine is made from 100 per cent Pinot Nero grapes and has a minimum alcohol content of 11.5 per cent.

Breganze Pinot Bianco: Pinot Bianco and Pinot Grigio grapes, processed together, produce a dry white wine with a minimum alcohol content of 11.5 per cent.

Breganze Vesparolo: The Vesparolo is a local white grape which produces a dry white wine with a minimum alcohol content of 11.5 per cent.

In the cases that the Cabernet, the Pinot Nero, the Pinot Bianco and the Vesparolo have a minimum alcoholic content of 12 per cent and they are suitably aged, they may be designated Superiore.

Cabernet di Pramaggiore (244 – 27.9.1971)

A dry red wine made from 90 per cent Cabernet with 10 per cent Merlot, has a yield of 100 quintals per hectare, and a minimum alcohol content of 11.5 per cent. With three years' ageing in the barrel and 12 per cent minimum alcohol content, the wine may be called Riserva. Produced by:

G. G. Conti di Porcia, Pordenone

La Braghina, Lison di Portogruaro, Venezia

Sant'Anna, Loncon di Annone Veneto, Venezia

Sant'Osvaldo, Loncon di Annone Veneto, Venezia

Villa Frattina, Ghirano, Pordenone

Zignago, Santa Margherita, Portogruaro, Venezia

Colli Berici (32 – 4.2.1974)

All the Colli Berici wines are produced by Zonin of Gambellara, Vicenza.

Berici Cabernet: A dry red wine, made from Cabernet Franc and/or Cabernet Sauvignon, at 120 quintals per hectare, with a minimum alcohol content of 11 per cent. With 12.5 per cent and three years' ageing, the wine may be labelled Riserva.

Berici Garganego: A dry white wine, at 140 quintals per hectare, made from the Garganego grape with 10 per cent of Trebbiano di Soave, and with a minimum alcohol content of 10.5 per cent.

Berici Merlot: A dry red wine, at 130 quintals per hectare, provides an 11 per cent alcohol content.

Berici Pinot Bianco: A dry white wine, at 120 quintals per hectare, made from 15 per cent Pinot Grigio, to provide a minimum alcohol content of 11 per cent.

Berici Sauvignon: A dry white wine, at 120 quintals per hectare, with a minimum alcohol content of 11 per cent.

Berici Tocai Bianco: A dry white wine, at 120 quintals per hectare, made from Tocai and 10 per cent Garganego, and with a minimum alcohol content of 11 per cent.

Berici Tocai Rosso: A dry red wine, at 120 quintals per hectare, with 15 per cent of Garganego, provides 11 per cent of alcohol content.

Colli Euganei (281 – 6.11.1969)

The white is made from the Garganega, Serpina and Tocai vines, with a yield of not more than 120 quintals per hectare, to produce a wine with a minimum of 10.5 per cent alcohol. If aged suitably, and with 11–12 per cent of alcohol, the wine may be labelled Superiore.

The red is obtained from a blend of Merlot, Cabernet, Barbera and Verona Raboso; it has a minimum alcohol content of 11 per cent. With suitable ageing and more than 11 per cent of alcohol, the wine may be labelled Superiore.

The Moscato, with, like the white, a 120-quintal-per-hectare yield, produces a sweet white wine. It has a minimum alcohol content of 10.5 per cent. This wine may be used, as also the other two, for the making of sparkling wines.

In this area is the Luxardo winery at Torreglia, near Padova, which produces fine wines and liqueurs. Produced by the Consorzio Vini DOC, Albano Terme, Padova.

Gambellara (132 – 29.5.1970)

The DOC covers a white table wine, a sparkling Recioto and a Vin Santo. The basic wine for all three is from the Garganega vine blended with a little Trebbiano di Soave. These wines are all produced by Zonin of Gambellara, Vicenza.

Gambellara Bianco: This dry wine has an alcohol content of 11 per cent. If aged suitably and of 11.5 per cent alcohol content, the wine may be qualified as Superiore.

Gambellara Recioto: Produced by the Valpolicella semi-dried grapes method to reach 12 per cent of alcohol, this wine is customarily processed to be both sweet and sparkling.

Gambellara Vin Santo: Also produced from semi-dried grapes, this wine, which reaches 14 per cent of alcohol, must be aged for two years in the wood. This wine is also produced by Cantina Sociale di Gambellara of Gambellara, Vicenza.

Merlot di Pramaggiore (244 – 27.9.1971)

Wine made from 90 per cent Merlot with a 10 per cent blend of Cabernet, and with a 110 quintal yield per hectare. It has a minimum alcohol content of 11.5 per cent. If the wine is aged for at least two years and reaches 12 per cent of alcohol, it may be qualified as Riserva. Produced by:

La Braghina, Lison di Portogruaro, Venezia   Santa Margherita, Fossalta di Portogruaro,
Russolo, Pramaggiore, Venezia   Venezia
Sant'Anna, Loncon di Annone Veneto,
   Venezia

Montello e Colli Asolani (304 – 8.11.1977)

Cabernet di Montello: This is produced from 85 per cent of Cabernet with the addition of Cabernet Franc, Cabernet Sauvignon and Malbec grown in the same vineyards. 100 quintals per hectare is the permitted yield to obtain an 11 per cent alcohol. This dry wine, with two years' ageing and 12 per cent of alcohol, may be qualified as Superiore. Produced by Cantina Sociale Montelliana dei Colli Asolani, Montebelluna, Treviso.

Merlot di Montello: This is produced from 85 per cent Merlot with the addition of either Malbec, Cabernet Franc or Sauvignon, which must be grown in the same vineyard. 120 quintals per hectare is the maximum yield permitted to obtain a 10.5 per cent alcohol content. With two years' ageing and more than 11.5 per cent alcohol, the wine may be qualified as Superiore.

Prosecco di Montello: This is produced from 85 per cent of Prosecco wine with permitted blending of Pinot Bianco, Pinot Grigio, Riesling Italico, Verduzzo Trevigiano, and Bianchetto Trevigiana from the same vineyards. 120 quintals per hectare is the maximum yield permitted to obtain a 10 per cent alcohol content. This Prosecco may be processed into an *amabile* sparkling wine.

Prosecco di Conegliano – Valdobbiadene (141 – 7.6.1969)

This legislation deals with the Prosecco, both as a still and as a sparkling wine, as well as in its dry, *amabile* and sweet characteristics. It also distinguishes between Prosecco and Cartizze, the classic zone.

The Prosecco is made from 90 per cent of Prosecco grapes with additions of Verdiso; the yield per hectare must not exceed 120 quintals. The Prosecco has an alcohol content of 10.5 per cent and the Cartizze of 11 per cent: in the sparkling varieties of these wines, the percentages alter – 11.5 per cent for Prosecco and 11 per cent for Cartizze. In the case of *bruts* made by the Champagne method, Pinot grapes are the major ingredient. Produced by:

Bertollotti, Conegliano, Treviso
Canella, San Dona di Piave, Venezia
Carpene Malvolti, Conegliano, Treviso
Cosulich, Collabrigo di Conegliano, Treviso
De Bernard, Conegliano, Treviso
D. Deroa, San Polo di Piave, Treviso
Ruggeri, Valdobbiadene, Treviso
Pino Sardetto, Conegliano, Treviso
Valdo Vini Superiore, Valdobbiadene, Treviso

Soave and Recioto di Soave (269 – 22.10.1968; 227 – 27.8.1976; 72 – 14.3.1975)

Soave: Approximately 80 per cent Garganega and 20 per cent Trebbiano di Soave form the Soave white wine, produced from a yield of not more than 140 quintals per hectare, to give a 10.5 per cent alcohol content. The wine may be qualified as Superiore with an alcohol content of 11.5 per cent and Classico is produced in the original delimited area of Soave.

Recioto di Soave: This wine is made with semi-dried grapes to reach an alcohol content of at least 14 per cent; it is customarily sweet and may be fortified. Soave is produced by:

G. B. Bertani, Verona
Bertolli, Lucca
Biscardo, Bussolengo, Verona
Fratelli Bolla, Soave, Verona
Cantina del Castello, Soave, Verona
Cantina Sociale della Valtramigna, Cazzano di Tramigna, Verona
Cantina Sociale di Soave, Soave, Verona
Castagna, San Bonifacio, Verona
Lamberti, Lazise sul Garda, Verona
Marcato, Ronca, Verona
Montresor, Verona
Pasqua, Verona
Pegaso Premiovini, Brescia
Pieropan, Soave, Verona
Santi, Illasi, Verona
Pietro Sartori, Negrar, Verona
Sterzi, San Martino Buonalbergo, Verona
Tenuta Masi, Cantina di Soave, Marano, Verona

Tocai di Lison (220 – 1.9.1971)

The Friuli Tocai vine, at 95 per cent with the balance of unspecified other vines, produces a dry white wine of 11.5 per cent alcohol content. There is a classic zone offering a superior wine at 12 per cent minimum alcohol content. Produced by:

Canella, San Dona di Piave, Venezia
Di Porcia Conti, Pordenone
La Braghina, Lison di Portogruar, Venezia
I. and C. Russolo, Pramaggiore, Venezia
Santa Margherita Tenuta, Fossalta di Portogruaro, Treviso
Sant'Osvaldo Cantine, Loncon di Annone Veneto, Venezia
Villa Frattina, Ghirano, Pordenone

Valpolicella and *Recioto della Valpolicella* (268 – 21.10.1968; 72 – 14.3.1975; 271 – 11.10.1976)

Valpolicella: This wine is made up from 85 per cent Corvina Veronese, Rondinella and Molinara and Rossignola, Negrara, Barbera and Sangiovese contribute the remaining 15 per cent. The maximum yield permitted is 120 quintals per hectare and the minimum alcohol allowed is 11 per cent. With 12 per cent of alcohol and suitable ageing, the wine may be called Superiore. The wines from the smaller and original Valpolicella growing area are labelled Classico.

Recioto: This wine is made with semi-dried grapes to reach an alcohol content of at least 14 per cent. The Recioto is usually considered to be the sweet dessert wine while the dry version, the Amarone, is considered to be a strong table wine. Valpolicella is produced by:

Allegrini, Fumane Valpolicella, Verona
Belcamin, Bussolengo, Verona
G. B. Bertani, Verona
Biscardo, Bussolengo, Verona
Fratelli Bolla, Verona
Cantina Sociale della Valpantena, Quinto Valpantena, Verona
Cantina Sociale di Soave, Soave, Verona
La Masua, Marano Valpolicella, Verona
Pio Longo, Buttapietra, Verona
Giacomo Montresor, Verona

Pasqua, Verona
Pegaso-Selezione Premiovini, Brescia
Santi, Illasi, Verona
Pietro Sartori, Negrar, Verona
Arturo Scamperle, Fumane Valpolicella, Verona
Speri, Pedemonte Valpolicella, Verona
Sterzi, San Martino Buonalbergo, Verona
Tedeschi, Verona
Tenuta Masi, Marano Valpolicella, Verona
Villa Girardi, San Pietro Incariano, Verona

Vini del Piave or *Piave* (242 – 24.9.1971)

This DOC covers four styles of wine – Merlot, Cabernet, Tocai and Verduzzo. The former two red wines may be aged; the Merlot with one degree of alcohol more and two years' ageing, is qualified Vecchio, and the Cabernet with three years of ageing becomes Riserva.

Piave Cabernet: This wine with a yield of 110 quintals per hectare, is dry and red with 11.5 per cent of alcohol. Produced by:

Botter Cantine, Fossalta di Piave, Venezia
Luciano Canella, San Dona di Piave, Venezia
Cantina Sociale Cooperativa di Campodipietra, Campodipietra di Salgareda, Treviso

Cantina Sociale di San Dona di Piave, San Dona di Piave, Venezia
Gaggiato, Noventa di Piave, Treviso
Rechsteiner, Piavon di Oderzo, Treviso
Antonio Verga Falzacappa, San Vendemiano, Treviso

Piave Merlot: This wine with a yield of 130 quintals per hectare is dry and red with 11 per cent of alcohol. Produced by:

Ciani Bassetti, Roncade, Treviso
Bianchi di Kunkler, Mogliano Veneto, Treviso
Botter, Fossalta di Piave, Venezia
Luciano Canella, San Dona di Piave, Venezia
Cantina Sociale di Campodipietra, Campodipietra di Salgareda, Treviso
Cantina Sociale di San Dona, San Dona di Piave, Venezia

D. Deroa, San Polo di Piave, Treviso
Liasora, Ponte di Piave, Treviso
Italo Maccari, Treviso
Mason, Gorgo al Monticano, Treviso
Rechsteiner, Piavon di Oderzo, Treviso
Antonio Verga Falzacappa, San Vendemiano, Treviso

Piave Tocai: This dry white wine with a yield of 110 quintals per hectare, has a minimum alcohol content of 11 per cent. Produced by:

Cantina Sociale di San Dona, San Dona di Piave, Venezia

Liasora, Abbazia di Busco, Ponte di Piave, Treviso

D. Deroa, San Polo di Piave, Treviso

Mason, Gorgo al Monticano, Treviso

Gaggiato, Noventa di Piave, Venezia

Rechsteiner, Piavon di Oderzo, Treviso

Piave Verduzzo: This dry white wine with a yield of 120 quintals per hectare, has a minimum alcohol content of 11 per cent. Produced by:

Carlo Botter, Fossalta di Piave, Venezia

Luciano Canella, San Dona di Piave, Venezia

Cantina Sociale Cooperativa Campodipietra, Campodipietra di Salgareda, Treviso

TRENTINO – ALTO ADIGE (South Tyrol)

1979 vintage – good quality and generous yield.

Alto Adige (190 – 18.7.1975)

This sixteen-varietal legislation for the South Tyrol permits that labels may also describe the wines as Südtirol wines; and that the German names for the vines be used also. These will be mentioned in the various sections that follow. The whites are grown at above 900 metres, the reds at 700 metres.

Alto-Adige Cabernet: With a yield of not more than 110 quintals per hectare, the Cabernet produces a dry red wine of 11 per cent alcohol content. If aged for two years, the wine may be labelled Riserva. Produced by:

Rudolf Carli, Nalles, Bolzano

Vaja, Egna-Neumarkt, Bolzano

G. Kettmeir, Bolzano

Schloss Kehlburg (Bellermont Wangen), Appiano, Bolzano

Alto-Adige Lagrein Rosato (Lagrein Kretzer): The Lagrein Rosato, with a yield of not more than 140 quintals per hectare, produces a dry red wine with an alcohol content of not less than 11 per cent. If produced in the commune of Bolzano, the wine may be called Grieser Lagrein or Lagrein de Gries. Produced by:

Rudolf Carli, Nalles, Bolzano

Vaja, Egna-Neumarkt, Bolzano

G. Kettmeir, Bolzano

Alto-Adige Lagrein Scuro (Lagrein Dunkel): The Lagrein Scuro, with a yield of not more than 140 quintals per hectare, produces a dry red wine with an alcohol content of not less than 11 per cent. With one year's ageing, this wine may be labelled Riserva. It may also be called Lagrein de Gries or Grieser Lagrein if produced in the commune of Bolzano. Produced by:

Cantina Sociale Gries, Gries, Bolzano

Schloss Kehlburg (Bellermont Wangen), Appiano, Bolzano

Lageder, Bolzano,

Muri, Bolzano

Alto-Adige Malvasia (Malvasier): The Malvasia produces a dry white wine with a yield of not more than 110 quintals per hectare. It has an alcohol content of not less than 11 per cent. Produced by:

Cantina Sociale Gries, Gries, Bolzano

Lageder, Bolzano

G. Kettmeir, Bolzano

Alto-Adige Merlot: The Merlot produces a dry red wine with a yield of not more than 130 quintals per hectare. It has an alcohol content of not less than 10.5 per cent. If aged for one year, the wine may be qualified as Riserva. The producer is Kettmeir of Bolzano.

Alto-Adige Moscato Giallo (Südtiroler Goldenmuskateller or Goldenmuskateller): The Moscato, with a yield of 80 quintals per hectare, produces a sweet white wine of a minimum alcohol content of 10.5 per cent. Produced by:

Brigl, Cornaiano, Bolzano
Cantina Sociale Terlano, Terlano, Bolzano
Rudolf Carli, Nalles, Bolzano
J. Hofstatter, Termeno, Bolzano
G. Kettmeir, Bolzano
Kupelwieser, Bolzano
Lageder, Bolzano
Rametz, Merano
Vaja, Egna-Neumarkt, Bolzano
Walch, Termeno, Bolzano

Alto-Adige Moscato Rosa (Rosenmuskateller): The Moscato Rosa produces a sweet red wine, with a yield of not more than 60 quintals per hectare. It has a minimum alcohol content of not less than 12 per cent. Produced by:

Brigl, Cornaiano, Bolzano
Rudolf Carli, Nalles, Bolzano
Kunburg, Bolzano

Alto-Adige Pinot Grigio (Rülander): The Pinot Grigio, with a yield of not more than 130 quintals per hectare, produces a dry white wine with a minimum alcohol content of 11 per cent. Produced by:

G. Kettmeir, Bolzano
Kupelwieser, Bolzano
Lageder, Bolzano
Lun, Bolzano
Rametz, Bolzano
Vaja, Egna-Neumarkt, Bolzano

Alto-Adige Pinot Nero (Blauburgunder): The Pinot Nero is produced from not more than 120 quintals per hectare. The wine has an alcohol content of not less than 11 per cent. If aged for one year, the wine may be qualified as Riserva. It may be used for making sparkling wine. Produced by:

Brigl, Cornaiano, Bolzano
Hofstatter, Termeno, Bolzano
G. Kettmeir, Bolzano
Lageder, Bolzano
Lun, Bolzano
Schloss Kehlburg (Bellermont Wangen), Appiano, Bolzano
Vaja, Egna-Neumarkt, Bolzano
Walch, Termeno, Bolzano

Alto-Adige Riesling Italico (Welschriesling): This Riesling Italico, with a yield of not more than 130 quintals per hectare, produces a dry white wine with a minimum alcohol content of 10.5 per cent. The producer is Kettmeir of Bolzano.

Alto-Adige Riesling Renano (Rheinriesling): The Riesling Renano, with a yield of not more than 120 quintals per hectare, produces a dry white wine of not less than 10.5 per cent. Produced by:

Brigl, Cornaiano, Bolzano
G. Kettmeir, Bolzano
Kupelwieser, Bolzano
Lageder, Bolzano
Lun, Bolzano
Rametz, Merano
Schloss Kehlburg (Bellermont Wangen), Appiano, Bolzano

Alto-Adige Riesling x Sylvaner (Müller-Thurgau): The Müller-Thurgau, with a yield of not more than 110 quintals per hectare, produces a dry white wine of not less than 10.5 per cent alcohol. Produced by:

Abbazia Novacella (Neustift), Chiusa, Bolzano
Cantina Sociale Isarco, Chiusa, Bolzano

Alto-Adige Sauvignon: The Sauvignon, with a yield of not more than 120 quintals per hectare, produces a dry white wine with a minimum alcohol content of 11.5 per cent. Produced by:

Abbazia Novacella (Neustift), Chiusa, Bolzano
Cantina Sociale Terlano, Terlano, Bolzano
Lageder, Bolzano

Alto-Adige Schiava (Vernatsch): The Schiava is produced from not more than 140 quintals per hectare. The wine has a minimum alcohol content of not less than 10 per cent. Produced by:

Brigl, Cornaiano, Bolzano

Hofstatter, Termeno, Bolzano

G. Kettmeir, Bolzano

Kupelwieser, Bolzano

Lageder, Bolzano

Lun, Bolzano

Nuova Cantina Sociale di Caldaro, Caldaro, Bolzano

Walch, Termeno, Bolzano

Alto-Adige Sylvaner: The Sylvaner, with a yield of not more than 130 quintals per hectare, produces a dry white wine with a minimum alcohol content of 10.5 per cent. Produced by:

Abbazia Novacella (Neustift), Chiusa, Bolzano

Cantina Sociale Isarco, Chiusa, Bolzano

Alto-Adige Traminer Aromatica (Gewürztraminer): The Traminer, with a yield of not more than 120 quintals per hectare, and not growing higher than 853 metres, produces a dry white wine of not less than 11 per cent of alcohol content. Produced by:

Brigl, Cornaiano, Bolzano

Hofstatter, Termeno, Bolzano

G. Kettmeir, Bolzano

Kupelwieser, Bolzano

Lageder, Bolzano

Lun, Bolzano

Schloss Kehlburg (Bellermont Wangen), Appiano, Bolzano

Vaja, Egna-Neumarkt, Bolzano

Walch, Termeno, Bolzano

Caldaro or *Lago di Caldaro (Kalterersee)* (115 – 9.19.1970)

This wine may be produced from one of the following vines or a blend of all three: Schiava Grossa, Schiava Gentile, and Schiava Grigia, which locally are called Grossvernatsch, Kleinvernatsch and Grauvernatsch. There may be up to a 15 per cent contribution of Pinot Nero (Blauburgunder) and Lagrein. The yield per hectare may not exceed 140 quintals and the resulting alcohol content must not be less than 10.5 per cent. If the wine's alcohol content is above 11 per cent, the wine may be labelled Scelto (selected) or Auslese. Produced by:

Josef Brigl, Cornaiano, Bolzano

Cantina Sociale, Colterenzio, Bolzano

Cantina Sociale, Cornaiano, Bolzano

Cantina Sociale, Cortaccia, Bolzano

Cantina Sociale Lavis Sorni Salorno, Lavis, Trento

Cantina Sociale San Michele Appiano, Bolzano

Cantina Sociale Schreckbichl, Cornaiano, Bolzano

Cantina Sociale Termeno, Termeno, Bolzano

Rodolfo Carli, Castel Schwanburg, Nalles, Bolzano

Cantina Viticoltori, Ravina di Trento, Trento

G. Kettmeir, Bolzano

Lechthalter, Mezzocorona, Trento

Anton Lindner, Appiano, Bolzano

Alois Morandell, Appiano, Bolzano

Karl Schmid, Merano, Bolzano

Tiefenbrunner, Cortaccia, Bolzano

Von Elzembaum, Termeno, Bolzano

Vaja, Egna-Neumarkt, Bolzano

Walch, Termeno, Bolzano

Casteller (257 – 3.10.1974)

This composite wine is made up of at least 30 per cent Schiava Grossa and Schiava Gentile, and not more than 20 per cent of Merlot; and up to a maximum of 40 per cent Lambrusco. A yield per hectare is permitted up to 135 quintals and not less than 11 per cent of alcohol is required for this dry red wine. Produced by:

Cantina Viticoltori, Ravina di Trento, Trento

Liberio Todesca, Mattarello, Trento

Colli di Bolzano (291 – 3.11.1975)

A dry red wine obtained from the Schiava (Vernatsch) vine with 10 per cent of Lagrein and Pinot Nero, from a maximum yield of 130 quintals per hectare. Its minimum alcohol content is 11 per cent. Produced by:

Maloyer, Bolzano   Rotensteiner, Bolzano

Meranese or *Meranese di Collina (Meraner)* (188 – 26.7.1971)

This wine is produced from the Schiava Grossa (Grossvernatsch), Ledia (Mittervernatsch), Piccola or Gentile Schiave (Kleinvernatsch), Schiava Grigia (Grauvernatsch) and the Tschaggele (Tschaggelevernatsch). In view of the altitude in the Alps, 15 per cent of cutting-wines may be added. This dry red wine has a 10.5 per cent of alcohol content. It may also be labelled Burgravio or Burggrafler. Produced by:

Cantina Sociale di Merano, Merano,   Castel Rametz, Merano, Bolzano
  Bolzano   G. Kettmeir, Bolzano

Santa Maddalena (Magdalener) (245 – 28.9.1971)

Made with the four varieties of the Schiava vine, with a yield of 125 quintals per hectare, this dry red wine has an alcohol content of 11.5 per cent. Produced by:

Josef Brigl, Cornaiano, Bolzano   G. Kettmeir, Bolzano
Cantina Sociale, Cornaiano, Bolzano   Lechthaler, Mezzocorona, Trento
Cantina Sociale Santa Maddalena, Bolzano   Anton Lindner, Appiano, Trento
Cantina Sociale, Terlano, Bolzano   Schreckbichl, Cantina Sociale, Colterenzio-
Rodolfo Carli, Castel Schwanburg,   Cornaiano, Bolzano
  Nalles, Bolzano   Vaja, Egna-Neumarkt, Bolzano
Hofstatter, Termeno, Bolzano   Walch, Cantina Vini, Termeno, Bolzano

Sorni (280 – 13.10.1979)

A Schiava, with some Lagrein and Teroldego, and with a yield of 140 quintals per hectare, produces a dry red wine. Its minimum alcohol content is 10.5 per cent. If aged for one year and with 11 per cent of alcohol, the wine may be labelled *Scelto* (selected). Produced by Cantina Sociale Lavis Sorni, Sorni, Trento.

Teroldego Rotaliano (139 – 3.6.1971)

Made entirely from grapes from the Teroldego vine, with a yield of 130 quintals per hectare, this wine has an alcohol content of 11.5 per cent. A Superiore Teroldego Rotaliano has 12 per cent of alcohol and at least two years' ageing in the wood. A rosé is also made. Produced by:

Barone De Cles, Maso Scari,   Dolzan, Mezzolombardo, Trento
  Mezzolombardo, Trento   Pierfranco Donati, Mezzocorona, Trento
Bossi Fedrigotti, Rovereto, Trento   Foradori, Mezzolombardo, Trento
Cantina Sociale, Mezzocorona, Trento   Girelli, Trento
Cantina Viticoltori, Ravina di Trento,   Roberto Zeni, Grumo di San Michele
  Trento   all'Adige, Trento

Terlano (Terlaner) (17 – 17.6.1975)

The Terlano legislation offers seven white wines, each with a minimum yield of 130 quintals and varying alcohol contents: Terlano – 11.5 per cent; Terlano Pinot Bianco – 11 per cent; Terlano Riesling Italico – 10.5 per cent; Terlano Riesling Renano – 11.5 per cent; Terlano Sauvignon – 12 per cent; Terlano Sylvaner – 11.5 per cent; Terlano Müller-Thurgau – 11 per cent. A 5 per cent in volume use of cutting-wines is permitted. The Pinot Bianco is called Weissburgunder locally. Produced by:

Josef Brigl, Cornaiano, Bolzano
Cantina Sociale, Cornaiano, Bolzano
Cantina Sociale, Terlano, Bolanzo
Cantina Sociale Colterenzio, Cornaiano, Bolzano
Cantina Sociale San Michele, Appiano, Bolzano
Rodolfo Carli, Castel Schwanburg, Nalles, Bolzano

Di Pauli, Caldaro, Bolzano
G. Kettmeir, Bolzano
Alois Legeder, Bolzano
St Florin, Caldaro
Von Elzembaum, Termeno, Bolzano
Walch, Termeno, Bolzano

Valdadige (Etschtaler) (194 – 7 23.7.1975)

Two wines, a Valdadige red and a Valdadige white, of a very eclectic nature, are permitted under this legislation. The white must be made up of more than 20 per cent from one of or a blend of Pinot Bianco, Pinot Grigio, Riesling Italico and Müller-Thurgau; the difference must be made up from one of a blend of Bianchetta Trevigiana, Trebbiano Toscano, Nosiola, Vernaccia, Sylvaner and Veltliner. The result must be a wine made from a grape yield of not more than 140 quintals per hectare and with a minimum alcohol content of 10.5 per cent. A 15 per cent in volume use of cutting-wines is permitted; also for the red.

The red wine must be made up of at least 20 per cent of Schiava and 10 per cent of Lambrusco; the difference may be made up with Merlot, Pinot Nero, Lagrein, Teroldego and Negrara as required. The minimum alcohol content is 11 per cent. Produced by Cantina Viticoltori, Ravina di Trento, Trento.

Valle Isarco (Eisacktaler) (299 – 16.11.1974)

The DOC legislation allows for the production of five dry white wines. The aromatic Traminer (Gewürztraminer) and the Pinot Grigio (Rülander) may not have a yield of more than 100 quintals per hectare nor less than 11 per cent of alcohol; the Veltliner – a yield of 120 quintals and 10.5 per cent alcohol, the Sylvaner and the Müller-Thurgau – a yield of 130 quintals and 10.5 per cent of alcohol content. In all cases, 10 per cent by volume of cutting-wines may be added. The wines may be given a geographical denomination of Bressanone or Brixner. Produced by:

Abbazia di Novacella, Novacella di Varna, Bolzano

Cantina Sociale Valle Isarco (Eisacktaler Kellereigenossenschaft), Chiusa, Bolzano

Vini del Trentino (221 – 2.9.1971 and 324 – 28.11.1979)

Cabernet Trentino: This is made from 90 per cent of Cabernet, and has a minimum alcohol content of 11 per cent. A wine for ageing, although no legislation exists. Produced by:

Baroni a Prato, Segonzano, Trento
Cantina Viticoltori, Ravina di Trento, Trento
Dolzan, San Michele all'Adige, Trento
Fratelli Endrizzi, San Michele all'Adige, Trento
Girelli, Trento

La Vinicola Sociale, Aldeno, Trento
Lechthaler, Mezzocorona, Trento
Pisoni, Pergolese, Trento
Saiani Albino Cantine, Rovereto, Trento
Liberio Todesca, Mattarello Trento, Trento
S. A. V. Vallagarina, Sant'Illario Rovereto, Trento

Lagrein Trentino: A light red wine with 11 per cent minimum of alcohol and a yield of not more than 120 quintals per hectare. There is also a Lagrein Kretzer (rosé) from Mezzocorona at 12.5 per cent, produced by Dorigati, Mezzocorona, Trento. Produced by:

Barone de Cles, Mezzolombarda, Trento
Bossi-Fedrigotti, Rovereto, Trento

Cantina Sociale di Mezzocorona, Trento

Marzemino Trentino: A dry red wine, with a yield of 90 quintals per hectare, a minimum alcohol content of 11 per cent; with 12 per cent and two years' ageing, the wine may be called Riserva. Produced by:

Bossi-Fedrigotti, Rovereto, Trento
Cantina Sociale, Nomi, Trento
Cantina Viticoltori, Ravina di Trento, Trento
Fratelli Endrizzi, San Michele all'Adige, Trento
Girelli, Trento, Trento
La Vinicola Sociale, Aldeno, Trento
Saiani Albino, Rovereto, Trento
S. A. V. Vallagarina, Nogaredo, Trento

Merlot Trentino: A dry red wine, produced at an 11 per cent alcohol content, has a yield of 125 quintals per hectare. Produced by:

Barone de Cles, Mezzolombardo, Trento
Bossi-Fedrigotti, Rovereto, Trento
Cantina Sociale, Mezzocorona, Trento
Cantina Sociale, Nomi, Trento
Cantina Viticoltori, Ravina di Trento, Trento
Fratelli Endrizzi, San Michele all'Adige, Trento
Girelli, Trento, Trento
La Vinicola Cooperativa, Aldeno, Trento
Pisoni, Pergolese Sarche, Trento
Saiani Albino, Rovereto, Trento
S. A. V. Vallagarina, Rovereto, Trento

Moscat Trentino: A sweet white wine, produced from semi-dried grapes, to give a minimum alcohol content of 13 per cent. Produced by:

Cantina Viticoltori, Ravina di Trento, Trento
Fratelli Endrizzi, San Michele all'Adige, Trento

Pinot Nero Trentino: A dry red wine with an alcohol content of 11.5 per cent. Produced by:

Baroni a Prato, Segonzano, Trento
Cantina Sociale Lavis Sorni Salorno, Lavis, Trento
Cantina Viticoltori, Ravina di Trento, Trento
Fratelli Endrizzi, San Michele all'Adige, Trento
Lechthaler, Mezzocorona, Trento
Saiani Albino, Rovereto, Trento

Pinot Trentino: A dry white wine with an alcohol content of 11 per cent. It is much used as an apéritif and for converting into sparkling *spumante* wines. Produced by:

Barone de Cles, Mezzolombardo, Trento
Cantina Sociale Lavis Sorni Salorno, Lavis, Trento
Cantina Sociale, Nomi, Trento
Cantina Viticoltori, Ravina di Trento, Trento
Dorigati, Mezzocorona, Trento
Fratelli Endrizzi, San Michele all'Adige, Trento
Girelli, Trento, Trento
La Vinicola Sociale, Aldeno, Trento
Lechthaler, Mezzocorona, Trento

Riesling Trentino: A dry white wine with a minimum alcohol content of 11 per cent. Produced by:

Cantina Viticoltori, Ravina di Trento, Trento
Dolzan, San Michele all'Adige, Trento
Fratelli Endrizzi, San Michele all'Adige, Trento
Girelli, Trento, Trento

Traminer Aromatico Trentino (Gewürztraminer): A dry white wine with a minimum alcohol content of 12 per cent. Produced by:

Castel Rametz, Merano, Trento
Castel Schwanburg, Nalles, Bolzano
Josef Hofstatter, Termeno, Bolzano
G. Kettmeir, Bolzano
Von Elzembaum, Termeno, Bolzano

Vin Santo Trentino: A sweet white wine made from semi-dried grapes to reach a total alcohol content of 16 per cent. Produced by Fratelli Marchelli, Arco, Trento.

FRIULI-VENEZIA GIULIA

1979 vintage – good quality and generous yield.

Aquileia (290 – 31.10.1975)

All the Aquileia wines are produced by the Cantina Sociale Cooperativa del Friuli Orientale, Cervignano, Udine.

Aquileia Cabernet: A dry red wine with 11.5 per cent of alcohol content is produced from a maximum yield of 120 quintals.

Aquileia Merlot: A dry red wine with 11 per cent of alcohol content is produced from a maximum yield of 130 quintals.

Aquileia Pinot Bianco: A wine of 11.5 per cent alcohol content, produced from a maximum yield of 120 quintals per hectare.

Aquileia Pinot Grigio: A wine of 11 per cent alcohol content, produced from a yield of not more than 130 quintals per hectare.

Aquileia Refosco: A dry red wine, with 11 per cent of alcohol content, is obtained from a maximum yield of 130 quintals per hectare.

Aquileia Riesling Renano: A wine of 11 per cent alcohol content, produced from a yield of not more than 130 quintals per hectare.

Aquileia Tocai Friulano: A dry white wine of 11 per cent alcohol content, produced from a maximum yield of 130 quintals per hectare.

Collio Goriziano or *Collio* (178 – 15.7.1968; 153 – 6.6.1979)

The yields of none of the Collio wines may exceed 110 quintals per hectare.

Collio Cabernet Franc: A dry red wine with an alcohol content of 12 per cent. Produced by:

Attems, Lucinico, Gorizia	Arcangelo Pavan, San Quirino, Pordenone
Livio Felluga, Brazzano di Cormons, Gorizia	Roncada, Cormons, Gorizia
Marco Felluga, Gradisca d'Isonzo, Gorizia	Giovanni Scolaris, San Lorenzo Isontino, Gorizia
Conte Michele Formentini, San Floriano del Collio, Gorizia	Villa Russiz, Capriva, Gorizia

Collio Goriziano: Produced from the Ribolla, Malvasia and Tocai grapes this is a dry white wine, with an 11 per cent alcohol content. Produced by:

Conti Formentini, San Floriano del Collio, Gorizia	La Viticoltori, San Floriano del Collio, Gorizia

Collio Malvasia: A dry white wine with 11.5 per cent of alcohol. Produced by:

Angoris Sacta, Cormons, Gorizia	La Viticoltori, San Floriano del Collio, Gorizia
Attems, Gorizia Lucinico, Gorizia	
Azienda Agricola della Roncada, Cormons, Gorizia	Santa Caterina, Scrio di Dolegna, Gorizia
	Valle Aziende Vitivinicole, Buttrio, Udine
Formentini, San Floriano del Collio, Gorizia	Villa Russiz, Capriva del Friuli, Gorizia

Collio Merlot: A dry red wine with a 12 per cent alcohol content. Produced by:

Attems, Lucinico Gorizia, Gorizia
Azienda Agricola della Roncada,
    Cormons, Gorizia
Cantina Produttori Vini del Collio e
    dell'Isonzo, Cormons, Gorizia
Carlo Drufovka, Oslavia, Gorizia
Enofriuli, Capriva, Gorizia
Livio Felluga, Cormons, Gorizia
Marco Felluga, Gradisca d'Isonzo, Gorizia

Formentini, San Floriano del Collio,
    Gorizia
La Viticoltori, San Floriano del Collio,
    Gorizia
Ercole Pighin, Risano, Udine
Santa Caterina, Scrio di Dolegna, Gorizia
Subida Di Monte, Cormons, Gorizia
Valle Aziende Vitivinicole, Buttrio, Udine
Villa Russiz, Capriva, Gorizia

Collio Pinot Bianco: A dry white wine of 12 per cent alcohol content. Produced by:

Azienda Agricola della Roncada,
    Cormons, Gorizia
Cantina Produttori Vini del Collio e
    dell'Isonzo, Cormons, Gorizia
Enofriuli, Capriva, Gorizia
Marco Felluga, Gradisca d'Isonzo, Gorizia

Giovanni Ferlat, Cormons, Gorizia
Formentini, San Floriano del Collio,
    Gorizia
La Viticoltori, San Floriano del Collio,
    Gorizia

Collio Pinot Grigio: A dry white wine of 12.5 per cent alcohol content. Produced by:

Attems, Gorizia Lucinico, Gorizia
Azienda Agricola della Roncada,
    Cormons, Gorizia
Marco Felluga, Gradisca d'Isonzo, Gorizia
Formentini, San Floriano del Collio,
    Gorizia
La Viticoltori, San Floriano del Collio,
    Gorizia

Ercole Pighin, Risano, Udine
Santa Caterina, Scrio di Dolegna, Gorizia
Giovanni Scolaris, San Lorenzo Isontino,
    Gorizia
Subida di Monte, Cormons, Gorizia
Villa Russiz, Capriva, Gorizia

Collio Pinot Nero: A dry red wine of 12.5 per cent alcohol content. Produced by:

Livio Felluga, Cormons, Gorizia
Marco Felluga, Gradisca d'Isonzo,
    Gorizia

Giovanni Scolaris, San Lorenzo Isontino,
    Gorizia
Villa Russiz, Capriva, Gorizia

Collio Riesling Italico: A dry white wine with 12 per cent of alcohol content. Produced by:

Attems, Gorizia Lucinico, Gorizia
Enofriuli, Capriva, Gorizia

Marco Felluga, Gradisca d'Isonzo, Gorizia

Collio Sauvignon: A dry white wine of 12.5 per cent alcohol content. Produced by:

Attems, Gorizia Lucinico, Gorizia
Azienda Agricola della Roncada,
    Cormons, Gorizia
Marco Felluga, Gradisca d'Isonzo, Gorizia
Formentini, San Floriano del Collio,
    Gorizia

Ercole Pighin, Risano, Udine
Subida Di Monte, Cormons, Gorizia
Valle Aziende Vitivinicole, Buttrio, Udine
Villa Russiz, Capriva, Gorizia

Collio Tocai: A Tocai white wine with a 12 per cent minimum alcohol content. Produced by:

Angoris Sacta, Cormons, Gorizia
Attems, Lucinico Gorizia, Gorizia
Catemario, Gramogliano di Corno di
    Rosazzo, Udine

Carlo Drufovka, Oslavia Gorizia, Gorizia
Livio Felluga, Cormons, Gorizia
Marco Felluga, Gradisca d'Isonzo, Gorizia

Schloss Schwanburg, at Nalles near Bolzano in the Alto-Adige/Süd Tirol,
where the Carli family makes elegant red and white wines

Formentini, San Floriano del Collio,
  Gorizia
Pighin, Risano, Udine
Produttori del Collio e dell'Isonzo,
  Cormons, Gorizia
Santa Caterina, Scrio di Dolegna, Gorizia

Giovanni Scolaris, San Lorenzo Isontino,
  Gorizia
Subida di Monte, Cormons, Gorizia
Valle Aziende Vitivinicole, Buttrio, Udine
Villa Russiz, Capriva, Gorizia

Collio Traminer: A dry white wine of 12 per cent alcohol content. Produced by:

Buzzinelli, Cormons, Gorizia
Enofriuli, Capriva, Gorizia

Subida Di Monte, Cormons, Gorizia

Colli Orientali del Friuli (4247 – 30.9.1970; 166 – 19.6.1979)

All the following wines have a maximum yield of 110 quintals per hectare.

Colli Orientali del Friuli Cabernet: A dry red wine with an alcohol content of 12 per cent. If aged for two years, the wine may be labelled Riserva. Produced by:

Colli di Manzano, Ronchi di Manzano,
  Udine
Colli di Spessa, Ronchi Sant'Anna,
  Cividale, Udine
Conti di Maniago, Soleschiano, Udine
D'Attimis Maniago, Sottomonte di
  Buttrio, Udine

Genagricola, Poggiobello, Manzano, Udine
Ronchi di Manzano, Manzano, Udine
Valle Aziende Vitivinicole, Buttrio, Udine
Volpe-Pasini, Togliano di Torreano,
  Civicale, Udine

Colli Orientali del Friuli Merlot: A dry red wine with 12 per cent of alcohol content. If aged for two years it may be labelled Riserva. Produced by:

Collavini, Rivignano, Udine
Colli di Manzano, Ronchi di Manzano,
  Udine
Colli di Novacuzza, Prepotto, Udine
Colli di Spessa, Cividale, Udine
Colutta, Bandut, Manzano, Udine
Conti di Maniago, Soleschiano, Udine

D'Attimis Maniago, Buttrio, Udine
Girolamo Dorigo, Buttrio, Udine
Livio Felluga, Cormons, Udine
Ronchi di Manzano, Manzano, Udine
Valle Aziende, Buttrio, Udine
Villa Frattina, Ghirano, Pordenone
Volpe-Pasini, Togliano di Torreano, Udine

Colli Orientali del Friuli Picolit: An *amabile* or sweet wine with an alcohol content of 15 per cent. If the wine is aged two years, it may be labelled Riserva. Produced by:

Cantina del Friuli Centrale, Beriolo, Udine
Conti di Maniago, Soleschiano, Udine
Florio Maseri, Buttrio, Udine

Bernarda Rocca, SMOM, Ipplis, Udine
Ronchi di Manzano, Manzano, Udine
Valle Aziende, Buttrio, Udine

Colli Orientali del Friuli Pinot Bianco: A dry white wine with a minimum alcohol content of 12 per cent. Produced by:

Colli di Novacuzza, Prepotto, Udine
Livio Felluga, Cormons, Gorizia
Ronchi di Manzano, Manzano, Udine

Valle Aziende, Buttrio, Udine
Villa Frattina, Ghirano, Pordenone
Volpe Pasini, Togliano di Torreano, Udine

Colli Orientali del Friuli Pinot Grigio: A dry white wine with 12 per cent of alcohol content. Produced by:

Colli di Manzano, Ronchi di Manzano,
  Udine
Colli di Novacuzza, Prepotto, Udine
Colli di Spessa, Ronchi Sant'Anna di
  Cividale, Udine
Conti di Maniago, Soleschiano, Udine

Girolamo Dorigo, Buttrio, Udine
Livio Felluga, Cormons, Gorizia
Florio Maseri, Pavia di Udine, Buttrio,
  Udine
Ronchi di Manzano, Udine
Volpe Pasini, Togliano di Torreano, Udine

The vineyards of Cacchiano, a very large estate owned by members of the Ricasoli family, showing the traditional mixed nature of a Chianti Classico estate with vines and olives growing side by side

Colli Orientali del Friuli Pinot Nero: A dry red wine with an alcohol content of 12 per cent. If aged for two years, the wine may be labelled Riserva. Produced by:

Girolamo Dorigo, Buttrio, Udine
Ronchi di Manzano, Manzano, Udine
Volpe-Pasini, Togliano di Torreano, Udine

Colli Orientali del Friuli Refosco: A dry red wine with an alcohol content of 12 per cent. If aged for two years, the wine may be labelled Riserva. Produced by:

Colutta, Bandut, Manzano, Udine
Conti di Maniago, Soleschiano, Udine
Ronchi di Manzano, Manzano, Udine
Valle Aziende, Buttrio, Udine

Colli Orientali del Friuli Ribolla: A dry white wine with a minimum alcohol content of 12 per cent. Produced by:

Valentino Butussi, Corno di Rosazzo, Udine
Genagricola, Poggiobello, Manzano, Udine
Valle Aziende, Buttrio, Udine

Colli Orientali del Friuli Riesling Renano: A dry white wine with 12 per cent of alcohol content. Produced by:

Giovanni Collavini, Corno di Rosazzo, Udine
Livio Felluga, Cormons, Udine
Ronchi di Manzano, Manzano, Udine
Valle Aziende, Buttrio, Udine

Colli Orientali del Friuli Sauvignon: A dry white wine with 12 per cent of alcohol content. Produced by:

Giovanni Collavini, Corno di Rosazzo, Udine
Colli di Manzano, Ronchi di Manzano, Udine
Colli di Novacuzza, Prepotto, Udine
Colli di Spessa, Ronchi Sant'Anna di Cividale, Udine
D'Attimis Maniago, Buttrio, Udine
Livio Felluga, Cormons, Gorizia
Rubini Cantina, Spessa di Cividale del Friuli, Udine

Colli Orientali del Friuli Tocai: A dry white wine of 12 per cent of alcohol content. Produced by:

Accordini, Campeglio, Udine
Collavini, Corno di Rosazzo, Udine
Colli di Manzano, Ronchi di Manzano, Udine
Colli di Novacuzza, Prepotto, Udine
Colli di Spessa, Ronchi Sant'Anna, Cividale, Udine
Colutta, Bandut, Manzano, Udine
Conti di Maniago, Soleschiano di Manzano, Udine
D'Attimis-Maniago, Buttrio, Udine
Girolamo Dorigo, Buttrio, Udine
Livio Felluga, Cormons, Gorizia
Florio Maseri, Buttrio, Udine
Bernarda Rocca SMOM, Ipplis, Udine
Ronchi di Manzano, Manzano, Udine
Valle Aziende Vitivinicole, Buttrio, Udine
Villa Frattina, Ghirano, Pordenone
Volpe Pasini, Togliano di Torreano, Udine

Colli Orientali del Friuli Verduzzo: A dry white wine of 12 per cent alcohol content; when the wine is made sweet it is called Ramandolo. Produced by:

Colli di Manzano, Ronchi di Manzano, Udine
Colli di Spessa, Ronchi Sant'Anna, Civicale, Udine
Colutta, Bandut, Manzano, Udine
Conti di Maniago, Soleschiano di Manzano, Udine
Girolamo Dorigo, Buttrio, Udine
Livio Felluga, Cormons, Gorizia
Genagricola, Poggiobello, Manzano, Udine
Ercole Pighin, Risano, Udine
Bernarda Rocca, SMOM, Ipplis Udine
Ronchi di Manzano, Manzano, Udine

Grave del Friuli (244 – 26.9.1970; 166 – 19.6.1979)

Grave del Friuli Cabernet: A dry red wine with 11.5 per cent of alcohol content. Produced by:

Cantina Sociale Cooperativa di Casarsa, Casarsa della Delizia, Pordenone

Friulvini, Porcia, Pordenone

Antonio Furchir, Felettis di Bicinicco, Udine

Arcangelo Pavan, San Quirino, Pordenone

Plozner, Spilimbergo, Pordenone

Russolo, Pramaggiore, Venezia

Valle Aziende, Buttrio, Udine

Grave del Friuli Merlot: A dry red wine with 11 per cent of alcohol content. Produced by:

Cantina Sociale Cooperativa Casarsa della Delizia, Pordenone

Conti G. G. di Porcia, Pordenone

Friulvini, Porcia, Pordenone

Antonio Furchir, Fellettis di Bicinicco, Udine

Arcangelo Pavan, San Quirino, Pordenone

Pighin, Risano, Udine

Plozner, Spilimbergo, Pordenone

Grave del Friuli Pinot Bianco: A dry white wine with 11.5 per cent alcohol content. Produced by:

Cantina Sociale Casarsa, Casarsa della Delizia, Pordenone

Collavini, Rivagnano e Corno di Rosazzo, Udine

Friulvini, Porcia, Udine

Pighin, Risano, Udine

Plozner, Spilimbergo, Pordenone

Grave del Friuli Pinot Grigio: A dry white wine with an alcohol content of 11 per cent. Produced by:

Canella, San Dona di Piave, Venezia

Cantina Sociale Casarsa, Casarsa della Delizia, Pordenone

Friulvini, Porcia, Pordenone

Plozner, Spilimbergo, Pordenone

Villa d'Arco, A Pavan, San Quirino, Pordenone

Grave del Friuli Refosco: A dry red wine with 11 per cent of alcohol content. Produced by:

Friulvini, Porcia, Pordenone

Antonio Furchir, Felettis di Biciniccio, Udine

Plozner, Spilimbergo, Pordenone

Grave del Friuli Tocai: A dry white wine with 11 per cent of alcohol content. Produced by:

Cantina Sociale Casarsa, Casarsa della Delizia, Pordenone

Friulvini, Porcia, Pordenone

Arcangelo Pavan, San Quirino, Pordenone

Plozner, Spilimbergo, Pordenone

Grave del Friuli Verduzzo: A dry white wine with an alcohol content of 11 per cent. Produced by:

Cantina Sociale Casarsa, Casarsa della Delizia, Pordenone

Conti G. G. di Porcia, Pordenone

Friulvini, Porcia, Pordenone

Isonzo (65 – 8.3.1975; 287 – 20.10.1979)

Isonzo Cabernet: A dry red wine, produced from less than 120 quintals per hectare and with an alcohol content of at least 11 per cent. Produced by:

Marco Felluga, Gradisca d'Isonzo, Gorizia   Giovanni Scolaris, San Lorenzo Isontino,
Giovanni Ferlat, Cormons, Gorizia   Gorizia
Prandi d'Ulmhort, Romans d'Isonzo, Gorizia

Isonzo Malvasia Istriana: A dry white wine is produced from 130 quintals per hectare. It has a minimum alcohol content of 10.5 per cent. Produced by:

Marco Felluga, Gradisca d'Isonzo, Gorizia   Prandi d'Ulmhort, Romans d'Isonzo,
                                                                      Gorizia

Isonzo Merlot: A dry red wine, produced from a yield of less than 130 quintals per hectare, has an alcohol content of more than 10.5 per cent. Produced by:

Silvio Cosolo, Fogliano, Gorizia   Marco Felluga, Gradisca d'Isonzo, Gorizia

Isonzo Pinot Bianco: A dry white wine is produced from less than 120 quintals per hectare and with more than 11 per cent of alcohol content. Produced by:

Sergio Cosolo, Fogliano, Gorizia   Giovanni Scolaris, San Lorenzo Isontino,
Marco Felluga, Gradisca d'Isonzo, Gorizia   Gorizia
Prandi d'Ulmhort, Romans d'Isonzo, Gorizia

Isonzo Pinot Grigio: This dry white wine, with a minimum of 11 per cent of alcohol, is produced from a yield of less than 120 quintals per hectare. Produced by:

Marco Felluga, Gradisca d'Isonzo, Gorizia   Giovanni Scolaris, San Lorenzo Isontino,
Prandi d'Ulmhort, Romans d'Isonzo,   Gorizia
  Gorizia

Isonzo Riesling Renano: This dry white wine, produced a yield of less than 120 quintals per hectare, has an alcohol content of at least 11 per cent.

Isonzo Sauvignon: A dry white wine is produced from a yield of 120 quintals per hectare. It has a minimum alcohol content of 11 per cent. Produced by Giovanni Ferlat, Cormons, Gorizia.

Isonzo Tocai: A dry white wine is produced from a yield of 130 quintals per hectare. It has a minimum alcohol content of 10.5 per cent. Produced by:

Sergio Cosolo, Silvio, Orietta,   Giovanni Scolaris, San Lorenzo Isontino,
  Fogliano, Gorizia   Gorizia
Marco Felluga, Gradisca d'Isonzo, Gorizia

Isonzo Traminer Aromatico: This dry white wine with a minimum of 11 per cent of alcohol content, is produced from a yield of less than 120 quintals per hectare.

Isonzo Verduzzo Friulano: This dry white wine, with a minimum of 10.5 per cent of alcohol, is produced from a yield of less than 120 quintals per hectare. Produced by Marco Felluga, Gradisca d'Isonzo, Gorizia.

Latisana (292 – 5.11.1975)

All the Latisana wines are produced by the Cantina Sociale di Latisana, Latisana, Udine.

Latisana Cabernet: A dry red wine, which may be blended with Cabernet Franc and Cabernet Sauvignon, and produced from not more than 130 quintals per hectare, has an alcohol content of 11.5 per cent.

Latisana Merlot: This dry red wine, with 11 per cent of alcohol, is produced from a yield of less than 120 quintals per hectare.

Latisana Pinot Bianco: A dry white wine produced from a maximum yield of 120 quintals per hectare. It has 11.5 per cent of alcohol content.

Latisana Pinot Grigio: A dry white wine produced from a maximum yield of 130 quintals per hectare. It has 11 per cent of alcohol content.

Latisana Refosco: This dry red wine, with a maximum yield of 130 quintals per hectare, has an alcohol content of 11 per cent.

Latisana Tocai Friulana: This dry white wine is produced from a maximum yield of 130 quintals per hectare. It has an alcohol content of 11 per cent.

Latisana Verduzzo Friulano: A dry white wine is produced from a maximum yield of 130 quintals per hectare. It has 11 per cent of alcohol content.

EMILIA – ROMAGNA

1979 vintage – average-quality but reduced-yield.

Albana di Romagna (209 – 21.8.1967; 253 – 6.10.1969; 63 – 6.3.1975; 15 – 15.1.1978)

Produced at a maximum of 140 quintals per hectare, the Albana is a white wine that is made both dry (at 12 per cent) and *amabile* (12.5 per cent). The legislation permits it being turned into a sparkling wine by natural methods. Produced by:

Colombina, Bertinoro, Forli
Cooperative Riolo Terme Baldrati,
  Lugo, Ravenna
Fattoria Paradiso, Bertinoro, Forli
Ferrucci, Castelbolognese, Ravenna
Guarini Matteucci, San Tome, Forli
Pantani Torino e Edo Casa, Mercato
  Saraceno, Forli

Pasolini Dall'Onda, Montericcio, Bologna
Poletti, Imola, Bologna
Sociale Cooperativa Produttori Vini Tipici,
  Modigliana, Forli
Tenuta Amalia, Villa Verucchio, Forli
Zerbina, Marzeno di Faenza, Ravenna

Bianco di Scandiano (37 – 9.2.1977)

This wine is made from 85 per cent of Sauvignon (locally called Spergola or Spergolina), with the balance from Malvasia di Candia or Trebbiano Romagnolo. Its maximum yield per hectare is 130 quintals. It is made as *dolce*, *semi-secco* and as *secco*; in all cases, the alcohol content is 10.5 per cent. It is mostly made as a sparkling wine, when it has an alcohol content of 11 per cent. Produced by:

Consorzio Vini Scandiano, Reggio Emilia,
  Reggio nell'Emilia

Cooperativa Colli di Scandiano, Scandiano,
  Reggio nell'Emilia

Colli Bolognesi di San Pietro (318 – 2.12.1975)

Also known as 'Colli Bolognesi – Monte San Pietro' or 'Colli Bolognesi dei Castelli Medioevali'.

Colli Bolognesi Barbera: A dry red wine produced from a maximum yield of 120 quintals per hectare to provide an 11.5 per cent alcohol content. With a 12.5 per cent alcohol content and three years' ageing, of which one must be in the wood, the wine may be called Riserva. Produced by:

Cantina Consorziale Comprensorio
  di Monte San Pietro Cooperativa,
  Zola Predosa, Bologna

Sassoli, San Martino in Casola, Bologna
Torre Ca Bianca, Zola Predosa, Bologna
Vallania, Zola Predosa, Bologna

Colli Bolognesi Bianco: A dry white wine made from 60 per cent Albana and 40 per cent Trebbiano. The yield may not exceed 130 quintals per hectare and the alcohol content may not be less than 11 per cent. Produced by:

Cantina Consorziale Comprensorio
  di Monte San Pietro Cooperativa,
  Zola Predosa, Bologna

Sassoli, San Martino in Casola,
  Bologna
Vallania, Zola Predosa, Bologna

Colli Bolognesi Merlot: A dry red wine produced from a maximum yield of 120 quintals per hectare to provide an 11.5 per cent alcohol content. Produced by:

Cantina Consorziale Comprensorio
  di Monte San Pietro Cooperativa,
  Zola Predosa, Bologna

Sassoli, San Martino in Casola, Bologna
Torre Ca Bianca, Zola Predosa, Bologna
Vallania, Zola Predosa, Bologna

Colli Bolognesi Pinot Bianco: A dry white wine produced from a maximum yield of 110 quintals per hectare to provide a 12 per cent alcohol content. Produced by:

Cantina Consorziale Comprensorio
  di Monte San Pietro Cooperativa,
  Zola Predosa, Bologna

Torre Ca Bianca, Ponte Ronca, Zola
  Predosa, Bologna
Vallania, Zola Predosa, Bologna

Colli Bolognesi Riesling Italico: A dry white wine produced from a maximum yield of 120 quintals per hectare to provide a 12 per cent alcohol content. Produced by:

Cantina Consorziale Comprensorio
  di Monte San Pietro Cooperativa,
  Zola Predosa, Bologna

Sassoli, San Martino in Casola,
  Bologna
Vallania, Zola Predosa, Bologna

Colli Bolognesi Sauvignon: A dry white wine produced from a maximum yield of 120 quintals per hectare to provide a 12 per cent alcohol content. Produced by:

Cantina Consorziale Comprensorio
  di Monte San Pietro Cooperativa,
  Zola Predosa, Bologna

Sassoli, San Martino in Casola,
  Bologna

Gutturnio dei Colli Piacentini (203 – 14.8.1967)

A dry red wine made with 60 per cent Barbera and the rest, Bonarda, is produced from a yield of 120 quintals per hectare to offer 12 per cent of alcohol content. Produced by:

Azienda Agricola Giuseppe Molinelli,
  Ziano Piacentino, Piacenza
Bonelli, Rivergaro, Piacenza
Cagnoni, Niviano Castello, Piacenza
Celso Berte, Piacenza Settima, Piacenza
La Solitaria, Ziano, Piacenza
Montesissa, Cascina Buffalora, Travazzano
  di Carpaneto, Piacenza

Celio Piacentini, Ziano, Piacenza
Pusterla, Vigolo Marchese, Piacenza
Quattro Valli Cantine, Piacenza
Valtidone Cantina Cooperativa,
  Borgonovo Val Tidone, Piacenza

Lambrusco Grasparossa di Castelvetro (203 – 12.8.1970)

A sparkling red wine, produced both dry and *amabile*. It has a maximum yield of 140 quintals per hectare and a minimum alcohol content of 10.5 per cent. Produced by:

Cavalli, Scandiano, Reggio nell'Emilia
Cavicchioli, San Prospero, Modena
Chiarli, Modena
Consorzio Interprovinciale Vini, Modena

Contessa Matilde (Selezione Premiovini),
  Brescia
Angelo Giacobazzi, Nonantola, Modena
Val Panaro, San Cesario, Modena

Lambrusco Reggiano (223 – 4.9.1971; 32 – 1.2.1979)

A sparkling red wine, produced both dry and *amabile*. It has a maximum yield per hectare of 150 quintals; minimum alcohol content 10.5 per cent. Produced by:

Cantine Cooperative Riunite di Reggio-Emilia, Reggio nell'Emilia
Cavalli, Scandiano, Reggio nell'Emilia
Donelli, Ilario d'Enza, Reggio nell'Emilia
Ermete Medici, Villa Gaida, Reggio nell'Emilia
Ina Maria Pellerano, Ravarino, Modena

Lambrusco Salamino di Santa Croce (204 – 13.8.1970)

A sparkling red wine, produced both dry and *amabile*. It has a maximum yield per hectare of 150 quintals; minimum alcohol content 11 per cent. Produced by:

Cantine Cooperative Riunite di Reggio-Emilia, Reggio nell'Emilia
Cavicchioli, San Prospero, Modena
Chiarli e figli, Modena
Severi Vini, Baggiovara, Modena
Val Panaro, San Cesario, Modena

Lambrusco di Sorbara (206 – 17.8.1970)

A sparkling red wine, produced both dry and *amabile*. It has a maximum yield per hectare of 140 quintals and a minimum alcohol content of 11 per cent. Produced by:

Cavicchioli, San Prospero, Modena
Chiarli e figli, Modena
Consorzio Interprovinciale Vini, Modena
Contessa Matilde (Selezione Premiovini), Brescia
Angelo Giacobazzi, Nonantola, Modena
Severi Casa Vini, Baggiovara, Modena
Val Panaro, San Cesario, Modena

Monterosso Val d'Arda (321 – 9.12.1974)

A dry white wine made from nearly 50 per cent of Malvasia di Candia and a blend of Moscato Bianco, Trebbiano Romagnolo and Sauvignon. Its maximum yield per hectare is 90 quintals and the minimum alcohol content is 11 per cent. It is also made *amabile*. Produced by:

Enoteca Castellarquato, Castell'Arquato, Piacenza
Gino Innocenti, Bacedasco Alto, Piacenza
Pusterla, Vigolo Marchese, Piacenza

Sangiovese di Romagna (203 – 14.8.1967; 253 – 6.10.1969; 343 – 27.12.1976)

A dry red wine from the Sangiovese vine, with a maximum yield of 110 quintals per hectare and a minimum alcohol strength of 11.5 per cent: if aged for two years, the wine may be qualified as Riserva. With 12 per cent it may be labelled Superiore. Produced by:

Luigi Baldrati, Lugo, Ravenna
Camerone, G. Marabini, Castelbolognese, Ravenna
Cantina Sociale Sangiovese, Predappio, Forli
Cantina Braschi, Mercato Saraceno, Forli
Colombina, Bertinoro, Forli
Cooperativa Agricola, Riolo Terme, Ravenna
Emiliani, Sant'Agata sul Santerno, Forli
Fattoria Paradiso, Capocolle di Bertinoro, Forli
Ferrucci, Castelbolognese, Ravenna
Guarini Matteucci, San Tome, Forli
Pasolini dall'Onda, Montericcio di Imola, Bologna
Poletti Casa Vinicola, Imola, Bologna
Tenuta Amalia, Villa Verucchio, Forli

Trebbianino di Val Trebbia (100 – 15.4.1975)

This dry white wine, based on 35–50 per cent of Ortrugo vines, 10–30 per cent of Malvasia di Candia, 15–30 per cent of Trebbiano Romagnolo or Moscato and 15 per cent of Sauvignon, is an 11-per-cent-content of alcohol wine that may be processed either as completely dry or as *abboccato-frizzante*. Produced by Fratelli Bonelli, Rivergaro, Piacenza.

Trebbiano di Romagna (327 – 20.12.1973; 15 – 16.1.1978)

A dry white wine produced from 100 per cent Trebbiano grapes at 11.5 per cent alcohol content. This may also be made as a *spumante* sparkling wine by natural methods. Produced by:

Luigi Baldrati, Lugo, Ravenna

Emiliani Casa Vinicola, Imola, Bologna

Pasolini dall'Onda, Forli

Poletti Casa Vinicola, Imola, Bologna

Tenuta Amalia, Villa Verucchio, Forli

TUSCANY

1979 vintage – good quality and very generous yield.

Bianco della Val-di-Nievole (Valdinievole) (140 – 28.5.1976)

This dry white table wine is made from the Trebbiano, with 25 per cent Malvasia di Chianti and Vermentino. The maximum yield per hectare is 130 quintals and the minimum alcohol content is 11 per cent. A Vin Santo is also included in this legislation which is made in three versions – dry, semi-dry and sweet.

Bianco Vergine Val di Chiana (310 – 29.11.1972)

This wine contains 75 per cent Trebbiano with a contribution of Malvasia del Chianti. It is a dry white wine, with at least 11 per cent of alcohol content, produced from a grape yield of not more than 130 quintals per hectare. Produced by:

Mario Baldetti, Terentola, Petraia, Arezzo

Mancini Griffoli, Foiano, Arezzo

Il Poggetto, Rigutino, Arezzo

S. A. V. Spaletti, Rufina, Firenze

Brunello di Montalcino (132 – 30.5.1966)

This famous wine is made from the Sangiovese Grosso vine at not more than 100 quintals per hectare. Its minimum alcohol content is 12.5 per cent. It must be aged for four years in the wood; if it is aged for more than five, it may be denominated Riserva. This Brunello became DOCG in 1980. Produced by:

Barbi, Colombini, Montalcino, Siena

Biondi-Santi, Il Greppo, Montalcino, Siena

Casale del Bosco, Montalcino, Siena

Castiglione del Bosco, Montalcino, Siena

Col d'Orcia, Montalcino, Siena

Il Colle al Matrichiese, Montalcino, Siena

Fattoria Camigliano, Montalcino, Siena

Lisini, Sant'Angelo in Colle, Montalcino, Siena

Poggio alle Mure, Montalcino, Siena

Villa Banfi, Sant'Angelo Scalo, Montalcino, Siena

Bianco di Pitigliano (132 – 30.5.1966)

This dry white wine is produced in volcanic soil in the province of Grosseto. It has a yield of 125 quintals per hectare and 11.5 per cent of alcohol content. It is made from the Trebbiano Toscano, Greco, Malvasia Bianca Toscana and Verdello vines. Produced by:

Cantina Sociale di Pitigliano, Pitigliano, Grosseto

Vinicola Toscana Agricola Immobiliare, Pitigliano, Grosseto

Carmignano (222 – 21.8.1975)

Carmignano was a Chianti that withdrew from the Chianti discipline to formulate one of its own. Its style is individual due to its unusual blend: Sangiovese (45–60 per cent), Canaiolo Nero (10–15 per cent), Cabernet (Uva Francesca 6–10 per cent), Trebbiano Toscano, Canaiolo Bianco, Malvasia del Chianti (10–20 per cent), Mammolo, Colorino, and Occhio di Pernice up to 5 per cent. It has a minimum alcohol content of 12.5 per cent and a minimum ageing in the wood of two years; with three years' ageing, of which two in the wood, the wine may be termed Riserva. Produced by:

Artimino, Artimino, Firenze
Bacchereto, Carmignano, Firenze
Contini-Bonacossi, Capezzana, Carmignano, Firenze
La Farnete, Carmignano, Firenze

Il Poggiolo, Carmignano, Firenze
Sasso Podere, Santa Cristina a Mezzana, Carmignano, Firenze
Sghedoni, L'Albanella, Verghereto, Carmignano, Firenze

Chianti Classico (217 – 30.8.1967; 253 – 6.10.1969)

A composite wine, based on Sangiovese, made in the historically delimited zone of central Tuscany. It has a minimum alcohol content of 12 per cent and, if aged for two years, may be called Vecchio. If with a 12.5 per cent alcohol content and aged for three years, it may be labelled Riserva. Almost all producers make an aged, completely dry, Vin Santo dessert wine. More than 90 per cent of the producers belong to the guild, called the Consorzio del Chianti Classico but only 50 per cent of the wine reaches the quality to get the Black Rooster seal on the bottle.

ESTATE/BRAND NAME	PRODUCER
Antiche Fattorie Isole e Olena	Società Immobiliare Agricola Alto Chianti Spa, Barberino Val d'Elsa, Firenze
Azienda Agricola Riecine	Palmina and John Dunkley, Gaiole in Chianti, Siena
Azienda Agricola San Felice	Agricola San Felice Spa, Castelnuovo Berardenga, San Gusmè, Siena
Badia a Coltibuono	Piero Stucchi Prinetti, Gaiole in Chianti, Siena
Casa Vinicola Fossi	Cav. Duilio Fossi, Compiobbi, Fiesole, Firenze
Castello di Brolio	Barone Bettino Ricasoli, Piazza V Veneto, Firenze
Castello di Cacchiano	Elisabetta Balbi Valier and Ricasoli Firidolfi, Gaiole in Chianti, Siena
Castello di Fonterutoli	Lapo Mazzei, Castellina in Chianti, Siena
Castello di Montefioralle	Pecchioli, Greve in Chianti, Firenze
Castello di Promiano Villa Le Corti/ Le Corti Corsini	Principe Corsini, San Casciano Val di Pesa, Firenze
Castello di San Polo in Rosso	Cesare Canessa, San Polo in Rosso, Gaiole in Chianti, Siena
Castello di Uzzano	Conte Castelbarco Albani, Greve in Chianti, Firenze
Castello di Verrazzano	Cappellini, Localita Greti, Greve in Chianti, Firenze
Castello di Vicchiomaggio	John Matta, Greve in Chianti, Firenze
Castello di Volpaia	Stianti, Radda in Chianti, Siena
Fattoria Ama	Giovanni Ginanneschi, Ama in Chianti, Siena
Fattoria di Campalli	Francesca Ricci Campana nei Giani, Castellina in Chianti, Siena
Fattoria Il Casalino	Casa Vinicola Tenuta di Angoris Spa, Quercegrossa, Siena
Fattoria Castell' in Villa	Principessa Coralia Pignatelli della Leonessa, Castell' in Villa, Castelnuovo Berga San Gusmè, Siena
Fattoria Castello di Cerreto	Marchese Emilio Pucci di Barsento, Pianella, Siena
Fattoria Castello di Gabbiano	Dr Arnaldo La Cagnina, Mercatale Val di Pesa, Firenze

ESTATE/BRAND NAME	PRODUCER
Fattoria Castello di Meleto	Viticola Toscana Agricola Immobiliare Spa, Gaiole in Chianti, Siena
Fattoria Castello di Rencine	Fratelli Brandini-Marcolini, Castellina in Chianti, Siena
Fattoria Castelvecchi	Marchese Carmen and Isabel Gutierrez de la Solana, Radda in Chianti, Siena
Fattoria Catignano	Dott. M. Sergardi Biringucci and Ved. Marmoross, Pianella, Siena
Fattoria di Cerbaiola	Aroldo Barsottini and Maria Teresa Fedeli, San Donato in Poggio, Firenze
Fattoria Fortilizio Il Colombaio	Contessa Isabella Bonucci, Quercegrossa, Siena
Fattoria di Gaggiano	Chianti Melini Spa, Poggibonsi, Siena
Fattoria Il Caggio	Rivella e Fideli, Castellina in Chianti, Siena
Fattoria Il Guerrino	Ornella Loretelli Taddei, Montefioralle, Greve in Chianti, Firenze
Fattoria La Capraia	Uiragricola Spa, Castellina in Chianti, Siena
Fattoria La Casaccia	Ing. Luigi Socini-Guelfi, Pianella e San Gusmè, Siena
Fattoria Agricola la Pagliaia	Agricola La Pagliaia Spa, Castelnuovo Berardenga, Siena
Fattoria Le Bocce	Le Bocce Spa, Panzana, Firenze
Fattoria Le Lodoline	Contessa Radicati di Brozzolo, Vagliagli, Siena
Fattoria Monsanto	Fabrizio Bianchi, Barberino d'Elsa, Firenze
Fattoria Montaglieri	Giovanni Cappelli, Panzano in Chianti, Firenze
Fattoria di Montepaldi	Marchese Corsini, San Casciano Val di Pesa, Firenze
Fattoria di Nozzole	Ruffino Spa, Pontassieve, Firenze
Fattoria dei Pagliaresi	Alma Biasotto Sanguineti, Borgo San Gusmè, Siena
Fattoria Palazzo al Bosco	Renzo Olivieri Eredi, Chiesanuova, Firenze
Fattoria Pian d'Albola	Pian d'Albola Spa, Radda in Chianti, Siena
Fattoria Rocca delle Macie Villa Banfi	Agricentro Spa, Castellina in Chianti, Siena
Fattoria San Leonino–I Cipressi	San Leonino Spa, Castellina in Chianti, Siena
Fattoria di Sicelle	Conti Rucellai, San Donato in Poggio, Firenze
Fattoria di Sizzano	Sizzano Spa, Castellino in Chianti, Siena
Fattoria Tizzano	Conte Filippo Pandolfini, San Polo in Chianti, Firenze
Fattoria di Vignamaggio	Conte Ranieri Sanminiatelli, Greve in Chianti, Firenze
Fattoria Villa Cafaggio	Villa Cafaggio s.a.s., Panzano in Chianti, Firenze
Machiavelli	Conti Serristori, San Casciano Val di Pesa, Firenze
Podere La Puzzola	R. Grierson, Castellina in Chianti, Siena and London
Selecru Selections	Roberto Pandolfini, Via San Gallo 74, Firenze
Soc. Coop. Agricoltori del Chianti Geografico	Produttori Chianti Geografico, Gaiole in Chianti, Siena

ESTATE/BRAND NAME	PRODUCER
Società Cooperitiva Castelli	Fattorie e Coltivatori Diretti Riuniti del Chianti Classico, Mercatale Val di Pesa, Firenze
Villa Antinori/Fattoria San Cristina	Marchesi L. and P. Antinori, Palazzo Antinori, Firenze
Villa Calcinaia	Conte Neri Capponi, Greve in Chianti, Firenze
Villa Terciona	Lina Capri Saccardi, Mercatale Val di Pesa, Firenze

Chianti

Like the Chianti Classico, Chianti is a composite wine made from the same four varietals – Sangiovese, Canaiolo, Trebbiano and Malvasia del Chianti. However, if aged for two years and with an alcohol content of 12 per cent, instead of its regular 11.5 per cent, it may be labelled Vecchio; and Riserva if aged for three years and more. Almost all producers make an aged, completely dry Vin Santo dessert wine.

ESTATE/BRAND NAME	PRODUCER
Cantina Vini Tipici Arctini	Cantina Vini Tipici Aretini, Ponte a Chiani, Arezzo
Castello di Poppiano	Conte Gucciardini, Montespertoli, Firenze
Fattoria I Pieri	Biondi Santi, Montalcino, Siena
Fattoria Il Borro	Amedeo di Savoia Aosta, San Giustino Valdarno, Arezzo
Fattoria La Selva	Carpini, Montebenichi, Arezzo
Fattoria Nippozzano/Pomino	Marchesi de'Frescobaldi, Palazzo Frescobaldi, Firenze
Fattoria Pancone	Pancone, Capannoli, Arezzo
Fattoria Poggi Dormicello	Vannucci Zauli, Poggi Dormicello, Empoli, Firenze
Fattoria Poggio Reale	Conte Spalletti, Rufina, Firenze
Fattoria San Fabiano	Borghini Baldovinetti, San Fabiano, Arezzo
Fattoria Santa Vittoria	Conte Mancini Griffoli, Foiano della Chiana, Arezzo
Stravecchio Monnalisa	Melini Spa, Pontassieve, Firenze
Vecchia Cantina di Montepulciano	Vecchia Cantina di Montepulciano, Montepulciano, Arezzo
Villa Capannoli	Gotti Lega, Capannoli, Pisa
Villa Capezzana	Contini Bonacossi, Carmignano, Firenze
Villa Cusona	Guicciardini Strozzi, San Gimignano
Villa Lilliano	A. Malenchini, Antella, Firenze
Villa Pasolino	Pasolini dall'Onda Borghese, Barberino Val d'Elsa, Firenze

Elba Bianco and Rosso (200 – 10.8.1967)

A dry red and a dry white wine are covered by this legislation; the red is a Sangiovese at 90 quintals per hectare and 12 per cent minimum alcohol content. The white is a Trebbiano at 90 quintals per hectare and with a minimum alcohol content of 11 per cent. Produced by:

Antinori, Portoferraio, Elba
La Pianella, Proccio Elba, Livorno

Tenuta Acquabona, Portoferraio, Elba

Morellino di Scansano (92 – 4.4.1978)

A Sangiovese wine (85 per cent), with 15 per cent of other approved red grapes grown in the same vineyards, with a yield of not more than 120 quintals per hectare. The minimum alcohol content is 11 per cent. If, however, the wine is aged for two years, one of which is in the wood, and the alcohol content is 12 per cent, the wine may be labelled Riserva. Produced by Cantina Sociale del Morellino, Scansano, Grosseto.

Montecarlo Bianco (283 – 8.11.1969)

This dry white wine is made from a blend of grapes including the Tuscan Trebbiano, Sémillon, Pinot Gris, Pinot Bianco, Vermentino, Sauvignon and Roussane. The maximum yield is 100 quintals per hectare. Minimum alcoholic content is 11.5 per cent. Produced by:

Carrara Vasco, Chiesina Uzzanese, Pistoia   Mazzini Franceschi, Montecarlo, Lucca
Fattoria Buonamico, Montecarlo, Lucca

Montescudaio (37 – 9.2.1977)

The Montescudaio DOC offers a red and a white wine; the red wine a Sangiovese (65-85 per cent), with a balance of either or both Tuscan Trebbiano and Malvasia del Chianti. The white wine is 70-85 per cent Trebbiano Toscano with the balance made up of Malvasia del Chianti and Vermentino. Both wines have a maximum yield of 120 quintals per hectare and a 11.5 per cent minimum alcohol content. A Vin Santo of 14 per cent may also be made.

La Parrina (246 – 29.9.1971)

The Parrina DOC allows for both a red and a white wine. The red is Sangiovese and the white, Trebbiano. The red wine has a maximum yield of 120 quintals per hectare and 12 per cent of alcohol content; and the white wine has a 110 quintal yield and a minimum total alcohol content of 11.5 per cent. Produced by La Parrina, Albinia di Orbetello, Grosseto.

Rosso delle Colline Lucchesi (186 – 23.7.1968)

This red is made from 49-60 per cent of Sangiovese with a maximum yield of 120 quintals per hectare, with the contribution of 5-15 per cent of Canaiolo, 10-15 per cent Ciliegiolo and Colorino, 10-15 per cent Trebbiano Toscano, and 5-10 per cent Vermentino and Malvasia Toscano. It offers an 11.5 per cent alcohol content. Produced by:

Leoni, San Gennaro, Lucca   Scola Camerini, Pieve, San Stefano, Lucca

Vernaccia di San Gimignano (110 – 6.5.1966)

Produced from the Vernaccia vine, with a yield of 100 quintals per hectare, this dry white wine offers a minimum alcohol content of 12 per cent. A Riserva is permitted if the wine is aged for one year in the bottle; this also may be fortified. Produced by:

Azienda Riccianello, San Gimignano, Siena   Dott. Giulio Frigeni, San Gimignano, Siena
Fattoria La Torre, San Gimignano, Siena   Strozzi e Guicciardini, Fattoria Clusona,
Fattoria Pietrafitta, San Gimignano, Siena   San Gimignano, Siena

Vin Nobile di Montepulciano (233 – 19.9.1966)

Produced from the Sangiovese Grosso (Prugnolo) grape, with some Canaiolo Nero, Malvasia del Chianti and Tuscan Trebbiano and not more than 8 per cent of

Grechetto Bianco and Mamolo, at a 100 quintal per hectare yield, this Vin Nobile provides a 12 per cent alcohol content. The legislation requires two years of ageing in the wood; should ageing be for more than three years, the label may state Riserva; if for over four years, the wine may be categorized Riserva Speciale. Produced by:

Fassati, Montepulciano, Siena	Sant'Agnese Fanetti, Montepulciano, Siena
Fattoria di Gracisano, Montepulciano, Siena	Vecchio Fattoria, Montepulciano, Siena

Some recommended non-DOC wines in Tuscany: The Pomino reds and whites by Frescobaldi; and the Sassicaia and Tignanello reds by Antinori.

Some recommended non-DOC Tuscan whites:

ESTATE/BRAND NAME	PRODUCER
Villa Antinori	Marchesi L. and P. Antinori, Firenze
Bianco del Beato	Giovanni Colombini, Montalcino, Siena
Pomino	De'Frescobaldi, Firenze
Lacrima d'Arno	Melini, Pontassieve, Firenze
Tizzano	Conte Filippo Pandolfini, San Polo, Firenze
Brolio	Barone Bettino Ricasoli, Firenze
Trebbiano	Ruffino, Pontassieve, Firenze
Stigliano	Guiseppe Vannucci Zauli, Empoli

MARCHES

1979 vintage – good-quality and generous-yield.

Bianchello del Metauro (143 – 10.6.1969)

Made from the Bianchello grape, with a 5 per cent addition of Malvasia Toscano and with a yield of 140 quintals per hectare, this dry white wine has an alcohol content of 11.5 per cent. Produced by Anzilotti-Solazzi, Fano, Pesaro.

Bianco dei Colli Maceratesi (177 – 5.7.1975)

This dry white wine must be made with more than 50 per cent of Trebbiano Toscano with a balance of Maceratino, Malvasia Toscana and Verdicchio. Its maximum yield per hectare is 140 quintals and its minimum alcohol content is 11 per cent.

Falerio dei Colli Ascolani (226 – 26.8.1975)

A dry white wine made with not more than 80 per cent of Trebbiano Toscano grapes; the balance may be Passerina, Verdicchio, Malvasia Toscana or Pinot Bianco, either singly or blended, with the option of using Malvasia Toscana up to 7 per cent. The maximum yield per hectare is 140 quintals. The minimum alcohol content is 11.5 per cent. Produced by:

Consorzio Agrario Provinciale, Ascoli Piceno	Constantino e Rozzi, Ascoli Piceno
Pennesi, Sant'Elpidio a Mare, Ascoli Piceno	Giovanni Vinci, Cupramarittima, Ascoli Piceno
Tatta di Ciarrocchi, Porto San Giorgio, Ascoli Piceno	

Rosso Conero (210 – 22.8.1967; 128 – 12.5.1977)

Produced from the Montepulciano vine, to which may be added up to 15 per cent of Sangiovese, and with a 140 quintal yield per hectare, this dry red wine provides an alcohol content of 11.5 per cent. Produced by:

Castelfiora, Loreto, Ancona
Enopolio di Osimo Stazione, Ancona
Gioacchino Garofoli, Loreto,
   Ancona

Mario Marchetti, Pinocchio Pontelungo,
   Ancona
Torelli, Cupramontana, Ancona
Umani Ronchi, Osimo Scalo, Ancona

Rosso Piceno (245 – 26.9.1968)

This dry red wine is made from a blend of 50 per cent Sangiovese and 40 per cent Montepulciano with a balance of Trebbiano or Passerina. Its maximum yield per hectare is 140 quintals and its minimum alcohol content is 11.5 per cent. With 12 per cent alcohol content and one year's ageing, the wine may be labelled Superiore. Produced by:

Aurora, Cupramontana, Ancona
Consorzio Agrario Provinciale, Ascoli
   Piceno
Consorzio Agrario Provinciale, Macerata
Giuseppe Pennesi, Sant'Elpidio a Mare,
   Ascoli Piceno

Tatta di Ciarrocchi, Porto San Giorgio,
   Ascoli Piceno
Emidi Vigneti, Montalto Marche, Ascoli
   Piceno

Sangiovese dei Colli Pesaresi (207 – 9.8.1972)

This dry red wine is made from 85 per cent Sangiovese grapes, with the addition of up to 15 per cent Montepulciano and Ciliegiolo. It has a maximum yield of 110 quintals per hectare and a minimum alcohol content of 11.5 per cent. Produced by:

Cantina Colli-Vigneti Mancini,
   Pesaro

Fattoria San Cristoforo, San Lorenzo in
   Campo, Pesaro

Verdicchio dei Castelli di Jesi (245 – 26.9.1968; 79 – 21.9.1979)

This dry white wine is produced from 80 per cent Verdicchio and up to 20 per cent of Trebbiano Toscano and Malvasia Toscana. With a yield of 150 quintals per hectare, it provides a 12 per cent alcohol content. Made from grapes produced in vineyards in the historically limited zone, the wine may be labelled Classico. Produced by:

Aurora, Cupramontana, Ancona
Castelfiora, Loreto, Ancona
Consorzio Agrario Provinciale Ancona,
   Enopolio di Majolati, Ancona
Fazi Battaglia Titulus, Castelplanio
   Stazione, Ancona
Gioacchino Garofali, Loreto, Ancona

Giuseppe Pennesi, Sant'Elpidio a Mare,
   Ascoli Piceno
Staphilus, Staffolo, Ancona
Torelli, Cupramontana, Ancona
Umani Ronchi, Osimo Scalo, Ancona
Val di Nevola Cantina Sociale, Corinaldo,
   Ancona

Verdicchio di Matelica (211 – 30.8.1967; 157 – 9.6.1979)

This wine closely resembles the Verdicchio di Jesi in composition and characteristics. The DOC legislation permits the making of sparkling wines from this base by natural methods. Produced by:

Consorzio Agricolo di Macerata, Enopolio   La Monacesca, Matelica, Macerata
   di Matelica, Matelica, Macerata

Vernaccia di Serrapetrona (222 – 4.9.1971; 142 – 25.5.1979)

An *amabile* or sweet *spumante* wine made from Montepulciano grapes, with up to 20 per cent Sangiovese and Ciliegiolo. It has an alcohol content of 11.5 per cent. Produced by Attilio Fabrini, Serrapetrona, Macerata.

UMBRIA

1979 vintage – good quality and average yield.

Colli del Trasimeno (84 – 29.3.1972)

There is a Sangiovese red and a Trebbiano white permitted under this DOC.

Colli del Trasimeno Bianco: The Trebbiano white may be blended with Malvasia del Chianti, Verdicchio, Verdello and Grechetto. The maximum yield per hectares is 125 quintals. The minimum alcohol content is 11 per cent.

Colli del Trasimeno Rosso: The Sangiovese red may be blended with 40 per cent of Ciliegiolo, Gamay, Malvasia del Chianti and Trebbiano. The maximum yield per hectare is 125 quintals and the minimum alcohol content is 11.5 per cent. Produced by:

Cesare Brunelli, Corciano, Perugia

Cantina Sociale Trasimeno, Castiglione del Lago, Perugia

CO. VI. P, Ponte Pattioli, Perugia

Gino Massini, Corciano, Perugia

Sovereign Military Order of Malta, Magione, Perugia

Orvieto (219 – 31.8.1971)

The Trebbiano Toscano, with the addition of some Verdello, Grechetto, Drupeggio and Malvasia Toscana, produces a dry and an *abboccato* white wine with a minimum alcohol content of 11.5 per cent. If the grapes are harvested inside the original growing area, the wine may be labelled Classico. Produced by:

Marchesi L. and P. Antinori, Firenze

Barberani, Orvieto, Terni

Luigi Bigi, Orvieto, Terni

Cantina di Torriti, Civitella d'Agliano, Viterbo

Cooperativa di Orvieto, Orvieto Stazione, Terni

Cottarella, Monterubiaglio, Terni

Le Velette, Orvieto Canale, Terni

Achille Lemmi, Montegabbione, Terni

Littorio e Todini, Castiglione Teverina, Terni

Petrurbani, Orvieto, Terni

Vaselli, Orvieto, Terni

Torgiano (132 – 25.5.1968; 75 – 16.3.1973)

Torgiano Bianco: The white wine is a Trebbiano Toscano blended with some Grechetto which, with a maximum yield of 125 quintals per hectare, has an alcohol content of 11.5 per cent.

Torgiano Rosso: The red wine is a Sangiovese blended with some Canaiolo and Trebbiano Toscano which, with a maximum yield of 120 quintals per hectare, has an alcohol content of 12 per cent. If the wine is aged for three years, it may be called Riserva. Produced by:

CO. VI. P, Ponte Pattioi, Perugia

Dott. Giorgio Lungarotti, Torgiano, Perugia

ABRUZZO AND MOLISE

1979 vintage – average quality and satisfactory yield.

Montepulciano d'Abruzzo (178 – 15.7.1968)

This dry red wine is produced from 85 per cent Montepulciano grapes, with a balance of Sangiovese, and has a maximum yield of 140 quintals per hectare. Minimum alcohol content of 12 per cent. The Cerasuolo version of this wine is slightly rosé. Produced by:

Azienda Vinicola Pepe, Torano Nuovo, Teramo

Nestore Bosco, Pescara Colli, Pescara

Cantina Sociale di Tollo, Tollo, Chieti

Consorzio Aprutino, Roseto, Teramo

Consorzio Vini d'Abruzzo, Ortona, Chieti

Cooperativa San Vitale, San Salvo,
   Chieti
Madonna dei Miracoli, Casalbordino
   Stazione, Chieti
Gaetano Petrosemolo, Miglianico, Chieti

Colella Santoro, Pratola Peligna, L'Aquila
Casal Thaulero, Roseto degli Abruzzi,
   Teramo

Trebbiano d'Abruzzo (221 – 25.8.1972)

This dry white wine, made from 85 per cent Trebbiano, with the balance of suitable
local wines, has a maximum yield of 140 quintals per hectare. It has an alcohol
content of 11.5 per cent. Produced by:

Azienda Vinicola Pepe, Torano Nuovo,
   Teramo
Consorzio Aprutino, Roseto degli
   Abruzzi, Teramo
Consorzio Vini d'Abruzzo, Ortona,
   Chieti
Di Prospero, Bagnaturo, L'Aquila

La Vinicola di Angelucci, Pescara
Madonna dei Miracoli Cantina Sociale,
   Casalbordino Stazione, Chieti
Casal Thaulero, Roseto degli Abruzzi,
   Chieti
Valentini, Loreto Aprutino, Pescara

LAZIO

1979 vintage – average quality and above average yield.

Aleatico di Gradoli (217 – 22.8.1972)

A red dessert wine produced from the Aleatico grape, with a yield of not more than
90 quintals per hectare, it has a total minimum alcohol content of 12 per cent. A
fortified version is permitted with a total of 17.5 per cent. Produced by:

Bigi, Orvieto, Terni
Cantina Sociale di Gradoli, Gradoli,
   Orvieto, Terni

Bianco Capena (292 – 5.11.1975)

A dry white wine made from a maximum of 55 per cent of the three Malvasias
(Candia, Lazio and Toscana) with up to 25 per cent Trebbiano and 20 per cent of
local wines such as Bellone and Bombino (locally called Spanish grapes). It has a
maximum yield per hectare of 130 quintals and a minimum alcohol content of 11.5
per cent. With a minimum alcohol content of 12 per cent, the wine may be labelled
Superiore. Produced by Cantina Sociale di Capena, Capena, Roma.

Cervetri (64 – 7.3.1975)

This legislation provides for a dry red and a dry white wine.

Cervetri Rosso: This red wine is made up from a blend of Sangiovese and Montepulciano, exceeding 60 per cent; Cesanese may contribute to the extent of 25 per
cent and other grapes such as Canaiolo Nero, Carignano and Barbera make up the
balance. The yield per hectare is 140 quintals and the alcohol content not less than
12 per cent.

Cervetri Bianco: The white wine is made up of at least 50 per cent Trebbiano, to
which may be added 35 per cent Malvasi di Candia or Lazio; the balance is made
up of Verdicchio, Tocai, Bellone and Bombino. The yield per hectare is a maximum
of 150 quintals and the minimum alcohol content is 11.5 per cent. Produced by
Cantina Sociale di Cervetri, Cervetri, Roma.

Verdicchio vineyards in the DOC *of Castelli di Jesi near Corinaldo in the Marches*

Cesanese di Affile, di Piglio and *di Olevano Romano* (225 – 31.8.1973; 216 – 22.8.1973; 221 – 28.8.1973)

A dry red wine which is also made *amabile* and *spumante* is produced from the Cesanese vine with a yield of 125 quintals per hectare. It has 12 per cent minimum alcohol content. Produced by:

Cantina Sociale di Piglio, Piglio, Frosinone

La Selva, Paliano, Frosinone

Colli Albani (280 – 5.11.1970)

A Castelli Romani dry white wine made from the red Malvasia, various Trebbiano strains, Malvasia del Lazio and small quantities of Bonvino and Cacchione. The maximum yield per hectare is 150 quintals. The minimum alcohol content is 11.5 per cent. An *amabile* version is also made. Produced by:

Cantina Sociale Colli Albani, Cecchina, Roma

Vinoro, Roma

Colli Lanuvini (182 – 20.7.1971)

A dry white Castelli Romani wine made from Malvasia di Candia and Trebbiano, with an addition of Bellone and Bonvino. The maximum yield per hectare is 140 quintals and the minimum alcohol content is 11.5 per cent. Produced by Cantina Sociale di Genzano, Genzano, Roma.

Cori (243 – 25.9.1971)

Cori Bianco: The white wine is made up from a blend of Malvasia di Candi, Bellone, Trebbiano Toscano, and Trebbiano Giallo. It has a maximum yield of 110 quintals per hectare and an alcohol content of 11 per cent. The wine is made in three versions – dry, *amabile* and sweet.

Cori Rosso: The red wine is made up of a blend of Montepulciano, Nero Buono di Cori and Cesanese. It has a maximum yield of 110 quintals per hectare and an alcohol content of 11.5 per cent.

EST! EST! EST! di Montefiascone (111 – 7.5.1966)

A dry white wine, produced from the Trebbiano Toscano and the Malvasia Toscana, with a maximum yield of 130 quintals per hectare. The minimum alcohol content is 11 per cent. Produced by:

L. and F. Bigi, Firenze
Cantina Cooperativa di Montefiascone, Viterbo

Colle di Montesola, Montefiascone, Viterbo
Italo Mazziotti, Bolsena, Viterbo

Frascati (119 – 16.5.1966)

A dry white wine is made from Malvasia Bianca, the Malvasia del Lazio and the Greco, blended as wines or fermented together. The maximum yield per hectare is 130 quintals and the minimum alcohol content is 11.5 per cent; if this is 12 per cent, the bottle may be labelled Superiore. Produced by:

Cantina Produttori Frascati, Frascati, Roma
Cantina Sociale di Marino, Frattocchie, Roma
Cantine S. Marco, Monteporzio, Catone, Roma
De Sanctis, Frascati, Roma

Fontana Candida, Frascati, Roma
Valle Vermiglia, Frascati, Roma
Conte Zandotti, Frascati, Roma

Vineyards on the slopes of Mount Etna in Sicily showing the rich black volcanic soil which is excellent for growing vines

Marino (279 – 3.11.1970)

A dry white Castelli Romani wine made from red or white Candia Malvasias, Tuscan Trebbiano and Malvasia del Lazio, with a maximum yield per hectare of 150 quintals, provides an 11.5 per cent of alcohol content. Produced by:

Cantina Sociale di Marino, Frattocchie, Roma

Azienda Agricola Cantamessa, Frattocchie, Roma

Merlot di Aprilia, Trebbiano di Aprilia, Sangiovese di Aprilia (174 – 16.7.1966)

These wines are all single-grape varietals, with a yield of 80 quintals per hectare and with 12 per cent of alcohol content. Produced by:

Cantina Sociale Tres Tabernae, Cisterna di Latina, Latina

Colli del Cavaliere, Campoverde, Latina

Cooperativa Enotria, Aprilia, Latina

Montecompatri Colonna (212 – 17.8.1973)

A dry white wine produced from up to 70 per cent Malvasia di Candia with the balance made up of Trebbianos; Bellone and Bonvino are permitted in small quantities. The maximum yield per hectare is 150 quintals. The alcohol content must be at least 11.5 per cent; if it is 12.5 per cent, the wine may be categorized as Superiore.

Velletri (190 – 22.7.1972)

Velletri Bianco: The dry white wine is made from Malvasia di Candia and Tuscan Trebbiano Toscano with small additions of Bellone and Bonvino; it has a maximum yield of 140 quintals per hectare, and a minimum alcohol content of 11.5 per cent.

Velletri Rosso: The red wine is a blend of Sangiovese, Montepulciano and Cesanese, also with a 140-quintal yield, but with a minimum alcohol content of 12 per cent. Produced by Consorzio Produttori Vini, Via Oberdan, Velletri.

Zagarolo (215 – 21.8.1973)

This dry white wine is made from grapes from the Malvasia di Candia and Trebbiano vines, with small additions permitted of Bellone and Bonvino. The maximum yield is 150 quintals per hectare and the minimum alcohol yield is 11.5 per cent. With an alcohol content of 12.5 per cent, the wine may be labelled Superiore.

SARDINIA

1979 vintage – A fair quality and a generous yield.

Cannonau di Sardegna (248 – 21.9.1972)

The Cannonau is the major wine of Sardinia and is processed variously to produce different wines, thus: as a table wine it is made both dry and *amabile* with a 13.5 per cent alcoholic content; it may also be made as a rosé wine. In either case, it must be aged for one year in the wood. If it is aged for three years, it may be called Riserva. A Cannonau with 15 per cent of alcohol content may be labelled Superiore and prepared as Naturale Secco, Naturale Amabile, or Naturale Dolce; in the case of the sweeter varieties, the wine requires two years' ageing, instead of one.

A fortified (*liquoroso*) version is permitted which is either Secco or Dolce Naturale. The former is of at least 16 per cent alcohol and the sweet of 16 per cent, with 2 per cent of sugar. In all cases, the maximum yield per hectare is 110 quintals. The Oliena and Capo Ferrato special zones specialize in making strong, dry table wines. Produced by:

Cantina Sociale di Capo Ferrato, Capo
  Ferrato, Cagliari
Cantina Sociale di Jerzu, Nuoro

Deiana, Oliena, Nuoro
Mereu, Tortoli, Nuoro
Sella e Mosca, Alghero, Sassari

Campidano di Terralba or *Terralba*

This dry red wine is produced from Bovale (both Bovale Sardo and Bovale di Spagna) grapes with the addition of up to 20 per cent of Pascale di Cagliari, Greco Nero (locally called Gregu Nieddu) and Monica from the same vineyards. The wine must have an alcohol content of not less than 11.5 per cent. Produced by:

Cantina Sociale di Arborea, Arborea,
  Cagliari

Cantina Sociale di Campidano, Terralba,
  Cagliari

Carignano del Sulcis (281 – 14.10.1977)

A dry red wine and a dry rosé wine, produced by the Carignano vine, with a maximum yield of 160 quintals per hectare, along with grapes from the Monica, the Pascale and the Alicate Bouschet, singly or together, but from the same vineyards. The minimum alcohol content for both the red and the rosé wines is 11.5 per cent; the red may be labelled Invecchiato if matured for one year. Produced by:

Cantina Sociale di Calasetta, Calasetta,
  Cagliari

Cantina Sociale di Sant'Antico, Cagliari

Giro di Cagliari (249 – 22.9.1972; 274 – 6.10.1979)

This red dessert wine is produced from the Giro vine, with a yield of less than 90 quintals per hectare. It is produced as sweet, dry, fortified and Riserva. As a dessert wine, it has a 15.5 per cent alcohol content, of which 2.5 per cent for the sweet and 1 per cent for the dry is left in sugar form, and not developed into alcohol. The fortified versions – Liquoroso Dolce Naturale and Liquoroso Secco – have a 17.5 per cent minimum of alcohol content. If aged for two years, they may be called Riserva. Produced by:

Cantina Sociale di Monserrato,
  Monserrato, Cagliari

Efisio Meloni, Selargius, Cagliari
Zedda-Piras, Cagliari

Malvasia di Bosa (255 – 28.9.1972)

This is a white dessert wine produced from the Malvasia di Sardegna vine with a yield of not more than 80 quintals per hectare. It is produced in the following versions: Dolce Naturale, Secco, Liquoroso Dolce Naturale and Liquoroso Secco. The dessert wines have a total alcohol content of 15 per cent, while the fortified versions reach 17.5 per cent. Produced by Deriu Mocci, Bosa, Nuoro.

Malvasia di Cagliari (228 – 1.9.1972; 164 – 16.6.1979)

A white dessert wine produced from the Malvasia di Sardegna vine with a yield of not more than 90 quintals per hectare. It is made in the following versions: Dolce Naturale, Secco, Liquoroso Dolce Naturale and Liquoroso Secco. The dessert wines have a total alcohol content of 14 per cent, while the fortified versions reach 17 per cent. Produced by:

Cantina Sociale di Campidano,
  Serramanna, Cagliari
Cantina Sociale di Dolianova,
  Dolianova, Cagliari

Sella e Mosca, Alghero, Sassari
Vinalcool, Cagliari
Zedda-Piras, Cagliari

Monica di Cagliari (217 – 22.8.1972)

This red dessert wine is produced by the Monica vine at a yield not exceeding 90 quintals per hectare. It is produced in the following versions: Dolce Naturale,

Secco, Liquoroso Dolce Naturale and Liquoroso Secco. The dessert wines have a total alcohol content of 15.5 per cent and the fortified versions, 17.5 per cent. Produced by:

Cantina Sociale di Campidano di
  Serramanna, Serramanna, Cagliari
Cantina Sociale di Campidano di
  Terralba, Terralba, Cagliari

Cantina Sociale di Villacidro, Villacidro,
  Cagliari
Zedda-Piras, Cagliari

Monica di Sardegna (309 – 28.11.1972)

This red table wine is produced from 85 per cent of the Monica vine and, for the remainder, a blend of Pascale di Cagliari, Carignano, Bovale Grande and Bovale Sardo. The maximum yield per hectare is 150 quintals, and the minimum alcohol content is 12 per cent. If the wine has one year's ageing in the wood and a minimum alcohol content of 13 per cent, it may be called Superiore. Produced by:

Cantina Sociale Marmilla, Sanluri, Cagliari
Cantina Sociale del Campidano
  Serramanna, Cagliari
Cantina Sociale della Riforma, Santadi,
  Cagliari

Cantina Sociale di Sant'Antioco, Cagliari
Vini Classici di Sardegna, Pirri, Cagliari

Moscato di Cagliari (222 – 25.8.1979; 164 – 16.6.1979)

This amber-coloured dessert wine, produced exclusively from the Moscato Bianco vine, with a maximum yield of 90 quintals per hectare, is processed as a Dolce Naturale with a minimum alcohol content of 16 per cent – of which 3 per cent remains as sugar, and as Liquoroso Dolce Naturale with a minimum alcohol content of 17.5 per cent. Produced by:

Vini Classici di Sardegna, Pirri, Cagliari   Zedda-Piras, Cagliari

Moscato di Sorso-Sennori (193 – 26.7.1972)

A sweet dessert wine, produced exclusively by the Moscato Bianco vine at a maximum of 90 quintals yield per hectare. It has a minimum alcohol content of 13 per cent, and a 2 per cent sugar residue. Produced by Cantina Sociale di Sorso Sennori, Sorso, Sassari.

Nasco di Cagliari (220 – 24.8.1972; 153 – 6.6.1979)

A white dessert wine, produced exclusively from the Nasco vine, with a maximum yield per hectare of 90 quintals. It is made in four versions: Dolce Naturale, Secco, Liquoroso Dolce Naturale, and Liquoroso Secco. The first two have a total alcohol content of 15.5 and 15 per cent respectively, while the fortified versions stand at 17.5 and 16.5 per cent. If aged for two years in wood, these latter may be qualified as Riserva. Produced by:

Sella e Mosca, Alghero, Sassari   Zedda-Piras, Cagliari

Nuragus di Cagliari (66 – 10.3.1975; 160 – 19.6.1979)

This dry white wine is obtained from the Nuragus di Cagliari vine, with 15 per cent permitted from the Trebbiano Toscano, the Romagnolo Trebbiano, Vermentino, Clairette and Semidano vines, with a maximum yield of 200 quintals per hectare. Its minimum alcohol content is 11 per cent. Produced by Cantina Sociale Mermilla, Sanluri, Cagliari.

Vermentino di Gallura (173 – 2.7.1975)

This dry white wine is obtained from up to 95 per cent Vermentino grapes, with the addition of not more than 5 per cent of locally approved grapes. The maximum yield is 140 quintals per hectare and the minimum alcohol content is 12 per cent. With an alcohol content of 14 per cent, the wine may be sold as Superiore. Produced by:

Berchidda, Monti, Sassari

Cantina Sociale del Vermentino, Monti, Sassari

Sella e Mosca, Alghero, Sassari

Vernaccia di Oristano (247 – 30.9.1971)

This dry white dessert wine is produced exclusively from the Vernaccia grape with a maximum yield of 80 quintals per hectare. The wine has an alcohol content of 15 per cent. If this is 15.5 per cent or more, and the wine is aged for three years, it may be labelled Superiore. Produced by:

Cantina Sociale della Vernaccia, Oristano Rimedio, Oristano

Silvio Carta, Baratili San Pietro, Oristano

Attilio Contini, Cabras, Oristano

Produttori Riuniti, Baratili San Pietro, Oristano

Josto Puddu, San Vero Milis, Oristano

Sella e Mosca, Alghero, Sassari

CAMPANIA

1979 vintage – average quality but a below average yield.

Capri (339 – 14.12.1977)

This DOC permits a red and a white wine, both dry.

Capri Rosso: The red wine is made from more than 80 per cent Piedirosso and the balance from other locally authorized wines. The maximum yield is 120 quintals per hectare. The minimum alcohol content is 11.5 per cent.

Capri Bianco: The white wine is made approximately with half and half of Falaghina and Greco. The maximum yield is 120 quintals per hectare and the minimum alcohol content is 11.5 per cent. Produced by Adolfo Patrizi, Capri, Napoli.

Fiano di Avellino (241 – 29.8.1978)

A dry white wine, produced from 85 per cent Fiano and from a blend of Greco, Coda di Volpe and Trebbiano Toscano for the remainder. A maximum yield of 100 quintals per hectare and a minimum alcohol content of 11.5 per cent. Produced by Michele Mastroberardino, Atripaldi, Avellino.

Greco di Tufo (130 – 25.5.1970; 157 – 9.6.1979)

The Greco vine (or Greco di Tufo), with a 20 per cent addition of Coda di Volpe, produces a dry white wine of 11.5 per cent alcohol content. Maximum yield of 100 quintals per hectare. Produced by Michele Mastroberardino, Atripaldi, Avellino.

Ischia (112 – 9.5.1966)

Ischia Rosso: The Ischia red is made from a blend of Guarnaccia, and Piedirosso (locally called *Per'e Palummo*) with not more than 10 per cent Barbera. The yield must not exceed 100 quintals per hectare; minimum alcohol content is 11.5 per cent.

Ischia Bianco: The white is made from the Forestera and Biancolella vines, with a yield of not more than 100 quintals per hectare. The minimum alcohol content is 11 per cent. If the wine is made from a yield of 80 quintals per hectare and has an alcohol content of 12 per cent, it may be labelled Superiore. Produced by:

D'Ambra, Panza di Ischia, Naples

Perazzo, Naples

Solopaca (28 – 30.1.1974)

Solopaca Rosso: The red wine is made from 45-60 per cent Sangiovese with a balance of Aglianico, Piedirosso and other varieties. The maximum yield is 130 quintals per hectare. Its minimum alcohol content is 11.5 per cent.

Solopaca Bianco: The dry white wine is made from up to 70 per cent Trebbiano Toscano, 20-40 per cent Malvasia di Candia and some Malvasia Toscano and Codadivolpe. The maximum yield is 150 quintals per hectare. Its minimum alcohol content is 12 per cent. Produced by:

La Guardiense Cantina Sociale, Guardia   La Vinicola Ocone, Ponte, Benevento
   Sanframondi, Benevento

Taurasi (129 – 25.5.1970)

A dry red wine chiefly made from the Aglianico vine, with a yield of 110 quintals per hectare. Its minimum alcohol content is 12 per cent. All Taurasi wines must be aged for three years, of which at least one must be in wood; if aged for four years, the wine may be labelled as Riserva. Produced by Michele Mastroberardino, Atripaldi, Avellino.

PUGLIA

1979 vintage – average quality and generous yield.

Aleatico di Puglia (214 – 20.8.1973)

This sweet dessert wine is produced in two versions, natural sweet and fortified. It is made from 85 per cent Aleatico grapes, with the balance made from Negro Amaro, Malvasia Nera and Primitivo. As a sweet red wine, it has a minimum total alcohol content of 15 per cent and as a fortified wine, 18.5 per cent. If aged for three years, the wine may be qualified as Riserva. Produced by Centrale Cantina Riforma, Cantina di Corato, Bari.

Cacc'e Mmitte di Lucera (82 – 29.3.1976)

This dry red wine is a composite, including 35-60 per cent Troia, up to 35 per cent Montepulciano, Sangiovese and Malvasia Nera of Brindisi and a balance of Trebbiano Toscano, Bombino Bianco and Malvasia del Chianti. The maximum yield is 140 quintals per hectare and the minimum alcohol strength is 11.5 per cent. Produced by Cantina Cooperativa di Lucera, Lucera, Foggia.

Castel del Monte (188 – 26.7.1971)

This legislation covers three types of wine – red, rosé and white. The first two are of the same origin with a maximum yield of 120 quintals per hectare: Uva di Troia with Bombino Nero, Montepulciano and Sangiovese where required; the red has 12 per cent and the rosé 11.5 per cent of alcohol content. If the red has 12.5 per cent and three years' ageing in the wood, it may be labelled Riserva. The white is made from the Pampanuto vine, with additions of Trebbianos (Grallo and Toscano) Bombino Bianco and Palumbo as required. This has a maximum yield per hectare of 130 and a minimum alcohol content of 11.5 per cent. Produced by:

De Corato, Bari   Premiovini, Brescia
Fattoria Torricciola, Andria, Bari   Rivera, Andria, Bari

Copertino (27 – 29.1.1977)

This wine comes in two versions – red and rosé. Both are made from Negro Amaro grapes alone, at a maximum yield of 140 quintals per hectare. The red and the rosé wine both have a minimum alcohol content of 12 per cent, but the red wine, if aged for two years and with an alcohol content of 12.5 per cent, may be labelled Riserva. Produced by:

Barone Fabio Bacile di Castiglione, Copertino, Lecce

Cantina Sociale di Copertino, Lecce

Locorotondo (211 – 19.8.1969)

The Verdeca and d'Alessano grapes produce the Locorotondo dry white wine, with a maximum yield of 130 quintals per hectare and a minimum alcohol content of 11 per cent. Produced by:

Cantina Emmigi, Locorotondo, Bari
Cantina Sociale di Locorotondo, Locorotondo, Bari

Premiovini, Brescia

Martina or Martina Franca (211 – 19.8.1969)

This dry white wine is produced from the Verdeca and the Bianco d'Alessano vines, with a yield of not more than 130 quintals per hectare. The wine has a minimum alcohol content of 11 per cent. Produced by:

Centrale Cantina Cooperativa di Puglia, Lucania and Molise, Bari

Vinicola Miali, Martina Franca, Taranto

Matino (187 – 24.7.1971)

This legislation permits two versions – red and rosé – of a Negro Amaro wine, which may be blended with some Malvasia Nera and Sangiovese if required. Both versions have an 11.5 per cent alcohol content and a maximum yield per hectare of 120 quintals. Produced by:

Leone de Castris, Salento'Lecce Renna, Squinzano'Lecce

Ruffino, Pontassieve, Firenze

Moscato di Trani (63 – 6.3.1973)

A sweet white wine is produced from the Moscato di Trani (or Moscato Reale) vine, with a maximum yield of 90 quintals per hectare to provide a total alcohol content of 15 per cent of which 2 per cent remains in sugar form. A fortified version is permitted at 18 per cent, with the same 2 per cent of sweetness. Produced by:

Gennaro Marasciulo, Trani, Bari

Nuovo Vinicola Picardi, Barletta, Bari

Ostuni (83 – 28.1.1972)

Ostuni Ottavianello: The Ostuni Ottavianello is a dry red wine, made from grapes of the vine of the same name, with a yield of 110 quintals per hectare, to provide 11.5 per cent of alcohol content.

Ostuni Bianco: The white Ostuni is made from Impigno and Francavilla grapes and Bianco di Alessano and Verdera if required. It has a maximum yield of 110 quintals per hectare and an 11 per cent alcohol content.

Primitivo di Manduria (60 – 4.3.1975)

This is a red dessert wine, produced at a yield of 90 quintals per hectare, to provide a natural sweet, a fortified sweet and a dry fortified wine: at 16, 17.5 and 18 per cent of total alcohol content respectively, of which 3, 2.5 and 1.5 per cent are left in sugar form. Produced by Cantina Sociale di Lizzano, Lizzano, Taranto.

Rosso Barletta (278 – 12.10.1977)

A dry red wine produced from the Troia vine, with a yield of 150 quintals per hectare. The minimum alcohol content is 12 per cent. If aged for two years, the wine may be labelled Invecchiato. Produced by Fattoria Torricciola, Barletta, Bari.

Rosso Canosa (198 – 20.7.1979)

A dry red wine made from 65 per cent Canosa-Troia and 35 per cent of Montepulciano grapes. The maximum yield is 140 quintals per hectare. The minimum alcohol content is 12 per cent. With three years' ageing, of which two are in the wood, the wine may be labelled Riserva. Produced by Giudice Rossi, Canosa, Foggia.

Rosso di Cerignola (285 – 31.10.1974)

This dry red wine comes from grapes of the Troia vine (55 per cent) and the Negro Amaro (15 to 30 per cent), with optional contributions of a maximum of 15 per cent of Sangiovese, Barbera, Montepulciano, Malbec and Trebbiano Toscano. The maximum yield per hectare is 140 quintals and the minimum alcohol content is 12 per cent. If the wine is aged for two years in wood, and has a 13 per cent alcohol content, it may be labelled Riserva.

Salice Salentino (224 – 25.8.1976)

A red and a rosé dry wine are permitted under this legislation. They are both made from Negro Amaro grapes, with a maximum yield of 120 quintals per hectare. Permitted additions to this wine are Malvasia Nera di Brindisi and Malvasia Nera di Lecce to the extent of 20 per cent. The minimum alcohol content is 12.5 per cent. Both the red and the rosé may be aged: in the case of the red, it may be called Riserva after two years' ageing, of which one must be in the wood. The rosé, after one year's ageing, may be called *prodotto invecchiato* (aged product). Produced by Leone de Castris, Salice Salentino, Lecce.

San Severo (138 – 1.6.1968)

This legislation covers red, rosé and white wines, all of which have a maximum yield of 140 quintals per hectare. The red and the rosé are produced from the Montepulciano d'Abruzzo and Sangiovese vines and the white from Bombino Bianco and the Trebbiano Toscano. The red and the rosé have an 11.5 per cent and the white an 11 per cent alcohol content. Produced by:

D'Alfonso del Sordo, San Severo, Foggia

Cirillo Farrusi, Cerignola, Foggia

Squinzano (230 – 31.8.1976)

This legislation covers a red and a rosé wine, produced with a maximum yield per hectare of 140 quintals. Both also have the same alcohol content, which is 12.5 per cent. The red wine may be called Riserva if it is aged for two years, of which six months are in the wood and it reaches more than 13 per cent in alcohol content. Produced by Renna, Squinzano, Lecce.

BASILICATA (LUCANIA)

1979 vintage – good quality and generous yield.

Aglianico del Vulture (129 – 22.5.1971)

This dry red wine is made from grapes of the Aglianico vine, with a maximum yield of 100 quintals per hectare. It must normally provide 11.5 per cent of alcohol content. When aged for three years, two of which are in the wood, and with a 12.5 per cent alcohol content, it may be labelled Vecchio. If it has five years' ageing, it may be called Riserva. Produced by:

Azienda Botte, Barile, Potenza

Azienda Vinicola del Vulture, Rionero, Potenza

Centrale Cooperativa Riforma Fondiaria Puglia, Lucania, Molise – Centrale di Rionero, Potenza

D'Angelo, Rionero, Potenza

Armando Martino, Rionero, Potenza

Napolitano, Rionero in Vulture, Potenza

Paternoster, Barile, Potenza

Premiovini, Brescia

Sasso, Rionero, Potenza

Ente Sviluppo, Enopoli di Rionero, Maschito e Acerenza, Potenza

CALABRIA

1979 vintage – a good quality and normal yield.

Ciro (139 – 4.6.1969)

This DOC covers a dry red, a dry rosé and a dry white wine.

Cirò Rosso and Rosato: These are produced by grapes from the Gaglioppo vine, with up to 5 per cent of Trebbiano Toscano or Greco Bianco, with a maximum yield of 115 quintals per hectare. They have a minimum alcohol content of 13.5 per cent. If aged for three years, and with a minimum of 13.5 per cent alcohol content it may be labelled Riserva. There is a long-established limited zone around the town of Cirò from which wines produced in it may be designated Classico.

Cirò Bianco: The Cirò white is made from the Greco Bianco and up to 10 per cent of Trebbiano Toscano, with a maximum yield of 135 quintals per hectare, and a minimum alcohol content of 12 per cent. Produced by:

Cantina Sociale Torre Melissa, Torre Melissa, Catanzaro

Caparra e Siciliani, Cirò Marina, Catanzaro

Fratelli Caruso, Catanzaro

Cirovin, Cirò Marina, Catanzaro

Vincenzo Ippolito, Cirò Marina, Catanzaro

Donnici (225 – 25.8.1975)

A dry red and a dry rosé wine are permitted under this legislation. These wines must contain at least 50 per cent of Gaglioppo (locally called Mantonico Nero), 10 to 20 per cent of Greco Nero and not less than 20 per cent of Malvasia Bianca, Mantonico Bianco and Pecorello, either singly or together. The maximum yield per hectare is 120 quintals and the minimum alcohol content is 12 per cent. Produced by Cantina Sociale Donnici, Donnici, Catanzaro.

Lamezia (96 – 5.4.1979)

This dry red wine is made from the Nerello grape (30–50 per cent), the Gaglioppo (25–35 per cent) and the Greco Nero (25–35 per cent), with a yield of 120 quintals per hectare. It has a minimum alcohol content of 12 per cent.

Melissa (326 – 28.11.1979)

This dry red wine is made from Gaglioppo grape, with a small contribution of Greco Nero, Trebbiano Toscano *et al*, and with a yield of 110 quintals per hectare. It has a minimum alcohol content of 11.5 per cent. If this is 12.5 per cent, it may be labelled Superiore. The white Melissa wine comes from the Trebbiano Toscano and Malvasia Bianca, with a yield of 120 quintals per hectare. It has a minimum alcohol content of 11.5 per cent. Produced by Cantina Sociale di Melissa, Torre Melissa, Cantanzaro.

Pollino (291 – 3.11.1975)

A dry red wine produced from not less than 60 per cent of Gaglioppo (locally called Arvino, Aglianico, Aglianico di Cassano or Lacrima) and with at least 20 per cent of Greco Nero, Malvasia Bianca (locally called Verdana and Iuvarella), Mantonico Bianco and Guarnaccia Bianca either singly or together (these whites should not exceed 20 per cent). The maximum yield per hectare is 110 quintals and the minimum alcohol content is 12 per cent. The wine may be labelled Superiore with two years' ageing and a minimum alcohol content of 12.5 per cent. Produced by Cantina Sociale 'Vini del Pollino', Castrovillari, Cosenza.

Sant'Anna di Isola Capo Rizzuto (158 – 11.6.1979)

A dry red wine made chiefly from the Gaglioppo vine, with some Nerello and Nocera. The maximum yield is 120 quintals per hectare and the minimum alcohol content is 12 per cent. Produced by Cantina Sociale di Sant'Anna, Isola Capo Rizzuto, Catanzaro.

Savuto (291 – 3.11.1975)

A dry red and a dry rosé wine, produced from 35-45 per cent of grapes from the Gaglioppo vine (locally called Magliocco and Arvino); to this may be added between 35 and 45 per cent of Greco Nero, Nerello, Cappuccio, Magliocco Canino and Sangiovese – however, there must not be more than 10 per cent of Sangiovese; Malvasia Bianca and Pecorino may also be added singly or together, for a maximum of 25 per cent. The maximum yield per hectare is 110 quintals and the minimum alcohol content is 12 per cent. However, if the wine has two years' ageing and a minimum alcohol content of 12.5 per cent, it may be labelled Superiore. Produced by G. B. Longo, Azienda Vitivinicola, Marina di Cleto, Cosenza.

SICILY

1979 vintage – a good quality and good yield.

Alcamo (249 – 22.9.1972)

This dry white wine is produced from the Catarratto Bianco with a permissible addition of 20 per cent of Damaschino, Grecanico and Trebbiano Toscano, to yield not more than 120 quintals per hectare. Its minimum alcohol content is 11.5 per cent. Produced by:

Aurora Cooperativa, Salemi, Trapani	Cooperativa Paladino, Alcamo, Trapani
Consorzio Produttori, Alcamo, Trapani	D'Angelo, Alcamo, Trapani

Cerasuolo di Vittoria (221 – 28.8.1973)

Produced from the Frappato and Calabrese grapes with the addition of Grosso Nero and Nerello Mascalese if required, at a maximum yield of 100 quintals per hectare. Its minimum alcohol content is 13 per cent; the wine is noted for its long ageing. Produced by Giuseppe Coria, Villa Fontane, Vittoria, Ragusa.

Etna (244 – 25.9.1968)

Etna Bianco: The white Etna wine comes from the Carricante and Catarratto vines, with a 15 per cent contribution of locally permitted grapes. It has a minimum alcohol content of 12 per cent.

Etna Rosso and *Rosato*: The red and the rosé are made from the Nerello Mascalese with an addition of some Mantellato and up to 10 per cent of approved, neutral white grapes. The red and rosé wines have a minimum alcohol content of 12.5 per cent. Produced by:

Cantina Sociale Le Vigne dell'Etna, Linguaglossa, Catania

ETNEA Vini, Catania

Barone Nicolosi di Villagrande, Milo, Catania

Faro (61 – 4.3.1977)

A dry red wine, produced from the following vines at not more than 100 quintals per hectare: Nerello Mascalese 45-60 per cent, Nocera 5-10 per cent, Nerello Cappuccio 15-30 per cent and, permitted also up to 15 per cent, Calabrese (locally called Nero d'Avola), Gaglioppo (Mantonico Nero) and Sangiovese. The minimum alcohol content is 12 per cent. Produced by Spinasanta, Messina.

Malvasia delle Lipari (28 – 30.1.1974)

A sweet dessert wine produced from the grapes of the Malvasia delle Lipari and 5-8 per cent of Corinto Nero. Three versions are available – a sweet wine at 11.5 per cent of alcohol content; a *passito* (made with semi-dried grapes) at a total of 18 per cent; and a *liquoroso* (fortified) at 18.5 per cent total alcohol content – part of this alcohol content is not developed and remains in the wine in the form of sugar. Produced by:

Cantina Sperimentale di Milazzo, Milazzo, Messina

Duca di Salaparuta, Casteldaccia, Palermo

Marsala (143 – 10.6.1969)

This dessert wine is produced from the Catarratto, Grillo and Inzolia vines, yielding white grapes at not more than 100 quintals per hectare. This is a fortified wine with a complex process of vinification and ageing. Its colour varies from amber to tawny. Its alcohol content is rarely less than 17 per cent. The wine is variously aged, the younger Marsala being the sweeter. Amongst the versions will be found the following categories: SOM – Superior Old Marsala; COM – Choice Old Marsala; OP – Old Pale; PG – Particularly Genuine; GD – Garibaldi Dolce; LP – London Particular. There are also Extra and Stravecchia Marsalas as well as others with fruit flavourings. Produced by:

Antonio Buffa, Marsala, Trapani
Di Giuseppe, Partinico, Trapani
Florio, Marsala, Trapani

Lombardo-Marchetti, Marsala, Trapani
Mirabella, Marsala, Trapani
Diego Ralli e Figli, Marsala, Trapani

Moscato di Noto (199 – 30.7.1974)

A sweet amber-coloured dessert wine, produced from the Moscato Bianco grape (incorrectly called locally the Moscatella) at 125 quintals per hectare. This has a total alcohol content of 11.5 per cent: the fortified (*liquoroso*) version has a total alcohol content of 22 per cent, of which 6 per cent remains undeveloped as sugar. Produced by Cantina Sperimentale, Noto.

Moscato di Pantelleria and Passito di Pantelleria (239 – 22.9.1971)

The Pantelleria comes in four versions. An amber white, sweet dessert wine is produced from the Zibibbo (Moscatellone) vine, with a yield of 70 quintals per hectare. It has a total alcohol content of 12.5 per cent, of which 4.5 per cent remains in sugar form. The naturally sweet (made with semi-dried grapes) reaches 17.5 per cent total alcohol of which 4.5 per cent remains as sugar.

The Passito di Pantelleria is amber-coloured and has an alcohol content of not less than 14 per cent and a sugar content of not less than 11 per cent. The Extra

Passito is aged for at least one year and has a total alcohol content of 23.5 per cent, of which 8 per cent is left in sugar form. A sweet sparkling wine is also permitted by this legislation. Produced by:

Cossyra Maccotta, Marsala, Trapani   Diego Rallo e Figli, Marsala, Trapani
Carlo Pellegrino, Marsala, Trapani   Tanit, Via Volta 33, Palermo

Moscato di Siracusa (315 – 6.12.1973)

A sweet amber-coloured dessert wine with a minimum alcohol content of 16.5 per cent obtained through the processing of semi-dried grapes. Produced by Giovanni Bonvicino Aretusa, Siracusa.

Some recommended non DOC-*Sicilian wines:* Over and above the well-known but non-DOC production of Regaleali and Corvo di Salaparuta, should be included Castelvecchio by the Aurora Cooperativa of Salemi; the Mamertino of the Cantina Sperimentale of Milazzo; the Medoro by the Consorzio Produttori Bianco Alcamo of Alcamo; the Carboj by the Cantina Sociale Enocarboj at Sciacca; the Grecanico of the Cantina Sociale Europa of Mazara del Vallo; Donzelle by the Cantina Sociale La Vite of Partanna; Etna Nibbio by the Cantina Sociale Le Vigne dell'Etna at Linguaglossa; an Alcamo Bianco by the Paladino Cooperativa of Alcamo; the Draceno by the Cantina Sociale Saturnia of Partanna; the Settesoli (Bianco di Menfi) by the Cantina Sociale Settesoli di Menfi; the Grecanico of the Cantina Sociale Valdelia of Marsala; the Rapitala by the Adelkam of Palermo; the Marsala Superiore Secco by Curatolo Arini; the Cerdese by the Azienda Agricola Fontanarossa of Palermo; the Faustus Bianco by the Azienda Vinicola Grotta of Palermo; the Solimano by M.I.D. of Palermo; the Marsala Superiore Secco of Carlo Pellegrino of Marsala; the Alcamo Bianco of Enosicilia of Palermo; the Riserva Egadi Marsala by Cantine Florio; the Solunto by Solunto, Palermo; Birgi Rosso by the Cantina Sociale of Birgi, Marsala; Fenicio by the Cantina Sociale di Mozia, Eloro by the Azienda Vinicola Siciliana of Noto; Normanno by Diego Rallo e Figli, Marsala; Gebbia by D'Angelo, Alcamo; Saturno by Cantina Sociale di Saturnia; and Alcamo and Zibibbo by the Agricoltori Associati di Pantelleria.

The Tablewines of Spain and Portugal

JAN READ

Jan Read has long been established as an expert on Spanish and Portuguese wines and has written many books and articles on the subject, including *The Wines of Spain and Portugal*, published by Faber, London, and by Hippocrene Books, New York, and *Guide to the Wines of Spain and Portugal*, published by Pitman Publishing, London, Monarch Books, New York, and Elsevier Press, Amsterdam. He also helps the Rioja Wine Information Service in London.

It is customary to write of the wines of the Iberian Peninsula as a whole, though perhaps the most striking similarity is that both Spain and Portugal are best known for single, highly individual wines, Sherry and Port, described elsewhere. Some experts profess to distinguish a generic 'Iberian taste' in the table wines, but I have found that in the upshot this simply refers to the somewhat 'earthy' taste of the more ordinary wines, grown in the hotter regions of the countries and possessing a high degree of alcohol. There are, of course, striking similarities between the 'green wines', the *vinhos verdes* of northern Portugal and the *vinos verdes* of Galicia from the other side of the Minho river. In the past the reputation of the finer wines from both countries has suffered from a preoccupation with bulk exports of cheap wine; but to compare, for example, the Riojas or Penedès wines with the Dãos is singularly profitless. The product of different grapes and soils, they are made by markedly different methods and are quite unalike. Spain and Portugal first made their wines under the tutelage of the Romans; but the countries parted ways in the thirteenth century, and it is often a matter of pride to accentuate their differences.

THE WINES OF SPAIN

Spain has the largest area of land under the cultivation of vines of any country in Europe, where three-quarters of the world's wine is made. In terms of production, it nevertheless ranks third after Italy and France; this is because much of the soil is barren and many of the vines are old and in need of replacement by better and more fruitful types and because insufficient precautions are taken for checking rot in humid conditions. In recent decades it has been best known for the bulk export of inexpensive table wine to northern Europe and, to a lesser extent, to the United States, for direct consumption as carafe wine or for blending with wines less strong in alcohol from northerly countries such as Switzerland. With increasingly large amounts of cheap wine from new sources such as South America coming on to the world market, there is, however, a growing awareness among knowledgeable growers in Spain that, rather than with cheap bulk wine, the future lies in producing better quality bottled wine, which the country is well-placed to make. The purveyors of branded wine in large bottles buy wherever a product of reasonable quality is least expensive, and areas such as California and the Argentine are more suited to the production of wine in bulk by mechanized methods than Spain, with its patchwork vineyards, often located in mountain terrain, difficult to cultivate and worked by peasant farmers without the capital to invest in modern equipment.

It is perhaps worth mentioning that, as regards Spain in general (but not the Rioja, which suffered from late rains), the 1979 vintage was one of the largest ever to be recorded, amounting to some 43,000,000 hectolitres. Production was up by 30 to 40 per cent in Aragon and Catalonia, by 60 to 65 per cent in Navarra and Alicante, and by 50 to 60 per cent in La Mancha. No doubt prices will move accordingly, and there may well be an upsurge in shipments of carafe wine.

There has already been a very marked growth in the export of fine Spanish table wine, especially from the Rioja and Catalonia. To the United Kingdom alone, shipments of bottled Rioja rose threefold during 1975–77, again tripled during 1978, when they stood at 235,000 cases a year, and are currently running at about 325,000. The rise in exports of quality wines from the Penedès has been even more remarkable. The strength of wines such as Rioja is that they provide honest quality in the middle-to-upper bracket at prices the customer can still afford. This is also particularly true of the sparkling wines made by the Champagne method in the Penedès, one of whose largest customers is now Italy; and it would seem that for the foreseeable future Spain is assured of its place after France, Italy and Germany as an exporter of fine wines to the world in general. The current trend in Spain is, on the one hand, to the scientific reorganization of the larger cooperatives and, on the other, to the demarcation of favoured districts making fine wines by individual methods. There is one important fact that should not be overlooked: since the introduction of the closed vat and methods for controlling the temperature of fermentation, the sunnier hotter regions of the world, including the Mediterranean, are now better placed for making good quality wine.

Geography and Wine Regulations

Spain is one of the most rugged countries in Europe and is criss-crossed by great mountain chains and their associated spurs, where it is not possible to grow vines; but, very broadly, it may be divided into three areas:

1. The north, with temperate climate and plentiful rainfall.
2. The drier and sunnier central zone, embracing the great Castilian plateau.
3. The south, with its low rainfall and scorching summer sun.

The world's best table wines are produced along a belt lying between the latitudes of 30° and 50° in both hemispheres and particularly in the cooler part of this belt; and it is therefore not surprising that the best Spanish table wines come from the Rioja and the Penedès in the north, lying in the centre of this zone, but cooler than average because of their high altitude. The wet and often sunless north coast produces no wine except for the thin and acid Chacolí from the Basque country; and the characterful 'green wines' of Galicia, like the *vinhos verdes* of northern Portugal, undergo a secondary malolactic fermentation to eliminate acid. The hotter central part of the country, embracing New Castile, Valencia, La Mancha, Valdepeñas, Alicante and the Extremadura, makes sound, but less delicate wines for everyday drinking. Andalusia, in the south, with its extreme heat, has great apéritif and dessert wines, such as Sherry, Montilla and Málaga, vinified by entirely individual methods.

Wine regions **1** Ribeiro **2** Valdeorras **3** Valle de Monterrey **4** Méntrida **5** Navarra **6** Rioja **7** Cariñena **8** Ampurdán-Costa Brava **9** Conca de Barbera **10** Alella **11** Tarragona **12** Priorato **13** Penedès **14** Terra Alta **15** Mancha **16** Valdepeñas **17** Manchuela **18** Utiel-Requena **19** Jumilla **20** Cheste **21** Valencia **22** Alicante **23** Yecla **24** Almansa **25** Montilla-Moriles **26** Condado de Huelva **27** Jerez-Xérès-Sherry/Manzanilla Sanclúcar de Barrameda **28** Málaga **29** Vinhos Verdes **30** Port **31** Dão **32** Colares **33** Bucelas **34** Moscatel de Setúbal **35** Carcavelos

The regions that have been demarcated and make wines conforming to a *denominación de origen* (roughly corresponding to the French *appellation d'origine*) are shown on the map. Standards of quality are controlled by a central Instituto Nacional de Denominaciones de Origen (INDO), which delegates its authority to *Consejos Reguladores* operating in the twenty-four demarcated regions. Each *Consejo* includes representatives from the Ministry of Agriculture and local growers and merchants, and lays down its local requirements for matters such as the boundaries of its area, cultivation and grape varieties, yield per hectare, methods of vinification, ageing, alcohol content and freedom of the wine from defects and contaminants. Their regulations are policed by inspectors, who pay frequent visits to vineyards and wineries. Samples of all wine for export are carefully checked in government laboratories.

Since the time of the great phylloxera epidemic, which swept the European vineyards in the late-nineteenth and early-twentieth centuries, it has been the custom in Spain, as in all other European countries, to graft cuttings from the native varieties of *Vitis vinifera* onto the resistant root stocks of the American *Vitis riparia* or *Vitis rupestris*, or the *berlandieri*. The cultivation of hybrids evolved by cross-pollination of American and native vines is forbidden in all parts of Spain on the score that they yield 'foxy' wines, sometimes containing a toxic substance, 'malvina'. Another provision of the *Estatuto de la Viña, del Vino y de los Alcoholes*, which lays down a basic code of practice for all the *Consejos*, has recently met with criticism. This is the embargo on the irrigation of vineyards, now employed to such good effect in California and Australia. It has been argued that judicious irrigation of vineyards in the hotter and more arid regions would lead to better wines and that in this respect the *Estatuto* has been modelled too closely on regulations obtaining in Bordeaux and Burgundy, where conditions are very different.

Above-average wines meeting the requirements of the local *Consejo* are granted a *Denominación de Origen*, either printed on the label, sometimes, as in the case of the Rioja, in the form of a small facsimile stamp, or alternatively on the *precinto*, a narrow paper band stuck across the cork. This is a guarantee that the wine originates from a definite region and meets the basic standards of its *Consejo Regulador*; but there is again a feeling among some of the makers of the finer Spanish wines that the time has come for a classification based on systematic tasting of the different wines and more directly related to quality.

The North

THE RIOJA

For many people, good Spanish wine is synonymous with Rioja – though this is to do an injustice to the fine wines of the Penedès in Catalonia. The Rioja's traditional export market is South America, but in recent years its wines have been increasingly shipped to northern Europe, the United States and Canada, and have won widespread recognition for their outstanding quality and consistency. They are characterized by their softness, fruitiness, body and good balance and, above all, by their pervading vanilla-like flavour of oak. In fact, the practice of maturing the wines for long periods in oak has been criticized as old-fashioned, a fact of which knowledgeable Rioja growers are well aware; and the current trend is to cut down or to eliminate oak in maturing the white wines and to extend the bottle-ageing of the reds.

There were vineyards in the Rioja long before the Romans colonized Spain in the second century BC, and one of the main centres of production, Cenicero, meaning an 'ashtray' in Spanish, was so-called because the Roman legions cremated and buried their dead near the town. It was one of the first regions to be recaptured during the slow reconquest of the country by the Christians after the Moorish invasion of 711, and after the lifting of the Koranic ban on wine, the vineyards were rapidly developed and later sent wine to the New World for the enjoyment of the Conquistadors. By 1790 a 'Royal Society of Harvesters' had been founded; but it was as a repercussion of the phylloxera epidemic of the late-nineteenth century and with the interest and help of French *vignerons* in search of alternative supplies that the wines were evolved in their present style.

Soil and Climate

The Rioja is a hilly and most picturesque part of Spain, dotted with walled, hill-top townships, former bastions against the Moors. The vineyards, which are often small and dotted among the fields of potatoes, peppers and wheat, comprise some 45,000 hectares and extend for about 100 kilometres on either side of the River Ebro, flowing from west to east from the high pass of the Conchas de Haro to Alfaro in the flatter east of the region. Logroño, near the centre, the provincial capital and commercial headquarters, stands at 384 metres.

The *Consejo Regulador* divides the Rioja into three subregions: the Rioja Alta and Rioja Alavesa to the west, and respectively south and north of the Ebro, and the Rioja Baja to the east. The first two make the best wines; grapes from the hotter and drier Rioja Baja contain less acid and more sugar and produce coarser, stronger wine, often used for blending and to confer body.

In the west, the Ebro valley is flanked by mountains on either side and is never

'Bombonas', open to sun and rain,
are used for making a local apéritif in the Penedès

more than forty kilometres wide, and the vineyards are sited along the river and on the lower slopes of the hills. The soils are sedimentary and of three main types: calcareous clay, ferruginous clay and alluvial silt from the Ebro and its tributaries. The vineyards of the Rioja Alavesa are entirely planted in calcareous clay, which Manuel Ruiz Hernandez, the Director of the Estación de Viticultura y Enología in Haro, considers to be the best for viticulture; the soils of the Rioja Alta are of all three types; while in the Rioja Baja there is a preponderance of silt, together with large areas of ferruginous clay. The climate is well-suited to viticulture. The winters are not severe; the springs, mild; the summers short and hot; and the autumns long and warm. The pattern is fairly predictable, though there have been years such as 1971 and 1977 when sudden hailstorms or prolonged spring and summer rain, bringing in its train mildew and oidium, have wreaked havoc. But, in general, vintage years, while still important, are less so than in more northerly regions, such as Bordeaux.

Grape Varieties and Cultivation

The official booklet of the Ministry of Agriculture, *Vides de la Rioja*, lists fourteen varieties of vine grown in the Rioja, but of these only six are now regularly used for making fine Riojas.

For the red wines, the basic grape is the native Tempranillo, producing wines of 10.5 to 13.5 per cent alcoholic strength with good acid balance. It is unfortunately very susceptible to oidium and, on its own, yields wines without sufficient life. In the Rioja Alta it is therefore used in combination with the Graciano, highly resistant to disease, conferring freshness, flavour and aroma on the wine, but giving rise to musts low in alcohol; and the Mazuelo, whose musts are rich in tannin, important for wines that are matured for so long in wood. Small quantities of the Garnacho Tinto (akin to the Grenache of the Rhône Valley), the grape *par excellence* of the Rioja Baja, may also be used to contribute body and alcoholic strength; but wine

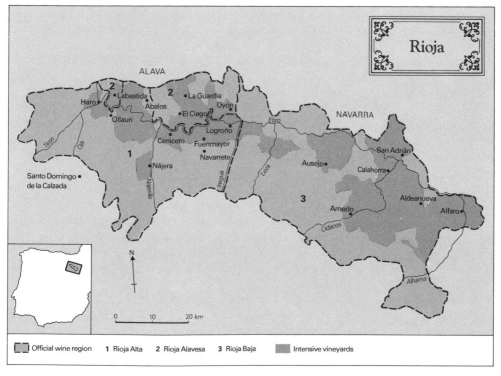

(*Above*) *Rockets charged with silver iodide are used in the mountain vineyards of Bodegas Torres in the high Penedès to disperse hailstorms*
(*Below*) *A small private 'bodega' high in the Priorato region of Catalonia*

made from the Garnacho oxidizes very easily and is short-lived, so that it must be employed with care. (Incidentally, it is almost impossible to gauge the age of Garnacho wines by colour alone, since, owing to oxidation of the anthocyanins, they very rapidly turn from purplish-violet to brick-red.) The make-up of a typical Alavesa wine is very different, so accounting for the marked contrast in style and flavour between wines from the Rioja Alta and Rioja Alavesa. Some *bodegas* use 90 per cent of Tempranillo and 10 per cent of the white Viura, while others may add a proportion of Garnacho Tinto. Only two white grapes are regularly used in the Rioja, the Viura and Malvasía, though small amounts of the Garnacho Blanco may also be employed.

A vineyard in the Rioja looks very different from those in Bordeaux or the Côte d'Or, since the vines are grown low, *a la castellana*, without supporting wires and stakes, and are pruned *en vaso* ('goblet-shaped'). This method involves the retention of three main stems of the resistant stock, onto each of which are grafted two *sarmientos* (or shoots) bearing two bunches of grapes, i.e. twelve in all. The yield is less than if the grapes were grown Bordeaux-style in the Rioja, but it is considered, given local conditions, that the quality is better. Different types of wine were traditionally planted together to produce fruit in the proportions used in vinification, but since individual varieties do not ripen at the same time, modern practice is to plant them in separate parcels, to vinify the wine separately and to blend it at a later stage.

Most of the *bodegas* in the Rioja are vastly bigger than the châteaux of Bordeaux or the domains of Burgundy and require very large quantities of fruit. The older-established may grow as much as 40 per cent in their own vineyards and buy the remainder from independent farmers, as far as possible obtaining it from the same *viticultores*, whose vineyards and methods are carefully supervised. Some of the huge new *bodegas* buy in the open market, and a less desirable practice is to buy wine ready-made from local cooperatives and simply to blend and mature it. It is perhaps a legitimate criticism of the Rioja that more emphasis is sometimes placed on the 'elaboration' of the wine than on viticulture and vinification.

Vinification and Ageing

The age-long method of making wine in the Rioja was to empty the grapes, stalks and all, into an open stone trough (or *lago*), where they were lightly trodden. Tumultuous fermentation began, and the *vino de lagrima* was drawn off into a second chamber. A firmer pressing of the grapes and renewed vinification produced a larger quantity of *vino de corazón*; the *marc* was then pressed, and all three types of wine were mixed and aged in oak casks. A certain amount of wine is still produced in this fashion and sold locally, but it is short-lived and not suitable for export.

The making of wine by Bordeaux methods after prior removal of the stalks was first undertaken by the Marqués de Riscal, who engaged a French *maître de chais* to construct a *bodega* along Bordeaux lines in 1868. It was at this period that the oak fermentation vats and 225-litre casks for maturing the wine were introduced to the Rioja, and during the 1870s and 1880s a group of *bodegas*, including López de Heredia, the Compañía Vinícola del Norte de España (CVNE), Bilbainas and La Rioja Alta, sprang up around the new railhead in Haro and began making wine in the now traditional Rioja fashion.

Apart from a little sparkling *cava* wine made at Bodegas Bilbainas by the Champagne method, three main types of wine are made in the Rioja: red (the full-bodied *tinto* and lighter *clarete*), rosé (*rosado*) and white, dry, semi-sweet and sweet (*blanco seco*, *abocado* and *dulce*). The tradition in the Rioja has been to employ nothing but oak for all the vessels used in making the wines; and this is still the case with some of the older *bodegas* and also at Muga, a small firm producing wines of the greatest distinction in a *bodega* of fairly recent origin. The main difference between production methods in the Rioja and Bordeaux is that the red Riojas are often aged in oak *barricas* or *bordelesas* for much longer than the eighteen months usual in Bordeaux and – until recently – have spent less time in bottle.

The new generation of *bodegas*, some with a capacity of 30,000,000 litres, constructed by interests as different as the Sherry firms, banks and Basque steel companies, all use stainless steel or cement vats, coated with epoxy resin, for fermentation. All age their red wines in the traditional 225-litre oak *bordelesas* and later in bottle.

Most Riojas are blended, and the year stated on the label refers to the predominating vintage; but this is not always true of the *reservas*, which are basically vintage wines made in especially good years. In Spain itself, Rioja is often labelled, for example, 3° *año* or 5° *año* rather than with the year of vintage, and these descriptions mean that the wine was bottled in the third or fifth year after the harvest – the bottle age being unspecified. Whatever its type, red, white or rosé, the *Consejo Regulador* stipulates that a good quality wine entitled to the description of *crianza* (i.e. 'educated' or 'aged') must be matured for at least two years, one of which must be in 225-litre *barricas*; the red *reservas* spend years more in cask. Undoubtedly, the long period in wood and a slow process of oxidation and esterification gives old Riojas, like tawny Ports, a lightness and fragrance; they throw their deposit in wood and rarely need decanting at table. White Riojas, on the other hand, are apt to lose their freshness through prolonged contact with oak, and the new trend is to age them in wood more briefly or to dispense with oak casks altogether.

The Wines

In the Rioja Alta the *bodegas* are mostly grouped in and around Haro, Logroño, Ollauri, Fuenmayor and Cenicero; and in the Rioja Alavesa around Elciego, Laguardia and Labastida. Over the last years control of some of them has passed from the original owners to international firms, such as Crofts, Schweppes, Seagrams, Schenley, Pepsi-Cola, Pedro Domecq and Rumasa. A list follows.

LA RIOJA ALTA

AGE, Bodegas Unidas, S.A., Azpilicueta, Cruz Garcia and Entrena (Fuenmayor and Navarrete)

Bodegas Berberana, S.A. (Cenicero)

Bodegas Beronia (Ollauri)

Bodegas Bilbainas, S.A. (Haro)

Bodegas Campo Viejo (Logroño)

Bodegas Carlos Serres, Hijo (Haro)

Bodegas Castillo de Cuzcurrita (Rio Tirón)

Bodegas Cooperativas Santa María la Real (Nájera)

Bodegas Corral (Navarrete)

Bodegas Delicia (Ollauri)

Bodegas Federico Paternina, Vinos Riojas, S.A. (Ollauri and Haro)

Bodegas Francisco Viguera (Haro)

Bodegas Franco Españolas (Logroño)

Bodegas Gómez Cruzado, S.A. (Haro)

Bodegas La Rioja Alta, S.A. (Haro)

Bodegas Lafuente, S.A. (Fuenmayor)

Bodegas Lagunilla, S.A. (Cenicero)

Bodegas Lan (Fuenmayor)

Bodegas López Agos (Fuenmayor)

Bodegas Olarra (Logroño)

Bodegas Marqués de Caceres (Cenicero)

Bodegas Marqués de Murrieta (Logroño)

Bodegas Martínez Lacuesta Hnos., Ltda (Haro)

Bodegas Montecillo, S.A. (Fuenmayor)

Bodegas Muga (Haro)

Bodegas R. López de Heredia, Viña Tondonia (Haro)

Bodegas Ramón Bilbao (Haro)

Bodegas Rioja Santiago, S.A. (Haro)

Bodegas Riojanas, S.A. (Cenicero)

Bodegas Velazquez, S.A. (Cenicero)

Bodegas Vista Alegre, S.A. (Haro)

Compañía Vinícola del Norte de España, S.A. (CVNE) (Haro)

LA RIOJA ALAVESA

Bodegas Alavesas, S.A. (Laguardia)

Bodegas Cantabria, S.A. (Laguardia)

Bodegas Cooperativa Vinícola de Labastida (Labastida)

Bodegas Faustino Martínez (Oyon)
Bodegas Real Divisa (Abalos)
Bodegas Rojas Cía., s.r.o. (Laguardia)
Bodegas Palacio (Laguardia)
Bodegas Viña Salceda (Elciego)

Rioja Alavesa s.m.s.
Sociedad General de Vinos, s.a. (Elciego)
Vinos de los Herederos del Marqués de
    Riscal, s.a. (Elciego)

LA RIOJA BAJA

Bodegas Gurpegui (San Adrián)
Bodegas Latorre y Lapuerta (Alfaro)
Bodegas Muerza, s.a. (San Adrián)

Bodegas Palacios, Vino Rioja, s.a. (Alfaro)
Bodegas Rivero (Arnedo)
Savin, s.a. (Aldenueva de Ebro)

At the outset, a distinction must be made between Riojas labelled '*crianza*' or '*sin crianza*', both of which may be shipped with a *Denominación de Origen* and which are labelled as such either on the *contra etiqueta*, a small label stuck on the back of the bottle, or on the *precinto*, a paper strip over the cork. The wines *sin crianza* are not aged in oak, but simply bottled (and sometimes hot-bottled at 50°C or pasteurized) after secondary fermentation and are often no better than inexpensive young wines from other regions.

With the fine Riojas the great divide is between those from the Rioja Alta and Rioja Alavesa. In general, the wines from the Rioja Alta are fresher, more definite and assertive and age better. The Alavesa wines, with their much higher proportion of Tempranillo, tend to be more fragrant when young. With age the nose becomes sweeter and a little cloying, and the wines lose body, remaining soft and very gentle with a lingering finish of great charm. Both types of wine have their devotees, and with practice it is soon possible to distinguish between them simply from the nose.

In theory, there are two basic types of red Rioja: the *claretes*, sold in Bordeaux-type bottles, are said to resemble the wines from that area in their lightness, dryish flavour, slight acidity and longevity; the *tintos* (or 'Burgundy-type'), which remain longer in contact with the grape skins during fermentation, are deeper in colour, fuller and of softer flavour and greater body. In fact, the style varies so much from *bodega* to *bodega* that one firm's *clarete* might be another's *tinto*.

As regards vintage years, there is general agreement among the *bodegas* that the best recent years were 1964, 1966, 1968, 1970, 1973, 1975, 1976 and 1978; but over this period there has not been a single year, with the possible exception of 1977, when some of the *bodegas* have not made good wine. For example, much of the 1973 Rioja is first-rate, but the Marqués de Riscal made a much better wine in 1971, a year in which 65 per cent of the harvest was lost because of the onset of oidium.

Red Riojas

The youngest of the *crianza* Riojas and those with the widest sale, especially in Spain itself, are bottled in the third year after the harvest (i.e. 3° *año* or of a vintage corresponding to this). Among the biggest sellers and least expensive are the Paternina Banda Azul, which went through a bad period after the transfer of the *bodega* to a large new plant at Haro, but is now an improved wine; Campo Viejo, made by the large firm of Savin, a big, full-bodied wine; Berberana's Carta de Plata, smooth and fruity, like all the wines from this very well-run modern *bodega*; and Cumbrero from Bodegas Montecillo, a subsidiary of the sherry firm of Osborne, light, elegant and excellent value. Somewhat more expensive are the well-made 3° *año* reds from the old-established and medium-sized *bodegas* in Haro, López de Heredia, La Rioja Alta and CVNE, all of them wines of style and breeding. One might add that there are expert tasters abroad who consider that the long years of ageing in oak leaves some of the *reservas* with good initial taste and bouquet and a long aftertaste, but a little lacking in flavour in between. For this reason they prefer to drink these younger Riojas.

As regards the four- and five-year-old wines, there is an *embarras de richesses*. In the past, Spaniards have considered that the aristocrats were the wines from the Marqués de Murrieta and the Marqués de Riscal. The former tend to be fruitier and more fully bodied, while the Riscal wines are lighter, more nervous and more in the style of Claret (and vary very considerably from harvest to harvest). One of my own favourites is the 1973 Muga, a beautiful wine, aromatic and fruity, well-balanced and with a long aftertaste. Both the velvety and full-bodied Ardanza and the lighter Arana from La Rioja Alta are lovely, well-balanced, fruity wines with a fairly pronounced oak nose. The 1973 Marqués de Caceres, from a *bodega* where French influence is strong, since its technical adviser is from Bordeaux, has been much admired for its deep blackcurrant taste by foreign critics. Oddly enough this goes to show that it is possible to make excellent Rioja by blending and maturing, since its red wine comes from private growers or cooperatives near Cenicero. Viña Zaco from Bodegas Bilbainas has always been a light, dry, fully flavoured wine; while the newer *bodegas* with their modern technology are also capable of making most satisfactory wine. I would particularly instance the Carta de Oro from Berberana and the Olarra Tinto 1973, both full, velvety, deeply coloured wines, full of fruit and aftertaste. Much to be commended among the Alavesa wines are the 1973 Solar de Samaniego, with its pale orange colour, perfumed Tempranillo nose, its taste of raspberries and soft and lingering finish, and also the Monte Real wines from Bodegas Riojanas, an old family firm established in Cenicero since 1890, which still makes some of its wine by the traditional *lago* method.

Of the still older wines, the *reservas* must be aged for six years or more in the *bodega*, and the *gran reservas* for upwards of eight years. It is impossible to write of all those to which I should like to do justice. The Imperial *reservas* from CVNE and the Reserva 904 from La Rioja Alta, currently available in the 1968 vintage, are beautiful old wines, intense and silky with deep bouquet and long finish. The Muga 1970 Prado Enea, with its lovely Alavesa-type nose, is exceptionally smooth and mellow. If I were to single out one or two quite exceptional older *reservas*, not, unfortunately generally available, I would mention the 1957 Paternina, still full of flavour and life; the Viña Tondonia, blended from six-year-old wines in 1972, then bottled and released in 1977 to commemorate the first centenary of the *bodega*, a wine reminiscent of an old Claret, light, fully flavoured and with a strawberry flavour and none of the astringency so typical of the younger Tondonia wines, made with no concessions to modernity, to last and to appeal to purists of Rioja; and finally the glorious 1934 Murrieta Castillo Ygay, at its peak when I drank it a year or two ago, a wine whose full complexity emerged as it warmed in the glass, and again with overtones recalling a really good old Claret.

White and Rosé Riojas

By general agreement the best wines to come from the Rioja are the reds, but much of the white wine is also of good quality and, especially when bottled young, is dry, fresh and fruity. The danger is to mature the white wines too long in oak, when they sometimes become pronouncedly yellow in colour, rather tired and flat, and without much finish. But there are exceptions to every rule; I recently drank a white Tondonia which had spent no less than seven years in oak and another seven in bottle. Surprisingly, it emerged remarkably fresh and without an overpowering taste of oak; and, in fact, perhaps the best white to come out of the Rioja in recent years has been the 1971 Viña Tondonia from López de Heredia, described recently (Spring 1979) by a leading English shipper as 'perfectly dry, beautifully balanced,

deep gold in colour and with a long finish in which the oak and the fruit seemed to
be in perfect harmony. Other dry white Riojas to look out for and to drink young
are the fresh and aromatic Cumbrero from Bodegas Montecillo, the 1978 Marqués
de Caceres, the big-selling Monopole from CVNE and La Rioja Alta's Metropole
Extra. The semi-sweet Diamante from Bodegas Franco Españolas, so popular in
Spain, is an excellent wine with a dessert, elegant and flowery, round and well-
balanced, with a refreshingly dry finish. Among the rosés (or *rosados*), that from the
Marqués de Riscal is of good standard, both dry and refreshing.

THE PENEDES

Thanks to its soil, climate and geographical position, the Penedès district, a little
to the south of Barcelona, makes a larger range of wines than any other part of
Spain. They include red, white and rosé table wines; dessert wines such as Sitges;
a maderized *rancio* in the style of Sherry; a *vino de aguja* with a slight natural sparkle;
and, of course, vast amounts of sparkling wine made by the *cava* or Champagne
method. It was probably the Greeks who introduced the Malvasía grape used for
making the dessert wines of Sitges. Vilafranca del Penedès, the centre of the region,
was founded by Hamilcar Barca; and after driving out the Carthaginians during the
Second Punic War, the Romans laid firm foundations for a wine industry which
has flourished ever since. Catalan brandy has been exported to England and elsewhere for centuries, and brands like the excellent Torres 'Black Label' or Mascaro,
made by the Charentais method, compare with the best, as blind tastings have
proved. Several of the large *bodegas* can trace back their history for centuries:
Cordorníu, now the largest concern in the world to produce wine by the Champagne method – its *cavas* have been declared a national monument – was already
making still wines in 1551; and the Torres family has owned vineyards since the
seventeenth century.

Soil, Climate and Grape Varieties

The Penedès is a limestone area with soils very suitable for viticulture; the climate
is temperate and the rainfall ideal for growing vines. There are three subregions:
Bajo Penedès, Medio Penedès and Alto Penedès. The Bajo Penedès, bordering the
coast, is wild, rocky and rugged. The climate is hotter than in the other zones, and
it is therefore particularly suitable for the cultivation of the black Cariñena, Garnacha, Ojo de Liebre (alias the Tempranillo) and Samsó grapes, and has been making
good red wines for centuries. The Medio Penedès is responsible for almost 60 per
cent of the wine from the area as a whole, mainly white and made from the Xarel-lo
and Macabeo grapes for use in sparkling wines. The bases for the best sparkling
wines are in fact white wines without overmuch personality, but at the same time
light and well-balanced.

The Alto Penedès, rising to a height of some 700 metres in the hills around the
monastery of Montserrat, is almost entirely given over to the cultivation of the
white Parellada grape. Here, the sun shines through the clouds, and the climate is
humid and cooler. It produces some of the best Spanish white table wines, light,
delicate and aromatic.

There is another native and 'noble' grape, the black Monastrell, and a number of
foreign grapes have been introduced to the Penedès, where they have been successfully acclimatized and grown in the vineyards of Bodegas Torres. These include the
white Gewürztraminer from Alsace, the Chardonnay from Burgundy and the
Riesling from Germany; also the red Pinot Noir from Burgundy and Cabernet
Sauvignon from Bordeaux. It is of special interest that, at Bodegas Torres, the
foreign vines are necessarily staked and trained on wires, and pruned by the Guyot

method – a marked departure in Spain, where the native vines are elsewhere grown low and pruned *en vaso*.

The Wines

Apart from the dozens of *cavas* making sparkling wine, there are numerous well-equipped modern *bodegas* in the Penedès producing still table wines of high quality.

Among the most modern are the recently completed Bodegas Bosch-Guell, owned and operated by the Bosch family, who make good Clarete fino and Blanco selecto wines. The *bodegas* of Masia Bach, now owned by Codorníu, began as an appendage to a vast Florentine-style mansion, built by two elderly brothers from Barcelona, who had made a fortune by selling uniforms to the British and French armies during the First World War. As the wines became better known, the *bodega* grew to its present capacity of 3,000,000 litres, with 1,000 metres of cellars housing some 8,500 oak *barricas*. Extrísimo Bach has long been famous as one of the very best white Spanish dessert wines, lush and fragrant, with a pronounced oak nose and long finish; and the *bodega* also produces a refreshing dry white Masia Bach and a red wine, ruby-coloured, dry and fruity, but uncomplicated and without much nose or aftertaste. The best recent vintages were 1970, 1974 and 1978, which, as elsewhere in Spain, promises to be outstanding.

The Marqués de Monistrol is another family firm which has recently been taken over – by Martini & Rossi. It has been making excellent sparkling wine by the Champagne method since 1882, and red, rosé and white wines since 1974. The most individual is the Vin Natur Blanc de Blanc, made with 60 per cent Parellada grapes and 40 per cent Xarel-lo and bottled only two months after they are picked. Light, refreshing and fruity with a typically aromatic Parellada nose, it is incipiently *pétillant* and is presented in bottles with corks held by hooks. The other still wines are aged in oak, the pleasantly fruity red *reserva* for three to four years, with another one-and-a-half in bottle. Its medium sweet Tinto abocado is something of a rarity and goes well with oily food when well-chilled.

The still wines which have most gained the Penedès its growing reputation outside Spain are those from Bodegas Torres, scrupulous both in the culture of the vines and the vinification and maturing of its wines. In the past, as in the Rioja, the must was vinified by Bordeaux methods in large oak *cubas* (or vats), some of which survive in the old *bodega*, where they are now used for blending the contents of individual *barricas* before the wine is bottled. Fermentation of all the wine is now carried out in thermostatically controlled stainless steel tanks. Most of the white wine is not now matured in oak, since it has been found that it emerges lighter and fresher without such treatment. The reds are aged in 300-litre oak *barricas* for one to two years; and one of the most impressive sights at the *bodega* is the underground galleries, tunnelled beneath the vineyards and two kilometres in length, with capacity for 20,000 casks, all new – they are subsequently transferred to the brandy store.

Miguel Torres Jr, who trained at the Department of Oenology at Dijon University, is one of the most gifted and forward-looking wine-makers in Spain – not the least of his innovations are the electronically controlled rockets used to disperse approaching hailstorms in the high mountain vineyards, where many of the white grapes are grown. With him it is an article of faith that all the wines should carry a label stating the year of vintage and not simply a description such as 4° *año* – meaning that the wine was bottled during the fourth year after the harvest – and all Torres wines are therefore labelled according to vintage. There is a large range, both of whites and reds.

The dry Viña Sol and semi-sweet San Valentin, both made from the native Parellada grape, are light and fruity white wines with an agreeable bouquet. In addition to the Parellada, the 1977 Gran Viña Sol contains some 30 per cent of the newly introduced Chardonnay grapes, and since these wines benefit from longer bottle age, they are kept in the *bodega* for some two years before shipment. Fresh, fruity and well-balanced with a long finish and remarkably flowery nose, it is a very good dry white wine. The same characteristics are even more pronounced in the Gran Viña Sol 'Green Label', a wine made in small quantity with grapes picked in the most select vineyards of the estate and containing 25 per cent of Sauvignon. This is the only white wine from Torres to be aged in oak, which contributes to its complex flavour. Newcomers to the Torres range are a remarkably fresh Riesling and the semi-sweet Esmeralda, made with 30 per cent Gewürztraminer and 48 per cent Muscat d'Alsace, an extraordinarily round wine in which one has the impression of chewing the fresh grapes. There is also a *rosado*, De Casta, light, fresh and crisp, with plenty of fruit.

The youngest of the red wines, the Tres Torres, made from the native Garnacha and Cariñena grapes, is full-bodied, deep ruby in colour, with a smooth finish and characteristic fruity aroma. The better wines made from these grapes are given more bottle age – some three to four years for the Gran Sangredetoro, which emerges as a very big wine with an even more pronounced bouquet. The Coronas *reservas*, containing a high proportion of Cabernet Sauvignon, spend even longer in bottle – up to five years for the Gran Coronas and more for the 'Black Label'. They are both distinguished wines, well-balanced, velvety and full of flavour, with a long finish and a nose reminiscent of violets. The Torres reds are sometimes criticized as being on the oaky side but it is not something which disturbs me (I have, no doubt, drunk far too much Rioja). More to the point is that at a recent blind tasting in Paris, in which French experts and a group of English Masters of Wine took part, the 'Black Label' was actually voted superior to the Château Latour 1970; the two wines were obviously at very different stages of development, but the verdict is indication enough of the quality of the Torres. Completely different in character is the beautiful Santa Digna, the first fruit of the plantings of Pinot Noir grapes, light and dry, with a restrained cigar-box nose carrying through into the glass.

Sparkling Wines

Manufacture of sparkling wine by the Champagne method in the Penedès was begun in 1872 by Don José Raventos, whose family firm of Codorníu is now by far the largest concern in the world making such wines. Its sales amount to 35,000,000 bottles a year, of which 4,000,000 go for export; and the reserves amount to some 75,000,000 litres, stored in the eighteen kilometres of cellars occupying five floors beneath the decorative gardens. Between them, Codorníu, Freixenet, Gonzalez y Dubosc, Monistrol, Segura Viudas, the Marqués de Caralt and the other dozens of *cavas* scattered around the little town of San Sadurní de Noya are responsible for 85 per cent of all Spanish sparkling wine, the balance coming from the provinces of Gerona and Lérida.

The grapes used for these *cava* wines are the native Parellada, Xarel-lo and Macabeo, but in all other respects they are made exactly as they are in Reims. As in the Champagne district, there have, of course, been certain changes in technology during recent years. The must is now fermented in large, cooled stainless steel tanks; during secondary fermentation the bottles are closed with Crown corks and plastic inserts instead of ordinary corks held by hooks; and experiments are in progress with large octagonal metal frames, known as *girasols* or 'sunflowers', holding 504 bottles and promoting the gradual descent of the sediment into the neck of the bottle in the same way as the traditional *pupitre*.

The best of the wines, the *brut natural* and *brut*, are light, clean and dry, with a delicately fruity nose, long-lasting bubble and character of their own. They are first-rate value at about half the price of French Champagne. Now that the Chardonnay grape has been introduced to the Penedès, it will be interesting to see whether it is taken up by the *cavas* – but any large-scale usage would be a matter of decades in view of the huge plantations of native grapes, which have already proved their worth.

OTHER CATALAN WINES

Tarragona produces large amounts of wine, both white and red, most of it for bulk export and blending, and exports 'altar wine' to the world in general. Tarragona *classico*, made in various styles and aged for long years in *solera*, is reminiscent of fine old Oloroso Sherry or tawny Port. Tarragona is also closely involved in the manufacture of Chartreuse. Originally made in France by the Carthusian monks of the monastery of La Grande Chartreuse near Grenoble in 1764, it is a liqueur with a long and romantic history; and in 1903, when the brothers were expelled from France, its fabrication was transferred to Tarragona. Production is now shared between their distilleries there and at Voiron. Chartreuse from the two establishments is practically indistinguishable – apart from price – the Spanish, perhaps, being a shade drier.

Priorato, which takes its name from the ruined monastery of Scala Dei high in the mountains, is a small enclave within the demarcated region of Tarragona and makes characterful red wines from the Cariñena and Garnacha grapes. Almost black in colour, dry to the point of astringency, high in alcohol and so full-bodied that one can almost chew them, they are much used for blending.

Alella, to the north of Barcelona, another area with Roman traditions, is one of the smallest demarcated regions in Spain. The best of its wines, matured in oak for one to two years and aged in bottle for another, are made by the local cooperative, which sells and exports them under the trademark of 'Marfil' ('Ivory'). The Marfil seco is an excellent dry white wine, refreshingly crisp and delicate; while the medium-dry, smooth and golden-yellow, has a nose which has been compared with peaches. The cooperative also makes a decent, but unremarkable red.

Ampurdán-Costa Brava, near the French border and the Pyrenees, is the most recent of the Spanish regions to be demarcated. The beautiful and historic castle of Perelada, the home of one of the best wine museums in Spain – the other is at Vilafranca del Penedès – is well known for its good sparkling *cava* wines; and a subsidiary company, the Cavas del Ampurdán, makes large quantities of wine by the *cuve close* process, once the target of a famous law suit undertaken by the French Champagne companies. Perelada also produces a range of still wines, including the drinkable young red Tinto Cazador and a well-balanced, fruity Reserva Don Miguel, matured for one-and-a-half years in oak and another five to six in bottle.

NAVARRA

The red wines from Navarra have something in common with those from the Rioja, which it borders to the east, and are sometimes made from the same grapes: the Tempranillo, Graciano, Mazuelo and Garnacho. A name to look out for is the Vinícola Navarra, whose full-bodied and fruity five-year-old Castillo de Tiebas is excellent value.

The best *bodega*, the Señorio de Sarría, near Pamplona, has a sizeable capacity of 100,000 cases of wine a year and 6,000 oak *barricas* and, like Masia Bach, was begun as a rich man's hobby by the Huarte family, with interests in building and construction. The model winery now makes a variety of red and white wines, all of good quality.

The fruity and full-bodied red Viña del Perdón, which spends two or three years in cask and two in bottle, has rapidly established itself as a favourite in export markets. I particularly like the Reserva 1973, a soft, well-balanced red wine with an oak-vanilla bouquet; and the bright, pale-pink *rosado*, which, with its flowery nose and light, fruity flavour is arguably the best rosé to be made in Spain.

VEGA SICILIA

Vega Sicilia is a legendary name in Spain, and the estate and house to the east of Valladolid, dating from 1864, resemble a small French château in Bordeaux. The vineyards, set back somewhat from the River Duero, are on gently sloping chalky land fringed by pine trees and are planted with native vines (including the Garnacho and a little of the white Albillo) and vines acquired, after the devastation of the area by phylloxera in the late-nineteenth century, from Bordeaux, and still propagated in the *bodega*'s nurseries. After removal of the stalks, the fruit is very lightly crushed between the rubber rollers of a machine modelled on the nineteenth-century original; there is no second pressing, and only the must which separates from the *marc* of its own accord is transferred, first to oak *tinas* (or vats) and later to 225-litre *barricas* for slow and prolonged maturation. The *bodega* makes only red wine, and no Vega Sicilia is sold less than ten years old, the 'younger' wine being marketed as 'Valbuena'. It is a wine with an enormous reputation in Spain and one of which I am personally very fond, though one hears the odd complaint about a bottle which is corked or suffers from too much volatile acidity. A doyen of the London wine trade once ventured the opinion that it had been made from the Douro grapes used for Port, fermented to completion without being brandied and this, interesting in view of its similarity to the beautiful Portuguese Ferreirinha (see page 356), perhaps better than anything conveys an impression of its deep cedarwood nose and its richness and complexity of flavour. Annual production amounts to only 80,000 bottles, of which a little is exported, and it is expensive and difficult to find even in Spain, where supplies to the best hotels and restaurants are strictly rationed.

GALICIA AND THE FAR NORTH

Along the whole length of the often wet north coast only one wine is made, the Basque Chacolí. It is an astringent, slightly *pétillant* 'green' wine of only 8 to 9 per cent strength, available in two varieties, red and white, the best coming from around Guernica, Guetaría and Zarauz, and should be drunk young, on the spot and cold. With the superb shellfish from the north coast, it can, at its steely best, be pleasant.

Despite its often wet climate, Galicia in the far north-west produces a vast amount of wine, most of which is consumed locally or by Galician expatriates in Madrid; and to try its wines in any variety you will have to go to Galicia itself – no great hardship in summer, since, with its secluded Atlantic beaches and mountain slopes fragrant with eucalyptus and wild thyme, it is one of the most picturesque and unspoilt parts of Spain.

Valdeorras, Monterrey and Verín, to the east of the region, produce well-balanced, bone-dry, dark-red wines and some refreshingly dry white, now being exported, but the typical growths of the region are slightly *pétillants* and are made in much the same way as the Portuguese *vinhos verdes* by the secondary or malolactic fermentation (see page 352) of grapes from high-growing tree-vines, supported on wires strung between tall chestnut stakes or granite pillars.

The largest *bodega* in Galicia is the huge cooperative at Ribadavia, just across the Minho river from Portugal. In addition to a potent *aguardiente* (or *marc*), it makes a variety of wines, white, rosé and red, all with a slight sparkle, of which the best is the white 'Pazo' (a Galician word for a seigneurial residence), light, dry and with a bouquet reminiscent of Moselle, and made principally from the Treixadura, Godello and Turuntes grapes.

The choicest Galician wine is made from the white Albariño grape, akin to the famous Alvarinho from Monção across the Portuguese border, and comes from the region bordering the Atlantic on the west. Most reputed is the Fefiñanes Palacio made by the Marqués de Figueroa in a tiny *bodega* housed in his splendid palace. Since it is aged in oak for some years, it is a deeper yellow and has less sparkle than most Galician wine, such as the Albariño del Palacio, made by his brother (though not at the Palace), which is very pale in colour, extremely dry and somewhat acid, with a flowery bouquet that bounces at one out of the glass. These and other Albariños may be sampled at the Parador at Cambados near Pontevedra or at the annual *Fiesta del Albariño* held in this pleasant little seaside town during August.

In general, the Galician reds are raspingly dry and somewhat acid; they should be drunk stone cold.

LEÓN

To the south-east of Galicia the ancient kingdom of León produces both red and white wines. Its full-bodied red *sangre de toro* (no relation of the wine from Torres) was a favourite with the dons from Salamanca University; and the *Tierra del Vino*, nearer Valladolid, has long been famous for Rueda, a dry, golden, *flor*-growing wine of up to 17 per cent strength with a Sherry-like flavour. The Marqués de Riscal is now making and shipping an agreeable dry white wine (though not in the traditional style) with grapes grown in the Rueda area, and the Planta de Elaboración y Embotellado de Vinos – with a total capacity of some 8,000,000 litres and equipped with the most modern plant – produces and exports red, white and rosé wines, surprisingly fresh and light in comparison with the heavyweights which, during the Peninsular War, incapacitated the troops of both British and French armies for days at a time.

CARIÑENA

Cariñena is made in Aragon, rather to the south of Saragossa and the River Ebro. Production is dominated by the reds and *rosados*, made from the Bobal, Cariñena, Juan Ibañez and Garnacho grapes. Like Toro, which it resembles, Cariñena was in the past, when tastes were evidently heartier, one of the most sought-after Spanish wines. Sound, but not particularly delicate, its wines, particularly those from the Cooperativa San Valero, are a popular standby for visitors to the Mediterranean coast and for everyday drinking.

The Centre

VALDEPEÑAS AND LA MANCHA

The great plateau of La Mancha, south of Madrid, is the most prolific of Spanish wine-growing areas. Comprising the demarcated regions of Méntrida, Mancha, Manchuela and Valdepeñas, this huge area, with its seas of vines stretching unbroken to the horizon, supplies most parts of Spain that do not produce wine themselves. Apart from providing most of the often excellent carafe wine drunk in Madrid, Valdepeñas ships vast amounts for blending and export and, in the form of *holandas*, supplies much of the spirit used for making Spanish brandy and subsequently matured in the *soleras* of Jerez.

The grapes most frequently used for the red wines are the Cencibel, Monastrel and Tintorera; and for the whites, the Lairen. They grow in a sub-soil compounded of gravel, chalk and clay; and the three-metre high earthenware *tinajas*, in which the wines were traditionally vinified and matured (the newer *bodegas* use cement vats) were made from this same clay. The wine is drunk young and generally sold during the spring following the vintage, quantities also going to the great export houses in Valencia or Tarragona, where it is matured in oak and used for blending.

The *claretes* and red *aloques*, made from a blend of black and white grapes, which established the fame of Valdepeñas in the sixteenth century, are dry, deep in colour, contain little acid and from 13 to 15 per cent of alcohol. One is frequently and pleasantly surprised by their light taste and freshness.

THE LEVANTE

Bordering La Mancha to the east and stretching along the Mediterranean coast from the Ebro delta in the north to Almería in the south, the Levante is a scarcely less prolific source of wine for everyday consumption and blending. If the description 'Iberian' has any meaning in regard to wines so much at variance, I would say it applies to these. The hot sun and rich, loamy soil in areas such as Valencia and Castellón de la Plana, so suitable for growing oranges, lemons and vegetables, militates against delicacy in the wines, which tend to be 'earthy', heavy and high in alcohol. The better growths come from the mountainous hinterland, among them the lighter *tintos* and *claretes* from Utiel-Requena in the hills to the west of Valencia on the rim of the central plateau and those from two demarcated regions in the hills of Murcia, further south: Yecla and Jumilla. Both of the latter are now enjoying some success in export markets, thanks to the astuteness of their shippers. The inky-black Yecla goes well with a *paella* from the region, but induces deep somnolence, to which a *siesta* is the only answer. The traditional red wines from both regions were, and still are, *poderosos por su densidad* (of powerful density) and contained up to 18 per cent of alcohol, at which point the yeasts are paralysed and further fermentation ceases. What the shippers have done is to add some 10 per cent of white wine, so making a quite acceptable *vin de table* of more character than much from other sources. The whites have a faint, but flowery nose, are fresh and fairly full and better value than the average white carafe wine.

THE EXTREMADURA

The Extremadura, bordering the western frontier with Portugal, straddles both the central and southern areas; and the crowded *bodegas* of Almendralejo, almost as numerous as those of Valdepeñas, produce seas of undemarcated wine on a commercial scale. The best of the Extremaduran wines are made in tiny peasant *bodegas* and are not generally available. Salvatierra de Baros makes a brilliant, intensely coloured and aromatic red wine from Garnacho, Almendralejo and Morisca grapes. Cañamero, a characterful *flor*-growing white wine in the style of Rueda, may be sampled in the Parador and bars of Guadalupe, the shrine of the Conquistadors; while the big surprise is a peasant-made Montánchez – the only red wine in my experience to grow a *flor*.

THE ISLANDS

The Canary Islands do not make wine of particular interest; and the *vino corriente* of Majorca, earthy in the style of the heavier wines from the Levante, is produced in insufficient amount to supply the countless visitors. The wines of one *bodega* are, however, well-worth drinking. On his estate at Binisalem, José L. Ferrer makes a young and very fresh red 'Autentico' from the local Montenegro grape and also some excellent, rather spicy *reservas*, which should be tasted on the spot, as they are not exported.

The South

Apart from some minor table wines from the province of Huelva adjoining Portugal, southern Spain is, of course, famous for Sherry, and produces another good apéritif wine, Montilla-Moriles, and a classical dessert wine from Málaga.

MONTILLA-MORILES

This region, one of the sunniest and hottest in Spain, lies south of Córdoba and centres on the small towns of Montilla and Moriles. Although the demarcated area is half as big again as that of Jerez, it produces only about two-thirds as much wine, very similar in style to Sherry, but not as well known abroad, since before demarcation in 1933 much of its wine went for blending in the *bodegas* of Jerez de la Frontera.

The predominant grape is the Pedro Ximénez, grown in chalky-white Albero soil. In contrast to Jerez, where it is used for making sweet wines, it is here picked when ripe, but still waxy white, and is then fermented without delay and to completion, so that all its sugar is converted to alcohol. The musts yield wine of from 15.5 to 16.5 per cent strength.

Vinification and maturation is along the same lines as in Jerez, with the important difference that the wine is made in large earthenware *tinajas*, resembling in shape the Roman amphorae or orcae, from which they are descended. The liquid clears after a few months, when it 'falls bright' and is either sold as *vino corriente* or removed to the oak butts of one of the large *bodegas* in Montilla or Córdoba for education in a *solera*. The wines emerge as *finos*, *amontillados*, *palos cortados* or *olorosos*, but the most typical type is the *fino*, pale in colour with a greenish tint, fragrant, light and dry, and containing some 14 to 17.5 per cent of alcohol. It is not fortified, except occasionally for export, and in the south of Spain it is drunk with *tapas* or throughout a light meal.

MÁLAGA

Málaga is a wine which is not as popular as it was in its nineteenth-century heyday.

The vineyards, small in size and threatened by tourist developments, are mostly in the hills to the north and west of the city – hence the old name 'Mountain Wine' – and the principal grapes are the Moscatel and Pedro Ximénez. The wine is made either in the small *bodegas* of the hill villages or from grapes brought into Málaga for vinification in one of its large *bodegas* – where it must in any case be matured to qualify for the *Denominación de Origen*. The *Consejo Regulador* lists sixteen types of Málaga, ranging from the very sweet wines made with Pedro Ximénez or Moscatel grapes to a medium-sweet *amontillado*, made from the Lairen and aged for some ten years in wood, and the *seco* with its dry aftertaste. One of the best Málagas to be exported is the Solera Scholtz 1885, a wine comparable to tawny Port, though with overtones of a good *oloroso* Sherry and a refreshingly bitter-sweet flavour and dry finish.

THE WINES OF PORTUGAL

Portugal has been shipping wine since the fourteenth century, when the first of a series of treaties giving her preference was signed with the country's oldest trading partner, England. The trade received a great stimulus as a result of the famous Methuen Treaty of 1703, of which the effect was virtually to exclude French wines from England; and exports were for long dominated by Port, evolved during the decades that followed to meet the tastes of English drinkers.

Today, only two out of every hundred bottles of wine produced in Portugal are

Port. In more recent times the largest volume of exports to the world in general has been of sparkling rosés, such as Mateus and Lancers; but Portugal produces table wines in great variety and has a great deal more to offer. Wine is the country's largest export; and with the precipitate rise in the price of Bordeaux and Burgundy, the better Portuguese wines, such as the honest and often excellent Dão and the refreshing 'green wines', so suitable for summer drinking with their elusive tingle on the tongue, are breaking into foreign markets.

Portugal has been described as a country for wine romantics, and nowhere does the mantle of the Romans lie heavier. In the north, where one cannot move without seeing vineyards, a fresh green in the spring and splashed with oranges and reds in the autumn, the high-growing tree vine of classical days still predominates. The slow-moving lines of creaking ox-carts with their tubs of purple fruit have disappeared from the main roads, but are still to be seen in country districts; and off the beaten track the stone-built houses crowding the cobbled streets of the villages often hide tiny peasant *adegas* (or cellars), each with its granite *lagar* for fermenting the grapes. The reverse of this idyllic coin is that the small farmers are loath to abandon the traditional grapes in favour of better modern varieties and that their wine, made in contact with the stalks, is often tannic and harsh. Over the centuries the Portuguese, among the most inveterate wine-drinkers in Europe, have developed a taste for excessively dry and astringent wines; and there has been some difficulty in adjusting to foreign markets, where the taste is for something a little more comforting and sweeter. Progress in modernization has, however, been rapid in recent decades; and cheek by jowl with the small *adegas* one finds large modern establishments equipped with the latest in horizontal presses, stainless-steel vats and spotless analytical laboratories. These are often the creation of industrialists with an instinctive feeling for their native countryside and the traditions of their forebears.

Geography and Wine Regulations (see map page 335)

Most of the wine is made north of Lisbon and the River Tagus or Tejo, where the ground rises progressively from a narrow coastal strip to the high mountains along the Spanish border. Except for the hot summer months of June, July, August and September, the climate is humid and wet. Tradition apart, there is therefore good sense in training the vines well clear of the ground so as to minimize rot and mildew. There is also another and socio-economic reason. Few regions of the world support a denser rural population than the Minho and north-west Portugal. This has resulted in a polyculture, in which the small farmer makes the best possible use of his plot by festooning the vines along the edge or training them on high granite posts, so releasing the rest of his land for food crops.

A little south of this region of *vinhos verdes* or 'green wines' and the Douro Valley, famous for Port, lies the upland enclave of the Dão, producing some of the best of Portugal's still wines. Another prolific source is the broad plain of the Ribatejo, just north of Lisbon. Further to the south, between the Tagus and the holiday coast of the Algarve, lies the great tract of the Alentejo. Despite its more Mediterranean-like climate it produces very little wine. There are historical reasons for this, in that its vines were uprooted by the Moors and never replanted when the region was parcelled out among the nobility after the Reconquest and devoted to wheat and olives. It has remained the preserve of the often absentee landowner and during the 1974 Revolution much of it was taken over by agricultural workers without the skill or resources for planting vineyards.

Such was the overwhelming importance of Port, that the regions producing table wines were not demarcated until the early 1900s. The government then took action to improve quality by defining the areas making the better wines, introducing safeguards for the consumer along the lines of the French *appellation d'origine* or Spanish *denominación de origen* and, as time went on, by constructing cooperatives, to which the farmers could take their produce to be vinified and marketed. Today, there are still only seven such demarcated regions: Douro (Port), Vinhos Verdes, Dão, Moscatel de Setúbal, Colares, Bucelas and Carcavelos.

Government control of the industry is now shared between four autonomous *gremios*: the Instituto do Vinho do Oporto, dealing with Port; the Comissão de Viticultura da Região dos Vinhos Verdes; the Federação dos Vinicultores do Dão; and the Junta Nacional do Vinho. The last, which embraces Madeira, has recently assumed direct responsibility for the small regions of Colares, Bucelas, Carcavelos and Moscatel de Setúbal, which formerly possessed controlling bodies of their own. The time is, in fact, ripe for thoroughgoing reorganization of the demarcated regions, since much of the best table wine is nowadays produced in undemarcated areas. Regions likely to be demarcated in the near future are the Ribatejo, Bairrada, Upper Douro (for table wines as distinct from Port), Borba (near the Spanish frontier) and the Algarve. The *gremios* do a great deal more than issuing guarantees of origin – in the form of a narrow paper band affixed to the cork before capsuling. Among their many activities, they maintain skilled inspectorates, advise the growers, authorize the planting or replanting of vineyards with approved types of grape, plan and arrange loans for cooperatives, and carry out fundamental research into wine-making. To obtain a *selo de origem* the demarcated wines must not only conform to the specification of the regulating body, but must also be approved by its expert tasters.

VINHOS VERDES

Portuguese wine lists always distinguish between *vinhos verdes* ('green wines') and *vinhos maduros* ('mature wines'), listing them separately; and this is logical, because the *vinhos verdes* account for some 25 per cent of the country's production. The description does not refer to the colour; contrary to what is often thought abroad, they are produced in the proportion of 70 per cent of red wine, almost all of it for domestic consumption, to 30 per cent of white wine, more familiar to foreign drinkers. Both are characterized by a light sparkle or *pétillance*, resulting from a secondary malo-lactic fermentation appropriate to the highly individual method of viticulture. Light, delicately perfumed and bone-dry in their natural state, the white wines contain only some 9 to 11 per cent of alcohol. Ideal for summer drinking with light food and most acceptable as an apéritif, of all Portuguese table wines they are perhaps the most distinctive.

The demarcated region, one of the most beautiful in the country, with its scented pine and eucalyptus, banks of hydrangeas and leafy pergolas, covers the north-west of Portugal from the Galician border to somewhat south of Oporto. The most striking geological feature is the universal presence of granite, both in the soil and outcropping from the hills. There are six subregions, Monção, the Basto, Lima, Braga, Penafiel and Amarante, differing in micro-climate and in the method of growing the vines – either up trees, in pergolas or, in the more modern plantations, trained along wires supported by tall 'T'-shaped *cruzeiros* of wood or granite.

The four most commonly used black grapes are the Vinhão, Borraçal, Espadeiro and Azal Tinto. Chief among the white grapes are the Azal Branco, Loureiro and Trajadura; but the most famous of all (commanding a higher price than any other) is the Alvarinho, grown only in small amount in the Minho and giving rise to exceptionally fruity wines of some 12 to 13.5 per cent. It is often stated that the grapes are picked early and while not fully ripe, but this is a misconception. In a good year, such as 1979, they are sweet, full of sugar and completely ripe. The need for malolactic fermentation results from growing them so far removed from the ground and reflected sunlight. This favours a higher than average content of malic acid, which is converted to the smoother-tasting lactic acid during secondary fermentation.

Vinification

All wines undergo a slow secondary fermentation, during which residual sugars are partially broken down and malic acid is largely eliminated. The musts of the *vinhos verdes* contain so much malic acid (about 7 grams per litre) that a specialized malolactic fermentation is employed to reduce the level. Traditionally, the grapes were pressed in open stone troughs and the must was left in wooden casks until the following spring, when naturally occurring yeasts and bacteria converted most of the malic acid into the more acceptable lactic with the simultaneous release of the carbon dioxide which gives the wines their slight natural sparkle.

Nowadays most of the wine is made in one of the twenty-one cooperatives operated by the Comissão, with capacities ranging from 500,000 to 3,000,000 litres annually, or in modern, privately owned *adegas*. In either case, the wine is fermented in large cement or stainless-steel vats. After malolactic fermentation in the presence of selected strains of yeast or bacillus, it is cooled to $2°-3°C$ and left to stand for a week or more in a cork-lined cold store, so that all the solid matter is deposited. It is then filtered, and before bottling a little carbon dioxide is pumped in to make good the loss of gas during malolactic fermentation in bulk.

The Wines

The wines are ready for drinking in February or March of the year after the harvest. They should be chilled before serving and should not be kept for long, as they will otherwise lose their natural freshness and *pétillance*. The great bulk of the red *vinho verde*, fermented in the presence of stalks and skins, is consumed locally. Tart and astringent as it often is, it goes well with the rich *cozidos* (stews) of the region or with oily dishes such as grilled sardines. It seems a pity that so little is shipped abroad, where it would surely acquire a following.

White *vinhos verdes*, fermented *en blanc*, with their pale lemon-yellow colour, flowery nose and delicious prickling freshness, are fortunately shipped in great variety. Some of the bigger-selling brands are artificially sweetened for foreign markets. In the case of the very fragrant Gatão from Borges & Irmão this is achieved by adding a sweet must, whereas with the more discreet Aveleda, fermentation is checked by filtration and centrifugation of the yeasts, so leaving a little sugar in the wine and reducing the alcoholic strength to some 9 per cent. The purist will probably prefer his wines unsweetened, though the traditional bone-dry wines, such as the stylish Quinta da Aveleda, tend to be a little less fruity and to possess a more restrained bouquet.

The wines from the subregions vary in style and quality, but it is a little profitless to discuss the variations, since most of the commercially available wines are blends. The large plant at Santo Tirso, for example, which markets its wines under the label of 'Vercoope', blends, bottles and sells the whole production from some thirteen different cooperatives north of Oporto. Among the most individual growths are those from the smaller private *adegas*, such as the Quinta de San Claudio at Esposende, a beautiful and delicately flowery wine with a somewhat astringent finish, made exclusively from the Loureiro grape. The Alvarinho wines from Monção, on the Minho river dividing Portugal from Galicia, fragrant, fruity and elegant, are higher in alcohol than the others and have traditionally been regarded as the best from the whole region. Names to look out for are Cépa Velha, whose

Harvesters at work in the vineyards of Quinta de Aveleda east of Oporto near Penafiel; its 'green wine' is one of the best-known Portuguese wines abroad

wines are made in Monção itself and aged briefly in chestnut casks, and the Palacio de Brejoeira, a splendid Manueline residence equipped with the latest in horizontal presses and stainless-steel vats, and surrounded by its own vineyards.

THE DÃO

In terms of quality and general availability, the Dão wines are to Portugal what the Riojas are to Spain – though there the comparison must end, since the wines are entirely different in style and flavour.

The Dão (roughly pronounced 'Dawng') is an upland region in central Portugal, cut off from the rest of the country by the high chains of the Serra da Estrela and the Caramulo mountains. The area covers some 376,000 hectares, of which only 15,000 hectares, or one twenty-fifth, are under vines; the highest parts reach 1,900 metres, but it is in the land lying between 200 and 500 metres that the best grapes are grown. Its summer aspect is of shimmering green vineyards, splashed by dark belts of pine trees and broken by expanses of the ever present granite; and the rocky soil must often be broken up with crowbars before planting the vines. The most important are the Tourigo, Tinto Pinheira and Alvarelhão for the red wines and the Arinto and Dona Branca for the whites. In general, the vineyards are small and scattered and are cultivated by smallholders.

There is a significant difference between the Dão and regions in most other countries with a reputation for their table wines. The Dão has, in effect, progressed direct from the era of the peasant farmer to that of large-scale modern technology without the intermediate stage of the sizeable privately owned winery, so typical, for example, of the Rioja; and there is a positive government embargo on private firms vinifying grapes which they have not themselves grown. As far as I know, the only estate-made wines are those of the Conde de Santar, happily available both as red and white abroad.

Vinification

As late as 1949, most of the wine was vinified by the farmers in granite troughs, stalks and all, for the first thirty-six or forty-eight hours and was then pumped into wooden barrels, where tumultuous fermentation continued more slowly in the cool of a cellar. With the onset of cold weather, transformation of grape sugar into alcohol was delayed, so promoting the formation of glycerine, so typical of the wines. As a result of government reforms, a União Vinícola do Dão was formed in 1934 and was replaced in 1942 by the present Federação dos Vinicultores do Dão, with its headquarters in Viseu at the centre of the region. One of the first reforms of the Federação was an energetic programme for the construction of cooperatives, where the farmers could take their grapes to be vinified by more sophisticated methods. Of these there are now ten, strategically situated over the area, and some, like that at Silgueiros, with its great cement *cubas da fermentação*, its underground *depósitos* for the storage of the young wine during the winter and its annual output of 7 million litres, are very large.

The white wines, made in much smaller amount than the reds, are fermented *en blanc*, without stalks, skins and pips; but a criticism sometimes voiced by the private firms which buy and mature the cooperative-made wine, is that the reds remain in contact with pips and skins overlong, thus acquiring the deep ruby colour and astringency so popular with domestic consumers, but necessitating lengthy ageing if less tannic wine is to be supplied for foreign consumption.

Of the many private firms marketing excellent and individual Dãos under their own label, only two, J. M. da Fonseca and the Vinícola do Vale do Dão, actually own establishments in the region for maturing and bottling the cooperative-made

Vila Mateus, near Vila Real, producer of the famous Mateus Rosé wine

wine. The others, having made their selection from different cooperatives, take the wine by road tanker to their *adegas* near Oporto or Lisbon, where it is carefully blended to achieve an established house style and then run into oak casks to be aged. The Federação lays down that all red Dão sold under a *selo de origem* must be aged in wood for at least two years. Since the casks are much larger than the 225-litre *barricas* used in the Rioja (ranging from 7000 to 30,000 litres in large establishments) there is not the same degree of exposure to oak or of oxygenation, and the *reservas* must be aged for long periods if they are to develop the nose and mellowness of which they are capable. (In this, it is only fair to say that I disagree with some of the producers, who maintain that only the best of the wine in good vintage years will stand more than six or seven years ageing between cask and bottle.)

The Wines

The red Dãos are dry, strong in alcohol (up to about 13.5 per cent), deep in colour and full-bodied. The young wines tend to be on the hard and astringent side, without much bouquet and somewhat 'earthy'; but as time passes, they develop a fragrant nose, a silkiness and velvety character deriving from the presence of glycerine, and good aftertaste. To my mind the small extra expense of buying a *reserva* or *garrafeira* – a wine with a plain white label set aside in the bottle store – is always worthwhile. Vintage years are less important than in Bordeaux or Burgundy; but the 1970 red Dão was outstanding, and one would not go wrong in buying any of the better-known Dãos of this vintage, such as Grão Vasco from the Vinícola do Vale do Dão, Terras Altas from J. M. da Fonseca, the *reservas* from Caves Aliança, the Real Vinícola or Caves Velhas, or, of course, the exceptionally velvety and full-bodied estate-made wine from the Conde de Santar, matured and marketed by Carvalho, Ribeiro & Ferreira. Some of these firms made excellent wine in 1972, 1973 and 1974; but 1975, the year following the Revolution, was patchy, owing to abrupt changes in the management of the cooperatives and the departure of some of the senior staff for Brazil. During a recent visit to Portugal, the red Dão which I liked best of all was a 1958 Grão Vasco Tinto Garrafeira, rusty in colour, with only slight astringency, a taste of blackberries, and a nose and softness of style reminiscent of an Alavesa from the Rioja.

The white wines, far less numerous than the reds, are underrated and much their superior when young. They quickly develop a pronounced, flowery nose and are clean, dry and refreshing. Some of the 1976s and 1977s, the Grão Vasco in particular, are fresh and attractive wines and remarkably good value at their modest price. There is, however, an Iberian propensity for ageing white wines overlong in oak and for overdosing them with sulphur dioxide. I have drunk some most characterful older white Dãos, but in general they are apt to develop a golden yellow colour and to become somewhat tired and flat.

DEMARCATED WINES OF THE CENTRE

The four small regions in the immediate vicinity of Lisbon, Bucelas, Carcavelos, Colares and Moscatel de Setúbal, were among the first to be demarcated in the early 1900s. All produce classical wines, but in minuscule amount, and two of them, Carcavelos and Colares, are threatened with extinction in the face of urban sprawl.

Bucelas, whose white wines were popularized in England by Wellington's officers returning from the Peninsular War and which are still shipped to the United Kingdom, is fortunately in no immediate danger. The 180 hectares of vineyard, situated in the Trancão valley, inland of Lisbon and 25 kilometres to the north, produces some 7,000 hectolitres of wine annually, made by two firms, João Camiles Alves Lda. and Caves Velhas. The Arinto grape, often but mistakenly supposed to be a Riesling, gives rise to agreeably fresh white wines, light, dry and slightly acid. Carcavelos has all but been engulfed by the explosive growth of the fashionable seaside resort of Estoril, and only one vineyard, that of the Quinta do Barão, producing an annual average of 270 hectolitres, now survives. It seems appropriate to quote H. Warner Allen's description of this fortified dessert wine in its heyday from the previous edition of this book: 'The first impression of luscious sweetness which it gives is promptly saved from excess by a curious nutty flavour, vaguely reminiscent of Amontillado, but quite distinct. . . .'

Colares, which in its day made the most distinguished of Portuguese red wines, is another small and diminishing region in danger of disappearance. Its vineyards lie on the coast beyond Sintra, and the vines are grown in dune sands, sheltered from the salt sea winds by pallisades of woven cane and willow. They are planted in a layer of Mesozoic clay some three to nine metres below the surface, and a deep trench must first be excavated. As the sides are liable to collapse without warning, the man at the bottom works with a basket over his head to avoid the risk of suffocation. Protected by the deep layer of sand, the creeping Ramisco vines were among the few in Europe to escape the ravages of phylloxera; and even today there is no need for grafting. The red wines – the whites are of little importance – are therefore typical of the pre-phylloxera growths of the nineteenth century and earlier. Averaging 11 to 12 per cent of alcohol, the younger wines are rich in tannin, acidic and highly astringent. With prolonged ageing they develop an onion-skin colour, extraordinary intensity of bouquet and a flavour which has been likened to that of 'one of the fuller Beaujolais such as Juliénas'. Unfortunately it is now extremely difficult to find any wine of this age and quality.

Moscatel de Setúbal

Today, the most important of the wines from these small demarcated regions is the Moscatel de Setúbal, made by J. M. da Fonseca at Azeitão in the Arrábida Peninsula, rather south of Lisbon across the great suspension bridge. Production is happily on the increase, and it remains one of the world's great dessert Moscatels.

The white Moscatel grapes (known as Alexandria in France), from which most of the wine is made, are grown on the northern limestone slopes of the sunny Arrábida hills. Fermentation is stopped by the addition of brandy when the sugar content reaches 5° Baumé – sulphur dioxide is never employed, since it spoils the taste of Moscatel wines. The must is then transferred to 12,000-litre cement *depósitos*, and lightly crushed grapes and skins are steeped in it. In February the wine undergoes its one and only pressing and is then left in large containers for a year, after which it is filtered and matured in 600-litre casks. The evaporation rate is high and the casks are topped up at intervals with wine of the same age. Over the years the degree Baumé increases from 5° to 20° and the alcohol content from 18 to 20 per cent. It is bottled only shortly before dispatch.

The wines available commercially in the United Kingdom and elsewhere are the six-year-old, with its extraordinarily fresh bouquet and flavour of grapes, and the twenty-five-year-old, richer, sweeter and more honey-like. I was, however, recently privileged to take part in a remarkable tasting of old Moscatels at Fonseca's Old Winery in Azeitão, and my impressions may interest connoisseurs.

The wines, drawn straight from the barrel, ranged from the 1978 vintage to that of 1900 and were chosen at ten-year intervals. The 1978 was characterized by its strong grapy bouquet and intensely fruity flavour and aftertaste; the brandy was not completely amalgamated, and the wine a little turbid. The 1968 wine resembled an *oloroso* Sherry in colour and was soft and very fruity with some oak in the nose. Over the next few decades the wines smelt somewhat of *oloroso*, but were completely different in flavour – smooth, rich, sweet and soft with overtones of burnt sugar. Between the 1928 vintage, which tasted of cherries and caramel, and that of 1918, there was a striking change of colour, and thereafter the wines became almost black. Maderized and intensely sweet, I felt that they could only be compared with vintage Ports. Senhor Soares Franco finally produced a wine *hors d'age*, the 'T.V.' (Torna-Viagem), shipped to and from the tropics in the manner of Madeira. Pitch black and 'chewy', with a nose that was not so much maderized as perfumed, it tasted of an unctuous cherry liqueur.

UNDEMARCATED WINES

The most significant development in the Portuguese wine industry over the last decades has been the increasing importance of wines from regions yet to be demarcated.

The North

It is only comparatively recently that the Upper Douro Valley, at present demarcated only for Port, has begun making good quality table wine. In the past, a fast and furious fermentation in open stone tanks carried away most of the bouquet, and the resulting wine was harsh and without trace of residual sugar. The introduction of closed vats or *automaticos* has transformed the situation. Among the best of the red wines made by this method are the very drinkable Vila Real *claretes* from SOGRAPE, vinified at a winery which also produces base wine for Mateus Rosé, and Evel from the Real Companhia Vinícola do Norte de Portugal. These wines improve greatly with bottle age, and an Evel which I drank recently, non-vintage but about five or six years old, was a soft and pleasant wine, orange-ruby in colour, with a raspberry nose, fruity flavour and long finish. The Quinta do Corval near Pinhão also makes good wines of this type.

In a class of its own is the famous red Barca Velha, made by the Port firm of Ferreira and named after the sailing boats which formerly ferried the young port from the *quintas* to the lodges. First produced in 1951, it is made at an *adega* near the Spanish border from two Port wine grapes grown in the Ferreiras' own vineyards, the Tinta Roriz and Touriga Francesa, lightened by the admixture of more acid grapes bought from local farmers. These contain less sugar and make possible the production of a good table wine without excessive alcohol. After removal of the stalks, the grapes are lightly crushed and fermented in oak vats. The wine is later taken to Vila Nova de Gaia, matured in half-pipes of 250 litres and bottled with long corks. The wine reminds me irresistibly of Vega Sicilia which is not surprising, since there are marked similarities in the elaboration. Dark orange-red, with a fragrant cigar-box nose, it is an intensely fruity wine with complex flavour and long finish. Senhor Jorge Ferreira considers that his best vintages are the 1957 and 1964. Of the more recent, the 1965 has the deeper nose, but the 1966 is a softer and fruitier wine and quite beautiful. Like Vega Sicilia, it is made in very limited quantities and is not at present available outside Portugal, although there are plans for increasing production.

The Upper Douro is also making some good white table wines, of which one of the pleasantest is the Monopolio from Constantino (now a subsidiary of Ferreira), a pale yellow wine with a flowery Riesling-like nose (albeit with a hint of sulphur), both fresh and fruity. The Bairrada, the coastal region immediately south of Oporto, produces red wine in bulk, some of which, when aged in cask, is very drinkable. It is also a major source of the wine used for making the big-selling rosés and is noted for sparkling wines made by the Champagne method.

To the south-west of the Dão, but still a long way north of Lisbon, is the forest of

Buçaco, where Wellington defeated Marshal Masséna in 1810. Tucked away among the ginkgos, Himalayan pines and other exotics stands a vast hotel, once a royal hunting lodge, in exuberant pastiche Manueline style. Its cellars contain an extraordinary collection of vintage wines from the locality, production of which was begun by a former proprietor, Alejandro Almeida. The wines are vinified in a nearby *adega*, then taken to the hotel to be aged in oak and bottled. The old red wines in particular are beautiful: orange-coloured, with a light fruity nose, full flavour, good balance and long finish. For the benefit of readers who wish to stay for a few days and sample them – and I can imagine nothing pleasanter in the silvan surroundings – the best vintages still available are 1927, 1940, 1945, 1947, 1951, 1953, 1959, 1962, 1963 and 1970.

The Centre

The alluvial, sun-baked expanse of the Ribatejo, north-west of Lisbon, with its vines growing in endless rows to the horizon, is the source of most of the inexpensive *consumo* wine drunk in the capital, of which the sound, but unexciting red and white Cartaxo is typical.

In a different class, one of the best wines to come from the area is the 'Serradayres' from Carvalho, Ribeiro & Ferreira, who also mature and market the estate-made Dão from the Conde de Santar and are the largest manufacturers of Portuguese brandy. 'Serradayres' was first made at Borba, on the Spanish frontier near Évora – hence the name, which means 'Mountain of Air'. After acquiring the brand name, the firm set its oenologists to work to reproduce the wine by skilful blending of wines from the Ribatejo, with such success that it is now a household word – indeed, I prefer it to the original. Though dark in colour, the red 'Serradayres' is noticeably lighter in taste than Dão, more like Claret in style in a country whose wines tend to be on the heavy and astringent side. It is aged for some three years in wood, and after a year or two more in bottle can be a mellow and delightful wine. Carvalho, Ferreira and Ribeiro also make an acceptable white 'Serradayres' and some good old *garrafeira* reds from the Ribatejo grapes.

The other undemarcated wines of most distinction from the central area are those from near Setúbal (the region is demarcated only for the Moscatel de Setúbal). The local grape *par excellence* is the red Periquita ('Little Parrot'), named after the farm where José Maria da Fonseca started his wine-making business in 1834. Fonseca is now the second largest wine concern in Portugal and, apart from the Moscatel and sparkling rosés, makes a range of good red and white table wines. The biggest-selling of these, available abroad, is the red Periquita, made entirely from this grape, grown in sandy soil near Palmela. Dark ruby in colour and full-bodied, it is aged in oak for some years and is a satisfying and well-made wine, sometimes on the astringent side, with a raspberry nose. Camarate, formerly sold as 'Palmela', is a lighter, more Claret-like wine, made from Periquita and Merlot grapes with the admixture of a little Cabernet-Sauvignon, now being grown in small amount in the region. Fonseca have, in fact, plans for making a little straight Cabernet Sauvignon from grapes grown privately at the adjacent Quinta de Bacalhoa and have already laid down a *chais* with 225-litre chestnut casks for maturing it. The *adega* also produces the pleasant red Pasmodos and various older *garrafeira* wines from blends of Alentejo grapes.

The South

The only wines of any note to come from southern Portugal are the stout, full-bodied reds from Borba and some run-of-the-mill cooperative-made wines from the Algarve for undemanding holiday-makers.

Rosé Wines

Any review of Portuguese wines would be incomplete without mention of the carbonated rosés, which have made such an impact on foreign markets. At the time of writing, SOGRAPE alone is sending some 1,300,000 cases of Mateus rosé to the United States each year, and large quantities of Lancers, Lagosta and others are being shipped. Although sales in the United States have slipped in comparison with the leading branded wine, the German 'Blue Nun', in terms of volume they are still on the increase.

The wines used for Mateus, made by SOGRAPE, Portugal's largest wine firm, controlled by the Guedes family, which also owns the Quinta da Aveleda and the Vinícola do Vale do Dão, originate from Vila Real and the Dão and may be made either by vinifying red and white grapes together or from red grapes pressed in a horizontal press and fermented in the manner of a white wine. Lancers is made in the latter manner from red grapes grown in the Setúbal area.

Both firms elaborate the wines in establishments which are models of hygiene and sophisticated modern technology, with their gleaming stainless-steel vats and vast tiled containers. The wine passes from epoxy-lined storage receptacles, made by inflating enormous rubber balloons and spraying them with concrete, to the blending tanks and is then cooled to precipitate solids. After filtration it is aerated by pumping in carbon dioxide at five atmospheres. Wines destined for the American market are sweetened by the addition of must, in which fermentation has been checked by treatment with sulphur dioxide.

The final style is adjusted to the tastes of the consumer. Lancers for the American market is a great deal sweeter than the wine destined for Europe, of which the Baumé degree is slightly less than that of Mateus. Fresh, fruity, sparkling and more than a little sweet, the Portuguese rosés are calculatedly made for people who are not regular wine drinkers, and they have undoubtedly done a great deal to popularize the drinking of wine with food. There are now plans afoot to demarcate the regions producing these rosés and to upgrade the wines by reducing the sugar content and degree of aeration, as consumers grow more sophisticated in their tastes.

Sparkling Wines and Spirits

Portugal also produces sizeable amounts of sparkling wine by the Champagne method, most of it from the Bairrada, south of Oporto; but perhaps the best of these sparkling wines is Raposeira from Lamego. The dry or *bruto* wines are clean and fresh, nevertheless lacking the distinction and finish of the French original. Those labelled *seco* or *meio seco* ('dry' and 'semi-dry') are liable to be as sweet as 'dry' white port, and the pink *espumantes* are sweet indeed.

Brandy (*aguardente de vinho*) and marc (*bagaceira*) are produced on a large scale. Most of the *adegas* operate small distilleries, while the Comissão de Viticultura da Região dos Vinhos Verdes maintains large establishments at Amarante, Arcos de Valdevez, and Palmeira, near Braga, for converting red *vinho verde* produced in excess of demand into spirit. It is there distilled by the continuous process in large vertical columns resembling those used for grain whisky and sold to AGE (Administração Geral de Alcool), which disposes of it to private firms for elaboration as *aguardente de vinho* or to the Port companies for brandying their wine. Like the big-selling Spanish brandies, the cheaper marks often have a pronounced flavour of caramel and vanilla. The better brandies are made by the Charentais process in small pot stills, and some, like the Adega Velha, distilled from *vinho verde* at the Quinta da Aveleda without addition of caramel and flavouring essences, are very good indeed.

Sherry

JULIAN JEFFS

Julian Jeffs has had a long association with Sherry, working as a Sherry-shipper's assistant in Spain in 1956. He was Editor of *Wine and Food* from 1965 to 1967; on the Committee of Management for the International Wine and Food Society from 1965 to 1967, and again since 1971. He was also Chairman from 1970 to 1972 and has been Vice-President since 1975 of the Circle of Wine Writers. Julian Jeffs has twice been winner of the Glenfiddich Wine Writers Awards in 1974 and in 1978, and is also General Editor of the very successful Faber Wine Series. His books include: *Sherry*, published in 1961 (second edition 1971) by Faber, London; *The Wines of Europe*, published in 1971 by Faber, London, and by Taplinger, New York; and *Little Dictionary of Drink*, published in 1973 by Pelham Books, London.

Sherry is one of the greatest wines in the world – and certainly the most underrated. Too often taken for granted, bought by price rather than quality, and badly served, it is not surprising that only too seldom does it give of its best. But only a fine wine is worth imitating and no wine has been flattered with so much imitation. Some of the imitations are excellent in their own way and have something of the Sherry style. It is more the pity that, many years ago, their growers saw fit to try and cash in on Sherry's great reputation rather than to compete fairly as an alternative, which some of them could well do.

Real Sherry comes from the extreme south of Spain, from Andalusia, roughly from a triangle between Jerez de la Frontera, inland, and Puerto de Santa Maria and Sanlúcar de Barrameda, both on the coast. It is a part of Spain that is rich in history. The Phoenicians, the Romans, the Vandals, and the Visigoths all ruled there before the Tarik Ben Zeyad, leading the Saracens, defeated Roderick, last king of the Visigoths at the battle of Guadalete, fought in the Sherry country in AD 711; and the long period of Moorish rule began, creating one of the greatest civilizations in the history of Europe. During this period the town of Jerez was called Šeriš, a name that was later corrupted to Jerez by the Spanish and Sherry by the English. Despite their religion, the Moors were far from teetotal, and even then the region was noted for its vineyards. Eventually the Moorish domination came to an end with the Christian reconquest and it is generally accepted that Jerez fell to Alfonso x in 1264, but it remained at the frontier of the Moorish and Christian kingdoms, and in 1380 King Juan 1 granted it the privilege of adding *de la Frontera* to its name, in honour of the part the people played in the continuous struggle. Parts of the old walls still remain. The local archives contain records, going as far back as 1485, of wine being exported to England.

The finest vineyards are on *albariza* soil which, as its name suggests, can be almost as white as snow and is very high in calcium, but when looked at closely it is seen to contain many earth-coloured particles and is very finely grained; a very few are found on poorer, darker soils known as *barro* or *arena*. The even texture of the soil is very important in the climate of Jerez. In February, March, and April there are heavy rains which the earth absorbs like a sponge, and when the blazing sunshine follows in May, the surface is baked into a hard layer without cracks, which traps the water beneath to feed the roots of the vines throughout the semi-tropical summer. The vines penetrate deeply into the soil in search of water, and anyone digging a well in a vineyard commonly finds the roots going down to a depth of nine metres. Thus the sub soil feeds the roots and matters just as much as the soil higher up. The best vineyards contain about 25 per cent of limestone at the surface, 40 per cent at about 60 centimetres down, and as much as 60 per cent at 80 centimetres, continuing in a similar proportion for many metres of depth. Not surprisingly the yield is low.

As the hills slope only gently, giving in that southern latitude an ample exposure to the sun on all sides throughout the months in which the grapes are ripening, in Sherry vineyards, unlike those of northern Europe, the aspect does not matter much and the hills are planted with vines all over. Nevertheless, the micro-climate varies from place to place and, as a general rule, grapes from a vineyard near the coast give about a degree less sugar (and therefore less alcoholic wines) than those well inland. The vineyard area is carefully limited by an official state organization, the Consejo Regulador, which only allows vines to be planted on suitable soils, and which also controls and supervises all the stages in growing and maturing the wine. By no means all the best sites are planted, though, and (as in the Douro) there is still ample scope for expansion without loss of quality.

The classic Sherry vine is the Palomino, of which there are two varieties, related but different. Historically the vineyards were planted with the Palomino de Jerez, now known as the Palomino Basto, which is still found growing in the older ones. This has now been supplanted by the Palomino Fino, originally found growing in the vineyards of Sanlúcar. It is clearly the better of the two, both in the quality of wine it provides and in the yield. Nowadays the Sherry growers, like most wine-growers, practise clonal selection, selecting the finest vines and propagating them. This has led to an increase in yield, but the main object has been to secure freedom from disease: a matter of consistency rather than simply of quantity, so the increase in yield has only been incidental and the quality has been maintained. Historically, the Pedro Ximénez grape was also planted on a large scale and was particularly noted for its sweet wines; but it is harder to cultivate and more prone to disease, so it is rarely planted now and only forms a very small proportion of the whole. As the Palomino Fino is also capable of yielding excellent sweet wines, it is doubtful whether much more Pedro Ximénez will be planted. The third vine found is the Moscatel, which is grown exclusively for making sweet wines.

The vintage takes place in the middle of September and is carefully timed to begin at the moment when the grapes are completely ripe; they are checked for ripeness daily for several days beforehand. The climate is ideal for wine growing and remarkably consistent, so there are no vintage years. Although occasionally the quality fails to come up to standard or the vintage suffers in quantity owing to bad climatic conditions, these disasters are rare indeed compared with those faced by the more northerly wine-growers.

Until as late as the 1960s, the bulk of the grapes were still crushed by foot; not by bare feet, as in the Douro, but by men wearing special cowhide treading boots with tintacks knocked into the bottom at an acute angle, so that stalks and pips collected between them, forming a soft mat with the grape skins that spread the pressure very

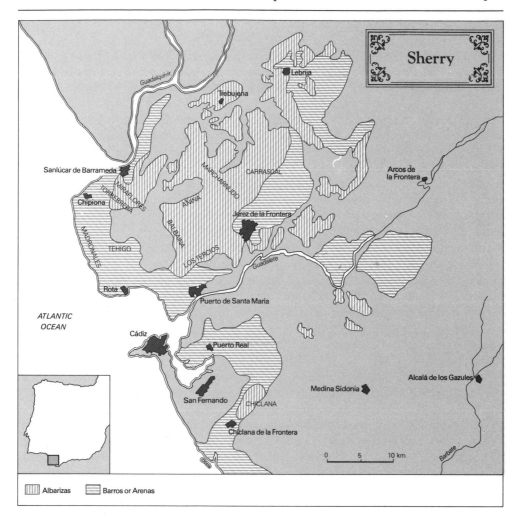

evenly and prevented pips and stalks from being crushed. Crushing the stalks would not matter much, resulting only in a small increase in tannin, but the pips contain 'essential' oils which, if released, give a most unpleasant flavour to the wine that can never be got rid of. The pressing used to take place all through the night so that the labourers could rest during the hottest hours and were less troubled by wasps, which find freshly crushed grapes almost as attractive as jam.

The massive increase in wages has made such labour-intensive work completely out of the question; but man's ingenuity has been equal to the problem, and the latest kinds of presses (which are nowadays essentially the same in all the vineyards of Europe) are so gentle and so effective in their operation that the quality is in no way jeopardized. Before the pressing is started, the grapes are sprinkled with a small amount of gypsum, or *yeso*: 1.5-2 kilograms for 680 kilograms of grapes. The effect on the must is that cream of tartar from the grapes combines with the gypsum to produce potassium sulphate, calcium tartrate, and tartaric acid, the calcium falling into the lees and the tartaric acid usefully increasing the acidity in a most natural way, the attainment of enough acidity often being a problem with wines grown in very hot climates. It is a technique that is certainly centuries old, though its origin is veiled in obscurity.

The must traditionally used always to be fermented in new casks, which fed it with wood tannin, while in turn it matured the casks and made them fit for shipping wine, after which they were usually sold to the whisky distillers and used for maturing whisky. This method of fermentation is still widely used, but it is no longer by any means universal. The demand by the whisky distillers is so high, though, that they now regularly supply casks to Jerez wine-growers specifically to have must fermented inside them.

After the newly pressed must has been poured into the cask, there is a short delay while the yeasts begin their work; then there is 'tumultuous fermentation', which goes on for three or four days, and is so fast that the wine tends to bubble from the bung hole in the cask, which has a big funnel inserted to give room for expansion and to avoid waste – though it is by no means always successful. The fierceness of the fermentation is the only snag with this traditional method, so that although the best casks are magnificent, the fermentation sometimes gets out of hand, the must gets too hot, and the quality of the wine suffers. Although the old methods are still widely used, and some houses prefer them, more and more must is being fermented on a large scale. This is done in great fermentation tanks made of glass fibre, reinforced with resins, or stainless steel. These give the advantage that they can be very carefully monitored and the temperature controlled within close limits by a spray of water which runs down the outside of the tanks in what ever quantity may be right to keep the temperature at its ideal level. This system did not originate in the Sherry country and it is the one that is becoming favoured in all the major vineyards of the world, even as far north as Champagne, where temperature problems are much less likely to arise than they are in Spain. A slow, cool fermentation produces the best, most fragrant wine. By using these modern techniques, it is the worst casks of wine that are lost, not the best.

By the end of September, the Sherry towns reek of fermenting must. After the tumultuous fermentation is over, a slower fermentation continues for many months. Throughout all this time, the containers, be they large or small, are not kept full. Unique among the great wines of the world, Sherry is matured on *ullage*: that is to say, there is an empty space for air above the wine. Indeed, the method of maturation is so different from other wines that not only is a gap left at the top of the cask, but it is also essential that there should be an easy access of air, with a free flow of air around the casks. This is thanks to a special gift of providence: the Sherry *flor*. *Flor* simply means 'flower', but it is not a flower at all. It consists of a rather repulsive-looking film of yeast cells that covers the surface of the must about a couple of months after the vintage, and rapidly grows into a white layer with a surface having a mass of irregular wrinkles, so that it looks rather like an old-fashioned farmhouse cream cheese. It has a number of remarkable effects. One of them is that of protecting the wine against oxidation into vinegar. But some casks grow much more *flor* than others, and the amount that is grown has a profound effect on the way in which the wine develops.

The existence of *flor* calls for a very special technique in sampling. Wine is taken from the casks with a form of cup called a *venencia*, which is unique to Spain. One kind – perhaps the older – consists of a bamboo cane cut away so that there is a complete cup at the end with a very thin stem attached to it to give flexibility. The other kind is a silver cup attached to a long whalebone handle, so that it looks rather like an antique candle snuffer, cathedral size; but even in Spain things are no longer what they were, so that the cup nowadays is more often made of stainless steel and the handle of plastic. To get the wine from beneath the *flor*, the *venencia* is plunged straight in through the surface and then drawn out quickly, so that the yeast is dispersed over a small area and none gets into the cup. After it has been pulled out, the handle is deftly swung upwards so that the wine falls neatly into a waiting glass.

It sounds easy, it looks easy, but anyone who has tried it will know that it calls for a great deal of skill.

All the wine is matured in oak casks, including that which is fermented in large containers. These are made of oak and are called bodega butts. They hold more than a shipping butt – about 730 litres as compared with 490 – so as to contain a full measure of wine and still leave an ample air space over the surface. Experiment over the centuries has shown that this is exactly the right size to get perfect development of the wine.

Types of Sherry

After six months or so, when the wine has begun to show its style, samples are taken out with a *venencia* by the *bodega* foreman or *capataz*, and are classified. This is done entirely by smell, and divides the wine into four categories which are distinguished by the following marks:

/	*una raya* (light and good)
/·	*raya y punto* (slightly less promising)
//	*dos rayas* (musts with less style)
///	*tres rayas* or quema (coarse or acid)

Then it is racked off the lees, or in other words decanted from its sediment into another cask. Its strength is then likely to be 14 to 16 per cent of alcohol by volume, strong by the standards of most wines. Wines of the first category, which are showing a good growth of *flor*, are at this stage very slightly fortified by an addition of alcohol, to bring them up to 15 or 15.5 per cent, but those of the lower categories, which tend anyhow to be rather stronger and which often grow little *flor*, are fortified more strongly, to a strength of 17.5 or 18 per cent, which kills off the *flor* and decides the way in which the wine will continue its development. Wines that grow *flor* develop as Finos, those that do not, as Olorosos.

After this has been done, the wine is allowed to rest for a few weeks and is then classified again, using rather more precise signs:

Y	*palma* (a wine breeding *flor*)
/	*raya* (a rather fuller wine with no *flor*)
//	*dos rayas* (inclined to be coarse)
#	*gridiron* (no good at all)

But although these signs give a very good indication of the way in which a wine will develop, it remains its own master and is notoriously perverse, so that a continuous watch has to be kept on it. Each cask is matured at first separately from the others and the wine is then known as *añada*, derived from the word *año* meaning 'year', or in other words a vintage wine that has not been blended with one of another year. It stays like that normally for a minimum of nine months though occasionally for as many as three years, and during that time it is classified at regular intervals. These are typical of the marks that are used when a wine is mature enough to be classified more exactly:

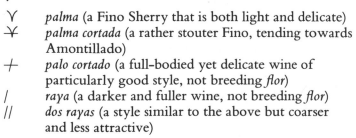

Y	*palma* (a Fino Sherry that is both light and delicate)
⅄	*palma cortada* (a rather stouter Fino, tending towards Amontillado)
+	*palo cortado* (a full-bodied yet delicate wine of particularly good style, not breeding *flor*)
/	*raya* (a darker and fuller wine, not breeding *flor*)
//	*dos rayas* (a style similar to the above but coarser and less attractive)

Different butts of wine, pressed and matured from grapes grown in the same vineyard, mature very differently. Some time ago I counted the marks on the butts in two bodegas. All told there were 25 butts of *palma*, 68 of *raya*, 73 of *dos rayas* and one each of *palo cortado* and *palma cortada*. There used to be more *palo cortado* produced in the nineteenth century before the phylloxera devastated the vineyards and the vines had to be grafted on to American roots – as happened in nearly all the vineyards of Europe. From the grafted vines, it is rare indeed. But that is the main difference. The controversy about pre- and post-phylloxera wines is one that looks as if it will rage for ever, and the effect of grafting has undoubtedly been different in some areas as compared with others, but in all major vineyards it has at least had one good result: inferior kinds of vine were replaced with the best. This certainly happened in the Sherry country and those who lived through this period were generally agreed that the post-phylloxera wine was no whit the poorer; rather the reverse, though sadly with less *palo cortado*.

Mature Sherry falls into three basic classes: Fino, Palo Cortado, and Oloroso. These mature in different ways and with different nuances that make exact description difficult. It is made all the more difficult in that some of the words used in the earlier classifications are used quite differently in describing the mature wine. One essential point must be made at this stage, though: all mature Sherry unblended in the cask is absolutely bone dry. To say – as is often said – that Fino is dry, Amontillado medium, and Oloroso sweet, is a pronouncement of folly and utter ignorance. If a sweet wine is required, it has to be sweetened, and that will be discussed at a later stage.

Fino is the lightest and most delicate of Sherries with a penetrating, fresh aroma and a delicate, subtle flavour. Although described as straw-coloured, the tincture of colour is often so slight that Finos look more like hay. The term *palma* (Y) is used by some shippers to distinguish their best Finos and, as the wines age, these become *dos palmas*, *tres palmas*, or *cuatro palmas*, though the dividing line between one and another is completely arbitrary. When left to mature in cask as nature dictates, a Fino will always grow darker over the years and will become stronger in flavour. Just occasionally it will go on being a Fino in style and become that very rare wine, an old Fino, which may be almost black in colour and yet retain a Fino's pungency and delicacy. Such wines, owing to their age, are of course expensive, and relatively cheap Finos which are sometimes seen labelled 'Fine Old Fino' by United Kingdom merchants, are laughably short of the real thing. Indeed, usually their greatest merit is in their fresh youthfulness. More often with age a Fino gains in body and develops a somewhat different style of bouquet, becoming first a Fino-Amontillado and then an Amontillado, so named because these wines resemble those grown in the hills around Montilla, near Córdoba. The Amontillado Sherries are, however, subtler and more distinguished. The flavour of an Amontillado has been described as 'nutty', though such similes rarely mean very much. Genuine Amontillado, though, is a supremely fine wine; and again, because it is old, it is necessarily expensive. Most of the wines that usurp its magnificent name in the United Kingdom and other export markets are nothing of the sort. They are bastardized and sweetened Finos.

Palo Cortado is often classed as a style of Oloroso, and so it is, but it is really a law unto itself, with a flavour of a light Oloroso but with an aroma more like an Amontillado. It is a rare thing, a connoisseur's wine that is very hard to come by. As it ages, it may be classed as *dos cortados* (≠), *tres cortados* (≢), or *cuatro cortados* (≣) but, as with the *palmas*, the classification is arbitrary. Very little is exported.

Oloroso, in Spanish, means 'fragrant' and the term may come as a surprise to those who are familiar with the far greater fragrance of Fino. However, it is a term founded in history, for in the distant past far more Oloroso was produced than

Fino and the term Oloroso was used to distinguish the finer wines from their coarser and less fragrant brethren, the *rayas*. These wines, as has already been indicated, are completely dry. Some, though, have so much glycerine in them, as a natural product of their fermentation, that they are known as *pata de gallina*, or hen's foot, perhaps because they were supposed to be nourishing.

The various classes of Sherry can therefore be represented roughly by a family tree, thus:

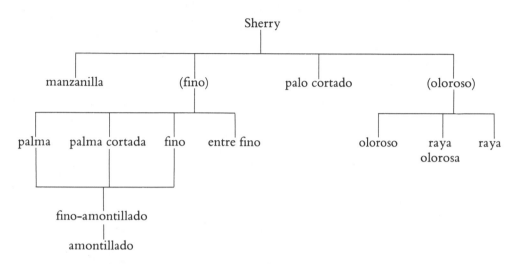

The vast variety of the ways in which Sherry develops is a nightmare for the shipper. Fortunately, though, he has his answer. He matures his wine by the *solera* system. A *solera* consists of a number of butts of identical wine. If a butt of Sherry is taken, of a style that the shipper particularly likes, and a proportion of the wine – perhaps a third – is taken out, and the cask is then refreshed by the same amount of wine of similar style but a little younger in age, then after a period of time – perhaps six months – the wine in the cask goes back to its original style and tastes as it did before. The *solera* system uses this peculiar attribute on an enormous scale. The *solera* itself consists of a large number of casks of identical wine, from which wine is drawn from time to time. The casks in the *solera* are refreshed from the last scale of a *criadera*, or nursery, of wine, which is similar in style to the *solera* but a little younger. This in turn is refreshed from the second scale of the *criadera*, which is refreshed from the third, and so on. There may be seven or eight in all, or even more. In this way, the shipper can ensure a continuous supply of wine of unvarying style.

One wine that is very popular throughout the world has not yet been mentioned: Manzanilla. The reason for this is that it can only be produced by means of the *solera* system. Moreover, it can only be matured in the relatively cool atmosphere of Sanlúcar de Barrameda. It is, therefore, a comparatively recent invention, as the *solera* system only came into being in about 1800. To make Manzanilla, the grapes are usually picked a little earlier than in the main Sherry vineyards, so that they are less ripe and rather more acid. The wines then enter the *solera* system when still young and are passed through a large number of scales very rapidly, being moved more often than a Fino Sherry, and they grow an extremely abundant film of *flor*. The term Manzanilla Simpliciter is synonymous with Manzanilla Fina – the Fino version of Manzanilla, lighter than an ordinary Fino Sherry, having a fragrance of its own and a slightly salty tang. As it ages, it becomes a Manzanilla Pasada, which is equivalent to a Fino-Amontillado, and then a Manzanilla-Amontillada. Likewise, Oloroso is produced in Sanlúcar de Barrameda from the musts which do not have a strong tendency to grow *flor* and is similar in style to the Olorosos produced in the other Sherry towns, but with a rather more piquant flavour.

Just a few of the bone-dry Sherries sold in the United Kingdom are straight *solera* wines, but the vast majority of them are blended from a large number of wines. Wines from the *solera* system form the basis of them all: the mature Sherries of varying ages, qualities, and styles, which are the base wines. Sometimes (to make the cheapest Sherries) these are blended with young wines that have never been in a *solera* at all. At the other end of the scale, to make the most expensive Amontillado and Oloroso Sherries, small quantities of wine of tremendous age are included in the blend. These exceptionally old Sherries are quite undrinkable by themselves. They are so powerful in flavour that they shrivel the mouth; but a small proportion of them in a blend will completely transform it.

Visitors to the Sherry country are often shown how this is done. If some very old wine is poured into a glass, swirled round, and then poured out again, a small amount clings to the glass, and when a younger wine is added it blends with the old, gets deeper in colour and, to a dramatic degree, in flavour and aroma. This very small proportion will do the trick. The art of the Sherry shipper lies in knowing how much of each wine to use in creating the finest blends on which the reputation of his house for quality ultimately depends.

The sweetening wines are made in the same way as Port. In other words, the must, just as it has started fermenting, is put into casks that already contain a certain amount of alcohol, so that when the fermentation is complete and the young wine has attained the strength at which the ferments cease to work, there will still be a considerable amount of unused sugar left in the wine to give it sweetness. To add to the sweetness, the grapes for making such wine may be left out in the sun for several days or even for two or three weeks, so that they are shrivelled, almost like raisins, and attain a great concentration of sugar and flavour. Or they may be picked late. The great traditional sweetening wine was Pedro Ximénez, made from the grapes of that name, and it used to be imported in large quantities from Montilla-Moriles where the Pedro Ximénez grape particularly flourishes. However, with an increasing awareness of the geographical significance of names, the importation of wine from outside is being completely phased out, and this has already eliminated another sweetening wine, the *dulce apagado*, which used to be produced from grapes grown in the region of Los Palacios, just outside the Sherry area. However, this has now begun to be replaced by a new version of *dulce apagado*, and a very good one, made from Palomino grapes grown within the Sherry area, though not on the finest sites. Moscatel is produced in the same way. The fourth sweetening wine is *dulce de almíbar* which is a blend of invert sugar (which is the same as natural grape sugar) and Fino Sherry. The first three sweet wines all have their distinct (and often splendid) flavours, whereas the fourth is used in more delicate blends or those in which the colour must be kept pale.

Just a few of the best and most expensive Sherries sold on the export markets are straight *solera* wines or blends from various *soleras* but contain no sweetening wine at all. Being completely dry, they are something of an acquired taste, and this particularly applies to the completely dry Amontillados and Olorosos. Most of the wines that are sold, though, are blends of wine from several *soleras*, sweetening wines, and occasionally special wines that are used to add colour, and are made from boiling down unfermented must, which is then mixed with fresh must and fermented.

The final stage of making the blend is to add a small amount of alcohol. Pure alcohol is rarely used, but rather a mixture of one half pure alcohol and one half sherry, called *mitad y mitad* – 'half and half'. This gives the wine less of a shock and blends in better. This final fortification is largely a matter of tradition. In the past, when no doubt the wine was less well made than it is today, the fortification helped it to travel, protecting it from the hazards of infection and oxidation which could well afflict a lighter wine on a long sea journey in cask. Nowadays no such mishaps are expected, and they should never happen to a well-made, fully mature wine. But the taste for a strong wine remains and Sherry is still fortified by one or two per cent, the exact amount depending on the taste of the importer and the fiscal laws of the importing country, as countries tend to have higher rates of duty for very strong wines.

There is an additional reason for fortifying Finos. If they are imported in their natural state, and the cork is removed from the bottle for a time, tiny fragments of *flor* remaining in the wine may spontaneously grow. A real Sherry lover would greet this with joy, for he would shake the *flor* off and know that the wine beneath it would be in perfect condition. But in these days of mass markets, people do not even seem to understand that good table wines throw a deposit and need decanting. Faced with a bottle of Sherry growing *flor*, they might well become hysterical and sue the importer. So Fino Sherries have to be fortified to prevent it from happening.

The misplaced horror that affects the public on finding any deposit has brought about another change. Since the 1960s, practically all Sherry for export has been ultra-cooled: reduced to a very low temperature for several days so that any deposit likely to be thrown comes out of the wine, which is then filtered clear. It has been commercially very successful and it is rare indeed today to find any deposit in a Sherry bottle. But more is the pity. A certain, small element of flavour is also left behind. Happily a few murky bottles are still exported for the enlightened.

Serving Sherry

No wine is more regularly ruined by being served badly. As with all good wines, one of the most attractive features of Sherry is the bouquet. It is therefore essential that this should be given the opportunity to develop. It is no good serving the wine in a thimble, and the worst glasses of all are those dreadful things that are narrow in the middle and wide at each end. The best glass of all is a dock glass, or tasting glass: a big glass that is broad at the bottom and narrows gradually towards the top. The Spanish *copita*, which is now easily available nearly everywhere, is a small version of the same thing and is almost as good. With either, the wine should only fill about a third of the height of the glass, so that it can be swirled round and the aromatic elements collected in the space contained above the wine. They add a whole dimension to the pleasure of drinking Sherry. But if the wine is second-rate, its deficiencies will all the more readily be shown up. Failing glasses of this kind, a good tulip wine-glass is excellent – or indeed any glass that narrows towards the top and gives plenty of air space above the wine.

Fino Sherries, like practically all white wines, taste better if they are served chilled; chilled but not frozen stiff. Cellar temperature is usually very satisfactory, or they can be kept in the door of the refrigerator. Amontillado and Oloroso Sherries, on the other hand, are generally best served at room temperature.

Like all wines, Sherry oxidizes if left open in contact with air. It is a complete myth that it can be put in a decanter and left for weeks or even days. It is fair to say, though, that the oxidation is scarcely noticed if the wine is a sweet one, particularly if it is a cheap sweet one, which is likely to have been rather coarse even to begin with. But a really fine, very dry Sherry will noticeably deteriorate with time, and it is generally unwise to keep it open for more than about three days if you want to drink it at perfection. In practice, the best Sherries are so good that this point is usually academic, as there is no possibility of their being kept as long as that; but if the sherry is not wanted for immediate drinking, it is unwise to decant it (which can only increase the speed of oxidation) and it is often a good idea to keep a spare, empty half bottle, decanting half the Sherry into the waiting half bottle as soon as it is opened, and then tightly corking it. This gives very little exposure to the air and the half bottle lasts just as well as if the wine had never been opened. The remainder of the Sherry can then be drunk in a more leisurely way. Oxidation is also reduced if a Fino Sherry is kept continuously chilled after it has been opened, and if the cork is always meticulously put back immediately after the wine has been poured. In that way it can be kept perfectly satisfactorily for up to a week. Fino Sherry does not like bottles. There is certainly no point at all in laying it down. The longer it is kept, the less delightful it will be. A sensible thing is to buy your Sherry in modest quantities from a merchant who has a quick turnover. This type of trading is nowadays much more common than it used to be, encouraged by the cash flow demands of accountants. It is the one useful contribution they have made to the trade. If you are keeping Sherry in your cellar, it can be stored vertically (unlike unfortified wines), as the stronger alcoholic strength protects it against oxidation, and some of the corks are not good enough to support constant contact with a fortified wine of 17 or 18 per cent. But in practice corks are rarely attacked seriously and experience has shown that bottles generally come to no harm even if kept on their sides for twenty years or more.

Sometimes one hears that Sherry – particularly Fino Sherry – is 'not what it was'. There is some truth in it, too, for the Sherries that receive and deserve this criticism are usually those sold in pubs. They have been kept for some time by the brewer, then for some months or even years by the publican, left in the form of a half-drunk bottle under the hot floodlights of the bar for weeks more, then served in an abominable little thimble, lukewarm. Indeed the Fino is not what it was! But it is not the Sherry shipper's fault.

Dry Amontillado and Oloroso Sherries, on the other hand, change very little in bottle and can safely be kept for many years. If such wine has been sweetened, it can actually improve materially in bottle, becoming steadily less sweet as the years go on, so that occasionally a very sweet dessert Sherry finishes up tasting bone dry. At the same time it develops a new depth of flavour and a distinctive, somewhat musty aroma which has been graphically described as 'widow's weeds'. This type of aroma is one that the Sherry shippers themselves do not approve of. They are firmly of the belief that their wine should be drunk soon after it is bottled. However, it is a perverse taste which has long found favour in the United Kingdom and which serious wine-drinkers will hotly defend.

Fino Sherries are dry white wines. They stimulate the appetite and therein lies one of their great virtues as apéritifs; but once the appetite is stimulated, it needs to be satisfied. In Spain, such Sherries are invariably drunk with *tapas* – the word means 'lid' and it may be that historically these little snacks were brought on top of the Sherry glass: a bit of bread with some fish or cheese on it, for instance. The best bars in Spain vie with one another in the excellence of the *tapas*, which include all sorts of seafood, slices of sausages, small meat dishes (sometimes hot), bits of omelet and so on, apart from the inevitable nuts and crisps. All of this demonstrates the supreme versatility of the wine, and it is quite wrong to suppose that Sherry can only be good as an apéritif or perhaps with the soup – though it is excellent in both places. It is, in fact, delicious with those foods with which white wine is regularly drunk: most sorts of seafood, including oysters, and white meats.

Amontillado Sherries also make admirable apéritifs, particularly in winter, where a bigger-bodied wine can feel more warming, especially if it is slightly sweetened. A light, dry Oloroso or Palo Cortado likewise. But these Sherries also

A vineyard near Jerez showing the chalky white 'albariza' soil needed for making the finest Sherry

find their place after a meal. We drink dry brandies after a meal, so why not dry Sherries? – provided that they have enough body to taste well at that stage. Palo Cortado and Oloroso wines do have enough, but Finos do not. And they are less sleep-inducing than are the sweet wines, especially Port, so they can be enjoyed after an alfresco lunch in the summer without ruining the subsequent croquet.

The sweet wines taste their best with the dessert or after the meal. A fine sweet Sherry is wonderful with such food as plum tart or a baked apple, and a very sweet brown Sherry will even stand up to the impact of a treacle pudding. But the finest, oldest, and grandest sweet Sherries are best of all taken after the meal and treated with the same sort of attention and respect that you would devote to a vintage Port. This especially applies to the finest old bottled Sherries.

The following houses are amongst the leading shippers of Sherry and Manzanilla:
Barbadillo, Bertola, Agustin Blazquez, Bobadilla, Bodegas Internacionales, Burdon, Caballero, Croft, Cuvillo, Diez-Merito (formerly Diez Hermanos), Pedro Domecq, Duff Gordon, Garvey, Gonzalez Byass, John Harvey, De La Riva, Emilio Lustau, O'Neale, Osborne, Palomino & Vergara, Pemartin, Real Tesoro, Rivero, Zoilo Ruiz-Mateos, Sandeman, José de Soto, Fernando A. de Terry, Valdespino, Varela, Williams & Humbert, Wisdom & Warter.

Some shippers supply wine to importers for sale under their own name – Diez-Merito, Cuvillo, Lustau, Valdespino and de Terry are noted in this field. Many wine merchants throughout the world sell excellent wines under their own labels obtained from sources such as these. It should be remembered that heavily promoted, world-wide brands of Sherry are not necessarily always the best, and most shippers and importers have other Sherries, less well-known, that are of more interesting quality. It is worth asking for true Amontillado, aged Fino, and genuine dry Oloroso, as all Sherry houses have these fine wines – even if the British market is the most likely export market in which to find them. Remember that Fino Sherry is sold at a lighter strength in Spain itself. Sometimes there are slight differences in blends between the importing countries, but with greater standardization, and the need for travellers to find their favourite brand the same everywhere, these differences are largely ironed out.

It should also be pointed out that some brands that are bone dry in Spain itself are slightly sweetened for the export market. Not all of the recommended Sherries in the list that follows can be obtained on all markets, but demand for them can only increase their availability.

Some Recommended Sherries

SHERRY	BRAND NAME	PRODUCER
Manzanilla	Solear Manzanilla Pasada	Barbadillo
	La Lidia	Garvey
	Manzanilla	Harveys of Bristol Ltd
	La Guita	Ramiro Perez Marin
	Manzanilla	Don Zoilo
Very Dry Fino	Duke of Wellington Fino	Bodegas Internacionales
	Carta Blanca	Blazquez
	Fino	Croft
	Tres Palmas	De la Riva
	Palma	Diez-Merito
	San Patricio	Garvey
	Tio Pepe	Gonzalez Byass
	Elegante	Gonzalez Byass
	Bristol Fino	Harveys of Bristol Ltd

Sherry matures in large butts placed in rows in the cathedral-like 'bodegas' of Jerez

Some Recommended Sherries continued

SHERRY	BRAND NAME	PRODUCER
	Luncheon Dry	Harveys of Bristol Ltd
	Dry Lustau	Lustau
	Fino Quinta	Osborne
	Tio Mateo	Palomino & Vergara
	Apitiv	Sandeman
	Fino Campero	de Soto
	Inocente	Valdespino
	Fino Oliver	Wisdom & Warter
	Fino	Don Zoilo
Old Fino	Fino Imperial	Diez–Merito
Very Dry	Tio Guillermo	Garvey
Amontillado	Guadalupe	De la Riva
	El Duque	Gonzalez Byass
	Amontillado Extra Tonel	De la Riva
	Fine Old Amontillado	Harveys of Bristol Ltd
	Amontillado Viejisimo Reserva	De la Riva
	Tio Diego	Valdespino
Amontillado	Royal Palace	Wisdom & Warter
	Finest Old Amontillado	Cuvillo
	Botaina	Domecq
	Amontillado del Duque	Gonzalez Byass
	Reina Victoria	Harveys of Bristol Ltd
	Los Cisnes	O'Neale
	Royal Esmeralda	Sandeman
	Amontillado	Don Zoilo
Very Dry Oloroso	Oloroso Seco	Barbadillo
	Cartujo	Bobadilla
	Dry Lustau	Lustau
Pale Cortado	Solera Palo Cortado	De la Riva
	Capuchino	Blazquez
	Palo Cortado	Cuvillo
	Palo Cortado	Harveys of Bristol Ltd
	Palo Cortado	Lustau
	De Luxe Sherry	Sandeman (sweetened dessert wine)
	Dos Cortados	Williams & Humbert
Oloroso	Fabuloso	Cuvillo
	Victoria Regina	Diez–Merito
	Flor de Jerez	Garvey
	Matusalem	Gonzalez Byass
	Royal Corrigidor	Sandeman
	Imperial Corrigidor	Sandeman
	Solera 1804	Valdespino
	Walnut Brown	Williams & Humbert
	Oloroso Extra Tonel 1806	De la Riva
	Oloroso	Don Zoilo
Cream Sherry	Sanlucar Cream	Barbadillo
	Nectar Cream	Gonzalez Byass
	Casilda Cream	O'Neale
	Armada Cream	Sandeman
	Choice Cream of the Century	Wisdom & Warter

Port

WYNDHAM FLETCHER

Wyndham Fletcher's lifelong career has been spent in the wine trade and he is a recognized authority on Port. He joined Cockburns in 1930 and spent more than forty years with them, witnessing at first hand the many changes in methods of production and marketing. From 1970 to 1975 he was Managing Director of Cockburns and he still acts as a consultant to the firm. He has also served for some years on the Committee of the Port Wine Trade Association and became Chairman in 1973. His acclaimed book on Port, *Port: an Introduction to its History and Delights*, was published by Sotheby Parke Bernet in 1978, London and New York.

> Port, Port,
> No Briton ought
> Consider that he's done his duty
> Until he's felt
> Beneath his belt
> A bottle of the old and fruity.

Although the quantity prescribed in this jingle is perhaps excessive these days when we move about hunched behind a steering wheel rather than jogging healthfully on horseback, it does imply the age-old connection between Port and the British, and no account of Port today is quite complete without some brief historical notes.

Apart from a passing contact during the Crusades, when an English contingent helped to capture Lisbon from the Moors, the first milestone in the relationship between the two countries came in 1373 with the signing of a Treaty of Perpetual Friendship, the six hundreth anniversary of which was celebrated in London in 1973 with the visit of the then Portuguese Prime Minister to London amid suitably convivial junketings. It was this treaty that was invoked by Winston Churchill in 1943 during some of the darkest days of the Second World War to secure the use of the Azores as a British and American naval and air base.

Cromwell's Commonwealth strengthened the commercial ties, in spite of the natural reluctance of the Portuguese king to have dealings with a regicide, and at this time English merchants were granted 'most-favoured nation' privileges laying the foundations of the trade which have endured to this day.

The interminable wars with France gave a great opportunity to the wines of Portugal, and in 1678 the first entry was inscribed in the Oporto Custom House of *vinho do porto* shipped over the bar of the Douro. The English had discovered that the fuller and more robust wines of the Douro were more to their taste than the thinner wines of the Minho from the extreme north of the country, which had hitherto been shipped. But it must be emphasized that the Douro wines of those days differed markedly from the Port of today.

The next landmark was the Methuen Treaty of 1703, Portugal taking English wool free of duty against a preferential duty of one third given by England on Portuguese against French wines. In 1727 the British Association was formed from the British factory or trading factors, and their factory house for business and meetings was completed in 1790. Both Association and factory house are very much in evidence to this day.

By the middle of the eighteenth century, mutual recriminations between shippers and growers alleging the adulteration of the Douro wines led to the intervention of the Marquis of Pombal, virtual dictator of Portugal, who set up a wine monopoly, the 'Old Company' or Companhia Velha da Agricultura dos Vinhos do Alto Douro, to control quality and through which all wine had to be bought at fixed prices. Pombal also fixed for the first time the boundaries of the Douro district which, with small modifications, have endured to this day. However, political interference with the trade led to such graft and inefficiency that, with the death of Pombal, the controls were gradually relaxed and the monopoly powers of the 'Old Company' finally abolished. By the beginning of the nineteenth century, large quantities of Port were being shipped to the United Kingdom, big generous wines made from the pre-phylloxera national grape; and the presence of the British army in Portugal during the Peninsular War gave a great fillip to demand. At about this time, the present cylindrical-shaped bottle was rediscovered so that Port could be binned away and matured. Most important of all, the addition of brandy (grape spirit) to the fermenting must came into general use, thus stopping the fermentation and retaining some sugar in the wine. Certainly, by about 1840 all Port shipped was in the style of the wine we know today.

The phylloxera devastated the Douro vineyards, as it did the rest of Europe, but in Portugal, too, grafting on to the American root stock saved the day. Port flourished in the golden age up to the First World War and made a good recovery after it. But the economic and political consequences of the Second World War were much more far-reaching and the trade took longer to recover; however, now the picture is far brighter, there are few countries that are not increasing their imports of Port, and the future looks much rosier.

THE DOURO REGION

By Portuguese law no wine, other than that produced within the geographically defined delimited Douro region, may be made into and be called Port (*vinho do porto*). A protective ring of granite hills and mountains virtually surrounds the whole area, which comprises about 320,000 hectares. Starting about 100 kilometres east of Oporto at Mesão Frio, it continues right to the Spanish frontier at Barca d'Alva, with the administrative capital of the whole district at Regua and the local capital of the fine wine area, the Upper or Cima Corgo, at Pinhão. The principal districts which make up the region are Vila Real, including Pinhão, Bragança, Viseu and Guarda. Of this area 25,000 hectares are under vines.

The composition of the soil is mostly schistous sandstone, with granite predominating towards the outer boundaries of the region. Schist is the best soil for both red and white grapes and comprises the greater part of the total area, particularly along the south bank of the Douro. The granite produces good whites but poor reds, while further down the scale is a calcareous earth giving rather poorer wines. Lastly, the alluvial soil at the base of the valley makes for a still coarser product. Variations in soil within the same area will give subtle differences in the styles of wine from the same grape.

Great extremes of climate exist, the variations in rainfall being inversely related to the average temperature. Moving upstream, eastwards, the temperature rises, and at Regua the rainfall can reach 60 centimetres, half as much at Tua and half as much again at the Spanish frontier. The total distance is only about 80 kilometres.

Snow is a rarity, but frosts in early winter are frequent and can be severe, though happily spring frosts seldom do any damage. High summer temperatures of around 40°C are not uncommon, and 44°C has been known. There are, in fact, three micro-climates in the region, Atlantic, Atlantic-Mediterranean and Mediterranean, the ideal being the one affecting the middle reaches of the Douro and producing the finest Ports. Below Barqueiros, at the western boundary, the Douro makes a sharp bend between two hills, which serves as a protective barrier against the damp Atlantic winds. On the north and south banks of the Douro, high mountains give further protection and the whole configuration of the terrain leads to unique climatic conditions peculiar to the Douro alone.

Grape Varieties

There are about eighty-five varieties of grape grown in the Douro district. Because of the remarkable range of micro-climates, it has been found that this great range of vines is necessary to cope with the differences between one valley and the next. Indeed, one vineyard or *quinta* will normally have growing three or four varieties which will all be blended together at vintage time to make a balanced wine.

The main varieties of vine, including some fairly recent crossings, are as follows:

Recommended

Red: Bastardo, Donzelinho Tinto, Mourisco, Tinto Cão, Tinta Francisca, Tinta Roriz, Touriga Francesca and Touriga Nacional. *White:* Donzelinho, Esgana-Cão, Folgasão, Gouveio or Verdelho, Malvasia Fina, Rabigato and Viosinho.

Authorized

Red: Cornifesto, Malvasia Preta, Mourisco de Semente, Periquita, Rufete, Samarrinho, Tinta Amarela, Tinta da Barca, Tinto Barroco and Touriga Brasileira. *White:* Arinto, Boal, Cercial, Codega, Malvasia Corada and Moscatel Galego.

Tolerated

Red: Alvarelhão, Avesso, Casculho, Castela, Coucieira, Moreto, Tinta Bairrada, Tinta Carvalha and Tinta Martins. *White:* Branco sem Nome, Fernão Pires, Malvasia Parda, Pedernão, Praca and Touriga Branca.

American root stocks extensively used have been Riparia 3309, Monticola, Cordifolia, Aramão and, more recently, two new developments of Berlandieri, R99 and R110. Production can vary according to the situation of the vines; those in the steepest and stoniest vineyards will yield as little as a hogshead (half a pipe) per thousand vines, those on easier slopes up to six pipes, and soil variations will also play a part. With the advent of the tractor and increased labour and upkeep costs, the preparation of vineyards has changed. Prior to this, everything was done by hand. In the Cima (Upper) Corgo, the fine wine area, the slopes are so steep that drystone walls had to be built which sometimes retained only sufficient soil to take one row of vines, all the work being done with hand spikes and crowbars. The schist can be broken with comparative ease to the required depth for planting, but small charges of dynamite are often used to get the work started. New vineyards are now made on a much more gradual slope supporting many rows of vines, allowing tractors and other mechanical aids to be used.

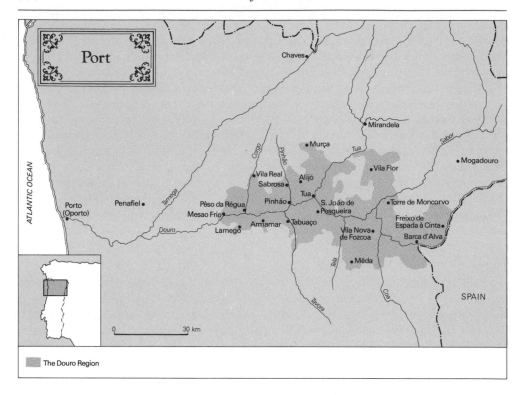

The root stocks used depend on the situation of the vineyard; Berlandieri Riparia strains 420A and SO4 on the cooler lowlands and Rupestris E99 and RI 10 on the hot, dry hillsides. Grafting takes place during February and March, traditionally *in situ*. The American stock having been planted a year earlier, the head of the year-old vine is cut off, the stem split and the shaped scion inserted. The stem is then bound with bass and covered with earth to keep it moist and free from damage. Before insertion, each graft is put into the mouth of the grafter who has frequent recourse to a bottle of table wine. Without this precaution the graft would not take! During the last few years ready-grafted vines have been prepared under glass in France, the scion having been sent over from Portugal. So far, the experiments have been quite small, but the results appear satisfactory.

Pruning takes place from December until the end of February. Usually a form of double Guyot is used and the two arms of the vine are left with about fourteen to sixteen buds each. The vines are trained along wires two or three to each row at varying heights. The main stem of the vine is normally tied to the lowest wire, about 32 centimetres above the ground. When the new shoots reach the second wire they are bent over and secured.

Spraying is an essential part of the year's work to combat cryptogamic diseases and insect pests. To prevent oidium, sulphur powder applications are made from April onwards, and against mildew, depending on the dampness of the season, a mixture of copper sulphate and lime, called Bordeaux mixture, is sprayed on the vines between three and ten times a season, with an average of six. From March to May weeding may be necessary, by hoe or plough or, today, treatment with herbicides. In July, depending on the situation of the vineyard and the weather, some of the vine leaves will be removed to help the ripening of the grapes.

Other worries the Douro farmer may face during the season are such pests and diseases as *Altica ampelophaga*, which occurs in very wet years. If the vine is sprayed with an organic pesticide at the time of the first application of Bordeaux mixture, the insect will be killed before it lays its eggs on the underside of the leaves. The grape moth has also appeared in recent years in the Douro. Usually two sprayings with a phosphoric compound will prevent the eggs from hatching, but if allowed to go unchecked the larvae will eat the young grapes and the affected bunches will rot. In about 1948 a disease called maromba reappeared in the Douro. It had been noted as far back as 1845 and wrongly diagnosed as a virus. It is, in fact, due to a deficiency of boron in the soil, and by the application of borax according to the level of acidity, the yield per hectare is markedly increased. From August onwards there is little or nothing to do in the vineyards until the vintage, which usually starts about the middle of September and lasts for three to four weeks.

Production in the biggest *quintas* in the Baixo (Lower) Corgo varies from 600 to 700 pipes (950 kilograms of grapes per pipe) down to two or three baskets of grapes (70 kilograms per basket) in the thousands of small holdings in the Cima Corgo. In between these two extremes are a number of *quintas* producing from 100 to 250 pipes, many of twenty to eighty, and hundreds from one to fifteen pipes. Very few medium and smaller *quintas* now make their own wine; the grapes are bought by the big farmers, shippers, or the government-sponsored cooperatives.

Due to the almost total stoppage of shipments during the Second World War, many new regulations regarding grafting, planting and the amount of Port each property can make, came into force. A points system was devised taking all relevant factors into account, and this is set out below.

The River Douro itself has changed and is changing. This is due to the series of great dams built and projected, which have in places raised the water level to a very considerable height. It is too early to say to what extent this will affect the climate and therefore the wine produced, but government-inspired studies have been inaugurated to look into the question.

The Register

I am deeply indebted to Senhor José Antonio Rosas of Adriano Ramos-Pinto, Vila Nova da Gaia, and his colleagues for permission to refer to their most detailed study. The whole object of this most exhaustive registration is to correlate quality to quantity produced, with overwhelming weight given to quality. The full details of every vineyard in the Douro have been amassed, involving in 1973 approximately 26,000 growers, owning 86,000 properties planted with 165,500,000 vines. Between 1969 and 1973 production averaged 100,925,486 litres, of which 35,304,085 litres were authorized to be made into Port. The figure is arrived at for each vineyard by considering the factors affecting quality on a marks basis as follows:

Factors considered	Minimum points	Maximum points	Spread	%
Altitude	−900	150	1,050	20.6
Productivity	−900	120	1,020	20.0
Nature of the land	−600	100	700	13.7
Locality	−50	600	650	12.7
Methods of training vines	−500	100	600	11.8
Qualities of grapes	−300	150	450	8.8
Slope	−100	100	200	3.9
Aspect	−30	100	130	2.5
Density	−50	50	100	1.9
Soil and degree of stoniness	0	80	80	1.6
Age of vines	0	70	70	1.3
Shelter	0	60	60	1.2
Totals	−3,430	1,680	5,110	100.0

Properties are then grouped in classes:

Class A: over 1,200 points   Class D: 601–800 points
Class B: 1,001–1,200 points   Class E: 401–600 points
Class C: 801–1,000 points   Class F: 201–400 points

In any given year the total quantity of wine to be made into Port is fixed by the Instituto do Vinho do Porto and then allocated to each property in terms of per thousand vines. As an example, the average quantity for 1963–73 was 29,865 hecto-litres allocated to Classes as under:

Class A: 595 litres per thousand vines   Class D: 300 litres per thousand vines
Class B: 580 litres per thousand vines   Class E: 175 litres per thousand vines
Class C: 467 litres per thousand vines

Port Production

Until the early 1950s and the advent of the first modern wineries in the Douro, the making of Port had changed very little over the past 150 years. Traditionally the wine was, and to some small extent still is, made as follows.

After picking, the grapes are tipped into a shallow stone trough or *lagar* holding between 2,250 and 15,900 litres. The grapes are crushed by foot or by simple roller crushers and fermentation usually starts within twenty-four hours. During fermentation, colour extraction in the case of red wines is obtained by regular treading, so that the skins of the grapes are kept in close contact with the must. This regular movement also prevents the pomace from becoming a breeding ground for acid-producing bacteria. Fermentation in the *lagar* is allowed to continue until the must contains 4 to 6 per cent alcohol, after which it is run off and fortified with brandy (grape spirit) at 77 per cent. The pomace is then pressed either by simple vertical basket presses, or, in some cases, by more primitive wooden presses. The red-wine pressings, which are rich in colour and tannin, are then recombined with the already fortified must, or fortified and kept separate for blending. As the concentration of alcohol after fortification is between 17 and 19 per cent, and the specific gravity of the wine between 1,015 and 1,030, the natural fermentation slows down and finally stops within forty-eight hours.

Although the traditional *lagar* is still used to make a considerable percentage of Port, modern wineries have existed in the Douro for the last twenty years. They are owned either by shippers, individual farmers or farmers' cooperatives and, if properly run, provide wine-making facilities where grapes can be transformed into wine under hygienic conditions with the minimum involvement of labour. Because of the geography of the Douro region and its poor communications, in order to avoid undue delays between picking and crushing, small wineries are distributed over the region as a whole, ranging in capacity from about 500 to 10,000 pipes.

Nowadays, the majority of grapes are transported by road to the winery in mild-steel resin-painted containers holding approximately 1,000 kilograms of grapes, or in traditional wickerwork baskets, and samples of grape must will be taken for density analysis to determine roughly how much fermentable sugar the grapes contain.

After weighing, the grapes are discharged into open concrete tanks with sloping sides. A continuous Archimedes screw then transports the grapes to the crushers. Although there are still some roller crushers at wineries, the tendency is to use centrifugal crushers which will automatically remove either part or all of the stalks. Sulphur dioxide is added to the grapes, either before crushing in the form of sodium metabisulphite, or after in the form of a solution of the gas in water. After the crushing, the grapes are transported to the fermentation area by a large-bore piston pump, connected to a permanent pipeline system, normally of plastic.

Fermentation tanks are constructed of concrete, resin-painted concrete, resin-painted mild steel or of stainless steel, of a capacity normally ranging from ten pipes to forty-five pipes. This is equivalent to about 5,040 to 22,680 litres.

In the main, two types of fermentation tank now exist, the open-tank system and the closed tank, the latter developed from the Algerian autovinification system. The open-tank system is open to the atmosphere, and to achieve colour extraction during fermentation, must is withdrawn from the bottom valve and pumped up to the top of the tank, where it is sprayed over the grape skins. In the closed system the pressure exerted by carbon dioxide gas is used as a means of motive power to withdraw must from the fermentation tank and to cascade it back down over the grape skins. The closed system is automatic only when fermentation has started, whereas the open system does allow pumping over at any time before or during fermentation.

The more modern fermentation tanks are fitted with a conical bottom. When the fermentation has produced the required amount of natural alcohol, the must is run off and fortified in the usual way. The pomace that remains, which accounts for between 20 and 25 per cent of the volume, can then be discharged by opening a large manhole in the bottom of the tank. This obviates the necessity of emptying the tanks by hand, which is both a dangerous and time-consuming operation.

The pomace is either discharged into a dejuicer, which gives a light pressing, and then into a basket or other type of press, or, in more automated wineries, falls into another cement trough with a continuous screw in the bottom, which then transports the pomace to the pressing section. It is normal practice in the pressing section to pass the pomace through a dejuicer, before it is processed by continuous or Vaslin-type presses. Yield of must from the pomace after fermentation varies, but in an average year, 60–70 per cent of the total is free-run from the pomace by gravity, 15–20 per cent is expressed by the dejuicer and 5–15 per cent by the final pressing.

The continuous press tends to be more favoured in modern wineries. It is simple to operate and, once set up, requires little or no attention during the vintage. Yield of pressed juice is high, and in most models pressings can be separated into two or three fractions, according to tannin content and astringency.

The length of fermentation is short; hence the period of colour extraction is limited, therefore efficient pressing is very important if maximum colour yield is to be obtained. Unlike production of red table wines, where the pressings are often kept separate and used for distilling material, the colour and body of red Port depends to some extent on the inclusion of these pressings in the finished wine.

White Port can be made either by fermentation with the skins, or by the fermentation of free-run juice without the skins. Free-run juice can be produced by holding crushed grapes in tank until natural draining produces enough must, or by the use of proprietary dejuicers linked to a continuous Vaslin or basket press. Better quality musts are probably produced by holding crushed grapes in a draining tank, as they are exposed to much less physical maceration than they would be if dejuiced by mechanical means.

White Port produced from free-run juice results in a rather neutral wine, devoid of many of the intrinsic characteristics of the grape, whereas fermentation in the presence of skins does give the wine more flavour and vinous characteristics. After pressing, the pomace is sold or stored in silos until after the vintage, when it is steam-distilled to produce a fiery spirit called *bagaçeira*. Finally, the remains are used as vineyard manure, and the pips for chicken food.

Fermentation of sugar results in the liberation of large quantities of heat. In small containers most of this heat is lost by radiation, but in fermentation tanks part of this heat is retained and as a consequence the temperature is raised. High fermentation temperatures of 36°–38°C result in the wine yeast losing its fermentative abilities, and loss of flavour and aroma in the finished wine. Apart from damage to the flavour of the wine, high fermentation temperatures lead to the growth of heat-resistant spoilage bacteria, and unless sufficient levels of sulphur dioxide are maintained in the must, acidification will take place with the consequent production of large quantities of acetic acid (vinegar) and ethyl acetate. The more sophisticated Douro wineries have refrigeration equipment to control the fermentation temperatures, and it is generally considered that for red wines fermentation temperatures should be between 26° and 27°C, and for white wines two or three degrees lower. Refrigeration equipment normally consists of small compressors which chill water down to 0° to 5°C. This water is then circulated against wine in tubular heat exchangers, or circulated in cooling coils or heat exchangers actually within the fermentation vat. It can be calculated that wine made in the traditional *lagar* took about twenty man-hours per pipe, whereas in a modern winery this period can be reduced to approximately thirty man-minutes per pipe.

Wine-making

In an average year, 750 kilograms of grapes yield approximately 550 litres of must, and if 450 litres of fermented must, which contains 4–6 per cent alcohol, are mixed with 100 litres of brandy at 77 per cent, the resulting wine will have an alcohol content of approximately 17 to 19 per cent.

As grapes are received at the winery they are visually examined to ensure that they are free from mould, bruising, leaves and other debris. A sample of the grapes is crushed, and the juice is examined by a refractometer or weighed with a hydrometer to ascertain the Baumé or specific gravity, which is normally between 11° and 13°, or between 1.083 and 1.100 in gravity. From these readings the wine-maker can judge the maturity of the grapes, and have an approximation of the percentage of alcohol after fermentation. Obviously, the sweeter the grape the less brandy has to be added on fortification. Centrifugal crushers will then remove automatically the required percentage of stalks. Immediately before or after crushing, sulphur dioxide is added to the must. Very little is needed when the grapes are in perfect condition and cool; in practice 100 to 200 milligrams per litre is used.

Once the fermentation tank is full, with the open tank, the must is pumped out of the bottom and sprayed over the pomace at intervals to keep the skins and solid matter fresh and moist. In the case of the Algerian closed tank, there is very little to do except wait until fermentation starts. If the grapes were received under hot conditions, some cooling may be used to reduce the temperature of the must to 25°C. Fermentation should normally start within twenty-four hours.

During fermentation, must in open tanks is pumped over frequently to encourage good colour extraction and to keep the skins free from acetifying bacteria. In the closed tank, the frequency of must withdrawal and its re-entry over the pomace can be controlled with a simple pressure valve. Ideally, this occurs every twenty to thirty minutes during the height of fermentation.

Fermentation is continued under normal conditions for about thirty-six hours, by which time the Baumé will have dropped from, for example, 12° down to the level required by the wine-maker; this depends on the degree of residual sweetness wanted in the final wine, but most normal wines are run off between 6° and 7°. The fermenting must is then run off into a vat together with the required amount of brandy. Pressings from the pomace are added, and the contents thoroughly mixed to ensure that the brandy is not, because of its low density, floating on the must.

White wine can be made in a similar manner except that, if fermented with the skins, less pumping over is needed as no colour extraction is required. Sweet wines, which contain virtually all the grape sugar, are made by fermenting the must with the skins for very little time, so that there is hardly any drop in density. These are, in the case of red wines, naturally light in colour and are fortified with up to 150 litres Brandy to 400 litres must.

After the vintage, wines receive their first racking either in November or the spring, the lees are removed, and the wine is brought up to 18.5 per cent with the addition of more Brandy. Depending on the system of vinification used and the year, the first lees represent an average between 5 and 9 per cent of the total volume.

Racking as soon after the vintage as possible is to be recommended, as early removal of yeast prevents loss of colour, which occurs when the colouring matter is absorbed into the yeast cell wall, and the release into the wine from the breakdown of dead yeast of vitamins and growth factors that will stimulate the growth of spoilage bacteria. Regular racking and the addition of brandy during the first year is an important contribution to ensuring that the wine remains free of infection by acid-producing micro-organisms. The number of rackings a wine receives during its maturation very much depends on the ideas of the individual wine-maker. In some houses, wines are racked every three months in the first year, twice in the second and less frequently as the wine ages.

Brandies for fortification are selected by taste and smell, and those with a clean but aromatic character are preferred. They should be as colourless as possible. The shippers can only obtain the brandy they require at a fixed price through a government agency, the Junta Nacional de Aguardente. Final clarification of Port is achieved by filtration, fining or refrigeration.

White Wines

In wood, white wines gain colour, which has to be removed before the wine is shipped. This can be done by the addition of gelatine together with tannin, or the use of milk, isinglass or casein. After fining, a further treatment with bentonite is sometimes used to remove proteins, which have either been introduced by the fining agents themselves or which have not been removed by their action. To prevent the precipitation of the potassium and calcium salts of tartaric acid, refrigeration is the only suitable method currently available. Wine is chilled to within $2°$ of its freezing point and held at this temperature for sufficient time to allow precipitation of the tartrates. After this is achieved, the wine is either pad- or kieselguhr-filtered. In the case of white wines, refrigeration does little to remove colour, and complete stability of a wine can only be obtained by the use of fining.

Red Wines

Fining has always been the traditional method for clarification of red wines, gelatine being most used. Fining removes from the wine a certain amount of colour and tannin, which makes it softer and gives slightly more age. Although fining results in clarification, if wine is then bottled, especially young or dark wine, it will after a time throw a further deposit in the bottle. Although this is acceptable for crusting and vintage Ports, the customer for ruby and tawny requires the wine to be poured bright to the last drop.

Refrigeration of red wines down to within $2°c$ of their freezing point precipitates unstable colouring matter, which would cloud the wine after bottling. The wine is normally held for sufficient time at this temperature to allow precipitation to occur, and then cold-filtered through a pad- or kieselguhr-filter at the same temperature. The addition of small quantities of an antioxidant such as sulphur dioxide at this stage, when the wine is still cold, preferably before filtration, protects the wine against air, which could cause further instability. Careful use of refrigeration, followed by the use of sulphur dioxide, and storage in full tanks before bottling with minimum aeration, can give a young ruby wine a considerable shelf life.

Wood Port

To the shipper, his vintage Port, when declared, is a small but very welcome 'piece of cake'. But because of the comparative infrequency of declarations, probably averaging out at about 2 per cent of annual shipments, the shipper depends basically for his business and prosperity on regular shipments of wood Port to the various markets of the world. By definition, wood Port is a blended wine matured in cask until it is ready for drinking, and being a blend, it can be 'followed' year by year through the skill of the tasters, so that 'so-and-so's' Vintage Character drunk today will be the same tomorrow and was the same yesterday. The blending of each shipper's basic blends which he uses for his shipping 'marks' has the same objective as the Sherry *solera* system, though the way in which this is achieved is quite different.

After the vintage gathering is completed, the new wine is left up the Douro till the early spring of the following year, when it is racked and sent down to the shippers' lodges (*armazéns*) by road or rail. The lodges are huge airy sheds with their rows of casks and vats, and roofs blackened by the fumes of evaporation. There, the wines are tasted and categorized and a start is made with the blending, which lies behind the continuity of style of each shipper's various 'marks'. The distinctive style of each shipper will have been basically formed by the way the wines are made and handled at the vintage, and further blending will continue this process.

Because shippers have tended to buy from the same farmers year after year, they are familiar with the way each one makes his wine and, furthermore, the actual fermentations will be supervised by the shipper's representative who sees that instructions are carried out. As nowadays most of the wine is made in autovinification tanks with easier and more scientific control, it is probable that the task of the taster is that much simpler, especially as most shippers now concentrate on a comparatively few labelled brands.

As the young wine matures, and as basic quality and style are confirmed by tasting, it will be channelled into various lots from which the actual shipping 'marks' are made up. In the case of a young ruby this may take only two or three years, in the case of an old tawny, twenty years and more. Tasting is an art, not a science, and there is no short cut to a proficiency that requires time and experience. Most people with a reasonable palate can probably be trained to be average tasters, but the really great seem to run in families – the Smithes of Cockburn's, the Yeatmans of Taylor's.

There are three main types of wood Port: ruby, tawny and white, with subdivisions in each style. One of the difficulties is that these descriptions refer essentially to the colour and therefore to the body of the wine, and while there is no doubt what white Port is, ruby and tawny vary considerably depending on the ideas of the individual shipper. So far as the United Kingdom is concerned, ruby is the basic wine of the Port lover. Being young it is relatively inexpensive and has the full-bodied freshness so appealing to the palate. Before the Second World War, 'Port and lemon' was a favourite drink in the pubs, now happily being rediscovered, and for this a glass of dark ruby is added to a tall glass of fizzy lemonade.

A development of ruby that has become particularly prominent in recent years is Vintage Reserve or Vintage Character. This is a wine with the same basic characteristics, but of higher quality and more mature. In an appropriate year, some of the wines in the blend would find their way into the shippers' vintage lot. These wines, with the finest old tawnies, represent the acme of wood Port.

Tawny is a lighter style of Port than ruby. The word is descriptive of a wine aged for many years in wood which, when held in a glass, has a yellow, browny, in fact tawny, edge. Being a blended wine, only an approximate age can be given to it, but it is safe to say that a real old tawny will have some very old wine in it indeed. The wine has the wonderful soft yet crisp nuttiness that only age can offer, while the nose gives a concentration that again is the quintessence of quality and maturity.

In recent years 'Ports with an indication of Age' have come on to the market. These are tawnies aged in wood and may be offered as ten, fifteen, twenty, thirty or over forty years, with the date of bottling in Oporto on the label. The shipper's stock of these wines must have been registered with the controlling body of the trade, the Instituto do Vinho do Porto in Oporto.

For many years there has been a demand for cheap tawny Port. This type of wine is made by blending white Port as required with ruby. The result is perfectly sound and very drinkable but, naturally, lacks the quality and unique distinction of the real old tawny. In colour it is pink rather than tawny.

The popularity of white Port varies considerably from country to country. Most white is of the same sweetness as the average red, but of recent years dry white Port, drunk chilled as an apéritif, has made a very encouraging appearance.

The casks and vats used for maturing are normally made of oakwood, nowadays chiefly imported from Yugoslavia. Stainless-steel, glass-lined and concrete tanks, the latter totally lined with one of the resin-based inert materials, are extensively used for blending and for storage when maturing is not required. A shipping pipe is the standard cask of the trade, holding 522 litres, or 56 dozen bottles, a hogshead is half a pipe and a quarter cask half a hogshead.

To keep wood Port bright in bottle for as long as possible, a technique of chilling the wine before bottling has been developed; this should give several months of 'shelf life' without cloudiness. Once opened, a bottle of wood Port will come to no harm for a considerable time provided it is firmly re-stoppered. The bigger the air-space in the bottle, the quicker the oxidization, so when it is half empty, much better to finish it off!

The whole theory and technique of wood Port is to bring it to its peak in cask. The bottle, therefore, is merely a convenience to get it to your table and broadly speaking will not improve the wine. If kept too long in bottle it will lose its fresh-ness, this applying particularly to old tawnies, and develop a rather smoky taste and smell, called 'bottle age'.

A fine old tawny, or white Port, makes first-rate 'elevenses', and is much im-proved in hot weather by cooling in the refrigerator or serving 'on the rocks'. But do not use a full wine for this purpose, still less a vintage. France, which buys more Port than any other country, drinks it almost entirely as an apéritif and in the early evening.

Vintage Port

The turn of the eighteenth and beginning of the nineteenth century coincided with a series of remarkably fine vintages, culminating in the 'Waterloo' of 1815. Further-more, the presence of Wellington's army in Portugal brought to the attention of the right people at the right time just how good vintage Port could be. From this time, vintage Port became the standard-bearer for the whole Port trade, on which its prestige and reputation was built and enhanced.

What is vintage Port? To summarize, the Portuguese Wine Laws on the subject, approved by the Instituto do Vinho do Porto on 24 November 1970, and revised as from 1 January 1974, state:

1. Samples must be submitted by the shipper to the Instituto do Vinho do Porto between 1 January and 30 September of the second year.
2. The wine shall be offered in bottle only under the *Selo de Garantia* (Seal of Guarantee), and should be bottled between 1 July of the second year and 30 June of the third year.

A vintage is usually 'declared' to the trade in the spring of the second year after the harvest, and will be offered to the public that autumn when the wine is actually bottled.

Late-Bottled Vintage (LBV)

In general the same rules apply, but the year of bottling must be between 1 July of the fourth year and 31 December of the sixth year after the proposed vintage. The year of bottling must appear on the label. This style of vintage has achieved considerable popularity in recent years, particularly in the restaurant trade. Having had a minimum of nearly four years ageing in cask, it can be handled as a wood Port and should need no decanting. But a word of warning for the unwary, who may order a glass of vintage in a hotel or a restaurant, expecting a conventional two-year bottled wine, and may be served with LBV without comment. Because of its age in wood, it is much lighter in colour and body and without the distinctive nose and flavour given by bottle age. In general, shippers do not offer as LBV the same year that they declare their *crème de la crème* for two-year bottling. LBVs, therefore, are usually of good if not supreme quality.

Crusted Port

Though not a vintage, crusted Port has one attribute in common with two-year bottlings, that of maturing in bottle. Crusted Port is normally a young blended wine and can therefore be 'followed' like any other of the shipper's 'marks'. Moreover, the blend can be made up so that the wine comes round in bottle ready to drink in as little as three years. These wines are not of the superb quality of vintage, and being quicker maturing, are reasonably priced. They should be handled and decanted in the same way as vintage, and on the right occasion make a very acceptable substitute.

Port with date of vintage

Again, the basic rules apply, but the selected wine must be at least seven years old. The label must show the vintage year, an indication that the wine has been aged in wood, and the date of bottling. Although found in many other countries, this type of wine does not have a great following in the United Kingdom.

Sometimes bottles which bear on the label the word *garrafeira* will appear in the saleroom or may more often be seen in Portugal. It is difficult to translate *garrafeira* directly into English. Usually it refers to the wine of a Portuguese shipper or farmer of his own cellar, rather like the *Kabinett* wine of a German wine-grower in its original sense. The wine is of a vintage, but very often consecutive years will be bottled without regard to generally declared vintages. Traditionally, the bottles are binned vertically and mature probably more quickly. Certainly the corks are replaced with new ones at regular intervals.

Vintage Port is the wine of a year selected by the shipper as being outstanding, and the decision is that of the shipper alone; though in most vintage years several shippers will agree that the wine is worthy to be offered. It is usually a blend from several *quintas*, sometimes owned by the shipper or by various farmers, in a relationship often going back for generations. Some shippers have exceptionally large and fine *quintas* which are the backbone of their vintage lot, and these are in fact often declared by themselves. The size of each shipper's lot varies considerably, depending on the yield of the particular year and the likely demand from the trade. The shipper must also assess the size of his lot against his requirements for fine wood Ports, particularly the very high quality vintage character brands that are now such a feature of the market.

By recent decree of the Instituto do Vinho do Porto, all vintage Port must be bottled in the country of origin under the *Selo de Garantia* and, though it is to be hoped that the wine may still be bottled in the traditional way, it is not impossible that the bottling line may be used and the result be just as good.

The cork is of prime importance in a bottle of vintage Port in view of the time it may have to remain 'wine-proof'. 'Full-long' corks of the highest quality from Portugal's own cork forests are used, branded with the name of the shipper, the year, and sometimes the date of bottling. In the old days, the name of the bottler was also sometimes branded. The top of the cork and bottle is sealed with a capsule; lead is still the best material, though sometimes the old-fashioned melted wax is used. This seal finishes the job but, more important, protects the cork against the risk of cork weevil, though this is minimal in modern storage conditions.

Storage temperature should be about 13° to 16°C, but consistency of temperature is much more important than the exact degree. The wine should be stored with the label face up or, in the case of old Port of pre-Labelling Act days, with the white splash at the bottom of the bottle uppermost. The crust will then form on the underside of the bottle.

In the old days, 'shotted' bottles, pitted with shot from a cartridge shaken up by hand, were often used, and the crust was said to adhere more firmly to the uneven surface, but such refinements are now prohibitively expensive.

A lot of unnecessary mystery is woven round the question of decanting. The bottle to be decanted should be stood up for twenty-four to forty-eight hours, or as long as possible beforehand, so that all loose pieces of crust will fall to the bottom. The cork, unless the wine is very old, should draw without too much difficulty; the problem these days is to find a really long corkscrew with a good thread. With a steady hand and the label or splash on the upper surface of the bottle, pour the wine into a suitable receptacle, such as a water jug, taking care not to set up a surge. Stop decanting as soon as bits of loose crust begin to appear in the neck. It will help to have a fairly strong light on the other side of the bottle; the light will shine through the wine during decanting. It may be prudent, particularly if there is the risk of an old cork crumbling, to decant through a clean piece of muslin or a handkerchief. In any case, any 'floaters' in the jug can be extracted before the wine is poured into the decanter. Before using, rinse both jug and decanter with a drop of wood Port, to be sure they are quite clean and smell nice.

There is a trick, peculiar so far as I know to Cockburn's, in knocking off the neck of a bottle if the cork is too tight to draw or is very old and crumbly. Take off the capsule and insert the corkscrew in the normal way as far as it will go. Put the bottle on a table, for safety's sake with a cloth round it, and hold it firmly. Then, using a fairly heavy object with a flat edge, such as an old-fashioned carving knife (or better still, a cold chisel), hit upwards quite gently and with a loose wrist against the flange. If all goes well, the neck of the bottle will crack quite cleanly about half-way between the top of the neck and the shoulder, and with the cracked piece still held firmly in place by the lower third or so of the cork. Draw this small remnant of cork with the corkscrew already positioned, and it should come out quite easily, then decant in the ordinary way.

On the subject of decanting and decanters, it is worth knowing that, with ships' decanters, the ratio of the measurement of the circumference of the lip to the vertical height from the lip to the base is constant and is, in fact, for some inexplicable reason, always the same, or at any rate approximately so. Modest wagers can be won on this after dinner.

A question frequently asked is when should vintage Port be opened. There are divergent views on this, but personally I am a convinced early opener, and am sure that far more bottles fail to show up as well as they should because of too late rather than too early decanting. For a wine with some youth, I would decant many hours before use, sometimes the previous day, and even for an old vintage, two hours or so before drinking, leaving the stopper of the decanter out.

The time a wine will last once decanted, before becoming flat and uninteresting, is again a question of age. A young Port will last several days, an older one perhaps only a day or two, the common denominator being the air space in the decanter; the more air, the less time it will remain really enjoyable for drinking. A really old Port should be drunk at one sitting.

The age at which vintage Port is drunk is to some extent a question of fashion. Certainly when the wine first became popular in Britain, it was drunk very young, but nowadays the convention that vintage Port is laid down to be drunk at a son's twenty-first birthday party probably gives a rough idea of when it is at an all-round peak of perfection. But from an everyday point of view, it does seem that a particular vintage starts being drunk and receiving general acceptance at from ten to twelve years old. It should be remembered that vintage Port is less mellow when drunk as young as this, and the combination of alcohol and sugar is smoother if you can wait a little longer.

To drink a mature vintage Port is to experience one of the great vinous joys. First, roll the wine round in the glass to make the most of the concentrated bouquet, only developed by many years in bottle, then taste the wine, this time rolling it round the tongue with a sense of mellowness and well-being.

Vintage Port can still be much appreciated when it is old, or even very old. The colour will get steadily lighter and the spirit will tend to be more noticeable, but it will disappear on the nose and palate when the wine has been decanted a little time.

Some Vintage Years

I must emphasize, firstly, that these tasting notes represent my own personal opinion and, secondly, that in the case of the older wines they often refer to a tasting a few years back. Possibly I shall never taste some of them again!

1900: Of very great breed and delicacy, but perhaps rather light in colour and fine drawn. I remember in my younger days tasting the Cockburn quite frequently and recall its beautiful, fragrant and concentrated nose.

1904: This was an extraordinary vintage, as most farmers produced up to 30 per cent more wine than they had allowed for. Not for the first, nor indeed for the last, time there was administrative bungling over the supply of brandy, and spirit had to be imported from various sources. It was said that one shipper made his Port with grain spirit from Scotland.

In spite of these difficulties, good wines were made and generally the year was offered as a vintage, though the 1904 never achieved the *cachet* of a major classic. I remember a few years back sharing an exceptional bottle of Croft.

1908: A great classic. Not a very big wine, but superbly balanced with great vinosity, flavour and staying power. May still be enjoyed and lingered over. (See also notes on 1912.)

1911: Sandeman shipped a famous vintage. Also declared by Martinez and Rebello Valente.

1912: Bracketed with the 1908 as very much one of the leaders and, as such, shipped

The small town of Pinhão, capital of the Cima Corgo district on the River Douro, is surrounded by steeply terraced vineyards from which come the finest Port wines

by all. Certainly bigger and fruitier than the 1908 and therefore perhaps 'easier'.

During all my time in the trade it has been fascinating to compare these two great wines, preferring first one, then the other. But the last time, not so many years ago, and maybe it really was the last time, I tasted them 'side by side' and came down on the side of the 1908. It just seemed to have the edge in quality and 'grip', now that the fruit is fading in both wines.

1919: A fair year with some houses offering the vintage.

1920: Attractive wines were made and most firms shipped.

1922: Originally rather an underrated year, but as the wines grew older they developed a delightfully attractive silky smoothness. I have enjoyed several bottles of Martinez, and just after the Second World War, a bottle or two of Rebello Valente and Tuke.

1924: A small yield but an excellent vintage. From my own experience, I would say that Taylor 1924 stood out as a very great wine.

1927: Has proved to be one of the finest and was generally shipped. The wines were light when first made and some thought they lacked staying power. With development, their superb quality has taken them to the top. I have never seen a better 1927 than the Cockburn.

1931: A fine year which would undoubtedly have been generally shipped had it not coincided with the depths of the world slump. As it was, Noval 1931, made both from the grafted vines and the very rare 'Nacional', is numbered among the historic vintage ports. It certainly brought Noval into the modern 'top ten'.

1934 and 1935: Both very fine years, though perhaps not quite tip-top classics and almost equally split between the firms declaring. As Cockburn shipped 1935, I originally supported that year, though never really coming to terms with it until recently, with the wine and the drinker in the autumn of their years.

A friend of mine recently had the wonderful privilege of drinking side by side Cockburn and Taylor 1927 and 1935. The Cockburn had the edge in the 1927 and the Taylor in the 1935. But what an experience!

I have seen some very fine 1934s and the Fonseca particularly comes to mind.

1945: A very great classic year, Oporto-bottled because of the Second World War, and almost universally shipped.

1947: Shipped under the government concession, the quantity offered was small. Possibly because the wines were light in colour and body, they have never quite achieved their due recognition. The fine delicate quality, reminiscent of the 1900s, has tended to be overlooked.

In 1975 in San Francisco, after a superb meal served with Californian wines in a private house, the guests, including myself, were asked to taste blind what turned out to be no fewer than four 1947 vintage ports, Warre, Dow, Vargellas (Taylor-shipped under their *quinta* name to the United States; the wine was not shipped to the United Kingdom), and Cockburn. I managed to keep very quiet during dinner while the Californian wines were under discussion, but was then forced into the open. Mercifully I did not entirely disgrace myself. On this occasion, the Cockburn and the Vargellas were outstanding. I wonder at how many dinner tables you could expect to see four vintage Ports at the same sitting!

1948: Taylor, Graham and Fonseca shipped the 1948 rather than the 1947. Originally rather coarse, it has developed well, big, full and fruity. Graham is a wine I have particularly enjoyed.

1950: Shipped by most of those who did not declare 1948. The wines were rather light, and it could be summarized as a useful rather than a great year.

1955: Generally shipped, they are magnificent wines of the very first class: big, fruity and vigorous. My personal favourite in 'modern' vintages. The one I have

*(Above) Harvesting with music at Quinta da Roeda, Croft's well-known vineyard,
just upstream of Pinhão in the Douro*
(Below) View of the Port lodges from the high river bridge at Vila Nova de Gaia, Oporto

seen recently is Cockburn which is quite superb.

1958: The number of shippers and the quantity offered was small, but they were good average wines, rather light but attractive to drink.

1960: Shipped by most firms and have proved very popular. Starting with no particular *réclame*, they have done remarkably well and turned out better than most shippers expected. This is a lightish, well-balanced year.

1963: Generally acclaimed as a great year. I must confess to having been in a minority of one against the universal chorus of praise, as in the wine's younger days I was never particularly struck with it. However, as the vintage reached maturity, my opinion changed markedly, and I have recently drunk some quite beautiful bottles of Cockburn's. Fonseca and Croft are superlative wines.

1966: With one or two exceptions, generally declared. Big wines but perhaps a little coarse.

1967: It is very difficult, in fact impossible, for me to be impartial about this year, as Cockburn's so very definitely preferred it to the 1966s. The wines are not very full but firm, with 'grip' and very great breed and style.

1970: The weather was perfect for the vintage and a very great wine resulted, to be enjoyed to the full in the mid-1980s. A considerable quantity of this vintage was bottled in Oporto.

1975: The first vintage to be bottled in Oporto in its entirety, as required by Portuguese law. On the light side, but of very good quality, it should develop well for drinking in about ten years. Generally declared.

1977: Most shippers are offering, though with one or two famous exceptions. Early reports speak of this as a fair, though not a great, year. I have had an opportunity of tasting four shippers' samples and was particularly impressed with Graham's, though not particularly with the other three.

1978: The quantity was considerably smaller than hoped for at the start of the vintage. Quality was on the whole good with one or two outstanding wines being produced. Noval have recently declared 1978 as a vintage wine.

A new departure in single *quinta* vintages is the declaration in the autumn of 1980 of Eira Velha, the vineyard largely managed by Cockburn's and the sales handled by Harvey's. Certainly one of the finest *quintas* in the Cima Corgo for quality wine it could claim to have scenically the finest of all the views over Pinhão and the surrounding hills and valleys.

1979: A large amount of wine could have been produced but the Portuguese authorities only authorized the making of enough port to cover approximately the year's shipments (126,000 pipes). Unfortunately rain fell in the middle of the gathering, giving considerable variations in quality so that on the whole the wines are rather below average and lack colour and body.

Some Wood Port Tasting Notes

I should make it clear that, apart from some obvious exceptions, these notes are based on fairly infrequent tastings.

COCKBURN'S

All these wines are Bristol-bottled for the United Kingdom market; wines for nearly all other foreign markets including the United States are bottled in Portugal.

Fine Old Tawny: A 'commercial' tawny, i.e. blended red and white but fresh and invigorating.

Special Reserve: Probably the greatest success in post-war Port brands. A vintage character of great breed and quality and, not carrying a date, it has the advantage of continuity of style.

Director's Reserve: I cannot pretend impartiality as this has been my Port for daily drinking for the last fifty years. There are older fine tawnies but none that combine the requisite age with such life, breed, character and charm. The lot was started in 1865 when Cockburn's purchased a parcel of old tawny which they refreshed with the 1863s, a fine year; ever since then, the blend has only been refreshed with the finest of fine vintage years.

Dry Tang: This white apéritif is really dry and is made by fermenting out the must with the wine spirit added afterwards. Served well chilled, it makes a first-rate alternative to conventional pre-prandials.

CROFT

Distinction*: An old tawny, but seems to lack 'grip' and fades on the palate.
Choice Old Ruby: Rather ordinary but very fair in its class.

FONSECA

Bin 27*: A vintage character with body and colour; perhaps showing rather 'hard' on the finish.

GRAHAM

Late-Bottled Port (Finest Reserve)*: A quality port of a single year, but undated, it has the Graham rich fruitiness. Rather too brown in colour.

NOVAL

L.B.*: Could be described in colour as a light ruby, but has a distinct vintage-character style on the 'nose' and on the palate. A wine of quality, although it should be remembered that this is not late-bottled vintage and does not have that weight.

SANDEMAN

Partners*: A very drinkable, medium-full tawny of no great age. Perhaps rather lacks character.

TAYLOR'S

Ruby*: A very good example of this style. Fresh and full.
Atlantic*: An excellent light medium quality tawny.
L.B.V.*: Being dated vintage, these wines naturally vary, but on the whole show the quality expected, with an acceptable fruit and body.

WARRE

Warrior Finest Vintage Character*: I was not impressed. Seemed brown, worn, and spirity.

Notes on Port Houses

COCKBURN SMITHES & CO.

Robert Cockburn, younger brother of Henry, Lord Cockburn, the famous Scottish judge who made his name as an advocate in the trial of Burke and Hare, founded this great firm in 1815 with his friend George Wauchope of Leith. He married Mary Duff, a lady much admired by Lord Byron.

Robert Cockburn died in 1854 leaving his two sons to carry on the business with Henry Smithes, who brought his younger brother J. T. into the business, leaving him in Oporto while Henry returned to the London office.

*Oporto-Bottled

J. T. Smithes married twice, first a Teage and secondly a Cobb, thus bringing both families into the firm. On the retirement of the two Teages, W. M. Cobb took over, to be succeeded by his son R. M. (Reggie) Cobb, only fairly recently retired as Chairman. He had as his colleagues, first A. C. Smithes, son of J. T., and then John H. Smithes, the son of A. C. It may be said with certainty that in their respective epochs, there were no finer tasters of Port than A. C. and J. H. Smithes, father and son. John Smithes is still active as a consultant, visiting Portugal twice a year. His knowledge of the Douro district is quite unrivalled, and he has recently visited California to study types of vine stocks there.

After the Second World War, retirements became inevitable. Antonio Filipe is currently Managing Director, and the team includes Peter Cobb, nephew of R. M. Cobb, Gordon Guimaraens, originally with the sister firm of Martinez Gassiot, and John Graham and, on the technical side, an American graduate of Davis University, Kevin Hamel, probably the first American member of the Port trade since Mr Camo of Taylor's in the early nineteenth century.

It became obvious, too, that the firm must look for friends with whom to consolidate the business. Harvey's now handle the brand brilliantly and, while greatly increasing the sales, they have preserved the essential reputation for quality on which the name of Cockburn is founded. Though possessing a fine and expanding *quinta* at Tua, it has not so far been Cockburn's policy to ship single *quinta* wines; though perhaps their recent acquisition of the production from the great *quinta* of Eira Velha might lead to a reappraisal. The style of Cockburn's is a vigorous freshness, full without being heavy on the palate.

CROFT & CO.

Certainly one of the oldest Port houses, founded as Phayre & Bradley in 1678. The first Croft appears in 1736 when the name of the firm had been transformed to Tilden Thompson & Croft. John Croft came from York, where he continued to carry on his business as wine merchant.

Another John Croft went to Portugal during the Peninsular War. There he met his old friend William Warre and later married Warre's sister, Amelia. At considerable personal risk, he carried on intelligence work in north Portugal, concerned with the movements of the French armies. For these services he was created a baronet. He was responsible for organizing the distribution of the British gift to the Portuguese who had suffered from the war.

Shortly after the First World War, the firm was merged with Gilbeys, which has now expanded into International Distillers and Vintners Ltd. Croft's own the well-known Quinta da Roeda vineyard, which is sometimes shipped as a single *quinta* wine.

DELAFORCE SONS & CO.

John Fleurriet Delaforce, of Huguenot descent, came to Oporto in 1834 as manager for Martinez Gassiot & Co. His second son, George Henry, started the Delaforce business when he began trading under his own name in 1886, and his two sons, Henry and Reginald, formed the partnership of Delaforce Sons & Co. in 1903.

The firm is still a family business, with Henry's sons Victor and John being eventually succeeded by the present Delaforces, John's sons David and Richard. In 1968 Delaforce became part of the International Distillers and Vintners Ltd of London.

DOW & CO.

See Silva & Cosens.

A. A. FERREIRA

Founded in 1761, the firm had no more than a local reputation until the famous widow Dona Antonia Ferreira took up the reins. Born at Regua in 1810, she died at an advanced age, worth the equivalent of more than £3,000,000.

Twice married and twice widowed, she married first her cousin A. B. Ferreira, one of the richest men in Portugal at that time. On his death, she married the very able manager of the properties, Francisco Torres. When she became a widow for the second time, she took the whole administration into her own hands. Dona Antonia was in the Douro boat with Baron Forrester when the latter was drowned in the Cachão rapids in 1862. She was kept afloat by her expanse of crinoline, and happily saved.

Still the owners of several beautiful properties, of which the Quinta do Vesuvio is probably the best, the firm is one of the largest and best-known of the Portuguese Port shippers.

FONSECA

See Guimaraens.

GUIMARAENS VINHOS S.A.R.L.

The firm of Fonseca Monteiro & Co. existed well back into the eighteenth century. In 1822 it was acquired by Manuel Pedro Guimaraens who, moving to England and marrying an Englishwoman, built up an all-round business, using the name Fonseca as his vintage brand.

In 1949 the Yeatman family of Taylor Fladgate & Yeatman bought the firm, Bruce Guimaraens continuing to represent the founder's family in the business. In style, Fonseca vintages are full, dark and rich.

W. J. GRAHAM & CO.

Graham's was founded as a dry goods and, in particular, textile business in the early 1820s. The firm also had extensive interests in India. Legend has it that in 1826 the Oporto office accepted payment of a debt in Port, thereby entering the trade and becoming Port shippers.

The firm was particularly strong in Scotland where for many years it had its own office. At one time, on the Glasgow board of five directors, three were holders of the Victoria Cross. The Graham vintage is very well known, big, dark and luscious wines. The firm was recently bought by the Symington family of Silva & Cosens.

MARTINEZ GASSIOT & CO. LTD.

This fine old firm was founded in 1797 by Sebastian Gonzalez Martinez. Joined by J. P. Gassiot in 1822, the business was taken over by the Gassiot family on Martinez' retirement in 1849. The Gassiots were remarkably gifted in various fields, and Charles was a notable benefactor to St Thomas's Hospital, London. The last two Gassiots left no children, and the firm was floated as a public company in 1902. One of the firm's offices in the City of London had cellars running under the old house of Dick Whittington, the famous Lord Mayor. After the Second World War, facing the same difficulties as many other firms, Martinez decided to come under the Harvey umbrella.

OFFLEY FORRESTER LTD

This is one of the oldest firms, founded in 1761. Its title enshrines the name of J. J. Forrester, without doubt the most gifted individual in the history of the trade, who was drowned in tragic circumstances in the River Douro he loved so well. In

1962 the firm was sold to Sandeman's who, in 1965, sold 50 per cent to the St Raphael Company of France. Offley vintages with their unmistakably scented 'nose', have been traditionally based on the famous Quinta Boa Vista.

QUINTA DO NOVAL VINHOS S.A.R.L.

Until recently known as A. J. da Silva & Co., this well-known house was founded in 1813 by J. A. da Silva. In 1920 the da Silva family brought their son-in-law Luiz Vasconcellos Porto into partnership, and it was he who developed the magnificent Quinta do Noval into one of the great show places of the Douro; work that has been most ably carried on by his grandsons, the van Zeller brothers.

GEORGE G. SANDEMAN & CO. LTD

George Sandeman of Perth founded this great firm in 1790 in London and soon extended his interests to Oporto. The family line has continued to the present day, though the firm has recently been bought by Seagrams. Sandeman was the first Port firm to sell its wines solely under its own brand, an example since widely followed!

SILVA & COSENS

A. F. da Silva came to England from Oporto in 1798, and married an English lady. His grandson was joined by F. W. Cosens, thus founding the firm. In 1868 a member of the Warre family became a partner, followed by J. R. Dow whose name is perpetuated in the vintage brand.

In 1912 the firm became virtually amalgamated with Warre, and both were managed in Oporto by A. J. Symington, the first of the clan which now plays such a large part in the Port trade. The family own the Quinta do Bomfim at Pinhão.

TAYLOR FLADGATE & YEATMAN

This great house goes back to 1692 under the title of Job Bearsley. The Bearsley family was connected with the firm up to the French invasion of Portugal in the Peninsular War when, prudently, an American neutral, Mr Camo, was admitted into partnership. Mr Camo, however, disappeared from the scene in 1812 when the United States declared war on England. The Taylors, Fladgates and Yeatmans came into the firm between 1816 and 1844, eventually leaving only the Yeatmans whose descendants run the firm to this day. The firm owns the famous Quinta de Vargellas, often shipped as a single *quinta* wine, and its vintage Ports in general have the highest reputation.

WARRE & CO.

The first Warre entered this old firm in 1729. In 1905 A. J. Symington joined the firm and, with the Warre family concentrating on the London end of the business, the Symington family have since managed the shipping side with great success.

In 1965, with the growth of business in France, Warre's agents there, Dubonnet-Cinzano-Byrrh, were admitted into partnership.

7

Madeira Wine

NOEL COSSART

The name of Cossart, Gordon and Company Limited has been associated with Madeira wine since 1745. Beginning in 1924, Noel Cossart worked on the island of Madeira until 1939 and then after the Second World War in 1949 he became Managing Director of the firm. He was appointed a director of the Madeira Wine Association in 1952 and returned to London in 1953 becoming Chairman of Cossart, Gordon and Company Limited. During his fifty years in the Madeira wine trade, Noel Cossart has made a close study of the viticulture and viniculture of the Madeira Islands. He has written many articles on Madeira wine for newspapers and magazines all over the world. He is currently writing a book on the history of Madeira wine and its making taken from the Bolton Letters written from Madeira between 1695 and 1720 and the archives of Cossart, Gordon & Co from 1745 to date.

Geography and Climate

To the south west of Europe, 2,408 kilometres from England and to the west of the coast of Morocco, a most beautiful cluster of islands rises out of the blue Atlantic in latitude 32°N and longitude 17°W. Bermuda, Los Angeles and Jerusalem are on the same parallel, and in the southern hemisphere Buenos Aires, Valparaiso and Perth are on the same latitude. The main island, Madeira, covers an area of 731 square kilometres. Its greatest length is fifty-seven kilometres from east to west, and twenty-three from north to south. A ridge of mountains forms the backbone, dividing the island into two halves. The highest mountain, Pico Ruivo, towers 1,829 metres above sea level. The other islands are Porto Santo, seventeen by six kilometres, and the uninhabited Deserta Islands, the largest of which, Deserta Grande, is fourteen by 1.6 kilometres.

A warm current flows past the island south south west and the trade wind blows regularly from the north east, for an average of 300 days in the year. Madeira has a surface temperature of 21°C, and the mean annual temperature in Funchal, the capital, is 19°C. Summer temperatures rarely exceed 27°C, and in winter seldom are below 13°C. Along the coast, annual rainfall is seventy-six centimetres, most of which falls from November to April. However, in the last ten years there has been earlier rain, which accounts for the small vintages.

The island of Madeira is wholly volcanic and is composed of volcanic rock. Between basaltic strata there are deposits of brightly coloured red and yellow tufa, a granular deposit that originally poured from the craters when the volcanoes ejected triturated material mixed with steam in the form of mud instead of lava. This has produced a very fertile soil. The island of Porto Santo is of completely different structure, although only sixty-four kilometres away. The soil is rich in lime which is imported into Madeira where it is not found.

The Vines

The Madeira archipelago was discovered by the Portuguese sea captain João Gonçalves Zarco in 1418 and donated by the crown of Portugal to Prince Henry the Navigator, a grandson of John of Gaunt and a patron of nautical exploration. Prince Henry sent ships to bring plants of sugar cane from Sicily and sweet Malmsey from Crete to plant on Madeira. His object was to capture for Portugal the trade in sugar and sweet wines which the Genoese and Venetians had hitherto enjoyed, while not competing with produce grown on the Portuguese mainland. Sugar cane has become an uneconomic crop, but the vines have flourished as the climate and soil are eminently suited to their growth.

The first vines came from Crete, but originally derived from Monomvasia, a small town in the Bay of Epidaurus Limira in the Peloponnese. The name became Malmsey in English, Malvoisie in French and Malvasia in Portuguese. Another strain of Malmsey, called *Malvasia babosa*, was imported in 1515 from Minoa. The word *babosa* means flabby, as the grape is softer and less sweet than the Cretan Malmsey. Many other vines were introduced: these included the Bual or Boal; the Verdelho or Gouveiro, which is the Verdia of Tuscany; and the German Riesling, which was known as Cercal and is now called Sercial. The Negra Mole, which is thought to be the French Pinot Noir, produces a wine called Tinta, known in the United Kingdom as 'Tent'. Other vines which did not survive the phylloxera were the Terrantez, Bastardo, Listrao, Alicante and Muscatel.

Originally Madeira was an unfortified beverage wine. One reads of Madeira burgundy made from the Negra Mole grape. In England during the reign of Queen Anne there were rumours of wars, and ships bound for North America and the Caribbean did not call at the islands, so stocks of the wine grew. Merchants had encouraged the planting of vines and were morally obliged to buy from the growers. There were not enough casks and storage problems became acute, so they were forced to distil their surplus wines into brandy with which to fortify and preserve their stocks. When peace returned, more ships than ever before called at Madeira, but they loaded a wine of a very different character and much stronger, which gained an enthusiastic reception.

History

The history of Madeira wine-shipping is possibly the best documented of all wine-growing regions. It starts with the letters of the Englishman William Bolton of Warwick, who was shipping from Madeira from 1695 to 1720. Very early in the history of Madeira it was found that a long sea voyage, especially to a hot climate, greatly benefited the wine. This was not only due to the heat, but also to the movement of the ship. Ships called to take wine to the East and West Indies and back, and the wine was called *vinho da roda* or 'wine of the round voyage'. After mellowing in the heat of the hold, rolling and pitching over the sea, *vinho da roda* took on some of the character of the sailing ship itself; in America, it was customary to label Madeira under the name of the ship that brought it. *Vinho da roda* may have been romantic but it became very expensive. Normal ullage on the trip was calculated at over 6 per cent, and with pilfering by the crew it exceeded 15 per cent, so shippers tried to simulate the effects of a long sea voyage on shore. In 1794 a Portuguese abbot built a glasshouse in which his wine casks were stored. This was the first *estufa* or hothouse. Such *estufas* developed into hot stores in which the casks were placed and the room heated by hot-water circulation, the wine in the casks being frequently roused.

Wine has been made in Madeira since the fifteenth century, but only small quantities were exported until firstly Cromwell enforced on Portugal the granting of very special privileges to English merchants in Madeira in 1654 and secondly, in 1663, Charles II's Act banning the exports of European produce to the English plantations, unless shipped in English ships from English ports, except Madeira. These two events created a virtual monopoly for Madeira in the American colonies and West Indies – a vast market – the effects of which last to this day. Attracted by the possibilities of this trade, British merchants established themselves in the island, and Madeira-drinking became an American way of life. George Washington drank a pint at dinner every day. Officers and officials returning home to England after the American colonies gained independence brought with them the habit of drinking Madeira and the Prince Regent, the First Gentleman of Europe and a mirror of fashion, soon acquired the taste.

In the nineteenth century two great disasters struck Madeira's vines; the first occurred in 1851 when mildew, *Oidium tucheri* (known locally as *mangra*), attacked the vineyards after a French botanist had brought a collection of infected vines to Madeira. By the following year the disease had spread, causing havoc. The average production during the years 1849 to 1851 was 50,000 hectolitres, but in 1852 it fell to 8,000, and in 1853 to only 600 hectolitres. The cure was found to be dusting with sulphur, and by 1861 the *mangra* had been controlled. Almost all the long-established British shippers left for Spain, and it is to the courage, endurance and persistence of a handful of Englishmen and Scotsmen that we owe the present Madeira wine trade.

The second scourge was the vine louse, *Phylloxera vastratrix*, which came from America and hit Europe in 1860, quickly spreading and methodically bringing havoc and devastation to the vineyards. The louse was brought to Madeira direct from America in Isabella vines of the *Vitis labrusca* variety, which had been found to be resistant to mildew, and by 1872 it had become rampant, attacking the vine roots. Each louse produces between 25 to 30 million individuals in one breeding season.

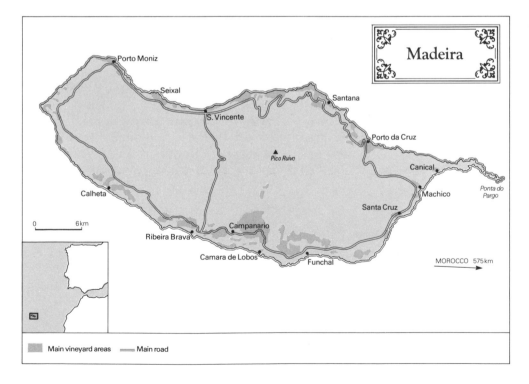

In Europe it had a winter hibernation, but in the warmth of the Madeira climate it bred continuously and the result was catastrophic. Before the oidium and phylloxera there were some seventy British merchants on the island, but in 1883 the number was reduced to ten, and now there are only four.

Fortunately, among these was Thomas Slap Leacock, a leading entomologist of the day who bequeathed his notes to Cambridge University. He identified the phylloxera, and in 1874 treated the roots of his vines with resin and essence of turpentine. Later, he used tar on the roots and sulphate of copper spray to combat the aerial form. By 1883 phylloxera was under control, but the vineyards were left sadly depleted. Before the phylloxera, 2,500 hectares were covered by vines, producing 16,000 pipes annually, but in 1883 the area was reduced to 500 hectares, producing 3,500 pipes.

The original Madeira vines were propagated by planting cuttings, but after the vine louse had been brought under control, phylloxera-resistant root stock was imported from America onto which scions of the original Madeira *Vitis vinifera* strains were grafted. This stock was mostly *Riparia* and *Rupestris monticola* which, owing to its robustness, is still used and called Silvado or Bramble. Now it has been found that, due to the low limestone content, such varieties as Solanis, Riparia x rupestris and the Berlandieri stocks are the most successful, as they accept the Madeira 'noble' strains well.

Prompted by the demands of the EEC and American markets, which take 75 per cent of Madeira's exports, the Portuguese government initiated a programme in 1972 to encourage and aid growers to replant the classic Madeira qualities. This has increased the production of the 'noble' strains by 75 per cent since its initiation. The programme is directed by viticultural experts at three experimental stations. Apart from free technical advice, there are more tangible incentives, such as cash grants per square metre of vineyard from which direct-producing hybrids have been uprooted, as well as annual grants for loss until the 'noble' vines are in full production. Between 1973 and 1980, these three stations distributed over one million plants of improved modern root stock, and registered over 700,000 grafts of traditional noble varieties. After the phylloxera in 1872, Madeira vintages were no longer declared owing to the shortage of wine and existing vintages were in most cases converted into dated soleras. These took the date of the original vintage prefixed by the word 'Solera'. When the casks were 25 per cent ullaged, or annually (whichever was less), they were topped up with a blend of old wine to suit the original vintage. Thus, Soleras 1815 and 1822 were actually vintaged in those dates, but were topped up after 1872. These vintages are interesting because 1822 was the better of the two, but 1815 became immortalized as the date of the Battle of Waterloo. A vintage 1815 would have been vintaged in that year and untouched afterwards. The advantage of a Solera is that any faults which may develop can be corrected.

Vintages

The exodus of shippers due to oidium and phylloxera enabled those that remained to secure stocks of old wine which they preserved to this day, and which are the origin of the pre-phylloxera vintages. There are two outstanding pre-phylloxera vintages made from the Terrantez vine: the 1846, bottled in 1900, and some as late as 1950; and the 1862, bottled in 1940. Both are exquisite. The vines did not fully recover until around 1900 and there are some excellent vintages after that date. Malmsey 1880 was possibly the best after the 1808, followed by 1893, 1914, 1916, 1920 and 1954. Bual 1895, 1914, 1926, 1941, 1954 and 1956 are the best, with preference going to the 1926 and 1941. There is no doubt that the Verdelho 1907 is the best post-phylloxera vintage, closely followed by the 1900, 1902, 1909, 1914 and 1934. Verdelho must be very robust when vintaged, to stand age well. Sercial had never been taken seriously, being thin and drier than other types of Madeira, until it was discovered, at the time of the Prince Regent, that it was an excellent palate cleanser after a bout of Port drinking; then it came into its own. The best post-phylloxera Sercial is the 1883, followed by 1900, 1905 and 1940.

Ageing

Madeira is *firmissima vinha*, that is it will live longer than any other wine. No other wines vintaged in the years of the battles of Valmy and Waterloo, or as Sir Winston Churchill pointed out when drinking the 1792 in 1950, vintaged when Marie Antoinette was alive, can be drunk today with any pleasure. The longevity of Madeira is attributed to the semi-pasteurization during *estufagem* or to the heat crossing the tropics. But most of the pre-phylloxera vintages known to us today were *canteiro*, not *estufado* or *vinho da roda*, so it is likely that the longevity is due to the volcanic soil, as well as to the time and labour given to bringing the wine to perfection. Unfortunately, due to very large sales to the United States after the Second World War, stocks of old vintages and dated Soleras are very low and pre-phylloxera vintages may be counted in bottles rather than dozens.

Viticulture

Madeira's terraced vineyards have been constructed on the mountainsides and represent enormous expenditure of labour. Supporting walls, sometimes six to nine metres high, are built of large blocks of basalt with no mortar to ensure free drainage. They are rarely known to collapse, even when torrents flow down the valleys. They are filled with tufa scraped from the mountainside higher up, or carted from the river beds. The vines are trained on trellises called *corredors* sloping from one to two and a half metres high. The main terminal branch, sometimes five to six metres long, is bent on to the *corredor* and tied with banana bark. Pruning is effected with the new moon at the end of March or early April.

Vinification

Officially the vintage should start every year on 15 August. Madeira has the longest vintage in the world, starting in mid-August at sea level and continuing up the slopes until the Sercial grapes, 457 metres above sea level, are picked at the end of October. A few grapes are always left to be picked, with a lot of junketing, on 11 November, the Feast of St Martin, Bishop of Tours and patron of wine-growers, when every self-respecting picker becomes drunk. The vintage is a social affair, with whole families involved, women, children, and old people picking, and the men packing and carting. The children fill small baskets at the lower ends of the *corredors*, and adults at the higher ends. Men fill *vindima* baskets with forty-five to fifty kilograms of grapes and carry them off to the presses.

A normal vintage should produce 110,000 to 120,000 hectolitres but due to recent weather conditions, only 80,000 have been produced. On average, one-third of the wine produced is exported as fortified wine. Approximately 70,000 hecto-litres are consumed locally in the form of unfortified *vinho seco*, in spite of shippers' efforts to induce the local population to drink table wine produced on the Portuguese mainland, of which there is a surplus. However, most of the *vinho seco* is derived from the *Vitis labrusca* (American fox grapes) variety Isabella, and is not suitable for shipping owing to its *moisi* flavour which Madeirans seem to like.

Shippers no longer buy must from the growers – they buy grapes which are selected and graded before they are pressed. Pressing by men's feet in a *lagar* is still used in outlying districts. It is undoubtedly the best method, but the mechanical press is mostly used today. The stalks and skins are removed before fermentation, and are fermented separately to make either *agua pé*, literally 'foot water', an unfortified table wine, or else distilled.

Fermentation is aerobic and takes from three to six weeks depending on air temperature; if it is very hot, the fermentation tanks have to be cooled. Malo-lactic fermentation never starts, because the wine is either fortified or heated in *estufas* before it is able to set in. The must is usually fermented right out to obtain the maximum of natural alcohol, and the sweetness is adjusted by the addition of *vinho surdo*, which is must of high specific gravity whose fermentation has been stopped by the addition of alcohol. Nowadays, however, rich Madeiras can be achieved by arresting the fermentation of the wine itself at the required degree of sweetness. The merits of both methods are still debatable. The writer put down some Bual for his son, David Cossart, vintaged in 1941, the year in which he was born, and its fermentation had been arrested. It is now lighter and more elegant than other Buals of the same year that were sweetened with *surdo*; only time will tell which will accept age gracefully.

After fermentation has ended, the *vinho claro* is racked off the lees, and at this point a selection is made. Madeira may be given four classifications: Current Madeiras; Reserves; Soleras; and Vintage Madeiras. These correspond to James Christie's old classification of wine sold on the London Docks, which were Common Madeira; London Market; London Particular; and East India Madeira. Current Madeira would include all wine up to those labelled 'Fine' or 'Fine Old'. Reserves include all wines labelled 'Reserve', 'Finest' or 'Finest Old'. But a 'Shipper's Reserve' is a lot not offered for sale but destined for topping up Soleras or reserved for observation with a view to becoming a vintage. Soleras have been explained, and vintages are self-explanatory.

The next step is the process peculiar to Madeira known as *estufagem*. If the wine has been selected to become a 'Shipper's Reserve', it is fortified before *estufagem* to 20 to 22 per cent of alcohol by volume. This is an expensive practice, as the loss in alcoholic content during *estufagem* is 2 per cent, added to *estufa* ullage of 10 per cent of volume, so current lots are processed unfortified.

There are two kinds of *estufas*. The *armazém de calor* (hot store) is heated by hot-water circulation. Pipes of wine are placed in it, and they are frequently stirred. The hot store is heated to an air temperature of 70°C, with a maximum time limit of six months, which means that the wine in the casks is kept at about 45°C. These hot stores, where the wines are processed in wood, are used for quality wines, or for finishing off Current wines.

The modern *estufa*, called *cuba de calor* (hot vat), usually holds 30 to 40,000 litres. The wine is heated by means of hot water circulating through stainless-steel coils at the bottom of the vat, so that the hot wine rising causes circulation. The wine is further activated by either a propeller or compressed air. Present legislation sets a maximum temperature for the wine in the vat at 50°C, but there is a tolerance of 5° each way. The minimum time allowed for *estufagem* is ninety days, and shippers may heat from 45° to 55°C, direct temperature of wine. Most prefer the lower temperatures and longer periods, with a finishing-off period in wood in an *armazém de calor*. If wine comes into contact with air at high temperatures it oxidizes, so the vats are not emptied until the wine is below 20°C. It has also been found that a brisk lowering of the temperature by refrigeration is beneficial and expedites turn-round of the vats. After the *estufagem*, the wine requires a resting period of twelve to eighteen months to recover from the shock. This period is called *estagio*. Wine which has not been *estufado* is called *vinho canteiro*.

Before the *estagio* period, the wine is fortified with alcohol rectified to 99.6 per cent as opposed to the brandy which is used in Port. There is considerable ullage in the alcoholic content due to evaporation during the *estagio* and storage afterwards, so Current Madeiras are fortified to 17 per cent and increased to 18 per cent before shipment. Fortified wine is called *vinho generoso*.

Madeira finishes the *estagio* when it is two years old, so it can only be used for blending with older wines after it is at least three years old. It is only shipped as a Current Madeira after its fifth year. Selected wines for Vintage and Solera Reserves are put aside in wood and carefully watched until they are declared as a vintage. If they do not live up to expectations, they are demoted and put back into the stock lots for blending. Some wines of certain years, and in particular Sercial, develop very fast for up to seven or eight years and then remain almost static. Sercial is rough and harsh when young; whereas other varieties are palatable at five years, Sercial cannot be drunk until it is at least seven years old.

Madeira Varieties

Nowadays, Madeira is mostly labelled under the names of the classic grapes from which it is made.

Sercial or *Cercal*: Pale, light-bodied, dry or extra dry (0.5° Baumé to 1.5° Baumé). Sercial is rather harsh when young, so shippers generally blend in some Tinta to soften it. Sercial should have a strong, nutty nose. With age, it becomes mellow and medium dark, the mellowness rather covering its dryness. Not recommended for laying down unless rather full and over 1° Baumé.

Verdelho: Golden, darkening with age. Medium dry (1.5° to 2.5° Baumé), medium-bodied and elegant, with a very dry finish. When old, becomes dry on the palate, retaining its fullness. Good for laying down, provided it has body and is over 2° Baumé.

Bual or *Boal*: Medium to dark, full-bodied, fruity and very fragrant. Medium rich (2.5° to 3.5° Baumé). Well-balanced and elegant; Cossart's Gunner Bual used to be a great favourite with officers' messes and clubs in India, being lighter than Malmsey or Port. It mellows quickly with age and is eminently suitable for laying down.

Malmsey, Malvasia or *Malvoisie*: Medium dark to dark. Full-bodied, fruity, luscious and very fragrant. Rich (3.5° to 6.2° Baumé). Some Malmseys reach 8°, which may seem too rich but is comparatively normal when tasted in the winter in, say Norway. Mellows fast with age, and tends to become drier and more elegant. Most suitable for laying down.

All the above four grapes are white, and all blends are based on these wines. Owing to the soil in which the vines grow, Madeira is naturally high in fixed acids. It also has a permissibly high volatile acidity, giving the richest wines the dry, almost bitter finish peculiar to Madeira.

Other types of Madeira:

Tinta or *Tent*: Made from the Negra Mole black grape. The wine is a deep colour, turning tawny with age and becoming the colour of medium-dark Madeira. Rich and very fragrant, but rather astringent. Mellows rapidly, losing its astringency. Tinta was a Madeira type some seventy years ago, but now it is mostly used for blending, sweetening (*surdo*) or colouring. Colouring wine is little used, because the wines are kept in American white oak and, in fact, shippers have difficulty in keeping their lots pale enough.

Rainwater: A blend, but the name has become generic. The wine is pale golden, light, soft and elegant. Medium dry (1° to 2.5° Baumé). The Portuguese call it *palhete*, 'straw-coloured'. The English name is derived from colonial America. An American merchant described it as 'the colour and softness of rainwater which has run over a straw roof into a butt'.

Madeira is also sometimes offered labelled under the names of districts such as Cama (or Camara) de Lobos, Campanario, Quinta da Paz, St Martin, and St John. If the name of the grape is not mentioned in the labelling, it means the wine comes from the Tinta grape.

Drinking Madeira

Old, dated Soleras and vintages not only offer joy, but are a considerable thrill to those who have the good fortune to experience them. They have usually been in the bottle for many years, some for half a century or more. When opened, they should be carefully decanted and allowed to breathe to eliminate the bottle stink Madeira acquires. One cannot overdo this breathing period, and a wine that has been in bottle for twenty years should be left open to breathe for at least six hours before drinking. Madeira will stand for months on ullage with no worse effect than becoming rather flat. It would, however, be wise to rebottle any valuable wine not drunk at the time in full, half or quarter bottles for the next occasion.

Madeira Wine Trade

Until the early part of the eighteenth century, the Madeira trade was almost exclusively in British hands. Thirteen houses were shipping in 1754, all of which were British except for Dr Richard Hill of Philadelphia. Two of the original firms are still trading today: Cossart, Gordon & Co., established in 1745; and Leacock & Co., established in 1760. During the succeeding years of the eighteenth century, production and export increased enormously – the annual shipments, which in 1774 amounted to about 7,000 pipes, reached upwards of 17,000 pipes in 1800. Many more British houses were established at this time, among them Blandy Brothers and Rutherford & Miles, founded respectively in 1811 and 1814 and both still in existence. Attracted by the substantial increase in trading, many Portuguese houses were founded; those operating today are T. T. da Camara Lomelino, established in 1820, Henriques & Henriques, 1860, and H. M. Borges, 1877. The most recent firm to be established is Vinhos Barbeito which, with Henriques & Henriques, possesses the most modern lodges and equipment in the island.

During the oidium and phylloxera, very little wine was exported. In the twenty-four years between 1881 and 1905, shipments averaged 5,000 pipes per annum. Madeira received a great blow with the collapse of the Russian market after the 1917 revolution, because it had been a favourite of the Imperial court. Today, yearly shipments average 10,000 pipes, which are distributed between thirty-nine countries. After France and West Germany, which take 30 per cent for cooking, Sweden, Norway, Denmark and Finland are the largest markets for quality wine, followed by the United Kingdom, United States, Belgium, Holland and Switzerland. However, shippers are encouraged by the marked recent increase in shipments of high-quality Madeira to the United Kingdom and to the United States, to the detriment of the French and West German markets. There can be no doubt that Madeira wine shipped today far surpasses in quality and style the wine of the past, entirely due to improved methods of viticulture and scientifically controlled vinification and ageing processes.

Other Vinelands
of the World

BILL GUNN MW

Bill Gunn MW is Buyer for two of the United Kingdom's largest and most important wine concerns, Grants of St James's Ltd and the Victoria Wine Company. He has written several articles on wine in British wine publications. He qualified as a Master of Wine in 1974 and has travelled extensively in the countries described in this chapter.

If this edition of *Wines of the World* was being published fifty years ago, in those uncomplicated days (for the wine trade) when the world of wine was bounded by Mainz, Marseilles, Bayonne and Nantes, the wines produced in 'Other Vinelands of the World' might have been regarded as at best eccentric and, with the solitary exception of Tokay, at worst irrelevant. The situation today is very different. Not only have the tastes of wine-drinkers encouraged by the growth in licensed supermarkets and 'self-service' wine stores, become more catholic in recent years but the standards of quality and value for money to be found in countries once regarded as 'outlandish' have improved so considerably in relation to the 'classic' areas of Western Europe that the share their wines enjoy of our western markets is continually increasing. Yugoslavia, to take but one example, has risen, as it would seem, from nowhere to take fifth place, no less, in the league of light wines imported into the United Kingdom, and this trend will undoubtedly continue as demand outstrips the supply available from nearer and more traditional sources. This section, then, is no mere afterthought as its title suggests, but a brief survey of wines which we can all expect to be drinking in the decades to come.

LUXEMBOURG

The first time I ever tasted a wine from Luxembourg was not in the Grand Duchy at all (something of a rarity in itself, since only one in four bottles is exported), but at Epinal in the foothills of the Vosges, some miles to the south. I remember that it was described as a Rivaner (contraction for a Riesling x Sylvaner cross), that it had an attractive flowery bouquet, a marked acidity and, though not without fruit, an austerity overall reminiscent of its German neighbours from the Saar. I have since tasted many Luxembourg wines, several of them of more exalted quality, but that first wine remains with me as a quintessential example. As one might expect from this tiny country's northerly situation and hilly, heavily wooded landscape, the Luxembourg vineyard is not extensive. It stretches from south-west to north-east along a forty-kilometre stretch of the Moselle from Remich near the French frontier, to Wasserbillig ('cheap water'), where the Sur flows into the Moselle from the north and marks the eastern border of the Grand Duchy. Along this narrow strip are packed some 1,200 hectares of vines, divided between 1,600 growers, this fragmentation is the legacy, as elsewhere, of the French Revolution and the Napoleonic laws of inheritance which followed in its wake. The vineyards face east, well-protected from the prevailing westerly wind by the slopes at their back, and look across to a similar landscape on the German side of the river: the valley of the Saar is only some five kilometres to the east. The well-drained soil is a little richer, and less schistous, than the vineyards down river, and the best sites are found on a mixture of chalk and marl. Alternating with vineyards are orchards, providing the same attractive patchwork that one finds further south in Alsace, and in the German Palatinate.

Like their German counterparts, the Moselles of Luxembourg are light in alcohol, crisp, fruity and acidic, and best drunk cool and young: they are also exclusively white, and made very largely from the same grape-types. The best of these are Riesling (always elegant, occasionally severe), Traminer (often excellent), Ruländer (Pinot Gris), Pinot Blanc, Auxerrois, Sylvaner, Riesling x Sylvaner (Rivaner, also called specifically Müller-Thurgau). The Elbling is also grown, but is gradually (and rightly) disappearing as the quality it produces is nondescript.

Production of Luxembourg wines is very largely in the hands of cooperatives, and the peaks and troughs of quality are thereby to some extent eliminated. The great majority of them are consumed locally, and only Belgium features to any extent as an 'export' market. Governmental controls of production and quality in Luxembourg date from just after the First World War, when the Grand Duchy was recognized as an independent state. The Government Viticultural Station at Remich is the fountainhead of an admirably strict regime, covering everything from new plantations to labelling: in the viticultural sphere it performs much the same role as a 'hothouse' of experiment as the celebrated school of Geisenheim in the Rheingau. The highest quality grade of Luxembourg wines, described as *appellation contrôlée* or *appellation complète*, is the subject of stringent examination and blind tasting under government auspices, an additional guarantee being provided in the form of a 'Marque Nationale' neck-label. It is possibly invidious to single out one or two sites of particular merit from such a compact vineyard area, but names which stand out in my experience are Grevenmacher, Wormeldange, Stadtbredimus, Remich and Schwebsingen, all names to conjure with. As one might expect, the Luxembourg wine-growing tradition is a blend of the French and German systems, and arguably incorporates the best features of both.

SWITZERLAND

Switzerland has a proud wine-growing tradition, and, in view of the country's size and contours, the remarkably high figure of 12,141 hectares under vine. The best vineyards of Switzerland lie in an extended sickle-shape in the south-western corner of the country, in the French-speaking Vaud and Valais. The 'handle' of the sickle is the Upper Rhône, cutting through the mountains in a broad valley south-west to Martigny, where it turns north to run into the Lake of Geneva: the 'blade' is a wide half-moon of vineyards stretching from Chablais, the district around Aigle on the eastern bank of the Rhône, through Lavaux, Vaud and La Côte along the northern shores of the lake, to Geneva at its south-western corner. Switzerland is a country of contrasts, and the vineyards in this first area I have described are a good

Estreito de Cama de Lobos church on the island of Madeira, 490 metres
above sea level, showing terraced vineyards of Bual grapes

example. We must also take into account the contours, and in these the vineyards vary enormously: the sunny shores of Lake Geneva at its western end are orchard country, where the slopes of the hills are gentle and undulating. East of Lausanne, the gradients become steeper, and once south of the lake the landscape is uncompromisingly Alpine. South of Visp, where the Zermatt railway branches up from the valley floor, lie the highest vineyards in Europe, steep terraces carved across the mountain slopes at an altitude of nearly 1,200 metres. It will easily be understood that the wines are correspondingly different in character.

Not all Switzerland's vineyards lie in the French-speaking cantons, though these do produce the lion's share of the total, and certainly that of the wines exported. The German-speaking north and east of the country, centred on Zürich, and the Italian Ticino in the south both have extensive areas under vine and quite distinct styles of production.

French-speaking Switzerland

The Valais: The Valais, as its name suggests (a derivation from the Latin *vallis*) is a typical Alpine valley, with meadows and orchards bordering the valley floor, vineyards on the lower slopes of the northern side, meadows on the south, rising to the tree line above and finally to snow-covered peaks. The vineyards lie on the northern valley wall in order to gain maximum exposure to the sun; the Valais, in fact, is one of Switzerland's driest areas. A greater problem even than the perennial threat of spring frosts is the provision of adequate water supplies for the vines, which have to be conducted by means of little wooden-walled canals (called *bisses*) from the snowfields and glaciers above.

The wines produced here are predominantly white, as they are throughout Switzerland (in quantitative terms at least), and predominantly from the Chasselas grape variety, or Fendant as it is locally called. The Chasselas is despised in France (notably in Alsace, where it is haughtily dismissed as 'un-noble') and regarded as primarily a table grape, but Switzerland, and the Valais in particular, provides the lie to such generalizations. Fendant, well-made, is a delightful wine; gentle and soft-scented on the nose, with a luxurious fullness in the mouth and clean, dry, grapy flavour. The only telling criticism one can make of it is that it finishes 'short' in the mouth, but perhaps that is a comment more for the academic than for the drinker! Fendants from the Valais are to be found with over 12 per cent alcohol, although many would think that the lighter, fresher wines are more appealing.

In smaller production than Fendant, but no less notable, is the Valais's (and Switzerland's) foremost red wine, Dôle, made from a mixture of Pinot Noir and Gamay. Dôle is generally distinguished by a rich, deep ruby colour, warm, scented bouquet and firm, grapy flavour – definitely Burgundian in type, but individual none the less. The name refers not to a place nor to a grape variety (although some authorities make it a local synonym for Gamay), but to the style of wine; wine of the same origins, but of lower standard (as determined by the local authorities) is sold as Goron. A similar wine is made in the Vaud, where it is known as Salvagnin.

Other wines of the Valais are: Johannisberger, reputed to have been introduced with cuttings from Schloss Johannisberg in the Rheingau. The vines are most probably a Riesling x Sylvaner cross, with the latter strain predominating; certainly parallels with German Rhine wines are not unacceptable. Malvoisie is a dessert wine made, improbably, from the Pinot Gris or Ruländer. An interesting speciality, especially when it is from a grower such as M. Louis Vuignier at Grimisuat, Sion.

The original vines of the Valais, with origins shrouded in the Alpine clouds, are Armigne, Petite Arvine (a good one is made by the Domaine du Mont d'Or at

Vineyards are planted widely on the south-facing slopes of Lake Geneva and profit from the radiation caused by the proximity of the lake

Sion) and Humagne, excellent from the Caves de Riondaz, rarely if ever seen outside the locality. Even stranger varieties, and names, exist, such as Reze and Heida
Paien, but it is a question of trying them on the spot before they disappear altogether
– the Caves de Riondaz at Sierre do produce them, but grapes like Reze tend to be
disease prone and do not seem to have a long future ahead of them. Familiar names
of more recent introduction are Riesling, and Hermitage (Red, from the Marsanne,
and White).

Vaud: Of the twenty-two cantons, Vaud is Switzerland's biggest wine-producer,
lying as it does around the fertile shores of Lake Geneva. It divides into several sub-
districts, the most important being (from west to east): La Côte: the lake-shore
from the outskirts of Geneva to those of Lausanne, producing mainly light red
Gamays and Chasselas whites. The latter variety is known here by the dialect name
of Dorin. Lavaux: the steeper eastern shore from Lausanne to Montreux, probably
the most attractive of all Swiss vineyards and the most immediately accessible to
visitors; certainly, too, the most photographed, as the backdrop to the Château de
Chillon. Here the grapes ripen easily with their southerly exposure and mirrored
radiation from the lake, but the terrain is far from amenable to the *vigneron*. Precipi-
tous terraces cling to the mountain-slopes, erosion from winter rains and melting
snows has to be repaired without mechanical aids, and all the other vineyard tasks
performed by hand. The fact that Swiss wines are generally expensive has as much
to do with difficulties such as these as with the soaring impregnability of the franc.
The main variety here, once again, is the Dorin, and a name to look for is Dézaley,
a vineyard just east of Lausanne whose wines are reported to be the best of the
region. Chablais: not to be confused with French imitations of similar pronuncia-
tion! This is the area linking Lavaux with the Valais, south and east of Lake Geneva
and centring on Aigle, with its splendid castle. The Chasselas again reigns supreme.
One famous vineyard here is the steep Clos des Murailles, which skiers pass on their
way up to Les Diablerets.

Neuchâtel: Produces some of the best-known Swiss wines, from vineyards lying in a
long, narrow strip south-west of the lake (with the French Jura only just over the
border at its back), and along its northern shore to the town of Neuchâtel and the
Bieler See beyond. Both red and white wines are produced, the former mainly
from Pinot Noir (the village wine of Cortaillod is reputedly the best), the latter
from the ubiquitous Chasselas, though here with a difference: Neuchâtel white
wines are often bottled *sur lie* to retain a distinctive *pétillance*, while the chalky soil
lends itself to the making of sparkling wines by the Champagne method.

German-speaking Switzerland

The area north of Zürich and its adjacent cantons produces some acceptable red
wines from the Pinot Noir, known here as Klevner or Blauburgunder, often vinified to retain a little sugar: *lieblich* or *suffig* wines in the vinous sense and on the
German pattern. White wines tend to be made from the main German varieties
such as Riesling, Müller-Thurgau and Ruländer (Pinot Gris), and a centre of
production is the Rhine-falls town of Schaffhausen.

Italian-speaking Switzerland

With Italy to the east, west and south, it is not surprising that the Ticino should look
thither for inspiration. One of Switzerland's most beautiful provinces, embracing
as it does the northern end of Lake Maggiore and almost all of Lake Lugano, it has
always been one of the poorest, and wine-growing here is on a small scale. The
more distinguished wines of the area are red, and made largely from the Merlot,

which is increasingly planted nowadays in preference to the ancient Bondola variety. Their main fault for the visitor is a certain dryness and astringency resulting from excessive ageing in wood, but producers are quick to point to the classic Lombard tradition on which their own methods are modelled. As the great majority are consumed and appreciated locally, one has little ground for complaint.

AUSTRIA

It is hard to understand why, with the exception of a handful of excellent, if uniform, 'branded' wines, the wines of Austria have failed to capture a bigger share of export markets. At the root of the problem, perhaps, is that one tends rightly or wrongly to associate them with German wines, which either overshadow them at the top end of the quality scale (for few Austrian wines, however good, can truly be classified as 'great') or undercut them with Liebfrauenmilchen at the lower end. However valid it may be in marketing terms, such a comparison is quite unfair, for Austria, home of Lenz Moser, of the unique and wonderful *Heurigen*, and of many other vinous innovators and innovations, has a wine-growing tradition and flavour entirely its own.

Viticulture in Austria goes back at least to Roman times: the Emperor Probus is credited with its introduction, though more probably it flourished under the Celts some centuries before. Although as a country today its glories lie mainly in the past, the wine-growing tradition has survived all the vicissitudes of history, and many of its facets (e.g. the *Heurigen*, established by the formidable Maria Theresa in 1780) remain unchanged to this day. Western, or Upper Austria, today makes negligible amounts of wine, and the country's vineyards are concentrated at the eastern end of Austria where the Alpine massif gives way to foothills and to the great plain of Pannonia, which stretches to the eastern borders of Hungary. They extend in a great half-moon from north-west to south-east of Vienna (Wien), where they straddle the shallow Neusiedlersee, and then continue in a series of smaller, separate zones down to the Yugoslav border south of Graz, in the province of Styria (Steiermark).

The majority of Austrian wines are white (some 80 per cent of the total), and the Grüner Veltliner produces 40 per cent of them; if not Austria's best wines, certainly the most distinctive and a taste, once acquired, not easily forsaken. After the Grüner Veltliner come Wälschriesling, Bouviertraube, Müller-Thurgau, Weissburgunder (Pinot Blanc), Rheinriesling, Zierfandler, Ruländer (Pinot Gris), (Gewürz) traminer and others, the proportions planted varying considerably from region to region. Production of red wines, of which one sees fewer abroad, is on the increase, the main varieties being Blauburgunder (Pinot Noir), Blauer Portugieser, St Laurent, Rotgipfler, Blaufränkisch (Gamay) and Zweigelt.

As one will readily gather from the daunting lists of grape-varieties, the diversity of Austrian wines is considerable. Though the reds in the main are fairly light in colour, smooth, perfumed and Burgundian in style (but often with a cuttingly dry or faintly bitter finish) and thus conform to something of a type, there are some broad distinctions that can be drawn between the white wines; generally speaking (and of course there are exceptions to any rule), the vineyards to the north of Vienna produce wines of lower alcohol and higher acidity than those from the central region around the Neusiedlersee, while the wines of Styria in the south fall intermediate between the two. Though the micro-climates of the three regions are also quite distinct, the central area being the hottest and driest, the critical factor behind the differences is geology. In the north of the country, the soil is generally stony, with schist, limestone and gravel all featuring in the make-up; in Styria it is predominantly clay, while in the Burgenland, the shores of the Neusiedlersee contain a high proportion of sand, producing wines of immediate attraction but little staying power.

The Austrian Wine Law divides the country viticulturally into four regions which are, in descending order of size, Lower Austria, Niederösterreich (33,387 hectares), Burgenland (30,351 hectares), Styria, Steiermark (2,226 hectares) and finally the capital, Vienna (607 hectares).

LOWER AUSTRIA

This, the largest region, embraces the whole of north-eastern Austria and, incidentally, the capital, although as we have seen, the latter is regarded separately under the Wine Law. It is itself divided into seven sub-districts, the majority of which lie between the Danube and the northern border with Czechoslovakia, though there are two important outlying districts to the south of Vienna. The seven are:

The Wachau: This, the most spectacular of the Austrian vineyards, rivals the Moselle for the beauty of its river scenery; the Danube, emerging here from an impressive gorge, flows under a wall of terraced vineyards on the northern bank, surmounted by the ruined castle of Dürnstein. It was here that Blondel found the imprisoned Richard Coeur de Lion in the closing years of the twelfth century, and the aspect can have changed little since. The best wines of the Wachau, which have considerable finesse, are made from the Rheinriesling, Grüner Veltliner and Muskat Ottonel. Their main hallmarks are an exceptional floweriness of bouquet, a firm balance of acidity and a length of flavour on the finish which set them apart from their less distinguished cousins from down river. Village names of the Wachau to look for are Spitz, Weissenkirchen, Dürnstein and Loiben.

Krems and Langenlois: The attractive riverside village of Stein marks the eastern extremity of the Wachau and the beginning of the Krems district. Here the northern wall of the Danube valley falls away to a low escarpment of loess. The vineyards, laid out in broad terraces, are penetrated by narrow, winding lanes known as *Kellergassen* marking the entrances of cellars cut deep into the hillsides. A few miles to the north of Krems is the town of Langenlois, which gives its name to the vineyards flanking the valley of the attractive river Kamp, which flows into the Danube east of Krems. The wines of these districts are similar to those of the Wachau, the Grüner Veltliner predominating, though in this Lenz-Moser stronghold (where the high-culture system was pioneered) there is constant experimentation with quality varieties from all over Europe, particularly on the stony plateau overlooking Röhrendorf.

The Weinviertel: This is the largest area in Lower Austria, embracing the whole north-eastern corner of the country – a landscape of low hills and mixed agriculture, supplying not only wine but grain, vegetables and even more important in this energy-starved era, petroleum. The most important sectors of the Weinviertel (literally the 'Wine Quarter') are the district known as Am Wagram, on the northern bank of the Danube, midway between Krems and Vienna, and the hinterland of the erstwhile Brünnerstrasse, the old imperial road from Vienna to Brünnen of the Hapsburgs, now Brno in modern Czechoslovakia. The wines are, in the main, light, dry and fruity in the Grüner Veltliner tradition, though good red wines are made both north-east of Vienna, and around Haugsdorf on the Czech border to the north-west. Retz, Pulkau, Falkenstein and Poysdorf are names to look for.

Klosterneuburg: Formerly Donauland, the 'land of the Danube,' this area lies west and east of Vienna in a long rectangle bisected by the river. Its heart is the great monastic complex of Klosterneuburg, whose well-marketed wines are gaining an ever-increasing foothold abroad.

Baden and Vöslau: These two districts adjoin each other south of Vienna on the line of the *Südbahn*, the southern railway. Their vineyards, covering the south-eastern slopes of the Wienerwald (Vienna Woods) look similar but their wines are very different – a function of the soil once again. Vöslauer is predominantly red, from the Blauer Portugieser, with a tangy flavour and a sharp bite of acidity, while the Baden district is best known for Gumpoldskirchener, a heady, generally medium-dry white wine made from Spätrot and Rotgipfler varieties: one of Austria's best-known wines for export.

BURGENLAND

The experience of a train journey from the Hungarian town of Sopron, surrounded on three sides by vineyards of the Burgenland, westwards across the Iron Curtain into Austria gives a vivid impression of how cynically politics can impose frontiers between areas whose geography, culture and traditions make them one. On both sides of this particular frontier wine-makers excel in the production of sweet wines, and the guiding influence is unmistakably Hungarian: indeed Burgenland was Hungarian until 1921. The central feature of the Burgenland is the shallow lake Neusiedlersee, surrounded by flat, sandy country which benefits from one of the warmest and driest micro-climates in Europe. The vineyard zones may conveniently be divided between those to the west, and those to the east of the lake and we will look at them in turn:

Western Burgenland: On a small hill overlooking the reedy western shores of the lake lies the old town of Rust. Ruster Ausbruch was once known as one of the great, sweet dessert wines of the world, and is still one of the most prestigious names of the Burgenland even if some of its erstwhile pre-eminence has been lost. Behind the lakeshore, vineyards rise to the slopes of the Leitha and Rosalien mountains where the soil, limestone now in place of sand, gives a favourable environment for the production of red wines as well as white. Pottelsdorf, a little way to the south, produces some pleasant reds of distinctive character.

The grape-varieties grown in the western Burgenland testify to its long Austro-Hungarian past. Furmint, the backbone of Tokay, features prominently among the whites, with Weissburgunder, (Gewürz) traminer, Wälschriesling and Muskat Ottonel, while Kadarka, a Magyar name to conjure with, appears with the Blaufränkisch (Gamay), and Blauburgunder (Pinot Noir) as the principal red varieties.

Eastern Burgenland: Here the wines are exclusively white, often from ungrafted vines planted in phylloxera-free sandy soil, and predominantly sweet *mit prädikat*, e.g. *Spätlesen*, *Auslesen*, *Beerenauslesen* and *Trockenbeerenauslesen*, the only star rarely found in the galaxy (as a result of the generally mild winters) being *Eiswein*. The principal villages of the area, from north to south, are Weiden, Gols, Podersdorf, Illnitz and Apetlon, the latter three comprising an area known as the Seewinkel, a narrow enclave squeezed between the Neusiedlersee and Hungary. The main fault of the wines from this area, which are excellent in every other respect (Oechsle readings especially), and are usually excellent value compared to German counterparts, is a premature tendency to oxidize: drunk young, they leave no grounds for complaint.

There is also 'southern' Burgenland, a series of outlying vineyards to the south of the Sopron corridor. Both red and white wines are made, but are of no particular eminence and are generally consumed locally.

STYRIA

As Burgenland is to Hungary, Styria is to Slovenia – Ljutomer is only just over the border. The landscape is one of rolling green pastureland, with vineyards interspersed with woods and meadowland. The pivot of Styria is the city of Graz, the vineyards lying in a wide semicircle to south-east and south-west, with the Yugoslav border at its base. The Styrians are a busily independent breed, and their wines tend in consequence to be many and individual. There are few cooperatives or big companies here, and consequently few wines are produced in sufficient quantity for export – though the pattern will doubtless change. Wälschriesling, Weissburgunder (Pinot Blanc), Traminer and Ruländer are the principal white varieties grown: the red wines are made from the same varieties as we have seen elsewhere, with one local speciality, the Schilcherwein of Stainz and Deutschlandsberg, made from the local Blauer Wildbacher, an interesting grape variety with a spicy, individual taste.

VIENNA

Few Viennese wines are seen abroad for the very good reason that they are consumed, with enormous enjoyment, in Vienna. If a visit to see the sights of this marvellous city were not enough in itself, it is also obligatory if one is to assess its wines. 'Assess', though, is perhaps too serious a word: the wines of Vienna are not such as lend themselves to 'assessment'.

The vineyards of Vienna are close to the city centre; stretching from the heart of residential suburbs up the slopes of the Vienna woods, they surround the western flanks of the city from Grinzing, Nussdorf and Sievering in the north to Perchtoldsdorf in the south, and are in every sense a vital part of the city's fabric. Unique to Austria, and to nowhere more than Vienna, is the institution of *Heurigen*. *Heurige* is new wine, green and prickling with the carbon dioxide of fermentation; *Heurigen* are the cellars-cum-wine gardens where this delicious product is consumed, amid the music, singing and general *gemütlichkeit* for which Vienna is famous. Under the law of Maria Theresa, each grower is permitted to sell the wines of his own vineyards for consumption 'on' or 'off' the premises: when a green bough appears outside his door, the wine of the year is ready; when it is taken down, the wine has all been sold and prospective customers must search for other *Heurigen*, or go home thirsty. It is clear that the *Heurige* tradition is one reason why not many Austrian wines are exported. Arguably, the best wines that this beautiful country produces are consumed on the spot and never see a bottle or an export certificate: 'gulping wines' in the best sense.

YUGOSLAVIA

Yugoslavia is the largest of the Balkan countries, an exotic compound of at least a dozen ethnic groups, six republics, four languages, three religions and two alphabets, until recently united under the forceful personality of one leader. With Tito's passing, it remains to be seen whether the very different elements of which Yugoslavia is composed will draw apart once again, or whether the unity he preserved for so long will be maintained.

The wines of Yugoslavia are a perfect illustration of the diversity of the country itself. The red wines come in every shade from deep pink through inky black to mahogany, the whites in every type from bone dry to luscious, not to mention a formidable breed of wine-based vermouths, *vinjaks* (grape brandies), and the heart-stopping national apéritif *slivovic*, made everywhere from the small blue plum.

Although production of Yugoslav wines is very largely in the hands of the dozen or so major cooperative groupings which operate independently from the State, and effectively compete with each other under the system known as self-management, the wide range of soils and micro-climates found in the different regions, the choice of grape varieties, and finally the varying methods of vinification all combine to give a breadth of choice to the wine-buyer that few other countries can match.

Yugoslavia today produces some 6½ million hectolitres of wine per annum from approximately a quarter of a million hectares of vineyards; these figures place her ninth in the world table, with Rumania her only rival in the Balkans on the basis of quantity. Four of the six republics account for the great majority of the wines produced, only minimal quantities being made in Bosnia-Herzegovina and Montenegro. The four are: Serbia, with some 45 per cent of the national total, Croatia with around 35 per cent, and Macedonia and Slovenia with under 10 per cent each. Qualitatively, the scale is somewhat different, with Slovenia traditionally accepted as producing the country's finest white wines (though some Serbian districts run very close behind), and Macedonia the best of the reds.

SERBIA

Serbia comprises most of eastern Yugoslavia, and has borders with Hungary to the north, and Rumania and Bulgaria in the east. It embraces a number of autonomous provinces: the most important of these for our purposes are Vojvodina and Kosmet. The heartland of Serbia lies around the capital, Belgrade; one of the country's biggest wine combines, Navip, has a huge central winery at Zemun on the outskirts of the city, to which they bring wines in bulk from outlying cellars all over Serbia for blending and preparation for export. Serbia produces both red and white wines, most of which are distinguished either by the name of their grape variety, or the region from which they come.

Vojvodina: This fertile province lies to the north of Belgrade. Important also as an agricultural centre (the fairs at Novi Sad draw many visitors every year), its vineyards lie in three main zones. The first of these is the Fruška Gora, a long, wooded ridge overlooking a west-east sweep of the Danube some eighty kilometres from the capital. At its eastern end, where an impressive bridge links the old Hapsburg fortress town of Petrovaradin with Novi Sad, the river flows south again past Sremski Karlovci (formerly Carlowitz, whose wine was popular in Britain a hundred years ago) and a Navip winery specializing in white wines. Approached from the south, the Fruška Gora offers welcome relief from the monotony of the Serbian plain. As well as a favourable alkaline soil, its slopes offer perfect exposure to a range of white grape varieties. The Wälschriesling (known in Yugoslavia as the Laski Riesling) predominates, here as elsewhere, though arguably the best wines of the Fruška Gora are made from aromatic varieties such as Traminer, Sauvignon and Sylvaner, together with Pinot Blanc and Sémillon. Plemenka and Smederevka (named after the town of Smederevo, near Belgrade) are local varieties producing rather neutral wines, dry and austere in style: the Smederevka features, however, in an interesting cross with Traminer known as the Neoplanta, which produces a wine of immediate attraction. Although the local preference is for dry wines of golden colour and slightly maderized flavour, crisper, fresher styles are being made in response to foreign demand, notably from the United Kingdom, often with a little residual sugar. Fruškagorski Biser is a pleasant sparkling wine.

The two other zones of Vojvodina are, respectively, the Banat and Subotica. The Banat is a flat, sandy region forming a corner of the great Pannonian plain: part of it lies in Rumania. Its wines are mainly white, and similar to those of the Fruška Gora without quite the same degree of finesse. The Subotica zone lies just south of the Hungarian border: it, too, is flat and sandy. Hungarian influence is seen in two of its grape varieties, the white Ezerjó and red Kadarka. Wälschriesling, Muscat Ottonel and Kevedinka are also grown. The best wines of Vojvodina are white, but good rosé known as Ruzica is also made as are respectable reds from the native Prokupac and recent plantations of Gamay and Pinot Noir. While the last-named varieties are assured of a future, the Prokupac is not without its attractions: a richly coloured, perfumed and very fruity wine with its own individual character.

Kosmet: This mountainous province, embracing the vineyard region of Kosovo, lies in the far south of Serbia, bordering Albania and Macedonia, and produces wines very different to those of Vojvodina. They are predominantly red, and made in the main from classic French varieties (Cabernet Franc, Gamay, Merlot and Pinot Noir) planted only in the 1960s following a severe outbreak of phylloxera earlier in the twentieth century. The Pinot Noir, in particular, exported under the brand name Amselfelder, enjoys enormous success in West Germany. The Žilavka produces the only white wine of note.

Župa: In the hills south of Belgrade, this is a large region making red and rosé wines, almost exclusively from Prokupac.

Venčac-Oplenac (Šumadija): This area lies on the Morava river, about an hour's drive south of Belgrade, and midway between Župa and the capital. It is a landscape of rolling hills, on one of which (above the town of Topola) sits a famous shrine of the former Kings of Serbia, the Romanesque chapel of St George, a landmark for miles around. The vineyards in this region are given over mainly to red vine varieties which flourish in the bituminous soil, rich in trace elements. Cabernet, both Sauvignon and Franc, are grown here, together with Merlot, Gamay, Pinot Noir, Prokupac and another local variety, Plovdina. Growing in a micro-climate rather more temperate than in Macedonia, these varieties produce wine of rather greater balance and finesse than those from further south.

Krajina and Timok: The last of the more important Serbian vineyards lies in the east of the republic near the town of Negotin, and a point where Yugoslavia, Rumania and Bulgaria meet. It produces mainly red wines. The area has seen significant replanting and expansion in recent years, and the quality of the new vineyards is promising. The Gamay is among the more successful varieties, though the influence of the heavy local soil is seen in the dark, powerful wine it produces – impossible under any circumstances to confuse with Beaujolais!

CROATIA

As we have seen, Croatia produces over a third of Yugoslavia's wines. These fall into two quite distinct categories: those from the inland vineyards north of the Danube, which fall midway in every sense between the wines of Slovenia and Vojvodina, and the wines from the Adriatic coast, from the Istrian peninsula in the north down the matchless Dalmatian coast to beyond Dubrovnik in the south.

Inland Croatia: Vineyards occupy much of the land between the Drava and Sava rivers as they flow eastwards to the Danube. This is the province of Slavonia, producing white wines of acceptable quality but of no particular distinction except on the borders of Vojvodina, where the best of them are excellent: Ilok, for example, produces some superior Wälschriesling (here known as Grasevina), and good wines are made from hill vineyards planted with Sauvignon, Traminer and Sémillon. Further west, between Kutjevo and Zagreb, vineyards on the plain are given over to blander varieties, such as 'Beli Burgundec' (Pinot Blanc) and Pinot Gris, producing heavy wines of higher alcohol, but lesser acidity and attraction.

The Coast: Yugoslavia's long Adriatic coast produces many of the country's most interesting and idiosyncratic wines. Clinging to the rocky islands and coastal hills, sheltered to the north and east by the Julian and Dinaric Alps, the vineyards enjoy an almost ideal micro-climate and produce wines of naturally high alcohol, both red and white. The grapes grown here are of bewildering diversity, and 'homework' on the part of the visitor is essential: the traditional Yugoslav wine-labels, their Spartan designs contrasting with the cheerful individuality of the wines within, give little clue as to the nature or degree of sweetness of the contents.

The Istrian Peninsula: At the northern end of the coastal strip lies the Istrian peninsula, formerly a province of Italy. The Italian influence is still seen both in the way many of the vines are trained on *pergolas*, and in the appearance of such grape varieties as the Refosco of Friuli, known here as the Teran. The best wines of Istria and the offshore islands of the Kvarner group are mainly red, made from Teran, Cabernet, Gamay, Merlot and Pinot Noir: often astringently tannic, they are full-bodied and fiery. The most prominent exception is the Istrian Malvasia, a rich dessert wine on the Malmsey pattern; similar wines are made from Muscat. Istria is also known for its sparkling wines, and an orange-based apéritif known as Istra Bitter.

Dalmatia: Moving southwards into Dalmatia, one passes first the ancient town of Žadar, centre for the production of Maraschino from the sour cherries which abound along this part of the coast, and then the resort of Šibenik. This northern part of Dalmatia again specializes in red wines, of which Plavina and Babic, both made from local varieties, are the best: light, dry and faintly bitter at the finish. When drunk fresh the local white, Maraština, is also pleasant, with a slightly herbal flavour. Opol is a rosé found throughout Dalmatia. Southern Dalmatia, from Šibenik southwards again past Split and Dubrovnik to Montenegro, produces a cluster of highly individual wines, many of them grown on the islands of the Dalmatian archipelago. A selection of the most interesting is as follows: Plavac is made from the Mali Plavac, the predominant grape variety throughout the region and is a deep ruby wine with perfumed bouquet, smooth palate with naturally low acidity, and refreshingly dry finish. Dingac is made from partially-dried Plavac grapes (along similar lines to the Reciotos of the Veneto). It is a dark, full-bodied, sweetish red from a delimited area on the Pelješac peninsula; it normally has around 15 per cent of alcohol. Postup is a red wine very similar to Dingač; the production area of Postup lies at the western end of the Pelješac peninsula. Prosek is the best-known dessert wine of Yugoslavia, made from a blend of red and white grape varieties. Thick, luscious and very sweet, Prosek has a natural alcohol of some 15 per cent of 16 per cent, and is normally unfortified. With the local Maraština which we encountered in northern Dalmatia, Pošip is the best of the Dalmatian white wines, made from a grape of the same name, grown on the island of Korčula. It is a full-bodied, straw-coloured wine with upwards of 13 per cent alcohol, excellent with local seafood, if perhaps a little heavy for Western tastes.

Grk, Bogdanuša and Vugava are three heady, aromatic whites from the islands of Korčula, Hvar and Vis respectively. Local taste favours a golden colour and maderized flavour, which provides an excellent complement to the Dalmatian diet.

MACEDONIA

The republic today is an important centre of red wine production, as well as of table grapes. The wines tend on the whole to be dark, powerful and alcoholic, often used to improve blends from further north, though the best of them are excellent in their own right. There are few new names to be remembered from Macedonia: the most widespread of the red grape varieties is Prokupac, while Smederevka and Zilavka head the limited production of white wines, all of which we have encountered in other regions. Perhaps the most exciting discoveries in Macedonian wines are to be found in the far south-west of the republic, amid the mountains and lakes near the Albanian border; here, some recent plantations of Cabernet, Merlot and Pinot Noir are producing wines of excellent quality and balance, which will doubtless gain a place on our shelves. Vranac and Kratosija are the best of the traditional reds.

SLOVENIA

This former Austrian province is in every sense a far cry from the minarets of Macedonia, and its traditions have been steeped in wine-growing from earliest times. Embracing the northern part of the Istrian peninsula, the foothills of the Triglav massif and the Alpine meadowland on the borders of Austria and Hungary, Slovenia's vineyards produce the most elegant of Yugoslavia's white wines, balanced with a marked natural acidity that the southern wines lack. They divide conveniently into three main zones, which we will consider in turn:

The Drava Region: This is the most important of the three zones, and certainly the one which has established the reputation enjoyed by Yugoslavia's white wines abroad, for it includes the famous districts of Ljutomer and Ormož. The heart of this zone lies around and between the valleys of the Drava and Mura rivers, in a rough square bordered by the town of Maribor at the north-west, and Ptuj, Ljutomer and Radgona at the other corners. It is gentle, hilly country, with terraced vineyards planted on an excellent subsoil of limestone, marl and clay.

The grape varieties grown in this zone are mainly of the Germanic type. Wälschriesling predominates, though arguably the finest wine of the area is made from its nobler cousin, the Renski (Rhine) Riesling, of which there is a regrettably small production: this is a wine of classic breed, with only perhaps a trace of softness and a higher alcohol content to distinguish it from the great growths of the Rhineland. After the two Rieslings come Sauvignon, Sylvaner, Muskat Sylvaner, Gewürztraminer, Ruländer and Beli Burgundec (Pinot Blanc), which all produce wines of excellent quality and pronounced varietal character. With their high acidity, these are wines with exceptional keeping qualities, even if we would normally prefer to drink them young and fresh: in the cellars of the Vinag cooperative in Maribor, for example, I have tasted some vigorous Rieslings, a Traminer, Sauvignon and a Pinot Blanc, all of which were at least twenty years old.

Vinification in Slovenia is carried out to a high standard. The Slovin combine, for example, has developed a form of model winery, built into the side of a hill in such a fashion that grapes arrive at the top, descend by gravitational flow through the wine-making process, and emerge as finished wine at the base: examples may be seen at Ljutomer and Ormož. While Ljutomer is justly the best-known name among the Drava wines, some other site-names are of interest. Jeruzalem, for example, marks a particularly agreeable spot among the Ljutomer hills, where Crusaders rested on their way to the Holy Land; today it produces some of the best of the Ljutomer wines. The neighbouring vineyard of Svetinje is famous for its Beli Burgundec: a late-harvested Svetinje of the outstanding 1971 vintage (a comparative rarity, as with few exceptions the Slovenes regard late-harvesting as unrewarding) I recall as being a wine of exceptional finesse and character, particularly from this generally rather neutral variety. Further afield, Ranina Radgona, a vineyard on the Mura, produces the sweetish white Tiger Milk, while from the slopes of the Pohorje, a mountain overlooking Maribor, comes Ritoznojcan, another fairly dry blend appreciated locally. Haloze, on the Drava produces full white wines on the Ljutomer pattern. At least as marketed for export, most of the wines from the Drava-Mura region are produced to contain a proportion of residual sugar to match their natural acidity. The most common exception is that produced from a local variety, the Šipon, which will appeal to the wine-drinker with a taste for the very dry.

The Sava Region: The white wines of this more southerly part of Slovenia, in the basin of the Sava river, tend to be overshadowed by their neighbours from the Drava but are respectable nevertheless. They are made primarily from Wälschriesling, Sylvaner, and some native white varieties such as white and yellow Plavac. Unlike the more northern vineyards, the Sava also produces red and rosé wines, of which the most noted is the dry, pink Cviček: light in alcohol, Cviček has a cutting acidity which is refreshing in summer, though perhaps rather austere in other seasons! The red wines of the region are distinctly Austrian in character; indeed the St Laurent features among the local grape varieties, along with Gamay and Red and Blue Portugieser. These are dark, fruity wines, hard in style and faintly bitter at the finish.

The Coastal Region: Western Slovenia looks to Italy, to which it used to belong, as the eastern part looks to Austria. It comprises the upper part of the Istrian peninsula, the hilly inland country east of the Trieste corridor and, a little further north, vineyards looking across the Isonzo to Gorizia and the Italian district of Collio. Much of the region is composed of barren limestone plateaux, a geological formation known as 'karst'.

Both red and white wines are produced in the region. The most noteworthy of the former are made from Cabernet, Merlot and 'Teran' (Refosco): Kraški Teran, from the 'karst', is a wine with a firm local following but possibly little appeal to export markets, a rugged, gutsy red, rich in trace minerals but more than a touch harsh at the edges. The Rebula of Brda (clearly a relation of the 'Robola' of Cephalonia, see Greece page 431 and the Ribolla of Friuli) is an individual white wine, a deep golden straw, pungent and very dry. Vipavac, from the town of Vipava, is an acceptable, lighter white from a blend of grapes including 'Rebula' and Wälschriesling. Tokay is also grown in the area, along with native white varieties called Pinela and Zelen: adequate wines, if not memorable. The more distinguished dessert wines of Istria, the Malvasia and Muscat, have already been noted.

BOSNIA-HERZEGOVINA

This large republic has a land surface of some 52,000 square kilometres, but only some 5,000 hectares of vineyard: a situation explained not only by its mountainous, afforested landscapes but by a long Moslem tradition. It does, however, in the region of Mostar (capital of Herzegovina) produce what many consider to be Yugoslavia's most distinguished white wine: Žilavka. The wine is produced from grapes of the same name, grown in the valley of the river Neretva. It is dry, pungent, and alcoholic (normally 12–14 per cent), but with an acidity and balance rare for white wines produced at this latitude and, at its best, an agreeable fruitiness akin to that found in the aromatic wines of Slovenia. The Žilavka vine is grown elsewhere in southern Yugoslavia, but the Mostarska Žilavka, the Žilavka of Mostar, is particularly recommended. Herzegovina also produces a red wine, Blatina, from a selection of grape varieties in which the native Blatina is predominant. It is acceptable but rather ordinary.

MONTENEGRO

This, the last of the republics of Yugoslavia, also produces a single wine of note, this time red: Vranac, which comes from the hills between Titograd and the coast, and around the northern shores of Lake Skadar. Vranac is a deep, complex red wine of powerful character, aggressively tannic in youth but mellowing with age to something not unlike the classic reds of the Rhône. If carefully vinified, this is a wine with some potential for the export market; as yet, it is rarely seen outside Yugoslavia.

It will be seen from the multiplicity of Yugoslav wines described in the foregoing paragraphs that Ljutomer Laski Riesling represents the tip (albeit a notable one) of a sizeable vinous iceberg. The potential for Yugoslav wines world-wide is enormous, particularly for the white 'varietal' styles of Slovenia and Vojvodina, and the reds of Kosovo, Macedonia and Montenegro. Measured on the price/quality scale, they rank as wines of exceptional value: given a greater commitment to marketing on the one side, and a consumer prepared to experiment on the other, we may expect to see a continuing growth in both the volume and the range of Yugoslav wines exported beyond the markets of the Eastern bloc.

Central Europe

Wine regions 1 Weinviertel 2 Langenlois 3 Krems 4 Wachau 5 Klosterneuburg 6 Baden 7 Vöslau 8 Eastern Burgenland
9 Western Burgenland 10 Eisenberg 11 Kisalföld 12 Transdanubia 13 Alföld 14 Vojvodina 15 Fruska Gora 16 Banat 17 Zupa 18 Kosovo
19 Dalmatia 20 Istria

HUNGARY

Visitors, comparing Hungary to its neighbours, Austria and Yugoslavia, should not be deceived by the prevailing drabness of appearances: underneath a very thin veneer is a rich wine-growing tradition second to none among the countries under review. The wines of Hungary, like the Magyars themselves, are fiercely individual: none more so than the country's most famous product, Tokay, the elixir of kings. Tokay is arguably the only truly classic wine to be found in this chapter of *Wines of the World*, and will merit a section of its own below; but while unquestionably in a class of its own, it should not be allowed to overshadow the many other excellent wines to be found in this fascinating country.

Hungary produces annually some 6 million hectolitres of wine from around 200,000 hectares of vineyards, spread throughout the country. These figures place her well down the production table behind Yugoslavia and Rumania, but quantity to us is of secondary importance to quality, on which basis she ranks at least on a par. This in itself is an achievement, given the fact that Hungary is a poor country, weak in natural resources and based on a struggling agricultural economy; central investment in viticultural and wine-making technology is low and irregular, and in no way compares to the organized programmes of the other Balkan countries of the Eastern bloc. The vineyards of Hungary fall conveniently into four main zones, determined by the main geographical features of this landlocked country. These are, respectively, the Great Plain (Alföld) which includes the whole of central and eastern Hungary from the Danube to the Rumanian border, the greatest concentration of vineyards being found between the Danube and Tisza, and around Debrecen in the east; the Small Plain (Kisalföld) of the north-west, in the angle formed by the borders with Austria and Czechoslovakia; Transdanubia, between the rivers Danube and Drava and centred on Lake Balaton; and finally what is known as the 'Northern Massif', where the Carpathian foothills cross into Hungary from Czechoslovakia in the far north-east of the country. It is these four zones that I will use as headings in describing the principal Hungarian wines, since they provide a more convenient classification than the fourteen registered sub-districts into which the latter were divided in an official post-war survey. But first a note on the colourful subject of Hungarian grape varieties, which are an ampelographer's dream.

Grape varieties

The great attraction of the numerous native grape varieties of Hungary is that all their names mean something, and the meanings are often highly descriptive. Here are a few of the principal ones:

Szürkebarát (white): 'Grey Friar', a cousin of the Pinot Gris or Ruländer.
Hárslevelű (white): 'Lime Leaf', a reference to the shape of the leaves. This is one of the three varieties used in the making of Tokay.
Kéknyelű (white): 'Blue Stalk', a characteristic of the vine.
Ezerjó (white): 'A thousand boons', a fair description of the contribution this variety makes to the wines of Mór.
Leányka (white): 'Young Girl', producing fresh white wines of sprightly charm.
Mézesfehér (white): 'Honey white', source of rich golden wines.
Juhfark (white): 'Lamb's Tail', a grape from the Somló district.

There are many more. The direct translations into Hungarian of the normal middle European varieties, 'Olaszrizling', for example, for Wälschriesling, or 'Fehérburgundi' for Pinot Blanc seem positively prosaic in comparison. 'Kékfrankos', incidentally, is the Hungarian term for Gamay, and the 'Médoc Noir' a strange synonym for that staunch progenitor of St Emilion and Pomerol, the Merlot.

THE GREAT PLAIN (Alföld)

Approximately half of Hungary's vineyards are planted on the vast sandy expanse of the Great Plain, which plays the same role as that of the Midi in France: a reservoir of honest but ordinary wines, red and white, produced for everyday domestic consumption, for blending, for export in bulk, for the production of sparkling wines or base wines for vermouth, or finally for distillation. They are made, in the main, from two grape varieties, one red, one white: the Kadarka and Wälschriesling respectively. The latter needs little introduction: the Kadarka, too, we will find growing in other countries described in this section, but it is in Hungary and on the Great Plain in particular that it gives of its best, a deep-coloured, flavoursome red wine with an aromatic, peppery finish.

The sandy soil of the Great Plain produces wines which, on the whole, are light in body and alcohol: we have noticed the same results in the Austrian Burgenland. There are, of course, exceptions, and wines of more powerful constitution are made in several areas of the Plain where richer sub-soils come closer to the surface: Kecskemét, south-east of Budapest, is one such area, and Szeged, near the Yugoslav border in the far south, is another. Near Kecskemét is the large state-controlled winery of Helvecia, whose name recalls a Swiss viticulturist of the last century who was among the first to master the art of planting vines in the drifting sands of the Plain. One advantage such pioneers enjoyed, equally valid today, is that sand is a disagreeable habitat to phylloxera: vine-roots established in sand are highly resistant in consequence, making grafting to a large degree unnecessary.

THE SMALL PLAIN (Kisalföld)

The pleasant town of Sopron, with a fine collection of baroque churches and other historic buildings, lies but a few minutes from the Austrian border, a small Hungarian enclave in the Burgenland. Surrounded by some 1,300 hectares of vineyard, Sopron enjoys a relatively cool micro-climate, the heat of summer being tempered by the proximity of Lake Fertő (the Austrian Neusiedlersee): I can testify that the winters are cold, recalling a December wind in the streets of the town which severed all feeling above the eyebrows.

The fame of Sopron rests on its leading red wine, Soproni [Hungarian possessives end in '-i' just as the German equivalents end in 'er', e.g. Piesport(er)] Kékfrankos, a light, fruity, eminently drinkable red made in the Beaujolais image from a strain of Gamay. It is not, generally speaking, a wine for keeping, but for drinking young and fresh. Soproni Kékfrankos is the only wine of any real significance from the Small Plain, an area more generally renowned for its associations with famous Hungarians of the past, such as Franz Liszt and the princely Esterházys. Modest but acceptable white wines, from Wälschriesling, Traminer and Veltliner, are also made in the region.

TRANSDANUBIA

Comprising the whole of Western Hungary apart from the Small Plain, Transdanubia contains several areas producing wines of 'outstanding' and 'excellent' quality in the terms of the official classification: eight of these fourteen districts, indeed, fall within its borders. Of these eight, six are white wine districts and two red. We will consider them in turn, beginning with the districts on and around the shores of Lake Balaton, the largest freshwater lake in Europe and often described as Hungary's 'inland sea'.

Badacsony: This district, a landscape dominated by the truncated stumps of extinct volcanoes, of which Mount Badacsony is one, produces the finest white table wines in Hungary. It lies on the northern shore of Lake Balaton, enjoying a perfect south-facing exposure and mild climate; the prevailing soil structure is of basaltic rock, with its characteristic 'columnar' appearance, in combination with loess and clay topsoils. The shallow waters of the lake provide a constant store of retained heat and reflected light, encouraging the terraced vineyards to produce grapes full of natural sugars and high potential 'extract' and degree. The grapes grown in Badacsony are primarily Szürkebarat and Kéknyelű, which make yellow, pungent, full-flavoured wines with considerable 'backbone' and finesse. Following the disastrous visitation of phylloxera in the 1870s, many of the vineyards were replanted not with the traditional varieties but with Wälschriesling, which here produces a wine of un-usual elegance for this variety. Furmint and Yellow Muscat (Sárgamuskotály) are also grown.

Balatonfüred-Csopak: Named after adjoining villages, this district lies eastwards of Badacsony, from which it differs principally in its soil structure. Red sandstone replaces loess, and an iron-rich sub-soil produces wines which are softer and broader than their neighbours, making up in charm what they lack, relatively speaking, in firmness. The north-east shore of Lake Balaton is favoured with a particularly warm micro-climate and its wines, like those of Badacsony, are rich, sweetish and full-flavoured. They are exclusively white and made from Wälschriesling, Sylvaner, Müller-Thurgau and Furmint, the last named a Hungarian speciality, whose provenance is the subject of conflicting legends: we will meet it again in Tokay.

Balaton: Some 3,250 hectares of vineyard on the north shore of the lake are entitled to the generic description 'Balaton'. Their wines are generally lighter and less dis-tinguished than those of the two previous districts, but sound, easy-drinking and attractive nevertheless. Wälschriesling, Sylvaner, Ezerjó and Mézesfehér are the grapes grown. While Lake Balaton provides a focal point for white wines of quality in Transdanubia, the outlying district of Somló to the north-west enjoys a reputa-tion of at least equal standing and antiquity.

Somló: Mount Somló is another extinct volcano, a little over 300 metres high with vineyards and a cluster of wine villages on its slopes. The total area is small, only some 400 hectares, but its wines have been famous ever since the days of St Stephen in the eleventh century. Two quite distinct styles are made, depending on the vine-yard site and exposure: those on the south and east-facing slopes, with the longer hours of sun, produce sweet dessert wines of the Tokay family from Furmint, Riesling (both styles) and Traminer, while from the cooler western slopes come lighter, drier wines made from native Hungarian varieties such as the Ezerjó. Somló wines are reputed to encourage both virility and longevity, a legend which the village registers reportedly substantiate, and to which the Hapsburgs and Esterházys certainly lent credence in past centuries.

Mór: The village of Mór gives its name to an important wine-growing district of some 1,100 hectares in the hills west of Budapest. The first vines were planted here some two hundred years ago, but the area first came to prominence at the time of the phylloxera epidemic of the late nineteenth century, which it largely escaped on account of its sandy soil structure. Even today the vines, planted in a mixture of sand, quartz and mica, are ungrafted. Mór is best known for its 'Móri Ezerjó', a dry white of pronounced character and flavour, the product of a happy marriage of soil, climate and vine variety. Nowhere else does the Ezerjó produce a wine of such obvious finesse: one thinks of the Gamay and Beaujolais as a parallel, albeit of a different colour. In exceptional years in Mór, the Ezerjó attracts botrytis and makes a wine of dessert concentration. North-west of Mór, on the borders of the Kisalföld, lies the smaller district of Barsonyos-Császár, producing wines of similar style.

Mecsek: Southern Transdanubia, the country lying between Lake Balaton and the Yugoslav border, produces both red and white wines. Mecsek, a district of attractive, rolling hills, specializes in white wines: Pécs (the district was formerly known as Pécs-Villány) is the best-known name, with a loyal following in the United Kingdom. The wines produced here come mainly from the Wälschriesling, though Furmint, Müller-Thurgau, Pinot Blanc, Chardonnay and the Austrian Zierfandler are also grown. They are generally of sound, attractive quality, without reaching the heights of excellence of the Balaton wines: made on the German pattern with a degree of residual sugar, they have a ready export market.

Villány-Siklós and Szekszárd: These two areas, Villány-Siklós lying to the south of Mecsek and Szekszárd to the north-east, are known for their red wines. Most authorities consider the best wine from the former district, Villányi Burgundi, as being the finest of the Hungarian reds, and I would not disagree. Villányi Burgundi is made from Pinot Noir (Nagyburgundi) which on the local clay and loess soils produces a deep-coloured, soft red wine with considerable perfume and elegance. It improves substantially after a few years in bottle.

Siklós produces sound red wines from Kadarka and Blau Portugieser, the former being the more immediately attractive, the latter tending to harshness. White wines are also made here from Wälschriesling and Hárslevelű, without attaining any particular distinction.

Szekszárd, the last of the Transdanubian districts, makes some excellent red Kadarka from some 2,000 hectares of vines. This was a favourite wine of the Austro-Hungarian court, and Liszt its most famous protagonist. In good years it attains an astonishing intensity of bouquet and flavour and, like the Pinot of Villány, is well worth laying down to mature.

THE NORTHERN MASSIF

North-eastern Hungary, from Budapest to the narrow border with Russia, is a continuous range of hills, at their western end known as the 'Mátra', in the centre as the 'Bükk', and the east as the 'Hegyalja', the district of Tokay. These names have more than a geographical significance as the areas they describe make quite different wines, and I will deal with them separately.

The Mátra: These rolling hills, which at one point reach over 900 metres, form the largest vineyard area in Hungary after the Great Plain (nearly 12,000 hectares in all). As well as large quantities of table grapes, the area produces mainly mass-consumption white wines from Wälschriesling and indigenous varieties such as Leányka and Mézesfehér, plus a little red Kadarka. There is, however, one wine of especial note from this region: Debrői Hárslevelű, a sweet, scented white wine of some 13 per cent alcohol, rich in extract and flavour. Aside from Debrő, the other main centre for the table wines of the Mátra is the tongue-twisting area of Gyöngyös.

Bükkalya and Eger: The baroque town of Eger lies on the southern edge of the Bükk hills. Its best-known, if not necessarily its best wine (for its Leányka and other white wines are also much esteemed) is the romantically named Egri Bikavér, 'Bull's Blood of Eger', a smooth full-bodied red made from a blend of different grape varieties. Authorities differ as to the exact recipe: that most commonly circulated

The north shore of Lake Balaton is one of Hungary's most important table-wine areas

is of 70 per cent Kadarka, 15–20 per cent Pinot Noir and 10–15 per cent Médoc Noir (Merlot), while other versions include Kékfrankos (Gamay), Cabernet and even Portugieser. Suffice it to say that the wine is generally harmonious and well-made, though its popularity at home and abroad means that it is generally drunk too young: old 'Bull's Blood' is a very different proposition, a wine of genuinely classic proportions, and one can readily understand how it fuelled the Magyar defenders to resist the assault in 1552 of the Turks under Ali Pasha (whence sprang that highly successful legend). The pure Kadarka of Eger is also worthy of note, racier than the Kadarkas of the plain and with more fruit, though here again some time in bottle is needed for it to reach maturity. The Kadarka is also used to make garnet-coloured rosés of the Siller type.

White wines account for over 60 per cent of the production around Eger and in the hill vineyards of the Bükkalya. Leányka, Wälschriesling and Mézesfehér are the most widely planted varieties: many of the best wines are dry, with an agreeable acidity resulting from the cool micro-climate of the hills, though the proximity of Tokay is seen in the more luscious dessert types which are also made. The volcanic tufa of the Bükk lends itself not only to the production of good quality wines but also the carving of extensive cellars: any visitors to Eger will remember the magnificent candle-lit galleries which lie under the town and honeycomb the surrounding hills. We will meet them again in Tokay.

Tokaj-Hegyalja

In considering the wines of this district, some 6,000 hectares in the far north-east of Hungary, we are dealing with the very stuff of which legends are made. Not even the leaden hand of the Hungarian State Monopoly has been able to stifle their past glories. Tokay (the spelling is anglicized from Tokaji) remains, as it has always been, one of the greatest (arguably the greatest) of the world's dessert wines. The district where this unique wine is made takes its name from the small town of Tokaj, past which flows the river Bodrog on its way to the Danube and the sea. It is a pleasant rural landscape, with vineyards rising from the river valley towards the wooded foothills of the Carpathians, and dotted with villages of which some twenty-nine are entitled to the Tokay denomination. The soil is volcanic, with a topsoil of decayed lava and loess: vital components in the making of Tokay, together with the temperate micro-climate, characterized by hot dry summers and long misty autumns. These are ideal conditions for botrytis to form on the grapes and draw off their water content, leaving a rich concentration of grape sugars and the perfect foundation for a natural dessert wine.

The grape varieties grown in the district are another indispensable part of the Tokay formula. There are three of them, all of which find near perfect conditions and realize their fullest potential. The first, and by far the most important, is the Furmint, a yellowish, thick-skinned variety, particularly prone to botrytis; next in proportion comes the Hárslevelü, whose juice is naturally sweeter and less acidic than that of the Furmint, and thirdly, contributing aroma and flavour, comes the Yellow Muscat (Sárgamuskotály).

If nature provides an ideal environment and raw materials for the making of Tokay, it is man who discovered the process which makes it unique, probably no earlier than the seventeenth century although vines had been grown here from earliest times. This process (I am referring here to the making of Tokay Aszú, since there are other types of Tokay) involves, firstly, the separation at harvest time of overripe grapes, affected by botrytis, from those grapes which have a normal ripeness and sugar content, and the subsequent addition to the fermenting must of measured quantities of a paste made from the first category, depending on the

Rozaki vines growing in the region of Heraklion in central Crete

degree of sweetness to be attained. Several factors make this system exclusive to Tokay, not least the traditional wine-making equipment and the measuring systems which are among its more colourful traditions.

The first of the special features of Tokay is the *puttony* (in the plural, *puttonyos*), a wooden receptacle containing some thirty-five litres. The uses of *puttonyos* are twofold. During the vintage, they are used to keep the overripe grapes separate from the remainder. Later, during vinification, they are used either in theory or in practice as a measure, as described below.

The paste made from overripe grapes is known as *aszú*: the same word in German is *Ausbruch*, which we found in the Austrian Burgenland (e.g. 'Ruster Ausbruch' see page 405). This paste is trodden carefully in order not to crush the pips and thereby add unwanted tannins to the must: machines have been developed to do this, though the human foot still produces the most satisfactory results. The paste is then added to the 'normal' must in proportions measured in *puttonyos* to ferment in open vats. After a pre-determined period, the mixture is then filtered and transferred to small wooden casks called *gönci* (each *gönc* contains only 140 litres, compared to a Bordeaux hogshead of 225) to continue a slow fermentation and maturation over several years (five or six is the norm). The *gönci* are left unbunged, and an ullage forms with evaporation: on the exposed surface of the wine there soon appears a thin film of fungus, not unlike the 'flor' of Jerez, which reduces the rate of oxidation, gives the wine a characteristic nutty flavour and if anything concentrates its rich natural aromas. There are several different types of Tokay, of which the four principal, in ascending order of quality, rarity and price are listed below.

Tokay Furmint: This Tokay must come to many 'first purchasers' as a disappointment, as its only resemblance to the 'real', dessert Tokay is in its basic flavour. It is a heavy, full-bodied table wine, made from the principal Tokay grape variety: it may be either dry or medium sweet.

Tokay Szamorodni: The suffix 'Szamorodni' means 'as it was grown', or in more popular parlance 'just as it comes'. It is made from grapes from which no selection of *aszú* berries has been made, and may therefore be either sweet or dry, depending on the nature of the vintage. Apart from the absence of sweetening *puttonyos*, the method of production is as described above.

Tokay Aszú: This is the style of Tokay which one most commonly associates with the term. It is made, as we have seen, by the addition during fermentation to the normal must (in which, incidentally, a proportion of grape stalks are included during the maceration to give additional 'backbone') of *puttonyos* of *aszú* paste, which in theory may range from one to six in number. In practice, the usual blends contain three, four or five *puttonyos*, the last obviously producing the richest wine of the three: it is composed, in fact, of a greater proportion of *aszú* paste (5 × 35 litres = 175 litres) than normal must (maximum 140 litres). The alcoholic percentage of Tokay Aszú will obviously vary according to the number of *puttonyos*, but is normally between 13 and 15 per cent. The taste of Tokay Aszú is evocatively described by Hugh Johnson in *The World Atlas of Wine*: '. . . a silky texture, a haunting fragrance and flavour of mingled fruit and butter and caramel and the breath of the Bodrog among October vines'. Its brilliant amber colour well seen through the white glass, Tokay Aszú, like Szamorodni and Eszencia, is sold in characteristic 'ninepin' bottles of half a litre: a perfect size, in fact, for a small dinner party of four to six, where a single glass is a perfect, uncloying complement to fruit or a rich dessert.

Tokay Aszú is not made every year, since the visitations of botrytis are as irregular here as they are in Sauternes or the Rhineland; neither can it be made throughout the Tokay area, since only vineyards of a certain altitude have the necessary combination of humidity and exposure. These very difficulties, and the limitations they impose upon its production, account for the esteem in which it is held worldwide.

Tokay Essence (Escenzia/Essencia/Eszencia): This is the purest and rarest form of Tokay, in past centuries reserved for the deathbeds of princes and the royal tables of Europe, and renowned for its miraculous restorative properties. Louis XIV described it as the 'Wine of Kings and King of Wines', and troops of Cossacks were employed solely to escort convoys of the precious liquid to the courts of the Tsars at St Petersburg. With such a history, it is hardly surprising that the true 'Essence' is now too rare and too expensive to be marketed commercially: the 'Essence' of modern vintages is basically *aszú*, with a small proportion of Essence in the blend, but the occasional bottle of the genuine elixir still appears at auction, and attracts willing buyers from all over the world. Tokay Essence is the juice of the *aszú* berries which leaks naturally from the grapes in the *puttonyos* or on the collecting table as they wait to be crushed into paste. The liquid, released simply by the natural pressure of the heaped-up grapes, is so rich in sugar that its fermentation will take years and will in all probability never be completed. 'Essence' is an entirely accurate description, for in this juice is concentrated all the aroma, fruit, flavour, character and pungency of Tokay. Each *puttony* will produce perhaps a litre, perhaps two, rarely more than this: a precious commodity indeed.

CZECHOSLOVAKIA

One does not associate Czechoslovakia with wine. The Czechs are primarily beer drinkers: Pilsen, after all, has become a sort of 'super appellation' for lager beer. But there are Czech wines to be found, and good ones too, though the Czechs consume more than they produce and in consequence few of them are seen abroad.

Many of the countries covered in this chapter are what might be described as 'agglomerates', states made up of a number of smaller components, each with its own cultural and ethnic roots. Czechoslovakia, an autonomous state only since 1918, is a prime example: its three provinces, Bohemia, Moravia and Slovakia, have their own quite individual and distinct traditions, in wine-making as in all other respects. Bohemia, in the north and west of the country, including within its borders the old Sudetenland with its tragic memories of the 1930s, looks to Germany as a guide. Moravia, in the centre, looks (metaphorically) south to the Austrian Weinviertel, while the easternmost province, Slovakia, a heartland of the old Hapsburg empire, looks south and east to what was once called Austro-Hungary.

Although some acceptable reds are made in one area of Bohemia, it is fair to summarize that the best Czech wines are white, and produced from the same, predominantly 'aromatic', varieties that one finds throughout this quarter of Europe: Riesling (both the classic Rheinriesling and its workhorse cousin, the worthy Wälschriesling – known in Czechoslovakia as the 'Vlassky' Ryzling), Müller-Thurgau, Sylvaner, Traminer, Ruländer (Pinot Gris), Sauvignon (or 'Muscat Sylvaner') and (Grüner) Veltliner. Leaving political geography aside, Czech wine-growing is dominated, as so often happens, by the country's river system: the Elbe, Danube and Morava all have a crucial role to play.

As far as viticultural practice is concerned, Czechoslovakia is close enough to Röhrendorf for the teachings of Lenz Moser to have taken root, and the majority of vineyards are transferring progressively to the high-culture system, more suited to mechanical cultivation. Sadly, as an erstwhile marketing man, I have to record that such wine-labels as I have seen of Czech origin have been uniformly drab and have done little justice to their contents: but then, this is a criticism that can be levied against most of the Eastern European countries, where marketing is not an important part of life, and good wine, as the saying goes, needs no bush in any case.

BOHEMIA

Thirty-two kilometres north of the Czech capital, Prague, the river Vltava joins the Elbe on its long journey to the Hamburg estuary. This confluence, at Mělník, marks the centre of the main Bohemian wine district: Litoměřice and Roudnice are the other main towns. Climatic conditions here are not unlike those of the German Rheinland, which lies on the same parallel, and the best wines are white, with Riesling, Müller-Thurgau, Traminer and Chardonnay predominating. Further south, from Mělník to the south of Prague, is the area specializing in red wines, made from 'Blauburgunder' (Pinot Noir), Blau Portugieser and St Laurent. Bohemian wines are generally of good quality (a visit to one of the cellars under the Hradčany citadel in Prague will confirm this), but production is relatively small and accounts for only a fraction of the national total. Sparkling wines are also made.

MORAVIA

The Moravian vineyard extends to some 12,000 hectares (compared to less than 400 in the whole of Bohemia), and may be divided into three main zones lying to the south and east of Brno: Znojmo-Mikulov, which lies along the border with Austria, Hustopeče-Hodonín a little further to the east, and a small area, Bzenec-Strážnice, to the north-east, a hilly zone noted for its romantic castles. White wines predominate, with the pronounced acidity and slightly sour finish so prized across the Austrian border: Rheinriesling, Weissburgunder (Pinot Blanc) and Traminer are among the best. Red wines are made from the same varieties as in Bohemia, plus some local variants known as the Neuberger (from Austria) and Frankovka.

SLOVAKIA

This is by some way the most prolific of the three provinces, producing some 70 per cent of the national total. The principal zone, around the towns of Modra and Pezinok a few kilometres to the north-east of Bratislava, extends to the slopes of the 'Little Carpathians', while other zones centre on the Danube plain around Nové Zámky and Hurbanovo, Skalica on the upper Morava, and Hlohovec – Trnava to the north-east. Finally, meriting a separate mention on its own, is a prestigious outpost in the far south-east corner of the country around Malá Trňa, which makes very acceptable Tokay.

I have mentioned that Slovakia looks to Austria and Hungary for its inspiration: perhaps Germany should be included too, as the most widely-planted grape (some 20 per cent of the total) is now Müller-Thurgau. From Austria comes the pattern for its light, crisp white wines and fruity, faintly bitter reds which together form the greater part of Slovakian production, but the influence on the making of 'Tokay' is of course of purely Hungarian origins, as are the grapes grown in this district (Furmint, Hárslevelű and Muscat).

Czechoslovakia now produces annually some 1.5 million hectolitres from a total vineyard area of 42,000 hectares; figures which are far from negligible. On the East European pattern, most wine-making is in the hands of state-owned cooperatives, which leads to a certain uniformity of quality, though at a respectable level. In every sense the country stands at a crossroads, open to influence from all points of the compass: the potential for experimentation and improvement is consequently considerable, and subject only to the maintenance of that political stability which has always proved such a precarious commodity.

RUMANIA

Rumania is a rich country, in terms of both human and natural resources: the latter include generous mineral deposits and the oilfields of Ploeşti, while as a people the Rumanians are energetic, resourceful and outward-looking, with strong historical and cultural affinities with the 'Romance' peoples of Western Europe. The potential for making good wines is considerable, and well on the way to realization with enthusiastic backing from the state: unlike its southern neighbour Bulgaria, however, where the wine industry has been completely 'collectivized' (with obvious success), state participation in Rumania accounts for less than a quarter of national production, with large local cooperatives accounting for the major share and personal holdings for the remainder.

The geography of this large, francophile country is dominated by two main features: the great, knee-shaped sweep of the Carpathians and Transylvanian Alps enclosing a high plateau to the west (the province of Transylvania), and the broad plains of Wallachia and Moldavia, the provinces to the south and east, through which the rivers Danube and Prutul flow towards the Black Sea. Its climate is 'continental', with soaring summer temperatures and bitter winters, softened only to a modest extent by the proximity of the Black Sea. It has a wide range of soils, alluvial and sandy in the east, stony and better drained in the environs of the Carpathian massif: a diversity well suited to experimentation and improvement, under the leadership of the state research stations and technical institutes of Dealul Mare, north of Bucharest, and Murfatlar near the Black Sea coast.

Producing an annual total in excess of 7 million hectolitres, the Rumanian vineyards are distributed widely throughout the country, with the majority of zones specializing, for reasons of their particular soil, climate and exposure, in the production of either red, white or dessert wines.

TRANSYLVANIA: NORTH-WEST RUMANIA

Western and north-western Rumania is composed of the eastern end of the great Hungarian (or Pannonian) plain, known as the Banat, and the high plateau of Transylvania, ringed by the Carpathians.

The Banat: The area of Arad and Timişoara produces both red and white wines, the former superior in quality, the latter in quantity. Grapes grown here are Cabernet, Merlot and, primarily, Cadarca (the Hungarian Kadarka) for red wines, and the ubiquitous Fetească for white wines, which are light and dry.

Tîrnave: This is one of the best areas in Rumania for white wines, developed comparatively recently; it takes its name from the River Tîrnave. The soil is predominantly sandstone, well-suited to the growing of aromatic varieties such as Wälschriesling, Traminer, Muskat Sylvaner (Sauvignon) and Muskat Ottonel, as well as two varieties of Fetească, Alba and Regala. A successful blend of these varieties is known as Perla, one of the Rumanian wines most commonly exported. The Ruländer (Pinot Gris) is also grown. Many wines of the area are produced with some sweetness, balanced by an agreeable acidity.

A little to the south of the main Tîrnave vineyards is the area of Alba-Iulia. The soil here is heavier, and the wines correspondingly so.

MOLDAVIA: NORTH-EAST RUMANIA

Rumanian Moldavia is the 'rump' of the large former province of Bessarabia, of which the greater part now lies in the USSR. Its most important area is still a name to conjure with:

Cotnari: On the eastern foothills of the Carpathians, on the other side of the range from Tîrnave, the Cotnari vineyards produce a rich dessert wine in the image, if without quite the complexity of, Tokay. It is made from a variety which the Rumanians call Crasă, which most authorities believe to be either Furmint, or a very close relation. We may safely pass over the argument as to whether the Hungarian or the Rumanian strain is the original one: the white of Cotnari is one of the classic wines of the world, with a natural harmony and distinctive flavour.

Focşani: Rumania's largest vineyard area follows the sweep of the Carpathians north of the Dealul Mare into southern Moldavia, overlooking the Wallachian plains, the valley of the River Siret and the Danube delta. The soil and exposure vary widely, from limestone on the upper slopes to loess and sand on the plain, and the wines themselves are correspondingly diverse: the area is also a centre of production for table grapes, particularly around Panciu, with the Chasselas Doré predominating.

   Though the zone takes its name from the town of Focşani, better known in the wine world are the names of Coteşti, Odobeşti and Nicoreşti. The first of this mellifluous trinity makes both red and white wines, with Pinot Noir, Merlot and Cabernet Sauvignon among the best of the reds, and Wälschriesling, Fetească and Muscat among the whites. I have also tasted an excellent Ruländer (Pinot Gris) from Coteşti. Odobeşti, in the centre of the region, is best known for white wines, with Traminer, Furmint and Aligoté to be added to the list found at Coteşti. Nicoreşti, to the east of the Siret, is renowned for red wines, particularly the Băbească Neagră, a local speciality: full bodied, faintly herbal with a good acidic bite, this is a wine of distinct and individual character.

WALLACHIA (SOUTHERN RUMANIA) AND THE DOBRUDJA

The loss of Bessarabia was an ill wind that blew some good to Rumania, for it provided the stimulus which led to the development of new vineyards, and to the expansion of old, traditional sites in a wide band to the south and east of the Carpathians, and inland from the port of Constanţa on the Black Sea coast. Today these vineyards account for the major proportion of Rumanian production. There are some five areas of note:

Sadova and Segarcea: East of the Iron Gates the Danube flows sedately through a sandy plain. A small area in the region of the two named towns, relic of a larger area ravaged by phylloxera in the 1880s, makes good red wines from Cabernet Sauvignon and Pinot Noir. Sadova is best known for its semi-sweet rosé.

Drăgăşani: This compact area lies midway between the Danube plain and the Transylvanian Alps, overlooking the valley of the River Oltul. Though some good red wines are made from Cabernet Sauvignon, Pinot Noir and native varieties such as Băbească Neagră and Negru Virtos, the best of the area are aromatic whites made, *inter alia*, from Sauvignon, Muskat Ottonel and a spicy local variant of the Muscat known as Tămîioasa. Often medium-sweet and occasionally a little short of acidity, these wines are agreeable and have character.

Argeş and Piteşti: Argeş with its main town, Piteşti, lies in the shadow of the Transylvanian Alps. Conditions and grape varieties grown are similar to Drăgăşani, but with greater emphasis on white wines. The Fetească Regala is the predominant variety, followed by the aromatic varieties listed in the previous paragraph. One of Rumania's many experimental stations is located here, at Stefaneşti.

Dealul Mare: This covers one of the most favoured sites in Rumania: the south-eastern slopes of the Carpathians, along which the vines extend for some sixty-four kilometres. Wines of high alcohol and heavy extract are easily attained here as a result of the excellent, south-facing exposure, and for Western tastes, this is some-times carried to excess. The best, most balanced wines are produced either from vineyards on the higher slopes, or under state supervision from experimental vine-yards such as the Valea Călugărească (Valley of the Monks); this latter site, rich in trace elements, produces some of Rumania's most prestigious red wines from the classic varieties of Cabernet Sauvignon, Cabernet Franc, Merlot and Pinot Noir. If these wines occasionally lack subtlety, they make up for it in overall roundness and harmony. Much the same applies to the white wines of the area, predominantly from Wälschriesling, Ruländer and Fetească (Regala) varieties: more popular on the home market are the heavier styles made from Grasă and Tămîioasa.

Dobrudja: Lies in the far south-east of Rumania. It is one of the oldest vineyard sites in Europe (wine was produced here for at least seven centuries BC), neatly defined by the Danube on two flanks and by the Black Sea coast to the east, which combine to form an 'island' of vines with a tradition all of its own. The vineyard extends to some 1,000 hectares, planted on a limestone plateau with good south-easterly ex-posure and tempered by the coastal micro-climate; at its centre lies the town of Murfatlar, which gives its name to a heavy, Muscat dessert wine much appreciated in Rumania. To Western tastes, the most promising wines of the Dobrudja are the white Chardonnays, and those made from classic aromatic varieties such as Pinot Gris, Muscat and Sauvignon. The first-named, in particular, have proved a most successful introduction, and I have been present on at least one occasion when expert tasters have placed 'blind' samples unhesitatingly into Burgundy. Red wines are also made here, the best from Cabernet Sauvignon, Merlot and Pinot Noir. The young plantations in the Dobrudja are but one example of the enormous strides which are being taken in Rumania to modernize and improve the wine industry. As with Bulgaria, the potential for improved exports is enormous and we can expect to see more Rumanian wines on our shelves in the 1980s.

BULGARIA

Wine-making in Bulgaria is both old and new: old, because ancient Thrace (part of which falls within the borders of modern Bulgaria) is where wine-making in Europe began, and new, because the modern, state-controlled wine industry of today is only some thirty years old. In between, accounting for some five hundred years of Bulgarian history to which the skylines of Sofia and of most other Bulgarian cities bear witness, came occupation by the Turks to whom wine is one of life's forbidden pleasures. Bulgaria achieved a state of semi-independence in 1878, but no real stability until the end of the Second World War.

The wines of Bulgaria are interesting and diverse, but not particularly easy to describe because one is forced to rely on names which are far from familiar. For the very same reason it is easy to make them sound more diverse than they really are! To some extent, therefore, I intend to stress their similarities to wines with which the average reader will hopefully be more familiar, though this is far from suggesting that the many wines of this enterprising and complex country do not each have a distinctive character of their own.

The Vineyard Areas

Just as Spain is a 'satisfying' country on a map, with its capital where it ought to be, at the centre, Bulgarian geography is comparatively simple, at least as far as the 'bones' of the country are concerned. It has five features of importance: two mountain ranges, two rivers and a coastline (such a gross simplification will suffice for our purposes). The two mountain ranges are, respectively, the Stara Planina, which runs west to east and bisects the country for most of its length (known also as the Balkan Mountains), and the great massif of the Rhodope, which covers the whole of the country's south-western corner. The two rivers are the Danube, which acts as the northern border with Rumania for much of its length, dominates this part of the landscape and governs its micro-climate, and the Maritsa which flows south-east towards the Aegean, creating a fertile plain between the two great mountain masses. The coastline, finally, is the Bulgarian shore of the Black Sea, whose wine-growing hinterland benefits from its special form of micro-climate. The groupings of the Bulgarian vineyards around these five salient features are more complex to describe, but the latter will serve as points of orientation. There are some nine zones, of which the most significant are:

North of the Balkan Mountains: Here, between the Yugoslav border and the River Yantra, are several large areas devoted to production of red wines, which will be described in a later section. They are named after their principal towns which include Pleven, Turnovo, Sukhindol and Lyaskovets.

The Upper Maritsa Valley: A sizeable zone extends from Plovdiv (ancient Philippopolis) south and west along the Maritsa basin to the foothills of the Rhodope. This again is a red wine area, with the Mavrud wines of Asenovgrad being particularly reputed.

Melnik: A small enclave hidden beyond the Rhodope in the far south-west, making powerful red wines much regarded for their colour and concentration.

Stara Zagora and Slavyantsi: These adjoining areas at the south-eastern end of the Balkan Mountains mark the transition between the western uplands, specializing in the main in red wines, and the flatter country inland from the Black Sea, where large-scale production of white wines begins.

Eastern Bulgaria: A large zone bordered by the Danube to the north, the border with Turkey to the south, and the Black Sea to the east. There are no hills of any size in this zone, which is given over in the main to widely spaced rows of vines and mechanical cultivation. Production is almost exclusively of white wines, the vineyards benefiting from the temperate climate; the best of them are light and dry, whereas in other districts there is a tendency towards the heavier, sweeter styles traditionally appreciated on the home market.

Vines and Wines

We are spared the necessity of further grappling with Bulgarian place names by the fact that Bulgaria's wines are in the main marketed by the name of the grape variety, or under recognizable brand names thoughtfully devised by the state export monopoly, Vinimpex. Often the grape names are qualified by the village or area of origin. The mastery of a short list of grape names, and of the types of wines they produce is, on the contrary, essential to an appreciation of the country's wines.

Red Wines

Mavrud: This is the most distinctive, and regarded by many authorities as the best of Bulgaria's red wines. From those I have tasted, I would agree with the former judgment, if perhaps no longer with the latter. The Mavrud is a native variety, producing a dark, gutsy wine with a tannic edge: a *vin de garde* certainly. The best sources of Mavrud lie south of the Balkan Mountains, particularly in the Maritsa basin.

Gamza: Another native variety (probably a relation of the Kadarka), this is the most widely grown red variety. The wine it produces is lighter and fruitier than the Mavrud, agreeable when young but rather prone to oxidation. The best regions for Gamza lie in the north of the country.

Kadarka: Among the best known of the Balkan varieties, usually associated with Hungary. The Kadarka makes a dark, aromatic red of distinctive character.

Cabernet: Samples I have tasted of Bulgarian Cabernet (both Cabernet Sauvignon and Cabernet Franc are grown, in relatively new plantations) suggest that this is the red wine of the future, where Mavrud is that of the past. These wines, if occasionally lacking a little backbone, are often well-balanced and stylish, with fine varietal flavour.

White Wines

Dimiat: Either the same as, or a close relation to, the Serbian Smederevka and to the West European Chasselas, this is the workhorse of the white varieties; widely planted, it produces a rather neutral dry wine of no particular finesse. It is also grown for table grapes, and for distillation.

Misket: The most distinctive of the native wines, this is made from a variety of red Muscat which produces a full-bodied, heavily scented dry wine of character. Sometimes a little clumsy by comparison, it is not too far removed from the dry Muscats of Alsace. The best Misket comes from Karlovo, the 'Valley of the Roses' (where musk roses are grown for the making of attar), under the southern slopes of the Balkan Mountains, and from Sungurlare near Slavyantsi.

Rcatsitelli: A grape of Russian origin, this produces an attractive but rather neutral white wine in the coastal region. It can be dry or sweet.

Chardonnay: My personal view is that this is the white wine of the future, as Cabernet is the red. Of comparatively recent introduction, the Chardonnays produced from large plantations in the coastal region are most impressive: firm, well-balanced wines of considerable extract and character, and the distinctive flavour of this classic variety.

Other Wines: A number of other white varieties are grown in Bulgaria, including the ubiquitous Wälschriesling, Sylvaner (another recent success story), the Hungarian Furmint and the Rumanian Fetească. Tamianka is a heavy, sweet dessert wine made in Stara Zagora. An adequate rosé wine called Pamid is made in the Plovdiv area, attractive when fresh. Sparkling wines are also popular, being generally found under the brand names Perla and Iskra. With the fascinating strawberry wine of Berkovitsa, we are probably straying beyond the scope of this book.

Branded Wines

Unlike many of their East European counterparts, the Bulgarians were quick to recognize the difficulties presented by Cyrillic script (they share this 'problem' with the USSR) and unfamiliar regional names to the proper development of export markets. Apart from the USSR, the most important of these has traditionally been West Germany, and for this reason the majority of the brand names they devised have a Germanic ring to them. Here is a brief list:

Donau Perle: Dry white from north-eastern Bulgaria, based on Fetească.
Sonnenküste: A blended wine from the Black Sea, based on Dimiat and Rcatsitelli.
Rosenthaler Riesling: A blend of Rhein' and Wälschriesling from Karlovo.

Euxinograd: A blend of aromatic white varieties, again from the Black Sea.
Hemus: Perhaps the best known, a sweet Misket from Karlovo.

The 'special relationship' between Germany and Bulgaria has been very much a two-way affair. German influence is clearly to be seen in cellar techniques and equipment, and in the gradual transfer of emphasis, in the making of white wines in particular, from the heavy, sweet dessert types formerly appreciated in the Balkans, to the lighter, fresher styles consumed in Western Europe. Providing that the trend continues, we are certain to see more Bulgarian wines in our Western markets.

USSR

The vineyards of the USSR, extending in a broad arc from the Rumanian border in the west to the shores of the Caspian Sea, and in scattered plantations eastwards to Samarkand and beyond, today account for over 10 per cent of the world's total acreage under vine, and their production, some 32 million hectolitres, places the USSR third in the volume table after Italy and France. It has not always been so: the growth of the wine industry in the USSR since the end of the Second World War has been nothing short of dramatic, spurred on by governmental determination to satisfy the prodigious Russian thirst with a national beverage less potent than vodka. Indeed, if growth were to continue at the post-war rate, it would not be long before the USSR became the biggest wine-producer in the world. Inevitably, in the process, some concessions have been made to the principle of quantity before quality, though there is evidence to suggest that the latter in general is improving, particularly under the enlightened influence of Rumania.

The Russians have a decidedly sweet tooth, and their wine-making techniques are very largely devoted to the production of sweet wines. The same preference is seen in viticulture; although the classic grape varieties of Western Europe are increasingly in evidence, the aim behind their introduction is the improvement of the sweet wines into which they are made or blended. Every style of wine is made, from still table wines through sparkling (accounting for a high percentage of production) to dessert types, often, with a cavalier disregard for Western legislation, labelled under the descriptions 'Port', 'Madeira' etc.

Production of wine in any of the southern republics of the USSR is not without its difficulties, the principal one being that of climate. For example, Moldavia, at the western extreme, suffers from torrential rainstorms (and consequent soil erosion), hail and frequent late frosts, while in the vineyards further east the winter temperatures are so cold (often below $-30°C$) that the vines need special insulation. Baking summers in the southerly latitudes make irrigation a necessity.

The vine is planted in eleven of the Soviet republics. East of the Caspian sea, in the remote provinces to the north of the Hindu Kush and Himalayas, production is mainly of dried and table grapes, and the main wine belt lies in the west around the northern and eastern shores of the Black Sea. From west to east, the wine-producing republics are Moldavia, with some 4.3 million hectolitres of wine per annum, Ukraine with 4.7 million hectolitres, Russia with 10.8 million hectolitres, Georgia with 1.7 million hectolitres, Armenia with 0.9 million hectolitres, and finally Azerbaijan on the Caspian with some 1.6 million hectolitres. Together these republics account for over 80 per cent of the total.

MOLDAVIA

This former province of Rumania produces the most 'western' of Soviet wines, and influence from across the border is evident both in the choice of grape varieties and the wines they produce. Prominent among the white varieties, for example, is the Fetească, the traditional backbone of Rumanian white wines, which in Moldavia produces one of the better dry wines of the USSR; often rather neutral and austere, but clean and refreshing nevertheless. Other white grape varieties grown in Moldavia include the Aligoté, Sauvignon, Traminer, Riesling (both Rhein- and Wälsch), Muscat and the indigenous Rcatsitelli. Most of the wines are made with at least 15 or 20 g/l of residual sugar (about as sweet as the average Liebfraumilch), though the proportion of drier wines is higher here than elsewhere.

Good red wines are also made in Moldavia and plantations of Cabernet Sauvignon, Merlot and Malbec are on the increase; in the zone of Romănești (Romanovka), these three varieties are used in combination to produce an above average red of the same name. Another good Moldavian red is Negru de Purkar, blended from the same three varieties with an addition of Saperavi and Rara Neagra.

The warmer climate of southern Moldavia provides a centre for dessert wine production, particularly along the lower reaches of the Dniester. Place names of note are Chumay (or Ciumaj) which produces an unlikely sweet red made from Cabernet and Grifesti (a Muscat-type sweet white).

UKRAINE AND THE CRIMEA

Production in the Ukraine is centred on three main zones. The first two, the coastal region south of the Dnieper and the eastern foothills of the Carpathians, are important only from the point of view of quantity; the third, in the central and southern Crimea, is one of the oldest centres of wine production in the USSR and is reputed to make the country's finest wines, particularly of the dessert type.

The vineyards of the Crimea lie in the hills around Simferopol, and in a long strip along the sunny, sheltered coastal riviera from Sevastopol to Feodosiya. The best-known name in the Crimea is Massandra, a former estate belonging to the Princes Vorontsov of the Tsarist era, which is now applied to the wines produced by a number of state cooperatives, mainly of the dessert type: the best of these are the amber-coloured Muscatels, which are one of the few wines of the USSR that are commonly exported. Sevastopol and Balaclava are centres of sparkling wine production: Kaffia is reputedly the best of these. Other Crimean wines of note are:

Livadia Muscat: Good sweet Muscatel.
Chërnyi or Chorny Doktor: A rich, red dessert wine from a zone known as 'The Valley of the Sun' (Solnechnaya Dolina). *Chërnyi* means black, e.g. also Chërniye Glaza (Black Eyes), a wine of similar style from the Russian republic.
Ay-Danil: One of the former Vorontsov estates, today a wider description for sweet white dessert wines.

RUSSIA

So often used as a synonym for the whole vast confederation, the Soviet republic of Russia forms the eastern coastline of the Sea of Azov. Its borders contain three major zones of production: the area around Rostov on the lower Don, which produces red, white and sparkling wines principally from indigenous grape varieties, and a rather more important area between Anapa and the port of Novorossiysk on the Black Sea coast and the city of Krasnodar inland. A third area, devoted to the production of dessert wines, will be considered with Azerbaijan. The second area described above is particularly noteworthy in that, apart from some good quality sparkling wines, it produces some sound dry table wines of styles more likely to appeal to Western tastes. The best of these are the Riesling and Cabernet from Anapa. Other Western grape varieties grown here are Aligoté, Sauvignon, Sémillon, Pinot Noir and Pinot Gris.

GEORGIA

Georgia enjoys a southerly latitude, protection from the winds and cold of the steppes by the great massif of the Caucasus, and a reputation for the quality of its wines equal only to that of the Crimea. Most of its vineyards lie in the broad valley of the river Rion in Central Georgia, which enjoys a particularly favourable micro-climate: hot summers and relatively mild, rainy winters. Georgia is particularly famous for its sparkling wines, often (as in other parts of the USSR) labelled in liberal fashion as Champanski. The Georgian capital, Tbilisi (Tiflis) is one of the centres of production. Pinot Noir and Chardonnay are among the varieties grown for base wines. East of Tbilisi are vineyards specializing in still wines, of which the Saperavi and Mukuzani are reputedly the best of the reds, and Tsinandali and Napareuli of the whites. The zone of Kakhetiya is particularly noted, and Cabernet Sauvignon is among the varieties planted. Eastern Georgia is the homeland of the white Rcatsitelli variety, which nowadays appears all around the shores of the Black Sea, and another native variety known as the Mtsvane: they both make rather heavy, neutral white wines, which vary from dry to sweet.

ARMENIA

This mountainous republic, bordering Turkey and Iran, is a centre of dessert wine production. Many of its vineyards lie within sight of Mount Ararat, whence Noah may once precariously have prospected for a suitable site; it is certain that the origins of viticulture here are ancient indeed, though the climate is one of extremes and the landscape rugged. Irrigation is widely used to improve yields. Grape varieties grown in Armenia include Verdelho and Sercial, Aligoté and Muscat, as well as a range of local varieties of which the most important is Voskheat: this last named produces a good quality wine of the sherry type known as Ashtarak. Other wines produced here do carry a distant resemblance to the 'Port' and 'Madeira' after which they are named, even if the labelling itself is to be deprecated. Armenia is also one of the main centres of brandy production in the USSR.

AZERBAIJAN

This, the final republic of our survey, lies south of the Caucasus on the western shore of the Caspian. As in neighbouring Armenia, and in the south-eastern zones of the Russian republic around Makhachkala and Derbent, the concentration is once again on dessert wines, of all shades from green-gold to mahogany. Most of the grape varieties grown here are indigenous, with the Rcatsitelli at their head, though since the area under vine is rapidly increasing one may expect to see a growing proportion of Western strains. Few of these wines are seen outside the USSR, though Matras and Shemakh from the region of Kyurdamir and Shemakha enjoy a high reputation on the home market.

   Although, as we have seen, the vineyards east of the Caspian, in the republics of Turkmenistan, Kazakhstan, Uzbekistan and Kirgizistan, are mainly devoted to purposes other than the production of wine, they may well assume a more important role in the future. Plantations in these areas have increased substantially in recent years, and with irrigation a standard practice the potential is enormous. In conclusion, however, it must be said that the many wines of the USSR remain of mainly academic interest to us in the West: a situation which is unlikely to change.

GREECE

The origins of wine-making in Greece are a colourful blend of the mythical with the historical. Virtually all the great writers of the classical period have something revealing to say on the subject, though few with more good sense than the 'father of medicine', Hippocrates, who commented some twenty-five centuries ago that 'wine is wonderfully wholesome for man in sickness and in health, provided that it is taken at the right time and in the right quantity to suit individual needs.' It is a little-appreciated historical fact that the glories of classical Greece were very largely financed by profitable exports of wine (and oil) to the Mediterranean world, a trade which after centuries of comparative inactivity (and, it must in fairness be added, of Turkish occupation) now shows promising signs of revival, for Greece is putting her house in order in thorough and enterprising fashion. With accession to the EEC in 1981, and her growing awareness of the needs of export markets, the potential for Greek wines abroad is developing fast.

The vineyards of modern Greece extend to nearly 200,000 hectares, of which only just over half produce wine; the balance provide table grapes and raisins. They are to be found throughout the Greek mainland and islands, from Macedonia and Thrace in the north, where the traditions lean towards the Balkans, to Crete and Rhodes at the mouth of the Aegean where the influence is that of the Levant. Soils vary between chalk, rock and tufa, generally poor and providing the necessary challenge for vines to flourish. Most of the Greek vineyards lie within zones moderated by the close proximity of the sea, tempering the extreme heat of summer and that extraordinary luminosity of light which is the country's famous asset.

Greek wines fall for administrative purposes under three main headings: 'own label' wines (a term used to describe the 'branded' blends marketed by such leading companies as Achaia Clauss and Andrew Cambas, with 'Demestica' at their head); 'country wines' (a category which one is unlikely to see on export markets, being in the main reserved for strictly local consumption); and finally 'typical wines', some twenty-five of which have controlled denominations and are subject to governmental guarantees. These latter, the highest quality grade of Greek wines, are easily recognized by the paper band with maroon serial numbers which forms a seal across the cork. To this three-tiered structure must be added one general class of wines, 'Kokkineli', which is the Greek term for rosé (often quite deep in colour) and a special category: Retsina.

Retsina: Impossible in any circumstances to ignore, Retsina has its critics and its devotees; both would agree that it is one of the most distinctive wines of the world though, sadly, it has probably discouraged many people from further exploration of the wines Greece has to offer. Retsina can be white or rosé, the major part being made from Savatiano and Rhoditis grapes. The best of it comes from the heartland of Greece, Attica (the region of Athens), Euboea and the Peloponnese, all regions where the Alep pine flourishes: it is resin from this tree, added to the must during fermentation and removed at the first racking, which provides the special flavour. It is a taste which has remained unchanged for at least 3,000 years, with its origins in the seal of mixed plaster and pine resin with which the ancients used to seal their winejars: cause and effect became confused, and the resin itself was at first believed quite erroneously to have a preservative effect. The discovery that the harshness of resinated wine provided a perfect match for oily Greek food must have followed later, but is certainly one of the main reasons for its continuing popularity today. It should be drunk cold. Metaxas, Achaia Clauss and Cambas all export very reliable examples. Courtakis Retsina is popular on the home market.

Our main consideration will be the Appellation of Origin wines which account for some 12 per cent of the country's total production of about 5 million hectolitres. This is the most interesting area for the amateur, even if branded wines will continue to dominate both the home and export markets as they have done hitherto.

THE PELOPONNESE

Exactly a third of the country's vineyards lie on this huge artificial island (divided from mainland Greece only by the Corinth Canal), but many of them produce only table grapes and raisins. Production of wine is just over 1 million hectolitres; it is the most important area in Greece, with at least three wines of international repute.

Mavrodaphne: Mavrodaphne is a rich, deep red dessert wine, strong in alcohol (around 15 per cent by volume) and sweet with unfermented grape sugar. After Retsina, it is probably the best known of Greek wines: unlike Retsina, it matures well, and needs several years in bottle to reach its best. I agree with Hugh Johnson's comparison of Mavrodaphne to the Recioto of Valpolicella. Mavrodaphne is also made on Cephalonia and other islands, but the best of it comes from Patras, at the north-western corner of the Peloponnese.

Patras: In addition to the Mavrodaphne, Patras gives its name to wines of other types. The Muscat of Patras is justly renowned: a rich, golden dessert wine with luscious bouquet and flavour. Other wines are in the main light and dry, made from the Rhoditis variety. Patras is the headquarters of the Achaia Clauss wine company, whose brands (Castel) Danielis (red), Santa Helena (white) and Santa Rosa (rosé), as well as the ubiquitous Demestica, are well known at home and abroad.

Nemea: This is one of Greece's finest red wines. Big, black, gutsy and tannic, it comes from an area near Corinth in the north-eastern Peloponnese. It is a hilly zone, with vineyards rising to nearly 900 metres. The grape variety here is the Agiorgitiko (the variety of St George).

Mantinia: Produced in the centre of the Peloponnese (Arcadia), this is a light, aromatic white wine made from the 'Moschofilero'.

CENTRAL GREECE

Central Greece is composed of the three provinces of Attica, Boeotia and Euboea (the last named being an island), which combined produce around 1.6 million hectolitres of wine per annum. It is predominantly white, made almost exclusively from the Savatiano grape (arguably the best of the native varieties), and destined for early consumption on the domestic market, much of it as Retsina for the Athenian tavernas. Some pleasant rosé is made from Rhoditis grapes, and light red from Mavroudi. A good dry white Hymettus is made from vineyards on the slopes of Mount Hymettus near Athens.

THE NORTH: THESSALY, MACEDONIA AND THRACE

These three northern provinces combine to produce some half a million hectolitres of wine per annum. The most noteworthy wine of Thessaly is Rapsani, a deep red wine made from a blend of local varieties grown on the slopes of Mount Olympus. Harsh in youth, it mellows to an agreeable softness with age. The higher rainfall and harsher climate which distinguish northern Greece from the rest of the country provide conditions well suited to the production of red wines of quality. Naoussa is the best known of these, a robust red of some finesse made from Xynomavro grapes grown on the hilly slopes of Mount Velia.

Phylloxera devastated the Naoussa vineyards in the early years of the twentieth century, and the vineyards, replanted and expanded, have an orderly look to them: a contrast with much of Greece, where vines sprawl haphazardly over open ground. Naoussa is one of the few Greek reds which does not have that characteristic 'baked earth' flavour that so many of them share: possibly as much a product of the climate as of careful vinification, though wine-making in this northern area is certainly in advance of the norm. The vineyards of Amynteon lie close to the borders of

Yugoslavia and Albania. This is another deep red, rather more astringent wine than Naoussa and less impressive, though still a wine of individual character.

THE WEST: EPIRUS AND THE IONIAN ISLANDS

Epirus produces only two wines of note: Zitsa, a fragrant semi-sparkling white, and Metsovo, where the Cabernet Sauvignon makes one of its very rare appearances in Greece: I have not (yet) found a sample to taste. Apart from the local wines appreciated by tourists in Corfu and the other islands, the main claims to fame of the western archipelago are the Mavrodaphne and Muscat of Cephalonia, and a strong, full-bodied dry white called Robola of Cephalonia after its native grape variety. The most reputed Robola is made by the Calligas company: I would rate it as one of Greece's finest white wines.

CRETE AND THE ISLANDS: THE AEGEAN, CYCLADES AND DODECANESE

Wines from the Greek islands account for around a fifth of the national total, Crete alone producing some 900,000 hectolitres every year. Monemvasia, a town in the Southern Peloponnese, has given its name to the style of wine which used to pass through its harbour to all corners of the Mediterranean world. The wine itself, known variously as Malvasia, Malvoisie, Malvagia and in the Duke of Clarence's homeland as Malmsey, was and still is produced in the islands, notably on Crete in the areas of Sitia and Daphnes, and on Naxos and Paros in the Cyclades. It is an amber, scented dessert wine, drunk locally as an apéritif and particularly agreeable when chilled. Crete is best known for its powerful red wines. Principal grape varieties are (Mavro) Romeiko, Kotsifali, Liatiko and Mandilari; Archanes and Peza are the two most reputed *appellations*, both from the region of Heraklion. The sweet Muscat of Samos has a worldwide reputation as being the finest of its type. The vineyards on this mountainous island, some 2,300 hectares, are devoted almost exclusively to its production, rising in narrow terraces from the plain to a height of some 800 metres on the mountain slopes. Harvesting, production and quality are all strictly controlled, and blending with other Muscat wines is forbidden. The typical Muscat of Samos is sweet and unfortified, though dry and fortified apéritif-type wines are also made from the same variety. Muscat wines are also produced on Lemnos which, from the point of view of wine production, is the only other island of significance in the Aegean group. Paros and Thera (Santorin), the two most important islands in the Cyclades, are swept by the violent 'Meltemi' winds of the Aegean. In self-defence they have developed a unique method of viticulture, whereby the vines are pruned in a basket shape, the grapes in the centre being protected by a wall of greenery. This system is not the only special feature of the stunningly beautiful island of Thera, whose cliffs rise 300 metres sheer from the sea. The combination of volcanic soils and a unique micro-climate produces wines with high natural alcohol (often up to 17 per cent), but with adequate acidity to match. The best of them are made from the white 'Assyrtiko' variety, and may be sweet or dry, the latter labelled 'Santorin', the former 'Santorin' or 'Vinsanto'. The largest of the Dodecanese, Rhodes produces a variety of wines of which the best are the dry whites grown in the north of the island around Embona, and some excellent Muscats of the Samos type. The dry white of Lindos is also pleasant.

Country wines

The 'Country Wines' of Greece are really too numerous to be catalogued here; a long list of names would seem to me to serve little purpose, and Virgil himself remarked that 'it would be easier to count grains of sand than the varieties of vines'. With the reflection that the best way to discover them is to travel in Greece (and what a marvellous excuse they provide), I will mention just a few of special merit:

Paros: Deep red, made from the Mandilari grape grown on this and many of the surrounding islands.
Santa Mavra: The local wine of Levkas, one of the Ionian islands. So dark it is almost opaque, it is made from the Vertzami grape.
Verdea: A 'green' (more properly yellow-green) wine from Zakinthos (Zante), off the western shore of the Peloponnese. A relation of the Verdelho found in other European vineyards.
Chalkidiki and Mount Athos: This trident-shaped promontory in northern Greece produces rich red wines from a variety known as Limnio, after the nearby island of Lemnos. Chalkidiki is also noteworthy as the site of the Carras estate: impressive model vineyards and an ultra-modern winery, created by an enlightened shipping millionaire to service his other creation, the 'Porto Carras' holiday village. The quality of the wines is excellent.

The many wines of Greece, at once bewildering in their variety and fascinating for their differences, will provide a happy hunting-ground for many of us in the 1980s.

CYPRUS

Wine has been made on Cyprus since the very beginnings of Mediterranean civilization: what is more, it has been made virtually without interruption, for although Cyprus, in common with many other European lands, spent a long period under Islamic rule, the rulers themselves were sufficiently enlightened to allow viticulture to continue, the first of them even rejoicing in the title of Sultan Selim the Sot! It is, perhaps, hardly surprising that even they should have been seduced by the beautiful birthplace of Aphrodite, and the wines once produced in her honour. Like lianas in an equatorial forest, the vineyards of Cyprus reach upwards for life: not, in their case, for light, but for the cooler temperatures and rainfall of the Troodos Mountains, which dominate the western end of the island. The baking plains to the north and east are unsuitable for vines, but the southern slopes of the Troodos provide ideal conditions for some 45,000 hectares of vines, often rising to the 900-metre contour and beyond.

In contrast to the complex local traditions which obtain among the Greek islands to the west, the pattern of viticulture on Cyprus is remarkably simple. There are, in effect, only three main grape varieties grown: the reason for this, apart from the innate conservatism of the growers, is the fact that Cyprus has hitherto succeeded in avoiding the depredations of phylloxera, and the introduction of new varieties to the island is only possible after the most rigorous selection, quarantine and trials. The three original varieties, still growing ungrafted, are respectively:

Mavron: This red variety (*mavro* actually means 'black') is by far the most widely grown and accounts for some 85 per cent of production.
Xynisteri: A white variety, accounting for some 10–15 per cent of the total production.
Muscat of Alexandria: Though only providing some 2–3 per cent of total production, the powerful scent and flavour of this Muscat variety announces its presence in a blend to an extent quite disproportionate to its volume.

The wines produced from these three varieties gained such a reputation in the early Middle Ages that there is a well-established tradition that cuttings from the vines were exported to Madeira, to Marsala in Sicily, and even to Tokay in Hungary. Cyprus produces over a million hectolitres of wine every year, the total being fairly constant in view of the predictable climate, and these fall into three main categories:

Cyprus Sherry: These wines have traditionally taken the lion's share of Cyprus's exports, though (at the time of writing) their future on the vital British market at least is rather uncertain in view of the United Kingdom's membership of the EEC, and the conflicting priorities this will continue to impose. Cyprus Sherry varies widely both in style and strength; for many years it was standard practice among British importers, for the savings that resulted, to ship sherries in bulk both at low and high strength and 'marry' them in this country after duty had been paid. The tendency in Cyprus today is towards production of higher strength wines more on the pattern of Jerez, though the low strength wines remain popular and are still, as yet, relatively inexpensive. As far as styles are concerned, Cyprus produces the whole spectrum from bone dry to lusciously sweet. For dry wines, experiments with *flor* yeast, the vital ingredient required for producing wines of *fino* style, have proved successful, and the principal sherry producers have built up *bodegas* and *solera* systems very much on the Spanish pattern. At the sweet end of the scale, grapes dried in the sun are used for the making of cream sherries, which often have an attractive hint of Muscat in the flavour; they are generally lighter in colour and texture than their counterparts from Spain, South Africa or Australia, and have a pleasantly fruity taste.

Commandaria: This most famous of Cypriot wines was given its name by the Knights Templar as long ago as the twelfth century: previously, it had been known locally as Nama. In 1363, at the Feast of the Five Kings at Vintners Hall in London, Commandaria was served in honour of the visiting King Peter I of Cyprus, and so won a special place in British wine-trade history. Commandaria is made from a blend of Mavron and Xynisteri grapes, which are dried in the sun to attain the maximum concentration of the natural grape sugars. Slow fermentation follows, and the result is a lusciously sweet, deep red or amber dessert wine of 25 per cent alcohol or more. For a wine with such a colourful past and reputation, the commercial Commandarias most commonly found on export markets tend often to disappoint: they are pleasant sweet wines, and no more. The true Commandaria is harder to discover, but the search brings its own rewards: as made in the mountain villages, some twenty of which, such as Zoopiyi, or Kalokhorio, are recognized as producing wines of the best quality, Commandaria is the uniquely concentrated, velvet wine of legend, often matured in earthenware amphorae clearly dating from medieval times. In the making of such wines as these, the proportion of white grapes in the blend is patently very small!

Light Wines: Cyprus produces a range of very acceptable red, white and rosé table wines which are widely exported. The Cypriot taste is for robust, tannic reds which are an excellent match for the local cuisine. The native Mavron variety is reputed to produce its best wines at Afames, a site in the Troodos near the village of Platres. Ophthalma and Maratheftika are other names to look for. Othello is a well-known brand on sale in the West. Cypriot rosés, like those in Greece, are known generically as Kokkineli. Made from the Mavron, they are generally quite full in colour, robustly alcoholic and never to be underestimated. Most rosés are dry, and are agreeable served chilled. The heat of the Cypriot climate, and the natural tendency of the Xynisteri to maderize, at once encourages the production of sherry-type wines and militates against the making of good natural table wines. Creditable dry white wines are made nevertheless, often quite yellow in colour, full-bodied and with the natural sugars fermented out to give a relatively high degree. Paphos is recognized as a centre of production. Aphrodite and Arsinoë are branded wines exported.

Wine production in Cyprus is very largely controlled by a handful of important firms, of which the most prominent are Keo, Sodap and Etko, incorporating Haggi-pavlu. Investment in new premises, equipment and technical expertise has been most impressive in recent years, and the quality of the wines exported has notably improved. Despite the island's troubled recent history, the export trade through the busy port of Limassol has continued to flourish, a trend which will no doubt be maintained through the 1980s.

TURKEY

Turkey as a wine-producer is a sleeping giant: a country of enormous potential, as yet unrealized. Although, at the height of the phylloxera 'epidemic' in Europe, Turkish wines found a ready market and were well distributed in the Western capitals, decline set in with the First World War and the pendulum is only now swinging back to growth. Like the countries of the Levant, Turkey produces enormous quantities of grapes, of which only a fraction are turned into wine: of some 800,000 hectares planted under vines, less than half produce wine-grapes. The national production per annum falls currently between 500,000 and 600,000 hectolitres, of which only minimal quantities are exported.

The Turkish state is committed to developing its wine industry, and since the 1950s serious efforts have been made both to increase production and to improve quality, following the example set by the regime of Kemal Atatürk in the 1920s and 1930s. It has not been an easy task: the Moslem tradition of abstinence dies hard, and apathy and lax standards abound at the local level. The traditions of wine-growing in Turkey are some of the oldest in the world (Sumerian and Hittite reliefs suggest a past of at least 4,000 years), and many of the native varieties grown and the methods of wine-making are similarly rooted in the past. Phylloxera is still a potent force in the more primitive country districts. There are, nevertheless, distinct signs that the government is prevailing in its battle of modernization and the standard of wines exported has improved noticeably in recent years. However, as in everything, political stability is needed for commercial and economic growth. One of the outward and visible signs of state intervention in the wine industry is the division of Turkey's vineyards into nine administrative zones: the bones of a full-scale wine regime, to which the enforcement of viticultural standards will in due course add flesh.

THRACE/MARMARA

This is one of the only two zones in Turkey which the map-makers shade in green, rather than the deepening brown and grey shades of mountain massifs. Zone III of the Turkish wine regime, it straddles the Bosphorus to embrace a roughly equivalent acreage in Europe and Asia Minor; production of wine from vineyards here is proportionally higher than in any other zone (some 40 per cent).

Both red and white wines are grown here, from a mixture of native and imported varieties. Of the red varieties, Papazkarasi, Adakarasi and Karasakiz are of local origin, the first named in particular producing a solid, drinkable red wine: among the newcomers are Gamay and Cinsault, and recent plantings have also included Pinot Noir and Cabernet Sauvignon. The white varieties are led by the Yapincak, a local cousin of the Sémillon: the Sémillon itself is also grown from imported stock, with Beylerce (one of the better native varieties) and new plantings of Riesling, Chardonnay and Sylvaner. The Chardonnay, in particular, shows similar signs of promise to those we have seen in Bulgaria and Rumania to the north. Place names of note in Thrace/Marmara are as follows:

Trakya: The Turkish name for Thrace, and applies equally to red and white wines.
Tekirdağ: A sweetish white wine made from Yapincak grapes on the northern shores of the Sea of Marmara.

THE AEGEAN

This, the second of the 'green' zones (Zone II), embraces the whole of Turkey's western coastline and 160 kilometres of hinterland. It produces over a quarter of the country's grapes, and is the home of the Sultaniye, the seedless table grape that we know in the west as the sultana. Wine is made from only 20 per cent of the grapes produced. Prior to 1912, the island of Samos belonged to Turkey, and the Muscat variety on which its renown is based is grown all along the coastline to the east. The Bornóva Muscat (or Misket) produces both 'natural' sweet wines, or fortified wines of the apéritif or dessert type, often very agreeable. The main production centre is Izmir, the ancient Smyrna.

CENTRAL TURKEY

This region, more properly described as Central Anatolia, is divided into three zones: I, VIII and IX in the regime, respectively Central-North, Central-East and Central-South. The Central-North zone, as its number indicates, is that surrounding the capital Ankara. Good red wines are made from Kalecik, Çubuk and Dimrit grapes, and whites from Hasandede, Narince, and Emir. Kalecik and Çubuk are named after the districts where they are grown. Central-East Anatolia is best known as the source of Buzbağ, a name with undeserved but faintly comical connotations for Westerners, but a serious wine in every sense of the word. Made from a tongue-twisting variety called Öküzgözü in the region of Elâziğ, this is a deep, complex red wine of high alcohol and full-bodied character, which many authorities have compared to the reds of Hungary and even of Burgundy. Perhaps because of its memorable name, it is one of Turkey's most exported wines and one of the best. Central-Southern Anatolia is the biggest producer of the three, embracing all inland Turkey to the South of Ankara. Grape-varieties are broadly the same as in Zone I; newly introduced varieties from Western Europe, such as Gamay, Carignan, Clairette and Riesling, are more in evidence, though as yet on a very small scale.

SOUTH-EAST TURKEY

Zone IV of the regime covers Turkey's Mediterranean coastline from west of Antalya to Antakya (Antioch) in the east, and inland eastwards to the Euphrates. While particularly noted for its table grapes (Mersin being the centre of production), some good red and white wines are made: the red Gaziantep, from Sergikarasi grapes, is probably the best. Horozkarasi and Boğazkerasi are two other red grape varieties producing sound wines of the Buzbağ type.

Turkey, it will be seen, produces a wide variety of wines, in all shades of colour from white through red to tawny, and in all shades of flavour from very dry to luscious. Production is very largely controlled by the nineteen wineries of the State Monopoly, and the wines exported reflect this, though the enthusiast would do well to make enquiries of such leading private firms as Kavaklidere in Ankara, or Kutman in Istanbul. Many of the wines show promise of better things to come, particularly those from Thrace and Marmara where European influences are more strongly felt. If the sleeping giant should truly awake, the results could well be memorable.

MALTA

Malta makes some excellent beer, a local challenger to Coke or Pepsi-Cola called Kinnie, and nowadays not a little wine, of which most is consumed by the semi-permanent invasion force of tourists.

Information on the wines produced on Malta and its neighbours, Gozo and Comino, is not very easily obtained. Experiment alone will tell, but caution should be the watchword: 'treat with respect' says a publicity leaflet sternly of the full-bodied red of Gozo. Malta's climatic extremes do not fit the island particularly well for viticulture, though archaeology reveals that the vine was grown here as long ago as the Phoenician period. The 2,000 or so hectares under vine are planted mainly in small scattered parcels along the western and southern sides of the island, with the greatest concentration around Rabat and Siggiewi; the vineyards on Gozo lie mainly in the north. The vines are largely native varieties, of which one, the Insola, provides grapes both for the table and for the making of wine. Though there has been some experimentation with classic table-wine varieties imported from France and Italy, the most promising results are being obtained from the Muscat, and some good dessert wines of this type have been appearing on export markets.

There are around 10,000 private growers on Malta and its neighbours, supplying grapes at vintage time to cooperative and private wineries. The largest and most enterprising of these is the Marsovin Company, which produces a wide range of 'branded' wines for mainly local consumption: the standards of wine-making applied by this company are noticeably in advance of the norm, and its standard rosé, Marsovin Verdala, makes for agreeable drinking.

ISRAEL

Despite biblical traditions wine-making in Palestine on the modern pattern is only a hundred years old. Long centuries of Islamic occupation permitted only limited cultivation of the vine, and the first steps towards a modern wine industry were only taken at the end of the nineteenth century. An agricultural school with an experimental vineyard was founded in 1870, but the more important stimulus came with the patronage of Baron Edmond de Rothschild in the 1880s. Under his enlightened guidance, a thousand hectares or so were planted with varieties chosen from France, and in the 1890s the foundations were laid of extensive new cellars at Richon-le-Zion, south of Tel Aviv, and at Zichron-Jacob between Tel Aviv and Haifa, in the shadow of Mount Carmel. By the early 1900s, the first influx of Zionist settlers was sufficiently established for Rothschild to hand over the two wineries as a gift: today, they produce between them nearly three quarters of the country's wine production (some 350,000 hectolitres), and the cooperative founded in 1906, the Société Coopérative Vigneronne des Grandes Caves, is still flourishing. The foundation of the modern state of Israel in 1948 provided a further stimulus to the industry, and another landmark was passed in 1957 with the foundation of the Israeli Wine Institute at Rehovot, among whose functions is the examination, for quality-control purposes, of all wines leaving the country for export. Against a difficult background of recurring Middle East tensions, the industry has continued to expand in recent years, and latest statistics show an annual production of some 430,000 hectolitres of wine. Some 9,000 hectares are under vine, but this figure includes sizeable areas devoted to table grapes and also to the production of wines for distillation. The United States is substantially the most important export market, followed by the

United Kingdom; in both countries, the Société Coopérative has established off-shoots trading as The Carmel Wine Company, who account for almost all imports. All wines exported are prepared and certified as Kosher. Although vineyards may be found throughout modern Israel, the most important zones are classified regionally as follows:

The North: The slopes of Mount Carmel, dominating the port of Haifa, are one of the country's most historic sites. The best vineyards look southwards, and the big Zichron-Jacob cooperative lies at their foot. Another important zone lies around the northern shores of the Sea of Galilee (Lake Tiberias).
Central Region: Substantial plantations extend over the coastal plains inland from Jaffa and Tel Aviv, and eastwards into the hills around Jerusalem. Many of the sweeter, dessert type wines originate from here.
The South: Southern Israel drives a great wedge shape into the Negev desert to reach the Red Sea at Aqaba. Most of the area is unsuitable for vines, but sizeable vineyards lie in the neighbourhood of Beersheba, and north and westwards towards the coast at Ascalon.

Grapes and Wines

Two grape varieties alone account for very nearly three quarters of the country's wine: these are the Carignan (41 per cent) and the Grenache (32 per cent), both red grape varieties which are vinified either to produce light table wines, or heavier dessert types such as those produced at the other end of the Mediterranean in Southern France and Iberia. Most popular of the white varieties are the Sémillon, with 9 per cent of the total, and then the Clairette and Muscat d'Alexandrie with 15 per cent between them. The final category in the official statistics I have quoted is 'others', and it is fair to say that many of Israel's most promising wines (in my own opinion) are to be found among this final 3 per cent. As we have seen in many of the other countries described in this chapter, it is the well-tried and classic varieties which offer the greatest attraction to Western tastes. In Israel, some excellent wines are beginning to appear from Cabernet Sauvignon and Sauvignon Blanc, and the country's close links with the United States are also bearing fruit in the form of varieties imported from California. The plantations are young, and only time will reveal the quality of these new wines: but the signs are promising.

Israel today produces a confusing multiplicity of wine styles, but the trend is away from the sweet, red and amber-coloured dessert types which used to account for the lion's share of production, towards lighter, drier red and white table wines on the patterns more favoured in Western Europe. I give a list below of the principal names under which the wines are commercialized:

White Wines: Carmel Hock (a legacy of German monks who planted cuttings from the Rhineland in the Carmel district in the 1880s) and Château de la Montagne are the two most widely seen.
Red Wines: Adom Atic (light and dry), and Château Windsor (smooth and full-bodied), are the leaders among the reds.
Red and/or White Wines: Avdat, Binyamina, Askalon, Arad and Mikveh-Israel may be either red or white.
Dessert-type Wines: Muscatel, Château Rishon, Partom (previously sold as 'Port'), Almog, Topaz, Toda, Maagal, Golden Cream, Caesarea, Independence, Poria, Hadar, Porath and Ashdod. The practice of marketing wines under 'borrowed' *appellations*, such as 'Malaga', 'Tokay', etc., is happily on the decline.

Israeli vermouth, fortified wines, brandy and arak may safely be considered as beyond the scope of this book, but I cannot pass on to Lebanon without a final mention of the excellent Champagne-method sparkling wine made in Israel and sold under the splendidly simple label 'The President's Sparkling Wine'. A similar alternative is known as Sambatyon.

LEBANON

References abound in the Bible to vineyards which fall within the borders of modern-day Lebanon, but the subsequent history of the vine has been similarly spasmodic. Following the relatively brief interlude of the Crusades, viticulture in Lebanon was effectively curtailed under several centuries of Islamic domination, though the resolute Christian community succeeded in keeping at least a few scattered vineyards in production for most of the period. It is the Jesuits who can largely be credited with founding the modern wine industry of Lebanon, with the construction of the winery at Ksara, in the Bekaa valley east of Beirut, in 1857. With its vast subterranean galleries, this is reputedly the largest cellar in the Middle East.

Lebanon has some 17,000 hectares under vine, which sounds an impressive total, but the great majority of the grapes grown are either produced for the table, dried as raisins, reserved to be sold as grape juice, or distilled for arak and other spirits; only a very small proportion is vinified (some 40,000 hectolitres) for consumption by the Christian population and, with at least one interesting exception described below, virtually no wine is exported. Sad political and religious strife also presents a difficult climate in which to expand. Lebanon has no formal wine regime on the lines found in most producing countries. It has been left to progressive and enthusiastic individuals to put Lebanese wines on the twentieth-century map. One such pioneer was Gaston Hochar, who in 1930 founded a family business known as the Caves Musar. The wines account today for at least a quarter of the national production, under the vigorous management of Gaston's son, Serge; at the Bristol Wine Fair in 1979, the red Château Musar in particular caused something of a stir, but it has to be admitted that novelty can play a part in these things.

The main vineyard area in Lebanon is the long Bekaa valley, cradled between two mountain massifs: Mount Lebanon, nearly 3,048 metres, forms its western wall, dividing it from Beirut and the narrow coastal plain. The valley floor is some 1,000 metres above sea-level with a constant micro-climate, and good vineyard sites on the slopes. The soil, of limestone with a gravel topsoil, is rich in trace elements.

Production on the Musar estates, which I will take as being representative, is 75 per cent of red wines, 25 per cent of white. The inspiration in terms both of the vine varieties planted and of the methods of elaboration is strongly French, as one would expect from the historic links that Lebanon has enjoyed with that country. The red varieties are headed by the Cabernet Sauvignon; Cinsault, Merlot, Carignan, Syrah and Pinot Noir are also grown. Chardonnay is the most promising of the white varieties, followed by Ugni Blanc, Sauvignon, Muscat and Chasselas. Maturation of the Musar red wines is carried out in traditional Bordeaux hogsheads of 225 litres. Many smaller Lebanese concerns, such as J. Nakad & Fils, based at Jdita in the Bekaa, still employ the original system of fermenting and storing in amphorae, reminiscent of the great stone *tinajas* of inland Spain.

From what I have seen of the Château Musar and other Lebanese wines, such as the Domaine des Tourelles of Pierre Brun, there is certainly some potential for export. I believe that the modern wine-makers are still at the 'trial and error' stage in finding the right balance between wood and bottle maturation, and in achieving consistency in their white wines. However, it is clear that the raw materials are excellent, and there is an impressive will to succeed.

EGYPT

The story of modern wine-making in Egypt is fascinating and is very largely the story of one man, Nestor Gianaclis, a pioneer like his counterparts in Lebanon who, in the early years of the twentieth century, set out to bridge a gap of some two thousand years and restore Egyptian wines of quality to the world. His work, so boldly undertaken, is still far from completion, but the results that have already been achieved are astonishing.

Although there were Egyptian wines to be found in the 1900s, they provided no basis on which to build and Gianaclis decided to start again from scratch. A soil suitable for vines had first to be found. After intensive research, the first site was planted in 1903 at Maryut (Mariout), west of the Nile delta near Alexandria, possibly (historians differ) the ancient source of the *vinum mereoticum* which Cleopatra served to Julius Caesar. The next stage was to find the grape varieties most suited to grow here, a patient process of trial and error extending over years, and arguably still incomplete, for experiments continue. Today, the principal varieties planted are Chasselas (for both table-grapes and wine-production), Pinot Blanc and Chardonnay, Pinot Noir, Gamay and Muscat Hamburg, plus locally developed varieties such as the Fayumi, Guizazi and Rumi.

The vineyards west of the Nile delta, extending from Alexandria towards El Alamein, run to some 18,000 hectares, though only about 4 per cent of the grapes produced are used to make wine. Annual production of wine runs to some 70,000 hectolitres, of which only a minimal amount is exported. The Gianaclis wines are commercialized today under brand names: Reine Cléopâtre, Cru des Ptolemées and Clos Mariout among the whites, and Gianaclis Abyad, Gianaclis Ahmar and Omar Khayyam among the reds.

With the exception of the last-named, I must in all honesty confess that I have not been impressed by the samples I have tasted in London of a range of Gianaclis wines, but I do not believe that these can have been truly representative. I am fully prepared to give them the benefit of the doubt, and recommend readers to do likewise, until such time as I, and they, are able to taste them at source. With the Omar Khayyam I have no such reservations; an interesting wine, this, smooth and scented on the palate, no doubt with a proportion of Muscat Hamburg in the blend, and the nearest taste I can imagine to liquid Turkish delight. Egyptian wines do tend to be heavy and overpoweringly flavoured. Some even are faintly resinated, a residue from Greek wine-growers in the past, perhaps.

NORTH-WEST AFRICA

All three countries of North-West Africa, Tunisia, Morocco and Algeria, produce wine. Indeed, only the stricter rule of Islam in Libya and the wide physical barrier of the Sahara, where the sand meets the sea, prevent the Mediterranean from being surrounded by a continous ring of vineyards, with only minor interruptions in the chain. Phoenicians, Greeks, Romans, and more recently the French, all passed through North Africa, and left their imprint on the land. Vines have always been grown here. Following the Moorish conquests of the early Middle Ages, the vineyards were devoted to producing table grapes and raisins, and the established rule of Islam is still the dominant factor in limiting modern-day consumption of wine on the domestic markets. Wines produced here today are destined, as they seem always to have been, primarily for export.

The modern wine industries of Tunisia, Morocco and Algeria have much in common, not least that their origins are of uniquely French inspiration. They all date from the hundred years of French domination and settlement which preceded the granting of independence in the 1950s and 1960s. During this period, they were all geared to the production of bulk blending wines for France, be they assigned to 'correcting' the thin, acid *ordinaires* of the South or, in the heady days before France's export customers felt constrained to heed the laws of *appellation contrôlée*, to fattening many a shipper's generic Burgundies with the colour, fire and warmth on which their reputation was deservedly founded. Political severance from France, the emerging economic hostility of the powerful growers' lobby in the Midi of France, and prohibition of the blending of North African wines with produce of the EEC, meant that each country had to seek new markets and a new production policy in order for its wine industry to survive. Retrenchment, and the upgrading of the quality of production were policies each country was forced through sheer necessity to adopt, but as a result, their better wines have been progressively establishing an identity and reputation in their own right. Today, enormous quantities of bulk wines still leave these countries for their new markets in the Eastern bloc and the francophone countries of Africa, but the interest of the consumer is focused on the wines of higher quality, whose light was hidden for so long under a bushel.

Algeria

Of the three wine-producing countries of North-West Africa, Algeria has always been the heavyweight. Partly, of course, this is the result of geography, for Algeria has five times the land area of Morocco and fourteen times that of Tunisia; a more potent factor, however, has been the nature and intensity of French settlement in the hundred years preceding the country's independence in 1962. French influence penetrated as deep as the vines planted by French colonists, and only partially diluted by the traumas of separation, remains entrenched to this day.

The history of modern wine-growing in Algeria is a short and eventful one. It began in the 1860s and 1870s, with an influx of *vignerons* from southern France on the run from two sources of menace: Prussian expansionism and phylloxera. They only succeeded in escaping the first of these, for phylloxera arrived a decade later. After extensive replanting of the vineyards, wine production regained its earlier momentum and increased steadily through the first half of the twentieth century. In 1961, on the eve of independence, Algeria stood fourth among the world's producers (behind only France, Spain and the Argentine), with an annual total of 15 million hectolitres, yielded from 360,000 hectares of vines. Since then, the pendulum has swung away from quantity as the main target of production, a policy dictated by the changing nature of Algeria's export markets. Today, the area under vine has fallen to some 230,000 hectares, and wine production to under 5 million hectolitres: a very substantial total, nevertheless, and sufficient to keep Algeria among the world's most important producers. Whether quality has improved in proportion to the reduction in the vineyards and their output is debatable. A state-controlled industry can never replace the commitment and collective hard-won expertise of individual growers, and the loss of the *pieds noirs* (France's gain) was a damaging blow indeed. The fall in standards which followed their departure in 1962 was a sharp one, but things have improved substantially again since then. In general, it is the vineyards on the flat, coastal areas, producing wines of lesser quality, which have not been replanted, and the prolific, inferior grape varieties such as the Aramon which have been disappearing progressively in favour of *cépages améliorateurs*. Although the emphasis today remains on the production of common wines for export in bulk (the home market accounts for only 2 per cent of the wine produced), the best of Algeria's wines are of excellent quality and fully live up to the reputation gained under the former administration. As in Tunisia and Morocco, the best of them are red.

When Algeria came within the scope of the INAO (The Institut National des Appellations d'Origine), some twelve vineyard areas were classed as VDQS (Vins Délimités de Qualité Supérieure). Today their superior status is rather less formally defined, though retained under the Algerian wine regime, and their labels continue to demonstrate their pre-eminence over the common wines of the plain. The great qualitative divide in Algeria is today, as it was under the French, between the vineyards in the hill-zones, rising to 1,219 metres on the northern slopes of the Atlas, which produce the better qualities, and those on the flat lands along the coast, which produce the majority of the common wines. Apart from a small, and commercially insignificant area on the southern slopes of the Atlas, overlooking the Sahara, Algeria's vineyards are all in the far north of the country, within one hundred kilometres of the Mediterranean. They extend for some 1,207 kilometres along the whole length of the littoral, from west of Oran to the borders of Tunisia in the east. Algeria's vineyards are divided into three main regions, subdivided into departments (four per region) and thereafter into numerous communes. The three regions referred to are (from west to east) Oran, with some 70 per cent of the total production, Alger, with 25 per cent, and Constantine, with the remaining 5 per cent. Of the last-named, suffice it to say that the wines produced are both red and white, the former of lighter alcohol and extract than the average in Algeria, and of unremarkable quality. The white wines of Constantine are regarded by the Algerians as the best they produce. I cannot recommend them, being in the main heavy, overalcoholic and fruitless and, in my experience, invariably oxidized. They account for around 15 per cent of the region's production. Place names of note are Bougie, Djidjelli, Philippeville, Daroussa, Guelma and Jemmapes.

ORAN

This region contains not only the greatest concentration of vineyards but also nine out of the twelve zones accorded VDQS status under the French. It may be divided physically into three categories: the mountain-slopes, the foothills and the plain, zones which differ from one another not only in altitude, micro-climate and exposure, but also in soil composition. The soil of the mountains is calcareous gravel, covering a layer of limestone, marl and sand. Here are produced some of Algeria's richest, most robust red wines, invariably deep in colour and often formidably high in alcohol: natural alcohol of 15-18 per cent is not uncommon. These are the very model of *vins médecins*, their traditional role in life, though the best of them, carefully vinified, are exceptional wines in their own right. The foothills are composed of a variety of soil types, ranging through silica, gravel, clay and sand to volcanic (the region of Ain Temouchent). Their wines are less robust, and of a lower alcoholic degree than those of the high mountain slopes. The soil of the plain, finally, with the exception of one area (Sebkra) where there is a salt lake, is a mixture of sand and marl. The wines here are much more commonplace, relatively lacking in backbone, and swift to oxidize. The following are the most notable of the upland vineyards:

Coteaux de Mascara: A mountainous zone south-east of Oran, producing red, white and rosé wines. The reds are substantially the best.
Mascara: The lower slopes of the same zone, producing wines of good quality, but without the finesse of the 'Coteaux'.
Haut Dahra: Formerly in the province of Alger, since 1962 these wines have been considered under Oran. Only red wines are produced, in a massif to the east of

Mostaganem. The villages of Rabelais, Renault, Ramanet Picard and Paul Robert are particularly reputed.

Monts du Tessalah: This zone lies south of Oran in the direction of Sidi bel Abbes. Red, white and rosé wines are made, the best being the first-named, as elsewhere.

Coteaux de Tlemcen: Overlooking the Tunisian border, these mountain vineyards rise to nearly 900 metres. They yield rich, perfumed wines which are longer-living than the average.

Mostaganem (and Mostaganem-Kenenda): The zone stretching inland from the port of Mostaganem. Mainly red wines, with a leavening of white and rosé.

The list of superior zones in the region of Oran is completed by A'in-el-Hadjar, south of Mascara, and Oued Imbert, a half-moon of vineyards between Oran and the Monts du Tessalah.

ALGER

In general wines from this region are lighter than those of Oran. What they lack in power, however, they often make up in delicacy and bouquet. As in Oran, soil, altitude and exposure are of cardinal importance in determining the quality of a vineyard's output. The best vineyards are again those of the uplands, where the subsoil is mainly limestone, with a covering of gritty sand and marl. One area, Miliana in the department of Medea, even has a soil of startling similarity to that of many slopes of the Burgundian Côte d'Or: a mixture of limestone and iron debris, rich in manganese and other minerals. The mountain wines in general are remarkable for a brilliant colour and pronounced fruity bouquet. Lower down the scale, the coastal hills of the Sahel are composed mainly of sandstone. Their wines are delicate and perfumed, lacking the finesse of the mountain wines, but palpably superior to the light, blending wines of the plain. The soil of the coastal areas is rich and alluvial, better suited to the production of quantity than quality. The most important area is the fertile Mitidja, an extensive plain to the west of the capital Algiers (El Djezair). Since the heights of Haut Dahra are now in the region of Oran, Alger is left with only three of the twelve vDQs zones of the French administration. Arguably, however, the first of these produces the best red wines of Algeria.

Medea: A mountain zone south-west of the capital. The wines have a lively colour, perfumed bouquet, and overall balance and harmony lacked by many of the 'bigger' wines from further west.

Côtes du Zaccar: Beyond the Mitidja, west of Algiers, the hills of Zaccar produce both red and white wines. The latter are unremarkable, the former rich and scented.

Aïn-Bessem-Bouira: This zone lies east of Algiers, on the borders of Constantine. The wines are marginally lighter and more delicate than those of the first two zones.

The best Algerian wines are red, and produced from the mountain vineyards. Their virtues are strength, suppleness and warmth of flavour, their shortcomings a lack of acidity and backbone, and an inherent tendency to oxidize prematurely. The most widely planted red varieties are Carignan, Cinsault, Alicante-Bouschet and Morrastel; though Aramon is on the decline, large plantations remain, particularly in the flat areas. In the hill-zones, Grenache, Mourvèdre, Pinot Noir and Syrah are among the red varieties grown, contributing much to the superior quality we have noted. The rosés of Algeria are mostly full-bodied, dry wines with good extract and flavour. They are generally short-lived, like the reds, and prone to oxidation, but drunk young and cool can be very agreeable. They are made usually from Cinsault, Grenache and Aramon. The white wines are less attractive. The principal grape varieties grown for these wines are Clairette and Ugni Blanc, with Maccabeo and the native Merseguera. Though these are all by their very nature somewhat neutral varieties, it is fair to say that the shortcomings of the Algerian whites are due as much to poor vinification as to the choice of grapes. Recent advances in the Midi of France have shown that the very same varieties can produce most appealing wines if only the proper techniques are employed, so there is certainly hope for the future. Production in most Algerian wineries is on a large scale, and the regular climate allows for little variation between vintages. In consequence, it is necessary, when seeking wines of truly individual personality, to look for the names of particular villages or domains. The list of hill-zones mentioned provides in itself a starting point for exploration and experiment, which will bring their own rewards.

Tunisia

Tunisia first produced and exported wines in the Phoenician era, when Carthage was one of the busiest trading stations of the Mediterranean. The revitalization of Tunisia's wine industry came with the French protectorate established in the 1880s, although Italian influence is also discernible as the legacy of colonists from Sicily and Pantelleria. A major turning point came with a disastrous epidemic of phylloxera in the 1930s, after which the vineyards were systematically replanted on resistant root stocks and assumed their present shape and size: some 47,000 hectares, approximately three quarters of which are devoted to wine production, and yield in the region of one million hectolitres per annum.

The Tunisian vineyards are concentrated in the extreme north of the country, extending in a broad half moon from Bizerta in the west, inland from Carthage and Tunis in the centre, to the holiday resorts of Sousse and Hammamet on the coastline facing east towards Malta. At the north-east corner lies the broad promontory of Cap Bon, famous for its Muscat wines, whose vineyards are the oldest in the country. Within this comparatively narrow enclave are several areas where vineyards are particularly concentrated. Grombalia, midway between Tunis and Hammamet is one of these, and Mornag, just south of Tunis, another. Kelibia, on the Cap Bon peninsula, is a centre of Muscat production. West of Tunis, towards Tebourba and Mateur, and in the valley of the Oued Medjerdah and Oued Miliane, lie vineyards producing the lion's share of the national total.

Since independence in 1956, production of Tunisian wines has been very largely controlled by the state, through the UCCVT (Union des Caves Coopératives du Vin de Tunisie), an organization which embraces some fourteen local cooperatives. The central cellars and headquarters of the UCCVT, at Djebel Djelloud on the outskirts of Tunis, are modern and business-like and the quality of the wines is strictly controlled. Among the best of the wines marketed under the standard labels of the UCCVT are Coteaux de Carthage and Haut Mornag, both robust, smooth, rather peppery reds (white and rosé wines are also produced under these labels, though are less impressive), Sidi Rais, an acceptable dry rosé, and the attractive Muscat Sec de Kelibia, a dry, scented Muscat with the true scent of the variety in the bouquet and a touch of Mediterranean warmth on the finish. Tyna is a five-year-old red, smooth and full-bodied with a dry end, Nahli, a sound inexpensive *ordinaire* (red and rosé). Other names of repute are Coteaux de Khanguet, Tebourba, Cap Bon, St Cyprien and Sidi Tabet. While the country's vineyards have never been formally delimited, and the geographical descriptions are thus rather loosely defined, the government's commitment to improving the quality of Tunisian wines is embodied in the classification *Vin Supérieur de Tunisie*, introduced in 1942 for vintage wines at least one year old which have passed the scrutiny of an official panel of tasters and analysts. Wines submitted for this award are not required to declare either their origins or the grape varieties from which they are made, so the system falls some way short of the ideal, but it is clear that both government and UCCVT are working hard behind the scenes to establish a proper balance between the quantity and quality of production.

The grape varieties are almost exclusively of French origin. Predominant among the varieties grown for red wines is the Alicante-Bouschet, a prolific variety giving a rather neutral-flavoured wine of intense colour when young; Carignan and Cinsault make up for the deficiencies of the Alicante-Bouschet in providing body and a necessary minimum of acidity. Red wines are normally made from a combination of these varieties, though Mourvèdre, Pinot Noir and Cabernet Franc are increasingly grown nowadays and may feature in the blend. Rosé in Tunisia is generally made from Alicante-Grenache and Cinsault: when drunk young and fresh, these wines have an agreeable balance and delicacy of flavour, reminiscent of good Gris from the Midi. White wines, apart from the Muscat types described later, are produced from a base of Clairette and Ugni Blanc, though Sauvignon and Sémillon have been more recently introduced to provide much needed qualities of aroma and acidity; Pedro Ximénez and a native variety, Beldi, are also grown. Tunisian white wines in general are menaced by oxidation, and the visitor would be advised to experiment first with the more successful reds and rosés. Apart from the notable dry Muscat from Kelibia, Tunisia also produces good dessert wines of the Muscatel type, which since 1947 may qualify for the *appellation, Vin Muscat de Tunisie*. They are made from any of three specific sub-varieties of Muscat (those of Alexandria, Frontignan or Terracina) and are fortified to at least 17 per cent.

Morocco

As with her neighbours to the east, wine-making in Morocco is a legacy of the French protectorate of the first half of the twentieth century. Modern wine-making can only be said to have begun in the 1920s with an influx of settlers from France, and many of the vineyards that the visitor sees today date from after the Second World War. Morocco is thus one of the youngest of the world's wine-producers, but she has been quick to learn new skills, and her wine industry today is vigorous and forward-looking. Since independence in 1956, government intervention has been both enlightened and restrained, devoted to providing essential controls for the development of a trade based on quality. Private companies have been encouraged to invest in new vineyards, equipment and expertise, competition between companies has been lively, and as a result the industry as a whole has prospered. Morocco's vineyards today extend to some 55,000 hectares, a notable reduction from the 75,000 hectares recorded in the 1960s and a reflection of a sensible policy of consolidation and qualitative improvements which has been followed in recent years. Production is normally just under one million hectolitres per annum of which, unusually for a Moslem country, only about half is exported, the balance finding a ready market at home, tourism accounting for a good deal of this.

Under the Moroccan wine regime, which extends to control of production and the regulation of market prices, wines destined for export must attain at least 11 per cent of alcohol: a target which, given the guarantee of long hours of summer sunshine, is not difficult to achieve. The quality grades awarded to Moroccan wines are broadly equivalent to those current in France, on which they have always been modelled; wines in the top echelon, for example, are described as of *Appellation d'Origine Garantie. Vin de Qualité Supérieure* is a description reserved for wines of superior quality to the everyday table wines, which are normally described as *Vins Selectionnés* or by some similar phrase.

Some of the oldest vineyard sites in Morocco are found on the slopes of the Zerhoun and Atlas mountains and also in the Rif Massif, but these are devoted almost exclusively to the production of table grapes. They are, moreover, continually menaced by phylloxera, since the native varieties grown here have never been grafted to resistant root stocks. Commercial attention is today focused on the 'new' vineyards, which may conveniently be divided into the following zones:

Meknes/Fes: The vineyards here lie at some 450–600 metres on the most northerly slopes of the Atlas (more precisely, the Middle Atlas), profiting from good conditions of exposure and drainage and a micro-climate cooler than that of the plain. A heavier soil structure here produces red wines which are among the best in Morocco, less intense in colour than those of the plain, and with a degree of firmness and general 'finesse' which sets them apart from the general run. Production in the Meknes region is very largely controlled by the private company, Meknes Vins SA, amounting to nearly a quarter of the national figure. The best wines are made from 700 hectares of vineyards in two zones south of Meknes, straddling the road southwards into the Atlas: to the west, Guerrouane, and to the east, Beni M'Tir. Both wines are awarded the AOG, and are broadly similar in style, based on Carignan, Cinsault and Grenache: full-bodied reds, with deep colour, scented peppery bouquet and soft, generous palate. The Guerrouane Les Trois Domaines emerged first in a class of eighteen red wines tasted at the Gault-Millau Olympiades du Vin held in Paris in 1979, and deservedly so: for me this is one of the finest Moroccan reds, with elegance and backbone to match its supple, easy-drinking style. A good dry rosé is also sold under the label of Les Trois Domaines.

The Coastal Plain (North): The Moroccan capital, Rabat, is surrounded by vineyards to north, east and south, zones known respectively as Dar bel Amri, Roumi and Sidi Larbi. All three zones specialize in red wines of the broad, soft style: rich in colouring matter, glycerine and sugars, these are powerful, heady wines which are agreeably smooth when young, but lack the acidity and tannin necessary for keeping. To some extent this is a function of the light, sandy soils of the littoral; partly, too, the higher proportion of Alicante grown here accounts for the faster-maturing style.

The Coastal Plain (South): South of Sidi Larbi, vineyards extend intermittently along the flat coastal strip past Casablanca almost to Essaouira, on the parallel of Marrakech. They lack the ordered look of the new plantations around Rabat and Meknes, and in general the wines produced here are less impressive, the techniques employed more traditional. The main exception to the general rule is the Gris de Boulaouane, an excellent, full-bodied, dry rosé from vineyards south of Casablanca, the best of a family of rosés which have always been made and appreciated in this area; El Jadida and Demnate (near Marrakech) are two other good sources of rosé.

The North-East (Taza, Oujda and Berkane): The ancient town of Taza commands the strategic pass between the Rif and Middle Atlas: it forms the centre of a small zone of red wine production, of no great significance. In the far north-east of the country the town of Oujda is little more than an oasis settlement in an arm of the Sahara, but gives its name to a sizeable production zone among the low coastal hills. The best wines here are of the dry rosé type, though some acceptable Muscats (mainly of the rich, dessert style) are also made, notably around Berkane.

French grape varieties predominate in Morocco. The best of the red wines are made from a foundation of Carignan, Cinsault, and Grenache, with Alicante providing quantity. Small plantations of two other classic varieties from the Rhône, the Syrah and Mourvèdre, are to be found in the vineyards of Meknes/Fes, and

Cabernet Sauvignon is also making an appearance. The best rosé wines are made from Grenache. Little mention has been made so far of the white wines made in Morocco, which are produced from Clairette, Ugni Blanc, Pedro Ximénez, Muscat and a score of native varieties, notably the Rafsai. The climate is an implacable foe to those qualities in white wines of freshness, fragrance, fruit and acidity that we value in our northern climes, and I cannot see that the problem will ever satisfactorily be resolved. With the red and rosé wines of Morocco, however, there need be little cause for complaint. The golden rule is to consume them young, and the rosés chilled. For the visitor, they make a delightful introduction to a country that is truly a frontier between civilizations.

THE FAR EAST

One of the many notable features of the great, unfathomable divide between East and West is the comparative importance of wine in the one, where it not only forms a staple of the diet and economy of many of the leading nations but everywhere plays a long-established social and cultural role, and its relative insignificance in the other, where to this day it remains little more than a curiosity. Nevertheless, though the traditions of centuries will not easily be overturned or replaced, it is clear that a vinous 'wind of change' is blowing in the Far East. The pace of experimentation is undoubtedly quickening, and nowhere more so than in Japan, spurred on by that nation's enviable capacity to pursue new ideas, once adopted, with singleminded enthusiasm. Nor is China, with the widening horizons of the post-Mao era, to be disregarded as a wine-maker of the future and with a potential home market of one-fifth of the world's population, what a momentous development that could be! With few exceptions it is difficult, as yet, to enthuse about the wines of China and Japan, or such of them, at least, as reach us spasmodically in the West. But they are unquestionably here to stay, must inevitably improve in both quality and appeal and, who knows, may one day dominate world markets.

China

The origins of wine-making in China can be traced back at least to 2140 BC, the date of the first recorded reference to a species of vine (*Vitis chunganensis*) still found in remote parts of the country to this day. For much of their subsequent history the wines produced in China were very foreign to those we would recognize today: in general they were produced for medicinal purposes, and since they were often made with exotic additives of a supposedly therapeutic nature, they cannot have had much to offer in terms of popular appeal. Wine-making on the European model began with the advent of the *Vitis vinifera*, which reached China during the second and first centuries BC. It travelled from its heartland in Persia and Mesopotamia along the caravan routes of Central Asia: remote Sinkiang, where China's oldest vineyards are to be found among the mountains, was one of the final staging posts along the way.

According to statistics published by the OIV (Office International du Vin) China has some 30,000 hectares under vine. When one subtracts even from this land area the vineyards producing raisins and table grapes, it will be seen that the scale of the Chinese wine industry is as yet extremely limited by European standards. Nevertheless, there are at least seven distinct vineyard areas, and these are, respectively: Sinkiang (in the far north-west), Kiangsu (north of Shanghai), Shensi and Shansi (near the city of Sian, on the Yellow River), the Shantung peninsula, Hebei (northeast Peking) and finally Liaoning (in Manchuria, near the Great Wall). With the exception of Sinkiang, all these areas lie in Eastern China.

For such a relatively small area under vine, the range of varieties grown in China is bewildering. Of the major European varieties, Pinot Noir, Merlot, Cabernet Franc and Riesling are to be found, though as yet on little more than an experimental scale. Many of the vines in production are of indigenous species, which have survived in parallel with *Vitis vinifera*: *Vitis davidii* and *Vitis amurensis* are two of the more important. The picture is further complicated by the various hybrids (crosses between *vinifera*, the American *labrusca* and the indigenous varieties) which have been bred by research stations at Peking and Nanking to suit specific local conditions. In general, this is a subject best left to the specialist researcher. As far as wines are concerned, the following list will provide an introduction:

P'u t'ao Chiu: The generic Chinese term for wine produced from grapes. Chaosing (or Shaohsing) is wine made from rice; Pai chiu is grain spirit, the best known being Maotai.
Chefoo: Named after a town on the Shantung peninsula. May be red or white, both being high in alcohol and reminiscent of Port and Sherry respectively.
Tsingtao: Also from Shantung, Tsingtao wines are both red and white, the latter being the more widely known and again reminiscent of Sherry: dry, straw-coloured wines, high in alcohol and with a good balance of acidity.
Meikuishanputaochu: A sweet, muscat-type wine made from a successful hybrid.
Great Wall: Christopher & Company, the old-established but enterprising London shippers, have recently added this white table wine to their list. It comes from Hebei, and is made from a grape variety called Loong Yan (Dragon's Eye). I find it most attractive: a scented bouquet, reminiscent of fresh fruit salad, and a tangy, well-balanced flavour with nice acidity and a hint of pine needles.

Japan

Wine-making in Japan began, as it did in China, for medicinal purposes, though its history is neither so long nor so well-documented. Research suggests that *Vitis vinifera* reached Japan from mainland China during the early medieval period, but it was destined from the outset to coexist with a number of other species of vines which, over the years, have proved as well (and in some cases better) adapted to cope with the naturally hostile environment of the Japanese islands. The problems confronting the Japanese as *vignerons* are twofold: a predominantly acid soil, and a damp and humid micro-climate, characterized by extended periods of continuous rainfall which reach a climax during the September monsoon. Such difficulties might well have deterred a people of lesser determination and resource.

The origins of the modern wine industry of Japan date only from the mid-nineteenth century, when the country was breaking from a long era of isolationism. From this period can be dated the first experiments with American and European grape-varieties, brought back by students returning enthusiastically from studies in the West, and the first tentative adoption of European *mores*, of which wine-drinking was one of the more significant. Although progress has been rapid in the years since 1945, corresponding to the growth of American influence, it would be premature to suggest that the wine-industry of Japan, as it enters the 1980s, is at any stage more advanced than adolescence. The main period of experimentation is over, although the techniques employed at every stage of production are still of a fairly primitive standard: something of an anachronism in such a thrusting economy. Four large companies virtually control the market: Sanraku Ocean, Mann's Wine, Godo Shusei and Suntory. Japan imports wine as well as producing it; not only as a luxury for consumption but also in bulk for blending in certain cases as *vins médecins* (corrective wines) with the local product. This latter practice, involving principally wines and musts from Australia and Chile, provides one element of doubt in one's assessment of Japanese labelling practice; another, and a far less acceptable, convention is the blatant apeing of French terminology and bottle presentation of which many Japanese producers are guilty. One Sanraku Ocean label, for example, declares 'Château Mercian, Grand Cru Classé, Mis en bouteille au château'. It is to be hoped that such practices are merely symptomatic of the insecurity of adolescence, rather than of a concerted design to infiltrate world wine markets by deception.

Vineyards are found throughout the Japanese archipelago, amounting to some 30,000 hectares in total: through the 1970s, new plantations have averaged 1,000 hectares a year. In total, the vineyards produce nearly 200,000 hectolitres of wine per annum, the balance being in grapes for the table. The greatest concentration of vineyards is found on the principal island, Honshu, the most important district lying in Yamanashi prefecture south-west of Tokyo, in the shadow of Fujiyama. Here, around the town of Kofu, lie some 6,000 hectares of vines, profiting from a relatively temperate micro-climate and good exposure on the walls of a sheltered valley. The soil, though volcanic in origin, is gravelly and well-drained. Japan's best wines are made here. Following Yamanashi (Kofu and Katsunuma) in importance, comes the district of Yamagata in northern Honshu with 3,500 hectares. Other major vineyards on Honshu are found in the areas of Nagano (west) and Okayama (south). The southernmost island, Kyushu, has one important area around Fukuoka, and on northern Hokkaido, vineyards are found in the area of Sapporo.

Five grape varieties alone account for some 90 per cent of Japanese vineyards, and their names will probably be unfamiliar. In order of importance they are Delaware (a variety of *Vitis labrusca*), Campbell's Early (a hybrid of *labrusca*), Neo-Muscat (a table grape), Muscat Bailey A (another hybrid of *labrusca*) and finally the native Koshu (a strain of *vinifera*). The grape varieties making up the remaining 10 per cent are responsible for the best of the Japanese wines, and their names will cause fewer surprises: Sémillon, Riesling, Müller-Thurgau and Chardonnay among the whites and Cabernet Sauvignon and Merlot among the reds. Plantations of all these classic varieties are on the increase, particularly in Yamanashi. Exports of Japanese wine are as yet insignificant, and the best of them are consumed on the spot. I have tasted various vintages of Château Mercian, which I found to be a pleasant, rather ordinary red, and a number of white wines made from Koshu, which were light, dry, sappy and acidic, not at all disagreeable with fish even though apparently prone to oxidation. Our Editor mentions being agreeably surprised by a Sapporo 'Polaire' Cabernet (1976 vintage), though her suspicions were aroused by its notable resemblance to a Chilean counterpart. On the strength of such slender experience, I can only counsel readers to experiment, and wish them good hunting.

Working in the vineyards on the arid, lower slopes of the Troodos mountains in Cyprus

9

The Wines of England

JACK WARD

Jack Ward is a director of the Merrydown Wine Company and Chairman of the recently formed Merrydown Vineyards Limited. He has been Chairman of the English Vineyards Association since its formation in 1967 and since then his work has mostly been concerned with the continuing development of the English wine industry.

Although it may come as a surprise to find vineyards planted in England, the vine is no stranger to her shores. There is some evidence to suggest that the Romans brought the plant to this country during their occupation but no one can be quite sure. It can be established, however, that vines were being grown in many parts of England during the Middle Ages. The Domesday Book records the existence of some forty vineyards at the time of William the Conqueror. With the exception of Sussex, Hampshire and Middlesex, the counties most favoured for the production of wine were almost the same as those that have been chosen today. This is no coincidence and is largely concerned with rainfall and other micro-climatic conditions. England has been a wine-producing country for much longer than has been generally understood and such considerations help to explain the present revival.

Much has been written about the subsequent decline of English viticulture. Some blame the weather; English summers are now cooler than they used to be. Others maintain that communications improved to such an extent that competition from overseas made wine production unprofitable. It is certainly true that the English occupation of Bordeaux for three centuries encouraged farmers to abandon the vine in favour of other crops. Existing vineyards were further reduced by the Dissolution of the Monasteries in 1536, where wine was used for religious purposes. By the following century viticulture in Britain had very likely been discounted as a sound commercial proposition, yet vineyards continued to exist on certain private estates. Among the most famous were those planted at Cobham in Surrey and at Castell Coch in South Wales. The first, belonging to the Hon. Charles Hamilton, existed in the middle of the eighteenth century; the second, planted by the Marquess of Bute, produced wine for nearly forty years until it was uprooted during the First World War.

Such conclusions, however, do not fully explain the remarkable revival that is now taking place. Part of the credit must go to the late Edward Hyams, whose scholarly book *The Grape Vine in England* has certainly helped to start the ball rolling. This was supported by the generosity of Ray Barrington Brock, who personally financed and conducted a research programme on his own premises for

An English vineyard, Wootton Vines, near Shepton Mallet in Somerset with six acres planted to Müller–Thurgau, Seyval Blanc and Schönburger; netting is used as a much-needed protection against birds

a period of at least fifteen years. It is maintained that the efforts of these pioneers persuaded another to plant the first post-war vineyard in Hampshire. It covered about an acre and belonged to Major General Sir Guy Salisbury-Jones. It was stocked with Seyval Blanc (Seyve-Villard 5276) a French hybrid, and also Müller-Thurgau, now recognized to be the most popular vine in Germany. Sir Guy embarked on this venture in 1952 and the vineyard, recently enlarged to five acres, has been successfully producing wine for a quarter of a century.

It was at least ten years before others followed suit. Margaret Gore-Browne, rather more ambitious, started with 5½ acres, and attempted to produce rosé wine as well as white. In order to achieve this, she added Pinot Meunier and Seibel 13053 to provide the colour. Margaret was a champion of English wine and will be remembered for the part she played in helping to create the English Vineyards Association and for generously donating a handsome silver trophy, a prize to be awarded annually for 'The Best English Wine of the Year'. The Association was registered in 1967 because by that time a handful of enthusiasts had decided to 'have a go' themselves. With only a dozen or so members and even less acres in production, the prospects of future development were not exactly promising. Nevertheless by the 1970s the revival had really got under way with vineyards being planted all over southern England, Wales and the Channel Islands, producing more than a hundred different wines for sale to the public. Total membership now exceeds 700 and the number of acres already planted must be approaching the 800 mark.

Grape Varieties

At first growers tended to play safe, following the recommendations of Barrington Brock and choosing vine varieties noted for their reliable performance. A few, however, experimented with new cultivars from the German research institutes. Classic French varieties such as Pinot Noir, Chardonnay and Pinot Gris were also planted with varying degrees of success. The Hop Department of Wye College, cooperating with the English Vineyards Association, planted groups of some twenty different vines on a four-acre plot, in an effort to discover which variety would do best in the sort of weather conditions endured in England. Similar experiments were conducted at Long Ashton near Bristol, Efford in Hampshire and on a smaller scale by the Royal Horticultural Society at Wisley in Surrey.

It soon became evident that varieties behave differently according to where they are planted, but soon some kind of pattern began to emerge. To pretend that climatic conditions are the same as, or even similar to, those prevailing in the Rhineland is misleading: latitude is not the only consideration. Müller-Thurgau for instance may well perform better in Germany than in England, where Reichensteiner or some other variety could in fact prove more consistent. The list of vines recommended by the EEC for cultivation in the United Kingdom, Müller-Thurgau, Pinot Meunier and Auxerrois, may have to be revised as a result of further experience. Varieties which are emerging for consideration are Madeleine Angevine, Reichensteiner, Regner, Huxelrebe, Bacchus, Würzer, Schönburger and Zweigeltrebe. All these have done well in different parts of the United Kingdom and could be regarded as suitable. The hybrid Seyval Blanc, though unlikely to be recommended by the EEC, will continue to be popular with the British grower.

Climate

All these varieties are harvested on the Continent in September and October, but in Britain where the summer is short and temperatures lower, they could ripen up to a fortnight or three weeks later. Those who want to make wine in the United

Kingdom must therefore take this into account and afford their vines the utmost protection. Perhaps the worst feature is not the lack of sunshine but the persistence of windy conditions which can only serve to reduce the prevailing temperature, thus retarding growth and even preventing pollination. English growers would do well to understand why the Germans have chosen river valleys in which to site their most northerly vineyards; at such latitudes it is important to conserve as much heat as possible, making the best use of any physical features available. Many of the vineyards in the United Kingdom can scarcely be described as sun traps.

It is unfortunate that the warmest part of Britain is also the wettest. Except for Somerset, part of which is dry enough, the whole of the southwest peninsula and Wales record an average rainfall above 30 inches per annum, rather too much for the successful production of grapes. It will be interesting to see whether modern fungicides will prove an effective answer to the problems of greater humidity.

It is important to realize also that the British climate has certain advantages. The incidence of winter frost damage due to excessively low temperatures does not readily occur in the south of England, nor can it be said that hailstones the size of golf balls are a common occurrence during summer. The slow ripening period and cool ambient temperatures during fermentation help to improve the quality of English wine by providing the maximum degree of fruit to the nose and the palate. Again it can be argued that Britain, possibly thanks to her climate, suffers less from insect predators, of which the most important must surely be *Phylloxera vastatrix*. Whether this grub would spread if it really got established in this country is problematical. Some think not, but the history of its progress throughout the viticultural world suggests otherwise. On the other hand, full recognition must be given to the problem of bird damage. Under present conditions, with isolated vineyards spread across the south of England, there is only one totally effective way of reducing this menace. Protective netting spread over the entire area and properly secured at ground level can effectively prevent the loss of fruit to blackbirds, thrushes, fieldfares, starlings, pheasants and other birds who find the taste of grapes irresistible.

The EEC

The United Kingdom, on the extreme edge of the European wine-growing belt, needs all the help it can get from the climate, the government and the EEC. Whitehall has so far been reluctant to provide financial help by way of grants, subsidies or research and is not in a position to allow a preferential rate of excise duty. As a result, the present rate of Value Added Tax, coming on top of the high cost of production, may cause the consumer to feel that English wines are overpriced.

The government has, however, made one important concession in respect of English wine used for domestic consumption. This consists of a special allocation amounting to 120 gallons per annum plus 10 per cent of production above that figure, up to a maximum total of 240 gallons. The concession means duty-free wine for the grower and his family, together with members of his staff. Untaxed bottles may be given away as trade samples or used for other promotional purposes, provided the owner of the vineyard has been registered as a British Winemaker for Sale. Such liberties are not enjoyed by other members of the wine trade.

Since the United Kingdom joined the Community, certain regulations affecting the production of wine must be observed by British growers. The Ministry of Agriculture, Fisheries and Food, together with the Wine Standards Board, are the authorities responsible for seeing that these measures are enforced. A few concessions have been granted by Brussels, in an effort to encourage an industry that could benefit the Community as a whole.

British growers, for example, are not obliged to plant the varieties authorized and recommended by the EEC, so long as the United Kingdom continues to be regarded as an experimental area. Again, the ban imposed by the necessity to reduce the wine lake has not yet been applied to the United Kingdom, where new vineyards may still be planted and those in existence extended.

There are, however, other causes for concern. English vineyards are known to provide an excessively high contribution to the Treasury in the form of Excise Duty, Value Added Tax, Corporation and Income Tax. As a member state of the Community, the United Kingdom cannot expect to discriminate in favour of English wine production by creating a preferential rate of duty. By the same token British growers should enjoy the advantages that are available to their European competitors. This does not always happen. By refusing to grant agricultural status to the production of wine, the government allows the Inland Revenue to assess buildings used by wine growers for rating purposes. This directly refutes Article 38, Clause 1 of the Treaty of Rome, which accepts that 'first-stage processing' is necessary for certain products and makes it clear that grape pressing, fermentation, bulk storage and bottling are not industrial activities. In a country where the production of wine is not fully understood, it is not appreciated that wine grapes have no sale as dessert fruit but are able to yield a valuable end product by processes as natural as the cultivation of the vines themselves. As with milk, wine must be put into some container before it can be offered for sale.

The English Vineyards Association

The English Vineyards Association, which was registered under the Industrial and Provident Societies Act 1965 on 8 March 1967, can be said to represent the vine-growers of the United Kingdom. Originally it was intended that it should act as a cooperative but it soon became apparent that its functions would be different. For this reason a change of constitution was suggested; this was achieved on 20 February 1979, when the Association was incorporated under the Companies Acts 1948 to 1976 and limited by Guarantee. Commercial growers, that is to say those who have planted at least half an acre, may join as members and pay an annual subscription related to the size of their vineyard; others who are indirectly concerned with the development of English viticulture may be included as associates, without voting rights. The Association supplies a journal annually, together with a series of news-letters circulated to members and associates every other month; these are in addition to the usual notices providing information about Association events, EEC directives, government legislation and other technical literature. Members and associates have opportunities to meet socially and discuss various technical theories. Special classes of instruction are arranged from time to time.

It was thought that among consumers the quality of English wine would be suspect from the start. The Association therefore decided to set its own standards and obtain official recognition for the excellence it hoped to achieve. Negotiations to obtain a certification trade mark that would serve as a guarantee for English wine were started in 1971, when a statement of case was prepared for submission to the Patents Office.

A self-imposed standard of quality such as this became significant when the United Kingdom joined the EEC and learned that the words 'table wine' had to appear on every bottle produced in the United Kingdom. Community policy insisted that English vineyards were required to show a 'track record' over a period of at least ten years before they would be permitted even to apply for quality status.

It was seven years before the Patents Office and the Department of Prices and Consumer Protection declared themselves satisfied with the proposals submitted by the Association, so it was only in 1978 that growers were able to apply for the use of the mark, which made its appearance a year later.

The seal, an EVA monogram partly encircled by the words 'Certification Trade Mark', was intended to provide a service for English growers that the Community was not prepared to undertake. Methods used by the French for granting *appellation contrôlée*, together with the German system for determining *Qualitätswein*, were all carefully studied. In addition EEC Council Regulation 817/70, aimed at creating standards for quality wines but irrelevant in the United Kingdom for the reasons stated above, was examined in detail. It was hoped that the best features from all these sources would be adopted and, with the help of experts, create a similar criterion, which would serve as a guarantee of good workmanship and be recognized by the wine trade and consumer public in this country.

To obtain the mark, a grower has to announce his intention of making an application before his grapes are harvested and has then to declare the weight of fruit and yield of must achieved. When the wine has been made and bottled, he must submit three samples to a specified laboratory for a series of stability tests. These examine the presence of iron, copper, protein, micro-organisms, free sulphur dioxide, acid, alcohol and extract. Wines that fail to pass any one of these tests are rejected. Successful samples are finally tested by a panel of judges, most of them Masters of Wine, who have generously offered their services for the occasion.

Is it possible to describe the nature of English wine or compare it with those that are being produced in other European countries? It is not at all easy because, as might be expected, vine varieties grown on the Continent tend to yield wines of a different character when planted in the United Kingdom. Although most Englishmen are growing German varieties, they seem to prefer a drier wine and are therefore inclined to use smaller quantities of *Süssreserve*, when it becomes necessary to adjust the balance of their product. As a result, English wines tend to resemble those of Alsace rather than those produced in the German Rhineland. Perhaps it could also be said that English wines possess the elegance, charm and flowery bouquet of wines usually associated with the river Moselle and its tributaries. Variety has been achieved by introducing Siegerrebe, Huxelrebe and Schönburger, all of which have succeeded in various parts of England.

Very little red wine has so far appeared, although some growers are making a determined effort to find cultivars likely to produce the best results under difficult conditions. Trials are being made with Zweigeltrebe, an early ripening Austrian variety, Gargarin Blue from the Soviet Union, and Léon Millot, a vigorous French hybrid.

Prospects for the immediate future seem to be favourable and the revival of the English wine industry may depend more on the depth of commercial demand than on the uncertainties of the climate. It has been established that a certain standard of quality can be achieved, it is hoped at not too great a cost; provided this standard is maintained, there is no reason why demand should not continue to grow. Marketing so far presents no problem and English growers are getting enormous help from the media without having to pay for it. Compared with France and Germany, nearest neighbours in the EEC, vineyards in this country suffer no competition. There is literally not enough English wine to go round. At first it was thought that prejudice would exist; of course it did and still does in certain quarters. As long as the volume of English wine continues to grow, however, and more people are able to taste it, the scepticism will gradually disappear, to be replaced by a sense of pride at this unexpected national achievement. British hotels and restaurants are already finding it necessary to include an English wine on their list, especially if they happen to be in tourist areas.

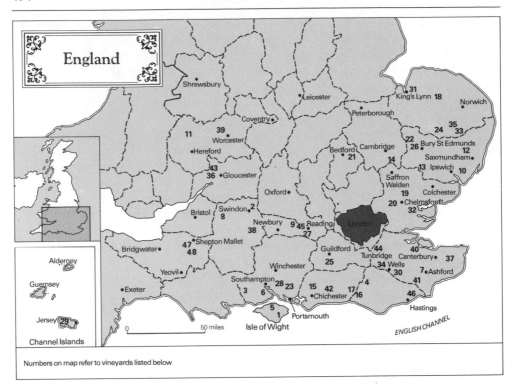

Numbers on map refer to vineyards listed below

A LIST OF SOME ENGLISH VINEYARDS

	Vineyard	Size	Name	Address
1.	Adgestone	8½ acres	K.C. Barlow	Locks Cottage, Adgestone, Sandown, Isle of Wight.
2.	Aeshton Manor	7½ acres	C. Stuart	Church Farm, Ashton Keynes, Swindon, Wiltshire.
3.	Aldermoor	6 acres	M.F. Baerselman	Aldermoors, Picket Hill, Ringwood, Hampshire.
4.	Barnsgate Manor	20½ acres	Pieroth Ltd	Barnsgate, Herons Ghyll, Nr. Uckfield, Sussex.
5.	Barton Manor	4½ acres	A.H. Goddard	Barton Manor, Whippingham, East Cowes, Isle of Wight.
6.	Beaulieu	4½ acres	Montagu Ventures Ltd	John Montagu Building, Beaulieu, Hampshire.
7.	Biddenden	14 acres	R.A. Barnes	Little Whatmans, Biddenden, Ashford, Kent.
8.	Bosmere	12 acres	G.H. Walton	Bosmere Farm, West Tytherton, Chippenham, Wiltshire.
9.	Bowden	3½ acres	M. Cardy	Lower Bowden Farm, Pangbourne, Berkshire.

	Vineyard	Size	Name	Address
10.	Brandeston Priory	6 acres	H.P.B. Dow, QC	The Priory, Brandeston, Woodbridge, Suffolk.
11.	Broadfield	9 acres	K.R.H. James	Broadfield Court, Bodenham, Herefordshire.
12.	Bruisyard St. Peter	10 acres	I.H. Berwick	Church Road, Bruisyard, Saxmundham, Suffolk.
13.	Cavendish Manor	10 acres	B.T. Ambrose	Nether Hall, Cavendish, Sudbury, Suffolk.
14.	Chilford Hundred	18 acres	S. Alper	Chilford Hall, Linton, Cambridgeshire.
15.	Chilsdown	11 acres	I.R. Paget	The Old Station House, Singleton, Chichester, Sussex.
16.	Ditchling	5 acres	D.D. Mills	Wick Farmhouse, Underhill Lane, Ditchling, Sussex.
17.	Downers	5 acres	Cdr. E.G. Downer, RN	Downers Vineyard, Clappers Lane, Fulking, Henfield, Sussex.
18.	Elmham Park	7½ acres	R.S. Don, MW	Elmham House, North Elmham, Dereham, Norfolk.
19.	Felstar	15 acres	J.G. Barrett	The Vineyards, Cricks Green, Felstead, Essex.
20.	Fyfield Hall	3 acres	R.J. White	Fyfield Hall, Fyfield, Essex.
21.	Gamlingay	8½ acres	G.P. Reece	The Vineyard, Drove Road, Gamlingay, Sandy, Bedfordshire.
22.	Genesis Green	4½ acres	M.H.C. Fuller	Wakelins, Genesis Green, Wickhambrook, Newmarket, Suffolk.
23.	Hambledon	5 acres	Sir Guy Salisbury-Jones, GCVO, GMG, CBE, MC	Mill Down, Hambledon, Hampshire.
24.	Harling	6 acres	J. Miljkovic	Eastfield House, East Harling, Norfolk.
25.	Hascombe	6 acres	Lt. Cdr. T.P. Baillie-Grohman, RN	Lodge Farm, Hascombe, Godalming, Surrey.
26.	Highwaymans	25 acres	Macrae Farms Ltd	Heathbarn Farm, Risby, Nr. Bury St Edmonds, Suffolk.
27.	Hillfoot	8 acres	R. Jones	Hillfoot Vineyard, Beenham, Nr. Reading, Berkshire.
28.	Hill Grove	8 acres	C.J. Hartley	Hill Grove Farm, Swanmore, Southampton, Hampshire.

	Vineyard	Size	Name	Address
29.	La Mare	4½ acres	R.H. Blayney	Elms Farm, St Mary, Jersey, Channel Islands.
30.	Lamberhurst Priory	28¾ acres	K. McAlpine	Ridge Farm, Lamberhurst, Tunbridge Wells, Kent.
31.	Lexham Hall	8 acres	N.W.D. Foster	Lexham Hall, Kings Lynn, Norfolk.
32.	New Hall	15 acres	S.W. Greenwood	New Hall, Purleigh, Chelmsford, Essex.
33.	Pennoyers	6 acres	I.J. Van der Zwan	The Grange, Pulham, St Mary the Virgin, Diss, Norfolk.
34.	Penshurst	7 acres	W.H. Westphal	The Grove, Penshurst, Kent.
35.	Pulham	6 acres	P.W. Cook	Mill Lane Farm, Pulham Market, Diss, Norfolk.
36.	Southfield	3 acres	A.G.E. Prins	Southfield, Solomons Tump, Huntley, Gloucestershire.
37.	Staple	7 acres	W.T. Ash	Church Farm, Staple, Nr. Canterbury, Kent.
38.	Stitchcombe	4 acres	N. Thompson	Grove Farmhouse, Mildenhall, Marlborough, Wiltshire.
39.	Stocks	11 acres	R.M.O. Capper	The Stocks Farm, Suckley, Worcestershire.
40.	Syndale Valley	5½ acres	J.H. Abbs	Old Thatch, Bistock, Doddington, Sittingbourne, Kent.
41.	Tenterden	6½ acres	S.P. Skelton	Spots Farm, Smallhythe, Tenterden, Kent.
42.	Thakeham	10 acres	J. Rice	Goffsland Farm, Coolham Road, Thakeham, Sussex.
43.	Three Choirs	17½ acres	A.A. McKechnie	Fairfields Fruit Farm, Rhyle House, Newent, Gloucestershire.
44.	Underriver	6 acres	B.S. Robinson	The Underriver Vineyard, Rooks Hill, Sevenoaks, Kent.
45.	Westbury	12½ acres	B.H. Theobald	Westbury Farm, Purley, Nr. Reading, Berkshire.
46.	Westfield	18 acres	D. Carr-Taylor	Yew Tree Farm, Westfield, Hastings, Sussex.
47.	Wootton	6 acres	C.L.B. Gillespie	North Town House, North Wootton, Shepton Mallet, Somerset.
48.	Wraxall	6 acres	A.S. Holmes	Vine Lodge, Wraxall, Shepton Mallet, Somerset.

The Wines of North America

NATHAN CHROMAN
with special assistance from Dr Ralph Hutchinson

Nathan Chroman is the wine correspondent of *The Los Angeles Times*, and is very involved with the Californian wine trade, which is the most important one in the United States. He has written *The Treasury of American Wines*, published in 1973 by Crown, New York, and is a regular taster at the big American wine fairs, as well as being a vineyard owner. He is also Chairman of the wine judges at the Los Angeles County Fair.

CALIFORNIA

Although many of the first European settlers on the eastern coast of North America came from wine-growing regions and from wine-drinking backgrounds, the development of a commercial wine industry in what later came to be known as the United States had to await California's entrance into the Union. It was not that the colonists did not try to grow grapes and make wine. They did. However, they discovered the wine they made from native American grapes, mainly *Vitis labrusca*, which they found growing profusely, unsatisfactory to their tastes, and their attempts to transplant the European wine varieties of *Vitis vinifera* were unsuccessful for a number of reasons. Partially, the failure was due to the harshness of the winters but much of it must be attributed to an almost invisible microscopic plant louse called *Phylloxera vastatrix*, which attacks and destroys the root system of the *vinifera*. This vicious little pest is native to the eastern part of the United States, and native American grapes had developed resistance to its ravages, but the more tender root system of the *vinifera* could not withstand its attack. Thus no significant American wine industry developed along the Eastern seaboard during the Colonial period.

The Spanish were more successful. When they landed on the coast of Mexico in the sixteenth century, they brought at least one European wine grape variety with them and, because there was no phylloxera in the western part of North America until it was brought there in the 1860s, grew grapes successfully everywhere they settled in Mexico. The vineyards which they founded around Saltillo, Torreón and Parras still flourish today. Because of the importance of wine in the sacrament, the Franciscan padres who came with the Spanish took the grapevine with them wherever they went, planting vineyards and making wine at each new mission. Eventually, by this process, the grape arrived in Baja California and was transported from there to San Diego in 1796. The grape they brought is still with us today. Variously known as the Criolla in Mexico and the Mission in California, it not only formed the basis of viticulture and wine-making during the Spanish and Mexican periods in California, but figured importantly in the earliest of commercial ventures in southern California, after the missions were secularized by the Mexican government in 1834. By the time California seceded from Mexico and joined the United States, a substantial commercial effort was underway in southern California, particularly around Los Angeles; and production had begun on a smaller scale in Sonoma and in the Napa Valley.

An early pioneer was Joseph Chapman who planted 4,000 grapevines in Los Angeles as early as 1824. Although his efforts were unsuccessful, those of a Frenchman, Jean Louis Vignes, were more prosperous. In the 1830s, he planted 400 acres on what is now the site of the railroad station in downtown Los Angeles, and prospered so much that he was able to bring two nephews to California and take them into his wine and brandy business. By the beginning of the 1840s, he had built up a substantial coastwide trade, extending as far north as Monterey, particularly with his brandy.

By the beginning of the 1850s, the centre of wine-making in California had already begun to shift to northern California. The Gold Rush of 1849 brought a rapid influx of population into the city of San Francisco as well as into the foothills of the Sierra Nevada mountains. The miners demanded table grapes and wine and were prepared to pay handsomely for both. Wine grapes were planted not only in the Sierras, but also in the Napa Valley, and plantings were expanded in Sonoma. The real driving force in the development and growth of wine-making and grape-growing in northern California, however, was a Hungarian immigrant, Agoston Haraszthy, who virtually singlehandedly transformed grape-growing and wine-making practices in California. He settled first in Wisconsin, founding the town now known as Sauk City, where he attempted to grow wine grapes. In 1849, he moved his family to California, settled in Mission Valley, north of San Diego, where he again planted grapes, having imported the vines from Europe. In 1852, he bought land near Mission Dolores in San Francisco and planted grape vines there also. When the grapes failed to ripen because of summer fog, he transplanted them to a site near Crystal Springs Reservoir, south of San Francisco, where they failed to ripen for the same reason. On a visit to Sonoma in 1856 he discovered that the *vinifera* vines planted there were flourishing, so he promptly bought a vineyard, named it Buena Vista, and settled down to a spectacularly successful, if somewhat brief, career as a grape-grower and wine-maker. By 1861, he was famous throughout the state for his work with grapes and wine. He had since his San Diego days imported vines from Europe and by 1858, had imported over sixty-five varieties. In 1862, he wrote and published *Grape Culture, Wines and Winemaking*, based on his experiences in Europe. He was willing to teach anyone who would listen what he knew about grapes and wine-making and demonstrated in his own vineyards that it was possible to make fine wine from grapes which had not been irrigated. He sent his son, Arpad, to France to study Champagne-making and when he had perfected the technique, he introduced sparkling wines into California. With the financial backing of a San Francisco banker, William Ralston, Haraszthy organized the Buena Vista Viticultural Society, and then donated his 6,000-acre ranch to it. For all these accomplishments and more, Agoston Haraszthy is known as the 'father of modern California viticulture'. He proved that it was possible to produce fine *vinifera* wines in California and in the New World.

It is, however, ironic that Haraszthy's imported vines, the basis of modern viticulture in California, also brought with them the greatest adversary of the *vinifera* in the United States, the phylloxera. It seems that in the 1850s phylloxera reached Europe on root stock of *Vitis labrusca* shipped there from the eastern part of the United States as part of an experiment to control powdery mildew (oidium) in

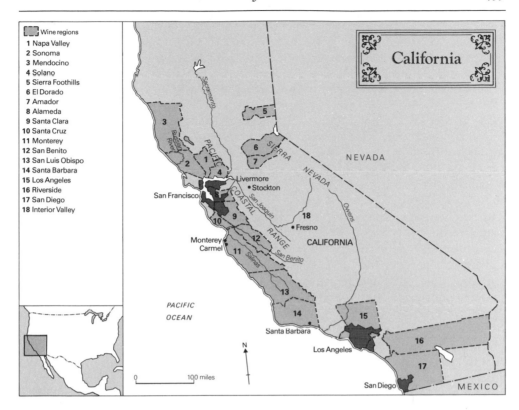

Wine regions
1 Napa Valley
2 Sonoma
3 Mendocino
4 Solano
5 Sierra Foothills
6 El Dorado
7 Amador
8 Alameda
9 Santa Clara
10 Santa Cruz
11 Monterey
12 San Benito
13 San Luis Obispo
14 Santa Barbara
15 Los Angeles
16 Riverside
17 San Diego
18 Interior Valley

French vineyards. There is double irony in the fact that *labrusca* roots later became the salvation of the *vinifera* vineyards throughout the world. By 1861, California vineyards were virtually decimated in the counties of Napa, Solano, Yolo, El Dorado and Placer. The solution to the devastation of the phylloxera turned out to be the grafting or budding of California or European *vinifera* vines on to *labrusca* root stock, which is apparently resistant to the insect. The technique is successful, and most of today's wines of the world are produced from vines so grafted.

Reconstruction of the California wine industry following the ravages of phylloxera was barely complete when the passage of the Eighteenth Amendment to the United States Constitution inaugurated National Prohibition. Fourteen years of the so-called 'Noble Experiment' of abstinence destroyed the commercial wine industry in California. Upon Repeal the rebuilding process commenced again. There was a grievous lack of equipment, experienced wine-makers, fine wine grape varieties and knowledgeable consumers. There was, however, a great rush into the industry by would-be wine-makers who, lacking experience, shipped immature and poorly made wine into retail markets. It was not long before consumers turned away from commercial producers and returned to their whisky bootleggers and to home-made wines. Commercial wineries were left primarily with a market for inexpensive California ports and sherries, with 20 per cent alcohol, made from raisin grapes grown in the state's hot Interior Valley.

Few wineries of the early Repeal period owned their own vineyards, so they had to rely upon purchased grapes. Grape-growers were reluctant to plant fine wine varieties for sale to the filtering wine market. They found it more profitable to plant the bountiful raisin and table grape, the Thompson Seedless, which was used in any one of three ways: as fresh table fruit, or as raisins, or fermented into wine. The latter use became the significant one for the Thompson, especially for inexpensive ports and sherries. Consumers were relatively unsophisticated and were content with the generic (a California term for the use of European names such as Burgundy, Chablis, etc, on domestic wine labels) table wines which formed the greatest portion of table-wine production and sales during the early years following the end of Prohibition.

However, following the end of the Second World War (which interrupted the rebuilding of the California wine industry for four years), Americans began to show greater interest not only in wine in general, but in finer wines. As Americans learned to appreciate wine as a mealtime beverage, they gained in knowledge and sophistication. They began to seek improved quality and their interest turned to varietal wines (wines which are labelled by the name of the dominant grape from which they are made are called varietal wines in California and in the other wine-producing states of the United States. At present the minimum requirement is that 51 per cent of the wine be made from the grape named on the label, but this will be increased to 75 per cent by 1983). Finally, when the long, slow but steady increase in consumption of table wines burgeoned in the 1960s into a 'Wine Revolution', California's grape-growers responded with a spirited rush to plant fine grape varieties. The heavy planting of new vineyards soon began to fill all the available space in such established areas as the Napa Valley and Sonoma County, which caused a spillover into new and untried regions such as the Salinas Valley in Monterey, Santa Barbara and San Luis Obispo Counties. Table wine sales, which had increased steadily but slowly since the 1950s, jumped to rates of increase of 25 per cent in 1965, 1970 and 1971, before levelling off to a more modest, but still dramatic, annual rate of increase of 10 per cent. Annual sales of table wine trebled during the 1970s. Sales of ports and sherries, which had declined steadily throughout this same period, continued to decline, accounting for less than one-fifth of sales of California wine by the beginning of the 1980s. There was also an equally dramatic increase in the number of wineries operating in California, from 227 in the mid-1960s to 406 at the end of the 1970s.

The inexplicable change in the pattern of consumption was the abrupt increase in one twelve-month period in the drinking of white wine. As consumers substituted white wine for other alcoholic beverages, consumption of white wine increased to 40 per cent from 30 per cent of total sales in the period 1977-78, and to over 50 per cent of table wine sales by the end of 1979. Because two-thirds of the new plant-ings of wine grapes during the period 1970 to 1974 were red, the change in com-position of demand for table wines from mainly red to mainly white, developed a shortage of white grapes. However, wine-makers responded by making white wines from red grapes – giving birth to a 'new' category of California wines: Blanc de Noirs. Such grapes as Zinfandel, Pinot Noir, Gamay Beaujolais, and even Cabernet Sauvignon, were tried with results ranging from poor to outstanding. The best slightly resemble the still wines of Champagne, especially those made from the Pinot Noir.

THE NAPA VALLEY

The Napa Valley is the best-known viticultural area in the United States. Located approximately one hour's drive north and slightly east of San Francisco, the Valley is about twenty-five miles in length from its mouth on San Pablo Bay in the south to the foot of Mount St Helena in the north, and varies from three to five miles in width. It is separated from Sonoma County, an adjacent wine region, by the Mayacamas Mountains in the west, and its eastern boundary is delineated by the ridge line of a range of low mountains.

Rainfall is concentrated mainly in the winter months of November, December and January, and is usually ample enough (twenty to thirty inches per year) to supply the moisture needs of the vines planted there without the need for irrigation. Rain during the harvest occurs only occasionally. However, frost during early and mid-spring can be a problem and various frost protection devices are employed. Large fans resembling aeroplane propellers move air to prevent frost from settling on the vines. Another technique is the use of permanently installed water sprinklers to protect the vines by spraying a fine mist over them; as the water freezes, it insulates the vines from freezing temperatures. In general, the Valley's soils, volcanic and alluvial in origin, are well-drained, an essential feature in a vineyard site; it prevents the build up of mineral salts which would be harmful to vine roots.

San Francisco Bay in the south and the Pacific Ocean to the west serve as regulators of the micro-climates in the Valley. Temperatures range from relatively cool in the south to relatively warm in the north. The temperature gradation is not smooth nor continuous. Thus, although it is possible to say accurately that on the University of California at Davis system of heat summation, Region I is to be found at the southern mouth of the Valley, Region II in the mid-section near Oakville, and Region III in the northern portion surrounding Calistoga, it is also true that there are pockets, in which temperatures differ from those of the surrounding area, scattered throughout the Valley. The University of California system of heat summation and regional classification is based on the concept of the 'degree day'. A degree day is a period of 24 hours during which the average temperature exceeds 50°F by one degree. An average temperature of 65°F over a twenty-four hour period is equal to fifteen degree days. Degree days are calculated over the period of April 1 to October 31, the growing season, to determine five climatic regions. 50°F is the base temperature because plants do not grow actively below that temperature. Region I is anywhere with less than 2,500 degree days; Region II, 2,501 to 3,000 degree days; Region III, 3,001 to 3,500 degree days; Region IV, 3,501 to 4,000 degree days; Region V, in excess of 4,001 degree days. However, early ripening grapes such as Chardonnay and Pinot Noir appear to do better in the southern Region I than elsewhere in the Valley. Cabernet Sauvignon thrives in a middle band centred on Rutherford, where they have produced some truly outstanding wines. Zinfandel and Petite Sirah produce well, in terms of both yield and quality, at the warmer northern end of the Valley. On the western hillsides, the cooling effect of higher altitude has permitted the planting of Gewürztraminer, Chardonnay and Riesling with undeniably good results. Much of the stretch of hills from Napa to Calistoga may be as cool as Region I. The eastern hills are warmer and drier and, as a result, heat-tolerant varieties such as Zinfandel do well there.

Napa Valley wine-growing suitability was recognized by the mid-nineteenth century and the discovery of gold in the Sierra foothills in 1848 attracted thousands of new settlers to California; as a consequence, the pace of viticultural development in the Napa Valley quickened. Acreage increased from less than 1,000 at the beginning of the Gold Rush to over 10,000 at the end of the 1870s. After 1860, the new plantings were of *vinifera* varieties other than the Mission due to the efforts of Agoston Haraszthy. By the beginning of the 1890s, there were 17,000 acres planted to vineyards in the Napa Valley; few were Mission vines.

When the gold was exhausted, many of the miners turned to other occupations, including wine-making and grape-growing. Additionally, many American immigrants must have gone to California and the Napa Valley specifically for the purpose of making wine. At the end of the 1870s, forty-four of the forty-nine wine-makers in the Napa Valley reflected European wine-making background and experience. Among these few were included such historically significant pioneers as Charles Krug, who in 1858 made the first European-style wine ever produced in the Valley, using a cider press to extract the juice from the grapes.

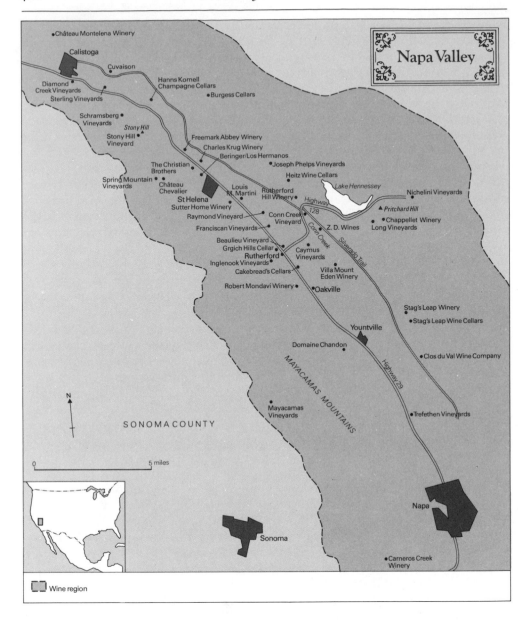

Château Montelena Winery
Calistoga
Cuvaison
Diamond
Creek Vineyards
Sterling Vineyards
Hanns Kornell
Champagne Cellars
Burgess Cellars
Schramsberg
Vineyards
Stony Hill
Stony Hill
Vineyard
Freemark Abbey Winery
Charles Krug Winery
Beringer/Los Hermanos
The Christian
Brothers
Joseph Phelps Vineyards
Heitz Wine Cellars
Spring Mountain
Vineyards
Château
Chevalier
Louis
M. Martini
St Helena
Sutter Home Winery
Raymond Vineyard
Franciscan Vineyards
Rutherford
Hill Winery
Conn Creek
Vineyard
Highway
128
Lake Hennessey
Nichelini Vineyards
Pritchard Hill
Chappellet Winery
Long Vineyards
Z. D. Wines
Conn Creek
Beaulieu Vineyard
Grgich Hills Cellar
Rutherford
Inglenook Vineyards
Cakebread's Cellars
Caymus
Vineyards
Silverado Trail
Villa Mount
Eden Winery
Robert Mondavi Winery
Oakville
Stag's Leap Winery
Stag's Leap Wine Cellars
Yountville
Domaine Chandon
Clos du Val Wine Company
Highway 29
MAYACAMAS MOUNTAINS
N
SONOMA COUNTY
Mayacamas
Vineyards
Trefethen Vineyards
0   5 miles
Napa
Sonoma
Carneros Creek
Winery
Napa Valley
Wine region

By 1890, commercial wine production was well and soundly established in the Napa Valley and its wines were receiving international attention. Then the disaster of the phylloxera struck, destroying 10,000 of the 17,000 acres of grapes. Wine production in the Valley had fallen from over 4,000,000 US gallons to less than 500,000 US gallons. Replanting of the devastated vineyards began at the end of the 1890s, but by the time it was completed and wine production was reaching its former peak, disaster struck again – this time in the form of National Prohibition, which all but completely destroyed commercial wine production everywhere in the United States. A few wineries in the Valley managed to survive by producing sacramental wines or by making wines to be used as bases for tonics.

At Repeal, in 1933, the Napa Valley suffered from the same difficulties experienced by the rest of the American wine industry. Equipment was in poor repair or non-existent; there were few experienced wine-makers and fine wine varieties of grapes were in limited supply. Moreover, an entire generation of Americans had grown up without the joy of wine as a mealtime beverage. Rebuilding was begun, only to be interrupted by four years of the Second World War shortages and disruptions. Even after the end of the war, reconstruction proceeded slowly. But the pace was steady: sales of table wines increased and varietal wines gained in relative importance. By the mid-1960s, Napa Valley wineries were beginning to experience shortages of such grapes as Cabernet Sauvignon and Chardonnay as the pace of consumer demand for table wines accelerated to annual rates of 10 to 15 per cent. Beginning in 1970, growers everywhere in California responded to increased demand for grapes by planting an additional 200,000 acres of wine varieties in the five-year period ending in 1974.

Vineyard acreage in the Napa Valley increased from 10,500 acres in 1970 to approximately 25,000 acres in 1974. By that time vineyards had displaced virtually every orchard or tree crop in the Valley, which had taken on the appearance of a virtually unbroken expanse of vineyards from Calistoga in the north to the city of Napa in the south. As vineyard acreage grew, so did the number of wineries – from fewer than forty in the early 1960s to 135 in 1980. New wineries also meant new wine-makers and an influx of capital.

In some instances the fresh approach, the new capital and the new techniques came from an experienced member of the industry, such as Robert Mondavi, who saw the bright future and opportunistically embraced it. In other situations, a flood of new capital came from large non-wine-making corporations seeking diversity or the glamour of the grape. Most of the corporate entrants were wise enough to engage the services of talented wine-makers such as Myron Nightingale at Beringer Vineyards, initially purchased by Nestlé who then had the good sense not to interfere in his wine-making decisions. Fortunately, in most instances, growth has not come at the expense of quality. If anything, quality has more than kept pace with growth in quantity, as a consequence of the updating of equipment and techniques.

Unfortunately, the growth in vineyard acreage in the Napa Valley during the 1970s has left little room for continued expansion at the rate at which growth has occurred in the past ten years. Even if vineyards are planted on the hillsides, they will not be so readily or easily developed as those on the Valley floor, and their development will be more expensive. Many of the vineyards in the Napa Valley are protected from urban encroachment by a county government ordinance designed to preserve the land for agricultural uses. Thus, there is no need to fear that Napa Valley vineyards will be removed to make way for housing tracts, but like all government edicts this could change. If Napa Valley wines become more difficult to obtain and more expensive, it will be as a consequence of rising demand rather than as a result of shrinking vineyards due to urban sprawl. The ever growing number of wineries will undoubtedly increase competition for the purchase of quality grapes.

BEAULIEU VINEYARD

For thirty-five years, from 1938 to 1973, André Tchelistcheff guided the fortunes of one of the Napa Valley's brightest stars, Beaulieu Vineyard. Now officially retired from Beaulieu, but working harder than ever as a consultant to several new wineries in California, Washington and Oregon, Tchelistcheff is still considered the 'Dean of California Wine-makers'. He has probably received more acclaim than any other single individual for shaping the course of California wine following Repeal. Born in Russia and educated in Czechoslovakia, he was brought to the Napa Valley in 1938 by the founder of Beaulieu, Georges de Latour, who discovered him working as a research oenologist at the Institut National Agronomique in Paris. When Tchelistcheff first tasted California wines, he promptly singled out Napa Valley Cabernet as offering the most promise. His tenure at Beaulieu Vineyard produced what many consider to be the finest Cabernets, Private Reserve; several have attained international acclaim. Even today, and in his absence, his techniques entrusted to a new Beaulieu Vineyard wine-making team still produce the most sought-after Cabernets in the United States. In 1969 Beaulieu Vineyard was sold to Heublein Inc. who, under the direction of Beaulieu Vineyard head, Legh Knowles, have continued the traditions established by the de Latour family and Tchelistcheff. Although Heublein have spent a considerable sum on modernization of crushing and fermenting facilities, annual output remains virtually unchanged and only modest increases are planned for the future. A cloud on the horizon appears, however, with the new Beaulieu Vineyard jug wines that, although of high quality, may portend future direction. Beaulieu Vineyard's best wines are still the Cabernet Sauvignons, regular as well as Private Reserve. The best buys on the list, however, may very well be the inexpensive generic burgundy and chablis, now available in a new 1.5-litre bottle.

BERINGER VINEYARDS/LOS HERMANOS VINEYARDS

An old Napa Valley name is Beringer Vineyards. The winery has produced wine in every vintage since 1879, including those during the Prohibition era. The winery was sold by the Beringer family in 1971 to the Swiss corporate parent of Nestlé, the famous chocolate producers. Nestlé immediately embarked upon a much needed modernization and restoration programme. A modern winery, filled with stainless steel, was built across the road from the old Beringer facilities, just west and south of Charles Krug. Storage capacity has been increased to a level just short of three million US gallons.

Perhaps the smartest move made by the new owners was to engage the services of Myron Nightingale, the creator of Cresta Blanca's fabled Premier Sémillon, as their wine-maker. While at Cresta Blanca in the Livermore Valley, Nightingale devised a laboratory technique for growing *Botrytis cinerea* mould, which is responsible for the great Sauternes of France and the *Trockenbeerenauslesen* of Germany. Spores of the 'noble mould' were sprayed on Sémillon and Sauvignon Blanc grapes which, when they had reached the appropriate degree of dehydration, were pressed and the juice fermented. The result was a wine which those fortunate enough to taste hailed as magnificent. Under Nightingale's direction, the Cabernets and Zinfandels have returned to significantly improved quality, while Chardonnays and Johannisberg Rieslings have achieved an intensity of varietal character and complexities never before attained in Beringer white wines. The reds, however, remain the more interesting wines. In 1973 the first significant amount of botrytis developed in Beringer's vineyards in Knight's Valley in Sonoma County, giving Myron Nightingale an opportunity to demonstrate that he had not lost his touch with grapes affected by the noble mould. His 1974 Johannisberg Riesling in the late-harvest style was delicately luscious and superbly balanced.

Beringer has acquired additional vineyards, increasing the total to an imposing 2,500 acres which provide Nightingale with a long-needed selection of grapes from which to produce and/or blend his wines. The varied grape-region selection has given rise to the practice of regional labelling for Beringer's varietals. Notable at the top of the list of vintage-dated varietals are the proprietarily labelled Traubengold, produced from Santa Barbara County Johannisberg Riesling grapes, and a port-styled wine made from Cabernet Sauvignon grapes. Beringer's line of generics and varietals, packaged in sizes up to four litres, is labelled Los Hermanos. Beringer

*An aerial view of the beautiful modern winery of Chappellet near
Pritchard Hill showing the contours of the Napa Valley*

was one of the first to bottle varietals in 1.5-litre size or larger, and these wines represent extremely good value considering taste and cost.

BURGESS CELLARS

Burgess Cellars is a winery that has quickly made a fine reputation and produces some of the Napa Valley's best Chardonnays and Cabernets. Other varieties include Johannisberg Riesling, Zinfandel, Petite Sirah, Chenin Blanc and Green Hungarian. The Cabernet Sauvignon and Chardonnay are outstanding, especially the 1977 Chardonnay from Winery Lake Vineyards (located in the Los Carneros district at the southern end of the Napa Valley) which was of monstrous proportions at 13.8 per cent alcohol and 0.73 total acidity. The wine was highlighted by concentrated varietal fruitiness and complex, buttery richness, resulting from fermentation in oak, and barrel ageing. It is a Chardonnay which should age for a decade. The 1976 Cabernet and the 1977 Zinfandel received Los Angeles County Fair awards. The Cabernet, produced in the first year of a two-year drought in California, reflects this is an attractive austere style, reminiscent of a St Julien. It has, however, a good varietal Cabernet nose and good Cabernet flavour which compensate for its steely backbone. The 1977 Zinfandel, produced in the second drought year, shows an intensity of the raspberry character of Zinfandel, which makes for a lush wine, with an ability to age for more than a decade. Also produced is a secondary label, Bell Canyon.

CAKEBREAD'S CELLARS

Jack Cakebread's initial wines were fascinating. From six-year old vines, Jack and his son Bruce produced an incredibly good 1974 Cabernet Sauvignon. Aged in wood and blended with 8 per cent Cabernet Franc, the wine is delightfully inky, concentrated with flavour and plenty of alcohol, too, at 13.5 per cent. The wine was neither fined nor filtered, just carefully racked and then bottled in May 1977. It will continue to age beautifully into a complex wine that by 1985 should be a Cabernet benchmark. The 1973 Chardonnay from purchased grapes was superb. Drinking it in 1979, I found the lusciousness and flavour outstanding. The 1976 Chardonnay has developed well, too. It was field crushed early in September, then fermented after four hours' skin contact which seems to give Jack's wines substance and power at 13.9 per cent alcohol. It has considerable flavour, delightfully not 'over-oaked', and is in good balance. It should reach its flavour peak in 1980. From fourth-year vines in the Yountville area, it is a wine for dedicated Chardonnay lovers, who like their wines crisp but with power.

CARNEROS CREEK WINERY

Los Carneros at the extreme southern end of the Napa Valley, as a Region 1, is the coolest region in the Valley, and also the home of Carneros Creek Winery. Balfour and Anita Gibson established the winery in 1972, a year not otherwise noted for great Napa Valley wine, to experiment with and to specialize in Pinot Noir. An attempt here has been made to challenge the California myth that fine Pinot Noir cannot be made. Twenty different clones on ten acres were planted to determine the best for both soil and micro-climate. The fifteen-year trial is funded by Carneros Creek, but is under the supervision of the Department of Viticulture and Enology at the University of California at Davis. While waiting for the experiment to be concluded, several fine Cabernets, Chardonnays, Pinot Noirs and Zinfandels have been produced from purchased grapes by the wine-maker, Francis Mahoney. Zinfandels have been especially interesting, dark and flavourful, which reveal clearly their Amador and Yolo counties' vineyard origins.

(Above) The reception area of Parducci Winery, the oldest winery in Mendocino County
(Below) Cellars at Clos du Val in the Napa Valley showing wooden vats
and in the foreground new oak Bordeaux-sized ageing barrels

CAYMUS VINEYARDS

In 1971, Charles Wagner established a winery, Caymus Vineyards, at Rutherford. His move was assisted by seventy acres of prime Napa Valley grapes, much of which has found its way into prime Napa Valley labels, including Beaulieu Cabernet Sauvignon. The winery produces Cabernet Sauvignon, Johannisberg Riesling and Pinot Noir from Caymus-owned grapes; Zinfandel and more Cabernet from purchased grapes are bottled under the label of Liberty School. Wines have been noteworthy, especially the 1974 abundantly flavoured Cabernet, mouthfilling, soft, with enough tannin for a long, prosperous, complex future. Pinot Noirs are also interesting. The 1972, in an otherwise unexciting year, displayed fine Pinot Noir aroma, medium body, dark colour and abundant flavour, the latter one of Pinot Noir's major shortcomings. Many believe it to be one of Napa Valley's finest.

CHAPPELLET WINERY

Rising dramatically above Lake Hennessey along Highway 128 in the Valley atop Pritchard Hill sits the beautiful, modern winery of Donn Chappellet. Notwithstanding the fine quality of the wines, the winery building is a wine tourist must. Production is limited to six varietal wines: Chenin Blanc, Chardonnay, Gamay, Johannisberg Riesling, Merlot and Cabernet Sauvignon; and three generics. The emphasis is upon dryness, especially for Chenin Blanc, and in earlier vintages, for the Johannisberg Riesling which in recent years has shown a bit of sweetness. The Chenin Blanc has been a remarkable wine. The vines were there when he moved on to the property, so the grapes were turned into wine while Cabernet and Chardonnay were planted. Not content to produce a casual fruity Chenin Blanc, Chappellet made it into a respectable dry white specifically for table use, completely different from the then popular sweet style of Charles Krug. The wine received the same treatment as Chardonnay, aged in wood, and reflected a heavier yet completely dry style that provided inexpensive relief from high-cost Chardonnay. It made immediate friends for the winery and allowed time for the Chappellet Chardonnays and Cabernets to bear and mature. It remains today as one of the driest and more interesting Chenin Blancs. Of special interest have been the big-styled Cabernets, topped by the 1969, which drinks today with vigour and demonstrates fruit and intensity that will make it last for decades. Chardonnays, while good, have not found as much favour as the Cabernets – perhaps not enough fruit to match the wood-ageing technique is the reason for this.

CHATEAU CHEVALIER WINERY

Château Chevalier, nestled nicely on a Spring Mountain site, is an old, efficiently remodelled Victorian house. In 1969, the Bissonettes purchased the château and rebuilt it from neglected disrepair. They cleared sixty acres, planted them to Cabernet Sauvignon and Chardonnay, and then literally hand-equipped a 25,000-US gallon winery facility. First crush was in 1973 from purchased grapes, which were bottled and released under the 'Mountainside Vineyards' label, reserved for non-estate bottling. The first wines from château grapes were made in 1974 and released in 1976. Notable were a 1974 Cabernet and a 1975 late-harvested Chardonnay. 1974 was a great year for Cabernet in Napa Valley and Chevalier's is no exception. A superb wine, dark, aromatic and lush, it drinks generously, although tannin and structure indicate a long life. Although fully assertive now, the wine may need at at least another decade or so before complexity. Proud of Californian wines, Greg Bissonette was amongst the first to champion 'boutique' exports to Europe and is at the head of a commercial venture so inclined.

CHATEAU MONTELENA WINERY

One of the publicized victors in the notorious Paris French-versus-California tastings is a winery with which destiny has taken a favoured hand, Château Montelena, north of Calistoga on Tubbs Lane. The Chardonnay finished first in the Paris tasting, ahead of France's best white Burgundies and five other California Chardonnays. The 1973 Chardonnay was a good wine produced by Miljenko Grgich, the experienced former wine-maker who had worked with Lee Stewart, founder of Souverain, Christian Brothers, Beaulieu and Tchelistcheff and Robert Mondavi. Grgich subsequently withdrew from Château Montelena to establish his own winery, Grgich Hills Cellars, north of Rutherford. In 1977, Jerry Luper, former Freemark Abbey wine-maker, assumed wine-making responsibility.

The winery was reactivated in 1972 by the new team of southern California attorney, James L. Barrett, and millionaire shopping-centre contractor, Ernest W. Hahn, joined by Lee Paschich, former owner of the property. Reflecting the new breed of winery proprietors, the team made its money elsewhere and has come to the Napa Valley to make wine for genuine sport as well as for profit. Because of the capital intensive nature of wineries, money made elsewhere is an indispensable commodity. Château Montelena produces only four wines, quite capably and, frequently, from grapes not grown on their own property. Chardonnay and Cabernet together constitute 90 per cent of their production, with lesser amounts of Zinfandel and Johannisberg Riesling. The long-term goal of Montelena is to concentrate most of their production in high quality Cabernet Sauvignon and smaller amounts of high quality Chardonnay. Sixty acres of vineyards around the château have been planted to Cabernet, and, interestingly, twenty-two acres are being planted to Chardonnay with the newest clone developed by the University of California at Davis. Chardonnays, in general, have been excellent and perhaps better than the Cabernet wines, which are robust, vigorous and full-bodied, but not yet of sufficient age to develop complexities. Zinfandels have been fresh, fruity and light, but not necessarily complex. Overall production is only 20,000 cases.

THE CHRISTIAN BROTHERS

The story of the Christian Brothers' involvement in California wine is fascinating and reaches back to 1882 to their original novitiate at Martinez. In the 1930s they decided to expand their altar-wine production to include commercial production and another ingenious move followed in 1937, when the Christian Brothers engaged the dynamic marketeers from Europe, Fromm and Sichel, as their exclusive world-wide representatives. The winery's name, then Mont La Salle, was changed to the Christian Brothers and their wines were successfully launched into world markets. Brother Timothy, the kindly teacher turned wine-maker, has for years been the national symbol of the Christian Brothers and under his guidance, they have produced quality wines in volume, without vintage dating, presumably to produce a mature taste that is good and always consistent. The Brothers have blended excellently, and on most restaurant wine lists their wines are welcome relief from high tannic, under-aged wines, particularly the reds. In recent years they have experimented with vintage dating, beginning with a special lot of 1976 Gewürztraminer released in 1977. The vintage-dated experimental line was expanded by the addition of Cabernet Sauvignon, Pineau de la Loire and Pinot St George also known as red Pinot (it bears no resemblance to Pinot Noir in vine, grape or wine, but the Christian Brothers have made it one of their prestige wines). All the vintage-dated wines are specially selected and are bottled under a special identifying label. A 1974 Cabernet, recently released, is without question characteristic of the new vintage-dating effort. The wine drinks generously and is in a soft pleasant style that is characteristic of Christian Brothers. A bit of tannin suggests longer ageing. Other special Christian Brothers' table wines are Brother Timothy's Special Selections, four non-vintage varietals which include Pinot Noir, Gamay Noir, Cabernet Sauvignon and Zinfandel. The wines are blends from different years and are judged to have special quality characteristics. Another wine worthy of interest is the nationally popular Château La Salle, produced from Muscat Canelli grapes, and for its type and cost it merits tasting. Brandies are also produced and in considerable quantity, including the largest selling brandy in the United States.

CLOS DU VAL WINE COMPANY, INC.

Along the Silverado Trail not far from Stag's Leap Wine Cellars is a Californian winery with close French ties. Clos du Val is a California corporation operated by wine-maker Bernard Portet (whose father André Portet is a former *régisseur* at Château Lafite-Rothschild) but who probably thinks of himself these days as more Californian than French. The first wines produced by the winery were made in 1972 from purchased grapes, while the first estate vintage from their own 120 acres of vineyard was produced in 1975. Clos du Val appears to enjoy the best of both worlds, Californian and French. The 1975 Cabernet was dark, intense, and full-fruited from its Californian origins, with elegant, good but not-overbearing flavour from its Médoc heritage. The Zinfandel 1975 was also dark and big, and long lived – perhaps too big and un-French-like. Its more than ample fruit, body and astringency suggest that lengthy ageing is in order. Portet is making excellent Cabernets, but by no means has he made his best. Perhaps the 1976 thus far lays a challenge, but it is obvious that great bottles will come. Recently, he has produced a Chardonnay which, although satisfactory, does not measure up to the Cabernets, a fact that will not go unnoticed and will direct Portet properly.

CONN CREEK VINEYARD

Conn Creek Winery was founded in 1974 by Napa Valley vineyardist, William D. Collins, and Stanford professor, William L. Beaver, who leased an 1886 stone winery, north of St Helena. A permanent structure at the intersection of Conn Creek Road and Silverado Trail east of Rutherford was later constructed with 1979 as its initial harvest. The wine-maker is Daryl Eklund. The list of wines includes Zinfandel, Cabernet Sauvignon (the 1976 is a fine wine), Chardonnay, Gamay Beaujolais and White Riesling. Early releases were pleasant, drinkable wines, especially the Chardonnays which have taken on a more serious character. The 1977 and 1978 were especially good, full-fruited, clean, with plenty of flavour somewhat intruded upon in 1977 by wood.

CUVAISON, INC.

Cuvaison is a Calistoga winery founded in 1970 by two engineers, Thomas Cottrell and Thomas Parkhill. It limits production to three wines: Chardonnay, Cabernet Sauvignon and Zinfandel. The limitation of the number of wines is another example of California's realization that a full line of wines does not mean a full line of quality. The equipment is up to the minute and new French oak cooperage is now utilized for maturing each of the wines. Today the 60,000 US-gallon winery is owned by Dr Stephen Schmidheiny and the wine-maker is Philip Togni. Togni's wine-making experience has produced some interesting wines, notably the 1977 and 1978 Chardonnays which are flavourful, generous, fully fruited wines. Assertive varietal character has attracted Cuvaison fans for these are not wines of restraint as evidenced by the reds which are big, dark, somewhat heavy wines that require a decade or more to develop suppleness and finesse. The Zinfandels have developed controversy over their peppery character which is not generally observed in most California Zinfandels. This characteristic was especially pronounced in a release labelled as '71–2', a blend of two vintages, 1971 and 1972. The 1977 Chardonnay was especially a favourite, a big wine with 14 per cent alcohol, it shapes up like a heavier-styled white Burgundy. A hint of oak is pleasant, with good balance and high alcohol, this wine displays staying power and it should be around in good style until the end of the 1980s.

DIAMOND CREEK VINEYARDS

Diamond Creek Vineyards, on the slopes of Napa Valley's western side, is owned by Albert Brounstein. Specializing in Cabernet, he planted on what he considers to be three distinctively different vineyard soils. The three sections produce three distinctly different wines, Red Rock Terrace, Gravelly Meadow and Volcanic Hill. Each is vinified and bottled separately. The wines are neither fined nor filtered and are generally considered so-called monsters of tannin, colour and flavour – perhaps too much so. These wines, in particular, need long-term ageing, but have a strong following, notwithstanding their 1980 price of $10.00 per bottle.

DOMAINE CHANDON

Domaine Chandon is fathered by France's prestigious Moët et Chandon. So as not to offend France's Champagne fraternity, the wine is known simply as Domaine Chandon. The fraternity is also not offended by the taste which each year becomes more French-like. Early bottlings produced a fruitier style because of California's often intensely fruited wines that form the blends. Initially, Pinot Noir, Pinot Blanc, Chardonnay and Ugni Blanc were variously blended, but it has taken time for the Moët wine-making team to find the exact combinations to produce a California sparkling wine against a Gallic technical background. Today, Pinot Noir is probably more employed than Chardonnay, which may be too fruity in the long run.

The enormous twenty-million dollar project, which includes a first-rate French restaurant, one of the best in the Valley, was entrusted to John Wright, formerly with the nationally known consulting firm of Arthur D. Little. Wright bought 600 acres in the cool Carneros region at the southern end of the Napa Valley, 200 acres on Mount Veeder in the hills to the west of the Valley, and one hundred acres just north and east of the Veteran's Home at Yountville. The first sparkling wines of Domaine Chandon were released in December 1976. These have aged extremely well and are drinking better now than when first released. Elegance and finesse have developed that did not seem possible earlier, while newer editions stress these characteristics more. Production is limited to four wines. There are two styles of sparkling wine, Chandon Napa Valley Brut, a white wine made from Chardonnay, Pinot Blanc and Pinot Noir grapes, and Blanc de Noirs, a coppery-hued wine, the colour of which may be described as *oeil de perdrix*. It is made 100 per cent from Pinot Noir grapes. These two are the bread and butter wines and have been received extremely well by American consumers and by touring Champenois who taste perhaps with a bit of envy and admiration. Make no mistake, the Chandon sparklers are entirely French influenced. It is not enough that the Champagne method is employed, but Moët lends its Champagne master, Edmond Maudière, who shuttles back and forth from Epernay to supervise harvesting and wine-making.

Also produced is a still white wine, labelled Fred's Friends because of its limited production and in honour of Comte Frédéric Chandon de Briailles, President of Moët-Hennessey, parent company of Moët et Chandon. The wine is not dissimilar from the high acid Côteaux Champenois of the region of Champagne. Another wine is Panache, made in the style of the Ratafia wines of Champagne (or the Pineau des Charentes of Cognac) from lightly fermented Pinot Noir juice fortified with brandy to 18 per cent alcohol. The style of the sparkling wines is still shaping. For the moment, the *brut* is made from 75 per cent Pinot Noir, 23 per cent Chardonnay and 2 per cent Pinot Blanc. Maudière prefers Napa Valley Pinot Blanc to Napa Valley Chardonnay for his wines. Therefore, future *cuvées* will contain a higher percentage (10 to 12 per cent) of Pinot Blanc. The Blanc de Noirs features 100 per cent Pinot Noir. The grapes are harvested at less than full ripeness (18 or 19° Brix rather than 22 to 23° Brix in a fully-ripe grape), and go directly to the press to reduce colour pick-up from the skins; the must is stained the colour of smoked salmon and so are the wines.

Although both wines are extremely dry and high in acidity, the Blanc de Noirs seems sweeter to the taste because Pinot Noir is fruitier than the *brut* with 23 per cent Chardonnay. Both wines are reminiscent of the Champagne made by Maudière at Moët et Chandon, illustrating the differences soil and climate can make. The wines have been so well accepted in the American market that Domaine Chandon has begun, over a year ahead of schedule, construction for winery expansion that will in effect double capacity.

FRANCISCAN VINEYARDS

After its founding, Franciscan Vineyards went through two changes of ownership before being purchased in 1975 by Colorado businessman Raymond Duncan and former Christian Brother Justin Meyer. With the acquisition came 30,000 cases of bottled wine and 265,000 US gallons in bulk, some of which was immediately sold wholesale. The balance was kept for ageing, blending and bottling under the Franciscan label. After much deliberation, it was decided to sell the bottled wine and to begin virtually anew. At the then unheard-of price of $1.00 per bottle, the wine was sold, causing the lifting of Napa Valley vintner eyebrows. But it is to Justin Meyer that the credit must go for restoration of Franciscan's fortunes. That he brought the winery back from financial and oenological despair is not only to his credit but also reflects a personality that does not wince at a challenge or two.

Meyer has made fine wines at low prices, a fact that won over the wine-consuming community. The 1976 Napa Valley Chardonnay, in a pleasant, generous, not especially complex style, sold for $5.00, while the 1975 Cabernet Sauvignon, more complex, sold for $4.50. An exceptional generic Burgundy Cask 316, sold for $2.50. Since these wines, others have followed. Notable under another label owned by Meyer, is Silver Oak, of which the 1974 Cabernet Sauvignon is one of California's best, a vintage that should speak articulately for California for at least a decade or two. Franciscan was sold to the Peter Eckes Company of West Germany in 1979, with Meyer still in command.

FREEMARK ABBEY WINERY

En route to Calistoga, Highway 29 runs past an old stone building on the ground floor of which is a candle factory and a restaurant, surrounded by one of Napa Valley's most prestigious wineries, Freemark Abbey Winery. Freemark Abbey, although reincarnated in 1967, first became a winery in the 1880s. In 1967, the current owners, Charles Carpy, Frank Wood, William Jaeger, Richard Heggie, James Warren, R. Bradford Webb and John M. Bryan, acquired the property and revived the name and operation. Their wine list at present is limited to only four varieties: Cabernet Sauvignon (including the special Cabernet Bosché made from the grapes of a single vineyard, the property of John Bosché), Chardonnay, Johannisberg Riesling and Petite Sirah. Early Pinot Noir wines were not fully satisfying, and production has been discontinued, as it has in many other Californian wineries. The winery is chiefly known for its Chardonnay and Cabernet Sauvignon (blended with a small amount of Merlot) which make up 80 per cent of their production. These wines are in short supply, and in special vintage years like 1973 and 1974 have been spectacular. The 1968 Cabernet was a hallmark. The Petite Sirahs have been especially noteworthy as they were amongst the first to produce clean intense wines of flavour that were not overbearing with wood or varietal character.

In 1973, by accident more than by design, a botrytized Johannisberg Riesling was made by Jerry Luper, who has since departed for Château Montelena. Because botrytis was heavy, a big full-flavoured wine from the botrytized Riesling grapes was produced, and may be some of the best bottles of its type ever produced. There are those who compare it to *Beerenauslesen* and I am inclined to agree. It is labelled 'Edelwein' and is still drinking well. In 1975, at the Los Angeles County Fair wine judgings, a prestigious American wine competition, it won a Sweepstakes Award, and thus was not only a new star born, but a style of wine which is increasing in strength of popularity. The Cabernet Bosché is a darkly coloured wine, rich in fruit and long-lived. Chardonnay shares top billing with Cabernet Sauvignon, and rightly so. It has gained in style and character with every vintage in the 1970s, and now ranks with the best. The 1973 was as intense with fruit as any Chardonnay yet tasted. The excellence of Freemark Abbey's wines are further proof that vineyards are at least as important as wine-makers. Three of the seven owners are grape-growers who control at least 600 acres of vineyards, most of which are of the best, thus providing Freemark Abbey with a good choice of grapes. Current production at Freemark Abbey is 23,000 cases annually, a maximum figure set by physical limitations. Fortunately, limited physical space does not also limit quality.

GRGICH HILLS CELLAR

Another in the 'new breed' is Grgich Hills Cellar. Housed in a small, simple, rectangular building, complete with small French oak cooperage and 42,000 US gallons of stainless-steel fermenters, the winery produces attractive Chardonnays, Johannisberg Rieslings and Zinfandels. The first Chardonnay produced in 1977 was not yet in the big, fruity complex style, but augurs well for the future. Whether future Chardonnays will be lavished with the fame and notoriety of Grgich's 1973 Paris-tasting wine remains a question.

HEITZ WINE CELLARS

Joe Heitz, the much admired, now patriarchal wine-maker, represents more than any other the so-called 'new breed' of wine-maker of the decades of the 1960s and 1970s. Joe is not shy of opinions, not the least of which is that he produces some of the world's finest wines, especially Cabernet Sauvignon from a special Oakville vineyard named Martha's Vineyard. Joe may be the first graduate of the University of California at Davis to establish his own winery from scratch, that is, with no personal funds and virtually no backing, armed only with his wine-making education and with experience gathered in the laboratory at Gallo Winery in Modesto, Wine Growers Guild in Lodi, Mission Bell in Madera, and then the coveted position as André Tchelistcheff's assistant at Beaulieu Vineyard in 1951. In 1957, he donned academic robes to build the Enology course at Fresno State College, where he taught for three and a half years. In 1961, Joe and Alice Heitz made the great invest-ment plunge, and with a few hard-saved dollars purchased a tiny vineyard and primitive winery south of the Louis Martini Winery, the present location of the Heitz Cellars' tasting room. In 1964, they purchased the old stone winery at the end of Taplin Road along the Silverado Trail and moved the wine-making operation to better, but still not modernly efficient, wine-making facilities. Because of the absence of capital, Joe purchased grapes and wine for his own label, not unlike Burgundy's *négociants*. He bought wine to augment cash flows, so that ultimately vineyards could be included in his own winery investment. Best early wines pur-chased, and no doubt best for Joe's still small reputation, were those of Hanzell, notably Chardonnay. Indeed, in the early 1960s, Joe's finest Chardonnays were those he acquired from Hanzell, and he turned them into some of California's best. Crisp, clean, luscious, these Chardonnays launched Joe's enterprise more than any other wines and sold for $6.00, the then astronomical sum for a California bottle. More important, it sent Joe's price considerations to loftier and loftier levels, and it was common in 1980 for Joe to sell a bottle for the controversial price of $20.00. To this day Joe still buys many of his grapes, and continues to produce fine Char-donnay, Johannisberg Riesling, Pinot Noir and Grignolino, a leftover grape from the predecessor-owner of the tiny first winery, while finding time to serve as the President of the Wine Institute, the trade association of wineries in California. His reds have always attracted me more than his whites. The Martha's Vineyard Cabernet has developed its own legends, an intensely varietal, minty style, deep in colour and with an ability to age slowly with a great many layers of complexities and nuances. The 1974 Martha's Vineyard, assisted by the great Cabernet vintage of that year, may turn out to be one of the ten best Cabernets that California has produced since Prohibition.

INGLENOOK VINEYARDS

Just across the road from Beaulieu is another member of the Heublein wine family, Inglenook, founded by Gustave Niebaum, a retired Finnish seaman in 1879. Under Heublein ownership, Inglenook facilities have been expanded while the label has been extended to cover a greater variety of wines. Wine-making facilities have been moved to Oakville, while on the old Inglenook property was constructed a huge barrel-ageing and bottling cellar, increasing storage capacity to three million US gallons. Inglenook is now making fifteen estate-bottled vintage-dated varietals. Red Pinot has been discontinued, but Gewürztraminer, a Blanc de Noirs and a Fumé Blanc have been added. Inglenook now makes a line of generics, sold under Inglenook Vintage and the Navalle labels, in sizes up to twelve litres. This is the major change which constitutes Inglenook as one of the largest of California's so-called premium wineries, but has diluted its impact as a small estate devoted to a limited number of varietals produced in limited quantities. While the Inglenook wines are sound, the inexpensive wines to date appear to have attracted more attention than the expensive estate-bottled wine. The Cabernets are fine, but have not yet attained the glories of yesteryear, though that may come. The talented wine-maker is Tom Ferrell.

HANNS KORNELL CHAMPAGNE CELLARS

A Napa Valley sparkling-wine producer is Hanns Kornell, third-generation mem-ber of a German wine-making family. In 1952, he leased the old Tribuno Winery at Sonoma and made his own sparkling wine which he sold literally door to door. In 1958 when he had saved adequate capital, he bought the old Larkmead Cellars on Larkmead Lane, north of St Helena and has been there ever since. His production constitutes seven different sparkling wines from purchased base wines, and are Brut, Extra Dry, Demi-Sec, Pink Rosé, Rouge, Sehr Trocken and Muscat of Alexandria. Sehr Trocken is unquestionably the star. It is completely dry, as its German name implies. Left on the yeast for as long as five years, it develops complexities stemming from yeast autolysis. It is good enough to win awards each time it is entered in the Los Angeles County Fair. The wine is made principally from Johannisberg Riesling grapes, which gives it a fruity, not too austere style that takes a bit of getting adjusted to. Obviously, Kornell prefers wines in a Germanic style, although he uses French production methods. His Sehr Trocken demonstrates a preference for Johannisberg Riesling, which results in a style unfamiliar to wine drinkers accustomed to French Champagne. For Muscat fans, a pleasant intensely Muscat sparkler is produced under the name of Muscat of Alexandria. Somewhat heavy-handed in style, not as delicate as Martini's Moscato Amabile, none the less the wine has ample fruit to stand as an independent dessert.

CHARLES KRUG WINERY

Across the road and a short distance to the north of Beringer is another claimant to the title of old Napa Valley winery, Charles Krug. The Krug winery was constructed in 1861 by a German immigrant, Charles Krug, who made his first wine in the Napa Valley in 1858, using a small cider press to make 1,200 US gallons of wine for John Patchett of Napa. It was notable because it was the first wine made in the Napa Valley by a process other than the old Spanish method of fermenting in skins.

In 1860 Krug planted a vineyard on the site of the current Krug facility and erected his first wine cellar in 1861, both of which were considered models of his day. His skill as a vintner no doubt resulted in his appointment to the state's first Viticultural Commission. Krug earned an international reputation as a fine wine-maker. His wines were sold in Mexico, Germany and the United Kingdom, as well as in the eastern part of the United States and California. Unfortunately, phylloxera destroyed most of his vineyard and dealt him a financial blow from which he had not recovered at the time of his death in 1892. In 1943 Cesare Mondavi, an Italian immigrant, bought the Charles Krug Winery from the Moffitt family and began to restore it to its early prestige. Cesare had two sons, Robert and Peter, who assisted in the shipping of bulk wines while they replanted the vineyards and updated the winery. They saved their best for the Charles Krug Label, and slowly, but persistently, built up a reputation for it. At the time of Cesare's death in 1959, the winery was one of the best equipped and most efficient in the state, and the Krug label and reputation for quality, firmly established.

The Cabernet Sauvignons were some of the best in the state, particularly during the 1950s when the 1951 and 1958 vintages were notably good. In later years, the 1968 and 1974 vintages were also excellent. The Vintage Selection Cabernets, bearing Cesare's signature on a red diagonal stripe on the label, are among the best produced anywhere. Krug's red wines are, in general, more interesting than their whites. Among the whites, the Chenin Blanc may have been the first to be made as a varietal in California. The reputation of the Chenin Blanc was based on a sweet style that is still popular today.

Under the secondary label of C. K. Mondavi is bottled some of the wine that in earlier years probably would have ended up as a jug wine under another winery's label. These wines are relatively inexpensive, and although originally bottled only in 1.5 litres and 4 litres, are now available in the 750-ml size as well. In 1965, disagreements over policy and the future of the winery split the brothers and

Robert Mondavi left Krug to establish his own winery at Oakville.

LONG VINEYARDS

The neighbour of Chappellet Vineyard on Pritchard Hill is Long Vineyards. Robert and Zelma Long are talented wine proprietors who have made wine-making their life. Zelma learned wine-making by working, notably at the Robert Mondavi Winery, where she produced some of Robert Mondavi's finest wines. The first two wines, although limited in production were 'long' on quality and overall character. A 1978 Chardonnay was superb, luscious and Montrachet-like. Aged in French oak, the wine was actually a judicious 'sipping Chardonnay' rather than one to be enjoyed at table. The botrytized Johannisberg Riesling was clean and fragrant, intense in nose and flavour in a semi-sweet Germanic style that was one of the best yet tasted from California. Decidedly in balance, the wine left complexities on the palate which expressed honey-like qualities that made Zelma's wine-making début a huge success.

LOUIS M. MARTINI

For years Louis M. Martini, the Italian wine-maker patriarch who founded his winery in 1922, was the senior statesman of the Californian wine industry. By 1933, he was nestled in the Napa Valley south of St Helena, where the winery stands today. In the first six years following Repeal, he smartly and quietly built up a stock of ready-to-drink, bottle-aged wines and put the entire line on the market in 1940, creating a sensation. Good, well-aged California wines were not plentiful then and Martini's new Napa Valley wines were an instant success. The emphasis today is still to bring the consumer good wines to be enjoyed at the table early on and at reasonable prices. No other winery of high premium standards has been able to maintain such a low-pricing policy; e.g. Cabernet at under $5.00 per bottle (1980). These low-priced wines, frequently produced from Sonoma as well as Napa grapes may not, when young, win compliments, yet they sell well, but more importantly, age gracefully. Hardly a month goes by when an older Martini Cabernet, say from the 1940s or 1950s, especially the 1958s, does not surface to confirm an unerring ability to capture Cabernet's complexities.

I have also been especially impressed with other reds, Zinfandel, Barbera and Pinot Noir, especially the latter, which has on occasion produced some of California's finest, notably the 1957. The reds have always impressed me more than the whites, although the Gewürztraminer is always outstanding, not necessarily an Alsatian, but with good flavour and a characteristic spiced nose. My favourite has always been, and continues to be, the fresh, fruity, delightful Moscato Amabile, the superb, refreshing Asti Spumante-style made from Muscat of Alexandria grapes. This is Muscat at its nunceful best, not sparkling, but slightly *pétillant*, and is one of the most sought-after wines in the United States. It needs to be refrigerated from production to delivery to the consumer; however, if more were available, this impeccable, delicate Muscat wine could lead America back to dessert wine-drinking. Martini also produced a 1978 Chardonnay which at last taste was pleasant, but without adequate fruit, viscosity and complexity. Knowing the Martini penchant for producing wines that age well, future Chardonnays can be expected to be in that mould. Of special interest are the Private Reserve and Special Selection Cabernets. The Private Reserve wines are those held back from regular releases, in 200-case lots, for extra ageing whenever a vintage of a particular wine is deemed to have special ageing potential. Special Selection wines are selected lots of wine, completely different from the regular releases, chosen because they are 'special'.

MAYACAMAS VINEYARDS

High on a Mayacamas Mountain ridge overlooking the Napa Valley, is Mayacamas Vineyards, run by Robert and Noni Travers. Today, small, efficient, and somewhat modernized, the winery produces some of the state's best Cabernets and Chardonnays, and a Zinfandel in a late-harvest style. Some of the early wines have already become classics, like the 1968 late-harvest Zinfandel that early in the 1970s sold for the highest price ever paid for this varietal, $40.00 per bottle. Beautifully made Chardonnays truly reflect the hillside-characteristic buttery richness and complexities that can come only with time. The Chardonnays are notorious slow-starters, austere and locked-in, but drop in on the wine in a decade or two and it has a delicious lusciousness. The Cabernets are in the same high styled mould. The past decade of Cabernets and Chardonnays has provided a spectacular track record that has led Travers to purchase grapes from other areas so that he can turn loose the hard-earned knowledge and experience that has made him one of the most interesting and highly stylized wine men of the day. Obviously not in it for profit, *per se*, Travers' vineyard produce small quantities.

ROBERT MONDAVI WINERY

When Robert Mondavi established his own winery at Oakville in 1966, he built the first new-from-the-ground-up winery to be constructed in the Napa Valley since Repeal. From the outside, it was, and has remained, one of the most handsome, modern, progressive and innovative wineries in California. The winery was one of the first to use temperature-controlled and stainless-steel fermentation tanks as well as to age red wines in small sixty-us gallon French oak barrels on a much larger scale than had been employed in California. Additionally, the winery was one of the first to use a centrifuge for must clarification and has set the pace not only for new wineries in the Valley, but also for new premium quality wineries in the state and, indeed, in the world.

The initial size of the winery was quite small but growth was rapid. From 100,000 US gallons in 1966, storage capacity has increased to nearly two million US gallons in 1980. Vineyard acreage has grown from twelve to 1,100, and more significantly, contains the largest amount of so-called estate acreage, that is, vineyards that surround and are adjacent to the winery. One winery was not sufficient and so in addition, a winery with five million US gallons of storage capacity at Woodbridge near Lodi in the Interior Valley has been acquired. The Robert Mondavi Table Wines, a secondary label, are now produced there. The list of varietal, vintage-dated wines produced at Oakville is limited to Johannisberg Riesling, Chardonnay, Fumé Blanc, Chenin Blanc, Gamay Rosé, Gamay, Zinfandel, Petite Sirah, Cabernet Sauvignon, Pinot Noir and Moscato D'Oro. All are interesting wines, although some have greater complexity than the others. Of particular note are the Cabernet Sauvignons, always full of varietal character, fruity and complex. The most famous of the whites has consistently been the Fumé Blanc; a dry wine made of Sauvignon Blanc grapes in the Pouilly Fumé style of the Loire Valley, it seems to improve with each vintage. Recent vintages have become a match for so-called low-end California Chardonnays. Mondavi's Chardonnays in a good vintage can rank with the best. They seem to enjoy a fine delicate balance between wood and fruit that makes for generous white-wine drinking that compares favourably with some of the better French white Burgundies. The Reserve Chardonnay, in particular, is a wine to watch and in due course will enhance the Mondavi name even more.

In May 1980, Robert Mondavi and Baron Philippe de Rothschild, owner of Château Mouton, announced a joint venture to produce Napa Valley wines with a

French accent. The first vintage of 1979 Cabernet Sauvignon blended with a small amount of Merlot (the exact proportions to be determined by frequent tasting) was made jointly by Tim Mondavi, now the chief wine-maker, and Lucien Sionneau, wine-maker at Château Mouton Rothschild. Release is scheduled for not sooner than 1983. Although existing Mondavi vineyards and winery were utilized for this first vintage, which in mid 1980 was ageing in French oak in the Mondavi cellars, plans call for a separate winery and vineyards.

NICHELINI VINEYARDS

Jim Nichelini, proprietor of Nichelini Vineyards, is the third generation to make wine in the stone cellar built by his Swiss grandfather in 1890. Most of the winery equipment is also seeing its third generation of use, helped along by mechanization such as electric must pumps. Wine-making methods are far from complex, and so are the wines. They are, however, good sound wines sold at reasonable prices for everyday drinking. A speciality is Sauvignon Vert, not generally produced as a varietal in California. Notable red wines include Zinfandel and Petite Sirah.

JOSEPH PHELPS VINEYARDS

A neighbour of the Heitz Wine Cellars is Joseph Phelps, the Colorado bridge builder who, in 1973, gave expression to wine-making dreams by the construction of a beautiful, modern redwood winery. Modern, efficient equipment was stressed, along with several thousand 600-US gallon barrels of both French and American oak. Most notable is the Johannisberg Riesling, which was amongst the first to be produced and accepted with a slight sugar residual that produced richness of body that could not be reached otherwise. It was a wine that literally revolutionized California Johannisberg Riesling producers' thinking, which to that day had been generally targeted to a dry style. Americans found that they could enjoy 'JR's that were well balanced, yet slightly sweet – and that these wines did not have to be simply for dessert. Walter Schug is most creative as a wine-maker. He believes that solar exposure is more important than heat summation during the growing season, and is currently locked in an experiment in matching grape varieties to it. Because soil types in the Phelps acreage are extremely varied, Schug places less emphasis on matching variety to soil type, but does stress that each vineyard site should be well-drained.

Other varieties with which he has good success are Gewürztraminer, Sauvignon Blanc, Cabernet Sauvignon, Zinfandel, Merlot, Pinot Noir and Chardonnay. Besides the Phelps Vineyard label, there are two proprietary labels, Le Fleuron, a secondary label, and Insignia (introduced in 1974), for wines considered extra-ordinary. One of Schug's great successes is the making of late-harvest Johannisberg Rieslings, that is, wines affected by botrytis and in a Germanic *Trockenbeerenauslese* style. Some have been magnificent, especially the 1978s and 1979s. Cost is less than *Trockenbeerenauslese*, at around $20.00 per bottle. Another exciting effort is with the Syrah. The latest approved French clones are being tested in twenty acres of vineyards in an effort to approximate the great Rhône Valley wines of Hermitage. Here, Schug is experimenting with cold fermentation and the addition of Grenache or white grapes to the fermenter to soften the aggressive character of the varietal. Eventually Schug hopes to be able to add Viognier, a white variety of the Rhône, to produce whites that are also comparable. A unique experiment at Phelps is with the Scheurebe, a Riesling x Sylvaner cross developed in 1916 at the State Research Institute at Alzey, Rheinhessen. Plantings of the variety are widespread in Germany, but Phelps Vineyards contain the only acreage of this grape here.

RAYMOND VINEYARD AND CELLAR

Raymond Vineyard and Cellar, a new winery, has ninety acres of vineyards south of St Helena with plans to produce no more than 20,000 estate-bottled cases annually. Vineyards are planted to Cabernet Sauvignon, Merlot, Zinfandel, Pinot Noir, Gamay, Chardonnay, Johannisberg Riesling and Chenin Blanc. A 1976 botrytized White Riesling in a luscious full-flavoured style won a gold medal in the 1977 Los Angeles County Fair. The 1977 Cabernet is intense, structurally big and should be a long keeper, a good example of the varietal for its area. Considering the wine-making experience, future releases should be well done.

RUTHERFORD HILL WINERY

South of Taplin Road along the Silverado Trail on a knoll overlooking the Napa Valley stands Rutherford Hill Winery. I must confess to prejudice here because of my small partnership interest which, for me, represents a lifelong dream of winery association. The first group of wines released in 1977 were not wines of which I could take exceptional pride. It was a period of getting to know the winery, the vineyards and the market. It did not take long, however, for this is an experienced team and the newer releases are much, if not outstandingly, improved, notably, the 1978 Chardonnay and the 1976 Cabernet. The 1976 Cabernet is beautifully balanced, intense with flavour and fruit, and should be one of California's finest of that vintage. It is Rutherford Hill's best wine to date and portends well for both the wine-maker and the vineyards. This Cabernet has that nice blend of tannin and the fruit to support it, so that ageing in the true sense of the word will make for an unforgettable wine. It is uniquely Cabernet and is truly what the varietal is all about, with no need to pay any homage to Bordeaux. The 1978 Chardonnay is far superior to the 1977, with fine balance and fruit, and a wine-making style that is coming together attractively to provide a nicely developing, luscious, viscous style. The Cabernet, however, is indeed the superior wine. Other wines are pleasant but not necessarily memorable, and include Gewürztraminer, Zinfandel, Pinot Noir, Merlot and Johannisberg Riesling. These wines will improve immeasurably because several of Rutherford Hill's partners own some of the choicest Napa Valley vineyards in increasing acreage. Not a few of the grapes found their way into the Napa Valley Chardonnays that won attention at the nefarious Paris tasting. As grape contracts with other wineries expire, these grapes will become available to Rutherford Hill and quality will rise accordingly.

A vineyard not owned by the partners is responsible for one of Rutherford Hill's best wines, a Napa Valley Zinfandel. Generally, Zinfandels do not do well in the Napa Valley. This one, from an Atlas Peak vineyard owned by famed museum curator Giles Mead, is first rate. The production is small from the several decades-old vines, and this wine is medium- to heavy-bodied in a somewhat spicy, full-flavoured style that is rare. A big, gutsy wine, it does need time. While I look to Rutherford Hill for pride more than for profit, I am convinced there is a bright future.

SCHRAMSBERG VINEYARDS COMPANY

Considered amongst California's finest wineries, perhaps in the first two or three sparkling-wine producers, is Schramsberg, founded by Jack and Jamie Davies, wine-lovers turned California Champagne-makers. In February 1972 Schramsberg became an overnight sensation when it was revealed that its Blanc de Blancs Brut was served at the first US–Sino banquet honouring the Chinese Premier, the late Chou-en-lai. As a consequence, sales accelerated and production was taxed. To this day, the availability of Schramsberg is limited. Other types of wine have been added, including Crémant, produced from the Flora grape, a grape crossing of Sémillon and Gewürztraminer. Of greater interest, however, has been the Blanc de Pinot, made principally from Pinot Noir grapes in a restrained, somewhat neutral style that makes it unquestionably one of the best American sparkling wines. In addition to these wines, Davies likes to produce Blanc de Blancs (principally of Chardonnay) with additional bottle maturity under a reserve ageing programme.

SPRING MOUNTAIN VINEYARDS

West of the city of St Helena, on a mountainside above Beringer, stands a relatively new winery, Spring Mountain, the creation of Mike Robbins. Although new, the winery is in its second home, located on the old Tiburcio Parrott Estate, Miravalle. Curving around the natural contours of the landscape, the building fits into the slope of the mountain and allows the use of gravity in some wine-making operations. Specializing at the outset, Spring Mountain has emphasized Cabernet Sauvignon and Chardonnay, although Pinot Noir and Sauvignon have also been produced. Attention to detail is obvious throughout the winery. The thirty 1,000-US gallon upright tanks from France and Yugoslavia are relatively tall, so as to aid in the natural clarification of wine stored in them, and with domed heads to reduce oxidation. The winery is designed and equipped to ensure that it can continue to operate without interruption throughout the harvest.

Spring Mountain's Chardonnay and Sauvignon Blancs have apparently been pleasing critics and consumers. The Sauvignon Blanc is crisp and flavourful, while the Chardonnay has varied, although it is ever improving, and indeed today it is clearly one of the finest. The Chardonnay receives considerable technical attention. It is partially fermented in stainless steel at relatively low temperatures until the sugar level reaches 10° to 12° Balling, and then moved to sixty-US gallon barrels to complete fermentation. Thus, it has good solid varietal character resulting from the initial fermentation, but it also benefits from the complexities added by the yeasts being in more intimate contact with the must in the barrels resulting in a slight spicy hint of oak. Given time, the wines generally develop considerable finesse and richness. Cabernet Sauvignons appear to be, but are not, overshadowed by the Chardonnays. Generally, they have been deep, round, full wines with good colour and excellent varietal character and with a good dose of that flavour shown by the Chardonnays. Of particular interest was a blend of three Cabernet vintages, Les Trois Cuvées, that argues favourably for selective blending. Not only was the wine intense with flavour, varietal character and decidedly in good balance, it drank with amazing generosity which seems characteristic of Robbins' Cabernets. Obviously striving for a Bordeaux-like taste, Robbins seems to be accomplishing this against a background of California's tannin and fruit.

STAG'S LEAP WINE CELLARS

Stag's Leap Wine Cellars, renowned throughout the world because of the Paris tastings of 1976 where it affronted major Bordeaux châteaux by capturing first place with its 1973 Cabernet is, in spite of its press clippings, a first-class winery operation. Warren Winiarski, the wine-maker-proprietor, is in the perfectionist mould, with heavy involvement in both vineyards and winery. His Cabernets, perhaps his best wines, are outstanding. His 1973 award-winning wine was no fluke, and his 1974 Cabernet is better yet, with an intensity that suggests a wine that is forever durable. In recent years, he has made Chardonnays that challenge the Cabernets. Johannisberg Rieslings, Pinot Noir, sometimes labelled Gamay Beaujolais, and Merlot are also produced. In order to ensure uniformity of grape ripeness, Winiarski's vineyards are harvested in five or six stages, an extremely time-consuming and costly practice. The vigour and degree of crushing are adjusted by a variable speed crusher, adjusted to grape size and condition. The choice of fermentation temperature is adjusted in accordance with what Winiarski has learned in the vineyard. Red wine skin contact is also determined by this method. Finally, wood-ageing in small Nevers oak cooperage is watched closely by frequent examination, tasting and topping. Winiarski's dedicated labours are best reflected in a continuing effort to upgrade Chardonnay to match his Cabernets. The best example is the 1978 Chardonnay from a significant Napa Valley vineyard, Haines, which should, with several years of ageing, turn out to be a wine of distinction. The wine is well-balanced with good fruit and that pleasant hint of oak that enhances both wine and a Chardonnay palate. Future bottlings should win a competition or two.

STAG'S LEAP WINERY, INC.

Carl Doumani's vineyard and label, Stag's Leap Winery, is the subject of a legal battle with Stag's Leap Wine Cellars. Carl and his wife Joanne purchased the old Stag's Leap Hotel, a 'Roaring Twenties' refuge and resort for the Bay Area and its environs. The old hotel has been remodelled into the Doumani residence. An old winery building nearby is not yet modernized nor rehabilitated. While waiting for capital to do so, wines have been made at Rutherford Hill Winery from Doumani's grapes and marketed under the Stag's Leap Vineyard label. At least a hundred acres of vineyards are owned by the Doumanis. Principal varieties are Chenin Blanc, Petite Sirah, Cabernet Sauvignon and Pinot Noir, sufficient to produce 10,000 cases of wine. While Doumani has not had the press glory of Winiarski, his grapes have produced two fine wines. His Petite Sirah is much favoured by fans of that variety and by restaurateurs who desire the big, inky, robust character for their fare. The blend of black pepper and cherry juice of Petite Sirah is there in full measure. As the wine ages, the body is almost velvety. The other fine wine is Chenin Blanc.

STERLING VINEYARDS

Just south of Calistoga, at the top of a wooded hill, stands Sterling Vineyards. With a structure that is frequently affectionately described as Napa Valley's Disneyland, the building, patterned after Greek Island architecture, is brilliantly white and virtually gleams in the sunlight of a summer's day. However, there is nothing Disneyland about the winery which is both serious and high quality, notwithstanding the fact that in 1977 the Coca Cola Company of Atlanta, Georgia, purchased it.

Inside, the Sterling Vineyards winery plant reveals its utilitarian nature by means of a self-guided tour, helped along by large graphic panels which explain every step of wine-making from crush to bottle. The wine-making equipment was set into place, and the building constructed around it, so as to make use of the gentle slope of the hilltop from north to south to allow gravity to assist in moving grapes, must and wine from one stage to another. Theo Rosenbrand is the wine-maker who has brought with him twenty-two years of experience at Beaulieu under the tutelage of three of the best wine-makers in California. While the early and present wines are satisfactory, especially the Cabernet and the Sauvignon Blanc (the latter is labelled 'Blanc de Sauvignon'), they have not been spectacular. With additional grape acreage and the strength of Coca Cola's capital, it is to be hoped that improvements will be seen under the leadership of Rosenbrand. Perhaps the greatest success has been in Cabernet. Two Cabernets are produced, a regular and a Reserve, the latter a barrel-selected wine which receives additional ageing (a total of two years) in Nevers oak in a separate *chais* built in 1979 especially to house the Reserve wines. These Reserve Cabernets have so much depth, flavour and body that the special treatment and extra care which goes into their production is obviously justified, but not the special price, I fear, which was $25.00 per bottle in 1980. The regular is perhaps a better buy, priced at around $7.00 in 1980. Merlot wine is one of Sterling's innovations, in as much as it was one of the first produced in the United States when Sterling made it at the beginning of the 1970s. Other wineries have copied, but at Sterling the wine has been big, dark, heavy and tannic. On occasion it has captured the charm and complexity of a St Emilion. Sterling's Chardonnay is barrel-fermented, a practice which may be discontinued by Rosenbrand. Generally, they are decent, but lacking in complexity, although recently I enjoyed a 1969 which provided superb survivability and a luscious flavour.

STONY HILL VINEYARD

What may be the finest Chardonnay winery in California is aptly named Stony Hill Vineyard started by Fred McCrea, who died in 1977, and now run by his widow, Eleanor. Located between Diamond Mountain and Spring Mountain high atop the Napa Valley, the winery is a gem. It is also one of the smallest. With a mere thirty acres of vineyards and 7,000 US gallons of storage capacity, Stony Hill produces only about 2,000 cases of wine annually, variously divided amongst Chardonnay, Gewürztraminer. White Riesling and Sémillon. Excitement and complexity is what these wines have in full measure. Several of the vintages of the 1960s still, today, drink with rich, soft and full-flavoured lusciousness and have, indeed, matched the delicious joys of white Burgundies. Vintages of the 1970s are no different, especially the 1973, 1974, 1976 and 1978.

What is surprising about Stony Hill Chardonnay is the characteristic it derives from its mountain-hillside soil, which gives the wine enduring power and complexity that takes a long time in coming. The wine starts slowly and austerely, but all Stony Hill Chardonnay watchers argue that this is only a hint of what is to come. Stony Hill has produced by far the best of Napa Valley Chardonnays. The style is unmistakably earthy when young, rich when old, with an excellent balance.

McCrea did not stint in employing the latest wine-making techniques and equipment. He liked to buy new equipment as one would buy a new toy, and was one of the first to use new Limousin oak in the ageing of his Chardonnay. Stony Hill Chardonnays are generally blessed with a great deal of fruit and seem to be able to handle the wood much better than most. The Johannisberg Riesling started in a dry style but was changed to one that is similar to the Germanic-charactered wines which are becoming more and more usual amongst California wine-makers. The Gewürztraminer is not in the classic Alsatian style, but is a good balance between the austere and the fruity with a good sugar-acid balance. A small amount of sweet Sémillon known as Sémillon de Soleil is also produced.

SUTTER HOME WINERY

The winery, founded originally in 1874, was taken over by John and Mario Trinchero in 1946. It grows no grapes of its own and is an amazing winery which is known principally for only one varietal, Zinfandel. Perhaps it is inaccurate to say the winery produces only Zinfandel, because a 'white' Zinfandel is also produced by fermenting only Zinfandel juice. The white Zinfandel, while interesting, is not the heavyweight, fine tasting wine that the red is. There is no question that some of the state's finest Zinfandels have been produced by Sutter Home. No doubt this can be attributed to Trinchero's wine-making skills, combined with the quality of non-Napa Valley Zinfandel vineyards in Amador County, notably the Deaver Vineyard. Napa Valley Zinfandels have not found much favour amongst American wine drinkers but those of Amador County have. The success of the Zinfandels of Amador County precipitated the founding of at least a dozen new wineries in Amador and El Dorado counties as 'new' areas, especially for Zinfandels. The dessert line is limited to one wine, Muscat, in an *amabile*, sweet, fruity style and in very small amounts.

TREFETHEN VINEYARDS

Trefethen Vineyards began more as a vineyard than as a winery. It was founded in 1973 by Gene Trefethen, but is run today by his son John, who also acts as wine-maker. The vineyards actually began in the 1850s, planted by Napa Valley pioneer Joseph Osburn. The large, 600-acre vineyard, is planted principally to Chardonnay, White Riesling and Cabernet Sauvignon, with small experimental test plantings of several other varieties. Early releases have been more than satisfactory. Of special interest are 1977, 1978 and 1979 Chardonnays, each showing considerable improvement in a rich fruity, drinkable style. The 1977, which won a dubious award in Europe, was perhaps the poorest, while the 1978 was the best. A 1974 Cabernet is outstanding as well as a 1978 Johannisberg Riesling. The latter is in a bone-dry style, though fruity, that is becoming extinct in California's 'JR' repertory. Trefethen was actually the launching pad for Moët et Chandon during the vintages of 1973 to 1976 while its sparkling-wine facility was being constructed at Yountville.

VEEDERCREST

A small winery managed by Alfred Baxter which has good Johannisberg Riesling and Chardonnay.

VILLA MOUNT EDEN WINERY

At Oakville Cross Road which parallels Conn Creek Road, a mile to the south, is Villa Mount Eden Winery. Acquired in 1970 by James McWilliams, the winery is situated on a nineteenth-century vineyard. Vineyard and wine-making duties are assigned to Nils Venge, a University of California at Davis graduate of the 1967 vintage, with early experience of Charles Krug, Sterling Vineyards and Heitz Cellars. Initial releases, all more than satisfactory, were Gewürztraminer, Chenin Blanc, and Napa Gamay, followed by Cabernet and Chardonnay, especially the 1977, 1978 and 1979 Chardonnays, which are intense, rich, beautifully balanced wines. The style is decidedly French-like, easy to drink and not overbearingly Chardonnay-ish. Cabernet, too, is French-like and developing its fruit intensity to the point that in five or more years it should become one of Napa Valley's best.

Z. D. WINES

California wine-making history is more and more punctuated by people with careers in other fields. No less so is Z. D. Wines on Conn Creek. Engineers, Gino Zepponi and Norman de Leuze, supported by home wine-making, started commercial wine-making in 1968 with six tons of grapes. They produced 900 US gallons with equipment that was primitive but the wines were more than acceptable. Pinot Noir and Chardonnay were barrel-fermented in whatever oak was available, e.g., Limousin, Nevers and American. Labels are precise, identifying the vineyard source and vintage date; back labels provide technical information such as acidity and sugar content. By 1979, they had outgrown their barn on Burndale Road in Sonoma's outskirts, and the winery was moved to the Silverado Trail in the Napa

Valley. Storage capacity and production have increased from 9,700 US gallons to 18,000 US gallons. The Pinot Noirs have been exceptional. They are produced from Los Carneros grapes into big, deep red and fruity wines that drink well, although not necessarily in the Burgundy manner. Chardonnays may be better yet, for they are rich, extremely luscious and fruity. Gewürztraminers are spicy and rich in the Alsatian style. Zinfandels are fully varietal, dark, delicious and drinkable when young, but gain finesse with age.

SONOMA COUNTY

The historical, tiny village now grown into the town of Sonoma is where wine-making began in northern California in the nineteenth century. Sonoma County is divided into three principal valleys, Alexander, Sonoma, and Dry Creek. The series of mountains and valleys which criss-cross the county break it into a set of micro-climates which differ considerably. Temperatures during the growing period range from a cool Region I to a fairly warm Region III in the University of California system of heat summation (see page 461). There is a wide variety of soil types, extending from clay loam to sandy loam; most are well-drained silty loams in which grape vines grow well. Rainfall is heavy, confined principally to the winter months, and varies from twenty inches annually in the valleys to over fifty inches in the mountains. These factors assure that every conceivable combination of soil, solar radiation, heat and rainfall can be found somewhere in the county.

The dominant weather characteristic of Sonoma during the growing season is the daily occurrence of a marine incursion from the Pacific Ocean. As temperatures of the great interior valley of California begin to climb above 90°F during the late spring and the summer, atmospheric pressure falls. This enables the fog bank lying off the coast throughout these months to push inland for a distance of thirty or forty miles each evening. The morning sun burns off the fog layer and the result is a moderation of temperatures during the summer's heat.

Following Repeal, most of Sonoma County's wines could be accurately described as Italian-style *vin ordinaire*. Today, Sonoma County is in the process of a rediscovery of its viticultural and oenological roots, which began with Haraszthy, were stopped by phylloxera and Prohibition, and resumed in the late 1960s during the so-called 'Wine Boom'. From fewer than ten which were well known, the number of Sonoma County labels has increased to more than forty, and is still growing. Vineyards have increased from 11,000 acres in the late 1960s to more than 20,000 at the beginning of the 1980s. Sonoma County now has a healthy rivalry with Napa County.

Sonoma is, in a sense, a study in contrasts. The old and the new frequently are found in close proximity. Long-established wineries, steeped in tradition, house a collection of stainless-steel fermenters, small oak barrels and centrifuges – the physical embodiment of the 'new' application of technology to the art of wine-making. Some are still family-owned and have been for several generations. Others are completely new: buildings that still smell of fresh paint and freshly cut wood, built especially to hold the newest and latest in crushers, fermenters, dejuicers and presses. The changes and modernization are impressive, but most spectacular is the combination of youth and talent in the county's wine-makers. They are returning Sonoma to the quality wine map of California.

ALEXANDER VALLEY VINEYARDS

The winery was started in 1963 by Harry Wetzel, Jr., his son and Dale Goode. Vineyards were planted to Cabernet Sauvignon, Pinot Noir, Merlot, Chardonnay, Johannisberg Riesling, Gewürztraminer and Chenin Blanc. The winery specializes in three vintage-dated, estate-bottled wines. Chardonnay, Johannisberg Riesling and Cabernet Sauvignon, all of which have been excellent models. Chardonnay, in particular, is crisp and clean, not as luscious as others, but drinks in a straight-forward style that is most attractive. The Riesling, especially the 1978, is dry and fruity, a bit high in acidity, but it has good varietal character and is a departure from the currently fashionable, slightly sweet style. Notable, too, is the 1975 Cabernet Sauvignon, blended with Merlot, in good balance and with an ability to age.

BUENA VISTA WINERY AND VINEYARDS

Buena Vista provides an excellent example of the contrast of old and new. Built by Agoston Haraszthy in 1857, the winery is the oldest in Sonoma Valley. Frank Bartholomew acquired the abandoned winery at an auction in 1941. He set about rebuilding the winery, replanted the vineyards and gradually turned Buena Vista into a dynamic enterprise. In 1968, Bartholomew sold the winery to Young's Market Company, a southern Californian food and wine purveyor, which purchased 700 additional acres lying about six miles away from the old Buena Vista, planted grapes and then built a new modern winery with 90,000 US gallons of storage capacity. The old site, with its 120-year-old tunnels, is still utilized to produce wines and as a visitors' centre and tasting room. Buena Vista's speciality has been Green Hungarian, a fresh, crisp, fruity California varietal, perhaps named after Buena Vista's first proprietor. Also produced are fruity, flavourful Gewürztraminers, that in their early years were admired by André Tchelistcheff, who made a habit of recommending them to me. Cask Pinot Noirs are also in the repertoire along with Zinfandel, Cabernet and Chardonnay. The Zinfandel is especially noteworthy. Buena Vista has now been sold to a major German beverage concern, the Racke Company, which appears to be making efforts to upgrade the wine quality.

CHATEAU ST JEAN INC

A few miles west along Highway 12 on the outskirts of the town of Kenwood is Château St Jean, Inc. Brothers Edward and Robert Merzoian, along with Edward's brother-in-law, Kenneth Sheffield, bought a 250-acre estate in 1973. They then hired a young energetic wine-maker, Richard Arrowood, whose task it was to design and develop a winery which would permit him to produce the finest wines possible. Originally, the plan was to build a winery which would permit the handling of a relatively large number of small separate lots of fruit so that grapes purchased from individual sites could be fermented, aged and bottled separately. This practice permits label identification giving significant recognition to the vineyardist. St Jean was one of the first Californian wineries to acknowledge publicly the importance of the resource material, even though it was not their own. This has increased the capital cost of the winery by increasing the number of fermenters required to accommodate each harvest. At first, it seemed confusing to market simultaneously several examples of a single variety from a given vintage year. In the final analysis, the confusion not-withstanding, Château St Jean fans applauded the opportunity to taste the differences between the wines from different vineyards, although the wine-maker was the same.

Production at St Jean is principally of white wines and is limited to Chardonnay, Sauvignon Blanc, Johannisberg Riesling, Gewürztraminer, Pinot Blanc and Muscat Canelli. A Pinot Noir has been made into a white wine. Red wines have included Cabernet Sauvignon, Merlot and Zinfandel, but plans are to limit red-wine pro-duction to Cabernet Sauvignon from Wildwood vineyard grapes (near Kenwood). Arrowood has developed a reputation for skill with botrytized grapes. There have been several examples of *Beerenauslesen* (BA) and *Trockenbeerenauslesen* (TBA) types produced from Rieslings and, surprisingly, Gewürztraminers. The federal government agency charged with approving wine labels has halted the use of German phrases on California wine labels. Now, St Jean must identify its so-called BA and TBA wines by descriptive phrases in English, such as late harvest and individually bunch-selected late harvest, etc. The quality of Château St Jean has indeed been recognized. Major wine judgings have lavished medal after medal on Arrowood and his wines and at the Los Angeles County Fair, Arrowood has reaped a harvest of gold, silver and bronze medals each year that he has entered since 1975.

One hundred and five acres owned by Château St Jean have been planted to Chardonnay, White Riesling, Gewürztraminer, Sauvignon Blanc, Muscat Canelli and Pinot Blanc. The winery will continue to rely upon grapes purchased from thirty growers to supply 70 per cent of the Château's needs for grapes. Another practice of the 'new breedists' places St Jean's vineyard manager at the growers' vineyards to control wine-growing practices and grape-picking ripeness. Growers are compensated for quality by a sliding scale of payments and especially for any yield-reducing vinicultural practices as suggested by the winery. Extremely notable in St Jean's repertoire are the 1977 Chardonnay from the Robert Young Vineyards – a noble bottle, rich with flavour yet with a nice balance and a 1978 *Trockenbeerenauslese*-styled Gewürztraminer. A candied nose and a rich luscious taste rarely found in Gewürztraminers mark its success. A separate sparkling-wine facility is now under construction. It will be built in stages, with the first completed in time for the 1980 crush, and upon completion in 1985, it will be able to crush 2,000 tonnes of grapes to produce 60,000 cases of finished wine each season. The Champagne method and a blend of Chardonnay and Pinot Noir will be used.

CLOS DU BOIS

Founded in 1976, Clos du Bois began as a vineyard rather than as a winery, with the incredible number of 1,000 acres in the Alexander Valley and Dry Creek regions. Proprietors Frank M. Woods, Thomas C. Reed and Dennis Malone all attended the renowned Ivy League school, Cornell, in the mid-1950s. Vineyards were purchased in the mid-1960s, but in the wine fiscal downslide of 1974, the partners were unable to sell all of their grapes, so they leased space at a Sonoma winery for wine-making. In 1976, wines were released under the Clos du Bois label. From there there was no turning back, and a modern winery was constructed across the road from Jordan Vineyard and completed in time for the 1980 crush. Despite rented wine-making quarters, wines have been decent. Of two recent Chardonnay vintages, the 1978 easily was better than the 1977, perhaps due to spring rains which broke California's two-year drought. Five months of oak ageing is not overdone, so that the wine easily qualifies as one of California's better Chardonnays, full flavoured and rich. The 1974 Proprietor's Reserve Cabernet Sauvignon is indeed the best wine Clos du Bois has made. Production was limited because of its hillside vineyard location overlooking Dry Creek which yielded only one tonne per acre. Aged for forty months in French oak barrels, only 100 cases were produced. The wine is huge and intense in a strong Cabernet assertive style that French palates may not like, but Californians do. Even now the wine has not displayed hoped-for complexities, one of the problems with these monster-like reds. If it happens here, this could be one of California's finest of the already acclaimed California 1974 Cabernet vintage. Clos du Bois's second label, River Oaks, is used for wines judged to be less complex or which receive less extended cellaring and ageing. The second label provides not only a different taste, but also lower prices reflecting lower costs of preparation. With the considerable acreage, Clos du Bois easily will be an important factor during the 1980s.

DRY CREEK VINEYARD, INC

Founded in 1972, an off-vintage year but not for this winery, Dry Creek has become one of the most quality-consistent of California's 'boutiques'. David Stare is proprietor and wine-maker. The first stage of the Dry Creek building was completed in time for the 1973 crush, with another structure completed in 1978. The vineyard's fifty acres surrounding the winery contains Chardonnay, Sauvignon Blanc, Chenin Blanc, and Cabernet Sauvignon, sufficient to supply about one-half of the needs of the winery. The first wines released after the winery was completed were a Fumé Blanc, clean, crisp, good, and a dry full-bodied Chenin Blanc which, too, is respected by wine-lovers and established Stare's reputation as a wine-maker. The reds, released in 1975, also demonstrated Stare's ability. Although the reds are good, I have preferred the whites. The Chenin Blanc is a particularly fine example of the dry style. The Fumé Blanc is far more restrained than others, and that is precisely why I prefer it, because it strikes a nice balance between grape flavours and the small oak cooperage in which it was aged. It is the Chardonnay, however, that has scored. Stare's Chardonnays are clean, full of varietal character and possess a crispness not usually found in Chardonnays in this region. While they do not develop the lusciousness that others may provide, the wines are easy to drink in a restrained style that makes for good drinking at table and have performed well at Fair competitions. Reds may indeed suffer from too much varietal intensity, although that may be unfair, because Stare's reds have not been around long enough for a definitive evaluation. His Zinfandels, Cabernets and Merlots should improve. Perhaps in five or more years with a new taste, Stare's reds will be the equal of his whites.

GEYSER PEAK WINERY

Schlitz Brewery, producer of the beer that proclaims itself to be the beer that made Milwaukee (America's important brewery centre) famous, is now trying to do the same for California wine with its Geyser Peak Winery. Purchased in 1972, production is now at one million US gallons. To gain that volume, it is difficult to make the very best wines, but what it has done with Geyser Peak after several false starts by others, is to search for special limited bottling from specific vineyards. This is best illustrated by four wines of the 1974 vintage: Pinot Noir, Sonoma County (limited bottling); Cabernet Sauvignon, Santa Maria (limited bottling); Chardonnay (regular) and Pinot Noir, Sonoma County (regular). All four are prestigious bottles, forerunners of the high quality to be found today. They represent good values that are not far removed from California's best, and are an obvious attempt to move away from the confusion which reigned when the winery jumped simultaneously into wine production with three different labels (Geyser Peak, Voltaire and Summit). All three represented different quality levels and pricing.

Low-priced generics under $2.50 (1980), some as low as $1.69, were produced under the name of Summit and were good everyday wines at bargain basement prices, a feat at which California excels. The Voltaire label was eliminated and the winery now concentrates on Geyser Peak, its vintage-dated, limited bottlings. Geyser Peak's turnaround was made thanks largely to Al Huntsinger, veteran wine-maker, who came to Geyser Peak after a twenty-year stint at Almaden. Today he is retired, replaced by Armand Bussone, also from Almaden.

GRAND CRU VINEYARDS

The picturesque town of Glen Ellen to the southeast of Château St Jean is the home of Grand Cru Vineyards. It is another study in the contrasts between the old and the new that marks the revival of Sonoma as a wine-growing region. In 1970, on the site of the eighty-year-old Lamoine winery, Robert Magnani and Allen Ferrara, with other partners, formed Grand Cru and installed custom-designed, temperature-controlled fermenters. These provide a vivid contrast with the old concrete storage tanks which, with newly cut doors, now serve as cellars for the small oak cooperage in which the wines are aged. Since its inception, Grand Cru has produced elegant-styled Zinfandel from twenty-five acres of eighty-year-old vines. These vines do not produce many grapes but have an intense fruitiness that surfaces beautifully in aroma and flavour. In 1977, the grapes from the old Zinfandel vineyard were allowed to hang on the vines until they became fully ripe, almost overripe. At harvest, the sugar level had reached 25.8° Brix. Fermentation was allowed to go to completion at ambient temperatures. The finished wine reached an alcohol level of 14 per cent and was bone dry; residual sugar was a mere 0.2 per cent. Aged in a combination of French and American oak, the result was a wine of unusual appeal. The nose was very similar to that of a well-aged Port, but on the palate there were no Port-like characteristics. Despite the high alcohol, the wine was balanced and had an abundance of fruit that exploded in the mouth.

Another wine that was produced in several vintages was a sweet Gewürztraminer, made so by a laboratory culture of botrytis mould that was sprayed on the grapes. In 1977, sugar level in the grapes was increased to 48° Brix from 24° Brix. Fermentation stopped of its own accord at 7.1 per cent alcohol and 32 per cent residual sugar, producing a wine with intense Gewürztraminer character punctuated by botrytis. The 1978 was excellent and could well be a harbinger for future Gewürztraminers and constitute a new role for the varietal. Rounding out the line is a Cabernet Sauvignon, a 'dry' Gewürztraminer, and a white wine made from Pinot Noir grapes. Grand Cru was one of the first to make a white wine from red grapes. With the increased consumer interest in white wines, this wine-making device will no doubt continue.

GUNDLACH–BUNDSCHU WINERY

A century ago, the Gundlach-Bundschu Wine Company was internationally famous for its varietal wines. It may soon be again if three brothers-in-law, Jim Bundschu, great-grandson of founder Charles Bundschu, John Merritt and Barney Fernandez (vineyard manager for Château St Jean), are successful with new wine-making operations. It has been a slow, painstaking process since 1970 when the three began restoring the old winery, which had been destroyed by fire after Prohibition. The winery is known for producing Kleinberger wine from the only commercial planting of this variety (known as the Elbling in the Rhine) in the United States. More notable, however, is its Cabernet Sauvignon, of which the Batto Ranch vintage 1977 won a gold medal at the 1979 Los Angeles County Fair judgings. Big, dark, rich, round, full-bodied, it is a statement of the new attitude at Gundlach-Bundschu and a fine example of California Cabernets. With fruit and tannin, it is a wine which should greet the twenty-first century and beyond.

HANZELL VINEYARDS

Along State Highway 12 is as unique a winery as can be found, Hanzell, founded by James K. Zellerbach. Hanzell has from the outset produced perhaps California's finest Chardonnay (along with Stony Hill Vineyard) and Pinot Noir. Zellerbach, a man of wealth and means, was a great wine-lover first. Enamoured of the wines of Romanée-Conti and Montrachet of Burgundy, he dreamed of producing wines of equal quality in California. In 1952, he planted ten acres of Pinot

Noir and nine acres of Chardonnay on a lovely undulating parcel. When the vines reached maturity, he built a gem-like winery with an exterior which architecturally resembled Clos de Vougeot. In the interior was enclosed the most modern wine-making equipment together with a collection of small French oak cooperage.

His Chardonnays, including the first in 1956, were spectacular. I have tasted every Hanzell Chardonnay since its inception, and they always impress me with balance, luscious vitality and generous drinkability. Recently, I tasted the early vintages of the 1950s and then the 1960s, and found them still filled with vigour and drinking as if they were made yesterday. Amazing? Perhaps not so, in the light of their bottling under nitrogen which gave them super ageing abilities.

Zellerbach is often credited with introducing French oak barrels to California wine ageing and sending California wine-makers off to assemble a collection of expensive French cooperage. He is also to be credited for successful Pinot Noir production that provided incentive for other Pinot Noir producers to push forward. Profit was not his motive, as he was one of California's richest individuals. Yet he sold his wine at the then (late 1950s and early 1960s) high price of $6.00 per bottle, proclaiming that a small, high-quality California winery could be made profitable and that he would prove it. His death in 1963 prompted the estate's executors to market grapes rather than wines until ownership passed to Douglas Day, former executive of Lucky Stores, a large Californian retail marketing chain. In 1975, Countess Barbara de Brye acquired the winery. The major change at Hanzell since then has been the planting of four acres of Cabernet Sauvignon, because she has a fondness for red Bordeaux wines. When these vines mature, the number of Hanzell wines will increase to three. Wine-making today is in the capable hands of Robert Sessions. The countess has given him broad range and Sessions has lapped it up, as confirmed by the 1974 Chardonnay which may well be amongst the top five ever produced in the state. The wine is so completely in balance, luscious to the point that a spoon may be more effective than a glass – outstanding and without question as good as the Chardonnays of the late 1950s on which the Hanzell reputation was justifiably based.

KENWOOD VINEYARDS

Near Château St Jean is Kenwood Vineyards, founded in 1905 by Julius Pagani, who produced Italianesque wines in red and white jug and bulk quality, until recently not atypical of other Sonoma County producers. In 1970, upon Pagani's death, the winery was purchased by a San Francisco group comprising Mike Lee, and his sons Marty and Mike, John Sheela, Bob Kozlowski and Neil Knott. Vineyards were replanted, principally to Johannisberg Riesling, while new equipment was installed. Wines produced are Chardonnay, Chenin Blanc, Cabernet Sauvignon, Pinot Noir, Petite Sirah and Zinfandel. The wines are not expensive and are generally high in quality, especially Zinfandel and Cabernet. The latter was one of the best of the 1972 vintage, a year that was generally deprecated because of two weeks of high daily heat. A vastly underrated vineyard!

F. KORBEL AND BROTHERS, INC

To the northwest of Santa Rosa, above a bend of the Russian River, stands Korbel, a top sparkling-wine producer that was one of the first to use the Champagne method. It was founded by three brothers from Bohemia in the late nineteenth century. The sparkling wines are today the speciality and mainstay, although several vintage-dated table wines are also produced. The Heck brothers arrived in 1954 with considerable sparkling wine experience. Under the aegis of the Hecks, the cellars have been expanded and modernized, the vineyards increased to 600 acres, and additions made to the number of sparkling wines produced. The list of sparkling wines now includes Natural (the first in America to be made with little or no *dosage*), Brut, Extra Dry, Sec, Rosé and Rouge. Table wine varieties produced are Chardonnay, Johannisberg Riesling, Sauvignon Blanc (called Sonoma Blanc), Chenin Blanc, Gewürztraminer, Zinfandel, Pinot Noir and Cabernet Sauvignon.

In 1962, the Hecks hired Alan Hemphill, the first oenology graduate of Fresno State University, as production manager. He stayed for seventeen years, before leaving to assume similar responsibilities with Château St Jean. During Hemphill's tenure with Korbel, the process of clarifying the sparkling wines was automated by the invention of racks which shake the bottles mechanically, sliding the yeast sediment into the neck. A second machine from France disgorges each bottle mech-anically. Although the two machines eliminate hundreds of hours of hand shaking and disgorging, Korbel can accurately label their sparkling wines as 'fermented in "this" bottle'. Korbel California Champagne for years had the market to itself. The Natural was perhaps the first premium sparkling wine to gain national atten-tion, a crisp, clean, austere wine that made good taste sense.

LAMBERT BRIDGE

Lambert Bridge was founded in 1975 by Gerard Lambert, heir to the Listerine mouthwash fortune, and his wife Margaret. With seventy-eight acres and a 40,000-US gallon capacity, the winery specializes in Cabernet Sauvignons and Chardonnays from their own vineyards. Notable are the 1977 and 1978 Chardonnays, which are a bit heavy in wood, but are nevertheless well-fruited, semi-luscious in style and eminently drinkable. The suppleness of the 1978 is probably better than that of the 1977.

LANDMARK VINEYARDS

Landmark Vineyards at Windsor was founded in 1974 by William Mabry, Jr., retired Air Force officer and architect, together with his son William III. Sixty-seven acres of Alexander Valley vineyards form the estate while a new winery was constructed in 1975. Wines include Chardonnay, Johannisberg Riesling, Gewürz-traminer, Cabernet Sauvignon and Pinot Noir. Reasonable pricing and high quality are the two themes here, especially for the Chardonnay, the 1977 and 1978 vintages of which sold for under $7.00 in 1980. The wine is not in a heavy, lush, fruited style. None the less, it is nicely balanced, clean, crisp and good table drinking at the price, perhaps similar to a fine Mâcon Blanc in a good vintage. Brad Webb consults.

J. PEDRONCELLI WINERY

North of Healdsburg is another interesting Sonoma town, Geyserville, where the J. Pedroncelli Winery is located nearby on the outskirts along Highway 101. Until 1955, Pedroncelli Winery produced mainly generic wines, such as Sonoma red, white and rosé. Then John, Sr. allowed sons, John and James, to take over the winery and to add vintage-dated varietals to the generic jug wines which had been the mainstay of the winery until then. Commencing with a Zinfandel rosé in 1958, the list of varietals has been expanded to include Cabernet Sauvignon, Pinot Noir, Chardonnay, Chenin Blanc, French Colombard, Gamay Beaujolais, Gewürz-traminer and Zinfandel. The winery, located at the periphery of the Dry Creek Valley, is surrounded by 135 acres of vineyards which supply many of the grapes used in the wines, while others are purchased from vineyards located in both the Alexander and Dry Creek Valleys.

Of special interest are Pedroncelli's Zinfandels and Cabernet Sauvignons, heavy-handed reds, assertive in nose and taste, perhaps a bit hard to drink early, they age far better than their low price would indicate. They are, however, a consumer's rather than a collector's wines, which cry out for drinking at table rather than storing and are remarkably good value.

SEBASTIANI VINEYARDS

Samuele Sebastiani, another in the long line of Italian first-generation immigrants, commenced wine-making in 1904. The third generation, led by Samuel, his grandson, carries on today. Sacramental wine saved the winery from extinction during Prohibition. At Repeal, Samuele's youngest son, August, entered the family business which constituted nothing other than bulk wine-making for the many wineries sporting such important names as Beaulieu Vineyard, Mirassou and Paul Masson. In the early 1950s, August assumed control of the winery and decided to sell wines under the Sebastiani label. Within a decade, the reputation grew, while his wines were picking up awards at the Los Angeles County Fair and California State Fair judgings. For years the winery was known for its Barbera, a varietal with a heavy-handed style. It became a kind of trade mark for the winery, full-bodied and sharp. The wine was gutsy and loaded with ageing ability. With time, smoothness arrived, as did full flavour. The winery has also made excellent Zinfandels, Cabernet Sauvignons and surprisingly good sherries which are baked in the sun within a *solera*-like system. I prefer the reds to the whites as being more complex and interesting. Note should be taken of a white Pinot Noir, appropriately labelled 'Eye of the Swan'.

Sebastiani retains old oak storage tanks, but in his drive to modernize, he has replaced the old fermenters with temperature-controlled stainless steel. Within the last five years, the winery has produced a range of varietals and generics that literally covered the United States. These wines show good quality, are moderately priced, and have made Sebastiani one of the United States' most prominent producers. In 1980 August died and his son Sam now assumes control.

SIMI WINERY

At the town of Healdsburg on the western side of Sonoma County, Simi is yet another winery in the old mould which has undergone complete rehabilitation under new ownership. Located midway between the Alexander Valley and Dry Creek Valley, the winery building in which Simi is housed reaches back to 1876 and was brought up to date by Russell Green in 1970. Green hired André Tchelistcheff as consulting oenologist, and Mary Ann Graf, the first woman oenologist to assume full charge of a major commercial winery. After putting the winery in ship-shape state, Green sold it in 1974 to Scottish and Newcastle Vintners, the American subsidiary of a Scottish beer and whisky producer. An appellation of origin of Alexander Valley was one of Green's accomplishments during his era, when the list of wines produced included Chardonnay, Johannisberg Riesling, Chenin Blanc, rosé of Cabernet Sauvignon, Gamay Beaujolais, Zinfandel, Pinot Noir, Cabernet Sauvignon and Gewürztraminer. Schieffelin, the well-known American importing house (Dom Pérignon and Blue Nun), is the proprietor today, with direction supplied by Michael Dixon and another new woman wine-maker, talented Zelma Long, who performed wine-making chores brilliantly at the Robert Mondavi Winery. A recent Simi release, a 1974 Cabernet Sauvignon, one of Sonoma County's finest, indicates the seriousness of Schieffelin's wine-making and ageing programme. It is ageing well against a background of tannin and ample fruit.

SONOMA VINEYARDS

Sonoma Vineyards is fortunate to have Rodney Strong as wine-maker. The winery is capable of nearly three and a half million US gallons of storage capacity. Production includes Cabernet Sauvignon, Johannisberg Riesling, Chardonnay, Pinot Noir, Ruby Cabernet, Chenin Blanc, Gamay Beaujolais, Grenache Rosé, Petite Sirah and California Champagne. Although the winery is large in comparison with most of its Sonoma County neighbours, Strong places great emphasis upon vineyards for such premium varietals as Cabernet Sauvignon, Johannisberg Riesling, Chardonnay and Pinot Noir, especially upon those produced from grapes grown on the winery-owned property. The best of these are produced from grapes grown in single vineyard plots identified on the label. For example, there are the outstanding Cabernet Sauvignons of Alexander's Crown (in the Alexander Valley), the River West and Chalk Hill Chardonnays, the River West 'Old Vine' Zinfandels, and the Le Baron Johannisberg Rieslings, produced in two styles: one which is dry, and one which is sweet, made from grapes from the same vineyard harvested several weeks later than the first and lightly touched with botrytis. In addition to these wines, which are designated as 'Estate Bottled', there are four wines which are barrel-selected by Strong and are released under a special label as 'Rodney D. Strong Signature' wines. These include a sparkling wine made 100 per cent from a specially selected Chardonnay *cuvée*, a Pinot Noir, a Cabernet Sauvignon and another Chardonnay. The first release of the Signature was made in October 1979. Quantities are small, and the Signature wines may not be available each vintage year but because Sonoma Vineyards own 1,200 acres of vineyards, there is ample choice for Strong.

The finest wine made to date is the much acclaimed 1974 Alexander's Crown Cabernet Sauvignon, a remarkable lush wine that reminded me much of the style of the finely made Beaulieu Vineyards Private Reserve. And yet Alexander's Crown has its own unique style. The soft, supple nature of the wine, with a magnanimous dose of fruit, proclaimed it a California-style, made for generous drinking early. This wine has aged beautifully up to now and will continue to do so for years; at present, its softness and charm are not unlike that of a Pomerol Merlot. The wine's beauty and grace are obvious, and remain a testament to Rod Strong's unrelenting determination to find small isolated lots of wine. The 1975 Alexander's Crown is doing well, too, but is not nearly the equal of the 1974. The 1976 shows amazing promise but only time and taste will tell.

Sonoma Vineyards, because of the hard-driving efforts of Strong to acquire the best of fruit, purchased or optioned to buy hundreds of acres, the cost of which nearly bankrupt the winery during the California economic wine doldrums of the early-to-middle 1970s. Reorganization, with the capital of his partner, Renfield, a national importing house, put Sonoma Vineyards well on its way, again, to financial security and wine-making excellence.

The table wines that sell in corked magnum bottles are another example of Strong's wine-making wizardry. The red contains Cabernet and is indeed fine value and has good taste, while the white has a percentage of Chardonnay, launched on a base of French Colombard and Thompson seedless. The latter is hardly discernible because of the dominance of Chardonnay. Not only are wine consumers convinced of Strong's wine-making ability, but so is Piper Heidsieck, the French Champagne producer. The French company has formed a partnership with Renfield to construct a 200,000-case sparkling-wine facility in Sonoma, with Strong as its wine-maker. It seems that Piper Heidsieck likes the style of Sonoma's sparkling wines. The new label will be Piper-Sonoma, a fact which will be viewed by the industry with envy and renewed interest.

SOVERAIN CELLARS

Soverain at Geyserville was formerly known as Soverain of Alexander Valley when it was owned by Pillsbury Milling Company, one of America's largest. A partnership of 179 north California coast grape-growers purchased the winery in 1976 and in so doing acquired one of the most striking new wineries (constructed in 1973), filled with the latest in efficient wine-making equipment. William Bonnetti, who brings experience from Conegliano, Italy, Gallo, Cresta Blanca and Charles Krug, was retained as wine-maker. The wines are nationally distributed. They are generally sound and cleanly made, but not, as yet, exciting. A 1978 French Colombard, one of the best I have tasted in a luscious, fruity style, won a gold medal at the 1979 Los Angeles County Fair wine judgings; with the excellent grape resources of 179 growers, this vineyard is expected to provide better.

JOSEPH SWAN VINEYARDS

In 1967, Joseph Swan purchased a thirteen-acre ranch on the outskirts of Forestville, in Sonoma County, on which grapes had grown since 1885, and replanted it with five acres of Chardonnay, five acres of Pinot Noir and half an acre of Cabernet Sauvignon. Swan has very little acreage but his reputation extends beyond his quantity. He makes 3,000 US gallons of wine annually, not only from his own grapes, but also includes six to eight tonnes of Zinfandel purchased from a grower in Dry Creek. It is the Zinfandel for which he has received his greatest acclaim. Emphasis is upon so-called classical methods with no filtering; clarification is achieved by careful racking and lengthy barrel-ageing in French oak prior to bottling. Wines receive four to six months of bottle-ageing prior to release. Pinot Noirs are not in the customary California style. They are usually big-bodied, intense wines that may not achieve the elegance for which Pinot Noir is sometimes known. There is no denying, however, that the wines have full-flavour, roundness and long-age potential.

MENDOCINO COUNTY

Although grapes were grown and wine was produced in Mendocino as early as the 1850s, it was not well known nor highly regarded for fine wine until the late 1960s and early 1970s. Most of the wine had been of the bulk table variety shipped out to wineries outside Mendocino. However, the 'Wine Boom' has brought Mendocino out of the closet with publicly acclaimed wineries and expanded vineyards. Viticulturally, Mendocino County is composed of three principal areas. The largest is the Ukiah Valley, a Region III, in which such well-known vineyards as Parducci, Weibel, Cresta Blanca and Milano are found. In nearby Redwood Valley, also a Region III, is Fetzer, while the newest wineries and vineyards are in Anderson Valley, a Region I. The latter includes Husch, Edmeades and Navarro.

CRESTA BLANCA WINERY

North of Ukiah is the century-old winery, Cresta Blanca, transplanted from the original winery site in the Livermore Valley in Alameda County. It is now owned by Guild Wineries. Although Cresta Blanca purchases grapes from numerous Mendocino County growers, many of its grapes are acquired from all over the state. The best wine yet produced under the Guild banner has been the Mendocino non-vintage Zinfandel which is a most satisfying wine, especially for its low cost. Cresta Blanca's sweet wines also deserve special attention. A sherry labelled Dry Watch, in the Amontillado style, has been extremely popular, but it has been their Triple Cream Sherry, not unlike Harvey's Bristol cream, which surprised the industry by capturing, several years ago, the Sweepstakes Award at the Los Angeles County

Fair. A new line of varietals, including Chardonnay and Cabernet Sauvignon that are rather pleasant and satisfying, has been introduced. Priced at under $5.00 in 1980, the wines represent the new intention to produce finer wines from the better grapes of their cooperative member-owners. While the wines are not exciting nor memorable, they are first-rate value.

EDMEADES WINERY

Another in the long line of southern Californians transplanted to north-coast vineyards is Dr Donald Edmeades who established Edmeades winery near Philo in Mendocino County in 1962. When he died in 1972, his son Deron took over operation of the winery. Jed Steele, an oenology graduate of the University of California and a young talented wine-maker, has been producing some wines that have been putting Edmeades on the map. In 1977, Steele produced one of the state's best Pinot Noirs, most unusual for Mendocino County. Produced from grapes grown at Garden Creek Ranch in the Alexander Valley of Sonoma County, it was a wine of good structure, with elegance and balance rarely found in California Pinot Noirs. Also produced are Chardonnay, Gewürztraminer, French Colombard, Cabernet Sauvignon, Zinfandel and Johannisberg Riesling. Especially interesting is the *Eiswein*-style wine that Steele made from French Colombard grapes in 1977. The frozen grapes were harvested at 38.7° Brix, and at fermentation's end the wine contained only 7 per cent alcohol and 16 per cent residual sugar nicely balanced with acidity.

FETZER WINERY

North of Cresta Blanca, in Redwood Valley, a former lumberman, Bernard Fetzer, launched his family-owned and operated winery in 1968. Two completely separate wineries have been built by the Fetzers, a white wine facility and a red. Fermenters in both are stainless steel. Ageing of the whites is in Yugoslavian oak. French oak is responsible for the reds. Since my initial Fetzer tastings, I have preferred the reds, especially the Zinfandels and Cabernets. The Zinfandel first captured my attention in 1968 with a wine that was forward in taste, full-fruited, but with heavy wood ageing. Cabernets are simple in style, lush big wines, but do not seem to develop complexities found in Napa and Sonoma county wines. Labels identify vineyards; frequently there are several versions of a given variety and vintage. The lengthy Fetzer wine list includes Cabernet Sauvignon, Carignano, Chardonnay, Chenin Blanc, Fumé Blanc, Gamay Beaujolais, Gewürztraminer, Johannisberg Riesling, Muscat Canelli, Petite Sirah, Pinot Noir and Zinfandel. In addition, there are three extremely good jug generics labelled simply as red, white and rosé. The red is perhaps the best, full flavoured and no doubt made from the ever-present Zinfandel. Whites in recent years have improved in flavour and concentration of more fruit, but it is the Zinfandel which has brought Fetzer its greatest fame, especially from the Ricetti vineyard in Mendocino County which has captured its fair share of state awards.

PARDUCCI WINERY, LTD

Oldest and best-known Mendocino winery is Parducci Vineyards. Teachers Management Institute purchased a majority interest in Parducci in 1973, providing funds for expansion and modernization of the winery. Old redwood tanks were replaced with stainless-steel fermenters, and a new storage warehouse and a separate tasting room were built. The old winery building received a face-lifting of stone and redwood, with storage capacity now totalling over one million US gallons.

Parducci's vineyards were expanded by stages to the present 350 acres, planted mainly to Chenin Blanc, Chardonnay, Johannisberg Riesling and Pinot Noir. The complete list includes, in addition to the vineyard varieties, Cabernet Sauvignon, Carignane, Charbono, Gamay Beaujolais, Zinfandel, Petite Sirah, French Colombard, a May Wine, Mendocino Riesling and three generics called chablis, burgundy and rosé. Although ageing cellars contain American oak barrels, all of the whites are aged in stainless steel, as are a portion of the reds, to test and support John Parducci's theory that wood ageing hides varietal flavours and that complexity will come with bottle age when the phenols begin to break down. This controversial theory has not been seriously tested to date and only time will indeed tell but there are several award-winning (in the Los Angeles County Fair) white wines such as the Silver Medal Chardonnay, French Colombard and Mendocino Riesling in support of this belief. The winery has perhaps produced better whites than reds, emphasizing intense, fruity flavours, such as Chenin Blanc and French Colombard. However, the Cellarmasters Cabernet Sauvignon is a very good wine.

WEIBEL CHAMPAGNE VINEYARDS

As urbanization confronted Weibel Champagne Vineyards at Mission San Jose, other prime vineyards were sought. Mendocino County was selected, and there a winery and a tasting room, shaped like an upside-down Champagne glass, were built on the northern outskirts of Ukiah in 1973. In Mendocino, 250 acres of vineyards were planted while some spilled over to Sonoma. Grapes are vinified at the Ukiah winery, but the wine is shipped in bulk to the Mission San Jose winery for finishing and bottling. Ultimately, the production of all Weibel's table wines will be moved to Mendocino County, while production of sparkling wines will continue at the other location. The new grapes have produced some very satisfactory still wines, though Weibel is chiefly in sparkling wines.

A full line of Chardonnay, Cabernet Sauvignon, Green Hungarian, Johannisberg Riesling, Pinot Noir, Gamay Beaujolais, Grey Riesling, Pinot Noir Blanc, Chenin Blanc, Zinfandel, Petite Sirah and the usual generics, chablis, burgundy and rosé, form an ever-improving group with fruit that abounds. The Chardonnay, for instance, is clean and fruity but without the complexities of other areas; nevertheless it is a most attractive wine. Others drink well too, namely the 1973 Cabernet Sauvignon, produced from North Coast grapes with ample good flavour. It is soft, nicely balanced and with complexities that are just developing. Ageing for several years will be beneficial.

SOLANO COUNTY

Geographically, Solano County lies adjacent to Napa County to the northwest, with Yolo County to the northeast and Contra Costa County to the south. The main, heavily travelled route of Interstate 80, between San Francisco and Sacramento, passes through Solano County. About midway between the two cities, the highway veers through to the north to go around the county seat of Fairfield.

CADENASSO WINERY

Along the Fairfield approach from the west, it is possible to view Solano County's oldest winery, Cadenasso Winery. The appearance of the winery building may be somewhat decrepit, and yet it houses a handsome collection of redwood tanks and oak ovals. Cooperage is not small here and equipment is simple, with only one stainless-steel storage tank. Proprietor Frank Cadenasso relies chiefly upon his theory that the wine-maker's most important tools are care and patience. He produces good, everyday wine; albeit some of the reds are complex enough to win awards at the Los Angeles County Fair, most of which he sells at the winery. Prices are so reasonable that customers frequently drive from Sacramento or San Francisco to buy. His reds are to be preferred over his whites (although his whites are improving, as is the case with many California wineries), and the best of these are Pinot Noir, and Cabernet Sauvignon, which won an award in the Los Angeles County Fair a few years back. His Zinfandel is also a sound, drinkable wine, especially with a plate of spicy pasta or sausages. He is also one of the few California wine-makers producing a Grignolino, which also received an award in the Los Angeles Fair judgings the last time he entered it. The wines are not vintage dated and by judicious blending, Cadenasso bottles at apparently the right moment without any trace of wood.

Prior to Prohibition, there were 2,000 acres of vineyards in Solano County. Upon Repeal, acreage dropped steadily until it had fallen to under 600 acres in the early 1960s. But the American 'Wine Boom' reached here, too, and plantings began to increase in 1965. By 1978, there were almost 1,300 bearing acres in the county, most of them protected from urban encroachment by agricultural preserve status. The increased interest in wine even prompted the second oldest winery in Solano County, Wooden Valley Winery, to plant its own vineyards and to produce its own wines.

The newest winery in Solano County, Diablo Vista, was established in 1977 in Benicia, formerly a military arsenal during the Second World War. It is a tiny winery, with only a 20,000-US gallon storage capacity, but it purchases grapes from vineyards in Placerville, Livermore, Lodi, Dry Creek and the Napa Valley. Little tasting experience does not allow for any significant evaluation of the quality of the wines as yet. This seems to be the problem with Solano County in general, that the wine-tasting track record is not yet long enough to form any strong opinions.

SIERRA FOOTHILLS

The Sierra Foothills represent an area which was more famous for gold than grapes. El Dorado County had more vineyards in 1860 than either Sonoma or Napa counties and by 1890, more than one hundred wineries were operating here. Prohibition put an end to the Gold Rush wineries, with no resumption until recently. The Sierra Foothills were ignored by growers and wineries adjacent to the Bay area, until urbanization and rising land tax rates forced a return to abundant vineyard lands here. Appropriately the Zinfandel grape, considered uniquely Californian, drew attention to the 'new' potential of the Sierra Foothills, especially at Amador County.

Amador County: The uniquely attractive and popular character of Amador County Zinfandels is an important factor in the blossoming of six new wineries in Amador County during the 1970s. Most are relatively small, with storage capacity of between 3,000 and 5,000 US gallons.

D'AGOSTINI WINERY

Located at Plymouth is one of Amador County's oldest wineries, operated by the D'Agostini family since it was purchased in 1911 by Enrico D'Agostini from the Swiss immigrant, Adam Uhlinger, who founded it in 1856. Closed by Prohibition but reopened at Repeal, D'Agostini Winery produced primarily generic wines, bottling their Zinfandel as burgundy, but the burgeoning consumer interest in

Amador County Zinfandels has changed that. It is now accurately labelled as a varietal, Amador County Zinfandel. Its storage capacity of 185,000 US gallons stamps D'Agostini as the largest Amador County winery, and the only one with guided tours. D'Agostini vineyards total 125 acres.

HARBOR WINERY

Charles Myers, the college professor who makes wine literally in his garage, is given not enough credit for the discovery of the production of the Zinfandel grapes grown in Shenandoah Valley in Amador County. His wines, like so many others, are intense in flavour and in aroma in a forward style that is uniquely Shenandoah Valley. His initial wines, so-called home-made, were produced from grapes grown in Deaver Vineyard and so impressed Darrell Corti, Sacramento wine-merchant, that he arranged for the Trincheros at Sutter Home Winery in the Napa Valley to produce and bottle Deaver Vineyard Zinfandel under the Corti Brothers label. The wine has been a regular part of Sutter Home's production since the early 1970s. Myers also produces wine from Napa Valley grapes, including Cabernet Sauvignon and Chardonnay. The latter drinks with superb deliciousness, especially the 1976. Production is small but includes one of the more interesting wines, Mission del Sol, a wine made from Mission grapes, in a style that Myers describes as exactly that in which wines were made in the early part of the nineteenth century. It is one of California's best dessert wines.

MONTEVINA

Established in 1973, Montevina is owned by Cary Gott who is also the wine-maker, his wife, Vicki, and father-in-law, Walker Field. Montevina Zinfandels are noted for relatively high acid and alcohol as well as deep colour, full body, flavour and aroma. Gott attributes these characteristics to the combination of the apparently perfect climate (warm days and cool nights) and the red volcanic soil, which he claims produces grapes of higher acid and sugar than Zinfandel grown elsewhere. The Zinfandel comes from two old vineyards totalling eighty acres. Since 1972, eighty acres of Cabernet Sauvignon, Sauvignon Blanc, Barbera and Nebbiolo have been added. A speciality is a Zinfandel produced by the Beaujolais technique of carbonic maceration. The resulting wine is light in colour, fresh and intensely fruity, with a strawberry-like aroma and flavour. Intended for early consumption, it has a short lifespan and a large fan-following. Several years ago Gott produced a Barbera, a variety not necessarily in favour today. It was so intense and lush with flavour, that blind tastings have shocked many, but it was a prime example of innovation and desire on the part of Gott to make the best out of Amador, irrespective of the grape.

El Dorado County: El Dorado County sprouted three wineries during the 1970s. The largest of the three is Boeger, which has begun to produce relatively heavy-style Zinfandels and Cabernet Sauvignons of some interest, complexity and appeal. Other new wineries which are too new to permit evaluation string the county line between Calveras and Tuolumne. The soils and climate of El Dorado County closely resemble those of Amador County. So it is not surprising if the wines also closely resemble those of Amador. The re-discovery of these areas has opened entirely new vistas and prospects for wine-growing in a different kind of gold search. This historical California Gold Rush country appears to provide ideal sites for Zinfandel, which may attain new heights of complexity, a characteristic which is frequently elusive for the variety.

ALAMEDA COUNTY-LIVERMORE

Livermore Valley, one of the most important California wine-growing areas for over a hundred years, is virtually synonymous with white wines, but is now making sound reds. For Alameda County, its greatest wine asset is Region III – Livermore Valley's gravelly soils, that are well-drained and closely resemble the soils of Graves in Bordeaux, France.

CONCANNON VINEYARD

Concannon Vineyard, a Livermore Valley gem, was founded in 1883 by James Concannon, an Irish immigrant. Altar wines are a significant portion of the winery's output and sales and there is pride in the fact that a Concannon bottle each year graces the table of the Pope. The 250 acres of Concannon vineyards are now protected as an agricultural preserve from residential housing tracts' encroachment. The population of Livermore has quadrupled since the Lawrence Radiation Laboratory was established there in 1962. Because of the preserve, Concannon is able to sustain a substantial portion of their grape needs from their own vineyards. Otherwise, Concannon probably would have found it necessary to move or to close its doors. Fifteen wines are produced. Notwithstanding Livermore's penchant for white wines, Petite Sirah may be the house's finest. Although it had always been used as a filler grape, possibly in generics, Concannon was the first California winery to produce Petite Sirah as a varietal and since 1963, the wine has been one of the most popular on the Concannon list. The Concannons have always liked to experiment with various grape varieties, the most interesting of which is a variety obtained from Russia, the Rkatsiteli, which produces a fragrant, fruity wine not unlike a Riesling, yet not as complex.

A strong belief was that Livermore could produce only fine white wines. Livermore can make reds as fine as whites, a fact confirmed by Concannon's 1968 and 1969 Cabernet Sauvignons. These wines were in a different style from Napa's, not too fruited, but with nicely developed suppleness and finesse. Perhaps some of the quality of those Cabernets may have been added by grapes from the late Chaffee Hall's Hallcrest Vineyards at Felton in the Santa Cruz Mountains. Another wine which has done extremely well is Sauvignon Blanc, and on occasion a limited edition provides the crispness of taste and restrained fruit that makes magnificent wine drinking. This is unlike the current rage of Fumé Blancs of unbridled fruit with taste that is overbearing. The winery is run today by James Concannon, although it has been sold to Noble Vineyards of Kerman, California.

VILLA ARMANDO

Villa Armando, located also at Pleasanton, ships 90 per cent of its Italian-country-style wines to the east coast. The winery is run by Anthony D. Scotto, a second-generation Italian. Acquired in 1953, the Villa Armando label was merged into the 1902 Frank Garatti Winery in 1961. In the early 1960s, the family began to produce wines for the Villa Armando label. The most popular of the line is Vino Rustico, which is a slightly sweet, fruity red wine fermented without skin contact by an unusual procedure, patented by Scotto under the name of 'Autovin'. Prior to fermentation, colour is extracted by heating skins and juice together. The technique extracts colour, but little tannin, thus the wine is ready to drink within six months following fermentation. The list of wines sold under the Villa Armando label includes Petite Sirah, Napa Gamay Rosé, Zinfandel, Chenin Blanc (dry and sweet), French Colombard, Pinot Blanc, Chardonnay, Sauvignon Blanc, Cabernet Sauvignon, Valdepeñas, a late-harvest Malvasia Bianca, and two generics, burgundy and chablis, as well as a rosé and a red Rustico.

WEIBEL CHAMPAGNE VINEYARDS

At Warm Springs, just south of Mission San Jose, Leland Stanford planted 100 acres of vineyards and constructed a winery in 1869. Until phylloxera reigned, 250,000 US gallons of wine were produced each year at Stanford's Warm Springs Winery. The winery was reactivated in 1945 by Rudolf Weibel, a Swiss immigrant who had been making custom-labelled champagne in San Francisco. Rudolf and son Fred planted their own vineyards and moved their champagne production from San Francisco to Warm Springs. There they produced sparkling wines, not only for themselves, but for other vintners and for hotel and restaurant private labels. Many American wine drinkers do not realize that when they pick up a bottle with a house label, it was probably produced by Weibel. Weibel produces sparkling wines that have been amongst the best in the state. The line includes Brut, Extra Dry, Chardonnay Brut, Muscat Spumante, Sparkling Green Hungarian, a Crackling Rosé and Crackling Duck.

The winery has now focused attention on table wine production as well. This has been coming for some time because of the maturing of new vineyards in Sonoma County and at Ukiah in Mendocino. These include Chardonnay, Johannisberg Riesling, Pinot Noir, Cabernet Sauvignon, Grey Riesling, Chenin Blanc, and Zinfandel. The new table wines may prove to be successful, considering the new, 1980 releases. Outstanding is the 1979 Johannisberg Riesling which is packed with intense flavour. At 1.25 per cent residual sugar, it is not too sweet, while the concentration of Johannisberg Riesling flavour from Mendocino County is attractively distinctive. Another winner is Grey Riesling 1979 from North Coast grapes. The wine is especially floral and fragrant and provides a delightfully fruity taste. The body appears heavier than that in other Grey Rieslings. Two Chardonnays were produced in the 1979 vintage. One is from Santa Clara grapes, the same *cuvée* used for Weibel's premium Champagne Brut Cuvée. A youthful apple taste is most attractive in a light Chardonnay style. Yet it is most assertive in varietal character. Perhaps a bit too assertive for now; bottle age may bring restraint. There is little oak in the wine, as oak is not one of Fred's loves. The second Chardonnay was produced from Mendocino County grapes. I found the floral fragrance and the unrestrained fruit not to my liking. Perhaps time will help, but not for me. Yet hard-core Chardonnay fruit lovers should like this one. In descending order of my preference, the other 1980 releases are Pinot Noir, North Coast, 1975, Pinot Noir Blanc, 1979, Chenin Blanc, 1979, Gamay Beaujolais, 1979, Zinfandel, 1977. Weibel's sherries and ports are also receiving greater attention these days. Their Solera Dry Bin Cocktail Sherry, Solera Flor Medium Sherry, Solera Flor Amber Cream Sherry and Solera Cask Rare Port won awards in the Los Angeles County Fair judgings in 1979.

WENTE BROTHERS

Almost directly across Tesla Road from Concannon is Wente Brothers, founded in the same year, 1883, as Concannon. The founder was Carl Heinrich Wente, an immigrant from Germany who learned wine-making from Charles Krug in the Napa Valley before moving to Livermore, where he bought a fifty-acre vineyard and set up wine-making on his own. Prior to Prohibition, only bulk wines were produced, with the entire output marketed at wholesale. Upon Repeal, the Wentes bottled Sémillon, Sauvignon Blanc and Grey Riesling. The latter, to this day, is the best-selling white varietal, and remains a first wine for millions of Americans. Interestingly, Grey Riesling is a misnomer, for it is, in fact, Chauché Gris. Chardonnay may have found its first California home at Wente Brothers. Long identified with this varietal, the Wentes are considered by Americans to have invented it. Produced early on with little or no wood, it was embraced eagerly by Chardonnay lovers. Subsequently, oak-aged Chardonnays made by a host of new wine-makers came into favour with wine-lovers; Wente Chardonnay quality may have waned and the popularity slipped a little. Today, however, the quality has improved immeasurably. Pinot Blanc has always been a model wine and the 1978 is no different, full and luscious, with a developing finish that suggests a wine that can challenge Chardonnays. Wente has also produced, lovingly, a Sauvignon Blanc that was probably the best in its day. With good flavour and, like Concannon's, not too fruited so as to compete with food flavours, a popular wine has been made for inexpensive wine drinking. Without complexity, it is perfect for neophytes. It is also of interest to note a wine that was full of Riesling character, the first naturally botrytized California Riesling made by Wente in 1969. Wente has long been identified with Sémillon in a Sauternes-like style made from vines originally obtained from the Lur-Saluces family of Château d'Yquem in Bordeaux.

As urbanization squeezed the winery, the Wentes, too, looked southward for vineyard land and, for a time, considered moving the winery, too. They planted vineyards, now totalling 550 acres, in the Arroyo Seco region of Monterey County. The winery was not moved because of the passage of an agricultural preserve ordinance by Alameda County. Today, much of the Wentes' wine carries a Monterey County *appellation*. The Johannisberg Riesling is an exceptionally good example of the variety. Pinot Noirs have also done well and the 1972 vintage is a good example. The future of Wente is assured, and the great old name will find new wine drinkers in much the same way that they have provided good low-cost wine-drinking for almost a hundred years.

With much gratitude I note that Alameda County is not yet finished as a California wine-producing region. Agricultural preserves offer protection from urban encroachment. After a long decline in bearing acreage, from nearly 2,500 acres in 1960 to less than 1,400 acres in 1977, there has been a slight increase to over 1,500 acres. It is hoped that the citizenry will agree that these vineyards should be protected for so long as they care to produce fine wines.

SANTA CLARA

Santa Clara County owes its oenological history to the Franciscan missionaries who planted grapes at Mission Santa Clara de Asis at the end of the 1770s. From a peak of 8,000 acres of grapes and over sixty wineries shortly after Repeal, the great post-Second World War westward migration, with its attendant spread of residential housing tracts, inundated nearly 6,000 acres of prime vineyards with uncontrolled sprawl, and reduced the number of wineries in the county to twenty-five or fewer. The urban sprawl forced the surviving wineries to look south to Monterey and San Benito counties for vineyard space.

Despite the journey to the south, Santa Clara County remains the headquarters for the Mirassous, the oldest wine-making family in America, and two of the largest wineries in the United States, Almadén and Paul Masson Vineyards. Urbanization, with its soaring land taxes, pressured all three to move south, Mirassou and Masson to Monterey County, and Almadén to San Benito County. Mirassou developed a unique system of mechanical harvesting, field crushing and transporting of must in order to assure that juice arrived in perfect condition after a two-hour transfer to their winery in San Jose, approximately a hundred miles from their vineyards. Masson constructed a winery near Soledad in Monterey County in 1967 to produce table wines. Sherry Cellars were constructed at Madera in 1974 for production of apéritif and dessert wines. Their Champagne Cellars headquarters, built in 1959, in Saratoga, California, remains, and is utilized now for production of sparkling wine by the transfer process. It also houses corporate headquarters and a visitors' centre. Almadén also constructed two wineries, one in San Benito County, south of Hollister at Cienega, and the second at Paicines, about twenty miles north of the Pinnacles National Monument. Nearly 5,000 acres of grapes, a size approximately equal to the whole of France's Chablis, are located in San Benito. There are 2,000 additional acres in Monterey County.

ALMADEN

Almadén's headquarters are on Blossom Hill Road between San Jose and Los Gatos. Most of the original vineyards have now disappeared, covered by a housing tract called Almadén Estates. Those that remain are merely a frame for the headquarters building and bottling cellars. Only sparkling wines are produced here, while table, dessert and apéritif wines are produced at two San Benito County wineries and at a third in Fresno. Finishing and bottling occurs in the Blossom Hill Road facility. Almadén is now the eighth largest winery in the United States, with twenty-seven million US gallons of storage capacity. Founded in 1847, the winery was small and not very well known until Louis Benoist purchased Almadén in 1941, and Frank Schoonmaker was hired as consultant. It then began to gain a reputation and a better following. The Benoist-Schoonmaker team, with Oliver Goulet as wine-maker, introduced a fine inexpensive line of varietals which included the first commercial Grenache rosé made in California. After the Second World War, a period of financial difficulty ensued, followed by a short-lived merger with Madrone Vineyards under the name of Almadén-Madrone. Pushed by suburban encroachment, Louis Benoist farsightedly led the southern vineyard move. In 1954, the winery planted vineyards in San Benito County.

The vineyards now total nearly 4,500 acres. Success accelerated for Almadén and Benoist, and the old Palmtag Winery in Cienega was acquired. A new winery and brandy distillery were constructed there. Almadén's greatest expansion has been under the banner of its present owner, National Distiller's. More vineyards have been acquired and an increase to the number and types of wine made.

The range includes inexpensive generic jug wines, together with a line of varietals and, more recently, expensive varietals under the name of the founder, Charles Le Franc. The latter hold great promise for the future, especially in Cabernet, where there is an attempt to provide both intensity and complexity. Recently, the 1977 'regular' Cabernet from Monterey County grapes exemplifies the new programme. It is a wine that sells for under $5.00 per bottle (1980). It is worthy of more, and the wine drinker's attention. Almadén probably sells more wine to and through restaurants than any other winery in the United States, no doubt aided by their bag-in-the-box dispenser which contains up to five gallons of wine in a collapsible pouch designed to prevent contamination by oxygen.

Critics prefer, however, a bronze-gold sparkling wine made with a large percentage of Pinot Noir and called 'Eye of the Partridge', or the Blanc de Blancs *cuvée*, both of which provide good, clean sparkling wine enjoyment at reasonable prices. Better yet is the 'Chardonnay Nature' sparkler, made with little or no dosage, a wine that confirms that a huge-volume wine-making enterprise can make more than satisfactory wine should they so choose. Also available is 'Le Domaine' sparkling wine that sells for under $4.00 per bottle (1980). Not to be confused with French or premium bottle-fermented Californian sparkling wine, this wine is clean, although a bit heavy in texture, and uniformly simple in taste – a pleasant, uncomplicated wine. Wine-maker Klaus Mathes can make literally any wine, from sound, commercial wine that spares American wine-drinkers' budgets, to the Le Franc line which showcases his talent. The programme will continue and should be encouraged.

LLORDS AND ELWOOD WINERY

Llords and Elwood Winery began as a retail wine shop under the wine-wise and watchful eye of J. H. Mike Elwood. During the period of 1933-61, he was considered in Los Angeles as the wine merchant *extraordinaire*, for he was not only selling but teaching wine as well. Customers came in for wine lessons as well as bottles, many of them from the Hollywood movie industry, including Ronald Reagan, then a successful actor. In the 1950s, convinced that finer wines could be produced, he began his own wine-making operation in Fremont. Early wines were California sherries and ports, which were Elwood-blended and aged until the first release in 1961. The store was sold, and Mike Elwood was in the wine business to stay. Today there are ten wines. Three styles of sherry range from very dry to very sweet. The Great Day D-r-r-y Sherry is the driest; the Dry Wit is medium sweet, and the Judge's Secret Cream Sherry is the sweetest. Ancient Proverb Port rounds out the list of apéritif and dessert wines. Without question, the four represent the finest of such wines made in California and generally are perennial medal winners in the judgings at the Los Angeles County Fair.

The table wines are also given intriguing names; such as the Rare Chardonnay, which is just that – rare. Relatively small quantities are produced, and frequently the wine is unavailable in retail channels. Perhaps the reason is that the wine is not unlike some of the simpler white Burgundies of France, and it is reasonably priced. The Magic Castle Johannisberg Riesling, characterized as a *Spätlese*, was one of the first California Rieslings to be produced in this relatively sweet, fruity style. When the wine was first entered in the Los Angeles County Fair more than a decade ago, the style had not yet turned into today's fashion, and several judges rejected it. How sad it is that Mike Elwood did not live to see the style become popular.

The Rosé of Cabernet, made exclusively from the Cabernet Sauvignon grape, is full-bodied with a fair amount of sweetness. Cabernet Sauvignon, aged in oak, has made remarkable improvement, but somehow does not yet show the complexities seen in other California Cabernets. The Velvet Hill Pinot Noir drinks extremely well but not necessarily like a Pinot Noir. There is also a sparkling wine, one of the first made with the assistance of Weibel, and it is easily one of the best sparklers. Clean and round, the wine has good flavour and a finish that belies its cost. The first Llords and Elwood wine began with the appropriate name of Grand Entrance Burgundy, that later became a classic. While Llords and Elwood table wines are favoured by many fine-wine drinkers, there are probably an equal number who do not so favour them. While this may suggest controversy, there is none in the dessert wines, which are easily amongst California's best.

MOUNT EDEN VINEYARDS

Mount Eden Vineyards operates out of the Saratoga hilltop winery which Martin Ray built after he sold his Paul Masson winery and vineyard site to Seagrams, Canadian-based distillers, in 1942. The winery, as well as the principal vineyards, were acquired by a group of investors in the early 1970s, who formed the Mount Eden Vineyards Corporation. As under the Ray management, the winery specializes in three estate-produced varietals, Cabernet Sauvignon, Pinot Noir and Chardonnay, grown on twenty-five acres of vineyards near the small, 9,000-US gallon winery. However, in recent years, for the crushes of 1978 and 1979, Mount Eden has purchased Chardonnay from Ventana Vineyards, now accounting for one-half of Mount Eden's total production. The balance of production is evenly divided between Cabernet Sauvignon, Pinot Noir and Chardonnay grown in Mount Eden's own vineyards, where yields are frequently no more than one tonne per acre.

Pinot Noir and Cabernet are fermented in stainless steel and aged in small French cooperage, while Chardonnay is barrel fermented, also in French oak. Thirty per cent of the barrels are replaced each year, with Nadalier, a Bordeaux cooper favoured, especially for the Cabernet. The barrels of Serge and François Frères, from Burgundy, are selected for Chardonnay and Pinot Noir.

Cabernet, a most interesting wine, is left on the skins for a total of two weeks, including the period of fermentation. It is not forward, but is lean and spare in a St Estèphe style – emphasizing elegance rather than robustness. Vineyards are located at 2,000 feet above sea level, which results in lower growing season temperatures than in other parts of the Santa Clara Valley, where lower acid and sugar levels are more likely. For example, in 1979 the Cabernet was harvested at 24.5° Brix and 0.9 per cent acidity; whereas, the Pinot Noir was picked at 25° Brix and at an acid level in excess of 1 per cent, resulting in grapes that show superb balance and full varietal character and likely complexity.

Availability of Mount Eden wines is limited as a consequence of low yields, supported by a winery policy to remain small. Plans called for 3,400 cases in 1980, with 5,000 cases as a peak. Dick Graff, the self-made, talented wine-maker and one of the founders of Chalone, has been consultant to Mount Eden since 1972 and assumed full wine-making control with the 1980 crush.

PEDRIZZETTI WINERY

Pedrizzetti Winery at Morgan Hill in southern Santa Clara County was founded by John Pedrizzetti in 1938. The winery today produces varietals including Barbera, Gamay, Zinfandel, Zinfandel rosé, Cabernet Sauvignon, Chardonnay, Gewürztraminer, French Colombard, Chenin Blanc and Green Hungarian. Notable is a Petite Sirah, 1977 Shell Creek Vineyards Special Release which won a gold medal at the Los Angeles County Fair in 1979. Zinfandel is generally of high quality. Edward Pedrizzetti and his wife, Phyllis, took over the winery in 1967 and have installed modern equipment in the form of stainless-steel fermenters.

MARTIN RAY WINERY

Martin Ray died in 1976, but the winery and the legend did not. His son Peter, continues to produce Ray-styled wines, and with experience – he has been active in the winery since 1959. Martin Ray was often controversial, but his wines were not. At a time when American wines had not yet become internationally acclaimed he probably was the first during the early 1950s to charge more than $5, sometimes as high as $8, for a bottle of California wine. It shook the very foundations of the industry. I doubt I shall ever taste Pinot Noir better than his 1960 vintage, nor his Chardonnay of 1962 and his Cabernet 1952 Centennial, which he naturally proclaimed as the greatest of all Cabernets. Peter Ray continues to accept his father's gauntlet and challenge of fine wine-making with a list limited to three varietals and a sparkling wine. Released in 1980 are 1979 Winery Lake Chardonnay (from Rene di Rosa's vineyard in Los Carneros in the Napa Valley), 1979 Dutton Ranch (at Sebastopol in Sonoma County) Chardonnay, 1977 Winery Lake Pinot Noir, and 1976 Howell Mountain (Napa Valley) Cabernet Sauvignon. Two non-vintage wines are also offered under the La Montaña label, Pinot Noir and a Cabernet-Merlot blend, and a Champagne-method sparkling wine. The latter is a rich, full wine, somewhat woody in flavour, which blends the same Chardonnay (which accounts for the oak in the taste) that goes into the table wine, with a Pinot Noir.

RICHERT AND SONS WINERY

Another producer of fine dessert wines in Santa Clara County is the Richert and Sons Winery of Morgan Hill, established by Walter S. Richert in 1954. His son Scott, after a stint with Paul Masson, assumed responsibility for the winery in 1976. Table wines were produced in the 1950s, but the dessert wines, now reduced to six in number, are the stars. The six are Pale Dry Sherry, Full Dry Sherry, Club Sherry, Triple Cream Sherry, Ruby Port and Tawny Port. The sherries are made by the system of baking base wines to achieve desired flavour and aroma nuttiness as well as a characteristic golden brown colour. (This technique is probably closer to that found in the production of Madeira, than it is to that of Sherry in Spain.) The wines have done well at the Los Angeles County Fair judgings.

SAN MARTIN WINERY

South of Morgan Hill is San Martin, the name of the town as well as the winery, which stands in the centre of town. In 1892 the winery started as a cooperative. In 1932, a remarkable Italian, Bruno Filice, acquired it and spent forty years expanding the capacity of the winery to over two million US gallons, the vineyards to 700 acres and the fruit orchards to 300 acres. By 1972, San Martin was one of the largest family-owned wineries. For many years, it was probably better known for its fruit wines than for its grape bottles. After several changes of ownership in the mid-1970s, and the retention of a new wine-maker, the product as well as the reputation of San Martin have changed radically. San Martin was acquired by a Norton Simon subsidiary, Somerset Importers, which had earlier purchased Alexis Lichine and Company and were now interested in moving into California wines. To an already expensive rehabilitation of the physical facilities at San Martin, Somerset added a vigorous marketing and sales promotion programme. Most important was the retention of the young innovative German wine-maker, Ed Friedrich, who joined San Martin in 1973 after fourteen years with Paul Masson and a brief stint with Wiederkeher Wine Cellars in Arkansas. He trained at the Viticultural Institute in Trier, Germany, his birthplace. His German and Californian training and experience well equipped him to shift completely San Martin's emphasis from fruit and berry wines to top quality vintage-dated varietals. His innovation came with the introduction of fresh, fruity, low alcohol 'soft' wines that are made for instant serving and generous drinking.

The changes were sparked by the ready availability of Monterey County grapes with intense varietal characteristics. Friedrich also used grapes from Amador and San Luis Obispo counties. The eminently successful 'soft' wines are inspired by the low alcohol wines of Germany. The 'soft' emphasis began with a 1975 Chenin Blanc with less than 10 per cent alcohol. In other vintages Friedrich added a 'soft' Johannisberg Riesling, a 'soft' Zinfandel and a 'soft' Gamay Beaujolais. Because California's minimum alcohol standards were 10.5 per cent for reds and 10 per cent for whites, it was legally necessary for Friedrich to secure special permission to market these wines. Fortunately, California's legislation was modified to federal standards, which permit wines with alcohol content as low as 7 per cent.

Of the four 'softies', the Johannisberg Riesling is by far the most successful. With sufficient acid to balance the sugar left unfermented at the arrest of fermentation (by chilling and centrifuging), it is an intensely fruity wine with a powerful aroma. An amazingly full-flavoured wine, it drinks perhaps too easily, but that is not a complaint. The Chenin Blanc exhibits pronounced varietal characteristics, too; however, it lacks the Johannisberg Riesling complexity. The Gamay Beaujolais is the lightest of the four, reminiscent of grape juice more than of wine, but slightly chilled it is a great boon for neophytes. All four wines are instructive and provide interest. Normal table wines at San Martin have shown great improvement since Friedrich's assumption of the wine-maker's chair. The reds, especially the Cabernets, are better, and indeed are beginning to show complexities. It appears probable that this improvement will continue and the future promises even better wines at San Martin. So as to avoid the label of a so-called 'soft' winery, Friedrich will continue to emphasize development of varietal table wines.

THE TURGEON AND LOHR WINERY

The Turgeon and Lohr Winery in San Jose was established in 1974 by Jerry Lohr, Bernie Turgeon and Peter Stern. Sporting well-drained and cool, gravelly acreage, the winery has made some interesting wines, now up to 25,000 cases per year. Although the winery is known as Turgeon and Lohr the label used for the wines is 'J. Lohr Wines'. Notable is a Johannisberg Riesling, which not unlike the style of others, is fermented slowly for at least forty-five days before it is stopped by chilling and centrifugation. This cold-stopped fermentation serves to preserve fruitiness and lightness and to keep alcohol low, producing a wine typical of the Mosel region of Germany, with unusually intense perfumy aroma, complexity and strong varietal character. Usually an outstanding wine, Gamay is produced in a fresh, fruity but full flavoured style, not *nouveau*, but not unlike a Beaujolais in a prime year. This wine is fascinating because it is created by the difficult French technique of *macération carbonique*, requiring hand-picking of grapes and hand-placement into a fermenter where, under inert gas atmosphere, whole berries begin a slow, intracellular fermentation within their own skins. Neither fined nor filtered, at $4.00 (1980) the wine is an amazingly good quaffing-style wine.

Also interesting was a late-harvest style Chardonnay of 1978, which was picked selectively for berries without any raisining effect. Growing conditions, as described by wine-maker Peter Stern, resulted in a concentration and shrinkage of the individual berries, with highly concentrated juice at a sugar level of $31.1°$ Brix. The grapes were pressed and the juice centrifuged prior to fermentation, which was held at $50°$F, and lasted nearly eight months before being stopped at $6.4°$ Brix. The wine has a deep golden colour with a sage and honey aroma, a complex character and a full buttery flavour, a fine change of pace as an apéritif or a dessert wine.

Santa Clara Valley vineyards and orchards, largely displaced by residential and commercial construction, have reached a stable plateau and the rate of decline is diminishing. The southward movement has helped beleaguered Santa Clara to survive with quality and pride. Mirassou, Paul Masson and Almadén hold on to important wineries in the Santa Clara Valley, yet for a decade or two their grapes have come from Monterey and San Benito counties. Tiny valley wineries also rely on Monterey County grapes, and in some cases on those of San Luis Obispo County. While the future lies to the south, Santa Clara County's present remains inexorably tied to the new vines of neighbouring counties.

SANTA CRUZ

It is difficult to demarcate precisely the geographic and viticultural limits of the Santa Cruz Mountains. In a petition filed with the Federal Bureau of Alcohol, Tobacco and Firearms, the eighteen-member Santa Cruz Mountain Vineyard Association proposed to designate an area twenty-five miles long and nearly as wide to constitute the Santa Cruz Mountain *appellation*. However, that proposal may be drawn more for geo-political considerations than for viticultural realities.

The *appellation*, if granted as proposed, would designate the upper elevations as Santa Cruz Mountain. The lowest elevation to be included would be 400 feet above sea level (in some stretches it would be higher), but the contours appear to be drawn so as to exclude the valley floor and all heavily concentrated urban areas. Although the delimitation as proposed seems somewhat arbitrary, nevertheless it is a fact that the Santa Cruz Mountains do exist and there were, as of 1980, nearly twenty wineries operating there. Together they jointly own a mere 250 acres of grapes and produce no more than 100,000 cases of wine annually.

BRUCE WINERY

Southeast of Ridge Vineyards is the winery of Dr David Bruce, a dermatologist from San Jose. In 1961 he planted twenty-five acres to Chardonnay, White Riesling, Cabernet Sauvignon and Pinot Noir. In 1964, he bonded a winery and began limited production. A 6,000-square foot concrete-block ageing cellar was completed in 1968, and in 1975 a second building was added, to house stainless-steel fermenters. Bruce wines are unique, even controversial, no less so than David Bruce himself, who has a flair for the unique and unusual. His wines are noted for body bigness and full flavour that lingers on the palate. But because fining and filtration are rarely employed, the Bruce wines must generally be decanted to rid them of the sediment which builds within even a relatively short bottle time. Noteworthy are Chardonnays and Zinfandels. His Chardonnays in 1968 and 1969 were so favoured that wine-lovers still recall them with praise. They were not long-lasting wines, almost gold in colour, but they had an older luscious taste that I found most appealing. Others thought that they were oxidized, but I must vehemently disagree. In recent years there has been less unrestrained enthusiasm for Dr Bruce's Chardonnays. Later vintages have not quite matched earlier ones and other wineries have multiplied the number of fine Californian Chardonnays. The grape repertoire of newer regions, such as San Luis Obispo County, has also provided an abundance of fine raw material.

FELTON–EMPIRE VINEYARDS

Felton-Empire Vineyards, west of Felton, occupies the historically famous Hallcrest winery site. Hallcrest was a fine vineyard, especially for red wine that was reminiscent of the strong earthy taste of Mouton. The late Chaffee Hall, a San Francisco attorney, was the founder of this important vineyard that had been planted in 1941 with the assistance of University of California at Davis viticulturists. The winery closed in 1964, but not before a dozen vintages of perhaps some of California's best Cabernets had been made. After Hall died in 1969, the winery lay idle while grapes were sold and on occasion found their way into Concannon Cabernets. In 1976, the winery was reactivated by three partners: James Beauregard, John Polard, Leo McCloskey, David Bruce, Calera and Richard Smothers. (A 1978 Gewürztraminer of Smothers made by McCloskey won the Sweepstakes in the 1979 Los Angeles County Fair wine judgings.) Concentrating principally on White Rieslings and Santa Cruz Cabernets, Felton-Empire utilizes 32,500 US gallons of storage capacity and thirty acres of leased vineyards. Of particular interest are White Rieslings, especially the 1976 vintage. *Auslese* in style, it brought together mouth-filling layers of Riesling and botrytis flavour, all in good balance.

RIDGE VINEYARDS

The largest Santa Cruz winery is Ridge Vineyards, nearing production of 30,000 cases per year compared to the smallest, Woodside, with a mere 500 cases. The winery was launched in 1962 by four partners from Stanford Research Institute in Palo Alto, led by David Bennion, who forsook his position there to work full time in the winery. Big, inky, Zinfandels were made that captured the imagination of wine consumers everywhere, as well as changing the style of Zinfandel from a fresh, strawberry-like taste to big, gutsy, late-harvested types that need endless bottle ageing. Originally believing them to be amateurish in approach, the industry soon realized the attractiveness of Ridge Zinfandels, frequently obtained from vineyards in Sonoma, Napa and Lodi, and now in Paso Robles and San Luis Obispo. Soon the industry followed with the sincerest form of flattery: emulation. Even in a white wine era, Ridge Zinfandels still sell easily. The style has softened and lightened a trifle with the addition of wine-maker Paul Draper to the team. It is Draper who is responsible for increasing production to 30,000 cases per year and for moving operations from the small cellar in which they began to the much larger cellars of the 100-year-old Monte Bello Winery dug into the hillside about a mile further up Black Mountain. Storage capacity is now 150,000 US gallons. Ridge's specialities remain Cabernet Sauvignon and Zinfandel, still big, gutsy wines, full of fruit, flavour and tannins. It was Bennion and Draper at Ridge who more than any other wine-makers demonstrated that the Zinfandel grape, treated with care and respect, can produce wines with character and finesse. To Ridge should go much of the credit for elevating Zinfandel to its current premium quality status. Cabernets are as big and as gutsy as the Zinfandels. Wines made from both grapes require ageing to round out to their full potential, although surprisingly, for wines so big, most vintages can be enjoyed when relatively young and full of fruit. The 1968 Cabernet is probably as fine a wine as Ridge has produced. A big year, it is indeed a big wine, rich and full with a nicely developing suppleness today that makes the wine eminently drinkable even though it will endure for many years.

The key to the Ridge style is what Draper refers to as his tradition, where it is his goal to make the finest wines possible with a minimum of man's interference with their natural development. Each wine is made without fining or filtration for clarification. Stabilization is achieved simply by racking. If necessary, fining or filtration will be employed only if stability and clarity cannot be achieved simply by racking alone. The tradition extends to the use of only the natural yeasts in fermentation. Ridge owns 50 acres of Cabernet Sauvignon in vineyards that surround the winery. When they mature, they will supply the grapes to produce 40 to 50 per cent of Ridge's output. The remainder will be Zinfandel made from grapes purchased elsewhere. Precise labelling has been a hallmark at Ridge. Labelling policy, which has been much copied, identifies exact percentage of each variety and the vineyard, alcohol content and bottling date. Some growers seek to sell to Ridge because of the special label credit their vineyards receive.

Ridge wines' earthy bigness is a mystery to the industry, perhaps due to soil or wine-making practice. An explanation is offered by Draper, who suggests that there are three practices which account for it. The first is submerged cap fermentation (with the cap held below the surface of the fermenting must by a stainless-steel latticework designed by Draper) at 75° to 85°F. The second is prolonged skin contact – an average of twelve days for Zinfandel and fourteen to twenty-five days for Cabernet Sauvignon, depending on the vintage and the grapes. The third is clarification solely by racking, which may also be a factor in generating complexities in the Zinfandels. Draper's explanation must be accurate since Ridge wines come from so many different vineyards with so much soil diversity. The wines have a style that commands attention and frequently respect. It is the lush, forward taste of soil and fruit that make the Ridge style unmistakable no matter which grape variety has been used.

ROUDON-SMITH WINERY

Robert Roudon and John Smith have operated a 35,000-US gallon winery at Santa Cruz since 1972. At first, the wines were made with purchased grapes, but in 1976 their twelve-acre vineyard produced Johannisberg Riesling. Especially interesting was the 1978 vintage, which was slightly sweet in a Germanic style, but well balanced and crisp with acidity – a most attractive wine. Also notable was a late-harvest Zinfandel which received a gold medal at the 1979 Los Angeles County Fair. Fruity and sweet in a ruby port-style, it had, nevertheless, a full measure of Zinfandel character in aroma and taste.

WOODSIDE VINEYARDS

Woodside Vineyards is tiny. It is no larger than the size of a large conventional garage, because it happens to be sited below the family garage of Robert and Polly Mullen but has the 'huge' storage capacity of 3,000 US gallons. Mullens' wines are exceptional. All three, Pinot Noir, Chardonnay and Cabernet Sauvignon, are produced entirely from vineyards which they own or control. Woodside sells wine under an old label and vineyard name, La Questa, which was very famous for the quality of its Cabernet when owned by Emmett H. Rixford in the nineteenth century. The three remaining acres of the old Rixford vineyards are the source of the Cabernets produced by the Mullens. Earlier, a Chenin Blanc was produced that was probably the biggest and most complex of all the state's versions of this varietal. Intensity of fruit and taste was not uncommon, and appears to be the *méthode* for the other varietals. Total production is 500 to 600 cases per year. The quality here is big, though the production is small, and Woodside is one more in a long string of so-called 'boutique' wineries whose importance belies their production.

Santa Cruz Mountain wineries are making their unique wine-making imprint. From hobby-like status into commercial production, these wineries are added proof of the vitality, professionalism and vigour of California wine-makers.

MONTEREY COUNTY

Monterey County is justly world famous for championship golf courses, fine restaurants, rugged coastline, gnarled cypresses, picturesque, sandy beaches and the little shops of Carmel, a quaint artist and tourist community. Now there is yet another reason for Monterey's world fame; the vineyards and wineries which have mushroomed during the 1970s. Two decades ago there were only thirty-five acres of wine grapes, as contrasted to 35,000 acres and six wineries today. Sprawling Santa Clara Valley urbanization in their home vineyard regions have forced Almadén, Paul Masson and Mirassou to seek and develop alternative regions. Under the leadership of Mirassou, test plantings were made in several locations in the Salinas Valley in the early 1960s. These grapes flourished and additional plantings were made. Wente Brothers, with 300 acres of vines near the Arroyo Seco, transports uncrushed grapes to its winery at Tesla Road in Livermore approximately 125 miles from the vineyards. Almadén, with 2,100 acres in two vineyards near King City and San Lucas are transporting both grapes and field-crushed fruit to either their Cienega or the Paicines wineries in San Benito County. Thus, several major wineries with facilities elsewhere are producing and marketing wines bearing a Monterey *appellation*.

CHALONE VINEYARDS

Senior winery in Monterey County is Chalone Vineyards. Now expanded to 125 acres, vineyards were planted on a unique limestone bench, where the soil is very similar to that of Burgundy, at the western edge of the geologic formation known as the Pinnacles, as early as 1919. The winery now belongs to a partnership, which includes Dick Graff as Chairman.

A new winery building was completed in 1974, and stocked with oak cooperage from the forests of France, in keeping with Dick's announced goal of producing Burgundian-style wines. To taste the Chardonnay and the Pinot Noir is to recognize the attainment of the goal; they have a strength and complexity of character reminiscent of the Burgundies of France. Other wines have done well too, such as the Pinot Blanc, the Chenin Blanc and French Colombard, the latter produced from Napa Valley grapes and released under Chalone's secondary label, which is reserved for wines made from grapes not grown in Chalone. The winery has made fine progress although the production remains small. Classified as one of California's finest vineyard gems, the winery has produced Chardonnays that are amongst the most sought after and Pinot Noirs that are full, round, rich wines, like the 1969 Pinot Noir which may have been one of California's finest. Not content with producing complex wines from their own vineyards, the owners have applied their wine-making technique to grapes from other areas, such as Edna Valley in San Luis Obispo County. They have produced a number of excellent wines under a variety of wine shop and restaurant labels, more particularly under their secondary label of Chapparal. Very fine wines have been made, including a 1977 Chapparal Pinot Noir which is remarkable for elegance and class and may well be a benchmark for the area. Frequently, the Pinot Blanc drinks as big and as well as the Chardonnay at one-half to one-third the price, and is especially sought after as the best available today for that varietal.

JEKEL VINEYARD

Newest of the Monterey County vineyards is Jekel Vineyard, located in Greenfield. The Jekels are seriously interested in wine-making and have 140 acres, planted in 1972 at the Arroyo Seco watershed. They are aided by William's son Rich as assistant wine-maker. Ten thousand cases were produced from the first crush, representing Johannisberg Riesling, Chardonnay, Pinot Blanc, Gamay Beaujolais and Cabernet Sauvignon. The 1978 Gamay Beaujolais was made from the very first grapes crushed at the facility. Made in the style of a French Burgundy, the wine was allowed to go through malolactic fermentation, which added complexity to its clean, fruity flavours. The 1978 Chardonnay is the best wine made yet, full of varietal character with an attractive oak resulting from seven months of sixty-gallon Limousin barrel-ageing. The Johannisberg Riesling and the Chardonnay may be the winery's two stars. The Johannisberg Riesling is impeccably clean, but has a delicacy that is hard to produce in the county, and a complexity of flavours that make it clearly attractive. Recently added has been a late-harvest style that is a joy to drink, full-flavoured and fragrant beyond belief – a delight for apéritif or casual sipping. A 1977 Cabernet is dissipating some of its herbaceousness and when completed, its fruit and suppleness will be most attractive.

PAUL MASSON

Paul Masson has 5,000 acres of Monterey County vineyards, divided into several areas: Pinnacles Vineyards I and II, Greenfield and San Lucas. The vineyards are located in Regions I and II. Although soil structures vary throughout, most are in decomposed granite, the balance is gravelly, sandy loam and coarse sandy loam. Vineyard slope increases from 4 per cent on the valley floor to 10 per cent near the foothills of the Gavilan Mountains. The combination of terrain slope and soil composition results in good drainage. By the end of the 1970s, all Masson white wines, except for Chenin Blanc and the generic Chablis, were produced entirely from Monterey County grapes. The red wines were generally blends of Monterey County and Sonoma wines. Monterey County rainfall is usually less than ten inches per year; consequently, the winery has installed a permanent sprinkler system for irrigation to supplement natural rainfall. The amount and timing of such irrigation is determined by means of tensionometers in the soil. All vines are trained on two and three wire trellises, not to accommodate machine harvesting, but to facilitate cultivation and to increase leaf exposure to solar radiation. All of Masson's grapes are harvested by hand and transported to the winery in two-ton gondolas. With the maturation of the Pinnacles Vineyards, Paul Masson initiated a programme of vintage-dating and of designating the wines produced from these vineyards, as Pinnacles Estate. Prior to 1977, none of Masson's wines were vintage-dated. However, as the vines in the Pinnacles Vineyards matured, the best wines from these vines were selected for bottling as vintage-dated estate wines. The first of these were released in April 1977, and include a 1975 Johannisberg Riesling, 1974 Gewürztraminer, 1975 Chardonnay and a 1974 Johannisberg Riesling sparkling wine. A subsequent release of Pinnacles Estate wines, in March 1980, included the 1978 Gewürztraminer, Sauvignon Blanc and Johannisberg Riesling, and the 1976 vintage of sparkling Johannisberg Riesling. These initial vintage-dated attempts are all much higher quality than the wines of the previous two decades. The Gewürztraminer, sporting an Alsatian character, may be one of the best produced in recent years. The Sauvignon Blanc was perhaps too concentrated in varietal character, with a green-grassy taste style that I find not appropriate for table fare. The Chardonnay, also intense in varietal character, was much better and bodes well for the future. The sparkling Riesling, made from 100 per cent Johannisberg Riesling, was much the best of the wines.

The estate-bottled programme is relatively small, and will remain small. It is expected that only 25,000 cases (out of an annual production of 6,000,000 cases) of the best wine produced each year from their Pinnacles grapes will be selected for the estate label. Paul Masson produces approximately fifty wines; a wide selection of table wines in their Soledad facility, and apéritif and dessert wines in their Sherry Cellars at Madera in the San Joaquin Valley. The latter, completed in 1974, was built especially to house the production of ports and sherries, of which Masson is one of the leading producers in the state. Here, 10,000 barrels hold ageing wine, which will not be released until it has a minimum of three years of age or five years for those labelled 'Rarity Treasure', which represent perhaps the best wines Paul Masson has produced in recent years.

MIRASSOU

Unlike Paul Masson, Mirassou chose not to move their winery operations to Monterey County, but elected to develop mechanical harvesting and field crushing to reduce the time lag between harvesting and crushing. Grape quality suffered from the four-hour journey to Mirassou's home winery. By 1969, Mirassou was in full production with machine harvesting and field crushing techniques that produced a Chenin Blanc from the first grapes to be so harvested and crushed which not only had lots of Chenin Blanc character, and drank as if it were pure fruit. I doubt that I have ever tasted Chenin Blanc with as much fruit character as Mirassou's. It was like biting into the grape. Machine harvesting and field crushing permitted Mirassou to harvest and crush grapes and place them under a protective blanket of inert gas in a 6,000-gallon tank truck within less than two minutes. Thus, the must arrives at the winery in a 'just-crushed' condition, with less oxidation than occurs with the conventional harvesting into gondolas. An apparent disadvantage with the technique is the inability to control desired skin contact time. During the ninety-mile journey, white wines may get more skin contact than desired.

Greatest in the Mirassou line are the wines labelled 'Harvest Selection', which are individual barrel selections for such varieties as Pinot Noir, Cabernet Sauvignon, Zinfandel and Petite Sirah. Chardonnay is specially made for the label. The Chardonnay and Cabernet have been especially successful. The Cabernets, notably the vintages of 1974 to 1979, are getting away from a hard taste that turned many consumers away from Mirassou Cabernets. The new wines have been specially made from Monterey County grapes, but some Cabernets have been produced from San Jose vineyards. The wines have developed complexities that are new to Mirassou. The style is minty, not unlike Heitz Cellars' Martha's Vineyard, a compliment that is well-deserved.

MONTEREY PENINSULA WINERY

Especially unique is Monterey Peninsula Winery, practically sitting in Carmel. It was founded in 1974 by two former amateur wine-makers, Roy Thomas and Deryck Nuckton. The innovative duo leased a former restaurant a mile east of Monterey Airport, where they used its four-foot thick walls, ideal for a winery. Zinfandels in the so-called 'Ridge tradition' are a speciality of Monterey Peninsula Winery. Here are made some of the biggest, fullest-bodied wines that have been made anywhere. Because the wine-makers neither filter nor fine, allowing gravity to do the job of clarifying the wines, sediment is as natural as the wines. In each vintage there are a number of versions of Zinfandel, not only from Monterey County but from elsewhere.

THE MONTEREY VINEYARD

Second in size to the Paul Masson winery at Soledad is The Monterey Vineyard at Gonzales, now owned by the Coca Cola Company of Atlanta, Georgia and with Dr Richard Peterson, formerly of Beaulieu Vineyards, as chief wine-maker. The winery may not own any vineyard acreage, but its vats are filled from 900 acres of contracted grapes. Peterson has been high on Monterey County wines, especially his 1974 and 1975 Pinot Noirs that are strong in varietal character with a hint of 'bitter-sweet' character in the finish. A pet wine concept is the 'December Harvest' Zinfandels of 1974 and 1975. Intensely varietal in character, but not too alcoholic, these wines develop well because Monterey County is the coolest wine-growing region in the United States, where grapes may reach maturity two months later than elsewhere in California. Hence, grapes ripen slowly, resulting in bonus vine time, so much so that the 1974 'December Harvest' Zinfandel was finally harvested on December 6. The wines are unlike any found in any other wine-growing area.

In addition to a long, cool growing season, botrytis is abundant, thus making it possible to produce Johannisberg Rieslings with a touch of the flavour of the mould. A fine-tasting botrytized Sauvignon Blanc, an apparent attempt at a French Sauternes style, was successfully made. Also, a November 'Thanksgiving Harvest' Riesling was produced from a section of Johannisberg Riesling that was slow in ripening and finally reached balanced maturity only in late November. The 1978 vintage wine was produced from slightly botrytized grapes, which tasted with good flavour, and satisfactory balance, an innovation that will no doubt continue.

Another innovation due to the cool climate in northern Monterey County resulted in the production of the first California wine of 1979. A small amount of Napa Gamay (the true Gamay grape which accounts for the fresh fruity wines of Beaujolais, France, not the strain of Pinot Noir called Gamay Beaujolais) was left on the vine to continue ripening until after the remainder of the 1978 harvest was completed. The grapes, a total of forty-five tonnes, were finally harvested on January 2, 1979, making them early harvest – very early harvest. The aim was to produce a Beaujolais *nouveau* style, using carbonic maceration. It was bottled, aged for two months in the bottle, labelled and released in the summer of 1979 at its flavour peak. After a year the wine was still fresh, fruity and flavourful, a triumph of Monterey climate and Dick Peterson's wine-making skills. This innovative process was repeated with Cabernet Sauvignon during the season of 1979, with the grapes harvested on January 4 and 5, 1980.

Production of wines under The Monterey Vineyard label reached only 60,000 cases in 1978 but, according to Peterson, growth is expected as vineyards mature and demand for Monterey County wines increases. In the meantime, The Monterey Vineyard uses its capacity, among the most modern and efficient in California, to produce wine for Coca Cola's Taylor California Cellars.

VENTANA VINEYARDS

Perhaps no other Monterey County winery has come so far so fast, chiefly due to the imaginative viticultural techniques of proprietor, Doug Meador. Meador modestly disclaims any dramatic wine-making techniques and sums up his skill in one word, 'farming'. However, his attention to detail and his understanding of grape vines are dramatic and 'magically' effective. Vines early in the season are encouraged to develop a leaf canopy so as to increase leaf surface area in relation to fruit. Moisture levels are decreased to arrest further vine growth. As part of soil-moisture management, the vineyard is clean cultivated until mid-August, when weeds are allowed to develop as ground cover and to compete with the vines for soil moisture, with the goal of keeping vines in a green leaf condition without further vine growth, and the elimination of excess water that would otherwise result in the take up of nitrogen from the soil and further vine growth. Permanent-set sprinklers permit compensation if soil moisture levels should fall too low. Different blocks of the vineyard are farmed differently to obtain qualities desired in grapes and even harvesting techniques are varied to fit individual grapes.

Meador describes Ventana as an experimental vineyard and winery. He notes that experiments with moisture levels in the vineyard have shown that the Monterey County bell pepper and/or vegetative aroma and taste character can be controlled by such management. In 1979 Ventana fermented eighteen different varieties of grapes, utilizing fourteen different yeast strains and three separate *lactobacilli* for inducing secondary malolactic fermentation. Furthermore, the wine was aged in barrels made by six different coopers. To accommodate grape customers, Meador is reducing the annual output of Ventana from 15,000 cases in 1979 to 5,000 cases in 1980. The 1978 Chardonnay, a Silver Medal winner at the Los Angeles County Fair, is as fine a Chardonnay as I have tasted from the area. It is not unbearably fruited, nor does it have the unpleasant herbaceous quality in nose and taste that all too frequently turns wine-drinkers away from Monterey County varietals. This wine is clean, lush, full-flavoured and, by all standards, exciting.

Meador makes good reds, too, in a light supple style, especially a 1978 Petite Sirah that is most attractive. It is the Chardonnay, however, that has attracted the attention. A late-harvested Chardonnay, infected with botrytis mould, is another of Meador's wine innovations. There have been few others in the late-harvest style, including the noted 'Alicia' made by Joe Heitz of the Napa Valley in honour of his wife. Ventana's wine is a unique, compelling combination of flavours – the honey-like character of the botrytis and the concentrated Chardonnay flavours and aroma, all overwhelm with intensity.

Monterey County is making its tasting points each vintage as the area's wine mysteries unravel. With such explorers as Chalone, Peterson, Monterey Peninsula, Jekel and Ventana, Monterey need not fear that it will be a northern California step-child. Cleaner and more restrained wines eventually will see Monterey County as one of California's most important and respected wine areas.

SAN BENITO COUNTY

CALERA WINERY

On the site of an abandoned limestone quarry and kiln in the hills eighteen miles north of the Pinnacles National Monument in San Benito County, Josh Jensen built his Calera Winery. Making use of the contours of the quarry, the winery utilizes gravity for movement of grapes, must and wine. While working in the 1970 and 1971 French grape harvests, Jensen was grape-smitten with the strange notion that he could make fine Pinot Noirs in California, patterned after those of Burgundy. His search for the appropriately chalky soil led him to his present winery and vineyard site twelve miles south of Hollister.

In 1974 and 1975 he planted twenty-four acres of Pinot Noir and built a 24,000-US gallon winery, completed in 1976. While waiting for mature Pinot Noir wines, he turned, like so many others, to Zinfandels. A first release of the 1975 vintage was most impressive, a robust, dark wine with good fruit, in the Ridge style. If that were not enough, he followed with a unique botrytized Zinfandel. This is a wine a European would not believe, for it is both big and fruity and displays Port-like virtues that are hard for the non-Californian to understand. None the less an excellent bottle, this kind of Zinfandel blends characteristic fruit flavours with the honeyed tones of botrytis, the latter tending to overpower the Zinfandel.

SAN LUIS OBISPO COUNTY

San Luis Obispo County, long dormant as a vineyard region, was literally rediscovered with California's 'Wine Boom' in the 1970s. Although grapes had been grown and wine produced in the county at Templeton during the nineteenth century, it was a viticultural unknown. Prior to the 'Wine Boom', the best-known vineyards of San Luis Obispo had been those of Polish pianist, Ignace Paderewski. At Prohibition's end, the number of wineries increased in the county but, regretfully, soon afterwards a decline set in, similar to elsewhere in the state. While the number of wineries has increased (there are probably still no more than six, but numbers keep changing as new wineries continue to enter the industry), vineyard acreage has increased nearly sixfold, from under 700 to over 4,000 acres during the 1970s. Many of these grapes find their way into north-coast wineries whose grape needs have been intensified by demand and urban developments. At the moment, the combined capacities of San Luis Obispo county wineries are insufficient to utilize all of the new vineyards' production, although the few old wineries of the county were joined by three new ones built in the 1970s.

ESTRELLA RIVER WINERY

A new winery, six miles east of Paso Robles, is Estrella River Winery. Housed in a spectacular winery structure, it was completed in 1977 just in time for the first harvest of grapes planted five years earlier, by Clifford Giacobine, his half-brother Gary Eberle and 'Rocky' Bleier. The varieties in the vineyard are Cabernet Sauvignon, Barbera, Zinfandel, the French Syrah, Muscat Blanc, Chardonnay, Chenin Blanc and Sauvignon Blanc. According to the University of California at Davis system of heat summation, the Estrella vineyards are located in a warm Region II or a cool Region III, similar to that of Hoffman Mountain Ranch. Nevertheless, Chardonnay, generally preferring a Region I, is performing beautifully, and it caught the eye of the judges in the 1979 Los Angeles County Fair. Perhaps the area is better suited to Cabernet Sauvignon, the 1977 vintage of which from Estrella took a gold medal in the 1979 Los Angeles Fair competition. This wine is marvellous for drinking now, although it should age well. It is fragrant and intense with good fruit and with a supple quality not generally found in wines from this area. The wines are produced by a talented young man, Gary Eberle, who with only a modicum of training makes wine as though technically trained. A fine Johannisberg Riesling has also been produced, but it is Cabernet and Chardonnay that will ultimately be the stars. The early Estrella River wines should attract other growers and wine-makers to the area.

HOFFMAN MOUNTAIN RANCH WINERY

The first of the new wineries was Hoffman Mountain Ranch, established in 1972 near the old Paderewski vineyards, Paso Robles. Another transplanted southern Californian, Dr Stanley Hoffman, a noted cardiologist, came to Paso Robles to blend country doctoring with gentlemanly wine-making. His skills as a cardiologist were sorely needed in Paso Robles, however, so responsibility for wine-making was assumed by his two sons, Michael (who serves as oenologist) and David, who is vineyardist. Both rely on consultations with André Tchelistcheff, the much-travelled wine consultant, whose hopes for this area are high. The vineyards are planted to Chardonnay, Pinot Noir, Cabernet Sauvignon, and Sylvaner. A Zin-fandel, a Cabernet Sauvignon Rosé, and a Chenin Blanc in two styles (dry and sweet) are produced from grapes purchased from other areas.

The soils, although shallow, are gravelly and well-drained and contain sub-stantial amounts of lime. Vineyards are located in a high Region II or a low Region III. The 1975 Pinot Noir has received considerable acclaim for its dark colour, intense aroma and flavour and full body. The wine is a bit heavy and coarse and may lose its rough edges with a bit more maturity in the bottle. Hopefully, it is a har-binger of better things to come and that the viticultural area around Paso Robles may yet prove to be a good one for Pinot Noir. The Chardonnay has not caught my fancy, nor have the other wines, but I suspect it may be too early for a con-clusive evaluation. Other palates that I trust suggest higher quality than I have found. No doubt the Hoffmans will prove them more correct than I.

Other vineyards in the area are Ascension Peak Winery, Lawrence Winery, York Mountain Winery, Pesenti and Las Tablas (formerly known as Rotta). San Luis Obispo County wine-making and vine-growing are like the young, spirited, talented child that may turn out to be an acclaimed prodigy or the mediocre, un-fulfilled brat. Most tastes promise the former. As the vineyards mature in the hands of dedicated, talented wine-makers, surely this will be so.

SANTA BARBARA

Grape-growing and wine-making are not new to Santa Barbara County, although by all standards it is considered part of the new wine wave in California. Fran-ciscan missionaries planted vineyards shortly after they built Missions at Lompoc, Santa Barbara and Santa Ynez. New are the 6,000 acres of vineyards and seven commercial wineries in the northern half of the county from Buellton to Santa Maria. The vineyards and the wineries are spread over several valleys which would logically appear to break the region into identifiable and meaningful viticultural areas. In common is the relatively cool climate which prevails through the growing season, constituting it a Region 1. Early ripening grapes do well. The success of the first Pinot Noir wines produced from Santa Ynez Valley grapes by Firestone Vineyards, Zaca Mesa Winery and by Sanford and Benedict Winery from Lompoc grapes suggest that the Pinot Noir may at last have found a home.

FIRESTONE VINEYARDS

At Santa Ynez Valley, a winery of showplace proportions, Firestone Vineyards, sits on the edge of a mesa looking out over the Valley to the south. The winery is the brainchild of Leonard K. Firestone and his son Brooks, both of Firestone Tyre and Rubber fame. A partnership was formed with a Japanese firm, Suntory, a producer of whisky as well as Japanese wines. Vineyards were planted in 1973, and the first wines, a rosé of Pinot Noir and a rosé of Cabernet Sauvignon, were produced in 1975 before the winery structure was completed. As the vineyards have matured, White Riesling, Chardonnay, Pinot Noir, Cabernet Sauvignon, Gewürztraminer and Merlot have been added to the list of wines produced. In some instances, the label identifies the vineyard in which the grapes were grown.

Thus far, the red wines show more promise than the whites, although Rieslings made from grapes lightly touched with botrytis have been attractive, aromatic and decidedly fruity. Fruit is one of the strengths of the area and on occasion may be more than necessary for nicely balanced table wine. Pinot Noirs are the most exciting. Even the 1975 vintage, made from the first harvest of the winery's vineyards, is impressive with its richness of aroma and flavour. Cabernet Sauvignon is another wine with promise. Although complexities have not yet developed, the variety has such intensity of character that one wonders whether it can be tamed. A vegetative quality in nose and taste suggest intensity that some may find objectionable. Time and taste will determine whether this will dissipate. If so, the wines have the potential of super quality.

What stands out in Santa Barbara County is the number of young, small wineries, each searching for style and prestige. If the Californian 'Wine Boom' continues as projected, these young vineyards will reach maturity, and so will the young winemakers but, as with all so-called new wine regions, only time is the real judge.

SOUTHERN CALIFORNIA

Wine-making was introduced into southern California by the Franciscan padres with the establishment of Mission San Diego, in 1769. Jean Louis Vignes, from Bordeaux, is credited with being the first to make wine and brandy a commercial business. He planted a vineyard of approximately one hundred acres and established a winery on the site of Los Angeles' huge rail passenger terminal. By the 1840s, he had built up a considerable trade, shipping both wine and brandy as far north as Monterey by coastal steamers. It also seems apparent that he was the first to import *vinifera* cuttings and to introduce the cultivation of *vinifera* varieties, other than the Mission grape. Although the new varieties were probably for experimentation more than for production, there is some evidence that several large shipments of cuttings sufficient for commercial production were imported during the 1830s. Vignes' operations prospered and represent a hallmark of southern California wine production. In 1855, he sold his business to two nephews, Pierre and Jean-Louis Sansevain, also from Bordeaux, who later established one of the first and best wine merchant operations in California.

Until mid-century, southern California continued as the centre of California wine production. The village settlement of Los Angeles was literally a vineyard. Grapes were grown and wine was produced virtually everywhere. To the southeast, in Anaheim, where Disneyland now reigns supreme, vineyards and a colony of German immigrant wine-makers flourished. By 1850, a series of developments, including the Gold Rush and Haraszthy's wine forays, resulted in the shift of the southern California wine capital to northern California. Nevertheless, Los Angeles continued to lead the state in production of viticultural products throughout the 1850s. Not until the early and mid-1860s did northern California come into full production and challenge the viticultural supremacy of Los Angeles. The most widely planted grape during this period was still the Mission, because of its high yields, ready availability and low cost. The Mission, however, does not produce wine of superior quality. Early growers realized its deficiencies and began importation of European varieties. The great *vinifera* planting impetus must be credited to Agoston Haraszthy. Another factor in the shift of viticultural leadership to northern California was the destruction of the Anaheim vineyards by the mysterious Pierce's Disease (sometimes called Anaheim Disease). It first struck in a corner of the vineyards and completely destroyed Anaheim vineyards within three years, eliminating it as a wine-producing centre. Other disease-like enemies of the grape, such as urbanization, smog and high real-estate taxes, all combined to force the marked decline of grape-growing and wine-making in southern California. As a consequence, no vineyards remain in Los Angeles County and nearby vineyards of Cucamonga have declined sharply from a peak of over 20,000 acres after Repeal to less than 10,000 today. There is one winery, San Antonio, still operating in downtown Los Angeles. With 80,000 US gallons of storage capacity, the Riboli family produce forty different wines from Cucamonga, Sonoma and Lodi grapes, selling them in their tasting room at the winery or in one of their chain of retail sales-tasting rooms scattered throughout southern California. Designated by the city of Los Angeles as Cultural Historical Monument Number 42, San Antonio Winery is protected from removal to make room for yet another of the warehouses which surround it. Other survivors elsewhere in southern California include The Cucamonga Vineyard (with bonded winery licence Number 1 in California), Brookside Vineyard Company (a subsidiary of Beatrice Foods of Chicago), Galleano Vineyards in Mira Loma and Filippi Vintage Company in Mira Loma, which also operates Thomas Cellar on Foothill Boulevard in Rancho Cucamonga. A new vineyard was established at Alta Loma in 1975 by Philo Biane: Rancho de Philo, which has produced a sweet-style sherry that may be one of the best in the state. Another, Opici Winery, located in Alta Loma, has no production facilities in southern California, preferring to make wine in Sonoma and the Central Valley.

All is not lost for southern California, however. Planting of vines and construction of wineries at Rancho California in southern Riverside County and in the San Pasqual Valley in northern San Diego County have provided compensation for shrinking grape acreage. The Rancho California development began in 1967 as part of a real-estate development being promoted by Kaiser-Aetna Company, a land development combine. Currently, vineyards are growing on 2,000 acres of former pastureland. Two wineries were constructed in nearby Temecula in the 1970s, but much of the Rancho California grape harvest is transported to Cucamonga and Guasti for crushing and fermentation by Cucamonga Vineyard Company and Brookside. Although 9,000 acres in San Pasqual Valley are protected by legislation designed to preserve the Valley for agricultural uses, there are in the Valley only one hundred acres of grapes, planted in 1974, and one winery, San Pasqual Vineyards, started in 1973, with a storage capacity of 76,000 US gallons. It is too early to make any predictions!

BROOKSIDE ENTERPRISES, INC

Until Brookside Winery was sold to Beatrice Foods in 1973, it had been a family enterprise operated continuously by the Bianes since early in the nineteenth century. Eighty wines and wine-based products are produced today by Brookside under four labels: Assumption Abbey, Brookside Estate, Brookside Cellar and Vaché. Top label at Brookside is Assumption Abbey which comprises principally varietals from Rancho California: Chardonnay, Johannisberg Riesling, French Colombard, St Emilion (Ugni Blanc), Vertdoux Blanc, Grenache Rosé, Gamay Beaujolais, Ruby Cabernet, Zinfandel, Petite Sirah, Pinot Noir and Cabernet Sauvignon. Good value more than greatness or complexity are the apparent features. I have always preferred the dessert wines which are frequent medal winners at the Los Angeles County Fair competition. The Muscatel, the Tinta Port, the medium and sweet sherries are perennial recipients of high awards. A unique commercial feature of Brookside is the mode of merchandising, a successful elaborate string of tasting room-retail stores. In California, as in many other states, no public tasting is permitted in retail shops. Wineries are permitted to offer tastes of their own products and Brookside is able to so license their stores so that tasting is permitted. Consumers are allowed to select a wine, taste it, and then purchase, a unique form of retail selling that has been especially effective. Recently, however, after twenty-five years of direct-to-consumer sales, Brookside has placed some of its wines into normal retail channels.

THE CUCAMONGA VINEYARD COMPANY

The second largest winery still operating in the Cucamonga region is Pierre Biane's, The Cucamonga Vineyard Company. The old winery has undergone a remarkable face-lift and modernization, partly the legacy of the National Drink Company who owned it from 1961 to 1974. Pierre continued the modernization programme by adding over a quarter-of-a-million US gallons of stainless-steel holding tanks and a tasting retail-sales room. Sparkling wines were the speciality for which Cucamonga was, and continues to be, justly famous. Sold under the Cuvée D'Or and Bonded Winery Number 1 labels, as well as under the private labels of numerous restaurants and hotels, all are bulk processed, and have been successful in this class at the Los Angeles County Fair competitions. Pierre has added to the line a Marsala and a sherry blended by Primo Scrosatto. There is also a line of generic table wines, and Pierre has begun direct importation from Bordeaux under the winery's own label. The wines, a red and a white, are made at Château Martouret in Bordeaux's Entre-Deux-Mers region. Another added attraction is the availability in the retail-sales room of Rancho de Philo cream sherry made by Pierre's father. Since Pierre's acquisition of The Cucamonga Vineyard, a major use of the capacity has been custom-crushing and fermenting of Rancho California grapes for wineries located elsewhere in the state. In the harvest of 1979, nearly 10,000 tonnes of Rancho California grapes passed through the Cucamonga crusher and fermenters on their way to be bottled and sold under the labels of other wineries. A major reason for the existence and success of a winery like Pierre's is its use for custom-crushing and fermenting.

Regretfully, the area continues to be in a state of diminishing vineyards. Perhaps the real culprit is the style of wines that were made rather than continuing urbanization. This area is blessed with soils and climates which probably would have produced, and did, some of the world's finest sweet wines. It would have been interesting if those styles of wines could have continued and, if so, maybe wineries would have, too. The consumer now looks to the area to the south, and more particularly to two wineries established at Temecula, Callaway Vineyard and Mount Palomar Winery.

CALLAWAY VINEYARD

Notable and successful is the winery of Ely R. Callaway, Jr., former president of Burlington Mills, the world's largest textile manufacturer. He planted his vineyards in 1969, and completed his winery in 1974. As the vines began to mature, experimental wines were made, first at the University of California at Davis in 1972, and then at a northern California winery in 1973. The wines showed such promise that Callaway, one of the shrewdest wine marketeers, decided to go forward with his own winery.

Rancho California, which includes Callaway's 140 acres of grapes, is Region III. Callaway maintains that wind chill effectively reduces the temperature of the vines to the equivalent of Region II or even Region I. It is true that throughout the growing season, an early afternoon breeze of 20 to 25 knots per hour flows from the Pacific Ocean, twenty-five miles away, through the vineyards on its way to the Salton Sea over one hundred miles to the east. It is perceptibly cooler on Callaway's hillside than at Temecula's valley floor four miles to the west. Production at Callaway is limited to seven grape varieties: Johannisberg Riesling, Chardonnay, Chenin Blanc, Sauvignon Blanc, Cabernet Sauvignon, Zinfandel and Petite Sirah.

Callaway's emphasis is upon dry white table wines; 70 per cent of sales are to restaurants, and a consequence is that winery personnel occupy much time assisting restaurateurs. The leading wine is a botrytized Chenin Blanc, 'Sweet Nancy', named in honour of Ely's wife. First produced in 1973, it created quite a stir but not success on my palate. The 1978 version has achieved considerable elegance for this style of wine. Thoroughly infected with botrytis, the grapes had reached 47.8 per cent sugar at harvest and fermentation lasted fifteen months at temperatures below 40°F. The finished wine contains only 10 per cent alcohol, with 16.5 per cent residual sugar and over 1.0 per cent total acidity. The result is indeed a liqueur-like wine, combining the intense fruit characteristics of Chenin Blanc, against a background of pronounced honey-like flavour, perhaps Callaway's best wine yet. Callaway is not known for his modesty. He has made great claims for his wines, and he is ever the intense merchant, clever, innovative and stylized. Also interesting are a Zinfandel called Noël, made in the *nouveau* style by carbonic maceration, an experimental port made according to classic Portuguese techniques, and botrytized Rieslings which are not made every year. The style intent here is bone dry, and wines are generally crisp, with good acidity and moderately low alcohol content. I have preferred the whites to the reds, because of apparent red stripping, which may have resulted from an earlier Germanic wine-making attitude. However, since Steve O'Donnell, former assistant wine-maker at Beringer, took over the wine-making chores, wine styles have changed for the better, especially the Petite Sirah and the Zinfandel. The Petite Sirah has begun to take on the complexity and a character reminiscent of an upper Rhône Valley wine, and the Cabernet Sauvignon, with reduced alcohol content, is becoming more Bordeaux-like in character. Best of the whites is a low-alcohol Johannisberg Riesling, made in 1979. The grapes were harvested at low sugar (18° Brix) and at high acidity (1.3 per cent) at the end of 180 days of the growing season, deliberately shortening the time on the vine from the usual California season of in excess of 200 days in order to permit the production of a fully dry, low-alcohol wine which would still have the desirable varietal characteristics of the Riesling grape. The finished wine was just over 10 per cent alcohol, having good fruitiness and flavour, and it makes an excellent seafood wine, the goal apparently achieved. Callaway has proved that it is possible to produce in southern

California, wines which, although different in style, are equal in quality to those of other more acclaimed areas.

There are three wineries located in northern San Diego County. Ferrara and Bernardo, with redwood tanks and basket presses, are monuments to a bygone era in wine-making. The third is San Pasqual, founded in 1973 with ninety-eight acres of vineyards. It is too early to make predictions here, although there is opportunity to produce wines in San Pasqual Valley, preserved by legislation for agricultural uses. Tearfully, I shall miss the vineyard areas surrounding Los Angeles. It is a bygone era that served the state and consumer well. Obviously, things are not entirely lost, for southern California appears to be in the good hands of the Rancho California-Temecula vineyards.

INTERIOR VALLEY

California's great Interior Valley, walled in by the towering Sierra Nevada Mountains on the east and the lower Pacific Coastal Range on the west, stretches from north of the capital city of Sacramento to south of Bakersfield, nearly two-thirds of the length of the state. Here is California's agricultural heartland, with deep fertile soils, abundant water for irrigation, and soaring summer-time temperatures to make this the most productive region in the United States. Here are planted nearly all California's raisin grapes, 53 per cent of the table grapes and over half of the state's wine grapes are grown here. Approximately 80 per cent of the wine produced in California is made here.

In the first decades following Repeal, the Valley's wines were mainly high alcohol dessert and apéritif wines, principally from the Thompson Seedless grape which then accounted for fully half of California's acreage. This hot inland valley allows grapes to ripen fully, building sugar to the high levels desirable for the production of California ports and sherries. Much of California's table wines of *vin ordinaire* quality (as much as three-quarters or more) were and are produced here. Make no mistake, here is not simply *vin ordinaire*. Authorities refer to it as *vin ordinaire-extraordinaire*. It probably represents the best value for money anywhere. Frenchmen would give anything to drink both the reds and the whites at prices under $2.00 per bottle and sometimes under $1.00 (1980). For greater wines, temperatures may be too high for acids to produce complexities.

Here storage capacity is more often than not reckoned not in tens of thousands of gallons but in tens of millions. In the 300 miles separating Sacramento and Bakersfield are perhaps no more than forty wineries (compare this to over one hundred in the twenty-five-mile length of the Napa Valley!) which together account for in excess of 60 per cent of the state's output of wine. However, there is also great diversity of size. The largest, Gallo Winery near Modesto, has a gigantic 250,000,000 US gallons of storage capacity; the smallest, Quady, can store only a mere 35,000 US gallons. Starting at Sacramento and travelling south, temperatures become progressively warmer. The region at Lodi is a warm Region III or a cool Region IV. Bakersfield is located in what is without question the hottest Region V. This, then, is port and sherry country, though as technology improves, more table varietals will fare better, including Cabernet and Chardonnay. Attempts are constantly considered, such as Ruby Cabernet (a Cabernet Sauvignon-x-Carignane cross), which flourishes in the Valley.

BARENGO VINEYARDS

Barengo Vineyards, noted as one of the first to produce Ruby Cabernet, was founded in 1935 at Prohibition's end. As a Central Valley winery, it is making a

serious effort to upgrade quality and image. In 1976, Ira and Kent Kirkorian purchased the winery and installed a row of jacketed, stainless-steel fermenters, and
a collection of small French oak cooperage. Premium wine production started from
purchased grapes from other, coastal vineyards, including Santa Barbara and San
Luis Obispo counties. The 1977 Santa Barbara Chardonnay, Tepusquet Vineyards,
clearly illustrates the winery's new thrust. Ample in fruit, it displayed a green
appley nose against a background of oak in a pleasant style and good finish. Also
featured are San Luis Obispo Cabernets and Santa Barbara Johannisberg Rieslings
that are far superior to Barengo's early offerings in bygone days.

J.F.J. BRONCO WINERY

Under the name of J.F.J. Bronco Winery, the young Franzias have quickly grown
to nearly thirty million US gallons' capacity, one of the largest in the United States.
The quality is not far removed from Franzias', with quality ever-improving because
of a blending of north coast and central coast grapes.

CALIFORNIA GROWERS' WINERY

California Growers' Winery, at Yettem, southeast of Fresno, another of the giants
of the state's great Central Valley, was founded in 1936 by Arpaxat (Sox) Setrakian
(now deceased), one of the leaders of the raisin grape industry. The Setrakian family
is heavily committed to the wine business in both bulk and bottled production.
Robert Setrakian, competent in wine-marketing and production, has introduced
a quality line of moderately priced varietals under several labels: Setrakian, LeBlanc,
Bounty Vineyards and Growers. Additionally, the winery does a substantial business in custom bottling for others. Generics are the principal thrust of the winery:
burgundy, sauterne, chablis, ports, sherries and sparkling wines. In 1965, however,
Setrakian planted 2,000 acres of 'varietals' that apparently are 'Valley proven',
Chenin Blanc, French Colombard, and Ruby Cabernet, together with some experimental plantings of Johannisberg Riesling. He believed that some delicate, early-
ripening varieties would, with appropriate vineyard practices, do well, of which
recent tastings confirm that they have. While the 'Valley varietals' now taste with
more fruit than ever before, they make for good casual sipping, but do not always
lend themselves to the table. The Ruby Cabernet is soft, sometimes ponderously
heavy, but on occasion, when balance is right, lusciousness makes for good, uncomplicated red wine drinking.

FRANZIA BROTHERS WINERY

Franzia Brothers Winery, located near Ripon, about fifty miles east of San Francisco,
is owned by the Coca Cola Company of New York. With thirty million US gallons
of storage capacity, this producer is part of the team of San Joaquin Valley giants.
Supplying thirty-three different wine types, Franzia is amongst the six largest
American wine producers. Although a bulk producer, Franzia Brothers is, like so
many other Italian establishments, a family affair and although the wines are among
the lowest priced in California, they are *vin ordinaire-extraordinaire*.

EAST SIDE WINERY

For me the best Californian port and sherry producer is the marvellous cooperative
of East Side Winery, one of the oldest and largest (130 members) surviving in
California. East Side Winery has employed varietal crosses developed by Professor
Harold Olmo at the University of California at Davis, such as Emerald Riesling

(a varietal cross of Muscadelle and White Riesling), Ruby Cabernet and Gold (a double crossing of Muscat Hamburg-x-Sultanina with Muscat Hamburg-x-Scolo-kertek Kiralynoje). The winery has been successful with wines made from these grapes, especially in the Middle West. East Side is best known, however, for dessert wines and brandy, many of them consistent medal winners at the Los Angeles County Fair including two Sweepstakes Awards. First given in 1972 for an East Side Dry Cocktail Sherry under the Royal Host label, it was bestowed a second time in 1979 for a Tinta Madeira tawny port under East Side's Conti Royale label. Both wines were of superb quality, the port, full-flavoured and intense, while the sherry is clean with a pleasant nuttiness that conjures up the memory of a similarly styled Amontillado. As a cooperative, East Side, in the capable hands of Ernest Haas as general manager and Lee Eichele as wine-maker, in recent years has fared well with table wines too. It has installed stainless-steel fermenters and small oak casks and the result has been great improvement in the varietals.

FICKLIN VINEYARDS

Another port producer asserts title to the best. Always fine, Ficklin Vineyards, a tiny winery by San Joaquin Valley standards, led today by David Ficklin, is literally a throwback to Portuguese wine-making. Production is principally of non-vintage Tinta port in a ruby style from a *solera* system for blending old and young wines together. On occasion, limited amounts of vintage ports have also been produced, discontinued for a time in the 1970s. Plans to resume are under consideration. Fine qualities of the Ficklin ports may be due in part to the soil and climate conditions that are unique to the area. I am inclined to believe that the finest dessert wines in the world could be made here if only the attention were given.

E. AND J. GALLO WINERY

The largest wine-maker in the United States, and maybe in the world, is the E. and J. Gallo Winery at Modesto. The winery is truly one of the great American success stories. The Gallo brothers, Ernest and Julio, began their wine-making careers in a rented warehouse at Prohibition's end with wine-making lessons gathered from the pages of early pamphlets, published by the University of California. Armed with this modest information, a few redwood tanks and a credit-purchased crusher, they sold their first vintages in bulk to eastern-coast bottlers. Not until the early 1940s did the Gallo name appear on a wine label. The Gallos persisted in bringing the consumer sound reliable *vin ordinaire-extraordinaire* wines at prices which represented an offer the consuming public could not refuse. The taste spectrum is wide, and varies from sherries to ports, to reds, whites, and pinks. The Gallos produce nearly one-half of the wine made in California and sell approximately one-quarter of all the wine sold in the United States. Gallo has introduced a number of firsts to California wine-making, including premiere flavoured wines (Thunderbird in 1957), and so-called 'pop' wines (Ripple in 1960). They were the first modern winery to build their own glass factory for bottle production.

The Gallos were amongst the first to replace wooden fermenters and tanks with stainless-steel and epoxy-lined tanks, and to sign with their growers long-term contracts with provisions to induce them to plant better grape varietals. The two most successful Gallo table wines are Hearty Burgundy and Chablis Blanc, introduced in the 1960s, which no doubt benefit from substantial amounts of Sonoma and Napa grapes. Gallo purchases 40 per cent of all the grapes grown in Sonoma County (and even bought a Sonoma County winery to turn those grapes into wine), 20 per cent of the grape production of Napa County, and 27 per cent of the grapes grown in the Coastal region from Monterey to San Luis Obispo. With Interior Valley grapes included, Gallo uses the output from 100,000 acres of grapes to produce their wines.

Most of the Central Coast grapes go into the new line of cork-finished varietals (the balance of the Gallo line is bottled under screw caps) introduced by Gallo in 1974 and re-introduced in 1979. The 1974 grouping did not fare as well as the Gallos had hoped. The seven varietals included no oak-aged wines nor any of the 'big four' varietals, Chardonnay, Cabernet Sauvignon, Pinot Noir or Johannisberg Riesling. So, beginning in 1977, Gallo constructed a huge underground cellar, filled with six hundred 4,000-gallon Yugoslavian oak tanks and began filling the tanks with Cabernet Sauvignon and Chardonnay to be released in 1980. In 1979, the first of the re-introduced varietals were released under a newly designed label featuring the winery's Modesto headquarters. Accompanied by a seven million dollar multi-media advertising campaign, the 'new' varietals were released reflecting substantial amounts of Monterey County and north coast grapes. Sauvignon Blanc, Gewürz-traminer, Chenin Blanc, French Colombard and Johannisberg Riesling were in-cluded in the 1979 release. All but the Gewürztraminer were packaged in a 1.5-litre 'Captain's decanter', as well as in the standard fifth (750-millilitre) size. The wines were good varietal examples, but Sauvignon Blanc and Gewürztraminer were slightly sweet. Decent wines at the price, they are aimed for a popular market that should receive them well. Released in 1980 were wood-aged Cabernet Sauvignon, Chardonnay, Zinfandel and Barbera. I have not always been a fan of Gallo wines, and yet the quality is undeniable. The Hearty Burgundy is a sound red wine that is no embarrassment and, indeed, is an asset to the table. Many American wine-drinkers' budgets and palate have been served by this Gallo staple. Gallo is also responsible for much California wine research. Important is the submerged-*flor* process which produces sherries with Spanish-like character including a pale dry cocktail and a very sweet one. The 'new' varietals place Gallo in a premium-priced bracket, which is another first for Gallo.

E. and J. Gallo Winery is so complex and gigantic that it is hard to envisage its size and production. Four wineries (at Livingston, Fresno, Healdsburg and Modesto) are required to produce all the wine sold under the plethora of labels owned by the Gallos. Its warehouse at Modesto covers twenty-five acres alone, from which wines are shipped to all fifty states. Five sets of railroad tracks service this warehouse, and at any given moment there are 2.5 million US gallons sitting in the loading area awaiting shipment. There is a research laboratory which not only rivals the best, but may surpass any that a university has to offer, while its several wine-makers read like a 'Who's Who'.

GIUMARRA VINEYARDS

Six miles east of oil-rich Bakersfield is Giumarra Vineyards, producer of bulk table and dessert wines. Founded in 1946, by a Sicilian called Giuseppe Giumarra, the winery owns 8,000 acres of vineyards and is now one of the largest shippers of fresh grapes in the United States. Mid-varietals include the 'heavyweights', such as Chardonnay and Cabernet Sauvignon. Cabernet Sauvignon, Pinot Noir and Gamay Beaujolais varieties, which generally are not supposed to do well in Region v, have performed satisfactorily. This varietal programme, instigated by Giuseppe's younger brother John, is supported by 1,000 grape-acres and a three-million US-gallon addi-tion to the main winery, which still produces bulk and custom-labelled wines. Huge quantities of generics are produced, together with varietals. While varietal character is not always dominant, the new varietals are sufficiently fruity to make them worthy of drinking.

ANGELO PAPAGNI VINEYARDS

Only a few miles north of Madera is Angelo Papagni Vineyards, a winery that emphasizes dry table wines including Chenin Blanc (one completely dry, one sweet), Muscat Alexandria, Chardonnay, Fumé Blanc, Alicante Bouschet, Barbera, Zinfandel, Charbono, Gamay Rosé, a proprietary blend called Bianca di Madera, and five sparkling wines (Brut, Extra Dry, Chardonnay, Au Naturel and sparkling Chenin Blanc). Papagni, who emigrated from Italy in 1912, put his money where his dream was and constructed a showplace with three million US gallons of storage capacity, the latest in modern technology, and an impressive collection of 50-US gallon barrels for ageing red wines. By the time the winery was fully complete in 1975, he had released his first wines: a 1973 Alicante Bouschet, a 1973 Barbera, a 1973 Zinfandel, a 1974 Chenin Blanc, a 1973 Muscat Alexandria and the first Spumante d'Angelo. Lo and behold, they were surprisingly good, considering their Region v origin. They have unexpected balance of acidity and fruitiness unusual for wines made in a hot climate. According to Papagni the secret is in the care of the vines: in pruning along with the timing and method of irrigation. Competitors suggest that he must be speaking to the grapes and convincing them that they are growing in a cooler region. My favourite Papagni is sweet, the Moscato d'Angelo produced from the Muscat Alexandria grape. It is one of the state's better wines for its type and, at a ridiculously low price, the wine is a unique success.

A. PERELLI-MINETTI AND SONS WINERY

At the southern end of the great Interior Valley lies the winery of A. Perelli-Minetti and Sons. The revered founder of the winery was Antonio Perelli-Minetti whose lifelong hobby was the development of a grape which would develop high acidity despite being grown in the Region v clime of Delano. By planting seeds from grapes in his vineyards which matured with high acidity, he eventually developed and patented one (a red) as 'Perelli' 101. It develops 1.12 acidity at 22° Balling, ripening in mid-November or later. The wine made from the grape is full bodied and tart, and has been blended with other varieties to increase their acidity.

The Perelli-Minetti winery sells its wines under a dozen well-known brands as a consequence of being the last operating member of the California Wine Association, which at its peak included sixty-four wineries. When Perelli-Minetti was left as survivor, it inherited such historic labels as Greystone, Guasti, Calwa, Ambassador and Eleven Cellars, as well as others. In September 1979, Perelli-Minetti, under their founder's name, released six premium varietals: 1974 Napa Zinfandel, 1975 Napa Cabernet Sauvignon, 1974 California Pinot Noir, 1974 Napa Chardonnay, 1978 Monterey Fumé Blanc and 1978 Santa Clara Johannisberg Riesling. The wines were typical of the area in which they were produced, but they were sold at prices which were untypical. They are drinkable, generous wines. This rapid entry into the premium end of the California wine market was accomplished by buying wine, engaging in some finishing operations, and bottling it. Perelli-Minetti today now covers the entire spectrum of California wines, from extremely low-priced to reasonably priced premium levels. The range of products includes apéritif, dessert, table and sparkling wines as well as two outstanding (for California) brandies, Aristocrat and J. R. Morrow.

SIERRA WINE CORPORATION

Another San Joaquin Valley winery giant, Sierra Wine Corporation, is located at Tulare, southeast of Fresno. It produces bulk wine that may find its way into top northern California labels. Many a well-known brand name probably has some Sierra wine flowing through its bottles. The 'Wine Boom' has had its impact on this winery, too. In the 1960s, 90 per cent of its output was ports and sherries shipped to eastern-coast bottlers, but since 1972, storage capacity has been expanded to 42,000,000 from 6,000,000 US gallons, with almost all production now table wine. Philip Posson, an unheralded competent wine-maker, continues to produce a superb sherry which carries his name. Introduced in 1975, the wine is made by the submerged *flor* process, that results in a flavourful, nutty-like style not unlike Spanish Amontillados in nose and taste. Production of submerged *flor* sherries was begun in 1964, a technique that is now widely used by California's finest sherry producers.

California Vintage Chart

To speak of meaningful vintage charts in California is difficult for a host of reasons. First and most important, California's vineyards are spread over a lengthy and broad area, with plantings stretching from San Diego County in the south to Ukiah in the north near the coast, and from Bakersfield to Sacramento in the hot central valley. In some instances, northern vineyards may be separated from southern vineyards by over 600 miles. Each region constitutes a completely different and distinct set of micro-climates and soils. It would be like trying to propose one vintage chart for the whole of France. Vineyards here differ from those of Europe in that they may plant several varieties in the same so-called viticultural area. Yet hundreds of miles away another vineyard might plant the same varieties under completely different climate and soil conditions. Chardonnay planted in the north will taste dramatically different from Chardonnay planted in the south, etc. Therefore, a comprehensive vintage chart would of necessity have to include evaluation of each variety.

Many wineries buy grapes from a variety of areas outside their own immediate estate. Therefore, it is difficult to evaluate in terms of vintage the products of the winery without precise information as to where the grapes are grown. The chart here is confined to broad regions only, the north coast, consisting of Napa, Sonoma and Mendocino counties, and the central coast, of Monterey County. (Neighbouring San Benito County experiences similar weather patterns, but most of the grapes appear to go into Almadén's non-vintaged wines, so exclusion of San Benito County may be justified.) Santa Barbara County to the south appears to parallel Monterey County; thus, with trepidation, Monterey ratings may be taken as an extremely rough guide to Santa Barbara, whose track record is indeed short. I have limited the chart to two varieties only.

Napa and Sonoma counties generally experience similar weather patterns and parallel growing conditions, despite the low range of mountains by which they are separated. Each benefits by the marine incursion from the Pacific Ocean, and approximately the same pattern of heat accumulations within sub-areas and received heat units that increase progressively from south to north. Mendocino County, to the north of both Napa and Sonoma counties and perhaps a trifle cooler, does not differ substantially in its weather pattern. Each county contains pockets in which micro-climates and soils are exceptions to the general patterns and where particular varieties will do better in one county as opposed to the others. A comprehensive vintage chart that purports to treat these special areas separately from the larger areas around them is at best risky, and probably not reliable.

San Joaquin Valley wineries, home of considerable California bulk wine production, frequently do not vintage date their wines, preferring to blend for taste uniformity. The valley's heat, combined with strong irrigation, serves to reduce or eliminate any significant differences from year to year, so that a vintage chart is not critical. San Luis Obispo County, the Santa Cruz Mountains and the Sierra Foothills are also hard to vintage chart. In many, indeed most, of the instances, wineries are recent, so much so that it is impossible yet to tie sufficient taste to vintage. Alameda and Contra Costa counties, destined now to limited production, may also be unchartable, since most wineries rely upon grapes from other counties.

In the interests of simplicity, the number of California varietals for vintage chart purposes has been reduced to Cabernet and Chardonnay. Since these two varieties are generally acknowledged to be California's most popular, perhaps her best, a vintage chart here may be of more interest. Rarely are the merits of vintages of other varietals as broadly discussed, such as Chenin Blanc, Gamay, Sauvignon Blanc, Zinfandel and Johannisberg Riesling. The latter is becoming more important, however, because of the proliferation of botrytized wines which are so heavily dependent upon correct climate conditions. Each vintage was rated on a scale of 0 to 9, with a score of 5 representing average quality. Cabernet vintages have been evaluated in this fashion for the past ten years; Chardonnay, for the last five. The time span covered by the central coast chart is limited to five years for both varieties; Monterey County did not begin production in any volume until the mid-1970s.

California Vintage Chart

Vintage Year:	1970	1971	1972	1973	1974	1975	1976	1977	1978	1979
North Coast										
Cabernet Sauvignon	8	6.5	5	7	8	8	7	7	8	7
Chardonnay						7+	7	8	8+	8
Central Coast										
Cabernet Sauvignon						8	5.5	9	8	8
Chardonnay						7	6	7	8	7

NOTE: Gratitude is expressed to Richard Peterson, wine-maker at The Monterey Vineyard, for his assistance in formulation of the scale herein used. Thanks also go to Zelma Long, wine-maker at Simi, Myron Nightingale of Beringer Vineyard, Timothy Mondavi, wine-maker at Robert Mondavi Winery, Don Alexander of Mirassou, and Legh Knowles of Beaulieu Vineyards for their cooperation in providing impressions of the vintages included here.

PACIFIC NORTHWEST

WASHINGTON

Wine-making began in the Pacific Northwest in the nineteenth century. However, until the 1960s the wines were principally from fruits (i.e., apples, cherries, etc.) and berries (raspberries, strawberries, etc.) with limited quantities from *labrusca* grapes, principally Concord. In 1872, on Stretch Island at Puget Sound, Washington's first vineyards were planted to native American varieties. Grape-growing concentrated there until after the completion of the Yakima project, a large-scale irrigation reclamation project, begun in 1906 by the United States Reclamation Service. Yakima Valley in eastern Washington is blocked off by the Cascade Mountains from the moisture-laden air which sweeps in from the Pacific Ocean. The Valley stretches eastward from the foot of the Cascades for 120 miles along the Yakima River until it flows into the Columbia River. An average of only eight inches of rainfall annually is received and, therefore, irrigation has been necessary in this semi-arid region. Not until 1950 were *vinifera* grapes planted in the Valley, when the National Wine Company began with Grenache.

ASSOCIATED VINTNERS, INC

Associated Vintners, like so many American wineries, began as a hobby of ten faculty members of the University of Washington. The scholarly vintners began with five acres at Sunnyside in the Yakima Valley in 1961. They cared for the vineyard and shared grapes, but because of independent style differences, fermented their wines separately. The move to commercial wine-making in 1967 was chiefly due to high praise given one of their Gewürztraminers by André Tchelistcheff. The crusher was moved from a member's garage into a small building in Kirkland, east of Seattle. For the next decade they operated much like a cooperative, working only at weekends. In 1976, production facilities were moved from Kirkland to larger quarters in Redmond's Overlake Industrial Park, with an expansion of vineyards from five to thirty acres. Six varieties are planted – Cabernet Sauvignon, Sémillon, Gewürztraminer, Chardonnay, Pinot Noir and White Riesling. Associated Vintners are not widely distributed, but they should be, especially their 1977 Chardonnay which challenges Château Ste Michelle's. It created a pleasant controversy amongst Washingtonians as to which was the better.

CHATEAU STE MICHELLE

Château Ste Michelle, at present Washington's leading producer of *vinifera* wines, survives two predecessor companies, National Wine Company and Pommerelle Company. Both companies in the 1930s produced apple juice and wines, and then merged in 1954 to form American Wine Growers. In 1967, *vinifera* wines were made, under the supervision of André Tchelistcheff, later released under the label of Ste Michelle. Initial wines were high in acidity and reflected their ageing in new American oak barrels. None the less it was a promising beginning. Promise fulfilment continued after American Wine Growers was purchased in 1973, by a group of Puget Sound investors led by Wally Opdycke, and resold in February 1974 to the United States Tobacco Company. The new company, able to provide necessary capital, constructed a new and expensive winery at Woodinville, fifteen miles northeast of Seattle. It is outstanding in design, resembling a French château, and the showplace of the area. The winery is 150 miles from the vineyards; therefore mechanical harvesting and field crushing have been utilized, the must treated with sulphur dioxide, and transported to the winery in closed stainless-steel tanks. A portion of the grapes are hand-harvested early in the morning, and because they are shipped over the 'cold' Cascades at elevations of 3,000 to 5,000 feet, the grapes arrive at the winery cool and in a sound state.

The vineyards' soils are volcanic in origin and well-drained, and on the same latitude as those of Burgundy, France. Temperatures during the growing season are cool and, because of the northern latitude, the vineyards receive up to sixteen or more hours of sunshine during the growing season. The long hours of sunshine plus cool temperatures combine to assure that the grapes ripen slowly, with good acidity, so as to retain high intensity of varietal character in nose and flavour. Grapes planted here are on their own roots, which ostensibly influences the character of the wines. Joel Klein is wine-maker. Upon the recommendation of André Tchelistcheff, he was chosen to design and construct the new winery at Woodinville.

Most of Ste Michelle wines are white and include Chardonnay, Sémillon, Sauvignon Blanc (in the Fumé Blanc style), Chenin Blanc, Johannisberg (White) Riesling, Gewürztraminer and Muscat Canelli. There are two rosés: Grenache and Cabernet Sauvignon; and two reds: Merlot and Cabernet Sauvignon. A sparkling wine made from Pinot Noir grapes is available at the winery. All of Ste Michelle's wines have shown improvement, especially the whites, which I prefer. Notable is a 1977 Chardonnay which was loaded with fruit, rich and round, assertive in nose with good viscosity. It should do well with bottle age and develop a long lingering finish in the next several years. It is probably as good a Chardonnay as has been produced in the State of Washington. This Chardonnay is only a forerunner of what is likely to be a series of fine Chardonnays because of additional vine age and Klein's better understanding of Washington's vintage vicissitudes.

Another exciting example is the 1978 Johannisberg Riesling in *Eiswein* tradition, an intense botrytized wine that was followed closely from late October and finally picked towards the middle of November. Also improving at long last are Ste Michelle's Cabernets. The 1975 appears more and more Bordeaux-like, with more fruit than any red from this region. I found an intense Cabernet nose and good tannin. The wine is coming around now, yet should be an excellent keeper for the next five years or so. It is an example of what Washington is able to do with Cabernet. The 1976 is in a softer more supple style that may not age as long but is eminently drinkable now.

Other wines also caught my interest, among them Sémillon 1978, which had both good taste and balance and is good drinking. The ability of a good Sémillon to age was clearly illustrated by the winery's 1972 version. Although developing a slight maderized character, it demonstrated considerable complexity. Not much California Sémillon is produced these days, and it is indeed a good wine for Ste Michelle to be making. The 1978 Chenin Blanc, which is much improved over the 1977, possesses an intense floral nose and is sweet in style, with decidedly good flavour and balance. At $4.25 (1980), it, too, is a good buy. A 1977 Johannisberg Riesling was most intriguing. It had exceptional flavour and was produced with 10.5 per cent alcohol from hand-selected botrytized grapes. Sold at around $10.00 (1980) per bottle, it is worth it. Rosé lovers should take to the 1978 Grenache Rosé, which is slightly sweet but in full varietal character, with a strong, berry-like nose. The wine is well made and should satisfy those who like their rosés in a little heavier, chewier style. Dessert-wine lovers will not be disappointed in the Muscat Cannelli with its restrained nose and generous flavour. It drinks extremely well, and is light in alcohol (11 per cent) and in price ($6.50 in 1980). What is interesting about Klein as a wine-maker is that he comes to the area with an open palate. Upon arrival he had apprehensions about wine-making there, but with the benefit of Tchelistcheff's enthusiasm and his own, he cannot now be prised away from the state and its wines. He acknowledges it may take some time to find the best style here because the area has such intense varietal character. In most wine-making countries that would not be considered a problem, but Klein is handling it well and in a few short years may make wines that match California's best.

PRESTON WINE CELLARS

William and Joanne Preston in 1976 started their original winery at the Columbia River Basin which is east of the confluence of the Yakima River with the Columbia. Preston is now the second largest Washington winery, with 110,000 US gallons of storage capacity and has the definite advantage of a location near its own vineyards. Thus it is unnecessary to transport grapes over the Cascades. Vineyards are planted to Cabernet Sauvignon, Pinot Noir, Chardonnay and White Riesling, with smaller amounts of Gewürztraminer, Gamay Beaujolais, Grenache, Chenin Blanc, Merlot and Sauvignon Blanc. A Chardonnay of 1977 was most impressive, but not the equal yet of Ste Michelle Associated Vintners.

Other Washington wineries are Griffin, Hinzerling Vineyards, The Manfred Vierthaler Winery and Mount Rainier Winery. Some are too new to have compiled a wine-making track record. They are Leonetti Cellar, begun by Garry and Nancy

Figgins in 1977 at Walla Walla, with storage capacity of 1,000 US gallons; in 1978, E. B. Foote Winery with 7,500 US gallons of storage capacity was founded in Seattle; Alex and Jeannette Golitzin started Cedar Ridge Vintners, Inc, with 2,700-US gallons' capacity in Snohomish, approximately seventy-five miles north of Seattle; John and Louise Rauner began Yakima River Winery with 8,000 US gallons of storage capacity at Prosser, in the Yakima Valley. It is apparent that production of *vinifera* wines is displacing fruit and berry types in Washington. In 1979, fourteen wineries were operating; nine of them were founded after 1975 as *vinifera* plantings matured. There were 4,000 acres of *vinifera* vineyards planted in the Yakima Valley alone at the end of the 1970s, but it is variously estimated that an additional 20,000 acres are suitable for the cultivation of *vinifera* grapes. Thus, the next decade or so should make for good, surprising competition for California and for America's wine growth in both the acreage in *vinifera* vineyards and the number of wineries producing wines from the grapes harvested from these vineyards.

OREGON

Vinifera wines were produced in Oregon's Willamette Valley during the latter part of the nineteenth century, but failed to make a come-back after Prohibition. Fruit and berry wines flourished until 1938, when sales of non-grape wines also languished. Revival of *viniferas* had to await increased wine interest by Americans in the mid-1960s. Today, Oregon's grape-growing and wine-making are centred in the Willamette Valley, with most wineries clustered in its northern end near Portland. Oregon's wine country is largely rural and its wineries are small, family-run enterprises, scattered about the countryside. The Willamette Valley stretches two-thirds of the length of the state from north of Roseburg in the south to the Oregon-Washington border in the north, lying between the low Coast Range of mountains in the west and the higher Cascades seventy-five miles to the east. The Cascades protect the Valley from cold air masses sweeping down from Canada through eastern Oregon. The Coast Range in the west is low enough to allow the Pacific Ocean to moderate the Valley's micro-climate. Rainfall varies between thirty-five and fifty-five inches per year, eliminating the need for vineyard irrigation. Although the Valley floor experiences some frost, most of the vineyards are planted on the hillsides above the risk of frost damage, eliminating the need for any special winter protection. Four men, William Fuller, Richard Sommer, David Lett and Charles Coury, deserve full marks for the rebirth of the Oregon wine industry. All studied oenology at the University of California at Davis.

THE EYRIE VINEYARDS

David Lett took two years alone searching for a site in Oregon on which to plant Pinot Noir, a grape which, for him, had become a kind of crusade. He selected the Red Hills of Dundee in 1966, where he trucked in cuttings, principally of Pinot Noir. The winery is located a few miles west of the vineyard, in the small town of McMinnville and it is Lett's intention to specialize in Burgundy-style wines. He ferments in small 200-US gallon fermenters and then ages in 60-US gallon Limousin barrels. His first love, Pinot Noir, stays in wood for two years, during which time it undergoes spontaneous malolactic fermentation. Lett also has a great love for Chardonnay on which he practises barrel-fermentation. Clarification is accomplished naturally for both wines, by racking each three or four times per year. On occasion the Chardonnay is filtered lightly before bottling, but the Pinot Noir is neither fined nor filtered. In addition to Pinot Noir and Chardonnay, he produces Sauvignon Blanc (from Washington grapes), White Riesling, Gewürztraminer,

Oregon Spring Wine (a blend of Muscat Ottonel and Pinot Blanc), and the only Pinot Meunier and Pinot Gris (about fifty cases of each annually) produced in the United States. Eyrie is small (storage capacity is only 15,000 US gallons) and is expected to remain so to permit Lett to continue to exercise close personal supervision over his wines. The wines are limited in distribution.

HILLCREST VINEYARD

Richard Sommer may be entitled to the most credit since he was the first to plant *vinifera* grapes in Oregon after Repeal. Like so many others, home wine-making led him to professional introductory oenology courses at the University of California at Davis in the late 1950s. In 1961 he planted his first vines on a ten-acre hillside ten miles northwest of Roseburg, naming it Hillcrest. By 1966, these vines had come into full production. Much of Hillcrest's wine production is White Riesling, which makes up 70 per cent of his total wine production. Cabernet Sauvignon accounts for much of the balance of the vines, along with smaller amounts of Merlot and Malbec (for blending with the Cabernet), Pinot Noir, Gewürztraminer, Chardonnay, Sauvignon Blanc, Sémillon and Chenin Blanc. Gamay Beaujolais and Zinfandel, which have not fared well, have been removed. Sommer's White Riesling is Germanic in style with 1 per cent residual sugar, ample fruit and with acidity in good balance. In certain years in which botrytis mould develops, Sommer also produces botrytized Rieslings in *Auslese* and *Spätlese* styles. A new winery building was completed in 1975, with storage capacity of 20,000 US gallons and a typical vintage yield of 15,000 US gallons. Eventual expansion will increase storage capacity to 50,000 US gallons.

TUALATIN VINEYARDS

Another Californian who migrated north to Oregon is William Fuller in partnership with Bill Malkmus. Seventy acres of vineyards were planted to White Riesling, Pinot Noir, Chardonnay, Gewürztraminer, Müller-Thurgau, Muscat and Flora. A winery structure was completed in time for the 1974 crush of purchased Washington grapes. Although Tualatin's vineyards produced a first crop in 1976, the winery will continue to buy Washington and Idaho grapes, as well as Oregon, to supplement its output. Tualatin's storage capacity makes it one of the largest of the new Oregon wineries, and it is indeed one of the most modern, with stainless-steel fermenters, a centrifuge and rows of Limousin barrels in which Pinot Noir and Chardonnay are ageing.

Oregon's *vinifera* revival is still in its infancy. Of the thirty-two wineries operating, twenty-four were founded in the 1970s, and five in the 1960s. Most remain family-run operations of 20,000 US gallons' or less capacity, and vineyards which range from five to twenty acres. Most, yet, do not grow sufficient grapes to satisfy production requirements, requiring purchase of grapes from other states, particularly Washington and Idaho. Several of the wine-makers, notably David Lett, are convinced that the Willamette Valley will prove to be America's home for the Pinot Noir; however, the experiment has only just begun. The fact that the *vinifera* are growing on their own roots may be a plus. Oregon's legislature may be as important to the industry as its wine-makers. No European place names, such as Burgundy or Chablis, are permitted on any Oregon label. Moreover, the minimum varietal requirement is 90 per cent on all varieties except Cabernet Sauvignon, which enjoys a 75 per cent minimum, allowing for the use of such blending varieties as Merlot and Malbec. Wineries are authorized to make wines from grapes grown in other states, but must identify the source on the back label. No doubt fine, even great, wine will be made not only as vines mature, but also because of the continuing influx of wine-makers displeased with, or unable to find, reasonably priced land in California. The Pacific Northwest region, including Washington, remains virtually an untapped resource.

IDAHO

Most Americans consider wine-making and grape-growing to be new to Idaho but, as in Oregon and Washington, vineyards were planted and wine was produced before Prohibition. Following Repeal, there was little grape-growing or wine-making activity in Idaho. A resumption had to await a change in Idaho wine-retailing law in 1971, which permitted the sale of wine in grocery stores and not exclusively in state-owned retail shops. Wine sales in Idaho have increased sixfold since.

CHATEAU STE CHAPELLE VINEYARDS

Increased interest in wine prompted William Brioch to establish, in 1976, Idaho's only winery, Château Ste Chapelle Vineyards. Located at Sunny Slope, which is about thirty-five miles west of Boise and nine miles west of Caldwell, Ste Chapelle's vineyards are planted on a ridge at an elevation of about 2,700 feet above sea level on soils of volcanic origin. They enjoy a long, cool growing season which, on the basis of the University of California at Davis heat summation (see page 461), can qualify as a Region 1. Vineyards that surround the winery are planted to Johannisberg Riesling, Chardonnay, Gewürztraminer, Pinot Noir and Merlot. In addition, some Cabernet Sauvignon acreage is owned in Washington State. Yields are relatively low, making it necessary to import grapes from Washington to supplement Ste Chapelle's grapes. Because the Washington grapes are harvested in October when the weather is cool, they can be hauled 300 miles from the vineyards to the winery and arrive in a sound state. Perhaps one of Ste Chapelle's problems is wines with relatively high acidity which may be due to the long, cool growing season.

The line includes Chenin Blanc, Gewürztraminer, rosé of Cabernet Sauvignon, rosé of Pinot Noir and Cabernet Sauvignon made from Washington State grapes, and Johannisberg Riesling and Chardonnay made from Idaho grapes. A Johannisberg Riesling labelled as American informs that it was a blend of both Washington and Idaho grapes. The best of Ste Chapelle's wines to date are a 1979 Idaho Johannisberg Riesling and a 1979 Idaho barrel-fermented Chardonnay. Although the Riesling has a strong resemblance to its German cousin, with high acidity and good fruit on the palate; it is lacking in aroma and, in spite of the acidity, seems somewhat flabby in the mouth. The 1979 barrel-fermented Chardonnay has possibilities because it has good fruit and seems to develop well on the palate, but is heavily yeasty (as might be expected in a barrel-fermented wine). But it is still not in the class of better California Chardonnays. A slight bitter finish may suggest new vines and, of course, that will change as vineyards mature. To date, the Chardonnay has been satisfactory, while the Johannisberg Riesling has been impressive. A late-harvest style produced from Idaho grapes was beautifully elegant, indeed, and superior to many wines of this type. Perhaps Idaho will prove eventually to be the Rhineland of the United States.

NEW YORK STATE

New York State stands second in American wine production to California. Although two-thirds of her grapes are still *labrusca* Concords, the planting of French-

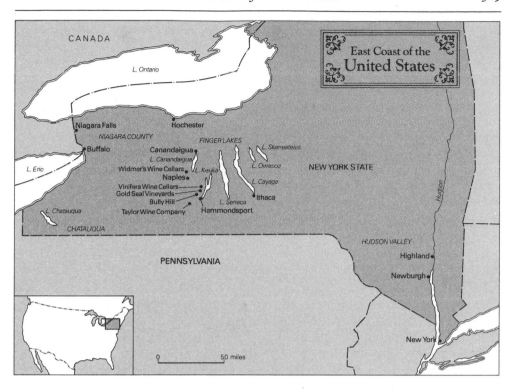

American hybrids is on the increase, as are *vinifera*. (French-American hybrids are the result of crosses of *Vitis vinifera* varietals with certain *Vitis* species native to America.) Four principal vineyard districts account for production. Best known is the Finger Lakes district; yet more significant acreage is in the Chatauqua district on the eastern shore of Lake Erie. Third in size is Niagara County, west of Niagara Falls, while the Hudson Valley accounts for the balance. A small fifth district is beginning to develop on the northeastern tip of Long Island at Cutchogue.

BENMARL WINE COMPANY

Approximately two hours' drive from New York City in the Hudson River Valley is Benmarl Wine Company, founded in 1971 by Mark and Dene Miller. Prior to the 1971 founding, Mark acquired an old winery and fifty-acre vineyard site overlooking the Hudson River near the town of Marlboro, where the Dutchess, an early hybrid of *labrusca* with *vinifera*, was developed by nineteenth-century grape pioneer, Andrew J. Caywood. Mark Miller planted French-American hybrids on approximately ten acres and Chardonnay on half an acre, and then invited fellow amateurs to join with him in an unusual cooperative – the Benmarl Société des Vignerons. Membership conveyed the privilege of harvest assistance for twelve bottles of personally labelled wine. After two years of amateur operation, the Benmarl Vineyard began commercial sales, even though much of the wine is still consumed by the 425 members of the Benmarl Société des Vignerons. Benmarl's seven wines, Seyval Blanc, Blanc Domaine, Rouge Domaine, Baco Noir, Rosé Domaine, Cuvée du Vigneron and Chardonnay, have made their mark on many a New York State wine list.

BULLY HILL

While the Taylor family is no longer in the Taylor Wine Company (see page 531), at least one Taylor still remains in wine. When he left Taylor Wine Company in 1970, Walter Taylor moved one and a half miles north of Hammondsport to open Bully Hill vineyards on the same farm site of the original Taylor winery and vineyards. Soon, Bully Hill wines became known for high New York quality. Walter Taylor is a staunch supporter of the French-American hybrids, as well as the native American *labrusca* types. From both hybrids and *labruscas*, he makes white, red and rosé, which are surprisingly clean and with good taste. Furthermore, he takes pride in the fact that his wines are 100 per cent from New York grapes without any addition of European or California juice. I recently tasted a 1976 bottle-fermented Bully Hill sparkling wine produced from Seyval Blanc whose excellence almost made me one of Taylor's supporters. Bone dry, it was clean and refreshing, with good flavour. Bully Hill's storage capacity has now increased to 96,000 US gallons, a decided jump from a 500-case beginning. The winery is an apparent blend of honest wines honestly made by a first-rate, vigorous New York State champion.

CANANDAIGUA WINE COMPANY, INC

New York's second largest winery is Canandaigua Wine Company, with storage capacity of 12,000,000 US gallons and 300 acres of vineyards, located at the north end of Lake Canandaigua. The winery is noted principally for Richard's Wild Irish Rose and their Virginia Dare wines, a line of wines that were universally popular throughout America following Prohibition. For a time it was the best-known American wine. Richard's Wild Irish Rose, a proprietary wine available with both 14 per cent and 20 per cent alcohol content, was created in the mid-1950s, when owners Marvin and Mack Sands bottled their wines at their Finger Lakes winery, a change in practice from solely bulk production. A definite *labrusca* flavour (a fragrant so-called 'foxy' flavour, raspberry to the Europeans) haunts the wine, yet it is one of the best-selling wines in America. The Virginia Dare line formerly applied only to a red and a white made principally from Scuppernong grapes, an American variety native to the southeastern United States. Today, the name is applied to a full line of generics: chablis, burgundy, sherry, etc., which are blends of principally New York and California grapes, with Scuppernong remaining for white and the rosé. In addition to the Canandaigua Winery, Marvin and Mack Sands also own Richard's Cellars in Virginia, Tenner Brothers Winery in South Carolina, and Bisceglia Brothers Winery in the San Joaquin Valley of California.

GOLD SEAL VINEYARDS

Just as staunchly as Walter Taylor defends and supports French-American hybrids and *labruscas*, so does Konstantin Frank argue vigorously for their replacement with *vinifera*. His own experimental vineyards are mindful proof that *vinifera* can thrive and do well in New York. Frank, a Russian émigré, had carried out research, both in Russia and in the United States on *vinifera* grapes and his research and logic came to the attention of Charles Fournier, then president of Gold Seal Vineyards, who hired Frank to develop a *vinifera* vineyard. Enthusiastically, Fournier accompanied Frank on an appropriate root-stock search throughout the northeast, which terminated successfully at Quebec, Canada. Back at Gold Seal, they grafted Chardonnay, Johannisberg Riesling, Gewürztraminer and Cabernet Sauvignon to these Canadian roots. For five years they persevered with grafts and plantings. In 1957, grafted Chardonnay and Riesling survived a temperature of $-25°$F with no apparent loss of vigour or reduction of crop. Fournier began planting *vinifera* at Gold Seal as fast as he could obtain root stock, and ultimately Gold Seal produced the first successful New York State *vinifera*. The first bottlings of Gold Seal intrigue me no end.

I still have several bottles of Chardonnay and late-harvest Johannisberg Riesling from the early 1960s which I serve blind to California's vintners, who, without hesitation, describe them as California. Despite the cost and limited production, the experiment constituted a successful breakthrough.

So far, only Gold Seal, among large Finger Lake wineries, has been willing to plant any important commercial *vinifera* acreage. Gold Seal and Fournier are entitled to considerable credit for Frank's research. Fournier, a visionary in his own right, remains active in the winery as a consultant, although he retired in 1967. The winery makes a full line of varietals and generics, including Chardonnay, Johannisberg Riesling, red, white and pink Catawba, burgundy, chablis and rosé, as well as *brut*, extra dry and blanc de blancs sparkling wines.

HERON HILL VINEYARD, INC

The third *vinifera* vineyard to be planted on Lake Keuka after Gold Seal's and Konstantin Frank's Wine Cellars' is Heron Hill Vineyard. Peter Johnstone and John Ingle planted thirty (now increased to forty) acres of White Riesling and Chardonnay in 1970. Upon the vines' maturity, a two-storey, 19,000-US gallon winery was completed in 1977. It is licensed under an interesting bit of New York State legislation, which permits a grower to bond a winery at an annual fee which is $800 less than that imposed on larger commercial enterprises, providing production does not exceed 50,000 US gallons per year. Located in an extremely cold site, Heron Hill's vineyard temperatures can fall as low as −27°F. Although vine canes can be damaged by the sub-freezing weather, roots are not, and the vines are regenerated sufficiently to produce small crops. The frigid location does, however, result in low heat accumulation during the growing season and low sugar levels at harvest. For example, the 1978 Chardonnay was harvested at 18.7° Brix, and the alcohol level was correspondingly low. Upon expert advice, the wines receive no wood ageing, which preserves delicacy and fruit character. The 1977 Chardonnay provided a good example of both delicacy and lightness, with good varietal character that was appealing and attractive, more for sipping than for quaffing.

THE TAYLOR WINE COMPANY, INC

The largest winery outside California and in New York is the Taylor Wine Company. The 31,000,000-US gallon storage capacity is indeed a far cry from the winery's humble origins, when it was founded by Walter and Addie Taylor on a seven-acre vineyard planted to native American varieties. Today, there are now in excess of 1,200 Taylor vineyard acres. The Taylors were the leaders in New York wine-making by employing the newest technological advances and introducing French-American hybrids in New York as well as mechanical harvesting in the vineyards. Taylor's bottle-fermented sparkling wines are still a significant part of the winery's sales today. Although bottle-fermented, the wines are clarified by the transfer process. In 1962 Taylor acquired Pleasant Valley Winery for the expansion of sparkling wine capacity and the noted 'Great Western Champagne' label. Pleasant Valley's claim to wine-making fame then was in sparkling wines that fared well in nineteenth-century European competition and whose admirers described it as a great Champagne of the Western World, hence the name: 'Great Western'. Upon the death of the last of the Taylor brothers in 1976, the Taylor Wine Company was purchased by the Coca-Cola Company of Atlanta, Georgia, which has continued the Taylor family production policies.

Table wines are not labelled varietally, but generically, as Taylor Lake County White, Taylor Lake County Pink and Taylor Lake County Red. Niagara grapes are employed in the white, the red relies upon a high percentage of hybrids, while the pink is substantially Catawba. Neither great nor complex, these wines are sound examples of *labrusca* and hybrids as grown in the New York State region. They are popular, but in a different taste character from European wines. It is an acquired taste that New Yorkers favour, but Californians do not. Under the name of Pleasant Valley, hybrid and *labrusca* table wines are produced. Best are Baco Noir burgundy (Baco Noir is a cross between Folle Blanche (*vinifera*) and *riparia* (American)), a Catawba varietal and a Chelois varietal (a crossing of Seibel 5163 with Seibel 5593, which are themselves crosses), a full-bodied red wine with distinctive flavour.

VINIFERA WINE CELLARS

Konstantin Frank, jubilant and obviously vindicated by the success at Gold Seal Vineyards, was motivated to plant his own vineyards and to erect a winery nearby. His own New York *vinifera* wines were released in 1965 and have proved to be clean, of good taste, and of high quality, especially the whites, but less so the reds. Chardonnay, Johannisberg Riesling and Gewürztraminer bottlings have been sound and bode well for New York *vinifera*. Frank's vineyards, Vinifera Wine Cellars, also produce Gamay Beaujolais, Pinot Noir and Cabernet Sauvignon.

WIDMER'S WINE CELLARS, INC

Another significant winery at Finger Lakes is Widmer's Wine Cellars with a capacity of 4,000,000 US gallons. The winery makes a full list of varietal and generic wines from both *labrusca* and French–American hybrids, such as burgundy, sauterne, port, sherry, Niagara, Salem, Dutchess, Elvira, Delaware, Vergennes, Moore's Diamond and Isabella. For a short period Widmer decided to go into *vinifera* and to California where 500 acres of vineyards were purchased, while Louis Martini produced wine for this New York winery. Regretfully, this experiment has now been discontinued.

NEW ENGLAND

NEW HAMPSHIRE

WHITE MOUNTAIN VINEYARDS

One lone winery operates in New Hampshire, White Mountain Vineyards. Founded in 1969 by John J. Canepa, a pharmacist turned wine-maker, and his wife Lucille, the 85,000-US gallon winery makes use of French–American hybrids from 150 winery-owned acres to produce estate-bottled, generically labelled table wines.

MASSACHUSETTS

CHICAMA VINEYARDS

In 1971, George Mathiesen, an electronics engineer, and his wife Catherine, home wine-makers from California, planted thirty acres of *vinifera* grapes on the island of Martha's Vineyard, located in the Atlantic Ocean, ten miles from the southern tip of Cape Cod. A small winery was built and has since been enlarged to 12,000 US gallons of storage capacity. Their Chicama Vineyards now produce Chardonnay, White Riesling, Cabernet Sauvignon, Pinot Noir, Gamay Beaujolais and Pinot Gris. The vineyards also include Rkatsiteli, a Russian variety employed also by Concannon Vineyards of California, and Mzvani, another Russian variety. Massachusetts' Farm Winery Law permits them to sell their wines directly to consumers from the winery at an annual licence fee of $22 per year. Also permitted are sales to restaurants and retailers.

COMMONWEALTH WINES

A recently established winery is Commonwealth Wines, founded after the 1977 passage of the Farm Winery Law. It is located at Plymouth, with 15,000 US gallons of storage capacity, and has Massachusetts Bonded Winery Licence Number 2.

RHODE ISLAND

PRUDENCE ISLAND VINEYARDS

The eldest of the three Rhode Island wineries is Prudence Island, founded in 1973 and located on Prudence Island in the middle of Narragansett Bay. Owners William Bacon, wife Natalie and their son Nathaniel produce principally Chardonnay and Gamay Beaujolais from twenty acres of *vinifera* plantings.

SAKONNET VINEYARDS

James and Lloyd Mitchell operate Sakonnet Vineyards in Little Compton, across the Sakonnet River from Newport, with 27,000 US gallons of storage capacity and thirty-six acres of French-American hybrids as well as *viniferas*. The wines have such imaginative labels as Rhode Island Red and America's Cup White.

SOUTH COUNTY VINEYARDS, INC

In the mid-1970s, H. Winfield Tucker and Don Siebert turned a dairy barn near Slocum, on the west side of Narragansett Bay, into a winery and began making small amounts of wine, principally from *vinifera* grapes brought from New York. They have only two acres at the winery, but they are planted to *vinifera*.

ATLANTIC COAST

NEW JERSEY

New Jersey has 1,000 acres of vineyards, yet produces 800,000 US gallons of wine, a lot from apples and from must and wine imported from California, which is frequently used as a base for vermouth. Much of the latter is produced at Lodi by Tribuno, whose 410,000-US gallon winery is now owned by Coca-Cola Bottling Company of New York. The largest winery in New Jersey is Laird, a company which has produced apple brandy and apple wine at Scobeyville since 1780. The best known winery is the Renault Winery at Egg Harbor City. Founded in 1864 by Louis Nicholas Renault, who represented the Duke of Montebello's champagne house in the United States, Renault has operated continuously since. With 125 acres of vineyards and 500,000 US gallons of storage, the winery specializes in sparkling wines and also produces some table wine from *labrusca* varieties.

PENNSYLVANIA

The State of Pennsylvania operates the largest alcoholic beverage wholesale and retail distribution system in the United States. Until 1968, no direct sales by producers of alcoholic beverages to consumers or restaurants were allowed. Thus was discouraged the establishment of wineries. Today, twenty-three wineries operate in Pennsylvania, with only three of them founded prior to the enactment of the state's Farm Winery Law that allows wineries which produce no more than 100,000 US gallons annually to sell directly to consumers and to restaurants.

CONESTOGA VINEYARDS, INC

This winery was founded in 1963 by Melvin S. Gordon, who sold his wine to the state stores. Now owned by David and Patricia Fondots, the 29,000-US gallon winery, located eight miles east of Valley Forge, produces its wines principally from French-American hybrids.

MAZZA VINEYARDS, INC

Mazza Vineyards was founded in 1972 by Joseph Mazza and his son Robert. They are experimenting with German, Alsatian and French *viniferas*: White Riesling, Chardonnay, Gewürztraminer, Pinot Gris and Cabernet Sauvignon. The 50,000-US gallon winery also produces wines from hybrids as well as from *labrusca*.

PENN-SHORE VINEYARDS, INC

Penn-Shore Vineyards, founded in 1969, has 125 acres of vineyards. Owned by a group of growers, led by wine-growers George Luke, Blair McCord and George Sceiford, the winery has 175,000 US gallons of storage capacity. The winery produces fourteen wines, including various shades of Catawba and sparkling wines.

PRESQUE ISLE WINE CELLARS

Presque Isle was founded by former home wine-maker Douglas Moorehead, who planted hybrids as well as *viniferas* in the family vineyards as early as 1960. In 1969, a 10,000-US gallon winery was built at the town of North East in Erie County. The winery owns twenty acres of vineyards planted to Aligoté, Gamay Beaujolais, Chardonnay, Cabernet Sauvignon and French hybrids.

MARYLAND

BOORDY VINEYARD

The most significant wine story in Maryland is Boordy Vineyard, which also parallels the life of Philip Wagner, one of America's most prominent wine-makers and viticulturists. He was an amateur wine-maker who, at the end of Prohibition, could no longer secure grapes from California and was unhappy with those he obtained from Delaware. Hybrid vines grown in France attracted him, and he began to import them and to plant his own vineyards at Riverwood, Maryland. Soon after that his home wine-making had outgrown the bounds of amateur, so he bonded his cellars in Riverwood and entered into commercial production. His success with both the hybrid vines and wines showed the way for the rest of an industry not too anxious to follow in the growing of wines of European character under the difficult climate conditions of the northeastern United States. He was so successful that a book followed called *American Wines and Winemaking*, that is still accurate and authoritative, retitled *Grapes Into Wine* in the fifth edition.

Four wines are produced under the Boordy Vineyard label. They are Boordy white, red and rosé, and Boordyblümchen, patterned after the Muskateller of Europe. Wagner does not regard any of his wines as great or complex, and thinks they are, at best, pleasant, young wines without any complexity pretensions.

SOUTHEASTERN UNITED STATES

Although North Carolina claims the native Muscadine family of grapes as her own, it grows throughout the southeastern United States, and is responsible for considerable wine-growing there. The southeast, humid coastal plains provide difficult conditions for *vinifera*'s bunch grapes that are subject to infection by moulds and Pierce's disease. Muscadines, however, grow in clusters and appear resistant to those grape ailments. Best known of the Muscadines is Scuppernong, which makes a light white wine favoured by eastern wine-drinkers, but not specially enjoyed in *vinifera* wine areas like California.

NORTH CAROLINA

THE BILTMORE COMPANY

In 1977, William A. Vanderbilt Cecil, grandson of the American philanthropist, George Washington Vanderbilt, planted three acres of French-American hybrids and built a 5,000-US gallon winery, both experimental, on the Biltmore Estate, near Asheville in the western part of North Carolina.

DUPLIN WINE CELLARS, INC

Duplin Wine Cellars, Inc at Rose Hill in southeastern North Carolina was founded in 1975 by eleven farmers who formed a cooperative 50,000-US gallon winery for production from seventy-five acres of Muscadines. Vintage-dated dry, semi-dry and sweet table wines are made from Carlos, Noble and Scuppernong varieties.

SOUTH CAROLINA

South Carolina's 2,000 acres of vineyards, principally of French-American hybrids and *labruscas*, yield 6,000 tonnes of grapes annually, most of which are shipped to New York, Virginia and Georgia.

TENNER BROTHERS, INC

Tenner Brothers Inc, owned by New York's Canandaigua Wine Company, produces Muscadine and *labrusca* wines from their 500 acres of vines under the labels of Hostess, Richard's Wild Rose and Richard's Peach.

TRULUCK VINEYARDS AND WINERY

At Lake City on the Coastal Plain, dentist Jim Truluck and wife Kay planted fifty acres of French hybrids in 1971 and built a three-storey winery, bonded in 1976, to produce red, white and rosé table wines which are sold locally.

GEORGIA

Muscadines also prevail in the 'Peach State' of Georgia, with much of the crop shipped to Virginia and New York. Largest winery is Atlanta's Monarch Wine Company, founded in 1936. Interestingly, with 2,000,000 US gallons of storage capacity, it is the largest producer of peach wine in the world.

FLORIDA

Historical speculation suggests that the first wine made in America was produced by French Huguenots from Scuppernong grapes at Fort Caroline in 1565. Yet the industry has never grown in any significant proportion, limiting itself to Muscadine, fruit and berry wines.

TODHUNTER INTERNATIONAL, INC

Todhunter International, Inc, also founded in 1972, produces table and dessert wines, all of which are sold in bulk. The 166,000-US gallon winery is located in West Palm Beach, a fashionable area for retired people and tourism.

ALABAMA

PERDIDO VINEYARDS

Alabama's lone winery is Perdido Vineyards, founded in 1979 at Perdido, a small town fifty miles northeast of Mobile. Wines include table and fruit produced from its fifty acres of vineyards, consisting principally of Scuppernongs and other Muscadine varieties planted in 1972. Founders of the 20,000-us gallon winery are engineer, Jim Eddins, and his wife biologist, Marianne, who is the wine-maker.

MISSISSIPPI

ALMARLA VINEYARDS

The newest winery is Almarla Vineyards, founded in 1979 by Dr Alex and Margaret Mathers at Matherville, near the eastern border of Mississippi in Wayne County. Dr Mathers was formerly director of scientific services for the Bureau of Alcohol, Tobacco and Firearms, the agency in the us Treasury Department responsible for regulation of the American wine industry. The 30,000-us gallon winery produces table wine from twenty acres.

THOUSAND OAKS VINEYARD AND WINERY

Thousand Oaks Vineyard and Winery, founded in 1978 near Columbus, is the property of William J. Burgin, who was the author of Mississippi's Native Wine Law, which reduced the state's winery licence fee from $1,800 to $10 annually and lowered the wine tax from 35 cents to 5 cents per us gallon on wine made principally from Mississippi fruit. The winery's storage capacity of 5,000 us gallons uses twenty-two acres of winery-owned grapes to make table wines.

THE WINERY RUSHING

The first Mississippi winery to take advantage of the new wine law was The Winery Rushing, founded in 1977. Ottis Rushing and his son Sam, an agronomist, converted their dairy barn into a 29,500-us gallon facility, equipping it with modern, refrigerated stainless-steel tanks and a centrifuge. The winery owns thirty-five acres of vineyards east of Merigold in the northwestern part of the state.

VIRGINIA

The State of Virginia has a rich wine history, dating back to Thomas Jefferson, who tried without success to plant *vinifera* at Monticello. Current vintners and wineries are Archie Smith of Meredyth Vineyards, Farfelu, which belongs to Charles and Lou Raney, La Abra, owned by Al Weed, Barboursville vineyards and Piedmont Winery. Two other ventures are also under way, notably by William Benton, who planted vines of both hybrid and *vinifera* varieties, and V. W. Lane who is planting a 600-acre vineyard. Smith's Meredyth Vineyards emphasizes Seyval Blanc and Villard Blanc among the whites and Chancellor and Villard Noir among the reds. Autrora, Foch and Rougeon are also employed. At Farfelu French-American varietals have been planted.

KENTUCKY

CANE RIDGE

Kentucky boasts one winery, Cane Ridge, located in an area with the unlikely names of Paris and Bourbon County. It is listed in official records as Kentucky Winery No. 1 and is situated on thirty-seven acres. Founded by Dr Carlton Colcord, French-American hybrids have performed well, with emphasis on Chelois and De Chaunac for reds. Whites are produced from Villard Blanc, Aurora, Seyval, Vidal and Baco. Grapes are hand picked and pressed in wooden basket presses. No sugar or water are added, contrary to established practice in other eastern wineries.

THE MIDWEST

MISSOURI

Wine has been made in Missouri since the nineteenth century, although Prohibition closed all wineries except for two monastery-operated ones. Today, there are thirteen wineries scattered along the Missouri River and its tributaries. The state's 2,500 acres of vineyards are planted principally in what is called the 'Big Prairie' section, better known outside Missouri as the Ozark Plateau, south of the Missouri River. The first official American *appellation* granted in June 1950 was to the Augusta viticultural area, located thirty miles west of St Louis. Montelle and Mount Pleasant are the two wineries which operate in this area.

MONTELLE VINEYARDS, INC

Founded in 1969 by Clayton and Nissel Byers, Montelle is limited to 2,600 US gallons of storage capacity and six acres of French-American hybrid vineyards.

MOUNT PLEASANT VINEYARDS

Mount Pleasant is a restoration of a nineteenth-century winery by Lucian Dressel. The winery has 60,000 US gallons of storage capacity and twenty-five acres of vineyards, planted to hybrids and native American varieties.

BARDENHEIER'S WINE CELLARS

The largest winery is Bardenheier's Wine Cellars, founded in 1873, operated by the four grandsons of the founder, and engages principally in blending and bottling of California wines for sale in thirty mid-western states. The four brothers planted their own seventy-five acres of vineyards to native American and French-American hybrid varieties in the early 1970s and now produce their own wines.

STONE HILL WINE COMPANY, INC

Stone Hill, situated on an old historical site in Hermann, west of Augusta, was founded in 1965 by James Hill. Wines are produced from Catawba, Niagara and Norton Seedling, native American varieties, planted on fifty-five acres belonging to the winery. The storage capacity is 110,000 US gallons.

WISCONSIN

THE WOLLERSHEIM WINERY, INC

Robert Wollersheim acquired in 1973 an old stone winery near Sauk City, which dates from the 1840s. He planted twenty acres of French-American hybrids and installed 30,000 US gallons of storage capacity. Subsequently, he discovered that the old winery had been owned in the 1840s by none other than Agoston Haraszthy, the Hungarian immigrant who later made grape-growing history in California. The winery building is now listed in the National Register of Historic Places.

ILLINOIS

Most of the state's 7,000,000 US gallons of wine annually are produced by Mogen David Corporation in Chicago, which uses grapes from Michigan, Missouri, Pennsylvania and New York.

THOMPSON WINERY

One small winery should be remembered, however. The Thompson Winery is located forty miles south of Chicago in the basement of an ancient Illinois Central Railroad station near Monee. The 18,000-US gallon winery sits in the midst of thirty acres of French-American hybrid grapes, amongst which are interspersed a few White Riesling and Chardonnay. Now owned by Dr John E. Thompson, the winery specializes in production of bottle-fermented sparkling wines. The winery produces two sparkling wines, a *brut* and a rosé-pink style. A line of table wines has been added, together with fruit and berry wines.

ARKANSAS

Arkansas is generally not considered a wine-producing state. However, wines have been produced there since the nineteenth century. Emphasis was upon *labrusca*, Scuppernong and Muscadine grapes, many of which grew wild. Five wineries now concentrate on the production of table wines, including Johannisberg Rieslings being made by one, Wiederkehr Cellars, near Altus in the west central portion of the state, which are as flavourful and enjoyable as many being made in California. During Prohibition, the nationally famed Welch Company built a grape-juice plant at Springdale with acreage planted to Concord. Protective tax legislation at Repeal encouraged the establishment of Arkansas wineries, and for a time the number increased, but the prosperity ended soon because of optional state legislation permitting local county Prohibition statutes. So many counties voted 'dry' that twenty-five years after Repeal, fewer than twenty wineries were operating in Arkansas.

MICHIGAN

Michigan ranks fourth among the states in grape growing and fifth in wine production. However, Michigan wines are not well known outside their immediate areas. The apparent reason is the protective tax legislation of the 1930s which attempted to preserve the Michigan wine market for Michigan wines. Under this law, table wines from outside the state are taxed at 50 cents per US gallon, and Michigan wines at only 4 cents per gallon, provided they are made at least 75 per cent from Michigan grapes. The result was that Michigan wineries made no attempt to compete with out-of-state premium wines. After the Second World War, some of the customers of Michigan wineries discovered that they preferred out-of-state wines to the local product, and so sales of Michigan wines began to shrink until, in 1965, they accounted for less than a third of total sales in the state. At that point, the Michigan Wine Institute and its members began a concerted effort to upgrade the quality of Michigan wines.

THE BRONTE CHAMPAGNE AND WINES COMPANY, INC

The first Michigan winery to improve quality significantly was the Bronte Champagne and Wines Company. Angelo Spinazzi, the wine-maker at Bronte, was among the first to work with French-American hybrids. He planted Bronte's first fifty acres of hybrids, beginning in 1953 and his Baco Dinner Wine, introduced in 1962, was the first commercial wine to bear the name of a French-American hybrid grape. By 1975, Spinazzi had replaced the rest of Bronte's Concord vines with hybrids and introduced two new wines made from the hybrids, Beau Blanc and Beau Rouge.

ST JULIAN WINE COMPANY, INC

St Julian, started in 1921 in Windsor, Canada, as Meconi Wine Cellars, is Michigan's oldest and largest premium winery. It was moved to Detroit upon Repeal, then to Paw Paw at the end of the 1930s. The winery produces forty different *labrusca* and hybrid table, sparkling and dessert wines. Modernization, which includes the addition of new cooperage and stainless-steel fermenters, began in 1980. Wines today are a decent Vidal Blanc sparkling wine, a Seyval Blanc table wine, and a *solera* cream sherry, produced under the *flor* process. The wine-maker since 1974 has been Charles Catherman, with experience at Giumarra Vineyards in California and Warner Vineyards in Michigan.

TABOR HILL VINEYARD

By contrast, Tabor Hill Vineyard has emphasized *vinifera* grapes and was the first new winery to be started in Michigan in twenty-five years when it was founded in 1970. Founder Len Olson firmly believed that *vinifera* grapes are necessary to the production of fine Michigan wines and was the first to grow White Riesling and Chardonnay in Michigan. His *vinifera* wines are consistently good and in blind tastings are frequently mistaken for California wines.

WARNER VINEYARDS, INC

The largest winery in Michigan is Warner Vineyards, which produces a long list of wines, mostly from hybrids. Notable in the assortment of hybrid varietals are Maréchal, Seyval Blanc, Aurora Blanc and Chancellor. Improvement has been steady in the Warner wines since 1973, when Richard Vine became Warner's wine-maker. Although he has now left the winery, the upgrading in quality has continued.

The American 'Wine Boom' has increased interest in table wines everywhere in Michigan. While proliferation of wineries has not been great, eight new wineries have been founded in the state during the 1970s. Consequently, over half the state's wineries are less than ten years of age, and if consumers provide the support, Michigan should make an impact on the American wine scene.

OHIO

CATAWBA ISLAND WINE COMPANY

Norman Mantey, president of Mantey Vineyards, is also president of Catawba Island Wine Company, which sell under the label name of Mon Ami Champagne Company. Mon Ami's wines include, in addition to several sparkling wines (made from *labrusca* and French hybrid grapes), a Chardonnay.

MANTEY VINEYARDS, INC

One of two wineries in Venice to trace its origin to the nineteenth century, Mantey Vineyards is a family enterprise operated by brothers Norman, Paul and Don, respectively, president, wine-maker and vineyard manager. The emphasis was always on Catawba until plantings of French hybrids and Johannisberg Riesling took over. Now there are Baco Noir, Seyval Blanc, Baco Rosé and Johannisberg Riesling wines.

MEIER'S WINE CELLARS, INC

Of the forty wineries operating in Ohio, the largest and best known is Meier's Wine Cellars at Silverton, northeast of Cincinnati. Meier's grapes are Catawba, but there are also plantings of Delaware and French-American hybrids, such as Baco No. 1 and Seibel, and experimental plantings of White Riesling, Gewürztraminer and Chardonnay. Approximately 1,000 tonnes of grapes are harvested from the vineyards of Isle St George annually, which are crushed near the boat dock with the must shipped by ferry in stainless-steel tanks across the Lake Erie channel and by truck to the winery for fermentation. Although the Catawba produces a distinctive wine, appreciated by many wine-drinkers, it appears that the future of Meier's wines may lie with *vinifera*, provided the plantings on Isle St George produce the desired quality.

THE STEUK WINE COMPANY

The Steuk Wine Company at Venice, four miles east of Sandusky, dating from 1855, claims to be the oldest winery in the United States still owned and operated by the founding family. Today Steuk has a small vineyard of four and a half acres and 10,000 US gallons of storage capacity. Responsibility for wine-making now lies with Timothy Parker, who was hired to work in the cellars following the death of Steuk in 1975. The winery continues to produce some of the country's finest Catawba wines: sweet, sparkling or dry, which can direct the serious wine-lover to understanding and appreciating the Catawba.

The American 'Wine Boom' appears to be reaching Ohio. Fourteen new wineries were founded during the 1970s. Experimental vineyards planted at the behest of the Ohio State Department, along the north bank of the Ohio River, have shown that good wine-producing vines could thrive along a stretch of the river from Cincinnati to Marietta. Although the grapes are mainly French-American hybrids, some good wines are being made, and it appears that Ohio is not to be discounted as a major American wine producer.

TEXAS

Approximately one hundred vineyards are producing wine grapes in Texas, most of them planted to Muscadines. One, Val Verde, the only pre-Prohibition winery to re-open upon Repeal, has produced wine every year, except during the Prohibition era, since it was founded in 1883. Of interest to Texans and wine-lovers alike are two experimental vineyards under way in widely separated regions of the state.

LLANO ESTACADO WINERY

The first to be established was the Llano Estacado Winery, founded near Lubbock by three professors from Texas Technical University in 1974. The 15,000-US gallon winery produces wine from fourteen experimental acres (the first seven of which were planted in 1971) of *viniferas*, French-American hybrids and Muscadines. Their first wines were released in 1978.

GLASSCOCK VINEYARD

A second experimental vineyard which should excite even more interest is that planted entirely to *vinifera* varieties by Gretchen Glasscock, an heiress to a Texas oil and cattle fortune, on Blue Mountain, 200 miles southeast of El Paso in western Texas. Planting of the forty-acre vineyard, situated at 5,000 feet above sea level, was to Sauvignon Blanc, Cabernet Sauvignon, Chenin Blanc and Merlot.

MEXICO

Successful *vinifera* wine-making on the North American continent began with the Spanish conquest of Mexico at the beginning of the sixteenth century. Commercial wineries in Mexico were amongst the first to be established in the New World in 1593 and 1626, at Parras, 500 miles north of Mexico. Both are still producing today. Wine-making progress in Mexico was interrupted, first by the 1595 edict of

Philip II against new vineyard planting or replacement of old, as a stringent measure to protect Spain's wine industry from competition. Mexico's governing viceroys repeated Philip's edict for the next 200 years and, indeed, some even went so far as to uproot established vineyards. Cultivation continued despite the order, and became an important factor in fomenting Mexico's revolution against Spain at the beginning of the nineteenth century. The revolution, itself, was the second factor to slow down Mexico's wine development. However, as the post-revolution turmoil subsided, commercial wine-making resumed with the help of two California wine pioneers. The first and earliest of these helpers from California was James Concannon of Concannon Vineyards, who received in 1889 a concession to introduce better grape varieties into Mexico. Concannon shipped several million Livermore cuttings along with Spanish-language pamphlets to provide vine care guidance. The entire project was completed in 1910, just as the second California pioneer, Antonio Perelli-Minetti arrived. He imported additional cuttings from California, namely Zinfandel, Petite Sirah, Malaga and Flame Tokay.

At the end of the Second World War, the Mexican government increased fourfold the tariffs on imported wines and placed quotas on wine importation. As a consequence, imported wines are priced to the consumer at levels which are two to ten times those of Mexican wines. Perhaps this encouraged plantings of grapes, and acreage increased from 4,000 acres in 1939 to 100,000 in 1977. Moreover, European and American companies were encouraged to establish plants for the production of brandy, and Pedro Domecq, Martell, Seagram and Osborne all have facilities there. Consumption of wine has not increased as rapidly as has grape acreage. Wine is still a relatively new product to beer-drinking Mexicans, who rely on the beverage to cool down their highly spiced diet.

There are nine main vineyard districts in Mexico described by Leon Adams as: 'northern Baja California, the Laguna district at the border of Coahuila and Durango, Parras and Saltillo in Coahuila, Aquascalientes, the San Juan de Rio region in Querétaro, the area around Fresnillo in Zacatecas, Delicias in Chihuahua and the Hermosillo-Caborca district in Sonora.' The best table wines produced in Mexico in recent years have come from Baja California, notably from Bodegas de Santo Tomas, whose cellars stretch along Avenida Miramar in Ensenada, approximately a two-hour drive south of San Diego. A unique period evolved during the 1970s when Beaulieu's consulting wine-maker, Dimitri Tchelistcheff, son of the great André, attempted to produce North-California-like wines such as Chardonnay, Chenin Blanc, Pinot Noir, Barbera and Cabernet Sauvignon. All wines have been expertly made. However, vineyard practices still leave much to be desired. Tchelistcheff did all he could to rectify this and probably would have succeeded had he remained. Wine progress has stopped at the level it had reached under Tchelistcheff's guidance. None the less, there are disciples that remain, and as they become more confident, perhaps the Tchelistcheff era can be expanded.

CANADIAN WINES

Two Canadian provinces grow wine grapes, Ontario and British Columbia.

ONTARIO

The Ontario district, located in the east, is on the Niagara peninsula connecting southeastern Ontario to New York's Niagara County. The wines resemble those of New York, utilizing many of the same grape varieties. Originally planted to *labrusca*, the region today emphasizes French-American hybrids and *vinifera*. Ninety per cent of Canada's vineyards, some 23,000 acres, are here, as are eight of her twenty-five wineries, which produce 75 per cent of her wines. The eight wineries are spread over a narrow strip thirty-five miles in length.

BRITISH COLUMBIA

Two thousand miles to the west is Canada's second viticultural region, British Columbia. This region grows a smaller portion of the grapes used to make the wines produced there, importing grapes from the State of Washington, and frequently from as far away as California. The wines tasted to date are uninteresting, but probably will improve as more grapes are imported from Washington. British Columbia's grape-growing district extends north from the Washington-Canadian border for 120 miles along a narrow strip from Osoyoos to Okanagan Lake.

Wines are produced in the other Canadian provinces of Nova Scotia, New Brunswick, Saskatchewan, Alberta, Manitoba and Quebec. Canadian wine consumption has increased during the past ten years, not unlike other parts of the North American continent. This has spurred an increase in test plantings of hybrids and *viniferas*, particularly in the Fraser River and the Okanagan valleys of British Columbia. Interestingly, half of the wine produced in Canada is of the home-made variety, largely due to the government control and operation of retail stores which frequently do not stock an adequate selection of wines from Europe and the United States. However, in recent years a greater professional attempt is underway to improve selections, allowing better French wines and a greater and better selection of California's wines. With Canadians visiting the United States, especially California, a thirst for California's wines has produced a telling effect on the government's foreign selections.

Technology

That Prohibition was disastrous for the American wine industry is without dispute. Certainly it accomplished what economic depressions and the phylloxera had been unable to do but, more importantly, it halted and no doubt regressed wine technology. Even the Volstead Act, the Prohibition-enforcement legislation, with its loophole which allowed the head of a household to make 200 gallons of wine per year for personal use, had negative results for the post-Repeal wine industry. The demand for home wine-making grapes that would stand shipping rigours grew, motivating grape-growers to graft vines to Carignane and Alicante Bouschet. These varieties were big, tough-skinned and would survive a trip to the east coast, but they were not as fine as the varieties they replaced. By 1925, despite Prohibition, there were nearly 630,000 acres of grapes growing in California, an all-time high until recent years. Although consumption of wine appears to have increased during the same period, commercial wineries did not benefit. At Prohibition's end, there was an immediate rush of consumers who preferred to drink wine, followed by a rapid influx of wineries into production. The new wine-makers were short of experience and equipment and what was available was poor and inefficient. Moreover, vineyards had been grafted over to coarser varieties; hence, coarse, uninteresting wines. Within two years after Repeal more than half the post-Repeal wine industry entrants had quickly departed as did the new customers, back to home wine-making or to their familiar bootleggers. The survivors were left with a commercial wine market in which some 75 or 80 per cent of sales soon turned out to be inexpensive 20 per cent alcohol dessert and apéritif wines. Dry table wines were generic blends labelled with European names. In the post-Second World War era, Americans became more and more interested in table wine. As a consequence, better wines were demanded. By the end of the 1960s, table-wine sales had come to account for half of a rapidly growing wine market as sales of 20 per cent dessert and apéritif wines declined. By 1968, the United States was clearly in the midst of a 'Wine Boom'. Increased demand for varietal wines soon led to increases in grape plantings. Thus, for the first time since Repeal, wine-makers had wine grapes in sufficient quantity to allow the production of wines without any significant supplement of raisin and table grapes. The 'Boom' brought with it not only an increase in wine-grape acreage, but an influx of new wine-makers, many of them very young. The young crop came particularly from the oenology programme at the University of California at Davis or at Fresno State University. Greater sales bought the new tools of an ever-increasing technology, such as temperature-controlled stainless-steel fermenters which replaced open-top redwood or concrete vats, centrifuges for clarification of both juice and wines by those who could afford them. Small oak cooperage for ageing was added, it seemed, everywhere.

Technology in the vineyard improved. New treatments developed by the Enology Department at the University of California at Davis provided virus-free grapevines, which improved quality and yield. Developments in grafting of *vinifera* canes or buds to *labrusca* roots resulted in higher survival rates. Additionally, mechanical harvesting and field crushing reached new highs in quality and effectiveness. Prior to the installation of temperature-controlled, stainless-steel fermentation tanks, temperature control during fermentation was largely a hit-or-miss proposition. Remarkable improvements in aroma and flavour, particularly of white wines, resulted, producing fruitier, livelier, more aromatic wines. Temperature-control flexibility has allowed wine-makers to stretch the length of fermentations to several months, by holding the must at temperatures which greatly reduce the metabolic rate of the yeast. Accurate temperature control has also permitted fermentation at elevated temperatures. Stainless-steel fermentation tanks have the added advantage of being essentially a neutral environment in which to conduct fermentations. Moreover, they can be kept immaculately clean in a way which redwood or concrete fermenters never could. Perhaps the centrifuge is the most useful tool in the hands of a skilful wine-maker. Employment of the centrifuge is to achieve greater clarity of juice as it goes into the fermentation tank and to regulate the speed with which a wine can be clarified following the completion of fermentation. Maturing in small oak barrels has added an extra dimension. Wood apparently aids in development of depth and complexity, as well as adding a condiment-like character of its own if it is used judiciously. André Tchelistcheff, the wine-maker at Beaulieu for over thirty years, must receive credit for introducing small oak ageing to wine-making in California. In addition, by 1966, he had begun the technique of small oak-barrel Chardonnay fermentation, as had Chalone. As Americans continue the practice of better wood usage, more and more French white Burgundy producers, especially in Chablis and the Mâconnais, have forsaken the wood. It is for Californians, then, particularly in Chardonnay production, to lead the way in barrel-ageing and barrel-fermenting, certainly where new oak is concerned.

Another important technical advance came during the mid-1950s when Hanzell Vineyards racked and bottled under inert gases to protect from oxidation. This practice was eminently successful, since older Hanzell wines, otherwise consigned to over-the-hill senility, taste as vigorous today as when produced. Vineyardists employed a similar technique with grapes by covering them with a layer of carbon dioxide in gondolas that move from the fields to the crushers. Mechanical harvesting and field crushing play important roles, too, especially in the light of necessity to move grapes long distances. It is not uncommon for wineries to reach up or down into other areas, perhaps one hundred miles or more, to secure the best of grapes.

Initially, field crushing was necessary to merge with mechanical harvesting. Since there were excessive delays in directing grapes into fermenters, a technique for field crushing became a natural by-product. It is not uncommon for grapes to be mechanically picked, field crushed in moments, and then transported under a layer of inert gas to the winery. While the evidence is not final, mechanical harvesting and field crushing have been a particular boon to Mirassou Vineyards, which pioneered in the utilization and perfection of these techniques as a matter of necessity.

Less obvious to the untrained eye are the advanced techniques that affect the planting of vineyards. At the University of California at Davis, researchers are convinced that plant viruses reduce vineyard yield and grape quality as well as the quality of wine made from the grapes from diseased vines. They have developed a heat-treatment technique which produces virus-free vines. Yields are improved as a result of the vines' virus-free state, as is quality. Even root stock has had the benefit of technological advances; the currently favoured root stock appears to be Rupestris x St George, an improvement over root stocks of earlier years. It is now common to graft vines in the nursery so that they go into the vineyard with at least a year's growth on them. Fewer failed plants result, and the vineyard begins to produce a not insignificant crop a full year ahead of field-grafted vineyards.

Technology of wine-making in California, although it is advanced and represents a high state of the art, is really relatively new. As wine hobbyists, professional vintners, and capital-intensive corporations merge their hard-earned knowledge with the academic world of the major oenology schools, California will be, as it appears to be already, the bastion of wine technology for the rest of the world.

Appellations

Historically and traditionally American wineries enjoyed the practice of giving European place-names to their wines, such as burgundy, chablis, rhine, etc. This practice is, at best, described as generic labelling, a labelling system that continues to this day, notwithstanding the great interest in and increase in use of varietal labelling. After the Second World War, as American wine consumers and producers became more familiar with such varietal names as Chardonnay and Cabernet Sauvignon, labelling grew more specific with the practice of identifying vineyards as well as grape variety. Today, it is not uncommon for a consumer to search out a particular, significant vineyard as well as the grape variety or the regional *appellation*. Notwithstanding this specification, industry and consumers desire yet more specificity in the use of geographic place-names which they believe need to be defined, delimited and officially sanctioned. The California wine industry, in particular, is in a state similar to that of pre-*appellation d'origine contrôlée* France. Legal codification of place-names in France evolved over hundreds of years, but it may not take quite as long as that in California. Such internationally known names as the Napa Valley, Santa Clara Valley and Livermore, will come under the scrutiny of the US Federal Bureau of Alcohol, Tobacco and Firearms within the 1980s.

Geographical designations have made their mark on American wine labels as the result of a more or less informal practice adopted by the Bureau, which authorized them to be used if 75 per cent of the wine had been produced from grapes grown in the geographic area so identified. However, the Bureau has grown more and more reluctant in recent years to approve labels containing geographic designations in the absence of formal delimitation of the geographic region. The key issue is the question of whether the regions are simply to be defined by geo-political and viticultural boundaries, or whether the wineries situated in these areas and utilizing specific viticultural names will be allowed to produce wines there without any relation of grapes to soil.

The three-storey winery at Trefethen Vineyards in the Napa Valley,
built in 1886, was constructed of huge timbers and redwood walls

11

The Wines of South America

DAVID STEVENS MW

A director of Matthew Clark and Sons Limited, London, David Stevens MW has contributed regular articles on wine to newspapers and magazines for the past thirty years. His work in the wine trade takes him regularly to South America, especially to Argentina. He is also a former chairman of the Wine and Spirit Education Trust.

Historical records indicate that, although the vine was indigenous to the northern continent, it was not until the middle of the sixteenth century, following the colonization of Mexico by the Spanish *conquistadores*, that it was introduced to what we have come to know as Latin America. In the reports and chronicles of the sixteenth and seventeenth centuries there are many references to wine-making in the New World by the settlers from the Old, but the native grapes that they used were almost certainly the forerunners of the *Vitis labrusca* which today support the massive wine industry of New York State and the province of Ontario.

Vitis vinifera, the European grape species, was first planted in Mexico around the year 1545 by Jesuit priests with the express purpose of providing wine for the sacrament, although it was not long before the entrepreneurial instincts of the rich Spanish merchants led to the introduction of vineyards on a commercial scale, first in the central part of the country and spreading eventually to the long, thin peninsula to the west that was to become Baja California. The actual grape that derived from these first cuttings was in all probability the Criolla which, like its Chilean counterpart, the País, was to predominate in South America for three centuries.

On the face of it, it appears something of a paradox that in the country where the European vine was first introduced to the Americas, the wine industry that one finds today is much less important than in countries far to the south, but the fact is that as the Spanish explorers and colonists leap-frogged their way through the Central American states – Peru and onwards into Chile and Argentina – they were to find lands far better suited to the cultivation of the vine. Also, it must be said that unlike these last two countries, Mexico never benefited to the same extent from the specialist viticultural knowledge which the immigrants from France, Germany, Italy and Spain brought with them towards the end of the nineteenth century. Mexico has about 52,000 hectares under vine, producing only about 140,000 hectolitres per annum, with Baja California remaining the centre of the industry; one of the best known wineries is Santo Tomas.

In Europe, and North America it is not widely known that South America today can boast of having the fourth biggest wine-producing country in the western world, namely Argentina:

Vineyards in the province of Mendoza in Argentina, with the Andes mountains in the background

	1973	1974	1975	1976	1977	1978	1979
France	82,425	75,482	68,454	73,035	52,345	58,170	82,000
Italy	76,716	76,867	69,814	65,850	65,000	69,960	79,500
Spain	40,000	36,190	31,496	26,400	22,190	29,031	40,000
Argentina	22,566	27,183	21,020	26,939	22,588	20,426	26,000

('000s of hectolitres)

South America also has a reviving, quality-based wine industry in Chile, who takes tenth place in the world league of wine producers, and an interesting and potentially very significant development in part of Brazil. Of the other South American countries, Peru, despite earlier associations with the original vines brought from Mexico, is too hot and arid for successful table-wine production, although a local brandy called Pisco is distilled from wine made from the País grape. A well-made Pisco sour can be an enervating experience! Very small quantities of rather inferior wine are made in Bolivia, Equador, Colombia and Paraguay for home consumption; Venezuela has no vineyards of its own, but imported grape concentrate is fermented and turned into 'made' wine; Uruguay, on the other hand, perhaps because of its proximity to the Rio Grande do Sul of Brazil, is beginning to expand its wine industry and the quality is improving.

THE WINES OF ARGENTINA

Some uncertainty surrounds the circumstances in which vines were first introduced to the country; it is known that in 1551, Don Bartolomé de Terrazas planted the first Criolla vines at Cuzco in Peru, the spiritual home of the Incas, who were taught the art of vine cultivation by this enlightened Spanish missionary. From there, vine cuttings were taken to Chile, and in 1557 settlers in Santiago del Estero probably introduced the first vines to Argentina, although some historians maintain that they came from Bolivia through the Humahuaca Pass. At first, vineyard planting was restricted, with convents and Catholic missionaries making just sufficient wine for the celebration of the mass and the spiritual well-being of the colonial communities for whom they felt responsible. Although Argentina was settled from the east as well as from the west, it was in the foothills of the Andes that the best conditions were found for the cultivation of the vine. The city of Mendoza was founded in 1561, and the first major vineyards there and in the province of San Juan followed between 1569 and 1589. Through the use of dams and irrigation systems, wine production increased rapidly until it far exceeded local demand. Because of the relative isolation of the Andean provinces from the growing centres of population to the east, it became vitally important to produce wine of quality which could reasonably be expected to survive long journeys by horse-drawn waggons in varying climatic conditions and the waggon trains often drew the unwanted and extremely hostile attentions of Indian tribes.

The beginning of the nineteenth century saw a big influx of European immigrants. The railway between Mendoza and Buenos Aires was completed in 1885, and it brought a new dimension to Argentina's growing wine industry. By 1900, a further wave of settlers had arrived, many from the traditional wine-producing countries of France, Italy and Spain. In addition to their customs and traditions, they brought with them up-to-date viticultural methods as well as their native vines; Cabernet, Malbec, Pinot, Barbera, Moscatel and Pedro Ximénez began to spread rapidly throughout the Argentine vineyards, and the old colonial ways became subject to the new technology: the modern Argentine wine industry was born.

Climate and Soil

Argentina's vineyards are situated in the west of the country at the foot of the Andes range, and extend from the Tropic of Capricorn in the north to 40°s. There are approximately 350,000 hectares under vine and the area is still growing. 72 per cent of all the country's vineyards are found in the province of Mendoza, 18 per cent in San Juan province, approximately 5 per cent in the Rio Negro and the rest spread through the northern provinces of La Rioja, Catamarca and Salta.

Apart from the Rio Negro and Neuquén districts to the south, the climate is of a semi-desert nature, with a very low annual rainfall of between 200 and 250 millimetres. The dry, clear air and lack of humidity ensure that the grapes always reach full maturity and the risk of cryptogamic disease of the vine is greatly reduced. Summer temperatures vary from 10° to 40°C, and the four seasons are well defined, with winter temperatures on or below 0°C, allowing the vines essential vegetative rest. What rainfall there is occurs mainly in the summer months; winter rain high up in the Andes is important because, throughout the area, the vineyards are irrigated and depend to a considerable extent on water from the melted snow.

Wine regions 1 Atacama 2 Coquimbo 3 Aconcagua 4 Valparaiso 5 Santiago 6 O'Higgins 7 Colchagua 8 Curicó 9 Talca 10 Maule 11 Linares 12 Nuble 13 Concepcion 14 Bió-Bió 15 Malleco 16 Cautin 17 Jujuy 18 Salta 19 Catamarca 20 Santiago del Estero 21 La Rioja 22 San Juan 23 Mendoza 24 Neuquén 25 Rio Negro 26 Salto 27 Colonia 28 Canelones 29 Montevideo 30 Rio Grande do Sul 31 Santa Caterina 32 Sao Paulo

This water is stored in strategically placed reservoirs and distributed throughout the vineyards by an intricate network of canals and ditches. The system is one of the most advanced of its kind in the world and is carefully regulated by a highly efficient water control board. In more recent years, this essential water supply has been augmented by the drilling of deep bore holes which has led not only to greatly increased production but also to a programme of extensive afforrestation. Tall trees now line the canals, ditches and roads, giving much needed shade to the vines during the heat of the summer. The overall landscape is unique, and the cultivated areas resemble oases in the otherwise barren surroundings. With ample water and sun available, it follows that the make-up of the soil is not such an important factor in the production of wine as it is in some countries, although the selection of vine species to suit the ground is encouraged by the Instituto Nacional de Vitivinicultura who have made a careful study of this aspect of cultivation in recent years. Soils vary slightly by regions, but a loose, deep, sandy texture predominates, as one would expect from reclaimed desert, although substrata of clay can also be found.

Cultivation of the Vine

Before the young vines are planted, the ground is levelled by bulldozer, with just a slight slope to facilitate the flow of water. Four methods of irrigation are used: simple flooding of the vineyards; the running of water along furrows in which the vines are planted; overhead sprinkling; drip irrigation to each vine from underground feeder pipes. The latter method allows for the more precise regulation of water supply depending on the state of the vine, but it is expensive to install. Once the ground is prepared, the grower must decide which system of vine training is to be used. The choice will depend largely on the type of grapes being grown and whether they are to be made into quality wine or *vino de mesa*. Over half the vines in Argentina are trained on the high or low Espalderos or Espalier system introduced by the European settlers of the mid and late nineteenth century, but there is a growing movement towards the Parral Cuyano or trellis system, particularly in the hotter areas. The advantages of the trellis are that it produces much higher yields, facilitates picking, protects the grapes from reflected heat from the soil and, in some areas, permits the growing of a secondary crop beneath the vine.

A wide range of grape species is grown, although that hardy original, the Criolla Grande, together with its near relative the Cereza, are still the most common and account for nearly 25 per cent of the total planted area. In common with the Ferral and Garnacha, they are neither black nor white, and can best be described as rosé grapes growing in huge bunches that can weigh as much as 10 kilograms each, producing vast quantities of juice. Black grapes account for 31 per cent of the total, with the Malbec predominant. Other red wine species are the Lambrusco, Barbera, Nebbiolo, Bonarda, Tempranillo, Pinot Noir, Merlot and, with the increasing demand for fine wines, the Cabernet Sauvignon. White grapes are grown in 18 per cent of the vineyards, the main varieties being the Palomino, Moscato d'Asti, Torrontes, Muscadelle of Alexandria, Sauvignon, Chenin Blanc, Sémillon and Riesling. Table grapes and raisin production account for the remaining 26 per cent.

The Harvest and the Making of the Wine

The vintage normally starts in mid-February, although some producers are experimenting with the picking of white wine species as early as late-January in order to increase the basic acidity. Because the various vines ripen at different times according to the area, the harvest extends until mid-April. The tremendous yields require massive crushing, fermenting and storage facilities – for instance, the

Mendoza firm of Peñaflor, which is recognized as being one of the biggest wine producers and distributors in the world, has at least forty vats of 10,000 hectolitre capacity, and they will proudly show you a cathedral-like blending tank, or Pileta, capable of holding 45,000 hectolitres of wine. The fact that it is built underground is a reminder that Mendoza has twice been destroyed by earthquakes and that the whole vineyard area lies atop the San Andreas Fault. Vintage time signals the arrival of many itinerant workers from all parts of the country and from neighbouring Bolivia and Paraguay. Because labour is cheap, mechanical picking has not yet become an economic necessity. The grapes are loaded onto lorries in the vineyards, taken in convoy to the *bodegas*, weighed and tipped into rows of hoppers for de-stalking and crushing before being pumped out into the fermentation tanks. Chaptalization is forbidden by law. A big firm like Giol, Peñaflor, Greco or Furlotti is capable of handling $2\frac{1}{2}$ million kilograms of grapes a day. Despite the political and economic uncertainties of recent years, the Argentine wine industry is uncommonly well equipped. The standards of cleanliness during the wine-making process are exemplary, and the techniques of wine storage and handling are in no sense inferior to the best that Europe, California or Australia can offer.

The Wine-Producing Areas

MENDOZA

To approach Mendoza by air on a clear day affords the traveller what must surely be one of the world's most inspiring sights: on the horizon, like ghostly sentinels, the tops of the snow-capped Andes with Aconcagua – at 7,010 metres the highest peak in the Americas – standing out; below, the startling green belt of irrigated vineyards and trees in the midst of scrub and sand. Mendoza itself is a pleasant, modern city with wide streets and lush green parks. It is also the centre of the Argentine wine industry, the headquarters of the Instituto Nacional de Vitivinicultura, and the place where most of the best-known firms have built their *bodegas*.

There are 32,000 separate vineyards in the province of Mendoza covering over 255,000 hectares. In 1890 there were just 6,000 hectares under cultivation, so progress has been rapid. The most important wine areas are in the departments of Maipu, Luyan de Cuy, San Rafael, Lavalle and San Martin, and it is here and in the city of Mendoza itself that most of the 1,300 *bodegas* are situated.

The climate and soil structure are the best in Argentina for grape production. Because the accent is on quality wine, two-thirds of the vines are trained on the Espalier system. The water for irrigation comes both from five mountain rivers rich in mineral deposits which have their origins in the Andean glaciers, and from 17,000 deep wells. The volume of water from these latter man-made sources is equal to the flow of two additional rivers, and the abundance of water is amply demonstrated by the long lanes of shady trees that make the high summer temperatures of up to 36°C quite bearable.

Mendoza is best known for its red wine, with the Malbec being the most common grape variety, but the Cabernet Sauvignon is being widely introduced alongside the Lambrusco, Barbera, Tempranillo, Pinot Noir and Syrah. Nonetheless, the ubiquitous Criolla, and to a lesser extent the Cereza, between them still account for 30 per cent of the total area, with white grapes covering only 15 per cent. The most common white varieties are the Pedro Ximénez, Chenin Blanc, Sémillon, Palomino, Moscatel and, more recently, the Chardonnay and Riesling.

SAN JUAN

The capital of the province, the town of San Juan itself, is situated about 150 kilometres north of Mendoza. Although the soil structure is similar, the climate is even drier and hotter, with rainfall averaging only 150 millimetres annually and peak summer temperatures of 42°C not uncommon. The vineyards are irrigated from the San Juan and Jachal rivers, supplemented by deep wells, and the best areas of production are in the Ullun Zonda and Tulun Valleys. The province has nearly 14,000 vineyards covering 60,000 hectares, and there are over 370 separate *bodegas*. Eighty-six per cent of the vines are trained on the Parral system. Pruning is kept to a minimum, allowing for 25 to 30 buds per plant, and the resulting yields are the highest in Argentina, averaging over 150 hectolitres per hectare.

The most important grape species are the Criolla, Cereza, Pedro Ximénez and Moscatel, with only 10 per cent given over to black varieties. Because of the climatic conditions, musts have an exceptionally high sugar content and a correspondingly low acidity which makes them ideal for concentrating. Until recently, large quantities of concentrated grape juice went to Venezuela, the United Kingdom and Japan for making into various types of wine in those countries. In 1977, the United Kingdom took over 4 million kilograms of concentrated grape juice – nearly 25 per cent of the total exports – but a big rise in prices in the following year greatly curtailed this trade. San Juan province is also the centre for the production of brandy, and of excellent sherry-style wines which are filled into wooden casks and left in the open to mature under the sun.

RIO NEGRO AND NEUQUÉN

In many ways these two attractive provinces are the most interesting of Argentina's wine-producing areas because the climate in its seasons more closely resembles Chile or even Europe. Situated on or around 39°s, the much cooler conditions produce wines with lower alcoholic degree but much higher acidity. Historically, this area has been the centre of Argentina's fruit-growing industry, to which the production of wine has taken second place. The two provinces have a combined population of about half a million people, and their relative isolation on the edge of Patagonia has not encouraged wine growers – until recently – to make good use of the excellent conditions. However, with domestic taste changing towards a more European style of wine, the future of this area looks much brighter. Producers are also beginning to realize that it affords the best type of white wine for the manufacture of so-called 'Champaña'.

Today, there are about 3,700 vineyards covering 17,500 hectares, mostly in the Alto Valle of the Rio Negro. Vines are irrigated by water from the Negro, Neuquén and Colorado rivers, and because of the lower summer temperatures and the emphasis on quality, over two-thirds of the vines are trained on the low Espalier system and Guyot-pruned. Among the black grapes, the most common is the Malbec, followed by the Barbera (most of the vineyards were started by Italian immigrants at the turn of the century), the Syrah, Pinot, Merlot and Cabernet; of the white grapes, the Torrontes is the most popular, followed by the Pedro Ximénez, Sémillon, Chenin Blanc, Pinot Blanc and Malvasia.

LA RIOJA

Although one of the oldest wine-producing areas in the country, production has been limited to approximately 8,000 hectares because of a fundamental lack of water for irrigation. White and rosé grapes predominate, with the Torrontes being the most popular species, followed by the Criolla, Cereza, Moscatel and Ferral. Very few black grapes are grown, and the exceptionally hot climate produces wines of high alcohol and low acidity with a very pronounced bouquet and some sweetness – a style of wine which finds much favour with the Argentines but which wine drinkers in the northern hemisphere would probably dismiss as oxidized and flabby.

SALTA, JUJUY AND CATAMARCA

These three provinces combined cover over 517,998 square kilometres, but there are only 5,500 hectares planted with vines, mostly in Catamarca, where the grapes are used for distillation, and in Salta where wine growing is concentrated to the west of the province in the Calchaqui Valley. Here, the climate is somewhat similar to that of Mendoza, but the soil is much richer. The Torrontes Riojana is the most popular grape species, and Salta wines – particularly the whites – have quite a following within Argentina.

The National Institute of Vitiviniculture

In 1959, the Argentine Congress passed an act unifying all laws relating to the production and distribution of wine, and the Instituto Nacional de Vitivinicultura (the INV) was set up to supervise and assist the industry. Its headquarters are in the city of Mendoza, and there are forty-two branches spread throughout the wine-producing areas, with ten regional laboratories. The INV performs a variety of functions: it concerns itself with research and development within the industry and, in this respect, it coordinates and assists the activities of both official and private organizations by means of grants and scholarships; INV inspectors supervise the wine-making process in all its aspects, from the selection of vines to the analysis of the finished product; the date for the beginning and ending of the harvest is decreed by the Institute; it lays down minimum alcoholic standards and decides when the new wine may be released onto the market; all production figures and stocks must be registered with the INV, and physical checks are carried out by inspectors at regular intervals. Article 17 of the Wine Law clearly defines the products that are subject to the Institute's control, and wine cannot be moved without the covering INV analysis which is printed on the tags and labels of the samples which must accompany each consignment. Wines destined for export are subject to even more stringent regulation and analysis. As interest in exporting grew, the INV set up a special bureau to deal with the specific problems that arose and to assist individual firms with the documentation and shipping of wine. A modern storage plant is being constructed in the dock area of Buenos Aires to facilitate the export of bulk wine and grape concentrate. All the information that stems from the Institute's activities is published annually in the INV's statistical review.

Argentine Wines – How do they Compare?

Traditional wine growers will tell you that irrigated vineyards seldom, if ever, produce great wines, although the advantages in terms of quantity are not in dispute; in the case of Argentina, the average yield per hectare is 70.5 hectolitres, compared with 47.5 in France and 40.4 in Italy. It must also be remembered that Argentina drinks at least 80 litres per capita, the third highest consumption in the world; wine with a meal is the rule rather than the exception for all the social classes and, despite the country's staggering rate of internal inflation, common wine has until recently remained absurdly cheap.

Because consumption was always slightly lower than one year's production, the incentive to export has been minimal, and with one or two notable exceptions, the few firms that did bother to seek customers abroad did so more as a way of gaining prestige and earning foreign currency than as a conscious effort to establish Argentine wines in the world market. Today, that situation is changing rapidly. Massive speculation in ordinary wine pushed prices up by 900 per cent almost overnight. Consumer demand in turn dropped by 15 to 20 per cent as desperate brand owners were forced to put up their prices, exports dried up, and the wine growers, burdened with a much bigger vintage in 1979 than had been anticipated, found themselves holding 40 million hectolitres – or nearly two years' stock.

This economic crisis came at a time when changes in Argentine drinking habits were becoming apparent. The emerging middle class had begun to demand something better for their *pesos*, and the recent influence of the female wine drinker had, in common with the rest of the world, started a swing toward white wine in the land where beef and full-bodied red were once synonymous. The 1980 vintage was bigger than expected and it is obvious even now that the Argentine wine industry will have to be much more outward looking if it is to prosper in the future, with greater emphasis being placed on quality wines both for export and for the ever more discriminating domestic market.

That such wines can be produced there is no doubt. While the Cabernet Sauvignons, Pinot Noirs, Sémillons, Chardonnays and Rieslings will never compare with the great wines of Bordeaux, Burgundy and the Rhine, they can and do compete favourably with the lesser generic wines produced in these countries, and at a price which makes European and Californian varietals look expensive.

At a tasting in September 1979 in London for the Circle of Winewriters, a Cabernet Sauvignon from the fine, old firm of Pascual Toso in Mendoza drew much favourable comment, and in the United States, recent tastings of a Chardonnay and Chenin Blanc from Trapiche also underlined the advances that had been made in white-wine vinification. Today, world demand is for light, dry, crisp white wine with relatively low alcohol and good acidity; the Argentine grower is able to produce white wines to this specification by picking the selected grapes at the end of January or early February and by using cold fermentation and early bottling. One firm that has been extremely successful in using more modern techniques of vinification, storage and bottling is a comparatively new one, Weinert of Mendoza. Financed by a Brazilian businessman, the wine-making is under the control of one of Argentina's leading oenologists, Raoul de la Mota, and the well-known Buenos Aires wine writer, Derreck H. N. Foster, recently put Weinert wines top in a list of the best ten red and white wines being sold today in Argentina.

There are many firms who can be relied upon to produce a good bottle of wine. Lopez S.A.C.I., whose *bodega* is in Maipu, produce an excellent red and white wine under the slightly misleading name of Chateau Montchenot. Adopted European names like 'Val de Loire', 'Oro del Rhin', and even 'Valdepeñas', 'Chablis' and 'Margaux' are often found on the labels of otherwise perfectly respectable wines (although there is talk of legislation to rule out this practice by 1981), but perhaps the most interesting description of the lot is the free use of the word 'Champaña' which appears on most Argentine sparkling wines, even when they are made by a wholly-owned subsidiary company of Moët & Chandon of Epernay, France! In fact, M. Chandon, as the firm is called in Argentina, produce excellent sparkling wine, and their top brand, 'Baron B.', made by the traditional Champagne method, is in no way inferior to many *marques* of the real thing. Arizu, Crillon and Toso also make very good sparkling wines.

Other notable red and white wines come from Bodegas Norton, Suter and Bianchi who are all under the control of Seagrams, from Calvet – one time subsidiary of the Bordeaux house, from José Orfila – a small but excellent independent – from Rural, and from the large, superbly equipped Peñaflor organization which controls Trapiche. In the main, the practice is still to age red wines in oak wood from three to six years, followed by a much shorter period in bottle, but as with the production of white wines, the thinking on this traditional method is beginning to change; the faded colour, the woody, slightly oxidized bouquet and flavour that it imparts to the wine does not find favour in the export markets of the world, and despite the problems of space, bottle ageing for red wine is becoming more prevalent.

Sparked off by the shortage of Cabernet Sauvignon in the United States during the late 1960s (a trend that seems to be repeating itself following the great white wine boom), several growers of quality wine with an eye on the American market began to produce straight Cabernet Sauvignons with varying degrees of success. Historically, the finest Argentine reds for domestic consumption had been made from a blend of two or more grape varieties. Lopez's Château Montchenot, for instance, combines Cabernet with Malbec, while Arizu's excellent Valroy is made from the Cabernet Sauvignon, Merlot and a small percentage of Pinot Noir – by French standards a most unlikely combination! Certainly Peñaflor's Andean Cabernet Sauvignon, which was produced specifically for export to the United States and is also marketed in the United Kingdom, has excellent balance, but one cannot escape the feeling that these single-grape wines, like their counterparts in South Africa and Australia, would benefit from the extra fruit and roundness that judicious blending with the Merlot, Syrah or Malbec seems to produce.

The Future for Argentine Wines

It is hoped that the crisis brought about by speculative accumulation of stock, which hit all sections of the Argentine wine industry in the middle of 1978, will resolve itself, although it is unlikely that prices will ever return to the exceptionally low levels of 1977. This is because many of the hundreds of small growers, who in the past used to sell their grapes by the kilogram to the big *bodegas* – often at very low prices – and who then had to survive for the rest of the year on the proceeds, have begun to see the advantages of holding stocks of wine instead. The astute vineyard owner still delivers his grapes to the state cooperatives or privately owned *bodegas* as before, but the finished wine – for which he pays a storage charge – remains his property, and he is able to release stocks as and when his own or market circumstances dictate.

The price explosion occurred when Argentina's exports around the world, both in bulk and in bottle, were beginning to take on significant proportions. In 1977 the United Kingdom imported over 1.5 million litres of red and white wine in bulk, and brands labelled 'Produce of Argentina' were to be found on the shelves of many wine stores and supermarkets. The National Association of Beverage Importers' 'Annual Statistical Report for 1978' shows that nearly 250,000 US gallons of Argentine wine in bottle found its way onto the American market. Since then, sales abroad have slowed to a trickle, but it will be surprising if Argentina does not assert itself again as a force in the world wine market.

Today the increasing demand for wine throughout the western world falls into three main categories: first, the vast 'commodity' wine market, often distributed as well-advertised brands which appeal to the novice drinker because they are instantly recognizable and inexpensive, rather than having an obvious association with a particular source; second, there is the more specialized, medium-priced range where the consumer may identify the wine with a specific country or grape variety; and third, there are the classic, mainly European wines which, because of their traditional quality, scarcity and high price, will always be sought after by the well-to-do minority.

Given a realistic approach to pricing, backed by official support for what is still regarded by some government departments as a non-traditional, non-essential export, there is no doubt that the Argentine wine industry is well placed to take advantage of those sectors where rapid growth can be expected over the next few decades. Argentina has the right climate, a large, even production, the equipment and the know-how; but in a country where historically, long-term confidence has been at a premium, the growers must first come to terms with themselves.

THE WINES OF BRAZIL

It might seem out of character for such an extrovert nation with all its natural wealth and awakening prosperity to do less than justice to one of its oldest industries, but the fact is that little has been made public about Brazil's growing wine production, and one suspects that until recently, the natives were not too proud of their viticultural effort in their vast land, and visitors who took the trouble to sample the local product could not find much to be enthusiastic over either. However, it is entirely in keeping with Brazil's amazingly rapid progress that its wine industry has suddenly taken on a completely new look.

Vines were brought to the Rio Grande do Sul in 1626 when the Jesuit priest, Roque Gonzales de Santa Cruz, established the first Christian colony at St Nicholau. The grapes they grew were almost certainly the Criolla, which had found its way from Argentina, and for the next hundred years the Spanish influence was to be maintained. When Portugal's grip on the country began to tighten at the beginning of the eighteenth century, a party of immigrants from the Azores settled in what is now Porto Alegre and the first Portuguese grapes were introduced, to be followed by other varieties of *vinifera* from France, Italy and Germany. The early settlers found wine-making heavy going in the hot, damp climate, with diseased vines and crop failures occurring all too frequently. In 1832, the Marquis de Lisboa, impressed by the success of hybrids in North America, sent cuttings of a species known as Isabel, or Isabella, to an English merchant named Messiter and these were planted out on the Marine Islands as an experiment. The American vine was found to be much better suited to the climate and it soon spread to all the other vineyards, to the almost total exclusion of the European species. During the 1870s, large numbers of Italians arrived in the south and set about improving and extending the vineyards. They founded the townships of Garibaldi, Bento Gonçalves and Caxias, which still remain the centre of Brazil's wine industry.

Most of Brazil's 70,000 hectares are to be found in the southern state of Rio Grande do Sul. Other areas of production are around the city of San Roque in Sao Paulo State, and in Santa Catarina where German influence is very strong. There is also an extraordinary viticultural experiment taking place in the interior of the State of Bahia, situated only fifteen degrees south of the Equator, where it is hoped that two crops of grapes a year will eventually be picked. If this proves successful, the implications for the rest of the world are incalculable.

Production has been rising rapidly in recent years, from 1.5 million hectolitres in 1973 to 2.8 million hectolitres in 1978. American and hybrid grapes still predominate, with the Isabel accounting for nearly half the total wine produced, but the Herbemont is extensively planted in Santa Catarina. Other hybrids to be found are the Bordo, Americanas, Concorde, Seibel and Niagara (white).

Vitis vinifera was reintroduced to Brazil after the First World War, and the red wine grape that best succeeds is the Barbera, although new techniques in cultivation and wine-making have greatly improved the wine made from Cabernet Franc. Other varieties beginning to appear are the Bonarda, Merlot and Syrah. Of the white *viniferas*, the Moscato accounts for two-thirds of the production, although there is an increasing amount of Riesling and Trebbiano grown. The emphasis on Italian grape varieties is a clear indication of the strong influence which immigrants from that country still exert on the Brazilian wine industry.

The vintage starts in January and is usually finished by late-February. Grapes are picked by hand and taken in trucks to wineries for fermentation; grapes from Santa Catarina are normally processed in the neighbouring state of Sao Paulo. It is at this point that the new technology is beginning to have the most effect. Much more care is being taken to prevent pre-fermentation before the freshly picked grapes reach the wineries, and modern firms such as Dreher s.a. (a wholly owned subsidiary of the American Heublein Corporation) use carefully selected strains of yeast to ensure a more even fermentation of the must. In the past, white wines were left in contact with the skins, and today's accepted practices of separation, clarification and temperature control were seldom, if ever, used.

Big advances have been made in the storage of wine, with a much greater use of steel tanks lined with epoxy-resin or glass, as opposed to the old, wooden vats where risks of tainting and oxidation were high. Clarification of the new wine with suitable fining agents, refrigeration to prevent the subsequent precipitation of tartrates, and sophisticated filtering methods – all common practices in the developed wine countries – are becoming the norm, and greater care is being exercised in the actual bottling process. Packaging too, never previously a Brazilian strong point, has been much improved by the arrival on the scene of international corporations like National Distillers, Martini & Rossi, Cinzano and Moët & Chandon.

At a 1979 tasting in London, three wines from the excellent house of Dreher s.a. surprised experts by their almost total lack of hot country characteristics. A white 1979 *vinifera* blend was pale in colour, with no hint of oxidation, clean tasting with excellent acidity; a 1979 Cabernet displayed remarkable fruit and balance; but the outstanding wine was a 1979 Barbera which compared more than favourably with many of the products of its native Italy. In addition to the firms already mentioned, one of the best known in Brazil is the Cia. Vinicola Rio Grandense, which distributes good red and white wines under the brand name 'Grandja Uniao'. Other major producers include the Cooperativa Aurora, the Cooperativa Garibaldi and the Companhia Monaco. Most Brazilian wines are sold domestically for, as in Argentina, consumption has until recently kept pace with production. But, with the growing surplus, serious efforts are being made to export, and in Canada particularly they seem to have found a ready market.

THE WINES OF CHILE

In keeping with the part played by the Catholic church in the early development of South America's wine industry, it seems likely that vines were first brought to Chile from Cuzco in 1548 by Father Francisco de Carabantes. At about the same time, a sizeable vineyard was planted by Don Francisco Aguirre in the region of Copiapo, some 800 kilometres to the north of Santiago, and we are told that he enjoyed his first vintage in 1551. By 1554, that great entrepreneur, Juan Jufré, best known perhaps as the founder of the Argentine city of San Juan, owned a significant stretch of vineyards in the Nunoa district just south east of Santiago. Under Spain's colonial rule, wine production increased, and Chilean wines began to acquire a reputation for quality as merchants sold them along the length of the Pacific coast. By the seventeenth century, records show that the Jesuits were already concerned about a problem that has bedevilled the Chilean wine industry since its inception, namely alcoholism. Cheap wine was bought in copious quantities by the Indians, who had no head or stomach for it, and death and disease from over-indulgence were commonplace.

In 1851 the 'father of Chilean viticulture', Silvestre Ochagavia, perceived that the climate and soil in his adopted country were ideal for the production of quality wine, and he lost no time in bringing experts from France along with cuttings of the finest French vines to plant in the fertile central valleys. Cabernet Merlot, Côt, Pinot and Sémillon began to take the place of País and Moscato as – encouraged by the government – other vineyard owners followed his example. It is one of life's little ironies that in the 1870s, when phylloxera swept through the vineyards of France, Chile was able to send cuttings of genuine, ungrafted French vines to restock the devastated French vineyards. The firm of Ochagavia and some of the other pioneers survive to this day, and Chile's wine industry has never lost its Gallic character.

In the twentieth century, Chile's wine-makers have suffered from the edicts and persuasions of governments bent on curbing alcoholism, on curtailing the planting of vines in favour of other crops and, more recently, on dispossessing the vineyard owners so that the land could be handed over to the peasants. Since 1974, however, the restriction on the use of better quality land has been lifted, and Chilean wine looks set for a period of stability and growth. Chile is over 4,828 kilometres long and at no point more than 322 kilometres wide. The area of wine production is so stretched out that it is impossible to generalize about soil and climate. There are approximately 110,000 hectares under vine and the main wine-producing areas extend from 27° to 39°s, a distance of nearly 1,448 kilometres. However, Chile's vineyards all have three important features in common: the searing hot deserts to the north, the Andean mountain range to the east, and the Pacific Ocean with its cold Humboldt Current close by to the west. It is reasonable to suppose that these natural barriers prevented that scourge of the vine, phylloxera, from ever having made its presence felt in Chile, and it is therefore one of the few countries in the world where the original vines can be planted directly into the soil without the need for grafting onto American root stocks.

THE NORTH CENTRAL ZONE

This covers the provinces of Atacama and Coquimbo and it is of a semi-desert nature. Rainfall is lower than one millimetre per annum, and so the vineyards must depend upon irrigation which comes from the few rivers that flow down from the mountains. The area is not suitable for the production of fine wine because the extreme heat and clear skies produce a high alcohol level in the must, along with a low acidity. It is, however, the centre of the 'Pisco' industry – that fiery brandy much loved by all South Americans, and Chileans in particular. There are approximately 2,500 hectares of mainly Moscatel and País grapes, producing an average of 70 hectolitres per hectare. A certain amount of sherry-style wine is also made.

THE CENTRAL VALLEY ZONE

This is the heart of Chile's wine production. Here all the finest wines are made and these were, until recently, mostly classic red varieties. The zone covers the provinces of Aconcagua, Valparaiso, Santiago, O'Higgins, Colchagua, Curicó and Talca, and between the Aconcagua River in the north and the Maule River in the south there are 37,000 hectares of irrigated vineyards. Perhaps the best wines come from the Maipo Valley around Pirque, Linderos and Santa Ana, and at least one famous vineyard is situated in Macul, almost in the suburbs of the city of Santiago itself. Other areas for quality wine are the Aconcagua Valley, Lontué and San Clemente in Talca Province. Rainfall varies from 360 millimetres in the northern part of the zone to 730 millimetres in the south; the much higher rainfall which Chile enjoys compared with, say, Mendoza or San Juan on the other side of the Andes, is certainly one reason why Chilean red wines have always been considered superior to their Argentine counterparts. The limestone soil, too, is much deeper and is admirably suited to the growing of the Cabernet Sauvignon, Cabernet Franc, Côt Rouge and Merlot. In line with French tradition, the early plantings were trained on the low or high Espalier system and the Guyot method of pruning is still used. Since 1974, however, when the flat, rich farmlands were freed for vine cultivation, many growers have introduced the Parral system because of the greater yields and, with changing tastes, white wine varieties such as the Sauvignon, Sémillon, Chardonnay and Riesling are becoming more prevalent. The Central Valley Zone accounts for 52 per cent of the total national production, which averages about 5 million hectolitres per annum.

THE CENTRAL UNIRRIGATED ZONE

Although this area falls within the same provinces as the Central Valley zone for administrative purposes, the actual wine-growing area is limited to unirrigated, roughish land in the coastal *cordillera*, and only the hardy País and Torrantel are grown; the total area under vine is about 9,000 hectares.

THE SOUTH CENTRAL VALLEY ZONE

This area extends from the south bank of the Maule River to the southern border of Nuble Province, with the best wines coming from the central valleys of Linares. Vineyards are irrigated despite the considerable rainfall, and summer temperatures are higher than in the Central Valley, with corresponding extremes in winter. Red wine made from the irrigated and heavily cultivated País is of particularly poor quality, but the climate and soil make the zone much more suitable for white wine and excellent Sémillons and Sauvignons can be found. The total planted area is about 6,500 hectares, and the heavy use of País produces a high yield of around 65 hectolitres per hectare.

SOUTH CENTRAL UNIRRIGATED ZONE

The area's 46,000 hectares are situated mainly in the foothills and valleys of the coastal *cordillera* that runs through the provinces of Maule, Nuble and Concepcion. Rainfall is very high, with an average of one metre per annum. The vineyards are unirrigated and for this reason, the País which predominates in the zone, makes much better wine than in the provinces to the north. The whole area depends on the production of wine for its livelihood, as the climate and soil are unsuitable for alternative crops. Nevertheless, yields are very low, at less than 30 hectolitres per hectare, and as there are more than 19,000 vineyard owners, these provinces pose particular socio- and economic problems for the government. Traditionally, this area has been the source of Chile's cheap wine, but consumption is not increasing, and recently farmers have been encouraged to grow Moscatel grapes for eventual distillation.

THE SOUTHERN VITICULTURAL ZONE

This lies in the provinces of Bió-Bió, Malleco and Cautin, and the total area of 8,000 hectares has the very low yield of nine hectolitres per hectare. The alcoholic strength of the wine is often below the minimum set for the rest of the country, and if consumed outside the zone, it must be blended with wines of greater degree.

Chilean Wines and their Place in the World

Before and after the Second World War, Chilean claret could be found on the lists of several respected English wine merchants. In those days, passenger liners regularly sailed between Liverpool and Valparaiso; there was a large British business community in Chile, and the booming nitrate trade meant a regular service between the Pacific ports and the United Kingdom.

Because of this and the historic connections with France and Spain, Europeans 'knew' about Chilean wines and respected them for their excellent quality and value for money. But as trade with the Old World dwindled, a sense of isolation set in and wine growers began to look to their own continent for the relatively small exports of wine that the restricted production and high domestic consumption allowed. By 1977, South American countries, with Brazil and Venezuela leading the way, accounted for 84 per cent of the total export value of Chilean bottled wines; the value of British imports was a derisory £10,455 or 23,000 US dollars, and even the United States could manage only £136,364 or 300,000 US dollars. In the world of wine political commentary is invidious, but even the most impartial observer would agree that under the Allende regime, the Chilean wine industry suffered a major setback. Vineyards were left untended, vineyard owners were dispossessed, plant and machinery deteriorated, and there was no money available for the introduction of new viti-vinicultural methods.

Today attitudes have changed. Freedom to plant new vineyards on previously prescribed agricultural land has induced the producers to look at exports in a new light. In 1978, the excellent firm of Concha y Toro exported nearly 3,785 hectolitres to the United States and there seems little doubt that, as production increases, Chile's wine growers will have to look further afield for their markets. However, if they are to be entirely successful, it will be necessary for them to reappraise the traditional ways of making white wine. Too often they suffer from woodiness and oxidation, and although the more forward-looking oenologists realize this, they are quick to point out that they must first persuade their own countrymen that white wine should be light in colour, fresh, fruity and clean to the taste.

Some Chilean Firms and their Wines

During April 1979 I was able to visit a number of firms in Chile and, while being impressed with the uniformly excellent quality of the red wines, I found many of the whites exceedingly disappointing.

Concha y Toro S.A.

Probably the biggest firm in Chile and certainly the largest exporter. One of the few companies to have understood the power of advertising. Under their German, Geisenheim-trained oenologist they are making good, commercial wine.

1977 Sauvignon: Medium-gold in colour; heavy rather flat bouquet; soft, well-rounded flavour, lacking in acidity and with a hint of oxidation.

1978 Riesling: Colour light golden-green; a good fruity bouquet but not obviously Riesling grape; some sugar with a reasonable if rather heavy flavour and a fair finish.

Cassillero del Diablo (Brand): Deep golden colour; strong oxidation on the nose; heavy, unbalanced taste lacking in acidity and finish.

St. Emiliana Cabernet: Fair colour; good strong Cabernet nose; firm, well-rounded body; good long finish.

1974 Cassillero del Diablo (Brand): Colour turning brown; rather woody bouquet; soft, mellow taste showing age, but lots of class.

1974 Marques de Casa Concha: Fair red colour going brown at edge; fine, fruity Cabernet bouquet; excellent balance of tannin and acidity; strong finish.

Viña Santa Helena/Viña San Pedro

Both companies are part of the Wagner Stein Group, Chile's third biggest exporters.

1979 Sémillon Santa Helena: Surprisingly pale in colour; fresh, fruity bouquet; crisp, dry taste and clean finish – an excellent example of how to make white wine.

1976 Riesling Santa Helena: Deep golden, almost brown; heavily oxidized bouquet and taste – very much an old style white wine.

1971 San Pedro White: Dark golden colour; rather 'closed' bouquet; very oxidized flavour and lacking in acidity; short finish.

Gato Blanco (60 per cent Sauvignon, 40 per cent Sémillon): Bright, medium golden colour; a rather 'silent' nose; nice crisp taste and dry finish.

1978 Cabernet Franc Santa Helena: Brightish red colour; good fruity bouquet; excellent balance and finish.

1978 Côt/Merlot Santa Helena: Good, deep red colour; excellent bouquet; tannic, good, strong, firm aftertaste.

Gato Negro (60 per cent Cabernet, 40 per cent Côt): Very bright, young red colour; strong, scented nose, rather sweet taste but an attractive, fruity wine.

1970 Cabernet Sauvignon San Pedro (one year in bottle): Good, deep red colour, strong bouquet rather lacking in finesse; firm, well-balanced taste; pleasant, lingering finish.

Viña Undurraga S.A.

A fine old family firm set in an elegant, landscaped park. The modern, highly sophisticated bottling plant is in striking contrast to the old oak vats used for storage. Their best wines are filled into *bocksbeutels*.

1978 Sauvignon: Pale green-golden colour; rather heavy nose lacking in fruit; strong, pungent flavour, low acidity and short finish.

1975 Sauvignon/Sémillon/Riesling: Deep golden in colour; strong taste of wood.

1977 Cabernet Sauvignon: Good, full red colour; fine, fruity bouquet; well-rounded, excellent balance; a delight to drink.

1975 Pinot Noir/Cabernet: Lightish red in colour; rather closed bouquet; a light but pleasant wine; a little short on the finish.

1973 Cabernet Sauvignon: Rich ruby colour, good, strong Cabernet nose; showing a little age on the palate and finish, but attractive to drink now.

Viña Cousiño Macul

Looked upon as Chile's leading producer of fine wine; very much in the French tradition as befits a family business whose founder, Don Luis, introduced French vines over 100 years ago. This firm makes classic wines only from its own vineyards – which cover nearly 300 hectares.

1978 Doña Isadora Riesling: Medium green-gold colour; fair fruit on the nose, but lacking crispness; fair flavour but a hint of oxidation.

1978 Chardonnay: Medium green-gold colour; good, fresh, fruity bouquet; light, dry flavour; a bit thin on the finish.

1978 Cabernet/Merlot: Good red colour; fine, fruity bouquet; nicely balanced if a little on the light side; fair finish.

1976 Don Luis Cabernet Sauvignon: Deep red colour; strong 'cedar-wood' bouquet, typically Cabernet; good firm taste, excellent balance and lingering finish.

1976 Don Matias Cabernet Sauvignon: Good red colour; strong Cabernet nose; tannic, rather unbalanced flavour; reasonable finish.

1974 Antiguas Reservas (two years in bottle): Colour shows signs of fading; fine if rather woody bouquet; odd, slightly bitter flavour; dry finish.

Viña Linderos S.A.

A small firm owned by the three dedicated Ortiz brothers. Their wines come exclusively from their own irrigated vineyards in the best part of the Maipo Valley.

1977 Cabernet Sauvignon: Astonishingly deep colour; superb, rich Cabernet bouquet; firm but full of fruit; a delightful wine with years ahead of it.

Other good firms are Viña Santa Carolina S.A., Viña Santa Rita S.A., Viña Santa Teresa S.A. and Viña José Canepa y Cia.

THE WINES OF URUGUAY

As in most South American countries, it seems probable that the vine was first introduced to Uruguay by the Jesuit priests, following the discovery of the country by the Spanish explorer, Juan Solis, in 1516. It was not until the mid-1870s, following a period of Portuguese domination from neighbouring Brazil, that serious attempts were made to grow vines commercially. In 1875 two important vineyards were established, one near Colonia in the south-west of the country and the other at Salto in the north-west. By 1880, eighteen vineyards had been established, and by the turn of the century the numbers had risen rapidly to over 1,400, covering 4,000 hectares, mainly in the provinces of Montevideo, Salto, Canelones and Colonia. Today, there are over 19,000 hectares under vine, and since 1904 the annual production has increased from 105,000 to 500,000 hectolitres. This yield per hectare is low by South American standards, but the soil and humid climate, particularly in the south, are not ideal for vine growing. For a while, hybrid American grape varieties predominated because they were found to be better suited to the conditions, but as the growers became more expert in their selection of vines, the *Vitis vinifera* was introduced on a much wider scale. Today one can find the Cabernet Sauvignon, Cabernet Franc, Pinot Noir, Merlot, Sémillon and Sauvignon from France, the Grignolino and Lambrusco from Italy, the Cariñena, Malvasia and Pedro Ximénez from Spain, and the Riesling from Germany.

The quality and size of the Uruguayan wine industry cannot be compared with that of Argentina, Chile or even Brazil simply because the country has not got the population or the wealth to sustain it. Of the total population of 3 million, one-third live in or around the capital of Montevideo and, historically, a poor peasant community has eked out a living on small-holdings or by working for the rich *estancia* owners who could well afford to buy the finest imported wines. Until recently, there was no affluent middle class to encourage the producers to raise their standards, but there are signs now of economic and social change in the country. Improved standards of living coupled with a considerable growth in the tourist industry have led to a greater demand for wine, and an all-round improvement in quality and presentation – which so often left much to be desired – is clearly discernible. Today, in the hotels and restaurants of Montevideo and Punta del Este an inexpensive but quite passable home-produced Cabernet Sauvignon can be found, and although white wines tend to suffer from the hot-country problems of oxidation and low acidity, the rosés are not unattractive and there is a limited amount of quite drinkable sparkling and sherry-style wine available as well. Plans to export wine are being considered and the government agricultural authorities say that production could be doubled in five years if demand continues to grow.

South American wines have much to offer the modern day wine drinker. Vintages are reasonably consistent, their wines are well made, and there is a growing acceptance by hitherto inward-looking producers that styles must be adapted to suit foreign tastes. No one who has seen the Argentine wine industry in depth would doubt for a moment that they can do this, although because of its very size, its best prospects in the long term may prove to be the inexpensive commodity wine market. Brazil is something of an unknown quantity, but big, successful international corporations are not in the habit of investing large sums of money in marginal projects. It is not beyond the bounds of possibility that the Rio Grande do Sul could vie with Argentina as a source of good, cheap wine in the future and one would expect to see the important grape concentrate business being developed there. The Bahia experiment, of course, could change the face of viticulture across the world. Chile's strength must lie in her ability to produce wines of quality to help fill the gap in the middle price range left by the inflationary trend of generic European wines. By the year 2000, South American wines will either be established firmly in the world or they will have disappeared without trace. At the time of writing, the first possibility seems the most likely.

A vineyard estate south of Santiago in Chile

The Wines of
Australia

LEN EVANS

Acknowledged to be the leading authority on Australian wines, Len Evans runs a large wine consultancy firm in Sydney and regularly travels throughout the country visiting vineyards. He has written many books on Australian wines including his classic, *The Complete Book of Australian Wine*, published in 1973, and is currently writing for *The Wine and Spirit Brewing Journal*, *The Wine and Spirit Buying Guide* (Chief Taster) and *The Australian Newspaper*.

To understand the Australian wine scene during the last decades of the twentieth century, one must understand change. Any writer on Australian wine faces a most unenviable situation. The moment a book is completed, it is out of date. Another three wineries have been built, another vineyard planted in highest quality varietals, while the galley proofs were being corrected. In 1959, 13,211,000 litres of table wine were sold, compared to 36,813,000 litres of fortified wine, most of the latter being cheap, wholesale sweet wine of the 'night-cap' variety. Fortified wine outsold table wine by 45 per cent in 1959. By 1969, consumption was 38,826,000 litres (table wine) and 47,743,000 litres (fortified) and many people saw that table-wine sales would soon exceed those of fortified wine. This occurred in 1971–2, and by 1979 sales of table wine were 143,209,000 litres compared to fortified sales of 47,935,000 litres: change indeed. The change is further emphasized by a couple of examples. By 1960, the famous Hunter Valley district of New South Wales, about 160 kilometres north of Sydney, had fallen into gentle decline. There were about seven companies left and less than 320 hectares were under vine. Within twenty years, 8,094 hectares were under cultivation, approximately forty new companies, partnerships or ownerships had been established, two major companies had gone into receivership and others had escaped that fate by being taken over or sold, often at a loss to the original developers. In McLaren Vale, a popular district south of Adelaide, South Australia, and within easy reach of that city, there were fourteen wine producers in 1960. By 1976 this had grown to thirty-three, and by the 1980s the figure was forty-five – in one, small district.

This change is reflected throughout Australia. Developments abound in every state. There are enthusiasts in Tasmania, devotees in Queensland, professionals who, having their practices in that state and not being able to commute the vast distances to recognized wine districts, made up a district of their own. In Western Australia there are separate new districts in the south-west corner, and other new districts have been established in South Australia, Victoria and New South Wales. There is even a vineyard near Alice Springs in the 'dead heart' of Australia.

A vineyard in the Barossa Valley, South Australia, one of the most famous of all Australian vineyard areas

To appreciate the quite dramatic extent of change that has taken place, it is necessary to be aware of the type of wines that were made for the first fifteen years after the Second World War. The styles of these wines varied considerably. The majority of wine made was of the sweet, wholesome fortified variety. McWilliams' Cream Sherry, Lindemans' Montillo Sweet Sherry, Penfolds' Invalid Port, plus another of the same style, quite wonderfully named Royal Reserve, were among the market leaders. Increasing quantities of finer, dry sherry were being made, due mostly to John Fornachon, who did a great deal of work helping develop *flor* cultures in Australia during that time. Reynella and Mildara were among the larger companies who took advantage of his work, and there was considerable market acceptance of their more elegant, and more expensive, efforts. Full-flavoured fortified reds were important – some very good wines of vintage port character were made, notably by Stonyfell and Hardy, and much of the rest of the material went into a favourite Australian wine, part matured in wood for many years. Not all of it was Tawny, however, for the hot maturation sheds of the Barossa Valley led to a deal of it becoming quite liqueurish. Since there was no control over names, labels could bear the legends Tawny Port, Liqueur Port, Liqueur Tawny, and in some circumstances when the wine was of one year, Vintage Tawny Port, leading to the confusion which still exists in some minds today. In north-east Victoria and, to a lesser extent, in Swan Valley in Western Australia and in the Barossa Valley in South Australia, some quite wonderful Muscats were still being made, from the various Frontignan varieties, which were largely unknown and certainly very much unappreciated except by a few.

In the Hunter Valley, Maurice O'Shea of Mount Pleasant dominated. Though taken over by McWilliams, one of the largest companies, in the early 1930s, he had been allowed to continue in his idiosyncratic way. He bought other wines from local makers such as Drayton, Tyrrell, Elliott and Tulloch. He was a skilful blender with a fine, developed palate and he was a good host who spread the word of table wine. Most of his wines sold for very few shillings. There are still many examples of his skill in private cellars, and a feature of them is that most open, still, in top condition. At their best, they are definitive examples of a distinctive type of red, a soft, fleshy, deep, earthy, almost smoky-flavoured wine that has no counterpart in the world of wine, with perhaps the single exception of some old Tain Hermitage wines the writer has tasted. No wonder, perhaps, since the grape variety is the same, the conditions were similar, and the wine-making methods, from what we can understand (O'Shea studied at Montpellier), were not that different. In that same district Lindemans and Tulloch also produced some fine bottlings during this time although, as stated, most of the smaller makers sold to merchants, or other wine companies, in bulk.

In the rest of New South Wales little else of table-wine quality existed. Mudgee 'Mud' was one unfortunate nickname given to a substantial dry red of the time. On the outskirts of Sydney, however, a small vineyard did exist, producing Traminer grapes. Penfold leased this vineyard, and from it came the famous Trameah. For some reason, this wine was not coarse, not overblown. It had all the Traminer characteristics, yet a subtle, fine manner. The wines were long-lived and built up considerable bottle character. One of the old connoisseurs declared one vintage 'the best Australian white wine I have ever seen'. Eventually, expanding suburbia and changes in company policy for ever removed the cork from the Trameah bottle.

In Victoria, there was a younger counterpart to Maurice O'Shea, making fine dry whites and quite wonderful dry reds. Incredibly, he was only 'allowed' to do so by an indulgent management, since his chief business was making sparkling wines – and what sparkling wines they were, the best Australia has ever seen. Colin

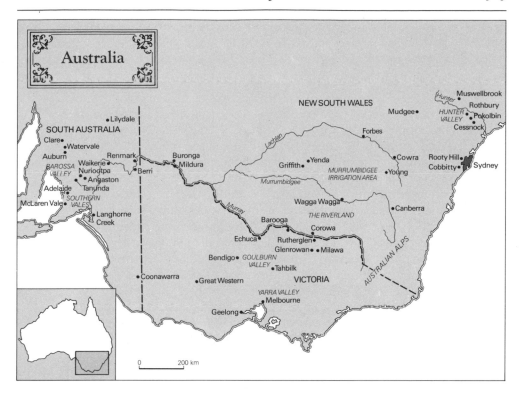

'Joe' Preece worked at Great Western until 1962 and for the twenty years prior to that date both sparkling and still dry wines were among the finest in the land. They have kept their condition and the dry reds, particularly, remain a collector's joy.

During the late-nineteenth century, Australian vineyards, like so many others all over the world, were decimated by the dread vine parasite, phylloxera. However, South Australia, like Chile, escaped entirely from attack. This, coupled with Federation in 1901, when all trade barriers between the various states were ended, established South Australia as the premium producer, in quantity terms. Quality was something else. The Clare district, north of the Barossa, produced some rather hard, long-living reds. The Southern Vale, particularly Reynella, produced many vintages that grew, in the bottle, to be outstanding. The writer has tasted forty- and fifty-year-old Reynella reds that opened in immaculate condition. This quality continued after the Second World War, and was appreciated by a small, mostly local group. To the south there was another area, Coonawarra, developed in 1861 when a far-sighted Scot, John Riddoch, recognized the potential of the region. Alas, the Penola fruit colony, which he founded in 1890, came to little. Some of the vineyards, and his old winery, remained until after the Second World War. Bill Redman, who started work in the area in 1901, the year of John Riddoch's death, became the sole wine-maker of the district. By the 1940s little was heard of Coonawarra. Then, one company was established which bottled and sold the Redman wine under a 'Treasure Chest' label. These labels, fine reproductions of early colonial prints and etchings, were said to have cost more than the wine. Today, they are collectors' items, sometimes achieving more than $100 per bottle at auctions. In the early 1950s, Wynn's, the Melbourne wine merchants, became interested in the area and bought the old Riddoch winery. They founded the Coonawarra Estate, and many notable wines have been made by that company – or by Redman, who, at the beginning made Wynn's wines as well as his own.

The scene was set for Australia's greatest boom in table-wine sales. Many things contributed to this boom. The technical side of wine-making improved vastly, and this led to greater public acceptance. In turn, public acceptance was fostered by the wine companies and the Wine Board. Among the factors were:

1. The introduction, in the early 1950s, of the so-called slow or cold fermentation of white wines. To Gramp, of the Barossa Valley, is due most of the credit for this. Previously most Australian 'Rhine' Rieslings were rather hard, lacked fruit and with bottle age developed a 'kerosene' flavour. The German methods introduced, soon to be copied by wine-makers all over the country, led to fresher, lighter, more flowery fragrant whites which, in fact, were to become precursors of the present white-wine boom.

2. The early experiments conducted by Penfolds, which led to the famous Grange Hermitage, centred around the use of small, new wood, *à la bordelaise*. This kind of maturation, especially for Cabernet Sauvignon, is now almost mandatory.

3. New varieties were introduced. Quality Australian table-wine production came mainly from four varieties: Shiraz (Hermitage) and Cabernet Sauvignon for reds, Sémillon and Rhine Riesling for whites. The 1950s and 1960s saw the importation of new vine stocks, better clones of those already in use, plus many of the other traditional varieties, Chardonnay, Pinot Noir, Merlot, Gewürztraminer, Chenin Blanc, Sauvignon Blanc and Müller-Thurgau. Propagation of these varieties in different areas together with different methods of wine-making and maturation has led to a wide range of new styles and flavours.

4. Immigrant influx has a great bearing on what happened in Australia during the three decades since the Second World War. Not only did the migrant have different habits which led to new requirements but, in many cases, he actually imposed his standards upon the existing situation by becoming a restaurateur or wine-maker, wine merchant or hotelier. Some of the best wines made during the wine boom were by the children of makers from Germany, Austria and Holland.

5. The promotional efforts of both company and industry were extensive. The Australian Wine Board, a statutory body, collected a levy from each company and cooperative based on the tonnage crush. This money was used to promote Australian wines overseas and at home. Local funds were disseminated through state associations and the Wine Bureau. Advertising campaigns of the Wine Board gave a cheerful, anti-élitist message that found great acceptance among the egalitarian Australians. Separate company advertising was very strong and the advent of television during the late 1950s provided further scope.

6. Press attitudes changed. At one time, the job of the lone press officer of the Wine Board was to prevent statements such as 'He was hit over the head with a wine bottle.' A bottle was enough surely? In 1962 Australia's first wine column appeared, this writer being responsible for Cellarmaster of *The Bulletin*, a title that helped mask the inadequacies expressed. Today, there are wine press clubs in almost every state, and the three main branches, Sydney, Melbourne and Adelaide, have up to 100 members each. This mass of wine commentators and critics has resulted in a coverage in book, magazine, newspaper, radio and television, probably unmatched, on a *per capita* basis, anywhere in the world.

All these, and other factors, contributed to a wine boom. Not unnaturally, the increase in red-variety plantings during the 1960s and early 1970s, a result of the demand at the time, led to a surplus of red wine. Much of the poorer material was distilled or discounted. Much of the better material was discounted too, and red-wine bargains abounded at the end of the 1970s. White wines of quality rose quite dramatically in price, although flagon and cask (the bag in the box) prices remained fairly stable. One reason for this is the availability of the sultana, or Thompson's

Seedless, variety, a dual-purpose grape grown in abundance in the irrigation areas of South Australia and Victoria.

The greatest phenomenon during all this time was the growth of cask sales. The glass flagon had been introduced in the late 1950s and early 1960s. It was followed a few years later by the cardboard cask with plastic bag liner which collapsed as the wine was withdrawn by tap, thus preventing oxidation. The cask rapidly became everyman's wine container. By the beginning of 1980, casks made up 37.6 per cent of Australian table-wine sales and approximately 25 per cent of total wine sales. Wine casks and reasonably priced wines such as Lindemans' Ben Ean Moselle, the nation's number one seller, dominated the market. At the top end, interest in top wines, vintages and varieties had never been higher. There was in truth a shortage of top wine. It was the middle market that was losing ground, as the wine-buying public seemed to want either a drink or the best. What was the rating of Australia's best wines at the beginning of the 1980s? There had been some overseas success, particularly with Chardonnay, Sémillon and Pinot Noir wines, but these successes were isolated, though well publicized, and did not reflect the true standing of Australia's top offerings among the world's best.

Grape Varieties (Red)

SHIRAZ (HERMITAGE)

The Shiraz (or Hermitage) has long been the work horse of the Australian industry. There are many different flavours and styles which emerge from its use throughout Australia. Of these, perhaps four could be offered in a broad sense for consideration. Both the Hunter Valley (New South Wales) and Coonawarra (South Australia) can produce light, balanced, intensely flavoured dry reds from the Shiraz grape. Though the final flavours can be different, and these wines of Coonawarra have more acid and tannin apparent on the finish, there is much in common between the two styles. At the other end of the wine spectrum, the variety can also produce 'blood and guts' dry reds, of substantial alcohol, body, raciness and depth. Again, these wines fall into two broad groups, divided by the use or non-use of small new wood. Of the wines matured, the best is almost certainly Grange Hermitage from Penfolds, which is more a company product than a specific vineyard one. Though Grange is a small area, almost surrounded by houses, in the foothills of Adelaide, no one pretends that all the wine comes from that area. Rather the company seeks to make a certain style of wine, from various vineyards, which is then matured in small new wood. The big, non-small wood dry red is likely to be the product of a smaller maker from, say, the districts of Clare in South Australia or north-east Victoria. These robust old-fashioned reds have much to offer, and one of the world's most distinguished wine men who visits Australia occasionally raves about them. 'If they could make these in the Rhône valley, every year would be a great year.' The Shiraz material is also often used to blend with Cabernet Sauvignon, to fill out with fleshiness some of the after-palate emptiness of the latter variety, an emptiness which does not prevent most wine-makers in Australia from regarding Cabernet Sauvignon as their top red variety, the one to which to tender the most devotion.

CABERNET SAUVIGNON

The Cabernet Sauvignon remains one of the enigmas of the Australian wine industry. At best, it can produce an elegant, fine, ethereal, light-bodied, deep-flavoured, balanced wine of considerable distinction. At worst, a heavy, almost 'burnt' wine, lacking finesse, coarse, imbalanced, and far too tannic. Most wine areas of Australia have abundant heat summation. The problem is not the lack of ripening of the variety; it is the over-ripening. Should the maker pick the fruit before it is fully ripe, he may get problems of 'greenness' or heavy malolactic activity. There seems, also, to be another problem. It may be that the thick Cabernet skins, hardened by the ever-abundant Australian sun, form too many tannins at the expense of fine fruit quality. The result may be a wine that shows good fruit aromas, of a reasonable bouquet if long bottle-aged, a full fore-palate and then a mysterious 'hole', a lack of substance, or fleshiness, which is even more emphasized by the abrupt tannic finish. The balance of sugar, acid and pH becomes therefore very important, and it would be safe to say that many Australian wine-makers have become extremely aware of those factors, and are now most anxious to see more finesse, perhaps less body and certainly finer fruit in their wines.

Grape Varieties (White)

The white wines pose fewer problems, if one is satisfied that certain varieties have achieved certain standards which are not now likely to be surpassed. On the other hand, other varieties offer vast scope for experimentation as far as area, and making- and maturation-methods are concerned.

RHINE RIESLING

The Rhine Riesling variety has come a long way in twenty years. At one time, the wines, made by antiquated methods, were cumbersome, thick, hard and lacking in fruit and finesse. Since the introduction of the cold fermentation methods, and all the new equipment that has followed, the wines have become lighter, finer, with more elegance and finesse and with floral characteristics and fruity palates. Yet there is still something lacking, a density, an intense complexity of flavour that sits lightly yet so deeply on the tongue. With haste, it must be added that it is felt that only the most celebrated of German wines has this quality. Most of the poorer German-style wines sold overseas do not compare with the best Australian offerings, but the best Australian wines do not compare with the best from Germany.

SEMILLON

With the Sémillon grape, it is another matter. Without equivocation, with pride (and, it is to be hoped, with complete justification), many Australian critics feel that one area of the country produces the best pure Sémillons in the world. Laville Haut-Brion, the celebrated white wine of Château La Mission Haut-Brion, is made from 50 per cent Sémillon, 50 per cent Sauvignon, so it goes into the category of a brilliant blend. When the Hunter Valley was settled in the early part of the nine-teenth century, many different types of white-wine varieties were planted. Some relics of these early endeavours exist to the present day – Aucerot (Aúxerrois), Montils, White Shiraz (Trebbiano, Ugni Blanc), Verdelho (Verdelhao), and Pinot Blanc (thought to be a variant of Chardonnay). As in other areas of the world, one white variety came to be used more and more, since it seemed to suit the area, and the wines made from it had a distinctiveness and quality unmatched by the others. The name Sémillon was disliked and the more euphemistic Hunter Riesling sub-stituted, a change of name that has caused endless confusion during the past twenty years. The Hunter wine-makers are not sympathetic on this point and many of them will use the name until they may no longer legally do so. Eventually, the grape became the basis of all the top whites of the district, a position held without challenge until the comparatively recent introduction of Chardonnay.

Throughout this period roughly from the 1860s to the 1960s, wine-making methods were fairly simple. The grapes were picked, de-stemmed, and milled, the skins were taken off, and fermentation took place in open vessels. After the Second World War, some changes were made here and there, notably a slower fermentation in enclosed vessels, even temperature assisted (i.e. cooled). The white wines had great flavour and depth, although some could be on the coarse side. One particular feature was their longevity. One example instances a batch of bottled wine sent by Lindemans to the United Kingdom after the Second World War. The wine was returned to Australia in the early 1960s. Fifteen years in the bottle and hot sea voyages of some 43,452 kilometres later, the wine was incredible, having a rich, developed nose, reminiscent of the best in Burgundy, a full, soft, complex-flavoured palate and a long smooth finish. There was no hint of oxidation or coarseness. The wine was a joy.

In the late 1950s and early 1960s, there was a change, and this was chiefly dictated by Lindemans. Up until this time, all the white wines had been stored in old wood for a period, generally a year to eighteen months. Lindemans saw no reason to do this, and also believed that some of the 'straw' character came from a form of oxidation. So the juice was settled overnight to remove solids, carbon dioxide was used in enclosed stainless steel to eliminate oxygen, the wine was slow fermented, and then bottled early to preserve freshness and life. They were fresher and had more initial flavour when young, and hence became very popular, being included on wine lists in their first year of making. Surprisingly, perhaps, they matured even better than the 'old-fashioned' style having a finesse, an elegance missing previously. The mature flavour was also different, and though flavours are almost impossible to describe, words used were 'vanilla', 'creamy', 'hazelnut'. These whites went on and on, and many of them were a joy for twenty years or more. Since then, other companies have developed their own styles, but along the same lines. Some pick earlier than others, because they desire higher acidity. Others 'strip' their wines thoroughly to make them even softer and more acceptable when young.

These four grape varieties dominated quality table-wine production for many years. In truth, they still do. But the advent of other varieties has made an important and exciting difference to the wine scene in Australia. Of these, the most spectacular advance has been made by the Chardonnay grape. The variety has been in Australia for many years, but the development of the table-wine industry over the last two decades, plus the importation of new clones of Chardonnay, led to an upsurge in interest which becomes more intensified each year. Although there are now only 195 hectares planted throughout Australia, more plantings take place each year. But not all is success. In some areas a rather 'blowsy', full, coarse wine is made. The irrigation areas produce a pleasant wine, but it lacks true Chardonnay depth and does not mature particularly well. Some of the most successful of the new introductions to the lists have come from an obscure area, Cowra, in New South Wales, which had no vineyard before a group of professionals got together to experiment with various varietals. Yet of all districts, at this stage, the Hunter Valley has taken most kindly to the variety. It has been there for some time, almost unnoticed, masquerading under other names (White Pinot or Pinot Blanc). Lindemans and Penfolds had patches of it. Often it finished up lost in a blend with the more ubiquitous Sémillon. Murray Tyrrell was perhaps the first to understand its potential, and he has been extremely successful with a series of very full, rich-flavoured wines which have a character of their own.

Not as successful is the Pinot Noir variety. It seems that we have not yet found the right area for the variety, or we do not have a sufficiently understanding and talented wine-maker in the area in which the grape is being favourably grown. Most efforts lack fruit, and lack that density and complexity of flavour, coupled with lightness, that is the hallmark of wine produced from the Pinot Noir at best. And although there has been some international recognition of the quality of some recent vintages, most serious Australian wine men feel that there is a long way still to go. What is so interesting, perhaps, is that our New World cousins, the Californians, are experiencing the same difficulty with the variety. Of the others, Merlot has had some attention, but thus far has produced nothing of excitement. Malbec has been in Australia for years and can combine with other varieties to produce an interesting dry red.

Of the whites, Chenin Blanc and Sauvignon Blanc have produced clean, well-structured dry whites with flavours typical of those varieties. So far, none has proved sufficiently distinctive for serious attention. The Traminer variety, of which 250 hectares are under vine, has proved to be very popular. Although many bottlings have been made of the single variety, it is safe to say that none has equalled the fame of the now extinct 'Trameah' from Penfolds. Single bottlings tend to be too intense in flavour, with 'hair oil' or spice overtones which are too coarse and cloying. It seems that our climate is too strong for the variety, until developments take place in southern Victoria or Tasmania, perhaps. However, there has been much success with blending Traminer and Rhine Riesling together, and several companies have such wines which are extremely popular.

One other comparatively recent development has been in style, rather than in variety. The late-picked wines, the *Spätlese* and *Auslese* of Germany, Austria and Alsace, the Sauternes, Barsac and others of France, have long held a place in the affections of serious wine lovers. Australia, particularly the Hunter Valley, has occasionally produced sweet table wines of quite formidable quality, as well as generic 'Sauternes' of lolly-water character. Interestingly, the cheaper sweet wines are called by that name, while the much better quality, more serious wines are not. Lindeman's 'Porphyry' is one example from the Hunter, of which there have been some excellent vintages. Most of these sweet wines were late-picked, although *Botrytis cinerea*, the noble rot, was not a factor in their quality. (The Hunter Valley can be affected by rot; it can decimate a vineyard in twenty-four hours in the warm humid conditions prevalent immediately post normal vintage. Many names are used for it at the time, none of which is noble.)

However, during the 1970s, there has been much interest in late-picked wines from other areas, particularly South Australia and Victoria, centring on the Rhine Riesling variety. These wines have various names, all so designated at the whim of the company or wine-maker in question. Most prefer 'late-picked', but some, wishing to differentiate between the degree of sweetness revert to the old *Spätlese*, *Auslese* and even *Beerenauslese* and *Trockenbeerenauslese* names. It is to be hoped that, in the future, the government will take sufficient interest in the industry to tell the makers to sort the whole business out, so that the necessary laws may be passed. The industry shows no desire to do this by itself, and to be feared is the kind of governmental implementation that gives little consideration to a well-functioning industry when it enacts regulations – which is a digression from wine qualities. Of these sweet wines, some are very good indeed, although few are affected by noble rot. But there does seem to be sufficient retention of complex fruit flavours augmented by grape sweetness to justify the development of the style. Lately, more Hunter Valley wine-makers, encouraged by the popularity of these wines among the wine-buff section of the consuming public, have been turning their attention to more bottlings of late-picked Sémillons in their district.

Some appreciation of the peculiarly fragmented nature of the wine industry of Australia should now be made. There are three broad groups of wine-making enterprises: the large 'across the board' company; the small, 'boutique', mostly specialist company; and the medium-sized company in between, which may offer all styles of wines or specialize in a few. The large companies, generally, are long-established enterprises that were solidly entrenched in the Australian market-place when the table-wine boom began. They may have their headquarters in Sydney and holdings all over the various wine states (Lindemans, Penfolds, Wynn's) or a head office in Adelaide, with branches all over Australia and important holdings in other states (Seppelt, Gramp), or a concentration of holdings in one state with branches elsewhere (McWilliams). These companies, however, have one thing in common: they offer, more or less, the same range of wine – quality sparkling, ordinary sparkling, top fortified, wholesome fortified, and all table-wine styles. The competition between them is intense (when there was surplus wine discounting was rife), and market share is everything. Yet, because of the favourable location of their vineyards and the high degrees of technical skill attained by them, many of Australia's best wines are theirs. And because of the range of these wines, no smaller company can possibly hope to win the greatest wine honour of the country, Best Exhibitor of Show. Some of the most interesting of Australian wines, as in California, come from the 'boutiques', small wine-making proprietorships of one chosen area, and often specialists in one or two grape varieties only. Their wines are much sought after by the consumers, who seem often to think 'small is beautiful'. In fact, small is often rather ordinary, since many of the makers have insufficient capital to buy the right equipment, or yearly new wood, for example. But there is a great deal to be said for the maker of a smaller quantity of wine, for care and attention can result in great quality. Between these two is an assortment of medium-sized companies ranging from the producer in one area who specializes in a limited range of table wine, to companies on the verge of becoming one of the big fellows. The latter may also have holdings in various areas, or may dominate a sub-area, buying up most of the locally produced grape material. One feels that as far as the future of these companies is concerned, much rationalization will have to take place. The production of some of the specialists is too much to permit easy marketing. It is difficult to achieve maximum prices, with the limited population of Australia, when production is of the 100,000–300,000–case level. Little mention has been made of the cooperatives, among whom are the largest crushers of material in Australia. Much of their produce is sold to other companies to be marketed under the label of the latter, although there is a tendency for market identification. Of the cooperatives, a couple have worked hard to make batches of quality wine, and these will be discussed in the area summaries.

New South Wales

THE HUNTER VALLEY

The vineyard area is divided into two parts: the traditional area, the Lower Hunter, centred around the parishes of Pokolbin and Rothbury near Cessnock, 160 kilometres north of Sydney, has had sections planted for over 120 years. The second area, the Upper Hunter near Muswellbrook, another 80-100 kilometres further north, is a product of the recent wine boom, and styles produced are different from the more famous region to the south. The Pokolbin-Rothbury area has seen many changes: boom to bust, bust to boom. The 1980s are a time of rationalization, as bigger companies consolidate their positions and smaller ones develop their styles. Not much planting is taking place and most of that is with the Chardonnay variety. Although there are 'relic' vineyards of obscure varietals, most table red wine is made from the Shiraz or Hermitage grape, though much recent work has been done with Cabernet Sauvignon. Pinot Noir has many supporters in the district, though most efforts have been unsuccessful, the final product lacking colour and fruit. The famous white wine of the district comes from the Sémillon variety, though some recent, voluminously flavoured Chardonnays have attracted much attention. Other white varietals have been planted, but of these only Traminer shows promise, and then presenting a wine quite different in style to the usual aromatic variety. The district stands secure in its almost total production of dry table wine, in the unique qualities of these wines, and in its proximity to Sydney.

Lower Hunter Vineyards

BROKENWOOD

A development of the 1970s by three Sydney lawyers, who have now been joined by other partners as the vineyards have been extended. They specialize in dry red wines with concentration on the Cabernet Sauvignon. Some fine wines have been made. When a year lacks full fruit, they are not afraid of repeating some of the earlier blending successes conducted by wine-makers in the 1950s; bulk wine from Shiraz is purchased from Coonawarra district for this purpose.

CHATEAU FRANÇOIS

A small vineyard planted variously in Shiraz, Cabernet Sauvignon, Pinot Noir, Sémillon and Chardonnay, by Don François, who makes good to very good wines from all varieties, consistently winning medals in local and interstate shows.

DRAYTON'S BELLEVUE

An old-established firm that has suffered the slings and arrows of Hunter adversity for over one hundred years. Of the various wines made, the best are full-flavoured dry reds from Shiraz, some quite soft, full, round wines from Cabernet Sauvignon which, surprisingly, drink very well when reasonably young, and some rather big, round, soft, white wines, of tremendous 'straw' flavour when developed, which are among the more traditional of the Hunter whites available today.

ELLIOTTS

Another old proprietorship of very good name, taken over during the boom years by a company that went into receivership. The Elliotts have now resumed their own affairs, centred around the old Oakvale property. The reds, from old vines, have a dimension of flavour, when mature, called 'earthy' or 'sweaty saddle'. The whites are long-lived and rich in flavour. At best, both are top examples of traditional Hunter qualities.

LAKES FOLLY

Owned by Dr Max Lake, one of the great characters of the wine and food scene in Australia. His small vineyard was planted by friends during the early 1960s, and was the first of the current expansion of the district. Dr Lake, always a great enthusiast for the Cabernet Sauvignon variety, was dismayed that none was available in the Hunter Valley, so, typically, he set about correcting the situation. His wines from that variety, matured in new wood, have attracted a great deal of favourable comment, and achieve among the higher prices for wines from the district. Recently there has been much enthusiasm for a white from Chardonnay, matured in small new oak, of which little has been sold. There have been some outstanding wines made of this variety and one looks forward to their peak of maturation in the bottle.

LINDEMANS' BEN EAN

One of the many vineyard holdings of the company with the largest sales in Australia, and one of the most important. The fortunes of Lindemans were founded in the Hunter Valley by a doctor of that name. The present winery was bought in 1912. Lindemans became a public company in 1953 and took over important wine companies in the Barossa Valley and Coonawarra, and was in turn taken over by Philip Morris in 1971. The Ben Ean winery has long remained the centre of the company's top quality wine-making, and the wines from it are a major reason for its success. Lindemans foresaw the table-wine boom. The company always had a large part of what table-wine market there was and, when demand rose, was in an ideal position to take advantage of it. Before and after the Second World War, Cawarra Claret and Cawarra Riesling Hock were celebrated table wines, and were entirely from the Hunter. The wines, named after the original Lindemans property, exist to this day, although no one pretends that anything but a minute percentage of Hunter material is in the bottlings. During the 1950s, the top wines were sold in a series of 'bin' numbers, authentic then though somewhat simplified these days. The whites made from Sémillon (and sold as Hunter Riesling, White Burgundy and Chablis), were consistently among the very best the Valley had to offer, having a finesse and a dimension of quality removed from the fuller wines of other companies. Many of the reds, too, were lighter and finer, and since every scrap of flavour was retained, this lightness seemingly intensified the complexity of developed fruit character. It is not unusual to taste both reds and whites that are over twenty years old and in prime order. During the 1960s there were seemingly endless progressions of quality dry reds and whites, plus the occasional sweet wine, which dominated the quality field in their categories, and led to the company enjoying great success at shows. During the 1970s, there seemed to be a falling away from the highest degree of quality. This may have been due to the extra demands for profitability imposed by the parent company, the greater demand for fine wine (and therefore subsequent increases in availabilities to match demand, resulting in a decrease in quality), poorer seasons, or the comparison against the rising qualities of wines of other companies. Whatever the cause, it is to be hoped that the Hunter wines of Lindemans revert to their full former glory. The whites, deep-hued, rich in golden green, huge-nosed, full of tremendous mouth-filling flavour, long in finish, among the very best from their variety in the world, and the reds, uniquely flavoured, deep and rich in complexity, balanced, with a character that is no shadow or imitation of any overseas style, but one that is assertively of the Hunter Valley, and one of which Australians can feel proud.

MCWILLIAMS MOUNT PLEASANT

The Mount Pleasant vineyard is one of the smallest operations of that large and prosperous company, and one of its most important. The company makes a number of distinctive varietal wines from its large wine-making plants in the Murrumbidgee irrigation area in New South Wales, but none is as important as the standard and special wines that come from their holdings in this district. There is a fairly large quantity of red sold under the Mount Pleasant Philip Hermitage label. Vintages of this vary. The best of this wine can develop in the bottle for ten to fifteen years, and show good reason for long keeping. The colour blends into a brick-garnet at a fairly early age, and then holds this hue for some years. The nose becomes full and redolent of the earthy, smoky character that is the hallmark of the district. The palate is soft, round and deep-flavoured, the whole smooth and balanced with a long finish. Lesser vintages showed some H_2S overtones, which dominate both the regional and fruit characters. A higher quality, generally more interesting wine is the Mount Pleasant Pinot Hermitage, a blend, fairly obviously, of Pinot Noir and Shiraz. The company has had the former variety since early days, though there is some clonal difference between it and newer importations. This wine is not blended every year. Sometimes, confusingly, it is blended under another 'special' label. It is higher in structure than others and has, at best, a particularly interesting flavour. There are various 'special' labels, of certain vintages which are almost too confusing to follow, that designate various vineyards (if the particular vintage offering is 'different' enough to excite), or various styles (if it happens to crop up that year). This is a fairly indulgent habit, practised only by a large company not making much money out of its pride and joy. Thus we may spot RH, P and OP, OP and OH, or Frederick, Charles or Richard. All of these wines command attention, and among them have been some of the most outstanding wines of the area (1954 Richard, 1952 Stephen, 1958 P and OP, 1959 RH, 1967 P and OP, and 1964 Robert).

Names crop up again with the whites of the company, although in a less spasmodic manner. One has tasted Florence and Margaret, but these old girls seem to have been laid to rest. Production now centres on what is said to be the largest single-selling wine from the area, Elizabeth Riesling, and its more expensive sister, Anne. Elizabeth is from both Mount Pleasant and Lovedale, a vineyard a few kilometres away next to Cessnock aerodrome. Generally speaking, the wine is rather full, sometimes a little coarse, and with a slightly 'cheesy' nose which is said to be its trademark. However, in latter vintages there has been a considerable degree of evolution into a lighter, fresher, more fruity style which has more finesse. On the other hand Anne remains a traditionalist. Since this wine, said to be the pick of Lovedale, is always sold after having spent four to five years (or even more) in the bottle, it is very much an old-fashioned 'style' of Hunter white, developed, full, with great richness of flavour on the middle palate – not everyone's style of wine perhaps, but highly regarded by serious critics because of its individuality. The company occasionally makes a sweet wine, unfortunately dubbed 'Sauterne' or 'Sauternes' which, although light, can develop lovely honey flavours.

SAXONVALE

A victim of the Gollin crash, purchased by the MacDougall brothers of Rugby Union fame, this company has vineyards, some forty kilometres away from the main Pokolbin-Rothbury area, at Fordwich. The reds, which are so far not totally proven, tend to be non-Hunter in character with the varietal fruit used playing the dominant part. Time will tell how both the Cabernet Sauvignon and Shiraz settle down. However, the whites are more interesting at this stage, since the company appears to be making an individual style of white, and since, also, it does not seem to be afraid of using small new wood. It makes two Chardonnays, one with, one without wood, and these seem to be more forward than others, almost to the point of being 'designed' to be enjoyed early. With age, early vintages tended to flatten and fill out fairly quickly. But even these wines were most attractive when young, having lovely fresh fruit qualities and being soft with good balance. The Sémillons are more typical of the district, although again on the short developing side. Strangely, the most interesting of the whites, from the point of view of future development, rests with the blend of the two varieties, which show more backbone.

THE ROTHBURY ESTATE

The writer must disclose his bias towards this property since he was among its founders and has remained its chairman since its inception. Founded in 1968, with high ideals, the company has had difficulties, the chief ones being under-capitalization, the swing to white wines (the vineyards have a red–white ratio of 2 to 1), a string of excessively wet vintages, and, probably, its chairman. However, it seems to have surmounted these most successfully, with most of the original ideals intact. Wines appearing under the Rothbury label must come from its own vineyards, which are the most extensive in the Valley, with over 300 hectares planted. There is a rigid selection programme after the wines have been made, and generally speaking, 60–70 per cent of the wines make the grade of one of the labels. The rest is sold in bulk or as 'quaffing' wine. Most of the wines are sold to members of The Rothbury Estate Society, which is at its most simple, a mail-order list. The wines are highly interesting, coming from three main varietals, Cabernet Sauvignon, Shiraz and Sémillon. There are also plantings of Pinot Noir and Chardonnay. Perhaps ideals can be set too high, but thus far the material made from these latter varieties has not been considered good enough to be sold under a style varietal label.

Each year all the individual containers of red wine are tasted at least three times by the panel, lesser wines being discarded each time. Prior to bottling, the reds are split up into three categories: Individual Paddock (IP), Individual Vineyard, Varietal. The IP wines must be of one particular variety from one particular vineyard. These are selected in small quantities only because of their degree of complexity and interest. The main quantity goes into the Vineyard range. There are four main vineyard areas, some kilometres apart (to minimize hail risk): Rothbury, Herlstone, Broken-back, and Homestead Hill. These wines may be blends of the various grape types grown depending on each year and the different qualities. A small quantity of 100 per cent varietals are offered as a cheaper line for those who wish to examine those styles each year. Many of the reds have been extremely good, though there has been much disappointment over the final, small quantity of top wine that emerges from a rather large vintage. Perhaps there was also some impatience, for vines planted in red varieties do take more time to mature and develop their full characteristics. Whatever, the best Rothbury reds are light-structured, round and soft, with complex intensity of flavour.

The whites have the same gradings. In the opinion of many people, the IPs (Individual Paddock) are among the very best the Hunter Valley has to offer each year. There is also a wood-matured IP, which has built up an almost fanatical following. Of the four vineyard wines, Rothbury is nearly always the finest, having an 'estery' delicacy that ages extremely well. The Brokenwood is the broadest, and matures the quickest, and the other two vineyards vary between the two. The IPs and the Individual Vineyards all age magnificently, the optimum character depending on the year. Top white years produce wines that will develop for ten to fifteen years, and even 'off' years (amusingly, perhaps, these can be the result of both wet and too hot years) will achieve very good wines which mature for up to ten years. In the view of the writer, Rothbury has taken over, to some extent, the role pursued by Lindemans in the area during the late 1950s and 1960s.

TULLOCH

Another old-established family company, which under the direction of the brothers Hector and Keith Tulloch did much to foster Hunter wine and, in fact, wine-drinking in general. The company was taken over by Reed Consolidated in 1969 and, although new equipment was purchased, buildings established and vineyards planted, there seemed to be some loss of wine-making direction. Fortunately, strong efforts were made to overcome this, and the position was further strengthened when Gilbeys took over from Reed in the mid-1970s. The reds had always been famous, and among them were some really great wines, deep-flavoured, well balanced, long-lasting. For some years these qualities were lost, and it was only in the mid- and late-1970s that the older characters, much beloved, seemed to re-emerge. The whites, on the other hand, seemed to undergo a metamorphosis, becoming lighter and finer, and having a depth of fruit character not previously apparent. Tulloch Sémillon wines, called Hunter Rieslings, especially the 'Private

Bin', are very sound and consistent and, like other top Hunter whites, repay cellaring – about three to six years in the bottle. They have also made a speciality of a blend of Sémillon and Chardonnay, matured in new wood, which is not quite so forward as others in the district, having a higher-acid, cleaner finish. Of the reds, the Private Bin Hermitage shows signs of maturing to former glories, and the Cabernet Sauvignon, a straight bottling, can be quite remarkably fine.

TYRRELL

Murray Tyrrell, the 'King of the Hunter', enthusiast, autocrat, advocate, is one of the most tenacious of wine men, and one of the most dissatisfied. In 1959 he took over the vineyards which were in good order, from his uncle but most of the wine was sold in bulk. As soon as Murray took over, the vineyards were hit by hail, and then again the following year. Murray realized that, in order to survive, he would have to develop the imported (that is, from other states) wine side of his business. He built tasting rooms and barbecues, and soon had a thriving business in cheap wine. Meanwhile, on the dirt floors of his cellar, many of Australia's top amateur palates and most eminent professional buyers were busy tasting from the casks the fine vintage wines made from the old-established vineyard, the reason for Tyrrell's wish for survival. Today, much of the rubbish has gone. Tyrrell still sells a lot of reasonably priced wine to the tourist trade, but much of it comes from his extended holdings in the area. In the meantime, his top wines have become among the best of their styles in the country: this statement may be better appreciated when one learns that, in 1978, his wines won the second highest number of gold medals in table-wine classes in major shows throughout Australia, an incredible feat for a small company against the 'big boys'.

Of the consistent medal winners, Tyrrell's Chardonnay has dominated. Picked early in vintage, matured in small wood for a year or more, the wines have an individuality of their own. They are not as full and 'early' as the Californian wines, nor as flinty as a top Chablis and not as 'nutty', perhaps, as a top Meursault. Yet they have something of all three, with a finesse often lacking in the Californians, and a strength of fruit lacking in all but the best French. After some years in the bottle, the wines become full of tremendous flavour – and indeed it may be wondered quite how long they will go on. There is only one point of criticism: some of the lesser vintages tend to flatten out on the back of the palate. However, it appears that as soon as Murray spotted this defect, he took steps, in both selection of grape-picking times and wine-making, to overcome it.

His Sémillon wines, called Hunter Riesling, are also outstanding. There are various vat numbers, the pick of which are generally Vat 1 and Vat 18. These wines are remarkable for their tremendous balance and freshness when young, qualities that make them extremely pleasant drinking. They mature slightly quicker than other Hunter whites, often achieving high-flavoured, developed characters within three to five years in the bottle. Since both varieties are made so well, perhaps it is not surprising that there is also an excellent Sémillon Chardonnay blend.

The reds have remained true to the traditional style, although there have been endless experiments with Merlot, Cabernet Sauvignon, Malbec and Pinot Noir. A vintage of Pinot Noir 1976, did particularly well in a Paris tasting, defeating all comers, including Tête de Cuvée Burgundies. However, the main and most popular of the quality reds are made from Shiraz, and again are sold in Vats. Vats 5, 9, 11, 12 spring to mind for their consistency. These reds are tasty when quite young, but need five to ten years in the bottle to show their real worth, a solid, straightforward rich, earthy flavour which many call 'old-fashioned'. Meanwhile, in the ever-growing winery, Murray Tyrrell marches on. This is where the dissatisfaction of the man appears. The Chardonnay is good, but could be better. The Pinot is a nice wine, but does not show enough fruit and is not deep enough. Why can't we make a sparkling wine out of Pinot Noir? So they made one. It's not fine enough, let's make another with Pinot Noir and Chardonnay. So they do. The experiments by this most imaginative of wine men go on and on – rosés, sweet wines, semi-sweet Sauvignon Blancs, Cabernet Malbec blends – and from them, undoubtedly, will emerge some highly interesting and even great styles.

Upper Hunter Vineyards

There has been some rationalization of both vineyard and winery properties of the Upper Hunter since those enthusiastic days of the late 1960s and early 1970s. Of those remaining, these would appear to be the most significant:

ARROWFIELD

The giant of the Upper Hunter with perhaps the largest single vineyard in Australia, most of which is drip-irrigated. After a promising launch, the company, a subsidiary of the giant W. R. Carpenter Holdings, experienced problems with its place in the market, attempting to sell all degrees of quality table wine, including cask and flagon, against the more entrenched companies. In the late 1970s this policy was discarded, and it is to be hoped that their new policy, of making and marketing top wine qualities, will be adequately rewarded. Of the wines that did make some impact, both Rhine Riesling and Sémillon produced lively, fresh and balanced styles, showing good varietal characteristics.

HORDERN WYBONG ESTATE

Owned by David Hordern and Dr Bob Smith. The winery is a reconstructed jail, all sandstone and heavy timber and the vineyards lie beneath its commanding site. Much of its wine is sold under merchant label in Sydney, but occasionally outstanding Sémillons are made of the more traditional style, having depth of fruit and taking kindly to considerable bottle ageing, building up rich, full flavours.

ROSEMOUNT ESTATE

Owned by Bob Oatley, Rosemount is run with an expected high degree of efficiency. The vineyards are well irrigated, the winery contains some of the most modern equipment available. The marketing approach has been sound, the advertising often brilliant. Consequently Rosemount, a relatively new company, got off to a very good start, and a couple of early award-winning wines helped this considerably. However, these wines tended to flatten out in character fairly quickly, and although public acceptance did not appreciate this as rapidly, many felt that there was a 'flash in the pan' element to the wines. Fortunately, there seemed to be a managerial change of heart about this time, and now some very pleasant wines, especially from the Rhine Riesling variety, are being made.

M.I.A. (RIVERINA)

The Murrumbidgee Irrigation Area, one of man's triumphs over the harshness of nature, is located in the Riverina district of New South Wales, around the main town of Griffith. Many kinds of fruit are grown under irrigation and, where the canal water flows, the land is rich and verdant. The vines spread wide and are of prolific growth. At vintage they are so heavy laden they seem on the point of collapse, and yields of up to fifty tonnes per hectare, for lesser varieties, are not uncommon. Penfolds, Gramp, Seppelt and Wynn's, big companies all, have large wineries there to take advantage of the amount of material available. Most of the grapes are grown by the original returned soldier-settlers, or their progeny, and large numbers of Italians who helped settle the area and who, through their industry, have given great vigour and spirit to the community. There are also a number of smaller wineries, some of which specialize in making light, fruity wines for the Italian community, and others that have more 'serious' wine aspirations. Among these various companies are Calamia, Calabria, De Bortoli, McManus (yet another wine doctor) Rossetto, San Bernadino (a strong and quality-oriented relative newcomer), Sergi and Toorak. However, one company dominates all, for this is the home of McWilliams, one of the largest wine companies in Australia, and said to be the largest family company of any kind.

MCWILLIAMS

McWilliams has three large wineries in the area at Yenda, Hanwood and Beelbangera. Total storage capacity is well over 50 million litres. Obviously, much of the wine made is of the reasonably priced fortified nightcap variety, for which there is still much demand, particularly in country areas. But McWilliams has triumphed with quality wine, concentrating on the best varietals. The vineyards are controlled carefully, and chosen growers are recompensed to lessen yields. Of all these wines, none has been as successful as the Cabernet Sauvignon, which is matured in new wood, and remains one of the 'safest' reds in the country, being of reasonable price and consistent character. What is more, the wines last. Although they settle down after two to three years in the bottle to provide quite substantially enjoyable drinking, the best need five to six years, and then they hold character for quite some years more. Incredibly, some of this character spreads down to very reasonably priced wines of the same variety, some of which appear in flagons and two-litre bottles: a straight Cabernet Sauvignon at a price not much different to bottled beer! There are also many successful whites, from Rhine Riesling, Chardonnay, Sauvignon Blanc, Traminer and Sémillon. There is a highly successful Traminer-Riesling blend, perhaps the best of its kind. It is not wise to attempt to mature these whites for years in the bottle, since one of their characteristics is freshness of varietal fruit when young. At their wonderfully modest prices they are therefore often a much better proposition than more highly touted, and much more expensive, wines from other areas. Climate and grape availabilities also bring about the making of a fine, wood-matured sweet red of the Tawny category. This wine, called Hanwood Port, can become liqueurish if the blend is an old one, but either way it is excellent fortification of both nature and fate.

MUDGEE

Another high-quality general fruit-growing area, about 225 kilometres north-west of Sydney. Very good table grapes are grown, among a wide range of other fruit. Although on much the same latitude as the Hunter Valley, the altitude is much greater (490–600 metres above sea level) and consequently the ripening cycle is slower and vintage starts four to six weeks later than in the Hunter. There have been vines in the area for well over 120 years, and until recently most of them were grown by descendants of the original planter, Adam Roth. At one time in the 1880s there were thirteen wineries in the district and six of the largest were separate Roth undertakings. The area went into depressed times later in the century and by the 1930s there were only two wineries left: one of them, Craigmoor, was run by Jack Roth, one of the modern promoters of the district, who died in 1969. Since the mid-1960s there has been a revitalization of the wines of the district, with the establishment of several new vineyards and wineries. The region is one of the first to drive towards a form of *appellation contrôlée*, and its own wine show is given much local prominence. Among the most interesting of the local makers are:

CRAIGMOOR

The old Jack Roth winery was taken over by Sydney businessman, Cyrile Van Heyst, in the early 1970s. There is a range of dry reds and dry whites made, as well as port and muscat styles (one favourite is Rummy Port, said to obtain its flavour from the rum casks used). The reds from Cabernet Sauvignon Shiraz and Pinot Noir can be on the heavy side, though attempts have been made to make a more elegant, lighter style. The whites have depth of fruit character, but can be broad and sometimes common. However, the Chardonnay, though rather big in structure, can be good drinking when young and the Sémillon Chardonnay blend is a very consistent and well-flavoured wine. Some big, pungent Traminers, with loads of typically musky or spicy fruit, have been made, as well as pleasant, fresh whites from Sauvignon Blanc and Trebbiano.

HUNTINGDON ESTATE

Felt by many wine critics to make the most consistent wines of the district. Bob Roberts, owner and wine-maker, is a dedicated enthusiast who has tried hard to bring more finesse into the local style. His Cabernet Sauvignons consistently win medals in open competitions and the whites, from Sémillon and Chardonnay, have a freshness, a cleanness of varietal character not impaired by broadness or coarseness. An old-fashioned heavy style of Shiraz is made to appease the regulars. All wines are made from the estate fruit, from over forty-five hectares of the varieties mentioned, plus Pinot Noir, Merlot and Sauvignon Blanc. The Roberts have a substantial private trade, run mostly by mail order by Wendy Roberts.

Other Vineyard Districts

There are various small vineyard areas scattered in many parts of New South Wales, and although these may not have a giant impact in the world of wine (though some have pretentions in that direction), their very diversity and range stress the availability of different soil structures and macro- and micro-climates in just one state of the Commonwealth. This in turn stresses the flexibility of the industry in Australia.

Rooty Hill

On the outskirts of Sydney, this was once an area of quite considerable vineyard holdings. Surrounding suburbia (plus an increased annual rainfall, apparently a result of such encroachment) has reduced their planting from more than eighty hectares to less than twelve. Traminer is grown, which used to be the source of the famous Trameah, but which is now used by Penfolds, the owners, in their popular Traminer Riesling blend.

Corowa

This area is on the northern banks of the great River Murray and therefore is the southernmost part of the State, and opposite the celebrated dessert wine district of north-east Victoria. It is famous, also, for its fortified wines. Lindemans is the company most associated with this subdistrict, and takes from it some of its better Muscats, port and sherry styles.

Young

This area, famous for its cherries, has ridges of fertile red soil which have a clay base. The clay absorbs and retains winter rain, and is therefore ideal as a storage unit for deep-rooted vines. Yields of up to twenty-two tonnes per hectare may be obtained from these outcrops, whereas two to three tonnes may be the maximum only metres away, off the soil structure. One local grazier, Peter Robertson, became interested, and has done so well, making full-flavoured, generous-bodied reds, and clean fresh whites, that others in the district are now following his example.

Cowra

In central New South Wales there is quite an extensive vineyard planted under the auspices of a number of local businessmen and professionals. The varietals are the 'usual now' vineyard mix, Cabernet Sauvignon, Shiraz, Chardonnay, Traminer, Sémillon, and Sauvignon Blanc. What makes it so interesting is that the altitude (549–610 metres above sea level) produces a slow ripening cycle, which has resulted in some outstanding material. Brown Bros of Milawa, Petaluma, now centred in South Australia, and The College of Wagga Wagga, have all used some of this material with outstanding success in spite of the huge distances the fruit has to be transported. The best Brown Bros Chardonnay, and the celebrated Petaluma's Chardonnays of 1977, 1978 and 1979, all came from Cowra fruit, resulting in competition that has produced some of the highest prices for grapes in the country. It does seem that Cowra has great potential as a quality wine area.

Namoi

In the heart of this well-known cotton district, a local man, Ron Radford, has developed a vineyard. His wines, called Cubbaroo, are most distinctive, being strong and heavy, and having a distinctive flavour. Their success has led to others planting vineyards.

Finally, among other small areas, there are various plantings as far apart as Cobbitty (not far from Sydney), Burong (near Mildura in Victoria), Barooga (near Rutherglen in Victoria), and Forbes (Central). And they all make a living.

Victoria

THE NORTH EAST

Another old-established area, another boom-and-bust region. It extends from just south of the border (with New South Wales) along the River Murray and then south to Glenrowan and Taminick. In the east the highlands rise to become the Australian Alps, and in the west the vast plains stretch into the dry country. Rutherglen, a small town of some 2,000, is said to be its centre. Incredibly, perhaps, in the late-nineteenth century, before phylloxera, there were nearly 6,100 hectares under vine at Rutherglen alone, plus another 4,059 in the immediate district. Add to this grape boom a gold boom, and it does become rather remarkable that the district can be so sleepy today. However, times change and recently there has been a fair amount of new wine activity.

The area is famous for its rich dessert wines and huge-flavoured robust reds. The former are a delight, especially the Muscat, made from various Frontignan varieties, and the Tokay, which ampelographists believe is not the Furmint variety, as may be expected, but the Harslevelu, which, of course, is also from Hungary. The liqueur Muscats are the best of their style in the world, according to many experts, and the writer agrees, having quested for years to other parts of the globe to see if there was adequate competition. He has yet to find it. Amazingly, these wines were almost totally unappreciated for years. In the early 1960s, a blend of liqueur Muscat with an average age of thirty years could be bought for shillings a bottle. Certain wine-makers did not know what to charge for even older samples and, embarrassed, gave away bottles of the 1890 and blends going back to the 1860s.

Luckily for them, and unluckily for the consumer, times have changed, and the very best of the great show-winning wines can auction for very high prices.

ALL SAINTS

The winery is said to be a scaled-down version of the Castle of May, and was built by the Scottish founder of the company, George Sutherland Smith. Run today by his descendant of the same name, the company has long been famous for its port styles and Muscats. Many of the latter were of the traditional viscous and concentrated style, though today a lighter, more elegant edition is sold at a reasonable price. A substantial red is also made, from Cabernet Sauvignon, as well as the solid Shiraz which is traditionally popular. In recent years there has been much effort to make a range of whites, from Chardonnay to Rhine Riesling and including some Marsanne, most of which reflect the hot vintage, being towards the broad side.

BAILEY

The wine is made now by Harry Tinson. The soil is very fertile and is said to have a ferrugineous quality, and this is certainly to be tasted in the unique reds. These are probably among the most individual in Australia, having been described as 'a meal with wine *and* a good cigar.' Some recent use of new oak has changed the style somewhat, and this has met with a mixed reception, some feeling that character has been lost. A great liqueur Muscat has been under a form of *solera* for years, and from time to time a release is made which is snapped up with alacrity. Lately, some whites have been attempted with mixed success.

BROWN BROS, MILAWA

Certainly the most dynamic of the older companies in Victoria. The material from the vineyards of Milawa is augmented by others from nearby Everton and also Mystic Park, an irrigated vineyard on the shores of Kangaroo Lake, in the heart of the 'River' country. The present owner, John Brown, has four sons, all of whom work in different areas of the company's business. Brown Bros wines fill a disproportionately large part of all 'selected wines' and 'wines of the year' lists. A recent 'Best of Year' book listed twenty-two wines from them, which was equal to that of Lindemans, a company many times the size. A perusal of that list gives some indication of the present scope attempted by the family and their enthusiasm for single varietals. Rhine Riesling (both dry and late picked), Chardonnay, Chenin Blanc, Traminer, Sémillon, Marsanne, white Frontignan, Sauvignon Blanc, Colombard, Cabernet Sauvignon, Shiraz, Mondeuse, Carignan, Verdelho and 'Tokay', all produced wines that were considered good enough to be mentioned before hundreds of others. Before this involvement, Brown Bros were celebrated for making lighter, less dense and gutsy dry reds than those from the district, and they uphold the quality of these still.

CHAMBERS

Another 'oldie' from the Rutherglen area, making rich, round, soft dry reds that are wonderful accompaniments to strong cheese and pasta dishes. Bill Chambers is one of the most experienced (and least assuming) wine judges in Australia, yet he continues with the old-style wine which, he feels, is what the area produces best. There is also a range of marvellous old fortified wines, an Amontillado, a Liqueur Muscat and a Liqueur Tokay: when available they are worth every cent charged.

MORRIS WINES

Another proud name of the Rutherglen district, now a subsidiary of Reckitt and Colman. This is probably the most famous of all the liqueur Muscat producers, and the Morrises (one still runs the operation) should know something of the style, as they have been making it since 1859. The best Muscats are a joy, having great vinosity and depth of flavour, superb balance and such length that one may still taste them the next day. Expensive now, though that may be a relative word, since the average age of the top blend can be twenty to thirty years, and some material is said to be over 100 years old. Outstanding Amontillado Sherry and Very Old Tawny Port styles are also produced, as well as the Liqueur Tokay style. Vigorous Cabernet Sauvignon is made, and an interesting soft dry red made from the Durif variety.

GOULBURN VALLEY

CHATEAU TAHBILK

One of the most picturesque wineries and sites in Australia. About 129 kilometres north of Melbourne, on the high banks of the Goulburn River, the place reeks with history and interest. Founded in 1860, Eric Purbrick took over Château Tahbilk in 1932 with no oenological experience at all, except drinking the stuff. He is still there, and it is to be hoped will be for many years to come. His son and grandson now run the property.

The wines are most interesting. Long before the current insterest in them, only table wines were made. The reds are famous, long-lived, substantial. Surprisingly, perhaps, the Shiraz made a firm wine, while the Cabernet style was softer and rounder. Indeed, at one time, the former was named 'Claret' and the latter 'Burgundy'. White wines were made, the chief of which was the Marsanne, although some rather thick Rhine Riesling appeared occasionally, plus a straightforward White Hermitage. Alister, Eric's grandson, makes the wine now, and has lightened and freshened the whites, while increasing the varietal distinction. A very good Sémillon style is now being made. But the reds of Tahbilk will always be its chief glory, and the best of them live for years, growing flavour and character.

GREAT WESTERN

SEPPELT GREAT WESTERN

Hans Irvine's former vineyard and winery, a piece of wine history in Australia bought by Seppelt and made more famous by Colin (Joe) Preece, who died in 1979. During the 1940s and 1950s, Colin Preece became one of the great figures of Australian wine-making. In this time he produced the sparkling wines that were named after the township and hence made it known all over the country. These were the best ever made, of this style, in Australia. They had a lightness and finesse plus depth of intense flavour, which was not similar to that of real Champagne but on a par with it. Indeed, at competitions, when given a rare chance of comparison, it often won first prize against French Champagnes. Colin also made a wonderful series of red wines, particularly from Cabernet Sauvignon and Shiraz and 'launched' the ubiquitous Chalambar Burgundy and Moyston Claret, the material for early vintages coming from the Great Western.

BESTS CONCONGELLA

Some pleasant 'old-fashioned' reds and whites come from the 'other' Great Western property. The reds may be full of power, the whites long wood-matured, round and silky soft. Both are amiable reminders that not all of Australia's wines should be made in the same way and appear out of the same mould.

YARRA VALLEY

Not a wine name, but a district. Lilydale, before phylloxera, was a most important wine area. Twenty years ago, it was all but forgotten. Today there are nearly twenty small concerns. (If a doctor, growing over forty hectares and crushing two to three hundred tonnes of grapes, is a 'small' concern.) Among them Yarra Yering, Yarinberg, St Huberts, and Mount Mary have produced some delightful reds. Again, most of these are from Cabernet Sauvignon, and show characteristics of deep colour, huge vinosity and complexity of flavour, long 'breed' and finish. Many of these mature excellently and will feature, in the years to come, at celebrated dinners and tastings. Another company, Fergusson, is making interesting Rhine Riesling as well, but again the Cabernet grape dominates, the wines being good enough to startle many better-known makers when the wines were exhibited. The Yarra Valley is today full of intelligent enthusiastic wine men, albeit that some are part-time. The wines vary for, apart from anything else, the area is susceptible to vintage change, but the best of the wines being made have a considerable future. That most of them are red and in demand, in times of surplus, points to their qualities.

BALGOWNIE

Near Bendigo, established in 1969 by a former chemist, called Stuart Anderson. Over eight hectares of Cabernet Sauvignon and Shiraz, plus a scrap of Chardonnay. The wines are eagerly sought, and of them the Cabernet Sauvignon has really captured the Wine-Buying Public's imagination, for it shows tremendous vinosity on nose, huge fruit flavours on palate, together with strong evidence of new oak maturation, a long persistent tannin finish and good balance. One of the best wines Victoria has to offer.

Other Districts

Victoria is enjoying something of a wine renaissance. Much of this is post-wine boom and much of it of the 'boutique' nature. There are some remarkably fine reds and whites coming from all corners of the State, and a summary of the more important districts and subdistricts, and the people making considerable contributions follows.

WATER WHEEL

At Bridgewater-on-Loddon, thirty-five kilometres north of Bendigo. This is a small company which seems to be specializing in red wines and, in spite of the surplus of these, is doing very well. The Shiraz wines are of the expected character, large, firm, fruity and both the Cabernet Sauvignon and Cabernet Franc have lightness and elegance.

VIRGIN HILLS

Famous restaurateur, Tom Lazar gave it all up to start a vineyard at Kyneton, south of Bendigo. Cabernet Sauvignon, Shiraz, Malbec, Pinot Noir, Traminer and Rhine Riesling are the grapes used. The vineyard seems ideally suited to the first mentioned, which appears to grow well everywhere in Central Victoria. Tom Lazar, has made some outstanding Cabernet Sauvignon, matured in Nevers oak, which has huge 'berry' fruit character and dense flavours. Wines of great potential.

TALTARNI

Dominique Portet is a member of a family that also has holdings in France and California (Clos du Val in the Napa Valley). His aim, in Australia, is to take full advantage of the climate to make full-flavoured, rich reds that will 'last for ever'. Varieties include Cabernet Sauvignon, Shiraz and Malbec. The first releases of the company showed that M. Portet had every hope of realizing his aims, for the wines have plenty of body and flavour, and are very well made.

IDYLL

An older established new boy, going as far back as 1966. A joyously idiosyncratic couple, Daryl and Nini Sefton, led the way in the Geelong wine revival. Daryl's great grandmother was a member of a Swiss wine-making family from Neuchâtel, who emigrated to Australia with the encouragement of Sophie de Montmillon, also of Neuchâtel, and was the wife of Charles Latrobe, Victoria's first governor. The Seftons love Cabernet Sauvignon and Traminer, because of the cooler climate of the district, and feel they make wines that are quite different to the rest of Australia. They are eagerly sought by hosts of fans.

TISDALL

A quite new enterprise located in a cheese factory in Echuca, in the central north of Victoria. The owner is a dynamic gentleman who is a doctor with a large practice, and a desire to make both great cheese and great wine. His wine-maker is John Ellis, formerly of Rosemount. The material comes from either Picola, near Echuca, or Mt Helen, near the Strathbogie ranges in central Victoria. Of various varietals made, from Chenin Blanc, Colombard and others, the most impressive has been a late-picked Rhine Riesling of most excellent character and flavour. The flavour has a depth which leads one to hope that this higher vineyard may have another dimension of flavour to add to the sometimes repetitious ranks of the variety.

MILDURA

This is quite a large company, which happens to have its wine-making and brandy distilling headquarters at Mildura, a large town to the north of the State on the River Murray. However, since most of its finest table-wine material comes from its large holdings at Coonawarra, these will be discussed under that heading. It would be churlish, however, not to mention its fine sherry-style wines, made by the *flor* process: these have been among the best wines of this type for many years.

South Australia

ADELAIDE

Originally, soon after the foundation of the free colony of South Australia, Adelaide was the centre of viticulture for that State, and many of the existing wine companies, who have long moved to other holdings, had their beginnings in the areas surrounding the city. Today, little remains. Inevitably, high rates and taxes have eliminated all but the most sentimental of those vineyards that still existed. However, some companies still have their headquarters in or near the city, and others seem reluctant to lose contact with it.

PENFOLDS

Once the colossus of the Australian wine industry and now just one of the larger companies. It started, in the person of Dr Christopher Rawson Penfold, at Magill at the foot of the Mt Lofty Ranges just outside Adelaide, in 1844. Penfolds was taken over by the giant New South Wales brewer, Tooth & Co., in 1976. However, although the company is run from Tempe, a suburb of Sydney, and though Nuriootpa in the Barossa Valley does most of the production, blending and maturation, Magill will always be the centre of Penfolds to many wine people since, apart from the historic aspect, many of the great wines of the company were made and matured here.

Of these, the Grange Hermitage is the most famous red wine in Australia, and one that most often excites the wine visitor. It is also the most expensive, generally selling for a price twice and three times that of other top reds. Grange is made from purple-black material, so full of concentrated grape flavour that it might be taken for pressings. However, there are none of those extractive qualities, oils and tannins, associated with such material. This is one of the secrets of the making, a well-kept family one, too. This material is then matured in small new hogsheads of American oak. On bottling, the oak is very assertive, but such is the depth of fruit flavour that the two generally harmonize to something delightfully distinctive.

If Grange was the big brother of the Penfolds range, there was a younger son who was liked more by a large number of people, the St Henri claret. Again coming from the early 1950s, it evolved when some very good red was blended at Auldana, near Magill. The essence of St Henri is elegance, finesse, a concentrated flavour and perfume, balance and this faint stalkiness. The wine is long-lived and seems to build character all the time in the bottle. And there are other labels which have established Penfolds as probably the single largest producer of top-quality red wine throughout Australia. There is the Bin 389, a blend of Cabernet and Shiraz variously from Coonawara and Kalimna in the Barossa Valley, known as 'Poor Man's Grange', not a derogatory title considering that it has the elements of that famous wine, to a somewhat less intense degree, and sells for a third of the price; Bin 28, a straight Kalimina Shiraz and Bin 707, a straight Cabernet Sauvignon, a label that disappeared when the company needed the material for the 389, but which now, happily, has been restored. These are all top reds, among the best available, and are consistently long-lived wines, which are enjoyable when fairly young, because of fruit and balance, but which grow in the bottle into something uniquely Australian. Perhaps, of all the companies, Penfolds has the most individual 'cellar' style, breeding flavours and characters that are easily identifiable as theirs. Interestingly, they have never repeated this success with white wine, and this may be one reason for the decline in their share of the market. Obviously, a company with their vineyards and branches must have some white sales. The Bin 202 Traminer Riesling has always been of great commercial acceptance, the Bin 365 Pinot Riesling (actually a Sémillon/Chardonnay mix) can mature into some quite fine wines, but they have never been near to usurping the white success of Orlando or Lindemans, for example. In the lower-priced ranges of bottle, flagon and cask wine, they have played their part, but one feels that Penfolds should be in a much stronger position, that the company should still dominate as it once did.

STONYFELL

Part of the Martin family holdings from the mid-1850s to 1972, which were later to include W. Salter and Sons (Saltram's) of the Barossa Valley. Sold to Dalgety Australia, a subsidiary of the English group, and resold in 1979 to Seagrams Vintners, the international giant. Prior to this, the company received wide recognition for the fortified wines made from material from various areas, particularly a Vintage Port – the 1945, from straight Cabernet Sauvignon, was probably the finest of its kind made before or since. There were also some old-style reds, burgundy and claret, rich, round, soft, and full of all sorts of flavours. The best Stonyfell red, however, came from material, approximately 40 per cent Cabernet Sauvignon and 60 per cent Shiraz, that comes from the company's Metala Vineyards at Langhorne Creek, an area to the south of Adelaide centred around the Bremer River. The line has been in existence for some time, since the early 1950s, and has always tended to the big style, being strong-bodied with firm tannin. However, as a keeper, it can achieve a quality of full, if slightly heavy, character which has appeal to a section of the hearty, steak-eating Australian red-wine drinkers.

WOODLEY

Situated at Glen Osmond, six kilometres south-east from the city, having a unique maturation cellar located in the workings of an old silver mine. One of the more celebrated innovations of Tony Nelson, who was in charge from 1940 to 1963, the Treasure Chest labels, is with us still as the Queen Adelaide Claret and Riesling label. They are the two main wines of the company today. The material is purchased from the Barossa Valley and marketed by a Melbourne chainstore company, Crooks National Holdings who are the present owners.

THE SOUTHERN VALES

One of the centres of viticulture nearest a capital city, and therefore a developing tourist area, and one of the most fragmented in that there are so many new enterprises, with numbers increasing each year. It was not always thus. When a new restaurant license was granted in the 1960s, and this was quite an event, one of the pleas was the lack of tourist facilities. At that time there was but a handful of wine operations. The large companies Hardy and Reynella exported much of their wine in bulk to the United Kingdom. Emu, the English company that has caused so much embarrassment to nationalistic Australians, had large holdings at Morphett Vale. There were smaller family companies such as Glenloth, Osborn, Kay, Ryecroft and Seaview, and that was about all. The various subdistricts of this fairly large area produced fortified wines of both high quality and general standard, and dry red wines of considerable body and strength. There were exceptions, of course, and some of the great old red relics of pre-boom days come from the cellars of the two largest companies; the Cabernet Sauvignons in particular have lighter qualities with, however, tremendous longevity.

The demand for red wine changed this sleepy hollow dramatically and there are now nearly one hundred different vineyard and wine operations in the district. Among the better names are:

CORIOLE

Having sixty-four hectares of vineyard opposite the well-established Seaview winery, this smaller producer had his first vintage in 1969. He specializes in full dry reds, although some dry whites are made.

DARINGA

Owned by Ken Maxwell. His dry reds, from Shiraz and some Cabernet Sauvignon, are typical of the best of the area, being soft, full-flavoured, generous, open, sunshiny in character, but without the heaviness and coarseness of past decades.

THOMAS HARDY & SONS

The dominant wine company of McLaren Vale. It has cellars and office headquarters in Adelaide, at Mile End, and a winery in the Barossa Valley. But the main vineyard holdings have always been in the Vale. The founder of the company, Thomas Hardy, a native of Devon, arrived in the colony in 1850. He died in 1912 in his eighty-second year, and the local people erected a memorial to him, the only one to a wine-maker in Australia. Today his great-grandson, also called Thomas Hardy, is managing director of the company, and his great-great-grandson, another Thomas Hardy, works in the Melbourne branch. Hardy's wines are 'across the board': casks, standard commercial bottled lines, varietal and regional specials, private bins, and common and classic fortifieds. One of the last-named, for example, the Vintage Port made at McLaren Vale, is definitive of its style in Australia. There are two types of very good quality Vintage Ports made, which appear at most wine shows. There are serious attempts, by some companies, to make an elegant, slightly tannic, clean liquorice fruit style, something along Oporto lines. Then there is the full fruit 'blackberry' style, of enormous power and flavour, corrected by fine brandy spirit, which is the Hardy hallmark. Its top Vintage Ports become collectors' specials which are auctioned for very high prices. The material for this wine is all Shiraz from the old Tintara vineyards.

Of the other Vale wines there are frequently specials made from Cabernet Sauvignon, which may include wine from elsewhere. This company has always been a blender; some Hardy wines of the past have contained Coonawarra, McLaren Vale, Victorian and Hunter material. This makes cataloguing difficult, under regional headings especially, but the wines can be quite remarkable. It is interesting to note that many of the greatest reds of Australia were blends of different regions. Hardy's seem to be doing less of this, as its large plantings at Keppoch, some 346 kilometres south of Adelaide, have come into full bearing. The famous Cabernet Sauvignon line is now likely to be from the Vale, or Keppoch, or a mixture of both. Of the other reds, the Nottage Hill Claret, from local Shiraz, is a big, fruity, ebullient, slightly old-fashioned wine; and a special tribute, largely unprocurable, deserves particular mention. This is the Eileen Hardy red, which can be either Shiraz or Cabernet Sauvignon, and which was started in 1970 in honour of the widow of Thomas Mayfield Hardy. Matured in new oak the wines chosen for this single honour are among the best in the land.

Of the whites, the best do not come from the Vale. The Old Castle Riesling, a generic blend, is the best seller. However, the best wine is Hardy's Seigersdorf Rhine Riesling, which comes from the winery of that name the company owns in the Barossa Valley (though it may be from Keppoch fruit as well as the Barossa – blends can be most confusing). This white is extremely aromatic, fresh and lively, made to be enjoyed young, and contains a scrap of residual sugar that lifts the palate. There are also standard reds, likely to be blends. It seems that the firmer, so-called claret styles are more difficult to handle these days, in that the style does not facilitate early consumption. Thus the St Thomas Burgundy, a softer, rounder wine appears as the best of the range.

INGOLDBY

Jim Ingoldby is one of the guiding lights of the district. Son of a First World War soldier who settled in the area and started making wines under the Ryecroft label, Jim now runs the company. Ryecroft prospered; and also McLaren Vale Wines, another operation which bought bulk wines from local makers, matured and bottled them and then used their names on the joint label. These were both taken over around the beginning of the 1970s, and now Jim has a small, pleasant winery, named after him, which features the familiar wines of the district, full, soft, deep-flavoured reds, and broad, clean whites, most from Rhine Riesling. Both styles, however, have the balance and degree of finesse that would be expected from such an experienced wine man.

MARIENBERG

Not actually in the Vale, but more in the hills south of Adelaide. Made famous for two reasons: the wine-maker is a lady, Ursula Pridham, and a very charming one at that, who was one of the first to compete in a male-dominated world. What is more, she competed so successfully that in 1970, after only three vintages, she was able to win a gold medal in Adelaide against all comers. Secondly, she adores small oak flavours for *both* red and white, with the result that the latter especially, which is usually of Rhine Riesling, is most distinctive.

OSBORN 'D'ARENBERG' WINES

d'Arry Osborn, son of the founder Francis, who bought the vineyard in 1912, is one of the spokesmen for the district, and has done as much as anybody to promote it. His bottled reds personify both his and the district's character, being high-coloured, round, full and soft – 'generous' is a word often used. Among them have been wines, particularly those called Burgundy, made from Shiraz with just an addition of Grenache to lighten them, which have scored extremely well at various shows. Indeed one vintage, the 1967, won nearly thirty gold medals and many special trophies for Best Red. Worthy of mention, too, is his flagon red wine, if only for the fact that it is of a high quality for the *genre* and is always at a most reasonable price, the very essence of an Australian *vin* not that *ordinaire*. d'Arry also persevered with a dry white, remarkable for its totally honest 'fat' and rather coarse character. Lately he has been buying Rhine Riesling from Clare which is sold under his label. This indicates that even the most chauvinistic of regional characters can be pragmatic too.

RYECROFT

Formerly the Ingoldby property, bought by Reed Consolidated in 1970 and sold to Gilbery in 1974. Over 100 hectares of vineyards and a fairly large winery make this among the most important in the McLaren Vale area. The emphasis is on red table wines and again the area characteristics – fullness, softness, roundness, and generosity of flavour – dominate.

SEAVIEW

Second to Hardy's in the area, with a wide, national acceptance. Established and made famous by Edwards and Chaffey: Benjamin Chaffey was a grandson of the pioneering brothers who did so much work for the Murray irrigation settlements. After making some splendid red wines from Cabernet Sauvignon in the period 1957–62, demand for his wines was so strong that fruit was obtained from other than the large Cabernet vineyards owned by the company. This did not deter the wine lovers who continued to endorse the name, so much so that Ben Chaffey sold out in 1971 to Allied Breweries in the United Kingdom, in conjunction with Tooheys, the New South Wales brewer. Eventually, the latter became the sole owners, and amalgamated the company with Wynn's, their major wine acquisition, though both labels have been retained. In fact, the Seaview name has such *cachet* that the sparkling wine operation, the Australian Wine Company, a subsidiary of Wynn's, changed its label name from Romalo to Seaview. The reds are still in demand, although the label is now more commercial, without quite the charisma once shown. There is also a Rhine Riesling made in large quantities which is very much in demand. This shows, generally, rather broad flavour and some residual sugar, but is very well made, clear and balanced. Seaview is now very much a popular name, although the older reds were among the best offered at the time.

SETTLEMENT WINE COMPANY

An ebullient Italian from Trieste, called Vincent Berlingieri, runs this new company, owned by him and Dr David Mitchell. The vineyards are not extensive, and are centred around an old 1840 homestead. The partners share a love for Australiana, and this appears to run over into their chosen style of wine, a huge, rich, ripe, full-bodied dry red of the older style. In spite of current trends, this is the type of wine they chose to make. Small new oak is used, and the wine has a high acid content and low pH. All the major wines made have been of this style, and sales have been good. Some huge fortified wines of the Vintage Port heavier type are also made.

SOUTHERN VALES

The lone cooperative of the district, enjoying one of the best sites in town on the main road. A charming old style winery, of bluestone and tile, it was called 'Wattles' and was built in 1896 to dispose of surplus grapes in the district. Penfolds acquired the cellars some fifteen years later and used it as that company's local centre until 1963. The cooperative was founded by 185 grape-growers in the district and the cellars bought from Penfolds. The first vintage was in 1965. Today the crush is over 5,000 tonnes. All styles are produced, equal amounts being sold in bulk and in popular casks and flagon lines. However, there has been considerable emphasis on bottled quality wine, and some excellent Cabernet Sauvignon and acceptable Rhine Riesling have been produced.

THE BAROSSA VALLEY

Perhaps the most famous of all Australian vineyard areas, and certainly the place that wine enthusiasts must visit. A brief history is necessary if one is to begin to understand the unity and solidarity of the area today. The valley was first explored by Europeans in 1837 and named (incorrectly) after an area in the south of Spain. George Fife Angas, a native of Newcastle, England, who helped fund the South Australian company to promote agriculture in the colony, decided to settle in the valley, and realized help was required to establish orchards and vineyards. At the time there was some religious persecution in Silesia, and Angas, a humanitarian as well as a businessman, provided the finance to bring three boatloads, comprising twenty-eight refugee families, to Australia. They settled in 1842, and were the first of many to do so. Some of the names of the early settlers are household words today, and the descendants of those men are among the most celebrated in the world of wine. The settlers prospered, built towns, planted vineyards, raised crops, and established traditions and customs that are still very much part of valley life. There is even a *patois*, Barossa Deutsch, still used by older people, and the cleanliness and order of the valley is a lesson to the rest of the country.

The Barossa Valley is actually in two distinct parts, and this is important to understand if the various qualities of wine are to be appreciated. The floor of the valley, from three to ten kilometres wide and nearly thirty-two kilometres long, is rather an arid area, quite hot and dry at times, with little summer rain. The environs of the valley, particularly the Barossa Ranges to the east, have a higher rainfall and a cooler summer climate. The floor of the valley was traditionally planted with fortified wine varieties, Shiraz, Grenache, Pedro, Mataro and Doradillo, while the hills were likely to grow a lighter yield of Shiraz and white varieties such as Rhine Riesling and Crouchen (Clare Riesling).

At the time of the beginning of the recent interest in table wine in the early 1960s, the Barossa Valley was the centre of the premium wine-producing state. It was prosperous, for the hard-working and thrifty farmers grew many crops, the principal being grapes, and were partly self-sufficient. The major companies among them, Burings, Gramp, Penfolds, Saltram, Seppelt and Yalumba, had some vineyard holdings but purchased most of their material from the hundreds of growers. The boom changed the emphasis of wine-making. The use of many varieties was converted: Grenache was now used for light reds and rosés instead of port, and the humble Pedro utilized for bulk dry white. Establishments such as the Barossa Valley cooperative, grew from a mass of tin sheds to a castellated complex of buildings as demand for the Kaiser-Stuhl wines grew. Family companies such as Yalumba established many hectares of production, maturation and storage buildings to cope with vastly increased annual grape crushes. New hotels, motels and restaurants sprang up, and though the area had always catered for tourists, it now became a tourist must. Happily, life for the average resident does not seem to have changed much. The Lutheran Church is still the centre of communal activity, the brass bands play, the Liedertafel Choir, full of local businessmen and burly farmers, still practices weekly. And every other year, the community puts on the Barossa Valley Vintage Festival, considered far the best of its kind in the country. The area has more large and medium-sized wine companies established than any other district, as well as some smaller enterprises which, although they have histories equally as long as some of the others, have chosen not to grow to any great extent. There are fewer 'boutiques' and 'hobby' wineries in evidence. Among the most celebrated of the valley names are:

BASEDOWS

A small winery in the heart of the Valley, actually situated in the town of Tanunda among the suburban houses. Owned by the Basedow family for four generations until 1971, when a group of local businessmen took over. Some good red wines have been made, using the Eden Valley (in the Barossa Ranges) fruit as well as local material. Consequently, an added degree of finesse has been accomplished.

CHATEAU YALDARA

An amazing enterprise owned and run by a German who was interned in Persia in 1941 and shipped to Australia for further internment. Hermann Thumm came from a wine-making family and had a degree in oenology so, naturally, after the war, he turned to wine. In 1947 he bought an old, almost ruined mill and built it into a replica of a German *Schloss*. He made sparkling wine, encouraged tourists and prospered. A French château, looking like a miniature Margaux, followed, then a Spanish *bodega*, and a Champagne cellar. It is now a most prosperous business, and undoubtedly Hermann's able sons, Robert and Dieter, will continue to expand it.

C. A. HENSCHKE AND COMPANY KEYNETON

In the Barossa Ranges, in an area once called North Rhine, is a relatively small operation that is the sole survivor of various wineries once there. The original Henschke settled in the valley in 1842, and soon had a farm holding at Keyneton, some miles away in the hills, which included a small vineyard. Subsequent generations of the family farmed, grew grapes, and made wine. During the 1950s and 1960s production was devoted to table wine only, which is quite rare in the Barossa Valley region. Two reds achieved fame, the 'Hill of Grace' and 'Mount Edelstone', the latter from Shiraz planted in 1900. Some delicate dry whites from Rhine Riesling and other premium varietals are also made.

HOFFMAN'S NORTH PARA WINES

The Hoffmans have long specialized in fortified and red wines. The former can be splendid, liqueur Muscats and sweet reds of the highest quality. Firm reds of typical Barossa style, now generally with some oak refinement, are made from blends of Cabernet Sauvignon and Shiraz. Some Rhine Riesling is now also made.

KAISER-STUHL

The name is that of the highest hill in the Ranges, so called because it reminded the original settlers of such a hill, 'The Seat of Emperors', in their home district, of Baden in Germany, and is used as the label for the wines of the Barossa Cooperative Winery Ltd. This was the new name, in 1966, of the old South Australian Grape Growers Cooperative Ltd, formed during the Depression in 1931. For years there was little prosperity. Wines were sold in bulk to the United Kingdom, then after the Second World War to other wineries. The advent of the winery's own label, in 1958, helped change this. There were also sales of thousands of dozens of sparkling wine (Buyers Own Brand) to other companies. Kaiser-Stuhl became a force in the flagon and cask market, although the premium quality market was not neglected. During the late 1960s and early 1970s there was much acceptance of their oak-flavoured, rather firm, red styles, and there were some delightful Rhine Rieslings. Of these, the best developed extremely well in the bottle for two to four years, one example being the Eden Valley U24 of 1976, which won several gold medals, plus special trophies for top white, in 1978 and 1979. Another remarkable wine made was the Purple Ribbon Auslese, which, with bottle age, can be among the best sweet wines available. The Green Ribbon, a dry Rhine Riesling, is the cooperative's always reliable commercial line.

LEO BURING'S 'CHATEAU LEONAY'

One of the favourites of the quality wine stakes. This company, in the heart of the Barossa Valley, was a concept of one of the grand old men of wine, Leo Buring, who died in 1961 aged eighty-five. As the originator of 'Rinegolde', the first table wine to be readily accepted by a wide range of Australians, he did much to set the trend that exists today. Buring was taken over by Lindemans in 1962. Among the assets was a young wine-maker, John Vickery, who in the years that followed made some of the most remarkable whites yet seen in Australia. From the Rhine Riesling variety, the source of which was generally the Barossa Valley and the higher-altitude districts of Watervale (to the north near Clare) and the Eden Valley in the Barossa Ranges. Sometimes the material was from one district, or it could be a blend of two, or even the three, districts. Whatever the composition, the best were of a unique style. Some of the higher-altitude examples of the variety are typified by a 'head and shoulders' character. All is lift, fruit and fragrance on the nose and fore-palate, the middle is thinner and then the wine tapers off. These wines do not take extended bottle age. However, the converse is epitomized by the Buring style. When young, the whites have an 'estery', rather delicate, almost steely nose which is not redolent of the variety. The palate is substantial, the finish firm. Though pleasant to drink, one is aware, through experience, that doing so at this stage would be wasteful of the wines' destiny. Some years in the bottle make an amazing differ-ence. This period could range from four to ten years, and fifteen-year examples are still in remarkable order. The colour is a brilliant gold-green, the nose is full powered, voluminous and quite distinctive, unmistakably Rhine Riesling and yet not like anything else in the world. The palate is full, generous in flavour, yet with that hint of steel, almost a Chablis flintiness, on the back of it; the finish is very clean and persistently long. It is unquestionably one of the top whites in the country. There is also a late-picked version of the variety which has the same qualities, with the added dimension of the complexities of character associated with residual sugar. Again these wines are long-lived.

Buring also makes a range of special reds, again from many different areas, and among them are some excellent examples of different regional styles. There is also a wide range of commercial bottlings. The Black Label range is one of the more consistent of the standard offerings, of which the Bin 33 Riesling is often the safest choice on the limited wine list that is the shortcoming of so many restaurants. A high quality sherry, Florita, is a fine delicate wine of much appeal.

ORLANDO – C. GRAMP AND SONS PTY LTD

In 1850, Johann Gramp made, from the first vineyard planted in the Barossa, an octave of hock-style wine. Appropriately Orlando wines are now the first, or close to it, in the valley, and much of their eminence is due, still, to hock-style wine. The Gramps ran and expanded the company, still near the original Jacob's Creek vineyard at Rowland's Flat, until it was one of the giants of the industry. Among innovations for which the whole of the rest of the industry should be grateful eternally were the installation of the so-called cold and pressure-controlled fermentation systems, and the 'Pearl' style of wine. The latter, launched in 1956 as Barossa Pearl, a Charmat-style of rather sweet sparkling wine, had an enormous impact in the market, and helped make Australians conscious of the joys of table wine. The company also helped pioneer such machinery as centrifuges, gravity separators, carbon dioxide presses, pure yeast strains, and thermomification. And, happily for them, much of this effort was in the white-wine direction, at times when fortified, and then red wines, were all the rage. In 1970, the family sold to Reckitt and Colman Australia Ltd, a subsidiary of the international group. Reckitt and Colman have helped Orlando tremendously, and have therefore placed themselves in the forefront of the wine market. The quality principles of the company have been retained, or even enlarged upon, with the result, to take one instance, that Orlando made a clean sweep of the major 1979 wine shows, taking out the trophy for the Best Exhibition on each occasion. This attitude is reflected throughout the company's range, for as well as the 'specials', the private bins, the vineyard series, the old 'families' (Barossa Riesling, Barossa Cabernet), the fortifieds, the flagons and the casks, all represent good value for money, and each is a leader in its division. The casks, especially, always feature extremely well in any such tasting, and are consistently among the market leaders.

But it is at the top end of the range that most international wine lovers will look. At this peak Orlando excels. There are many celebrated whites made from Rhine Riesling. The commercial lines can be excellent, and occasionally these contain a 'sleeper', wines costing less than $A3 a bottle. The ivs (Individual Vineyards) of which there are several (all numbered, too) contain outstanding wines. The dry style is interesting, having something of the Buring's 'steel' and something of the Clare 'Head and Shoulders', but yet not being quite of either. These wines take considerable bottle age, and may develop remarkable flavours and characters. There are also several sweeter wines made, the Green Ribbon late-picked, and the Gold Ribbon Auslese which, when made, is among the very best of the sweet Rhine Rieslings, having a lusciousness and depth of flavour beyond most German styles of the same predicate. There are also some notable varietals, from Traminer and Frontignan, and an occasional magnificent special from a particular vineyard. This is the Steingarten (Stone Garden), a planting hewn out of the rock on top of a hill over 460 metres high, skirting the valley. It is cool and windy there, and often vintage is a relative failure. But when this vineyard does grow ripe grapes, the wines have an elegance, a finesse, a degree of flavour complexity – not often met in Australia. The reds must not be entirely disregarded. From the rather gutsy, extractive style of the early 1960s, a lighter, more fruity style now exists. Although one feels that the valley makes rather straightforward reds, it has to be admitted that oak subtleties may be imported and balances achieved that add complexities. Perhaps, if red-wine sales surge again, the company will look to other areas. Finally, since the strength of the organization throughout all the experiments and innovations was its stocks of premium fortified wines, the best of these, particularly the old wood-matured Tawnies, should not be ignored.

ROSEWORTHY COLLEGE

Worthy of mention, since this is the main seat of oenology learning in Australia (Riverina College at Wagga Wagga is the other). Both colleges make small batches of wine as part of their educational programmes. Recently, both decided to sell, rather than store or drink, some of their better efforts. Wagga has had considerable success in this direction, and now Roseworthy is attempting to establish more direct contact with the public. This is to be commended, for much may be achieved when the heavy hand of commercialization is not apparent.

SALTRAM

A fine old family company, amalgamated within the Martin Group in 1941. Previously, the Salters had operated in the area since 1844, and had made wine since 1862. Peter Lehmann took over the wine-making in 1969 and helped establish a name for the dry reds of his company, which was not in the least hindered by his considerable hospitality. During the 1960s the Saltram reds were very much in demand. There were three main styles: the Mamre Brook Cabernet, named after the original holding of the founder, William Salter; Claret, which contained Cabernet Sauvignon, Shiraz, and, perhaps surprisingly, some 'Tokay'; and a Burgundy made from Shiraz, Tokay and Dolcetto. The last two wines had plenty of flavour, but avoided the usual heavy 'burnt' character of the decade because of the white material used (the grape blends were fermented together). Of the two, the Claret was perhaps the most interesting and complex style, extremely long-lived; but particular affection was held for the softer wine, some years of which were delightfully easy drinking. The Mamre Brook was the flag wine of the company, very much in demand for some years. Dalgety bought Saltram in 1972 and the wines seemed to lose direction. There seemed to be a wish to promote a Dalgety in 1979, and there is now much activity taking place in an attempt to re-establish this once eminent name.

SEPPELT

One of the largest of Australian companies, Seppelt, with extensive vineyards of its own, also has two old-established major wineries in the Barossa Valley. The first, Seppeltsfield, is the product of the drive and capacity of Benno Seppelt, the son of the original settler, Joseph, a Silesian. However, he was not a poor immigrant, for he headed the family company at Wustewaltersdorf (snuff, tobacco, liqueurs), and brought considerable capital to Australia in order to grow tobacco. He was not very successful, and so turned to wine. His son Benno took control when he died, aged fifty-five. From that year, 1868, until his retirement in 1916, Benno devoted himself to expanding Seppelt. The huge stone winery at Seppeltsfield was built and today it is a big tourist attraction. Indeed, so successful is the retail operation now established there that it is said to be Seppelt's best customer. Only fortified wine is made there today. Château Tannuda, another stone winery, built in 1889 and acquired by Seppelt in 1916, is responsible for local table-wine production.

The top fortified wines of the company, made from material grown in the district are classics, both Fino and Amontillado style sherries being consistently among the top wines in such classes at shows. The port-style wines have a formidable reputation and among them there is the celebrated Para Liqueur, a vintage wine that achieves the highest auction prices in Australia, a Tawny so long wood-matured that it may attain the viscosity of treacle. The Seppelt company has a charming conceit, as far as this wine is concerned, and retains hogsheads of each year from 1878. Each year they now bottle this wine when 100 years old, and much of the proceeds, at auction, go to the Seppelt Foundation, a charitable body.

Of the table wines, some interesting individual wines have been from Keppoch, the large holdings of the company, situated in the south some sixty-four kilometres north of Coonawarra. The best of these, from Rhine Riesling and Cabernet Sauvignon, give much hope that a consistently fine style of varietal will be produced. The company also makes a number of commercial table wines, Moyston Claret, Chalambar Burgundy, Arrawatta Riesling, Muroomba Moselle, which are consistent, pleasant drinking examples of their marque.

TOLLANA – TOLLEY, STOTT AND TOLLEY

Tolley, Stott and Tolley were old and respected brandy makers for many years, derived from the original East Torrence Winemaking and Distillation Company Limited, founded in 1858. In 1961 the concern was purchased by the Distillers Company of Edinburgh, who set about an expansion programme that still proceeds today. In a short time much has been achieved, with well over 400 hectares of vineyard planted, and millions of dollars spent expanding the winery at Nuriootpa in the heart of the Valley. One result was the new Tollana label which has met with a great deal of success, particularly the Woodbury Estate wines. The latter vineyard, in the Eden Valley, is likely to provide some outstanding wines in the future. Of those made today from the area, the most impressive have been the Rhine Rieslings, which have already established a firm reputation. Wine-maker Alan Hoey has achieved a style that balances the usual austerity and acidity of the district character with a freshness and lift of varietal flavour that is not usual. The company also appears to have a policy of maturing red wines for some years in the bottle before release, which is to be commended. Their flagon lines also indicate that they intend to offer value for money throughout the range.

YALUMBA – (S. SMITH & SON PTY LTD)

One of the larger family companies that has managed to resist the blandishments of stockbrokers and multinationals. The writer is grateful to the present Managing Director, Mark Hill Smith, a fifth-generation member of the family in Australia, for it was he who introduced him to the wine industry of Australia in the mid-1950s. Samuel Smith, a brewer from Wareham in Dorset, England, who began planting a vineyard in 1849, was the founder of the company, which still operates on the same site. History does play a part in what is Yalumba today. It is reflected in the establishment, just outside Angaston, which is full of old trees, well-tended lawns, gracious old buildings, horse paddocks, clipped hedges, with the old bluestone winery acting as a façade for all the technological activity taking place in acres of buildings behind it. It is also reflected in the attitude of the owners. At a time when their Pewsey Vale Rhine Riesling was in great demand they refused to raise the price to capitalize on that demand, a refreshing attitude in the industry. Employees of the company tend to stay for most of their working lives, and their efforts are recognized each year in a line of its very best red wines, the Signature series: the year's release is always named after one of them.

Yalumba crushes over 20,000 tonnes of grapes a year, some from its own vineyards but mostly from the local growers, and makes a range across the wide spectrum of fortified and table wines. Of them, the top appetizer and dessert wines should be mentioned. Chiquita is an extremely good Fino, and Galway one of the best-loved Tawny ports in all states. The table wines have market favourites among the mid-priced range, the Carte d'or Riesling, a vintage white of freshness and clean varietal character, and Galway Claret, a red that in some years can be considerably undervalued. The Pewsey Vale vineyard, high in the Ranges near the Kaiser-Stuhl hill, produces a Rhine Riesling of high quality, of great aromatic lift, a delicious, clean fruity flavour. Some contain a trace of residual sugar but the better vintages have enough depth of fruit to balance this. Further 'altitude' plantings at Heggies, a new development, show great promise, particularly the Rhine Riesling, Traminer, and Chardonnay. Of the reds, the Signature series can be outstanding, full-flavoured wines of some finesse, matured in small new wood, with some intensity and complexity of character, balanced by a soft persistent tannin finish, which mature extremely well after some years in the bottle. There is also a new range of varietals, Chenin Blanc, Sauvignon Blanc, and so on, which are extremely well made and reflect the skills of the team of wine-makers headed by the experienced Peter Wall. Yalumba wines are always tremendous value for money, completely honest, and uniformly reliable, and, at their best, may represent the finest Australia has to offer.

CLARE-WATERVALE

One of the most interesting of wine areas, and one that has long flourished, though times and perhaps emphases have changed. There were early vineyards in the district, of which Sevenhills and Quelltaler still exist. There were over 400 hectares under vine at Clare alone at the turn of the century, a considerable amount when the population of the country is taken into account.

The Clare-Watervale district covers a series of valleys about sixteen to twenty kilometres long. The countryside is pretty with hills, woods, farmland and streams, looking in some ways almost un-Australian. The main towns, Clare Watervale and Auburn, are small, well maintained, and progress has not removed a charming air of Victorian solidity. The wines of the district have long been famed, for the reds have tremendous stamina, and the whites were well known and appreciated when others were not. Today, the district is regarded very much as a high-quality table-wine area, and many regard it as a competitor to the Hunter Valley as the best 'double'-style region – that is, the best for both red and white quality, though of course the styles are quite different. Formerly, the Shiraz variety dominated, though there are now considerable plantings of Cabernet Sauvignon. The Rhine Riesling has long been the premium white variety, and there is much opinion weighted to the thought that wines from this grape may be the best of the type in Australia.

A. P. BIRKS, WENDOUREE CELLARS

A small operation, in the heart of the local bushland which, under the direction of the founder's grandson, 'Roly' Birks, maintained a solid reputation for very big reds. These live for many, many years, and may be regarded as classic examples of the old-fashioned Clare style.

CHATEAU CLARE ESTATE

Founded during the wine boom near the small town of Auburn. The reds quickly became quite celebrated, the Cabernet Sauvignon in particular, for the fruit was fine and the company spared no expense in its acquisition of new small wood. Numerous gold medals helped, and the estate, owned by the Taylor brothers of Sydney, seemed destined for success until the red surplus. Fortunately, the quality of the reds was sufficient to tide the company over until some good whites were produced, notably from Rhine Riesling, and now all seems set for further success.

MANRESSA SOCIETY – 'SEVENHILL' CELLARS

Run by the Brothers of the Jesuit College of St Aloysius in marvellous old cellars not far from the church. The main function of the wine-making side of the operation is the supply of altar wine to the Order all over Australia and overseas. However, successive brothers put in charge of the operation have made some marvellous bits and pieces, notably sturdy Cabernet Sauvignons of high colour, huge flavour and long life.

QUELLTALER WINES

Now owned by the Rémy Martin group of France, but operated for nearly one hundred years previously. Two energetic Germans, Carl Sobels and Hermann Buring, were the chief reasons for early successes, and by the 1960s the company was noted for its *flor* sherry, Granfiesta, and a ubiquitous hock. The Rhine Riesling and the hock have continued this success, and both wines are safe and can, in certain years, be of quite high quality.

ST CLARE

Owned by Jim Barry, who has always been strongly identified with the district. He built his own winery in 1973, and enjoys a reputation for good quality, reasonably priced Rhine Riesling and solid, well-balanced reds, mostly from Cabernet Sauvignon.

STANLEY WINE COMPANY

Heinz, the canned-food agglomerate, took the company over in 1971 and since then, it has become a major quality force, consolidating the considerable efforts of Tim Knappstein, particularly with table wines under the Leasingham label. Two styles of dry Rhine Riesling are made, Bin 5 and Bin 7, which have wide public acceptance. The Cabernet Sauvignon, Bin 49, became in the late 1960s a classic red of Australia, having wonderful colour, a huge 'berry' nose and flavour, balance and complexity, plus a fine addition of small new wood characters. There is also a Cabernet Malbec blend, Bin 56, which is softer, more forward in fruit qualities, and can be quite outstanding. The Stanley company also has a reputation for its bulk wines, sold in the flagon and cask, which are often among the 'best available' lists.

TIM KNAPPSTEIN ENTERPRISE WINES

A long title, but not inapt. Tim Knappstein left Stanley in 1976, having worked hard over the previous ten years to build up the reputation of the top wines of the company, achieving great success in particular with the Leasingham label. He acquired the old Enterprise Brewery building, at the north end of the township of Clare, and managed to obtain fruit from grower friends to augment his own vineyards. Since the white-wine boom was in full flood by that time, it is not extraordinary that his main aim has been to make top white wines from the Rhine Riesling in particular, both dry and 'late-picked'. His limited production is snapped up quickly, proof of his continued skill.

COONAWARRA

One of the most exciting of all Australian wine areas, though first sight does little to enthral. Indeed, the writer once flew there in a small plane and could not find it. Eventually, in a vast brown-baked plain, dotted with huge gum trees, there appeared a tiny oasis of vine-green. This was Coonawarra, one of the smallest of established regions. It is more than 400 kilometres south of Adelaide in South Australia. The climate is cool, and vintage is later than in any other part of the country. There is a strip of soil, Terra Rossa, and only this is suitable for grape-growing. A variable water table provides year-round irrigation. These factors combine to make this small region an anomaly, for high yields, up to twelve tonnes per hectare for Cabernet Sauvignon, for example, result in high-quality material. The place was 'discovered' for wine by a wealthy grazier who noted how well table grapes grew at the homestead. After almost a century of effort, the quality of the red wines of the district was finally appreciated during the mid-1950s. The wine boom did the rest, and now almost every hectare of available land is covered. The Cabernet

Sauvignon is still the key variety, though Shiraz is at its most elegant in Coonawarra and some fine Rhine Rieslings have been made.

Penfolds has holdings there, and the material is made in Adelaide. Petaluma has an important vineyard there, and again the wine is made at the Adelaide winery. Lindemans has a large winery there, built on the site of the old Rouge Homme shed, and has continued with that label, having bought the company from the Redmans in 1965. The remaining companies of major interest are as follows:

BRAND'S 'LAIRA' VINEYARDS

Eric Brand and his family are devoted to the area. The business is a comparatively new one, for Eric was a grape-grower and winery worker for Rouge Homme. In the late 1960s he set up his own establishment and has gone from success to success. His wines are more robust than most, having a depth and body that augment the classical 'lightness' or finesse of the district. The Cabernet Sauvignon and Cabernet Malbec Shiraz blend, can be outstanding. The Brand operation is a humble, but authentic 'Estate' of great interest.

HUNGERFORD HILL

This medium-sized public company is spread over various wine regions including the Hunter Valley and the Riverlands. Their Coonawarra holdings are over eighty hectares in extent. From them come some rather 'edgy' reds, from the usual varieties, which show strong oak influences. However, some fine, delicate Rhine Rieslings have been made, showing typical varietal fruit with an unusual finesse and elegance.

MILDARA

The late Ronald Haselgrove, OBE, was the force behind the acquisition of vineyards by his company in this area. Mildara now owns the largest vine area in Coonawarra, and crush up to 3,000 tonnes each vintage. Most of this is in red material, Cabernet Sauvignon being dominant. Some outstanding wines have been made, 1963, 1971, 1975 among them, the 1963 being regarded as one of the greatest reds ever made in Australia. There have also been some pleasant Rhine Rieslings, including some late-picked examples infected by an Australian version of noble rot.

REDMAN

Bill Redman, who died in 1979 when he was well over ninety years old, was the modern 'father' of Coonawarra. He had worked there since 1901, had established his own winery, made wines for other people, helped found wine dynasties and fought for recognition, always believing in the quality he knew the area could produce. Eventually, Rouge Homme (a whimsical translation by a label artist who thought Redman was too plain) began to prosper, bottling and selling its own wines. In 1965 it was taken over by Lindemans, and Bill's eldest son, Owen, who had been making the wines for some time, decided to set up for himself. After buying a vineyard, he made his first vintages at the Brands' establishment, opening his own Redbank Winery in 1969. Two reds only are made. A straight Cabernet Sauvignon, which is often bottled in Magnums and Imperials as well as normal bottles, and a claret made from Shiraz. These are among the best reds to be found in Australia. They have considerable Claret characteristics, being light, yet having great depth of flavour. Small oak treatment adds a further degree of complexity. The wines are beautifully balanced, with a 'long' soft, persistent tannin finish. Often, they appear too light and even thin when young, but this is a local characteristic, for there is a great degree of development in the bottle.

WYNNS

Although Wynns has been taken over by Toohey, the highly active brewers from New South Wales, the fame of its Coonawarra reds continues. This is but justice, for David Wynn was one of the strongest supporters of the area. Melbourne-based, he followed his father, Samuel, in bemoaning the fact that Coonawarra wines were not appreciated as they should be. So committed to this belief were they, that they acquired the old Riddoch winery, established by the founder of the area in the early 1950s. Pre-empting Owen Redman, they made a Cabernet Sauvignon and a claret from Shiraz. There have been many notable vintages of both, for one of the characteristics of the district is that often the Shiraz performs as well as its more noble counterpart. Generally speaking, the wines have plenty of fruit, but can be less elegant than others, having a more robust nature. This is said to occur because some of the vineyards are planted on the black, clay soils that border the Terra Rossa. However, lately, there seems to have been some rationalization, and the wines are achieving a degree of finesse not formerly apparent.

THE RIVERLAND

It is difficult to deal comprehensively with the vast fruit areas in South Australia that extend along the River Murray. Settled in the most part by returned servicemen who were granted blocks, the farms grow all manner of various fruits, among them table, dual-purpose and wine grapes. To help provide a market for the latter, huge cooperative wineries were established, at Berri, Waikerie, Loxton and Renmano, as well as private establishments such as Angoves, which use local material as well as their own produce. A huge quantity of fortified wine is made at these cooperatives, plus brandy and fortifying spirit. The table wines are sound, and can be extremely well made. They provide much of the bulk wine which is sold under other labels, and a lot of effort has gone into creating their own bottled brand images, particularly as far as Berri and Renmano are concerned. Yet one feels that the growing cask market will absorb most of their output, be it under the labels of other companies or their own. If, eventually, demand does outstrip supply, then it seems natural that these cooperatives will do more to assert their right to be strongly identified with their own produce.

Western Australia

With the arrival of European settlement in 1829 came the first viticultural initiatives in the western half of the country. The pioneers under Captain James Stirling brought vines and cuttings from England and South Africa. Western Australia has always been fortunate in having qualified viticulturalists available to guide *vignerons* in their endeavours. The first, and perhaps most famous was Adrian Despeissis who came to the west in 1894. His professional training and tireless field 'workshops' saw a dramatic advance in wine quality. He was also responsible for importing better clones of vines from Europe and for the production of an efficient handbook on horticulture. The arrival of Yugoslav and Italian migrants in the early 1920s boosted the State's flagging industry. The Swan Valley just north-east of the city took on a new lease of life with the immigrants zealously establishing model vineyards, albeit on a cottage-industry basis. Today, due to the influence of a typical Mediterranean climate, the style of wine is much akin to the Rhône Valley of France.

The quest for a more delicate style of table wine saw the industry focus on the cooler southern regions of the state in the 1950s and 1960s, such as Mount Barker 400 kilometres south of Perth and Margaret River on the south-west coast 300 kilometres from the capital. The more even summer temperatures and lower overall heat summation, coupled with large tracts of the attractive gravelly loam soil types, were major factors in favour of both these new areas.

Government viticulturalist, Bill Jamieson, was responsible for developing a pilot vineyard at Mount Barker in 1966, and Perth physician, Dr Cullity, established the first modern-day vineyard at Margaret River shortly afterwards. Both proved to be outstanding successes. Cullity's wines from his Vasse Felix winery have secured several top awards at the State's annual wine show, and the wine from the Mt Barker venture, the whites particularly, have been most elegant. Today, with urban pressure on the Swan Valley, most new industrial developments have taken place in these two areas with some 500 hectares now under vine.

The wine industry in Western Australia is still small by world standards. Indeed, it produces only one per cent of the national vintage. Most of the wine is consumed in the state, usually in the year of vintage. The general standard of wine is good with the usual crop of top wine. Technology has seen great advances in quality control. The industry is still very much in the hands of the small producer who tends to make a total range of styles, from sherries through to the table styles, to some very luscious liqueur-style fortifieds. The new southern regions have specialized in the lighter dry whites, which are very much in the Loire mould, and reds that are approaching a typical Bordeaux specification. The main wineries are:

SANDALFORD

This attractive Swan Valley property has been in the Roe family since 1840. (Lately Sandalford has taken in the Anglo-Thai corporation). In addition to the old Swan property there are nearly 150 hectares under vine at Margaret River. In recent times substantial capital has been ploughed into updating winery equipment and storage. Sandalford Wines has been the most successful larger winery at the Perth Wine Show for some years. The Swan Valley Cabernet Sauvignon is a rich elegant wine and has good depth of fruit. It is full-bodied and usually balanced with time in new oak; the Chenin Blanc is a full flavoured dry white style, rather full-bodied and with good varietal character. It develops well in bottle. The Verdelho is a dry table wine with good flavour and character. It is among the best of this varietal in Australia and develops up to five years with maturation. Sandalford has made a name for itself with its Cabernet rosé, a very dry crisp style. The Sandalford Liqueur Sandalera is made from the Pedro Ximénez grape. With its Margaret River Cabernet Sauvignon, Sandalford is perhaps making the most forward of the dry reds in this area, with almost Pomerol overtones. The cool climate gives a touch of elegance to the middle palate fruit. Judicious use of new oak has balanced the wine well. Both sweet and dry styles of the Margaret River Rhine Riesling have been made to date. The drier wines are more definite and should prove to rank with the better wines of Australia.

HOUGHTON/VALENCIA

Two lovely old properties that were developed in the late nineteenth century. Valencia for many years was the largest producer in the west. Both were acquired recently by the South Australian-based, Thomas Hardy & Sons. Houghton under the guidance of Jack Mann, who spent over fifty vintages as wine-maker, always had the reputation of being the state's best producer. It was Jack Mann who pioneered the Houghton White Burgundy in 1937. This full-bodied dry white took Australia by storm, and the company never looked back. Jack was also famous for his liqueur-style fortified wines – picked at over 30° Baumé, then crushed through an old mangle. Valencia added to its Swan Valley property the Moondah-Brook Estate at Gingin in the 1960s. North of Perth in a cooler climatic zone, Moondah-

Brook was established to provide top-quality fruit for its expanding table-wine market. The Houghton White Burgundy is made from a blend of Chenin Blanc and Tokay grapes. It is full-bodied, yet soft and elegant and is a style that has lightened out with recent introduction of cold, controlled fermentation. The Rhine Riesling is a well-made wine, considering the fruit is made in summer temperatures at times exceeding 40°C. It is varietally sound and shows the benefit of cool fermentation. The Cabernet Sauvignon is a full-bodied dry table wine. It has good depth of fruit, balanced with oak and acid. The Valencia Malbec rosé is light and elegant with a touch of residual sugar. It is consistently one of the best rosés in the west of Australia. The Valencia Moondah-Brook Estate Verdelho is an attractive alternative to the widely grown Chenin Blanc. Verdelho wines made in this full-bodied dry style are at their best with two to three years' bottle age. The reds from this new estate have taken time to show their best but patience has been rewarded with the Moondah-Brook Cabernet Sauvignon, a well-balanced flavoured wine which is well recommended.

WESTFIELD WINES

Under the guidance of John Kosovich, this small Swan Valley winery has established an enviable reputation – indeed it has been accorded the honour of being the top small winery in the state for the years 1978-9. It specializes in table wine from locally grown fruit. The Westfield Sémillon is light and elegant, yet carries a good measure of varietal flavour. It is well handled and attractive. The Verdelho is made lighter and more acid than most other producers'. Through early picking and cold fermentation, it marries the natural flavour with finesse. The Cabernet Sauvignon is consistently one of the best Western Australian reds. It has good balance of fruit, acid and tannin, and is normally given twelve months in new small oak.

GNANGARA WINES

Small well-run winery. Partners John Evans and John Tate are committed to the production of top-quality wine. The red wines from this property and their more recently developed Redbrook Estate at Margaret River are always among Australia's best. The Gnangara reds are a blend of Cabernet Sauvignon and Shiraz. The best French oak hogsheads are used for maturation. The Redbrook wines made to date are well away from the established style. Earlier-picked fruit has given the wine higher natural acid levels. Integration with oak and bottle age should produce a lighter-bodied style not unlike the wines of St Julien.

CONTEVILLE WINES

Paul Conti, a typical new generation wine-maker, took over the running of this winery and its vineyards at Wanneroo from his father with little knowledge of wine science. Determination and the willingness to re-invest much of his cash flow in modern technology reaped Conteville and Paul Conti substantial goodwill and show success. The Frontignan is a dry white table wine. Paul Conti has been able to capture the attractive bouquet and flavour of the grape without the usual attendant Muscat hardness. Several vintages made with a touch of residual sweetness have also been very drinkable. There is a very limited release of Cabernet Sauvignon. The fruit is grown on light, sandy soils over limestone. This produces a wine that is light-bodied yet balanced with good flavour and acid. Small oak maturation for twelve months finishes the wine off well.

OLIVE FARM WINERY

This unique old winery with its ancient cellar has been in the Yurisich family since 1933. Vince Yurisich is acknowledged as the state's most successful small producer.

Most of the grapes crushed are purchased from specialist growers. Total production is a mere 100,000 litres, mainly table wine. Vince also makes an attractive bottle-fermented sparkling wine from the early Madeline variety. The White Burgundy is made from Tokay and Sémillon varieties. It is among the best of the dry full-bodied wines made in Western Australia. The Chardonnay is a recent addition to the winery's list. It is full, rich wine showing varietal character and a hint of small oak maturation. It has potential to develop into well-rounded wine.

VASSE FELIX

The pioneering venture at Margaret River on the south-west coast of the state. Planted with predominantly Cabernet Sauvignon and Rhine Riesling. The early promise of the area has come to fruition and once growers become fully aware of the district's nuances, some surprises are in store for the Australian industry. The Cabernet Sauvignon is made with a small addition of Malbec and Shiraz. Since the first vintage in 1972, this wine has been very much sought by oenophiles. It is light and elegant with good natural acidity and has the potential to mature for up to fifteen years in better vintages. Close attention is paid to vintaging techniques and only Nevers oak cooperage is utilized. The Rhine Riesling is a light dry wine with crisp, natural acidity. It has good varietal bouquet and flavour. Fermented cold, the wine is always fresh and indicative of the Rhine variety.

MOSS WOOD

A small, ten-hectare vineyard in the heart of the gravelly loam country at Margaret River. Under the owner, Dr Bill Pannell, this property has established a reputation for producing fine wine since its inaugural vintage in 1973. The Cabernet Sauvignon has very good depth of Cabernet flavour and French oak. It usually peaks to its best with five years' age with the potential to hold for a further three years or so. It is possibly the best dry red produced in the area to date. The Sémillon has a typical light dry style with a certain Loire character about it. The variety has adapted well in this new region, and the Moss Wood style is the hallmark. The Pinot Noir is very much indicative of the famous Burgundian wines – perhaps a trifle more full-flavoured and carrying more body. The strawberry tone sometimes associated with Pinot Noir is evident.

CULLEN'S WILLYABRUP VINEYARD

Run by Di and Dr Kevin Cullen, well-known local professional people and neighbours of the Vasse Felix property. Cullen's Rhine Riesling is made with a small retention of residual sugar, the style has a wide appeal. Very good Rhine Riesling character throughout, with well balanced natural acidity. Cullen has produced a more closed, austere style of Cabernet Sauvignon than the Moss Wood and Vasse Felix. The wine has taken several years to develop and show the potential that was always evidenced within the wine. It has typical Cabernet characteristics throughout.

LEEUWIN ESTATE

A joint venture at Margaret River between a group of Seattle business friends and Western Australian businessman, Denis Horgan. The American syndicate has retained Robert Mondavi, of Napa Valley fame, as consultant. He, in fact, has participated in the initial vintages. The partners have some of the best land in the Margaret River area and have constructed a most technically advanced winery on the property. Two styles of Rhine Riesling are made, one containing a residual sugar component and the other dry. Very elegant, and a wine that has the fruit flavour and acidity to develop well in the bottle. The Cabernet Sauvignon is still very much in the experimental stage. The partners are endeavouring to work with the natural environment of the area to produce the best possible style. Initial wines have been outstanding. Elegant, yet carrying plenty of acid and tannin, with the prospect of improvement given further maturation.

FOREST HILL WINES

The initial venture into the Lower Great Southern Region of Western Australia, based on the town of Mount Barker. The government-sponsored trial was concluded in 1975 as an outstanding success. Property owners Tony and Betty Pearse have added significantly to the trial vineyard. Rhine Riesling and Cabernet Sauvignon are the principal varieties planted. Vintaged by Paul Conti at Wanneroo, the Rhine Riesling displays an excellent varietal bouquet, while the palate has the flavour and balancing acidity to make for a very complete wine. The Cabernet Sauvignon is a very well-made dry red style showing good Cabernet flavour and oak handling, medium-bodied with balancing acid. It will age and develop well.

GOUNDREY WINES

Michael and Alison Goundrey have developed a model vineyard at Mount Barker and were fortunate in acquiring an old milk-processing factory in the nearby town of Denmark which they have renovated into a most functional winery. Their Cabernet wines since the mid-1970s have improved markedly with each vintage. The awards won for this type would confirm his style as among the very top in the district. The 1978 wine has a light elegant character with good fruit and oak flavours throughout.

PLANTAGENET WINES

Partners Tony Smith and Rob Devenish have systematically developed their venture into the wine industry since 1969. Based on a farming property south of Mount Barker, they now have approximately twenty-five hectares under vine. The initial vintages were made under contract in Perth. Vintages since 1975 have been based on their Mount Barker winery. Like other local growers, they have principally committed the major efforts towards a high quality dry white style from Rhine Riesling, and a dry red from Cabernet. After several indifferent vintages from young vines, recent Rhine Riesling wines have been of the highest quality. Top awards have been won recently with the current vintage. The wine is typically Rhine. Light, elegant with good natural grape flavour and a crisp acid finish. The Cabernet Sauvignon has a typical Bordeaux Cabernet style. Good varietal bouquet with delightful oak integrated flavours and subtle nuances of elegance. It will develop and age beautifully.

CHATEAU BARKER

Developed by the Cooper family on their historic property just north of Mount Barker. Since the initial vintages in 1977 the wines have progressively attained greater depth and complexity. The Rhine Riesling is very much a cool-climate one. It has subtle grape character with elegant balancing crisp acid palate and finish. The Quondyp Gewürztraminer is possibly a misnomer, as it has not the richness of Alsace Gewürz wines. None the less, the Traminer character is evidenced, and future wine development and later-picking policies could see further character coming into the wine. It is light, elegant and pleasant drinking. The Tiger Eye Pinot Noir is one of the first Pinots from the southern vineyards. The initial vintage was picked a little too early. However, the elegance of the Pinot grape is much in evidence. Given ideal ripening conditions, a wine of more Beaune style could be possible.

The Wines of New Zealand

RON SMALL

Ron Small is an independent wine consultant in Auckland, New Zealand. He owns and edits a publication called *The Wine Report* and works as a wine judge and taster both in New Zealand and in Australia. He has also appeared on radio and television in both countries and writes the wine column in *Signature*, the Diner's Club magazine.

The New Zealand wine industry stemmed from Australia with the arrival of the Reverend Samuel Marsden who, in 1819, recorded in his diary that he had planted at Keri Keri 'about one hundred grape vines of different kinds brought from Port Jackson'. He also planted vines at Waimate. In 1831, James Busby, who had established vineyards in the Hunter Valley of New South Wales, noted 'that few vines are being grown in New Zealand', and he returned there in 1833 with cuttings of French and Spanish vines, planting them at the Bay of Islands. In 1840, Busby (the recognized pioneer of the New Zealand wine industry) produced what is thought to have been the first wine made in New Zealand. He was the official Queen's Representative, and this 'light white wine' was produced in sufficient quantity to sell to the military.

French immigrants settled in Akaroa (just outside Christchurch) in 1840; many of them were peasants from the wine districts of France, which they had left because of agricultural depression. They planted vines, harvested grapes and made wine. The Marist religious order brought vines to New Zealand which they cultivated at Hokianga, the Upper Wanganui and Poverty Bay before finally settling in Hawkes Bay in 1865, where they are still producing wines for the table and sacrament, and today lay fair claim to being the oldest wine-makers in New Zealand. In 1895 an Italian viticulturist, called Romeo Bragatto, arrived in New Zealand, on loan from the Victorian Government. In his tour of New Zealand his verdict for grape-growing was generally favourable, with Blenheim and Te Kauwhata being mentioned as ideal areas. The real development of the New Zealand wine industry has taken place over the last fifteen years, with the greater escalation being from 1970 onwards. New Zealand is not by tradition a wine-making country, and it has always suffered from a generally poor image. From a diet of rather 'gluggy' sherries and ports and some fairly ordinary whites and reds (made from inferior hybrid grapes) with noticeable faults, improvements over the last fifteen years have been made in grapes, in wine-making, in machinery and in technical advancement.

Wine-making in New Zealand is now a multi-million dollar business. There are four hundred commercial vineyards – over 5.5 million vines – producing in excess of thirty thousand tonnes of grapes – 79 per cent of which are *Vitis vinifera* with 97 per cent of this total being used for wine production.

The most recent figures released by the Department of Agriculture and Fisheries clearly indicate that sweeping changes have been made with selected vines and New Zealand is now growing more of the type which produces the better wines in other regions of the world that have similar climatic conditions. These varieties are known internationally as *Vitis vinifera* and although the *vin ordinaire* still comes from the American hybrid grapes, the Siebels and the Bacos, very little new planting of these vines is being undertaken.

The changes in grape production in more recent times clearly reflect the switch to higher quality grapes. During the last six years (from 1974) there has been a massive 75 per cent increase in vineyard-area – the most noticeable being the new plantings by Montana at Blenheim (the largest single block plantings in New Zealand), the development of the Mangatuna area of Tolaga Bay, Gisborne, by Corbans – and the new plantings on the East Coast, in particular around Gisborne by contract growers.

The top grape planted in New Zealand is the Riesling-based crossing, Müller-Thurgau (the name is used interchangeably with Riesling Sylvaner), with nearly twice as much planted as any other single variety. All New Zealand's better 'Riesling' wines are labelled Riesling Sylvaner or Müller-Thurgau, and many bottles carry a piece explaining the grape association. It has never been conclusively proved what the original clone was, and it is not possible to identify definitively the variety as Riesling Sylvaner or Müller-Thurgau. Experts do say, however, that the Müller-Thurgau in New Zealand produces definably different wine to that which the grape produces in Germany. Riesling Sylvaner/Müller-Thurgau is made into a plethora of styles, with the greater proportion being back-blended (the addition of small quantities of unfermented grape juice, or sweet reserve, to the wine after fermentation), arrest-fermented or freeze-concentrated. This results in unique, fruity wines that highlight the characteristic flavours of the grape in a style that is indigenously New Zealand. Then there is Palomino, the classic Sherry grape, producing some very fine *flor fino* and pale dry-style sherries which are a far cry from the bulk sherries produced twenty years ago. Other white *vinifera* varieties are Chardonnay which has a tremendous future potential, even allowing for its shy bearing habits, Grey Riesling, Chasselas (Gutedel), Pinot Gris, Chenin Blanc, and now new plantings of Gewürztraminer, Rhine Riesling and Sauvignon Blanc.

The most widely planted red grape is now Cabernet Sauvignon with the total amount of hectares (including new plantings) overtaking the prolific-bearing hybrids in such depth that the variety is bound to dominate this field. A great deal of the Cabernet area is in young vines, not yet in full bearing, and once these are producing and Cabernet becomes more plentiful, the red-wine outlook in New Zealand will be revolutionized. Other red varieties include Pinotage (a grape from South Africa purported to be a cross between Pinot Noir and Hermitage), which is produced as a straight varietal and also in blends with Cabernet. The very best Pinotage wines the grape produces have been said to lie somewhere between the styles of Rhone and Burgundy. Pinot Meunier has been around for a while; Pinot Noir has started to appear both as a single variety and in blends, as has Gamay de Beaujolais. There are some experimental plantings of Malbec, Merlot, Hermitage, Cabernet Franc, and Petit Verdot and these, with the exception of Hermitage, will probably be used in blends with Cabernet. However, all these varieties have yet to prove themselves under the maritime New Zealand climate.

Ninety per cent of all young vines in New Zealand are of the classic varieties, and the gradual replacement of existing plantings with vines free from known virus diseases will have a very significant effect on yields and wine quality. Improved viticultural and wine-making technology is probably the most important single factor in the New Zealand wine revolution. There has been a sweeping change in public attitudes towards wine. In the 1960s people were content if a wine was drinkable, by the mid-1970s premium table wines were being recognized, and identified for their quality and on their merits. The 1980s can be approached with confidence. A major study and development plan of the wine industry published in 1978 made mention of the emergence of major companies on the New Zealand wine scene becoming a natural development in the evolution of New Zealand wine-making, resulting in differences in the scale and economics of production and marketing. Numerically, there is an imbalance between the few wine-makers whose output comprises the substantial proportion of production, and the wine-makers comprising the remainder of the 107 holders of licences, most of whom are family units of immigrants or their descendants. It became evident that there was an immediate need for an effective wine-industry body to control policies and to undertake forward planning. This led to the formation of the Wine Institute of New Zealand Incorporated in September 1975, a move that was supported by the then existent wine-makers' organizations.

The Wine Institute is the national organization for all grape wine-makers, who are obliged to be members and are levied on a per litre basis. The Institute promotes the interests of its members through developing and improving the grape wine-making industry by assessing performance and prospects, formulating future policies and by investigating, testing and developing internal and overseas markets for wine. It also promotes the interests of consumers by its continuing obligation to establish, maintain and enforce among its members standards of quality and ethics in grape-growing, wine-making, packaging, distribution, and advertising. At the moment, vintages are not all that important in New Zealand, but they could become more significant with the reduction of hybrid grapes and the increase of quality grapes. The best vintages of the 1970s could be considered as 1970, 1974 and 1976, in that order. There is, however, a distinct trend towards regional character, and this probably will be more easily definable at the end of the 1980s.

A list of the major wine-producing companies:

MONTANA WINES

In 1943, a Dalmatian immigrant, Ivan Yukich, purchased a property high in the Waitakere Ranges, a few miles beyond Titirangi, Auckland, to carry on the 300-year-old tradition of family wine-making. As he stood on the new property, looking out over the Henderson Valley, to the upper reaches of the Waitemata Harbour, he said, 'This reminds me of the mountains at home, we will call this place Montana.' His words were to be prophetic: Montana, the Yugoslavian word for mountain, was the highest vineyard in New Zealand in terms of metres above sea level, and it was also to become the largest producer of wine in the country, as well as the fastest growing. By 1961, the vineyard had expanded to ten hectares. Two sons, Frank and Mate Yukich, formed a company, Montana Wines Ltd. They planted vines on a 121-hectare farm at Mangatangi, south of Auckland, and also arranged for contract growers in the rapidly developing grape-growing areas near Gisborne. By 1973 Montana was producing over 45,000 hectolitres of wine annually, to reach the top of the New Zealand industry – a position they hold to this day. Montana's success has been a result of meticulous but imaginative planning, intensive propagation of classic *vinifera* grapes and application of the most modern vineyard and wine-making techniques. In 1973, Montana bought Waihirere Wines, an old-established company in Gisborne and also that year, through affiliation with the giant American conglomerate, Joseph E. Seagram & Sons Inc. (40 per cent shareholding), they embarked upon the single most ambitious expansion programme in the history of the New Zealand wine industry. Montana purchased 1,620 hectares of smooth flats and rolling farmland in the Wairau Valley, Marlborough, and planted 202 hectares in vines. A severe drought in 1974 killed many of the young vines, but this initial setback was turned to advantage, as from the company's research and propagation centre an improved strain of indexed virus-free, well-rooted stock guaranteed the success of the replanting programme. This area around Blenheim has long held the record for the maximum sunshine hours in New Zealand. Its annual rainfall is less than 66 centimetres with the driest month being March, when the grapes are ready for harvest.

In 1976, the first harvests of the Marlborough vineyards produced grapes of remarkable quality even from the immature Riesling and Cabernet vines. Early in 1977, Montana revised its marketing policies, renamed Waihirere 'Ormond Estate', and developed regional identity of the premium wines from its two major wine-growing regions, Marlborough and Gisborne. Marlborough's classic table wines would be distributed under regional brand names and the Gisborne wines would be rationalized under one label, 'Ormond'. The Ormond range of wines has enjoyed good market success in the middle-range bracket. A number of wines under the Montana label, in particular a light medium white called Bernkaisler Riesling (later renamed Benmorven) which was the forerunner to back-blended Riesling styles and has been hailed by prominent wine experts as one of the New Zealand wine industry's great successes.

The first Marlborough wines, a Riesling and a Cabernet, were both highly acclaimed, and this was a major achievement for the Marlborough region as the vines had yet to reach maturity. More recently from the first selected pickings of Rhine Riesling and Gewürztraminer from Marlborough, Montana won gold medals at the 1979 National Wine Competition.

MCWILLIAMS WINES (NZ) LTD

In the early 1940s, McWilliams, who were already established in Australia, turned their attention to New Zealand. It was with a background of many years' experience that investigations were initiated to select the ideal vineyard location in New Zealand. This research pointed firmly to the Hawkes Bay area as being New Zealand's best grape-growing district. In 1947 the first vineyards were established at Te Awanga and Bay View. Today the company has fourteen vineyards and three wineries in Hawkes Bay. The first wines produced from the company's Hawkes Bay vineyards were marketed in 1953, and progress has been such that today McWilliams is one of the largest wine-producing companies in New Zealand.

Although a completely separate entity, predominantly New Zealand-owned, the company still has the advantage of the Australian company's skill and experience. McWilliams are credited with the introduction of varietal grapes into New Zealand and their Cabernet Sauvignon, Chardonnay and Riesling Sylvaner wines are always in demand. They have the largest small wood storage in the country (barrels of 245.5 litres) and are the biggest buyers of new oak (barrels of 500 litres) for the maturing of their premium wines.

McWilliams' Cabernet Sauvignon has enjoyed a reputation, since their celebrated 1965 vintage, as the top red wine in the country. This reputation is arguable, but McWilliams's track record is undeniable. In 1974, they produced a Chardonnay which won a gold medal at successive National Wine Competitions. More recently they have produced an Ice Wine and a Riesling Sylvaner 'late pick' – one freeze-concentrated, and the other arrest-fermented and slightly back-blended. Both enjoy success on the market.

McWilliams also produce a wide range of fortified wines and their top three commercial wines, Bakano (red), Cresta Dore (white) and a sparkling Marque Vue are so well known that the company name is very rarely mentioned for identification.

CORBANS WINES

In 1902 Assid Abraham Corban, a Lebanese, purchased a few hectares in Henderson, West Auckland. This was the start of Mount Lebanon vineyards and the Corbans' commune. Over the next fifty years Corbans firmly established themselves as the largest producers in the Auckland area and gave recognition to Henderson as a major grape-growing area. Like most of the early wine-makers, Corbans concentrated on sherries and ports, moving from these types into a wide range of table wines. With substantial plantings at Henderson and Whenuapai, Corbans expanded in Gisborne where new vineyards were established in 1968, and a second winery was built in 1971. Also in 1971 an interest was acquired in Corbans by the giant conglomerate Rothmans Industries, and over the next six years, Rothmans expanded their equity in the Corban Group to 80 per cent; it is reported that the company's sales have trebled during the same period. To meet the demand in New Zealand and in export markets (Canada, and the United States), Corbans' vineyards in Henderson and at Gisborne have been expanded. A new vineyard has been established at Tolaga Bay and nursery facilities have been enlarged to provide selected virus-resistant stock to plant out the extended total amount of hectares and replace older varieties. In addition, Gisborne Winegrowers Ltd, a Rothmans subsidiary, developed two vineyards at Gisborne and in 1979, in a joint venture, an eighty-nine-hectare vineyard was planted at Te Kauwhata. The seventy-fifth anniversary of the establishment of this major wine company was in 1977 and it seemed quite appropriate that they should produce an anniversary sherry and port to mark the occasion. Corbans have been in the forefront of the development of the New Zealand wine industry; with the introduction of the first pneumatic presses for the making of quality white wines, pioneering refrigeration in wine-making techniques and installing the first pressure tanks for the production of table and sparkling wines. They pioneered the bulk fermentation process for sparkling wines, were the first to produce *flor* sherry on a commercial scale, produced the first commercial quantities of Riesling Sylvaner and Chardonnay, and installed the first sterile-bottling room in New Zealand.

Cabernet Sauvignon is marketed as a straight varietal, and is also used in a blend with Pinotage for the company's well-known Claret. Riesling Sylvaner and Chardonnay have long been the top varietal whites but, as from the 1976 vintage, these have been joined by Chenin Blanc from grapes grown at Tolaga Bay and this variety is fast establishing itself as a market leader backed by impressive show results. The old tradition and name of Corbans, combined with the sales and marketing expertise of Rothmans, could well prove to be a happy marriage.

COOKS NEW ZEALAND WINE CO. LTD

Te Kauwhata is in so many ways the cradle of the New Zealand wine industry. It was Te Kauwhata that was chosen by Romeo Bragatto as the site for the Government Research Station; Bragatto was the viticultural expert who was called in to advise the Government of Richard Seddon in 1895. But it was not until 1968 that the district began to show its potential as one of the great wine-producing districts. In that year, the directors of Cooks commissioned a report from Professor Petrucci, an eminent Californian viticulturist, on the selection of a site for a vineyard and the grape varieties that would be most suitable. Petrucci was adamant; Cooks must plant classic varieties. And it was reported that the climate of Te Kauwhata had overwhelming advantages.

In 1969, the first twenty-four hectares were planted with Cabernet Sauvignon, Pinot Gris, Riesling Sylvaner, Golden Chasselas, Pinot Meunier and Pinotage. The first vintage appeared in 1972. Two years later Cooks received their first major New Zealand competition award at the 1974 New Zealand Easter Show – gold medals for Golden Chasselas and Cabernet Sauvignon, two wines which subsequently won gold awards in the International Wine and Spirit Competitions in the United Kingdom. Cooks have extended their operations beyond Te Kauwhata, with extensive plantings of selected white grape varieties in Gisborne and red grapes at Riverhead, north of Auckland.

Since, and indeed before, the first vintage at Te Kauwhata, Cooks were regarded as innovators. The winery is unashamedly modern, as is the equipment within it. Cooks were the first wine-makers in New Zealand to install a four-stage continuous press line. They were also pioneers with the installation of thermo-vinification equipment for heat treatment of red wines. But despite the march of modern technology, Cooks still follow the Northern European traditions of the wine-maker's craft.

VILLA MARIA WINES LTD

The estate covers an area of 7.6 hectares at Mangere and, with the addition of grapes from contract growers in Gisborne, Te Kauwhata, Henderson, Kumeu and Te Hana, George Fistonich has transformed one of the smallest wineries into one of the largest privately owned wineries in New Zealand. The winery has recently installed a carbon-dioxide storage tank and a new refrigeration plant for the cold fermentation of white wine; as well as the very latest Westfalia centrifuge (hermetically sealed – continuously saturated with carbon-dioxide) which assures the virtual elimination of oxidization. Centrifuging of juices after fermentation is quite common but this additional equipment will allow this to be done before the juice passes into the fermentation tanks. Centrifuging of the juice before it enters the fermentation tank keeps out all unwanted matter, ensuring a clean wine and giving the wine-maker far greater control over the fermentation process. This seems to have become evident with the style of white wines currently being produced by the winery.

Notable medal successes at the most recent National Wine Competition and the last two New Zealand Easter Wine Shows have lifted this company's image. Most notable have been a Private Bin Sauternes made from the Riesling Sylvaner grape with the addition of freeze-concentrated juice. This has filled out the wine and given it a full lusciousness. As well, the company is producing a good Traminer and has just produced a top quality Chardonnay from fairly young vines. A wide range of commercial whites (mainly Riesling Sylvaner) is made, with a tendency towards the addition of unfermented grape juice. In the reds, the company pioneered Melesconera as a commercial variety, and now produces Private Bin Pinotage and Cabernet Sauvignon wines.

VIDAL WINE PRODUCERS

In 1905, Anthony Joseph Vidal bought a racing stable standing on 0.5 hectares of land in Avenue Road, East Hastings. There, with his sons Leslie, Cecil and Frank, he established a reputation for producing fine sherries and table wines. In 1972, Vidals amalgamated with the Australian wine-making company, B. Seppelt & Sons Ltd. The trading name then became Seppelt Vidal Ltd. In 1976 another change took place, when the managing director, George Fistonich of Villa Maria, acquired the total interest and set about turning it into a showplace winery.

The company has been reconstructed, with the bottling and packaging now being carried out at the Villa Maria winery in Mangere, Auckland. The previous wine-maker, Warwick Orchiston, has been retained and he continues to produce semi-finished wine and operates the old winery in Hastings which acts as a bulk crushing, blending and wine maturation installation.

The top Vidal wine is Te Moana Riesling, a free-run premium white table wine, slightly back-blended and a consistent medal winner. Many fine sherries are produced from old wood-matured material at the winery, and a good tawny port, SV56 – which takes its name from the year of the vintage (1956) – is released in small quantities each year. More recently, the company has introduced a wood-finished Chardonnay and a Cabernet Sauvignon to its premium table-wine range.

Other Wine-producing Companies

The other remaining members of the 'big seven' are Penfolds and Glenvale. Established in 1963, Penfolds was 40 per cent owned by its Australian counterpart but in 1977, the controlling interest was gained by Frank Yukich, who was the driving force in the formative years of Montana. The winery is situated in Henderson, but only a small proportion of grapes come from there; the principal grape-growing regions are at Waimauku, with contract growers around the Henderson–Huapai area and at Gisborne. More recently, the company has embarked on a quality programme with better grapes replacing existing hybrids. From a reputation gained mainly on sherries, it is now producing wines of *vinifera* classes, including Chardonnay, Chenin Blanc, Gewürztraminer and Cabernet Sauvignon. In 1976 Penfolds produced an Autumn Riesling, a first for the company using a then new freeze-concentrate method, which basically expels water content prior to fermentation. It was awarded the Championship white wine of the 1976 Easter Show.

Glenvale, a Hawkes Bay winery, has until recently only been known as a producer of fortified wines but late in 1976 a Riesling Sylvaner and a golden Chasselas were released. These two wines from *vinifera* varieties add a new dimension to this label, and other varieties are expected in the future.

Delegats was established in 1947 by N. P. Delegat and have mainly been involved with fortified wines and with a medium-priced range of table wines. The founder died in 1973 and the company continues under the management and guidance of his son, Jim Delegat. The company has recently employed a young Australian wine-maker, John Hancock, who has made his presence felt immediately by showing a gold medal dry Riesling and a silver medal back-blended Riesling at the 1979 National Wine Competition. Vineyard and winery expansion stamp Delegat as one of the up-and-comers for the 1980s.

Other medium-sized wineries producing good wines include Babich Wines, Henderson, well-respected for their dry Riesling, Gewürztraminer, and Cabernet Sauvignon and Cabernet/Pinotage blend; another family vineyard. Nobilo Vintners of Huapai can justifiably claim to be leaders with Pinotage (major awards since 1970) and their estate-bottled Cabernet Sauvignon. Other wines of note include Gewürztraminer, Chardonnay, Riesling Sylvaner and Pinot Noir. Selaks Wines, Kumeu, is one of the only two producers of champagne made by the true Champagne-method process. It sells at a premium price and is always in short supply. The company is also known for its Riesling Sylvaner, a back-blended wine.

S.Y.C. Totara Vineyards in Thames (the only Chinese vineyard in New Zealand), San Marino in Kumeu, Lincoln and Soljans in Henderson, Mission Vineyards in Hawkes Bay (the vineyard of the Marist Brothers), all have their own distinctive wines and their admirers. But, finally, mention should be made of a group of smaller vineyards, all producing top-class varietal wines and in doing so ensuring that the industry giants keep them in mind. Collard Brothers (Sutton Baron Vineyards), with their policy of producing only top-quality table wines under the control of Lionel Collard and his two sons, Bruce and Geoffrey, have resulted in major successes in New Zealand wine competitions with particular emphasis on Gewürztraminer, Riesling Sylvaner, Rhine Riesling and a generous Cabernet Pinotage blend. Matua Valley produces Riesling Sylvaner, Sauvignon Blanc, Cabernet Sauvignon and Burgundy with style and determination as would be expected from Ross and Bill Spence. They are one of the more progressive wineries in the so-called 'ginger' group. Dennis Irwin of Matawhero, just outside Gisborne, has produced by himself varietal wines of a high standard, mainly Riesling Sylvaner and Gewürztraminer as straight varietals and as blends. Kim Selonius of Hawkes Bay is also a one-man show, and his early attempts at producing varietals are most encouraging. Rod Abel at Kumeu, with his single variety Pinot Noir, has quickly established a following, and wine-judges-turned *vignerons*, John Buck and Michael Morris, have acquired Te Mata Estate in Havelock North. They are committed to a ten-year plan based on classic varieties and the refurbishing of the oldest winery in New Zealand. Many more names are certain to surface in the 1980s and with the emphasis on quality, the future seems assured.

The Wines of
South Africa

JULIUS BARRATT

Julius Barratt has spent a period of ten years working for the Stellenbosch Farmers' Winery as a wine buyer, dealing with both cooperative wineries and with private estates. For eight years he acted as a judge at the regional young wine shows and at the Grand Championship show in Cape Town. In 1974 he won the winelands wine-tasting competition in Stellenbosch and the national competition in 1976. In 1979 he returned to the United Kingdom to work with Laurence Hayward Limited in the London wine trade.

A knowledge of the history of wine-making in South Africa is important if the reader is to understand fully the industry as it is today, particularly regarding why certain grape varieties are used, and why certain styles of wine are made.

The Cape of Good Hope was colonized by the Dutch in 1652 with the purpose of supplying ships on the long voyage from Europe to the East with many of the requirements of such a trip. Fresh meat, vegetables and, of course, water were probably the most important supplies, but the assistance that wine gave in the prevention of scurvy was already well known due to the success of people such as the Spanish and Portuguese in surviving very long periods at sea. It could well be this fact that prompted Jan van Riebeeck, the leader of this first expedition, to cultivate the vine. He was quick to realize that the Mediterranean climate of the Cape would be ideal for its production, and he soon planted the first trial vines on the slopes of Table Mountain. Following their amazing success, the planting of larger vineyards soon followed, and in 1659 the first South African wine was produced.

With the arrival of the first Governor, Simon van der Stel, in 1679, viticulture was put on a firm footing and he did much to improve the quality of the wine being produced. In the eighteenth century, the Cloete family started to produce fortified wines, and these proved to be of such exceptional quality that they were very well received in Europe. These were to become the famous wines of Constantia, a few bottles of which are still in existence today – and indeed some have appeared in recent auctions in London. During the nineteenth century, as a British colony, a very considerable export trade was built up with the United Kingdom, and production increased at a fast rate. In 1861 the British government abolished the preferential tariffs that had been set up to assist the importation of South African wines, and French wines once again became very much cheaper. With the disappearance of this very lucrative market overnight, the South African wine industry went into a steep decline that was to last for many years. In 1886 phylloxera, which had already destroyed many of the vineyards of Europe, was found to exist in two vineyards, and soon started on its relentless path of destruction. Grafting onto American root stock was started, and slowly the vineyards were replaced. It would seem that recovery here was faster than in parts of Europe, and for a short while market conditions improved, but it was not long before the old problem of over-production was back again. At this time, a certain C. W. H. Kohler advocated the formation of a cooperative system to combat this by attempting to control both production and prices, and after many initial setbacks, the Koöperatieve Wijnbouwers Vereniging (KWV) was established in 1918. In 1924, statutory powers were given to the cooperative, and over the years since then new legislation from time to time has given it extraordinary powers, such as:

1. To ensure a production quota for every farm producing grapes for the production of wine.
2. To determine annually a minimum price to be paid for both distilling and good wine, the latter being a term meaning any wine to be consumed in either a natural or fortified state.
3. To determine annually a figure of surplus production and, based on this, pay out proportionately less for all distilling wines. Money thus obtained can be used to subsidize the export market.
4. In years of a shortfall in production, to determine a purchasing quota for the various merchants buying from the producers.
5. To handle all financial transactions between merchants and producers.

During the last two decades, the industry has taken tremendous strides forward both in the fields of viticulture and wine-making. As well as many new methods of vine cultivation, many new varieties have been imported from overseas and, after extensive trials at the Government experimental station, have been put on general release to the farmers. On the wine-making front, South Africa has both learned from and taught many of the other wine-producing countries of the world, and today leads the field in many aspects of wine production.

In September 1973 South Africa's Wine of Origin legislation became law, brought about partly by the fact that her principal wine export market, the United Kingdom, joined the EEC. In order to continue exporting to the United Kingdom or any other country within the EEC, South Africa had to abide by certain standards as laid down by the Office Internationale de la Vigne et du Vin. The wine-producing region was divided up into fourteen main areas, several of which have since been further subdivided. This new legislation also makes it illegal for a wine to carry either a vintage year or the name of the grape variety on the label unless the producer can satisfy the Wine and Spirit Board that it is, in fact, of this variety and from this vintage. Only when the Board is satisfied that all the relevant paperwork is in order, and that the wine has passed a very strict quality-control test, is the wine eventually issued with a seal, which has to be affixed to the neck of the bottle. This seal confirms that any claim relating to origin, cultivar or vintage stated on the label is correct. A producer who believes that his wine is of a particularly good quality may submit it to the Board and ask that the word 'Superior' should appear on the label.

CONSTANTIA AND DURBANVILLE

This stunningly beautiful area has many of its vineyards situated actually within the boundaries of the city of Cape Town, and unfortunately many once famous vineyards have already been swamped by housing developments. The vineyards closest to the mountains have a very high annual rainfall, those at Constantia having a total of 848 millimetres per annum. Groot Constantia is by far the most important estate in this area, being government property farmed under the management of

Wine regions 1 Orange River Valley 2 Olifantsriver 3 Piquetberg 4 Malmesbury 5 Tulbagh 6 Constantia and Durbanville
7 Stellenbosch 8 Paarl 9 Worcester 10 Robertson 11 Klein Karoo 12 Swellendam

the Enological and Viticultural Research Institute in Stellenbosch. Over the years the Estate has built up a reputation for producing high-quality red wines, and in recent years has also been producing smaller quantities of excellent white wines. The main red varieties planted today are Cabernet Sauvignon, Shiraz and Pinotage, and for the whites Chenin Blanc, Kerner and Riesling.

STELLENBOSCH

This is the centre of wine production in South Africa, and is certainly the most beautiful region of all with its mountain ranges, many of them rising in places to over 1,520 metres. It is bounded on the south by False Bay (so called because early traders sailed into it thinking that they had rounded the Cape), to the east and north by mountains, and on the west by the Cape flats, a large expanse of sand dunes. The town of Stellenbosch, which houses the three largest wine houses, Stellenbosch Farmers' Winery, Distillers' Corporation and Gilbey's Distillers and Vintners, is situated slightly to the north east of the centre of the production area. It is a great centre for learning, the home of one of the oldest and most famous universities in the country. Stellenbosch University is the only one in South Africa that has a faculty of viticulture and oenology. The Government Research Institute for Viticulture and Enology, founded in 1955, is situated just outside the town, where large experimental wine cellars, laboratories and acres of experimental vineyards provide information that assists the wine-growers and wine-makers in their continual struggle to produce ever better grapes, and therefore better wines.

The soils vary from fairly heavy granite type close to the mountains, to sandy soils derived from Table Mountain sandstone further to the west. As a general rule, the heavier soils tend to produce the finest red wines, but this is not always the case, and many surprises come from the lighter sandy soils. Many of the finest red wines come from the slopes of the mountains on the coastal belt. The Stellenbosch area has the greatest concentration of estates, bottling their own wine for sale to the public. Today there is a total of twenty-four estates; there are also six cooperative wineries which now bottle a proportion of their own wine. These estate producers were the first wine-makers to establish a wine route offering tourists the opportunity to travel from estate to estate and to taste the various wines available.

White Varieties

In Stellenbosch, the main white grape varieties planted are Chenin Blanc, Clairette Blanche, Riesling, and Colombar, with small amounts of Palomino, and new varieties to South Africa such as Kerner, Müller-Thurgau and Sylvaner. The Chenin Blanc gives wines with a lot of fruit, usually well-balanced with acidity and, in the case of the increasing numbers that are now made dry, crisp on the finish. The Clairette Blanche produces a lighter style of wine and is marketed in very small quantities, as a varietal wine, usually found only on the South African market. It is, however, in this area, a very successful variety for several reasons. Being lighter and having a considerably lower acid content than many other white varieties, it is most useful to the cellar master when it comes to blending many of the very popular wines sold under brand names, both in the lower and higher price brackets. It is also a variety that ripens very much later than many of the others and is therefore particularly useful to the farmer. In a country where many of the farming units exceed 300 hectares, and several of them even 600 hectares, it is of the utmost importance that the grapes do not all ripen together. It is therefore possible, by planting both early and late-ripening varieties, to draw out the main harvesting season to about six weeks, a considerably longer time than in most parts of Europe.

Riesling production is increasing fast and with the utmost urgency, due to the fact that this has always been a popular variety among drinkers who like crisp, dry wines. This market has grown fast over the last few years, and it is a peculiarity of the South African market that Riesling has become synonymous with dry white wine. Before the Wine of Origin (Wyn van Oorsprong) legislation came into being in 1973, it is fairly certain that the amount of Riesling in many of these wines on the market used to be considerably less than 50 per cent. The Government took cognizance of this fact, and allowed the trade a certain breathing space to build up over a period of years from 30 per cent to the 80 per cent required. This was also done with a few other very scarce varieties, but it was in the case of Riesling where it was most important. The Riesling strain originally planted in South Africa has long been recognized as not producing wines of a particularly 'typical' style when compared to its relatives in Germany. They tend to be fairly full in body and lack the fruit often expected from this famous variety and a lot depends on the skill of the wine-maker in getting the grape to give of its best. However, much work has been done to improve the stock being planted and new clones have been imported. A good Riesling from this area should be fairly light, fresh in colour with a good greenish tinge, having a clear but delicate fruit and a crisp finish.

The Columbar is another late-ripening variety and, although now grown in fairly large quantities in Stellenbosch, is a relatively newcomer to this area. It was first imported some twenty years ago and planted in the Robertson area (see page 622). As a vine it is much favoured by farmers, being a vigorous grower, and is relatively resistant to many of the vineyard diseases. It produces wines with a pronounced fruit, but tends to have a very high acid content; it is therefore much used for blending. As a varietal 'wine of origin Stellenbosch' it has not met with tremendous success. The new varieties that are being planted here are still on a relatively small scale but show a lot of promise for the future. Weisser Riesling is doing particularly well on both fairly light and heavy soils, and the best of them have achieved all the character associated with this variety, being fairly light, but spicy, racy and full of flavour. Gewürztraminer is also doing well on a small scale, and I have tasted them with the very distinct nose of roses so often attributed to this variety. Sylvaner has been in the area for quite a number of years, but only in a very small quantity, producing very delicate fresh wine, fairly pronounced on the nose, with the ability to develop very well over a period of two or three years – a trait often difficult to find in South African white wines.

Red Varieties

This area over the years has certainly produced most of South Africa's greatest red wines. Cabernet Sauvignon is the most famous, but Pinotage, South Africa's own grape variety, is increasing. Pinotage was the result of a crossing of Pinot Noir and Hermitage, made by Professor Peroldt of the University of Stellenbosch in 1922. At the time, he was not particularly impressed with the result, and the fruit of his labour remained in the nurseries for many years, and it was not until 1952 that it was planted in a vineyard. Planted in a fairly light soil it soon proved to be an exceptional vine, an early ripening variety that produced well. In 1959 this almost unknown variety was awarded the Grand Championship at the Cape Young Wine Show and since then has been planted in large quantities, not only in Stellenbosch, but in many of the wine-producing regions. However, it is in Stellenbosch that it really seems to produce its finest examples. When young, it has a fairly deep colour, a very pronounced nose, certainly quite unlike any other variety, and once tasted it can never be forgotten. The best Pinotage wines are rich on the plate and have a good tannin and acid. There are many South Africans who consider this a variety to be drunk while young, and some will even claim that it does not age well. I do not agree, except possibly in the case of those wines of a lighter style made particularly for drinking young. Though certainly this very pronounced Pinotage aroma does fade with a few years in wood and bottle, in its place the wine develops a certain richness of character, a breeding that is unmistakable and, at the same time, becomes mellow and round on the palate, a characteristic never found when the wine is young.

The famous Cabernet Sauvignon does well in Stellenbosch, as it seems to in nearly all corners of the globe. It always appears to be one of the few varieties that manages to attain its distinct characteristics, made so famous in Bordeaux, wherever it grows. In South Africa it grows nearly always on heavier soils on a fairly high trellis. It is a very late-ripening variety, and in fact on many farms it is often the last to be harvested. It is also one of the smallest bearers of all vines grown in South Africa. Good examples of Stellenbosch Cabernet Sauvignon are deep-coloured, fairly full and rich wines, usually requiring one to two years in cask (nearly always French oak), and several years in bottle. Many visitors to South Africa often remark that they find the wines too alcoholic and rich, and I feel that it is in Cabernet Sauvignon that this trait shows up most. However, when aged well and for long enough – and often they need ten years or more – they are quite magnificent and can hold their own in the best of company. Regrettably, as with so many of the world's great wines, they are usually consumed many years before reaching their peak.

The Cinsaut, once by far the most widely planted red-grape variety in this area, and still so if looked at on a country-wide scale, is now declining in importance. A very prolific bearer, it only produces satisfactory red wines when grown under fairly rigid conditions. It likes a fairly deep and rich soil, should be pruned severely to give a relatively small crop, and the grapes must be allowed to become fully ripe before harvesting. It is often a variety that, even under South Africa's usually ideal production conditions, has difficulty in obtaining sufficient sugar. Very often a portion of the juice has to be drawn off prior to fermentation in order to increase the ratio of skins to juice, and in this way a darker, richer wine is produced. This white juice, and in many instances the total amount of juice, is drawn off immediately for white-wine production, although it often turns out to have a faintly pink colour. It makes a very agreeable soft, easy drinking wine for early consumption. The red is usually the softest and lightest of South African red wines, used in vast quantities in the many lower-priced table wines. Many of these wines are of an exceptionally high standard, particularly when the very low prices are taken into consideration, and it has been said by many visitors to South Africa that some of these wines are possibly the greatest value to be found in the world.

Gamay has been grown in small quantities, but to date does not in any way resemble its counterpart from the northern hemisphere. Small quantities of Pinot Noir, Zinfandel, Malbec, Merlot and Verdot have also been cultivated, but these are still very much in the experimental stage.

Main Producers in the Stellenbosch Area:

THE STELLENBOSCH FARMERS' WINERIES

The largest wholesale wine merchants in South Africa, and owners of several farms. A very modern pressing cellar receives grapes grown on these farms, and also those purchased from other farms – approximately 12,000 tonnes. Purchases vast quantities of wine – over 100,000,000 litres – from private farmers and cooperative societies. There are very large and modern cellars for the handling of this quantity, including a method of continuous cold stabilization and several cold, sterile bottling lines. Red wines are matured in casks and vats of French oak in temperature-controlled cellars. It also has important production units in Paarl and Goudini in the Worcester area. The company created the tremendous expansion in wine drinking in South Africa with its launching of a very good quality but cheap table wine called Lieberstein in 1959. Produces wines in all price categories from the famous Zonnebloem range at the top of the scale, down to a large selection of low-priced table wines.

Zonnebloem Cabernet Sauvignon: A fairly full and rich wine, distinctly Cabernet and known for its longevity. The 1945 is still quite remarkable and other particularly good vintages are 1965, 1967, 1970, 1971, 1975, 1976.

Zonnebloem Pinotage: One of the fullest and richest of Pinotages. The 1974 (the first year in which Pinotage was marketed in this range) was quite exceptional.

Zonnebloem Riesling: A fairly light and delicate wine, fine, crisp and dry. At its best very young.

Oude Libertas Pinotage: A wine in the Oude Libertas range that replaced the famous Lanzerac range in the early 1970s. Good wines slighter in style than the Zonnebloem. Good years include 1959 (the first Pinotage on the market), 1961, 1964, 1968, 1973.

Oude Libertas Dry Steen: One of the first Dry Steens (Chenin Blanc) to be marketed under its varietal name. When young it is very fresh with a good fruit and often a guava character.

Château Libertas: One of South Africa's most famous red wines. A blended wine usually of Cabernet Sauvignon, Shiraz and Cinsaut. I have tasted many superb vintages going back as far as 1936.

THE OUDE MEESTER GROUP

Incorporating Distillers' Corporation, Castle Wine, E. K. Green, the Bergkelder and Drostdy Cellars. The Distillers' Corporation is responsible for the production of a large range of red and white table wines; most of the top-quality wines are produced at the Bergkelder. Both establishments have modern cellars and produce excellent wines in the various price categories. The group was a great advocator of the marketing of estate wines and entered into agreements with many estates to undertake all bottling and marketing on their behalf; in several instances this has proved to be a success. Brandy is also a very important product, with the company having the lion's share of the South African market.

Fleur du Cap Riesling: A fairly light and crisp wine, but not quite dry.

Fleur du Cap Pinotage: A pronounced Pinotage aroma, medium to full in body, but recent vintages have tended to be a little more robust.

Fleur du Cap Cabernet Sauvignon: Here again recent vintages have been fuller and more robust than those of the early 1970s.

Fleur du Cap Shiraz: Full-bodied, dark and smooth with a hint of a smoky nose so typical of this variety.

Grünberger Stein: A blended medium-dry white wine, produced mainly from the Chenin Blanc. Packaged in such a way that it looks very much like a German wine from Franconia.

GILBEY'S DISTILLERS AND VINTNERS LTD

The third of the large wholesale wine merchants and producers. Owners of Bertrams and the Devonvale Estate, where the company's premium products are produced and bottled. Great success has been achieved in recent years in both the medium- and high-priced markets. Bertrams is noted particularly for Cabernet Sauvignon, Shiraz and Pinotage of exceptional quality.

Bertrams Dry Steen: A fairly full but dry Steen wine.

Bertrams Pinotage: Very pronounced on the nose, a wine that is bottled young and, unlike many other Pinotages, is not given any cask maturation.

Bertrams Shiraz: Full-bodied, dark and rich and certainly one of the most outstanding Shiraz wines sold. The 1971 was particularly good.

DELHEIM ESTATE

Situated high on the slopes of the Simonsberg, this estate has been bottling and marketing its wine for very much longer than most of the others. Good white wines are produced, particularly Riesling and Chenin Blanc, and fair reds, but these tend to be a little lighter than many others from the Stellenbosch area.

MURATIE ESTATE

Situated just below Delheim, this is the oldest of the estates and is owned by Miss Canitz. Old production methods produce some good red wines.

BLAAUWKLIPPEN ESTATE

Situated on the lower-lying ground between Stellenbosch and Somerset West, this estate has been transformed in recent years from a very run-down property into a modern and highly productive unit. Well-run vineyards and cellars produce both white and red wines of good quality that have established themselves on the South African market in a remarkably short space of time.

VERGENOEGD ESTATE

Situated on low land close to the sea, this estate was first made famous when the KWV bottled and sold Vergenoegd wines to members of the cooperative and on the export market. Today, much wine is still sold to the KWV, but small quantities of excellent Cabernet Sauvignon, Shiraz, and Cinsaut are bottled on the estate. The Cabernet Sauvignon is a full rich wine requiring several years' maturation, and has on several occasions been awarded the championship of the Cape Wine Show.

KANONKOP ESTATE

A large estate that is bottling an increasing quantity of wine under the estate name. Very well managed with superb vineyards. Particularly well known for its Cabernet Sauvignon and Pinotage wines.

SIMONSIG ESTATE

Owned by F. J. Malan, who was one of the main champions of the estate wine movement in the early 1970s; he has been very successful marketing his wines throughout South Africa. Produces good-quality whites and reds, but is more noted for his white wines particularly from new varietals, such as Kerner, Weisser Riesling, and Gewürztraminer.

UITKYK ESTATE

A large estate situated due north of Stellenbosch. It provides good wines, both white and red, which are bottled and distributed by the Bergkelder.

RUSTENBURG AND SCHOONGEZICHT

A magnificent farm in Idas Valley near Stellenbosch. Vineyards are planted on steep slopes producing good Cabernet Sauvignon – in many years, a wine that comes closer to a Claret than any other in South Africa. Red wines are sold under the name of Rustenburg and whites under the name of Schoongezicht.

OVERGAAUW ESTATE

Situated in a small valley some six kilometres south west of Stellenbosch, this estate has been well known for many years to those in the trade for its quality wines, but has only recently started to bottle a small part of the crop itself. The first estate in South Africa to plant Sylvaner, from which a very delicate but pronounced wine is made. Cabernet Sauvignon, Pinotage and Chenin Blanc wines of good quality are also made.

ALTO ESTATE

A name well known for many years for its rich and robust Cabernet Sauvignon and for a blended red wine. All wines are bottled and distributed by the Bergkelder.

SPIER ESTATE

A large estate west of Stellenbosch, with land spread over several different types of wine-growing areas, giving it vineyards on slopes and on flat ground close to the river. The majority of the crop is bottled on the estate and, unlike many of the other estates, it has achieved success not only with middle- to high-priced wines, but also

(Above) A typical early Cape Dutch homestead
(Below) The floor of the Hex River Valley in the Worcester area,
with intense vineyard cultivation, is a magnificent sight in the autumn

with a selection in the lower-priced range. Good Chenin Blanc, Colombar and Pinotage, although the last does tend to be a little light.

MIDDELVLEI ESTATE

Situated very close to Stellenbosch, and particularly well-known for full-bodied red wines which are bottled and distributed by the Bergkelder.

NEETHLINGSHOF ESTATE

Recent cellar modernization has started to produce wines of good quality, particularly Chenin Blanc and Colombar, and some of these are bottled on the estate.

KOOPMANSKLOOF ESTATE

One of the largest estates in the country, in fact comprising several different farms. Certainly the largest private crushing cellar. Wines are now all bottled and distributed by the Bergkelder.

MEERLUST ESTATE

Until fairly recently, all grapes were delivered to a local winery, but a new and modern cellar has now been installed. Much new planting has been carried out, including small quantities of Merlot. An interesting Cabernet Sauvignon/Merlot is made; one of the few Bordeaux combinations, but more will be appearing over the next few years.

UITERWYK ESTATE

A farm lying near the head of a beautiful valley. Some grapes are delivered to a local winery, but the majority are pressed in a fairly small and traditional cellar. A very mellow, round Cabernet Sauvignon is made and one of the best Colombars from the Stellenbosch area. The estate has a beautiful and classic Cape Dutch homestead.

VERDUN ESTATE

An estate made famous in South Africa as it is the only one to have some Gamay vines. Old production methods produce distinctive wines and the Gamay can be fair, but bears no likeness to any of the Beaujolais wines.

Other estates and cooperatives in the area are: (estates) Audacia, Bonfoi, Goede Hoop, Hazendal, Jacobsdal, Montagne, Mooiplaas, Oude Weltevreden, and Vredenheim; (cooperatives) Bottelary Cooperative Winery Ltd, Eersterivier-Valleise Cooperative Wine Cellar Ltd, De Helderberg Cooperative Winery Ltd, Koelenhof Cooperative Company Ltd, Vlottenburg Wine Cellar Cooperative Ltd, and Welmoed Cooperative Wine Cellars Ltd. These cooperatives, with their large and modern cellars, handling between 8,000 and 12,000 tonnes, produce both white and red wine of outstanding quality. Many of them are now bottling a small proportion of their crop for the local market, but they depend on the larger wholesale wine merchants for their livelihood.

PAARL

This fertile area has the broad Berg River, originating in the Franschhoek mountains to the south, flowing almost due north through its centre. The town of Paarl is situated in the centre, and Franschhoek lies in the south-east corner. Paarl is a very spread-out town, noted for the length of its main street, and it is here that we find the head offices and huge cellars of the KWV. There are still many vineyards within the town itself, giving it an unusual appearance. One of these is La Borie,

The headquarters of the KWV, the wine-growers' cooperative, in the centre of Paarl, behind which lie their vast cellars

a farm beautifully restored to its former Cape Dutch glory, including modern cellars built in the same style, and several hectares of well-kept vines. The area is bounded in the east and south by high mountains, and stretches away to the west to join with the vast plain that ends at the Atlantic coast. Three types of soil abound: most of it is a fairly light, sandy type; granitic soil is found close to the mountains; and to the north pockets of very slaty soil. The climate is considerably hotter than Stellenbosch during the summer months, and to the south has a slightly higher rainfall of approximately 650 millimetres to that of Stellenbosch's 500 millimetres.

Grapes are grown almost throughout the area, including large quantities of table grapes, the latter cultivated in conjunction with many other kinds of fruit. The main white-grape varieties are Chenin Blanc, Sémillon, Palomino, Riesling, small quantities of Clairette Blanche, and several new varieties. The Chenin Blanc does particularly well in Paarl and produces wines of varying styles. It forms the basis of many of the farming units and ripens during the main part of the harvest. When picked fairly early, and when made under perfect conditions, particularly with regard to refrigeration during fermentation, it often produces wines with a most unusual fruit on the nose, often likened by the locals to that of fresh guavas. This is a fairly recent phenomenon and is becoming much sought after, but is a characteristic that is found while the wine is young and fades quickly with age after eighteen months to two years. When allowed to become fully ripe, the Chenin Blanc, or Steen as it is often known in South Africa, produces very full, round wines often with a delightful honey-like bouquet. Both styles of wine are made, dry and semi-sweet; the former tends to have a higher acidity and crisper, longer finish. The term semi-sweet in South Africa means any wine with a sugar content in excess of 5 grams per litre and not exceeding 30 grams per litre. In order to produce a wine in excess of 30 grams of sugar per litre, special permission is required of the Wine and Spirit Board.

Sémillon is probably more popular here than in any other area and is planted essentially in the southern part around Franschhoek. It is a variety known in South Africa for many years and, until the Wine of Origin legislation, was nearly always referred to as green grape, or in Afrikaans *groen druiwe*. Sémillon is very rarely marketed under its varietal name and is used almost exclusively for blending in wines in the lower price bracket. However, although its wines do not resemble its namesake in France, they do often have a lot of merit. Sémillon wines are very easily recognized by their rather coarse and green nose, two adjectives that do not sound very complimentary, but in this particular case are intended to be so.

Palomino is a variety that is fast diminishing although still grown in large quantities. It is a plentiful producer and the wines at their best tend to be neutral, light and have a low acid. Used to a certain extent for the production of sherry, although Chenin Blanc is now usually the preferred variety for this purpose, its greatest use has been in the production of wines for the huge brandy market. But, as the table-wine market grew in the early 1960s, more and more Palomino was used for this purpose, probably reaching a peak towards the end of the decade, when farmers realized that to produce wines of better quality it was necessary to replant many of their vineyards with better varieties, chiefly Chenin Blanc.

Riesling, as in many of the other areas, is fast increasing in importance. The cooler mountain slopes are the areas mainly chosen for new planting, and the vines are trained onto high trellises and the foliage is encouraged to grow, thus shading these delicate berries from the often vicious African sun. It is probably a fair comparison to say that, whereas hail is the *vigneron*'s worst enemy in Burgundy, in South Africa it is two or three days of exceptionally hot weather just as the grapes are nearly nature; with temperatures exceeding 35°C the damage can be extreme.

Of the new white varieties planted in Paarl, Kerner and Buketraube have found particular favour: the former produces delicate, slightly spicy wines with a clean, crisp finish; the latter gives lovely fresh wines with a faint Muscat nose.

The important red varieties are Cinsaut, Cabernet Sauvignon, and Pinotage. The Cinsaut tends to produce slightly darker, fuller wines here, due in part to the hotter climate, and in certain small areas they develop a most unusual berrylike nose. I have never quite been sure if this is due to soil or wine-making. The Pinotage has done well here in recent years, and the wines are usually very robust, often having an alcohol content in excess of 13 per cent by volume. The Cabernet Sauvignon until recently was found in very small quantities, but is now being produced in much larger amounts. Characteristics of the Cabernet Sauvignon change more from area to area in Paarl than in Stellenbosch, those on the slopes being more typical, those on the flatter ground tending to lose some of the strong varietal character.

Main Producers in the Paarl Area:

NEDERBURG

Part of the Stellenbosch Farmers' Wineries Group. Extensive vineyards and large modern cellars that receive approximately 10,000 tonnes of grapes, many of which come from other farms belonging to the group and from private farmers. One of the most famous names in South Africa for top-quality wines. Under the founder, Johann Graue, many new innovations in wine-making were made, in particular, that of fermenting the white juice under refrigerated conditions, which in time was to revolutionize wine-making in South Africa. Made Riesling a household name in South Africa. Today, under the direction of the famous wine-maker, Günter Brözel, some of South Africa's finest wines are produced and great success has been achieved on the export market.

Nederburg Riesling: The wine that really made Riesling popular in South Africa. It is slightly more pronounced on the nose than Stellenbosch wines and is usually higher in acidity.

Nederburg Cabernet Sauvignon: Fairly full and fresh when first bottled after about twelve to eighteen months in oak vats and, although good drinking when young, it has the ability to age well. 1972 and 1973 are good vintages with lots of life ahead of them, and the 1966 and 1968 are now at their peak.

Nederburg Private Bin S333: One of my favourite South African semi-sweet white wines. A very pronounced nose, which is slightly Muscat in character, and a long full flavour. Sold only at the Nederburg Auction.

Nederburg Steen 1974: One of the exceptions to the rule about South African white wines not ageing well. A light golden colour, a rich sweet nose and luscious flavour.

Nederburg Edelkeur: One of South Africa's triumphs of wine-making in the 1970s. The name means 'noble choice' and the wine is made from Chenin Blanc grapes infected by *Botrytis cinerea* (noble rot). In most years it is closer to a good Sauternes than to a *Trockenbeerenauslese* wine. A steady improvement has been evident since the first wine of this type was produced in 1969; 1976, 1977 and 1978 are quite superb.

THE KOÖPERATIEVE WIJNBOUWERS' VERENIGING

The huge cellars of the KWV are situated close to the town centre, and it is here that vast quantities of sherry are aged and prepared for the export market. It is these sherries that constitute the majority of the cooperative's exports, both in bulk and bottle, many of which are bottled under the buyer's own name. The most famous is the very high quality range of Dry, Medium, and Cream Sherries produced under the name Cape Cavendish.

MONIS

A famous name in South Africa, now part of the Stellenbosch Farmers' Wineries Group. The winery in Paarl is now mainly used for bottling many of the group's lower-priced products, but its greatest importance is in the production and maturation of the popular range of sherries that carries the Monis name.

BACKSBERG ESTATE

One of the earlier estate wineries to bottle and distribute its entire crop. Well-managed vineyards and modern cellars ensure the production of good wines that are well known throughout South Africa. Particularly good are Chenin Blanc, Cabernet Sauvignon and Pinotage.

Other estates and cooperatives in the area are: (estates) Fairview, Landskroon, and De Zoete Inval; (cooperatives) Bergrivierse Wine Cooperative Ltd, Bolandse Cooperative Wine Cellar Ltd, The Bovlei Cooperative Wine Cellar Ltd, Drakenstein Cooperative Wine Cellar Ltd, Franschhoekse Wine Cellar Cooperative Co. Ltd, Perdebergwynboere Cooperative Co. Ltd, Pêrelse Wine Cellars Cooperative Agricultural Co. Ltd, Simonsvlei Cooperative Wine Cellar Ltd, Wamakersvlei Cooperative Winery Ltd, The Wellington Wine Farmers' Cooperative Co. Ltd, and Windmeul Cooperative Ltd.

WORCESTER

Travelling almost due east over the high Du Toitskloof Pass, which reaches a height of over 610 metres, and from the top of which the traveller has the most exquisite view of Paarl and Wellington, we enter the large Worcester area. Descending from the Du Toitskloof mountains, we pass through very wild countryside. As we come to flatter ground, we see the first vineyards, and immediately are struck by the fact that they look very different from those we have left behind. In this western area, nearly all the vines are grown as bush vines and are planted very close together. In fact, so close are they that on these farms the cultivation is still done by horse, but today when vineyards are replanted most farmers are turning to conventional distances so that mechanization becomes possible.

The Breede River, fed by many tributaries, flows through the centre of the region and it is beside these rivers that most of the vineyards are found. The fairly large spread-out town of Worcester has sprung up mainly to service the extensive agricultural community, and just to the south of the town the huge Brandvlei Dam is situated, providing irrigation water for farmers, not only in the Worcester area but also in the Robertson area to the east. Most of the soil is of a very fertile, sandy, alluvial type which, when given sufficient water, is extremely productive. Close to the mountains in the west the rainfall is very high, reaching an average of 720 millimetres per year, but this decreases very fast eastward: just to the east of Worcester, a distance of only some nineteen kilometres, the annual average falls to about 200 millimetres. Here, of course, irrigation is an essential part of grape production. Much of the water is fed in a main channel from the Brandvlei Dam, and much is pumped by farmers from the Breede River and other rivers into dams on their farms. In the far east of the area is the Hex River Valley, where large amounts of table grapes are grown, mainly for the export market. In autumn, when the leaves turn to the most magnificent colours on many of the table-grape varieties, this valley is a really wonderful sight.

The most important white varieties grown here are Chenin Blanc, Palomino, Sémillon, Muscat d'Alexandrie and Colombar. Until the 1960s, the area was chiefly noted for its production of dessert wines and wine for distillation into brandy, and for this purpose large quantities of Palomino and Cinsaut were planted – both heavy bearers, particularly under irrigation. The latter, when grown under these conditions, and if the juice is drawn off immediately, produces a nearly white wine which, like Palomino, is fairly neutral and is ideal for this purpose. Today, the area is producing huge quantities of table wine. Many of these wines are of excellent quality and compete very well in the championship wine show when put up against the wines from Paarl and Stellenbosch, traditionally regarded as the top-quality areas. Little red wine is made, most of it coming from the northern corner; the chief variety is Cinsaut, with a little Pinotage, although this is now increasing. The Cinsaut, when well made, tends to be fairly full, but round, and softens very much earlier than that from the Stellenbosch side of the mountain range.

The most important quality variety is certainly Chenin Blanc, and it is from here that the 'backbone' of many of the table wines drunk in South Africa is produced. Depending on harvesting, production and irrigation, many different styles are produced, some light with a good fresh fruit and a fairly high acidity – but to me the best are fuller in style, slightly darker in colour, with a good concentration of fruit and honeylike aroma. The Palomino is fast decreasing now and Chenin Blanc is taking its place to a large extent, but in addition to its importance as a brandy producer it does give many table wines of fair quality, still very much needed by the industry. The Sémillon is not of great importance but produces some fairly attractive wines, usually similar in style to those of Paarl, but they tend to be considerably more delicate. The Colombar is a relative newcomer to this area and is produced in small quantities over most of the region, but it is increasing fast and is certainly destined to become an important variety. Very small quantities of Clairette Blanche are grown which in most places does not produce wines equal to those of Stellenbosch.

The Muscat d'Alexandrie needs no introduction here. It is no doubt descended from the Muscat of the Old World and is grown extensively both for dry and dessert wines. Many of the dry wines, with their delicate Muscat aroma, are used in some of the most popular, lower-priced table wines, but a large quantity are harvested when fully ripe and, after a very short period of fermentation on the skins (only approximately 2° Balling) so as to obtain as much character as possible, are fortified with grape spirit to approximately 18 per cent alcohol by volume. The resultant wine is obviously very sweet, full and rich, with a very powerful Muscat aroma, and it is a superb dessert wine. It is to some extent bottled under its varietal name, but the bulk of it is used in various fortified wine blends that are so popular in parts of South Africa. The Muscat d'Alexandrie variety has been known for many years to most South Africans as Hanepoot, and is one of the most important grapes for eating, for raisin production, and for jam-making, and is grown in many South African gardens. The Chenin Blanc is also used extensively for the production of dessert wines. They are produced in the same way as the Muscat d'Alexandrie, and give very full and luscious wines, used extensively for blending and also in the production of sweet sherries. The Chenin Blanc is also the preferred variety for the production of South Africa's excellent *flor* sherries, many of which come from the Worcester area.

There are no estates bottling their own wine in the Worcester area. There are, however, numerous cooperatives, too many to list here. Many of them press in excess of 12,000 tonnes of grapes and make wines of good quality. In 1977 they formed a central bottling cooperative in Worcester. Here a small portion of the production of cooperatives in the Robertson as well as the Worcester areas is now bottled under very modern conditions. These wines are then returned to the cooperatives for distribution. Due east from the town of Worcester, is a very dry region where, from the road, no grapes are seen for several kilometres. But a short distance along one of the many side roads or farm tracks towards the mountains, vineyards are soon encountered again. Production is only possible with water collected in dams in the mountains or, on the south side of the road, from the Brandvlei Dam irrigation scheme.

ROBERTSON

Beyond a low range of hills, lies the Robertson area, considerably smaller in size but of great importance. Here again, production is confined to the river banks or other areas where there is an abundance of water, and many of the vineyards are irrigated from the Brandvlei Dam Channel. The area is bounded by mountains both to the north and south, and the Breede River flows through its centre from west to east. One peculiarity of the area is that it is one of the few areas in South Africa occasionally to suffer the ravages of frost. The vineyards most susceptible are those closest to the river, and they are usually struck in very small, selected areas. It is an incredible sight to see one row of vines whose buds have been almost totally destroyed and another, only a few feet away, almost untouched. The most fertile soils are the alluvial soils close to the rivers, but, in fact, much of this ground is planted with peaches (I have seen vineyards and peach orchards mixed!). The other main soil type originates from shale and is locally known as Karoo type. Many of the vineyards are planted on this type. The rainfall here is approximately 350 milli-metres per year.

As in the case of Worcester, this area until recently was chiefly a dessert-wine- and brandy-producing area, but it is increasingly becoming very important, not only for the quantity of wine produced, but also for its quality. Very little red wine is produced, and it need not concern us here, but large quantities of both white wine and dessert wine are. White-grape varieties are Chenin Blanc, Palomino, Colombar and Muscat d'Alexandrie. The Chenin Blanc, under the correct con-ditions and the control of a good wine-maker, produces wines of greater delicacy than in Worcester, lighter in body but with a lot of fruit, occasionally with the guava quality that is found in Paarl.

The Colombar has its real home here in Robertson and is becoming increasingly important. It was first brought into the country from Cognac to be planted here for the production of brandy, and was used for this purpose for some time. How-ever, after a few years it was discovered that this variety could, in fact, produce excellent dry white wines. This, coupled with the fact that it is a variety resistant to disease and also to rot, which is so often a problem in humid areas close to the river, meant that it soon became very popular. It is in this area that the Colombar tends to produce its most distinctive wines, very fresh in colour with a slight greenish tinge, a very strong varietal aroma, with a fairly high acidity and good long flavour. The acid content is usually lower than in Stellenbosch.

The quantity of Muscat d'Alexandrie produced is limited, and as a general rule its quality is not up to Worcester standards. Small quantities of Riesling are also now being produced, some of which is of an excellent standard, but the quality does seem to be somewhat erratic. Large quantities of very fine dessert wines are also produced, chiefly from the Chenin Blanc, and both white and red Muscadel varieties. The Chenin Blanc very often achieves very high degrees of sugar here and makes a wine even fuller and more luscious than those from Worcester. The Muscadel is a most rewarding variety producing wines that I always feel should, by world standards, become far more famous than they are at present, but these will be discussed at more length further on.

Production of wine for brandy distillation is still very important in this area, and huge quantities are produced by some of the cooperatives. This is fast becoming a highly specialized product, and quality-control standards seem to get higher each year and, as all wine for the production of brandy has first to be submitted to a Board of Control before distillation, in years when demand is not, perhaps, as high as in the past, it is only the skilled wine-maker who achieves any great measure of success.

Main estates in the Robertson area are: Dewetshof (good white wines, particularly Riesling, bottled and distributed by the Bergkelder), Excelsior, Goedverwacht, Rietvallei, Weltevrede, Zandvliet (the pioneer with regard to making red wines in this area; success has been achieved with Shiraz. Also good fortified Muscadels). There are nine cooperatives in the area, which have a small part of their crop bottled by the Central Bottling Cooperative in Worcester. The bulk of their products are, however, sold to the wine merchants.

KLEIN KAROO

The road to the north east leads to the very picturesque town of Montagu. To give the reader who is not familiar with South Africa an idea of distance, this is a little over 160 kilometres due east of Cape Town. This area is known as the Klein Karoo, and it is a very long but narrow region with mountain ranges on both sides, with the southern range separating it from the Indian Ocean. The wine-producing areas are spread out, being most concentrated around the town of Montagu. To the east, there are pockets of vineyards under the northern range of mountains, some around Calitzdorp, and a further pocket around Oudtshoorn, the famous ostrich-farming centre. Most of these vineyards are planted on alluvial soils close to the many small river banks. The rainfall is less than 300 millimetres per year, and production is therefore dependent on irrigation.

Once almost exclusively a dessert wine- and brandy-producing area, more and more table wines are now produced. With the exception of small quantities of Colombar, however, there is nothing particularly noteworthy from a quality point of view, and it is therefore for the dessert wines made from the Muscadel grape that the area is famous. This very pronounced Muscat grape thrives in the hot climate and produces wines similar in character to those in Robertson. Both the white and red varieties are harvested when fully ripe, having attained a very high sugar level, often above 24° Balling, and after crushing are pumped into vats and allowed to ferment for a short time before being fortified with grape spirit. Very often some of the juice of the red is drawn off in order to concentrate what is left, and this free-run juice produces a very much lighter style of wine, sometimes referred to as white – although in fact the true white Muscadel comes only from the white grape. The finished red Muscadel should be fairly dark in colour, with a very powerful, deep Muscat aroma and a rich, lingering flavour. The white is obviously far more delicate, but none the less a great wine. Although the total planting of this variety is very small when taken as a percentage of the whole, and nearly all of it is produced in Robertson and the Klein Karoo, it is a product of which South Africa can be justly proud. Many think Muscadel may have been the first grape planted by van Riebeeck, and most certainly it played an important role in the production of the famous Constantia wines. Maybe one day it will again be enjoyed by people throughout the world.

SWELLENDAM

The Klein Karoo is the most easterly wine-producing area of South Africa. To the south west lies the Swellendam area, in the northern corner of which is situated the town of Bonnievale, and around it are fairly extensive vineyards. These vineyards are the last to be irrigated by the Brandvlei Dam Scheme. With regard to the style of wine, and grape varieties produced, this area can be considered to be a part of Robertson.

TULBAGH

North west of Worcester is the Tulbagh area. There are two main producing areas: the first in the most southerly corner where the vineyards actually adjoin those of Worcester, and whose quality is very similar; the second to the north, where the most interesting vineyards are found. To the north, west and east of the town of Tulbagh in an area almost totally surrounded by high mountains, many excellent white wines are produced. Much of this area suffered badly as the result of an earthquake in 1969. The rainfall varies dramatically, and there are both irrigated and non-irrigated vineyards. Many of the vineyards are now planted fairly high up the mountain slopes in relatively cool areas. The main varieties are Chenin Blanc, Clairette Blanche, Palomino, Muscat d'Alexandrie, and very limited quantities of the red varieties, Cinsaut, Cabernet Sauvignon and Pinotage. The top-quality wines from this area are made from the first two varieties mentioned, and from some of the new varieties recently planted. The Chenin Blanc produces a lighter, finer style of wine here than anywhere else, with the exception of Stellenbosch. The new varieties include Kerner, Gewürztraminer, Sauvignon Blanc, and Frontignac; the last three have been particularly successful in producing wines very typical of their varietal.

There are three estates, all of which are well known throughout South Africa for the production of very high quality wines.

MONTPELLIER

Has had success in producing white wines that age well.

TWEE JONGE GEZELLEN

One of the first estates to plant commercial quantities of new varietals. Wine is bottled and distributed by Gilbey's Distillers and Vintners. Tremendous success has been obtained with Sauvignon Blanc and Frontignac, and several awards have been won in the Cape Wine Show. The very fine and fresh Riesling is a household name in South Africa.

THEUNISKRAAL

White wine bottled and distributed by the Bergkelder.

OTHER AREAS

The most important producing areas from a quality point of view have now been covered, but from a quantity point of view there are still four more major regions. It would be wrong to generalize and say that no noteworthy wine comes out of them: indeed it does, but expressed as a percentage it is very small. Due west of Tulbagh is the vast Swartland area, comprising a plain, mainly noted for its very high wheat production. The main vineyards are situated around Malmesbury and Riebeek. The climate is very hot in summer and the rainfall is low, only about 250 millimetres per year, and so irrigation is very necessary. Much of the water required is provided by the large Berg River. The most important varieties are Chenin Blanc, Palomino, Sémillon, Colombar and Cinsaut. One estate, Allesverloren, produces good, full-bodied red wines and port-type wines, which are bottled and distributed by the Bergkelder. Four cooperatives, some of which press in excess of 18,000 tonnes, receive the bulk of the grapes from this area.

To the north is the Piquetberg area – a smaller expanse, mainly of wheatfields and sheep farms, but fairly large amounts of grapes are grown in the southern corner, and also in the centre of the region close to the Piquetberg Mountains. The rainfall here is considerably lower, 175 millimetres per year, and the summer temperatures are very high. Table wines of reasonable quality are made from Chenin Blanc and Palomino for use in the lower-priced products. Large quantities of wine for brandy distillation are also produced.

Further north again lies the large and very fertile Olifantsriver area. Flanked by mountains to the east, the Atlantic Ocean to the west, and stretching from Citrusdal in the south to Lutzville in the north west, this area is highly productive due to its fertile alluvial and loamy soil and an abundance of water. This water is supplied from the Clanwilliam Dam, which in turn is fed by the Olifantsriver and conveyed to the farmers by means of a channel. Grapes were first grown here for the purpose of drying for raisins, and those planted were Muscat d'Alexandrie and Sultana (Thompson Seedless). More recently, wine cooperatives were built and the production of table wine has risen considerably. Production is carried out throughout the length of the river but only along a very narrow strip on either side, and the most concentrated area is to the north. The area is also a very important producer of citrus fruits of all types. In the last decade, a great effort has been made to plant better-quality varieties, and today Chenin Blanc and Colombar are also very important. Due to the abundance of water, production per hectare is very high and, unless checked, the wines of all varieties can be very neutral in character. The large quantities of Muscat d'Alexandrie are very important for the blending of some of the well-known, but well-priced, table wines. Because of the distance of this area from the main buyers in Stellenbosch and Paarl, producers here tend to be very much at the mercy of the size of the crop in the higher quality regions, and in years of plenty are only able to sell their better Chenin Blancs, Muscat d'Alexandries and Colombars as table wines; the other varieties all have to be used for either brandy distillation or distillation for grape spirit. The Colombar has done well here recently and produces wines of some considerable charm, light, with a fairly delicate fruit, suitable for early consumption. Very small quantities of red wines have been produced but without very much success.

A tour of the winelands of the Cape would be completed by travelling approximately 800 kilometres north of Stellenbosch to the Orange River, a journey best done by plane, arriving at the town of Uppington. It is an amazing sight to come in low over the river and see the narrow strips of vineyards on either side, and stretching into the distance on either side of these a region that is little more than desert. The main production area stretches both east and west of the town and, like the Olifantsriver region, was at one time exclusively a raisin-producing area. This aspect of the region is still of great importance and the quantity varies greatly, depending on world demand. The area is extremely hot and dry and production is only possible because of the abundance of water supplied by the great Orange River. Sultana and Muscat d'Alexandrie are still the predominant varieties, but in recent years much Chenin Blanc and Colombar has also been planted. The wines here also tend to be very neutral, but are useful in the production of lower-priced table wines. The area has one great advantage in that it is ideally suited for the Johannesburg market – at a distance of some 800 kilometres, as opposed to 1,600 kilometres from Stellenbosch to Johannesburg. Many of the table wines are taken directly there, and in recent years distilleries have also been set up in the area to prevent the transport of large quantities of wine only destined for distillation purposes.

With the exception of the large and very successful export market built up for

South African sherries, the amount of wine exported is relatively small (the total crop exported is less than 1 per cent and for table wine, the figure is less than 2 per cent), and when the excellent quality and value for money of these wines is taken into consideration the figure appears even more ridiculous. I have little doubt that during the next few years an ever-increasing quantity of the finer wines will find their way onto numerous markets around the world.

Production Figures (Source: KWV Annual Reports)

Year	Total Wine Production* Hectolitres	Table and Fortified Wine Production Hectolitres	% of Total
1928	818,567		
1938	1,410,726	462,810	33%
1948	2,336,362		
1961	2,871,768	1,342,910	47%
1971	4,736,499	2,703,095	57%
1975	5,004,496	2,969,754	59%
1976	5,190,609	2,736,667	53%
1977	4,169,487	2,194,444	53%
1978	5,158,626	2,859,346	55%
1979	5,345,916	2,789,977	52%

* Table wine, fortified wine, wine for distillation
into brandy, and grape spirit.

The above figures show one very major contributing factor accounting for the high quality of South African wines: the relatively low percentage used for the production of table and fortified wines. In particular, this accounts for the very high standard of the lower-priced wines not found on markets outside South Africa.

In 1977, 9.5 per cent of total production was produced on farms, the balance being delivered in the form of grapes to cooperatives and merchants.

A short Glossary of Afrikaans Words that may be seen on Labels:

droë	dry	*oesjaar*	vintage
effer-soet	semi-sweet	*soet*	sweet
laat oes	late vintage	*vonkelwyn*	sparkling wine
landgoed	estate	*wyn van oorsprong*	Wine of Origin

I have not included vintage notes, as it is my opinion that vintages only differ very slightly in South Africa when the total picture is examined. There are, of course, vintage differences in wines from a particular cellar or of a particular brand. Zonnebloem Cabernet Sauvignon was a little disappointing in 1969, and did not exist in 1968, but this does not mean that other Cabernet Sauvignons from Stellenbosch in those years were not of good quality, i.e. quality differs more from year to year depending on wine-making rather than on climatic conditions. This obviously is a very general statement; there are years when there may be a severe heat wave or excessive rain (very rare), but even these conditions tend to be localized. To be accurate, a vintage chart would have to be drawn up for nearly every estate and product.

Selected Bibliography

Adams, Leon D., *The Wines of America* 2nd ed. rev., New York, Houghton Mifflin Co., 1978

Ambrosi, Hans, *Wo Grosse Weine Wachsen*, Grafe und Unzer Verlag, Munich, 1973; *Where the Great German Wines Grow*, New York, 1976

Ambrosi, Hans and Becker, Dr Helmut, *Der Deutsche Wein*, Grafe und Unzer Verlag, Munich, 1979

Amerine, Maynard A., Berg, Harold W. and Cruess, William V., *Technology of Wine Making* 3rd ed., The Avi Publishing Co. Inc., Westport, Connecticut, 1972

Amerine, Maynard A. and Joslyn Maynard A., *Table Wines: The Technology of their Production* 2nd ed., University of California Press, 1970

Amerine, Maynard A. and Roessler, Edward B., *Wines: Their Sensory Evaluation*, W.H. Freeman and Co., San Francisco, 1976

Amerine, Maynard A. and Singleton, Vernon, *Wine: An Introduction* rev. ed., University of California Press, 1978

Arlott, John and Fielden, Christopher, *Burgundy, Vines and Wines* rev. ed., Davis-Poynter Ltd, London, 1978

Auswertungs Und Informationsdienst fur Ernahrung, Landwirtschaft und Forsten e. V., *Die Weinwirtschaft in der Bundesrepublik Deutschland*, Verlag und Druckerei, D. Meininger GmbH, Neustadt, 1979

Balzer, Robert L., *Wines of California*, Abrams, New York, 1978

Becker, Werner, Hleke, Eugen, Jargen, Heinz, and Sebastian, Richard, *Wegweiser durch das Weinrecht*, Gewa-Druck, Bingen-am-Rhein, 1977

Bradford, Sarah, *The Englishman's Wine: The Story of Port*, Macmillan London Ltd, London, 1969

Broadbent, Michael, *Wine Tasting* 5th ed., Christie Wine Publications, London and New York, 1979

Cardinali, Bartolomeo, *Vini d'Italia*, Bologna, 1978

Carvelho, Benot de, and Correia, Lopes, *Vinhos de Nosso Pais*, Junta Nacional do Vinho, Lisbon, 1978

Castillo, Jose del, *Los Vinos de Espana*, Proyeccion Editorial, Bilbao, 1971

Chroman, Nathan, *The Treasury of American Wine*, Crown Publishers Inc., New York, 1973

Cobb, Gerald, *Oporto Older and Newer*, privately printed, 1966

Cocks & Feret, *Bordeaux et ses vins classés par ordre de mérite* 12th ed., Feret, Bordeaux, 1949

Dallas, Philip, *The Great Wines of Italy*, Faber and Faber Ltd, New York, 1974; *Italian Wines*, Faber and Faber Ltd, London, 1974

Deutscher Weinwirtschaftsverlag, *Die Weinwirtschaft*, Meininger GmbH, Neustadt

Dumay, Raymond (Ed), *Les Vins de Loire et les Vins du Jura*, Editions Montalba, 1979

Evans, Len, *Australia and New Zealand: Complete Book of Wine*, Paul Hamlyn, Sydney, 1974

Faith, Nicholas, *The Winemasters*, Hamish Hamilton, London, 1978; Harper and Row Publ. Inc., New York, 1978

Fletcher, Wyndham, *Port: An Introduction to its History and Delights*, Sotheby Parke Bernet, London, 1978

Flower, Raymond, *Chianti: The Land, the People and the Wine*, Croom Helm, London, 1978; Universe, New York, 1979

Forbes, Patrick, *Champagne: The Wine, the Land and the People*, London, 1967; Reynal, New York, 1968

Gadille, Rolande, *Le Vignoble de la Côte Bourguignonne*, Les Belles Lettres, Paris, 1967

Galhano, Amandio Barbedo, *Le Vin Verde*, Commissao de Viticultura de Regiao dos Vinhos Verdes, Oporto, 1951

Garoglio, P. Giovanni, *La Nuova Enologia* 3rd ed., Florence, 1965

Gonzalez Gordon, Manuel M., *Sherry: The Noble Wine*, Cassell Ltd, London, 1972

Grossman, Harold, *Grossman's Guide to Wines, Spirits and Beers* 6th rev. ed., Scribner, New York, 1977; Muller, London, 1978

Gunyon, R.E., *The Wines of Central and South-Eastern Europe*, London, 1971; Hippocrene Books, New York, 1972

Hallgarten, S.F., *Alsace, Wine Gardens, Cellars and Cuisine*, Wine and Spirit Publications, London, 1978; *German Wines* Faber and Faber Ltd, London, 1976

Hallgarten, S.F. and F.L., *The Wines and Wine Gardens of Austria*, Argus Books Ltd, London, 1979

Hallgarten, Peter, *Guide to the Wines of the Rhône*, Pitman Publishing Ltd, London, 1979

Halliday, James, *Wines and Wineries of New South Wales*, University of Queensland Press, St Lucia, 1980

Halliday, James and Jarratt, Ray, *The Wines and History of the Hunter Valley*, McGraw-Hill Book Co., Sydney, 1979

Hillebrand, Walter, *Taschenbuch der Rebsorten*, Zeitschriften Verlag Dr Bilz and Dr Fraund KG, Wiesbaden, 1973

Hutchinson, Ralph, *The California Wine Industry*, University of California Ph.D. dissertation, Los Angeles, 1969

Hutchinson, Ralph and Susan, *The Vineyards of Anaheim*

Jakob, Dr Ludwig, *Taschenbuch der Kellerwirtschaft*, Zeitschriftenverlag Dr Bilz and Dr Fraund KG, Wiesbaden, 1977

Jeffs, Julian, *Sherry* 2nd ed., Faber and Faber Ltd, London, 1971

Johnson, Hugh, *The World Atlas of Wine* rev. ed., Mitchell Beazley, London, 1977; Simon & Schuster, New York, 1978

Klerk, W.A. de, *The White Wines of South Africa*, Tri-Ocean, Cape Town and San Francisco, 1967

Lake, Dr Max, *Hunter Wines*, Jacasanda Press, San Francisco, 1964; *Classic Wines of Australia*, Jacasanda Press, Brisbane and San Francisco, 1966; *Hunter Winemakers*, Jacasanda Press, Brisbane, 1970; *Cabernet: Notes of an Australian Wine Man*, Jacasanda Press, Adelaide, 1977

Larrea Redondo, Antonio, *Vides de la Rioja* 3rd ed., Ministerio de Agricultura, Madrid, 1978

Leglise, Max, *Une Initiation à la Dégustation des Grands Vins*, DIVO, Lausanne, 1976

Lichine, Alexis, *(New) Encyclopedia of Wines and Spirits* 4th rev. ed., Alfred A. Knopf Inc., New York, 1974; Cassell Ltd, London, 1979; *The Wines of France* rev. ed., Alfred A. Knopf Inc., New York, 1969; Cassell Ltd., London, 1969; *Guide to the Wines and Vineyards of France*, Alfred A. Knopf Inc., New York, 1979; Weidenfeld and Nicolson, London, 1979

Massel, A., *Applied Wine Chemistry and Technology*, Heidelberg Publishers Ltd, London, 1969

Moog, Dr Heinrich, *Einfuhrung in die Rebensortenkunde*, Verlag Eugen Ulmer, Stuttgart, 1957

Navarre, Jean-Pierre, *Manuel d'Oenologie*, J-B Baillière et Fils, Paris, 1965

Nicholas, Elizabeth, *Madeira and the Canaries*, Hamish Hamilton Ltd., London, 1953

Opperman, D.J. (ed.), *Spirit of the Vine*, Tri-Ocean, Cape Town and San Francisco, 1968

Panarella, Giancarlo, *Italian Wine and Brandy Buyers Guide*, Rome, 1975

Paronetto, Lamberto, *Enciclopedia dei Vini del Mondo*, Arnoldo Mondadori, Milan, 1979

Penning-Rowsell, Edmund, *The Wines of Bordeaux*, Penguin Books Ltd, London, 1979

Peppercorn, David and Cooper, Brian, *Drinking Wine*, Macdonald Futura, London, 1979; Harbor House Books, New York, 1979

Peynaud, Emile, *Oenologie Pratique, Connaissance et Travail du Vin*, Dunod, Paris, 1975

Poupon, Pierre and Forgeot, Pierre, *Les Vins de Bourgogne*, Presses Universitaires, Paris, 1977

Puisais and Chabanon, *Initiation into the Art of Wine-Tasting*, Interpublish Inc., Madison, Wisconsin, 1974

Read, Jan, *The Wines of Spain and Portugal*, Faber and Faber Ltd., London, 1973; Monarch Books, New York, 1974; *Guide to the Wines of Spain and Portugal*, Pitman Ltd, London, 1977; Monarch Books, New York, 1978

Reay-Smith, *Discovering Spanish Wine*, London, 1976; Transatlantic, New York, 1977

Ribereau-Gayon, Jean and Peynaud, Emile, *Sciences et Techniques de la Vigne* (2 vols.), Editions Dunod, Paris 1971

Rivella, Ezio, *Note di Enologia Pratica*, Rome, 1974

Roncarati, Bruno, *Viva Vino, DOC Wines of Italy*, Wine and Spirit Publications Ltd, London, 1976

Ruiz Hernandez, Manuel, *Estudios sobre el vino de Rioja*, Graficas Sagredo Haro, 1978

Saintsbury, George, *Notes on a Cellar-Book* rev. ed., Macmillan London Ltd, London, 1978; Mayflower Books, New York, 1978

Sanceau, Elaine, *The British Factory Oporto*, Barcelos, 1970

Sandeman, George, *Port and Sherry*, London, 1955

Sauerwald, Peter and Wenzel, Edgar, *Konige des Riesling*, Stuttgart, 1978

Schneider, Steven, *The International Album of Wine*, Holt, Rinehart and Winston, New York, 1977

Scholtz, Merve, *Wine Country*, Cape Town, 1970

Schoonmaker, Frank, *Wines of Germany*, Hastings, New York, 1956; London, 1957; *Encyclopedia of Wine*, Hastings, New York, 1979; A & C Black Ltd, London, 1979

Schoonmaker, Frank and Marvel, Tom, *The Complete Wine Book*, New York, 1934, 1938; London, 1935

Scott, Dick, *Winemakers of New Zealand*, Southern Cross Books, Auckland, 1965; *A Stake in the Country*, Southern Cross Books, Auckland, 1977

Siegel, Hans, *Guide to the Wines of Germany*, Pitman Publishing Ltd, London, 1978

Simon, André L., *The History of the Champagne Trade in England*, London 1905; *The History of the Wine Trade in England*, London, 1906–9; *In Vino Veritas*, London, 1913; *Wine and Spirits, the Connoisseur's Text-Book*, London, 1919; *The Blood of the Grape: the wine trade textbook*, London, 1920; *Wine and the Wine Trade*, London, 1923; *Bottlescrew Days*, London, 1926; *A Dictionary of Wine*, London, 1935; *Vintagewise*, London, 1945; *A Wine Primer*, London, 1956; *Know Your Wines*, London, 1956; *The Wine and Food Menu Book*, London, 1956; *Madeira*, London, 1938; *History of Champagne*, London, 1962; *The Commonsense of Wine*, The International Wine and Food Society, London, 1966; Bonanza Books, New York, 1971

Stabilisierungsfonds für Wein, *German Wine Atlas*, Davis-Poynter Ltd, London, 1977

Thompson, Robert and Johnson, Hugh, *The California Wine Book*, William Morrow and Co. Inc., New York, 1976

Thorpy, Frank, *Wine in New Zealand*, Collins, Auckland, 1971; *New Zealand Wine Guide*, Auckland, 1976

Torres, Miguel A., *Vinas y Vinos*, Editorial Blume, Barcelona, 1978; *Vino espanol, un incierto futuro*, Blume, Barcelona, 1978

Vedel, Charle, Charnay, Tourmeau, *Essai sur la Dégustation des Vins*, s.e.i.v., Mâcon, 1972

Winkler, A. J., *General Viticulture* rev. ed., University of California Press Ltd, London, 1975

Yoxall, Harry W., *The Wines of Burgundy*, Pitman Publishing Ltd, London, 1979; Stein and Day, New York, 1979

Editor's Acknowledgments

Over the years, a great many people have helped me learn about wine. This willingness to impart information and share experience has often been given from motives of pure altruism, and each and every person who has had the generosity to pass on some of his hard-earned knowledge has my deepest thanks. Those who have answered my questions and opened bottles for me probably amount to hundreds, in many different countries of the world. Special awards for patience go to M. Claude Bouchard, M. Christian Moueix and M. Jean Hugel.

The contributors who have worked with me on this book deserve warm thanks. Their professional approach and great interest in their respective subjects were a constant stimulus, and I only hope they found the collaboration as pleasurable as I did.

It is a tradition that writers battle with their editor or publisher. However, in Fiona Roxburgh, I could not have had a more understanding, unfailingly good-humoured or competent editor, and if all writer/editor relationships were like this, the tradition would die a natural death.

I would like to give hitherto unexpressed, personal thanks to my father for his unstinting encouragement and enthusiasm when I wished to change careers, join the wine trade and go back to taking examinations. And to my greatly loved mother I owe what tasting acuity I may have – she had one of the finest natural palates I have ever known.

Finally, I owe the greatest thanks to my husband, David Peppercorn. I have learnt more about wine from him than from any other person. He also gave me the happiness and confidence which enabled me to undertake this book.

Serena Sutcliffe, London, 1981

Illustration Acknowledgments

32   J. Allan Cash Ltd
33   (above) Scope Photothèque, Paris (Photo: Michel Guillard)
33   (below) Scope Photothèque, Paris (Photo: Michel Guillard)
48   Scope Photothèque, Paris (Photo: Michel Guillard)
49   The Rainbird Publishing Group Ltd
72   Guy Gravett, The Picture Index
72-3 Colin Maher
73   Denis Hughes-Gilbey
96   Guy Gravett, The Picture Index
97   Bernard and Catherine Desjeux, Paris
112   Denis Hughes-Gilbey
113   Reportages J. and M. Ribière, Perpignan
160   Robert Estall
161   Wines from Germany Information Service
176   Colorific Photo Library Ltd (Photo: Esmond Saqui)
177   Colin Maher
200   Colin Maher
200-1 Bavaria Verlag (Photo: Michael Jeiter)
201   Robert Estall
224   Ian Jamieson
225   Bavaria Verlag (Photo: R. Holtappel)
240   QED Ltd (Photo: Jon Wyand)
241   Vision International (Photo: John Sims)
280   The Rainbird Publishing Group Ltd (Photo: Erik van Houtern)
280-1 QED Ltd (Photo: Jon Wyand)
281   QED Ltd (Photo: Jon Wyand)
304   QED Ltd (Photo: Jon Wyand)
305   QED Ltd (Photo: Jon Wyand)

320   Guy Gravett, The Picture Index
321   Zefa Picture Library (UK) Ltd
336   Jan Read
337   (above) Jan Read
337   (below) Jan Read
352   Jan Read
353   Douglas Dickens F.R.P.S.
368   Guy Gravett, The Picture Index
369   Vision International (Photo: Paolo Koch)
384   Guy Gravett, The Picture Index
385   (above) Guy Gravett, The Picture Index
385   (below) The Rainbird Publishing Group Ltd
400   The Rainbird Publishing Group Ltd (Photo: Percy Hennell)
401   Zefa Picture Library (UK) Ltd (Photo: G. Ricatto)
416   John Topham Picture Library
417   Zefa Picture Library (UK) Ltd
448   Peter Baker Photography
449   John Topham Picture Library
464   QED Ltd (Photo: Michael Freeman)
465   (above) QED Ltd (Photo: Michael Freeman)
465   (below) QED Ltd (Photo: Michael Freeman)
544   Jack Cakebread, Cakebread Cellars, Napa Valley
545   Zefa Picture Library (UK) Ltd (Photo: W. Hasenberg)
560   Robert Harding Associates (Photo: Walter Rawlings)
561   Douglas Dickens F.R.P.S.
616   South African Tourist Corporation
616-7 South African Tourist Corporation
617   John Topham Picture Library

Index